To Antietam Creek

To Antietam Creek

The Maryland Campaign of September 1862

D. Scott Hartwig

JOHNS HOPKINS UNIVERSITY PRESS | *Baltimore*

© 2012 Johns Hopkins University Press
All rights reserved. Published 2012
Printed in the United States of America on
acid-free paper

Johns Hopkins Paperback edition, 2019
9 8 7 6 5 4 3 2 1

Johns Hopkins University Press
2715 North Charles Street
Baltimore, Maryland 21218-4363
www.press.jhu.edu

The Library of Congress has cataloged the hardcover edition
of this book as follows:

Hartwig, D. Scott.
  To Antietam Creek : the Maryland Campaign of
September 1862 / D. Scott Hartwig.
      pages cm
  Includes bibliographical references and index.
  ISBN-13: 978-1-4214-0631-2 (hdbk. : alk. paper)
  ISBN-10: 1-4214-0631-4 (hdbk. : alk. paper)
  1. Maryland Campaign, 1862.   I. Title.
  E474.61.H374 2012
  973.7'336—dc23   2012001585

A catalog record for this book is available from the
British Library.

ISBN-13: 978-1-4214-2896-3
ISBN-10: 1-4214-2896-2

Title page illustration: Battle of Antietam, Maryland.
1862. Edwin Forbes. Library of Congress Prints
and Photographs Division.

Special discounts are available for bulk purchases of
this book. For more information, please contact Special
Sales at 410-516-6936 or specialsales@press.jhu.edu.

Johns Hopkins University Press uses environmentally
friendly book materials, including recycled text
paper that is composed of at least 30 percent post-
consumer waste, whenever possible.

To my parents,

Ann Marie

and

G. Douglas Hartwig,

with love

and gratitude

CONTENTS

ILLUSTRATIONS

Figures

Maps

To Antietam Creek

Introduction

It was September 5, 1862, and Captain Henry Pearson of the 6th New Hampshire Infantry sat down to write to a friend at home about his recollections of the recent Union defeat in the Battle of Second Manassas. Near the end of this long epistle, Pearson gave way to a sense of despair and of the inevitability of Southern independence.

> The Northern people get not the faintest idea from the newspapers of the true state of affairs at the seat of operations. The lying reports of our general and reporters beat anything that ever existed among the rebels . . . You need not be surprised if success falls to the rebels with astonishing rapidity. They certainly have the force, the skill and genius to do it.[1]

Many in the army shared Pearson's feelings and expressed them in letters home. The American Civil War had taken an abrupt turn during the summer of 1862; it now seemed a real possibility that the Union would not be preserved and that the Confederate States of America would win their independence. Thus the month of September promised to be a critical watershed in the war's outcome. Across the nation Confederate armies were on the offensive. In eastern Tennessee separate armies under Generals Kirby Smith and Braxton Bragg were preparing to mount an invasion of the border state of Kentucky, while other Confederate forces farther west under Generals Earl Van Dorn and Sterling Price made ready to invade western Tennessee.

But much of the nation focused its attention on the east. The opposing capitals were situated there, as were the major newspapers that covered the war. The east also had been the scene of one of the war's most remarkable campaigns to date—the outcome of which remained in doubt. Its architect was Confederate General Robert E. Lee, who took command of the Confederate army in front of Richmond in early June 1862 and went on the offensive. In two months he defeated two Union armies in Virginia, and by early September his forces stood poised to push across the Potomac River into Maryland, a border state of divided loyalties, and perhaps beyond into Pennsylvania. Lee sensed that opportunity lay north of the Potomac. Confederate victory on Maryland or Pennsylvania soil would strike a powerful blow at Northern morale, which in turn might influence the upcoming fall elections. Confederate victory north of the Potomac might also lead to recognition of the Confederate States by England and France. But Lee saw the Northern voter, not the slim hope of European recognition, as the Confederacy's best hope for victory. These voters would have a clear choice to make that autumn, either "to support those who favor a prolongation of the war, or those who wish to bring it to a termination."[2]

The future of human freedom in America was at stake as well that September. Convinced that the policy of limited war had failed, President Abraham Lincoln was prepared to introduce a policy of emancipation of slaves in those states that were in rebellion, which would sound the death knell of slavery in America. But he needed a battlefield victory to issue his Emancipation Proclamation, lest it be seen as a pathetic gesture of a desperate administration and only embolden and empower his opposition.

Lee forced the issue on September 4 when he sent his army splashing across the Potomac into Maryland. The balance would now move one way or the other. The campaign that followed lasted only two and a half weeks, but it contained enough drama and twists and turns that it might have been conceived by a novelist. The climax came on September 17 in the Battle of Antietam, the single bloodiest day of the Civil War. Unsurprisingly, in the years since, Antietam has received the greatest attention in histories of the Maryland Campaign. Yet the first phase, from the Confederate invasion of Maryland to the eve of Antietam—from September 4 through September 16—saw Lee's first defeat in battle, at South Mountain on September 14, and the largest surrender of U.S. troops prior to World War II, at Harpers Ferry. The Union garrison's surrender represented the most complete victory by any Confederate force during the war. Yet these events have been only lightly touched on in previous histories. This volume is the first attempt to give appropriate attention to South Mountain, Harpers Ferry, and the campaign leading up to Antietam. It concludes on the night before the Battle of Antietam because, in a sense, that night marked the end of the first phase of the war, where a negotiated settlement—with slavery continuing intact—remained possible. September 17 and the Battle of Antietam slammed the door on a limited war; there would be no turning back. Either the South would be defeated and slavery in America destroyed, or what Lincoln believed to be "the last best hope on earth," the government and nation created by the Founding Fathers, would be in ruins and the independence of a Southern slaveholding republic a reality. A second volume will complete these events with an in-depth study of the Battle of Antietam, the close of the campaign, and its political and military implications.

This is in part a study of command in war, of Lee and George B. McClellan and their lieutenants. But leaders command men who must obey orders, risk their lives, endure untold misery, and sometimes die or suffer terrible wounds.

The collective experience of the men who made up the two armies that marched forth into Maryland is no less important to our understanding of these events than that of their commanders.

In the end the Maryland Campaign changed the war—and the nation. This is its story.

1

The Return of McClellan

"General, I am in command again"

August 30, 1862. Alexandria, Virginia. All day the distant growl of artillery thumped and rumbled in the direction of Manassas, 30 miles to the southeast. General George B. McClellan, commanding general of the Army of the Potomac, puffed his cigar while he listened to the guns. An unfinished letter to his wife lay on his writing desk. The sound of the far-off battle tormented him and reminded him of his personal humiliation. He commanded the most powerful army in the nation, but over the previous weeks it had been detached from him piece by piece and sent to reinforce John Pope, a man he detested intensely, until all he had left were some staff officers and orderlies. His men were now in a desperate battle without him. When the guns finally fell silent he resumed the letter. "I have been listening to the sound of a great battle in the distance. My men engaged in it and I away! I never felt worse in my life."[1]

An hour later, at 10:30 p.m., unable to restrain his emotions any longer, he telegraphed Army General-in-Chief Henry W. Halleck to request permission to join his men on the battlefield. "I cannot express to you the pain & mortification I have experienced today in listening to the distant sound of the firing of my men . . . If it is not deemed best to entrust me with the command even of my own army, I simply ask to be permitted to share their fate on the field of battle," he pleaded. Halleck did not reply, and McClellan was left to brood over the remarkable events that had brought him from the pinnacle of power to such an ignominious position in only 13 months.[2]

McClellan had been the man of the hour in July 1861. In the wake of the Union defeat at First Manassas, President Lincoln had summoned him from western Virginia, where he had recently concluded a successful campaign over the Rebels, to Washington to assume command of the defeated army and make the capital secure from attack. McClellan was only 34 years old. Jacob Cox, who served with him in western Virginia as a volunteer officer, described him as "rather under medium height, but muscularly formed, with broad shoulders and a well-poised head, active and graceful in motion." Born in Philadelphia, Pennsylvania, to a cultured family with influential friends, he received an appointment to the Military Academy at West Point at age 15 and graduated four years later ranked second in his class. His high class standing won him a position in the elite Corps of Engineers, with whom he served with distinction in the Mexico City campaign under General Winfield Scott during the war with Mexico. In the years after that war U.S. Secretary of War Jefferson Davis saw promise in the bright young engineer, and in 1855 Davis saw to it that McClellan was named to a three-man military commission that went to Europe to observe the armies fighting in Crimea. It was a prestigious appointment, and the experience in Crimea deeply impressed McClellan with the need for more professional training and organization of the U.S. Army.

Upon his return and the completion of his report, McClellan was to join his regiment, the 1st U.S. Cavalry, in Kansas, where they were occupied in the thankless task of keeping the proslavery and antislavery Kansans from slaughtering one another. This held little appeal for McClellan, and he had also heard negative comments about the regiment's colonel, Edwin V. Sumner. He decided to resign from the army and accepted a position as chief engineer for the Illinois Central Railroad Company. Within three years—by 1860—he was the Superintendent of the Eastern Division of the Ohio and Mississippi Railroad Company, drawing a generous salary of $10,000 a year. With his outstanding accomplishments in organization and logistics as a railroad man, as well as his splendid army record, McClellan was in demand when war broke out in 1861. The governors of New York, Ohio, and Pennsylvania all vied with one another to secure his services as commander of their state forces. Ohio prevailed. Within two weeks of the firing on Fort Sumter, McClellan was commissioned a major general of volunteers and accepted command of Ohio's volunteer forces. His talent for organizing and training soldiers shone as he quickly brought order to the chaos of the state's mobilization of its manpower. Recognizing his capabilities, the government broadened his responsibility. On May 13 he was placed in command of the newly formed Department of Ohio, which included Ohio, Indiana, and Illinois. Promotion to major general in the regular army came a day later. Only General Winfield Scott outranked him.[3]

Late that spring and into the summer McClellan took personal command of a campaign to wrest control of northwestern Virginia (later West Virginia), which had rejected secession, from Rebel forces. The campaign climaxed in the Confederate defeat at the Battle of Rich Mountain on July 7, with McClellan delivering the North's first real military success. It earned him the acclaim of the national press, as well as a joint resolution of Congress thanking him for his victory. Two weeks later the Confederates shocked the North with their victory at First Manassas. In the aftermath of the defeat, Lincoln sought someone who could restore discipline and morale to the demoralized Union army and render the capital secure from Confederate attack. McClellan possessed ideal credentials: military success as a field commander in western Virginia, administrative success in organizing and training Ohio's volunteers, and experience as an engineer in the regular army. A day after the debacle at Manassas, he received a telegram from the War Department to "come hither without delay" to Washington, D.C. His moment had arrived.[4]

McClellan looked the part of a successful general. Young, handsome, vigorous, strongly built, he moved with the self-assurance and ease of a man who had always known success. His warm and charming public personality easily won people over, and his powerful intellect and capacity for long hours of work were impressive. Jacob Cox recalled how "his manner of doing business impressed all with the belief that he knew what he was about." A member of the U.S. Sanitary Commission who met McClellan wrote that there was "an indefinable *air of success* about him and something of the 'man of destiny.'" McClellan, in short, had charisma.[5]

Few men in the army could rival his knowledge of military history, and his experiences in Crimea had exposed him to the organization, equipment, and methods of professional European armies at war. A careful student of strategy and modern technology, he advocated the use of sea power to move armies quickly and unexpectedly against strategic points and he appreciated early on the impact that the railroad and telegraph would have on warfare. He appeared to possess the qualities that mark notable leaders, and the government—as well as the entire North—expected great things of him. "By some strange operation of magic I seem to have become *the* power of the land," he wrote to his wife, Mary Ellen, soon after his arrival in the capital. "I almost think that were I to win some small success now I could become Dictator or anything else that might please me."[6]

McClellan's politics were moderately conservative. He had been a Whig—as had Lincoln—until that party dissolved. He then became a Stephen Douglas Democrat, enthusiastically supporting Douglas in his famous senatorial race against Lincoln in 1858. McClellan blamed the war on extremists on both sides: the abolitionists in the North and the reactionary secessionists in the South. Although he abhorred abolitionists, viewing them as radicals, he also believed slavery to be a "great evil" and supported gradual emancipation. While the slavery issue had sparked secession and the war, McClellan strongly opposed any notion that the war might provide a platform for an attack on slavery. He believed such a course would be extremist and dangerous, turning the war into a revolutionary struggle and serving only to further unite the slaveholding South against the North. He advocated a limited war that employed carefully applied, overwhelming military strength to convince Southerners of the hopelessness of their struggle. He explained his thinking in an August memorandum to the president: "By thoroughly defeating their armies, taking their strong places, and pursuing a rigidly protective policy as to private property and unarmed persons, and a lenient course as to common soldiers, we may well hope for the permanent restoration of [a] peaceful Union."[7]

McClellan was assigned to command the Division of the Potomac, which included all forces in northeastern Virginia and within the capital, as well as the field army recently defeated at Manassas. He vigorously applied his considerable energy to his new position, working unsparingly to organize and train his raw volunteers into the most well-equipped and disciplined army in American military history to that date. He named the army that assembled in its camps around the capital the Army of the Potomac. Along with giving structure to this army, McClellan also supervised the construction of a system of fortifications to ring the capital and render it impregnable to assault. Within days soldiers recognized the change that McClellan brought. There was a system to how things were done, and regularity. McClellan made sure that he was seen often by his troops, frequently spending long days in the saddle. It paid off in the loyalty of his men, who sensed that they had a commander who took a personal interest in them.

Yet even in these early, euphoric days there were warning signs of potential problems. Despite his cool, confident exterior, McClellan was sensitive and temperamental, and tormented by insecurities. He had a history of clashes with superiors during his earlier military service and in private industry. Within days of his arrival in Washington he was in conflict with elderly General Scott. In McClellan's opinion Scott did not appreciate the grave danger the capital was in from an advance by the Confederates gathered at Manassas. On August 10 he complained to Mary Ellen that "Genl Scott is the great obstacle—he will not comprehend the danger & is either a traitor or an incompetent." By August 14 he stated that "Genl Scott is the most dangerous antagonist I have—either he or I must leave here—our ideas are so widely different that it is impossible for us to work together much longer." McClellan made no effort to heal the rift, and it widened as summer slipped into fall. By early October Scott was his "inveterate enemy." But Scott was not the only superior to earn McClellan's private contempt, which he revealed in letters to his wife. On August 16 he complained that the president "is an idiot." Nearly two months later he described Lincoln as "nothing more than [a] well meaning baboon," adding that his Secretary of the Navy, Gideon Welles, "is weaker than the most garrulous old woman you were ever annoyed by" and Secretary of State William Seward was a "meddling, officious, incompetent little puppy." McClellan had little patience with people who questioned his judgment or did not see things his way. Stephen Sears, one of McClellan's biographers, thought that the general's abiding faith in predestination lay at the root of these conflicts. McClellan's belief that God had chosen him to save the nation was "at once the prop for his insecurity and the shield for his convictions. With Calvinistic fatalism he believed his path to be the chosen path; anyone who raised criticism or objections—whether president or cabinet officer or legislator or editor or fellow general—was at best ignorant and misguided and at worst a traitor."[8]

Some of his early clashes with Scott and frustration with Lincoln and his cabinet had to do with his perception that they utterly failed to comprehend the danger the Confederates at Manassas posed to the capital. McClellan convinced himself that he was overwhelmingly outnumbered by the Rebel army there. On August 8 he reported to General Scott that he believed the Confederate army "has at least 100,000 men in our front." On August 19, in a letter to Mary Ellen, he wrote that the count had now risen to 150,000. Union intelligence sources, however, had placed Confederate strength at approximately 35,000 before the Battle of First Manassas in July. Nonetheless, it is clear that McClellan believed *his* numbers, because his fear that the Confederates would attack Washington in mid-August is palpable in his private letters to his wife. What makes this so bizarre is that McClellan was a professional soldier who understood logistics and was intimately familiar with the means by which large numbers of troops, equipment, and provisions could be moved rapidly— namely, by railroad. As a railroad man he surely must have realized that the South did not possess the rolling stock and rail lines to achieve such a rapid mobilization in northern Virginia or to keep it supplied. The North, with its superior rail system and industry, could mobilize and equip troops faster than the Confederates. Yet he chose to believe otherwise, and this would come to shape his command of the Army of the Potomac.[9]

By the end of October McClellan had succeeded in wearing down Scott, and the 75-year-old general retired after 53 years of military service. On November 1 Lincoln named McClellan general-in-chief of all Federal armies. McClellan assumed this new position with his typical vigor. But the work to be done— training the Army of the Potomac for active operations while also planning and directing the strategic operations of the entire Union war effort—was more than one man could possibly handle. His staff could have helped if he had let them, but he lacked confidence in their ability to manage things to his satisfaction and instead burdened himself with administrative details. "I must ride much every day for my army covers much space, & unfortunately I have no one on my staff to whom I can entrust the safety of affairs," he complained to Mary Ellen. He named his father-in-law, Colonel Randolph Marcy, who was an experienced and competent regular officer, as his chief of staff, but McClellan delegated little authority to him. "I can do it all," McClellan said to the president when Lincoln told him his position would entail "a vast labor." And McClellan did do a great deal.

His correspondence during this period is voluminous, and no detail seemed to escape his attention. But in the first month of his new command McClellan's patience with the president began to wear thin. Lincoln had a habit of dropping by unannounced at McClellan's headquarters on Jackson Square. McClellan initially tolerated the interruptions, but he soon began to regard Lincoln as a nuisance and grew contemptuous of him. His most famous snub of the president was on November 13, when Lincoln stopped by McClellan's head-quarters accompanied by Seward and John Hay, one of Lincoln's personal sec-retaries. McClellan was at a wedding, so the president's party waited for an hour in the parlor. When McClellan returned he swept by the parlor without a word and ignored his orderly's announcement that the president and the secre-tary of state were waiting to meet with him. They remained for another half hour and then sent McClellan's orderly upstairs to remind the general that the president was still waiting to see him. The orderly returned to report that McClellan had gone to bed. Four days later McClellan complained to Mary El-len about having to visit the White House, "where I found 'the *original* gorilla,' about as intelligent as ever." Lincoln had a good sense for people and he prob-ably discerned McClellan's frustration with him (he could not have failed to perceive the intended slight in the November 13 incident), but he remained patient and retained his trust in the general's military abilities.[10]

November passed into December and the Army of the Potomac remained in its camps, drilling and training, with the Confederate army less than 30 miles away at Manassas. As the weeks ticked by with no movement, criticism rose, emanating principally from the more radical Republicans in Congress, who were impatient to take the war to the Rebels. McClellan refused to be hurried or to reveal his plans for the army to anyone. He continued to drive himself relentlessly, and in late December he fell seriously ill with typhoid fever. The problem with having a single individual carry responsibility for the entire war planning of Union military operations was keenly felt as the Federal war effort stalled while the general lay ill. Senator Ben Wade of Ohio, one of a growing number of McClellan's critics, growled, "How can this nation abide the secret counsels that one man carries in his head, when we have no evidence that he is the wisest man in the world?" McClellan was not oblivious of the need to do something to quiet his critics. In mid-January, while recovering from his illness, he wrote to General Don Carlos Buell, commanding the Department of Ohio, that "you have no idea of the pressure brought to bear here upon the government for a forward movement." He advised Buell that he should undertake a move-ment into eastern Tennessee that McClellan had previously recommended, in order to both place Union forces in a region known to possess Union sentiments and seize the rail line running from Knoxville to Memphis. McClellan consid-ered this as a preliminary movement to a planned grand offensive to strike both the Confederate capital at Richmond, Virginia, and the strategic railroad junc-tion at Nashville, Tennessee. But this movement, which McClellan believed would be decisive, could not be hurried. Hasty action, he felt, was unproductive. "I have ever regarded our true policy as being that of fully preparing ourselves &

then seeking for the most decisive results—I do not wish to waste life in useless battles, but prefer to strike at the heart," he wrote to new Secretary of War Edwin Stanton in early February.[11]

There was logic in McClellan's thinking. It took time to assemble, equip, organize, and train armies for active operations. Yet he never seemed to fathom that he could win support and time for his plans if he had shared them with the president, who, if more fully informed, might have been able to calm the radicals' growing suspicions about the general. McClellan was delighted by the appointment of Stanton, whom he saw as an ally, considering it "a most unexpected piece of good fortune." Stanton was as unlike McClellan as was possible to be. The secretary of war was a brilliant, vigorous man but, as McClellan's biographer Ethan Rafuse related, he also "did not hesitate to lie, double-deal, bully, or play the sycophant to get what he wanted." McClellan's satisfaction with Stanton's appointment would be brief.[12]

Lacking any specific strategic plan from McClellan, a frustrated Lincoln finally issued President's General War Order No. 1 on January 27. He commanded that on February 22, Washington's birthday, the land and naval forces of the United States would "move against the insurgent forces." Four days later he followed this up with Special War Order No. 1, which instructed the Army of the Potomac to move against the rail communications of the Confederates at Manassas on or before February 22. If Lincoln issued these orders in the hope they would prod McClellan, they worked. The general hurried to the White House as soon as he received the General War Order and asked if he might submit his objections to the president's operational ideas and present his own plans in writing. Lincoln agreed, and on February 3 McClellan submitted a 22-page paper to Stanton that first summarized what had been accomplished since his arrival in Washington and then turned to the president's preferred plan of moving against the Confederate forces at Manassas. McClellan argued that even if successful against the Confederates, "these results would be confined to the possession of the field of battle, the evacuation of the line of the upper Potomac by the enemy & the moral effect of the victory." All, he agreed, were important results, but they were unlikely to be decisive, as the enemy army could simply withdraw to a new line of operations and would have to be attacked again. The weather at the latitude of Manassas, he explained, "will for a considerable period be very uncertain, which would render [it] impossible to fix a date that operations could commence." In the final part of the paper McClellan at last presented his own plan for the Army of the Potomac. "The second base of operations available for the Army of the Potomac is that of the lower Chesapeake Bay, which affords the shortest possible land routes to Richmond, & strikes directly at the heart of the enemy's power in the East," he began. The roads, he continued, "were passable at all seasons of the year." What McClellan suggested was a water-borne turning movement. The Army of the Potomac would be transferred via the Potomac River and Chesapeake Bay to Urbana, Virginia, near the mouth of the Rappahannock River, inserting them into the rear of the Rebels at Manassas. With the Federal army closer to Richmond than their own, the Confederates at Manassas would be forced to hastily abandon their position there and attack McClellan in a position of his own choosing. McClellan contended that "this movement if successful gives us the Capital, the communications, the supplies of the rebels; Norfolk would fall, all the Chesapeake would be ours; all Virginia would be in our power & the enemy forced to abandon Tennessee and North Carolina." McClellan closed by restating his opinion that little could be gained by the move on Manassas, but of the Urbana line of operations, he dramatically wrote: "I will stake my life, my reputation on the result—more than that, I will stake upon it, the success of our cause."[13]

Lincoln took time to digest and consider McClellan's plans. While McClellan waited, Federal troops were on the move elsewhere in the country, winning laurels for the Union cause. In mid-January a force under General George Thomas, dispatched by General Buell into southeastern Kentucky, routed the Confederates in the Battle of Mill Springs. In February a Union army under General Ulysses S. Grant captured Fort Henry on the Tennessee River, then marched overland and in four days surrounded and captured Fort Donelson, on the Cumberland River, and over 12,000 Confederate soldiers. At nearly the same time a Union amphibious operation McClellan had dispatched to coastal North Carolina under the command of his friend Brigadier General Ambrose Burnside captured Roanoke Island and some 2,500 Confederate defenders. On February 25 General Buell occupied Nashville, Tennessee. On all fronts Union armies were winning victories—except along the Potomac. Although McClellan had encouraged the strategy that led to these victories, he received no credit for them, for all eyes in the capital were focused on the large but inert army he had assembled but seemed reluctant to use. In late February McClellan at last marched up the Potomac toward Harpers Ferry with some 40,000 troops.

The purpose of this advance was to deposit a garrison in the lower Shenandoah Valley that would both threaten the valley and protect the western line of the B&O Railroad. To supply this force in the valley, new bridges had to be built over the Potomac at Harpers Ferry. On February 26 a pontoon bridge was laid amid much fanfare, but a second, more substantial bridge, designed to carry heavy army traffic, hit a highly embarrassing snag. The bridge would rest on a number of canal boats that were to be floated up the C&O Canal and then moved over to the Potomac by way of a lift lock. But upon their arrival it was discovered that the boats were a few inches too wide to pass through the locks, which brought everything to a halt. Both Lincoln and Stanton were furious when they heard of the snafu. Lincoln voiced his frustration to Randolph Marcy, McClellan's chief of staff, with an anger he rarely displayed. "Everything seems to fail. The general impression is daily gaining ground that the general does not intend to do anything." Despite this initial setback the expedition ultimately succeeded in repairing and opening the B&O railroad bridge, and General Nathaniel Banks established a Union presence at Winchester, Virginia, in the lower Shenandoah Valley. But in the short term McClellan looked foolish, particularly in light of the Union successes occurring elsewhere in the nation.[14]

On March 8 Lincoln met privately with McClellan. They discussed the Harpers Ferry debacle, and then Lincoln brought up what he termed a "more serious—or ugly—matter." He related that powerful people in the capital were suggesting that McClellan's plan to take the army to Urbana had traitorous designs, so as to deliberately leave the capital defenseless. This implication shocked and infuriated McClellan. He related that he rose to his feet and, "in a manner perhaps not altogether decorous towards the chief magistrate," asked him to retract the statement, "telling him that I could permit no one to couple the word treason with my name." Lincoln replied that he took no stock in the rumors; he was merely repeating what others were saying. He was also trying to tell McClellan that unfounded and outrageous as the rumors might be, the fact that they were circulating at all was dangerous, and that the general needed to be aware of the powerful forces growing against him. Lincoln could only do so much to protect McClellan. Action and success were what would silence his enemies.[15]

McClellan had called a meeting of a dozen of his division commanders for that afternoon to discuss an operation intended to clear Confederate batteries along the lower Potomac that had effectively closed the river to commercial traffic. He told Lincoln that he would instead submit his Urbana plan to the generals and let them each give their professional opinion of its merits or dangers. Lincoln agreed, and that afternoon, for the first time, the army's senior commanders heard McClellan's plan. Eight of the 12 endorsed it and 4 opposed it. The vote failed to allay Lincoln's concern about the Urbana line of operations, and that afternoon he issued two General War Orders. Order No. 2 declared that the Army of the Potomac should be immediately organized into army corps, and it named the four senior generals who would command them: Irvin Mc-Dowell, Edwin V. Sumner, Samuel P. Heintzelman, and Erasmus D. Keyes. Of the four, only Keyes supported the Urbana plan. A fifth corps was to be formed from the troops around Harpers Ferry and commanded by General Nathaniel P. Banks, a former congressman, Massachusetts governor, and loyal Republican, but an amateur soldier. The troops to be retained to defend the capital were placed under the command of another political appointee, Republican philanthropist Brigadier General James Wadsworth. General Order No. 3 stipulated that the army could not embark on a campaign without leaving a force deemed adequate by both McClellan and all his corps commanders to render the capital secure. Lincoln still sustained McClellan, but the general orders were evidence

THE RETURN OF MCCLELLAN | 13

of two important things. First, after four months Lincoln had concluded that McClellan could not do it all and that he himself needed to take a more active role as commander-in-chief. Second, although seniority dictated the selection of the first four corps commanders, Lincoln hoped that the overall selections would help appease McClellan's enemies within the Republican Party.[16]

The Confederates did the unexpected on March 9. Joseph E. Johnston's army evacuated Manassas, falling back to a new line below the Rappahannock River. McClellan was taken by surprise. He ordered an immediate advance on Manassas, and the army slogged forward along muddy roads in a cold rain. With a good 24 hours' head start, the Confederates got clean away without a particle of damage, and the grand advance sputtered out in anticlimax. Wrote one reporter who accompanied the army, "I return from this visit to the rebel stronghold, feeling that their retreat is *our defeat*." McClellan attempted to put the best face on the affair: the enemy had also departed from their positions along the lower Potomac and destroyed their artillery positions that had closed the Potomac to shipping. McClellan argued that the army's earlier move to Harpers Ferry had turned the enemy's flank and precipitated the collapse of the Confederate front in northern Virginia, but his reasoning did not convince those who wondered how the enemy had slipped away undetected. "Upon the whole it seems as if our genl. went with his finger in his mouth on a fool's errand and that he has won a fool's reward," wrote Attorney General Edward Bates.[17]

The Manassas affair may have clinched a decision the president had been contemplating, possibly since the Harpers Ferry debacle—that shouldering the duel burden of the duties of commander-in-chief and commander of the Army of the Potomac were more than George McClellan, or any man, could manage. On March 11, while McClellan was still in the field examining the Confederate works at Manassas, Lincoln told his cabinet that he had prepared a new general order relieving McClellan of his position as commander-in-chief. No one was named to replace him, leaving the way open for his return to the post should his upcoming campaign be successful. McClellan took his demotion gracefully enough, after the reasons were explained to him by Ohio Governor William Dennison—the emissary selected by the administration to deliver the news to the general—and he wrote to the president on March 12 to acknowledge receipt of the orders. "You will find that under the present circumstances I shall work just as cheerfully as ever before, & that no consideration of self will in any manner interfere with the discharge of my public duties."[18]

With his Urbana plan compromised by the Confederate withdrawal from Manassas, McClellan moved swiftly to preserve its general intent by changing the point of debarkation to Fortress Monroe, at the tip of the Virginia peninsula. On March 13 he submitted the revised plan to his four corps commanders, all of whom approved it. He reported the results of the meeting to the president through Stanton, who, in turn, swiftly returned Lincoln's reply. Lincoln made no objection to the new plan but dictated two important provisions: (1) a garrison must be placed at Manassas Junction, strong enough to "make it entirely certain that the enemy shall not repossess himself of that position and line of communications"; and (2) "leave Washington secure." Whether the army chose a base at Fortress Monroe or anywhere between there and Washington was immaterial, so long as McClellan moved "such remainder of the army at once in pursuit of the enemy by some route."[19]

At long last McClellan's grand effort to win the war in a single campaign was at hand. "I believe that we are now on the eve of the success for which we have been so long preparing," he wrote *New York World* reporter Edmund Stedman on March 17. Success would disarm his now numerous enemies in Washington and hopefully preserve the limited war he believed in. Just how dangerous his enemies were growing was underscored on the same day McClellan wrote to Stedman, when Republican radicals attempted to bring to a vote on the Senate floor a resolution calling for the general's removal from command. The effort was defeated, but it reflected the growing power of the anti-McClellan cabal. In a bizarre twist two days before this, without Lincoln's knowledge Secretary of War Stanton offered command of the Army of the Potomac to 63-year-old General Ethan Allen Hitchcock, then serving as a special military advisor to the secretary. Hitchcock declined, but the incident reflected Stanton's disillusionment with McClellan. George Gibbs, a longtime friend of McClellan's and brother of the general's West Point roommate, wrote to McClellan on March 13 that it was vital that he make some gesture to reassure moderate and conservative Republicans that he was not an agent of the Democrats. "You have secluded yourself from political associations and interests. I and others who know you, understand this, but the country don't," wrote Gibbs. "This is a popular war," he continued, and McClellan needed to acknowledge this, even if "you do not bow to popular feeling." Francis P. Blair Sr., one of McClellan's few Republican friends, suggested that McClellan take on Blair's son as a chief of staff to help smooth McClellan's relations with the administration. "No general can succeed without proper relations with the Administration," warned Blair. McClellan, however, ignored Blair's and Gibbs's advice. Military victory would silence his critics. To Samuel L. M. Barlow he wrote, "Do not mind the abolitionists—all I ask of the papers is that they should defend me from the most malicious attacks—tho' to speak frankly I do not care to pay much attention to my enemies."[20]

But the abolitionists—who, in McClellan's view, meant the Republican radicals—were gaining power and momentum in their efforts to alter the direction of the war. On March 13 Congress approved an act prohibiting officers in the U.S. service from employing any of their forces to return fugitive slaves to their owners, noting that "any officer who shall be found guilty by a court-

martial of violating this article shall be dismissed from the service." Back in
November, McClellan had written his ally Barlow: "Help me dodge the nigger—
we want nothing to do with him. I am fighting to preserve the integrity of the
Union & the power of the Govt—on no other issue. To gain that we cannot afford to raise up the negro question—it must be incidental and subsidiary." Yet
as Frederick Douglass observed in a February speech in Boston, "Is it not plain
as the sun in the heavens that slavery is the life, the soul, the inspiration, and
power of the rebellion? Is it not equally plain that any peace which may be secured which shall leave slavery still existing at the South, will prove a hollow
and worthless peace, a mere suspension of hostilities, to be renewed again at
the first favorable opportunity?" There were men in power who were beginning to see things as Douglass did, and they threatened to disrupt the tidy war
George McClellan hoped to fight.[21]

The leading elements of the Army of the Potomac embarked for the Virginia Peninsula from Alexandria, Virginia, on March 17. Over the next 20 days
the rest of the army followed: 121,000 men, with all the equipment attendant to
such a vast army. On April 1 McClellan boarded the steamer *Commodore* and
departed for the Peninsula. "Officially speaking, I feel very glad to get away from
that sink of inequity," he wrote to Mary Ellen. Free from the venomous atmosphere of the capital, he looked forward eagerly and confidently to the commencement of his carefully planned campaign to capture Richmond and deliver
a mortal blow to the rebellion.[22]

The grand campaign bogged down before it had fairly begun. Rather than
taking the time to meet with Lincoln, on the day of his departure from Washington McClellan submitted a report to the War Department detailing the
forces he had left to meet the president's orders to occupy Manassas and leave
the capital secure. By McClellan's arithmetic the total force available for the
capital's security was 73,000 men, yet when the president and Stanton examined
the document carefully they found McClellan's numbers did not add up: 35,000
of the 73,000 were in the Shenandoah Valley, 80 miles from the capital. There
were other errors in the report—one brigade was counted twice—and some of
the troops included in the capital's garrison were recruits from Pennsylvania
who had not yet left that state. What Lincoln and Stanton deduced was that only
26,700 men were actually left in the Washington–Manassas area, and many of
these were brand new units with little or no training. Lincoln acted promptly,
and on April 3 he instructed Stanton to detach one of the two corps still waiting
to embark for the Peninsula to serve as a covering force for the capital. Stanton
selected McDowell's corps of 33,000 men.[23]

McClellan learned of McDowell's detachment on April 5, which had not
been a good day for the general. The army was on the second day of its advance
toward Yorktown, the first objective of the campaign. It rained hard during the
day and turned the roads, which McClellan had assured Stanton "were passable

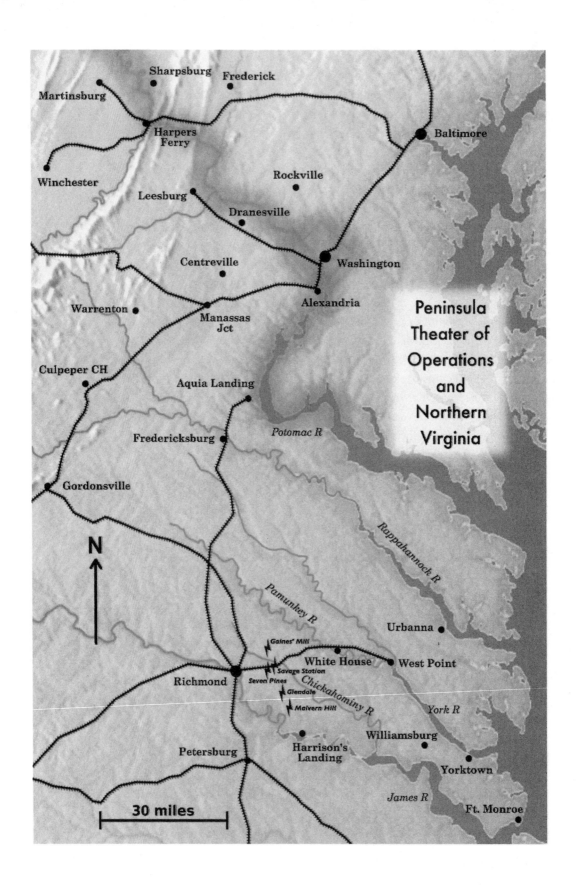

Sharpsburg   Frederick

Martinsburg

Harpers
Ferry

Baltimore

Winchester

Rockville

Leesburg

Dranesville

Centreville

Washington

Warrenton

Manassas
Jct

Alexandria

Culpeper CH

Aquia Landing

**Peninsula
Theater of
Operations
and
Northern
Virginia**

Fredericksburg

Potomac R

Gordonsville

Rappahannock R

N

Pamunkey R

Urbanna

Gaines' Mill

White House   West Point

Savage Station

Richmond

Seven Pines

Chickahominy R

Glendale

Malvern Hill

York R

Williamsburg

Petersburg

Harrison's
Landing

Yorktown

James R

Ft. Monroe

30 miles

at all seasons of the year," into quagmires that brought movement to a near stand-still. Then he discovered a line of enemy fortifications stretching from Yorktown all the way across the Peninsula, and they appeared to be well manned with Confederate soldiers. McClellan had anticipated that Yorktown would be defended by some 15,000 Rebel troops and that he could easily turn their position. In reality the Confederates had only 8,000 men, but their commander, Major General John B. Magruder, marched his men about so cleverly that he fooled the Federals into believing the enemy lines were strongly held. McClellan made no effort to test Magruder's lines to see if he were bluffing, concluding that if the works appeared formidable then they must be well manned, and he ordered up his siege train from Fortress Monroe. Now, in a single stroke, the president had deprived him of one-quarter of the force he anticipated to have available. To his wife McClellan wrote that he considered the president's action "the most infamous thing that history has recorded." To the president he begged "that you will reconsider the order" detaching McDowell. "In my deliberate judgment the success of our cause will be imperiled when it is actually under the fire of the enemy," he stated.[24]

The loss of McDowell's corps was serious, but hardly the crushing blow McClellan claimed it was. His logisticians were struggling to supply the troops already on the Peninsula, let alone having to provision an additional 33,000 troops. He also might have avoided losing the corps had he taken the time to fully explain the forces he left to defend the capital with the president and Stanton before leaving for the Peninsula, as McClellan had not planned on embarking the 1st Corps for at least two weeks. Finally, he had already made the decision to proceed with siege operations before he learned of the 1st Corps' detachment. The decision to undertake siege operations without any attempt to carry the enemy works by assault sacrificed the advantages the movement to the Peninsula had given McClellan. For a brief window of time he possessed superiority in numbers and held the initiative. But that window closed rapidly as the Confederates shifted troops to the threatened sector. No rail line fed the Peninsula, so while McClellan could receive reinforcements relatively quickly by water, Confederate reinforcements had to march down the Peninsula to Yorktown. A siege worked to the Confederates' advantage by granting them time to react, improve their defenses, and concentrate their forces. The president saw this, and on April 6 he cautioned the general that the Confederates "will probably use *time*, as advantageously as you can." They did. By April 11, Magruder had been reinforced to 34,400 men.[25]

McClellan's failure to test the Confederates' Yorktown defenses surprised his opponents. General Magruder noted gratefully how the Federals "permitted day after day to elapse without an assault." And Joe Johnston quipped that "no one but McClellan could have hesitated to attack" in the early days of the siege. On April 11 Lincoln released William B. Franklin's division of some 11,000 men from McDowell's corps to reinforce McClellan and promised to send George A. McCall's division, also from the 1st Corps, if the safety of the capital permitted. McClellan, in turn, had promised that if these divisions were sent to him, he would "invest & attack" Gloucester Point at once. Gloucester Point sat opposite Yorktown on the York River. Rebel guns emplaced there, along with those at Yorktown, prevented Union naval vessels from steaming up the York to the Confederate rear. If it could be captured, the way would be open for the Union navy to attack Yorktown in reverse. Franklin's division embarked on April 18, but McClellan reconsidered the risk of an attack on Gloucester Point. Instead, he decided to hold the division as a floating reserve. When Yorktown fell it could be dispatched up the York River to capture West Point, where McClellan intended to establish his depot to support the advance on Richmond. And so McClellan continued with his methodical preparations, confident that the enemy would permit him to execute his plans for a massive, crushing bombardment by his heavy siege artillery.[26]

The Yorktown siege reprised McClellan's proclivity for exaggerating the enemy's strength and capabilities and underestimating the abilities of his own army. Allan Pinkerton, a Chicago-based private detective whom McClellan had met while working for the Illinois Central Railroad, directed the general's intelligence-gathering services. Pinkerton and the others McClellan had relied on to obtain intelligence about the Peninsula had not served him particularly well. Maps supplied to the army were inaccurate. Reports that the roads on the Peninsula could sustain army traffic in all weather had proven to be a cruel joke. The enemy's defensive works along the Warwick River were unknown, and enemy strength was routinely overestimated. Based on Pinkerton's work, McClellan estimated enemy strength at "probably not less than 100,000 men & probably more" on April 7. Less than one month later Pinkerton gave Confederate strength at Yorktown at between 100,000 and 120,000 and considered this under the mark of the actual enemy strength. By this time the actual enemy strength was only 56,600. With implicit faith in Pinkerton's work and his own willingness to believe the enemy capable of fielding and supplying these large numbers, McClellan accepted the reports without question. Some have suggested that McClellan did not really believe the strength figures that Pinkerton provided, but used them to lobby for reinforcements. As Stephen Sears points out, the problem with this theory is that in his private letters to his wife, McClellan never once doubted that the enemy outnumbered him.[27]

That the enemy might not wait patiently while the Federals hauled up and emplaced their siege artillery never seemed to occur to McClellan. He had decided that the Confederates would stake their all on the upcoming battle and any evidence to the contrary was discounted. When a reporter came to Chief of Staff Marcy with news from an escaped slave that the Rebel wagon trains were pulling out, he was told that headquarters had "positive intelligence" that the enemy intended to fight. McClellan promised the president that he could "see the way clear to success & hope to make it brilliant, although with but little loss of life." Plans were made for the grand bombardment of the Rebel positions to begin on May 5. But for the second time Joe Johnston did the unexpected. On the night of May 3 he began to withdraw his army from its Yorktown lines and march up the Peninsula. In a reprise of Manassas, McClellan was again taken completely by surprise. He moved quickly to put a positive spin on his anticlimactic occupation of Yorktown, as he had done after Manassas. "Their works prove to have been the most formidable & I am now fully satisfied of the correctness of the course I have pursued. Our success is brilliant & you may rest assured that its effects will be of the greatest importance," he wrote to Stanton. He considered Yorktown "a great result gained by pure skill & at little cost."[28]

McClellan scrambled to organize a pursuit. The enemy's retreat from Yorktown and Gloucester Point now made it possible to use the York River to insert a force across the enemy's line of retreat. Unfortunately, in anticipation of the determined enemy resistance he foresaw in the assault on Yorktown, McClellan had unloaded Franklin's big division from their transports on May 3 so that they could support the attack. He now ordered Franklin's division back on the transports, intending to send them up the York River to outflank Johnston's retreating army, and tabbed three other divisions to support Franklin if he were successful in establishing a bridgehead. For the overland pursuit he dispatched his cavalry, horse artillery, and five infantry divisions. McClellan believed his waterborne flanking operation to be the most decisive and important of the two concurrent operations, so he personally supervised the time-consuming loading of Franklin's division. On May 5 he heard the sounds of fighting from the direction of Williamsburg during the day but presumed that it was no more than a rearguard action. In the early afternoon reports began to come in that things were not going well at Williamsburg. Gathering up some of his staff, he galloped to the battlefield, arriving late in the afternoon. The battle was largely over by the time he reached the field. He claimed that "I found everybody discouraged—officers & men—our troops in wrong positions, on the wrong side of the woods—no system, no cooperation, no orders given, roads blocked up, etc.," which was all true, but his assertion to Mary Ellen that he "saved the day" was hardly accurate. He restored order to his disorganized forces and arranged them to meet an enemy attack in the morning, but since the Confederates were fighting a rearguard action, no day needed to be saved. "I shall run the risk of at least holding them in check here while I resume the original plan," he assured Stanton, meaning he would hold at Williamsburg while the flanking column went up the York River and cut off the Rebels.[29]

The reembarkation of Franklin's division was not completed until May 6. The division steamed up the York River and disembarked that night at Eltham's Landing, near the junction of the York with the Pamunkey River. The Confederates were not surprised, and they attacked Franklin's beachhead the next day. Franklin, a cautious officer similar to McClellan, quickly abandoned any offensive ideas and reported back, "I congratulate myself that we have maintained our position." The flanking movement failed to achieve any important results, and the rest of the army remained mired in mud at Williamsburg, short on supplies and licking its wounds from the May 5 battle. Peter Michie, one of McClellan's biographers, concluded that the Confederates had achieved their objectives while the Federals had not. They had "evacuated their Yorktown lines with the loss of some heavy artillery and worthless impedimenta, had with a greatly inferior force held in check five divisions of the Union army for an entire day, inflicting on them greater loss than they themselves had sustained, and had succeeded in getting their stalled trains off in safety to continue their retreat unmolested. The honors of war were clearly theirs. Excuses and explanations, however abundant and conclusive, can not affect the fact of their superior generalship."[30]

Yet despite the failures of the flanking movement and the overland pursuit to damage the Rebels, in the days following the evacuation of Yorktown and the Battle of Williamsburg the general situation brightened. On May 9 the Confederates began to evacuate Norfolk and Portsmouth, and two days later the crew of the C.S.S. *Virginia* scuttled the vessel. Johnston's army retreated to within 5 miles of Richmond. The Army of the Potomac slowly followed him, their movements hampered by frequent rains that slowed them to a crawl and further strained the army's logistical support. As his army inched its way forward, McClellan renewed his requests for reinforcements. He had nearly 100,000 men with him on the Peninsula, but he warned Stanton that the coming battle would be a "life and death contest . . . Those who entertain the opinion that the Rebels will abandon Richmond without a struggle, are, in my judgment, badly advised, and do not comprehend their situation, which is one requiring desperate measures."[31]

The administration responded, and on May 17 ordered the balance of McDowell's 1st Corps to advance from Fredericksburg to the Pamunkey River. A day later they granted McClellan permission to create two new provisional army corps, due to his complaints about the performance of the other corps' commanders at Williamsburg. He used this authority to create the 5th and 6th Corps, to which he assigned his favorite generals, Fitz John Porter and William B. Franklin. On May 20 the army began to cross the Chickahominy River, the last great natural barrier before Richmond. McClellan selected White House Landing, on the Pamunkey, as his supply base, largely because the Richmond and York River Railroad ran from the landing to Richmond, and he needed the railroad to haul supplies and bring up the heavy guns he required for a siege of Richmond. But to cover the supply line to White House Landing and reach out to make a connection with McDowell's expected approach, it was necessary to hold part of the army north of the Chickahominy River, which meant that this sluggish stream split the army. Then McClellan fell ill with dysentery in late

May, and Major General Thomas J. "Stonewall" Jackson erupted in the Shenandoah Valley. On May 23 Jackson defeated Banks's small army at Front Royal. Two days later he whipped Banks at Winchester and churned northward down the Valley. This alarmed the president, and he suspended McDowell's advance from Fredericksburg. Rain fell on the Peninsula on the 29th, then heavy rains occurred on the 30th, causing the Chickahominy to swell over its banks, washing out bridges and threatening to isolate the two separate wings of the army. A day later, on May 31, Joe Johnston suddenly struck at McClellan's exposed left wing, which had advanced to within 10 miles of Richmond at Fair Oaks and Seven Pines.

The result was the two-day Battle of Seven Pines. Johnston's plan was sound, but its execution was awful, and the Confederates were unable to bring their superior numbers to bear on the battlefield. McClellan lay sick in bed most of the time and played a relatively minor role in the battle. He ordered up Sumner's 2nd Corps as reinforcements, which proved crucial; visited with the 3rd Corps commander, Major General Samuel Heintzelman, who directed most of the May 31 fighting by the Federals; and monitored reports of the battle as they came in, but he was too ill to do more. The army lost ground on the 31st, but on June 1 they repulsed Johnston's attacks and even recovered most of the lost ground, but no more. The two days of fighting cost 5,031 Union and 6,134 Confederate casualties. One of the latter was Joe Johnston, who was seriously wounded on the evening of May 31. Jefferson Davis named Robert E. Lee as his replacement. McClellan did not hold a high opinion of Lee as a general. Back in April, when McClellan received a report that Lee was in overall command of the Confederate forces opposing him, with Johnston serving as one of his subordinates (Lee actually was only Davis's military advisor at the time), he wrote to the president, stating that "I prefer Lee to Johnston," as "the former is *too* cautious & weak under grave responsibility—personally brave & energetic to a fault, he yet is wanting in moral firmness when pressed by heavy responsibility & is likely to be timid & irresolute in action." He would learn soon enough how wrong his judgment of Lee was.[32]

On May 21 McClellan related to his friend, General Ambrose Burnside, that "I feel very proud of Yorktown; it and Manassas will be my brightest chaptlets in history; for I know that I accomplished everything in both places by pure military skill. I am very proud and grateful to God that he allowed me to purchase such great success at so trifling a loss of life." This is illuminating in understanding McClellan's view of making war. He favored a methodical style of warfare over closing with the enemy and slugging it out. He sought to minimize casualties and carefully control his forces so as to ensure success, which was in keeping with his political view of the war. The less blood spilled, the easier the reunification of the country would be. Since he believed his army was consistently outnumbered, McClellan used fieldworks and the Union's superiority in modern heavy artillery to overwhelm the enemy or force their retreat. It is not surprising that he counted Manassas and Yorktown as his brightest successes. In both instances he believed that he had forced the enemy to evacuate powerful defensive positions at a trifling cost in men. Yet, while he might congratulate himself that he had gained ground at a small human price, this positional strategy had done relatively little damage to the Confederates, nor had it worked all that well. At Manassas and Yorktown, and then at Williamsburg and Seven Pines, the enemy stole the initiative. In the first two instances the Confederates escaped unscathed, and their withdrawal caught McClellan by surprise. While he might have felt proud of Yorktown, the product of a month's work in digging entrenchments and hauling up and emplacing heavy artillery to blast the enemy to pieces proved to be a spectacular fizzle. Johnston's army marched away undamaged, giving up a position that strategically was not critical to the Confederates. McClellan did not anticipate the rearguard action at Williamsburg, and Johnston's attack at Seven Pines also took him by surprise. In short, McClellan behaved predictably, which enabled the enemy to seize the initiative, and his army suffered from poor reconnaissance and faulty intelligence work, which explained the surprises. Joe Johnston, a soldier nearly as cautious as McClellan, had not exploited these defects, but a more enterprising commander now led the Army of Northern Virginia.[33]

Following Seven Pines, McClellan resumed his complaint that his army was too small for the coming decisive battle he anticipated would be fought before the gates of Richmond. The day after Seven Pines, he boasted to Stanton that "the morale of my troops is now such that I can venture much & do not care for odds against me." But two days later he wrote to Lincoln that "I have to be very cautious now," because of his losses in the battle. Despite the contradiction of such statements, Lincoln and Stanton reinforced him with all the troops they felt could be safely spared. They placed Fortress Monroe under his orders, and McClellan promptly ordered up nine regiments from there as reinforcements. On June 6 McCall's division of McDowell's corps was ordered to the Peninsula, and Stanton found seven other regiments in Washington and Baltimore to send to McClellan. In all, these amounted to two large divisions of reinforcements, nearly 20,000 men, more than making good the losses of Seven Pines. On June 8 Stanton sent orders recalling the balance of McDowell's corps from a futile mission to capture Stonewall Jackson in the Valley, sending them back to Fredericksburg and then on to operate in the direction of Richmond while still covering the capital. McClellan was thankful for the reinforcements. "I am glad to learn that you are pressing forward reinforcements so vigorously," he wrote to Stanton on June 7. "I shall be in perfect readiness to move forward to take Richmond the moment that McCall reaches here & the ground will admit the passage of artillery."[34]

Rain again hindered the planned advance. "I am quite checked by it," McClellan wrote to his wife. "First the Chickahominy is so swollen & the valley so covered with water that I cannot establish safe communication over it—then again the ground is so muddy that we cannot use our artillery—the guns sink up to their axle trees." But McClellan's conviction that he was heavily outnumbered also infused caution into every movement the army made. He wrote to the president on June 20, stating that "by tomorrow night the defensive works covering our position on this side of the Chickahominy should be completed. I am forced to this by my inferiority in numbers so that I may bring the greatest possible numbers into action & secure the Army against the consequences of unforeseen disaster." Two days later he confided to his wife that "the rascals are very strong & outnumber me very considerably—they are so well intrenched also & have all the advantages of position—so I must be prudent." Between June 12 and June 15, while McClellan complained about the abysmal weather, a Confederate cavalry force under General James E. B. "Jeb" Stuart rode completely around the army. McClellan paid little attention to the raid and failed to divine its purpose, which was to determine if the Federal right flank was vulnerable and if their main supply line was the York River Railroad. Stuart confirmed that both were true. The day after Stuart's raid ended, Lee ordered Stonewall Jackson to quietly move most of his small army to the Peninsula. Throughout the campaign Lee had not failed to take McClellan's measure as a general, and he understood the strategy the Federals would employ. "McClellan will make this a battle of posts," he wrote. "He will take position from position, under cover of heavy guns, & we cannot get at him without storming his works, which with our new troops is extremely hazardous." Lee intended to steal the initiative and strike before McClellan could complete his preparations, while the Federal army straddled the Chickahominy River.[35]

McClellan's first warning of Jackson's approach came on June 24, via a deserter who related that Jackson and 15 brigades were at Gordonsville, Virginia, on June 21 and were moving to attack the army's right and rear. McClellan passed the report along to Stanton, asking him for the latest information from the War Department on Jackson's whereabouts. But he did not cancel a planned advance on the 3rd Corps' front, set for June 25, to seize Confederate positions along the Williamsburg Road just west of Seven Pines.[36]

Sharp fighting ensued that sputtered on all day. The Federals only achieved small gains, but McClellan was satisfied. Then, toward the end of the action, he received a telegram from Porter, who reported that a contraband (an escaped slave) had come into his lines with a report that he had seen a "large portion" of General Beauregard's army in Richmond. He had also heard that the Rebels had 200,000 in the Richmond area and that Jackson was moving to attack the army's rear. McClellan's composure was shaken. He returned to his headquarters and telegraphed Stanton with the news from Porter. "I shall have to contend against vastly superior odds if these reports be true," he wrote. Later that evening McClellan telegraphed Stanton again. "The information I received on this side tends to confirm the impression that Jackson will soon attack our right and rear," he wrote. With a flourish of the melodramatic, he continued:

> I regret my great inferiority in numbers but feel that I am in no way responsible for it as I have not failed to represent repeatedly the necessity of reinforcements, that this was the decisive point, & that all the available means of the Govt should be concentrated here. I will do all that a General can do with the splendid Army I have the honor to command & if it is destroyed by overwhelming numbers can at least die with it & share its fate. But if the result of the action which will probably occur tomorrow or within a short time is a disaster the responsibility cannot be thrown on my shoulders—it must rest where it belongs.

This bizarre outburst of self-pity and finger pointing on the eve of what portended to be a great battle surely shook what little confidence Stanton retained in McClellan and raised a question regarding the general's emotional stability. A second telegram sent nearly five hours later, at 10:40 p.m., did nothing to reassure Stanton about McClellan's state of mind. "Every possible precaution is being taken," McClellan wrote. "If I had another good division I could laugh at Jackson." In a span of just over four hours McClellan went from envisioning defeat and destruction due to the enemy's overwhelming numbers to suggesting that the addition of a single division would enable him to laugh at the enemy.[37] "Every possible precaution" did not include reinforcing Porter's 5th Corps, the only corps north of the Chickahominy River and the certain target of Jackson's advance, because with such supposedly vast numbers McClellan imagined the enemy possessed the manpower to strike all along his line. The corps commanders south of the Chickahominy were ordered to receive the anticipated enemy attack in their entrenchments. Thus the entire army went into a defensive posture, fully surrendering the initiative and enabling Lee to execute his plans at will.[38]

It was as well for Lee that McClellan thought only of defense, for the first day of Lee's offensive against the Army of the Potomac went badly. Poorly coordinated attacks against Porter's corps—in position behind Beaver Dam Creek, just east of Mechanicsville—were easily repulsed with heavy losses to the attacking Confederates. McClellan initially effused euphorically. "Victory of today complete and against great odds. I almost begin to think we are invincible," he wired to Stanton. But then he learned that the forces repulsed that day were not Jackson's. He and Porter concluded that the 5th Corps should be withdrawn from its exposed position to a more secure one. McClellan's engineers selected a powerful position north of the Chickahominy River, near the grist-mill of Dr. William G. Gaines and behind Boatswain's Swamp.

The position covered four military bridges spanning the Chickahominy. The operations on the 26th had convinced McClellan of the need to transfer his base of operations from White House Landing to the James River. The enemy maneuvering north of the Chickahominy would surely sever his communications with White House Landing, cutting off the army's supplies. He ordered the quartermaster at White House to prepare the depot for destruction and forward to the army all the supplies that the rail line and wagons could carry. The rest could be moved by water to a new depot to be established on the James River. Headquarters were ordered to break camp and prepare for immediate movement. Engineers were dispatched to determine crossing points through the White Oak Swamp to the army's rear. In McClellan's mind, retaining Porter's 5th Corps north of the Chickahominy River was necessary "in order to cover the withdrawal of the trains and heavy guns, and to give time for the arrangements to secure the adoption of the James River as our line of supplies in lieu of the Pamunkey." Porter knew none of this. He operated under the assumption that by making a stand north of the Chickahominy, his 5th Corps might "so cripple our opponents as to make the capture of Richmond by the main body under McClellan, the result of any sacrifice or suffering on the part of the troops or myself."[39]

Since he believed the enemy capable of attacking in force at any point along his front, McClellan only made limited arrangements to support Porter if he were attacked on the 27th. He ordered Franklin to send one of his 6th Corps' divisions as reinforcements and issued a circular to the corps commanders south of the river asking how many troops they could spare from their front to reinforce Porter if necessary. But on the morning of 27th, as the 6th Corps' division was crossing the river to Porter's position, McClellan reconsidered his decision of the night before and ordered them back to the south bank. Enemy activity south of the river seemed to herald a potential attack on this front. Waffling between his belief that the enemy might still attack south of the river and Porter's request for an additional division, McClellan waited for events to dictate where Franklin's troops would be needed most.[40]

The Battle of Gaines' Mill began in the early afternoon of June 27. Lee concentrated over 60,000 men to crush Porter, who faced Lee's onslaught with just 27,000. The battle raged furiously all day, but due to an oddity in the acoustics, caused by the weather, the fighting could not be heard at McClellan's headquarters. Expecting attacks all across his army's front, the general remained at his headquarters, where he might react to an emergency at any point. At 2 p.m. Porter requested that Franklin's 6th Corps division reinforce him, and McClellan promptly set the unit in motion. Although he was less than 2 miles from Porter's headquarters, McClellan did not venture over to see for himself how the battle went. He relied on Porter's telegrams, which, as the day progressed, assumed a more ominous tone. Around 5 p.m. Porter telegraphed that he was very hard pressed, had committed every regiment to the fight, and expressed the fear that "I shall be driven from my position." Rather than order troops from the five corps south of the river to Porter's aid, McClellan asked his corps commanders what they could safely spare without endangering their defensive front. Sumner sent two 2nd Corps brigades, but they arrived too late to stave off defeat. At 8 p.m., with the battle still raging across the river, McClellan prepped Stanton for the potential of bad news, wiring the secretary that the army was being attacked by "greatly superior numbers in all directions" and, although they were holding their own, that "I may be forced to give up my position during the night, but will not if it is possible to avoid it." By late that evening Porter was retreating to the south bank of the Chickahominy. McClellan believed a retreat to the James River was now imperative, and at 10:30 p.m. he wired the Navy that "we have met a severe repulse to day having been attacked by vastly superior numbers, and I am obliged to fall back between the Chickahominy and the James River," noting that he would need their support on the James to help cover the withdrawal. Losses for the day were 6,836 Federals and 7,993 Confederates.[41]

Having slept little in two days, McClellan's nerves were on edge. Self-pity, anger, and his belief that he was outnumbered and had not been sustained by the administration boiled over late that night as he composed a telegram for Stanton about the outcome of the day's fighting. Porter was "overwhelmed by vastly superior numbers," McClellan maintained. It was "the most desperate battle of the war." Yet despite the enemy's vast numbers, McClellan claimed that if he had 20,000 or even 10,000 fresh troops "to use tomorrow I could take Richmond." The battle had been lost "because my force was too small. I again repeat that I am not responsible for this & I say it with the earnestness of a General who feels in his heart the loss of every brave man who has been needlessly sacrificed today. I still hope to retrieve our fortunes, but to do this the Govt must view the matter in the same earnest light that I do—you must send me very large reinforcements, & send them at once." McClellan accepted no responsibility for Porter's defeat. He bluntly advised Stanton that it occurred because "the Govt has not sustained this Army." He saved his angriest outburst for the final sentence: "If I save this Army not I tell you plainly that I owe no thanks to you or any other persons in Washington—you have done your best to sacrifice this Army." Unknown to McClellan, this insubordinate sentence so appalled the head of the War Department's telegraph office that he deleted it and had the dispatch recopied before it went to Stanton.[42] The grand campaign to take Richmond was over. McClellan now thought only of saving his army.

McClellan later described the retreat after Gaines' Mill as a change of base, from White House Landing, on the Chickahominy River, to Harrison's Landing, on the James River. A change of base is a planned movement, while a retreat is a movement an army is forced to undertake. Despite McClellan's rephrasing, the Army of the Potomac's movement to the James was a retreat in every sense of the word. Nearly 2,500 wounded and sick were left behind, along with their medical attendants. Vast quantities of supplies, camp equipment, and ammunition, stockpiled for the advance on Richmond, could not be transported and had to be destroyed or abandoned to the Rebels.[43]

Had Lee known McClellan planned to retreat to the James River, he might have administered a decisive defeat to the Army of the Potomac, but he initially thought that the Federals would fight to reopen their communications with their supply base at White House Landing. Therefore Lee kept the main body of his army north of the Chickahominy River during most of the 28th. The delay in ascertaining that the Federals were retreating to the James enabled McClellan to get nearly a 24-hour head start. It was good thing, for the army's 4,000 wagons and 2,500 beef cattle had only a single road and bridge to follow across White Oak Swamp, a process that took the entire day. On June 29, Lee caught up with the rear of the army and a sharp action ensued at Savage's Station. While the rear engaged the enemy, McClellan busied himself with supervising the passage of his trains across White Oak Swamp, important, to be sure, but a duty more appropriate to a staff officer than the commanding general. Meanwhile, his corps commanders fought without direction from headquarters, which was too far from the action to impact the battle. They managed well enough to deflect the Confederate attacks, and the retreat continued.[44]

Now fully aware of the Army of the Potomac's whereabouts and intentions, Lee planned a concentration of his army on June 30 at Glendale, a crossroads through which the entire Union army would have to pass to reach the James. If he could affect his concentration and seize the crossroads, the Federal army would most likely be destroyed. As one of McClellan's early biographers, Peter Michie, observed, McClellan had to be aware that Lee would strike him at Glendale and the White Oak Swamp bridge on June 30, "and that the crisis of the retreat had arrived." But McClellan was 5 miles away, at Haxall's Landing on the James River, examining the approaches to nearby Malvern Hill, the key terrain covering the landing. At 4 p.m., while his men literally fought to save the army, he boarded the gunboat *Galena* and steamed upriver to shell an enemy column sighted west of Malvern Hill. That evening he enjoyed "a good dinner with some good wine" aboard the gunboat. He again failed to appoint anyone to direct the defense of Glendale and left his corps commanders without any semblance of a plan. According to the 3rd Corps' commander, General Samuel Heintzelman, the three corps commanders who had men engaged in the battle "fought their troops entirely according to their own ideas." In bitter fighting they held off the Confederate attacks, but it was a near-run thing. Only the courage of the Union soldiers and the failure of Lee's divisions to properly coordinate their attacks averted a catastrophe. McClellan's behavior that day is indefensible. "This is the first time we ever had reason to believe that the highest and first duty of a general, on the day of battle, was separating himself from his army, to reconnoiter a place of retreat," wrote his chief engineer, John G. Barnard. Stephen Sears believed that McClellan "had lost the courage to command," a damning statement but, in light of the evidence, an accurate one.[45]

The army retreated again during the night to the positions McClellan had selected for it on Malvern Hill. The troops were exhausted from the daytime fighting and nighttime marches, and McClellan believed that they were "in no condition to fight without 24 hours rest." Yet, after riding the front lines to inspect his army's positions, he again climbed aboard the *Galena*, this time to personally inspect Harrison's Landing, where he intended to withdraw the army during the night of July 1 if Lee did not attack. As he had during the retreat from Gaines' Mill and at Glendale, McClellan chose to perform the duties of a staff officer rather than that of the army's commander. Fortunately, Lee was unable to assemble his troops for an attack on the Malvern Hill position until late afternoon. By this time McClellan had returned to the army and met with Porter, whose corps held the left of the line. Porter assured McClellan that he could manage any attack on his front and recommended that the army's commander position himself on the right of the line, which protected the army's line of retreat. Lee attacked late that afternoon on Porter's front and was easily repulsed, with the Confederates sustaining severe losses. Throughout the action McClellan remained content to monitor the battle from his position on the right, which was distant enough from the fighting that the musketry firing could not be heard. From Williamsburg to Seven Pines and through the Seven Days (the six battles between June 25 and July 1), McClellan's presence—and therefore his impact—on the battlefield had been largely insignificant. Not once had he been present at the critical moment of any of the battles on which his campaign turned. By the end of the Seven Days he thought not in terms of whipping the enemy but of saving his army from certain destruction from the Rebel masses he imagined they had concentrated against him. In McClellan's mind, to save the army was a victory. So despite the repulse of Lee's attacks at Malvern Hill, and Porter's assurance that he could hold the hill if attacked again, McClellan ordered a retreat during the night to Harrison's Landing.[46]

"I have succeeded in getting this Army to this place on the banks of the James River," McClellan wrote to the president at 5:30 p.m. on July 2. "I have lost but one gun which had to be abandoned last night because it broke down." And, he assured Lincoln, "I have not yielded an inch of ground unnecessarily but have retired to prevent the superior force of the Enemy from cutting me off—and to take a different base of operations." In truth, the army had lost an enormous quantity of material, hundreds of stragglers, and a good bit of its confidence in George McClellan. He remained popular with much of the rank

and file—who accepted without question reports that they faced overwhelming enemy numbers—but his failures as a general were apparent to those of
a fighting bent. General Philip Kearny, a division commander and one of the
army's most aggressive leaders, sensed a "want of nerve" in McClellan and complained on July 10 from the army's camps at Harrison's Landing that "McClellan's
want of Generalship, or treason, has gotten us into a place, where we are completely boxed up." Francis Barlow, a tough volunteer colonel in Sumner's 2nd
Corps, was scathing in his criticism. "McClellan issues flaming addresses though
everyone in the army knows he was outwitted + has lost confidence in him. His
statements that he lost no materials of war or ammunition are simply false . . .
We are surprised to learn from the New York papers that we gained a great victory. We thought here that we had made a disastrous retreat leaving all our
dead + wounded + prisoners + material + munitions of war in the hands of the
enemy." Two days later Barlow wrote home, "I have not seen one officer or man
(+ I have talked with many) who has any confidence left in him. The stories of
his being everywhere among the men in the fights are all untrue. I fought in
three divisions at the most critical times + in the hardest fights + never saw him
but once + then not under fire. I have found no one else who saw him. I hope
McClellan will be removed."[47]

In McClellan's mind his Peninsula Campaign had failed, although he would
never characterize the retreat to Harrison's Landing as a failure or a defeat. In
his version victory was impossible, because the enemy possessed overwhelming
numbers and the administration had not sustained him. "It is now clear beyond
a doubt that 20,000 more men would have given us a glorious victory," he noted
to General John Dix on June 29, after Gaines' Mill. "I for one can never forget
nor forgive the selfish men who have caused the lives of so many gallant men to
be sacrificed." He wrote to his wife the day before, "I thank my friends in Washn
for our repulse." Although Lincoln had upset his initial plans by withholding
McDowell's corps, over the course of the campaign the president and Stanton
had worked vigorously to strengthen the Army of the Potomac, first by sending
Franklin's division, then McCall's, and enough individual regiments to constitute a third division. In sum they were nearly the size of McDowell's corps. But
no matter how many troops Lincoln and Stanton sent, McClellan claimed that
there were never enough men. With 20,000 more men he would have won at
Gaines' Mill. A day before, he wrote to Stanton that with only 10,000 more men
he would take Richmond. On June 25 a single division would have enabled him
"to laugh" at Jackson.[48]

Throughout the campaign, from Yorktown to the Seven Days, McClellan
possessed the resources and the manpower to succeed. That he had not managed
this had little to do with the "selfish men" in Washington. The campaign's failure
to capture Richmond and defeat the Rebel army rested firmly on his shoulders.
The list of his failures is long: excessive caution, poor reconnaissance, miserable

intelligence that produced absurd enemy strength figures, and failure to seize opportunities at critical moments in the campaign. In every important engagement he surrendered the initiative to the enemy. At Seven Pines and during the Seven Days his army possessed an edge in overall manpower, yet the Confederates succeeded in massing superior numbers at the point of attack on both occasions. At Manassas, Yorktown, Williamsburg, and Seven Pines, the enemy had surprised him. Tactically, he was a nonfactor in each battle his army fought, and at two critical moments in the retreat to Harrison's Landing from Gaines' Mill he abandoned the army and left his corps commanders to fend for themselves. His emotional collapse after Gaines' Mill reflected a lack of the mental toughness and psychological stability necessary for high command in the field. Secretary of the Navy Gideon Welles offered an apt summary of the general in his diary when he noted, "To attack or advance with energy and power is not in him . . . He likes show, parade, and power . . . Wishes to outgeneral the rebels, but not to kill and destroy them."[49]

On July 3 McClellan wrote to Stanton and asked for reinforcements, "rather much over than much less than 100,000 men." Lincoln responded to this message the next day, saying that the government was doing everything it could to reinforce the army, but that the troops that could be scraped together at best numbered only about 25,000 men. "To reinforce you so as to enable you to resume the offensive within a month, or even six weeks is impossible," he stated. This, of course, presumed that the Confederate army in McClellan's front was as large as the general reported. Lincoln decided that a visit to the army was in order. He arrived at Harrison's Landing on July 8, reviewed the army, and met with McClellan on board the steamer *Ariel*, where the general handed him a letter he had completed the day before and about which he wrote to his wife, "if he [Lincoln] acts upon it the country will be saved." It was not a plan for resuming the offensive against Richmond; rather, it was a document representing McClellan's views on the conduct of the war. Lincoln's biographer, David Donald, observed that the letter "was couched in respectful language, and there was nothing insubordinate about it." The rebellion, McClellan wrote, had "assumed the character of a War," and it was necessary that "the Government must determine upon a civil and military policy." It was this policy on which McClellan sought to comment. He had undoubtedly followed the recent debate in Congress on the Second Confiscation Act, which would define those supporting or participating in the rebellion as traitors, ordering confiscation of their property and the freeing of their slaves. To McClellan this was madness, certain to harden Southern resolve and resistance and prolong the war. "It should not be a War looking to the subjugation of the people of any state," he wrote to Lincoln. "Neither confiscation of property, political executions of persons, territorial organization of states, or forcible abolition of slavery should be contemplated for a moment." He devoted an entire paragraph of his letter to the handling of slavery. "Military power should not be allowed to interfere with the relations of servitude," he advised. Although he acknowledged that military necessity would allow the government to execute the compensated emancipation of slaves in a particular state, he warned that "a declaration of radical views, especially upon slavery, will rapidly disintegrate our present armies." He concluded the letter by recommending that the position of commander-in-chief of the army be re-created. "I do not ask for that place myself. I am willing to serve you in such position as you may assign me and I will do so as faithfully as ever subordinate served superior." This last sentence would be put to the test in the coming weeks.[50]

Lincoln read the letter, thanked McClellan for it, placed it in his pocket, and said no more. Its contents were unsurprising to him and adhered to the conservative Northern Democrats' position on how the war should be prosecuted. But as David Donald notes, it was a policy that had been pursued for over a year, "and Lincoln was convinced that it had failed. He was ready to move on." McClellan sensed something when the president inquired of him and his corps commanders whether the army could be safely removed from the Peninsula, but he failed to fully understand the impending change Lincoln was contemplating. "I do not know to what extent he has profited by his visit," McClellan wrote to Mary Ellen the next day. "Not much I fear, for he really seems quite incapable of rising to the height of the merits of the question & the magnitude of the crisis."[51]

But Lincoln had seen what he needed to. Two days later he named Major General Henry W. Halleck as general-in-chief. Halleck's appointment, wrote David Donald, "signaled a repudiation of McClellan, and of McClellan's view of the war." The news was not made public until July 20, but McClellan suspected the change, for he wrote to his wife on July 18 that he thought Lincoln would make Halleck commander-in-chief "& that the first pretext will be seized upon to supersede me in command of this army." Despite his promise to the president to serve faithfully in any position assigned, McClellan revealed that this was conditional. If Halleck were made commander-in-chief, "I will remain in command of this army as long as they will allow me to, provided the army is in danger & likely to play an active part . . . I am tired of being dependent on men I despise from the bottom of my heart. I cannot express to you the infinite contempt I feel for these people." When Halleck's appointment was confirmed, McClellan confided to his wife that "it is grating to have to serve under the orders of a man whom I know by experience to be my inferior," and declared that "I cannot remain permanently in the army after this slight."[52]

Halleck's appointment was not the only personnel decision by the administration that grated on McClellan. He found little to like in John Pope, the major general that Lincoln summoned to the east in late June to organize the forces that had been chasing Jackson into a cohesive army. Pope had made something of a name for himself back in April with a skillfully executed operation that seized New Madrid and Island No. 10, which opened the Mississippi River through Tennessee and Missouri. He was West Point trained, aggressive, and a Republican. The combination made him appealing to Lincoln and Stanton. Pope talked a good game and he impressed the Republicans, who favored taking the gloves off against the Confederates. He spoke before the House of Representatives on June 25, denouncing slavery and deriding McClellan's estimates of the Confederate strength in front of Richmond. On July 8 Pope appeared before the Committee on the Conduct of the War, ostensibly to discuss the strategy his newly formed Army of Virginia would pursue, but it turned into a sharp critique of McClellan's Peninsula Campaign. All this could not have gone unnoticed by McClellan, but he was amiable in his first communication with the westerner. He thanked Pope for "your cordial offer of support" and encouraged regular communication between the two. But relations between them soured quickly.[53]

Pope, it turned out, was cut from the same cloth as McClellan when it came to being duplicitous. Far from seeking to cooperate with and support the Army of the Potomac and its commander, during his testimony Pope recommended to the Committee that McClellan's army should be withdrawn from the Peninsula and combined with his army to advance on Richmond by the overland route. And to Secretary of the Treasury Salomon P. Chase, and perhaps to Lincoln and Stanton as well, he recommended that McClellan should be relieved, due to his "incompetency and indisposition to active movements." On July 14, in an effort to inspire his newly formed army, Pope issued an address to the troops that came off as bombastic and insulting to the Army of the Potomac and its commander. "Let us understand each other," it began. "I have come to you from the West where we have always seen the backs of our enemies . . . Meantime I desire you to dismiss from your minds certain phrases, which I am sorry to find so much in vogue amongst you. I hear constantly of 'taking strong positions and holding them,' of 'lines of retreat,' and of 'bases of supply.' Let us discard such ideas." The latter was a clear shot at the operations of the Army of the Potomac. McClellan made no public response, but to his wife he expressed delight over a report that Stonewall Jackson was moving against Pope. "I see that the Pope bubble is likely to be suddenly collapsed—Stonewall Jackson is after him, & the paltry young man who wanted to teach me the art of war will in less than a week either be in full retreat or badly whipped. He will begin to learn the value of 'entrenchments, lines of communications & of retreat, bases of supply, etc.'— they will learn bye & bye." What McClellan did not know was that Stanton had helped Pope with the contents of the address and Lincoln had approved it.[54]

The narrowly focused war that George McClellan believed the United States should fight was spinning out of control that July. His failure on the Peninsula did not end his hope for a limited war, but it was increasingly unlikely that the country would follow such a course. Pope issued a series of general orders to his army over the course of the month, approved by the president, that permitted the army to lay a heavier hand on the civilian population than had been previously permitted. On July 17 Congress had passed the Second Confiscation Act, which heralded a harsher war against the Rebels, who were now to be treated as traitors whose property could be seized and whose slaves could be freed. Lincoln initially intended to veto the legislation as too severe, but after some modifications were made he signed it. Nonetheless, he included an unprecedented signing statement indicating his objections to the bill. The president had his own plans on the slavery issue, and he kept them close to his chest.

Lincoln had previously submitted a plan for gradual, compensated emancipation in their states to the border states' representatives in Congress, but they rejected it. Lincoln had hesitated in moving against slavery early in the war for fear that it would drive the border states into the Confederacy, that the Northern public was not ready for it, and that a legal challenge was certain to come from a conservative Supreme Court, headed by Chief Justice Roger B. Taney. But his thinking changed as the war took its course, and in late June he began work on a proclamation that would emancipate the slaves in the states in rebellion as a military measure, invoking his power as commander-in-chief to do so. On July 22 he assembled his cabinet and read them a first draft of his proposed Emancipation Proclamation. Reactions were mixed, but Secretary of State William Seward argued strongly against issuing the proclamation after the military defeat on the Peninsula. He thought it would be viewed at home and abroad "as the last measure of an exhausted government, a cry for help." Lincoln agreed. Emancipation would wait for a victory on the battlefield.[55]

Henry Halleck arrived in Washington on July 23 and left for Harrison's Landing the next day to meet with McClellan. Before departing, Halleck met with the president, who told him that he could reinforce McClellan with 20,000 men. If these were not sufficient for the army to resume the offensive, then Halleck was authorized to order the Army of the Potomac from the Peninsula, a decision that Lincoln clearly favored. The president also told Halleck that he "was satisfied that McClellan would not fight" and that Halleck could retain him in command or remove him at his own discretion. Halleck was a cerebral fellow. West Point trained and with a Phi Beta Kappa from Union College to his credit, he had won the nickname "Brains" (and the less flattering appellation "Wooden Head") in the prewar U.S. army. But it was his translation of Baron Von Jomini's four-volume treatise on war and his own *Elements of Military Art and Science* that won him notice. Winfield Scott had wanted Halleck, not McClellan, to succeed him as general-in-chief.

As a field commander, Halleck exceeded McClellan's caution. Following the Battle of Shiloh, it took him 26 days to move his army the 24 miles to Corinth, Mississippi. Halleck was an advocate of concentration of force, and the separation of Pope's and McClellan's armies disturbed him. If McClellan's reports of enemy strength were true, then the Union army was defying the basic principles of warfare and handing the enemy a wonderful opportunity to defeat the Federal forces in detail. But while Halleck harbored doubts about McClellan as a strategist, he respected his former commander and felt the embarrassment of a former subordinate whom circumstance had placed in the position of the superior officer.[56]

He and McClellan met at Harrison's Landing on July 25. McClellan proposed a plan to move the army to the south bank of the James River and then advance on Petersburg and enemy communications with Richmond. Halleck considered this too risky an operation, as it increased, rather than decreased, the distance between Federal forces in the Virginia theater, with the massive enemy force still holding the central position. He told McClellan that the army should be withdrawn and combined with Pope's army in northern Virginia, where it could cover the capital and resume an overland advance on Richmond, unless McClellan thought he could resume the offensive against Richmond from his current position with the 20,000 reinforcements the government could provide. This would give McClellan 110,000 men. McClellan repeated his estimate that the enemy in his front numbered 200,000 but agreed that he was "willing to try it" with the offered reinforcements.[57]

On July 26, McClellan wrote to Halleck that in the day since the general-in-chief had left, McClellan had met with many recently exchanged sick, wounded, and prisoners who had observed activity behind Confederate lines, and they reported enemy reinforcements "pouring into Richmond." This altered the circumstances in which he had agreed to renew the advance on Richmond with the 20,000 reinforcements promised by Halleck. Now McClellan asked that all of Burnside's 9th Corps, on the North Carolina coast, and General David Hunter's command, then operating along the South Carolina coast, reinforce him. Burnside's and Hunter's combined commands numbered 35,000. McClellan also requested an additional 15,000 to 20,000 men "from the West to reinforce me temporarily. They can return the moment we gain Richmond." Apart from the fact that it would take weeks to move 15,000–20,000 troops from the west to the Peninsula, further delaying offensive operations against Richmond, this was a deal breaker. When Halleck did not immediately respond to the reinforcement request, McClellan sensed that his enemies in Washington were at work. "I have nothing as yet from Washn, & begin to believe that they intend & hope that I & my army may melt away under the hot sun," he wrote to his wife on the 29th. The silence from Halleck aroused McClellan's ire toward the president and his administration. "I am confident that he would relieve me tomorrow if he dared do so," he fumed to Mary Ellen. "His cowardice alone prevents it. I can never regard him with other feelings than those of thorough contempt—for his mind, heart, and morality." To Samuel Barlow he expressed the opinion that "I do not believe there is one honest man among them & I know what I say—I fear none of them wish to save the Union." He fantasized to Mary Ellen that "if they leave me here neglected much longer I shall feel like taking my rather large military family to Washn to seek an explanation of their course."[58]

Halleck's answer came on August 3: "It is determined to withdraw your army from the Peninsula to Acquia Creek." McClellan was stunned. He wired Halleck that the orders "cause me the greatest pain I have ever experienced, for I am convinced that the order to withdraw this Army to Acquia Creek will prove disastrous in the extreme to our cause—I fear it will be a fatal blow." He then proceeded to argue the logic of keeping the army on the Peninsula; it was only 25 miles from Richmond at Harrison's Landing, but it was 75 miles to Richmond from Aquia Creek. The army could not be withdrawn from Harrison's Landing, so it would need to march 70 miles to Fortress Monroe to reembark. Therefore, he argued, it would have to complete a 145-mile journey to come back to a point that the army in its current position could reach in two days. The logic was sound, but McClellan had compromised himself. All the empty promises for action, the constant demand for reinforcements, and the reports of overwhelming enemy numbers had undone him at last. And McClellan timidly let slip away the one opportunity that presented itself to alter the withdrawal orders. Halleck had advised him on July 30 that Pope had received reports that the enemy was moving out of Richmond and the force defending the capital was "very small." Six days later, on August 5, McClellan sent 17,000 men under General Joseph Hooker to Malvern Hill to probe the enemy defenses. Hooker easily occupied the position but Lee dispatched a strong force to meet the Federals. McClellan had made no preparations to support Hooker, and now he chose to avoid the risk of a battle. "Should we fight a general battle at Malvern it will be necessary to abandon the whole of our works here & run the risk of getting back here should the enemy prove too strong for us," he wrote to Hooker. The troops were withdrawn from Malvern Hill, and the last chance to avoid an overall withdrawal from the Peninsula was lost. Stephen Sears aptly summarized this final sputter of the campaign: "In the fumbling direction and obsessive caution and anticlimactic result, the Malvern Hill episode was a clear reflection, in miniature, of George McClellan's entire Peninsula campaign." It confirmed that McClellan was unlikely to accomplish anything meaningful if left on the Peninsula.[59]

McClellan commenced the withdrawal in a bad humor. "Halleck is turning out just like the rest of the herd," he complained to his wife. "The affair is rapidly developing itself, & I see more clearly every day their settled purpose to force me to resign." Of John Pope, with whom he would soon need to cooperate, or possibly command, he wrote, "I have a strong idea that Pope will be thrashed during the coming week—& very badly whipped he will be & ought to be—such a villain as he is ought to bring defeat upon any cause that employs him."

Halleck sought to sooth McClellan's fragile ego with a friendly August 7 message in which he assured the general that "it is my intention that you shall command all the troops in Virginia as soon as we can get them together." It was a promise that Lincoln probably knew nothing about and of which he would not have approved. With Halleck now lumped in with the rest of the "herd," McClellan doubted Halleck's sincerity, but advised his wife that he would "accept no less place" than as commander of the combined forces.[60]

The withdrawal from Harrison's Landing began slowly. Although McClellan intended to march the army to Fortress Monroe, Yorktown, and Newport News for embarkation, he needed first to remove his sick and wounded, and the accumulated supplies and other equipment. The limited wharf facilities at Harrison's Landing permitted only a few vessels at a time to dock, and some larger transport vessels drew too much water to reach the landing, so the process went slowly. The main body of the army did not get underway until August 14 but, once begun, the movement proceeded quickly and efficiently. Fitz John Porter's 5th Corps reached Newport News on August 18, and by the 20th the entire corps was on transports to Aquia Creek. They were followed by the 3rd Corps, who sailed to Alexandria, Virginia, and then were sent to the front by rail. By August 23 both the 2nd and the 6th Corps were ready to embark as soon as transports were available.[61]

Events elsewhere were moving swiftly. Pope had assumed a position behind the upper Rappahannock River, where he faced a buildup of Confederate forces. Lee first met Pope's threat in northern Virginia by dispatching Stonewall Jackson, with 14,000 men, to the rail junction at Gordonsville in mid-July. When McClellan failed to stir from his position at Harrison's Landing, Lee reinforced Jackson with A. P. Hill's large division, raising Jackson's force to nearly 30,000. On August 9 Jackson attacked and defeated two of Pope's divisions at Cedar Mountain, near Culpepper. Meanwhile, McClellan's hasty withdrawal from his Malvern Hill reconnaissance, combined with other intelligence, convinced Lee that the Army of the Potomac was to be withdrawn from the Peninsula. Its most likely destination was to reinforce Pope. He also learned that Ambrose Burnside's 9th Corps was en route for northern Virginia from the North Carolina coast. Once all these forces were concentrated, Lee would be heavily outnumbered. Characteristically, Lee sought to seize the initiative. It was imperative to defeat Pope before the Federals could concentrate their might. On August 13 he ordered James Longstreet, with over 25,000 men, to Gordonsville. Lee joined Longstreet there two days later, leaving behind only some 25,000 troops to watch McClellan and defend Richmond. It would be a race now to see whether the Federals could complete their concentration of superior numbers in northern Virginia or Lee could defeat them in detail first. Lee possessed two important advantages: unity of purpose and calculated daring; the Federals had one great disadvantage: a command structure beset by jealousy, distrust, and confusion.[62]

Henry Halleck viewed the aggressive Confederate movements in northern Virginia with alarm. If McClellan's estimates of Confederate strength in Virginia were accurate—and Halleck had no reason to doubt them—then Pope was in grave danger of being overwhelmed before he could be reinforced. On August 21 Halleck advised McClellan that Pope and Burnside (who was now at Falmouth, across from Fredericksburg) were "hard pushed, and require aid as rapidly as you can send it." He also asked that McClellan "come yourself as soon as you can." McClellan's reaction spoke to his self-absorbed view of the situation. "I believe I have triumphed!!" he exulted to his wife. "Now they are in trouble they seem to want the 'Quaker,' the 'procrastinator,' the 'coward' & the 'Traitor.'" Two days later, after seeing to it that Franklin's 6th Corps was embarked and that Sumner's 2nd Corps was waiting only for its transportation, McClellan climbed aboard the *City of Hudson* and sailed for Aquia Creek. What his position would be weighed heavily on his mind. While underway, he wrote to Mary Ellen that when he reached Aquia Creek he would telegraph Halleck for orders. "I take it for granted that my orders will be as disagreeable as it is possible to make them—unless Pope is beaten, in which case they may want me to save Washn again. Nothing but their fear will induce them to give me any command of importance or to treat me otherwise than with discourtesy."[63]

When McClellan reached Aquia Creek that night, he knew little of Pope's situation, and the only news he could learn from Burnside and Fitz John Porter, who met with him, was that Pope had abandoned the line of the Rappahannock and fallen back. On the afternoon of the 24th McClellan wired Halleck for information about Pope's plans and clarification on his own position. "Until I know what my command & position are to be, & whether you still intend to place me in the command indicated in your first letter to me, & orally through Genl Burnside at the Chickahominy I cannot decide where I can be of most use. If your determination is unchanged I ought to go to Alexandria at once. Please define my position & duties." Halleck dodged the question of command. He could see things more clearly now then when he first arrived in Washington and better understood the administration's mood toward McClellan. If he could sideline the general and bolster Pope's chances for success, the administration would quietly approve. As for Pope's status, Halleck telegraphed back to McClellan: "You ask me for information I cannot give. I do not know where General Pope is or the enemy in force is." This did not bode well for Union arms.[64]

At the front, Lee was moving rapidly and decisively. When an effort to turn Pope's left flank on the Rappahannock line failed, on August 25 Lee sent Stonewall Jackson, with 24,000 men, on a wide flanking march to circle around Pope's right and fall on his rear. Pope learned of the movement, misjudged it as a feint, and continued to hold his Rappahannock line, in the belief that this was Halleck's desire until the Army of the Potomac joined him. Jackson covered over 50 miles in 40 hours, and on the evening of August 26 he fell on Pope's communications on the Orange and Alexandria Railroad at Bristoe Station, then marched north and captured the massive Union supply depot at Manassas Junction.[65]

While Jackson severed Pope's communications, McClellan was en route by water for Alexandria, Virginia. Halleck reported that "very great irregularities are reported there," and he wanted McClellan to supervise the disembarkation of troops and their movement to Pope. McClellan landed at Alexandria late on the 26th. There were reports of an enemy cavalry raid that had burned the railroad bridge at Bull Run, but otherwise McClellan found himself "terribly ignorant of the state of affairs and somewhat anxious to know." If he knew little about the situation at the front, he felt some satisfaction that he knew the position of his own corps: Porter's 5th Corps and Heintzelman's 3rd Corps were on or near Pope's Rappahannock line, Sumner's 2nd Corps was arriving at Aquia Creek, and Franklin's 6th Corps was in position near Alexandria.

Meanwhile, rumors filtered in that something was amiss at Manassas Junction. "I can get no satisfactory information from the front," complained Halleck in a telegram to McClellan on the morning of the 27th. "There seems to have been great neglect and carelessness about Manassas. Franklin's corps should march in that direction as soon as possible." There was news from Fitz John Porter, received via Burnside, that a battle was imminent near Warrenton. McClellan contemplated this and concluded that should things go badly in the battle, Sumner's 2nd Corps would be without support at Aquia, so he suggested to Halleck that it would be prudent to bring his corps to Alexandria and mass it with Franklin's before advancing toward Manassas. The more McClellan pondered the situation, the more it aroused his concern. There was too little known about Pope's situation to risk sending Franklin forward alone. Halleck approved Sumner's transfer to Alexandria but repeated his orders for Franklin to march. A general battle was imminent. "Franklin's troops should move out by forced marches," he wired to McClellan.[66]

Then, in the early afternoon, McClellan learned that a New Jersey brigade of Franklin's corps that had been sent out that morning to Manassas Junction had been ambushed and roughly handled by an enemy force estimated at 5,000 and "receiving reinforcements every minute." This confirmed McClellan's misgivings about sending Franklin forward before he had his full complement of artillery and cavalry, which were still arriving from the Peninsula. "I think our policy now is to make these works perfectly safe, and mobilize a couple of corps as soon as possible but not to advance them until they can have their artillery and cavalry," he telegraphed to Halleck. Franklin remained where he was.[67]

That evening McClellan went up to visit Halleck in person, arriving around midnight. The late night meeting seems partly intentional, to avoid any possible encounter with Lincoln or Stanton. "I shall keep clear of the Presdt & Cabinet—endeavor to do what must be done with Halleck alone," he confided to his wife. Both men left the meeting with very different ideas of what they had decided. Halleck thought that he had made clear the "importance of pushing forward Franklin as early as possible" on the 28th, while McClellan believed they had agreed that Franklin would not march until his artillery and cavalry were ready.[68]

Halleck spent the 28th trading telegrams with McClellan in a futile effort to get the 6th Corps moving. "The moment Franklin can be started with a reasonable amount of artillery he shall go," wrote McClellan at 1 p.m. Nearly four hours later he replied to yet another order from Halleck, which told McClellan to lose no time in opening communications with Pope, that "neither Franklin nor Sumner's corps [which started arriving at Alexandria on the 28th] is now in condition to move and fight a battle. It would be a sacrifice to send them out now." At 7 p.m. McClellan had the "honor to report" that the batteries of one of Franklin's divisions was complete but breathed not a word about moving Franklin. In response, an exasperated Halleck commanded, "There must be no further delay in moving Franklin's corps toward Manassas. They must go to-morrow morning, ready or not ready." McClellan at last relented and replied that Franklin would march at 6 a.m. on the 29th, but he warned of "reports numerous, from various sources, that Lee and Stuart, with large forces, are at Manassas; that the enemy, with 120,000 men, intend advancing on the forts near Arlington and Chain Bridge, with a view to attacking Washington and Baltimore." This was based on intelligence no more reliable than a camp rumor, but McClellan was plucking out any report that might delay the movement of the 6th Corps into an uncertain situation at Manassas. He advised that the "great object is to collect the whole army in Washington, ready to defend the works and act upon the flank of any force crossing the Upper Potomac." While he advocated retreating into fixed fortifications and surrendering the initiative to the enemy, John Pope's army was marching hard northward toward Manassas, hoping to catch and crush Jackson's force. They found him, or, more accurately, Jackson found Pope that evening. Battle near Manassas was joined.[69]

The next afternoon, August 29, Lincoln was monitoring the news at the War Department and wired McClellan to inquire, "What news from direction of Manassas Junction? What generally?" McClellan replied that news from the front was unreliable and that one of two courses should be adopted: either to concentrate all forces to open communications with Pope (which Halleck had been unsuccessfully trying to get McClellan to do for two days), or "to leave Pope to get out of his scrape & at once use all our means to make the Capital perfectly safe. No middle course will now answer." A shocked Lincoln replied that the first alternative "is the right one but I wish not to control. That I now leave to Genl Halleck aided by your counsels." As Stephen Sears notes, the phrase "to get out of his scrape" was one McClellan "used often and without particular malice." But Lincoln interpreted it otherwise and angrily presumed that McClellan wanted Pope to be defeated. This, of course, was not McClellan's wish. He loathed Pope and certainly would have felt some satisfaction in his failure, but part of McClellan's beloved army was fighting at Manassas, and he cared deeply about their fate. Lincoln and McClellan simply saw the situation at Manassas entirely differently. Where Lincoln saw an opportunity for victory by pushing troops toward the battle, McClellan saw risk, uncertainty, and potential disaster. He revealed just how wildly exaggerated his sense of the situation was when he wrote to his wife on the morning of the 31st: "I do not regard Washn as safe against the rebels. If I can quietly slip over there I will send your silver off?" He also directed that the Chain Bridge over the Potomac be prepared for destruction. That order was countermanded, presumably by Lincoln. It is not surprising, considering McClellan's exaggerated assessment of the situation toward Manassas, that he urged concentrating a large force in front of Washington, even at the expense of further reinforcement of Pope, whom he believed strong enough to take care of himself, or "get out of his own scrape," as McClellan so crudely worded it. Furthermore, if Pope was defeated—and McClellan had no accurate idea of Pope's situation when he wrote to the president—McClellan believed Pope's army would have a secure line of retreat by way of the Occoquan River. But if Pope was defeated, and Franklin and Sumner were sent to reinforce him and shared in that defeat, then the capital would be defenseless.[70]

After two days of prodding by Halleck, McClellan finally ordered Franklin to march on the 29th but, exercising the discretion that Halleck's indefinite orders afforded him, McClellan halted the 6th Corps at Annandale, after only covering 7 miles. More dispatches flew back and forth between the two men, Halleck angrily demanding to know why Franklin had halted at Annandale and McClellan replying with heat that he was responsible and had simply "exercised the discretion you committed to me," which was true. Halleck had ordered Franklin to accomplish no more than "to go far enough to find out something about the enemy," and he had granted McClellan authority to "dispose of all troops as you deem best." They sorted things out that evening and the next morning, and by the afternoon of August 30 both Franklin's and Sumner's corps were marching in the direction of Manassas. McClellan remained at his headquarters camp near Alexandria, alone except for some orderlies and aides. His army was gone, sent to Pope. All day he listened to the sound of heavy firing from the direction of Manassas. In a depressed mood he continued a letter begun that morning to his wife. "I have sent up every man I have, pushed everything, & am left here on the flat of my back without any command whatever. It is dreadful to listen to the cannonading & not be able to take any part in it—but such is my fate." His fall from the pinnacle of power to humiliation in a year's time now seemed complete. Later the next morning he saw an order from the War Department, published in the *Washington Chronicle*, defining the commanders of the armies in Virginia. McClellan commanded "that portion of the Army of the Potomac that has not been sent forward to General Pope's command." This order had been the work of Secretary of War Stanton and was intended to mortify McClellan. "I am left in command of *nothing*—a command I feel fully competent to exercise, & to which I can do full justice," he wrote unhappily to Mary Ellen.[71]

The fragmentary news filtering into the War Department from Manassas on August 30 suggested that things were going well for Union arms. Pope reported a "terrific battle," and although the enemy remained in his front, they were "badly used up" and might even be retreating toward the mountains to the west. But this happy news faded on August 31 as rumors trickled into the city of a Union defeat at Manassas. A staff officer who McClellan sent to the front for news reported in at 3 a.m. "that we were badly whipped." As if to underscore this message, a stream of stragglers and wounded flowed into the city throughout the day bearing rumors of calamity. Halleck remained optimistic, but then came news from Pope himself that the battle had gone against him, although it was coupled with the reassurance that "we will hold our own here." But Pope's subsequent report on August 31 shook Halleck. Pope calmly asked, "I should like to know whether you feel secure about Washington should this army be destroyed . . . You must judge what is to be done, having in view the safety of the capital." The combination of lack of sleep accompanied by constant stress over the days of the Manassas crisis left Halleck emotionally and physically exhausted. Pope's dispatch was the tipping point, and shortly after 10 p.m. Halleck wired McClellan: "I beg of you to assist me in this crisis with your ability and experience. I am entirely tired out." McClellan replied immediately: "I am ready to afford you any assistance in my power, but you will readily perceive how difficult an undefined position such as I now hold must be. At what hour in the morning can I see you alone, either at your house or the office?"[72]

Washington was muggy and warm when McClellan rode into the capital on the morning of September 1 to confer with Halleck. He found the president there as well. According to McClellan, he arrived at the meeting "mad as a March hare" and had "a pretty plain talk with him & Abe." The contents of a dispatch he sent to Halleck the night before offer some idea of what he might have said. In it he bluntly stated that he no confidence in the dispositions that Pope had made since his defeat at Manassas and then continued: "To speak frankly & the occasion requires it, there appears to be a total absence of brains & I fear the total destruction of the Army." An August 30 letter he received from Fitz John Porter, and the verbal report of the officer who bore the letter, largely shaped McClellan's opinion. Porter said nothing about an absence of brains, but he did make it clear that the army had been badly whipped and was demoralized. After hearing him out, Halleck asked McClellan to take charge of the capital's defenses, although his authority would not extend to the forces under Pope. It was less than McClellan desired or expected but he agreed, "reluctantly," by his own account. Halleck added that he questioned the accuracy of McClellan's report on the state of the army; it was at odds with what Pope reported. McClellan suggested that Halleck should visit the army and see things for himself. Halleck declined, though not for the reasons that McClellan would later state—"that he was so much occupied with office-duty." It was simply unwise for the general-in-chief to leave his communications when he was responsible for coordinating the activity of all resources to both protect the capital and safely extricate Pope from danger. Instead, it was agreed that Halleck's adjutant general, Colonel J. C. Kelton, would go.[73]

Before Kelton returned, Halleck received a deeply troubling dispatch from Pope containing serious accusations. "Many" officers of the Army of the Potomac had exhibited "dangerous and unsoldierly conduct," reported Pope. "Every word and act and intention is discouraging and calculated to break down the spirits of the men and produce disaster . . . Their constant talk, indulged in publicly and promiscuous company, is that the Army of the Potomac will not fight; that they are demoralized by withdrawal from the Peninsula, &c . . . These men are mere tools or parasites but their example is producing . . . very disastrous results." Pope recommended that Halleck "draw back this army to the intrenchments in front of Washington, and set to work in that secure place to reorganize and secure it. You may avoid great disaster by doing so." Halleck carried the shocking dispatch to Lincoln. The president was alarmed. If what Pope said was true, then it might follow that the army would not fight for Pope or any general but McClellan; that the army, as some claimed, owed its loyalty and allegiance to the Pennsylvanian and not to the government. McClellan was summoned back into the city late that afternoon to meet with the president and Halleck. Without revealing his source, Lincoln told the general that he believed the Army of the Potomac was not "cheerfully cooperating with and supporting General Pope," and asked if McClellan would use his personal influence to correct the situation. McClellan replied that the army would "do their whole duty" under General Pope's command, irrespective of their opinion of him. Lincoln asked if McClellan would telegraph Fitz John Porter, or others of the army, and "try to do away with any feeling that might exist," adding, as McClellan recalled it, "that I could rectify the evil, and that no one else could." McClellan took this as flattery that Lincoln surely did not mean. The president's personal opinion of McClellan was that "unquestionably he has acted badly toward Pope. He wanted him to fail." But if McClellan had the heart of the army, then Lincoln must use him to help hold it together.[74]

McClellan composed a telegram to Fitz John Porter, asking the 5th Corps commander "for my sake, that of the country, and the old Army of the Potomac, that you and all my friends will lend the fullest and most cordial cooperation to General Pope in all the operations now going on." But the last sentence had the most impact: "I am in charge of the defenses of Washington, and am doing all I can to render your retreat safe should that become necessary." It announced that McClellan had survived the effort to marginalize him and had reemerged in the chaos of defeat.[75]

Late that afternoon the dull thump of artillery from an engagement at Chantilly, accented by a dazzling electrical storm that heralded the arrival of cooler weather, sounded clearly in the capital, creating renewed apprehension and fueling wild rumors. Stragglers and wounded from Pope's army continued to pour into the city in increasing numbers. During the night, Colonel Kelton returned from his ride to the front and reported to Halleck that the situation was serious. The army was retreating toward the capital, preceded by a large number of stragglers. Halleck forwarded Kelton's report to the president, who was now forced into a difficult decision. He needed someone to organize the capital's defenses and reorganize the army, which was not only disorganized by defeat but, in the case of the Army of the Potomac, apparently reluctant to fight under John Pope. There was only one choice. McClellan was both familiar with the capital's defenses and overwhelmingly popular with the army. It was painful to seemingly reward McClellan after the Peninsula debacle and his conduct during the Second Manassas Campaign, but Lincoln could see no alternative. He would preserve the Union with whatever tools it took and accept the consequences.[76]

September 2 dawned cool and windy. Shortly after 7 a.m., Lincoln and Halleck walked the few blocks from the War Department building to McClellan's quarters on H Street, where the general had spent the night. McClellan was eating breakfast when the two men arrived. The president explained that the army was defeated and falling back on Washington and, as McClellan recalled 11 months later, then Lincoln "instructed me to take steps at once to stop and collect the stragglers, to place the works in a proper state of defense, and to go out and meet and take command of the army when it approached the vicinity of the works; then to place the troops in the best position—committing everything to my hands." McClellan claimed that he accepted the command "reluctantly" and considered it a "terrible and thankless task." What seems more credible is that he was thrilled to have prevailed over his enemies in the administration and humbled the president, who had endeavored to discard him but now needed him. "Nothing but their fear will induce them to give me any command of importance or to treat me otherwise than with discourtesy," he had written to his wife on August 23.[77]

That afternoon Lincoln shared his decision with his cabinet. To a man they disagreed with it. "There was a more disturbed and desponding feeling than I have ever witnessed in council," Gideon Welles penned in his diary. The leading dissidents were Stanton and Secretary of the Treasury Salmon P. Chase. Stanton had hoped the cabinet meeting would be his moment of final victory over McClellan, as he had been building a case against the general. On August 28 he wrote to Halleck, asking a series of questions regarding whether McClellan had obeyed orders from the general-in-chief "as promptly as the national safety required." The tenor of Halleck's response was that McClellan had not acted with the swiftness and spirit the situation required. With Halleck's letter to strengthen his case, Stanton, acting with Chase (who thought McClellan should be shot), drew up a petition that amounted to an ultimatum to the president, demanding McClellan's removal or the possible dissolution of the cabinet. Interior Secretary Caleb B. Smith agreed to sign the petition, as did Attorney General Edward Bates, but only after getting Stanton and Chase to tone down its contents. Only Gideon Welles refused to sign; Seward was out of town. Lincoln's announcement about McClellan preempted Stanton's plans. He left the petition in his coat pocket undelivered, but he and the others freely vented their displeasure with the president's decision, Chase declared that restoring McClellan to command was the equivalent of "giving Washington to the rebels." Stanton seethed with anger. Lincoln felt his cabinet's disapproval. Attorney General Bates thought "he seemed wrung by the bitterest anguish—said he felt almost ready to hang himself." But though he understood his cabinet's displeasure, he did not change his mind. McClellan knew the ground to be defended and could be counted on to fight defensively. He might have "the slows," as the president put it, but there was no one better at bringing organization to dispirited and disorganized troops. His decision stood.[78]

Stanton and Chase may have accepted McClellan's appointment on the grounds that they believed it to be a temporary measure. After the Peninsula Campaign and McClellan's behavior during the crisis of Second Manassas, Lincoln lacked confidence in the general's ability as a field commander. But the capital first needed to be rendered secure from attack; then, while the army was reorganized to retake the field, Lincoln could select a new commander. However, the president did not take into consideration that Robert E. Lee and his Confederates were not likely to grant him the comfort of time.

While Lincoln and his cabinet met, McClellan was hard at work. Immediately after his morning interview with Lincoln and Halleck, he collected his staff and arranged to have supplies and ammunition pushed forward to meet the retreating troops. In order to keep confusion to a minimum, as each corps arrived from the front he planned to place them in essentially the same position they had occupied the year before during the formation of the army. Having briefed his staff, they departed to guide the corps into the designated areas or see that supplies and ammunition were moving forward. McClellan planned to ride to the front, hoping "to assume command as far out as possible," but his wishes for a Napoleonic moment were dashed by a message from Halleck, stating that it was Lincoln's intention that McClellan should not assume command until the troops had reached the immediate vicinity of the fortifications. McClellan obeyed, but he intended to have his moment of glory.[79]

That morning Pope's weary army had started the march to reach the security of the capital's fortifications. There was no panic, as there had been after First Manassas, but defeat had weakened the bonds of discipline and there were many stragglers who preceded the main body of the army. Colonel Charles S. Wainwright, an observant artillery officer, described their arrival in his diary.

> It seems as if the whole of Pope's army were poured in upon us today as stragglers. Such a sight I never saw before and never want to see again. I rode two or three miles out the Fairfax pike, a fine wide road, to see what I could see. It was full of wagons and wheel vehicles of all sorts coming in, mostly empty, or with men in them. Many of the drivers seemed not to have got over their fright yet, and were driving as if all Stuart's cavalry were after them. There were runaways from every corps and division in the army, if not from every regiment. All these are stopped at the line of forts, organized into provisionary companies, and set to man the works. Rumsey went up to see General Slough this afternoon, at Fort Lyon. He is in command at this point, and told Rumsey that 13,000 stragglers had already been picked up, and placed in the works.[80]

The main body of the army retired in relatively good order. "There is nothing of the defeated or disheartened among the men," wrote Colonel Rutherford B. Hayes of the 23rd Ohio, who observed the retreating troops from his position at Upton's Hill. "They are vexed and angry—say they ought to have had a great victory, but not at all demoralized."[81]

Disgust appropriately described the mood of most soldiers, and they directed it chiefly at army commander Pope and the unlucky 3rd Corps commander, Major General Irwin McDowell. "I dare not trust myself to speak of this commander [Pope] as I feel and believe," wrote Brigadier General Alpheus Williams, a division commander in Pope's 2nd Corps. "A splendid army almost destroyed, millions of public property given up or destroyed, thousands of lives of our best men sacrificed for no purpose . . . Suffice it to say (for your eyes only) that more insolence, superciliousness, ignorance, and pretentiousness were never combined in one man." Lt. Colonel Edward Bragg of the 6th Wisconsin infantry, in McDowell's corps, echoed Williams's sentiments: "Pope is a braggard & a villanous preverter of facts—& McDowell, too fusey [sic] & confused, to have any combination succesful." These were the judgments of respected officers in Pope's own Army of Virginia, and thousands shared their feelings. In the Army of the Potomac Pope's condemnation was loud and universal. Major General Joseph

Hooker, who had no great love for McClellan, thought Pope handled the battle at Manassas badly: "If they had left McClellan in command this never would have happened." Gouverneur Warren, a brigade commander in Porter's 5th Corps, expressed the opinion that "a more utterly unfit man than Pope has never been seen."[82]

The setting for McClellan's return to command could not have been better than if he had enlisted a theater director to stage the scene. Accompanied by several aides and a small cavalry escort, he crossed the Potomac that afternoon and rode out to Upton's Hill, about 3 miles from the Chain Bridge, as far as he could go and still be considered within his area of command. Here he joined Brigadier General Jacob D. Cox, a Republican state senator from Ohio now commanding a division of Ohio troops recently transferred to the theater from western Virginia, who had established his headquarters at Upton's Hill. The two men had served together during McClellan's West Virginia campaign. McClellan had been rather hard on Cox then, but it had not dampened the Ohioan's enthusiasm for the general or the otherwise cordial, friendly relations between the two men. A dust cloud in the distance indicated the approach of the retreating army, and McClellan waited anxiously, in anticipation of their arrival. This was to be his reward for his recent humiliation, to hear the cheers of the troops when they learned that he was in command again.[83]

Cox immediately noticed that McClellan wore his yellow sash and sword, something he had not done since his arrival at Alexandria, and was in high spirits. He greeted Cox with "Well, General, I am in command again." Cox congratulated him "with hearty earnestness for I was personally rejoiced at it. I was really attached to him, believed him to be, on the whole, the most accomplished officer I knew, and was warmly disposed to give him loyal friendship and service."[84]

At about 4 p.m. McClellan and Cox rode to the brow of the hill, where there was a good view down the Fairfax Road. The head of the column could be seen, led by Brigadier General John P. Hatch's division of McDowell's 3rd Corps. Pope and McDowell, accompanied by a small cavalry escort, preceded the column. Dust clung to the moving mass of tired men, and both generals and their escort were covered with it. Cox observed that Pope and McDowell appeared "worn and serious, but alert and self possessed." McClellan rode forward to meet them. The generals exchanged greetings and McClellan explained that he would assume command of the troops as they came within the fortifications. He informed Pope of the positions his corps was to occupy. Pope acknowledged his orders and both parties moved on.[85]

The meeting of generals would have been completely unremarkable if it had not been for General Hatch. Hatch nursed a grudge against Pope, who relieved him from command of a cavalry brigade for a subpar performance earlier in the campaign and reassigned him to command of an infantry brigade. He overheard the conversation between McClellan and Pope and seized the opportunity for some revenge. Riding to the head of his column, he shouted, "Boys, General McClellan is in command again; three cheers!" The cheers were given "with wild delight" and quickly resounded along the entire length of the column. Pope ignored the affront. He simply lifted his hat to McClellan in a parting salute and rode on. McClellan remained there for some time, savoring the moment and the cheers that burst from the throats of the passing troops; then he and his staff and a small escort rode northward toward Vienna.

The news of McClellan's return to command swept rapidly through the army. Its effect, except in some isolated instances, was instantaneous, electrifying, and jubilant. "Everywhere the joy was great, and was spontaneously and uproariously expressed," noted Rutherford Hayes. "It was a happy army again." George Kimball of the 12th Massachusetts later recalled. "The scene that followed [the announcement of McClellan's return] can be more easily imagined than described. From extreme sadness we passed in a twinkling to a delirium of delight. A deliverer had come." Wrote Lieutenant William H. Powell of the 4th U.S. infantry, "The effect of this man's presence upon the Army of the Potomac—in sunshine or rain, in darkness or in daylight, in victory or defeat—was electrical, and too wonderful to make it worth while attempting to give a reason for it." From the point of view of the fighting men—and perhaps the future of the Union—Lincoln had made the correct decision.[86]

The smoke of the Second Manassas debacle had cleared and McClellan had emerged triumphant. The president's efforts to shelve him, and Stanton's to destroy him, had been thwarted. Yet his victory was tenuous. Because of the relationships he had fostered—or, more accurately, failed to cultivate—and the history of the past year, an atmosphere of mutual distrust and a lack of confidence cast a pall over his relations with the administration and extended now to include Halleck. But McClellan resumed command with confidence and set to work with his characteristic energy to ready his forces to defend the capital if necessary, as well as to reorganize the army. A great deal needed to be done, but the luxury of time he enjoyed in the summer of 1861 would not happen again. There were fresh reports that Robert E. Lee's Army of Northern Virginia had disappeared from in front of Washington and was concentrated in the vicinity of Fairfax Court House and Dranesville, with the possible intention of invading Maryland. If this were true, an army would need to be placed in the field soon. The question was, who would command it?

2

The Army of Northern Virginia

"Who could not conquer with troops such as these"

When Confederate President Jefferson Davis appointed Robert E. Lee to assume command of the Rebel army outside of Richmond on June 1, 1862, few in the army or the public saw the change as a positive event. The wounded Joseph Johnston had been the army's commander for nearly a year and was well known. Lee was a question mark. "There was really very little known about him," recalled one officer. Lee was 55 years old. Although he had enjoyed a lofty reputation in the prewar U.S. Army, most of his 32 years of service in that organization had been with the engineers or as a staff officer. To many observers his experience with the Confederate States Army in 1861 and 1862 was unremarkable, if not downright unsuccessful. Jefferson Davis employed him as a military advisor until the late summer of 1861, when he sent him to western Virginia to assume command of Confederate forces there. His campaign failed, largely due to wretched weather and incompetent subordinates. But the press held Lee responsible and pitched into him, particularly for his apparent penchant for having his men dig entrenchments, which was considered a cowardly way of making war. A reporter from the *Charleston (SC) Mercury* complained, "The people are getting mighty sick of this dilly-dally, dirty digging, scientific warfare; so much so that they will demand that the Great Entrencher be brought back to pay court to the ladies."[1]

Davis dispatched the "Great Entrencher" from the debacle in western Virginia to assume command and improve the defenses of a department that encompassed the coastal areas of South Carolina, Georgia, and eastern Florida. Lee performed competently, but his service on the coast only strengthened the impression that he was wedded to fortifications and to the defensive. In March 1862, Davis brought him back to Richmond as his military advisor, a duty Lee neither sought nor particularly enjoyed; he wished to command troops in the field. Lee performed ably, however, and exhibited skill as a strategist. For example, Stonewall Jackson's famous Valley Campaign was set in motion by Lee, but this was unknown to the public or the army. In the eyes of both groups, Lee remained a timid, irresolute general, an opinion that was shared by his adversary, George McClellan.[2]

Given Lee's largely undistinguished record in the war, it is unsurprising that there was little enthusiasm within the Confederate army at the news of his appointment to command. The Richmond papers assailed him at every opportunity. Edward P. Alexander, the army's chief of ordnance, thought the motive was "to break him down with the troops & to force the president to remove him." Even Alexander questioned Lee's capacity to command the army. One day he encountered Colonel Joseph C. Ives, a member of Jefferson Davis's staff and a former member of Lee's staff. When Alexander expressed his concern, wondering whether Lee would have the audacity to overcome the odds the Federals could bring against the Confederates, Ives responded that Alexander—and the army—were in for a surprise. "Lee is audacity personified. His name is audacity and you need not be afraid of not seeing all of it that you will want to see," he told Alexander.[3]

Lee named the army he assumed command of the Army of Northern Virginia, a sign that he did not intend to fight his battles in Virginia's interior. Within three months to the day of his assignment as head of the army—an army inferior in nearly everything to the enemy, except spirit—he had accomplished this goal by waging a brilliant campaign of aggressive attack and maneuver that defeated two Federal armies—the Army of the Potomac and the Army of Virginia—and drove them within the fortifications of their capital. The derisive nickname "Great Entrencher" was heard no more. Lee's victories disrupted the entire Union war effort in the eastern theater. The Federals stripped all their garrisons within 100 miles of Richmond, except for Norfolk and Fortress Monroe, to reinforce the operations in northern Virginia. The bulk of the forces operating along the North Carolina coast and in West Virginia were also withdrawn to confront Lee. The Federals were knocked off balance, a posture Lee wished to keep them in as much as possible. "As long as the army of the enemy are employed on this frontier I have no fears for the safety of Richmond," Lee wrote to the Confederate president on September 3. But, he cautioned, this respite should also be used to strengthen Richmond's land and water defenses. He might also have added that the longer he maintained the war on the frontier, the greater the political pressure on Lincoln. Lee held the initiative, and the question he now pondered was how best to exploit it.[4]

Whatever new operation the army embarked on would have to be started without delay, for the army's supply situation bordered on desperate. Fairfax County, where the army paused to rest after Second Manassas, was completely stripped of food and forage, due to its proximity to Washington and its constant occupation by troops since 1861. The line of supply to Richmond extended 110 miles. The Orange and Alexandria Railroad and the Virginia Central Railroad could haul supplies for the first 50–60 miles, as far as the Rapidan River. But the railroad bridges over this river and the Rappahannock had been destroyed during the Second Manassas Campaign, which meant that the army's insufficient and badly overworked wagon train had to haul the army's subsistence and other supplies the remaining 50–60 miles. There was simply not enough transportation to perform this task. Lee had to move the army to a location in which it could subsist by itself, but where?

An assault on Washington was out of the question. "I had no intention of attacking him in his fortifications, and am not prepared to invest them," Lee wrote to Confederate President Jefferson Davis on September 3, adding that even "if I possessed the necessary munitions, I should be unable to supply provisions for the troops." There were two possible lines of operation open for serious consideration. The less productive of the two was to withdraw to the vicinity of Warrenton. This would shorten the army's supply line and, once the bridges over the Rapidan and Rappahannock were repaired, rail service would be available. The Warrenton position placed the army on the flank of any force that might advance overland on Richmond. But the negatives of this move outweighed the positives. It surrendered the initiative to the Federals, and it applied no pressure to compel them to abandon the security of Washington's fortifications and depots until they were reinforced and reorganized. It sacrificed all the blood and sweat that had been expended to drive the enemy to the frontier, and it relaxed the political pressure on Lincoln. The enemy had also demonstrated that they could easily outflank a defensive position in northern Virginia with an amphibious movement. A retirement to Warrenton or points south not only relieved the pressure on Lincoln, as Lee's aide, Charles Marshall, observed, but "the Northern people would have seen in such a result solid reasons for expecting ultimate and not very remote success." Lee believed the Confederacy's best hope for winning their independence was to undermine Northern morale. If he relinquished the initiative to the enemy now, the gains he had won on this front at great cost would be lost. With the November elections approaching, it was imperative to maintain the pressure on the enemy. An additional incentive for a bold move was the news—although exaggerated—that 60,000 newly raised Union soldiers had arrived in Washington. If Lee delayed, or went over to a defensive posture, the enemy forces could train and organize these new recruits at their leisure and lead an even more powerful army against him.[5]

Lee considered it bad policy to relinquish the initiative to the enemy. Under the circumstances he faced in northern Virginia after Second Manassas, he believed that the best line of operations was to advance into Maryland and, if possible, into Pennsylvania. Such a movement permitted him to retain the initiative and feed his army at the same time, and it forced the enemy to react to his movements and keep the main body of their army north of the Potomac. It was also in keeping with his general strategy, which Charles Marshall articulated: "General Lee's policy was not to capture any portion of Federal territory, but to protract the war by breaking up the enemy's campaigns and so bringing about the pecuniary exhaustion of the North." Marshall might have added the exhaustion of Northern morale to Lee's policy, for by prolonging the war and inflicting heavy losses on the Union armies, he tested the mettle of the North's resolve. Lee was confident that moving his army into the slaveholding border state—whose loyalty to the U.S. government had been suspect enough to prompt Lincoln to suspend the writ of habeas corpus—would provoke a swift reaction from that administration. "We expected to derive more assistance in the attainment of our object from the just fears of the Washington Government than from any active demonstration on the part of the people [of Maryland]," observed Lee in his official report of the campaign. There were risks with such a move, but there were risks with any move Lee made. The possibilities offered by a foray into Maryland made the risks acceptable.[6]

The question Lee considered was not *whether* the army should enter Maryland, but *where* it should enter. Stonewall Jackson advocated that the army should march west, presumably via Aldie and Snickersville, and invade by way of the Shenandoah Valley. This was certainly the safest invasion route, and it placed the army in close proximity to the valley's rich farming district. Lee rejected this approach—although it was essentially the route he later used in the Gettysburg Campaign—because he was not certain that it would apply the pressure necessary to lure the Federals out of Washington. There was also the possibility that the enemy might counter this more distant turning action by moving across northern Virginia, occupying territory freshly won, to strike at his communications. The Union army might even feel bold enough to detach a new force to threaten Richmond.

Under the circumstances, Lee thought it better to enter Maryland east of the Blue Ridge Mountains. This invasion route posed a more immediate threat to both Baltimore and Washington and their communications, and it was more likely to draw the Union army into the field. An approach east of the Blue Ridge also isolated Union garrisons at Harpers Ferry and Winchester. Lee hoped to establish a new depot at Winchester and a line of communications down the valley into western Maryland. Those two Union garrisons stood squarely on this line, but, once isolated, he anticipated that they would be withdrawn. If things went well, and the entire army was able to enter Maryland, Lee intended to remain east of the mountains only long enough to draw the Union army out of Washington. Once this had been accomplished, he intended to cross the Catoctin Mountain and South Mountain ranges—the two principal mountain ranges in central Maryland—and march to Hagerstown. This town of just over 4,000 residents was ideally situated to serve as a staging point for an invasion of Pennsylvania, which Lee intended to undertake if circumstances permitted. An invasion of Pennsylvania offered even greater political advantages, and the army could supply itself from the rich bounty of the state's farms and communities, but these were secondary to Lee's primary objective, which was to draw the Union army out of the capital—and away from their base of supplies and their fortifications—where the Army of Northern Virginia could administer a smashing blow. After the war, in giving his reasons for the invasion of Maryland, Lee stated bluntly, "I went into Maryland to give battle."[7]

If his campaign of maneuver in Maryland failed to yield a decisive victory, Lee believed that, at the very least, his army would "annoy and harass the enemy" and disrupt their plans. The army, he acknowledged, was "not properly equipped for an invasion of an enemy's territory," but he believed it strong enough "to detain the enemy upon the northern frontier until the approach of winter should render his advance into Virginia difficult, if not impracticable." The question was whether the army could maintain itself on the frontier this long. Edward P. Alexander, Lee's chief of ordnance, noted that "no army large enough to meet the Federal army could support and supply itself by wagon-trains from Staunton [Virginia, the nearest railhead in the valley] nearly 150 miles away, for any length of time. Whenever, therefore, we crossed the Potomac going northward, we were as certain to have to re-cross it coming southward, in a few weeks, as a stone thrown upward is certain to come down."[8]

There were other fruits that might fall into the Confederates' lap by invading Maryland. Union east–west communications across Maryland, particularly the C&O Canal and B&O Railroad, could be cut. Although Lee did not anticipate that Maryland's population would make any active demonstration against the U.S. government or for the Confederate cause, due to the temporary presence of his army on her soil, he did believe that by entering Maryland he gave its citizens the *opportunity* to express themselves freely. Some recruits might be added to his army's ranks, and any unrest that might occur benefited the Confederates.

Many Southerners still held out hope of European recognition that summer. Lee was not among them. He personally did not anticipate that any European nation would intervene on behalf of the Confederacy. Lee may have known that the British House of Commons had debated mediating an end to the hostilities in America, but it had not yet amounted to anything, and it is doubtful that he took the Europeans into account in his decision on whether to enter Maryland. This is not to say that he completely discounted the possibility of European recognition; he simply understood that a collapse of Northern morale was far more likely to occur first.

Lee possessed a more sophisticated appreciation of the political implications of his army's move into Maryland than is generally acknowledged. He reflected this in a dispatch to Davis from Frederick, Maryland, on September 8. Lee rarely ventured into the political arena in his correspondence with Davis, but he sensed that the offensive into Maryland offered the Confederacy a unique opportunity. Showing an acumen not often credited to him, Lee wrote: "The present posture of affairs, in my opinion, places it in the power of the Government of the Confederate States to propose with propriety to that of the United States the recognition of our independence." By making such a proposition when the

Confederate tide was riding high, it could "in no way be regarded as suing for peace," and Lee thought it would "show conclusively to the world that our sole object is the establishment of our independence, and the attainment of an honorable peace." If Lincoln rejected such a proposal, and Lee expected that he would, this rejection "would prove to the country that the responsibility of the continuance of the war does not rest upon us, but that the party in power in the United States elect to prosecute it for purposes of their own." With elections approaching in November, Northern voters would have the opportunity to decide "whether they will support those who favor a prolongation of the war, or those who wish to bring it to a termination, which can but be productive of good to both parties without affecting the honor of either."[9]

What Lee could not know was that his offensive into Maryland also threatened to bury or at least delay release of Lincoln's Emancipation Proclamation. This document, if issued, threatened to unravel the limited war that men like Lee and McClellan hoped for and send it spiraling in unknown and unexpected directions. It would also strike a blow at the Confederate States' slim hope of European recognition. Nations that had already abolished slavery were unlikely to recognize a nation fighting for its preservation. But Lincoln needed a battlefield victory to issue his proclamation; otherwise, it would be perceived as an act of desperation. If Lee could keep the pressure on and win a victory north of the Potomac, Lincoln's proclamation might well remain in the president's desk.

Besides the military and political advantages, there were practical reasons for an advance into Maryland. The border state could solve Lee's acute supply problem—or at least Lee thought it could—for its fields and orchards, untouched by the war, were laden with fruits and vegetables ready for harvest. While Maryland provided the food and forage his army needed, northern Virginia would be able to collect the fall harvest without the burden of occupying armies. There was a question, though, about how the food in Maryland was to be procured and whether enough could be purchased to sustain the army. Major General James Longstreet advised Lee that during his service in Mexico they were sometimes compelled to subsist wholly on roasted ears of corn, and that so long as Maryland's fields were loaded with "roasting ears" the army would not starve. Lee acknowledged Longstreet's advice, but he pondered how the army would pay for those roasting ears. He anticipated that Marylanders might be reluctant to sell supplies to his army, and he did not want his army to burden the people. "There may be some embarrassment in paying for necessaries for the army, as it is probable that many individuals will hesitate to receive Confederate currency," he warned President Davis in a letter on September 7. He expressed a desire that arrangements be made to ensure that any debts Marylanders incurred by supplying his army would promptly be made good. But such arrangements would take time, and Lee had to trust that initially his army would somehow be able to obtain the supplies necessary to sustain it. To help relieve the doubts of the citizens as to his army's purpose, he asked that former Maryland governor Enoch Lowe "or some prominent citizen" join the army in Maryland. This would all eventually come to naught, since the army spent so little time in Maryland, but Lee's instincts were sound.[10]

Lee acknowledged in a September 3 dispatch to Davis that an advance into Maryland "is attended with much risk." The army was neither equipped nor adequately supplied for an invasion, and after a spring and summer spent largely in the field, much of that time in active campaigning, it showed the strain of the hard service it had endured. Although he was well aware of the army's dilapidated condition, it was ammunition, particularly artillery ammunition, and subsistence that caused Lee "uneasiness." While subsistence could be found in Maryland, artillery ammunition could not. Although the army's batteries had been able to replenish their limbers and caissons after Second Manassas, another major engagement would dip into the ordnance reserves and necessitate refilling them. Lee wanted a forward depot established to provide resupply in the event operations on the frontier extended into the fall. By September 5, after learning that the Union garrison had evacuated Winchester, he selected this town as his forward depot.

Lee believed that two factors offset the risks entailed in crossing the Potomac. First, there was the condition of the Union army. He thought that it "was much weakened and demoralized" by the Peninsula and Second Manassas campaigns, and that the thousands of new recruits pouring into Washington would take time to train and organize. This assessment of his enemy, which proved to be an inaccurate estimate, prompted Lee to take risks in the campaign that he might not otherwise have attempted. The second factor was the Army of Northern Virginia. Even in its tattered condition, Lee thought it to be superior in almost every way to the Federal army. "I need not say to you that the material of which it is composed is the best in the world, and, if properly disciplined and instructed, would be able to resist any force that could be brought against it," he wrote to Davis. With this formidable weapon, Lee was confident he could accomplish much.[11]

In the short time since Lee had assumed command, the army had compiled a proud record and earned a reputation for toughness, aggressiveness, swift marching, and hard fighting. It had been forged in the fires of Seven Pines, Gaines' Mill, Savage Station, White Oak Swamp, Malvern Hill, Cedar Mountain, and Second Manassas. In some of these actions the army had fought awkwardly and ineffectively, but its rank and file consistently fought with spirit and courage. Despite the hardships of campaigning, hard fighting, and heavy casualties that had marked the three months under Lee, morale in the Confederate army had soared. The duel triumphs over McClellan and Pope had imbued it with confidence and a sense of superiority over the Yankees. "I am proud to have borne even my humble part in these great operations," wrote Lieutenant John "Ham" Chamberlayne, an artillery staff officer, "to have helped, ever so little to consummate the grand plan whose history will be a text book to all young soldiers & whose magnificent, bewildering success will place Lee at the side of the Greatest Captains, Hannibal, Caesar, Eugene, and Napoleon." Major Thomas Elder, the quartermaster of Pryor's brigade, echoed Chamberlayne's sentiments: "If we can only get enough for our men to eat up here I don't believe Genl. Lee's army can be whipped."[12]

Repeated successes generated confidence in the army's senior leadership. "Jackson, next to Lee is the favorite here," wrote Major Elder. After the victory at Second Manassas, Brigadier General William Dorsey Pender (known as "Dorsey") proclaimed to his wife that "Gen. Lee has shown great Generalship and the greatest boldness. There never was such a campaign, not even by Napoleon . . . Gen. Lee is my man." Besides Lee and Jackson there was a long list of leaders who had shone on the Peninsula and Valley battlefields or at Manassas: James Longstreet, A. P. Hill, D. H. Hill, John B. Hood, Jubal Early, and others. They were aggressive, confident men; most of them were graduates of West Point and had experience in the old U.S. Army. Their combativeness trickled down through the ranks, instilling a tough, self-confident spirit throughout the numbers of volunteers who formed the backbone of the army.[13] Yet the stunning victories of that summer had come at a heavy price. From the time Lee assumed command through the end of the Second Manassas Campaign, the army suffered 30,874 battle casualties, including 5,080 dead. Many excellent officers had been killed or wounded. "We were lavish of blood in those days," wrote D. H. Hill, "and it was thought to be a great thing to charge a battery of artillery or an earth-work lined with infantry."[14]

The nonbattle casualty lists were also lengthy. The horrors of combat, the grind of campaigning, forced marches, poorly enforced discipline, inefficient logistical support, and an often unhealthy and less than bountiful diet led to long sick lists, numerous desertions, and heavy straggling. The natty uniforms men had sported at the beginning of spring were now dirty, worn, and frayed. On many of the soldiers they were little more than rags. Thousands were without shoes. Even units that had seen less field service than others and should have been relatively well off often were not. Major General Lafayette McLaws's division—which had been in the vicinity of Richmond from after the Seven Days battles until it was ordered to join Lee in northern Virginia in late August, and ought to have been better off than others—reflected this. McLaws complained to his wife in a letter on September 4: "Many of our men are without shoes and all of them are very ragged, in addition we have seen marching for the last three days with nothing to eat but fresh meat and green corn one day with nothing to eat but corn and that not in abundance. One day there was nothing to eat." The condition of those units that had participated in the

Manassas Campaign was even more desperate. Jackson's command had received no issued rations from the time they captured the huge supply depot at Manassas Junction on August 27 until September 2, when they were issued a ration of "boiled fresh beef, without salt or bread . . . with an ear or two of green corn roasted by a fire." Longstreet's command was perhaps in worse shape than Jackson's, for they had not shared in the plunder from Manassas. What food the men did get, often nothing more than green corn, left many afflicted with diarrhea and unable to stay in the ranks.[15]

Despite the army's excellent morale, straggling was a serious problem. General Dorsey Pender called it "the curse of the army, and unless Congress pass some law to stop it there is no telling where it will end." The cause was only partly rooted in inadequate logistical support and diet, and often came from poorly enforced discipline at the company and regimental levels. The First Conscription Act, passed by the Confederate States Congress on April 16, contained, among other things, a provision that directed regiments already in the field to reelect their field and company officers. One of Lee's staff officers, Charles Marshall, observed that "the worst consequences anticipated by the opponents of the elective system were realized." Officers who had been strict in enforcing discipline and soldierly habits were often voted out of their positions, and those "who wished to retain their commissions, to seek favor for popularity at the expense of discipline" frequently filled their places.

The results were predictable. Officers ignorant of their duties or neglectful of their responsibilities contributed to massive absenteeism from the ranks. Immediately after the Maryland Campaign, Lee wrote to Confederate Secretary of War George W. Randolph: "There is great dereliction of duty among the regimental and company officers, particularly the latter, and unless something is done the army will melt away." General Cadmus Wilcox declared that "we have no discipline in our army, it is but little better than an armed mob." The infantry division of Major General Lafayette McLaws, a professionally trained soldier and good administrator who took excellent care of his command, offered a stark example of the army's problems. On July 20 the division mustered 532 officers and 7,188 men for duty, but by September 13 there were approximately 360 officers and 3,700 men present for duty. This was a difference of 3,660 men, almost 50 percent of the July 20 strength. The remarkable thing about this figure is that McLaws's division had done *no fighting* during this time period. In units that had participated in the Second Manassas campaign, conditions were generally worse.[16] Dorsey Pender, an excellent officer and former U.S. Army regular, commanded a brigade in A. P. Hill's division that had seen hard service from the Peninsula through Second Manassas. In a letter from Maryland to his wife, he offered an idea of how bad things could be in units that had been continuously in the field.

My dear such a filthy and unprincipled set of villains I have never seen. They have lost all honor or decency, all sense of right or respect for property. I have had to strike many a one with my sabre. The officers are nearly as bad as the men. In one of my Regts. the other day when they thought they were going to get into a fight, six out [of] ten officers skulked out and did not come up until they thought all danger over. More than half my Brigade went off the same day.[17]

In an effort to curb the problem, Lee issued General Orders No. 94 on August 11. The order created a divisional provost guard, to be composed of 1 commissioned and 2 noncommissioned officers and 10 men from each regiment, who were to march in the rear of each division, accompanied by one of the division's medical officers, and collect stragglers. The surgeon would determine which ones were really sick or disabled, and they would be given a ticket for transportation in an ambulance or wagon. The others would be marched into camp under guard. But the order was indifferently enforced, and straggling continued to drain the strength of the army. Stragglers reduced the combat strength of the army's regiments and taxed their commissary, for many stragglers appeared when rations were issued but vanished during hard marches or when signs of a fight were imminent. Lee also worried that stragglers would be likely to commit depredations against Marylanders, something that might turn the populace against his army and its cause, and he sensed that stricter discipline and sterner measures were in order when the army was in Maryland. On September 4 he issued General Orders No. 102, which essentially outlined preparations for the invasion of Maryland, but also created a provost guard under the command of Brigadier General Lewis Armistead, a tough infantry officer with many years of service in the old U.S. Army, who had the power to "arrest stragglers, and punish summarily all depredators, and keep the men with their commands."[18]

The army suffered 9,474 casualties at Second Manassas, leaving Lee with about 50,000 men of all arms. However, substantial reinforcements reached the army on September 2. When he moved north with the bulk of the army to confront Pope, Lee had left behind the divisions of D. H. Hill, Lafayette McLaws, and John G. Walker; four battalions of reserve artillery; and the cavalry brigade of Wade Hampton to watch McClellan's army on the Peninsula. By mid-August, when it became apparent that McClellan was evacuating the Peninsula, President Davis approved Lee's request to move Hill's and McLaws's divisions, Hampton's brigade, and the four battalions of the reserve artillery under Brigadier General William N. Pendleton to the vicinity of Hanover Junction. This left only Walker's division, four other infantry brigades, some home-guard units, and newly arrived green regiments in the immediate vicinity of Richmond and Petersburg. Lee wanted the Hanover Junction force to join the main body of the army in northern Virginia promptly, but the fear of leaving Richmond nearly bare of first-line troops caused the Davis administration to hesitate. Davis, Secretary of War George Randolph, Major General Gustuvas W. Smith (in command of Richmond's defenses), and Brigadier General Pendleton met on the night of the 25th and the morning of the 26th to discuss the perils and merits of forwarding the Hanover Junction force to Lee. The meeting resulted in Davis not only agreeing to release the entire Hanover Junction force to Lee, but also ordering Walker's division to reinforce the main army. Davis wrote to Lee on the 26th that "confidence in you overcomes the view which would otherwise be taken of the exposed condition of Richmond, and the troops retained for the defense of the capital are surrendered to you on a renewed request."[19]

The reinforcing column consisted of some 22,600 infantry, 1,509 cavalry, and six battalions of artillery (four of the reserves, and Hill's and McLaws's divisional artillery). It set out to join Lee in three separate columns. Two of D. H. Hill's brigades had been moved to Orange Court House before the rest of the division was ordered to Hanover Junction, so they started from Orange on August 27 and reached Manassas Junction on August 30. Hill led the main column from Hanover Junction, consisting of the remaining three brigades of his division, McLaws's division, Hampton's brigade, and the reserve artillery. Impatient to join Lee and the main army, which he knew were involved in important operations, Hill started on August 26 and set a blistering pace. On September 2, eight days later, his column joined Lee at Chantilly. They had covered 120 miles in 6 days, a brutal pace indeed.[20] The march left a vivid impression on a member of the 14th North Carolina.

> In our march the dust was atrocious, stifling; canteens long since empty—no water, wells drained by those in front—we substituted a bullet or piece of lead, which causes saliva, and in some measure allays thirst. For once no talking, no joking, no chaffing, no song. It would not do to open the mouth and breathe the fiendish dust to corrode the throat. Our vocabulary is unequal to picturing the hardship, the endurance, the suffering, of the private soldier.[21]

Brigadier General Howell Cobb, commanding a brigade in McLaws's division, was furious with Hill, describing the pace of the march as "inhuman" and noting that "men absolutely fell and died by the side of the road from the heat." He described Hill to his wife as "a weak, self-conceited heartless and cruel ass," and added that if he could have brought Hill to trial, Cobb would have charged him "with incapacity and inhumanity—and relieve the service of as despicable a wretch, as ever disgraced any army." The hard pace, combined with high heat, insufficient rations, a "want of shoes," and "inefficient officers," caused massive straggling. Colonel Francis Parker, commanding the 30th North Carolina in Hill's division, wrote to his wife that "our ranks have been somewhat thinned" by those who fell sick during the march, broke down, or gave out from sore feet. The greatest losses fell on the infantry. It is difficult to assess how many men straggled or were lost to sickness and did not rejoin their commands until after the Antietam Campaign was over, but it may have amounted to several thousand. In Hill's defense, he knew that important operations were taking place in northern Virginia and that there was an urgent need for his men.[22]

The third column, composed of Walker's division of two brigades, had an easier go of it. They moved by rail on August 27 from Richmond to Rapidan Station, where they arrived early in the morning on the 28th. Here they remained until September 1, waiting for their wagon trains to catch up. Walker set out promptly once his trains arrived and came to within 6 miles of Leesburg on September 5.[23]

The army received some additional manpower from the First Conscription Act. The South had not been more resolute than the North in enacting conscription after the war began, and the Conscription Act was passed because of dire necessity. Volunteering had dried up, and many regiments in the army had enlisted in April 1861 for only 12 months of service. The Confederacy faced the prospect of having its army melt away just as the spring campaign season opened. Under pressure from President Davis, the Confederate States Congress passed the act, which made all men between the ages of 18 and 35 liable for military service and reenlisted those men already in the service for three years or the duration of the war. Independent-minded Southerners objected to the act as an assault on their personal freedom (much as Northerners would do in 1863 when the U.S. government enacted conscription), but it kept the already-trained 12-month volunteers in the Confederate army. It was only partially successful, however, in sending conscripts to the army. The act was riddled with exemptions, and some states proved to be less than enthusiastic in enforcing its provisions. By August 22, North Carolina had conscripted only 5,066 men. Georgia had raised 2,718 by September 26. Many of the North Carolina conscripts evidently were sent to Lee's army, for a number of North Carolina regiments reported receiving large numbers of conscripts before and during the early stages of the Maryland Campaign. South Carolina also forwarded a contingent in early August. A liberal guess would place Lee's manpower gains from conscription at between 2,000 and 3,000 men. Some of these men reported unarmed, and nearly all of them were untrained. Discarded weapons collected from the Manassas battlefield probably equipped most of the unarmed men, but training was nearly impossible while on the move, and many conscripts were physically unprepared for the demands of campaigning. Some were also emotionally unprepared. Constantine Hege, a conscript in the 48th North Carolina of Walker's division, wrote to his family soon after joining his regiment: "I am not satisfied here, I do not like to hear of going to face the cannon and the muskets[.] I would be very glad if you could hire a substitute in my place because I cannot stand such a life with any enjoyment at all." His family would find no substitute, and Hege unhappily marched into Maryland with his regiment. A sergeant in the 5th North Carolina recalled that the 400 conscripts his regiment received "could not load a gun," a situation that had not improved by the time they went into combat at South Mountain on September 14. Nevertheless, the lot of the conscripts, who were being sent into veteran units where they quickly learned the ways of soldiering, was considerably better than that of the new recruits in the Union army, whose story will be told later.[24]

With the reinforcement of McLaws, Hill, Walker, Hampton, and the conscripts, Lee's army now numbered approximately 68,400 infantry and artillerymen, 5,300 cavalry, 1,300 artillerymen in the reserve artillery, and upwards of 280 or more guns. This is a significantly more formidable army than Lee has traditionally been credited with. The slim numbers frequently attributed to the army when it entered Maryland reflect the postwar efforts of the Lost Cause to select the lowest possible strength for the Confederate army while inflating the strength of the Federals. One wit from the Union army quipped after the war that in "a few more years, a few more books, and it will appear that Lee and Longstreet, and a one-armed orderly, and a casual with a shotgun, fought all the battles of the rebellion, and killed all the Union soldiers except those who ran away." But this was the pinnacle of Confederate army's strength that fall, for each day the army leaked men; once it entered Maryland, the losses from sickness and straggling were immense.[25]

The army entered Maryland with its order of battle still in transition. The division remained the largest formation provided for by Confederate law, although Lee had anticipated the authorization of army corps by the Confederate States Congress. A division had no standard table of organization and equipment, and it might contain anywhere from two to six brigades of infantry, although three to four brigades was the most common arrangement by Second Manassas. Lee did not hesitate to change the divisions' composition to meet the needs of the situation at hand, nor to test the abilities of his officer corps to see who had the capacity for higher command. He juggled his divisions again in the early stages of the Maryland Campaign by transferring Brigadier General Cadmus Wilcox's three-brigade division to Major General Richard H. Anderson's division, creating a six-brigade unit under Anderson's command. He did the same thing with Brigadier General James Kemper's three-brigade division, transferring it to Brigadier General David R. Jones's command, creating another six-brigade division. A six-brigade division was an unwieldy organization, but Lee may have felt it necessary to make the transfers for several reasons. Some of the brigades in these divisions were very small, due to battle casualties, straggling, and sickness, and he had to make the transfers to maintain combat power. Lee also may have wanted to reduce the number of divisions for efficiency, and Kemper's and Wilcox's performances at Second Manassas might have disappointed him. The consolidations gave the army nine infantry divisions, one cavalry division, and an independent infantry brigade.

The division was an administrative unit, serving to coordinate the operations of the infantry brigade. The brigade, consisting of an average of four to five regiments, was the basic tactical fighting unit of a Civil War army. Lee carried 40 brigades into Maryland. At full strength a brigade contained 4,000 to 5,000 men, but no brigade in either army ever maintained itself at full strength. Due to the varying severity of the service they had seen, the number of conscripts received, or the administrative ability of their commander in looking after their health and other needs, brigades ranged widely in size. At the upper end were the brigades of Walker's division, which contained over 2,000 men at the beginning of the campaign. At the lower end of the range were several brigades that numbered less than 1,000 men, and by the time the army made its stand on Antietam Creek, some counted no more than 200 men, the size of an under-strength regiment.

The fumbled opportunities and high casualties during the Seven Days revealed numerous flaws in the army's organizational and command structure. Among them was the fact that Lee and his small headquarters staff, with the primitive communications available to a Civil War commander in the field (which were no more advanced than those of Alexander the Great), could not effectively exercise command and control over nine or more divisions. There were too many units and commanders with whom to communicate and coordinate. The result was confusion, fumbled marches, dissipated strength, and lost opportunities. Lee recognized the need for a corps organization, both to decentralize his command structure and to make the army more responsive. Since no legal authority existed to create this organization, Lee improvised. During the course of the Second Manassas Campaign he grouped his divisions into two "wings," or "commands," under the command of his two most capable subordinates, Major General James Longstreet and Major General Thomas J. "Stonewall" Jackson. Lee did not seek to achieve balance with his wings. Jackson commanded three divisions at Manassas and Longstreet commanded five, which may have also reflected Lee's estimate of their respective executive capabilities at this stage. Lee also did not assign all of his divisions to the wing commands. McLaws, D. H. Hill, and Walker were never formally attached to either command during the Maryland operation. Joe Harsh, in *Taken at the Flood*, his study of the Confederate strategy in the Maryland Campaign, suggests that Lee might have contemplated forming a third corps, and was considering McLaws and D. H. Hill as candidates to command it, but he wanted to see how they performed first. Whatever Lee might have been thinking, the informality of his command structure led to some confusion. Lines of command were not always clear. For instance, during Second Manassas, Hood's division of two brigades was temporarily placed under the command of Brigadier General Nathaniel G. Evans. Hood apparently paid little attention to his attachment. When his division captured several Union ambulances, and Evans then demanded that Hood turn them over to his control, Hood refused. Evans pressed the issue and Hood was placed in arrest. When the army entered Maryland, Evans continued to operate with the belief that he was still in command of a three-brigade division, including Hood's two brigades. Lee evidently considered Hood's attachment a temporary one, necessary to meet the situation on August 30, but no one at his headquarters, or Longstreet's, notified Evans that his authority over Hood's brigades ended after the battle. Clear lines of authority are critical in a military organization. When the lines become fuzzy or uncertain, mischief, and sometimes of dangerous consequences, can result. As an experienced soldier, Lee certainly understood this, so the problem may have been sloppy staff work.

Despite its imperfections, Lee's new command structure performed effectively at Second Manassas. Pope had more men than Lee, but Lee's small command team, consisting of himself, Jackson, and Longstreet, proved to be more flexible and able to react more quickly and decisively than Pope and his subordinates. This flexibility enabled the Confederate army to be more maneuverable and responsive than Pope's. Jackson's and Longstreet's wings were large formations to command by Civil War standards, where staffs were small and often lacked training, and communications were conducted by written or verbal instructions carried by a horse-mounted courier or staff officer. But Jackson and Longstreet were exceptional officers, and during the Manassas Campaign both demonstrated that they were quite capable of handling large numbers of troops. Lee's command system was simple. He planned operations, often after consultation with Jackson or Longstreet, and then these two generals executed the plans. There was a cohesiveness and symmetry to the team, despite the fact that Longstreet and Jackson had no particular fondness for one another, and Longstreet was not yet sure that he favored Lee over Joe Johnston. This harmony, trust, and unity of purpose of Lee's high command contrasted starkly with the disharmony and distrust existing in the command structure of the Army of the Potomac (and between its commander and his political leadership as well). It gave the Army of Northern Virginia an important operational advantage over their Union adversaries.

Staff

To assist him with coordinating the operations of the army, Lee maintained a small personal staff of seven men, in addition to a larger general staff. Lee preferred a small staff, probably because he believed it to be more efficient and because it suited his command style. His model had been Winfield Scott in Mexico, on whose staff Lee served as an engineer officer. But Scott never had an army larger than 20,000 men. Despite his staff service, Lee had no innovative thoughts on the use of his staff. This, however, was not unusual. Few American officers yet understood how the size of Civil War armies and advances in technology rendered the staff systems of the Mexican War and the prewar U.S. Army insufficient for the tasks they now had to perform. Lee used his staff to attend to the burdensome administrative details of running the army, not for ideas or for planning combat operations. Lee was his own operations officer, although he left the details of executing operational plans to Jackson and Longstreet or to independent division commanders. The staff's principal duties were to conduct reconnaissance, transcribe and transmit orders, act as a liaison between headquarters and the wing and division commanders, prepare reports and returns, conduct inspections, and deal with the mountains of paperwork attendant to running a large army. In battle they might be called on to carry verbal orders to division and corps commanders or perform liaison service, but Lee did not yet use them to supervise the execution of orders. This was not a problem while Lee had subordinates of the caliber of Jackson and Longstreet.

Since the best officers were needed to command combat units, none of Lee's personal staff were gifted leaders or possessed charismatic, powerful personalities. Except for Colonel Robert H. Chilton, the chief of staff, who had been a captain of dragoons and U.S. Army paymaster before the war, and Colonel Armistead Long, Lee's military secretary, who had served in the prewar army as an artillery lieutenant, all came from civilian life. Lee selected them on his judgment of their ability, intelligence, and personality, for he needed men he could get along with. He worked them hard and, from the perspective of one of his aides-de-camp, Major Walter H. Taylor, showed little appreciation for their labors. "I never worked so hard to please any one, and with so little effect as with General Lee," he complained at one point in the war. Behind Lee's back, the staff referred to their chief as the "Tycoon."[26]

The seven men who started the Maryland Campaign on Lee's personal staff consisted of a chief of staff, a military secretary, an assistant adjutant general, an engineer, and three aides-de-camp. Colonel Robert H. Chilton was the chief of staff, although this was not an official title. Chilton gave his position as assistant adjutant general in the orders he wrote during the Maryland Campaign. On paper he was a good choice. Lee knew him from the old U.S. Army, and he had administrative experience as a former army paymaster. In modern armies the chief of staff is the ramrod of the commander, assuring that his intent and will are understood and carried out by subordinates. He also runs the headquarters and relieves the commander from details, allowing him to focus on the important decisions. Although Chilton performed some of these duties, an assistant adjutant general's responsibilities were largely administrative, which is how Lee used him. Chilton did not possess a forceful personality, and the letters of Walter Taylor indicate that he shirked some of his responsibilities. Taylor once described Chilton as "a very good fellow in his way, & certainly one would not be troubled much who served under him, if he knew how to manage his cards."[27]

Colonel Armistead L. Long, Lee's military secretary, handled Lee's official correspondence and sometimes drafted orders. Long was an 1850 graduate of West Point and the son-in-law of Union 2nd Corps commander Edwin V. Sumner. He had served in various positions as a staff officer and as chief of artillery—his branch of service—in the Confederate army before Lee selected him as his military secretary during Lee's tenure as Davis's military advisor. When Lee assumed command of the Army of Northern Virginia, Long came with him. Lee had great confidence in Long and sometimes consulted him on questions pertaining to the army's artillery. The assistant adjutant general was Captain Arthur Pendleton Mason, a Virginian and an attorney in Arkansas before the war. Mason was one of only two members of Joe Johnston's staff who remained to serve Lee after Johnston was wounded at Fair Oaks. Major Walter H. Stevens, the army's chief engineer, was the other, although Lee left him at Richmond to supervise work on the city's defenses. Major Thomas Mann Randolph Talcott was the only engineer on Lee's personal staff in Maryland, although his official status was as an aide-de-camp. The Philadelphia-born Talcott had been an engineer on the Ohio and Mississippi Railroad before the war and served as Gen. Benjamin Huger's engineer officer before joining Lee's staff in April. Engineers were among the most well-trained and intelligent men in the army, and Talcott appears to have been a capable soldier.[28]

There were three aides-de-camp: Major Walter Taylor, Major Charles Marshall, and Major Charles Venable. All were capable, bright, energetic men. Taylor had attended the Virginia Military Institute, although he had not graduated, and was a successful Norfolk businessman before the war. He had been with Lee since December 1861. The 31-year-old Marshall was the great-nephew of Chief Justice John Marshall. He held a Master of Arts degree from the University of Virginia and was practicing law in Baltimore when the war came. He joined Lee's staff in March 1862. Charles Venable was possibly the most well-educated member of the staff. A graduate of Hampden-Sydney College at age 15, he subsequently studied and taught at his alma mater, the Universities of Virginia and Georgia, and South Carolina College. He had also spent two years abroad studying mathematics and astronomy in Berlin and Bonn. Venable joined Lee's staff in April 1862. Aides-de-camp performed their most important work on campaign and in battle, when they were responsible for delivering orders, and sometimes for writing them. They were also expected to understand the intent of Lee's orders so that they could interpret them for subordinates if there was confusion. They did whatever the chief of staff or Lee wanted them to do. In camp or on campaign that meant piles of paperwork, which Lee disliked and Chilton sought to avoid.[29]

Lee's general staff consisted of the more specialized staff positions, such as ordnance, medical, commissary, and the like, and was larger than his personal staff. Although all the officers on the general staff were important to the day-to-day operations of the army, there were three who figured prominently in Maryland, both in the positive and negative sense. They were the chief of artillery, Brigadier General William N. Pendleton; the chief of ordnance, Lieutenant Colonel Edward P. Alexander; and the surgeon general, Lafayette Guild. Pendleton's resume was the least impressive, but he had the confidence of President Davis. He graduated near the top of his class at West Point in 1830 and served three years in the coastal artillery before resigning to pursue a career in the clergy. When the war came he had settled comfortably into a position as the rector of Grace Episcopal Church in Lexington, Virginia. Although 51 years old, Pendleton promptly donned the Confederate gray and helped raise the Rockbridge Artillery, a battery that would earn fame in the war and of which he was elected captain. Joe Johnston named him his chief of artillery in July 1861 on the recommendation of the Confederate president. Pendleton did not distinguish himself at First Manassas, but his standing with Davis remained unshaken and he won promotion to brigadier general in March 1862. He continued as Johnston's artillery chief and then as Lee's after Johnston was wounded. He was a capable administrator and had sound opinions on artillery organization, but the Peninsula Campaign revealed a critical weakness: he lacked energy, decision, and aggressiveness in combat. He was, wrote one artilleryman, "Lee's weakness. P[endleto]n is like the elephant, we have him & and we don't know what on earth to do with him, and it costs a devil of a sight to feed him." Major G. Moxley Sorrel of Longstreet's staff judged him a "well meaning man, without the qualities for the high post he claimed—Chief of Artillery of the army." Behind his back the young soldiers called him "Old Mother Pendleton," and the officers in the artillery reserve had little respect for him. He had contracted malaria before the war and continued to suffer its effects occasionally. In August either a viral bug or his malaria struck and prostrated him with what he called a "crisis of a diarrhea." He missed Second Manassas but recovered sufficiently to accompany the army into Maryland, although in a weakened physical state. Lee appreciated Pendleton's administrative ability but understood his limitations as a combat officer, and in Maryland he reduced Pendleton's tactical responsibilities by detaching three of the six reserve battalions to infantry commands.[30]

The chief of ordnance, Lieutenant Colonel Edward P. Alexander, contrasted sharply with Pendleton. The 28-year-old Georgian had graduated third in the West Point class of 1857. Alexander combined a keen intellect with vigorous energy and excellent executive abilities. The day after First Manassas, Joe Johnston named him his chief of ordnance. Alexander organized the department from scratch, providing system and order to ordnance supply down to the regimental level. He did his job so well that he was kept at it when Lee took command of the army, even though Alexander was a superb artilleryman. Alexander's duty as chief of ordnance was to keep the army supplied with small arms and artillery ammunition. "It does not sound like very much to do, but there was an infinity of detail about it," he wrote. The normal demands of his post were further complicated by "the great variety of arms with which our troops were equipped both in small arms & artillery." Nevertheless, Alexander had his department so efficiently organized that through the Seven Days battles he could boast that "there was never a breath of complaint anywhere of our men's ever being short of ammunition—either for small arms or artillery."[31]

Although his system worked during the Seven Days, Alexander was not satisfied. After that campaign he overhauled the ammunition supply service of the entire army and increased the size of the reserve ordnance train. Many small arms, some artillery, and artillery ammunition had been captured from the Federals during the campaign. "We had a great swapping around both in infantry & artillery, after the battles, for many weeks," wrote Alexander, as he hastened to replace as many obsolete weapons as possible. Although much work remained to be done to bring the army to anything approaching parity with the Federals in armaments, Alexander's efforts and accomplishments were impressive and greatly improved the army's firepower. In the opinion of the historian of the Army of Northern Virginia's artillery, "without an ordnance officer of Alexander's ability, it is difficult to see how the invasion of Maryland in 1862 could have even been possible."[32]

The medical department of the army was in charge of Medical Director Lafayette Guild, a man who shared Alexander's considerable intellect, energy, and administrative abilities. And, like Alexander, he had to organize the army's medical services virtually from scratch. The 36-year-old Alabama native graduated from Jefferson Medical College in Philadelphia in 1848, after which he took a position as an assistant surgeon with the prewar U.S. Army. He remained with the army until July 1861, when he was dismissed for refusing to take the oath of allegiance. The Confederates happily offered him a surgeon's commission and Lee selected him as his medical director. The army's medical services were poorly managed under Joe Johnston, and a fellow surgeon recalled that upon assuming his new post, Guild had "an extensive and immediate work of organization devolved upon him—appointments, instructions, supplies to be secured, medical and hospital trains to be arranged, hospitals to be established. All this work of immense importance was to be done in the midst of active campaigns, with the army in motion, and often in battle." Guild set to his work "without instructions of any kind and without knowledge of the previous orders and assignments of medical officers of an army already engaged in action." He revamped the ambulance system, which he found to be a wholly "impromptu" arrangement that failed to meet the demands the Seven Days fighting placed on it. Getting the wounded to the ambulances was another problem. Litters were provided to regiments, but no one was specially assigned to carry them in battle. Consequently, when bullets started to fly, an overabundance of volunteer litter bearers appeared. To address this problem, Lee issued an order on August 11 directing every company in the army to detail two men as litter bearers. This system did not satisfy Guild—he wanted an ambulance corps—but it improved the evacuation of the wounded.[33]

Guild also found that there were not enough surgeons to meet the army's needs. He requested that every regiment on active service have at least one surgeon and two assistant surgeons, an ideal the army did not attain by the time of the Maryland Campaign. There was also a general lack of discipline within the department, and administrative laziness and ignorance. Surgeons either neglected to file casualty returns or made incomplete reports. For instance, by mid-August, when Guild forwarded the casualty returns for the Seven Days battles, he still had not received the returns from two of the army's divisions. Guild gradually improved the efficiency of his department, and the care of the wounded and sick, but much work remained to be done by September 1862. Shortages in personnel, ambulances, and medical supplies afflicted Guild's department throughout the Maryland Campaign.[34]

Quartermaster and Commissary

Deficits in transportation and supplies also plagued the quartermaster and commissary departments. Their duties had been difficult enough in the Second Manassas Campaign, although the captures of Union supplies had eased the commissariat's burden somewhat. Maryland promised to be a greater challenge. Quartermasters would be even farther from their depots, while commissary officers could not impress supplies; they had to be purchased, and there was no guarantee that Marylanders would accept Confederate money or receipts. Major Thomas Elder, the quartermaster and apparently also the acting commissary officer of Pryor's brigade, described his duties in Maryland as both "laborious" and "disagreeable." It took 105 tons of food to feed 70,000 men a standard ration each day. Each horse required 14 pounds of hay and 12 pounds of grain daily. A rough estimate would place the number of horses and mules with the army at 10,000 to 12,000, which meant that at least 156 tons of forage were necessary every day to feed these animals. Well might Major Elder complain that his duties in Maryland were laborious and disagreeable. The army simply did not have the transportation necessary to sustain itself, and despite their best efforts Elder and his fellow logisticians were unable to meet its needs in food, clothing, or shoes. As the campaign progressed, procuring food became more problematic. Rations were sometimes nothing more than corn and apples, a diet that caused diarrhea and cramps. E. P. Alexander complained that these rations "weakened the men, caused sickness & had much to do with the straggling." Clothing was another issue. Many of the regiments that had taken part in the Manassas Campaign entered Maryland with their uniforms in tatters. Weeks in the field, in all types of weather, and without a resupply of clothing caused one of Longstreet's men to quip of his regiment: "What a set of ragamuffins they looked." Nearly everyone except those in the Richmond reinforcing column could have made the same comment.[35]

The Confederates enjoyed one small advantage over the Federals in logistics. While the Army of the Potomac had to detail men from line regiments to serve in the commissary and quartermaster departments, the Confederates had several thousand slaves, both contracted and body servants, who could drive wagons and gather food and prepare it, freeing soldiers to serve with their regiments.[36]

Senior Command

With the exception of E. P. Alexander and Lafayette Guild, an overall assessment of Lee's personal and general staff on the eve of the Maryland Campaign is that they were generally competent, but there were not enough of them. Alexander felt that throughout the conflict, Lee's staff was "insufficient to keep him in touch with what was taking place." This had been true on the Peninsula and at Gettysburg, but once Lee delegated greater responsibility to Jackson and Longstreet, and while those two men were alive, the size and quality of Lee's staff was not a hindrance in combat operations. Jackson and Longstreet were outstanding soldiers who more than compensated for the shortcomings of the army headquarters staff. There was not a corps commander in the Army of the Potomac yet that matched their ability. The more famous of the two was Thomas J. "Stonewall" Jackson. Newspapers fairly gushed with praise about him and soldiers held him in awe. He was 38 years old, nearly 6 feet tall, and, "with an frame angular, muscular, and fleshless, he was, in all his movements, from riding a horse to handling a pen, the most awkward man in the army." Taciturn, eccentric, self-confident, honest, intensely ambitious, and deeply religious, Jackson had a conflicting and enigmatic personality. He was also an unforgiving soldier who drove himself hard and demanded much from his officers and men. Too much, some thought. "He forgets one ever gets tired, hungry or sleepy," complained Brigadier General Dorsey Pender. As Brigadier General Alexander Lawton recalled:

> He had no sympathy with human infirmity. He classed all who were weak and weary, who fainted by the wayside, as men who were wanting in patriotism . . . He was the true type of great soldier. He did not value human life where he had an object to accomplish. He could order men to their death as a matter of

course. Napoleon's French conscription could not have kept him supplied with men he used them up so rapidly. Hence, while he was alive there was more pride than truth in the talk of his soldier's love for him. They feared him, and obeyed him to the death; faith they had in him, a faith stronger than death. But I doubt if he had their love, though their respect he did command."[37]

Jackson pushed his men with a purpose, as he explained once to a colonel who suggested Stonewall rest his men for an hour or so during the Valley Campaign. "Colonel," Jackson answered, "I yield to no man in sympathy for the gallant men under my command; but I am obliged to sweat them tonight, that I may save their blood tomorrow." His ability to rapidly maneuver his forces won dazzling successes during the spring campaign in the Shenandoah Valley, but when Lee brought him east with his Valley army to participate in the offensive against McClellan, he performed poorly. There are two possible explanations for this. First, Jackson needed more sleep than the average person to function at his peak. Supervising the movement of his command from the Shenandoah Valley to Richmond to take part in the Seven Days offensive left him exhausted and ill. There was no time to rest before the offensive commenced, and Jackson's body simply ran down until he was literally unable to function. "Jackson was mortal," wrote one of his officers, "his endurance simply gave out." Second, when exhaustion claimed Jackson, he did not have the staff capable of running the operations of the command without him. Part of this was a condition created by Jackson himself. He delegated poorly and often shouldered details that could have been better handled by subordinates or staff. And his chief of staff, Robert L. Dabney, a professor and Presbyterian minister Jackson had known and admired before the war, proved to be utterly unfit for his position.[38]

Despite Jackson's disappointing performance on the Peninsula, Lee evidenced no lack of confidence in his stoic subordinate, and when he dispatched a force to confront Pope, he selected Jackson to command it. Initially, when he faced elements of Pope's army at Cedar Mountain, Jackson stumbled again. Commanding three divisions, the largest force he had directed thus far in the war, he handled them clumsily and won the action principally through superior numbers. But after this he returned to his old form, brilliantly executing Lee's orders to march around Pope's flank and fall on his rear, then maneuvering his forces with a skill that left John Pope baffled. When Pope finally attacked, Jackson fought his command with fierce tenacity and an indomitable will that refused to be whipped.

Jackson was obsessed with secrecy. He rarely shared information or explained his plans to his staff or subordinates. They were told only what he thought they needed to know, a system that prevented security leaks but nurtured confusion. It did precisely that in the movement of his command from the Valley to Richmond in June, again at Cedar Mountain, and in other, less serious occasions.

When General Richard Ewell was asked what the destination of the command was on the morning of the Battle of Cedar Mountain, he reflected the ignorance of Jackson's subordinates when he responded, "I pledge you my word that I do not know whether we will march north, south, east or west, or whether we will march at all." General Richard B. Garnett, whose experience with Jackson was not a happy one, complained that while under his command, "I was kept in as *profound ignorance* of his plans, instructions, and intentions, as the humblest private in his army." Jackson's stern, uncompromising, and unforgiving style of command did not make him an easy chief to work under. As historian Robert K. Krick noted, "what he expected was nothing more nor less than unquestioning, rote, mindless, obedience to orders, without any hope of understanding their context or intent." Yet despite these shortcomings, Jackson achieved results.[39]

For the invasion of Maryland, Jackson's wing consisted of three divisions—A. P. Hill's, J. R. Jones's, and Richard Ewell's, commanded by Alexander Lawton since Ewell's wounding at Second Manassas—the same three that he had commanded throughout the Second Manassas Campaign. D. H. Hill's division would fall under his orders for several days in the early stages of the campaign, but it was subsequently detached.

Solid, broad-shouldered Major General James Longstreet led Lee's other wing. Although he did not enjoy the fame of Jackson, a point of jealousy for Longstreet, he emerged from the Seven Days and Second Manassas as the army's most able senior commander besides Jackson. He was 41 years old that September, and he had lost three of his four children to scarlet fever in January, an event that left him grief stricken but did not impair his ability to command. "He was like a rock in steadiness when sometimes in battle the world seemed flying to pieces," wrote Major Moxley Sorrel, one of his staff officers. Thomas Goree, who served as an aide-de-camp to Longstreet, described him as a "very fine officer, and is as brave as Julius Caesar. His forte though as an officer consists, I think, in the seeming ease with which he can handle and arrange large numbers of troops, as also with the confidence and enthusiasm with which he seems to inspire them." Lee respected and admired him. He often established his headquarters besides Longstreet, probably not, as some of Longstreet's detractors have suggested, because he needed to keep an eye on the Georgian, but because he liked the more jovial atmosphere that prevailed at Longstreet's headquarters and liked Longstreet personally. The image of Longstreet, and his relationship with Lee, has been so greatly colored and obscured by the debate between the anti-Longstreet and pro-Longstreet factions, and by Longstreet's own clumsy postwar writings, that arriving at an objective estimate of their relationship is difficult.[40]

Longstreet's greatest strengths were tactics and an ability to manage large formations on the battlefield, as Goree had observed as early as December 1861.

At Second Manassas Longstreet skillfully managed five divisions in a devastating attack that swept Pope's army from the field. He read ground well and knew how to post his infantry and artillery to draw the greatest advantage from the terrain. But he was largely unimaginative at strategy, although he fancied himself a strategist. He was not slow, as his critics have so frequently claimed, but he preferred making war in a more predictable manner than Lee or Jackson. Lee's deviations from the accepted strategic maxims of the day (such as dividing his army in the face of a superior enemy) disturbed Longstreet, and he preferred his old friend Joe Johnston, a true textbook soldier, to Lee as a commander. Even after the Maryland Campaign, he still expressed a hope that Johnston would return to command the army. Like Jackson, Longstreet could be obstinate with subordinates, and he possessed a disagreeable trait of seeking to transfer blame when things went wrong, as he had done after he bungled the attack at Seven Pines and then successfully painted General Benjamin Huger as the scapegoat. But he worked well with Lee. Although Longstreet did not hesitate to express his opinion to Lee, as he did at Second Manassas when he counseled against attacking when Lee thought they should, during their three months' service together he did not overstep his bounds in their relationship.[41]

At Manassas, Longstreet's wing had consisted of five divisions. Each division was composed of three brigades, a table of organization he evidently favored. But the heavy losses at Manassas, combined with sickness and straggling, reduced several of his brigades to skeleton size. This necessitated a reorganization to maintain divisional strength, and perhaps, as suggested earlier, to consolidate the brigades under more efficient leaders. The five divisions were reorganized into two six-brigade divisions, one two-brigade division, and an independent brigade.

Longstreet and Jackson were rivals, but they worked well together under Lee's leadership and shared a common desire to whip the enemy above all else. Such a cohesive, talented command structure enabled Lee to attempt things McClellan could not, and it gave him an army that was more responsive and maneuverable than the Army of the Potomac.

Division Command

Of the nine division commanders with the army in Maryland, seven were West Pointers, one was a Virginia Military Institute graduate, and the ninth was a 15-year veteran of the old U.S. Army. Their average age was 38. Six of the nine had commanded a division in at least one battle. Of the six veteran commanders, Major General Ambrose P. Hill, leading what was called the Light Division, was probably the most talented. An 1847 West Point graduate, he had seen service in the 1st U.S. Artillery before the war. His slender frame disguised a fiery, sensitive spirit and aggressive instincts. On the Peninsula he rose from brigade to divisional command on his ability. Lee considered him to be the best division commander in the army. After Antietam Lee wrote to Davis that next to Jackson and Longstreet, "I consider A. P. Hill the best commander with me. He fights his troops well and takes good care of them." High praise and well deserved, but Hill could be impatient and impetuous, which were not necessarily negative virtues if controlled. He was a prideful man and did not hesitate to butt heads with superior officers whom he decided were a bit too full of themselves. During the Seven Days and immediately after those battles, he fell under Longstreet's command. The two men clashed when John M. Daniel, the editor of the *Richmond Examiner*, who was serving as a volunteer aide on Hill's staff, published a column that highlighted the fighting of Hill and his Light Division while slighting the army's other commands. Longstreet, and other officers and men in the army, were all furious. Longstreet had Major Moxley Sorrel of his staff write a response to Daniel's column, with Sorrel's piece appearing in the *Richmond Whig*. Hill took immediate offense, and relations between Hill and Longstreet deteriorated until they reached the point where Longstreet placed Hill under arrest. Hill challenged Longstreet to a duel, whereby Lee finally intervened and transferred Hill to Jackson's command.[42]

The situation was no better there. Hill and Jackson had a dislike for one another extending back to their days at West Point. Further complicating their relationship was Hill's opinion that Jackson was overrated. On three occasions—at Mechanicsville, Gaines' Mill, and Frayser's Farm—Jackson had failed to arrive on time, with the result that Hill's division was repulsed at Mechanicsville and suffered heavy losses in the other two actions. Hill performed superbly at Cedar Mountain, and his division made a magnificent defensive stand along the unfinished railroad bed at Second Manassas, yet Jackson harbored doubts about the fiery Virginian. On several occasions during the Second Manassas Campaign the Light Division had not marched well or had moved late. More than one of these incidents, however, had been of Jackson's making; his failure to communicate with his subordinates led to the confusion that resulted in Hill's late starts. Nevertheless, as Hill's biographer noted, Jackson was "convinced that Hill could not be trusted to move promptly." Hill reciprocated with a thinly veiled disgust for Jackson's secrecy and his piety. Their relationship was like a pot ready to boil over. It would on September 4.[43]

Brigadier General Alexander R. Lawton led the second of Jackson's three divisions. The 44-year-old Georgian was an 1839 West Point and an 1842 Harvard Law School graduate. By 1860 he enjoyed success in business and politics and had accumulated eight slaves and nearly $65,000 in property. Not surprisingly, he strongly supported secession. But when war came he left politics and the comforts of his home to return to soldiering. He led a brigade in Richard Ewell's division. When Ewell lost a leg from a wound received at Brawner's Farm on

August 28, command fell to Lawton by seniority. Lawton belonged to that class of soldiers who are more effective administrators than they are combat leaders, and Jackson clearly held reservations about his ability for division command. Before the Battle of Cedar Mountain, by seniority Lawton should have commanded Jackson's division, but Jackson detached him and his brigade to guard trains, so that Charles Winder could take command of the other three brigades of the division. Winder was killed in the battle, so Jackson transferred Lawton and his brigade to Ewell's Division to keep him from division command. But then Ewell went down. There was nowhere to safely tuck Lawton, and no one available with the necessary rank or seniority that Jackson could reassign to the division, so Lawton led it through Second Manassas and into Maryland.[44]

Problems with casualties and seniority also afflicted Jackson's third division, his old command. The Second Manassas Campaign hit the division's leadership hard. Its commander, Charles S. Winder, who was handpicked by Jackson, was killed at Cedar Mountain. Jackson transferred Lawton, the senior brigadier, to allow Brigadier General William B. Taliaferro to take command, but Taliaferro went down with a wound at Brawner's Farm. Brigadier General William E. Starke, a prewar cotton broker in New Orleans and Mobile, took command and performed solidly at Second Manassas. But Brigadier General John R. Jones, absent since July 1 to recover from a wound received at Malvern Hill, returned just as the army was entering Maryland and, by seniority, took command of Jackson's division (to avoid confusion, hereafter in the text it will be called J. R. Jones's division). Jones was an 1848 Virginia Military Institute graduate. Before the war he taught school in several different states, and he had participated in some fashion in the Florida Militia. His private life was rather tumultuous for the times. He had been married twice, and his second marriage ended in divorce after one year, perhaps because Jones had a mistress, a former slave who came to work in Jones's household and by whom he had two children. When the war began he returned to Virginia and raised a company of the 33rd Virginia, which became part of Stonewall's brigade. Jones rose through the ranks and won the approval of Stonewall himself, who recommended his promotion to brigadier general. Although Lee and Jefferson Davis approved the promotion, the Confederate Senate had not confirmed Jones's rank by the time of the Maryland Campaign, and it never would. Jackson had many talents, but judging command ability was not among them, and Jones proved to be one of his numerous failures.[45]

Longstreet had one outstanding officer and two competent soldiers commanding his three divisions. His brightest star was Brigadier General John Bell Hood, 31 years old, a tall, rangy Kentuckian who had adopted Texas as his state of record. He graduated from West Point in 1853 and spent most of his prewar army career with the 2nd U.S. Cavalry in Texas. In 1861 he was named colonel of the 4th Texas Infantry. A year later he was selected to command the Texas

Brigade, which consisted of three Texas regiments, one Georgia regiment, and a South Carolina legion (essentially a battalion). On the Peninsula he earned a reputation as a hard-hitting and fearless commander, but it was at the Battle of Gaines' Mill that Hood emerged as one of the army's finest combat leaders. In that engagement he led his brigade in a fierce attack that penetrated the formidable Union defenses and helped secure a Confederate victory. Jackson, who was sparing in his praise, described Hood's attack as "this rapid and almost matchless display of daring and valor." Hood was a natural leader and inspired his men to deeds of valor.[46]

On July 26 Hood's division commander departed on a medical furlough, and Hood, as the senior officer, assumed command of the two-brigade division. At Second Manassas on August 30, he led his division in a furious attack that demolished the Federal left flank and helped drive Pope's army from the field. In two major engagements Hood had demonstrated consummate tactical skill at both the brigade and small-division level, and he exhibited the courageous personal leadership volunteers expected and needed. But his victories did not come cheaply. At Gaines' Mill the Texas Brigade sustained 572 casualties, and at Manassas his division suffered over 900. Despite these heavy losses, his men "were devoted to him and believed in him absolutely . . . and he was as popular and trusted by his officers as his men."[47]

Hood entered Maryland in the rear of the division, in arrest, the result of a squabble over captured Union ambulances with Brigadier General Nathaniel Evans, who temporarily commanded Hood's division at Second Manassas. Longstreet ordered Hood to Culpepper, Virginia, to wait there until his case could be heard—a rather bizarre decision, given the circumstances of the offense and the important operations the army was then engaged in. Lee prudently intervened and rescinded Longstreet's orders, allowing Hood to remain with his command, although still in arrest. Lee did not want some petty offense depriving him of one of his finest combat leaders in the operations ahead.[48]

Major General Richard Heron Anderson led the second of Longstreet's divisions. An 1842 West Point graduate, Anderson saw considerable service in the Mexican War and subsequently spent much of his career in the dragoons. He remained in the army until his native South Carolina seceded, when he resigned and offered his services to the Confederacy. As a brigadier general he distinguished himself at Williamsburg and fought well during the Seven Days. His overall performance on the Peninsula earned him promotion to major general on July 14, along with command of a three-brigade division. He stumbled leading this larger command at Second Manassas. At the peak of the battle, when the Union line atop Henry Hill wavered and might have been driven from the field, Anderson failed to press home the attack. Yet neither Lee nor Longstreet lost confidence in the affable South Carolinian, and in the reorganization after Second Manassas, Anderson received command of the three brigades that had been Wilcox's division, raising the size of Anderson's division to six brigades. Although personally brave, Second Manassas revealed a certain lack of energy in Anderson. Colonel Micah Jenkins, who served with Anderson at the brigade level and as a brigade commander after the latter's promotion to division command, found him a friendly fellow but an "indifferent officer." Moxley Sorrel, of Longstreet's staff, knew Anderson well and wrote that "his capacity and intelligence were excellent, but it was hard to get him to use them." Longstreet apparently understood this about Anderson and, according to Sorrel, knew how to "get a good deal out of him, more than anyone else."[49]

Brigadier General David R. Jones, a courtly South Carolinian, led the third division of Longstreet's command. Jones enjoyed powerful connections from birth: he was Zachary Taylor's nephew and Jefferson Davis's cousin. The military path of his uncle and cousin most likely steered Jones to West Point, where he graduated 41st out of 59 cadets in the class of 1846. He saw service in Mexico as an infantry officer and remained in the U.S. Army until South Carolina's secession, when he resigned. Jones distinguished himself early on, serving initially as Beauregard's chief of staff during the events at Fort Sumter, and then as commander of a brigade in the victory at First Manassas. In March 1862 he won promotion to major general and command of a small division, which he led with quiet ability and competence throughout the Peninsula and Second Manassas campaigns. Lee thought highly enough of Jones's performance in the latter battle to warrant enlarging his division to six brigades by combining it with Kemper's. Sorrel described him as "a very agreeable, loveable man, tall and stately, he made a brave appearance, and well merited the sobriquet of 'Neighbor Jones,' as they pleasantly called him at West Point." Although only 37 years old, Jones suffered from heart disease, and its effects were beginning to tell on him.[50]

Of the three independent division commanders, Daniel Harvey Hill was the most battle experienced. An 1842 West Point graduate, Hill compiled an outstanding record in the Mexican War. But the peacetime army held little appeal for him, and he resigned his commission in 1849 to pursue a career as an educator. At the outbreak of the Civil War he was commissioned a colonel and organized the 1st North Carolina infantry. In less than a year he was a major general. He led a division on the Peninsula, fighting at Williamsburg, Seven Pines, Gaines' Mill, and Malvern Hill, and earned a reputation for being a tough, fearless fighter. Moxley Sorrel described him as "a small, delicate man . . . and positively the bravest man ever seen." Another staff officer who served under Hill considered him "a man of considerable capacity and always seemed to go from choice into the most dangerous place he could find on the field." But, observed Sorrel, Hill was also known to fight "furiously for some time and then something weakened about him."[51]

Hill was not popular in the army. A fellow officer, one of the few who actually liked Hill, related that he had a reputation of "being cross, impulsive, and often gives offence." He possessed a sharp, caustic personality, and no one was immune from the sarcastic comments that rolled off his tongue or his pen. Cavalrymen were a favorite target of his. Hill once quipped that he "had yet to see a dead man with spurs on," a comment that won him no friends in the mounted branch. Lee valued his fighting qualities but personally disliked him, finding his temperament "queer." Lee tolerated many personality quirks among his subordinates, but his concern about Hill went beyond personality. Lee wrote to Jefferson Davis in mid-August that while Hill was "an excellent executive officer, he does not have much administrative ability. Left to himself he seems embarrassed and backward to act." Hill's days with the Army of Northern Virginia were numbered, but he would last through the Maryland Campaign, where his qualities as a combat officer served Lee well.[52]

The second of the independent division commanders, 41-year-old Major General Lafayette McLaws, was as yet undistinguished and largely untested in this role. He graduated with D. H. Hill in the class of '42 at West Point and had seen routine service. After nearly 20 years in the old U.S. Army he was only a captain when the war began, although this was hardly unusual in the small peacetime army, where promotions came painfully slowly. Advancement for McLaws was swifter in the Confederate army; by May 23, 1862, he was a major general. He had few opportunities on the Peninsula to exhibit his ability, and during the Seven Days battles he only commanded a two-brigade division. Lee apparently felt that McLaws had performed well enough, for he enlarged the Georgian's division to four brigades in the reorganization after the Seven Days. From Moxley Sorrel's perspective, McLaws was "not brilliant in the field or quick in movement there or elsewhere, [but] he could always be counted on." He was also known for his attention to detail and for keeping his command "in excellent condition." A stern test of his abilities awaited him in Maryland.[53]

Forty-year-old Brigadier General John G. Walker commanded the third of the independent divisions. Although Missouri-born, Walker, like Hood, had adopted Texas as his native state. He enlisted in the prewar U.S. Army at the outbreak of the Mexican War and rose to the rank of captain by 1861. His support of secession did not burn as fiercely as the others', and he did not resign from the army until 10 days after First Manassas. After service with the 8th Texas Cavalry, he was promoted to brigadier general in January 1862 and received command of a North Carolina brigade, which he led during the Peninsula Campaign. His command saw little action and reported only 12 wounded during the Seven Days. When Davis dispatched the Richmond reinforcements to Lee, he sent two of the three brigades that had been in Holmes's division during the Peninsula Campaign. As the senior officer, Walker assumed command of this new division, consisting entirely of North Carolina troops. Although said to have a "high reputation among those of his acquaintance," Walker's abilities at division command were unknown.[54]

Major General James E. B. "Jeb" Stuart commanded the cavalry division. As such, he was also Lee's chief intelligence officer, since the cavalry, among its other duties, was responsible for maintaining contact with the enemy and gathering information. A 31-year-old former West Pointer, Stuart was, wrote Longstreet, "endowed with the gifts that go to make a perfect cavalryman." A rugged build and boundless energy were two of his natural assets, as were intelligence, fearlessness, and daring. He could also be vain and arrogant. By the end of the Second Manassas Campaign he was without par as a cavalry officer in the eastern theater. In both the Peninsula and the Second Manassas campaigns he made the Federal cavalry look foolish and inept. As an intelligence officer he demonstrated the vital ability to both gather information—by aggressively making contact with the enemy—and exercise good judgment in screening it, so that Lee received reasonably accurate reports about enemy activity. But his successes bred contempt for the enemy and overconfidence. Some of his positive results during the Peninsula and the Second Manassas campaigns had been because the enemy was poorly led and dispersed its cavalry, while Lee concentrated his. That would begin to change in Maryland, and success would not come so easily. Stuart would also display some questionable judgment at key moments in Maryland. But that lay in the future.[55]

Brigade Command

The army's nine infantry divisions contained a total of 39 brigades. Evans's independent brigade rounded out the number to an even 40. The authorized rank of a brigade commander was a brigadier general. But the summer campaign had taken a heavy toll of brigade commanders, and colonels now led 16 of the 40 brigades. Seven of this group of 40 had never led a brigade in combat, which was not unusual, given the number of vacancies each battle produced. Eight were West Point graduates, and four others had been commissioned directly into the regular army before the war. Another 15 possessed some prewar military education or Mexican War experience. Thirteen had no professional training or prewar military experience. Several of the leaders, such as Jubal Early, Robert Rodes, and Dorsey Pender, were superb soldiers and destined for higher command. There were also several who lacked competence or the ability to head a brigade, such as Howell Cobb and Roger Pryor. But the majority were capable soldiers and well suited to brigade command, where leadership and courage were of greater importance than executive and administrative ability. Compared with the Army of the Potomac's brigade leadership, Lee's brigade commanders enjoyed an overall edge in ability and experience.

Staff work was a weak link at the wing, division, and brigade levels, but particularly at the latter two levels. The need for placing trained officers in combat positions meant that staffs were composed of volunteers who learned their duties on the job. Most had no prior military education or experience, and many were prewar friends or relatives of their commander. Lee recognized the problem and brought it to Confederate President Davis's attention on March 21, 1862. "If you can fill these positions with proper officers," he wrote, "not the relatives and social friends of the commanders, who, however agreeable their company, are not always the most useful—you might have the finest army in the world." After assuming command of the army, Lee made some progress in this area by tightening the casual atmosphere that had existed under Johnston's leadership, but he could not pick his subordinates' staffs, and the problem of inefficient or incompetent amateurs in staff positions continued. Experience gained in the Peninsula and Second Manassas campaigns had improved staff work, but there still remained considerable room for improvement. Almost one year later, at Gettysburg, Colonel Edward P. Alexander complained that "scarcely any of our generals had half of what [staff] they needed to keep a *constant & close supervision on the execution of important orders*" (Alexander's italics).[56]

The consequences of the April 16 Conscription Act on regimental and company-grade leadership still lingered in the army that made ready to enter Maryland. Many of the new field and line officers elected as result of the reorganization did not lack courage, but as Robert L. Dabney, Jackson's chief of staff on the Peninsula, noted, courage did not compensate for their other deficiencies.

> In many there was not an intelligent comprehension of their duties nor zeal in their performance. Appointed by the votes of their neighbors and friends, they would neither exercise that rigidity in governing, nor that detailed care in providing for the wants of their men, which are necessary to keep soldiers efficient . . . It was seldom that these officers were guilty of cowardice upon the field of battle, but they were often in the wrong places, fighting as common soldiers when they should have been directing others. Above all was their inefficiency marked [by] their inability to keep their men in the ranks. Absenteeism grew under them to a monstrous evil, and every poltroon and laggard found a way to escape.[57]

The Peninsula and Second Manassas Campaigns were a mixed blessing for regimental leadership. They provided a litmus test for the new field and line officers elected in the April–May reorganization and exposed some of those who might have been nice fellows but were not combat leaders. These individuals often departed, complaining of some illness. Others simply proved incapable of enduring the physical rigor of campaigning. Yet some incompetents still slipped through the winnowing process. Henry R. Berkeley, an artilleryman in the Hanover (Virginia) Artillery, confided to his diary immediately after the Seven Days battles that his captain and every other officer except one—all of whom were elected in the spring—"have proved themselves totally incompetent to command a battery. The company is going to the dogs, and unless something is done, and done very soon, it will go all to pieces." His battery commander, Berkeley added, was a very brave man, "but bravery alone will not keep up a battery." The company did go to the dogs, and it was broken up before the army entered Maryland. A South Carolina officer complained in a letter to his wife of some of examples of poor leadership he had observed: "You need not think *all* that come out here are entitled to their country's praise, and you would be astonished to know how many officers are dodging behind some various pretexts. I know of a great many." For those who did not belong to the brand of officer described by the South Carolinian—and this was the majority—the Peninsula and Second Manassas campaigns seasoned them and gave them an understanding of the discipline necessary to survive the harsh realities of campaigning and combat.[58]

The summer campaigns had decimated the regimental field and line officers. A regiment with its full complement of officers had 3 field officers (colonel, lieutenant colonel, and major), an adjutant, 10 captains, 10 first lieutenants, and 10 second lieutenants. By the beginning of September many regiments were commanded by majors and captains, and second lieutenants or sergeants frequently led companies. In two of Jackson's divisions, Lawton's and J. R. Jones's, out of the 43 regiments and battalions in the 2 divisions, captains commanded 15 and a lieutenant commanded 1. This was 37 percent of the regimental leadership in these two divisions. The situation was not as severe in the other divisions of the army, but few regiments counted more than one field officer. This meant that there were a considerable number of junior officers bearing responsibility for duties that they were unfamiliar with or untrained for.

The noncommissioned ranks—the backbone of discipline in any army—did not escape the damaging effects of the election system allowed by the Conscription Act. Charles Marshall observed that "under the election system, it is apparent that these officers not only had no encouragement to do their duty faithfully, but if they desired promotion, they were positively encouraged to neglect it. Strictness with the men would certainly debar them from promotion by their votes, and to gain popularity, they were tempted to tolerate conduct subversive of discipline, or to great indulgence inconsistent with the efficiency of the army." Probably many of the army's disciplinary and straggling problems were rooted at the company level, where company officers and noncoms were either unwilling, ignorant, or too lazy to see that discipline was enforced.[59]

Shortcoming in discipline and leadership at the regimental level were partially compensated for by the high quality of the men who made up the rank and file of the army. Except for a sprinkling of conscripts, they were all volunteers and represented some of the most dedicated men in the South to the Confederate cause. They were independent minded and chaffed under regular army discipline, but their spirit in battle was superb. They earned Lee's respect on the Peninsula and on the fields of Manassas. "I need not say to you that the material of which it is composed is the best in the world," he wrote to Davis on September 7. "Nothing can surpass the gallantry and intelligence of the main body."[60]

Infantry

The army's infantry carried the burden of the battle in the Seven Days, where terrain and an inefficient organization reduced the role of the artillery. At Gaines' Mill in particular, sheer élan and courage had carried the day. Lee's infantry prevailed, but not because they were better trained or disciplined than their Northern foes. It began with Lee, who cultivated an aggressive spirit and encouraged initiative in his subordinates. This trickled down the chain of command and, combined with battlefield success, helped imbue the foot soldier with a sense of superiority over his countrymen; aggressiveness; and confidence in his cause, its justness, and its ultimate victory. "They all believe in themselves as well as in their generals, and are terribly in earnest," wrote a northern doctor in Frederick, Maryland, of his encounter with men of Lee's army. Captain George Noyes, a staff officer in the Union 1st Corps, expressed similar sentiments after encountering a Maryland farmer who contemptuously described the rebels who had passed his home as "half-clothed and dilapidated." "But I knew how well these men fought," wrote Noyes, "and his statement elicited, not my contempt, but rather my respect for men who under such difficulties and want of food and clothing have stood up bravely and persistently in a bad cause. Such men must be sincere."[61]

Although the Federal troops fought bravely on the Peninsula and at Second Manassas, on the offensive their attacks apparently rarely possessed the violence and "shock" that characterized an attack by Lee's infantry. Union General Joe Hooker, a good judge of the fighting qualities of both armies, described a Confederate infantry assault as a "blow," so great was its impact and its severity. He believed the rank and file of the Army of Northern Virginia to be "vastly inferior to our own, intellectually and physically," but that its discipline was such that it had "acquired a character for steadiness and efficiency unsurpassed, in my judgement, in ancient or modern times. We have not been able to rival it, nor has there been any near approximation to it in the other rebel armies." Confederate officers would have howled at Hooker's statement that their army had achieved a level of discipline unsurpassed in ancient or modern times on the march or in camp. But in battle—on that they would agree.[62]

An incident between Stonewall Jackson and a wounded infantryman at Second Manassas, witnessed by Henry K. Douglas, of Jackson's staff, reflected the spirit that Hooker admired and Lee lauded. While riding along his lines after the fighting had subsided, Jackson noted a wounded soldier struggling out of the unfinished railroad cut that much of his command had occupied during the fierce fighting. Jackson stopped and asked if the soldier was wounded. "Yes, general, but have we whipped em?" the soldier replied. Jackson answered that they had, and then he asked the soldier what regiment he belonged to. "I belong to the 4th Virginia, your old brigade, general. I have been wounded four times but never before as bad as this. I hope I will soon be able to follow you again." Such men were not easily defeated.[63]

Due to the efforts of the Ordnance Department, supplemented by captures from the Federals, the quality of the small arms carried by the infantry had been significantly improved since the early days of the war. Then, 9 out of 10 Confederate infantrymen were armed with a variety of .69-caliber smoothbore muskets (some even had .70-caliber smoothbores). Obsolete by 1861 standards, the .69-caliber was accurate out to about 75 yards, although when firing buck and ball (three buckshot and a round ball) it was deadly at that range. The mission of the Ordnance Department was to replace these smoothbores with rifles. The Confederate government had adopted the muzzle-loading .58-caliber rifle-musket as its standard infantry arm. The .58-caliber was an excellent weapon, accurate out to 200 yards and capable of still killing a man at 1,000 yards. There were several models available, including the Model 1855 "Harpers Ferry" rifle, the Model 1861 Springfield, and the Model 1853 British-manufactured Enfield rifle, which came in both .577- and .58-calibers. The Springfields and Enfields were the finest rifles then available, but obtaining them in sufficient numbers to equip all the Confederate infantry proved impossible. Many men ended up with the "Harpers Ferry" rifle or the .54-caliber U.S. Model 1841 "Mississippi" rifle, as well as the Austrian-made Lorenz rifle, which came in calibers from .54 to .59. The excellence of the firearm depended largely on the manufacturer and the quality of its ammunition. Although the Springfields and Enfields tended to be the most reliable and serviceable of the small arms available, their quality was sometimes dependent on which contractor assembled it. The same applied to ammunition. Cheaply manufactured ammunition fouled weapons sooner, which made them difficult to load. Another wrinkle involved the Enfield. The .577 Enfield would accept .58-caliber ammunition, but it caused the weapon to foul quickly, and after several rounds it, too, became difficult to load. Such were some of the dilemmas Lee's ordnance officers dealt with.[64]

Between purchases overseas and captures from U.S. armories and from the Union army during the Seven Days battles and the Second Manassas Campaign, approximately 70 percent of the Army of Northern Virginia's infantry carried rifled muskets into Maryland. The remainder were armed with smoothbores. Ammunition supply remained a problem, however, since there was still little uniformity in caliber, and ordnance officers of nearly every brigade had to maintain ammunition for three or more calibers of weapons. Sometimes regiments even carried more than one type of small arms. Although ordnance officers like E. P. Alexander bemoaned the fact that not all of their army's infantry were armed with rifles, they would have taken heart had they known that the Union army's infantry were not much better off.[65]

The Federals, however, were considerably better uniformed and equipped than Lee's infantry. "A musket, cartridge box with forty rounds of cartridges, cloth haversack, blanket and canteen made up the Confederate soldier's equipment," recalled a sergeant in D. R. Jones's division.[66] But not all Confederate infantry traveled so light. Many had picked up knapsacks on the Peninsula, at Cedar Mountain, or at Second Manassas and carried them into Maryland, along with various other pieces of Union equipment, such as belts, haversacks, cartridge boxes, and the like, all of which were far superior to anything their state or the Confederate government provided. Except for the troops of the reinforcing column from Richmond, who were fairly well uniformed and shod, the uniforms and shoes of the infantry who had participated in the Second Manassas Campaign were in pitiful condition. Alexander Hunter, a private in the 17th Virginia, described his and his comrades' sorry shape when they were in Maryland.

> It seemed as if every cornfield in Maryland had been robbed of its scarecrows and propped up against that fence. None had any underclothing. My costume consisted of a ragged pair of trousers, a stained, dirty jacket; an old slouch hat, the brim pinned up with a thorn; a begrimed blanket over my shoulder, a grease-smeared cotton haversack full of apples and corn, a cartridge box full and a musket. I was barefooted and had a stonebruise on each foot. Some of my comrades were a little better dressed, some were worse. I was the average, but there was no one there who would not have been "run in" by the police had he appeared on the streets of any populous city, and would have been fined next day for undue exposure.[67]

The uniforms and shoes supplied by the Confederate government did not stand field service well, and a campaign as arduous as Second Manassas told severely on these items. Poorly made shoes wore out quickly. Although some men were able to obtain footwear from dead or captured Yankees at Manassas, the shortage of shoes in the infantry remained a serious problem, contributing to straggling and a considerable temporary loss of manpower when the army shed its ineffectives at Leesburg before entering Maryland.

One important advantage Lee's infantry enjoyed over their Federal opponents was that aside from the few thousand conscripts, they were all veterans. Twelve percent had participated in five major battles, and approximately 48 percent had seen action in three or four battles. Only 19 percent had been in just one battle. And the conscripts either quickly learned from the veterans around them or became casualties. The Army of the Potomac, in contrast, would enter the Maryland Campaign with nearly 20 percent of its infantry strength composed of raw recruits, in new regiments, with little or no training. The Confederate infantryman also possessed the edge in motivation to fight. They would straggle badly and maintain indifferent discipline on the march and in camp, but their battle discipline and enthusiastic spirit were such that even their enemy acknowledged it. It was these qualities—élan, courage, and motivation—that moved the typically dispassionate Jackson to exclaim during the Second Manassas Campaign, "who could not conquer with troops such as these."[68]

Artillery

While the Army of Northern Virginia might have had the edge in the quality and experience of its infantry, their artillery, in ammunition and equipment, was greatly inferior to that of the Federals. After the Richmond column reinforced him, Lee had 80 batteries of artillery, each battery generally being composed of four guns, although there were exceptions to this, some having more guns and some less. When the army reached Leesburg it shed seven batteries, or about 28 guns, that were unfit for service. Using the average of four guns per Confederate battery, this gave the army approximately 292 guns. In his memoirs, Edward Alexander recalled that there were 67 batteries, consisting of 284 guns, that entered Maryland. Alexander was incorrect on the number of batteries, but he may have been right about the number of guns. We shall probably never know the exact amount. It is possible that even Lee did not know the precise number of guns he had in Maryland, since his artillery was being reorganized before and after the Maryland Campaign. Batteries in the Army of Northern Virginia consisted of four guns, rather than the six that were standard in the Union army, because shortages in horses and equipment made it nearly impossible to fit out and maintain a six-gun unit. In the Army of the Potomac each battery, with only a handful of exceptions, consisted of the same caliber and type of field-piece. The Army of Northern Virginia had no uniformity of caliber, again because of shortages in quality ordnance. Two and, on occasion, three different-caliber field pieces might be found in a battery. One example was the Pee Dee (South Carolina) battery of Captain David G. McIntosh that served in A. P. Hill's division. McIntosh had one 10 lb. Parrott rifle, one 3-inch rifle, one 12 lb. howitzer, and one Napoleon. At ranges of over a mile, only two guns of the battery could engage, and the howitzer was only effective out to about three-quarters of a mile. Such mixed batteries created tactical issues and created headaches for the ordnance officers, who attempted to have an adequate ammunition supply on hand for the different-caliber guns.[69]

Despite the vigorous efforts of Chief of Ordnance Josiah Gorgas to meet the equipment and ordnance needs of the Southern artillerymen, nearly half of the Army of Northern Virginia's artillery in September 1862 was obsolete, and it was out-ranged by nearly every gun in the Army of the Potomac. Approximately 71 guns (24% of 292) were 6 lb. guns and howitzers, which were useful in the Mexican War but which became outdated by the introduction of the 12 lb. Napoleon, the 3-inch ordnance rifle, and the 10 lb. Parrott rifle. The 6-pounder had an extreme range of about 1,500 yards firing solid shot, but its range when firing the more effective shrapnel (also called case shot) was less. The missiles it discharged—solid shot, shell, and shrapnel—were half the weight of those from the Napoleon, and it fired a small canister charge, due to its smaller bore. The shell and shrapnel available for it were poorly manufactured—a common problem with all Confederate artillery—and tended to burst prematurely or not explode at all. Every field piece in the Federal arsenal outgunned the 6-pounder in both range and weight of metal.[70]

During the Maryland Campaign the Confederates had 59 Model 1841 12 lb. howitzers and 6 Model 1841 24 lb. howitzers, which represented 22 percent of the army's long arm. Howitzers had a higher trajectory than guns and were designed to lob shells or shrapnel on an enemy who might be out of the line of sight. The 12 lb. howitzer fired a nearly 9 lb. shell just over 1,000 yards. The 24 lb. howitzer could hurl an 18.4 lb. shell 1,300 yards. Both guns fired shell, shrapnel, and canister. Although howitzers had excellent hitting power, their limited range placed them at a distinct disadvantage against the Federal artillery, all of which out-ranged them. The weight of the 24-pounder—the tube and carriage weighed 2,446 pounds—also limited its mobility. The 12 lb. howitzer was only useful if it could not be seen by Federal artillery, which rendered it almost useless. When the howitzers could be deployed to engage enemy infantry with canister they were murderous, particularly the 24-pounder, which had a nearly 6-inch bore. But such opportunities rarely presented themselves on the battlefield, for the Union batteries generally sent the howitzers hunting for cover before a chance to deal canister presented itself.[71]

Of the Army of Northern Virginia's remaining guns, 32 were the popular 12 lb. Napoleon smoothbores, and around 112 were rifled pieces. Among the rifled guns, there was a smattering of excellent imported models: the Blakely, the Hotchkiss, and the breech-loading Whitworth. The workhorses among rifles, however, and the most numerous, were the 3-inch ordnance rifle and the 10 lb. and 20 lb. Parrott rifles, although there were only six of the latter. These guns could hit targets at ranges of up to 3,500–4,000 yards. They were invaluable for counterbattery fire and for disrupting enemy formations at long range. The quality of the rifled guns varied with the origins of their manufacture. Those captured from the Federals were of excellent quality, but a number of the rifles, principally the 3-inchers, were cast in the South. E. P. Alexander wrote that these weapons "were all adapted to the same ammunition, but were not of uniform length or shape, and varied in weight from a thousand to twelve hundred pounds." All of the rifles were capable of firing solid shot, shrapnel (or case), shell, and canister. The quality of the shrapnel and shell also varied, depending on where it was made. Union ammunition was first rate. Rifled shrapnel and shell produced by Southern factories bordered on worthless. According to E. P. Alexander, three out of four shells fired from the rifled pieces failed to take the grooves of the tube. Many shells exploded either in the gun or soon after they left the muzzle. Those that did catch the rifling often tumbled, which reduced their range, and "not one-fourth exploded at all." Alexander wrote that "against an enemy in the field it [the ammunition] was of little real value." There was also a lack of certain types of ammunition. Timed-fuse shell and solid shot were the principal long-range ammunitions available. Percussion shell, invaluable for getting the range, was extremely scarce, and shrapnel, the most effective rifled ammunition, was not manufactured in the South, due to a scarcity of lead.[72]

The Model 1857 12 lb. smoothbore bronze Napoleon was extremely popular with both armies. It was durable, maneuverable, and could fire a 12.3 lb. shot to an extreme range of 1,600 yards. Like the rifled guns, it could fire solid shot, shrapnel, shell, and canister. The Napoleon could be devastating when firing the latter type of ammunition. With its 4.62-inch bore, it delivered a potent canister charge. A single canister round contained 27 large balls, which could be delivered out to about 600 yards. At 200 yards and below, a gun might fire double canister, delivering 54 balls downrange. Thus a four-gun battery, in one discharge, could unleash 216 golf-ball sized balls into an attacking formation. Beyond canister range, ammunition quality hampered the Napoleons' effectiveness. The fuse used in Confederate manufactured shell turned out to be notoriously defective. Alexander wrote that "premature explosions of shell were so frequent that the artillery could only be used over the heads of the infantry with such danger and demoralization to the latter that it was seldom attempted." Improvements were eventually made, but not until 1863.[73]

Besides defective ammunition and obsolete equipment, the Confederate army's artillery had also borne the burden of inefficient organization during the Seven Days. This had been partly corrected when the army entered Maryland. When Lee inherited the army from Johnston, slightly less than half of its batteries were distributed to the infantry divisions. The rest were grouped into a large, unwieldy army reserve under Pendleton. Lee promptly granted Pendleton greater independence and administrative authority than he had enjoyed under Johnston and tasked him with increasing the artillery's efficiency. Pendleton managed to reorganize the reserve artillery into five battalions before the Seven Days offensive, but he was unable to make significant changes in the divisional artillery structure, which had serious defects. Divisional commanders, who were inevitably infantryman, regularly attached their individual batteries to infantry brigades. These brigade batteries received their orders directly from the brigade commander and depended on the brigade staff for their ammunition, rations, forage, and all supplies. With batteries dispersed to brigades, and brigade commanders loathe to part with their guns, the arrangement virtually guaranteed the impossibility of massing batteries for concentrated fire on a specific point.[74]

The consequences of this inefficient organization were felt throughout the Seven Days fighting. Coordination and concentration of artillery firepower was absent on every field, and "that when fought at all, it was put in only in inefficient driblets." The lack of adequate gun support contributed to heavy casualties in the infantry. The Battle of Malvern Hill was the most melancholy example. In this engagement Lee intended to precede his infantry assaults with a massive artillery preparation, but as the brigade batteries swung into action, one or two at a time, the excellent Union artillery, employed en masse by the Union's brilliant chief of artillery, Brigadier General Henry J. Hunt, easily silenced or knocked out the Confederate guns. D. H. Hill thought the artillery preparation preceding the infantry attack was "of the most farcical character." It was, but there was nothing farcical or comical in the massacre of Lee's infantry, who followed this inadequate artillery preparation and attempted to carry the strong Union position.[75]

Pendleton addressed the dismal performance of the army's artillery in a frank postcampaign report.

> I would commend to the consideration of the commanding general what seems to me to have been a serious error with regard to the use of artillery in these several fights—too little was thrown into action at once, too much was left in the rear unused. One or two batteries brought into position at a time to oppose a much larger artillery force well posted must greatly suffer, if not ultimately yield under the concentrated fire. This was in several instances our experience.[76]

Lee acknowledged these problems and, following the Seven Days, took steps to improve the situation. On June 22 he had already issued an order essentially directing that the artillery batteries of each infantry division were to be grouped into a single battalion under the command of an artillery chief. An experienced artilleryman could keep a sharper eye on the equipment, discipline, and training of his batteries than an infantry brigade commander would. In the few days before the Seven Days battles began, the army was unable to carry out this change, and it did not begin to do so in earnest until after that campaign concluded. Lee also reduced the size of Pendleton's reserve by transferring a battalion to Longstreet's command as a general reserve. The effect of these changes was immediately evident at Second Manassas, where the army's long arm, despite its problems with ammunition quality and subpar equipment, served the army well and had a direct impact on the successful outcome of the battle. This more efficient organization allowed batteries to be massed at critical points more easily. During Longstreet's counterattack against Pope on the 30th, his batteries moved forward with the infantry in a combined arms effort that would have been impossible on the Peninsula.[77]

Second Manassas also demonstrated that good organization could help offset inferiority in guns and ammunition. But improvements in organization were still necessary, and Lee planned additional changes before the army entered Maryland. The reassignment of batteries from attachment to brigades into divisional artillery battalions continued, as did a reduction in the size of the general reserve. The army reserve was to be pared down to three battalions, with a reserve battalion attached to each wing as a general reserve, all subject to the directions of the wing commander and his chief of artillery.[78]

Due to the speed with which events developed after Second Manassas, the army was unable to complete this reorganization before it entered Maryland. Jackson's wing did not receive a reserve battalion, and the artillery reserve entered Maryland with five battalions, although during the course of the campaign Lee detached one battalion to support D. H. Hill's division and another to Longstreet's wing, which gave the latter two reserve battalions. The changes were not balanced, but Lee managed to get more guns out of the general reserve to serve with the main combat units.

The army did complete a thorough inspection of its batteries on the eve of its entry into Maryland. General Orders No. 102, issued on September 4, stipulated that "those batteries with horses too much reduced for service will be, men and horses, temporarily transferred by General Pendleton to other batteries." The resulting inspections revealed a number of batteries that were unfit for service, due to personnel losses, the condition of their horses and equipment, or just general inefficiency by their officers. Rather than take them into Maryland, where they would be a hindrance, those deemed unfit for service were instructed to temporarily transfer their healthy horses and some of their equipment and men to other batteries. The residue were ordered to Winchester, where Lee intended to establish a depot. The net result of this shakedown was that it strengthened some batteries, but also reduced the firepower of some artillery battalions, such as D. R. Jones's divisional battalion, which was left with only a single battery.[79]

Although the organization of the Confederate artillery remained imperfect, it was now superior to that of the Army of the Potomac, whose long arm had not recovered from the confusion attendant on the withdrawal from the Peninsula and the consolidation of forces after Second Manassas. Although good organization did not completely compensate for poor quality ammunition and inferior firepower, it had narrowed the gap. So, too, did the men who manned and commanded the army's batteries. Energetic young men like John Pelham, William Nelson, Hilary P. Jones, Stephen D. Lee, and Henry C. Cabell had emerged as talented leaders. Under their direction, and with improved organization, the Army of Northern Virginia's long arm would perform respectably in Maryland.

Cavalry

The army's cavalry was organized into a division of three brigades. This was the largest cavalry force yet assembled in the Army of Northern Virginia, numbering about 5,300 officers and men. Three batteries of horse artillery under Major John Pelham—an excellent officer—provided gun support. Although on paper Pelham commanded a battalion, in practice his three batteries were attached one each to separate brigades. Overall, the cavalry division was a superb outfit, well led and mounted, experienced, and confident.[80]

By concentrating his cavalry into a division under an aggressive soldier like Stuart, Lee gave his mounted arm the strength to make an impact. The cavalry was vital in screening the movements of the army, covering its flanks, guarding its trains, and maintaining contact with the enemy to gather information. When concentrated, it could also serve as a mobile strike force that could threaten or disrupt the enemy's supply lines and communications, or keep them off balance and divert their attention from other maneuvers the army might make. This aggressive use of cavalry was in keeping with the temperament of Stuart, who delighted, sometimes too much so, in bold and daring operations.

Two of the three brigades were led by cavalrymen of proven ability, Fitzhugh Lee and Wade Hampton. Lee was a West Pointer. Hampton was a wealthy South Carolina planter and politician, but he turned out to possess natural skills as a cavalry officer. Their talents were one of the reasons why Lee reorganized his cavalry, so that they could be promoted to brigadier generals. The commander of the third brigade, Brigadier General Beverly H. Robertson, had disappointed Stuart. His brigade had been Turner Ashby's during Jackson's Shenandoah Valley campaign. After Ashby's death, Robertson was assigned to command it. The 36-year-old Virginian was a former captain in the prewar Army, with service with the 2nd Dragoons and the 5th U.S. Cavalry. Robertson was a good disciplinarian and excelled at drilling cavalry, but he lacked the aggressive qualities Ashby had and Jackson valued. When his brigade came under Stuart's command during the Second Manassas Campaign, Robertson displayed no improvement in his combat performance. According to William W. Blackford of Stuart's staff, Robertson "lost all self-possession and was perfectly unreliable" in the face of the enemy. Stuart requested that he be transferred. Lee agreed, and on September 5 Robertson was ordered to report to the Department of North Carolina for duty. Command of his brigade passed to its senior colonel, Thomas Munford, a soldier of considerable talents, but one who, for some reason, never won Stuart's confidence. There was no time to name a new commander before the army entered Maryland, so Munford commanded the brigade—quite competently—throughout the campaign.[81]

The superiority of the Southern horsemen over their Northern counterparts throughout the Peninsula and Second Manassas campaigns was partially due to their more efficient organization. Federal cavalry were parceled out to infantry commands, where they became wagon guards, couriers, headquarters guards, and the like. Consequently, they never were concentrated in numbers that could challenge Stuart. Added to this was the fact that the apart from the regular cavalry regiments, the Confederate cavalrymen, man for man, were superior horsemen. George C. Eggleston of the 1st Virginia Cavalry recalled that the men of his regiment, "if not actually born in the saddle, had climbed into it so early and lived in it so constantly that it had become the only home they knew." The same was true for most of Stuart's regiments. Their horses were generally of better blood than those of the Federals, because the Confederate troopers supplied their own mounts, while the U.S. government provided the Union cavalry with horses. This arrangement came about because there had been more cavalry who volunteered for service than the Confederate government could possibly supply mounts for. The system they adopted was one where the government would accept the cavalryman's horse at fair valuation, provide food and shoes, and pay a per diem of 40 cents per day for its use by the army. If the horse was killed in action, the government would pay its owner the horse's muster valuation, but if the animal was lost through disease or capture, the loss fell on the owner. "The adoption of such a policy was a misfortune," wrote cavalryman John Lamb, but the government retained it throughout the war.[82]

The impact of what proved to be a disastrous policy was felt keenly after the severe summer campaign of 1862. The owner of a horse killed during the summer would be compensated at its muster-in value, which probably was some time in 1861, so he did not receive sufficient compensation to replace the lost mount, due to inflation. Owners whose horses were wounded or disabled were forced to return home with the injured mount to seek a replacement, since only one mount could be kept at the government's expense. In the case of a South Carolina or North Carolina trooper, this trip involved considerable expense and time. "At some periods half of the command were away at one time on horse details, as they were called," recalled John Lamb, "and many noble fellows were reported 'absent without leave' because they were unable to purchase a horse and return to their commands within the time prescribed. To punish them would have been an act of injustice, so this led to a relaxation of discipline and the cavalry became too much a volunteer association."[83]

Although Stuart's troopers were generally well mounted and at ease in the saddle, they were not particularly well armed. Many companies had entered the service carrying only pistols and sabers. Some companies had only sabers;

others toted shotguns for extra firepower. By the Maryland Campaign this situation had improved, due principally to the capture of Federal weapons and equipment on the Peninsula and in northern Virginia. Crudely manufactured Confederate carbines were also supplied in some quantity, but there was nothing approaching uniformity in weaponry. In any regiment one would find a mix of variously manufactured carbines, shotguns, smoothbore muskets, rifled muskets, and pistols, besides the heavy cavalry saber. The carbines and muskets that were issued were often distributed to the best companies in the regiment (or to the companies with the senior captains), and these companies were trained to skirmish dismounted. It is unclear how many companies might have been so equipped, as it apparently depended on the luck or resourcefulness of their commander in acquiring weapons.[84]

THIS WAS THE Army of Northern Virginia in September 1862, as it prepared to embark on its most ambitious and important operation yet in the war. There were weaknesses, particularly in logistics and other areas common to an evolving volunteer army, but in many critical aspects that influence the outcome of battles, this army was superior to their foe. The army's leaders and men were nearly all combat veterans, its organization was more responsive and flexible than that of the Army of the Potomac, it had superior senior commanders in Jackson and Longstreet, and it had Lee. Wrote a Georgian on the very eve of the invasion, "Gen. Lee stands now above all general in modern history. Our men will follow him to the end." And the victories in the Shenandoah Valley, in the Seven Days, at Cedar Mountain, and on the fields of Second Manassas had imbued the army with an abundance of confidence and a sense of superiority over their enemy. "This is an important crisis," Captain William G. Morris, of the 37th North Carolina, wrote to his wife in the early days of the campaign. "Now is the pinch. We have the enemy terible frightened." William Elder, with Pryor's brigade, had seen enough in three months to convince him that they could not be beaten by the Yankees. "If we can only get enough for our men to eat up here I don't believe Genl. Lee's army can be whipped."[85]

3

The Army of Northern Virginia Enters Maryland

"Our movements will be rapid"

The camps of the Army of Northern Virginia near Chantilly hummed with activity before sunrise on September 3. The day before, those troops that had them prepared three days' rations, consisting of some boiled beef and "roasting ears," to carry them through until the army reached Loudoun County, which offered the prospect of more abundant food and forage. The army's order of march for the day called for Jackson and Longstreet to march north from the Little River Turnpike along roughly parallel country roads to Dranesville, about 10–12 miles distant. By directing his march close to the capital's defenses, General Lee hoped to maintain his army's threat to Washington, so as to keep the Federals guessing about his intentions and focus their attention south of the Potomac. His cavalry, bivouacked near Fairfax Court House, would play a more active part in the deception. Fitz Lee's brigade was ordered to demonstrate toward Alexandria. Hampton's brigade was told to march by way of Hunter's Mill Station to the Leesburg Turnpike, where his command could cover the right flank of the army's main body, while Robertson's brigade would go through Vienna to the Leesburg Turnpike and then probe toward Falls Church. D. H. Hill's and Lafayette McLaws's divisions, which had overtaken the army on the 2nd and camped north of the Second Manassas battlefield near Sudley, were commanded to travel by a different route to Leesburg, where they could secure that vital point as a staging area for the crossing into Maryland.[1]

Jackson started "very erley" in the morning, marching north from Ox Hill to the Ox Road, which his columns followed northwest to the Lawyers Road, where they turned east for about 1 mile before heading north to Thornton Station and Dranesville. The command went into camp 1 mile west of Dranesville, near Sugarland Run. Longstreet went west on the Little River Turnpike for about 1 mile before turning north on the road to Frying Pan. Here his column took the Ox Road to Guilford Station on the Loudoun and Hampshire Railroad, near which they then turned north on a country road to the Leesburg Pike. At the pike the column headed east, marching to the west bank of Sugarland Run, where Longstreet put his command into bivouac.[2]

The march of D. H. Hill's and McLaws's divisions was more difficult. With McLaws leading, the two divisions went from north of Sudley Ford on Bull Run to the village of Gum Springs. From here they probably took a country road running northwest to the Old Carolina Road, which they followed to Leesburg, arriving around 5 p.m. William Hill, of Barksdale's brigade, thought that they traveled 22 miles. McLaws himself only noted that the march was "very fatiguing." There was also considerable straggling. "Our men do not grumble," wrote McLaws, "they only straggle." But when the dusty column reached Leesburg, the residents lifted their spirits with a "very enthusiastic" reception. "The ladies in particular were demonstrative," wrote McLaws. "They all seemed to be rejoiced at the reoccupation of the country by our army, and their deliverance from Yankee rule," observed William Hill in his diary. The two divisions passed through Leesburg and marched 2 miles north on the road to the Potomac River, to the farm of George W. Ball and his 25-foot-diameter limestone spring—called the Big Spring, or "Double Spring"—where they bivouacked. This was familiar ground to Barksdale's men, for it had been their campsite in the fall of 1861.[3]

Although Lee certainly hoped to invade Maryland with the full weight of his army, it is not certain that on September 3 he had firmly settled on where he would enter the state, as he did not know if the enemy were guarding the Potomac fords near Leesburg. To determine the latter, plus cause some minor mayhem with Federal communications and commerce and generate confusion, he sent orders sometime on the 3rd to D. H. Hill at Big Spring to advance his three brigades (Ripley and Colquitt were still at Dranesville) to three different Potomac crossings: the Berlin Ferry (opposite present-day Brunswick, Maryland), Noland's Ferry, and Cheek's Ford (both near the mouth of the Monocacy River). The brigade at Berlin Ferry could harass rail traffic on the B&O Railroad, while the brigades at Noland's Ferry and Cheek's Ford could not only secure those crossing points, but also cut the C&O Canal. Spread out across a front extending some 10 miles, the Confederates would also confuse the enemy as to where the main body of the army might cross. Most importantly, the incursion would determine if the enemy were defending the Potomac fords, and in what strength.[4]

Jackson and Longstreet were told to continue their march to Leesburg on the 4th. Stuart's orders were to demonstrate with part of his force toward Falls Church and the Union forts south of the Potomac, and to follow the main body of the army to Leesburg with the balance of his force.[5]

During the night, some of the army's commissary wagons rejoined their commands at Dranesville, and on the morning of the 4th Lee allowed the hungry troops an opportunity to cook up their rations. "It would have done one good to sit down by one of the fires and watch the men," wrote John Worsham of the 21st Virginia. "As one 'spider' of biscuits and one frying pan of meat was cooked, they were immediately divided and eaten; then another was cooked and eaten; and thus we disposed of most of the rations for the twenty-four hours." But not everyone was so fortunate. In D. H. Hill's division, no commissary wagons had reached Ripley's brigade, and his men had nothing to eat all day on September 4. Such was the uneven state of Confederate subsistence.[6]

Jackson's command led the march, again followed by Longstreet. Spirits in the ranks were high, buoyed in part by the rumor that the army was destined for Maryland. But most of the veterans had learned not to trust rumors. "Wee don't know what wee are going to do never know untill its over," confessed Shepard G. Pryor of the 12th Georgia to his wife.[7] The weather was delightful, with a high near 70 degrees. "A very fine day," Jackson's cartographer, Jedediah Hotchkiss, recorded in his diary. But despite the excellent weather, the marching was unpleasant, with nearly an entire army confined to one road. Even under ideal circumstances, Confederate units shed stragglers, and on September 4 they left the column in droves. Alexander Hunter of the 17th Virginia painted a grim picture of the conditions that contributed to straggling.

> Our underclothes were foul and hanging in strips, our socks worn out, and half the men were bare-footed, many were lame and were sent to the rear; others, of sterner stuff, hobbled along and managed to keep up, while gangs from every company went off in the surrounding country looking for food, and did not rejoin their commands until weeks after . . . The ambulances were full, and the whole route was marked with a sick, lame, limping lot, that straggled to the farm-houses that lined the way."[8]

The sheer number of stragglers encountered apparently was more than Brigadier General Roger Pryor could stand, and at one point on the march he ordered his brigade to fire into a group of them.[9]

The only incident of note on the march to Leesburg occurred in Jackson's command. Displeased by the straggling he had observed on the 3rd, Jackson summoned his three division commanders to his headquarters that night and gave clearly understood instructions for the march on the 4th: he set a specific hour ("soon after daylight') for it to begin and directed that the troops were to march for 50 minutes and rest 10 minutes of every hour of the march. So Jackson was highly irritated when he rode up the Leesburg Pike early on the 4th and found half of A. P. Hill's division, which was to lead the column, still preparing to march and already a half hour late. Hill was not about, so Jackson pitched into the first brigade commander he came upon, Brigadier General Maxcy Gregg. There was little warmth between the two men, and when Jackson demanded to know why Gregg's brigade had not marched, the South Carolinian replied with some heat that his men were filling their canteens. Furious, Jackson exclaimed loudly, "there are but few commanders who appreciate the value of celerity!"[10]

Leaving Gregg, Jackson rode ahead to overtake the van of A. P. Hill's division. He discovered that Hill, instead of supervising the march of his division, had ridden some 200 yards in advance, out of sight of the head of his column. Jackson joined Brigadier General Edward Thomas, whose brigade of Georgians was leading the division column. Dismounting, he walked with Thomas until it was time for the 10-minute rest. Jackson directed Thomas to halt, which he did. When the 10 minutes had elapsed and the Georgians resumed the march, Hill and his staff suddenly came charging down the road. Without even acknowledging Jackson, Hill went directly to Thomas and demanded to know why he had halted his brigade. Thomas replied that he was ordered to do so. Hill then angrily drew his sword and offered the hilt to Jackson, stating, "I submit my resignation, sir!" Jackson controlled his own anger and simply responded by telling Hill to consider himself under arrest for disobedience of orders. While Hill rode to the rear, Jackson directed Brigadier General Lawrence Branch to assume command of the Light Division.[11]

While Jackson's and Longstreet's brigades tramped along the Leesburg Pike, D. H. Hill sent Brigadier General Robert Rodes's brigade, with some artillery support, roughly 7 miles north from Big Spring to cross the Potomac at Cheek's Ford. The Alabamians reached the south bank of the river around 4 p.m. Rodes halted the brigade and reconnoitered. There were some Federal troops on the opposite shore. Perhaps through locals, Rodes learned that they were Maryland Home Guards—37 men of Company E, 1st Maryland Potomac Home Brigade, under Lieutenant J. A. Burk. Deploying three companies of infantry and unlimbering his artillery, Rodes ordered them to fire into the woods on the opposite bank. D. H. Hill, who had apparently accompanied the expedition, ordered Rodes to ford the river. The honor of leading the crossing fell to the 3rd Alabama. The men stripped off their pants and plunged into the cool waters, holding their rifles ready. Captain John R. Simpson was in the van, with three companies of the 3rd following as skirmishers. Lieutenant Burk and his detachment beat a hasty retreat, leaving their tents and "all their clothes" behind.[12]

Captain Simpson was the first man in the Army of Northern Virginia to set foot on Maryland soil. One member of the 3rd Alabama wrote home that "it was quite an amusing sight to see us crossing," since so many men were pantless. With loud cheers spurring him on, the 3rd's color-bearer, clad only in his shirt, dashed up the river bank "and stuck his colors firmly in the ground." The Alabamians lost no time in looting the camp of the Yankee picket post and rushing up to a small nearby store to use their Confederate money to buy boots, sugar, and coffee. "In about 15 minutes his stock was sold," wrote one Alabamian. The troops also intercepted a canal boat on the C&O Canal laden with flour and bacon. This treasure, recorded Otis Smith of the 6th Alabama, "nearly disorganized the entire command." There was a sour note to the otherwise frolicsome crossing, however. A member of the 3rd who wrote home to describe his regiment's glorious passage of the Potomac River noted glumly at the end of his letter that "very few men crossed the Potomac with us—out of 82 in our company only two officers, two non-commissioned officers and nine privates crossed with us." For reasons unspecified, 84 percent of this one company did not cross.[13]

After stocking up on whatever supplies they could buy or scavenge, Rodes's men went to work destroying the bank of the C&O Canal, until its waters began to run into the Potomac River. They also tackled the canal aqueduct over the Monocacy River, but this proved impervious to all their efforts. Rodes's foray onto the Maryland shore was more successful than he could have imagined. Lieutenant Burk apparently sent a wildly exaggerated report of the encounter to Colonel Henry B. Banning, whose 87th Ohio, a three-month regiment, was garrisoning Point of Rocks. Banning panicked, abandoning Point of Rocks and reporting that 30,000 Rebels had crossed the river below him and were marching on him.[14]

About the same time that Rodes's men were crossing the Potomac, Jackson's command reached Leesburg. "The citizens of the town appeared very glad to see us, and many had biscuits & C. for the soldiers as we passed through," wrote one of A.P. Hill's men. Jackson marched his divisions to Big Spring, where they joined McLaws's division and Hill's two brigades. Longstreet's command, having to march in Jackson's wake, endured a fatiguing day of starting, then stopping, and then starting again. A diarist in the 16th Mississippi described the miserable march: "Fell in at noon, marched a mile & halted till dark. Then started and marched till midnight. Many stragglers." Longstreet halted his divisions at Newton Hall, 2 miles south of Leesburg.[15]

While the infantry made their way to Leesburg, Stuart's cavalry both screened the rear and conducted a demonstration toward the capital's defenses south of the Potomac. Stuart selected his smallest brigade and least efficient brigadier, Brigadier General Beverly Robertson, for the hardest work: a reconnaissance in the direction of Falls Church. Robertson had only two small regiments, the 7th and the 12th Virginia Cavalry, and three pieces of horse artillery from Captain Robert P. Chew's battery. He pushed eastward, skirmishing with enemy pickets until he reached Lewinsville, about 3 miles north of Falls Church. Here he unlimbered his artillery and, with two pieces, lobbed shells at the Federals. They responded with two pieces, and both sides kept up their noisemaking until "nearly sundown," when Robertson learned that several enemy regiments were moving toward his position. Having accomplished his mission of stirring up trouble, Robertson limbered his guns and withdrew toward Dranesville under the cover of night.[16]

The bulk of Fitz Lee's and Hampton's brigades enjoyed a day of rest near Dranesville, although elements of Hampton's brigade apparently conducted a scout east along the Georgetown Pike and skirmished with some Federal cavalry west of the Chain Bridge.[17]

General Lee reached Leesburg around noon on the 4th, covering the distance from Dranesville in an ambulance. On September 1 he had fallen while reaching for the reins of his horse, severely spraining his right wrist and breaking a bone in his left hand. With bandaged hands he could not mount, ride, or dismount from a horse without assistance. Lee established his headquarters at Henry T. Harrison's house, a graceful home some two blocks north of the courthouse. Any doubts Lee may have harbored about moving the army into Maryland had vanished by the time he reached Leesburg. The only question remaining was whether the army would enter Maryland east or west of the mountains. Sometime that afternoon Lee dictated a fresh dispatch to Davis, informing the president that "I am more fully persuaded of the benefit that will result from an expedition into Maryland and I shall proceed to make the movement at once, unless you should signify your disapprobation." Because of the long delay in communications with Richmond, Lee knew that it was impossible for any disapproval from Davis to reach him before the army entered Maryland. It is also unlikely that Lee would have ventured forth on such an operation unless he was confident that the Confederate president approved. Thus Lee probably included the statement as a gesture of respect for Davis's position.[18]

Perhaps even before Lee dictated this dispatch, orders had been drawn up to ready the army for its expedition. General Orders No. 102 directed all commanders to "reduce their transportation to a mere sufficiency to transport cooking utensils and the absolute necessaries of a regiment." All animals not in use by the artillery, cavalry, or army trains were to be left in charge of the army's chief quartermaster. The troops were advised that they were "about to engage in most important operations, where any excesses committed will exasperate the people" and possibly actively turn them against the army. Quartermasters and commissaries were to make all arrangements to purchase supplies, "thereby removing all excuses for depredations." Since it was unlikely that everyone in the army would abide by this provision, Brigadier General Lewis A. Armistead, a tough former regular, was detailed to command a provost guard to follow in the rear of the army, armed with the authority to "arrest stragglers, and punish summarily all depredators, and keep the men with their commands." Besides Armistead's provost guard, brigade commanders were charged with forming a rear guard under "efficient officers" to "prevent men from leaving the ranks, right, left, front, or rear." Lee intended to keep his army on a tight rein in Maryland.[19]

Besides reducing its transportation to the minimum necessary, the army paused at Leesburg to shed its sick and barefoot men—anyone, it seems, who was not likely to be able to keep up—and Chief of Artillery William Pendleton conducted a hasty and onerous reorganization of the army's artillery. All 80 batteries with the army were inspected between September 4 and 7 to determine whether they were in condition to cross the Potomac. Those batteries deemed too inefficient, or reduced by service, had their best horses transferred to other batteries, and some gave up personnel to fill depleted ranks. Altogether, seven batteries were deemed unfit to make the Maryland Campaign and were left in Leesburg. Major Charles Richardson assumed command of this derelict collection of "broken down horses . . . some guns, wagons and other plunder" and marched it to Winchester. Pendleton's efforts, given the brief time he had to make changes, were merely patches to get by. Numerous brave but inefficient officers remained, and despite the transfers of men and animals, many batteries entered Maryland understrength in both respects. A major reorganization was necessary, but this would have to wait until a period of extended rest could be had.[20]

Although no official order excusing barefoot men from remaining in the ranks has ever been discovered, there is evidence that, at least in Longstreet's command, an order was issued detaching barefoot and sick men from the campaign in Maryland. The historian of the 17th Virginia recorded that "many of the men, for want of shoes, were ordered to remain on the Virginia shore." David Johnston, a noncom in the 7th Virginia, wrote that at Leesburg "an order came for all sick and shoeless men to remain there." He thought it an unfortunate order, for "it was construed by a great many of the men to mean just anyone who did not want to go over the river into Maryland . . . Judging other commands by my own, I can state that much too large a number of men remained at Leesburg, stretching the pretext to cover far more than was intended by the order." How many sick or shoeless men, or men who just did not want to take part in the campaign for any reason, were left behind in Leesburg? Lieutenant Alex Erwin in the Phillips (Georgia) Legion thought there were "about 5,000." This same officer wrote that when his regiment reached Leesburg, "Gen Longstreet issued an order here that all barefooted, weak and inefficient troops of each regiment be left with the baggage in charge of an officer." The lieutenant took 150 men of his regiment who fell into the above categories with him to Winchester when Lee broke up his line of communications through Leesburg. This probably did not reflect an average drainage from the army's infantry regiments, but H. C. Kendrick, of the 9th Georgia, who had attempted to rejoin his regiment after the army entered Maryland and was directed to Winchester, wrote on September 15 that they were forming "brigades" of 3,000 to 4,000 men to march to Harpers Ferry or Martinsburg. If Lieutenant Erwin's estimate was accurate, then Lee carried about 70,000 men into Maryland, but the evidence from H. C. Kendrick indicates that the number of men that did not accompany the army there was greater than 5,000, so Lee's actual strength was probably below 70,000, and possibly as low as 65,000.[21]

During the march of Jackson's command to Leesburg, Jackson had summoned Colonel Bradley T. Johnson, the acting commander of a brigade in the division led by J. R. Jones, to ride with him and provide a "detailed description of the country in Maryland on the other side of the Potomac." Johnson was a bright fellow, having been educated at Princeton and Harvard Law School. As a native of Frederick, Maryland, and former state district attorney, Johnson knew the country the army was destined to operate in very well. That evening Jackson took Johnson to a meeting with Lee at the Harrison home. Lee questioned Johnson closely about the topography "of the banks of the Potomac between Loudoun County, Virginia, and Frederick County, Maryland, and those about Harpers Ferry and Williamsport." Johnson also stressed that in western Maryland "a large portion of the people were ardent Unionists," and that, while there were a number of Confederate sympathizers, they would not afford any material aid until they were assured of an occupation "promising at least some permanence." He may have also pointed out that Frederick County and Washington County, Maryland, were among the richest agricultural counties in the state and offered the prospect of abundant supplies for the army. Johnson recalled that Lee, sitting "straight, solemn and stern" throughout, declared at the end of their conversation of "several hours" that when Lee left Richmond, he had told Davis that he would relieve Virginia of the pressure of the two Federal armies in the state. Now, with the army poised to enter Maryland, Lee pondered whether to cross east or west of the Blue Ridge. "If I cross here [near Leesburg] I can do so at the cost of men, but with the saving of time," Johnson recalled him saying. "If I cross at Williamsport, I can do so with saving of men, but at a cost of time." Jackson sat through the meeting bolt upright and sound asleep.[22]

If Johnson remembered Lee's words accurately, then Lee believed the army might encounter some resistance crossing so near to Washington. But sometime that evening he must have received a report from D. H. Hill that Rodes had encountered only token resistance crossing the Potomac River. This, or some other report, eased Lee's mind and he chose to use the fords near Leesburg to cross the Potomac into Maryland. He decided to make the main crossing at one of the more obscure fords, White's Ford, situated about 5 miles north of Big Spring. Jackson's command would cross here, while Longstreet's wing would move up and occupy Jackson's camps at Big Spring. To draw attention away from the main crossing, D. H. Hill was ordered to send G. B. Anderson's brigade north to the Berlin Ferry—about a 17- to 18-mile march, depending on the route taken—to conduct a demonstration opposite Berlin, Maryland, and to have Samuel Garland's North Carolina brigade cross the Potomac at Noland's Ferry, where it could secure a lodgment on the west bank of the Monocacy River.[23]

Lee also learned on the 4th that the Federals had evacuated Winchester. This was good news, for it would allow a more secure line of communications and a forward depot to be established to support the operations in Maryland. On the 5th, Lee ordered his old and now vulnerable line of communications to be broken up as far back as Culpeper Court House and a new line, more secure from raids by Federal cavalry, established to run via Culpeper to Luray, then north down the Valley Turnpike to Winchester. Winchester would be the army's forward depot, and all trains, ammunition, stragglers, and the like, were to be directed to that point.[24]

The only threat to this new line of communications was the Federal garrison at Harpers Ferry. Lee did not yet know that the Federals also had a brigade-sized garrison at Martinsburg. The Harpers Ferry garrison did not greatly concern Lee, for he expected that it would be withdrawn when his army moved north of the Potomac. He thought Major General William W. Loring's small army of 5,000, operating in western Virginia, might afford some help. Lee also repeated an earlier request to Davis in a September 5 letter to the Confederate president, asking that Loring's force clear the Kanawha Valley if possible, and, in all events, move via Romney to a point near Martinsburg, where Loring could cover Winchester and provide security for Lee's line of communications. Considering the distances and the geography involved, as well as the opposition Loring would have to overcome, Lee should not have expected any material aid from Loring quickly. What Lee could hope for was that Loring would at least be active and keep the Federals on his front occupied and unable to move against Lee's communications down the Shenandoah Valley while the Army of Northern Virginia was in Maryland.[25]

Sunrise on Friday, September 5, came at 5:37 a.m., but the camps of Jackson's command were active before this. It promised to be a bright, warm, late summer day. The three divisions began falling into column "about sunrise" and wending their way north toward the Potomac. The 10th Virginia infantry of Colonel E. T. H. Warren's brigade led the column. A band, proudly carrying the flag of Virginia, preceded the 10th, anticipating the moment its members could plant the colors on the soil of Maryland and strike up the Confederate battle hymn "Maryland, My Maryland." Behind the 10th marched (in order) the divisions under J. R. Jones and Lawton, and that of A. P. Hill (still under Branch). Jackson rode prominently near the head of the column on a cream-colored horse, no doubt intense and full of anticipation.[26]

As the sun rose into a cloudless sky and dissipated the morning mists, the soldiers in the long column must have marveled at the lush green landscape that greeted their eye. The contrast with the grim fields of Manassas that they had recently left behind was striking. The surroundings en route to the Potomac River were unscathed by war. Between 9 and 10 a.m. the head of the column reached the southern bank of the Potomac. To Shepard Pryor of the 12th Georgia, the river looked to be about 800 yards across. In preparation, the troops stripped off shoes, socks, and pants. The band played "Maryland, My Maryland," prompting cheers, shouts, and laughter. Then the 10th Virginia, followed by the rest of J. R. Jones's division, plunged into the Potomac. The infantry were delighted to find that the water was only about three feet deep. To Lieutenant

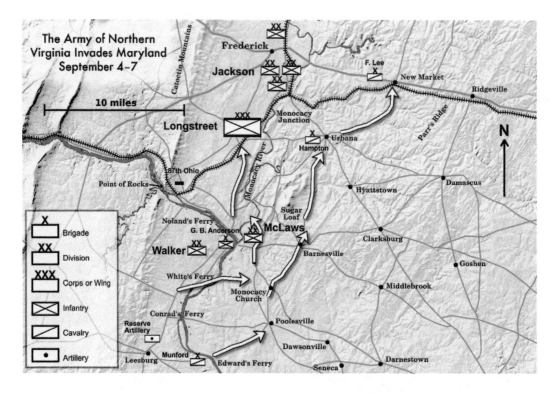

The Army of Northern Virginia Invades Maryland September 4–7

10 miles

N

Brigade
Division
Corps or Wing
Infantry
Cavalry
Artillery

Catoctin Mountains
Frederick
Jackson
F. Lee
New Market
Ridgeville
Monocacy Junction
Longstreet
Urbana
Hampton
Parr's Ridge
Damascus
87th Ohio
Point of Rocks
Hyattstown
Monocacy River
Sugar Loaf
Noland's Ferry
G. B. Anderson
McLaws
Clarksburg
Walker
Barnesville
Goshen
White's Ferry
Monocacy Church
Middlebrook
Conrad's Ferry
Poolesville
Reserve Artillery
Dawsonville
Darnestown
Leesburg
Munford
Edward's Ferry
Seneca

John Riley of the 31st Virginia, the scene was inspiring. He wrote in his diary that day: "Never in my life did I feel more proud than on this occasion that I was a Virginian." Shep Pryor simply thought "something more [than] I ever expected to do was to enter this state by wading the river." What struck Draughton Haynes of Thomas's brigade were the pale legs of thousands of men splashing across the river. "Never did I behold so many naked legs," he penciled in his diary.[27]

The infantry had no trouble fording the river, but its banks were too steep for the wagons and artillery vehicles to cross. This was a surprising development, and one that probably displeased Jackson. The Virginia side of the ford was on the farm of Captain Elijah White, who commanded a company of scouts accompanying Jackson. It seems likely that it was White who recommended the ford to Lee and Jackson, and he may have misjudged how difficult the banks of the river would be for the army's transportation to negotiate. Whatever the cause, it impeded Jackson's progress while the banks were dug down to allow vehicles to pass. Due to this delay, and probably others that went unrecorded, it was nearly 2 p.m. before J. R. Jones' division completed crossing the river. A. P. Hill's turn did not come until sunset, and Ripley's and Colquitt's brigades (of D. H. Hill's division) crossed during the night, something Thomas D. Boone of the 1st North Carolina never forgot. He and many others had removed their shoes to ford the Potomac, unaware that "the river was full of concealed rocks, doubly treacherous because it was dark." The crossing left Boone's feet "cruelly gashed," and he and his comrades reached the opposite shore "worn out, wet and completely disgusted by our first impression of Maryland."[28]

Jackson's timetable suffered an additional interruption when the front of his column, following the C&O towpath, encountered a set of canal locks. The towpath here ran across a culvert that was easily negotiated by the infantry, but not by army wagons. Forward movement halted until the culvert was bridged. But all was not lost. A canal boat loaded with melons was intercepted en route for Washington. The troops eagerly purchased the entire boatload. Someone even managed to keep one to present to Stonewall and his staff when they reached the Maryland shore. Perhaps it eased the frustration of the time-consuming river crossing.[29]

Lee wished to destroy the B&O railroad bridge over the Monocacy River. The delays of the river crossing concerned Jackson, who worried that he might not reach the bridge, which was his objective for the day, in strength by that evening. Lacking more than a token cavalry force, Jackson knew little about what enemy forces were in his front, and he prudently, but incorrectly, assumed that they would defend the bridge. At 1:55 p.m. he sent a dispatch to D. H. Hill, who was still in the vicinity of the aqueduct near the mouth of the Monocacy, and inquired, "Can you at once move forward to reach the Baltimore and Ohio Railroad bridge over the Monocacy this evening?" Jackson deemed it important that the two commands effect a junction, "as we may meet with opposition before we can destroy the bridge." The bridge was garrisoned by the green 14th New Jersey Infantry, but they had no intention of offering opposition and scrambled for Baltimore when they heard the Rebels were crossing the Potomac in large numbers.[30]

Rather than send a courier with a response to Jackson's message, Hill rode over to meet with him personally. He found Jackson with Lige White, examining a map of the area around Frederick. Jackson informed Hill that his division had been placed under his orders. "I wish your division to join me, to-night, near Frederick." Hill probably explained to his new boss that his division was scattered, and that he had only two of his five brigades on hand.[31]

By early afternoon the C&O Canal had been bridged and Jackson resumed his march with J. R. Jones's division, taking the Furnace Road north toward Buckeystown. As the column reached the top of the bluffs above the river, they observed dust rising from cavalry pickets of the 1st Massachusetts Cavalry, who were careful to keep their distance from the invaders. Maryland citizens emerged in considerable numbers, curious for a look at the vaunted Army of Northern Virginia. They were surely disappointed, for the dirty, gaunt, ragged soldiers they beheld looked more like vagrants than members of an invading army. But with few exceptions, the Marylanders were friendly toward the graycoats who streamed up from the Potomac. Among them was one enthusiastic individual who presented Jackson with what Henry Kyd Douglas recalled as a "strong-sinewed, powerful, grey mare, more suitable for artillery than the saddle." Jackson accepted the horse graciously.[32]

The delays in crossing the river and bridging the canal prevented Jackson from reaching Monocacy Junction with his main body. He pushed on as far as he deemed prudent, marching his command until nearly midnight (and beyond that time for troops at the tail of the column) before calling a halt at Three Springs, near Buckeystown, 6 miles south of the B&O railroad bridge and 9 miles from Frederick. There were no rations to issue, since the commissary wagons were far to the rear, so he purchased a nearby cornfield and fence rails to provide food and fuel for J. R. Jones's division, and issued orders for his other commanders to do likewise for their commands. Although the main body could not reach the B&O railroad bridge, Jackson refused to be denied a chance to cause some mischief. He ordered half of his cavalry force, Captain Robert Randolph's Black Horse Troop of the 4th Virginia Cavalry, to ride on to Monocacy Junction and cut the telegraph line, capturing the operator if possible. Appearing in the middle of the night, Randolph completely surprised Company G, 1st Maryland Potomac Home Brigade, who were defending the junction, and they withdrew without firing a shot. The Virginians accomplished their objectives without incident and withdrew.[33]

About the time A. P. Hill's brigades were crossing the Potomac at White's Ford, Jeb Stuart, with Fitz Lee's and Wade Hampton's brigades, were crossing the river some 7 miles below at Edward's Ferry. Both of these brigades had enjoyed a day of badly needed rest near Dranesville on the 4th. Robertson's brigade was not as fortunate. They did not return from their reconnaissance toward Falls Church until 10 p.m. Stuart allowed them only three hours' rest and then sent them marching to Leesburg. Fitz Lee's and Hampton's troopers rose at 3 a.m. on the 5th to the notes of "Boots and Saddles" sounding through the camps of the various regiments. The troopers were mounted before daylight, en route for Leesburg, with Fitz Lee's brigade in front. By daybreak the column had covered 8 miles and reached Frankville, where it halted to allow the men to feed their horses. Then the two brigades continued on to within 1 mile of Leesburg. The troopers observed great clouds of dust hanging over the town, raised by the feet, horses, and vehicles of Longstreet's command, moving to Big Spring. Stuart discovered that the streets of the town were "so compactly filled with troops, artillery, and wagon-trains" as to virtually block his way. He passed back the welcome orders to dismount while he rode into town to find General Lee and get his orders. The troopers used the break to breakfast on roasted corn and apples. Stuart found Lee at the Harrison home; the cavalryman's Prussian aide-de-camp, Heros von Borcke, recalled that Jackson and Longstreet were also present. It was probably around 10 a.m., so if von Borcke truly saw Jackson, he had a double, for at that moment Stonewall was

miles away, supervising his command's crossing of the Potomac. Lee's orders
for Stuart were to backtrack to Edward's Ferry; ford the Potomac; proceed in
the direction of Poolesville, Barnesville, and Hyattstown; and establish a cavalry screen to protect the army's right flank as it crossed the river and marched
north to Frederick. The two generals undoubtedly discussed General Beverly
Robertson, whom Stuart considered unfit for combat command. Lee evidently
agreed, for that afternoon orders were issued relieving Robertson of command,
which left the senior colonel, Thomas Munford, the fine leader of the 2nd Virginia Cavalry, as the acting brigade commander.[34]

At about 2 p.m. Stuart returned and started his two brigades backtracking
for the Edward's Ferry crossing. Robertson's brigade, now Munford's brigade,
marched to Big Spring on the 5th and remained there until sunset, when they
returned to Leesburg and went into camp. Perhaps they remained there to
await the arrival of their new commander. Munford was busy that day gathering stock in Loudoun County with his 2nd Virginia Cavalry, and he did not return until the 6th. Fitz Lee's and Hampton's troopers might have been puzzled
by the direction of their march—east, the direction from which they had come
that day. A two-hour march that von Borcke described as a "dusty and very
much impeded march . . . winding through infantry columns, and compelled
frequently to halt," brought the command to Edward's Ferry, some 7 miles below White's Ford. The 5th Virginia led the way into the river. The seemingly
inevitable band struck up "Maryland, My Maryland" and the men sang along
enthusiastically, forgetting their fatigue. By the time Hampton's brigade's turn
came to cross, night had fallen. "We were shrouded in darkness," wrote an officer in the 2nd South Carolina as they passed through the wooded banks of the
Potomac. But when they emerged at the edge of the river, a bright moon lit the
entire scene, revealing the long column of horseman winding their way across.
It was "a beautiful sight on that clear moonlight night," wrote James K. Munnerlyn Jr. to his sister. "The water reached our saddles & some small horses had
to swim." The scene evoked vivid images in von Borcke's mind when he penned
his memoirs. He recalled how, when Lee's regiments were crossing the Potomac, "the evening sun slanted upon its clear placid waters, and burnished
them with gold, while the arms of the soldiers glittered and blazed in its radi-
ance." It was one of the rare moments of beauty in the usually drab, toilsome
life of a soldier. Losses amounted to some saddlebags disappearing in the river
and a few delays in getting the horse artillery across. Otherwise the river crossing was uneventful.[35]

It took nearly two hours for the two brigades and the horse artillery to ford
the river, so Stuart ordered Fitz Lee's brigade to move ahead and secure Poolesville before Hampton and the artillery were over the river. Fitz Lee's Virginians
rode on through the fading light, past civilians who expressed no particular
enthusiasm for the gray horsemen, perhaps because they were unaware that the

riders were Confederates. The brigade approached Poolesville about nightfall. Elements of three companies of the 1st Massachusetts Cavalry, under Captain Samuel E. Chamberlain, were deployed at the village, sent there to harass enemy forces reported to be crossing the Potomac. Chamberlain was unfamiliar with the area. His regiment had only arrived from South Carolina on September 3, and it was dispatched to picket the Potomac fords and the C&O Canal the next day. The captain probably did not realize the strength of the approaching force, and he had not been in Poolesville long enough to understand that its citizens were not friendly to bluecoats. While Chamberlain and his command prepared to defend the western approaches to the town, some of the townsfolk busily piled stones and other obstacles in the road behind the troopers. Fitz Lee sent the 5th and part of the 3rd Virginia forward on the attack. It was quickly evident to Chamberlain that there were more Confederates than he and his men could handle, and he ordered a retreat at the gallop. The troopers came roaring through Poolesville, expecting to escape their pursuers, when they ran into the obstacles placed by the locals. Horses and men went tumbling about. Chamberlain's horse was among those that went down, pinning him to the ground. The delay allowed Fitz Lee's troopers to catch up and, according to a newspaper account, they "began firing into and sabering the prostrate men." The Federals defended themselves, for Fitz Lee had 3 men killed and 4 wounded, but Chamberlain soon recognized that his men were outmatched and called out for the Confederates to stop shooting, which they did. Chamberlain and 30 of his men were taken prisoner, and 8 or 9 were wounded. They were the first casualties in the Maryland Campaign.[36]

The Southern-sympathizing citizens of Poolesville gave Fitz Lee and Stuart an enthusiastic reception when the two cavaliers rode into town. The sight of so many dashing cavalrymen proved too much for some of the village's young men. They returned mounted on their horses and, a staff officer recalled, "insisted upon joining our ranks." Two of the town's merchants sold their entire stock of groceries to the Virginians, as well as boots, gloves, and hats ("at very low prices," noted one cavalryman), accepting Confederate money "without any hesitation." The Prussian von Borcke, contemplating this amusing scene, noted that "soldiers, on such occasions are like children. They buy everything, and embarrass themselves with numberless articles which very soon afterwards are thrown away as useless." The cavalrymen bought out the two merchants "to the last pin," after which the businessmen resolved to enlist in the Southern horse. This frolicsome interlude ended an hour later, when Stuart ordered Fitz Lee to move on. The column marched about 2 miles north of Poolesville, probably to near the tiny village of Beallsville, and bivouacked for the night. Meanwhile Hampton came up and occupied Poolesville, so that Stuart's two brigades interdicted both roads leading west from Dawsonville to the Potomac, affording some security for the army's main crossing points.[37]

Longstreet's command spent the 5th marching through Leesburg to Big Spring, in preparation for their own crossing into Maryland on the 6th. Jackson's command had not worn out the welcome of Leesburg's citizens, and they were out in force to cheer Longstreet's veterans as they passed through the streets. "I never saw so many women, according to the size of the town, in my life . . . Every one seemed to have a white handkerchief, and how they did wave those handkerchiefs at us! and how they did cheer us!" recalled Jonathan Stevens of the 5th Texas. "Cheer after cheer is being given by the soldiers in return," wrote a commissary officer in the town. As the troops went into bivouac, officers received orders that the march would be resumed at 4 a.m. on the 6th. Hodijah L. Meade, a private in the Richmond Howitzers, paused to write a letter home before turning in for the night. Meade was excited about the prospects of invasion: "It is a glorious thing to think that we are on the road straight for Yankeedom."[38]

Lee must have been satisfied with his army's September 5 accomplishments. He had a bridgehead of four divisions north of the Potomac River, within a short day's march of Frederick. Stuart was positioned to establish blocking positions on the main roads to Frederick from Baltimore and Washington the next day. G. B. Anderson's brigade had arrived near or at the Berlin Ferry. Longstreet's divisions, along with McLaws's division, were in place to start crossing the Potomac in the morning. Walker's large division had arrived within 7 miles of Leesburg. The reserve artillery were completing their reorganization and refitting and hoped to be ready to cross the Potomac behind Longstreet and McLaws. Enemy resistance had been negligible, spirits were high, and the future seemed to brim with potential.

Rumors that the Confederates were crossing into Maryland drifted into Frederick all day on September 5, creating a stir of uneasiness. "The citizens were in the greatest trepidation," wrote Dr. Lewis Steiner, a U.S. Sanitary Commission inspector who had been in Washington that day and caught a B&O train to his hometown when he heard the rumors. It turned out to be the last train to reach Frederick that day. Steiner found that most of the citizens positively dreaded the advent of the Confederate army. "Invasion by the Southern army was considered equivalent to destruction," he wrote. By nightfall reliable news reached the city that the rumors were true: a large Confederate force had crossed the Potomac near the Monocacy River and was marching toward Frederick. Urgent telegrams instructed the Federal army officers to immediately remove all stores and burn those that could not be moved. "Here began a scene of terror seldom witnessed in this region," observed Steiner in his diary. There were nearly 600 sick at the city's U.S. Army General Hospital No. 1, located on the grounds of the old Hessian barracks of 1777. Robert F. Weir, the head surgeon, assembled transportation for 398 patients who were ambulatory, as well as two wagonloads of valuable medical supplies, and put them on the road for

Gettysburg, Pennsylvania, under the care of Assistant Surgeon C. P. Harrington. Meanwhile the assistant quartermaster, Lieutenant George T. Castle, set fire to a large quantity of his stores at the depot, and Dr. Robert Weir, in charge of the general hospital, burned his storehouse and the most valuable parts of his surplus bedding. Captain W. T. Faithful, a resourceful fellow who commanded the town's provost guard, consisting of Company C, 1st Maryland Potomac Home Brigade, managed to collect an engine and enough rail cars to send a trainload of supplies to Baltimore. He then marched off with his company by way of Jefferson and Knoxville to take refuge with the garrison at Harpers Ferry. The 14th New Jersey, entrusted with protecting the railroad bridge over the Monocacy—the one Jackson had hoped to reach—gathered their belongings and boarded a train for Baltimore. Company G, 1st Maryland Potomac Home Brigade, guarding Monocacy Junction, also withdrew in the direction of Harpers Ferry. "Thousands of men, women, and children" also joined the nighttime exodus. "Many of our prominent citizens, fearing impressment, left their families and started for Pennsylvania in carriages, on horseback, and on foot," recorded Steiner. The *Baltimore American* reported that "the roads leading toward Pennsylvania and Baltimore are represented as having been lined with fugitives." Those that remained perhaps feared what the next day would bring.[39]

Jackson Occupies Frederick

Jackson's camps at Three Springs stirred at their typically early hour on September 6 as his three divisions and D. H. Hill's division prepared for the day's march. A sparse breakfast—probably consisting of parched corn and some cooked flour (if the particular mess were lucky)—was devoured, blankets were rolled, and the brigades assembled to take up the line of march for Frederick. Jackson decided that he would ride the horse presented to him the day before and had her saddled. "He mounted her and she seemed stupid about starting," recalled his aide, Major Henry Douglas. Then a band nearby struck up a tune. The horse, according to Douglas, then "rose on her hind feet into the air and went backward, horse and rider, to the ground." Jackson's cartographer, Jedediah Hotchkiss, thought the saddle girth broke when the horse reared up. In either case, Jackson was thrown hard on his back. He lay there, stunned, for more than a half hour. Finally he recovered enough to be raised up and placed in an ambulance, but he did not feel well enough to exercise command, so he directed D. H. Hill to take command of the movement on Frederick. Despite his discomfort, Jackson issued a stern reminder to his staff to make certain that Marylanders and their private property were not disturbed. By the end of the day he was well enough to ride again and resume command.[40]

The march to Fredrick was uneventful. Jackson's four divisions marched up the west bank of the Monocacy River, with J. R. Jones's division again in the lead. Lawton's and A. P. Hill's (still under Branch) divisions halted near Monocacy Junction. Lawton took up positions to cover the approaches from Baltimore, while Branch established A. P. Hill's division to guard the B&O railroad bridge and the Georgetown Pike from Washington. D. H. Hill's two brigades marched to within 2 miles of Frederick and bivouacked on the Best farm, close to the Monocacy River. J. R. Jones's division continued on to Frederick, preceded either by Captain Randolph's company of the 4th Virginia Cavalry or Lige White's scouts. Their advance riders, described by Dr. Steiner as "two seedy-looking individuals," rode into the city along Market Street around 9 a.m. "as fast as their jaded animals could carry them." At the intersection of Patrick and Market streets they raised a shout for Jeff Davis, then rode on to the intersection of Church and Market streets, where they repeated their cheer. The locals looked on silently. Having either accomplished their mission or fulfilled a wish, the two men rode back through town, where they met Randolph's or White's company, accompanied by Colonel Bradley T. Johnson and D. H. Hill—in all about 50 to 100 horsemen. Some "feeble shouts" from a handful of Confederate sympathizers greeted them, but most citizens watched silently or remained indoors, anxious about what the arrival of the Confederate army might herald for them.[41]

One of the Confederate troopers behaved as if the Southern occupation might be severe. He rode up to Sergeant Crocker, an older man in charge of the hospital stores in one building, and inquired whether he was a Yankee. Crocker replied, "No, I am a Marylander." "What are you doing in the Yankee army?" the trooper asked. Crocker answered proudly, "I belong to the United States Army." At this the Confederate waved his saber over Crocker's head, warning that "if you don't come along with me, I'll cut your head off." "This display of chivalry did not infuse great admiration of the Southern army into the hearts of the bystanders," remarked Dr. Steiner.[42]

But this trooper proved to be the exception rather than the rule. The Confederate occupation of Frederick was quiet and orderly. Around 10 a.m. J. R. Jones's division marched into town along Market Street. Only Bradley Johnson's brigade remained in Frederick. The balance of the division marched through town and out the Emmitsburg Road to a point about 3 miles north of the city, where they went into camp. Dr. Steiner found little to like in Frederick's occupiers, and he penned an unflattering description of Jackson's soldiers.

> A dirtier, filthier, more unsavory set of human beings never strolled through a
> town—marching it could not be called without doing violence to the word.
> The distinctions of rank were recognized on the coat collars of officers; but all

were alike dirty and repulsive. Their arms were rusty and in an unsoldierly condition. Their uniforms, or rather multiforms, corresponded only in a slight predominance of gray over butternut, and in the prevalence of filth. Faces looked as if they had not been acquainted with water for weeks; hair, shaggy and unkempt, seemed entirely a stranger to the operations of brush or comb.[43]

They may have looked rough and ragged, but Steiner could make no complaint about the Confederates' discipline. With one or two exceptions, the behavior of Jackson's men was exemplary. Jackson appointed Bradley Johnson as provost marshal, with his brigade serving as provost guard, and directed them to keep order. To calm the fears of the town's citizens, Johnson repeatedly announced that the Confederates were "no marauders," but were "Southern gentlemen" and would respect private property.[44]

Jackson himself did not enter Frederick. He had his headquarters established at Best's Grove, a majestic grove of oaks located about 2 miles southeast of Frederick. Foraging parties fanned out across the countryside, gathering up "droves of sheep, hogs, beeves, cows, and horses," which were reportedly paid for with Union greenbacks. Provost Marshall Johnson directed the shopkeepers of Frederick to open their doors to the soldiers, and by afternoon "the streets were thronged with Rebel soldiers" of Jackson's and D. H. Hill's divisions, who were about to enjoy their first shopping excursion of the summer.[45]

While Jackson's divisions established themselves near Frederick, Stuart moved his cavalry brigades to screen the army's right flank east of the Monocacy River. Stuart had his column in motion before sunrise, with Hampton's brigade in front and the 1st North Carolina in the lead. A halt was made at Barnesville to feed the horses. Leaving a squadron of the 9th Virginia Cavalry behind to picket the area, Stuart continued on, but rather than directing his men to Hyattstown, he marched toward Sugar Loaf Mountain, a large, isolated hill mass about 6 miles south of Monocacy Junction, the summit of which offered excellent observation from Leesburg to Frederick, a fact the U.S. Signal Corps had not ignored. On September 3 a signal party, commanded by Lieutenant Brinkerhoff N. Miner, ascended the mountain, and for three days the lieutenant observed the movements of the Confederate army and signaled his observations to stations that relayed the news to Washington. Miner spotted Stuart's column winding its way in his direction and, gathering his party, made his way down the mountain to avoid capture. At the mountain's base he and his party intercepted a Confederate officer and a courier bearing dispatches from Jefferson Davis for Lee, who had ridden ahead of the cavalry. These two men apparently intended to find Lee near Frederick. Miner took the officer prisoner, but the courier escaped and rode back to the advance guard of the 1st North Carolina. Miner, meanwhile, did not bother to examine the contents of the portmanteau hanging from the pommel of the Confederate officer's saddle. Instead, accompanied only by a private and his prisoner, Miner rode on to a farmhouse about 4 miles away, where some people he knew resided. Thinking he had shaken any pursuit, the lieutenant halted here. But his pursuers proved more resourceful than Miner expected, and a group of Tarheel troopers shortly rode into the farmyard and made him their prisoner.[46]

Stuart, no doubt leaving a detachment to occupy Sugar Loaf, continued on to Urbana, arriving about noon. Von Borcke established headquarters in the "very centre of the village," while Hampton's and Fitz Lee's brigades bivouacked nearby. Stuart rode to Frederick, where he met with General Lee and Jackson and learned that the army would remain around Frederick for several days, resting and gathering supplies, and observing the reaction of the Union army. Stuart's mission was threefold: to screen the army's front, gather intelligence on the movements of the Federals, and deceive the enemy as to the army's true intentions by implying a threat to both Washington and Baltimore. Lee hoped that such a threat, combined with the presence of his army at Frederick, would encourage the Union army to leave its fortifications and come out into the open. Returning later in the day, Stuart ordered Fitz Lee to march to New Market, a small village located on the National Road, about 6 miles northeast of Urbana. Hampton remained at Urbana, which sat astride the other principal road serving Frederick from the east, the Georgetown Pike. The South Carolinian posted strong outposts at Hyattstown and as far east as Middlebrook, some 8 miles from Hyattstown and only 23 miles from Washington. Fitz Lee also pushed his pickets well out, some of them being observed on September 7 at Poplar Springs, 10 miles east of New Market; 18 miles from Frederick; and within 7 miles of Westminster. By the end of September 6, the Confederate cavalry screen stretched from Barnesville to New Market, a distance of some 14 miles. By the 7th, Confederate patrols would range across more than a 30-mile front, from the Westminster Pike to Barnesville. While the National Road and Georgetown Pike were the most heavily guarded avenues of approach, detachments had to patrol the secondary roads as well, going as far north as the Westminster Pike.[47]

Stuart's third brigade, under Munford, crossed the Potomac River on the 6th, traveling through what George M. Neese of Chew's battery described as dust so thick it was "impossible to discern a man three rods distant." They found the river fords clogged by "the vast number of wagons and artillery there waiting for an opportunity to ford," so they were unable to make their crossing until midnight. They marched through the night and arrived near Frederick around 2 p.m. on the 7th.[48]

While Stuart's cavalry maneuvered to screen the army's eastern flank and Jackson's command closed up on Frederick and Monocacy Junction, Longstreet's divisions forded the Potomac at White's Ford. The march was routine but uncomfortable, due to the weather. The temperature climbed to 80 degrees and dust hung heavily in the air, but the troops endured it, for they were in high spirits and full of anticipation about what good things Maryland's rich farms and towns might have to eat.

Longstreet had his brigades in motion by 4 a.m. and reached White's Ford between 6 and 7 a.m. His column consisted of the divisions of D. R. Jones, Hood, and R. H. Anderson, and Evans's brigade. They were joined at the river by McLaws's division. As the head of the column reached the river's edge, it halted to allow the men to remove their shoes and socks and roll their pant legs up, and in some instances to remove their pants. Regimental bands moved to the front and assembled on the riverbank. Once they were stripped down, the regiments plunged into the cool, waist-deep water to the accompaniment of "Dixie" and "Maryland, My Maryland." The surgeon of Jenkins's brigade's 6th South Carolina noted how clear the water was and that he "could see every rock in the bottom and they were not a few—the bottom was covered with round rocks." A member of the Texas Brigade recalled that there was "yelling and singing [of] all sorts of war and jolly songs . . . the drums beating, the horns a tootin' and the fifes a screaming, possibly every one of them on a different air." An immense traffic jam developed at the ford, and Lee sent orders for McLaws to take his division north and cross the river at Cheek's Ford. Even with McLaws out of the way, the crossing of the three divisions, plus artillery and trains, went on until nearly midnight.[49]

When Lee and army headquarters entered Maryland is not known, but it must have been early, so that he could avoid the heavy troop and wagon traffic that would clog the roads when Longstreet's main body started to cross the river. Still unable to ride a horse because of his injured wrists, Lee entered Maryland in an ambulance. He paused briefly after crossing into the state to dictate a dispatch to Davis, informing the president that two divisions had crossed the Potomac (presumably he meant two of Longstreet's divisions), the C&O Canal's service had been interrupted (D. H. Hill's and Jackson's men had destroyed the banks of the canal along nearly 25 miles), and "efforts will be made to break up the use of the Baltimore and Ohio Railroad."[50]

Longstreet caught up with Lee, probably after headquarters had crossed the Monocacy River. The big Georgian rode beside Lee's ambulance and, while he did so, the sound of artillery fire could be heard in the direction of Berlin and Point of Rocks. It was G. B. Anderson, sparring with the 87th Ohio and a section of howitzers from the Union garrison at Harpers Ferry. This prompted some discussion between the two generals about the Union garrison, and Lee suggested that it might be possible to organize an expedition to descend on and capture the garrison. He offered command to Longstreet, or at least inquired as to what he thought of the idea. Longstreet believed it was too risky. The troops were worn down with hard marching and short rations, and they would be operating in enemy territory, where their movements would be quickly reported to the Union army. That army, Longstreet warned, though defeated at Manassas, "was not disorganized, and would certainly come out and look for us." Longstreet thought the Confederate army should rest and recruit itself for a time, build up supplies, and "then we could do anything we pleased." Lee made no response, and Longstreet assumed his chief had dropped the idea of a Harpers Ferry expedition.[51]

Lee and Longstreet continued on to Best's Grove, where they established their headquarters near Jackson's and D. H. Hill's divisions. Army headquarters soon produced General Orders No. 103. Lee wished to make certain that his army understood that he would tolerate no lapses of discipline, particularly toward civilians, while it was in Maryland. The orders also announced news of General Kirby Smith's victory over Union General William B. Nelson at Richmond, Kentucky, on August 30. Lee had read about the battle in a Baltimore newspaper on September 4, but he probably learned more details from the dispatches from Davis that had nearly been captured at Sugar Loaf Mountain. He now understood that his army was not acting alone and that Confederate troops were on the offensive in the west. Knowledge of Smith's actions may also have caused Lee to attach even greater importance to his own campaign. Success on the frontiers of the Confederacy in both the east and west might demoralize the North enough to fracture the support for Lincoln's war effort.[52]

Along Maryland's roads, the euphoria of treading on her soil evaporated in Longstreet's ranks as the blazing sun and choking dust clouds took their toll on the marching men. "I do not remember any march that so prostrated me as that of this first day of our invasion of the North," wrote John Dooley of the 1st Virginia. Probably because of the delays incurred in the river crossing, Longstreet's divisions did not reach Buckeystown, where the exhausted brigades bivouacked, until after 10 p.m.[53]

McLaws's division had an easier day of it. They crossed at Cheek's Ford without incident. But probably because it took so long for Longstreet's command to pass, they remained along the banks of the Potomac on the Maryland shore and bivouacked there for the night. By the end of the day, eight of the army's nine divisions were north of the Potomac, spread out from Frederick to near Cheek's Ford. Stuart had two brigades fanning out east of the Monocacy River to screen the army, and a third reached Frederick that day. All of the infantry, except for McLaws's division, were west of the Monocacy. Jackson had one division in the vicinity of Frederick and two other divisions, plus D. H. Hill's, at Monocacy Junction. Longstreet's three divisions (D. R. Jones's, R. H. Anderson's, and Hood's) were at Buckeystown. Only Walker's division, the reserve artillery, and G. B. Anderson's brigade remained south of the Potomac River. Walker's division spent the 6th making a hard march that brought them to within 4 miles of the Potomac, above Leesburg. The distance covered was only 12 miles, but for some reason the march was made in the heat of the day and the men suffered greatly from the high temperatures and the dust. An officer in the 35th North Carolina recorded that nearly two-thirds of the men in his regiment fell out because of the heat. G. B. Anderson completed his brigade's diversion at Berlin, Maryland, and they marched to Cheek's Ford, where they camped for the night. The reserve artillery completed their reorganization and prepared to enter Maryland on the 7th.[54]

The first phase of the campaign, the river crossing and concentration of the army, had proceeded smoothly. Enemy opposition had been insignificant, which strengthened Lee's impression that the Federals were demoralized by their defeat at Manassas. He still held the initiative, and his position at Frederick—threatening Baltimore, Washington, and Pennsylvania—pressured the enemy to react. While he waited to see how they would do so, Lee gave his army a badly needed rest and an opportunity to refresh themselves and gather supplies.

September 7 promised to be another warm, cloudless day. By sunrise (5:40 a.m.) both McLaws's and R. H. Anderson's divisions were on the move. Anderson's division, marching "at a rapid pace," left Buckeystown behind and reached the vicinity of Monocacy Junction "shortly after noon." McLaws apparently followed a different route than Longstreet, probably to avoid the latter's trains. His division either marched along roads that roughly followed the east bank of the Monocacy River, or they crossed the Monocacy at a ford above Licksville. Either way, the division forded the river at Buckeystown and continued on to near Monocacy Junction. Hood followed Anderson to Monocacy Junction at an unspecified hour, and D. R. Jones's brigades stirred from their Buckeystown bivouac "late in the day." According to one diarist in the division, they crossed the Monocacy River twice, probably at Buckeystown and again at Monocacy Junction, and "early in the evening arrived in the vicinity of Frederick City."[55]

Walker's division set out from its camp north of Leesburg by 6 a.m. and reached Cheek's Ford "about 10 a.m." Here Walker encountered G. B. Anderson, who apparently had crossed first, followed by Manning's brigade, and then Ransom's. A member of the 48th North Carolina found it amusing to watch "the boys wading like cranes over the rocky ford and cringing as their tender feet struck the rocky bottom." The 3rd Arkansas and the 30th Virginia regimental bands played the men across with the now standard favorites, "Dixie" and "Maryland, My Maryland." Everyone raised the usual shout when they touched the Maryland shore, followed by a halt to put on their pants, socks, and shoes. Dust and heat assailed the men again, but a breeze provided some relief, so that, as one North Carolinian wrote, they did not feel "the march as much as the day before." A march of 9 more miles brought Walker to Buckeystown, where his division camped. G. B. Anderson continued on to rejoin his division at Monocacy Junction.[56]

Pendleton and the four battalions of the reserve artillery did not leave Leesburg until late afternoon. They reached the Potomac River either at Noland's

Ferry or Cheek's Ford around sunset. It was dark by the time all the battalions were across, and Pendleton had them bivouac near the ford. A sergeant in Captain John Ansell's battery of Major William Nelson's battalion wrote that "the horses had hardly been unhitched, and the fires kindled, when Major Nelson came riding down and frantically exclaiming to John, who was sitting on the ground by the fire drying his feet, 'Captain, are you sitting down when the Yankees are only two miles off? Hitch up at once.'" The sudden panic seems to have originated at Pendleton's headquarters. Four squadrons of the 8th Illinois and the 3rd Indiana Cavalry had descended on Poolesville that day and captured the videttes posted there. News of this evidently reached Pendleton, accompanied by a warning that the Yankees were moving in his direction (which they were not). The numbers of Federal cavalry had also been greatly inflated. The report evidently caused Pendleton to lose his composure and become overly excited, ordering the battalions to hitch up and march at once. There was much grumbling at this, for most of the men had not eaten their dinner, but eventually everyone moved off, marching until 1 a.m., when they went into camp, probably near Buckeystown, where they had the protection of Walker's division.[57]

Pendleton's worries were justified, since his batteries lacked infantry or cavalry support and were highly vulnerable to enemy cavalry. Why no arrangements were made to provide an escort is an unanswered question. At least a regiment of cavalry, if not a whole brigade, such as Munford's, should have been assigned to Pendleton. Walker's division had passed through Leesburg on the 6th and could have detailed a regiment of infantry as escort. This important detail seems to have been overlooked both by army headquarters and by Pendleton. What disturbed some of Pendleton's battalion and battery commanders was their chief's lack of composure during the emergency. One battery commander complained that "Gen. Pendleton displayed an utter want of confidence & fearlessness."[58]

"We all had a really grand time"

For most Confederate infantrymen or artillerymen, September 7, 8, and 9 were precious days of rest, a pause in what had been a tremendously arduous spring and summer of campaigning. "We have been out of Richmond a full month and we have on the same clothes; pants, jacket and shirt, nothing more, through the dust and mud marching, fighting and sleeping on the ground," wrote one of Hood's veterans. Frederick and its environs offered these weary campaigners a city with plentiful goods and clothing, where something tastier than "roasting ears" might be found to eat. The days were sunny and warm. Whole brigades and divisions at a time enjoyed bathing in the cool waters of the gentle Monocacy. In Jenkins's South Carolina brigade, the men were read orders that "soap would be issued to us and it was required of us to wash both ourselves and clothes." Hood's brigades did likewise, the men plunging in with their clothes on, apparently to clean both their bodies and their garments.[59]

Being the first to reach Frederick, Jackson's men (and D. H. Hill's) got early pickings. While Longstreet's brigades were marching up from the Potomac on the 6th, Jackson's and Hill's troops enjoyed a shopping spree in the city, crowding into merchants' shops, which Bradley Johnson had ordered to be opened, eager to buy clothing and other goods. With a population of over 8,000, Frederick was the largest city Jackson's men had been near since July, and, unlike the towns and cities in Virginia, the shelves of its stores (unless the merchants had managed to get off some of their goods) were full. "They literally swept garments and shoes from the town," stated one resident. Dr. Steiner observed that "the shoe stores were most patronized, as many of their men were shoeless and stockingless. The only money most of them had was Confederate script, or shinplasters issued by banks, corporations, individuals, etc.—all of equal value. To use the expression of an old citizen, 'the notes depreciated the paper on which they were printed.'"[60]

When Longstreet's troops began to filter into the city on the 7th and 8th, they were disgusted to find that Jackson's men had already cleaned out the most coveted items from the shops. But they eagerly scooped up the leftovers, paying for goods with their hard-earned but largely worthless Confederate money for goods until, as the *Baltimore American* reported, "the entire stock of boots and shoes in Frederick were bought out." Although some soldiers found other items in scarce supply, good food could still be had, and, if a soldier was lucky, so could liquor. "Our houses were besieged by hungry soldiers and officers," wrote Dr. Steiner. "They ate everything offered them with a greediness that fully sustained the truth of their statement, that their entire subsistence lately had been green corn, uncooked, and eaten directly from the stalk." Although many soldiers found Frederick's citizens to be Unionists and not particularly enthusiastic about their presence, many would have agreed with the judgment of Captain Greenlee Davidson, one of Jackson's battery commanders. They "have received us cordially," he wrote. Another of Jackson's battery commanders, Captain William T. Poague, enjoyed meals with some of his comrades at the home of a local family. He recalled that they "were not ardent Confederates, but all the same they took our Confederate money and gave us the best they had. I never enjoyed good things to eat, as much in my whole army experience . . . we all had a really grand time." Poague's sentiments were by no means unique in the Confederate army. In the opinion of Napier Bartlett, a member of the famous Washington Artillery, abundant food and full stomachs "effectually banished the memory of hard marches."[61]

Liquor also banished the memory of hard marches, and, despite the efforts of Bradley Johnson's provost guard, soldiers found ways to elude them and sneak into Frederick's saloons. Napier Bartlett recalled that the doors of the saloons "from time to time would mysteriously open and shut, . . . and the jingling of spurs, sabres and glasses, and the faint aroma of tempting drinks, would be borne to the senses of the envious lookers on." In Jackson's camps the men of Raine's and Carpenter's batteries managed to lay their hands on a quantity of spirits, and, after imbibing "rather freely," the two units erupted into "a sort of a free fight." Lieutenant Baxter McCorkle, a powerful fellow from Poague's battery, waded into the brawl and broke it up.[62]

The rumpus between Raine's and Carpenter's men was unique, because it stood out from the otherwise uneventful Confederate occupation. For all their rough demeanor, the Southern soldiers were well disciplined and well behaved during their stay. This is not surprising, as all knew Maryland was a slave state and many believed it to be sympathetic to the Confederate cause, only held in the Union by Lincoln's firm grip. The wife of a Frederick shopkeeper found the Rebels "ragged filthy, worn out men," yet "every one (to our astonishment), respectful and polite." Union medical officer C. E. Goldsborough, who wandered the streets freely after having been paroled when the Confederates occupied the city, observed that "rarely did any act of outrage or disturbance occur . . . the strictest discipline was enforced in every case." Only two small incidents marred what was a model occupation of a city by an invading army. On the 6th, as J. R. Jones's division passed through, some men of the Stonewall Brigade gave way to "brutal excesses" directed toward several young ladies, which probably meant that they spoke some uncouth words to the ladies. The "brutes" were broadly described as "foreigners," which, to Stonewall Jackson, meant that they belonged to the Louisiana brigade of Brigadier General William E. Starke. Starke's brigade had some tough sorts: Irishmen from New Orleans's wharves and docks, and French Creoles. Without conducting an investigation of the incident, Jackson ordered Starke to march his brigade into the city so that the guilty "brutes" might be identified. This offended Starke and his sense of justice, and he refused to obey the order, which probably pleased his men but did not impress Jackson, who placed the brigadier under arrest. But Starke did convince Jackson that perhaps he should conduct an investigation. It uncovered, to Starke's satisfaction and Jackson's embarrassment, that the "foreigners" were Virginians of the Stonewall Brigade. The "brutes" apparently were not as bad as they had been made out to be, for they were subsequently released without punishment.[63]

The second incident occurred in the early hours of the Confederate occupation. A mob of Southern-sympathizing citizens made a rush on the offices of the city's two Unionist newspapers. The mob managed to drive in the door of the *Examiner* and began to throw the contents of its office into the street. Bradley Johnson's provost guard hurried to the disturbance and quickly put an end to the rioters' fun, which may have surprised the rowdies. But the guard did not stop at merely restoring the peace. They put the mob to work cleaning up the mess they had made. Then, after everything had been returned to the *Examiner*'s office, the troublemakers were marched off to the guardhouse.[64]

While Lee's soldiers carefully respected the personal possessions of Maryland's civilians, they actively carried out the destruction of communications and transportation that might benefit the Federals. The C&O Canal had been damaged at the beginning of the invasion. On September 8, the army's engineers blew up the B&O railroad bridge over the Monocacy, an event that was marred by the death of a member of the 17th Virginia, who was bathing in the river when he was struck by flying debris.[65]

"They were the roughest looking set of creatures I ever saw"

The physical appearance of the Army of Northern Virginia's soldiers left a deep impression on Frederick's Unionist citizens and probably shocked those sympathetic with their cause. "The troops are all in a most filthy condition," wrote the *New York Herald*'s Frederick correspondent. "It is positively offensive to be near them. They look as if they had not washed themselves or changed any of their clothing since they entered the service." A local citizen concurred: "I have never seen a mess of such filthy, strong-smelling men," he wrote. "They were the roughest looking set of creatures I ever saw, their features, hair and clothing, matted with dirt and filthy, and the scratching they kept up gave warrant of vermin in abundance." Another man thought that "it was almost impossible to distinguish the officer from the privates; all were victims of poverty and rags-rich in nought else, save desperation, dirt and Confederate script." To Dr. Steiner it seemed that "a motlier group was never herded together. But these were the chivalry—the delivers of Maryland from Lincoln's oppressive yolk." For C. E. Goldsborough the Confederates' ragged condition elicited not contempt, but grudging admiration: "How men famished and footsore could fight as they did was a question I asked myself over and over again."[66]

A single look at Lee's soldiers wilted the ardor of many a would-be recruit, who arrived in Frederick probably expecting to see well-fed soldiers in bright, neat uniforms. Perhaps 500 or so potential volunteers from the Frederick area and nearby communities wandered in to have a look at the army. "After seeing the character of the army and life which the men led, many of them refused to join," testified one Frederick resident. A correspondent reported that one potential recruit lost his eagerness to join the Confederate army after "seeing and smelling" the Southern soldiers. "If ever suicide were contemplated by any one it must be by those civilians who propose to attach themselves to Jackson's corps," commented Dr. Steiner. Few did. Less than 200 actually enlisted. Lee left at least 800 sick in Frederick when he departed, so his accessions from recruits did not nearly make good his losses from illness alone.[67]

Lee had anticipated that Marylanders might be reluctant to accept Confederate notes or receipts, causing difficulty in procuring supplies, and this proved to be the case. Abundant supplies were at the army's fingertips, but the farmers, millers, and others who were approached by commissary officers hesitated to sell. Lee sought the Marylanders' sympathy with his cause, and seizing supplies risked generating opposition and resistance. The consequence was that his army only managed to purchase a small amount of flour, a relative handful of cattle, 1,000 pairs of shoes, and some clothing, far short of what Lee needed and hoped to procure. Only forage for the army's animals was obtained without difficulty.

Lee also understood that the people might question why his army had occupied Maryland soil, and that some might fear its intentions. Enoch Lowe, whom he hoped might join him at Frederick to alleviate these fears and assist his army's efforts to purchase supplies, was unable to reach the army. Lowe was a Maryland Democrat, who had been its governor from 1850 to 1853. When the war broke out his sympathies were with the Confederates, and he took up residence in Richmond. Lowe set out to join the army at Leesburg in company with Jefferson Davis on September 7, but Davis turned back when he learned that the army had left Leesburg and broken up its line of communications across northern Virginia. Lowe continued on to Winchester, but he played no role in the campaign. In the absence of Lowe, Lee thought Marylanders deserved an explanation for his army's entry into their state. "I waited on entering the State for the arrival of ex-Governor Lowe; but finding that he did not come up, and that the citizens were embarrassed as to the intentions of the army, I determined to delay no longer in making known our purpose," he explained to Davis on September 12. On September 8 Lee had issued a proclamation that mainly sought to calm the fears of Marylanders. It explained that the army had entered Maryland to aid the state's citizens in throwing off the oppressive rule of Lincoln's government and to restore "independence and sovereignty to your state," a reference to Lincoln's suspension of habeas corpus in Maryland. The people were also reassured that whether they rejoiced or skulked at the Confederate army's presence, it knew "no enemies among you, and will protect all, of every opinion. It is for you to decide your destiny freely and without constraint. This army will respect your choice, whatever it may be."[68]

Marylanders reacted indifferently to the proclamation, which did not surprise Lee. Neither did it surprise his men, who, although appreciative of the willingness of Frederick's citizens to feed them, sensed that they were not among friends. "Yes, that Maryland is foreign evidences accumulate," wrote Lieutenant "Ham" Chamberlayne. "People are kind enough generally, but they fear us with a mortal terror . . . Frederick, it is as Yankee as Hartford or Cape Cod." William Y. Mordecai, serving in one of the Richmond howitzer companies, wrote that "the country is most picturesque and beautiful and the farms more productive and better cultivated than in any place I have ever seen," but the farmhouses were filled with "fat Dutch looking people who won't take Confederate money and tell you they have nothing to sell—this is the rule, but there are pleasant exceptions." A Mississippian in Barksdale's brigade noted of Frederick in his diary, "we found many friends there, but the Union element is also very strong," a sentiment with which many in the army would have agreed.[69]

"General Jackson's Command will form the advance"

While his army enjoyed their chance to rest and refit, Lee studied the operational picture and contemplated his army's next move. He also took the opportunity to correspond with President Davis on administrative and political issues. In a September 7 letter, Lee addressed the subject of straggling and the need for legislation that enabled the army to deal more effectively with the problem. On the 8th he deviated from his typical policy of never advising the Confederate president on political issues by suggesting that it seemed to be a most opportune moment for the Confederate States government to "propose with propriety to that of the United States Government the recognition of our independence." Nothing ever came of this proposal, however. The failure of all the Confederate offensives that fall killed it, even if Davis had seriously considered such a move, but Lee's thinking was sound. The Confederacy had nothing to lose, and might even accrue some political benefit from it.[70]

The strategic situation in Maryland developed much as Lee anticipated and hoped it would. Union cavalry probed Stuart's line at Poolesville on the 7th and again on the 8th, resulting in some sharp skirmishing (see chapter 5). Lee learned that behind these cavalry probes, the enemy had placed strong forces in the field. He reported almost casually to Davis on the 9th, "I believe that the enemy are pushing a strong column up the Potomac River by Rockville and Darnesville, and by Poolesville toward Seneca Mill. I hear the commands of Sumner, Sigel, Burnside and Hooker are advancing in the above mentioned direction." It was what he had hoped the Federals would do in reaction to his occupation of Frederick.[71]

But there were two surprises. President Davis provided the first. On the 9th Lee received a letter from Davis with news that he had started from Richmond with Enoch Lowe to join the army at Leesburg. Lee could not leave the army in the midst of the campaign to meet with Davis, which meant that the Confederate president would have to join the army in Maryland. Such a prospect was simply too fraught with unnecessary risk. If a roving Federal cavalry patrol captured Davis, the consequences would be disastrous. In a delicately worded dispatch Lee strongly discouraged Davis's journey. "I cannot but feel great uneasiness for your safety should you undertake to reach me," he wrote. "You will not only encounter the hardships and fatigues of a very disagreeable journey, but also run the risk of capture by the enemy." To ensure that he did not make the attempt, Lee dispatched Major Walter Taylor, of his staff, to intercept Davis and politely turn him back.[72]

The Union garrisons at Harpers Ferry and Martinsburg provided the second surprise. Here the enemy did not behave as Lee expected they would. Lee had only learned about the garrison at Martinsburg after the start of the Maryland invasion, and he had assumed that both of these garrisons would be withdrawn when his army occupied Frederick. By the afternoon of the 9th Lee knew that, against military logic, both garrisons remained in place. Their presence posed a problem that had to be dealt with. Lee planned to move the army from Frederick to Hagerstown on September 10 or 11, both to threaten Pennsylvania and to open communications with the Shenandoah Valley. The army's stay in Frederick had convinced him that he could not rely on Maryland to fully supply his food and forage needs, and supplies hauled down the Valley might need to make up the shortfall. But as long as the Union garrisons remained in place, his Valley communications were not secure. Characteristically, Lee viewed this not as a problem but as an opportunity. He thought it possible to capture or destroy both garrisons and reunite the army near Hagerstown well before the slowly moving Army of the Potomac posed a threat. Lee knew just the man to lead such an expedition, someone with experience in independent command who was familiar with the area in which the expeditionary force would operate: Stonewall Jackson. On the afternoon of the 9th Lee summoned him to headquarters.[73]

Before Jackson arrived, General John G. Walker's division marched up to Monocacy Junction and Walker reported to Lee. Walker apparently arrived before Lee had solid evidence that the Union garrisons in the Shenandoah Valley still remained, for Lee told the division commander that the main body of the army would march on the 10th to Hagerstown. Lee's orders to Walker were to essentially retrace his steps back to the mouth of the Monocacy River and destroy the C&O Canal's aqueduct over that river. When this work was finished, Walker was to march by way of Jefferson and Middletown to rejoin the army. Lee orders are puzzling. If he wanted the aqueduct destroyed, he should have sent orders to Walker either when Walker reached Leesburg or after he crossed the Potomac River. Why Lee waited until Walker's men had marched all the way to Frederick before telling them to turn back is oddly uncharacteristic of him, as he knew that this division had been marching hard for over a week. What seems likely is that Lee sent Walker back to the mouth of the Monocacy not only to destroy the aqueduct, but also so that his division would be in place to move against Harpers Ferry from the south if Lee's sources confirmed that the Union garrison there remained in place. If the enemy withdrew, then Walker could accomplish something productive for his marching by smashing up the aqueduct and drawing the attention of the advancing Army of the Potomac away from the main body of the Confederate army. With the Monocacy River between his division and the Federals, Walker could easily get away safely and rejoin the army at Hagerstown.[74]

After the war, in an article for *Century Magazine*, Walker claimed that during their meeting Lee explained his campaign plans to him in great detail, including Lee's intention to attack and capture the Union garrisons in the Shenandoah Valley. Recent scholarship has questioned Walker's account, and with good reason; it does not agree with his official report of the Maryland Campaign, which he wrote on October 7, 1862. Walker's report clearly states that he did not learn about the Harpers Ferry operation until the early-morning hours of September 10. If this important fact, which conflicts with his alleged conversation with Lee, is true, then the credibility of the rest of the discussion, as Walker related it in his article, must be regarded with skepticism.[75]

Special Orders No. 191

Sometime after Walker left headquarters, Lee must have received reliable intelligence about the Union garrisons in the Shenandoah Valley. When Jackson arrived at headquarters, the two generals retired to Lee's tent and closed the flaps. Lee explained that rather than march the entire army to Hagerstown, as he had originally planned, he intended to divide it, sending part of it in several separate columns to attack the Valley garrisons. The details of Lee's original plan are unknown, for we are only privy to what Lee and Jackson together produced. Jackson thought Lee's plan was too risky and suggested, as Longstreet had earlier, that they should deal with the Army of the Potomac first; then Harpers Ferry and Martinsburg could be taken care of. Lee disagreed. He believed that the Confederate army could destroy or capture both garrisons and reunite at Hagerstown well before the Army of the Potomac came up. Then, with secure communications, that army could be attended to. Lee's sources reported the strength of the Harpers Ferry garrison at between 7,000 and 8,000, although he thought its actual strength was considerably less, and Lee knew the Martinsburg garrison was much smaller than the one at Harpers Ferry. Lee was confident that both garrisons could be overwhelmed quickly. His arguments won Jackson over, and the lieutenant's mind "settled firmly upon the enterprise."[76]

The two generals developed a plan that divided the army into four parts, with over one-half of the army's strength dedicated to attacking the Valley garrisons. Walker's division would cross the Potomac back into Virginia at Cheek's Ford; secure Loudoun Heights, which overlooked Harpers Ferry from the

Virginia shore; and, in the unlikely event the Federals attempted to escape along the south bank of the Potomac, block the nearby escape routes. Lafayette McLaws and his division would capture Maryland Heights, the key terrain that commanded the Harpers Ferry position. Jackson's three divisions composed the third column. They would march to Sharpsburg, cross the Potomac at some "convenient point," and occupy the B&O Railroad. Here Jackson could intercept any elements of the Harpers Ferry garrison fleeing west to escape from McLaws and Walker and, somehow, capture the Union garrison at Martinsburg, although that force would be west of Jackson and have an escape route to the north and northwest. Of the remaining four divisions, D. H. Hill's would halt at Boonsboro to serve as a rear guard and scoop up any escapees from Harpers Ferry who eluded McLaws, while Longstreet marched with the remaining three divisions to Hagerstown. Stuart's three brigades would screen the army's rear and provide timely notice of an advance by the Army of the Potomac. The general plan was fairly settled by the time James Longstreet happened to show up at headquarters.[77]

Why Lee had not asked Longstreet to attend the planning meeting is unknown, but it was probably because Longstreet's command was not part of the strike force Lee intended to send against the Valley garrisons, and Longstreet was not familiar with the area of operations. But when Lee heard Longstreet's voice outside his tent, he called out for the Georgian to come in and join him and Jackson. Longstreet had not changed his opinion about dividing the Confederate army in the face of the enemy, and he disapproved of the plan that Lee now outlined for him, but it was evident to him that Lee and Jackson were firmly set on the operation and "that it seemed useless for me to offer any further opposition." But this did not deter Longstreet from suggesting that the three brigades of R. H. Anderson's division reinforce McLaws, and that he halt his own command at Boonsboro rather than further divide the army by marching it to Hagerstown. The first suggestion proved to be fortuitous, for Lee both underestimated the strength of the Union garrison at Harpers Ferry and the difficulty of McLaws's mission. Longstreet's second recommendation reflected his advocacy for concentration of force. Longstreet recalled that Lee approved both of his suggestions, which is only partially true, for privately Lee was neither convinced that McLaws needed reinforcements nor that Longstreet's command should not occupy Hagerstown, where vitally important supplies might be secured.[78]

Shortly after the meeting with Jackson and Longstreet broke up, Lee sent for McLaws. When he arrived, Lee explained that the next morning the army would march west on the Old National Road and that R. H. Anderson's division would be attached to McLaws's command. McLaws would form the rear of the army in the movement, marching to Middletown, where he would then turn south and go on to Harpers Ferry, securing Maryland Heights by

September 12 and attempting to capture as many of the enemy as he could. As McLaws recalled, "I remarked to the General that I had never been to Harper's Ferry nor vicinity. He replied, intimating that it did not matter, and then went on to inform me that it had been reported there was a force of 7000 or 8000 men in garrison at Harper's Ferry, but he did not believe there was that many, and asked if I did not think my division alone, or with some addition from Anderson's would be enough for the purpose." McLaws had slightly over 5,000 effectives in his division, and he did not share Lee's optimism that he could overcome an enemy who might be stronger than he. McLaws replied that he would undertake the operation with whatever force Lee ordered, "but that as the force of the enemy was unknown, but reported to be larger than my division, my preference would be to have the whole of Anderson's division with me." Lee listened but gave no indication as to whether he agreed. He sent McLaws back to his division with instructions to be ready to march early the next morning, and to reduce his baggage to one wagon per regiment.[79]

McLaws's and Longstreet's arguments had nearly convinced Lee that he needed to send R. H. Anderson's division with McLaws, but before committing to this he called Anderson to headquarters. Lee went over the details of the operation with the South Carolinian, who was unaware of Lee's earlier meeting with McLaws. Whatever Anderson said removed any doubts Lee had about whether Anderson's division should accompany McLaws, for he dispatched him with orders to attach his division to McLaws and insisted on the importance of carrying out the operation swiftly.[80]

That afternoon and evening the orders for the operation were drafted by Colonel Chilton and copies were made for Jackson, Longstreet, McLaws, D. H. Hill, Walker, and Jeb Stuart. They were Special Orders No. 191, destined to become some of the most famous orders of the Civil War.

SPECIAL ORDERS,   HDQRS. ARMY OF NORTHERN VIRGINIA
No. 191   September 9, 1862

*III. The army will resume its march to-morrow, taking the Hagerstown Road. General Jackson's command will form the advance, and, after passing Middletown, with such portion as he may select, take the route toward Sharpsburg, cross the Potomac at the most convenient point, and by Friday morning take possession of the Baltimore and Ohio Railroad, capture such of them as may be at Martinsburg, and intercept such as may attempt to escape from Harper's Ferry.

* Parts I and II are omitted since they did not deal with the active operations of the army. Part I placed Frederick off-limits to the troops except in cases of army official business. Part II noted that Major Walter Taylor would proceed to Leesburg to arrange for transportation of the sick and lame to Winchester, and stated that all soldiers returning to the army were to be directed to Winchester.

IV. General Longstreet's command will pursue the main road as far as Boonsborough, where it will halt, with reserve, supply, and baggage trains of the army.

V. General McLaws, with his own division and that of General R. H. Anderson, will follow General Longstreet. On reaching Middletown [he] will take the route to Harper's Ferry, and by Friday morning possess himself of the Maryland Heights and endeavor to capture the enemy at Harper's Ferry and vicinity.

VI. General Walker, with his division, after accomplishing the object in which he is now engaged, will cross the Potomac at Cheek's Ford, ascend its right bank to Lovettsville, take possession of Loudoun Heights between the end of the mountain and the Potomac on his right. He will, as far as practicable, co-operate with Generals McLaws and Jackson, and intercept retreat of the enemy.

VII. General D. H. Hill's division will form the rear guard of the army, pursuing the road taken by the main body. The reserve artillery, ordnance and supply trains, &c., will precede General Hill.

VIII. General Stuart will detach a squadron of cavalry to accompany the commands of Generals Longstreet, Jackson, and McLaws, and, with the main body of the cavalry, will cover the route of the army, bringing up all stragglers that may have been left behind.

IX. The commands of Generals Jackson, McLaws, and Walker, after accomplishing the objects for which they have been detached, will join the main body of the army at Boonsborough or Hagerstown.

X. Each regiment on the march will habitually carry its axes in the regimental ordnance wagons, for use of the men at their encampments, to procure wood, &c.

By command of General R. E. Lee

R. H. CHILTON
Assistant Adjutant General[81]

The plan reflected Lee's boldness and his affinity for doing what was least expected. The initial disapproval of his plan by both of his senior lieutenants may have served only to encourage him to undertake it. Both Jackson and Longstreet advocated the textbook move for the army's situation—concentration. It stood to reason that the enemy would expect him to do the same thing. The division of his army into a multipronged rapid movement against the Valley garrisons would be what the Federals least expected. The element of surprise, Lee hoped, would allow him to catch both garrisons unprepared and confuse the Army of the Potomac long enough to destroy the garrisons and reunite the army. Lee clearly did not anticipate a stubborn resistance by the Federal garrisons or a siege of either position. McLaws came to this conclusion after he read the orders. "It was, doubtless, assured that the enemy upon hearing of our approach would leave the place and attempt to escape," he wrote. The most likely route they would take to escape would be west, directly into Jackson's force. Out in the open, the outnumbered Harpers Ferry troops could be smashed. One of the errors students of the Maryland Campaign have fallen into is interpreting Special Orders No. 191 through what actually occurred when the Confederate army executed the plan. What happened and what Lee anticipated were quite different. Lee's confidence that the operation could be wrapped up by September 12 was predicated on the belief that the enemy would flee and be caught in the open. Had Lee expected both garrisons would hole up in Harpers Ferry, rendering a siege necessary, he might have designed both the operation and the forces involved differently. Lee expected the enemy to try to escape from a trap, not deliberately step into it, as they indeed would.[82]

The orders also reflected Lee's belief that the hardest and most important fighting would be done by Jackson. He had the largest force and was the most experienced commander. McLaws and Walker were both inexperienced in independent operations. Lee may well have been testing them, but it is apparent that he saw Walker's role as simply providing a blocking force to discourage the Harpers Ferry garrison from attempting to slip into Virginia to escape. McLaws would (1) render the Harpers Ferry position untenable by capturing Maryland Heights, and, because he held Maryland Heights, (2) herd the enemy toward Jackson.

The plan was not without its flaws. For one, Lee lacked accurate intelligence about the enemy. He apparently had no inkling that the Federals had some 1,300 cavalry between the two garrisons. The orders called only for a squadron of cavalry each to accompany Jackson, Longstreet, and McLaws, although Lee later modified this and attached the 7th Virginia Cavalry to Jackson and the 1st Virginia Cavalry to Longstreet. Walker received no cavalry, and Lee reinforced McLaws reluctantly, which is curious.[83] Lee knew the Harpers Ferry environs from his service there in 1859, and from his discussions with Jackson he knew that Maryland Heights was the key to Harpers Ferry. Why he did not believe the enemy would defend this position with their strongest force possible, as they had done when Jackson threatened the post in the spring, is puzzling. A plausible explanation is that Lee recognized that cut off as they were, the only way the Harpers Ferry garrison could save itself was to run for it. Defending Maryland Heights merely increased their peril, so Lee did not think they would make a fight of it. Perhaps this was his thinking, but if the enemy were unaware that Jackson was cutting across their best line of retreat, then it stood to reason that the enemy would defend Maryland Heights vigorously.

The plan also had no margin for delay in the movements of both McLaws and Walker. McLaws in particular had a highly ambitious timetable to meet, and an unusual placement in the army's order of march, given Lee's desire for speed. McLaws would follow Jackson and Longstreet, which meant that six divisions would precede him, guaranteeing that the Georgian's command would get a late start. His two divisions had to march about 20 miles to reach Maryland Heights, and he was restricted to using the National Road to Middletown before he could turn off toward Burkittsville and the gaps through South Mountain. "I could have reached Pleasant Valley early on the 11th," McLaws later complained, "and by the 12th have had Maryland Heights," had he been placed in front of Longstreet's divisions. Another, and probably better option would have been to have routed McLaws on the road to Jefferson, and then to Burkittsville, which only entailed a march of 1 mile more than the Middletown route. Here McLaws would have had a clear road to travel on and could have made better time.[84]

It is unclear how Jackson was to capture the enemy at Martinsburg if he crossed the Potomac River near Sharpsburg. As his objective was to reach the B&O Railroad, the most likely place Jackson would cross was at Shepherdstown, east of Martinsburg. The enemy could easily escape north along the Valley Pike to Williamsport, and from there march to Hagerstown or Pennsylvania. This fact could not have eluded Lee, and he probably expected the Martinsburg garrison to do the sensible thing and withdraw when they learned of Jackson's approach. Lee was after bigger game, the larger Harpers Ferry garrison, with its supplies and equipment. However, if the Martinsburg garrison did not withdraw on Jackson's approach, there is strong evidence that Lee had granted his lieutenant the flexibility to modify his orders and act as he saw fit.[85]

Perhaps Lee's greatest miscalculation, beyond factoring in no time for unforeseen delays, was that he expected the enemy to behave predictably. He knew from Stuart that the enemy had at least four corps in the field and had advanced in the direction of Poolesville. Union cavalry had driven Stuart's troopers out of this village in sharp skirmishing on the 7th and 8th, and they had skirmished again with the troopers of Munford's brigade at Barnesville and those of Hampton's brigade at Urbana on the 9th. The Federals were advancing on him, but Lee had the advantage of surprise and the barrier of the Catoctin Mountain and South Mountain ranges to screen his movements. There was good reason to assume that the Army of the Potomac, still recovering from the withdrawal from the Peninsula and the defeat at Second Manassas, was unlikely to move the nearly 40 miles over a river and two mountain ranges in three days. He also knew that until the Federals could repair the railroad bridge over the Monocacy River, they would have to haul their supplies by wagon west of that river, which would further restrict their mobility. Lee understood that he had a window of time to operate in comfortably and still reunite his army. But if anything went wrong in the Valley garrison operation—if the Federals resisted rather than fled at Harpers Ferry, if bad weather struck, if the Union garrison at Martinsburg withdrew to Harpers Ferry, and numerous other scenarios that might occur—and delay ensued, then the window of opportunity would shut and the Army of the Potomac might become a serious threat to Lee's divided army.

The operation entailed considerable risk. No military movement that seeks success can avoid it. But it was no more hazardous than Jackson's long flank march to gain Pope's rear had been, or the division of the army at Gaines' Mill. In both of those instances parts of their army had been highly vulnerable, but the Confederates held the initiative, employed the element of surprise, and kept the Federals off balance and unable to execute their own plans. Lee now hoped to duplicate tactics that had worked before. Given his successes that summer, Lee had good reason to be confident once more of achieving his goals.

Five divisions, consisting of 23 infantry brigades and 31 artillery batteries, composed the operational strike force. Jackson led the most powerful arm, consisting of 3 divisions totaling 14 brigades with approximately 14,700 men, 1 cavalry regiment, and 19 batteries. McLaws had 2 divisions with 7 brigades, numbering about 8,400 infantry, 1 cavalry squadron (2 companies), and 10 batteries. Walker's division contained 2 brigades with about 4,500 infantry and 2 batteries. The Boonsboro force consisted of Longstreet's command, which included D. R. Jones's division, Wilcox's division, Hood's division, Evans's brigade, the reserve artillery, and D. H. Hill's division. There were 17 brigades with about 21,000 infantry in the 4 divisions, along with 36 batteries of divisional artillery and the reserve artillery. The infantry strength of these columns represented roughly what they had contained when they left Frederick on September 10. From this point on their numbers steadily declined, due to straggling, lax discipline, and sickness.[86]

When Jackson received his copy of Special Orders No. 191, he noted that D. H. Hill, who had been attached to his command since the army crossed the Potomac, would be detached for this operation. As was typical in the Army of Northern Virginia then, Jackson received no official notification of the detachment from army headquarters. He had to extrapolate this information from the army's operational orders. Unaware that army headquarters had prepared a copy of the order for every named commander in it, Jackson personally wrote out a copy for Hill, omitting the first two sections, and sent it to him immediately. Hill received Jackson's copy of the order first, for after reading it he carefully tucked it away. It still exists today in the North Carolina State Archives. What happened to the headquarters copy is the great mystery of the Antietam Campaign. That someone wrapped it around three cigars, placed it in an envelope, and subsequently dropped it is all that we know for certain. Any number of individuals might be responsible for losing it. The only two men at divisional headquarters who would sign for so important an order were Hill and his assistant adjutant general, Major J. W. Ratchford, but they both made sworn statements that they never laid eyes on the headquarters copy of Special Orders No. 191. Therefore we must consider the possibility that Hill's headquarters did receive it and, through the carelessness of someone on his headquarters staff, lost it. It is also possible that someone at army headquarters lost the order, despite Colonel Chilton's statement after the war that headquarters couriers were trained to return the signed delivery envelopes for orders issued by headquarters, and that "this order was so important that violation of that rule would have been noticed, & I think I should certainly recollect if delivery had been omitted." Finally, a courier might have dropped it, although this seems the least likely scenario. The real culprit was the fluid organization of the army, and the lack of a clearly defined chain of command. This caused confusion in more than one instance during the campaign. This time its consequences would be serious.[87]

"Strike terror into the souls of the Yankees"

The stars were still shining brightly when the camps of Jackson's divisions began to stir on September 10. By 3 a.m. all three divisions had broken camp and formed up to march. J. R. Jones's division led the way, with three of his brigades marching south along the Emmitsburg Road to join Bradley Johnston's brigade in Frederick. The column moved down Market Street, then turned west on Patrick Street to follow the Old National Turnpike, or National Road, west. Lawton's division, followed by A. P. Hill's (still under Branch's command), both marching up from Monocacy Junction, entered the city from the south and followed Jones. It was about daylight by the time A. P. Hill's brigades reached Market Street, and the noise made by thousands of troops and vehicles had awaked the city. People emerged in large numbers to watch the army pass through. "Some few of the people cheered us and a great many ladies welcomed us by waving handkerchiefs and flags, but a large proportion of the people looked sullenly upon us," observed Captain Greenlee Davidson of A. P. Hill's division.[88]

Jackson rode into Frederick with his staff about the time Hill's division arrived. The large numbers of civilians who were out provided Jackson with an opportunity to practice some deception. He loudly asked his engineer, James K. Boswell, for a map of Chambersburg, Pennsylvania, and inquired of the nearby citizens "the distances to sundry places and about various roads" leading to points where the Confederates were not going. Jackson then rode to the Presbyterian manse of Dr. John B. Ross, the minister of Frederick's Presbyterian church, whom Jackson had known when both men lived in Lexington. Jackson had missed the minister on Sunday, when the former had ridden into the city in an ambulance to attend services at the German Reformed church, and he wished to pay his respects to Ross before departing. It was 5:15 a.m. A servant at the house informed Jackson that Ross and his wife were still asleep. Jackson chose not to awaken the couple and simply wrote a note expressing his regrets at not being able to see them. He then rode off with his staff along Mill Street to overtake the head of his command.[89]

During the night Longstreet had given more thought to the strength of McLaws's column and decided that even with R. H. Anderson's three-brigade division, the Georgian lacked the necessary manpower to ensure his success. He also may have spoken with Anderson and learned that his three brigades were all understrength. Whatever influenced Longstreet's thinking, he sought out Lee early on the 10th and urged him to further reinforce McLaws by attaching Wilcox's three-brigade division to Anderson, thus giving Anderson a six-brigade division. Lee agreed. Wilcox had perhaps 4,000 men in his 3 brigades, and these increased McLaws's force to 10 brigades, numbering about 12,400 men. The Boonsboro force was decreased to 14 brigades in 3 divisions, and around 17,000 men.[90]

Longstreet recalled that his command enjoyed a rollicking march through Frederick, with bands playing "The Girl I Left Behind Me." Bands may have provided a festive atmosphere, but the army's passage through Frederick was maddeningly slow, accompanied by tremendous clouds of dust. J. Evans Edings, the assistant adjutant general of Drayton's brigade, noted in his diary that his brigade reached Frederick at 4 a.m. but did not leave the city until 3 p.m. Captain Henry L. P. King of McLaws's staff succinctly summarized the day for his division in two words, "eternal halts." D. H. Hill took advantage of the interminable delays and ordered his men to bathe in the Monocacy River. McLaws did not clear the road until after 6 p.m., and Hill gave orders for his brigades to follow. After marching perhaps 1 mile, Hill apparently concluded that he would do his men more good and make better time if he returned to camp and started early on the 11th. He ordered his division back to their camps at Monocacy Junction. But this did not end the confusing, frustrating day for his men. When the men went to prepare their evening meal, the cooking utensils were in the divisional trains, which the details sent to hunt them up found were some 2.5 miles ahead. James Shinn, a second lieutenant in the 4th North Carolina, accepted the maddening events of the day with good humor. "So we had a good deal of confusion," and "some mad boys," he recorded in his journal.[91]

Despite the frustrations, incessant delays, and dust, the troops enjoyed their passage through Frederick. Many men noted the number of pretty women among the crowds along the street, and some of them were waving "Secession flags." Dr. Boulware of Jenkins's brigade recorded that "I was caught lifting my cap, and not a few times either," at these fair maidens. Lieutenant John Dooley of the 1st Virginia acknowledged that "there was a good deal of noise and cheering among our particular friends on this occasion," but he added that "it was not difficult to discern that this enthusiasm was roused only for the display, and that the large majority of the people were silent in regard to giving demonstrations of opinion." The men of the 17th Virginia encountered several young

Confederate infantry on Market Street in Frederick, Maryland, on September 10, 1862. This photograph was taken about 10 a.m. These men are possibly a unit from D. R. Jones's or Hood's divisions, given the time of the photograph, but a positive identification of the unit is impossible. Whatever unit it might be, the men are well uniformed and equipped. Courtesy of the Historical Society of Frederick, Maryland.

women who were not bashful about expressing their views. They appeared wearing red, white, and blue cockades on their breasts. A member of Company E stepped out of the ranks, tipped his hat, and politely said, "If you will take the advice of a fool, you will return into the house and take off those colors; some d———d fool may come along to insult you." The ladies withdrew.[92]

Dr. Lewis Steiner was among the crowds on the sidewalks of Frederick. But Steiner did not join the throng out of curiosity; he was there to gather information about the enemy. He provided a trained observer's glimpse of the Army of Northern Virginia on campaign. Steiner recorded that the enemy entered town at 4 a.m., and that Jackson's force had the advance. The passage of the Confederate army lasted 16 hours, with the last of the army leaving town at 8 p.m. "The most liberal calculations could not give them more than 64,000," he noted. Steiner's estimate of strength, while perhaps high by several thousand, was remarkably accurate. Included in this number, he wrote, were "over 3,000 negroes." These men were "clad in all kinds of uniforms, not only in cast-off or captured United States uniforms, but in coats with Southern buttons, State buttons, etc. These were shabby, but not shabbier or seedier than those worn by white men in the rebel ranks. Most of the negroes had arms, rifles, muskets, sabres, bowie-knives, dirks, etc. They were supplied, in many instances, with knapsacks, haversacks, canteens, etc., and were manifestly an integral part of the Southern Confederacy Army." Indeed they were, but as slaves, not as enlisted soldiers, as some modern mythmakers would have us believe. The African Americans with the Army of Northern Virginia, although slaves, often had to forage for food, and some were allowed to arm themselves to obtain food and protect themselves when they did so. They also could provide additional security for the army trains in the event of a Union cavalry raid, yet another reason for the Confederates to allow them to bear weapons.[93]

Steiner wryly noted that the nearly 150 guns that went by him bore U.S. markings, and that the army "seemed to have been largely supplied with transportation by some United States Quartermaster," for "Uncle Sam's initials were on many of its wagons, ambulances, and horses." Some of the Confederate regiments were down to 150 men, and not one that passed contained over 500. The men Steiner encountered "were stout and ragged, anxious to 'kill a Yankee.'" And they seemed glad to be departing Frederick, which some dubbed "a d——d Yankee hole." Steiner thought that his friends were equally glad to see the Confederates depart and "to get rid of them and of the penetrating ammoniacal smell they brought with them."[94]

There was much speculation in the ranks as to the army's destination. But there was also confidence that they would be successful wherever they might be going. Many would have nodded in agreement with Captain Greenlee Davidson's sentiments: "When we leave here our movements will be rapid and will, I trust, strike terror into the souls of the Yankees."[95]

4

The Army of the Potomac

"If we fail now the North has no hope"

Since daylight, September 5, Lieutenant Brinkerhoff N. Miner, of the U.S. Signal Corps, had been carefully observing the Potomac fords in the vicinity of Noland's Ferry from his lofty observation post on Sugar Loaf Mountain. The day before he had reported massive enemy wagon trains in the vicinity of Leesburg and large concentrations of troops. Now, scattered along the river on the Maryland side, from the C&O Canal aqueduct to Noland's Ferry, he estimated there were 2,000 Rebel soldiers, principally cavalry, he thought. He observed no other bodies of troops besides this force, although he had heard many rumors that large numbers of Confederate troops were in the vicinity of Leesburg. At 9 a.m., he signaled his report to the station at Poolesville, where Lieutenant Ephraim A. Briggs promptly telegraphed the news to Washington.[1]

Miner's report provided the War Department with some of the first reliable news that the Confederates had crossed into Maryland. The night before, Colonel Dixon Miles, commanding the Harpers Ferry garrison, forwarded a dispatch from one of his officers stationed at Point of Rocks stating that 30,000 Rebels forded the Potomac there. Throughout the day reports of enemy incursions into Maryland multiplied. At 3:30 p.m. J. W. Garrett, president of the B&O Railroad, telegraphed that his operators were notifying him that "very large forces of the enemy" were passing over the Potomac River into Maryland, "chiefly near the mouth of the Monocacy."[2]

The increasing quantity of reports that large numbers of Confederate troops were entering Maryland pressured President Lincoln into confronting the army's unsettled command situation. He needed a field commander, a decision he had hoped to put off while McClellan reorganized the army for active campaigning. But Lee's movement into Maryland forced Lincoln's hand. On September 3 he wrote out an order under Stanton's name directing Halleck to organize a field army, but Lincoln did not name a field commander. Perhaps he hoped that Halleck would either assume command himself or choose a commander. Halleck did neither. He simply passed the order on to McClellan to ready a force to take the field.

The list of qualified candidates available to Lincoln was a short one. Pope was not an option. The feelings against him in the army were far too strong, so he was transferred to Minnesota to deal with the Sioux uprising there. Other than McClellan, Ambrose Burnside—38 years old and an 1847 West Point graduate—appeared to be the most well qualified. Burnside had a winning personality; was a generous, likeable man; and, to those who did not know him well, inspired confidence. As overall commander he received the credit for the successful amphibious operation that captured New Berne, North Carolina, although it largely belonged to his subordinates and his naval commander. Lincoln was among those deceived by Burnside's impression of competence. Moreover, the Rhode Islander was politically neutral. Two weeks after his visit with McClellan at Harrison's Landing, Lincoln and Stanton offered Burnside command of the Army of the Potomac. But if few other people understood his limitations as a commander, Burnside himself did, and he declined the offer. "I had always unreservedly expressed that I was not competent to command such a large army as this," he testified later. Now, with a fresh crisis at hand, Lincoln tried Burnside again. When the general arrived in Washington from Aquia Creek on September 5, Lincoln called him to the White House and once more offered him command of the army about to take the field. Burnside turned the president down for the second time, repeating what he had told Lincoln initially, "that I did not think there was any one who could do as much with that army as General McClellan could, if matters could be so arranged as to remove their objections to him."[3]

With Burnside out of the picture, Lincoln saw no other alternative to McClellan. His lack of enthusiasm for the general was evident in what the president told John Hay, his personal secretary: "We must make do with the tools we have at hand." McClellan enjoyed the confidence of the army, which counted for a great deal at the moment, and he did not shrink from the responsibility of leading it against Lee. The point at which Lincoln made the decision to restore McClellan to field command is a question with no satisfactory answer. The president later claimed that he could not bring himself to do so, and that Halleck did it. But Halleck, in testimony before the Committee on the Conduct of the War, maintained that the choice was Lincoln's. Halleck stated that the president discussed who would take command "for two or three days" before making a decision, and that he himself did not know who it would be until the day Lincoln placed McClellan in command. On the morning of September 7 Halleck accompanied Lincoln to McClellan's home on H Street "about 9 o'clock in the morning." Halleck recalled that at first there was some discussion between the three men, and then the president told McClellan, "General, you will take command of the forces in the field." With this simple order the question of command was settled.[4]

McClellan had contemplated stipulating the removal of Stanton and Halleck as a condition of agreeing to take command, but Burnside dissuaded him, arguing that if McClellan "imposed such conditions at a time of national peril, the country would turn against him." McClellan later claimed that he received no orders to take charge of the army in the field. "I determined to solve the question myself," he related in a *Century Magazine* article, "and when I moved out of Washington with my staff and personal escort I left my card with P.P.C. written upon it, at the White House, War Office, and Secretary Seward's house, and went on my way." As McClellan told it, he took a grave risk in assuming command without authority. Had he failed in Maryland, he wrote, "I would probably have been condemned to death." P.P.C. stood for *pour prendre congé*, a French military phrase requesting formal leave to go on campaign. He might have left these cards when he departed (although it would have taken some time to ride to all of these places), but the idea that he took command on his own authority, or would have been condemned to death had he been defeated, was a figment of his active imagination. The facts were that he had never been formally relieved of command of the Army of the Potomac, and he had already received written orders to command all the troops within the fortifications of Washington, which eventually covered all available troops. All that was necessary was a verbal order for him to resume command of the forces taking the field.[5]

McClellan had not sat idly by while waiting for a field commander to be named; instead he had worked vigorously to organize a field army. Between September 3 and September 6 he assembled a force of some 60,000 troops and 313 guns, consisting of five army corps, two detached divisions, and a hastily organized cavalry division. While it marched forth under the name "Army of the Potomac," it was actually a potpourri of units from the eastern theater. Pope's Army of Virginia contributed its 1st and 3rd Corps, which McClellan renumbered as the 12th and the 1st Corps, respectively. The Army of the Potomac from the Peninsula contributed the 2nd and the 6th Corps, George Sykes's division in the 5th Corps, and Darius Couch's division from the 4th Corps. Burnside's 9th Corps, reinforced by Jacob Cox's Kanawha division of Ohio troops (recently transferred from western Virginia), completed the army. It was, in fact, three separate armies combined: Pope's, McClellan's Peninsula army, and Burnside's expeditionary force.[6]

Given the uncertainty of whether the Rebel advance into Maryland was a full-scale invasion or a diversion, a Federal force almost equal in number to the field army remained behind to cover the capital. This included the 3rd Corps, the 5th Corps (minus Sykes's division), the newly designated 11th Corps, garrison troops, the city guard, and a provisional brigade of new regiments. On paper it consisted of some 73,000 troops, 120 field guns, and 500 heavy guns. But the 3rd and the 5th Corps had borne the brunt of the Army of the Potomac's fighting at Second Manassas, and the 11th had lost heavily there as well. In addition, the 11th was commanded by Franz Sigel, one of Lincoln's political generals, which might have factored into the decision to leave that corps behind. Precisely who determined how much of the overall force, and what formations, would be assigned to guard Washington is unanswered, but it was probably a joint decision between Halleck and McClellan. Given the recent scare the capital had experienced, and the uncertainty of the whereabouts of the main body of Lee's army, it is unlikely that McClellan would have contemplated leaving a weaker force around Washington until the situation became clearer.[7]

The work to organize these forces into a mobile field army capable of engaging and defeating Lee's veterans was a challenge. The army's transportation was in disorder. The artillery was "much disorganized." The medical department was in "a most deplorable condition." There was a critical shortage of serviceable cavalry, and what did exist was in need of reorganization and leadership. The strength and the organization of the various army corps were not uniform. Many of the units from the Army of the Potomac still lacked their transportation and extra equipment, which had not yet arrived from the Peninsula. As Chief Quartermaster Brigadier General Rufus Ingalls noted, an army that had taken one month to be fully transported to the Peninsula could not be "brought back in a day." Nonetheless, the army was not in chaos; it could have taken the field two days after Second Manassas. But whether it could have fought successfully is in doubt. It lacked efficiency and organization, which make an army effective in battle. Because of Lee's invasion of Maryland, these deficiencies would have to be mended while the army was on the march. To fully understand the Army of the Potomac's performance in the Maryland Campaign and the coming battles, let us first pause to assess its strengths and weaknesses, and evaluate how it matched up against its opponent.[8]

While the summer's battles had imbued the Army of Northern Virginia with confidence and a sense of invincibility, they left the Army of the Potomac discouraged and caused morale to sag. The malaise affected officers and men alike. There was universal condemnation of the conduct of the war by what the men believed was a bumbling administration and incompetent generals. After Second Manassas, Captain Henry Pearson of the 6th New Hampshire wrote:

> Of all the brave boys who came out from N. H. with me only 9 followed me into Alexandria. The rest are all dead, sick, wounded or prisoners. And all to no purpose . . . All who have been engaged in the events of the past two months know with what desperation the Southern troops fight & with what bad generalship our efforts are conducted have no hopes whatever of ever subduing them. The Northern people get not the faintest idea from the newspapers of the true state of affairs at the seat of operations. The lying

reports of our generals & reporters beat anything that ever existed among the rebels. The whole army is disgusted . . . You need not be surprised if success falls to the rebels with astonishing rapidity.

Uriah Parmelee of the 6th New York Cavalry echoed Pearson's sentiment.

It is true, all the newspapers in the country to the contrary notwithstanding, that the soldiers in this corps [9th] at least have lost spirit & confidence. Not that they would not fight well if a chance were given them, but they would fight expecting to be driven & lose their position. They seem to expect nothing but long marches & that to the rear . . . You cannot expect me, then, to remain with this army as it is, if it does not change soon either in its principles or its actions, I trust in God that I shall have the courage to desert it.

Brigadier General Marsena Patrick, a brigade commander in the 1st Corps, confided gloomily to his diary: "There is a general feeling that the Southern Confederacy will be recognized & that they deserve recognition."[9]

Straggling, absenteeism, and lax discipline were the byproducts of the defeatism that afflicted the army. Captain Richard B. Irwin, an aide-de-camp on McClellan's staff who was serving in the Adjutant General's Department, observed that "there was quite an army of officers and men who had somehow become separated from their regiments . . . The number continued to be so enormous as to be quite unmanageable by any existing method." Colonel J. S. Belknap, who served at a convalescent camp near Alexandria, estimated that 20,000 men passed through his hands by September 17, which was the size of a very large army corps. Brigadier General John P. Slough, who commanded the convalescent camp, judged that 13,000 stragglers came through his camp on September 2 alone. The army's rolls carried nearly as many men on special duty, absent, sick, or in arrest as it did present for duty. The August 10 returns for the Army of the Potomac, before the Manassas defeat, showed 36,682 men absent and 22,704 on special duty, sick, and in arrest, which represented 35 percent of the army's total strength.[10]

Straggling was nearly as serious in the Army of the Potomac as it was in Lee's army. Part of the cause was the same: officers and noncommissioned officers who, for a variety of reasons, failed to do their duty and keep the men in the ranks. But Lee's straggling was also due to the failure of Confederate logistics to keep the men adequately supplied, and this was generally not a problem in the Army of the Potomac. Instead, low morale and poorly enforced discipline were the principal contributors. Defeat weakens the bonds of discipline. Brigadier General Philip Kearny, one of the more experienced and aggressive combat officers in the Army of the Potomac until his death at Chantilly, did not believe that the Federal army came close to the Confederates in discipline. He considered 50,000 well-disciplined troops superior "to double the number of our ordinary run of badly disciplined, badly officered, unreliable regiments now entrusted with the fortunes of the North." The North, he believed, "is not steadfast. Look at our list of absentees, tolerated at home, instead of being hissed at. I have hardly eight officers to a Regiment. Scarcely a field officer and only two Generals. Look elsewhere and it is worse. This is what I call demoralization . . . Elsewhere I fear, that the army is a mere crust, ready to play us some bad tricks." Colonel Charles Wainwright, helping disembark troops, guns, and equipment from the Peninsula during the fighting at Manassas, complained that although over 1,000 men of his division landed on August 30, "most of them went off and got drunk so soon as they landed."[11]

G. F. R. Henderson, a British soldier and critical observer of the Civil War, wrote that "an ill-disciplined army lacks mobility. Marching . . . makes the greatest demands on the subordination of the men and exertions of the officers." Thus far the Union army in Virginia had not marched as well as the Confederate army, and it consistently straggled badly. McClellan, like Lee, understood that straggling reflected poor leadership, usually at the regimental level, and he scolded his officers in a circular distributed on September 9: "The general commanding has observed the frequent absence from their commands while in camp, and from their columns on the march, of superior officers. These laxities must be remedied. Inattention and carelessness on the part of those high in rank has been one fertile source of the straggling and want of discipline which now obtain in the various corps." To combat this straggling, he issued General Orders No. 155. Its substance was to arm field officers with procedures to control straggling and the authority to punish stragglers by a regimental court-martial. The orders also gave specific measures to be employed while the army was on the march, so as to make it more difficult for soldiers to straggle. However, McClellan's efforts to curb his straggling problem, like Lee's, largely failed, and the army leaked soldiers all across Maryland.[12]

Not all units straggled badly. Some officers vigorously enforced McClellan's orders. Others employed their own innovations to deal with the problem. One such was Brigadier General Darius Couch, a division commander in the 4th Corps, who made an example of those who straggled. On September 11 he requested his regimental commanders to provide a list of all their "professional stragglers." He organized these men into a provisional battalion consisting of all the "scallywags of the division," so he could keep better track of them. Brigadier General John Gibbon, commanding a brigade in the 1st Corps, had excellent success in preventing straggling in his brigade by encouraging his men to jeer and laugh at stragglers they encountered along the route of march. "Very soon, news of what we were doing spread and the stragglers began to disappear from the sides of the road in our vicinity," wrote Gibbon. He also noted that within his brigade "it became an honorable ambition to remain in the ranks." No doubt the same was true in Couch's division, where most men wanted to avoid the humiliation of banishment to the "scallywag" battalion.[13]

The poor physical condition of many of the troops also contributed to straggling, absenteeism, and sickness. The men of the 1st, the 9th, and the 12th Corps, who had participated in the entire Second Manassas Campaign, were marched hard and fed badly by Pope. Brigadier General Alpheus Williams, a 12th Corps division commander, described the plight of his command on the eve of the Maryland Campaign to his daughter: "Suffice it to say that for over three weeks we have been scarcely a day without marching—for at least seven days without rations . . . Our horses fed on the grass of the countryside." A soldier attached to the 9th Corps wrote that they "have had a foot sore job for the last month marching continually back & forth. Many are entirely destitute of shoes & they are often without proper food." Samuel W. Crawford, a 12th Corps brigade commander and prewar army surgeon, complained on September 9 that his brigade of four regiments was reduced to 629 effectives. He reported that "every day adds to the report of the medical officers of these regiments, and they unanimously show that it is owing to the nature of the service to which we have been subjected, the great exposure they have suffered, the deprivation of proper food, and the want of absolute rest that the present condition has been induced . . . There are many men belonging to the command who cannot, from absolute want of muscular tone, follow in its marches."[14]

Even units from the Peninsula, who had not seen the hard marching or experienced the short rations that Pope's men had, reported large numbers of sick and absent. General George Sykes's division of U.S. Regulars, considered to be a crack unit, reported on August 31 that only 3,985 men were present out of 6,995, and only 3,352 were present for duty equipped. In other words, 52 percent of the division was absent for various reasons or not equipped for combat. The 2nd Corps, another outfit with an excellent reputation, noted on August 20 that 6,905 men were absent sick or without leave from a total strength of 24,652. The 2nd Corps had seen no combat since the Seven Days battles in early July, but the unhealthy climate at Harrison's Landing had taken a far more severe toll of its strength through illness than combat had.[15]

Equipment losses—principally shoes, clothing, and blankets—also contributed to straggling and sickness. When Brigadier General Abner Doubleday submitted requisitions to replace equipment and clothing in his brigade after Second Manassas, he reported that "owing to the great number making requisitions, mine were not filled and we were soon obliged to take the field deficient in everything." Captain James Wren, in Jesse L. Reno's division of the 9th Corps, wrote on September 5 that the men of the division "looked very bad, being Lousey, Dirty & Almost naked & worn out." The popular image of a well-fed, well-clothed, Union army in the Maryland Campaign is one of its myths. Although the army was generally better clothed, better fed, and better equipped than the Confederates, there were plenty of "ragged Yankees."[16]

McClellan had more success in restoring the morale of his army than he did in controlling straggling. Simply knowing that he was in command again gave the army renewed confidence. "McClellan is now with the army in the field," wrote Brigadier General Oliver O. Howard on September 10. "We cannot help feeling well about the matter. His fortifications saved Washington and his system gives us something to hope for and for some indescribable reason the army loves him." Charles F. Johnson of the 9th New York Infantry, writing the same day, observed: "McClellan seems to have put new life into everything, and I hope we will only get a fair shake at the enemy." Men who had served under Pope immediately sensed a difference in how things were managed under McClellan. One of them was Colonel David Strother, who had served on Pope's staff and then joined McClellan's on September 9: "I am suddenly transformed from the Dramatic to the Methodical school of war." For soldiers who had experienced Pope's "dramatic" school of war—consisting of short rations, forced marches with no apparent purpose, and no mail—McClellan's restoration to command was a godsend. Colonel Edward Bragg of the 6th Wisconsin, who had served under Pope, immediately noticed and appreciated the difference between the two commanders. Under McClellan the army seemed to be "in order, as if commanded and directed—before it was all 'helter skelter' bustle and confusion—Each man, & each corps & each wagon in the way of somebody else." A 7th Wisconsin lieutenant concurred: "Our army feels more confident and in better spirits . . . the men are not marched to death running back and forth, they feel more confidence in their commander, and will fight better." Even general officers welcomed the change. Brigadier General Alpheus Williams, whose morale flagged under Pope's leadership, found renewed hope with McClellan at the army's head. He wrote to his daughter: "I have great confidence that we shall smash them terribly if they stand, more confidence than I have ever had in any movement of the war. We move slowly but each corps understands the others, and when we do strike I think it will be a heavy blow." McClellan, as General Howard had noted, gave the army renewed hope and confidence. For all his deficiencies as a field commander, McClellan's impact on army morale was remarkable, and it would provide a surprise for Robert E. Lee.[17]

McClellan also needed to increase the strength of his army, as well as its morale. Many regiments were reduced to a fraction of their authorized strength. Battle casualties, and particularly sickness, had exacted a heavy toll. The units composing the field army in Maryland had sustained 15,364 casualties in the Seven Days battles and at Second Manassas. These losses were fairly evenly distributed, except for the 1st Corps, which lost 4,685 men during the Second Manassas Campaign. The 12th Corps suffered 2,154 battle casualties at Cedar

Mountain, but it lost many more to illness, mustering only some 5,800 effectives in its two divisions. The entire field army at this point numbered about 60,000 effective soldiers, hardly the Union juggernaut that is typically described in Maryland Campaign studies.[18]

McClellan added a handful of trained but untested garrison regiments as reinforcements, as well as Jacob Cox's Kanawha division of Ohio troops, who were attached to the 9th Corps. But the primary source of reinforcements were the numerous new regiments who were pouring into the city daily, raised in response to the president's July 2 call for 300,000 more volunteers. Rather than recruit volunteers to rebuild veteran regiments, it proved more politically expedient for most governors to attract recruits by raising new regiments. Many of these did not complete their recruiting and organization until August, when they were then hurried off to the capital in response to the crisis caused by the Second Manassas campaign, having only the most minimal training or, in some instances, no training at all. There were 36 new regiments in Washington by September 6. McClellan selected 24 of them to reinforce the field army. Of the 24, only 18 actually joined the brigades they were assigned to during the Maryland Campaign, but these regiments totaled between 15,000 and 16,000, or about 20 percent of the army's infantry. Some states, principally Massachusetts, New York, and Pennsylvania, recruited some volunteers for veteran regiments, and during the first 10 days in September around 3,000 to 4,000 of these recruits joined their regiments. These men typically lacked even rudimentary training, and sergeants had to provide what they could while the army was on the march. A 2nd Massachusetts lieutenant offered some sense of the problem of receiving untrained recruits during an active campaign. His regiment had 150 of them, whom he deemed "utterly useless, as they cannot be armed, much less drilled, unless we rest somewhere." The inexperience of a significant part of his army's infantry certainly influenced McClellan's strategic thinking for the campaign. Ezra Carman, who served as the colonel of the 13th New Jersey and was one of the campaign's most careful students, believed that because of the number of new recruits and the general overall condition of the army, McClellan hoped to avoid a general battle with the Rebels except under the most favorable circumstances, and wished to drive them from Maryland by maneuvering rather than by fighting. Histories of the Maryland Campaign rarely fail to highlight the Army of the Potomac's superiority in numbers, but at the outset of the campaign that advantage was rather slight, and the qualitative edge went to the Army of Northern Virginia.[19]

McClellan sought to balance out the strength and organization of his army in his assignment of the new regiments and additional reinforcements he scraped together from other theaters of operations. On the Peninsula he favored a corps organization of two three-brigade divisions. The exception to this had been the 5th Corps, which had three divisions, probably reflecting his confidence in Fitz John Porter. Pope had followed the same organization in the Army of Virginia, except for the 11th Corps (Pope's 1st Corps), which had three divisions. The three-division army corps apparently won favor with McClellan, for he made an effort in his hasty reorganization to make this the new standard in the army. Brigadier General John Reynolds's division of Pennsylvania Reserves, which had served with the 5th Corps on the Peninsula, was transferred to the 1st Corps, giving Hooker three divisions. A third division was created for the 2nd Corps by organizing a brigade of new regiments, forming a second brigade from garrison troops brought up from Fortress Monroe, and seasoning it with a third brigade composed of veteran regiments. Darius Couch's single division of the 4th Corps cooperated with the 6th Corps, although throughout the campaign Couch's orders came directly from army headquarters. After the campaign ended and McClellan reorganized the army, this division was permanently assigned to the 6th Corps, to give it three divisions.[20]

The 9th Corps initially consisted of two two-brigade divisions. McClellan reinforced it with two more two-brigade divisions, one formed from fresh troops from the North Carolina coast and the other consisting of Cox's Ohio division, transferred from the Kanawha Valley in western Virginia. The 12th Corps retained its three-brigade, two-division organization, but McClellan assigned it five new regiments, which more than doubled its strength.

McClellan's efforts raised the strength of his field army to some 87,000 men. This represented aggregate present for duty, which included men detailed to noncombat duties, such as teamsters, hospital orderlies, clerks, and the like. To arrive at an accurate combat strength in the Union army, approximately 17 percent should be deducted from the aggregate strength to account for noncombatants. Still, this gave McClellan approximately 72,000 combat effectives, an edge over Lee, but hardly an overwhelming one.[21]

Leadership

McClellan confronted a crisis in leadership as he assembled his field army. In the aftermath of Second Manassas, Pope had preferred charges of misconduct against Fitz John Porter, William B. Franklin, and Charles Griffin, a 5th Corps division commander. Because of the charges, Lincoln ordered that all three officers be relieved of duty on September 5. He also directed that Joseph Hooker be assigned to command the 5th Corps, and that Franklin's corps be attached to the 3rd Corps. The next day he ordered Major General Jesse L. Reno of the 9th Corps to assume command of the 1st Corps, from which Irvin McDowell had asked to be relieved of command. The situation required all of McClellan's tact and diplomacy. He understood the fragility of his position with the administration, but he also realized that the president needed him at the moment, so he could use the current crisis to his advantage. On September 6 he wrote to Halleck that Sumner reported "the enemy moving toward Rockville" and that, under the circumstances, "it will save a great deal of trouble and invaluable time if you will suspend the operation of the order in regard to Franklin and Porter until I can see my way out of this difficulty." To prevent a change in Burnside's command while on the march, McClellan also requested that Hooker, rather than Reno, be assigned to command the 1st Corps. He concluded his message by stating that "I really feel it is necessary for me to ask these things at once." Lincoln and Halleck agreed to all of his requests: Porter and Franklin remained in command of their corps, Griffin remained with his division, Hooker took command of the 1st Corps, and Reno remained with the 9th Corps.[22]

For reasons never officially explained, McClellan grouped the army into two wings and a reserve. One wing, also called the Right Wing, consisted of the 1st and the 9th Corps and was commanded by Burnside. Major General Edwin V. Sumner commanded the other wing, containing the 2nd and the 12th Corps. The reserve, which was never a formal command, included Major General William B. Franklin's 6th Corps, Major General Darius Couch's division, and Brigadier General George Sykes's division from 5th Corps. Until September 14 the wing command arrangement was an informal structure, and McClellan never offered an explanation of why he created these wings. Ezra Carman wrote that it was because of "an arrangement" between McClellan and Halleck that the army would be divided into two wings and a reserve, with Sumner and Burnside each commanding a wing and Franklin in charge of the reserve. The two corps of Pope's army would be separated, one to each wing. If such an arrangement was made, it was a verbal one, as no official document exists before McClellan published an order on September 14 naming Burnside and Sumner as wing commanders. It seems probable that McClellan organized the wings as a concession to Halleck, for he had a low opinion of Sumner's ability as a general and it is unlikely that he would have selected him as a wing commander. Halleck may have pressed the wing structure as a way to provide Burnside with an opportunity to distinguish himself, of which the president surely would have approved. But this is pure speculation.[23]

The two acting wing commanders were not destined to take a place beside the great captains of American military history. Recalling his first encounters with Ambrose Burnside that September, Jacob Cox wrote that "his large, fine eyes, his winning smile and cordial manner, bespoke a frank, sincere, and honorable character, and these indications were never belied by more intimate acquaintance." His abilities, however, were another matter. Burnside had resigned from the old U.S. Army in 1853 to go into business manufacturing a breech-loading rifle that he had designed, but the business failed and Burnside was burdened with a heavy debt. In 1858 McClellan, Burnside's old army friend and West Point classmate, secured a position for him with the Land Department of the Illinois Central Railroad, since McClellan was then its vice president. This proved to be a happy arrangement. Burnside emerged from his debt and he and McClellan grew quite close.

When the war began, Burnside immediately offered his services and was commissioned colonel of the 1st Rhode Island Infantry. He led a brigade at First Manassas, and was promoted to brigadier general a month after that battle. In January 1862 McClellan dispatched him with a division to conduct an amphibious operations against the coast of North Carolina. Burnside was blessed with some outstanding subordinates, and the operation was successful, capturing Roanoke Island, Newbern, Fort Macon, and Beaufort, and establishing a firm Union presence at this key point on the North Carolina coast. It was this operation that brought him to Lincoln's attention and convinced the president of Burnside's leadership ability. His reward for success was promotion to major general in March 1862 and, within the next seven months, two offers to command the Army of the Potomac.[24]

Although a Democrat and personally opposed to the Republican administration, Burnside was an extremely loyal soldier, highly devoted to his country, and devoid of the personal ambition that marred some of the personalities in the Union army. He was also a loyal subordinate and friend to McClellan. The two men addressed much of their correspondence to one another with "Dear Burn," or "Dear Mac." During McClellan's descent from power after the failure of the Peninsula Campaign, Burnside never wavered in his support. Because of his later failures as commander of the Army of the Potomac, Burnside has been characterized as something of a simpleton. He was, in fact, an average soldier, something he recognized and attempted—unsuccessfully—to communicate to the president. Nor was he particularly energetic or imaginative, but he was more capable than he has been given credit for and would perform credibly through most of the campaign.

Edwin Vose Sumner had been a soldier since 1819. The 65-year-old, Massachusetts-born major general was the oldest officer of his rank in the entire Federal army. He was a soldier of unquestioned bravery and integrity. During the war with Mexico, where his courage was conspicuous, he earned the nickname "Bull Head" because a spent musket ball allegedly bounced off his forehead during the battle of Cerro Gordo. Sumner was promoted to colonel of the 1st U.S. Cavalry in 1855, and to brigadier general in 1861, one of only three in the entire army at that time. His seniority gave him command of the 2nd Corps when it was organized in March 1862. His management of the corps through the Peninsula Campaign and the Seven Days battles left much to be desired. Although always courageous and a model subordinate, he displayed poor judgment on more than one occasion. McClellan appreciated his bravery but thought little of him as a general. After the army's first significant fight at Williamsburg on May 5, McClellan complained to his wife: "Sumner has proved that he was even a greater fool than I had supposed & had come within an ace of having us defeated." Major General Philip Kearny, never one to mince words, wrote that Sumner "has neither capacity, nor sane judgement. He is a proverbial blunderer." Artillery colonel Charles Wainwright was equally stinging in his evaluation of Sumner's leadership, writing after Williamsburg: "He [Sumner] is a great general, but I do not want to serve under him in another fight if this is a specimen." Sumner lacked imagination, and he had difficulty grasping the complexities and demands of high command, but he did have some positive attributes. In an army marked by conservative, defensive-minded officers, he was aggressive and unafraid of a fight. But wing command was quite beyond his ability. Nonetheless, Army seniority dictated otherwise.[25]

Major General Joseph Hooker, the new commander of the 1st Corps, was a supremely confident man. He was also vain, occasionally arrogant, highly ambitious, and frequently outspoken, often about his superiors. The 47-year-old soldier had been born in Massachusetts, attended West Point, and graduated in the middle of his class in 1837. He won three brevets for bravery in Mexico and then left the army in 1853 to seek his fortune in California. Settling eventually in the Sonoma area, he tried his hand at farming, but failed. The war offered him an opportunity to escape his circumstances. Hooker traveled to Washington to offer his services but received only a cool reception. It is said that after First Manassas (also known as First Bull Run) he met with Lincoln and told the president bluntly: "I was at the battle of Bull Run, the other day, and it is neither vanity nor boasting in me to disclose that I am a better general than you, sir, had on that field."

Whatever he actually said to the president, Hooker soon received a commission as brigadier general of volunteers, to date from May 17, 1861. He led a division in the 3rd Corps through the Peninsula and Second Manassas campaigns. Apart from Philip Kearny, no one in the army compiled a better combat record during this period. He fought his division aggressively and, some thought, recklessly. Kearny believed that Hooker had badly botched his division's attack at Williamsburg. "He is an ass," Kearny decided. Although deeply committed to the Union cause, Hooker was not a team player, and his penchant for criticizing his superiors irked many who knew him. His chief of artillery on the Peninsula wrote that while he found Hooker "a delightful man to serve with, I do not, however, like the way he has of always decrying the other generals of his own rank, whose every act he seems to find fault with." No one, it seemed, escaped Hooker's critiques, including McClellan, whom he openly criticized when the army failed to move on Richmond in early August.[26]

McClellan overlooked Hooker's faults because of his fighting abilities, which McClellan highly valued. He specifically wanted Hooker to command the 1st Corps, whom he believed after Second Manassas "are in bad condition as to discipline & everything else." Hooker, he thought, "will however soon bring them out of the kinks, & will make them fight if anyone can."[27] Besides Jesse Reno, Hooker was McClellan's best corps commander.

The 6th Corps commander, William B. Franklin, was a soldier cut from the mold of George B. McClellan. Both were Pennsylvanians, were outstanding students at West Point (Franklin graduated number 1 in his class in 1843, McClellan number 2 in 1846), served in the elite topographical engineers, were politically conservative, and believed in a systematic method of making war. Franklin was 39 and had been a soldier for 19 years, although he had spent little time with troops before the war. He led a brigade at First Manassas and performed bravely. McClellan and Franklin knew one another from the old U.S. Army (both were assigned to West Point in 1848) and McClellan valued his old comrade's loyalty as he built the Army of the Potomac. As McClellan wrote later, "Franklin was one of the best officers I had; very powerful. He was a man not only of excellent judgement, but of a remarkably high order of intellectual ability." McClellan gave Franklin a division and, when the army transferred to the Peninsula and McClellan received approval to create two new army corps, he gave one to Franklin. But Franklin's performance on the Peninsula did not sit well with McClellan. He confided to his wife on August 22 that Franklin had "disappointed me terribly," that he had "little energy" and that "his efficiency is very little." Hard-bitten Phil Kearny had a typically blunt assessment. "Believe me, that Franklin is no soldier," he wrote. "With all his mind he feels it, and in the hour of need, he dreads to show it." But Franklin was loyal, a good administrator, and an experienced corps commander, all qualities McClellan needed when the army took the field in Maryland. So, despite his misgivings about Franklin's command ability, McClellan reached out and protected him from a court of inquiry to keep him with the army at this vital time.[28]

Giving Burnside a wing command provided an opportunity to place Major General Jesse L. Reno in command of the 9th Corps. The 39-year-old Reno had been born in Wheeling, (now West) Virginia, but at a young age he moved with his family to Pennsylvania. He graduated from West Point in 1846 with McClellan and Thomas J. Jackson, and he served with distinction in Mexico. Within seven months of the outbreak of the Civil War, Reno was a brigadier general commanding a brigade in Burnside's North Carolina expedition. Reno proved himself an active and aggressive soldier in this campaign; he won promotion to division command and, by mid-July, to major general. John Pope, who had relatively few good things to say about many of the officers who served him during the Second Manassas Campaign, lavished praise on the Pennsylvanian. Reno, he wrote, "was always cheerful and ready; anxious to anticipate if possible, and prompt to execute with all his might, the orders he received. He was short in stature and upright in his person, and with a face and manner so bright and at all times cheerful." General Alpheus Williams of the 12th Corps thought that "of all the Major Generals he was my beau ideal of a soldier." The soldiers Reno led, particularly those who had served with him in North Carolina, offered similar estimates. In the opinion of Captain James Wren of the 48th Pennsylvania, Reno "was well liked" and "was a brave and wise general." Although Reno's experience in corps command was limited to the Second Manassas Campaign, he performed well, and none doubted that he was up to the task. By choosing Reno, along with Hooker, McClellan now had two corps commanders he could rely on to exhibit energy and act aggressively.[29]

When McClellan appointed General Nathaniel Banks as commander of the defenses of Washington, by seniority Brigadier General Alpheus S. Williams assumed command of Pope's old 2nd Corps, now the 12th Corps. The 51-year-old Williams was born and raised in Connecticut. He attended Yale University and Yale Law School. In 1836 he moved to Detroit, Michigan, and established a successful law practice there. Within three years he was elected judge of the Wayne County probate court. Williams possessed qualities that gained peoples' respect, and his years in Detroit were happy, successful ones. During the Mexican War he secured a commission as lieutenant colonel of the 1st Michigan Infantry. After the war he returned to his prosperous peacetime pursuits.

When the Civil War began, Williams, although a Democrat, was the one of the first from his state to offer his services. In December 1861 he was commissioned a brigadier general and went east to serve with the Army of the Potomac. Initially he led a brigade in Nathaniel Banks's division, but in March 1862 he moved up to division command when Banks was elevated to corps command. During the operations in the Shenandoah Valley that spring, Williams showed that he was imperturbable in times of crisis, and his stubborn and skillful delaying actions against Stonewall Jackson during Banks's retreat down the Valley were the only bright spot in the Union army's generally dismal performance there. At Cedar Mountain Williams's division again did the best fighting. Ezra Carmen, who served as one of his colonels in Maryland, wrote that Williams "was not a brilliant soldier, but a safe one, he never sacrificed his men for the mere sake of winning to himself the attention of the newspaper correspondents and the plaudits of the public, but whenever hard work was to be done or hard knocks to be received he was ready." Williams, in short, was a solid soldier, but he had three strikes against him with McClellan: he had not served on the Peninsula, he did not graduate from the West Point, and McClellan did not know him well.

McClellan wanted a professional soldier commanding the corps.[30] His first choice was Major General John Sedgwick, a steady and experienced division commander in the 2nd Corps. But Sedgwick declined McClellan's offer of promotion in order to remain with his beloved division. The War Department settled McClellan's search for a commander on September 8 by assigning Major General Joseph K. Mansfield to lead the corps. Mansfield graduated second in the West Point class of 1822. The 58-year-old professional soldier had spent most of his 40 years in the army as an engineer or on staff duty as an inspector general. He and McClellan had what might be termed a working relationship, not a friendly one. Mansfield had been less than enthusiastic when McClellan took command of the army in July 1861, and McClellan perhaps indicated his opinion of Mansfield by dispatching him to duty along the North Carolina coast and at Suffolk, Virginia, rather than with the Army of the Potomac. But this assignment may also have reflected McClellan's thoughts about Mansfield's proven abilities as an engineer. Mansfield had little experience with troops and had not even led so much as a regiment in combat. He would not reach the army until September 15 to take command. Until that time, Williams commanded the corps.[31]

Despite his service in the cavalry, McClellan revealed no modern thinking about its employment on the Peninsula. He parceled his cavalry force out in detachments, and the Southern horsemen literally rode rings around them. McClellan apparently recognized the need for reorganization, for in Maryland he placed his cavalry into a four-brigade division, although this was largely an administrative, not a tactical organization. He selected Brigadier General Alfred Pleasonton, a 38-year-old West Pointer, to command this cavalry force. Pleasonton had spent nearly his entire 18-year U.S. Army career in the mounted service, principally the dragoons. He came to McClellan's attention on the Peninsula while commanding the 2nd U.S. Cavalry, which was attached to army headquarters. McClellan gave him command of the cavalry in a reconnaissance toward Malvern Hill on August 5, and then put him in charge of the rear guard during the army's withdrawal from the Peninsula. Pleasonton's performance in both operations impressed McClellan. "I am glad to inform you that your friend Pleasonton has done splendidly," he wrote his wife on August 18. "He is a most excellent soldier & has performed a very important duty most admirably."[32]

Those who served with Pleasonton through Maryland were not as enthusiastic about his merits. Charles F. Adams of the 1st Massachusetts Cavalry considered him "the bête noire of all cavalry officers . . . He is pure and simple a newspaper humbug. You always see his name in the papers, but to us who have served under him he is notorious as a bully & a toady . . . Yet mean & contemptible as Pleasonton is, he is always _in_ at headquarters." Charles R. Lowell of the 2nd Massachusetts Cavalry doubted his ability to gather accurate information. "I can't call any cavalry officer good who can't see the truth & tell the truth. With an infantry officer this is not so essential, but cavalry are the eyes & ears of the army & ought to see & hear & tell the truth truly; & yet it is the universal opinion that P[leasonton]'s own reputation & P's late promotions are bolstered up by systematic lying." But these were opinions formed after the experience of the Maryland Campaign. In the early days of September 1862, Pleasonton appeared to be a solid choice.[33]

McClellan's senior leadership matched up poorly against Lee's. His wing commanders were mediocre. Two of his corps commanders—Hooker and, later,

Mansfield—were new to the job. Hooker was a known fighter, but Mansfield was a question mark. Reno had only led a corps for several weeks. Williams was solid, although he had not commanded a corps before and did not have the confidence of McClellan. Franklin was loyal and experienced, but lacked energy. Other than the loyalty and friendship of Burnside and Franklin, McClellan also did not enjoy the type of relationship that Lee had with Jackson and Longstreet. Nor did he seek to cultivate trust or confidence in his subordinates, as Lee did. McClellan generally encouraged caution and discouraged initiative, except in the case of Hooker, to whom he granted an unusual amount of freedom. McClellan's style of leadership favored a group of obedient soldiers who minimized risk—except for the headstrong Hooker—and did not exceed their orders, even if opportunity knocked.

Staff

McClellan's remarkable effect on the morale of the army contributed greatly to the rapid recovery of the Army of the Potomac after Second Manassas, but it offers only part of the explanation. Sorting out the logistical chaos; replacing equipment; reorganizing batteries, brigades, divisions, and even corps; and the myriad other tasks that were necessary to field an effective force required more than charisma. McClellan was served by an able, talented staff who helped him accomplish these things. Although he did not use his staff as effectively as he might have, McClellan was one of the few generals who understood from the outset that the small staffs that had been sufficient to manage the Mexican War armies of 20,000 men would not do for the large armies this war would produce. His extensive reading on military history and his experience as a military observer of the French and British armies in the Crimean War, both of which had well-developed staff organizations, helped shape his opinions on army staffs. Shortly after assuming command of the army around Washington in July 1861, McClellan created the position of chief of staff, naming his father-in-law, Colonel Randolph B. Marcy, to the post. The 60-year-old colonel had spent 34 years as a soldier. At that point he had as much experience for the position as anyone in the regular army did, which in itself was not a ringing endorsement, as no one in the army had done the type of staff work that managing an army of 100,000 required. Marcy spent the first two months of the war as inspector general of the Department of Ohio, then filled the same post for his son-in-law until his appointment as chief of staff in September. Marcy's staff appointment earned him a promotion to brigadier general, so he enjoyed a rank that his Confederate counterpart Chilton did not.[34]

Marcy brought no new ideas to his job, and, although he performed his duties competently, he was no Berthier (Napoleon's superb chief of staff) to McClellan—or even an equal to Andrew A. Humphreys, Marcy's contemporary who later held his same staff position under General George Meade. Peter Michie, one of McClellan's biographers (and a soldier as well), believed that Marcy "was a weak spot in his [McClellan's] armor, for it was not by any means conceded by those in a position to know, that Marcy was gifted with those rare and varied attainments that such an officer should possess so as to particularly distinguish him for selection to this office." While this may have been true, Marcy had greater authority and played a more active role in the army's day-to-day operations than Chilton did for Lee. McClellan also made use of Marcy as the eyes of headquarters, such as during the battle of South Mountain, when he had Marcy accompany Hooker's 1st Corps in its attack.[35]

The other members of McClellan's personal staff consisted largely of men who were devoted to the general and of similar, politically conservative views. Nearly every man, including the aides-de-camp (one of whom was Captain George A. Custer), were West Pointers handpicked by McClellan for their cool judgment, intelligence, energy, and ability.

McClellan's general staff was excellent. Brigadier General Seth Williams, his assistant adjutant general, was possibly the best staff officer in either army during the war. Williams executed the duties of his office with such quiet competence that every succeeding commander of the Army of the Potomac retained him in his position. He had been with McClellan since his service in Ohio at the start of the war. McClellan wrote that "I never knew a more laborious and conscientious man," and credited him with much influence "in bringing about the excellent organization of the Army of the Potomac."[36]

Lieutenant Colonel Rufus Ingalls, who served as a quartermaster in the Peninsula Campaign, now returned to his post as the chief quartermaster. Moving the army without Ingalls was unthinkable. The 44-year-old graduated in the class of 1843 from West Point. Shortly after the Mexican War he entered duty with the Quartermaster's Department and remained in this branch to the end of his military career. Ingalls performed his job with masterly skill. Theodore Lyman, who served with him in 1864, marveled at his ability to move the unwieldy trains that accompanied the army on campaign. "How these huge trains are moved over roads not fit for a light buggy, is a mystery known only to General Rufus Ingalls, who treats them as if they were so many perambulators on a smooth sidewalk!" wrote Lyman. Sorting out complicated, complex problems of logistics was something of a specialty with Ingalls. McClellan lavished well-deserved praise on him for his role in the difficult movement of the army from Washington to the Peninsula by water earlier that spring. He carried out his duties, wrote McClellan, with "remarkable skill and energy."[37]

The combination of the withdrawal of the Army of the Potomac from the Peninsula and the defeat at Second Manassas left the army's logistics in chaos. Now, with the need to field an army quickly, Ingalls faced a fresh challenge. Until the army reached Frederick and established rail communications, supplies for man and beast would have to be transported by wagon from depots around Washington. This meant that as the army moved away from Washington toward Frederick, the round trip of the supply trains increased accordingly, until supplies would have to be hauled nearly 40 miles to keep the army provisioned. This was no trivial matter. The army's daily needs for food and forage amounted to over one million pounds. It required an immense wagon train to lug this quantity of comestibles, as well as to transport the army's baggage, equipment, and ammunition. Supplies were plentiful, but Ingalls's main problem was the army's trains, which were in a muddle after the retreat from Manassas. Many wagons from the Army of the Potomac were still in transport, or waiting for transport, from the Peninsula. There were several thousand wagons within the fortifications of Washington, but Ingalls's efforts were unsuccessful in getting an accurate count of just how many there were in the few days he had to organize the army's trains. Many of the quartermasters he questioned simply did not know how many vehicles belonged to their commands; as for Pope's army, Ingalls sarcastically remarked that "it does not appear that the commander of the Army of Virginia ever knew how many wagons there were, nor what quartermasters were on duty."[38]

Ingalls worked tirelessly to arrange transportation and organize it efficiently to meet the army's needs, yet despite his efforts there were shortages. From September 2 to 20, the army's cavalry division received no forage, and the horses were fed almost entirely on "green corn stalks," which, one cavalryman noted, was a "very poor feed" to maintain a horse's strength. As late as September 9, requisitions sent to the depot in Washington for supplies could not be filled, simply because the depot quartermaster had no wagons with which to haul them. Part of the problem was that some regiments, brigades, and divisions, principally in the 1st and the 12th Corps, had somehow acquired more wagons than were authorized to them, and they used these wagons to transport an excessive amount of baggage. Ingalls's orders for all surplus wagons to be turned in to the depot quartermaster met with mixed results. "Many have actually been turned in," he reported on September 10, but in general "the order has been evaded, to the public detriment." The supply situation gradually improved as more wagons arrived from the Peninsula and as Ingalls gained a firmer grip on what transportation he actually had and found the time to organize it more efficiently, but the active part of the campaign was nearly over by then. Nevertheless, Ingalls ensured that there was adequate food and ammunition on hand, and he performed a Herculean task in patching together the army's logistics as quickly as he did. It has been said that Lee could not have undertaken the Maryland Campaign without an ordnance officer of E. P. Alexander's caliber. It can also be said that McClellan could not have moved beyond Washington as soon as he did without a quartermaster of Ingalls's ability and energy.[39]

McClellan's return to command restored Jonathan Letterman to the post of medical director of the army. Letterman was perhaps the most brilliant and energetic medical officer in either army during the entire war. Many a Union and quite a few Confederate soldiers who survived wounds or disease owed their lives to procedures and changes implemented by this remarkable man. Letterman joined the Army of the Potomac as medical director on July 1, at the end of the Seven Days battles. He promptly made common-sense changes in diet and sanitary conditions that dramatically improved the army's health. He also tackled the inefficient method for evacuating the wounded from the battlefield. Ambulances were the primary means of transport, but Letterman found that "no system had anywhere been devised for their management." Both medical officers and quartermasters were responsible for ambulances, with the result that each expected the other to look after the equipment. There also was misuse of the vehicles, both in battle and on the march. To remedy the problem, Letterman drew up a plan to organize an ambulance corps. Each corps, division, brigade, and regiment would have its own ambulance personnel and assigned ambulances. A clear chain of command and organization was defined to avoid confusion and make sure ambulances were placed where they were most needed to evacuate the wounded to field hospitals promptly. In short, Letterman introduced a system where essentially none existed. McClellan approved the plan, but there was a delay in distributing the order for its implementation, so the army did not receive it until several days before it began the evacuation of the Peninsula. Although Letterman worked to initiate some changes on the march, the plan was not fully in place when the army departed for northern Virginia.[40]

As the army was gradually detached to Pope during the month of August, Letterman was temporarily displaced. When he returned to his post on September 2 he found the department in a "deplorable condition," disorganized and deficient in many medical necessities. The shortages in supplies, equipment, and ambulances resulted from the limited transportation available to move the Army of the Potomac from the Peninsula. Medical supplies and ambulances were deemed of secondary importance to combat troops, and they were often left behind for later transport. "The labor expended at Harrison's Landing in rendering this Department efficient for active service, seemed to have been expended in vain, and it required to be completely refitted before it would be again in proper condition," wrote a discouraged Letterman. Complicating his problems, Letterman was unfamiliar with the medical personnel in the 1st, the 12th, and the 9th Corps, as well as with the state of their supplies, equipment, and organization. A complete refit and reorganization of the medical department was needed, but this was impossible with the need to put the army in the field quickly. Letterman worked indefatigably to make what changes he could on the march, and to see that medical supplies and ambulances were forwarded to relieve the shortages existing in every corps of the army. By the time the Federal army met the Army of Northern Virginia at South Mountain on September 14, only 12 days after Letterman returned to his post as medical director, he had the medical services in good enough condition to meet the enormous strain the battles of South Mountain and Antietam would place on them. This was no small achievement, and Letterman's efforts preserved many lives that might otherwise have been lost.[41]

McClellan appointed the immensely talented Colonel Henry Hunt to fill the position of chief of artillery, which had been vacant since Brigadier General William F. Barry had requested and been granted a transfer to an administrative post on August 27. The 42-year-old West Pointer had commanded McClellan's Artillery Reserve on the Peninsula and been instrumental in the deployment of the guns that destroyed the Confederate attacks at Malvern Hill. Hunt was a meticulous individual who understood the use of artillery on the battlefield like few other men in either army. "I regarded him as the best living commander of field-artillery," wrote McClellan. "Hunt's merits consisted not only in organizing his command to the best advantages, but in using it on the field of battle with the utmost skill and power." Hunt was a vocal and forceful advocate of massed artillery fire and of placing artillery batteries under the command of trained artillery officers, rather than subjecting them to the orders of infantry officers who did not understand how to use them. Because of his strong opinions on these matters, Hunt hesitated to accept McClellan's offer, since General Barry's position had been largely administrative, with no real tactical authority. Hunt not only wanted full authority over the artillery's administration, supply, and instruction, but he also wanted to supervise its battlefield deployment—not merely the Artillery Reserve, but the entire long arm of the army. Perhaps to Hunt's surprise, McClellan agreed to his conditions and named him chief of artillery on September 5. Within 10 days Hunt was promoted to brigadier general.[42]

Due to the speed with which the Maryland Campaign developed, there was no time to prepare the necessary orders to provide Hunt with the tactical authority he wanted. Hunt had his hands full anyway, simply learning what artillery the army had and putting it in fighting trim. "I was compelled to obtain on the roads the names and condition of the batteries and the troops to which they were attached," he reported. He found much confusion, with shortages in men, horses, and ammunition. Hunt attacked the problems with characteristic vigor, arranging for several hundred wagonloads of ammunition to be delivered, taking horses from the baggage trains for his gun teams, and finding volunteers from the infantry to fill the vacant positions in the batteries. He accomplished all this in nine days, with the army on the march, spread over miles of road. The organization of the army's artillery remained imperfect, but Hunt accomplished miracles in putting the army's batteries in fighting condition.[43]

Brigadier General John Buford Jr. was named chief of cavalry, an administrative position, on September 10. He was a West Point graduate and 14-year veteran of the old U.S. Army, with most of his service with the dragoons. Buford had been a regimental quartermaster for three years of his prewar army service, but his true strength was as a field commander. Pope gave him a cavalry brigade and Buford did well. While McClellan displayed good judgment in selecting Buford, he would have done better to name him rather than Pleasonton as commander of the cavalry division. Little is actually known about what Buford did during the Maryland Campaign, but the cavalry had considerable logistical problems over the course of the campaign and they probably occupied Buford's full attention.[44]

Fighting Men

INFANTRY | The Army of the Potomac matched up well against their opponents at the divisional, brigade, and regimental levels of leadership. When the army left Washington it was composed of 1 cavalry and 16 infantry divisions, and all but 2 were commanded by West Pointers. Of these men, 11 had led a division in battle; and of those who were new to division command, all but Isaac Rodman, heading up one of Reno's 9th Corps' divisions, were professional soldiers. Moreover, 11 of the 17 would eventually rise to corps command. Of the 47 infantry and 5 cavalry brigades that participated in the campaign, 18 were led by professional officers. Lee counted only 8 West Pointers among his brigade commanders; McClellan's group contained 4 future corps commanders—John Gibbon, Winfield Hancock, Oliver O. Howard, and George Crook—and one future army commander, George G. Meade. There were some mediocre leaders as well, and at least one outright incompetent, but Lee bore the same burden.

Regimental leadership in the Federal army largely mirrored that of the Army of Northern Virginia, although the ranks of McClellan's field officers had not been hit as hard by the summer's fighting as Lee's had. Among the veteran regiments, the number of incompetent field and company-grade officers had been whittled down by the summer's campaigning. The new regiments were a different story; many of their colonels were green. Ezra Carman described an encounter he had on September 7 with Colonel Samuel Croasdale of the 128th Pennsylvania: "The colonel was evidently green on military matters as he asked me how to form line of battle, not knowing himself and giving as an excuse that he had no time since being commissioned to buy a copy of tactics." Ten days later Croasdale led his regiment into combat at Antietam. It was just as bad at the company level in the new regiments, where company officers and noncommissioned officers had little or no experience in their duties and responsibilities and knew nothing of tactics. "To make any maneuver they fell into inextricable confusion and fell to the rear," wrote General Alpheus Williams. Williams added that the men were easy to rally and "of excellent stamp, ready and willing, but neither their officers nor men knew anything, and there was an absence of the mutual confidence which drill begets." Upon learning that the 13th New Jersey, which Carman commanded, had never loaded or fired their weapons or conducted a drill before embarking on the Maryland Campaign with his 12th Corps brigade, Lieutenant Charley Mills of the 2nd Massachusetts observed: "I do not imagine that they will prove very valuable auxiliaries in the field."[45]

Infantry regiments formed the backbone of brigades. The 13 new regiments, with an average strength of 960 officers and men, added raw numbers to the army. The strength of veteran regiments varied widely, depending on the severity of their service, and the difference could be significant between the reported aggregate present (the number carried on the regimental rolls) and those actually present for duty (what a regiment would carry into combat). For example, the aggregate present of the 16th Michigan, a 5th Corps regiment, was 241 officers and men, but its present for duty strength was 112. The 83rd Pennsylvania, in the same brigade, counted 513 in their aggregate present but only 101 present for duty. The adjutant of the 2nd Massachusetts Infantry explained why there was such a disparity between aggregate and actual combat strength: in his regiment, "some 200 or 300 men are detailed as Hospital nurses etc., and we shall never get them again." So, while the 2nd Massachusetts may have carried 551 men on its roles as present for duty, only about 250 to 300 were actually present for duty equipped in the field with the regiment; of these, 150 were recruits the regiment received during the Maryland Campaign. The 6th Corps commander, William B. Franklin, stated that to arrive at the effective fighting strength of a Union formation, it was necessary to deduct one-fifth to one-quarter from its present for duty strength. Although the Confederates also had to detach men to noncombat duties, they could reassign fewer than the Federals, since slaves could be used for some of the extra tasks, freeing up more men to carry rifles.[46]

One advantage that McClellan's infantry supposedly enjoyed over their adversary—superior small arms—was not true, or at least not to a degree that had a significant impact. Although the U.S. Army had adopted the rifled .58-caliber muzzle-loading rifle as its standard firearm, the Army of the Potomac's regiments took the field equipped with a wide variety of small arms. The outbreak of the war caught the U.S. government unprepared to supply first-rate arms to the numbers of volunteers who came forward. Of the 437,433 rifles and muskets on hand, roughly 100,000 were rifled, and only about 40,000 of these were the new model .58-caliber rifle. There were only two government armories, and one of these, at Harpers Ferry, Virginia, was destroyed at the beginning of the war. The remaining armory, at Springfield, Massachusetts, could turn out only about 40 Springfield rifles a day as of August 1861. Expansion of the armory began immediately, but its effects were not felt until late 1862. The government contracted with a number of private manufacturers to make arms, but these firms were simply not large enough in 1861 to meet the needs of the rapidly expanding volunteer army. Purchasing agents were therefore sent abroad to procure arms from Europe. They returned with thousands of weapons, but these were of varying quality, caliber, and reliability. The Europeans quite naturally took the opportunity to unload their poorest weapons first on the desperate Americans. Even those arms that were of acceptable quality had often been in storage for several years and, as a result, had various defects. Rigid inspections would have weeded out the problem weapons, but the U.S. Ordnance Department was pitifully small, able to examine only a small number of the guns that were received before they were issued to troops.[47]

Politics, and the general confusion that marked the early war effort, also had their influence on the arms McClellan's infantry carried into battle. The first volunteer regiments received the best weapons, even though many of these early regiments were three-month volunteers. By the time many of the three-year volunteer regiments were mustered, they were issued second- and third-rate arms. Brigadier General James W. Ripley, the U.S. chief of ordnance, had wanted to arrange things so that the regiments likely to do the most fighting received the best weapons, but this proved impossible to implement. The upshot was that McClellan's regiments went forth unevenly armed. Many of them still carried .69-caliber smoothbore muskets they had been issued in 1861. And there were a wide variety of calibers in the rifled weapons the soldiers carried—from .52 to .54, .577, .58, and .69—all of which made the ordnance officers' duty a nightmare. On September 8 an inspection of the veteran 11th Pennsylvania Reserves found five different types of small arms in the regiment. Even the new regiments, organized and equipped over the summer, offered proof that problems with issuing quality infantry small arms were unresolved. Austrian rifles, probably the .54-caliber Lorenz rifle, were issued to an entire brigade of 3,600 men in Andrew A. Humphreys's division of Porter's 5th Corps. The Lorenz was a reliable weapon, but Humphreys's officers discovered that in this batch at least 900 weapons had broken nipples or hammers, and the remainder were entirely unserviceable in some other way. The 118th Pennsylvania Infantry, another rookie regiment in the 5th Corps, were issued .577-caliber Enfields, more than half of which proved to be worthless when the regiment went into combat at Shepherdstown on September 20. Sometimes the fighting men took matters into their own hands and purchased, traded, or scavenged weapons from the battlefield. At the Battle of Crampton's Gap, the 4th New Jersey Infantry were able to exchange all of their smoothbore muskets for Springfield rifles captured from the Confederates.[48]

McClellan fielded more infantry than Lee, but the edge in quality went to the Army of Northern Virginia. Every one of Lee's regiments had been in at least one battle, and some 80 percent had been in two or more. Nearly 20 percent of McClellan's effectives—12,613 infantrymen—had yet to see action.

Experience counts for a great deal on the battlefield, which Lee's veterans would illustrate in Maryland.[49]

CAVALRY | On paper McClellan fielded the strongest cavalry force ever assembled, with the Army of the Potomac containing 14 regiments of cavalry and 4 batteries of horse artillery, totaling some 4,300 mounted men and 22 guns. During the campaign, 11 of these regiments were formed into 4 brigades. Of the other 3, 2 remained attached to corps headquarters (the 3rd Pennsylvania Cavalry with the 1st Corps and the 6th New York Cavalry with Burnside) and one, the 1st Maine Cavalry, was unattached. But the concentration of 11 regiments into a division seemed to indicate that McClellan had learned some important lessons about the most effective employment of cavalry from his experience on the Peninsula. In that campaign his cavalry had been "scattered about and used as escorts, strikers, dog-robbers and orderlies for all the generals and their numerous staff officers from the highest rank down to the second lieutenant." The consequence of this, according to one of the foremost authorities on Union cavalry in the war, was a "crippling effect on the discipline and training of units that had not been together long enough to acquire much of either, or to develop the esprit de corps that is an essential ingredient in the success of any military organization." So, while McClellan's creation of a cavalry division showed promise, few of the regiments and none of the brigades had yet operated as tactical formations.[50]

When the army first took the field on September 7, the cavalry division did not yet exist. It assembled as the campaign progressed, and the various cavalry regiments caught up with the army. On the 7th Pleasonton fielded only five regiments, and they had to picket a front extending from Seneca Mill, on the Potomac River, to Cooksville, on the National Road, a distance of over 25 miles. Several cavalry regiments were still disembarking from the Peninsula, and Pleasonton did not complete the formation of his division until September 12. Even then, most of the brigades were administrative, not tactical. Only Colonel John F. Farnsworth's 2nd Brigade operated as a tactical unit throughout the campaign, but even it rarely had all four of its regiments together.[51]

The brigade commanders were mostly able men, but just two had prewar cavalry experience and none had seen service above the regimental level. No one wore a general's star; three were colonels, and a regular army major led the brigade of regular cavalry. The latter was Charles J. Whiting, commanding the 1st Brigade, which consisted of the 5th and the 6th U.S. Cavalry. A West Point graduate and veteran of regular cavalry service on the frontier before the Civil War, Whiting was a tough, no-nonsense soldier. At Gaines' Mill he led a near-suicidal charge to cover the Union retreat there, losing 150 of his 250 men. He was captured, but an exchange returned him to the army in August. His bravery was unquestioned. Colonel John F. Farnsworth led the 2nd Brigade. A two-term Republican congressman from Illinois and an ardent supporter of the prewar antislavery movement, Farnsworth left politics to raise the 8th Illinois Cavalry in 1861. He was stalwart and aggressive, but owed his position as a brigade commander to seniority—he was the only colonel in the brigade. Colonel Richard Rush of the 6th Pennsylvania Cavalry and Colonel Andrew T. McReynolds of the 1st New York Cavalry commanded the 3rd and the 4th brigades, respectively. An Englishman by birth, Rush was a West Pointer whose prewar service had been in the artillery. McReynolds, an Irishman, served with the 3rd Dragoons as a captain in the Mexican War, but he left the service in 1848. When the Civil War began, McReynolds was 55 years old and practicing law in Michigan. The 1st New York Cavalry needed a colonel. They wanted Philip Kearny, but he recommended McReynolds, whom Kearny recalled from his service in Mexico, which was a testament to McReynolds's soldiery qualities and courage, for Kearny had high standards.[52]

The old habit of detaching cavalry companies for escort, orderly, and provost guard duty with the corps and with army headquarters continued in Maryland: 25 companies, numbering approximately 715 officers and men, were detached from regiments in the cavalry division for escort and provost duty. This was in addition to the 21 companies that were already attached to army and corps headquarters. Thus the equivalent of four cavalry regiments were scattered to serve as personal escorts, couriers, provost guards, and the like. This left Pleasonton with an effective cavalry force of only some 3,600 men.[53]

But even this figure for effective cavalryman is probably high, as an epidemic of "greased heel" struck the army's horses during the campaign. An officer in the 1st Massachusetts Cavalry blamed the outbreak on the horses' diet in Maryland, which was principally green cornstalks. Regular supplies of forage were not received, due to the tangled snarl army logistics were in, and the cavalry were constantly on the move during the first 11 days of the campaign. But it was a viral infection—hoof-and-mouth disease—not the horses' diet, that caused the outbreak, although their poor diet and the hard work the horses were called on to perform did not help matters. "Horses reported perfectly well one day would be dead or lame the next," wrote Rufus Ingalls. He estimated that 4,000 horses either died or were rendered unserviceable. Benjamin Crowninshield, in the 1st Massachusetts Cavalry, considered the disease's effect "disastrous" and thought that upwards of one-half of the horses in the Army of the Potomac were put out of action. Crowninshield may have exaggerated the numbers, but the disease's effect was serious.[54]

The opening of the campaign found most Union horsemen armed principally with a saber and pistol, the traditional weapons of a cavalryman. McClellan and others understood the value of arming troopers with carbines, but not enough were being produced to equip all regiments. McClellan's ordnance officers were able to outfit some regiments from stocks of weapon recently delivered to the Washington arsenal. The 6th New York, for instance, were armed on September 6. A day later the 1st Massachusetts received theirs. But there were not enough on hand to equip everyone, and when Pleasonton requested additional weapons from headquarters for his troopers, Chief of Staff Marcy could only suggest to the cavalry commander that he take the carbines out of the hands of the regiments that did have them and place them "temporarily into the hands of the serviceable regiments to relieve those that have been overworked."[55]

Those troopers lucky enough to be issued carbines carried a variety of single-shot, breech-loading weapons, all of which were superior to the muzzle-loading carbines with which Stuart's horseman were armed. This might have given the Federals an edge in combat, but carbines were most effective when troopers fought dismounted, and only a handful of Union regiments had any training or experience in these tactics. A member of the 4th Pennsylvania noted that at this stage of the war "the use of cavalry as dismounted skirmishers was not then thought of." This was generally true in September 1862, with the exception of the 8th Illinois and the 3rd Indiana, who both effectively fought dismounted with their carbines throughout the Maryland Campaign. But most of the other regiments had no training or experience in maneuvering and fighting this way. Dismounted combat for cavalry was not a novel idea. The U.S. Army had maintained a dragoon regiment—essentially mounted infantry—on the frontier for many years before the war, and there was a long history in Europe of mounted troops fighting dismounted with muskets or carbines. The problem in 1862 was that, with the exception of Pleasonton, the senior leadership of the Army of the Potomac did not yet understand the potential of employing cavalry as an offensive weapon, and no general doctrine for dismounted fighting had been embraced by the army at that time.[56]

The role of Pleasonton's cavalry in Maryland—particularly in the early stages of the campaign, when it was necessary to gather intelligence about enemy strength, position, and intentions—was critical. The duty of establishing contact with the Confederates fell on their shoulders, because Allan Pinkerton, McClellan's intelligence chief, did not have an established organization in Maryland. This meant that Pleasonton and his cavalry would be the army's chief source of intelligence about enemy strength and movements. Much was expected—and needed—from the army's mounted force, but they labored under disadvantages that almost guaranteed that they would not succeed. There was not enough cavalry to perform all the missions that had to be carried out, and the outbreak of hoof-and-mouth disease during the campaign meant that the number of mounted troopers decreased as the campaign progressed. The one advantage a Union trooper might have enjoyed over the enemy, that of firepower, evaporated from the shortage of carbines. Although the formation of brigades and a division were positive steps, units were still parceled out for miscellaneous duties, so their combat power was dispersed. Most regiments had relatively little combat experience. Leadership, although improving, remained uninspiring, unaggressive, and, in some cases, inexperienced. Pleasonton had not yet managed large cavalry formations, and his ability to provide accurate intelligence about the enemy was untested. Overall, Jeb Stuart and his horsemen remained their superiors in the field. "The truth was," wrote Captain W. W. Blackford of Stuart's staff, "that their cavalry was afraid to meet us . . . Up to this time the cavalry of the enemy had no more confidence in themselves than the country had in them, and whenever we got a chance at them, which was rarely, they came to grief." Troopers of the hard-fighting 8th Illinois or the 3rd Indiana cavalry would have taken exception to Blackford's braggadocio, for they never shied away from coming to grips with Stuart's horsemen in Maryland. But Blackford was not entirely wrong; the 8th Illinois and the 3rd Indiana were the exceptions among the Federal army's cavalry, not the rule. The rest of Pleasonton's regiments were not yet the equals of the Confederate cavalry.[57]

ARTILLERY | When Henry Hunt assumed his duties as chief of artillery, he found the army's long arm in a deplorable condition. The combination of the army's transfer from the Peninsula to northern Virginia plus the battle and defeat at Second Manassas played havoc with organization. When batteries embarked from the Peninsula, drivers and horses traveled in one class of transports, while cannoneers and guns went in another. When either arrived at Aquia Creek, they were hurried off to the front with whatever division was ready to march, without regard to their parent organization. The Artillery Reserve of 18 batteries, organized by McClellan and used with such deadly effect by Hunt at Malvern Hill, was largely broken up by this practice, with most of its batteries being attached to divisions and corps in the two Federal armies, the Army of the Potomac and the Army of Virginia. The extent of the disorganization was such that Hunt spent much of his time in the early days of the campaign simply trying to find out who had which batteries. He also discovered little uniformity in organization between the different corps. McClellan had attempted to establish a standard organization in his army corps: four batteries to each infantry division, with the batteries consisting of one regular and three volunteer batteries. But Hunt found few divisions that met this standard; many had three, and some had only two. Rodman's division in the 9th Corps had just one. In the 12th Corps they grouped all their batteries together into one battalion or brigade (an organization that would become the standard in the Army of the Potomac by June 1863). In the 1st Corps, its 1st Division made a practice of attaching one battery to each of its four infantry brigades, although this was against orders.[58]

Refitting and reorganizing the army's artillery posed the most formidable challenge Hunt had yet faced in the war, because the reorganization had to take place while the army was on the march, spread across a broad front. Hunt had a staff of seven officers to assist him. All of them, along with Hunt, were constantly in the saddle in the early days of the advance from Washington, locating batteries and assessing their condition. Hunt found that many batteries "had not been refitted since the August campaign; some had lost more or less guns; others were greatly deficient in men and horses, and a number were wholly unserviceable from all these causes combined." He also found that batteries that had been engaged at Second Manassas often did not have a full supply of ammunition.[59]

Hunt and his staff worked tirelessly to correct the deficiencies they encountered. Three hundred wagonloads of ammunition were ordered up from the Washington arsenal to correct the ammunition shortage. Batteries that were deemed unserviceable were ordered back to Washington to recruit and refit. Replacements for horses lost in combat or to disease were appropriated from the baggage trains. Manpower losses were partially replaced by appealing for volunteers from infantry regiments. Artillery service tended to be comparatively safer than the infantry, so finding willing volunteers was often not difficult. Hunt also transferred batteries from the Artillery Reserve to corps or divisions that were short of artillery support, but he was unable to achieve any uniformity in how many guns were assigned to each division and corps before the end of the campaign. Although the situation was far from ideal, by September 15 Hunt felt that "considering the condition in which the campaign in August had left it," the army's long arm was "very respectfully provided."[60]

Once the weeding out of unserviceable batteries was complete, Hunt counted 64 batteries—22 regular and 42 volunteer—totaling 323 guns. On paper this represented formidable firepower, but inefficient organization virtually guaranteed that it would be dispersed on the battlefield, a violation of a basic principle of war, that of mass, or concentration. The Artillery Reserve consisted of only seven batteries, four of which were equipped with 20 lb. Parrott rifles. These heavy guns packed punch, but their weight limited their maneuverability. The seven batteries of the Reserve were the only guns Hunt had available to reinforce an attack or bolster the defense of a threatened sector. The rest of the army's batteries, with the exception of those with the 12th Corps, were assigned to infantry divisions and subject to the orders of the division commander, who was usually an infantry officer unschooled in the proper use of artillery. Each division had a chief of artillery, who was the senior captain. It was an administrative position, not a tactical one, unless the chief's division commander granted him this authority, which was rare. But in battle the chief rarely could bother with the other batteries, for he was still responsible for directing his own battery. It was a classic case of increased responsibility without commensurate rank or pay. The response was unsurprising, as most chiefs did little more than forward "a few reports" to their superiors.[61]

The way this ineffective organization played out in battle is that division commanders tended to adopt a parochial attitude toward their batteries. The artillery chief could not arrange for cooperation, as he was subject to the orders of his division commander. Only the corps commander possessed the authority to order all batteries under his command to a certain point, and he was often too busy with his infantry to do this effectively. Even if someone were able to mass a number of batteries, each battery was dependent on its own division's ordnance trains for ammunition resupply. It was a patently bad system, and it would not be improved until just prior to the battle of Gettysburg, when the artillery was reorganized into brigades subject to the corps commander's and artillery chief's orders.

Although hampered by poor organization, Union artillerymen enjoyed superior guns and ammunition over the Confederates. Federal batteries usually consisted of six guns, compared with an average of four in the Army of Northern Virginia, and the guns were typically of the same caliber and type. With the exception of a pair of mountain howitzers that accompanied Jacob Cox's Kanawha division, every gun in the army was either a rifle (a 3-incher, a 10 lb. Parrott, or a 20 lb. Parrott) or a Napoleon, which made ammunition resupply considerably less complicated than it was for the Confederates. There was also the backbone of 21 regular batteries, whose drill, discipline, and experience was excellent. Most of their battery commanders were West Point trained, and many of the noncommissioned officers were experienced regulars. The volunteer batteries, while generally not yet on a par with the regulars, aspired to match or better them, and the volunteers were steadily improving. Ammunition and fuses were of a superior manufacture than those issued to Lee's gunners from Southern ordnance factories, resulting in far fewer duds or premature explosions. There was also a plentiful supply of shrapnel, the most effective long-range artillery ammunition.

THE ARMY OF THE Potomac marched into Maryland as a powerful but imperfect force. It was better equipped, uniformed, and supplied than its adversary, and it had a slim advantage in numbers. But the negatives outweighed these advantages. Mutual suspicion and a lack of confidence marked the relationship of its commander with the president, his cabinet, and the army's chief of staff. Two of the corps commanders were facing a potential court-martial at the end of the campaign. The senior leadership lacked the unity and trust in each other that Lee's command structure had, and McClellan generally discouraged any initiative by his subordinates. There were no leaders at corps command who were of Jackson's and Longstreet's caliber. The infantry contained large numbers of new recruits with little training. The army's overall organization remained incomplete, and some branches, such as the artillery, were downright inefficient. Lee may have had the smaller army, but it was an army with superior organization, morale, and leadership, which invariably proved to be more flexible and responsive, as well as capable of concentrating troops more rapidly.

Still, for all its imperfections, there was something magnificent about this Army of the Potomac. It had shown its resilience and dedication in the speed with which it shook off the disaster at Manassas. Defeat had washed away the starry-eyed optimism that had once buoyed the army, and it viewed the future with the grim knowledge that whatever lay ahead would be hard and bloody. The rank and file knew with what determination their foes fought. "I can't tell you of the future," confided General Alpheus Williams to his daughter, adding that "if we fail now the North has no hope, no safety that I can see." In the 6th Wisconsin, Major Rufus Dawes prepared his mother for what lay ahead. "Do not feel our task is easy or sure of successful accomplishment. The battle will be desperate and bloody, and upon very equal terms." So much rode on the shoulders of this army: the preservation of the Union, and the future of freedom in America. The Army of the Potomac would determine on the battlefield whether the document in the president's desk remained locked away or shed its light on the nation's future.[62]

5

The Army of the Potomac Advances to Frederick
"You may be sure that I will follow them as closely as I can"

McClellan considered the possibility that Lee might push a force into Maryland as early as September 2. He received a dispatch that morning from Brigadier General Jacob Cox at Upton's Hill, who reported that a captured Federal surgeon, who had been released by the Confederates, had passed through Jackson's command, encamped just north of Fairfax Court House. The doctor had overheard the Rebels talking about the main army "pushing for the Potomac." More reports followed this one, with similar circumstantial evidence. That afternoon McClellan wrote to the president and expressed the opinion that the enemy might "venture to cross the upper Potomac," but he considered this only one of several approaches the enemy might use to threaten the capital.[1]

McClellan sent orders late that night to Major H. L. Higginson, commanding the 1st and 2nd battalions of the 1st Massachusetts Cavalry at Alexandria, to draw two days' rations and march at once up the Potomac River. Higginson was to distribute his command to observe the fords between Great Falls and Harpers Ferry and provide warning should the enemy mount a raid or invade Maryland in strength. It was a tall order for two battalions of cavalry. "The service entrusted to you is of the highest importance and not a moment must be lost in proceeding to the scene of your duties," wrote Seth Williams, McClellan's assistant adjutant general. The mission, continued Williams, was not to engage the enemy, "but simply to watch carefully his operations, and give the commanding general timely notice should he appear in the quarter to which you are sent."[2]

No midnight dash into Maryland occurred, but an accumulation of reports on September 3 suggested that the Confederates were moving in that direction. A paroled Union cavalry major reported that on September 1 he encountered large Confederate forces marching west on the Little River Turnpike, bound, some of the Rebels told him, for Harpers Ferry. The following day, while working his way back to Union lines, the major observed numerous Confederate troops bivouacked west of Fairfax, between the Little River Turnpike and

Warrenton Turnpike. An escaped prisoner who belonged to a New York regiment corroborated the major's story, but added to the confusion by reporting that the Confederates talked of marching on Washington. Later that night a dispatch arrived from Colonel Dixon Miles, commanding the garrison at Harpers Ferry, reporting that a division of 12,000 Confederates was said to be in the vicinity of Leesburg. This report came on the heels of news that Brigadier General Julius White had abandoned Winchester on September 2 before an allegedly superior Confederate force, which added weight to the possibility that the enemy were indeed moving against Harpers Ferry. But there remained too many rumors, and too little hard intelligence about the Confederate army, to draw any conclusions about where they were heading next. McClellan nevertheless took the precaution of shifting the 2nd Corps to Tennallytown, Maryland, and ordering the 12th Corps to move there as well on the 4th.[3]

In the early hours of September 4 McClellan's headquarters received a terse message from Jacob Cox at Upton's Hill. "Evidence accumulates that the main body of the rebels have gone in the direction of Leesburg," reported Cox. As if to substantiate Cox's intelligence, an 8:20 a.m. dispatch from Pleasonton reported that one of his squadrons, scouting in the direction of Vienna and Dranesville, found the area clear of enemy troops until they neared Dranesville and Springvale, where "considerable numbers" of Confederate cavalry were reported to be present. Pleasonton added that "numbers of Union men" were coming into Federal lines from the direction of Dranesville "and report that that the enemy is going to cross the Potomac at Walker's Landing."[4]

With the 12th Corps on the march to join Sumner's 2nd Corps at Tennallytown, McClellan felt that he could handle any raid the enemy might mount on the Maryland side of the Potomac against the capital. Cox's and Pleasonton's intelligence caused him to make no other moves, other than to order the 4th Corps division of Darius Couch to Fort Ethan Allen, where it could help cover the Chain Bridge. He hesitated to make any additional redeployments until his cavalry scouts and other intelligence sources provided more information.[5]

At 1:30 p.m. Pleasonton's scouts on the Vienna Road reported Confederates approaching "in some force" in their front. The Federal troopers skirmished with the Southerners (Fitz Lee's cavalry), who seemed more inclined to make noise than to force a fight. Pleasonton offered his opinion that "the enemy is only making a show of force to conceal his movements on the Upper Potomac." McClellan thought so, too, even though the enemy probe carried on into the late afternoon. By that time McClellan had decided to shift Pleasonton's more mobile cavalry into Maryland and replace them with Bayard's and Buford's used-up cavalry brigades to screen and patrol the approaches to the capital's defenses on the Virginia side. Pleasonton was ordered to march at once to Tennallytown with his entire brigade, without waiting for Bayard to relieve him at Falls Church. To make certain Pleasonton understood the urgency of the situation, McClellan closed his message by stating, "the duty about to be entrusted to you is of the utmost importance."[6]

The shift of his only available fresh cavalry from Virginia to Maryland signaled that McClellan anticipated a Confederate invasion of Maryland. In what strength, and aimed at what objective, were questions he hoped Pleasonton's horseman might reveal. Heavier forces were slated to follow Pleasonton into Maryland. Orders went out to Burnside's 9th Corps to cross the Potomac at the Long Bridge and march out Seventh Street to Meridian Hill, and for Couch's division to join the 2nd and the 12th Corps at Tennallytown.[7]

As early as September 1, Nathaniel Banks, then commander of Pope's 2nd Corps (now the 12th Corps), anticipated that the Rebels might attempt a crossing at the Potomac fords near Leesburg, and he sent a party of four signal officers from his command to occupy sites where they could keep these crossing points under observation. Captain Louis R. Fortescue was ordered to Maryland Heights, while Lieutenant Brinkerhoff Miner went to Sugar Loaf Mountain. These two locales afforded a view of every Potomac ford above and below Leesburg. To hasten any communication these stations might signal, Lieutenant Ephraim Briggs was posted in Poolesville, where he could telegraph reports from Maryland Heights and Sugar Loaf to Washington.[8]

McClellan benefited from Banks's foresight when, late on September 4, Lieutenant Briggs telegraphed a signal from Lieutenant Miner on Sugar Loaf. Miner reported that he could see large wagon parks around Leesburg and what appeared to be bodies of troops. He said the Rebels advanced some forces and shelled the Union pickets near the mouth of the Monocacy River, in an apparent attempt to force a crossing into Maryland. The latter part of Miner's report was confirmed by a series of telegrams from Colonel Dixon Miles, commanding at Harpers Ferry. Miles stated that his officer in command at Point of Rocks, Colonel Henry B. Banning of the 87th Ohio Infantry, had abandoned his position there because 30,000 Rebels had crossed the Potomac and were advancing on him. Banning had telegraphed General John Wool, commanding the Middle Department, at his headquarters in Baltimore earlier in the day, stating that a "perfectly reliable" man up from Leesburg reported a "very large" Confederate force under Longstreet's command had been passing through Leesburg since midnight, marching west toward Winchester, and that this fellow had counted 60 pieces of artillery.[9]

Early morning on September 5 found Pleasonton and his cavalry on the march from Tennallytown to scout in the direction of the Potomac fords east of Poolesville. He reached Darnestown by 11:30 a.m., reporting that he had explored the River Road thoroughly and found no enemy. He had learned, however, that the enemy had crossed some cavalry over the river the night before and attacked a company of the 1st Massachusetts Cavalry picketing the mouth of the Monocacy, but the Rebels then returned south of the Potomac. Based on the country he had seen between Tennallytown and Darnestown, and his exaggerated opinion of himself as a strategist, Pleasonton added his opinion that he did not think the Rebels "will cross the Potomac in large force below Harper's Ferry."[10]

Just how wrong Pleasonton was became apparent as the day progressed. At 10:15 a.m. Dixon Miles telegraphed General Wool to reiterate his earlier report that some 30,000 Rebels had crossed the Potomac on the 4th, and that others were now fording it some 3 miles below Point of Rocks. General Wool took the initiative and sent Colonel Thomas J. Cram of his staff out on the B&O Railroad to see if he might discover "the truth of the various rumors and reports." Just how far Cram went is unknown, but he wired Wool at noon from Monocacy Junction confirming "that 30,000 Rebels crossed at the mouth of the Monocacy River last night." Wool also received a wire from B&O Railroad President John W. Garrett, who had his own men out to gather information, that 30,000 Confederates under the command of General Hill had crossed into Maryland during the night, with "more to come." Garrett also wired McClellan at 3:30 p.m. to report that "our telegrams continue to state the passage over the Potomac by very large forces of the enemy chiefly near the mouth of the Monocacy." News from Lieutenant Miner, perched atop Sugar Loaf Mountain, eventually made its way to Washington as well, but it was delayed because Lieutenant Briggs was absent from his telegraph post in Poolesville at 9 a.m., when Miner signaled that the Confederates had forded the river the previous night at Noland's Ferry.[11]

While the intelligence told McClellan that the enemy had crossed the Potomac near the mouth of the Monocacy in force, it remained unclear whether this was a full-scale invasion or a raid. If it was an invasion, what was the Confederates objective? Halleck advised McClellan to "dispatch General Sumner and additional forces to follow" the Rebels. To where, McClellan might have asked, for no one had yet divined the enemy's intentions. But McClellan agreed that it was necessary to push a force out beyond the capital's defenses north of the Potomac River to block two potential avenues of advance. Orders were issued for the 2nd and the 12th Corps to advance from Tennallytown to Rockville, about 10 miles northwest on the Georgetown Pike. Couch's 4th Corps division received orders to march to Offut's Crossroads, 8 miles west on the River Road. All of these forces were granted the freedom "to intercept a force crossing the river," provided that they could do so "without incurring any great risk," a warning that would literally become a doctrine during the campaign. But this was a defensive move, not an offensive one. Since Pleasonton had already scouted well beyond both Rockville and Offut's Crossroads and found no enemy, there was little chance that either advance would encounter any Confederates. The rest of the army was ordered to prepare three days' rations and hold itself in readiness to march. But until the still vague intelligence picture revealed more information, McClellan's headquarters issued no more marching orders.[12]

Reports that the Rebels were marching west of Leesburg, as well as crossing at the mouth of the Monocacy, created uneasiness about the security of the Union garrisons at Harpers Ferry and Martinsburg. According to McClellan, Secretary of State Seward visited him, probably on the evening of September 4, and expressed great concern about the safety of Harpers Ferry. McClellan offered his opinion that the garrison could do no good there; it should abandon the position and join the main army. If it did remain in that area, then the entire garrison should be withdrawn to Maryland Heights. At Seward's suggestion the two men then went to Halleck's home, where they woke the general so that he might hear McClellan's idea on what to do with the Harpers Ferry garrison. "Halleck received my statement with ill-concealed contempt; said that everything was all right as it was; that my views were erroneous, etc., and soon bowed out, leaving matters at Harper's Ferry precisely as they were," McClellan recalled. Like many things McClellan wrote in his memoirs, this was both ungenerous and untrue. Halleck did not agree that the Harpers Ferry garrison should be withdrawn, but he did accept McClellan's suggestion of removing it to Maryland Heights. Halleck wired General Wool on the 5th to advise him that it would take several days to place the army in the field, and that during this time "Harper's Ferry may be attacked and overwhelmed." Although he properly left the dispositions of the forces there to Wool's "experience and local knowledge," Halleck suggested the "propriety of withdrawing all our forces in that vicinity to Maryland Heights."[13]

Important news from Pleasonton reached headquarters in the early morning of September 6. Captain Casper Crowninshield and part of the 1st Massachusetts had scouted to Edward's Ferry and found no enemy there, but they did pick up a Rebel deserter who told them that "Jackson, Longstreet, Smith, and Hill were crossing, and that they had sixty pieces of cannon, and a force of between 30,000 and 45,000 men." From what he had seen and learned, it was clear to Pleasonton that the enemy "has a large force on this side of the river." Crowninshield had seen dust kicked up at White's Ferry, and from the direction of the dust "it is thought the enemy is moving toward Frederick." By this time McClellan may have already learned that an exodus of citizens and Federal property had started from Frederick because of reliable reports that the enemy were approaching. If he had studied a map, McClellan would have seen that if the enemy were crossing the Potomac River from White's Ford to a ford 3 miles below Point of Rocks, then it may have been because they wished to use the Monocacy River to protect their flank as they marched north to Frederick. From this city they could either advance on Baltimore or move on to Pennsylvania.[14]

Pleasonton's cavalry was too weak in numbers to do much more than picket roads and observe. His main force remained behind Muddy Branch, near Darnestown. The drubbing Fitz Lee's troopers administered to the 1st Massachusetts in Poolesville on the evening of the 5th left many of Pleasonton's men jumpy. "Some of my cavalry are so nervous I cannot make much out of their reports," he wrote to headquarters. Someone kept their cool, though, for at 8:30 a.m. on the 6th Pleasonton reported that he had "just learned that Lee's corps, said to number 30,000, crossed above yesterday, and moved down in the direction of Poolesville; and that Jackson is to move by the Frederick road, the design being an attack on Washington. This looks probable, for a flank movement by them to Baltimore would expose them fatally." This was the second report that put Jackson in Maryland, which was important. But the reference to "Lee's corps" (which was in fact Fitz Lee's cavalry brigade) might have puzzled them at headquarters, for as far as anyone knew there was no such organization in the Confederate army. And Pleasonton did not reveal how he had learned the enemy's designs.[15]

Pleasonton requested more cavalry to cover the growing front, and McClellan responded by reinforcing him with the 1st New York Cavalry, which reached Rockville on the 5th, and a squadron of the 1st U.S. Cavalry, detached from duty as the army's quartermaster's guard. Pleasonton ordered the New Yorkers to advance to Middlebrook and push their scouts out toward Clarksburg. The Regulars were dispatched to reconnoiter north from Rockville to Brookville and on to Unity, Cracklintown, and Goshen. The 8th Illinois and the 3rd Indiana of Pleasonton's brigade sent their pickets out in the direction of Poolesville. These movements learned very little, however. The Regulars encountered no enemy on their forays. The 1st New York advanced four companies to Clarksburg and pushed scouts out toward Hyattstown. Colonel Andrew T. McReynolds, commanding the 1st, interviewed two "respectable Union citizens," one of whom had left Barnesville before daylight that morning, and they said that Jackson and some 30,000 to 40,000 men were in and around that village. Some alert pickets along the Potomac River picked up "an Irishman" from Leesburg who had left the village that morning, crossed the river at Point of Rocks, and was apparently making his way down the River Road. He told Pleasonton that there were no enemy troops at Leesburg when he left, and only two regiments of cavalry at Barnesville. The main Confederate army—"some 60,000 strong, so the soldiers told him," and under Jackson—"are going to Baltimore." He also said that the enemy soldiers "were running over the country hunting something to eat, and are a hard-looking set, with a large number of stragglers."[16]

These two reports reflected the problems Army headquarters had in sifting the wheat from the chaff in the intelligence that came across their desks. Was the Irishman to be believed, or the respectable Union citizens? Fortunately McClellan had other intelligence sources against which to check the information Pleasonton was providing. General Sumner, at Rockville, reported that a spy "in whom I have confidence" had just returned from Poolesville and said that the Confederates had passed that town and were on their way to Frederick; he estimated their strength at 50,000. A supervisor with the B&O Railroad provided information that corroborated the spy's report that the Rebels were marching on Frederick. This man managed to get within a half mile of Monocacy Bridge, located 3 miles southeast of Frederick. There he met a railroad maintenance foreman who had been sent out to meet the supervisor. The foreman told him "that the enemy were advancing to Frederick in large force, by the Georgetown Road, and that 5,000 had then passed, and still more were following." The Rebels "were quiet and orderly," with "many barefoot and clothes worn out." "This information is correct," the supervisor added to his telegram, lest anyone on the receiving end doubt its veracity.[17]

Three things were emerging from the mass of reports accumulating at army headquarters. First, enemy strength in Maryland was increasing. On September 5 several reports gave the enemy strength as 30,000. Now there were reports that 50,000 to 60,000 were in the state. Second, the Confederates were poorly supplied. Third, they were advancing not on Washington but on Frederick. But where they intended to go from there remained a mystery. These reports, combined with the lack of enemy activity south of the Potomac River, convinced McClellan that this was not a raid. The Confederates had invaded Maryland in force and would have to be met. He and his staff spent much of the day on September 5 issuing orders and making the necessary preparations for the army to take the field. McClellan, as noted previously, had appealed to Halleck and the president to suspend the order relieving Porter and Franklin from command, and he asked that Hooker be put in charge of McDowell's 1st Corps so that Reno could command the 9th Corps, while Burnside headed a wing consisting of both of these corps. Meanwhile, marching orders were dispatched that afternoon to the 1st and the 6th Corps, and to George Sykes's 2nd Division in the 5th Corps. Other instructions went to the formations that would remain to defend the capital: the 3rd Corps; the 11th Corps; Porter's 5th Corps, now reduced to one division; Buford's and Bayard's cavalry brigades; and the unattached troops in the city. The Maryland Campaign was about to begin for the Army of the Potomac.[18]

The citizens of Washington heard the tramp of thousands of troops passing through the city all night on September 6. The men of the 1st Corps had just finished pitching tents and preparing their supper that evening when their marching orders arrived. "All surprised and not very well pleased," wrote Lieutenant Sam Healy of the 56th Pennsylvania. Men grumbled and cursed as they dropped their tents and packed their belongings. Lieutenant George Breck and the men of Battery L, 1st New York Light Artillery, took the orders more philosophically. "We didn't take it very seriously at heart, because we had become perfectly inured to marching orders," he wrote. In the 6th Corps camps around the Fairfax Seminary, Colonel Joseph Bartlett, commanding one of the corps' brigades, recalled that the men received their orders "with enthusiastic cheers along the whole line, and the camps were all bustle and cheerful excitement from that moment until the heads of our column drew out on the road toward Long Bridge."

It was a pleasant evening for marching. The temperature hovered in the low seventies and the moon shone "almost as bright as day." The 6th Corps crossed the Potomac River on the Long Bridge, and their journey toward Tennallytown took them up H Street, where they passed McClellan's headquarters. Cheers burst forth from the troops as they marched by, and as each brigade approached headquarters they began to sing: "McClellan is our leader, he is gallant and strong / For God and our country we are marching along." People crowded the streets to cheer on the bronzed veterans. "Even the despairing patriot officials of Washington seemed hopeful and buoyant once more," observed Colonel Bartlett.[19]

By the time Hooker's 1st Corps reached Georgetown and the Capitol Hill area, the pretty girls and cheering crowds had retired to their beds. John Vautier, in Ricketts's division, was struck by the "deep silence" of the marching column and recalled that all that could be heard was the "tramping of steady feet and the hoarse commands of the officers" as they marched through the city's deserted streets. They, too, used the Long Bridge to cross the Potomac, but their progress took them by the White House and out the Seventh Street Road. Around 2 a.m. a halt was called and the soldiers, numb with fatigue, threw themselves down on the sidewalks to sleep. The men of General Abner Doubleday's brigade found themselves in front of the White House. Despite their exhaustion, many must have pondered what "Old Abe" was thinking about all of this. Who could have imagined seven months ago, when McClellan embarked with his splendid army for the Virginia Peninsula, that it would have come to this: a Union army marching through its own capital to see to its defense.[20]

Hooker let his men sleep for an hour and then ordered the march resumed. The column wound its way out the Seventh Street Road. As the men in the 76th New York Infantry passed by Fort Massachusetts, where they had departed on the summer campaign four months earlier, they were struck by what a change those four months had wrought. They had left the fort 800 strong, "with clean, new uniforms; the men in excellent condition, with happy faces, and panting for a fight." Now, as they plodded along on through the early morning of September 7, they counted 200 "ragged, gaunt, foot-sore and jaded" men.[21]

Hooker's orders were to continue his march to Leesboro, 7 miles north of the capital. He gave his troops another break around 8 a.m. to boil coffee and eat some breakfast, and then pressed on. Of all of the marches the Army of the Potomac made during the Maryland Campaign, the one on September 7 was the toughest. "All nearly exhausted," recorded Lieutenant Healy in his journal, adding that he "could not stop my horse without sleeping." Samuel Webster of the 13th Massachusetts complained that the sun was "almost intolerably hot." The dust rose in clouds, so thick that one soldier wrote, "I could hardly see sometimes." The high that day was 81 degrees, and the heat took its toll. Stragglers left the ranks in droves. Jacob Cox, whose Kanawha division followed the 1st Corps out the Seventh Street Road, "was shocked at the straggling" he witnessed. "The 'roadside brigade,' as we called it, was often as numerous, by careful estimate, as our own column moving in the middle of the road."[22]

The 1st Corps' troops were not the only sufferers that day. Two-thirds of the army was on the move. Reno's 9th Corps was ordered to follow Hooker to Leesboro. The 6th Corps and Sykes's division were both ordered to continue to Rockville, 10 miles from Tennallytown. Only the 2nd and the 12th Corps, at Rockville, and Couch's division, at Offut's Crossroads, were spared from having to travel in the scorching heat. Sergeant Thomas Evans of the 12th U.S. Infantry in Sykes's division offered a picture of the march's severity.

> On Sunday, September 7, 1862, we left our camp at Tennallytown, just north of Washington, and made the worst dry march of the campaign; yet we did not go above ten miles [it is approximately 10 miles from Tennallytown to Rockville]. But the road was fine white sand, the heat intense, and the perspirations started in gushes at every pore. I cannot adequately describe it; sweat did not stand like beads on the surface, but it ran off us in streams. We wrung our blouses as we would have done after a shower, and moisture trickled from every finger end. The clouds of dust clung to the wet clothes and made us look like millers. Water was rushed for the moment it was seen, and drunk in enormous quantities. It was useless trying to hinder this; remonstrance was useless against the overpowering thirst. After that men could not keep in the ranks, they had either to fall out or fall down . . . When we reached Rockville, two-thirds at least of the brigade were behind on the road, but almost the whole were up by tattoo.[23]

Many regiments merely mustered a handful by the end of the day. Samuel Webster counted just three stacks of muskets with his 13th Massachusetts when they halted. In the 56th Pennsylvania there were only 25 men present.[24]

McClellan's redeployment of the army did not signal the start of offensive operations; the movements were defensive in design. The three corps and Sykes's division at Rockville, as well as Couch's division at Offut's Crossroads, covered Washington, while the two corps at Leesboro discouraged the Confederates from mounting an attack on Baltimore. McClellan left Washington the afternoon of the 7th to transfer his headquarters to Rockville. In contrast to the claim he made after the war that he fought the battles of South Mountain and Antietam with a noose around his neck, a note he jotted to his wife before departing the city brimmed with self-assuredness. "I have now the entire confidence of the Govt & the love of the army," he wrote. "My enemies are crushed, silent & disarmed—If I defeat the rebels I shall be the master of the situation." As his large headquarters group clattered out Pennsylvania Avenue that evening, they encountered Secretary of the Navy Gideon Welles walking with his son. McClellan reigned up and rode over to shake Welles's hand. When Welles asked where he was going, McClellan answered that he was off to assume command of the "onward movement." "Well," replied Welles, "onward, General, is now the word, the country will expect you to go forward." "That is my intention," McClellan said, and rode off toward Rockville. That evening Welles wrote in his diary: "He has now been placed in a position where he may retrieve himself, and return to Washington a victor in triumph, or he may, as he has from the beginning, wilt away in tame delays and criminal inaction."[25]

During his absence from the capital, McClellan named Major General Nathanial Banks as commander of the forces designated for its defense. He had no illusions about Banks's ability as a general, but he also had no choice; Banks was the senior major general of the troops left behind. McClellan probably reasoned that leaving Banks in command posed minimal risks. In the unlikely event that the capital was attacked, McClellan anticipated being near enough to return and assume command. If the main body of the Rebel army had entered Maryland, then Banks was out of harm's way. There was even one positive benefit to Bank's appointment: it relieved the 12th of a poor corps commander.[26]

Although he moved his headquarters to the field, McClellan remained unconvinced that the Rebels had invaded Maryland in strength, or that it was not a diversion to draw attention away from a larger force concealed in northern Virginia. The reports that streamed into his headquarters muddied the picture rather than clarified it. Pleasonton, with his cavalry stretched to the limit, offered little useful intelligence. He remained persuaded—on unconvincing evidence—that Baltimore was the Confederates' objective. "I think I ought to be over at Mechanicsville [northeast of Rockville]," he wired to Marcy at 10:15 that morning. An hour later he reported that an Englishman picked up by pickets at Clarksburg had been brought in, who said that he had crossed the river on the 6th with "Longstreet's division," who had a "good deal of artillery and many wagons." This man also repeated what others had said, that the Rebel soldiers were "badly cared for, many of them without shoes." At 2:30 that afternoon Pleasonton forwarded news from paroled prisoners who stated that the Confederates "are moving on the road to Frederick, and are tearing up the rails on the road as they go." The Rebels had also occupied Sugar Loaf, which, although probably expected, was a blow nonetheless, as it now afforded the Confederates the advantage of that mountain's excellent observation point. Pleasonton also added—without revealing the source of this intelligence—that as of September 5 the Confederates had 50,000 men at Dranesville. He speculated that "this body may be kept there, to cross in this direction after we get engaged elsewhere."[27]

At 7:30 a.m. came authentic news from General Wool that the enemy had arrived in Frederick: "Brig. Gen. B. [T.] Johnson, with 5,000 infantry, came into Frederick about 12 p.m. yesterday," and "General Jackson followed with 25,000 at 2:30 p.m." Wool also added a new and alarming twist: "General Bragg was advancing up the Shenandoah Valley for Pennsylvania, with 40,000 troops." Brigadier General Julius White, now commanding the Martinsburg garrison, seemed to corroborate this report when, late that morning, he informed Wool that his outposts were being attacked. Although White later told Wool that the attack had been beaten off, the prisoners he questioned claimed that they were the advance of a column that "came through Manassas Gap and reached Winchester yesterday." An hour later, further questioning of his prisoners revealed that the Southerners "all agree that they are the advance of a column which left Leesburg three days ago for Winchester, to march thence in this direction, to support the column already in the vicinity of Frederick." It was not Bragg, then, but the enemy at Leesburg who apparently had the numbers to mount a multi-pronged offensive into Maryland.[28]

Intelligence also came in from Pennsylvania Governor Andrew G. Curtin, who had his own agents out seeking information. At 2 a.m. on the 7th he wired Wool a report from one of his agents who had an eye for detail. This stated that the Rebels had arrived in Frederick at 11 a.m. Some 3,500 troops were seen with 19 pieces of artillery. They "were shoeless, unclad," and "taking possession of all stores having shoes, army goods, or other supplies." Some announced their destination as Baltimore, but Jackson himself told an intimate friend of Curtin's informant that "he designed crossing into Pennsylvania, through Adams, York and Lancaster, to Philadelphia." Curtin's agent, however, believed Jackson intended to invade the Cumberland Valley to gather supplies, although the man did not say whether this was deduction or intelligence obtained from a Confederate source.[29]

The enemy seemed to be everywhere, headed for nearly every point on the compass: Baltimore, Philadelphia, Harpers Ferry, Martinsburg, the Cumberland Valley, and Washington. Among the reports were many pieces of highly accurate information. A good intelligence officer could have gleaned some consistent information from the diverse reports, but McClellan had no such person on his staff. Further compounding the problem of divining the accurate from the inaccurate was McClellan's own estimate of enemy strength before Second Manassas at 200,000. If the enemy had an army that immense, then they could have 50,000 men in Frederick, be threatening Harpers Ferry and Martinsburg, and still have a large army in northern Virginia.

One question was answered on the 7th—whether the enemy occupied Poolesville in force. Colonel John Farnsworth, commanding the only operational cavalry brigade in the field—consisting of the 8th Illinois, the 3rd Indiana, and the 1st Massachusetts—organized a reconnaissance by a detachment of the first two regiments to probe the Rebel defenses. He placed his nephew, Captain Elon J. Farnsworth, a brave and aggressive officer from the 8th Illinois, in command. The detachment made its way undetected from near Darnestown to Poolesville. Farnsworth led his command into the village at the gallop, taking troopers of the 5th Virginia Cavalry who were picketing the town completely by surprise. Farnsworth rode down two Virginians himself and took them prisoner. Only some 60 Confederate cavalry were discovered, and they beat a hasty retreat out of town. There was no evidence that any substantial enemy forces were nearby, and Farnsworth withdrew his troops after this brief skirmish.[30]

Pleasonton's report of 50,000 Confederates at Dranesville caught both McClellan's and Halleck's attention. After reading it, Halleck wired McClellan immediately, warning him "about stripping too much the forts on the Virginia side. It may be the enemy's object to draw off the mass of our forces and then attempt to attack from the Virginia side of the Potomac." McClellan thought so, too, and had already sent orders to Brigadier General George D. Bayard, at Upton's Hill, Virginia, to push his cavalry scouts out toward Dranesville to investigate.[31]

McClellan planned only minor adjustments to his position on the 8th. Until he heard from Bayard's reconnaissance, he did not wish to move the army too far from Washington. The 6th Corps were ordered to continue their march about 4 miles west of Rockville, to Muddy Branch, where they could support Pleasonton's cavalry operating there. Burnside was ordered to head to Brookville with both the 1st and the 9th Corps, but this movement was delayed until September 9. The cavalry performed the bulk of the work on September 8, as it had done on the previous days of the campaign. Pleasonton was called to headquarters very early to discuss the latest information about the enemy and help outline the cavalry's mission. McClellan wanted his mounted force to advance along a broad front to Barnesville, Hyattstown, Damascus, and Unity, as well as to picket the Potomac fords and scout the C&O towpath.[32]

Farnsworth's skirmish at Poolesville on September 7 and the earlier reports of enemy activity made it likely that the advance to Barnesville would meet resistance. Pleasonton gave this mission to Colonel Farnsworth. He was ordered to take his 8th Illinois and the 3rd Indiana, along with a section of Battery M, 2nd U.S. Horse Artillery, and move on Barnesville by way of Poolesville, dropping off detachments at the latter town to picket the nearby Potomac fords. Pleasonton planned to follow Farnsworth with the 1st Massachusetts, moving either on the direct road to Poolesville or by way of the road from Dawsonville to Bealsville. Farther north, Colonel McReynolds of the 1st New York was ordered to advance to Clarksburg and push four companies out to Hyattstown from there, send one to Damascus, and proceed toward Barnesville with his remaining five companies. The 1st U.S. presumably drew the mission of conducting the scout to Damascus and Unity, while the 6th New York, which was attached to Burnside's wing, marched that day to Brookville. The shortage of cavalry was still acute, but reinforcements were being sent forward. Elements of Colonel William W. Averell's old brigade were arriving daily from the Peninsula, and the 5th and the 6th U.S. Cavalry had also disembarked; parts of all of them were moving toward the front.[33]

The advance on Barnesville felt its way cautiously, so Farnsworth's task force did not approach Poolesville until midafternoon. Confederate scouts observed the Union column and sent warning to Stuart at Urbana, who ordered Colonel Munford to march to Poolesville and "drive them [Federals] from the place." Dropping off Lieutenant Colonel Richard H. Burks's 2nd Virginia Cavalry at Monocacy Church, Munford continued on with the 7th and the 12th Virginia, both of which were quite small, and a section of Captain R. P. Chew's Virginia Horse Battery. Munford beat Farnsworth to the crossroads, for as his advance guard rode into the village Farnsworth's column appeared, approaching from the direction of Dawsonville. Munford hastily selected some high ground northeast of town and unlimbered his two guns, a howitzer and Blakely rifle. He kept his two regiments mounted, placing the 12th Virginia in the rear of the Blakely and the 7th Virginia supporting Chew's howitzer.[34]

Chew announced his presence by opening with his Blakely when the Union troopers came within range. Farnsworth ordered up the two 3-inch rifles of Battery M. They swung into action and were soon bellowing away. While the guns thundered, Farnsworth maneuvered the 3rd Indiana, under Major George Chapman, to strike Munford's left. Chapman moved unobserved and his regiment suddenly burst over a hill and charged on Chew's two pieces. The howitzer crew managed to swing their gun around and deliver two rounds of canister into the Yankee horsemen, which caused Chapman's troopers to disperse to avoid the iron greeting. This, in turn, gave Major S. B. Myers, commanding the 7th Virginia, time to wheel his regiment around and charge the Federals. The 12th Virginia, which numbered only 75 effectives under Colonel A. W. Harman, also went forward against Chapman's Hoosiers. A stone fence checked the 12th's charge, but they worked their guns and pistols at the Federals on the other side. Then some of the more aggressive members of Harman's regiment opened a gap in the wall, and he led his men through to close with the enemy. But Farnsworth had brought up the 8th Illinois, and they suddenly appeared in the 12th Virginia's rear. The pursuers suddenly became the pursued. The rush to the rear threatened Chew's Blakely rifle, but some members of the 12th rallied momentarily to allow the gun to be limbered and withdrawn. The collapse of the 12th—which Munford, with disgust, reported as having "behaved very badly"—forced the Virginian to beat a retreat with his command toward Monocacy Church, leaving behind 8 killed, 16 wounded, and 6 prisoners. Farnsworth counted 1 dead and 12 wounded, all from the 3rd Indiana.[35]

Farnsworth sent two squadrons to follow Munford, and they had pursued the Confederates for nearly 3 miles when they came on Burks's 2nd Virginia.

Burks dismounted some sharpshooters, who turned back the Federals, but one man was killed and one wounded in so doing. Darkness put an end to the skirmishing. Farnsworth collected his command at Poolesville, while Munford reorganized his brigade at the crossroads at Monocacy Church.[36]

Some 9 miles to the northeast, McReynolds's 1st New York, advancing along the Georgetown Pike, rode into the chain of hills known as Parr's Ridge and occupied Clarksburg without incident by nightfall. Per his orders, McReynolds then sent four companies the 3 additional miles along the pike to Hyattstown, where they encountered pickets from Hampton's brigade and traded a few shots. Another company advanced 5 miles to the northeast and occupied Damascus.[37]

McClellan remained at his headquarters in Rockville on the 8th, monitoring the intelligence reports that arrived throughout the day and into the night. He was particularly anxious to hear from Bayard about his scout out toward Dranesville. If Bayard found no enemy, then the reports might be true that the main body of the Rebel army had entered Maryland. But until he had confirmation of this, McClellan dared not move the army farther from Washington. The news that did come in proved to be "vague and conflicting" and did not clear up the uncertainty of situation. Halleck telegraphed at 1:05 p.m. that Bayard had reported to him, through Chief of Staff Marcy, that Bayard had found no enemy soldiers at Dranesville and "that they have gone to Leesburg to cross." Halleck added his opinion that if the enemy had crossed at Leesburg, "it seems to me that a sufficient number of your forces to meet the enemy should move rapidly forward, leaving a reserve in reach of you and Washington at the same time." But this report was at odds with one from Fitz John Porter. McClellan had earlier telegraphed his trusted subordinate to see if he could get any news about Bayard. Porter replied that Bayard reported that the enemy "are in large force between there [Dranesville] and Leesburg." With this conflicting news at hand, McClellan telegraphed Halleck: "I am by no means satisfied yet that the enemy has crossed the river in any large force."[38]

Certainly some elements of the Army of Northern Virginia had forded the Potomac, and McClellan believed correctly that they were concentrated behind the Monocacy River. Their objective remained unknown, but McClellan felt more confident that his dispositions would block their movement toward any strategic point. He wrote to General Wool: "This army is now massed between Rockville and Brookville, in position to move on the enemy, should he attempt to go toward Baltimore from any point above here, to advance into Pennsylvania, or attack Washington." But McClellan remained concerned about the safety of Harpers Ferry. Although he felt prepared to follow the Confederates into Pennsylvania, he doubted that they intended to do anything so risky and ambitious. "I can scarcely believe that such is their purpose," he reassured a very nervous Governor Andrew Curtain of Pennsylvania, who was frantically attempting to organize a defense of his state's borders. McClellan considered it more likely that the Confederates would move toward Baltimore, to isolate and cut communications with the capital. To defend against this, it would be necessary to push the right flank of the army farther north and position it to strike the flank of the most likely enemy axis of advance—the National Road. Late that afternoon McClellan initially ordered Burnside to send a division forward to occupy Brookville, Goshen, and Seneca Bridge, with Sumner to move a division toward Middlebrook. After some deliberation, or perhaps on the receipt of intelligence that never made its way into the official records of the war, McClellan decided instead to order a general advance of the army. Burnside's wing was commanded to proceed to the line of Goshen, Cracklintown, and Brookville; Sumner's wing would move to Middlebrook; Franklin to Darnestown; Couch to the mouth of Seneca Creek, while leaving one of his brigades at Offut's Crossroads; and Sykes to probably follow Sumner, although his movements would depend on circumstances. The cavalry were to continue probing forward. On the right, McClellan hoped they could reach as far north as New London and Liberty. On the left, Pleasonton would continue his advance toward Barnesville and the mouth of the Monocacy River. It was a modest move forward, but McClellan primarily sought to better position the army to check a move against Baltimore or Washington, yet not move too far from the Potomac, thus denying any Confederate force concealed west of Dranesville access the army's rear.[39]

Shortly after McClellan had decided on a general advance, a 9:45 p.m. dispatch from Pleasonton arrived with news that the "most reliable information has been obtained": the Confederates had crossed the Potomac with over 100,000 troops, and they intended to press forward to Frederick; then to Gettysburg and York; and then, strangely enough, on to Baltimore. Who had provided this information? What was their evidence? Why in the world would the enemy march to York and then head back down to Baltimore? Pleasonton, typically, offered no clue as to where or how this "reliable information" had been obtained.[40]

Pleasonton's report piqued McClellan's interest. It was the largest strength figure yet for enemy forces in Maryland. He queried the cavalryman as to who or what was the source of the 100,000 figure. Even if the enemy had moved 100,000 men into Maryland, which McClellan continued to doubt, it remained possible, by his calculation of Confederate strength, that they could have that many men in the state and still have a formidable force in Virginia. The only significant Confederate leaders identified in Maryland thus far were Longstreet and Jackson. Lee remained unaccounted for. McClellan's overestimation of enemy strength and capabilities received some confirmation from a report that reached headquarters either late on September 8 or in the morning of September 9. Lieutenant John A. DeFord, a captured signal officer who had recently been exchanged, reported that during his imprisonment at Salisbury, Confederate officers he spoke with there told him that their forces around

Richmond during the summer campaign amounted to between 150,000 to 200,000. One "very intelligent officer" DeFord talked to said that the Confederates had 170,000 men available during the Seven Days battles, with the officer stating that he had obtained this information from the adjutant general's office in Richmond.[41]

Possession of Sugar Loaf Mountain would be a key to helping clear up the mystery about how many Confederates were in Maryland and where they were. Major Albert J. Myer, the army's chief signal officer, brought this to McClellan's and Chief of Staff Marcy's attention (the latter had left Washington and rejoined the army) on the morning of September 9. Myer pointed out that it would be of "great importance" if Sugar Loaf could be captured; so long as it remained in enemy hands it was of "great benefit" to them. McClellan—who, strangely, had seemed until then to be unaware of the observational value the mountain's summit offered—agreed, and he had Marcy send a note to Pleasonton asking whether it would be "possible to get possession of it without incurring much risk."[42]

Pleasonton was moving toward Sugar Loaf well before Marcy's note left headquarters at 10 a.m.; he had sent Colonel Farnsworth's brigade marching north from Poolesville at an early hour on September 9. The tough 8th Illinois led the way, accompanied by a section of Battery M, 2nd U.S. Horse Artillery, and (presumably) the 3rd Indiana. As they neared the crossroads at Monocacy Church, 2 miles north of Poolesville, Farnsworth saw what he took to be a squadron of Confederate cavalry drawn up to dispute its possession. This was the 12th Virginia Cavalry, which only numbered 60 to 70 officers and men. Farnsworth detached a squadron of the 8th Illinois under his nephew, Captain Elon Farnsworth, to see if he could get to the Confederates' rear and cut them off.[43]

Captain Farnsworth maneuvered his two companies to a position that offered a promising direction of attack and then advanced to strike Harman's Virginians. Colonel Harman re-formed his line and moved to meet the Federals, with the two forces colliding in a general melee. The horses churned up so much dust that one of Harman's men wrote, "We could see nothing." For a "few moments" Harman's horsemen held their own, but a Yankee bullet felled a Virginian's horse, and in the close quarters of the fight its death caused chaos. Several other men's horses were either hit by the falling horse or stumbled over it in the swirling dust, and these collapsed "into heaps." This event, and superior Union numbers, apparently turned the tide. Harman's men broke and scattered through fields and woods, leaving behind one dead, several wounded, eight prisoners, and their regimental guidon. It was a total victory for the Illinois horsemen, as they counted no casualties among their men or animals.[44]

Having easily cleared the crossroads, Colonel Farnsworth then relieved his nephew's squadron with another from the 8th Illinois, commanded by Captain John A. Kelly. They continued the march toward Barnesville, 3 miles to the north. At the edge of the village Kelly's troopers encountered a 10-man outpost from Captain Thomas Waller's squadron of the 9th Virginia Cavalry in Fitz Lee's brigade. The Federals surprised the outpost and captured them to a man. Someone managed to sound a warning of the Yankees' approach, for Captain Waller attempted to organize a defense, but Kelly's troopers drove them through the village. The Virginians fell back on the road to Urbana, "contesting every foot of ground on the way." On two occasions the fighting was hand to hand, but each stand by Waller's command was "frustrated and broken up." By the time Waller reached the eastern base of Sugar Loaf Mountain, 3 of his men were killed, 5 wounded, and 19 captured. Fortunately for the Confederates, Colonel William H. F. Lee, Robert E. Lee's second son, arrived at this point with the balance of the 9th Virginia, which included a squadron armed with carbines. Waller dismounted them in a skirmish line on a wooded slope, to cover the flanks of his mounted force. Kelly halted in front of this more formidable array and waited for Colonel Farnsworth, who brought up his horse artillery and had them lob shells at the enemy. Then Farnsworth sent Kelly forward to test Colonel Lee's strength. Lee's dismounted line nearly collapsed under the artillery fire. Captain Oscar Knight, commanding the skirmish line, began "leisurely retreating from the woods." Lee rode up and asked if Knight were wounded. Knight said no, but offered his opinion that the "enemy are in such force we can't hold this position." Lee thought differently, and he ordered the captain to hold the line, which Knight did for the rest of the day. But for Lee's timely arrival and bold front, Sugar Loaf might have fallen to Farnsworth that day.[45]

Denying the Federals Sugar Loaf Mountain provided some salve to the pride of the Confederate horsemen. But they could not ignore the fact that they had suffered hard knocks at the hands of the heretofore hapless enemy cavalry. The day's losses amounted to 4 dead, 5 wounded, and 27 captured. Farnsworth had not lost a single man.[46]

While Farnsworth fought his way to Barnesville, Pleasonton transferred his headquarters to Poolesville. Before his departure from Dawsonville, McClellan's dispatch asking for the source of Pleasonton's intelligence that 100,000 Rebels had entered Maryland reached him. Pleasonton replied that it had been "Captain [Elijah] White, a noted Secessionist who is a guide to the rebel army." White spilled the details after he "had been drinking a little," but, added Pleasonton, "they are firmly believed to be true by those acquainted with him." If McClellan had any questions about Pleasonton's ability to sift and gather accurate information, this correspondence should have settled them.[47]

The movement of the main body of the Federal army occurred without incident. Couch advanced two brigades of his division to the mouth of Seneca Creek, while Franklin made an easy march to the vicinity of Darnestown. Sumner occupied Middlebrook with the 2nd and the 12th Corps, and Burnside reached the vicinity of Brookville and Mechanicsville with the 1st and the 9th

Corps, except for Cox's division, which occupied Goshen and picketed Seneca Bridge and Cracklintown. Sykes's division was given a respite and remained at Rockville as a reserve. McClellan felt that his dispositions placed the army "in condition to act according to the development of the enemy's plans and to concentrate rapidly in any position." Should the Confederates move on Baltimore, he could throw his army on their flank. If Pennsylvania were their objective, he could move on their rear. If they proceeded toward Washington, his forces were well placed to meet all possible avenues of advance. Now, even though substantial enemy forces were present in Maryland, McClellan wrote to his wife that he hoped for "a little breathing-time to get them [his troops] rested and in good order for fighting." As for his strategy, he disclosed to Mary Ellen that "I hardly expect to equal the genius of Mr. Pope, but I hope to waste fewer lives & to accomplish something more than lame defeat." Having arranged his forces to cover the capital and Baltimore, McClellan wanted to hold his position for several days, straighten out his transportation situation, and allow reinforcements to join him. There were still several cavalry regiments slated to join him in the field, and he thought that General John J. Peck's division of the 4th Corps would be arriving from the Peninsula and could be sent to him.[48]

Pleasonton spent a busy day questioning loyal citizens of Poolesville and, one would suppose, some of the POWs Farnsworth had captured. Pleasonton learned of more rumors of large enemy forces still remaining south of the Potomac River. During the morning some of Poolesville's citizens told him of a large Confederate force near Arlington, Virginia, who were left behind "to menace Washington." They were probably the same "loyal folk" who had placed obstructions behind Captain Chamberlain and his 1st Massachusetts troopers during their September 5 skirmish with Fitz Lee and then welcomed the Confederates into town as heroes. That afternoon someone else spoke of a large force that remained in the Leesburg area. How someone in Poolesville would know of a Confederate force at Arlington, and how the Confederates could maintain a large force that close to the capital without being detected, either eluded Pleasonton or he was simply passing along everything he learned. Nevertheless, McClellan wired Fitz John Porter, whose 5th Corps was positioned south of the Potomac in the capital defenses, and asked him to investigate these reports.[49]

Pleasonton also learned more details about the composition of the Confederate forces at Frederick, which he related to headquarters. His sources told him that Jackson had crossed the Potomac at White's Ford with 80,000 men and that Longstreet had followed with 30,000. Included in this force were the two Hills (D. H. and A. P.) and R. H. Anderson. The officers and men who spoke to the residents of Poolesville said their objective was Pennsylvania. "They will not injure Delaware or Maryland," wrote Pleasonton, "but when they get into a free state they will lay the country to waste." McClellan received additional

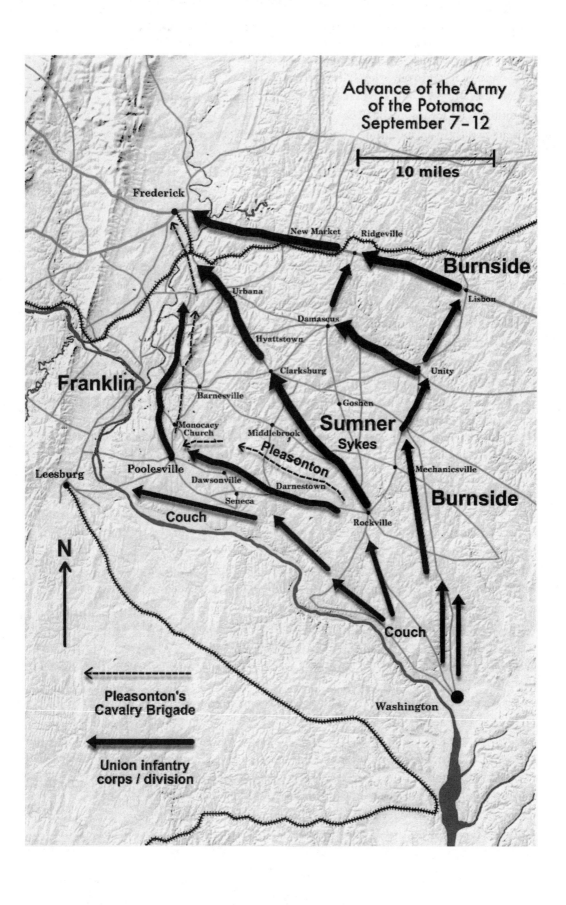

Advance of the Army
of the Potomac
September 7–12

10 miles

Frederick

New Market   Ridgeville

Burnside

Lisbon

Urbana

Damascus

Hyattstown

Clarksburg   Unity

Franklin

Barnesville

Goshen

Sumner
Sykes

Monocacy
Church   Middlebrook

Pleasonton

Poolesville   Mechanicsville

Leesburg   Dawsonville   Darnestown

Seneca   **Burnside**

Couch   Rockville

Couch

N

Washington

- - - →
**Pleasonton's
Cavalry Brigade**

→
**Union infantry
corps / division**

evidence that the enemy force at Frederick numbered over 100,000 from Thomas A. Scott, former assistant secretary of war and currently employed by the Pennsylvania Railroad. Scott wired word that the telegraph operator at Hanover, Pennsylvania, reported the Rebel army "to be over 100,000 strong" and within a few miles of Frederick. The operator had apparently formed this estimate from refuges that had fled the Frederick area, as well as a Confederate deserter who had made his way to Hanover.[50]

McClellan's hope for a "little breathing-time" was upset by a wire from Pleasonton, which reached headquarters at 7:30 p.m. The cavalryman reported that he had learned Jackson's headquarters that day were located at New Market, and Stuart's were at Urbana. From the sketchy picture McClellan had formed of the Rebel army in Maryland, he had concluded that Jackson commanded the main force—some 80,000, according to Pleasonton—at Frederick. If Jackson had moved his headquarters to New Market, 8 miles east of Frederick, it implied an enemy advance on Baltimore. At 10 p.m. Marcy wired Burnside with urgent instructions to drive in the Confederate pickets to Ridgeville "and beyond if possible," and to reconnoiter north as far as Westminster. If Burnside should find the enemy moving on Baltimore, he was to "let the column get well in motion, and then attack him vigorously on the flank."[51]

The events and reports of September 9 put an end to McClellan's skepticism about a significant number of the enemy having invaded Maryland. At 3:30 p.m. he wired Halleck that his latest information from the front "indicates the enemy are in large force near Frederick." Twenty minutes later Pleasonton's report arrived, giving the Confederate strength at 110,000. If McClellan questioned Pleasonton about his source for this report it did not survive, but presumably the cavalrymen's sources were more reliable than "the notorious Captain White," or the citizens of Poolesville. Thomas Scott's dispatch regarding 100,000 Rebels at Frederick added credibility to the intelligence Pleasonton had gathered. At 7:30 p.m. McClellan telegraphed Halleck that from such "information as can be obtained, Jackson and Longstreet have about 110,000 men of all arms near Frederick, with some cavalry this side." Characteristically, McClellan chose the larger of the two figures, and he omitted the fact that this information was gathered principally from Poolesville citizens and refugees from Frederick, not from stragglers and POWs. There was little science or logic in intelligence gathering at Army of the Potomac headquarters.[52]

Although McClellan acknowledged that the Confederates were in large force at Frederick, he continued to believe that his army had two separate Confederate forces to contend with: those at Frederick, and another group somewhere around the Leesburg area. Robert E. Lee had not yet been accounted for, and he might be leading this other force. "So McC has a difficult game to play," he confided to his wife, "but will do his best and try & do his duty." When McClellan penned his memoirs years later, he downplayed his uncertainty and his concern about a second Confederate army south of the Potomac, but these were very real at the time.[53]

When McClellan issued his instructions to Burnside, he may not have realized the fine defensive position Parr's Ridge offered his army, should the Confederates advance on Baltimore along the National Road. Parr's Ridge was a line of hills between Frederick and Rockville that ran north from Poolesville to Barnesville and on through Clarksburg, Damascus, and Ridgeville. The latter village was the key point on this line, for the National Road crossed Parr's Ridge here. Under the belief at headquarters that the Rebels were planning to march on Baltimore, Ridgeville suddenly loomed large. If it could be occupied before the enemy arrived, their drive on Baltimore might be blunted there. Headquarters bustled with activity in the middle of the September night as Chief of Staff Marcy drew up orders for a general advance of the army. The lynchpin for the plan was Burnside's wing. As if to underscore this, McClellan wrote out these instructions himself, while Marcy prepared those for the other corps. Burnside's orders required him to "occupy Ridgeville in force as soon as possible" by moving two columns, one by way of Damascus—although the route was left to Burnside's discretion—and the other via Cooksville. "No time is to be lost," wrote McClellan, for "I regard this movement as decisive, if successful." Meanwhile Sumner would move one of his corps to Damascus and the other to Clarksburg. Franklin was instructed to march to Barnesville; Couch, after leaving sufficient detachments to watch the Potomac fords near Poolesville, was to occupy that village.[54]

Had Jackson really been at New Market and planning an advance on Baltimore, it is difficult to imagine that Burnside could have beaten the Confederates to Ridgeville. Cox's division was the closest force Burnside had to that village, and they were some 12 miles away. The rest of his wing was nearly 18 miles distant. New Market, however, was only 7 miles from Ridgeville. Perhaps McClellan thought that by starting his army before dawn he could steal a march on the enemy. In any event, the entire plan—and McClellan's belief that the army's movement would prove decisive—merely demonstrated the poor quality of Union intelligence and how thoroughly baffled McClellan and his staff remained about enemy intentions.

Of course no battle developed for possession of Ridgeville. An enterprising captain, A. S. Cutts of the 6th New York Cavalry, attached to Burnside's wing, scouted from Damascus to Ridgeville on the 9th and drove out a few pickets from Fitz Lee's brigade. Two of Cutts's troopers forayed ahead to within 5 miles of New Market and found no evidence of a large Confederate force. Citizens that the New Yorkers questioned along the way said that the only Confederates in the area were Fitz Lee's cavalry brigade, which they estimated—with civilians' normal inflation factor—at between 5,000 to 15,000, and added that these horsemen occupied New Market. As for the main body of the South-

THE ARMY OF THE POTOMAC ADVANCES TO FREDERICK | 183

ern army, Cutts was told that it was "under Lee and Jackson" and remained around Frederick. Cutts's report reached Burnside around 4 a.m. on the 10th, moments after he received McClellan's orders. The Rhode Islander forwarded the Captain's report to McClellan and added that his scouts had uncovered no apparent movement of large bodies of troops in the direction of Unionville or Liberty, north of the National Road. "We cannot hear of their having moved in the direction of Hagerstown in force."[55]

Precisely when headquarters received this dispatch from Burnside is unknown. It was sent by telegraph and should have been received relatively quickly, but there was no reaction from headquarters until 10:30 a.m. on the morning of September 10. McClellan ordered an immediate halt to the forward movement, despite the fact the all the columns, except for Burnside's, which had been detained to await its overdue supply train, were marching toward their destinations. By the time the halt orders were received, Couch had arrived at Poolesville, the head of Franklin's column was entering Barnesville, Sumner had the 12th Corps closed up nearly to Damascus, and the 2nd Corps had arrived within 3 miles of Clarksburg. McClellan never explained his reasoning for halting the army's advance. He clearly considered it to be a risk, since the question of whether enemy forces remained in northern Virginia was still unresolved, but one that had to be taken to check a drive on Baltimore. It also seems evident that he did not yet consider the Federal army ready to fight a battle, and thrusting it forward might precipitate one.[56]

Instead of an advance by the entire Right Wing to Ridgeville, McClellan changed Burnside's orders to conducting a reconnaissance in force to Damascus and Ridgeville "for the purpose of ascertaining if the position at Ridgeville can be turned on the right, or if the ridge between Ridgeville and Damascus admits of the passage of the enemy between the two places, and whether your command and Sumner's can hold the two points against a large force of the enemy." Thirty minutes later McClellan amended Burnside's orders and instructed him that should he find Ridgeville to be a strong enough position to enable a division to make a vigorous defense, he had permission to keep one there.[57]

While attention at headquarters was focused on the army's right flank, Pleasonton sent news of developments on the left. At 8:20 a.m. on the morning of September 10 he reported from Barnesville that his scouts had learned of an apparent movement of enemy troops crossing back into Virginia from Maryland. He had no details but stated that a detachment (from the 8th Illinois) had been sent to investigate. Two hours later Pleasonton heard from the scout. There were no enemy troops at Monocacy Ferry (where the Monocacy River empties into the Potomac), but some 6,000 Confederates were reported to be at Licksville. This was Walker's division. The Illinois troopers investigated further, and at 1 p.m. they sent word that the enemy force numbered between 5,000 and

6,000 infantry, supported by 12 rifled guns, and was moving to occupy Sugar Loaf Mountain. Later that afternoon Pleasonton reported that the enemy force had marched down from Frederick on the 9th for the purpose of destroying the aqueduct at the mouth of the Monocacy River, but had failed to do so. These were the most accurate intelligence reports Pleasonton had yet managed to gather.[58]

The effort to take Sugar Loaf continued on the 10th. Pleasonton had been reinforced by the 6th U.S. Cavalry, commanded by Captain William P. Saunders, and he sent this small regiment, along with one or two companies of the 8th Illinois and a section of horse artillery, on a mission that bright September morning to capture the mountain. Munford's brigade drew the assignment of defending Sugar Loaf. Munford still only had two small regiments: the 2nd and the 12th Virginia Cavalry, with about 400 effectives at most, since the 7th Virginia Cavalry had been detached to accompany Jackson's column in the Harpers Ferry operation. Yet Munford made the most of the good defensive terrain and placed his men well. The 2nd Virginia took position behind a rail barricade that they threw up at a crossroad southeast of the mountain's base, and the 12th deployed on its right and rear. Saunders's Regulars came up against Munford's barricade, had one man killed and four wounded, and, to the disgust of the supporting 8th Illinois companies, "beat a hasty retreat." Part of the 2nd Virginia were armed with rifles for dismounted skirmish and sharpshooting duties, and they were so handy with these weapons that Pleasonton concluded that he was up against infantry. He dispatched a request to headquarters for infantry supports. McClellan had left to visit Burnside, so Marcy responded by ordering Couch to "hurry forward a brigade" from Poolesville to Pleasonton's support. "The mountain must be carried," Marcy added, even if it meant that Couch committed his entire division to the operation. Franklin—who Marcy thought had not left Darnestown, per the halt orders of that morning—was alerted as well to move to Couch's and Pleasonton's support should they encounter trouble.[59]

By the time the various communications made their way back and forth, the head of Franklin's 6th Corps arrived in Barnesville, making Couch's participation in the Sugar Loaf operations unnecessary. Franklin himself arrived at 3 p.m. and spoke with Pleasonton, who reported that the enemy defending Sugar Loaf was infantry in brigade strength, supported by 12 pieces of artillery "strongly posted" on the mountainside. The cavalryman believed the Confederates were disposed to make a "strong stand" in defense of the mountain. Franklin investigated and disagreed with Pleasonton. The enemy, he advised McClellan in a dispatch timed at 3:30 that afternoon, were a delaying force whose motive was "to protect their flank and rear from an attack by us at the Monocacy crossing at Greenfield Mills and to hold Sugar Loaf as a signal station." Franklin apparently felt that the day was too far advanced to make an effort to capture the mountain. He ordered up some of his infantry to relieve Pleasonton's cavalry and put his men into bivouac. It was unfortunate that McClellan did not organize a stronger effort to capture Sugar Loaf earlier in the day, for it would have been possible from its summit to have observed Lee's army marching west from Frederick and Walker's division marching south to cross the Potomac, so the mystery of where the Confederates were and where they were headed would have been resolved.[60]

The disappointment in not capturing Sugar Loaf Mountain was partly offset by the receipt of reliable intelligence about Confederate forces south of the Potomac River: there were none to be found. A 9 a.m. telegram from Fitz John Porter reported that as of September 8 there were no enemy at Fairfax Court House and only two mounted pickets were observed around Dranesville. Two hours later the 5th Corps' chief of staff, Colonel Alexander Webb, wired news from a cavalry squadron's reconnaissance that there were no Confederate soldiers for 10 miles out between the Orange and Alexandria and the Loudoun and Hampshire railroads. A telegram from Nathanial Banks arrived soon after Webb's, relating that an officer sent out to retrieve the body of General Bohlen, who was killed at Second Manassas, stated that there were no Confederate forces at Fairfax, Centreville, Manassas Junction, Warrenton Junction, "or at any intermediate point this side the Rappahannock." Banks offered his opinion that in light of this and other evidence, it "seems most probable that the main body of the enemy is between Leesburg and the mountains," by which he meant the Catoctin range in Maryland.[61]

By the afternoon of September 10 McClellan shared Banks's opinion. McClellan was now convinced that the main body of the Confederate army was in Maryland and that they were behind the line of the Monocacy River, massed near Frederick. Around midafternoon he composed a lengthy dispatch to Halleck with his assessment of the situation. The mystery of the Confederates intentions, he wrote, "exists no longer. All the evidence that has been accumulated from various sources since we left Washington goes to prove most conclusively that almost the entire rebel army in Virginia, amounting to not less than 120,000 men, is in the vicinity of Frederick City." McClellan estimated that he was outnumbered "by at least 25 percent" and asked for reinforcements from the garrison left behind to defend the capital. "I believe this army fully appreciates the importance of a victory at this time, and will fight well," but, he warned, "the result of a general battle, with such odds as the enemy now appear to have against us, might, to say the least, be doubtful." To even the odds, McClellan requested that one or two of the three corps defending Washington be sent to him, as well as Colonel Miles's Harpers Ferry garrison. If there were any Confederate troops south of the Potomac River, McClellan believed that they were so few that one corps plus the garrison troops could handle them. "But even if Washington should be taken while these armies are confronting each other," he wrote, "this would not, in my judgement, bear comparison with the ruin and disaster which would follow a signal defeat of this army. If we should be successful in conquering the gigantic rebel army before us, we would have no difficulty in recovering it."[62]

Since his restoration to command, McClellan had exhibited evidence that he was maturing and improving as a commander. He cooperated and communicated with his superiors, and when he led the army from Washington he kept behind a powerful garrison and made no complaints that his field army was too small. From the moment he arrived in Rockville he communicated daily—and frequently several times a day—with Halleck or the president to keep them informed of the situation at the front. His correspondence was businesslike, free of the bombast or the gloomy estimates of overwhelming enemy numbers coupled with demands for reinforcements that had marked his Peninsula Campaign posts. It seemed that McClellan had learned some lessons from his experience on the Peninsula and his temporary exile during the Manassas Campaign. But now, as contact with the enemy drew near, the familiar refrains from the Peninsula were sounded again: the overwhelming numbers of the enemy, the "momentous consequences" of the coming battle, the urgent need for reinforcement without which victory was "doubtful," and absurd counsel to his superiors. That an intelligent man, and a professional soldier of considerable experience engaged in a civil war, would profess that the fall of his nation's capital would not "bear comparison with the ruin and disaster which would follow a signal defeat of this army" can only be described as either marvelously naïve or preposterous.[63]

The strength figure of 120,000 was not derived from hard-nosed intelligence work at headquarters. It agreed with McClellan's thinking, so he accepted it. The 120,000 enemy soldiers and the belief that they intended to "hazard all upon the issue of the coming battle" in the Frederick area were based on a report from a church elder and the governor of Pennsylvania. Governor Curtin had telegraphed that morning that the aforesaid elder had passed through Frederick on Sunday, September 7, and reported that the Confederates numbered "not less than 120,000 men, and the part under Lee had not joined that army." "From all we can learn," Curtain concluded, "the enemy has selected his ground and massed his force near Frederick, to give you battle, the result of which will probably decide the future of our country." McClellan chose to agree.[64]

If Curtin was right and the enemy intended to hazard all in a battle near Frederick, then Burnside's Right Wing, which was nearest the city, was most likely to make the first contact. With a momentous battle possibly in the offing, McClellan felt the need to speak personally with "Burn." Shortly after completing his dispatch to Halleck, McClellan left for Brookville to visit Right Wing headquarters, leaving Marcy at army headquarters to monitor incoming dispatches and telegraphs. What McClellan and Burnside discussed can only be surmised, for neither left any record of it, but their decision was to thrust the Right Wing forward to New Market on the 11th. The orders for the remainder of the army were not nearly so daring. McClellan wired Marcy to issue orders to Sumner to occupy Clarksburg and Damascus with his wing and push a strong advance guard to Hyattstown. Franklin should take Sugar Loaf "if possible," but otherwise keep his corps at Barnesville. Couch was left at Poolesville, where he could support Franklin and picket the nearby Potomac fords. Sykes's division, with the pontoon train and reserve ammunition, was ordered to march to Clarksburg. Shortly before midnight, while still at Burnside's headquarters, McClellan wired Halleck: "I have ordered a general advance to-morrow. Send me up all the troops you can spare."[65]

McClellan's caution up to September 10 had some justification. He lacked reliable intelligence about enemy strength, location, and intentions. The tangles in his logistics were still being straightened out. He was short of cavalry, and he could not proceed too far from Washington until he was certain where the main Rebel army was; indeed, his superiors would not have approved a rapid advance that exposed the capital. But there is less excuse for the caution of the advance he ordered on September 11. He did not believe "that there is any large force of the enemy's infantry this side [east] of the Monocacy," yet he maneuvered his army as if there were. Ezra Carman thought that McClellan's caution was caused by the failure to capture Sugar Loaf Mountain on the 10th, since the enemy could view the movements of much of his army from its summit. McClellan recognized the importance of retaking Sugar Loaf, yet his orders to Franklin were to capture the mountain "if possible," hardly the orders a commander gives to a subordinate when a position must be taken.[66]

McClellan also had strong evidence that major elements of the Confederate force at Frederick had departed and were marching west, away from him. Colonel Dixon Miles wired from Harpers Ferry that afternoon that a column of 5,000 Confederates was marching on Hagerstown, Maryland. An hour later Governor Curtin forwarded a report received from a Hagerstown telegraph operator. "Jackson's advance within 3 miles of this place. He has only his own corps," the telegram announced. At 3:30 p.m. Curtin wired with news from a "paroled Union man" who had arrived in Hagerstown that day from Frederick and had passed "General Jackson, with a large force, on the National Road, between Middletown and Boonsborough, at 9 this morning." More reports confirming that a large Confederate force was on the move west of Frederick came in later that night. A scouting party from Harpers Ferry encountered the enemy "in considerable force" at Boonsboro, and a spy in the employ of General Julius White reported that "not less than 15,000" Confederate troops of all arms had marched through Boonsboro, probably destined for Hagerstown. In short, abundant evidence and multiple reasons existed for why it was high time to push the advance to the Monocacy River and make contact with the enemy, in order to find out what they were doing. McClellan failed to do so, partly because of his natural caution, but also because he believed that he was outnumbered and did not wish to precipitate an engagement until he had been reinforced.[67]

In his ignorance of enemy intentions and plans, McClellan believed that the army's movements on the 9th and 10th had foiled a Confederate advance, either on Baltimore or in the direction of Gettysburg or York, Pennsylvania. This was why he considered Burnside's advance to occupy Ridgeville to be decisive. Late that night he confidently expressed his opinion to Governor Curtin: "I think the enemy are checked in the directions of Baltimore and Gettysburg." If the Confederates were now moving toward Hagerstown, as reports indicated, then it seemed likely that they intended to enter Pennsylvania via the Cumberland Valley. "You should concentrate all the troops you can in the vicinity of Chambersburg, not entirely neglecting Gettysburg," he advised Curtin. "I will follow them up as rapidly as possible, and do all I can to check their movements into Pennsylvania. Call out the militia, especially mounted men, and do everything in your power to impede the enemy . . . You may be sure that I will follow them as closely as I can, and fight them whenever I can find them." The advice was sound, but if McClellan intended to follow the enemy as closely as he had in Maryland, then Governor Curtin had good reason to fear for the safety of his state.[68]

The army resumed its march on the 11th, in high spirits. After the months of campaigning in the hostile and depressing countryside of war-ravaged Virginia, the troops gloried in Maryland's lush, rolling landscape, with its tidy farms laden with fruit and crops ready for harvest and its clean, neat villages populated by people who smiled and cheered when they passed through. "We march through a well-cultivated, beautiful region," wrote Colonel Rutherford B. Hayes of the 23rd Ohio. "I never saw the 23rd so happy as yesterday. More witty things were said as we passed ladies, children, and negroes (for the most part friendly) than I heard in a year before." Lieutenant Charley Mills of the 2nd Massachusetts found Maryland "a paradise compared to Virginia." William Olcott, in Meade's division, enjoyed the "open doors, and happy cheerful faces," as well as "the hearty welcome everywhere extended to us." What a contrast, he thought, "to the vast and desolate fields, broken fences, and deserted dwellings we had been accustomed to in Virginia." The troops were delighted to find that most of the civilians they encountered were strongly pro-Union. "In this part of Maryland almost the universal sentiment was in favor of the Union," observed Isaac Hall of the 97th New York. To John Vautier of the 88th Pennsylvania, "it cheered our hearts to see the smiles of welcome bearing on us from every house by the way." It was no wonder, noted Hall, that "the spirits of the men became buoyant."[69]

The short daily marches (except for the grueling march of September 7, which no one ever forgot) also sat well with the men. "Things seem to be conducted with some system," wrote a 2nd Massachusetts lieutenant, "unlike Pope's style of doing things." Another infantryman, Captain Henry B. Young of the 7th Wisconsin, also found McClellan's leadership a refreshing change from Pope's. "I can tell you our army feels more confident and in better spirits, we have had something to eat and good wholesome water to drink, the men are not marched to death running back and forth, they feel more confidence in their commanders, and will fight better." The management of the army gave acting 12th Corps commander Brigadier General Alpheus Williams "more confidence than I have ever had in any movement of the war. We move slowly but each corps understands the others, and when we do strike I think it will be a heavy blow." The enlisted men agreed. "I believe the farther the army advanced into Maryland, the more warlike the division felt," wrote a member of the Pennsylvania Reserves. "Such was the feeling in my own case, at least, so much so that I arose from the bivouac one moonlight night and walked some distance out a sandy lane thinking of how beautifully we would 'whale' those fellows in the next engagement."[70]

The thousands of new recruits with the army did not find the daily marches to be the holiday stroll described by the veterans. "Much could be written about the discomfort of these marches," related Adjutant Fred Hitchcock of the 132nd Pennsylvania. The historian of the 16th Connecticut boasted with pride that their regiment made the 19-mile September 7 march in eight and a half hours. This, he noted, "was good marching for new troops." It was, but he failed to mention that only about 20–30 men out of nearly 1,000 in the regiment completed the march. Most of the soldiers subsequently caught up, but one member of the regiment wrote to a friend five days later that there were "a number we have not yet seen."[71] A captain in the 121st New York recalled how the rawness of both the officers and the men contributed to the massive straggling all the new regiments experienced in the first few days of marching.

We, in our inexperience clung to our knapsacks, blankets, overcoats, rubber blankets, and all the trinkets and 'whatnots' we had brought from home, and these made such heavy loads that they wore many a poor chap out; and by nightfall he was many miles in the rear, hurrying to catch up as best he could, generally with poor success. The weather was very warm, and the dirt roads, cut deep with the artillery, ammunition, supply and baggage trains, were shoe deep with powdered clay, and dust of a dark red color, and it would completely envelop a column of troops marching on each side of the roads, which were occupied by the cavalry and artillery portion of the army, because the infantry could go anywhere. So, loaded too heavily, and unused to work, the men would pluckily keep up until overcome by heat, or choked with thirst, smothered by dust, discouraged and exhausted, they would throw themselves down, and many a fine fellow perished in this way.[72]

The veterans offered little sympathy to the struggling recruits. Instead, they delighted in taunting them and found humor in their misery. "Day after day the regiment marched side by side with the Irish Brigade," wrote Henry P. Goddard of the 14th Connecticut, "and well do the men of the Fourteenth remember how they were jeered and guyed by the Irish Brigade, who called them blue-legged devils and assured them they could not be seen for the dust they would kick up getting away from Bobby Lee when he once got after them." The 121st New York were annoyed by the "constant shouting and ridicule we received from the old regiments," who referred to the New Yorkers as "paid hirelings," "two-hundred-dollar men," and "sons of Mars."[73]

The chief complaint of the rookies, as well as the veterans, was dust. From September 3 to September 16, no rain fell and the temperature climbed each day to the high 70s or low 80s. The roads dried to a "fine dust, which arose in almost suffocating clouds" when the army marched. Lieutenant Sebastian Duncan Jr. of the 13th New Jersey noted in his journal after one particularly toilsome march that "the dust [was] often so thick that we could scarcely breathe, or even see before us." Fred Hitchcock wrote that there were times when a man could not be seen a dozen yards away. Under such conditions a soldier needed plenty of water. But with thousands of troops on the move, water was often difficult to come by. Hitchcock recalled that "the water we could get was always warm, and generally muddy and filthy." Competition for water could become ugly. Hitchcock wrote that on their second or third day's march a fight broke out between the troops at the front of the column; one man was accidentally pushed into a well head first and killed. With so many thousands of troops competing for water—and often polluting what they found—it was not uncommon for men to have to travel up to 3 or 4 miles to find clean drinking water.[74]

Each day, though, the recruits grew stronger and wiser, so there was less straggling on the march. "This is the fifth days march for us over a hilly country through woods most of the time," Lieutenant Duncan wrote his mother on the 11th. "I have stood it much better than I expected and should feel first rate if we had a little more to eat." The men did better, partly because their bodies were growing accustomed to marching, but also because they learned to empty their knapsacks of everything except what was absolutely necessary. Andrew N. Terhune of the 13th New Jersey found that by September 9 he positively enjoyed being a soldier. "We have bully times out here," he wrote to his cousin. "We went out yesterday and caught four hogs and skinned them and roasted them over the coals this morning we fetched in another hog and some ducks and chickens we live first rate out here . . . Who would not be a soldier."[75]

Private Terhune's boast of stealing hogs, chickens, and ducks to supplement his army diet underscored a problem with both veteran and rookie regiments. The bonds of discipline, unformed as of yet in most new regiments, also broke down in many older troops as they marched through Maryland's bountiful countryside. The temptation of so many good things to eat proved irresistible, and soldiers drifted away from the ranks in large numbers. Sometimes food was bought. The men of the 61st New York made an effort on several occasions to purchase what they took. Charlie Fuller, a member of that regiment, recalled that one of his comrades "expressed his contempt" toward some Maryland farmers "for their simplicity in not charging more than they did for the amount furnished." James M. Perry in the 6th Wisconsin, who also paid for what he received, encountered a more business-wise farmer. He purchased some biscuits, cream, and meat from the man, but "Oh at what a price." Many, however, did not offer anything for what they took. On September 15, the day after the battle of South Mountain, the 83rd New York's historian recorded unashamedly that "as soon as the column halted the neighboring houses and gardens were ransacked for fruit and vegetables, and such other eatables as could be obtained." While lying under fire in the opening phases of the Battle of Crampton's Gap, members of the 96th Pennsylvania "stole milk, hams & preserves" out of a nearby house. Lieutenant Albert A. Pope of the 35th Massachusetts recorded in his diary on September 8: "All the hens within a mile have been bagged by our men. One man in the vicinity had forty hens, and boys took them all besides a pig. This morning some of the men went off at half past three o'clock and milked all the cows in the neighborhood." "Of course there is considerable foraging," wrote one New Jersey lieutenant, "and chickens, ducks, geese, pigs, and cows have to suffer."[76]

There were standing orders against this practice, but many officers simply looked the other way. Some even participated in it. J. Edward Shipman wrote that his colonel, Francis Beach of the 16th Connecticut, "and all the other officers steal everything they want to eat." Nonetheless, the more conscientious officers attempted to enforce the orders and uphold discipline. On the evening of September 7, when the men of Brigadier General Jacob Cox's Kanawha division made camp, they promptly raided nearby haystacks to feed their horses or use the straw for bedding. "I saw it and made no objection," wrote Colonel Rutherford B. Hayes. But when Major General Jesse L. Reno suddenly rode onto the scene, he was furious and pitched into Hayes's men, calling them "you damned black sons of bitches." He summoned Hayes and had sharp words for the colonel, but Reno was unable to make Hayes understand that as they were in a loyal state, foraging must be strictly controlled. Although Reno took no official action against Hayes, in Sumner's corps Colonel Oliver H. Palmer of the 108th New York was placed under temporary arrest for allowing his men to take straw from a haystack. Palmer submitted gracefully to his arrest, but, like Hayes, he did not understand its purpose: "I did not think there was any harm for the boys to get a little straw to lay upon, instead of in the mud."[77]

McClellan attempted to curtail straggling with a September 9 circular that provided very specific instructions on its prevention, as well as methods to be employed in dealing with stragglers. These general orders, and those already on the books, "were strict enough," observed Samuel Fiske, an intelligent New Englander who was serving in the rookie 14th Connecticut, but he thought that a "strict enforcement of the great principle of obedience seems to be utterly repugnant to the spirit of our citizen soldiers." Fiske believed the worst offenders were the veterans. From what he could tell, "the older the regiment, the more bold and expert in petty larceny," and, he opined, "the more undisciplined and disorderly." But Fiske only saw a part of the army, and there were regiments that behaved well in Maryland. Nevertheless, McClellan's orders, like Lee's, had little effect. The units with strong leadership upheld their discipline, while others continued to allow their men to descend on the good people of Maryland "like a cloud of locusts."[78]

September 11 dawned "gloomy," with a threat of rain. The army crept forward along a 30-mile front. Sumner's wing reached Clarksburg by 11 a.m., and Sumner advanced the 2nd Division of the 2nd Corps to Hyattstown, where they encountered some pickets from Hampton's brigade who were easily chased off. The 12th Corps peeled off and marched to Damascus. The movement of Sumner's wing was so uneventful that around noon McClellan pondered having Sumner continue his advance to Urbana. He sent a note to both Sumner and Burnside asking for their opinions. Before he received an answer from either, though, a dispatch from Sumner, timed at 11 a.m., arrived with news that Confederates "in heavy force" were reported around Urbana. This was only Hampton's brigade, but the words "in heavy force" killed any aggressive notions McClellan may have had. He wired Burnside that he had decided not to advance Sumner or Franklin on Urbana until the Right Wing's movement toward New Market "was decided." This was followed by what was becoming the standard caution to the wing and corps commanders: "Should you think that the taking [of] that place [New Market] will be likely to bring on a general engagement, you will not make the attack." Burnside was beginning to tire of the timidity of the army's advance. When he received McClellan's dispatch, Burnside took the initiative to loan Alpheus Williams some of his cavalry and suggested that he use it to scout toward Urbana.[79]

Burnside put his columns in motion at 6:30 a.m. that day, and by 4 p.m. Cox's hard-marching Ohioans, who led the way, had polished off a 14-mile march and occupied Ridgeville without incident. By early evening Burnside had two divisions at Ridgeville, Cox's and Willcox's, with Sturgis's and Rodman's 3.5 miles north of Damascus, on the road to Ridgeville. The 1st Corps moved from their camps around Brooksville and Mechanicsville and marched north to Cooksville on the National Road, where they then turned west and continued on to a point midway between the latter village and Lisbon. McClellan's noon message to Burnside, besides requesting any information the wing commander might have had about Urbana, also contained a warning, passed along by Franklin, that the main body of the Rebel army might be between Frederick and Liberty. Burnside received the standard message to move with "great care, feeling your way cautiously." But the Rhode Islander was properly suspicious of the report's accuracy, and he replied that evening that a company of cavalry had scouted to within 2 miles of New Market "without meeting any pickets." Locals told the company commander that the Confederates who had been there had left. Far from finding an army strung out between Frederick and Liberty, Burnside instead believed that "everything would seem to indicate the enemy have left the neighborhood." He nevertheless promised that "in accordance with your directions I shall move more carefully." His patience was growing thin, however, and at 5:30 a.m. the next morning he wrote to his chief: "In your communication of yesterday you spoke of a movement upon Urbana. My opinion is that a direct movement upon Urbana and the line of the Monocacy would develop the strength of the enemy, and in all probability drive him beyond it."[80]

The anticipated battle that day for possession of Sugar Loaf Mountain proved anticlimactic. Pleasonton worked out an elaborate plan with Franklin to outflank the mountain's defenders and trap them. Farnsworth's entire cavalry brigade, the 8th Illinois, the 3rd Indiana, the 1st Massachusetts, the newly arrived 12th Pennsylvania Cavalry (which was nearly half of Pleasonton's available cavalry), and Franklin's infantry corps were committed to the endeavor. But Munford spoiled everything by pulling out before the jaws of Pleasonton's trap could close around him. Although Pleasonton claimed to have "intercepted" the Confederates, the "fight" consisted of one of Pleasonton's horse batteries lobbing a few shells after Munford's retiring brigade and a volley fired in celebration by a party from Farnsworth's brigade when they reached the summit of the mountain. Franklin sent word to McClellan at 1:20 p.m. that Sugar Loaf was again in Union hands. The affair did not reflect credit on the Federals, particularly considering the small force the Confederates had left behind to defend Sugar Loaf. Everyone, from McClellan down to Pleasonton, had operated with entirely too much caution, and it did not reflect well on the ability of Pleasonton's cavalry to reconnoiter. This may not have been the fault of the troopers, but rather of their leader for failing to encourage his cavalry commanders to act aggressively.[81]

A signal party made their way to Sugar Loaf's summit late in the day and reported that they could see two regiments of Confederate cavalry in the vicinity of Frederick, along with a large force encamped opposite Point of Rocks (Walker's division). Except for these two forces, they could spot "no other sign of enemy in Maryland." This seemed to confirm the communications that had been steadily arriving at headquarters since September 10, namely, that the Confederates had departed from Frederick. General Wool forwarded a report from a civilian who had been in Frederick on the 10th, who stated that the Rebels broke camp at 1:30 a.m. "and marched in the direction of Hagerstown, Stonewall Jackson leading." This individual watched the Confederate army pass through Frederick from 5 a.m. to 9 p.m., when he left for Baltimore. Later in the afternoon, Colonel Miles sent word from Harpers Ferry that Jackson and Lee had camped at Boonsboro on the 10th "with 40,000 to 60,000 men," and that "the enemy is leaving Frederick." Governor Curtin reported at 11 a.m. that the telegraph operator in Hagerstown informed him that Rebel cavalry had arrived there at 9 a.m. on the 11th. Curtin wired again that evening with more details. "We have advices that enemy broke up whole encampment at Frederick yesterday morning, 3 o'clock, and marched in direction of Hagerstown, with over three hundred pieces artillery, large bodies of infantry and cavalry, Stonewall Jackson leading. Jackson is now at Hagerstown."[82]

Hagerstown was the gateway to the Cumberland Valley, and Curtin had no doubt that the reported arrival of Jackson there signaled an invasion of his state. He wrote to the president that "I have information this evening of a private character, which I deem entirely reliable, that the whole of the rebel army has been moved from Frederick, and their destination is Harrisburg and Philadelphia." Curtin requested that Lincoln "send here [Harrisburg] not less than 80,000 disciplined forces, and order from New York and States east all available forces to concentrate here at once." To McClellan he pleaded, "We shall need a large portion of your column in this valley [Cumberland Valley] to save us from utter destruction." Curtin called out the state militia with orders to assemble at Harrisburg, but he needed "an active, energetic officer . . . and one that could rally Pennsylvanians around him" to command this force. The governor wanted Brigadier General John F. Reynolds, then commanding the division of Pennsylvania Reserves in the 1st Corps, and he sent a note to Halleck requesting Reynolds. Halleck passed this on to McClellan, who made an effort to keep Reynolds with the army by asserting that his division was then supporting an attack on New Market—which was not entirely true—and that McClellan could not "see how his services can be spared at the present time." Halleck caved in to the pressure from Harrisburg and responded that someone else could command the Pennsylvania Reserves. Reynolds would go to Harrisburg and take command of the state's defenses. Reynolds's detachment infuriated Hooker, who fired off a letter to headquarters. "I request that the major-general commanding will not heed this order," he wrote. "A scared Governor ought not to be permitted to destroy the usefulness of an entire division of the army, on the eve of important operations." It was not quite that bad, however. Reynolds's replacement as division commander was George G. Meade.[83]

McClellan understood the potential danger Pennsylvania faced, but he was not as certain as Governor Curtin that this was the destination of the Rebels. Jackson's reported position at Hagerstown was just as well suited to a move on Martinsburg and Harpers Ferry as it was toward Pennsylvania. The enemy could destroy or captured the two garrisons, including all their supplies and equipment, and retire back into Virginia without a major battle. This would have seemed more logical to McClellan, who always thought in terms of conventional lines of operation. An advance into Pennsylvania would expose the Confederates lines of communications with Virginia. There was also sound reasoning in this; the enemy were highly unlikely to invade Pennsylvania with two Union garrisons on their lines of communications. Some evidence that Harpers Ferry, and not Pennsylvania, was the enemy objective arrived that afternoon from Captain William P. Saunders, commanding the 6th U.S. Cavalry. Saunders had conducted a reconnaissance to Licksville, Maryland, in the morning and met a member of an irregular Union organization called the Loudon County Rangers, who had just come in from Frederick. This man said that Jackson had left the city "for Harper's Ferry and that all the rebels are making for that point to capture General Wool." General Wool was, of course, not in Harpers Ferry, but Saunders's report offered some explanation for the Confederate force that was observed camped opposite Point of Rocks. It was known that this force had marched down from Frederick, attempted to destroy the aqueduct at the mouth of the Monocacy River, and then crossed the Potomac at Point of Rocks. If they intended to return to Leesburg, they could more easily have forded the river near Licksville. Crossing at Point of Rocks made it probable that they intended to threaten Harpers Ferry from the south. This was Chief of Staff Marcy's opinion. Marcy told another officer on the staff that he thought "to envelop and destroy this force [the Harpers Ferry garrison] was doubtless part of the enemy's plan."[84]

McClellan shared Marcy's concern for the safety of Harpers Ferry and Martinsburg. He also wanted reinforcements for his army, and the garrisons at these places, particularly Harpers Ferry, could add some 9,000 men. McClellan wired Halleck that morning and suggested that Colonel Miles's garrison be ordered to join him, for Miles could "do nothing where he is." It was a logical request, but the opportunity for Miles to safely evacuate his troops and equipment from Harpers Ferry and join the main army had evaporated the day the Confederates occupied Frederick. Halleck understood this and responded to McClellan's note by stating that "there is no way for Colonel Miles to join you at present." Miles's best course was to defend his position until McClellan could open communications with him. When that happened, Miles's command would be subject to McClellan's orders. Halleck offered up other reinforcements instead. McClellan had been counting on the 4th Corps division of General John J. Peck to arrive from the Peninsula. Halleck wrote that Peck's arrival had been delayed, but that he had ordered a large brigade of some 1,800 garrison troops under Brigadier General Max Weber to be sent forward the moment they had arranged their transportation. In reference to McClellan's dispatch of September 10, Halleck then asked that if the main body of the enemy were in Maryland, "why not order forward Porter's corps, or Sigel's? If the main force of the enemy is in your front, more troops can be spared from here." A clerk confused Halleck's last sentence, so that McClellan received it as "I think the main force of the enemy is in your front, more troops can be spared from here."[85]

McClellan lept at Halleck's offer of reinforcements. He wired back: "Please send forward all the troops you can spare from Washington, particularly Porter, Heintzelman, Sigel and all the other old troops." This raised eyebrows in Washington, for McClellan's request represented some 47,000 of the 73,000 troops in the capital's defenses and included all of the veteran troops. Halleck avoided the responsibility of this decision and passed McClellan's message on to the president, who patiently explained to the general that "if Porter, Heintzelman, and Sigel were sent you, it would sweep everything from the other side of the river, because the new troops have been distributed among them, as I understand. Porter reports himself 21,000 strong, which can only be by the addition of new troops. He is ordered to-night to join you as quickly as possible. I am for sending you all that can be spared, and I hope that others can follow Porter very soon."

Although McClellan surely wanted all the troops he asked for, Porter and his 5th Corps were favorites of his and their addition was most welcome. But the president's numbers for the 5th Corps were well off the actual mark. The 21,000 figure Lincoln gave was an aggregate number, not present for duty equipped, and it included Sykes's division, which was already with the army. Porter had two divisions besides Sykes's. They were Brigadier General George Morell's veteran division of some 4,700 effectives, and a new division that had not yet completely formed, composed of about 6,400 newly raised Pennsylvania regiments under the command of Brigadier General Andrew A. Humphreys. Thus the actual reinforcements totaled about 13,000, consisting of 11,100 from the 5th Corps and the 1,800 men of Weber's brigade. They were not nearly the force McClellan hoped for to meet an enemy that he believed substantially outnumbered him, but—perhaps reflecting a lesson learned on the Peninsula—he accepted them without complaint or a demand for more.[86]

The army's advance on September 12 was designed to bring about a concentration of force east of the Monocacy River, in the area from Urbana north to the National Road. If the reports of the enemy departure from Frederick proved false, then the army would be in position either to force passage over the Monocacy or defend behind it. But plentiful evidence had been accumulated that the enemy were gone, and Burnside received orders to "push on toward Frederick by the national pike and railroad as rapidly as possible." Yet at the same time he was instructed to be "extremely cautious" in his advance and keep flankers well out on his right toward Liberty and Westminster. Sumner's orders were to advance with the 2nd Corps to Urbana at daylight, and to send the 12th Corps to a crossroads south of Ijamsville, a tiny hamlet on the B&O Railroad southwest of New Market. Sumner also received the standard warning not to take for granted the reports that the enemy was gone, and to "be very cautious and careful to push out skirmishers and advanced guards well to the front."[87]

The operations around Barnesville and the mouth of the Monocacy River had drawn most of Pleasonton's cavalry toward the army's left. The main body of the 1st New York and the 8th Pennsylvania Cavalry, along with a section of horse artillery, were stationed at the mouth of the Monocacy. Several miles north of them, the 1st and the 6th U.S. Cavalry and another section of guns occupied Greenfield Mills, on the Monocacy. The rest of Pleasonton's command—the 8th Illinois, the 3rd Indiana, the 12th Pennsylvania, the 1st Massachusetts, and a battery of horse artillery—were at Barnesville. Pleasonton had intended to march to Licksville with his main body, then advance north on the west bank of the Monocacy to Frederick. But his orders instructed him to report early on the 12th at Clarksburg with whatever force he could assemble. Pleasonton ordered everyone to Clarksburg, save a squadron left at the mouth of the Monocacy and the 6th U.S. Cavalry, accompanied by a section of guns. This latter force he ordered to scout the west bank of the Monocacy from Licksville west to Point of Rocks, probing the possibility of establishing communications with Harpers Ferry, and then march north to Adamstown and Buckeystown.[88]

Franklin's 6th Corps were ordered north from Sugar Loaf to occupy an intersection about 2 miles west of Urbana, where they could cover Sumner's flank. To replace the departed cavalry and the 6th Corps, Couch was ordered to move one of his brigades to Barnesville. His other two were strung out between Offut's Crossroads and the mouth of the Monocacy, where they could keep an eye on the Potomac fords in that area. McClellan ordered Banks to send eight regiments from the capital's defenses to relieve these two brigades, so that Couch's division might be reunited. Halleck intervened and forbade Banks to move the regiments. The gradual shift of the Army of the Potomac away from the Potomac River toward Frederick, along with the departure of Porter's corps, left the general-in-chief nervous about the capital's safety, and he continued to worry about the possibility of another Rebel army lurking south of the Potomac. "No more troops can be sent from here till we have fresh arrivals from the north," he wrote to McClellan.[89]

The early morning of September 12 bore promise of another warm day; it was 70 degrees at 7 a.m. But it had rained during the night and settled the often-cursed dust, so at least the troops would not have to endure this particular misery on the march. Jacob Cox's division led the advance of Burnside's Right Wing. The division broke camp at Ridgeville, and they were on the National Road by 7 a.m., preceded by the 6th New York Cavalry and elements of the 1st Maine Cavalry. The night before, Jesse Reno took the initiative to send a cavalry squadron to New Market. They returned with "positive information" that Fitz Lee's brigade of four regiments and one battery "had left the area at 5 p.m.

that day [September 11], on its way to Liberty." There were no other Rebels nearby, although citizens told the squadron commander that Jackson "had been there with a very strong force" but had left for Hagerstown. Reno ordered Cox to press on and occupy Frederick. With the cavalry scouting ahead, Cox's Ohioans, marching with their "easy swinging step" and a good road to travel on, made excellent time. They reached New Market around noon. Here, all but three companies of the 6th New York Cavalry were detached to head north and investigate reports of "heavy bodies" of enemy cavalry in the Liberty area.[90]

With three companies of the 6th New York and six companies of the 1st Maine Cavalry leading the way, Cox pushed on toward Frederick. They met no opposition until around 2 p.m., when the cavalry approached the stone bridge that carried the National Road over the Monocacy River. Wade Hampton had arranged a reception here. Hampton was alerted about noon that the enemy was approaching on the National Road in "heavy force." Besides other pickets on the various roads approaching Frederick, Hampton had two squadrons east of the Monocacy on the Urbana Road. It was critical that he defend the bridge to cover the withdrawal of these squadrons and prevent them from being cut off. He had two guns already in position to cover the bridge, but he reinforced them with a rifled piece, supported by a squadron of the 1st South Carolina Cavalry under Lieutenant John Meighan. When the Federal cavalry and Cox's division came into view, Hampton's guns opened fire. Cox brought up some of his own artillery. The ground east of the bridge was higher, and the Federals had the advantage; their return fire killed two of Meighan's men. Using the artillery fire for cover, Cox advanced both of his brigades: Colonel Augustus Moor's 2nd Brigade and Colonel Eliakim Scammon's 1st Brigade. Moor's brigade led the way, dashing across the bridge, while the 30th Ohio of the 1st Brigade crossed at a ford a quarter mile north of the bridge. Moor deployed the 28th and the 36th Ohio in line on either side of the National Road. The 11th Ohio formed on the road in column, with a single gun of Simmond's Kentucky Light Artillery and a company of the Chicago Dragoons, an independent cavalry company attached to the brigade, in front. Scammon's brigade set up as a second line in support of Moor.[91]

While the Federals formed in his front, Hampton learned that his squadrons on the Urbana Road had safely pulled back. He ordered Meighan to slowly withdraw, commanding his artillery to limber and fall back through Frederick to a position at the base of Catoctin Mountain, where they could cover the National Road as it emerged from the city. It took time for Cox to get his division over the Monocacy and set in battle formation, so that it was 5 p.m. (or shortly after) before it resumed the advance. Moving at the quick step, the Ohio regiments advanced toward Frederick. Colonel Moor rode in front of the 11th Ohio, at the head of his brigade, accompanied by the Chicago Dragoons and Simmonds's single gun. Both sides of the turnpike were enclosed by stout post-and-rail fences that restricted the frontage the 11th could present. About a quarter mile from the city, a young staff officer from 9th Corps headquarters rode up beside Cox and his staff and made some remarks "in a boisterous way" about why the advance was not moving faster. Cox upbraided the impertinent young fellow with some sharp words, or at least he thought he had. Undeterred by Cox's rebuke and unseen by the general, he rode ahead to Colonel Moor and repeated his disapproval of the speed of the advance. Moor knew the officer was from corps headquarters and thought his words implied Reno's personal displeasure with Moor's handling of the advance. Stung by this criticism, Moor suddenly dashed ahead of his brigade line, leading the Dragoons and Simmond's gun into Frederick.[92]

Moor's party came thundering into the eastern edge of the city and quickly unlimbered the gun. Then, to the horror of Hampton and with what the South Carolinian described as "unparalleled atrocity," the gun crew opened fire on Hampton's troopers retiring down the busy city street. Hampton reacted at once and sent Lieutenant Meighan's squadron, plus the brigade provost guard of 40 men under Captain J. F. Waring, straight at Moor and his Dragoons. Either surprised by the ferocity of the Confederate charge or unwilling to cross sabers with the enemy, the Federals "scattered in every direction." Such was the hurry of the Chicago horsemen to get away that one "stupid trooper" rode between the gunner and the taut lanyard he had attached to Simmond's gun. The blow jerked the lanyard and discharged the gun, which was loaded with canister, killing two Federals and wounding six. Meighan's and Waring's men scooped up seven prisoners, including Colonel Moor, who was unhorsed in the melee and unable to escape. Moor's capture, oddly enough, would prove a benefit to the Federals two days later.[93]

The 11th Ohio rushed forward to Moor's rescue, but by the time they reached the scene of the brief melee Hampton's horsemen had vanished with their prisoners. Frederick's brief occupation under Confederate rule was over, and the people poured out into the streets to welcome the Union Army. The 11th Ohio led the march into the city, and they were greeted with the "most enthusiastic demonstrations of joy." Citizens emerged with "cakes, pies, bread, coffee, apples, peaches," and other delicacies. The men in the 12th Ohio were delighted to find that there were plenty of pretty women in the city and that they seemed enthusiastic, "even to wildness," at the troops' arrival. The suntanned and dusty soldiers, tired from their 17-mile march, were suddenly reinvigorated by hugs and kisses from pretty girls. One young woman, caught up in the excitement of the moment, declared loudly that she could kiss the whole army, whereupon a sergeant suggested she could begin with him. The sergeant's looks—and perhaps his body odor—apparently curbed her enthusiasm for kissing any other soldiers. U.S. flags appeared everywhere. Lewis Steiner, the staunch U.S. Sanitary Commission doctor, thought that "a new life seems to have infused into the people."

Colonel Rutherford B. Hayes mentioned the "fine ladies, pretty girls, and children [who] were in all the doors and windows waving flags and clapping hands." He concluded, as did many, that "it is pleasant to be so greeted."[94]

Shortly after Cox's men made their entry into Frederick, McReynolds's cavalry brigade arrived on the Urbana Road, and around 6 p.m. Pleasonton came in with Farnsworth's brigade. The cavalry passed through the city and went into camp a mile west of it, astride the National Road and within sight of the campfires of Hampton's brigade on nearby Catoctin Mountain. The rest of the army made their bivouac east of the Monocacy River. Burnside's wing encamped along the National Road, stretching from the Monocacy to Ridgeville. The 2nd Corps occupied Urbana, and the 12th Corps moved up to nearby Ijamsville Crossroads. Franklin reached his destination, the crossroads 2 miles west of Urbana, by 4 p.m., and Couch arrived at Barnesville with those element of his division that were not scattered to watch the Potomac fords.[95]

"The enemy have retired in the direction of Hagerstown," wrote Brigadier General George Meade to his wife that evening. "Where they have gone, or what their plans are, is as yet involved in obscurity, and I think our generals are a little puzzled." Meade was right. McClellan was deeply perplexed. At 10 a.m. that morning, McClellan had telegraphed Halleck that he felt "perfectly confident that the enemy has abandoned Frederick, moving in two directions, viz, on the Hagerstown and Harper's Ferry roads." Later that afternoon McClellan revealed to his wife that he thought that the "secesh is skedadelling & I don't think I can catch him unless he is really moving into Pennsylvania. I begin to think he is making off to get out of the scrape by recrossing the river at Williamsport—in which my only chance of bagging him will be to cross lower down & cut into his communications near Winchester. He evidently don't want to fight me—for some reason or other." Reports accumulated during the day to strengthen this opinion. Governor Curtin wired the president late that afternoon that "I have advices that Jackson is crossing the Potomac at Williamsport, and probably the whole rebel army will be drawn from Maryland." Lincoln forwarded this message to McClellan, with the additional news that the telegraph line to Wheeling had been cut and nothing had been heard from either Harpers Ferry or Martinsburg. Captain Saunders, commanding the 6th U.S. Cavalry, reported from his scouting mission to Point of Rocks that Walker's division had crossed back into Virginia. Were the enemy "skedadelling" or attempting to encircle Harpers Ferry? "My movements tomorrow will be dependent upon information to be received during the night," McClellan wired to Halleck that afternoon. But who would provide this information? The cavalry was not in contact with the enemy. The only other sources were civilians or Governor Curtin's agents. McClellan either needed to close more rapidly with the enemy and force them to reveal their intentions, or be the beneficiary of an intelligence-gathering breakthrough. Neither seemed likely on that warm September evening in Maryland.[96]

Although McClellan promised Halleck that "everything moves at daylight to-morrow [September 13]," he did not know in which direction to send his army, so he planned only minor movements by the main body while his cavalry searched for information. Pleasonton's small cavalry force drew multiple assignments. He was to advance over Catoctin Mountain to Pleasant Valley, which lay between Catoctin Mountain and South Mountain, with his main force and attempt to ascertain the situation at Harpers Ferry. At the same time he was to determine whether the main body of the Rebels had used the National Road when they left Harpers Ferry, and verify, if possible, whether Jackson had crossed the Potomac at Williamsport. McClellan also ordered Pleasonton to send a force north of Frederick to investigate the reports of Confederate troops supposedly moving through Lewistown and Mechanicstown—approximately 8 and 14 miles north of Frederick, respectively—and determine whether they were attempting to threaten the army's rear. McClellan anticipated that the enemy would leave some force to defend the pass where the National Road crossed Catoctin Mountain, so to clear the way for Pleasonton, McClellan ordered Burnside's 9th Corps to march at daylight and secure the pass.[97]

While Pleasonton and the 9th Corps probed ahead to Pleasant Valley, the 1st, the 2nd, and the 12th Corps were ordered to move up and mass around Frederick. Franklin's orders were to cross the Monocacy River and occupy Buckeystown, 5 miles south of Frederick. Couch, after looking to the security of Edward's and Conrad's ferries, would march to Licksville, where he could cover Noland's Ferry as well as the River Road. When this concentration was complete, the army would be poised to move in any direction from the Frederick road hub.[98]

It had taken the Army of the Potomac six days to march the approximately 45 miles from Washington to Frederick. The speed of this movement gave McClellan's critics an opportunity to claim that it was the Peninsula all over again, with the army creeping forward at a glacial pace. But this ignores the circumstances under which the advance was made and fails to give McClellan credit where credit is due. He reorganized two defeated armies in five days and put them in the field in a serviceable condition, although not in the condition that McClellan would have liked. Some historians have treated this as a trivial event, but it was no simple accomplishment. Unlike his demeanor on the Peninsula, McClellan made no complaint about the size of his force or its condition. He led it forward. His logistics were still in knots, and he lacked sufficient cavalry to scout the Maryland front, particularly the Virginia front. Largely because of McClellan having only a few cavalry, until September 11 it was unclear whether the main body of the Confederate army had invaded Maryland or remained south of the Potomac River. Even if McClellan had wanted to go charging off after the Confederates he knew were at Frederick, Halleck (and probably Lincoln) would have forbidden such a rapid advance until the question of what Rebel forces remained south of the Potomac was solved. McClellan testified to this before the Committee on the Conduct of the War, stating that he and Halleck had agreed before he left Washington that the army would "proceed carefully until we gained accurate information about the enemy, and to follow such a direction as would enable us to cover Washington, and, if necessary, Baltimore."[99]

By September 11, when McClellan was certain that the main Confederate army was in Maryland and that no large forces remained in Virginia, there is less excuse for his caution. He failed at first to appreciate the importance of capturing Sugar Loaf Mountain, and then, when the attack finally began, it was ridiculously timid. Elsewhere, no real effort was made at any point on the line to push or press the enemy to develop their position, or to determine their strength. Every move was made with defense in mind. Even Burnside, no great lion of offensive action, grew frustrated at the crawling pace his commander set. That the army finally did advance to the line of the Monocacy on September 11 was not due to a sudden burst of aggressiveness by McClellan. Instead it was Jesse Reno's forceful movement along the National Road that revealed how weak the Confederates in Frederick really were and led to the army's entry into the city. An advance to the Monocacy River that day might also have rendered help for the soon-to-be-encircled garrisons at Martinsburg and Harpers Ferry. Once the Potomac fords in the Leesburg area were denied to the Confederates, Lee had to shift his communications to the Shenandoah Valley, which meant that the Valley garrisons were in great danger. But it also meant that until Lee did something about them, the Valley garrisons were on Lee's rear and on his communications lines. Pressing assertively on Lee's rear would have taken advantage of this situation and might have upset Lee's carefully laid plans. Halleck bears the responsibility for leaving these garrisons in highly vulnerable positions, but McClellan did not take advantage of the opportunity their presence offered, nor did he afford them the support they surely needed with his tentative advance on Frederick.[100]

McClellan had displayed growth as a general, but the same careful and methodical commander of the Peninsula Campaign reemerged as the army moved closer to contact with the enemy. Just as Lee's aggressive style trickled down to his men, so did McClellan's tentativeness, cultivating timidity and caution in his subordinates. Constant warnings to "feel their way cautiously"; capture a position "if possible," "without the risk of losing your command"; and other such warnings promoted an atmosphere of defensive thinking and discouraged independent action and initiative. With a group of highly aggressive, head-strong subordinates, keeping a tight rein on them might have been necessary, but with the likes of Burnside, Franklin, and Sumner, it encouraged rigid and unimaginative leadership and defeated the flexibility the wing command structure provided.

The occupation of Frederick on September 12 by the Army of the Potomac marked the end of the first phase of the Maryland Campaign. McClellan had achieved his defensive mission: he had relieved the capital and Baltimore from the danger of attack. Now he had to ensure the security of Pennsylvania, clear Maryland of the enemy, and, since Halleck had insisted on leaving the Valley garrisons intact, relieve them. McClellan assuredly would have been satisfied if he could accomplish these objectives by maneuver rather than by battle, but the president reminded him that damaging the Confederates was also part of his mission. Lincoln wired McClellan that afternoon: "Please do not let him get off without being hurt." Given the excessive caution the general had evidenced in the final advance on Frederick and his modest plans for September 13, it was unlikely that the Confederates could be brought to battle, unless it was by their choice or by some stroke of great fortune.

6

Harpers Ferry

"To the last extremity"

arpers Ferry sits at the junction of two mighty rivers, the Shenandoah and the Potomac. In 1733 Peter Stevens came and settled here from Pennsylvania, establishing a ferry service across the rivers. It came to be called Peter's Hole, because Stevens' settlement sat at the bottom of three elevated locales: Loudoun Heights to the south, Maryland Heights to the north, and Bolivar Heights to the west. Robert Harper, an architect and millwright from Philadelphia, arrived in 1747, purchased the land, improved the ferry service, and built a gristmill. Harper's improvements attracted others and a small village grew. Growth and progress were slow at what became known as Harpers Ferry until 1794, when President George Washington selected this scenic setting as the site for one of the new United States government's armories. Washington considered Harpers Ferry "the most eligible spot on the [Potomac] river" for this facility. It had the necessary water power, with iron ore deposits nearby and large hardwood forests that could supply the charcoal to fuel the forges. Construction on the armory began in 1796. Buildings sprang up along the shelf of land that hugged the Potomac and ran down nearly to the point where the rivers met. Over the next six decades the armory thrived and grew, so that by 1859 it included 20 workshops and offices, and more than 400 employees. As the armory expanded, so did Harpers Ferry. The B&O Railroad and C&O Canal both served the community, arriving in the 1830s. Besides the armory, the town and surrounding environs now boasted a flour mill, an iron foundry, a cotton mill, machine shops, and some 3,000 residents, of whom roughly 1,250 were "free coloreds" and 88 were listed as slaves. The town spread uphill from the river-bench land to Camp Hill, which sits 300 feet above the rivers. A mile west of Camp Hill the town of Bolivar was established, near the eastern base of Bolivar Heights.[1]

The happy, uneventful pace of life in Harpers Ferry was shaken in the fall of 1859 by John Brown's raid. The good times unraveled permanently in the weeks after the nation plunged into Civil War in 1861. The Confederates moved quickly to seize the armory and arsenal, and to cut the railroad line and the canal. U.S. soldiers stationed at the armory attempted to destroy the buildings before they pulled out, but they did not do a very thorough job of it; the Confederates salvaged much of the machinery—which they transported to Richmond and North Carolina—and many of the small arms. A stern, humorless Virginia colonel named Thomas J. Jackson soon arrived to take command of the Confederate force assembled there. They remained until mid-June, when the approach of an 18,000-man Union army under Major General Robert Patterson caused Jackson to withdraw, but not before destroying the railroad bridge spanning the Potomac.

Federal soldiers took the place of the Confederate troops. They repaired the railroad bridge and the B&O resumed operations, but the long railway line was exposed at many points to forays by Confederate horsemen, using the Shenandoah Valley as a base. To protect the B&O, the Union army formed a unit called the Railroad Brigade on March 9, 1862, with headquarters at Harpers Ferry. The mission of this unglamorous outfit was to protect nearly 380 miles of railroad track. The brigade commander was a hard-bitten, prewar regular army colonel named Dixon Stansbury Miles.[2]

By 1862 Dixon Miles was 58 years old and had been a soldier for 43 years. He left his home in Maryland at age 15 to attend West Point. He graduated five years later, in 1824, and joined the infantry. In the war with Mexico he proved to be a brave and tough leader, earning brevets for gallantry at Palo Alto and Monterrey. His postwar service landed him principally on the frontier, in New Mexico Territory, where he saw service in campaigns against the Apache and Navajo. William W. Averell, who served with Miles in New Mexico in 1858, found him "surprisingly vigorous in action" despite his stooped shoulders and grizzled hair. Averell also learned that Miles was "undaunted in the face of hardships," was "ready to accept any responsibility," but "was nevertheless a strict constructionist of orders," which would reveal itself at Harpers Ferry. Sigmund Elble, another officer who served with Miles around the same time, recalled that Miles liked his liquor. After an 1857 expedition against the Apache, Elble brought charges of drunkenness against Miles. A court-martial convened and Miles was cleared, which, according to Elble, was because the prosecuting witness did not "drink out of the same bottle" as Miles and so could not prove he was drinking alcohol.[3]

In January 1859 Miles was promoted to colonel, one of only 22 in the U.S. Army, and awarded command of the 2nd U.S. Infantry. He led his regiment east after the outbreak of the Civil War and, because of his seniority in the army, was assigned to lead the 5th Division of Major General Irvin McDowell's army. Miles's division was held in reserve during First Manassas, but the action proved ruinous to his army career. Miles suffered from dysenteric diarrhea, for which his medical director prescribed opium, quinine pills, and brandy. The colonel apparently imbibed the later more liberally than the doctor ordered; combined with opium, it is not surprising that some of his subordinates observed him reeling in the saddle late in the day, seemingly incapable of commanding his division. Colonel Israel B. Richardson, one of his brigade commanders and an old adversary from Miles's New Mexico days, accused him of being drunk. McDowell relieved Miles of command after learning of the confusion existing in his division. The charge of drunkenness spread rapidly through the army and in Washington, and Miles requested a court of inquiry to clear his name. The court found that although Richardson was justified in declaring Miles to be drunk, there was insufficient evidence to convict Miles before a general court-martial, and that such a court "could only be organized in this army with the greatest inconvenience at present." In other words, the Army had no interest in making a public spectacle of a soldier who had given them four decades of service. Instead, they would tuck him away somewhere safe. That place was Harpers Ferry, in command of the Railroad Brigade, where the routine, garrison-type duty seemed better suited to Miles's limitations.[4]

Miles's new command consisted principally of second-line units and new units in need of some seasoning before they were sent to the active front. They were expected to garrison key points on the B&O Railroad and fight off an occasional Confederate cavalry raid. If the real war ever approached Harpers Ferry, the active field army was supposed to relieve the Railroad Brigade from the need to do any serious fighting. Although the armory no longer existed, Harpers Ferry still possessed strategic value. Besides the B&O Railroad, the Winchester and Potomac Railroad connected Harpers Ferry with Winchester, making it a suitable point as a base of operations in the lower Shenandoah Valley. The bridges there provided an important crossing point of the Potomac for operations in Maryland or Virginia. Situated as it was—at the lower end of the Shenandoah Valley and the base of the Cumberland Valley, which extends into Pennsylvania—Federal troops positioned at Harpers Ferry also threatened the communications of any Confederate force that attempted to move north of the Potomac River west of the Blue Ridge.

The problem with Harpers Ferry is that it was difficult to defend, since it is surrounded by high ground. Maryland Heights, which forms the southern end of Elk Ridge, rises to 1,380 feet and completely dominates the Virginia town. Whoever held Maryland Heights controlled Harpers Ferry. Across the Potomac and Shenandoah rivers, Loudoun Heights also commands the town. At 1,200 feet high, it forms the northern end of the Blue Ridge. Bolivar Heights is about a mile west of Harpers Ferry. It is a ridge of high ground, reaching 700 feet at its highest elevation, running south from the Potomac to the Charlestown Turnpike. South of the pike the ridge declines into broken terrain cut up by ravines running down to the Shenandoah. Thus properly defending Harpers Ferry from attack meant occupying Maryland, Loudoun, and Bolivar Heights, a perimeter of some 6–7 miles. It also meant that geography would divide the defender into three separate groups, with a river between each force. As one Union officer observed, "Harpers Ferry is not defensible by a force inferior to that attacking it, unless the surrounding heights be well fortified, and each of them held by a force sufficient to maintain itself unsupported by the other."[5]

The real war arrived unexpectedly at Harpers Ferry's doorstep in late May 1862, when Stonewall Jackson led his Army down the Shenandoah Valley to the front of Bolivar Heights. Washington quickly dispatched Brigadier General Rufus Saxton to take command at Harpers Ferry and organize its defense, a clear statement of the War Department's level of confidence in Miles. Saxton's actions at Harpers Ferry were a textbook example of how to defend the position. With a force of some 7,000 men and a naval battery of Dahlgren guns, Saxton placed the heavy guns on the western slope of Maryland Heights, where they commanded Bolivar Heights, and swept the ground between these heights and Camp Hill. He deployed his infantry on Bolivar Heights. When he received a report that enemy troops were observed on Loudoun Heights, Saxton promptly sent a force over to investigate. They were fired on, so the next day Saxton shelled the heights with the naval guns, causing the enemy to withdraw. Saxton also kept his cavalry force constantly probing and reconnoitering, and discovered that Jackson planned to execute a flanking movement, sending one division across the Shenandoah to occupy Loudoun Heights, and another across the Potomac to threaten Maryland Heights and Saxton's communications.

Saxton responded by withdrawing his troops from Bolivar Heights and deploying them on Camp Hill. Contracting his line freed up a brigade, which he sent to Maryland Heights to protect the naval battery from an attack on its rear. The shortened line on Camp Hill gave Saxton two advantages, which he listed in his after-action report. First, "being much less extended, it could be held by a smaller force, the enemy from the nature of the ground being unable to bring into action a larger force than our own." Second, "it would enable us to bring our naval battery on the Maryland Heights to bear on the enemy as they advanced down the declivity of Bolivar Heights into the valley which separates it from Camp Hill." Jackson probed Saxton's position the next day, but with reports of two different Union forces converging on him, he decided to withdraw. Saxton's defenses were not tested, but this was a testament to his dispositions. He gave Jackson no opening to exploit. Among those who served Saxton and witnessed his skillful handling of the Harpers Ferry defense was Dixon Miles, but, as events would demonstrate, he learned very little.[6]

With the threat over, most of the troops that were rushed to Harpers Ferry's defense were withdrawn. Miles was left with a brigade consisting of the 8th New York Cavalry (who had not yet received their horses), elements of the 1st Maryland Potomac Home Brigade, the 11th New York State Militia (whose enlistments were about to expire), and a squadron of the 1st Maryland Potomac Home Brigade Cavalry. All told he had 1,176 foot soldiers (including the 8th New York) and 182 cavalry. The naval guns remained on Maryland Heights, but there were no artillerymen to serve them. Miles was obliged to scatter his forces to protect the railroads. The 11th New York State Militia were distributed between Harpers Ferry and Winchester, and the 1st Maryland Potomac Home Brigade was parceled out in company outposts between Harpers Ferry and Edward's Ferry and north to Frederick. The 8th New York Cavalry, disgruntled over their long wait for horses, turned mutinous and positively refused to do any work until they received them. On June 9, 78-year-old Major General John Wool assumed command of the Middle Department, which included Harpers Ferry. Wool wanted a regular in command of a post he considered to be as important as Harpers Ferry. Of such leaders available in his department, Wool considered Miles "one of the best officers I had" and "the only one I could place there [Harpers Ferry]."[7]

Being unfamiliar with Miles's position at Harpers Ferry and his responsibilities, Wool requested a strength report from the colonel and an explanation of Miles's duties, as well as any suggestions Miles might have regarding his command. Miles apparently responded that he needed more men, for between June 17 and 20 Wool scraped up three three-month regiments, the 12th and the 22nd New York State Militia and the 87th Ohio, along with a company of artillerymen from the 5th New York Heavy Artillery as reinforcements. He also relieved Miles of the 8th New York Cavalry, transferring them back to Baltimore to receive their horses as well as a new colonel.[8]

The daily administration in running the Railroad Brigade occupied most of Miles's time and attention, but he did not entirely neglect the defenses of Harpers Ferry. In early July he sent two of his officers to inspect the approaches to the rear of naval battery on Maryland Heights. They reported that Solomon's Gap, a saddle in Elk Ridge about 6 miles north of the summit of the heights, offered an accessible approach and should be defended by infantry and artillery. Miles made up requisitions for guns but never received them.[9]

In August Wool traveled to Harpers Ferry to meet with Miles and inspect the defenses there. He found the post "in a very indefensible position," which meant that its prepared defenses had been neglected. In mid-June Wool had ordered Miles to complete entrenchments and artillery embrasures on Camp Hill that had been partially finished during Saxton's defense, and he discovered that Miles had accomplished nothing in two months. Wool ordered the colonel to finish these works, build an entrenchment on Bolivar Heights, and construct a blockhouse on the summit of Maryland Heights to protect the rear of the naval battery. The old general thought Miles seemed "very zealous" and "determined to do everything," and he departed for Baltimore satisfied that his orders would be carried out.[10]

Wool and Miles very likely discussed the nature and strength of the forces available to defend Harpers Ferry and guard the railroads. Most of Miles's force was made up of three-month volunteers, and the men of the 11th New York

State Militia were about to be discharged. There was also a shortage of cavalry, which was necessary for scouting and pursing rebel raiders. Whatever faults Wool may have had, a lack of energy was not one of them. Soon after his return to Baltimore, reinforcements began pouring into Harpers Ferry. The 3rd Maryland Potomac Home Brigade was ordered there, and in the last week of August three newly organized New York regiments came in: the 111th, the 115th, and the 126th New York. Several days later the fully mounted 8th New York Cavalry—commanded by Colonel Grimes Davis, a regular officer—arrived to bolster Miles's mounted arm. Wool also sent Major R. S. Rogers of the 2nd Maryland Potomac Home Brigade to help construct the blockhouse on Maryland Heights. By September 3, Miles's force counted six regiments of infantry, numbering 5,913 effectives; one regiment and three independent companies of cavalry, at 876 men; and two companies of the 5th New York Heavy Artillery. Not a single regiment had any combat experience. The three New York regiments had been mustered into Federal service less than two weeks before they were sent to Harpers Ferry. They were green—untrained and undisciplined. Miles complained that the first of these regiments he received, the 111th New York, "never had a gun in their hands until the boxes were opened and the muskets issued to them yesterday." Officers did not "know anything about the drill," and Miles had to borrow several officers and noncoms from his three-month volunteers simply to instruct the men on the manual of loading. Of his three-month volunteers, the 11th and the 22nd New York State Militia regiments' enlistments expired and they were sent home. The enlistment of their comrades in the 12th New York State Militia expired on September 1, and they were clamoring to be sent home as well. Davis's 8th New York Cavalry were still becoming accustomed to being mounted, and the other cavalry detachments were "nearly broken down" by constant hard work. As an offensive force, Miles's command was useless. On the defensive, behind prepared defenses they could offer some resistance, but against veteran troops they were completely outclassed.[11]

Miles needed all the men he had to properly protect the railroads, one of his two primary missions, and carry out the work on the defenses at Harpers Ferry. His garrisons in Maryland extended for 13 miles along the B&O, from Harpers Ferry to Point of Rocks. In Virginia, his infantry and cavalry patrolled or garrisoned the B&O for nearly 9 miles to Kearneysville, and for 21 miles along the Winchester and Potomac Railroad. His cavalry also watched the fords along the Shenandoah River to Snicker's Ferry, 16 miles south of Harpers Ferry. Even with 6,800 men Miles was stretched thin, and his cavalry were in the saddle constantly.[12]

In the days following the Union defeat at Second Manassas, General Halleck grew uneasy about the exposure of the 3,000-man, combined-arms brigade stationed at Winchester, commanded by Brigadier General Julius White. Halleck sent his chief of staff, General George W. Cullum, to visit Winchester and meet with White to discuss the garrison's situation and what it should do if a large Confederate force moved into the Shenandoah Valley. White was uneasy about his position, and so was Halleck, for on September 2 he ordered White to "immediately abandon the fortifications" at Winchester and withdraw to Harpers Ferry. At the same time as he received Halleck's order to withdraw, White also received a report that a force of 20,000 Confederates were moving down the Valley on his position. White wired to Halleck for instructions. If the reported enemy force were real and not just a rumor, an immediate withdrawal would oblige White to destroy a large quantity of food and ammunition. Should he do this, he asked Halleck, "or endeavor to defend it or move it?" Halleck replied that White should use his discretion, but guerrillas had cut the wires and White never received the message. He waited until nearly 10 p.m. for orders; then decided he could wait no longer and ordered his brigade to withdraw. The march was unmolested and White arrived in Harpers Ferry on the afternoon of the 3rd. His command consisted of four infantry regiments (the 39th New York, the 32nd Ohio, the 60th Ohio, and the 9th Vermont), two batteries of light artillery, and two small cavalry formations (the 1st Maryland Cavalry and the 7th Rhode Island squadron). The infantry added 2,947 offices and men to Harpers Ferry's defenses, and the New Yorkers and Ohioans provided seasoned troops with combat experience.[13]

General White's arrival at Harpers Ferry came as a surprise to General Wool, who was unaware that Halleck had ordered his retreat, and it confronted him with a command problem, for White now fell within Wool's command (Winchester was outside his department) and was the ranking officer at Harpers Ferry. The 46-year-old White was a personal friend of President Lincoln. He had resigned from a comfortable and profitable position as Chicago's collector of customs after First Manassas to raise the 37th Illinois Infantry. Although lacking any military education, White was clear headed and learned quickly. He served with some distinction in the battle of Pea Ridge, Arkansas, which, with his political connections, helped earn him promotion to brigadier general. When Halleck and Pope were reassigned to the eastern theater, White came, too, to command the brigade at Winchester. Wool knew little about him. What he did know he learned from Miles, who considered White a jumpy volunteer. "General White abandoned Winchester night before last, and, with his troops, arrived this point yesterday afternoon," Miles wired to Wool on September 4, failing to mention that White had pulled out under orders from Halleck. Then, in obvious reference to White's report of 20,000 enemy moving down the Valley, Miles added: "No enemy that I can hear of in the valley of the Shenandoah, nor do I know if Winchester is occupied by them." If there had been a question in Wool's mind, Miles's message answered it; White had to go, but his troops would stay at Harpers Ferry. On September 5 Wool ordered White to turn his brigade over to Miles and go to Martinsburg to assume command of the 2,500-man garrison there. White received his new orders "with astonishment and regret," and soon after arriving in Martinsburg he wired to Cullum and Halleck asking that he be restored to his former command, or relieved of command and reassigned "to duty in the front." Halleck responded that when White arrived at Harpers Ferry he came under Wool's command, and it would not be proper to change the general's orders during the current crisis. The order stood, and White remained at Martinsburg.[14]

The report on the night of September 4 from Colonel Henry B. Banning of the 87th Ohio, stationed at Point of Rocks, stating that 30,000 Rebels had crossed the Potomac River and were marching on him, combined with other reports of enemy crossings into Maryland, increased the possibility that Harpers Ferry might be isolated and attacked. It was this danger that prompted McClellan to advise Halleck that the forces there be withdrawn. When Halleck refused, McClellan, who was familiar with the topography of the place, suggested that the garrison should at least be withdrawn to Maryland Heights.

Halleck never explained why he was so reluctant to abandon Harpers Ferry. His biographer speculated that he recognized the threat a force stationed there posed to Confederate communications down the Shenandoah Valley into Maryland, so he wished to hold it for this purpose. But this presumes that on September 5 Halleck knew that the Confederate movement into Maryland was a full-scale invasion by the Army of Northern Virginia, and that the Confederates planned to establish their line of communications down the Valley. Halleck's correspondence during the campaign reveals that he fathomed no more of the Confederates intentions than any other man in the Union Army. Up through September 14 he continued to think the enemy movement in Maryland toward Pennsylvania was a feint, and that the main blow would be directed toward Washington by an army concealed in northern Virginia. It is more likely that Halleck was unwilling to abandon Harpers Ferry because of the supplies and other government property stored there. He knew nothing personally about the topography of the area or the composition and quality of the garrison there, and there is no existing evidence that he did anything to educate himself on this issue. On September 5 Halleck wired to Wool, informing him that it would be a day or two before the Army of the Potomac could take the field, and that "in the mean time Harper's Ferry may be attacked and overwhelmed." He left "all dispositions there" to Wool's experience and local knowledge, but suggested "the propriety of withdrawing all our forces in that vicinity to Maryland Heights."[15]

There is really nothing to criticize in this message. Halleck properly deferred the details of defending Harpers Ferry to Wool, but he also showed that he had heeded McClellan's advice to withdraw the garrison to Maryland Heights. Wool, unfortunately, ignored this suggestion. He wired two sets of instructions to Miles that same day, which would have fateful consequences. Miles was directed "to be energetic and active, and defend all places to the last extremity. There must be no abandoning of a post, and shoot the first man that thinks of it, whether officer or soldier." Later that day Halleck again urged Miles that "activity, energy and decision should be used," and then added the most crucial sentence: "You will not abandon Harper's Ferry without defending it to the last extremity." Wool clearly worried about Miles. Twice he felt it necessary to urge him to be energetic and active and to defend first "all places," and then specifically "Harper's Ferry," to the last extremity. Wool was apparently unaware of Miles's reputation for being a strict constructionist of his orders. In the narrow sense, Wool's last orders to the colonel forbid the withdrawal of the garrison to Maryland Heights, as this meant the physical abandonment of Harpers Ferry. And this was precisely how Miles interpreted his orders.[16]

Two days later, on September 7, Halleck reaffirmed Wool's rigid orders in a wire to Miles: "Our army is in motion. It is important that Harper's Ferry be held to the latest moment. The Government has the utmost confidence in you, and is ready to give you full credit for the defense it expects you to make."[17] Julius White received the same stand-fast orders from Wool, being instructed on September 6 to "defend yourself to the last extremity." Miles never questioned his orders. White did. He only had 3,000 troops at Winchester when Halleck had ordered him to retreat; at Martinsburg he commanded just 2,500 men. White asked if he was being ordered to stand against any number of troops. What if 20,000 men should attack him? "If 20,000 men should attack you, you will, of course, fall back," Wool replied, suggesting Harpers Ferry as the nearest safe haven. Had Miles questioned his orders like White did, Wool would not have approved a withdrawal, but he might have provided Miles with more flexibility in managing a defense than to simply defend Harpers Ferry "to the last extremity."[18]

Miles lost no time in organizing his command to carry out Wool's orders. On September 5 he grouped his force into four brigades, with a few assorted unattached units. He had only three veteran regiments, and he assigned one each to his first three brigades. Besides stiffening each brigade with some experienced men, it also assured that their regimental commanders, by seniority, would be the brigade commanders. Experience, alas, did not translate into ability, for Miles's brigade commanders were a mediocre lot. Colonel Frederick G. D'Utassy of the 39th New York led the 1st Brigade. An Austrian by birth, D'Utassy was brave but pompous, and less of a soldier than he liked to think. His major remarked that D'Utassy "gave great personal attention to our supplies, and the men were well fed and well clad; but beyond this he did little. In matter of discipline he was practically useless." But D'Utassy had a mark in his favor with Miles, as he had provided sympathetic testimony for Miles at the latter's court of inquiry after First Manassas.[19]

Command of the 2nd Brigade went to Colonel William H. Trimble of the 60th Ohio. Trimble was 51 and, judging from his subsequent testimony before the Harpers Ferry Commission, was a man of personal courage but felt his lack of experience as a soldier. He owed his colonelcy largely to political clout. His father was a former governor of Ohio, his brother was a congressman, and he had been a state legislator.[20]

Colonel Thomas H. Ford, commander of the 32nd Ohio, led the 3rd Brigade. A 47-year-old Ohio attorney, Ford had been lieutenant governor under Salmon P. Chase. But when Chase joined the Republican Party, Ford did not; it cost him political capital, which he sought to regain as a soldier. He served in the Mexican War as a volunteer and had seen action as a regimental commander in western Virginia and the Shenandoah Valley. Julius White, Ford's commanding officer at Winchester, found no man "more zealous in his duties, more courageous and efficient in the discharge of those duties" than Ford. Ford had only recently rejoined his regiment, having been absent for 60 days to have a fistula removed from his buttocks. He returned before it had fully healed and was "almost utterly unable to ride a horse." Walking was no better, which only helped to inflame the wound. Ford was really incapable of active service, but he was a conscientious man and thought his services were needed, so he endured the pain and attempted to do his duty.[21]

The 4th Brigade went to Colonel William G. Ward of the 12th New York State Militia. Ward was of the New York elite, counting among his relatives Revolutionary War General Nathanael Greene and Julia Ward Howe of "Battle Hymn of the Republic" fame. His regiment's three-month enlistment had expired; despite the emergency that now faced the North, the men wanted to go home and were "greatly dissatisfied at not being discharged." Miles thought them more trouble than they were worth and recommended that they be discharged. Wool appealed to Ward's sense of honor and courage and asked that the regiment remain "a few days." Ward revealed some measure of his leadership when he responded that unless Wool gave him a specific date when the regiment would be sent home, Ward would be unable to control them.[22]

Miles retained the 8th New York Cavalry, the 1st Maryland Potomac Home Brigade, and the detachment of the Maryland Potomac Home Brigade Cavalry as independent units, subject to his orders. The latter two forces were stationed at Sandy Hook, and Miles employed the New Yorkers for scouting, patrolling, and picketing the Virginia approaches to Harpers Ferry. Having organized his forces, Miles then considered their deployment. He expected any attack on Harpers Ferry would follow the same approach Jackson had used in May, moving down the Shenandoah Valley and against Bolivar Heights from the west. But with enemy forces in Maryland, there was the possibility that they might attack Maryland Heights, which he considered "the key to his whole position."

Harpers Ferry in 1862. The B&O railroad bridge and the pontoon bridge, which the cavalry used to cross the Potomac on the night of September 14, gave Harpers Ferry strategic importance. Courtesy of the Historic Photo Collection, Harpers Ferry National Historic Park.

Unlike Saxton, Miles dismissed Loudoun Heights from his defensive considerations. He did not believe the enemy could plant artillery on the heights or on the tablelands below them.[23]

Given these assessments, Miles determined to form his defense around Bolivar Heights and Maryland Heights. The key to this defense, as he admitted to some of his subordinates, was Maryland Heights and the three-gun naval battery, mounting one 5-inch and two 9-inch guns that were all located on a plateau down the mountain's western slope. These guns could reach targets at Bolivar Heights and beyond, and easily hit Loudoun Heights. Maryland Heights' chief vulnerability was from an attack on its rear, via Solomon's Gap, which the enemy could access from Pleasant Valley, situated between South Mountain and Elk Ridge. No defensive preparations had been completed there. Miles had also not built the blockhouse on the summit of Maryland Heights, which Wool had ordered and had even sent Major Rogers to help construct. Miles gave the idea of a blockhouse "no countenance" and sent Rogers back to Baltimore. Having neglected this aspect of Maryland Heights' defense, Miles now gave responsibility for its security to Colonel Ford and his brigade. Miles's selection of Ford's brigade was peculiar. It was the smallest of the three brigades of volunteers, and Ford was physically unfit to command. The brigade numbered approximately 1,150 men, of which somewhat over 800 were infantry in Ford's own 32nd Ohio and Major John A. Steiner's battalion of the 1st Maryland Potomac Home Brigade. Ford also had two small cavalry units—Major

Augustus W. Corliss's Rhode Island battalion, and Captain Charles H. Russell's squadron of the 1st Maryland Cavalry, about 135 and 146 men, respectively—who were available for scouting; and Company F, 5th New York Heavy Artillery, about 100 strong, who manned the naval battery and three 12 lb. guns.[24]

The size of Ford's brigade might have dictated Miles's selection. Although Miles acknowledged that Maryland Heights was the key to his position, he anticipated that the enemy attack, if it came, would be against Bolivar Heights. Miles needed his strongest brigades to man this extended front, which stretched for nearly 2 miles. He assigned D'Utassy's 1st Brigade and Trimble's 2nd Brigade, a total of 5,411 officer and men, to its defense, supported by Captain John C. H. Von Sehlen's 15th Indiana battery (six 3-inch bronze and iron rifles) and Captain Benjamin F. Potts's Ohio Battery (two Napoleons and four 3-inch rifles). The two brigades and two batteries covered about 1.3 miles of the Bolivar Heights front, from the Potomac River to the Charlestown Pike. Miles considered the rough, wooded ground south of the pike "impassable" to troops, so he left this three-quarter-mile stretch of ground undefended.[25]

Ward's 4th Brigade might have filled in this gap in the Bolivar Heights line, but Miles placed most of it on Camp Hill, probably to provide additional security for the pontoon and railroad bridges over the Potomac, and to serve as support to the Bolivar Heights line. The bridges gave Harpers Ferry much of its military importance, particularly the B&O railroad bridge. Spring floods washed it out twice, and it had only recently been repaired. Just the 12th New York State Militia and part of Battery A, 5th New York Artillery, manned the Camp Hill position. Miles detached most of the 87th Ohio and Potts's Ohio battery to reinforce Colonel Maulsby, who, with five companies of his 1st Maryland Potomac Home Brigade, were stationed at Sandy Hook and ordered to defend the eastern approach to Maryland Heights, as well as to provide security for the Potomac bridges on the Maryland side and supply detachments to observe the Potomac fords as far east as the mouth of the Monocacy River.[26]

Miles's initial dispositions were not quite as bad as some of his critics made them out to be. He could have posted three brigades on Camp Hill and not occupied Bolivar Heights. This would have shortened his line and allowed the heavy guns on Maryland Heights to fire on a force descending from Bolivar Heights. But this gave Miles no depth to his defense. Leaving the ground from near the Charlestown Pike to the Shenandoah River undefended was not a good idea, but besides thinking the ground impassable to formed troops, Miles did not have any men available to deploy there other than the 12th New York State Militia. If he moved them, then he had no infantry left to guard the Virginia side of the B&O railroad bridge and the pontoon bridge. And the 12th's reliability as a front-line unit was questionable. It should also be remembered that Miles had very little information about the enemy at this point, and what he did know indicated that they would probably approach from Winchester.

August 1862 view of Maryland Heights from Camp Hill. The Naval Battery is visible in the clearing midway up the mountain. Courtesy of the Historic Photo Collection, Harpers Ferry National Historic Park.

Miles's personnel selections for brigade command were adequate for what he had to work with, but there was no reason why he could not have assigned D'Utassy and his experienced 39th New York to the 3rd Brigade, and placed the 32nd Ohio—with Ford in command of the 1st Brigade—on Bolivar Heights. D'Utassy may have been more talk than action, but at least he was mobile and was physically able to command on Maryland Heights, as opposed to Ford, who was limited by his infirmity.

As Miles's brigades assumed their positions and examined the ground they were assigned to defend, they discovered virtually no prepared defenses. Camp Hill had an earthwork and two bastions left over from Saxton's previous defense, which were oriented to guard against an attack from the direction of Bolivar Heights. Captain W. Angelo Powell, an engineer officer assigned to Harpers Ferry, considered these works so poorly constructed as to be "of no account." There were no defenses on Bolivar Heights and none on Maryland Heights. The readiness of Harpers Ferry's defenses had been the topic of discussion between Miles, Powell, and General White before he was ordered to Martinsburg. Both White and Powell recommended that Loudoun Heights be fortified, and that several bodies of woods on Bolivar Heights and around the naval battery on Maryland Heights be cut down to clear fields of fire and prevent the enemy from using the woods for cover. Since Miles thought artillery could not be hauled up to Loudoun Heights and was convinced that the enemy would approach Harpers Ferry from the direction of Bolivar Heights, he dismissed the first recommendation. He also refused to remove the woods Powell wanted cleared. Miles thought it unnecessary to clear the trees on Maryland Heights near the naval battery, even though they were within 100 yards of the guns, and—against all military logic—he chose to keep the woods on Bolivar Heights, as he thought they would "mask what we were doing."[27]

Subsequent efforts by Miles's brigade commanders to improve defenses and obtain the necessary tools to build fortifications met with bizarre stubbornness, outright denial, or no response at all from Miles. On the day he assumed command of the 2nd Brigade, Colonel Trimble carefully studied the ground his men were assigned to defend on Bolivar Heights with Colonel George Stannard, commander of the 9th Vermont and an excellent officer. They found the place where the left of the brigade rested, near the Charlestown Pike, to be a vulnerable point and suggested to Miles that a belt of trees about a half mile from the position be cut down, as well as some cornfields that stood between the woods and Trimble's front line. They also recommended that breastworks and rifle pits be constructed along Bolivar Heights and the undefended part from the Charlestown Pike to the Shenandoah River. Miles refused all their requests. Colonel D'Utassy asked permission to cut down woods in a hollow northeast of the Heights to provide a field of fire for the naval guns on Maryland Heights. Nothing was done.[28]

On Maryland Heights, Colonel Ford submitted requisitions for entrenching tools and axes. Repeated requests got him 10 axes. Ford also asked for additional artillery, since the naval guns were placed to cover Harpers Ferry and were of little help in defending Maryland Heights. Miles denied Ford's repeated requests for a battery to guard Solomon's Gap. Ford "gave up that mode of defense" and next asked for a section of guns to place at a point called the Lookout, a cribbed-log observation structure on the summit of the mountain. Ford thought that with artillery support "I could make a stand at that point and probably prevent the enemy from ascending the mountain, either on the eastern or northern slope through the gap [Solomon's]. Miles replied that if Ford and Captain McGrath had their way, "we would have all the artillery at Harper's Ferry on Maryland Heights." On September 10 Miles finally agreed to send them two 12 lb. guns from Graham's Battery A, 5th New York Artillery, and he sent two more on the 11th when the threat to Maryland Heights became apparent. All were placed around the naval battery. While the extra firepower was welcome, these guns did nothing to help Ford defend Maryland Heights from an attack from Solomon's Gap. For this, he would have to rely on the 10 axes he had been allotted, and his infantry.[29]

By September 6 Miles knew that large numbers of Confederates had crossed the Potomac River below Point of Rocks and occupied Frederick, and that a

Confederate division, believed to be A. P. Hill's—but in fact G. B. Anderson's brigade of D. H. Hill's division—was at Lovettsville, Virginia, 3 miles south of Berlin. There were also rumors of an enemy force marching for Winchester from Leesburg. Miles may have been negligent in some aspects of his defensive preparations, but he proved vigilant in preparing his subordinates at their outposts for action and in using his cavalry to gather information. He ordered Colonel Maulsby to draw in the five detached companies of his regiment and concentrate them at Sandy Hook. Miles considered it critical to hold this area, for it controlled not only the approaches to the Harpers Ferry bridges, but also the eastern approaches to Maryland Heights. Miles wrote to Maulsby that he intended to hold the place "if it takes half of the force at this point." Maulsby's orders were clear: "You will not abandon it [Sandy Hook]." The three-month volunteers of the 87th Ohio Infantry, with two guns from Graham's New York battery, were at Berlin, now the extreme eastern post for the Harpers Ferry garrison. Banning, who was leading the 87th, was green and jumpy and had stampeded on September 4, retreating from Point of Rocks to Berlin when the Rebels first began crossing the Potomac. Miles ordered him back to Point of Rocks the next day, but he retreated again on the 6th, falling back once more to Berlin, when he feared the Confederates at Lovettsville might cut him off. Miles now ordered Banning to put up a bold front. "Defend your place as long as you can," Miles commanded, but, if forced to fall back, "stop at Sandy Hook; that place is to be defended at all hazards." Banning did not even last the day. G. B. Anderson shelled him from the south bank of the Potomac and Confederate pickets probed his front on the north bank. Banning and his men decamped so swiftly for Sandy Hook that he left behind a limber, equipment, and ammunition. When Miles learned of this he ordered an engine and platform car to go to Berlin and retrieve what Banning had left in his flight. The engine and car made the trip without incident, recovering all the lost items.[30]

September 7 brought news from two fronts. Julius White wired to Miles at 10:30 that morning, stating that his outposts were under attack from a force whose size he could not yet estimate, and that there were fresh reports of a large force of Rebels at Winchester. These concerned Miles, but he particularly desired information about the enemy in Maryland. Where were they? How strong were they? Where were they bound? To find some answers, he ordered two cavalry reconnaissances. A squadron of the 8th New York Cavalry was ordered to reconnoiter east along the River Road. Miles ordered a smaller party from Cole's Maryland cavalry battalion, under an intrepid lieutenant named Hanson T. C. Green, "not to return until he [Green] had felt the enemy and ascertained something definite." The New Yorkers marched as far as Berlin, where, according to Miles's aide, Lieutenant Henry Binney, they heard rumors of enemy forces and returned. Green, on the other hand, established himself as a man to be counted on. He led his party to Petersville, then north through Pleasant Valley to Middletown, and on to within 2.5 miles of Frederick. He probed the Confederate picket line at several points, captured some prisoners, and departed without a clash or loss. What Green reported to Miles, or what he learned from the prisoners, is unknown, but certainly he confirmed that the enemy occupied Frederick in large force. This was important, but it did not shed light on the enemy's intentions.[31]

While Miles's horsemen probed to the east, Julius White dispatched elements of the 12th Illinois Cavalry and the 65th Illinois Infantry to confront the force that had attacked his outposts at daybreak. It proved to be a squadron of the 12th Virginia Cavalry and the 17th Virginia battalion, the only Confederate force of any size operating in this part of the Shenandoah Valley. The Virginians retreated before the Federals until they reached Darkesville, Virginia, about 7 miles south of Martinsburg. Here they attempted a stand, but it dissolved before a charge of the Illinois horsemen. The fight then turned into a rout, with the Federals pursuing the Rebels almost to Winchester. The 12th Illinois counted 13 wounded and 1 captured in the fight but reported 25 Confederate dead and 41 prisoners. White closely questioned his prisoners and learned both that they were the advance of a column that had left Leesburg three days earlier for Winchester, and that they were to continue their march north to "support the column already in Frederick." Perhaps this is what the prisoners believed, or maybe it was what they wanted White to believe. But their account supported a report White had received before he left Harpers Ferry for Martinsburg, saying that a "heavy column" had passed from Leesburg in the direction of Harpers Ferry. White was convinced that the enemy "will, doubtless, be in this vicinity tomorrow, if the statement is true."[32]

White and Miles worked together to mount a coordinated reconnaissance to determine whether the reports of the enemy at Winchester were true. Miles agreed to send Colonel Davis and elements of the 8th New York Cavalry, as well as a detachment of the 1st Maryland Cavalry, who were stationed at Kearneysville. White pledged elements of the 12th Illinois Cavalry. The three forces arranged to meet at Smithfield, but something went amiss, for although Davis's New Yorkers and apparently the Marylanders arrived at the rendezvous at the appointed time, White's horsemen failed to show. Davis proceeded anyway and led the command to Bunker Hill on the Valley Turnpike, then on to Summit Point on the Winchester and Potomac Railroad. Apart from capturing a few pickets, they found no evidence of the enemy.[33]

A reconnaissance by some of Miles's scouts that same day was more successful, confirming the maxim that a few men can often learn more than a large body. These bold fellows ventured to (or close enough to) Winchester to learn that there was "but one regiment of about 400 cavalry" stationed there, and that other than this handful of horsemen there was "no enemy in the Shenandoah Valley." That much of their report was accurate, but they also stated that

Confederate General William W. Loring, at the head of 15,000 to 20,000 men, was en route for the Valley from Leesburg. This was a rumor without substance— Loring, at the head of a much smaller force, was actually then approaching Charleston, Virginia, many miles away—but Miles had to take it seriously and keep his scouts and cavalry busy watching the fords over the Shenandoah for evidence of its approach.[34]

Rumors also came to Miles from Lieutenant Colonel Stephen Downey, commanding the 3rd Maryland Potomac Home Brigade at Kearneysville, that enemy troops at Frederick were advancing west toward Boonsboro or Hagerstown. Miles dispatched scouts to investigate and sent orders for Ford to have his cavalry reconnoiter toward Frederick. Ford sent both Major Augustus Corliss's Rhode Island squadron and a 50-man force from the 1st Maryland Cavalry under Captain Charles Russell on separate reconnaissances. Corliss led his Rhode Islanders into Pleasant Valley by way of Solomon's Gap, then rode east, marching through Jefferson and to within 2 miles of Frederick before turning back. The Rhode Islanders picked up 25 prisoners and learned that the Southern army had not stirred from Frederick.[35]

Captain Russell led his detachment along the Potomac River to Knoxville and then turned northeast, marching through Petersville and Jefferson. At the latter village he captured the sergeant-major of a Louisiana regiment. From here he left the road and started cross-country until he reached the National Road about 3 miles west of Frederick. Russell prowled east, jumping a party of enemy pickets, whom they then pursued to within 1.5 miles of the city. With 50 men Russell had accomplished what all the cavalry of the Army of the Potomac had been trying to do without success: get a close look at the Army of Northern Virginia. Unfortunately, Russell's position west of Frederick did not permit him to see the main camps of Lee's army southeast of the city. But he did gather some useful information. The Confederates appeared to be either poorly supplied or stripped down for rapid movement. "The enemy evidently has no supply train," he wrote to Colonel Ford. "I could see only a very few wagons, not more than enough to supply transportation needs for officers, sick, and wounded." Russell also observed that there were few tents in evidence and that Confederate soldiers "could be seen sleeping on the sidewalks and cellar-doors about the street." He saw two columns of troops on the move, but neither was moving west. One was approaching Frederick from the Potomac River, which may have been Walker's division, and another was seen marching east in the direction of Baltimore. Perhaps due to inexperience, Russell failed to provide an estimate of their strength, but he had confirmed that the enemy remained at Frederick and displayed no sign of moving west.[36]

September 9 stayed relatively quiet on all fronts. The telegraph was cut west of Martinsburg in the morning but was repaired by afternoon. There was no news of General Loring in the Shenandoah Valley, and although there was a report of enemy troops near Boonsboro, nothing could be learned to confirm it. Miles spent the day inspecting his lines, visiting Sandy Hook, Maryland Heights, and Bolivar Heights.[37]

September 10 proved more eventful. Miles had the 8th New York in the saddle again, scouting south toward Winchester. They found the Shenandoah Valley quiet, with no evidence of an enemy force approaching from Leesburg. Scouts dispatched into Maryland sent word that an enemy column, 5,000 strong, was marching from Frederick in the direction of Hagerstown. Either Miles or White wired to Lieutenant Colonel Downey at Kearneysville (there was some dispute between White and Miles as to who commanded Downey—Wool settled it on September 11 and said it was White) and ordered him to investigate. Downey selected 19 men of the 1st Maryland Cavalry and trotted off to see what he could rustle up. Their specific route is not known, but they probably took the most direct course, crossing the Potomac at Shepherdstown and then proceeding through Sharpsburg to the Boonsboro Pike.

It was late afternoon when Downey and his party neared Boonsboro. As they rode into the western end of the village they observed three or four gray-clad horsemen entering the town from the east, along the National Road. Thinking he had come upon some careless Rebels who could be easily captured, Downey set his command on them. Downey's 19 horsemen came thundering into Boonsboro with pistols blazing. The Confederates whirled and fled east along the pike as fast as their horses could carry them, with Downey's Marylanders in hot pursuit. But a short distance east of the village Downey realized that his party had stirred up a body of troops—Downey described them as a "considerable force"— that could swallow them in an instant. A company of Confederate cavalry came furiously charging down on them, and now it was Downey's turn to be the pursued. He and his men spurred back through Boonsboro with bullets snapping the air around them. One of them creased Downey's head, and another killed his horse. Others also scored hits, for Downy reported one killed and three wounded. He thought his men killed 9 or 10 of the enemy, but apparently the only Confederate casualty was one of their horses, which a Marylander shot in the leg as they were leaving town.[38]

Despite losing his horse, Downey managed to escape and send a report to White, but the details were slim. He could only say that the enemy force was one "of all arms," and he did not know whether they were marching toward Shepherdstown or Hagerstown. White passed this news along to Miles, recommending that the colonel strengthen Shepherdstown with cavalry and Kearneysville with infantry and artillery. Miles had no interest in dividing his command to respond to potential threats, so he informed White that "to divide my command would lead to the loss of this place and destruction of the detachment I would send out." If the enemy were in large force—15,000 or more—then Miles believed "our united forces could do no more than take position, or [if] separated to dodge." Miles firmly believed that McClellan (Miles thought McClellan was the general-in-chief and believed that Halleck was the secretary of war) would drive the Confederates across the Potomac. When this happened it would be his and White's duty to "retard and harass" them. The idea that his and White's garrisons might themselves be an objective of the enemy seemed a remote prospect to Miles.[39]

Jackson Advances: "A hearty welcome"

The force that Downey and his stout band of 19 horsemen had stirred up was the advance guard of Stonewall Jackson's three divisions. Jackson's command had the longest march of the three columns designated to fall on Harpers Ferry, so his divisions led the march of the Confederate army from Frederick on the 10th. To facilitate rapid movement, transportation was reduced to one wagon per regiment to haul camp equipment and quartermaster and commissary stores. Jackson had little difficulty complying with the order, for his divisions already traveled on the barest of essentials. Captain Greenlee Davidson, one of his battery commanders, wrote that even "all knapsacks have been thrown away and the men have no clothes except those on their backs." Lee desired swift movement, but not more stragglers and broken-down men who might be lost to the enemy if left behind in Maryland. Orders were issued that the rate of march was to be 3 miles an hour and no more, "except in great emergencies." A 10-minute rest would be observed each hour, and the sick "and those otherwise unable to march were to be transported in the ambulances." An officer in Brigadier General Maxcy Gregg's brigade observed that "this last provision seemed superfluous, but it was required in countermand of Gen. Jackson's rule while in Virginia, to leave the foot-sore by the way."[40]

In the march west from Frederick, Jackson rode about a half mile in advance of his infantry, along with his staff and cavalry escort (the Black Horse Cavalry, Captain Robert Randolph's troop of the 4th Virginia Cavalry). Captain Randolph and a small squad of troopers rode a mile or more ahead of this group to ensure that no one passed to the front to warn of Jackson's approach, and that no one came toward the column without encountering Randolph's men. Jackson also had the 7th Virginia Cavalry attached to his command, but he placed them at the rear of the column, probably to pick up or prod along any stragglers.[41]

The long column made the laborious passage over Catoctin Mountain through Hagan's Gap and descended into the beautiful Middletown Valley. The temperature climbed to a high of 77 degrees, certainly tolerable, but Jackson's men, plodding along in the bright sunshine, thought it "very warm," and the march set no records for speed. Around 10 a.m. they reached Middletown, a clean, tidy village located about midway between Catoctin Mountain and

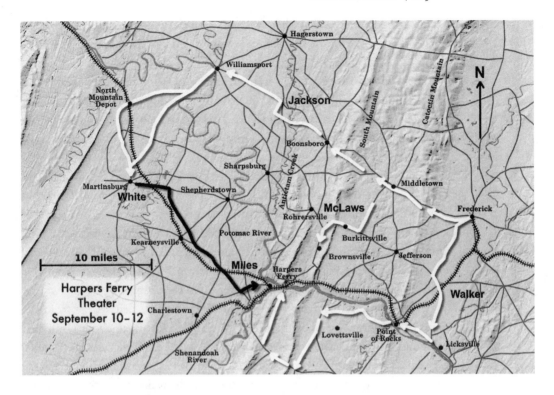

South Mountain. Captain Greenlee Davidson was unimpressed. "It has the reputation of being the bitterest abolitionist hole in the state," he wrote to his father. When Jackson rode into the village, his aide Henry K. Douglas recalled that two "very pretty girls" with ribbons of red, white, and blue in their hair and small Union flags in their hands "came out of their house as we passed, ran to the curb-stone, and laughingly waved their colors defiantly in the face of the general." Certainly they were not aware that this was the famous and terrible Stonewall Jackson before them. Jackson paused, politely bowed to the young ladies, then lifted his cap and "with a quiet smile said to his staff, 'We evidently have no friends in this town.'" Either the realization that these men were Confederates or Jackson's reaction deflated the girls' enthusiasm; lowering their flags, they beat a retreat to their home.[42]

The troops continued west along the National Road from Middletown and began the arduous uphill climb to Turner's Gap through South Mountain. Captain Davidson found time to admire the beauty of the country. Farms spread out in every direction across the valley, "and every farm has a barn almost as large as Noah's Ark." It seemed impossible for a soldier to go hungry in such a place, but Davidson discovered that this was indeed the case. "I visited nearly a hundred farm houses during the day and did not succeed in buying a pound of meat or a bushel of corn," he wrote in disgust. Some of the homes were deserted, but occupants who remained at others would sell nothing to the Confederates.

Davidson concluded (as had thousands of other Confederate soldiers) "that the people of this section of the State are as hostile to us as if we were north of Mason and Dixon line."[43]

The climb to Turner's Gap was long, slow, and tiring for men and animals, and it was late afternoon before A. P. Hill's and J. R. Jones's divisions were over the summit. Jackson called a halt to the day's march before the head of the column reached Boonsboro. Hill and Jones put their men into bivouac between the village and the mountain, and Lawton camped on the eastern side of the mountain, somewhere between Middletown and Turner's Gap. The front of the column had covered only about 18 miles, and some daylight remained. But before proceeding beyond Boonsboro, Jackson needed information about whether the Union garrison at Martinsburg remained in place or had withdrawn. The answer to this would dictate whether his command marched via Sharpsburg or Williamsport to cross the Potomac. He apparently anticipated receiving this information from scouts or spies that afternoon or evening.[44]

Jackson ordered his headquarters' tents pitched in a field across from the home of Mr. John Murdock, located along the National Road about 1 mile east of Boonsboro. While the tents were being unloaded from the baggage wagons, Lieutenant Douglas proposed to ride into Boonsboro to see some friends and try to get some information about the Potomac fords. Jackson advised his young aide not to go into town but did not forbid him from doing so. Colonel S. Bassett French of Virginia Governor Letcher's staff, who was accompanying Jackson as a volunteer aide-de-camp, joined Douglas, as did two or three troopers. French stopped at the United States Hotel at the corner of Main Street and the Sharpsburg Pike, hitched his horse, and started inside, no doubt in search of some refreshment. It was at this moment that Lieutenant Colonel Downey and his party came tearing up the Sharpsburg Pike and, as Douglas recalled, "proceeded to make war on us." French darted into the hotel and was concealed—in a meal box, in the coal cellar, or under a pile of rubbish, depending on who was telling the story—by a black man who worked there. Douglas and the others "went at once," escorted in their haste to depart from town by Downey and company. The shots and shouts aroused Jackson's headquarters staff, who were lounging under shade trees near Murdock's house. The Black Horse Cavalry went forward, and an infantry regiment was ordered up for good measure. The sight of the Black Horse pounding down the road put the Yankees to flight, although one of them managed to shoot French's tethered horse as he passed by. When the dust had settled, French emerged from his cellar. As a measure of thanks, he gave the man who had saved his skin a $10 Confederate note. "I doubt whether you will ever find him [French] again in advance of our lines," quipped one of Jackson's battery commanders.[45]

Jackson's infantrymen and artillerymen enjoyed a more serene encampment. They kept busy preparing three days' rations, but some found time to admire the striking natural beauty of the area. Draughton S. Haynes of Colonel Edward L. Thomas's Georgia brigade gazed on "one of the prettiest vallies I have ever seen. The sun is setting behind another mountain [North Mountain]. The scene is magnificent."[46] During the night Jackson learned that White's garrison was still at Martinsburg. This settled the question of which route the command would follow on the 11th. The longer march by way of Williamsport would be necessary to cut off the garrison's escape routes to the north and flush them in the direction of Harpers Ferry.

With important work imminent, A. P. Hill swallowed his pride and visited Jackson that night to request that he be restored to command of his division. Jackson agreed, but the charges against Hill still stood. They would be settled later.[47] Reveille sounded through Jackson's camps at 3 a.m. on September 11. It was humid with a threat of rain. No one, save a handful on Jackson's staff, knew where they were bound. At 4 a.m., nearly two hours before sunrise, the column swung onto the National Road. A. P. Hill's division led for the first half mile, apparently enough to clear the way for Lawton and J. R. Jones, whose divisions filed past to take the lead. Jackson led his command through Boonsboro, passing the Sharpsburg Pike and continuing north for approximately a mile and a half, when he turned them west on the Williamsport Turnpike. "We knew at once that we were destined for Martinsburg and H. F. where a considerable force of the Yankees were stationed," wrote Captain Davidson.[48]

The route of march took Jackson's Confederates "through a rich and fertile country in the highest state of cultivation," but the Yankee-hating Captain Davidson found no reason to change his opinion of the people who "almost without exception are soul and body Union shriekers." His low opinion of Marylanders may have revealed itself to those he encountered, for although he again expended great energy in hunting up something to eat, he found no one willing to sell him a morsel. "If we stay in this part of Maryland we will soon starve, unless the system of impressment is resorted to," he complained. The column passed through Jones' Crossroads and St. James College before reaching Williamsport around noon. A march through town led to Lights' Ford on the Potomac. Bands struck up "Carry Me Back to Old Virginny" as the troops plunged into river, which ranged from waist- to knee-deep at the ford. The cool water no doubt felt good on that warm day, and there was also delight to be returning to Virginia soil. "Every company gave a good cheer as it formed on the south bank of the River and I doubt whether there was a man in the army that did not rejoice that he was out of Maryland," opined Captain Davidson.[49]

Jackson's column reached Harmony Church, 2 miles south of Lights' Ferry. The road forked here, with the Valley Pike continuing south to Martinsburg, 10 miles away, and the North Mountain Depot Road branching west. The Depot sat square on the B&O Railroad and on Martinsburg's communications to points west. Anticipating that the Martinsburg garrison might attempt to escape in

this direction, Jackson directed both J. R. Jones's and Lawton's divisions to occupy this point and hem in the Federals from the west. The 7th Virginia Cavalry
were sent with these two divisions, with orders to push south of the railroad
and keep the roads leading west from Martinsburg under observation. While
Jones and Lawton made their end run, A. P. Hill's division would advance
directly on Martinsburg along the Valley Pike.[50]

The march continued until dark. J. R. Jones and Lawton reached the vicinity of North Mountain Depot without incident and captured some pickets
there, and the 7th Virginia Cavalry advanced a detachment to cover the turnpike from Martinsburg to Berkeley Springs. A. P. Hill's division bivouacked 8
miles north of Martinsburg. It had been a difficult march, but not one for the
record books. Lawton's division had the hardest route, traversing some 23 miles
and having to cross South Mountain at the beginning of the march. Hill's
brigades had the shortest journey, at around 17 miles. But all who wrote about it
noted that that it took a hard toll on the troops. "All very nearly broken down,"
wrote Captain Michael Schuler of the 33rd Virginia in his diary. A diarist in
Hill's division agreed. "This has been a hard day's march," he wrote. "Our troops
are very tired and some of the boys have failed to come up." But their hard
marching had sealed off the western escape routes for the Martinsburg garrison. The only practical move left for them was to retreat to Harpers Ferry.[51]

While Jackson's brigades swept up through Williamsport and across the
Potomac, Lieutenant Henry B. Curtis Jr., aide-de-camp to General Julius White,
wrote to his wife Lucy, explaining that their position at Martinsburg "is very
exposed, but our safety consists in their having too large game afloat to attend
to us except incidentally. They [the enemy] are all in our rear, near Hagerstown,
Williamsport, Boonsboro & . . . Our position is very uncertain, however, &
we may pull up stakes almost any hour." Curtis had no idea how soon that hour
would arrive.

Scouts had sent word to the Federals late that morning that the enemy were
crossing the Potomac at Williamsport and had dispatched forces in the direction
of the North Mountain Depot. White suspected that this latter move might
be to cut off his retreat to the northwest, and also that his garrison might be the
Confederates' quarry. At noon he assembled a task force to investigate: three
companies of the 65th Illinois; a section of Captain John C. Phillips's Battery M,
2nd Illinois artillery; a half company of the 12th Illinois cavalry; and two wagons loaded with axes and other tools, under the command of Colonel Daniel
Cameron of the 65th Illinois. Cameron's mission was to advance along the
Williamsport Turnpike, assess the enemy's strength, and "obstruct the roads,
tear up bridges, and, in every way possible, retard the advance of the enemy."[52]

Cameron's expedition made it as far as Falling Waters when they discovered
the Rebels across the Potomac "in overwhelming force." White also learned that
the enemy had occupied North Mountain Depot and cut White's communications. It was apparent that his small garrison would be crushed if it remained,

so he ordered the garrison to prepare to evacuate. With the Rebels moving along the Williamsport Turnpike and at North Mountain Depot, his only option was withdrawal to Harpers Ferry; with the enemy only 7 miles from Martinsburg, there was no time to lose. There were only 16 wagons for transporting baggage, ammunition, and equipment. White had ordered a train of 11 cars to be detained at Martinsburg for just such an emergency, but the Martinsburg railroad agent, in an act either of defiance, stupidity, or disloyalty, sent the empty cars off on the 10th, leaving White desperately short of transportation. A six-car train arrived from Harpers Ferry during the day, and White had his men seize it and fill the cars with camp equipment, surplus weapons, ammunition, and clothing. At 7:30 p.m. he wired to Miles: "As near as I can learn I am being surrounded, and shall make immediate preparation to move toward you." He asked that Miles move a support to Kearneysville. "Don't fail me," he added, an implication that he thought Miles might. "Miles is, as everybody knows, a fool & won't help us out," wrote Lieutenant Curtis that day, which possibly reflected the prevailing opinion at White's headquarters and offered an explanation for White's statement.[53]

White waited to move until Colonel Cameron's detachment returned. They arrived around 2 a.m., after a 14-mile round-trip march. There was no time to allow these men to rest, and White put the entire command in motion at once. In the hurry of their departure large amounts of hardtack and "a considerable quantity of quartermaster stores" were left behind, which Jackson's quartermasters were delighted to discover.[54]

White's exact route is unknown, but his column took a circuitous route to Harpers Ferry, for his command approached Harpers Ferry along the Charlestown Pike and his men were unanimous in saying that they marched 22 miles (36+ for the men who had been with Cameron's scouting detachment). It proved a rough go for these mostly green soldiers. "It was rendered harder by the fact that the men labored under the impression, usual to recruits, that they must carry as much luggage as they could well load on their persons," observed the 125th New York's historian. Before long the men began to lighten their loads, and cast-off clothing and equipment littered the line of march. Some Confederate pickets—probably from the 12th Virginia Cavalry—were encountered west of Halltown, but they were easily driven off. Then a report came from the front of a strong enemy force approaching from the direction of Harpers Ferry. White deployed his brigade into line and prepared to defend himself. The "enemy" proved to be a detachment of the 8th New York Cavalry, which Miles had sent out to support White. The march continued, and White's men struggled into Harpers Ferry around 4 p.m. They would soon discover that their grueling journey had simply transferred them from the frying pan into the fire.[55]

White evacuated Martinsburg not an hour too soon, for Stonewall Jackson had his divisions moving on Martinsburg by dawn on September 12. Jackson marched with J. R. Jones's and Lawton's divisions, who advanced on Martinsburg

by way of the village of Hedgeville. The troops moved slowly, since they anticipated enemy contact. Major Myers, scouting ahead with his 7th Virginia Cavalry,
soon sent word back that the enemy had departed. The infantry stepped up
their pace, for it was now a race to see who could get the pick of what the Yankees
had left behind. A. P. Hill's division had the better road and his brigades won
the race, arriving around 10 a.m. Martinsburg's friendly population "received
us cordially," noted Greenlee Davidson, "and soon nearly every house was
crowded with weary and broken down soldiers." An officer in Gregg's brigade
wrote that "in addition to the sutler's goods and government provisions, which
were in abundance, the citizens of the place brought us baskets of food, and
invited large numbers of us to go home and dine with them." Jackson arrived
soon after and received "a hearty welcome." Martinsburg had a reputation of
possessing Union sympathizers early in the war, but the Unionists either had
been run off or knew to keep quiet, and most of the town's residents rejoiced to
see Confederate soldiers. They flocked around Jackson, who sought refuge in
the Everett Hotel so that he might compose a dispatch to Lee undisturbed. But
the curiosity seekers of "both sexes, and of all ages and social condition," crav-
ing a look at the famous Stonewall, crowded around the hotel. Jackson ordered
the doors locked and the windows closed, but the citizens rattled the shutters
and called at the windows. "He wrote and gave no heed to the appealing sounds,"
observed Henry Kyd Douglas. A few young ladies among the crowd somehow
managed to pry open the shutters of one window near Jackson. They pressed
their lips against the glass and called out, "Dear, dear General." After their having
penetrated Jackson's defenses, someone assisted the young woman and forced
the window open a crack. Red and white roses were tossed into the room.
Douglas observed a smile break over Stonewall's stern face, "for there is a point
beyond which to resist the pleadings of woman is not a virtue." The dispatch
was finished and Jackson relented to the public onslaught. "Now admit the
ladies," he said to Douglas.[56]

Jackson's fans pressed up to and about the general. The fierce warrior stood
there "blushing, bowing, almost speechless" before them. "They were saying
everything and asking everything," Douglas recalled. "One little girl who had
forced her way in, was saying, 'Oh, can't Papa come home just till tomorrow,
please Sir?' and a boy not much larger, 'Ain't I big enough to be a soldier?'" One
young girl asked for a button off his coat. Jackson agreed and was promptly set
upon by girls and boys who cut half the buttons off the front of his jacket and all
of his coattail buttons. Someone produced some paper and Jackson answered
the cries for his autograph, but when one young lady asked for a lock of his hair,
he drew the line and called an end to the interview. He and his staff departed
Martinsburg that afternoon, halting some 5 or 6 miles southeast of Martinsburg
and established headquarters at the bivouac of A. P. Hill's division.[57]

Jackson allowed his divisions a nearly three-hour respite in Martinsburg,
perhaps to allow time for the quartermasters to allocate and distribute the

captured Union rations, but he also may have been waiting for his cavalry to report on what the Union garrison at Harpers Ferry was doing. His command had met the timetable of Special Orders No. 191 and seized possession of the B&O Railroad. They had not destroyed or captured the Martinsburg garrison, but that unit was on the run. If McLaws and Walker had captured Maryland Heights and Loudoun Heights, as called for in Special Orders No. 191, then the Martinsburg and Harpers Ferry garrisons might attempt to escape the trap closing around them and make a dash for Maryland. If they did, the only crossing on the Potomac open to them was Shepherdstown. By 4 p.m. Jackson probably learned that White had retreated to Harpers Ferry and that the garrison there remained in place. He ordered A. P. Hill's and Lawton's divisions to resume their march. They tramped "over a most wretched road," for nearly 6 miles "toward Harpers Ferry" before a halt was called and the two divisions camped for the night. Exactly where they halted is unknown, but given the distance marched, it was probably Walpers' Crossroads or Travelers Rest. The former point sat astride the Shepherdstown Pike, only 3 miles southwest of that town, and the latter locale was only a mile from the pike and 6 miles southwest of Shepherdstown. Either site placed these two divisions in position to intercept the enemy should they attempt a night march to Shepherdstown. J. R. Jones's division, for reasons that are not clear, remained near Martinsburg, camping just southeast of the town. Hundreds of barefoot men were also left behind, part of the steady drip of manpower exacted by the army's every move.[58]

As night spread across the lower end of the Shenandoah Valley, if Jackson had assessed the situation he would have had reason to be partially satisfied. His divisions were in position to intercept the enemy if they fled. If the Federals remained at Harpers Ferry, he could have two divisions in front of that place by late morning, and his third by the afternoon. But Jackson must have wondered how McLaws and Walker were faring. He had not heard from either. Were they in position? Had they encountered delays? These were questions that would have to wait until morning for answers.

McLaws and Walker: "All are cheerful and hopeful"

Brigadier General John G. Walker cut a trim and handsome figure as a soldier. Born in Missouri, his grandfather had served on George Washington's staff during the Revolution. Perhaps raised on the stories of that seemingly glorious time, Walker enlisted in the old U.S. army when war with Mexico began. By the war's end he had a wound received at Molino del Rey and a brevet captain's rank. He remained in the regular army after the war, but Walker was a cultured, intelligent man, and during one of his leaves he toured the great capitals of Europe. A sense of and taste for politics also ran in his family, and he spent part of his time in Europe in the company of Illinois Senator Stephen A. Douglas.

Secession did not immediately appeal to Walker, for he did not resign his commission in the U.S. Army until July 31, 1861. By January he was a brigadier general in the Confederate Army. He led a brigade of principally North Carolina troops in Theophilus Holmes's division on the Peninsula. After the Seven Days, when other employment was found for Holmes, Walker was elevated to command the division, which now counted only two brigades composed of seven North Carolina regiments, the 3rd Arkansas, and the 30th Virginia; life for the latter two in a nearly all–North Carolina outfit must have been interesting.[59]

Called up from the Richmond defenses after the victory at Second Manassas, Walker's march was delayed to wait for transportation, and his division did not reach the Confederate army until September 7, when they arrived at Buckeystown. They moved up closer to Monocacy Junction on the 8th, and his men enjoyed a chance to bathe and wash dirty clothes in the Monocacy River. According to Walker, he reported to Lee on this day and found him alone in his tent. Walker said that because Lee intended Walker's division to operate independently and be subject to orders directly from army headquarters, Lee proceeded to confide his plans for the campaign north of the Potomac in great detail to Walker. Walker was a gallant soldier, but either his memory failed him here or he had a flair for historical fiction, for this meeting with Lee probably never happened. If they did meet at all, the meeting was brief, for Lee did not yet know what assignment he would give the Missourian. Proof of this was revealed on September 9, in the apparent confusion over what it was headquarters wanted Walker's division to do. He was first ordered to march about 3 miles north toward Frederick. But around noon he received orders directing him to hurry his division back to the camp they had left that morning. They arrived around 2 p.m. and spent the next three hours drawing rations. By this point Walker knew his mission: return to the mouth of the Monocacy and destroy the aqueduct of the C&O Canal. Lee certainly knew how he intended to use Walker's division in the Harpers Ferry operation, but there is no evidence that he shared this with Walker. What he did communicate to the Missourian was a sense of urgency to complete the destruction of the aqueduct quickly, for Walker's division hurriedly decamped at 5:30 p.m., before the men had time to cook their rations.[60]

The division marched through a "pitch dark" night and arrived at the Monocacy River around 11 p.m. The 24th North Carolina had the advance, and they sent two men across the river to see if there were Yankees about. There were—probably a detachment of the 1st Massachusetts Cavalry. Whoever the Federals were, they captured both scouts. When the two men failed to return, it was decided to move the entire 24th and 25th North Carolina to the east bank, to protect the destructive work to be done to the aqueduct. As the two regiments established their positions in the inky darkness, someone called out a challenge. Captain George Duffy of the 24th went forward to investigate. Duffy was considered the best captain in the regiment, despite a drinking problem. Shots rang out and Duffy fell with a wound in his spine. A "bitter skirmish" ensued, resulting in two privates from Company K being taken prisoner but no other casualties. The Yankees departed, and there was no more trouble that night.[61]

Walker organized details to attack the aqueduct, but the structure was formidable. Walker found it so thoroughly "cemented that it was found to be virtually one solid mass of granite." Engineers tried to drill holes to plant blasting charges, "but the drills furnished . . . were too dull and the granite too hard." The work continued until nearly 4 in the morning before Walker concluded that the job would take days, not hours. Someone had informed him that a large force of Yankees under Nathanial Banks were at Poolesville, only about 6 miles away. Moreover, Lee had told Walker that the army would march west from Frederick on the 10th. If he remained to complete the destruction of the aqueduct, Walker fretted that his division was "in a most exposed and dangerous position." He ordered the engineers to pack up their tools and had his regiments and batteries fall in. At 4 a.m. the division left the aqueduct behind. Lee had advised the Missourian that he could rejoin the main body of the army by marching via Jefferson to Middletown. The road through Adamstown was the most direct route to these two villages, and Walker marched his division to near where this road left the road to Frederick, slightly over 2 miles south of Buckeystown, where he called a halt. He never explained why he halted here, but it was probably to rest his men and place the division where it could either move to Frederick, if the army's departure had been delayed, or proceed directly to Middletown. It soon became a moot point when a copy of Special Orders No. 191 was delivered to him. Instead of joining Lee at Middletown, the orders required Walker's division to return to the aqueduct, cross the Monocacy there, and ford the Potomac at Cheek's Ford. Walker sensed potential danger. If the Federals were at Poolesville, it was likely that they had occupied both of the suggested points in the hours since his division left the aqueduct. He investigated before marching and learned that "a large force of the enemy," with artillery, was positioned to cover both the Monocacy crossing and Cheek's Ford. Who they were is something of a mystery, and the size of the force is irrelevant; Walker believed they were there and decided not to attempt two river crossings with hostile forces nearby. He determined instead to ford the Potomac at Point of Rocks. Waiting until morning to make that crossing was out of the question. Walker had no choice but to subject his men to another exhausting night march. Sometime after 7 p.m. he assembled his division and set out for the Potomac.[62]

Point of Rocks was only about 6 miles away, but to reach the ford the division had to cross the C&O Canal, which proved problematic. Colonel Banning's detachment from Harpers Ferry had destroyed the bridge over the canal several days earlier, and Walker's men discovered this when they arrived there at midnight. The leading regiment, the 30th Virginia, was put to work carrying railroad ties some 300 yards from the nearby B&O Railroad to build a bridge. It took over five hours to finish the bridge and move the division, with its artillery and trains, over the canal to the Potomac. Here Walker encountered a new problem. The banks of the Point of Rocks ford were steep, which made the passage of his artillery vehicles and wagons painfully slow. The infantry plunged into the river, which they discovered was "very cold." It was deep as well, coming "to the shoulders of the shorter men." And the river bottom was covered with a "multitude of boulders," which made footing tricky. A drizzly rain began to fall, but the weather was warm, and most of Walker's men were too exhausted to care about being wet. By the time he had his entire division across the Potomac, Walker realized that two nights without sleep had sapped the energy of his men, and he decided not to push them farther that day. The division made camp about a mile from the river, where they were observed by the newly established Union signal station on Sugar Loaf Mountain.[63]

The division broke camp and marched at 7 a.m. on the 12th. Walker's orders directed him to march to Loudoun Heights by way of Lovettsville, but the route from Lovettsville to Loudoun Heights was a winding road that approached the Heights along an easily defended, narrow defile between the Potomac River and Short Hill Mountain. Even if the enemy did not guard this point, the road paralleled the Potomac for nearly 4 miles, which would certainly reveal his approach to the Federals. Walker decided it would better to approach Loudoun Heights by way of Hillsborough. This required a longer march, but it avoided the Short Hill Mountain defile, the roads were better, and it would be easier for his division to approach the Heights undetected. With a good day's rest and full night of sleep, Walker's troops enjoyed a march through the unspoiled countryside. One of his North Carolinians thought the landscape they passed through to be "some of the most magnificent country in Virginia." Walker called a halt to the day's march at Hillsborough, which was fine with the men, for it was a small but friendly village with an unusual number of pretty girls.[64]

At Hillsborough Walker was 8 miles from Loudoun Heights and a full day behind the schedule laid down in Special Orders No. 191. He might have pushed his men closer to Loudoun Heights that day, but Walker needed to proceed carefully. The enemy garrison at Harpers Ferry outnumbered him and, lacking cavalry, he could not easily gather information about them. Were they defending Loudoun Heights? What if the approach of Jackson and McLaws flushed them out of Harpers Ferry and they sought escape by crossing the Shenandoah? The Confederates did not expect the Yankees to wait until they were boxed in at Harpers Ferry. But, if this happened, then the enemy's most likely path of escape led through Hillsborough, because the Hillsborough Pike offered the swiftest escape route to points east. Viewed in this light, Walker's decision to halt his division at Hillsborough makes sense. He held a good defensive position astride the enemy's best path of escape, and he could use using the evening and night to have his scouts gather information on the Federals.[65]

The success of the Harpers Ferry operation depended greatly on speed and coordination to meet the timetable set by Lee. The cornerstone of the operation was the capture of Maryland Heights. With it in the Confederates' possession, the Union garrison must either surrender or run for it. Curiously, then, the force assigned to capture it—General Lafayette McLaws's two divisions—was next to last in the army's order of march from Frederick. Five divisions (Jackson's three and two of Longstreet's), plus Evans's brigade, all with their attached artillery and trains, preceded McLaws. It was not until noon that the road was open for his divisions, and it was 4:30 p.m. before his 10 brigades, artillery, and trains cleared Frederick. Some of the officers used the idle time to imbibe spirits. A South Carolinian remembered Brigadier General Howell Cobb being "very drunk," and his own brigade commander, Brigadier General Joseph Kershaw, "had been drinking." The men found the road "horribly dusty" and experienced the maddening and fatiguing stopping and starting that units in the rear of a marching column inevitably encounter. Sunset came at 6:16 p.m., but McLaws pushed on. "Most fatiguing march since Barhamsville. Thought we would never halt," a weary Captain Henry L. P. King, an aide to McLaws and a graduate of Harvard Law and Yale, noted in his diary. When they reached Middletown it was midnight. McLaws had hoped to get farther, but his men were at the end of their rope and he called a halt to let them get some rest. They had marched 14 miles in 12 hours, barely over a mile an hour—the price of marching near the rear of a long column.[66]

The troops woke early on the 11th to a day that promised to be both warm and rainy. They also discovered what Jackson's men had found earlier—the Confederates had no friends in Middletown. A Mississippi infantryman found the place "entirely Union" and learned that the women "expressed their opinion quite freely." While his men attempted unsuccessfully to buy something to eat in the village, McLaws had his quartermasters reduce the trains accompanying the two divisions to what his aide Captain King described as "as little as possible." No division in the Army of Northern Virginia could be accused of having too many wagons hauling supplies, but the march on the 10th apparently convinced McLaws that he did, at least to execute the type of swift movement he anticipated was necessary to meet the timetable of Special Orders No. 191. By 9 a.m. preparations were complete and the column set out, turning southwest in Middletown on the road to Burkittsville. Between the heat and the rain showers, a Mississippian in Barksdale's brigade found the march "very disagreeable." But James Kirkpatrick, in Featherston's brigade, admired the "fine fruit country" they marched through, although he noted, no doubt with disappointment, that the orchards "are always strictly guarded."[67]

While the infantry and artillery toiled along through heat and rain, McLaws dispatched his two companies of cavalry, accompanied by his engineer, Lieutenant Duncan G. Campbell, the son of the Confederate Assistant Secretary of War, to scout forward. No doubt Campbell's mission was to ascertain which pass McLaws should use to cross South Mountain and determine whether or not it was defended. Part of Campbell's escort rode ahead into Burkittsville and surprised some Federal cavalry, probably from the 7th Rhode Island squadron. The Confederates captured five of them, but the others beat a retreat and took cover behind a stone wall; these were numerous in the area. By the time McLaws arrived at Burkittsville, Campbell had discovered a former resident who apparently belonged to a Texas regiment and happened to be visiting home (probably without leave). McLaws evidently lacked a good map of the region, for the Texan knew where one could be found and agreed to lead Lieutenant Campbell to it. Captain King and a courier joined Campbell and the Texan, and the four men set off to cross South Mountain. They rode alone, because McLaws's cavalry had taken another road. There were two gaps over the mountain west of Burkittsville. The one with a better grade, although still steep, was Crampton's Gap, directly west of the village. Brownsville Gap, or Pass, crossed the mountain southwest of the village. This was the more direct route toward Maryland Heights and Harpers Ferry, and it was the pass the four riders used to cross the mountain. On the summit King saw tracks of Federal cavalry, and he observed three videttes below. They withdrew when the Confederates descended the mountain, and the Rebel party entered the small village of Brownsville without incident around 4 p.m. The people gave the Confederates what Captain King thought was a "dubious reception," but they told him that the enemy's troops were in strong force on Maryland Heights, and King could see Union cavalry in Solomon's Gap. Some 30 minutes after their arrival, McLaws's cavalry came up, followed by Joe Kershaw's infantry brigade. Kershaw had Captain John P. W. Read's four-gun Georgia battery with him, which included a 10 lb. Parrott rifle and a 3-inch ordnance rifle, both of which had the range to reach Solomon's Gap. Kershaw ordered Read to deliver some iron compliments to their Yankee observers. Two shells sent them scattering.[68]

The valley the Confederates had entered was called Pleasant Valley, a beautiful place populated by neatly kept, prosperous farms. It sat snug between South Mountain to the east and Elk Ridge to the west. From mountain to mountain the valley averaged about 1.5 miles across, but it was narrower closer to the Potomac River and wider as its northern end near Rohrersville. Two roads traversed the valley floor. The better of the two—the Weverton–Rohrersville Road—hugged the base of South Mountain. The other, "very much out of repair and not much used" in 1862, paralleled the base of Elk Ridge on its way to Sandy Hook. There were four mountain gaps in the area that were of importance to McLaws. The first two were Brownsville Pass and Crampton's Gap through

South Mountain, both about 1 mile southwest and west, respectively, from Burkittsville. Weverton Pass, 4 miles south of Brownsville Pass, marked the southern end of South Mountain, where it stops abruptly before the Potomac River, leaving barely enough land between river and mountain for the tiny village of Weverton, the Harpers Ferry–Frederick Turnpike, the B&O Railroad, and the C&O Canal to be crowded in. The formidable mass of Elk Ridge, whose southern terminus is Maryland Heights, had only one gap that provided access to the rear of the Heights. This is Solomon's Gap, situated due west of Brownsville and approximately 4.5 miles north of Maryland Heights' summit. McLaws learned that an old charcoal road ran south from the gap along the spine of the mountain for some distance and provided a useable approach to the Heights. It was along this route that the Georgian intended to march his infantry, who would storm Maryland Heights.

McLaws and his staff made their headquarters at the home of Mr. Boteler, who received them with "great hospitality." From the reconnaissance conducted by his cavalry, the prisoners taken that afternoon, and the civilians who visited Boteler's house that evening, McLaws learned that the 10,000 Federals he was told made up the Harpers Ferry garrison had not fled as expected, but had taken "every possible measure" to defend the place.[69]

Until nightfall obscured their view, Union officers perched in the Lookout atop the summit of Maryland Heights observed McLaws's entry into Pleasant Valley. Before it became too dark to see, they estimated that as many as 10 enemy regiments had descended through Brownsville Pass into the valley. The enemy numbers and their shelling of Solomon's Gap left no question that they intended to make trouble for the defenders of Maryland Heights. In the seven days since being assigned command of the Heights, Colonel Ford had managed to construct some modest defenses with the 10 axes he was allotted by Colonel Miles. Captain John T. Whittier's Company F, 1st Maryland Potomac Home Brigade, had partially completed a breastwork located about 400 yards north of the Lookout, built of "large chestnut logs" and tree limbs piled together, "with rocks to shoot through," the same day that McLaws made his appearance. The right of the breastwork was securely anchored on a rock outcropping overlooking the steep eastern slope of the mountain, but the left remained unfinished and ended in the woods on the western slope. Whittier's detail also built a formidable abatis of "trees cut down and limbs sharpened at the ends and all piled up in a mass" in front of the breastwork. Several hundred yards north of this they cut a second, but less imposing abatis. At Solomon's Gap other details had created some obstructions, but they amounted to very little, and Ford had established a picket here, consisting of a dozen troopers from the 7th Rhode Island squadron and 22 infantry from the 32nd Ohio, when McLaws's approach was reported.[70]

Other than the picket at Solomon's Gap and another at the Lookout, Ford's infantry—the nine companies of the 32nd Ohio, and three companies of the 1st

Maryland Potomac Home Brigade, slightly less than 1,000 men all told—were camped near the naval battery on the mountain's western slope when McLaws reached Pleasant Valley. Ford ordered three companies—two of Marylanders and one of Ohioans, totaling around 200 effectives—to reinforce the picket at the Lookout. He also requested reinforcements from Miles, who responded immediately, ordering Colonel Trimble to send a regiment and Colonel D'Utassy to detach the 39th New York, under Major Hugo Hildebrandt, from his brigade. The selection of the 39th is significant. It was the smallest regiment on the Bolivar Heights line, but it was the most experienced one, and its arrival on Maryland Heights would give Ford the two best regiments (the 32nd Ohio being the other) in the Union garrison. Miles was no longer discounting the enemy threat. With the wire from White announcing that he would abandon Martinsburg that night and the arrival of the Confederates in Pleasant Valley, Miles was now fully aware that he might be the game the enemy were after.[71] Late that night he sent Halleck the last telegram from Harpers Ferry before Jackson's men cut the line.

> My eastern front is threatened. My pickets at Solomon's Gap shelled out. The ball will open to-morrow morning. Force opposed to me is estimated at ten regiments of infantry with proportionate artillery, before dusk; others have come into camp since. General White will abandon Martinsburg some time to-night, and I expect this will be the last you will hear from me until this affair is over. All are cheerful and hopeful. Good-bye.[72]

In Pleasant Valley, Lafayette McLaws made his plans for September 12. He selected two of his best brigades to capture Maryland Heights: Brigadier General Joseph B. Kershaw's South Carolinians, and Brigadier General William Barksdale's Mississippians. Kershaw had 1,294 officers and men, and Barksdale 960. As the senior officer, Kershaw would command the attack. His orders were to ascend Elk Ridge through Solomon's Gap in the morning, march south along the spine of the ridge, and "carry the heights." The attack would be made with infantry alone, since the difficult terrain precluded taking any artillery along. While Kershaw attacked south along Elk Ridge to Maryland Heights, Brigadier General Howell Cobb's Georgia–North Carolina brigade, numbering 1,341 officers and men, would follow the old road along the base of Elk Ridge. In the words of McLaws, their job was "to give support, if possible, if it was needed, and to serve as a rallying force should any disaster render such necessary." Two brigades were left at Brownsville to watch Kershaw's rear, as well as both Crampton's Gap and Brownsville Pass through South Mountain. They were Brigadier General Paul J. Semmes's Georgia-Virginia brigade of 700 effectives from McLaws's division, and a Virginia brigade from R. H. Anderson's division, commanded by Colonel William A. Parham, which was also about 700 strong.[73]

McLaws committed only one brigade to secure Weverton Pass, probably because he knew it was undefended. This was Brigadier General Augustus R. Wright's Georgia-Alabama brigade, somewhat less than 1,000 men, of R. H. Anderson's division. Supported by two mountain howitzers, Wright's orders were to advance along the crest of South Mountain and seize the point overlooking the Harpers Ferry Road and commanding the pass. With the remaining four brigades—Armistead's, Pryor's, Featherston's, and Cumming's, all from R. H. Anderson's division—and most of the artillery of both divisions, McLaws intended to advance down the valley along the Sandy Hook road, paralleling Kershaw's advance. This movement had two purposes. First, it threatened Sandy Hook, forcing the enemy to defend it and possibly preventing them from diverting forces to confront Kershaw. Second, if the enemy attempted to sortie from Harpers Ferry and escape, McLaws could meet them with a powerful force. To maintain communications, signal corps detachments were detailed to all the various commands. It was a solid, well-balanced plan, but the obstacles to be surmounted—both enemy defenders and the formidable nature of the terrain—promised that success would not come easily.[74]

September 12 dawned clear and warm. Preparations for the day's operations were not complete until 8:30 a.m., when Kershaw moved out with his two brigades. He deployed five companies of skirmishers: two from the 7th South Carolina, one from the 2nd South Carolina, and two from Barksdale's brigade. His own brigade, trailed by Barksdale's, followed the skirmishers. An hour and a half's march brought them to Solomon's Gap. The skirmishers pushed up the mountain, probing carefully for Yankees. "Our duty was very hard indeed," wrote one of them, "as we had no road like the rest of the army, but had to clamber over immense rocks and climb up the steep heights in order to discover if any of the Yankees lay in our way." Near the summit they encountered some pickets from the 7th Rhode Island squadron. A handful of shots were exchanged, and the Federals melted away. Kershaw reached the summit of the gap by 10 a.m. Here he discovered two roads, which were little more than paths, running south toward Maryland Heights. Kershaw permitted his men a short rest to catch their breath and then resumed the advance. He ordered handsome, blue-eyed Captain George B. Cuthbert, commanding the South Carolina skirmishers, to orient his advance along the right-hand road—"a dim path" according to one skirmisher—which sent his skirmish line extending down the western side of the mountain, and told Major J. M. Bradley, commanding the Mississippians, to guide his men along the left-hand road, or path, which apparently ran near the crest of the mountain ridge.[75]

Fifteen minutes into the movement south, Cuthbert's men received fire from what he estimated were three companies of Union cavalry. It was actually Union infantry. At 5 a.m. that morning Major Hugo Hildebrandt had reported to Colonel Ford at the naval battery. Hildebrandt was at the head of a force consisting of six companies of the 39th New York and two companies of the 115th New York, which were loaned to him because two other 39th companies were not available when he marched. Hildebrandt and his companies were a veritable ethnic melting pot. The 30-year-old major was a Hungarian with an adventurer's spirit and a soft spot for causes aligned with liberty. He fought with Louis Kossuth's Hungarian revolutionary army and with Garibaldi in Italy before enlisting in the 39th. The regiment, raised in New York City, consisted of three Hungarian, three German, one Spanish, one French, and one Swiss company, plus a smattering of Turks, Croats, and others. They referred to themselves as the Garibaldi Guard. Ford allowed Hildebrandt and his men a short rest after the long climb up the Heights, then ordered him to take four of his 39th New York companies, along with two companies of the 1st Maryland Potomac Home Brigade (who were attached due to their familiarity with the area), "to make a reconnaissance" toward Solomon's Gap and capture two companies of Rebels, whom Ford had been told were lying exhausted at the gap. Hildebrandt had some 400 men.[76]

At the Lookout Hildebrandt encountered some Rhode Island cavalrymen who had been picketing Solomon's Gap. They told him that they had been driven in from the gap by a "heavy force" of the enemy. "I paid not much attention to them," Hildebrandt testified, but he ordered two companies out as skirmishers. They found the woods so thick that it was impossible to deploy in the normal skirmish order. Instead they spread out along the "very narrow road" that ran to Solomon's Gap, which Hildebrandt found so rough and closed in that "it was nearly impossible to ride on a horse." The other companies followed the skirmishers as best they could. It was 10:45 a.m. when Hildebrandt's men suddenly ran into Cuthbert's South Carolinians. The Federals got off the first shots, but Cuthbert's men replied with a "very heavy fire" that hit six or seven of Hildebrandt's men. This convinced Hildebrandt that the Confederates were ahead in strong numbers, and he pulled his entire force back to a more defensible position south of the point of contact. The major thought the right flank of this new position was potentially vulnerable, so he placed part of his Maryland contingent as pickets near the crest of the mountain to cover it.[77]

The Confederates did not press Hildebrandt, for the terrain provided a major obstacle to any movement. Cuthbert's three companies lost their way "by the fault of the guide" who accompanied them, and they drifted away from the main column, which followed Major Bradley's Mississippians. But even Bradley's troops became separated for a short time when a "high stone ridge" intervened between his skirmishers and Kershaw's main body. The going was agonizingly slow. McLaws sent along his aide, Captain Henry L. P. King, to accompany Kershaw, and the captain noted the difficulties they encountered in his diary: "Almost impassable woods[,] rocks—no road—blind path & no path." There were frequent halts to send signal messages to McLaws in the valley. In just over two and a half hours the column had covered only "about a mile." At 12:45 p.m.

shots cracked from Bradley's skirmish line, which had found its way back to its proper place in front of the main body. The Major reported that an abatis blocked the way. This was the northernmost obstruction thrown up by Captain Whittier's Marylanders. Defending it were the pickets Hildebrandt had deployed to protect his flank. Kershaw sent back orders for Bradley to advance "and ascertain the force in front." The Marylanders fell back, and the Mississippians easily carried the position. Here Kershaw found that the narrow path his two brigades had been following passed down the western slope of the mountain, away from the summit of Maryland Heights. He had no choice but to leave the trail and follow the spine of the mountain south, which meant bushwhacking "along the crags on the ridge."[78]

Around 3:30 p.m. Bradley's skirmishers encountered more light resistance, probably offered by the companies picketing the Lookout: Captain Jefferson Hibbetts's company of the 32nd Ohio, and Companies H and I of the 1st Maryland Potomac Home Brigade. But it was the terrain, not the Union pickets whom Bradley's efficient skirmishers easily drove off, that kept Kershaw's advance moving along at a glacial pace. Hildebrandt's force might have caused him considerable trouble had the major been more aggressive, but after the initial clash near Solomon's Gap Hildebrandt steered clear of the enemy and eventually marched his men back to Ford's headquarters at the naval battery.[79]

The Confederates' creeping advance continued unchecked until 6 p.m., when suddenly Bradley's skirmishers opened a rapid fire. The major sent back a report that he had encountered an abatis that extended across the mountain ridge and was anchored at both ends on steep rock ledges. Flanking was not an option at this late hour of the day. Kershaw ordered Bradley to test the position. "A sharp skirmish ensued," which satisfied Kershaw that "the enemy occupied the position in force." He ordered Bradley to retire his skirmishers and arrayed his brigade in battle line. The mountain ridge offered space for only two regiments to deploy abreast. Kershaw placed Colonel John W. Henagan's 8th South Carolina (a small unit of 126 officers and men) and Colonel D. Wyatt Aiken's 7th South Carolina (the largest regiment in the brigade, with 466 effectives) in the front line. The 2nd and the 3rd South Carolina, 624 officers and men combined, formed the support line in their rear. Barksdale remained in reserve, probably formed in column. By the time the deployment was completed, darkness had descended. The men were ordered to sleep with their equipment on and their weapons beside them. Kershaw planned to attack at daylight.[80]

All the men in both brigades were drained by the day's labor. It had taken nearly eight hours to march slightly less than 4 miles. Captain King scribbled in his diary that the troops "had had no water since morning, almost famished—little to eat and no fires allowed. Horses destitute." In William Hill's regiment, the 13th Mississippi, the men's rations consisted of "nothing but apples." Everyone, he wrote, "suffered very much for water & food." Some relief was afforded by a detail that hauled water 2.5 miles up the mountain in the dark. In Kershaw's second line, Sergeant Robert Shand of the 2nd South Carolina was "tired, sick and despondent." The heat and hard day's march had taken their toll, but Shand feared the combat he knew was pending in the morning. He had already been wounded once, at Savage Station. His brother-in-law, James Edwards, lay beside him, and Shand told him what to do if he should be killed in the next day's fighting. Edwards harbored the same fears, and he pledged Shand to do the same for him. Robert Gault, a conscript who had joined the regiment in July, overheard the two men talking and shared his own tale of woe, which perhaps convinced Shand and Edwards that things could always be worse. Gault, an illiterate farmer, explained that he was over 35 years old and had been improperly conscripted. He had apparently proved his point, for he told Shand that his discharge had been ordered and he would get his papers as "soon as this fight was over." Gault would survive the next morning, but it was a Yankee, not Confederate authorities, who gave him his discharge, with a bullet through the heart at Sharpsburg five days later.[81]

Dixon Miles responded to Kershaw's steady advance toward Maryland Heights with additional reinforcements. He had intended to send Ford two regiments on the morning of the 12th, the 39th and the 126th New York, which Colonel Trimble had selected from his brigade. Most of the 39th did go, but when the 126th reached the pontoon bridge they were ordered to return to their camp on Bolivar Heights. Ford thought the untrained New Yorkers "would do me more harm than good," and he apparently sent a message to Miles that he did not need them. But by around midafternoon on the 12th either Ford changed his tune or Miles made the decision, for around 3 p.m. Colonel Trimble received orders to send a regiment to report to Maryland Heights. Colonel Eliakim Sherrill, the commander of the 126th New York, which was the largest (and also the rawest) regiment in the Union garrison, was with Trimble when the order arrived. Things were evidently handled casually at Trimble's headquarters, for, according to the adjutant of the 126th, he "left it to Colonel Sherrill to go if he saw fit." Sherrill had an abundance of courage, but he was also conscious of both his and his men's lack of training and experience. He replied that "he knew nothing about military; that he made no pretensions to military; that he was just in the field and green, but if there was to be fighting he was ready to go." This expression of confidence was good enough for Trimble, and he ordered Sherrill to move his regiment at once. Sherrill had about 830 men on hand, for 200 officers and men of the regiment were on picket duty and could not be recalled by the time the regiment marched. Loaded down with a day's rations and 80 rounds of ammunition, they formed up and marched down through Harpers Ferry to the pontoon bridge, then started the laborious climb up Maryland Heights. The ascent took its toll on the new recruits. It was hot (the high that day was near 79 degrees) and they were unused to the heavy loads they carried. "Many strong men fell, victims of sunstroke or faintness," recorded the regimental historian.[82]

Despite the heat and the difficulty of the climb, Sherrill's regiment made good time and arrived at Ford's headquarters around 5:30 p.m. Ford turned the regiment over to Major Sylvester M. Hewitt, who was commanding the 32nd Ohio, while Ford exercised brigade command. Hewitt led the 126th and five companies of his own regiment up the path toward the Lookout. When they reached the bridle path that ran along the crest of the mountain, Hewitt detached Companies A and F of the 126th to reinforce Captain Abraham Crumbecker's Company A, 32nd Ohio, who were picketing the path up the southeastern slope of the mountain from Sandy Hook. Hewitt detached three more companies of the 126th (C, D, and I) and left them at the Lookout. The sharp firing between Bradley's skirmishers and the Ohioans and Marylanders who manned the thin Union skirmish line could be heard clearly. Hewitt marched the balance of his command—the remaining five companies of the 126th and the five companies of the 32nd—toward the gunfire. The 126th's companies formed a line of battle in the rear of the skirmish line across the mountain crest. It must have been frightening for the new recruits of the 126th. Muskets were banging away rapidly on the skirmish line. The acrid smell of powder lingered in the woods. Combat was nothing like these men probably expected it to be. Nerves were on edge. Most likely everyone had forgotten their fatigue from the climb up the mountain. "We could hear the enemy in pretty large force, by their talk," recalled the regiment's major, William H. Baird. But the Confederates rarely revealed themselves to view. The left companies of the regiment opened fire, probably more at the sound of the enemy than at any good targets. The return fire seemed heavy enough that Sherrill sent for Companies C and I at the Lookout and ordered them to support the left flank. Darkness soon put an end to the shooting, and the New Yorkers, Ohioans, and Marylanders lay down on their arms to try and get what rest they could when the enemy is within speaking distance.[83]

Listening to the firing on the mountain summit, Colonel Ford concluded that Hewitt could use more reinforcements. He ordered Major Hildebrandt to take two companies of his own 39th New York and two companies of the 32nd Ohio and report to the major. The four companies made the climb, only to have Hewitt countermand Ford's order and send them back to the naval battery with orders to "stay the whole night under arms" to protect the big guns. Ford made no known objection when the companies returned, but he did send Company H of the 1st Maryland Potomac Home Brigade up to the Lookout during the night. This time Hewitt accepted the reinforcements.[84]

Because of Ford's immobilizing illness, Major Hewitt was the de facto field commander on Maryland Heights. Colonel Sherrill outranked him, but both Ford and Miles knew about his inexperience and bypassed him for Hewitt when communicating orders to the Heights. Still, Hewitt was in far over his head. Nightfall found him at the Lookout, trying to take some measure of the enemy's strength and intentions. A verbal order reached him from Miles, commanding him to ascertain if the Confederates were cutting a road up the eastern side of the mountain and to determine the size of the enemy force then on the Heights. Hewitt spent some time seeking answers to these questions, but the results evidently were unsatisfactory to him, for around 9 p.m. he sent Second Lieutenant Adam Carnes of his regiment forward to find Colonel Sherrill and bring him back to the Lookout. The pitch-black night and close proximity of the enemy made locating Sherrill an adventure, but Carnes found him and they returned to the Lookout. Both Hewitt and Sherrill agreed that the Rebels were on the mountain in strong force, and that they needed substantial reinforcements. Hewitt initially thought two regiments were necessary. Sherrill thought one would suffice, but Hewitt declared that "there are men to spare down in the valley; and we haven't got three regiments." Perhaps employing the logic that if they asked for more than they needed, Miles might send them something, both men agreed to request three regiments and two mountain howitzers. Hewitt started to write out a message for Miles, but then decided that it would be better to go see Colonel Ford and explain the situation in person before communicating with Miles.[85]

Hewitt reached Ford's headquarters around 11 p.m. and explained to the colonel that the Rebels were on the mountain in strong force, more than the troops of the 3rd Brigade could handle. The Confederates were close enough to the defenders at the abatis that the latter could hear them talking and listen to their canteens rattle. Ford agreed that they should ask for three regiments. Ford had already sent two couriers to Miles requesting reinforcements (which is probably why Miles sent the 126th New York at 3 p.m.), but he thought it important that Hewitt "lay the whole matter before Colonel Miles" in person. Miles was in bed when Hewitt arrived, but he rose and met the major in his office. Hewitt laid it on the line. He estimated that the enemy outnumbered the defenders on the mountain by 10 to 1—a wild exaggeration, but perhaps a deliberate one, intended to shake up the old man—and that a general engagement could be expected in the morning. Hewitt warned, "Nothing short of a force sufficient to just shove them right off the mountain will save that place." Miles must have been perplexed by Hewitt's situation report, for earlier in the evening Colonel Ford had sent over that he could "hold Maryland Heights against all hell," to which Miles was heard to comment, "Then what in hell does he want of more men?" But Hewitt seems to have convinced Miles that reinforcements were urgently needed, for he told the major that two regiments and two guns would be on the mountain at daybreak, and that he would send a third regiment up the west side of the mountain to hit the Confederate flank. Hewitt must have been pleased as he returned to Maryland Heights. Miles had given them everything they had asked for, or so he believed.[86]

Neither Miles nor Hewitt may have realized it, but the decisive moment of the battle for Harpers Ferry had arrived. If Maryland Heights fell, the garrison was doomed. Miles had fresh reinforcements on hand and an active officer he could use to replace Ford: General Julius White had arrived from Martinsburg around 4 p.m., with the 2,500 men of the Martinsburg garrison. Miles moved quickly to settle any question of command. When White reported to him, he showed him the September 7 dispatch from Halleck to Miles that concluded: "The Government has the utmost confidence in you, and is ready to give you full credit for the defense it expects you to make." In light of this dispatch, and the fact that when the two officers had been together after White's withdrawal from Winchester, Wool sent White to the post of lesser responsibility at Martinsburg, "it was manifest" to White "that the authorities intended to retain Colonel Miles in command." White was unfamiliar with the terrain at Harpers Ferry, and also felt his inexperience as a soldier in light of Miles's 40 years' service. He agreed that Miles should command and pledged himself to serve in whatever capacity Miles needed him.[87]

As his second-in-command, White asked Miles what his plan of defense was. Miles responded that his orders were to hold Harpers Ferry to the last extremity and that he did not have any specific plans beyond defending Bolivar Heights and the bridges. White suggested that Maryland Heights appeared to be the key to the position and offered "the only feasible line of retreat" if that became necessary. It also seemed to White that the bridges could be held just as well from Maryland Heights as from Camp Hill. Miles agreed that Maryland Heights was crucial to the defense of Harpers Ferry and said that "he had erected defenses" on the summit, a statement that, while technically true, had been accomplished in spite of Miles's neglect of the Heights. But Miles did not think that the bridges could be defended as well from Maryland Heights as they could from Camp Hill, and he pointed out that there was no water on the Heights. This was not completely true. There were some small mountain streams that had their origin on the Heights, but Miles's doubt could have been over whether they could supply the water needs of thousands of men and horses. In any event, by his response to White's questions, Miles revealed that although he deemed Maryland Heights important to his defense, in his opinion it did not supersede the greater necessity of protecting the Bolivar Heights line and the bridges. He proceeded to confirm that by asking White to take command not at Maryland Heights, where he was desperately needed, but at Bolivar Heights, where Miles expected the enemy to pose the greatest threat. Maryland Heights was thus left without an effective commander.[88]

Up on the Heights, the New Yorkers and the Ohioans at the abatis lay on their arms in the dense woods, with the pitch-black night leaving them unable to see more than a few feet around them. The Confederates were only about 100 yards away. "We could hear the enemy in pretty large force, by their talk, as I judged," testified the major of the 126th. Their adjutant listened to the South Carolinians speaking and "heard several remarks made as to what they were going to do in the morning." The green New Yorkers of the 126th, only three weeks from home, must have been anxious. To a man they were sharply aware of how poorly prepared they were for combat. They faced a tough, experienced enemy, yet barely knew how to load and fire their weapons. That they were manning the front line at the critical point on Maryland Heights speaks to the ineptitude of both Colonel Ford and Major Hewitt in managing their force and reading the situation.[89]

As night descended over Maryland Heights, Ford had its defenders scattered about in several defensive pockets, none of them being mutually supporting. He had the six companies of the 39th New York, five companies of the 32nd Ohio, two companies of the 1st Maryland Cavalry, and probably two companies of the 1st Maryland Potomac Home Brigade—a total of roughly 850 effectives—providing security at the naval battery. The two companies of the 115th New York and a company of the 32nd Ohio, some 260 men, were picketing a point called the "school house" some 3 miles from the battery, which may have been along the Harpers Ferry–Sharpsburg Road. Two companies of the 126th New York and one of the 32nd Ohio, about 240 strong, picketed the eastern slope of the mountain, watching the trail up from Sandy Hook. About 230 men in three different companies from the 126th New York, the 32nd Ohio, and the 1st Maryland Potomac Home Brigade were in the vicinity of the Lookout. The balance of the 126th New York—seven companies—and Company B of the 32nd Ohio, perhaps 640 effectives in all, were facing Kershaw at the abatis several hundred yards north of the breastwork. Ford's errors were not limited to dispersing his force. He retained the best troops on the mountain to provide security for the naval battery, while the least experienced troops in the entire garrison faced the known main Confederate force. The guns were central to Harpers Ferry's defense, but husbanding his best troops to protect them while leaving green troops to fight the battle that might decide possession of Maryland Heights stood logic on its head. Moreover, Ford compromised unit integrity for no good reason by detaching and mixing companies from different regiments. Even if Miles's promised reinforcements reached the mountain by daybreak, neither Ford nor Hewitt gave hope that they would be effectively used. The battle had barely been joined, and the outlook for the Federals already looked discouraging.[90]

In Pleasant Valley McLaws had easily secured his day's objectives. Wright's brigade spent the day pushing south along the spine of South Mountain to Weverton Pass, where they arrived around 2 p.m. At sundown McLaws moved Pryor's brigade forward and secured Weverton. At the same time he advanced Cobb's and Armistead's brigades across Pleasant Valley, with their right resting on Elk Ridge, toward Sandy Hook. That village was held by five companies of Colonel William P. Maulsby's 1st Maryland Potomac Home Brigade, eight companies of the 87th Ohio, and four guns. Maulsby's men were positioned along

Maryland Heights' eastern slope, where they could cover a road or trail from the valley that ascended the Heights, as well as the approaches to Sandy Hook. Maulsby had spotted McLaws's wagon train earlier in the day as it was snaking along Pleasant Valley, extending for what appeared to be 1–2 miles and supported by a strong guard of cavalry and infantry. He sent this news back to Colonel Miles and requested instructions. Curiously, Miles responded that Maulsby should ascertain if the troops were friendly or hostile, and he ordered Maulsby to send out Captain Cole's Maryland Cavalry to investigate. If they were the enemy, Maulsby was ordered to fall back to the bridges over the Potomac and obstruct the road as he did so.[91]

It was quite clear to Maulsby that the force under observation was the enemy, for he had watched Wright's men place a gun to command Weverton Pass. Without bothering to send out Cole, Maulsby wrote Miles a note indicating that it was the enemy, and even though his orders to retire were quite clear, he claimed that he did not recognize them as a direct order to retire and wanted something unequivocal. According to Maulsby it was several hours, probably near sunset, before he received a reply. Miles delivered it personally, ordering the Marylanders to fall back to the head of the Potomac bridges. The Federals quietly left the eastern slope of Maryland Heights and evacuated Sandy Hook. McLaws was initially unaware of the Federal withdrawal, for he only advanced Cobb's and Armistead's brigades up to a point outside Sandy Hook, where they established a blocking position astride the Sandy Hook road. Had he known the Federals had evacuated, he surely would have pressed forward to threaten the Potomac bridges and isolate the Maryland Heights defenders. Except for the poor quality and possibly unknown Harpers Ferry–Sharpsburg Road running north along the western base and shoulder of Maryland Heights, the Confederates had effectively sealed off the Maryland exit for the Union garrison. They could still move troops up to Maryland Heights, but the noose around them had begun to tighten.[92]

Although the Harpers Ferry operation had fallen slightly behind schedule, the Confederates had reason to be satisfied. Jackson had flushed White's command from Martinsburg and bottled them up in Harpers Ferry. His divisions were within a day's march of Bolivar Heights. Walker's division was poised to seize Loudoun Heights on the 13th. McLaws had sealed off Weverton Pass and cut the road from Sandy Hook, and his two brigades on Maryland Heights had made good progress during the day and were in position to contest control of the key position on the mountain. But it should not be imagined that McLaws, Walker, and Jackson were smug, envisioning a quick and easy victory. The Union garrison was large, and it still held two strong defensive positions at Bolivar Heights and Maryland Heights. None of the three Confederate commands were in communication with one another; they were separated by two rivers and unable to render mutual support. And they were unaware of developments on

246 | *To Antietam Creek*

the eastern front, where the Army of the Potomac was advancing. Had they been privy to affairs at that army's headquarters and learned how utterly puzzled McClellan was by the Confederate army's movements, everyone might have breathed easier. But Lady Luck would visit the Army of the Potomac on September 13, and the campaign would be turned on its head. The Army of Northern Virginia would find itself in a very precarious position, and operations at Harpers Ferry would assume great importance.

7

The Battle for Maryland Heights

"For God's sake, don't fall back"

As dawn crept over Maryland Heights the opposing skirmishers commenced popping away at one another, announcing that this was disputed ground and only fighting would settle its possession. At Ford's headquarters, Captain Charles Russell, an aggressive officer commanding Companies H and I of the 1st Maryland Cavalry, had dismounted his troopers and come to Ford for orders. Ford told the captain to take his men up to the Lookout and report to Major Hewitt. Soon after Russell departed, Ford then ordered Major Hildebrandt to take three companies of his 39th New York up. The anticipated reinforcements promised by Miles to Major Hewitt the night before had not appeared by the time these companies departed. What happened regarding them is difficult to fix precisely, but both Ford and Miles bear responsibility. The night before, Ford told Captain Russell that Miles had sent a message offering to reinforce him with some green troops (pretty much all that was left in the garrison). According to Russell, Ford said, "I have made no answer at all to Colonel Miles, because I don't want any raw troops. I would rather do what fighting I have got to do here with the little handful of men which I have confidence in." Although Russell did not place the time of this conversation, it must have taken place after Major Hewitt's visit to Miles, requesting reinforcements. If Miles posed his communication to Ford as a question (whether the communication was written or verbal is unknown), then he may have taken Ford's lack of reply for an answer, namely, that he had changed his mind and did not need the reinforcements. This, however, would be a highly unusual change of mind for an officer, requesting three regiments of reinforcements and then, a few hours later, deciding that he did not need any. It is also possible that Miles or his headquarters staff were negligent in having the necessary orders delivered for troops to fulfill Ford's request. Whatever happened, no reinforcements were moving toward Maryland Heights when the shooting started that morning.[1]

By around 7 a.m., with the firing on Maryland Heights continuing steadily, Ford changed his mind about making his fight with the "handful" of men he "had confidence in." Ford sent the adjutant of the 32nd Ohio, Lieutenant John B. Pearce, down to Miles's headquarters to request immediate reinforcement.

Pearce reached headquarters around 8 a.m. and made his report. Miles promptly wrote out an order for Lieutenant Colonel Stephen W. Downey, commanding the 3rd Maryland Potomac Home Brigade, with 546 officers and men, to report to Ford. Apparently Miles thought Downey had already been ordered to the mountain, for he said in Pearce's hearing that if Downey did not have his command underway in five minutes Miles would arrest him. But Downey had received no orders until that morning. As Downey marched by Miles's headquarters, Miles came over and told Downey that he desired him to "report to Colonel Hall on Maryland Heights." Then he gave three or four other names for the commander on the Heights before Downey said, "You mean Colonel Ford." Downey concluded from this bizarre conversation that Miles "was not in a condition to command."[2]

Lieutenant Pearce came to a similar conclusion from his conversation with Miles that morning. After writing out the orders for Downey's regiment to march, Miles told Pearce that "there was nobody on Maryland Heights but skirmishers, but that we should expect an attack on the plateau of the Rohrersville road [which ran on the west side of Maryland Heights]." Pearce, who knew that scouts had been out that road without encountering any Rebels, replied that no enemy was on the plateau, "but that there were two brigades on the mountain." Miles said, "There was not," to which the lieutenant stated that he then responded that Miles "would soon find out there was."[3] Miles's composure and grip on reality seemed to be slipping under the mounting pressure, or perhaps he was exhibiting the effects of opium and brandy. Opium is highly addictive, and one of its side effects is confusion.

While Pearce went in search of reinforcements, the troops at the front on Maryland Heights prepared to do battle with Kershaw. Around 7 a.m. Colonel Sherrill reinforced Captain Hibbets and his Ohioans on the skirmish line with Company B of the 126th New York, under Captain William Coleman, who deployed on Hibbets left. The limited drilling the New Yorkers had completed in their two weeks of soldiering had taken place on open ground, where everyone could see everyone else and movement was unhindered by nature. On Maryland Heights, the dense woods concealed the enemy and made maneuvering and coordination difficult. For green troops, it was impossible.[4]

Captain Russell and his dismounted cavalrymen, followed soon after by Major Hildebrandt with a mix of five companies from his regiment and the 32nd Ohio, reported to Major Hewitt at the Lookout. Hewitt sent them all forward. Russell's troopers, with carbines and pistols in hand, went forward to reinforce the skirmish line, while Hildebrandt's infantry formed on the main line of battle. When Hildebrandt's companies took their place, the main line consisted of Hildebrandt's three 39th New York companies on the left, three companies of the 32nd Ohio in the center, seven companies of the 126th New York on the right center, and Companies K and B of the 1st Maryland Potomac Home Brigade, which Hewitt had also sent forward, holding the extreme right flank. All told there were probably 1,150 men on this line. Directly in their front was the less formidable of the two abatis cut by Steiner's Marylanders on the 11th.[5]

Captain Russell led his dismounted cavalry through the thick woods to reinforce the skirmish line. His companies apparently moved forward in column, for before Russell could deploy them as skirmishers, one of Kershaw's skirmishers put a minie ball through the thigh of a sergeant who stood at the head of Russell's line and dropped him. Quite a few members of the 126th New York's Company B witnessed the scene, became unnerved, and bolted for the rear, followed by their comrades. Russell quickly dispersed his companies into skirmish order, taking advantage of the abundant available cover of rocks and trees, and ordered them to return fire. While they engaged the Confederates, Russell went back and found the New Yorkers in the rear. He "begged the officers to bring their men forward again." His appeal worked, and Captain Coleman and his two lieutenants succeeded in bringing their men back up to the skirmish line.[6]

The opposing skirmish lines traded fire for several minutes, and then the Confederate skirmishers withdrew. The men of Company B, naïve in the ways of battle and unaware that the firing was simply the enemy testing their strength and fixing their position, thought that they had fought off an attack and raised a shout that was taken up by their entire regiment in their rear. This gave away their position and provided the Confederates with a sense of the strength of the Union force. A tense silence then ensued, for what Major Baird of the 126th thought was at least a half hour. Then the sharp beat of the long roll by a Confederate drummer pierced the stillness. Shouts of "Forward" sounded, followed by the noise of many soldiers approaching through the dense forest. The Confederates could not be seen yet, but, said Captain Russell, "we could hear them tramp through the alders and undergrowth." It was 7:50 a.m., and the Confederates were moving to attack.[7]

Unnerved by the sounds of hundreds of men smashing their way through the thick woods toward them, Company B broke and headed for the rear. They fled toward the center of their regimental battle line, which created a ripple of excitement in the ranks; only the efforts of the officers prevented the men from opening fire before their own men could pass through. A hole was formed in the center of the regiment and the skirmishers streamed by. Some of the company did not stop until they reached the breastwork some 300 yards to the south; others were rallied behind the regimental line. Their flight left a large gap in the skirmish line, and both Captain Hibbetts and Captain Russell were forced to pull their companies back to the main line.[8]

Kershaw attacked with two regiments up front and two in reserve. Colonel D. Wyatt Aiken's 7th South Carolina formed the left of the assault; the brigade's smallest regiment, Colonel John A. Henagan's 8th South Carolina, was on the right. The 3rd and the 2nd South Carolina followed in support. Almost immediately the front line encountered a ledge of rock that crowded the 8th regiment out of the line and left the 7th facing the Federals alone, at nearly a three to one disadvantage in numbers. But the South Carolinians were about to demonstrate that experience, discipline, and training can overcome a larger number of undisciplined troops. As the Confederates emerged into view, the Union line opened fire, with their principal firepower being the 126th New York. Had the regiment been capable of firing by volley they might have demolished Aiken's attack, but as their major, William H. Baird, observed, "it is almost impossible to get green troops to fire by volleys." Instead they opened a far less effective, and less accurate, fire at will. The Ohioans, the Marylanders, and the 39th New Yorkers added the bark of their muskets, and the mountaintop roared with the crack and whine of bullets. Aiken's men fired back and slowly and doggedly pushed their way forward into the slim abatis in front of the Federals. For 15 to 20 minutes the two lines blazed away at one another. Then the Union line wavered. The break again occurred in the 126th New York. A lieutenant in one of Captain Russell's companies was shot in sight of some of the 126th. There may also have been other casualties, and these created unsteadiness in the regiment. Major Baird, who had seen service with the 38th New York at Fair Oaks and the Seven Days battles, did not help the situation; Adjutant Samuel A. Barras observed him dodging behind trees for cover. Once the break began it spread quickly along the line. Someone shouted an order to fall back, which a corporal in Company F thought was strange, "but 'twas not ours to reason why,'" and he followed his comrades to the rear. According to Major Hildebrandt, his companies and those of the 32nd Ohio, and probably the 1st Maryland Potomac Home Brigade as well, did not join in the retreat but continued to hold off the rebels. A member of the 126th, however, writing less than a month after the battle, thought that the entire line fell into disorder, with the men of the 126th following the example of the "Garibaldis" (the 39th New York) and joined them in making for the breastwork "by the shortest route." A *New York Times* correspondent reported that the 126th became disorganized, "and the whole line fell back to the barricade, fighting as they receded."[9]

Because of the underbrush, nearly everyone crowded onto the thin mountain path that led back to the breastwork. Colonel Sherrill and his adjutant, Lieutenant Samuel Barras, beat the larger part of the troops to the works. With revolver drawn, Sherrill positioned himself at a gap in the breastwork where the trail passed through. As the men reached this point Sherrill, with the help of Barras and some of the company officers, rallied and reorganized his companies and had them form behind the breastwork. But many men slipped past in the confusion, continuing to the rear and out of the fight. The men from the other regiments came tumbling back as well, with Aiken's yelling South Carolinians in pursuit. But the slashing that ran parallel to the breastworks slowed them up, and then the Federal rifles and muskets began to crack from the breastworks. Union bullets drew some blood, and it was quickly evident to Aiken that the Federals had rallied. He ordered his men back to cover and sent word to Kershaw that the enemy was in strong force behind a solid breastwork of logs.[10]

So far the battle had raged loudly, but the thick woods afforded good cover to both sides and losses were low. That was about to change. The Federals' position was intimidating and the stout log breastwork gave the recruits of the 126th a greater sense of security, helping to stiffen their morale. The abatis, running the length of the breastwork and some 100 yards deep, posed a difficult obstacle to a frontal assault. Directly behind the abatis was the area cleared to create it, so that when an attacker managed to pass through the obstacle he emerged into the open, directly in front of the breastwork. The right flank of the breastwork rested on a precipitous ledge of rock that could not be gotten around easily. The left flank, which rested in the woods on the west slope of the mountain, was more vulnerable, but only slightly so.[11]

At the opening of his attack, Kershaw ordered Barksdale to deploy his brigade down the steep eastern slope of the mountain on his left. Union skirmishers were seen on this slope the night before, and Kershaw seems to have placed Barksdale's troops here initially to keep the Federals from harassing the advance along the summit. But when Aiken sent word about the abatis and breastwork running across the mountain, Kershaw thought Barksdale might outflank it. He sent the Mississippian orders to "attack the enemy in flank and rear, while I pressed him in front." The 8th South Carolina, having navigated the ledge of rock that cut them off from the first engagement, moved up and took their place on the 7th's right flank. Kershaw waited to launch his frontal assault, hoping that Barksdale could gain an advantageous position on the enemy flank, but the initial report from the Mississippians was discouraging. Barksdale sent word that his men could not mount the ridge and that they were harassed by fire from Company K of the 1st Maryland Potomac Home Brigade. Kershaw could not wait any longer. At 9:45 a.m. he ordered Aiken and Henagan to assault the works. "Then," wrote Captain King in his diary, "began a terrible engagement of small arms."[12]

As Kershaw's regiments began to advance, the defenders at the breastwork received additional reinforcements. Lieutenant Colonel Stephen Downey reported to Colonel Ford with his 3rd Maryland Potomac Home Brigade around 9 a.m. Ford promptly shuffled Downey's command, detaching four of his companies and attaching three companies of the 32nd Ohio in their place. He reason for doing this was that he intended to send Downey's detached companies around on the "eastern road"—evidently to guard against a Rebel advance up from Sandy Hook. Why the 32nd's companies could not have accomplished this

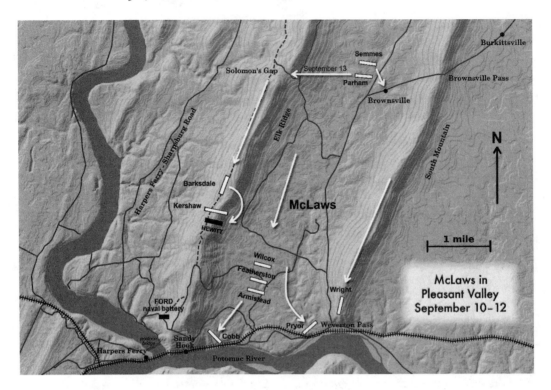

mission, instead of breaking up unit integrity, is a mystery. Downey had never been on Maryland Heights, so Ford provided him with a guide and instructed him to report to Major Hewitt at the Lookout. The companies struggled up the mountain, getting strung out along the trail. As the head of column reached the Lookout, Downey heard "a tremendous firing, and the bullets commenced rattling all around us"; several of his men were wounded. Downey could see the breastwork and the men behind it loading and firing. He met Hewitt, who kept to the Lookout during the entire fight and left the management of the battle at the breastwork to Colonel Sherrill. Hewitt apparently did not identify himself, for Downey did not know to whom he was speaking. Hewitt's instructions were simple: "You better reinforce Colonel Sherrill immediately." Downey had no idea who Sherrill was or where he was on the line, and Hewitt was not about to lead him forward to show him, but the little Marylander was made of stern stuff, and he strode forward, with his men following behind.[13]

The first officer Downy encountered was Adjutant Barras of the 126th, who introduced him to Colonel Sherrill. Downey ordered his companies in behind the breastwork wherever they could find room, while he and Sherrill decided on a hasty command arrangement. They split the line in half, with Sherrill commanding the left and Downey the right. Along the breastwork the Federals were pouring fire into the South Carolinians, but the Union troops were already in trouble. Unit cohesion had largely been lost in the retreat from the first abatis,

and the close pursuit by the 7th South Carolina did not allow a respite for officers to sort things out. The different commands simply fell in where they could
to meet the Confederate pursuit. Companies C, D, and F of the 126th New York
were near the center of the breastworks. Part of Company G was at the right of
the works, and its right was deployed between the breastwork and the Lookout. Companies K, E, B, and half of H were also at the works, but apparently
not connected with the three companies at the center. Sherrill deployed the
other half of H Company about 200 yards to the left of the breastworks to prevent a flanking movement. Some of the 32nd Ohio were along the works with the
126th, and probably elements of the other regiments as well. Those who could
not find a place along the works stood in the rear and fired over the heads of the
men along the front. According to the 126th's historian, some of these men
were careless with their aim, and after several close calls a few of the officers on
the line silenced the shooting by threatening to fire on the offenders. The same
historian also recorded that "there were quite enough men at these works to
fight to advantage." But the 126th's historian was not on Maryland Heights,
and he sought to vindicate the regiment's performance that day by redirecting
criticism at the other units there and at the management of the fighting force.
Captain Russell, who *was* there, thought that only about 450–500 men manned
the breastwork. If Russell was right—and we must assume he formed his estimate before Lieutenant Colonel Downey arrived—then 600 to 700 men of the
original force had left the firing line. Even if Russell underestimated the force
at the breastwork, a significant portion of the Union troops had abandoned the
fight during the retreat from the first abatis. The defenders remaining at the
breastwork were a confused and fragile crowd, and although inspired by the
bravery of Downey and Sherrill to keep fighting, they lacked cohesion and direction from an overall leader. Directing the battle was Hewitt's responsibility,
but he wanted no part of it.[14]

Colonel Ford believed Hewitt was tending to this duty, but the major clearly
did not think his task included managing the battle at the breastwork. His
remained at his headquarters at the Lookout throughout the fight. The most
damning indictment of his ineffectiveness came from Adjutant Barras of the
126th, who testified before the Harpers Ferry Commission that Hewitt "had
nothing particularly to do with the maneuvering. He was not very close to the
engagement."[15]

For the South Carolinians on the receiving end of the Federals' fire, there
was no hint of the confusion in the Union ranks. "A tremendous fire of musketry was encountered by our boys," wrote a *Charleston (SC) Daily Courier* correspondent who was with Kershaw. Captain Russell thought the 7th and 8th
South Carolina made three separate assaults on the breastworks. But the Carolinians could not traverse the open space between the works and the abatis,
and each assault was repulsed. Casualties piled up and ammunition began to

run low. Aiken's 7th regiment counted 13 dead and 100 wounded, nearly one-quarter of its strength. The 8th, percentage-wise, suffered just as severely. The regiment's color-bearer, Sergeant J. Strother, "a tall handsome man of six feet three in height," bearing a beautiful silk banner presented to the regiment by the ladies of Pee Dee County, was shot dead within 30 yards of the breastwork. The rest of the color guard were casualties as well, so Captain Andrew T. Harllee of Company I dashed forward to Strother's body, picked up the flag, and shouted to the men to rush the works. But he instantly drew fire, taking a bullet that passed through both his thighs and knocked him down. The 8th's commander, Colonel John W. Henagan, retrieved the flag from the fallen Harllee and tried to inspire his men to move forward, but he, too, was hit and wounded. The regiment wavered. But as a party bore Henagan to the rear, he commanded them to put him down and rallied his shaken men by shouting "in a loud, clear voice, 'About face! Charge and take the works.'" The regiment rallied, but the hail of Yankee bullets discouraged another frontal assault.[16]

Kershaw's attack had stalled. The 7th and 8th regiments were pinned down within 100 yards of the breastwork, low on ammunition, unable to reach the Union works and unable to withdraw without suffering severe losses. Kershaw ordered Colonel James D. Nance to take his 3rd South Carolina in and "pass over Col. A's Regiment and drive the enemy from his works." Only 24 years old, Nance was a tough customer. He had entered the 3rd as a captain, but the regiment elected him its colonel during the army reorganization in the spring. The brigade historian considered him "the best all around soldier in Kershaw's Brigade." He had about 340 officers and men, although quite a few of them were conscripts with only about two months' service, and this was their first battle. They dashed forward toward Aiken's prone line. Before they reached it, a volley burst from the breastwork and the bullets swept Nance's line. "My companies never faltered," he reported with pride, and as soon as his regiment had cleared Aiken's men they returned the fire. In the words of diarist Captain King, "a most terrific fight ensued." Nance found that due to the nature of the terrain, only seven of his nine companies could deliver their fire effectively. He quickly determined that the enemy breastwork and the approaches to it were so formidable that "I thought it unadvisable to attempt to carry the work at the point of the bayonet until I had engaged them by fire for a time, while I could discover more of their position and force." The 3rd traded fire with the Federals "for a considerable time" before Nance concluded that the enemy's left flank was vulnerable. From his perspective the 8th South Carolina, on his right, were "not very actively engaged" and could execute the movement. He ordered his adjutant, Lieutenant Y. J. Pope, to go back to Kershaw and convey this information to him.[17]

Behind the breastwork the men were gaining confidence. Captain Charles M. Wheeler, commanding Company K of the 126th New York, thought the men along the line "were very cool indeed, as a rule; dropping behind the breast-work to load, and then rising and firing coolly over the breastworks." The Con-federates had been repulsed three times and, thanks to the breastworks, losses along the line were light. The works also helped steady the 126th New York. In the open their lack of drill and their inexperienced officers shook their confi-dence, but behind the breastwork they had only to load and fire. Colonel Sherrill also inspired courage. What he lacked in military knowledge he compensated for with raw bravery. "I never saw a braver man than Colonel Sherrill in my life," testified Lieutenant Barras. Another lieutenant in the regiment watched Sher-rill mount the log works to direct the fire of his men, recklessly exposing him-self to enemy fire. He called up to the colonel pointing out this fact, to which Sherrill responded, "G——d D——m the exposure: no rebel ball can hit me." It was his elevated position that probably enabled Sherrill to see Confederates—the 8th South Carolina—moving to turn his left flank. He rapidly pulled Com-panies C and D of his regiment out of line and sent them double-quicking to the left. The companies formed a line running diagonally from the breastwork down the western slope of the mountain, "just in time to meet a strong party of the enemy working their way through the woods and tangled vines." While these companies traded fire with the 8th South Carolina, Nance's 3rd regiment con-tinued to blast away at the front of the Federal position. One of their bullets scored a lucky and deadly hit on Colonel Sherrill. While distributing fresh car-tridges to his men, a bullet struck him in the lower jaw and drove a piece of one of his teeth into the back of his tongue. It was a frightful, bloody wound, and demoralizing to inexperienced soldiers. Several of his men gathered Sherrill up and bore him to the rear.[18]

Although Companies C and D slowed the flanking attack of the 8th South Carolina, they failed to stop it, and some of the Confederates succeeded in gaining a position from which they delivered a flanking fire on the breastwork defenders.[19] Trouble threatened on the right at nearly the same time. Major Baird, who was near the extreme right, observed "large parties of men filing along, under cover of the woods, on the side of the hill below our right." It was Barksdale's Mississippians, and they were threatening to turn the right of the Union position. Some of Baird's men fired at them, as did some of the Mary-landers in Company K of 1st Maryland Potomac Home Brigade, who were sta-tioned to guard the flank. Captain Abraham Crumbecker had command of the skirmishers along the eastern slope. He also saw Barksdale coming and sent word to Major Hewitt that Confederated "were coming around that part of the hill in large force." Hewitt now completely lost his nerve and sent an orderly for-ward with orders for the breastwork defenders to fall back. When Lieutenant Colonel Downey heard the orders he demanded to know who gave them. The orderly replied that they were from Colonel Ford. Downey refused to believe it and told his men that "there certainly can't be an order to retreat from this position." They held. When no one obeyed his orders, Hewitt sent Lieutenant Adam Carnes, his adjutant, to deliver them again. Captain Russell saw Carnes ride up and wave his hat, motioning the men back. Russell was not aware of Hewitt's earlier order to retreat, so he ran over to Carnes and asked him what he wanted. Carnes replied that they were ordered to fall back. Without questioning the orders, Russell returned to the breastwork and repeated them. The men who heard him immediately began to fall back, and in moments the entire line began to unravel. Downey tried to stop them, shouting, "For God's sake, don't fall back; we must hold this position," but it had no effect. Convinced that someone had blundered, Downey commandeered Carnes's horse and rode off to find Ford.[20]

In the aftermath of the disaster that befell the Union garrison at Harpers Ferry, Hewitt and Carnes—and others—blamed the retreat from the breastwork on the poor behavior and performance of the 126th New York. Yet there is no evidence from those officers who testified before the Harpers Ferry Commission that the 126th caused the retreat from the breastwork. There had been confusion in the 126th, and a considerable number of its men left the battle during the retreat to the breastworks, but those who remained fought bravely. The two men who were in a position to know what happened, Lieutenant Colonel Downey and Captain Russell, both testified that the retreat began because of Hewitt's orders. The 126th simply provided a convenient scapegoat for Hewitt to cover his mismanagement of the battle.[21]

Moments before the Federals began to retreat from the breastwork, Kershaw heard from Barksdale that his brigade "with great labor" had reached the "desired position" on the enemy flank, but they could not advance to the crest of the mountain without running into the fire of Kershaw's regiments. He sent orders to Nance to cease firing. Almost simultaneously the enemy fire began to slacken, then sputtered out. The Yankees were clearing out. Nance's men rose and advanced to the works. They found them abandoned except for 5 prisoners, several dead soldiers, and discarded equipment. Nance sent back word to Kershaw that he had captured the works. Kershaw and others came forward to have a look at the enemy position that had defied them and cost so much blood to capture. Captain King was impressed: "It is wonderful how our men could have stood it, the place is so strong," he wrote. Kershaw thought so as well, and congratulated Nance "upon my success and safety and said my Regiment was an honor to its commander and State; all of which, of course, filled me with proper pride." Besides his commander's generous praise, Nance's reward was to have his exhausted regiment relieved by the 2nd South Carolina. It was 10:45 a.m. The battle for the breastwork and, so it would prove, for Maryland Heights was over.[22]

While Colonel Kennedy's regiment came forward and Barksdale's brigade completed its climb to the crest, the men of the 3rd, the 7th, and the 8th South

Carolina gathered up their dead and wounded: 36 dead and 163 wounded in the three regiments. Aiken's 7th regiment had been hardest hit, with 113 casualties. Nance's 3rd South Carolina counted 20 killed, the most of any regiment in the fight. Two-thirds of them were conscripts. Combat experience, even in the line-of-battle fighting of the Civil War, clearly made a difference. Barksdale had 2 killed and 15 wounded. The dead were buried "in the lofty cemetery of Maryland Heights," although there was a report from a Union soldier that they were cremated, since it was so difficult to dig graves on the mountain. No one wrote about the wounded, but their ordeal must have been awful. Water was in short supply, and each man had to be carried off the mountain.[23]

Thanks to the protection of the breastworks, the Union forces escaped with relatively light losses, considering all the lead the South Carolinians had fired at them. They reported some 21 killed, 88 wounded, and 5 captured. In retrospect the Federals, particularly the soon-to-be- much-maligned 126th New York, claimed that they had not been driven from the breastwork. In the opinion of the officers of the 126th, the order to abandon the breastworks was "unnecessary even if not criminal"; "the breastworks could have been held, and, in our opinion, should have been held, for a long time, if not altogether, by the force present." That Major Hewitt badly managed the fight is indisputable, but that he had prematurely ordered a retreat may not be. The claims of the 126th New York notwithstanding, when Hewitt ordered the retreat at least three companies of the 8th South Carolina had gained a position that enabled them to deliver a flanking fire on the left flank of the works. At the same time Barksdale's brigade threatened to turn the right flank of the position, a fact unknown to most of the breastwork defenders. Without reinforcements to relieve the men at the barricade and meet the threats to the flanks, the collapse of this position was only a matter of minutes. Hewitt believed "if we had remained there half an hour longer we would probably have been all taken prisoners."[24]

Down at Colonel Ford's headquarters, it was apparent from early morning that things were not going well on the summit of Maryland Heights. A steady stream of men trickled down the mountain after the initial skirmish with Kershaw's advance force. Many were from the 126th. They were the easiest to pick out, because the men wore the numerals of their regiment on the top of their caps. Lieutenant John B. Pearce, the 32nd Ohio's adjutant and an aide to Colonel Ford, encountered many of them while carrying orders up the mountain. "I met them running, and saw them in the bushes and behind trees and rocks and every place else," he said. "They appeared to be coming from every direction mostly." Ford ordered Pearce to take 20 men, rout those escaping from the battle out of the bushes, and drive them back up the mountain. Pearce did his best, but the stragglers "were in wild confusion and dismay," and despite his exertions to rally them, "we could never get them up to the top of the heights. They scattered in every direction." Captain John T. Whittier of the 1st Maryland Potomac

Home Brigade, who was ill in his quarters near McGrath's battery, attempted to help Pearce. "I tried all I could to get the men back," he testified. "I told them they must go back; that as we had but few men there, what men we had there must go back. They would not pay any attention to anyone. Nobody had any command over them. They were worthless; not worth anything." Although there is no evidence that Ford had yet received a situation report from Hewitt, he concluded from what he saw around him that disaster loomed. He ordered the three companies of Downey's 3rd Maryland that he had retained at his headquarters to march to the Lookout and report to Hewitt. The numerous demoralized stragglers from the 126th New York around his headquarters only confirmed his opinion of the quality of raw troops. He sent Miles a gloomy and quite inaccurate report.

> Colonel Miles:
> The One hundred and twenty-sixth New York has given way and straggling through the woods. All our forces are falling back.
>
> THOS. H. FORD
> Commanding Third Brigade

The battle for the breastwork had not yet begun when Ford wrote this, yet the commander of Maryland Heights already thought the battle lost. It did not bode well for the Union defense.[25]

The bearer of this dispatch also carried a request for reinforcements, which was Ford's standard reaction when things got tough. Colonel George Willard, commanding the 125th New York, visited Miles's headquarters shortly after Miles had received Ford's message. Miles was concerned, and Willard heard him say, "Ford is stampeded. He wants re-enforcements; and I am afraid we shall lose Maryland Heights." He sent orders for Colonel Simeon Sammon's 115th New York to march immediately to the Heights and alerted Colonel Daniel Cameron's 65th Illinois to ready his men in case they were needed as well. But before he sent more reinforcements to Ford, Miles decided to visit the colonel and see things for himself. Accompanied by his aides, Lieutenant Henry M. Binney and Lieutenant John L. Willmon, Miles left around 9 a.m. On the road to the naval battery, midway between the C&O Canal and the battery, they encountered nearly 200 stragglers, mostly from the 126th New York, making their way down the road and off the mountain. Miles accosted them and asked them where they were going. They responded that they had been ordered to fall back and that they had no officers. Miles said that there were no orders to fall back, and detailed Lieutenant Binney to bring them up while he rode up to Ford's headquarters with Lieutenant Willmon.[26]

When Miles and Willmon reached it they encountered "a great many stragglers." Miles demanded of them, "What are you men doing here?" By this time the battle at the breastwork was over, or at least in its last minutes. These men repeated what the others had told Miles: they had been ordered to retreat. Since most of the men seemed to be from the 126th, Miles told Willmon to go up on the mountain and see if he could re-form the regiment. Willmon came upon a disorganized force of nearly 500 men of the 126th and the 1st Maryland Potomac Home Brigade, as well as some men of the 39th New York who were attempting to prevent the others from descending the mountain. Willmon could find only four officers among the disordered group. "I appealed to them," Willmon recalled, "and they shirked and twisted and screwed about, and said they thought they could not get the men up." The lieutenant had better luck pleading with the noncommissioned officers in the group to lead the men to the front. "They had some energy about them," said the lieutenant, "and stepped out and said, 'Fall in, boys; come on, boys.'" It took nearly an hour of work for Willmon and the others to get the men into "some kind of ship-shape."[27]

Willmon turned the men he had rallied over to Lieutenant Samuel A. Barras, the 126th's adjutant, who came up while the lieutenant was busy trying to organize this group. He left Barras with instructions that there was no order to retreat and that Barras should march his men to the front at once. Willmon then rode back down to Ford's headquarters, where he reported to Miles: "Colonel, it is almost an impossible matter to get the men together. I have done all I could to form them in the best possible shape, and have handed them over to the adjutant, with instructions that they should be marched to the front and kept there." Miles responded, "Well damn them, they will run; just what I thought they would do."[28]

While Willmon worked to get his stragglers into some semblance of order, Lieutenant Colonel Downey arrived at Ford's headquarters to discover who had issued the orders to retreat from the barricade. He found Ford and Miles together at McGrath's battery and asked if either of them had given the order; both said that there had been none. Downey was now the ranking officer on the mountain, since Sherrill was wounded and Ford was physically unable to command. Ford and Miles instructed Downey to counterattack and retake the barricade. The absurdity of the order immediately struck the little lieutenant colonel, who asked what troops he could expect to support him. Ford— revealing how utterly out of touch he was with events—replied that the 126th New York would. Downey may have sensed at that moment that his mission was a hopeless one, but he was an optimistic fellow, so he left with an orderly, moving along a path running up the western slope of the mountain toward the Lookout, to see what could be done.[29]

Downey had already done some work toward stabilizing the front. After the retreat from the breastwork, when he seized Lieutenant Carnes's horse and rode off for Ford's headquarters, he encountered Major Charles L. Grafflin of his regiment, leading the three companies Ford had ordered up from McGrath's battery. Downey paused here long enough to rally the balance of his regiment on Grafflin's companies and then placed his now-united command on a slight ridge some 400 yards south of the Lookout. Leaving Grafflin with instructions to hold the position, Downey rode down for his meeting with Miles and Ford. When Downey struck this same ridge on his return up the mountain, he left the path and followed its course until he found Grafflin, dutifully holding his position. Besides the men of his own regiment, Downey discovered that nearly 300 men of other regiments had rallied on Grafflin's line. Among them was Major Hewitt, who had been carried along in the flotsam of retreat. Downey assumed command of this assortment of troops and conferred with Grafflin on their situation. It was not promising.[30]

Grafflin explained that during Downey's absence he had been ordered, probably by Major Hewitt, to advance back toward the Lookout. Grafflin deployed a company of skirmishers, supporting them with the entire regiment and some of the other men who had rallied on their line. Four hundred yards from the Lookout they encountered skirmishers of Barksdale's brigade, who drove Grafflin's skirmish line back on its supports. At the first fire the strangers from other units who had joined Grafflin fled. He called off the advance and pulled his Marylanders back to the "very good position" where Downey had found him. Downey was determined to carry out his orders from Ford, and he appealed to the collection of men who had stayed near his own regiment to advance and retake the lost position. The lieutenant colonel was enthusiastic but uninspiring, for his plea stirred no one. Several officers—who Downey thought were from the 126th New York—stepped forward from the group and told him that they had held a council of war and concluded that their men "will not fight." Despite this uninspiring verdict, Downey remained undaunted. He called out to the enlisted men, "if you have no officers to lead you, I will lead you myself, as your immediate commander." Only five soldiers, all from the 126th, stepped forward. It was no use. The fight was out of these men. Downey understood that he needed reinforcements simply to hold the position his regiment currently occupied, and even more assistance if Ford expected him to retake the breastwork. He sent his adjutant down to Ford's headquarters to explain the situation and the need for additional troops. While they waited, Downey was determined that every man he had on line was going to stay with him. He posted a guard behind the line with orders to "shoot any man who should attempt to go down to the battery."[31]

Reinforcements were scarce at that moment. Ford sent the two companies of the 115th New York, who were providing security for the naval guns, to reinforce Downey, but the rest of the troops on the mountain, other than those with Downey, were either scattered across the slopes in disconnected groups, demoralized, or struggling to gather up those who were in this condition. Major Hugo Hildebrandt, who had been ordered down from the mountain summit after the initial skirmish to assume command of Ford's headquarters area, posted men of his regiment with fixed bayonets in an attempt to check the flow of stragglers. Nearby, Captain McGrath, with his pistol drawn, set upon a group of stragglers and denounced them as "a set of cowards." Many men simply slipped around to the left of McGrath's artillery and Hildebrandt's infantry, forcing Hildebrandt to employ several companies to "hunt them up." "We had a very great difficulty to get them again in order," he later testified. Hard enough so that, until Maryland Heights was abandoned, Hildebrandt's companies did nothing else but chase stragglers and try to organize them.[32]

Lieutenant Barras had no better luck trying to herd the men that Lieutenant Willmon had collected back up the mountain. Barras ran into several company officers of his regiment when he neared Downey's position, and they told him what they had told Downey: their men would not fight, and they had decided to fall back. The demoralization spread quickly, and Barras's numbers steadily shrank the closer he came to the front. Barras soon gave up and rode back down to headquarters, complaining to Miles and Ford that he had been exerting himself "to the utmost" but that "it was almost impossible to rally his regiment." He added that the officers of the regiment, including Major Baird, were "all gone off somewhere," leaving him alone to try to get the men together. Barras was clearly rattled, and he exaggerated the situation. His report enraged Miles, who focused his wrath on the missing Major Baird, snarling out the order: "Arrest the major! Damn him! Shoot him the first moment you see him!" Baird, in fact, had simply been jarred loose from the main body of his regiment during the retreat, which was why Barras did not know where he was. The problem was not Major Baird or Adjutant Barras, but partly the rugged terrain, which made it extremely difficult to reorganize units once they were scattered by retreat. The other difficulty was Colonel Ford's lack of command and control, and his parceling of units, which helped destroy unit integrity.[33]

Around noon Colonel Simeon Sammon arrived at Ford's headquarters with seven companies of his 115th New York, about 630 men. Sammon immediately noticed things were not going well. He later said:

> I saw very many troops, soldiers standing about near Colonel Ford's headquarters. Not knowing where they came from, nor what they were doing there, I made the inquiry of Colonel Ford, in the presence of Colonel Miles. Colonel Miles stated that the One hundred twenty-sixth had behaved very badly, and confirmed it with an oath. Colonel Ford remarked that he had to place a guard across the roadway, or a company, I forget which, to stop them; but they could not stop them.

Sammon brought numbers, not experience, to the mountain, for his men were raw recruits. By this point both Ford and Miles had given up hope that the breastwork could be recaptured and were now thinking strictly defensively. Sammon was ordered to send two of his companies up to reinforce Lieutenant Colonel Downey. At the request of Captain McGrath, the other five companies were sent to Unsell's farm, situated in a valley north of McGrath's gun position, where they could cover a projecting knob off the mountain that offered a likely position where the Confederates could attempt to place a battery.[34]

Detailing Major Steiner of the 1st Maryland Potomac Home Brigade to guide Sammon and his five companies into position, Miles retired to Ford's headquarters with Ford and Lieutenant Binney to discuss the situation. It is impossible to know exactly what was said between these men, since Miles was killed two days later. Ford was desperately trying to defend his actions on Maryland Heights, and Binney sought to exonerate his chief. In his official report Ford claimed that Miles told him that if his men gave way again, "I must immediately withdraw my forces from Maryland Heights to Bolivar Heights." This may be what Ford thought he heard, or wanted to hear. The evidence indicates that Miles ordered Ford to hold the Heights as long as possible, but that if Ford was forced to retreat, not to do so without spiking the heavy naval guns and rolling them down the hill. Miles also advised Ford to use stringent means—which, if Miles's orders about Major Baird were a guide, meant shooting a few men—in order to get the 126th New York under control; otherwise they would panic all the troops on the mountain and cause the evacuation of the Heights. Ford, predictably, requested further reinforcements. Miles agreed to send more "if he could spare them from the front." The meeting probably concluded shortly after noon, and Miles rode back down to Harpers Ferry with his two aides.[35]

That Miles issued discretionary orders in the event the Maryland Heights defenders were defeated and forced to retreat from the mountain is not a reason to condemn him, but that he had left that discretion in the hands of Colonel Ford was unthinkable, tantamount to the certain and early loss of Maryland Heights. Ford was ill, demoralized, in over his head, and lacked confidence in his troops' ability to defend Maryland Heights any longer without reinforcements. Nor was he in any condition to retake control of the battle or inspire his troops to fight on. If Miles wanted to prolong the defense of Maryland Heights or win the fight for its control, either he had to give Ford peremptory orders to hold the mountain at all costs, or have replaced Ford with someone possessing more energy and determination, which meant General White. By noon on September 13 the loss of Maryland Heights was inevitable; the only question was how soon Ford would be stampeded. Miles was in a battle where hours, even minutes, might count in the end. Every strong point needed to be defended until it was absolutely untenable or the defenders were physically driven out. The key to survival was to disrupt the Confederates' timetable and buy time for a relieving force to arrive. A commander with more confidence and with some fire about him could have organized a defense that Kershaw may still have overcome, but not without more hard fighting. The terrain favored the defender, and the infantry had the close support of McGrath's light field pieces if the fight came near the naval battery. The infantry on the mountain had suffered a relatively small number of casualties. Many were scattered and some were demoralized, but they were not defeated yet. What Colonel Ford saw from the perspective of his headquarters, however, were running soldiers, confusion, and chaos, and he could envision nothing but gloom and defeat. Miles either did not notice that Ford was a whipped man or was unwilling to make the necessary change.[36] Miles's indecision, or poor judgment, whichever it was, earned him the condemnation of the Harpers Ferry Commission, which concluded: "This leaving the key of the position to the keeping of Colonel Ford, with discretionary power, after the arrival of the capable and courageous officer [General White] who had waived his rank to serve wherever ordered, is one of the striking facts illustrating the utter incapacity of Colonel Miles."[37]

On the mountain, the skirmishing continued after Miles's departure. At noon McGrath's heavy guns joined the battle, shelling the summit, but the gun tubes could not be depressed enough to hit their target, and the big shells sailed harmlessly over the heads of Kershaw's South Carolinians and Mississippians. At 1 p.m. Kershaw directed Barksdale to advance and clear the southernmost point of the Heights. The Mississippians bumped up against Downey's line south of the Lookout and the opposing skirmish lines sparred with one another. Downey's line held, but he realized he was outnumbered and sent an urgent note down to Colonel Ford saying he must have reinforcements to hold his position.[38]

Ford had several crises on his hands by the time Downey's request reached him. Between 1 and 2 p.m. he received a report from Captain Crumbecker, who was still manning the skirmish line on the eastern slope of the mountain, stating that they were being flanked on the right by a Confederate brigade. This was probably Cobb's brigade of McLaws's division, which McLaws had ordered to advance and occupy Sandy Hook that afternoon. By now Ford was inclined to think the worst about any situation, and Crumbecker's report spurred him to sent a dispatch to Miles: "The enemy are extending their lines from the top of the mountain down to the river."[39]

Downey's request for reinforcements probably arrived around the same time as Crumbecker's. An ammunition shortage in the 32nd Ohio added to Ford's list of woes. He sent over three times in the space of an hour and a half for a resupply, but by 2:30 p.m. he still had received no cartridges. They were en route. Miles had ordered Lieutenant Binney to provide three wagonloads of cartridges, but for some reason they were delayed and did not start out until 2:30 p.m. Even if the cartridges had arrived earlier, it is doubtful that they would have strengthened Ford's resolve. Around 1 p.m. Captain Russell came down the mountain. He gave Ford a gloomy report of the situation on the summit: the troops were running and the force under Downey was inadequate to hold its position. Confusion continued to swirl about Ford's headquarters. His aide, Lieutenant John Pearce, testified that "I did not see anybody standing their ground, as I thought, doing proper. I could hardly get through with an order as I was sent up the heights. It was almost impossible to get through the troops running down the steep mountain road."[40] Ford's nerve finally collapsed. He took his dispatch book and wrote to Miles: "I cannot hold my men. The One hundred and twenty-sixth all run and the Thirty-second Ohio are out of ammunition. I must leave the hill unless you direct otherwise."[41]

Miles's reply arrived shortly after 2 p.m. Unfortunately, Ford lost the message and no copy was retained in Miles's order book, but the apparent substance of his response was simply a repetition of his earlier orders: if Ford was pressed too hard his should spike the guns and withdraw his men. It seems likely that Miles also mentioned that he could not spare further reinforcements. The 65th Illinois had been alerted to go to Maryland Heights before Miles's visit there, but when he came down from the mountain he learned that Jackson had arrived in front of Bolivar Heights, so he canceled the 65th's orders. Mentally Ford had already lost the battle, and he was grasping for some excuse to pull out. The tenor of Miles's dispatch and the news that there would be no more reinforcements provided it. Ford rode over to McGrath's battery and read Miles's message to Captain McGrath, asking for his opinion. McGrath interpreted it as an order "to vacate." Ford felt the crushing burden of command and shrank before it. What should he do? McGrath answered that he was not ready to leave the mountain yet: "I was going to fight them yet a spell."[42] McGrath's pluck failed to bolster Ford's confidence or check the collapse of his will. Within the hour Ford drew up a brief withdrawal order: "You are hereby ordered to fall back to Harper's Ferry in good order. Be careful to do so in good order."[43]

Lieutenant Pearce carried the order up the mountain to Lieutenant Colonel Downey. Downey's name was not on the order and Ford had not signed it, so he pondered whether he should obey it. But 15 minutes later his orderly, whom he had sent down to Ford with his request for reinforcements, rode up with a copy of the same order, which he had received from Ford in person. When the order arrived Downey's command was "skirmishing some little" with Barksdale's skirmishers, but there was no pressure on his line from Barksdale's main body. Downey obeyed the orders and gave the command to withdraw. With the scattered condition of the various units on the mountain, delivering the order took time, and it was at least 4 p.m. by the time all the commands had received it and were withdrawing. McGrath worked his guns furiously to cover the withdrawal; then his crews spiked them and joined the solemn retreat.[44]

Miles was on Bolivar Heights when the evacuation began. He paused in his ride to study Maryland Heights through his field glass and observed troops coming off the mountain. The chaplain of the 115th New York, Reverend Sylvester Clemens, stood nearby, and he recalled that Miles exclaimed: "God Almighty; what does that mean? They are coming down. Hell and damnation!" He wheeled his horse and galloped off in the direction of Camp Hill. En route he encountered Colonel D'Utassy, who had also seen the retreat. D'Utassy offered to try and retake the position (with what force he did not say). Miles responded that first he had to learn why Ford abandoned it before there was any thought of retaking it. He met Ford coming down from the Heights on the Harpers Ferry side of the pontoon bridge, "on the rise in the armory yard." Miles took Ford's explanation for the evacuation with remarkable equanimity, considering the blow Ford's actions had dealt the defenders. The only remark Miles is known to have made about it was to comment to Colonel Maulsby that he thought Ford had abandoned the Heights "almost too soon." Ford's report that he had spiked the guns on the mountain nixed any ideas of making an effort to retake the position, for Miles erroneously believed that they were most important reason to hold Maryland Heights. If the guns were spiked, then—as Miles saw it—the only advantage the Confederates had gained by capturing the Heights was to block the garrison's Maryland avenue of escape. Since Miles had no intention of disobeying his orders by attempting to run for it, he did not see the loss of Maryland Heights as a decisive or irreparable turn of events.[45]

Few in the Union garrison shared Miles's opinion about Maryland Heights. General White's aide, Lieutenant Henry Curtis Jr., wrote that with its loss "the game was clearly up with us." The loss of the Heights was not a knockout blow—the garrison continued to hold out—but it did seal the fate of the garrison unless the Army of the Potomac relieved it. Miles either ignored or disapproved of Saxton's earlier defense of Harpers Ferry, which depended on holding Camp Hill and Maryland Heights. But it was control of the Heights and the heavy naval guns there that was the key to Saxton's strategy, for they commanded the important approaches to Harpers Ferry. Miles instead favored a defense with depth to it, and he centered his hope on holding Bolivar Heights and Camp Hill. The problem with this, besides the loss of morale associated with the enemy being located on the commanding terrain, is that Bolivar Heights could be enfiladed by guns on Loudoun Heights or on the plateau below the heights. The advantage of Saxton's plan was that it forced the enemy to assault Maryland Heights, for until they captured it they could not control Harpers Ferry and its strategically important bridges. Had Miles adopted this plan and staked his defense on Maryland Heights, he would have faced the full strength of McLaws's command. The Georgian later wrote that had Miles shifted his entire force to Maryland Heights, "I would have most certainly assaulted them, with all I had," and, "from the very feeble defense made against the two brigades which captured it from Colonel Ford, and from the character of the force, to judge of it from reading the published reports of the different commanders, and the failure to stand an assault in Harper's Ferry, I have reason to believe the Heights would have been carried." McLaws was probably correct. But it was never a question of *whether* the garrison could defeat the force brought against it; it was *how long* it could hold out against the assaulting force. The U.S. Army Commission that investigated the Harpers Ferry disaster did not equivocate in their judgment of the importance of Maryland Heights. They considered that the abandonment "was the surrender of Harper's Ferry."[46]

The Confederates scarcely troubled Ford's retreat. At 1 p.m. Kershaw ordered Barksdale to advance and "scour the lower & last point of the mountain," which apparently meant the area where the naval battery was located. Barksdale's advance encountered Downey's skirmish line and traded shots with it. Downey's bold front helped conceal the true state of the Union defenses, and Barksdale seems to have been content to spar and observe the Federals. The constant shelling of the summit by the guns at the naval battery may have also given Barksdale pause. At 3:30 p.m. Captain King and Kershaw's assistant adjutant general, Captain C. R. Holmes, decided that they would pay a visit to the "extreme point of the Mt" to see whether they had possession of it or not. Along the way they met a courier from Barksdale, who told them that they had secured this area. But when King and Holmes reached Barksdale's skirmish line, they continued on for what King thought was a mile before they reached the rocky precipice overlooking Harpers Ferry. Along the way they saw some Union stragglers, whom they fired at to hurry them along. Near the precipice they took two Federals prisoners, then had a regular skirmish with a larger party of stragglers. "We came near having trouble," wrote King, but the Yankees moved on and King and Holmes were able to enjoy watching the "Yankees hurrying into Harper's Ferry" down below them. They also observed the signs of a fight going on in the distance, beyond Bolivar Heights. It was 4:30 p.m. King took a moment to write a dispatch to McLaws to confirm that the enemy were retreating and that Maryland Heights was in Confederate hands; then they set out for Kershaw's headquarters.[47]

When McLaws learned that the Federals were abandoning Maryland Heights, he ordered Howell Cobb's brigade to advance and occupy Sandy Hook. Cobb's men discovered several hundred new muskets left behind by Colonel Maulsby's Marylanders when they withdrew the previous evening. With Cobb at Sandy Hook, the principal road east from Harpers Ferry was blocked. Only the Harpers Ferry–Sharpsburg Road remained open. This "rough road" ran north from the pontoon bridge over the western shoulder of Maryland Heights and then paralleled Elk Ridge on its way to Sharpsburg. McLaws may not have been aware of its existence, for he made no known effort that day to move troops to cut it, and he had other concerns that captured his attention.[48]

Throughout the day McLaws could hear "heavy cannonading" to the east and northeast, and cavalry scouts "were constantly giving reports of the advance of the enemy from various directions." But he could get "no authentic statements" about what the cannonading meant from any cavalry commander, nor "could anything definite" be learned from the scouts "as to the amount of firing or, as to the probable place the enemy were aiming at; whether at Weverton [Pass]," or toward Brownsville Pass or Crampton's Gap. By necessity McLaws had to defend all three points, but he expected the enemy would move on Weverton Pass, since it was the closest to Harpers Ferry, and he made preparations to defend this pass "with all the force I could bring to bear." He positioned two brigades, Wright's and Pryor's, for its defense. Four other brigades were within support-ing distance: Armistead's and Cobb's brigades, which were at or near Sandy Hook; and Wilcox's and Featherston's, which McLaws held in reserve some-where in the lower end of Pleasant Valley. Kershaw and Barksdale were also near enough to be summoned to help if necessary. Brownsville Pass and Cramp-ton's Gap were allotted one brigade each—Parham's and Semmes's—both of which were bivouacked at the village of Brownsville in the valley. In McLaws words, their mission if attacked was to hold "long enough to prevent an irrup-tion in my rear, without due notice."[49]

By nightfall McLaws knew that Walker had possession of Loudon Heights and that Jackson had arrived in front of Bolivar Heights. The Yankee garrison was trapped. "How can they get away?" Captain King wrote happily in his diary. But McLaws understood that the clock was ticking. He still needed to haul ar-tillery up onto Maryland Heights, no simple operation from the direction in which he approached the Heights There was also the question of whether the enemy were moving against his rear and, if they were, in what strength? A dispatch from Lee arrived late that night, signed by Major T. M. R. Talcott of Lee's staff, which shed some light on the situation east of South Mountain.

> General: General Lee directs me to say that, from reports reaching him, he believes the enemy is moving toward Harper's Ferry to relieve the force they have there. You will see, therefore, the necessity of expediting your operations as much as possible. As soon as they are complete, he desires you, unless you receive orders from General Jackson, to move your force as rapidly as possible to Sharpsburg. General Longstreet will move down to-morrow and take a position on Beaver Creek, this side of Boonsborough. General Stuart has been requested to keep you informed of the movements of the enemy.[50]

The movement of Longstreet down to near Boonsboro was evidence that Lee took the threat to the army's rear seriously. McLaws could derive some satisfaction in having already taken measures to defend his rear. Knowing that Stuart stood between him and the enemy provided additional comfort and, hopefully, a timely warning if the enemy advanced. But Lee offered no clue as to how close the enemy was to South Mountain. One day's march? Two days? What-ever the case, McLaws understood that he had to move quickly to position his artillery, as well as open communications with Jackson and Walker, since if the enemy barged into his rear before Harpers Ferry surrendered, then his com-mand might be isolated.

Later that night, in the early hours of September 14, McLaws received a sec-ond dispatch from Lee, this one signed by Lee's military secretary, Colonel

Armistead L. Long. It was almost certainly written before the Talcott dispatch but, for reasons unknown, arrived after the latter. This message briefed McLaws on the army's dispositions, warned him to "watch well" the road from Frederick to Harpers Ferry (which went through Weverton Pass), and twice urged him to expedite the operation against Harpers Ferry.[51]

There was not much McLaws could do that he had not already done. His command had possession of Maryland Heights, cut the road to Frederick, strongly garrisoned Weverton Pass, and made visual contact with Jackson and Walker. All that remained was to find a way to get artillery positioned on Maryland Heights to bring the Federals under fire. McLaws wasted no time in seeking a route by which he could haul guns up the mountain's steep slopes. After Captain King reported that the Heights were in Confederate possession, McLaws dispatched his engineers to examine the approaches and see if it was possible to cut a road to the summit. They returned that evening with disappointing news. The steepness of the ascent and the numerous rock walls that "could not be turned or passed" made construction of a road impractical. But when Major Abram H. McLaws, the general's brother and the division quartermaster, was returning from Kershaw's command that evening, he found an old wood road that ascended partway up the mountain. The rest of the ascent could be accomplished by lifting the guns and carriages over the remaining rock ledges and dragging them into position by hand. McLaws ordered Kershaw to detail work parties from his brigade and Barksdale's to assist the major in improving the wood road and hauling the guns into position. "Exhausted as they were" by the efforts of September 13, the parties nonetheless were at work before daylight on the 14th.[52]

Spirits at McLaws's headquarters were high the night of September 13. The operation was behind schedule, but bagging the entire Yankee garrison seemed inevitable. Even the reports of an enemy advance toward South Mountain did not shake their confidence. An unperturbed Captain King wrote in his diary that night: "Gen. Pryor brought some men from Washington" who "report enemy advancing and skirmishing up the river and by way of Frederick. D. H. Hill is in their way and we also, let them come."[53]

A reporter from the *Boston Transcript* was on Bolivar Heights when the evacuation of Maryland Heights took place. As he watched Ford's men filing down the mountain, "I could not but think they were marching to the funeral of Harper's Ferry." The soldiers around him were astonished. "Amazement filled their companions on Bolivar Heights, mortification and rage possessed the officers." Even the greenest private sensed the ominous implications in the loss of the Heights. A camp rumor started to circulate—probably to raise spirits— that Sigel was marching to the garrison's rescue. W. E. Scorsby of the 115th New York recalled how, in the twilight from Bolivar Heights, "we could see the glistening of the arms of troops moving up the road along the Potomac," and someone cried out, "That is Sigel!" The men of the Martinsburg garrison knew better, and the truth soon spread along the line: they were Confederates under Jackson's command taking up position to block escape along the Shepherdstown Pike. Flags were also seen waving on Loudoun Heights—Confederate signal flags. Captain Graham's battery of the 5th New York Heavy Artillery, situated on Camp Hill, opened fire and drove their bearers to cover. But in the opinion of Captain E. H. Ripley of the 9th Vermont, who watched Graham's guns blaze away from his position on Bolivar Heights, there "was a wicked waste of ammunition."[54]

Night closed on a despondent garrison. Nicholas DeGraff described himself and his comrades as "a sad company." The *New York Times* reporter, fresh from Maryland Heights, thought the troops retired that night "feeling that all was lost unless reinforcements arrive, and expected to be awoke on the morrow with the booming of artillery from the evacuated heights." It was evident to Colonel Grimes Davis, commanding the 8th New York Cavalry, that the garrison's nearly 1,500 cavalry were of little service under the circumstances they now faced, but the horses and equipment "would be of great value to the enemy if captured." He approached the commander of the 12th Illinois Cavalry, Lieutenant Colonel Hasbrouck Davis, and suggested that they should cut their way out of the trap. Davis agreed, and the two officers carried the idea to Julius White, who approved and asked them to accompany him to Miles's headquarters to present their plan.[55]

The discussion at headquarters turned to whether the entire garrison should attempt to break out. Miles rejected the idea for two reasons: his orders did not permit him to evacuate Harpers Ferry, and he did not think the infantry and artillery could keep up with the cavalry. He also expressed little enthusiasm for a breakout only by the cavalry, thinking such a plan impracticable and fraught with enormous risks. Grimes Davis refused to give up, pressing Miles. "After some hesitation and sharp words" between the two, Miles relented and agreed to issue an order for the cavalry to march the next night, September 14th. They then talked about the route the cavalry would follow. Grimes Davis favored marching up the west bank of the Potomac as far as Kearneysville and crossing the Potomac at Shepherdstown. Miles disapproved, as he thought there "was extreme danger in their going that way." After more discussion, all agreed that the column stood a better chance of escaping detection by the Rebels if they crossed the Shenandoah at a point about a half mile below its junction with the Potomac. The column could then strike east for Washington. The impracticability of this plan would not reveal itself until the next day.[56]

After the meeting with Davis and White adjourned, Miles summoned Captain Charles Russell to his headquarters, asking him if he thought he could lead the cavalry in the garrison out from Harpers Ferry. "I told him I was willing to try," Russell answered. Miles then wondered if Russell felt he could take two or three men, pass through enemy lines, and try to reach "somebody that had ever heard of the United States Army, or anybody that knew anything about the United States Army, and report the condition of Harper's Ferry." Russell believed he could do this. Miles then gave him a simple message. Harpers Ferry had subsistence to hold out for 48 hours. If they were not relieved in that time, Miles would have to surrender. He ordered Russell to find any general officer, or a telegraph station, or, even better, get to McClellan, whom Miles thought was at Frederick.[57]

Russell returned to his quarters and picked nine men from his command to accompany him. They made their preparations quickly and then rode out, traveling northwest over Bolivar Heights. After carefully threading their way through Jackson's picket line, Russell led them down toward the Potomac, which they followed north until they reached the point where Antietam Creek empties into the river. The party forded the river here and soon came upon another Confederate picket post. Spurring their horses, they dashed by the surprised Confederates and pushed on, riding east toward the dark mass of South Mountain along "by-roads" that they knew well.[58] The hopes of the Union garrison rode with them.

8

September 13

"My general idea is to cut the enemy in two"

Bugles echoed through the camps of the Union cavalry bivouacked on the western side of Frederick, rousing the troopers for what promised to be busy day. Eight regiments of cavalry, the largest concentration of Federal horsemen yet in one place in the eastern theater, were assembled there. But Pleasonton's orders required him to scatter his force to meet the multiple missions McClellan had assigned him: make contact with the main enemy force, attempt to open communications with Harpers Ferry, and investigate the enemy activity reported north of Frederick toward Westminster. For the latter mission, Pleasonton tabbed Colonel Andrew T. McReynolds's brigade, consisting of McReynolds's own 1st New York Cavalry and the 8th Pennsylvania Cavalry, reinforced by elements of the 12th Pennsylvania Cavalry and a section of Battery M, 5th U.S. Artillery. McReynolds's orders were to march to Adamsville and scout the road to Gettysburg, as well as toward Liberty and Westminster. Five hundred Confederate cavalry (from Fitz Lee's brigade) were reported in Westminster on the evening of the 11th, and McClellan wanted to make sure that this was not the advance of a larger force. The 6th Pennsylvania Cavalry were selected to scout in the direction of Jefferson and "follow up the road to Harper's Ferry." They would be supported in this endeavor by the 6th U.S. Cavalry, who were reconnoitering along the Potomac River, making their way toward Jefferson from the south. For the job of pressing ahead along the National Road toward Hagerstown, Pleasonton picked his best regiments: Farnsworth's stalwart brigade—the 8th Illinois, the 3rd Indiana, and the 1st Massachusetts—and two horse batteries from the 2nd U.S. Horse Artillery, Battery M and combined Battery B&L. The 1st Maine were lost to duty as provost guard of Frederick, as was part of the 12th Pennsylvania, who were detached for service with the 2nd Corps.[1]

For the reconnaissance to Jefferson and along the National Road, McClellan's arrangements were that Pleasonton could call on Burnside for infantry support. Pleasonton caught up with the wing commander around midnight on the 12th and Burnside agreed that Brigadier General Isaac P. Rodman's troops would provide it. One brigade of the division would support Colonel Rush and his 6th

Pennsylvania Lancers, while the other brigade backed Farnsworth. Pleasonton wanted the infantrymen as a backup he could call on as needed, so he did not have to wait for them to come up in the morning. His command was saddled and moving by daylight on the 13th.[2]

While Pleasonton's cavalry set out in search of the enemy, the balance of the Army of the Potomac made their way toward Frederick. McClellan entered the city at 10 a.m. The people were jubilant. "The whole city was fluttering with national flags," wrote a member of the staff, "while the sidewalks to the house-tops, shone with happy human faces. It seemed as if the whole population had turned out, wild with joy." They were particularly keen on getting a look at the young Napoleon. The crowd pressed him so closely that it brought he and his staff to a halt. McClellan and his horse "were absolutely covered with wreaths and boughs," and the crowd surged about with people jockeying for position to touch the great general. A *New York Daily Tribune* reporter recorded that "from the male citizens and soldiers a constant cheer" followed McClellan as he slowly made his way through the city.

McClellan found his reception both deeply gratifying and somewhat over-powering. "I was nearly overwhelmed & pulled to pieces," he wrote to Mary. "As to flowers!!—they came in crowds! In truth I was seldom more affected than by the scenes I saw yesterday & the reception I met with." But there was an enemy to find and fight, and McClellan still had little reliable information about him. As gratifying as it might have been to remain and enjoy the adulation of the crowd, he managed to break away and find his way to Burnside's headquarters on the Baltimore Pike.[3]

Burnside had little news to offer, although he probably mentioned that Rod-man's division had marched out to support Pleasonton. Both generals were aware that the cavalry had bumped up against some resistance, for the sound of artillery from the direction of Catoctin Mountain could be plainly heard. No doubt plenti-ful rumors about the Rebels circulated among Frederick's citizens and reached Burnside's men. Only the day before "a reliable gentleman" had visited Pennsylva-nia Governor Andrew Curtain after spending an entire day among Fitz Lee's cav-alrymen in Liberty, Maryland. The Confederates told him the plan was to invade Maryland with 190,000 troops, and that part of this force would capture Harpers Ferry and Martinsburg, while the main Rebel army took position between Wil-liamsport and Hagerstown, "from which they will move on the Cumberland Val-ley and other points in Pennsylvania." In addition to the 190,000 in Maryland, the Rebels had "about 250,000 men" in northern Virginia who were concentrated to menace Washington "while their forces in Maryland devastate and destroy Penn-sylvania." This was probably a sample of the type of information Burnside's scouts learned from Frederick's populace—bits of accurate information hidden within the utterly fantastic. McClellan needed some harder intelligence, and for this he counted on Pleasonton.[4]

"I was nearly overwhelmed & pulled to pieces," George McClellan wrote of the enthusiastic reception he received in Frederick, Maryland. Artist Edwin Forbes, however, recorded the wrong date; it was September 13. Courtesy of the Library of Congress.

Pleasonton had found the enemy but was having a difficult time moving him. Farnsworth's brigade marched 3 or 4 miles along the National Road without incident before a salvo of artillery fire brought them to an immediate halt. On the evening of September 12 Jeb Stuart had dropped off Lieutenant Colonel William T. Martin with his Jeff Davis Legion and a section of Captain J. F. Hart's South Carolina horse artillery battery to picket the National Road where it crosses Catoctin Mountain, while he continued on with the balance of Wade Hampton's brigade into Middletown Valley to the west. Martin picked his ground well, dismounting his troopers and unlimbering his guns at a point along the turnpike where "no other passage to the right or the left led across the mountain-spur." It was Martin's guns that greeted Farnsworth's bluecoats at 6 a.m. that morning. The Federal troopers moved out of harm's way to find cover, while Lieutenant Peter C. Hains's Battery M and Captain James M. Robertson's Battery B&L lashed their way forward and unlimbered both in and beside the turnpike. While Hains's and Robertson's gunners opened fire and engaged Martin's artillery, Pleasonton ordered several squadrons of the 3rd Indiana and the 8th Illinois to dismount, and he sent them scrambling up the mountain on either side of the National Road to see if they could outflank the Confeder-ate guns.[5]

On the night of the 12th Stuart had made his headquarters with Hampton's brigade at Middletown, about 2 miles from Catoctin Pass. Therefore he and Hampton's troopers were all in the saddle and marching toward Catoctin Moun-tain soon after the sound of Captain Hart's guns reached them. Stuart's orders were "not to retire too fast before the enemy," to keep Lee advised of enemy movements, and to prevent the Federals from discovering "our movements." Lee also wished him to guard the road from Harpers Ferry "through Maryland" and to keep McLaws informed of any enemy movements affecting him. Stuart interpreted his orders from Lee to mean the road from Frederick through Jeffer-son and Weverton, and he moved Munford's brigade to Jefferson on the 12th. Stuart was curious about the purpose of the enemy activity that morning, "whether a reconnaissance feeling for our whereabouts, or an aggressive move-ment of the army." The Federals had been careful not to expose any of their force at Frederick to observation from Catoctin Mountain, and Stuart was unable to gauge their strength. Whatever the Union army planned, Stuart in-tended to give them a check and "develop his force." Besides his orders, Stuart's impetus to do so was the knowledge that it was unlikely the Harpers Ferry op-eration had been concluded, for Lee had advised him that Jackson had only forced the enemy out of Martinsburg the night before and was moving down against Harpers Ferry that morning. Catoctin Mountain offered what Stuart considered a "very strong position" to accomplish his purposes.[6]

When Hampton's brigade reached the summit, Hampton posted two guns on a ridge commanding the road and dismounted part of his brigade, posting them "along the cliffs that overlooked the road" to reinforce Martin's Mississippi skir-mishers. Between the skirmishers and the artillery, Pleasonton's troopers could make no headway up the mountain. Pleasonton estimated enemy strength at 8 guns and 1,500 cavalry—which for Pleasonton was reasonably accurate—a force requiring infantry to clear it out of the way. He expected the brigade from Rod-man's division to be up shortly, but when they did not appear by 11 a.m., Pleason-ton sent back to Burnside and asked what had happened to his infantry supports. Rodman's 2nd Brigade had set out earlier to reinforce Pleasonton, but through some misunderstanding they followed the road to Jefferson instead of the Na-tional Road. Headquarters sorted out the mistake, and "around noon" Brigadier General Jacob Cox received orders to support Pleasonton with his entire divi-sion. As Cox left Frederick he met McClellan, who told him that if he met Rodman's 2nd Brigade along the way to take them with him.[7]

It was about 1 p.m. when Cox's column came tramping out of Frederick. The Confederates on the mountain saw them coming. One of Hampton's men, with a good dose of exaggeration, described it as an "immense column," and the "roads as far back as the city seemed to be one moving mass of infantry." Stuart accurately estimated Cox's strength at two brigades—more than he wished to tangle with. And the dismounted Federal cavalry had managed to gain a position that commanded Hart's guns as well as the turnpike. Hampton ordered his guns to withdraw and redeploy at Middletown; then he pulled in his cavalry, remounted, and everyone clattered down the mountain into the Middletown Valley. It was shortly after 1 p.m. The delaying tactics of the Confederates and a misunderstanding had cost the Federals seven hours.[8]

"As soon as the artillery left the ridge, all Pleasonton's cavalry started in pursuit," wrote a member of the 1st Massachusetts Cavalry. But as they descended to the western side of the hills, the head of the column again came under a "brisk artillery fire" from Hart's battery, which had unlimbered east of Middletown. Pleasonton ordered up Captain Horatio Gibson's Battery C&G, 3rd U.S. Artillery, which had joined the column. Gibson placed a section on either side of the turnpike and returned fire, while Pleasonton maneuvered his horsemen to turn the enemy flanks. Hampton held his ground for some 20 minutes and then ordered his guns and the main body of his brigade to withdraw. Colonel L. S. Baker's 1st North Carolina covered the withdrawal. Baker deployed one of his squadrons under the "brave and daring" Captain T. P. Siler to delay the enemy while he took the rest of the regiment back near Middletown. One of Siler's men recalled how "the enemy's cavalry advanced down upon us with files of infantry sharpshooters [probably dismounted cavalry] on each side." Siler dismounted part of his force and they opened fire on their pursuers with carbines. The Federals responded by dismounting elements of their force to fix Siler's line, while mounted elements of the 8th Illinois and the 1st Massachusetts were sent sweeping around to outflank the North Carolinians. Siler took a bullet that shattered his thigh, but he grimly kept in the saddle long enough to extricate his men and start them back toward Middletown. The 1st Massachusetts found their flanking maneuver frustrated not by the Confederates, but by the innumerable farm fences. Lieutenant Charles F. Adams wrote that they rode "as fast as we could go, over the hill, pulling down the fences, floundering through ditches, struggling to outflank them. But the fences were too much for us and we had to return to the road, all losing our tempers and I all my writing materials."[9]

As Captain Siler's men withdrew, Colonel Baker deflected an effort—by what was probably part of the 8th Illinois Cavalry—to cut off their escape over Catoctin Creek about a mile west of Middletown. Baker was assisted by Captain Hart, who had repositioned his field pieces on a hill west of the creek "that commanded the pike on the Middletown side." Hart helped keep the Federals back while the North Carolinians made good their escape across the covered bridge spanning the creek. Once everyone was across, Stuart ordered the bridge burned. Adam Koogle's house, barn, and all his other farm buildings, including one with 1,500 bushels of wheat he had recently threshed, stood close to the bridge. When Koogle saw Stuart's men making preparations to burn it, he emerged and implored Stuart to stop, telling him that a good ford existed just below the bridge where the creek was not more than six inches deep, so burning the bridge would not hinder the enemy. Stuart knew differently. The need to ford the creek, no matter how shallow, would slow the enemy down, particularly their artillery and wagons. The fire was set and flames were soon licking up the sides of the bridge. As Koogle feared, the fire spread to his barn and then began to consume his other buildings.

Meanwhile, Captain Gibson brought up two sections of his battery to the eastern side of Middletown and engaged Hart's guns. John Long, a young man living in Middletown, never forgot how a shell from Hart's guns struck Dan Rudy's barn and "glanced across the pike and knocked down a couple panels of fence." Mr. Koogle's home, threatened by the flames that were fast consuming his farm buildings, took several direct hits, probably from Gibson's guns. One shell went through the outer wall of his chimney and cracked his parlor wall. Another burst near the bake oven "just as Mrs. Koogle was taking bread from the oven," and a piece of shell went through the bread pan when she took the bread out to put it on a shelf. Yet another shell killed a 7-year-old African American girl who, along with her mother, were Koogle's slaves. A Confederate artilleryman, who had been wounded by the accidental explosion of a caisson on September 10 and left at Koogle's to recover, also nearly lost his life in the artillery duel and burning buildings. The family forgot about him in the excitement, but when a shell struck the house just below his room they remembered he was in the house, rolled him into a sheet, and carried him to the basement.[10]

Following the engagement on Catoctin Mountain, Stuart had communicated the details of the enemy's activity to D. H. Hill, who was at Boonsboro, as well as to Lee. As the action rolled back toward South Mountain, Stuart advised Hill that infantry were needed to occupy Turner's Gap. He thought no more than a single brigade was sufficient, since it was only necessary to give the enemy a check, and the Federals had revealed no more than their cavalry and two brigades of infantry. But Stuart also thought it quite possible that the Union advance along the National Road was part of a larger effort to relieve Harpers Ferry. The garrison there had probably been captured during the day, but if it had not—and there was no confirmation that it had—then Stuart considered Crampton's Gap to be the most likely point a relieving force would attack. He believed this pass "was now the weakest part of the line," since so far as he knew only Munford's small brigade of cavalry defended it. As Stuart neared Turner's Gap late that afternoon, he learned that Colquitt's brigade of D. H. Hill's division had arrived. With infantry now at Turner's gap, Stuart ordered Hampton to march at once for Crampton's Gap with his brigade and Hart's battery, leaving behind only the Jeff Davis Legion. For the time being Stuart remained with the legion, to keep the enemy at Middletown under observation.[11]

Despite Mr. Koogle's opinion that burning the Catoctin Creek Bridge would not slow the Federals down at all, it did. The good people of Middletown also contributed to the Union force's delay. When the troopers of the 8th Illinois rode down the streets in pursuit of Baker's retreating North Carolinians, ladies of the town emerged from their houses and plied the hungry bluecoats with "large slices of good bread well buttered." The 1st Massachusetts soon came galloping up with pistols drawn, having heard the crack of the 8th's carbines only moments before. "I was somewhat surprised at the number of women who were waving their handkerchiefs hailing us with delight as liberators and passing out water to our soldiers," wrote Lieutenant Adams. "In vain I looked for rebels, nary one could I see, and at last it dawned on my mind that I was in the midst of a newspaper battle—'a cavalry charge,' 'a sharp skirmish,' lots of glory, but n'ary a reb." Being green, Adams perhaps did not understand his luck at missing the fun, but the scrape had been sharp enough for the 29 North Carolinians killed, wounded, or captured in it.[12]

By the time the 8th Illinois reached the bridge, Mr. Koogle's buildings were ablaze and the troopers paused to help save his house from being consumed by the flames. Although the 8th, followed by the 3rd Indiana and the 1st Massachusetts, were able to cross the creek below the bridge easily, the artillery could not use the ford, a fact Stuart certainly knew. They had to wait until the fire could be extinguished and the bridge repaired. Soon after traversing the creek, Pleasonton or Farnsworth learned that part of the enemy force had turned south toward Burkittsville. A hastily assembled force—consisting of two companies each of the 8th Illinois and the 3rd Indiana, commanded by Major William H. Medill of the former regiment—were sent in pursuit.[13]

Medill did not catch up with Hampton until about a mile and a half north of Burkittsville. Here they caught sight of Hampton's baggage train, Hart's guns, and, as one 3rd Indiana trooper noted, "cavalry enough to eat us up" marching toward Crampton's Gap. Medill concluded that there were more Rebels than he wished to tangle with, and he ordered his column to turn about and start back to Middletown. The about-face took place near a country schoolhouse, known as the Quebec Schoolhouse, which sat at the northwest intersection of the Burkittsville and Quebec School roads. Corporal William Pickerill of the 3rd Indiana and his comrades noted that school was still in session, and "out of every window open in our direction were craned the necks of the curious urchins." But unbeknown to Medill and his men, Hampton had taken the Cobb Legion Cavalry, led by the aggressive Lieutenant Colonel Pierce M. B. Young, back to deal with his pursuers—probably along what today is called Picnic Woods Road, which parallels the Burkittsville Road—and concealed the horsemen in some woods overlooking the latter road. One of Medill's troopers recalled that the road in front of the Quebec Schoolhouse was narrow and "hemmed in on either side by a very crooked worm fence." When the Federals turned about and entered the constricted roadway, Hampton and Young struck. The attack was announced by two shots, which surprised the Yankees. Then, as Corporal Pickerill related, they "heard a yell, and over the little ridge and down upon us leaped a body of Confederate cavalry apparently twice our numbers, with drawn swords, wild-eyed, cursing us furiously and demanding our surrender." In a moment the Federals were in "a tussle for existence difficult to describe."[14] One of Pickerill's comrades, Charles N. Dawson, offered a picture of its deadliness.

> Nearly every one on both sides of him [Dawson's comrade Thomas] and I were either killed or wounded. During the hottest of the contest Thomas' horse was knocked down and at the same time he received a stroke on the left shoulder which fortunately proved to be a glancing lick as it did not cut but only bruised. Thomas all this time was busy fighting and was no doubt the means of saving my life. My carbine failed to go off when I had it aimed direct for the rebel Cols [Young] breast who was but a few paces from me leading his men on. When not more than ten feet apart Thomas fired his carbine the ball taking effect in the rebel Cols leg and killed his horse.[15]

It was over in a few moments, with both sides breaking off the action. Nearly 30 members of the 3rd Indiana and the 8th Illinois were casualties. The survivors withdrew with their dead and wounded toward Middletown. Pierce Young and eight of his men were wounded, and four were dead. The savagery of the close quarters' conflict seems to have put some of Young's men in an ugly frame of mind, for they attempted to kill one of their prisoners from the 8th Illinois, cutting him several times over the head with their sabers and leaving him for dead. But he survived and managed to make his way back to his regiment, swearing "vengeance on his would-be murderers." The circumstances that prompted such deadly behavior are unknown, for the other five prisoners who were taken were well treated and paroled the next morning.[16]

While Medill's detachment clashed with Young, Pleasonton and Farnsworth pressed ahead along the National Road toward Turner's Gap. Despite the nearness of the enemy, the troopers found time to admire the beauty of the landscape surrounding them. Lieutenant Adams thought it "the most beautiful valley I ever saw." The column moved swiftly across the valley and through the tiny village of Bolivar to the foothills of South Mountain. Here they came to a "dead stand." By Lieutenant Adams's account, "it was only a single man on horseback in the middle of the road some few hundred yards before us, but it stopped us like a brick wall." The men at the head of Farnsworth's column stood on the top of a hill, and before them the National Road ran straight across a small valley west of Bolivar before "disappearing in a high wooded range on the other side." This was Turner's Gap. The Federals could see several other Confederate videttes from the Jeff Davis Legion beyond the solitary rider, and on the mountainside someone observed an enemy battery of artillery. Where there was a battery there were inevitably supports. Pleasonton concluded that the enemy was present in "large force," and he sent a note back to Burnside requesting some infantry. Since the lateness of the day meant that any effort to seize the gap would have to wait until the next morning, Pleasonton used the remaining daylight to probe the Rebel defenses and reconnoiter the approaches to South Mountain. This revealed a "considerable force" north of the National Road, which was Colquitt's brigade, as well as two roads, north and south of the gap, that offered prospects for flanking Turner's Gap. Armed with this valuable information, Farnsworth's brigade went into bivouac near Bolivar to pass "a tedious night."[17]

While Farnsworth's brigade fought its way forward along the National Road to the foot of South Mountain, a simultaneous three-pronged reconnaissance toward Jefferson took place. Jefferson was a small village nestled at the western base of Catoctin Mountain. Spearheading the northern element of this movement was Colonel Richard Rush's 6th Pennsylvania Cavalry, also known as Rush's Lancers, because the troopers were armed with lances instead of carbines. Supported by Colonel Harrison Fairchild's brigade of the 3rd Division, 9th Corps, Rush approached Jefferson along the Frederick Road. At the same time the 6th U.S. Cavalry advanced on Jefferson from two directions—the road from Adamstown and along the western side of Catoctin Mountain, along the road from Point of Rocks.[18]

Stuart had assigned the defense of the approaches to Jefferson to Munford's brigade. They arrived at Jefferson on the 12th and encamped there. Munford's orders from Stuart were certainly a duplicate of Hampton's: delay the enemy, force him to reveal his strength, but avoid a real fight. The Virginian anticipated that the enemy's most likely avenue of approach was the Frederick Road, and he assigned Captain Holland's 2nd Virginia Cavalry and Chew's horse battery to its defense. That left him the 12th Virginia, part of which he charged with escorting his baggage wagons to Burkittsville, as well as securing that village at the base of the vitally important Crampton's Gap through South Mountain.[19]

The early morning artillery duel 4 miles north along the National Road put Holland's troopers and Chew's gun crews on alert. Holland dismounted part of his command and posted them in the woods and orchards that flanked the Frederick Road where it crossed Catoctin Mountain. Soon they saw the 6th Pennsylvania approaching, the red pennants on their lances fluttering with the movements of man and rider. Behind the cavalry came Fairchild's infantry. Chew announced his presence with several shells. Colonel Rush sent back for infantry support and Fairchild deployed a company of the 9th New York, a Zouave regiment that would make its mark at Antietam, south of the Frederick Road. Chew limbered his guns and rumbled off into Jefferson, then turned north toward Middletown. Captain Holland's skirmishers remained to dispute the pass, concentrating principally in the woods north of the road. Fairchild deployed two more companies of the 9th New York, and the force of mounted and foot soldiers probed forward carefully. One of the New Yorkers, Charles Johnson, recalled: "We started with the Lancers up an abrupt road leading toward the top of the Catoctin Ridge and went about a half mile to a sort of narrow ravine or gorge. Here we were attacked, six shots being fired in rapid succession from an invisible foe. The Lancers turned about in a hurry and we were immediately deployed as skirmishers." The infantrymen made their way forward over difficult terrain, but the Confederates simply melted away, falling back to their horses and slipping off, except for one unfortunate chap who had climbed a tree and was captured before he could make good his escape.[20]

The New Yorkers pushed on through woods and cornfields until they reached the mountain summit. The view was worth the hard climb. "Beneath us was ten miles of country checkered with fields of grain of various hues," and across the valley "the Blue Ridge [South Mountain] in its massive, dark-blue shade," wrote a New Yorker. The Federals spilled down over the mountain toward Jefferson. A company of the 6th Pennsylvania and four companies of Fairchild's 103rd New York were sent north along the Middletown Road to follow up Chew and Holland's 2nd Virginia, which also withdrew in this direction. The balance of the Union task force proceeded cautiously into Jefferson and out on the road to Burkittsville. The 12th Virginia was either handled with considerable skill or the Federals were overly cautious, for nearly a mile and a half west of the village Fairchild halted and deployed the 89th New York and an artillery battery. Here they remained until sunset, when orders arrived recalling the entire brigade to Frederick.[21]

The laurels of the day went to Munford, who, with an inferior force, managed it adroitly enough to fend off the Federals and prevent them from either getting into Stuart's rear along the National Road or reaching the base of South Mountain. The former was highly significant, for it kept the enemy from discerning how weakly held the passes at Burkittsville were. Munford left Jefferson with the 2nd Virginia, riding toward Middletown. The company of Lancers sent in pursuit followed closely—too closely, Munford decided—and he ordered Captain Holland to drive them off. With "a mere handful of men" Holland set on the Pennsylvanians. A brief clash ensued, resulting in the death of one of Holland's men, the wounding of another, and an unknown number of Union casualties. The Lancers pulled back to a more discreet distance and Munford continued his withdrawal unmolested. When they came within a mile of Middletown, scouts sent back word that Yankee cavalry had possession of the village. "Consequently we had to cut across the country on a narrow, lanc-like, hilly road, leaving Middletown a mile to our right," wrote a gunner in Chew's battery. They arrived in Burkittsville by late afternoon. Munford hurried his baggage train over the mountain at Crampton's Gap, then placed Chew's battery in position on the mountain slope where it could cover the Middletown Road, and waited for his pursuers to show themselves.[22]

The Federals were more interested in observing than fighting. Munford's pursuers, the 6th Pennsylvania Cavalry company and four companies of the 103rd New York, made camp at Broad Run Village, about 2 miles east of Burkittsville. The 6th U.S. also arrived in the area from Jefferson and threw out scouts to observe Crampton's Gap and probe south as far as Petersville.[23]

The only other significant cavalry operation that day, Colonel McReynolds's reconnaissance from Frederick to Gettysburg, discovered nothing. An important part of McReynolds's mission had been to find the Confederate cavalry that had descended on Westminster on the evening of the 11th, and make certain that this was not the advance of a larger force moving against the Union right flank. The Confederates McReynolds searched for were Brigadier General Fitz Lee's brigade, which Stuart had ordered to ride north of Frederick and try to gain the enemy's rear, both to confuse them and to gather intelligence about their strength and intentions. Fitz Lee left early on September 11 from New Market and rode north through Liberty and New Windsor. He arrived at Westminster around 7:30 p.m. and swiftly secured the town. Pickets were posted to prevent the escape of anyone who might sound the alarm. When one man tried to slip through, one of Fitz Lee's pickets shot him dead. With the town secure, Fitz Lee's troopers flocked into Westminster's shops and stores "to lay hands upon all the boots, shoes and clothing that they could find." Although a strong Union town, many of the young ladies found it all very exciting and, to the shock of the more staid residents, could not resist flirting with the bronzed and dashing cavalrymen.[24]

After assessing the situation from the vantage of Westminster, Fitz Lee concluded that advancing farther into the Union rear would court disaster. On the 13th he departed, marching to Middleburg, where he bivouacked for the night. McReynolds never found Fitz Lee, although the 8th Pennsylvania Cavalry of his brigade scooped up a picket of some 50 of Lee's horsemen during their march to Emmitsburg on the 13th. It may be that McReynolds did not relish the idea of finding Fitz Lee, for on the 14th, rather than divert his planned march to Gettysburg in order to hunt for the Rebels who had posted the pickets, he stuck to his orders and marched to the Pennsylvania town, where the entire command passed a pleasant evening in the company of loyal friends. While McReynolds moved north, Fitz Lee cut across his rear, marching from Middleburg through Creagerstown, then across Catoctin Mountain through Hamburg, and to South Mountain by way of Orr's Gap. He arrived at Boonsboro after nightfall on the 14th, with no damage suffered save the pickets lost to capture. His accomplishments were not great, but he had caused the Federals to divert a brigade of cavalry on a fruitless search for him and made McClellan cautious about his right flank.[25]

It was 3:30 a.m. on September 13 when the soldiers of General Alpheus Williams's 12th Corps were awakened in their camps around Ijamsville to ready themselves for the day's march to Frederick. The troops ate a hasty breakfast, packed their gear, and were formed up to march by 5 a.m. The first hour of the march was unremarkable. Then the thump of artillery fire from the direction of Catoctin Pass caught everyone's attention. Orders were barked out for the column to move more rapidly. At times the pace increased to a double-quick. Williams's two divisions went "up and down hill, through a splendid country," following the tracks of the B&O Railroad. The Confederates had destroyed the railroad bridge over the Monocacy River, so the column turned north on Reels Mill Road, which led to Crum's Ford.[26]

Brigadier General George H. Gordon's 3rd Brigade, 1st Division, led the advance of the corps across the ford to the west bank of the Monocacy. He deployed Colonel Silas Colgrove's 27th Indiana as skirmishers and followed with the rest of the brigade in line of battle, since it was thought there might still be enemy forces in the area. The Hoosiers splashed across the shallow river, pushed through the thin belt of timber along its border, and advanced to within a mile of the city, where it was learned that Frederick was securely in Union hands. Colgrove ordered his companies to halt and stack arms in a clover field. The time was around 9 a.m.[27]

Before the men had even stacked their weapons, several men in Company F spotted a package in the grass. Corporal Barton W. Mitchell picked the parcel up and discovered within it a piece of paper wrapped around three cigars. The paper was headed "Hdqrs. Army of Northern Virginia, September 9, 1862, Special Orders No. 191," but Mitchell was illiterate, so he handed the paper to his First Sergeant, John M. Bloss, and then, according to one account, divided the cigars between himself, Bloss, and a private, David Bur Vance. Fortunately for the Union army, Bloss was both well educated and more curious about the paper than the cigars. He began to read it aloud to the others. He did not get far before realizing that it was an order of importance. After wrapping it back around the three cigars—which Mitchell had to give up—Bloss and the corporal hurried over to show it to their company commander, Captain Peter Kop. Kop agreed with Bloss that the order might be important and the group made their way to Colonel Colgrove. The series of events happened so quickly that Colgrove had not yet dismounted when Kop, Bloss, and Mitchell presented him with their bundle—cigars and all. Colgrove studied the order for a moment, asked who had found it, then rode off to corps headquarters. General Alpheus Williams was not there when Colgrove arrived, so he gave it to Captain Samuel E. Pittman, Williams's assistant adjutant general. Captain Clermont Best, the corps' chief of artillery, and Captain Ben Morgan, the corps' provost marshal, were also present, and they gathered around Pittman to analyze and debate the authenticity of the document. It seemed so fantastic a find that either

Best or Morgan expressed the opinion that it was a *ruse de guerre* by the Rebels. But only a few years before, Pittman had been a teller at the Michigan State Bank in Detroit, where a prewar U.S. Army paymaster by the name of Robert Hall Chilton kept his account. Pittman paid many of Chilton's checks and knew his signature well. As Pittman recalled, "I was able to assert that I was familiar with Col. Chilton's signature and that the signature on this order was genuine." Pittman and Colgrove sought out General Williams who, after reading the order, told Pittman to send it to McClellan at once. When Pittman asked if he might carry it to McClellan in person, Williams said no, the corps was expecting orders to move at any moment and he needed his assistant adjutant general on hand. A "trusty courier" was selected, who was exhorted to "ride fast" and to deliver the order into McClellan's hands. Before he departed, Williams wrote a hasty cover note: "I enclose a Special Order of the Gen. Lee commanding Rebel forces which was found on the field where my corps encamped. It is a document of interest & also thought genuine." Then, ever mindful of giving credit where it was due, Williams added that "the Document was found by a corporal of 27 Ind. Rgt, Col. Colgrove, Gordon's Brigade."[28]

It is unknown when Williams's courier delivered Corporal Mitchell's discovery. The traditional version is that McClellan received it before noon because of the telegram he sent to the president at "12 m." ("m" being a standard nineteenth-century abbreviation for "meridian," or noon). But it is now known for certain that he did not write the president at noon that day; McClellan's original telegram to Lincoln was actually timed at *12 midnight*. This revelation occurred when McClellan's original telegram, bearing the above time notation, was recently found among Lincoln's papers.[29] The confusion appears to have been the work of the compilers of the Official Records, who abbreviated the word midnight.

The first evidence that headquarters had received the orders is a dispatch from Chief of Staff Marcy to Pleasonton at 3 p.m.

> General: The following order of march of the enemy is dated September 9.*
> General McClellan desires you to ascertain whether this order of march has
> thus far been followed by the enemy. As the pass through the Blue Ridge may
> be disputed by two columns [Longstreet and D. H. Hill], he desires you to
> approach it with great caution.[30]

Even if Williams's courier did not leave 12th Corps headquarters until 10 a.m., a reasonable estimate, it seems impossible that the courier could not find army headquarters, only about a mile away, until four to five hours later. One would think that an hour or two would be ample time to locate army headquarters.

---

*Paragraphs III through X from Special Orders No. 191 were included in the original message to Pleasonton.

What seems more likely is that Williams's courier delivered the orders to Marcy, or Seth Williams, and they may not have had an opportunity to show it to McClellan until nearly midafternoon.

At noon, following his meeting with Burnside, McClellan went to "near the end of town" to review the 2nd Corps, who were just arriving in the city. He found Frederick's citizens still filled with enthusiasm. The cheering, both of the people who thronged the sidewalks and the soldiers who marched by, "was incessant," wrote Colonel Strother. The soldiers were overwhelmed by their reception. "Many a sunburnt, ragged soldier blessed the kindhearted people of Frederic that day, and would have protected their property with their lives," recorded a member of McClellan's headquarters guard. McClellan reviewed his beloved Peninsula veterans until around 1:30 p.m., when it is known that he met Jacob Cox leading his division out to reinforce Pleasonton and told him of the misunderstanding with Rodman's division. Headquarters were probably established soon after this, "about a mile north of the city in a field near the reservoir." It is likely that this is where McClellan first learned of the existence of Special Orders No. 191. He was outside when the order was delivered to him, because some civilians who were visiting headquarters observed his reaction. According to one of them, when McClellan read the document he lost his typical composure and threw up his hands, exclaiming, "Now I know what to do." [31]

McClellan had possession of an order that, if genuine, handed him an opportunity to deliver a smashing blow and possibly a decisive defeat to the enemy. Most importantly, it cleared up the baffling question of the Confederates' intentions. They were not running to escape across the Potomac, but were moving to encircle and destroy the Martinsburg and Harpers Ferry garrisons. It also solved the puzzle of where Lee, Longstreet, and Jackson were. But there were still questions that needed answers before McClellan could set the army in motion. First, was the order genuine or was it an enemy ruse? Pittman's validation of Chilton's signature was reassuring, but McClellan needed more than the word of Chilton's former teller to set an entire army in motion. Second, although the order told him that the divisions of McLaws, R. H. Anderson, Walker and D. H. Hill were present, it also stated that the "commands" of Longstreet and Jackson were in the area, too. The order offered no clue as to what constituted a "command," but clearly it was larger than a division. Third, there were inconsistencies in the movements ordered compared with recent intelligence reports of enemy activity. The order placed no one at Hagerstown, but a substantial enemy force occupied that town, which meant that they might have modified or changed their plan. McClellan needed confirmation of the order's authenticity, and reliable evidence that Harpers Ferry still held out, before he could prepare a plan and set the army on a course of action. This explains the 3 p.m. message from Marcy to Pleasonton, but McClellan probably also sought help from the friendly local community to determine whether the Confederates had followed the order of march that was specified. Between 2 and 3 p.m. both

Willcox's and Sturgis's divisions of the 9th Corps received orders to march to the Middletown Valley [the oft-repeated criticism that McClellan did not order anyone to march until September 14 is untrue]. McClellan may have made this decision independent of Special Orders No. 191, but it seems likely that the order influenced what McClellan chose to do. If both D. H. Hill's division and Longstreet's "command" were at Boonsboro, then Cox's lone division and Pleasonton's cavalry at Middletown were mightily exposed and outmatched.[32]

While he waited for answers to his questions about Special Orders No. 191, McClellan studied the operational picture and considered his options. He recognized the situation as similar to that which confronted Napoleon in northern Italy in 1796, when he discovered the enemy had split their forces; Napoleon then seized the opportunity to defeat them in detail at Castiglione. McLaws was the most vulnerable to destruction, provided that Miles still held out at Harpers Ferry, for the former's two divisions could be pinned against the Potomac River and annihilated or scattered. But the force identified at Boonsboro—D. H. Hill's division; Longstreet's command; the reserve artillery; and the supply and baggage trains—was a juicy target. If part of this force included those who occupied Hagerstown, so much the better. It left the enemy even more divided and vulnerable. Two attack options presented themselves. One was to move against either McLaws or Boonsboro with the entire army. This offered sure numerical superiority, but the force that was not attacked would still be free to maneuver against McClellan's communications or come to the support of its beleaguered comrades. And, if the Boonsboro target were selected, it left Harpers Ferry to its fate—an unacceptable choice.

The better and more ambitious option was a two-pronged attack. While one force pinned and hopefully overwhelmed McLaws, thus relieving Harpers Ferry, the other would attack the Boonsboro force. This offered a larger payoff, with the destruction or defeat of a significant part of Lee's army. And, although the numerical superiority of either attack would not be as great as that offered by a single axis of attack, McClellan certainly understood that he still had an edge in both position and manpower at the point of attack. His entire army was closer to McLaws and Boonsboro than Jackson and Walker were—provided that Miles held out and denied the enemy the pontoon bridge over the Potomac. McClellan had five corps and one division to the three Confederate divisions and one command positioned north of the Potomac. There is evidence that McClellan equated Lee's "command" with a corps, which meant that the enemy could pit the equivalent of two corps against his five corps and one division.[33] If part of the Boonsboro force had moved to Hagerstown, the odds were even better. Hagerstown was over 10 miles from Boonsboro, which meant that supports would take at least three hours to arrive.

The most efficient route of attack against Boonsboro was along the excellent National Road. The principal problem with this route was geography. The troops had to cross two mountain ranges—Catoctin Mountain and South

Mountain—to reach Boonsboro, and the gap through South Mountain, called Turner's Gap, was unsecured. The move against McLaws had more questions associated with it. There were two possible approaches to be considered. The first was along the Knoxville–Frederick Pike through Weverton Pass, which had the advantage of striking McLaws only 4 miles from Harpers Ferry, so that the garrison there would hear the sound of the relief force's guns. But the distance from Weverton Pass to Turner's Gap was some 10 miles, too far for the two wings of attack to mutually support one another if it became necessary, and McLaws could easily reinforce Boonsboro. Some time that afternoon McClellan received information about this approach that further argued against it. The Rebels had reportedly established batteries on the south bank of the Potomac to enfilade the approaches, and the "road from that point winds directly along the river bank at the foot of a precipitous mountain, where there was no opportunity of forming in line of battle."[34]

The second approach against McLaws was via Burkittsville, the gateway to Crampton's Gap and Brownsville Pass through South Mountain. McClellan may not have been aware of Brownsville Pass, but Crampton's Gap was the better of the two anyway, and McClellan learned that it was practicable for artillery and wagons. The advantage of this approach was that once Crampton's Gap was carried and Pleasant Valley reached, McLaws would be cut off from Boonsboro and isolated. He could still attempt to escape by retreating along the Harpers Ferry–Sharpsburg Road, but if McClellan had any information about the condition of this road, he knew it was of poor quality for army trains and equipment. Unless McLaws abandoned these, his movement would be slowed to a crawl. If the attack at Boonsboro went well, McClellan had a fine road from Boonsboro to Sharpsburg that he could sweep down to cut off McLaws.[35]

Having settled on his approach, McClellan next considered the best balance of forces and the details of his offensive. He estimated enemy strength at 120,000, although there was plenty of evidence that contradicted this. A reporter with the *New York Daily Tribune* who questioned Frederick civilians on Confederate strength found that they "agree generally in saying 70,000 or 80,000, with about 200 pieces of artillery." U.S. Sanitary Commission surgeon Lewis H. Steiner, who was still in Frederick on the 13th, estimated Confederate strength at 64,000, and this number included 3,000 slaves.[36] Whether anyone from McClellan's headquarters spoke with Steiner is unknown, but the point is that there were many credible witnesses in Frederick who had observed the Rebel army, and it seems inconceivable that someone from McClellan's staff did not interview reliable sources like Steiner to get some idea of enemy strength. But whatever strength numbers McClellan believed were accurate, it was evident that the enemy force at Boonsboro was twice the size of McLaws's and commanded by Robert E. Lee. It also had the Rebel trains and reserve artillery with it, making it both the tougher nut to crack and the more appealing target. McClellan de-

cided to move against it with the entire force that had massed at Frederick—
the 1st, the 2nd, the 9th, and the 12th Corps; Sykes's division; and the reserve
artillery—about 61,000 men all told. McClellan selected Franklin's 6th Corps,
13,000 strong, and Couch's division of about 6,000 to deal with McLaws and
relieve Harpers Ferry. Franklin was positioned 5 miles south of Frederick at
Buckeystown, which put him approximately 13 miles from Crampton's Gap by
the most direct route. Couch was more inconveniently located at Licksville, 7
miles south of Buckeystown and 16 miles from Crampton's Gap. And elements
of Couch's division were detached to watch the Potomac fords above and below
the mouth of the Monocacy.

By late afternoon McClellan had answers to his most pressing questions:
firing from the direction of Harpers Ferry established that Miles still held out,
signal officers confirmed that McLaws was in Pleasant Valley, and the best evidence that could be obtained indicated that the enemy had followed the order
of march laid down in Special Orders No. 191. At 6:20 p.m. McClellan issued his
first orders, detailing the offensive he had spent the afternoon planning. They
went to Franklin, an officer that less than a month before McClellan had complained about, saying he had "little energy" and "disappointed me terribly." His
opinion of Franklin's initiative might explain the length of McClellan's orders.
But they were also the most complex ones McClellan issued for his September
14 offensive. After briefing Franklin on the positions and movements of the
enemy, McClellan explained that the main body of the army would march that
night and early the next morning to carry the Boonsboro position. Then he
turned to Franklin's mission. Franklin was told that Couch's division had orders to "join you as rapidly as possible." But, without waiting for Couch's entire
division to arrive, Franklin's orders were to move at daybreak with his corps,
going by Jefferson and Burkittsville "upon the road to Rohrersville," which ran
through Crampton's Gap. If he found the gap lightly defended, he was to "seize
it as soon as practicable, and debouch upon Rohrersville, in order to cut off the
retreat of or destroy McLaws's command." If Franklin found the gap defended
by the enemy in strength, "make all your dispositions for the attack, and commence it about half an hour after you hear severe firing at the pass on the
Hagerstown pike, where the main body will attack."[37]

After clearing Crampton's Gap, Franklin's first mission was to "cut off, destroy, or capture" McLaws's command and relieve Colonel Miles. If this was
accomplished, Franklin would add Miles's force to his command, destroy the
bridges over the Potomac, and, after leaving behind a sufficient garrison to guard
any ford the Confederates might use, "return by Rohrersville on the direct road
to Boonsborough if the main column has not succeeded in its attack." But, if
the attack on Boonsboro was successful, then Franklin's orders were to move by
way of Rohrersville to either Sharpsburg or Williamsport to cut off D. H. Hill
and Longstreet or prevent Jackson from reinforcing them. "My general idea is

to cut the enemy in two and beat him in detail," wrote McClellan. The order's last sentence perhaps reflected McClellan's concern about Franklin's initiative. "I ask of you, at this important moment, all your intellect and the utmost activity that a general can exercise."[38]

While writing Franklin's orders, McClellan received a dispatch sent at 4 p.m. by Major General William F. Smith, commanding Franklin's 2nd Division. Smith related that Colonel Rush, commanding the 6th Pennsylvania Cavalry, reported the enemy to be "in strong force at Petersville"—which was not true—and Franklin, when he endorsed Smith's report before sending it on to McClellan, suggested that the 6th Corps should attend to this force. McClellan pondered this and then wrote a postscript to Franklin's orders. The Pennsylvanian "was fully authorized to change any of the details of this order as circumstances may change, provided the purpose is carried out; that purpose being to attack the enemy in detail and beat him." If it were preferable to destroy the enemy at Petersville before executing the attack on Crampton's Gap, "you are at liberty to do so," but, McClellan cautioned, "you will readily perceive that no slight advantage should for a moment interfere with the decisive results I propose to gain." He added that Franklin should communicate with him every hour of the day on the 14th and frequently at night. Acknowledging the problem of straggling, McClellan encouraged Franklin to compel his colonels to prevent it "and bring every available man into action." The thought that Franklin might not think he had sufficient troops at hand for the work ahead may have caused McClellan to add that "the force you have is, with good management, sufficient for the end in view. If you differ widely from me, and being on the spot you know better than I do the circumstances of the case, inform me at once, and I will do my best to re-enforce you."[39]

Orders to the corps commanders involved in the Boonsboro wing of the offensive were distributed later that night. The order of march called for Hooker's 1st Corps, who were bivouacked 2 miles east of Frederick near the Monocacy River, to march at daylight (sunrise was at 5:49 a.m.), followed by Sykes's division, then the reserve artillery, and finally the 2nd and the 12th Corps. The timetable was both ambitious and unrealistic. Sykes and the reserve artillery were expected to follow Hooker at 6 a.m., and Sumner's wing was to start out at 7 a.m. To speed movement, only ambulances and ammunition wagons were permitted to accompany the column. Nonetheless, the National Road would bear the burden of this entire force.[40]

Orders went to Pleasonton, at the forefront of the strike force, to arrange with Burnside for a reconnaissance to ascertain enemy strength at Turner's Gap, and to "fire occasionally a few artillery shots (even though no enemy be in your front to fire at), so as to let Colonel Miles at Harper's Ferry know that our troops are near him."[41]

Elements of the plan were commendable. It realized several of the fundamental principles of war: *seizing the initiative; achieving mass* at the strategic or operational level by bringing five corps against the equivalent of two enemy corps; *flexibility* and *cooperation*, since the two wings of the advance were only about 5 miles apart and could easily reinforce and cooperate with one another, and Franklin was granted the freedom to make alterations in his orders based on changing conditions; *unity of effort*, as the entire army was committed to splitting the enemy in twain; and, lastly, *simplicity*. The plan was uncomplicated. The army marched forward on two roughly parallel lines of advance and pitched into the enemy. And, in his orders to Franklin, McClellan exhibited a refreshing vigor and offensive spirit, the like of which had been noticeably absent in the advance to Frederick.

But other aspects of the plan—security, logistics, and surprise—fell short of the mark. Except for the 9th Corps, no troops were moved over Catoctin Mountain that night, even though the weather was beautiful and the march that day had been an easy one for most of the soldiers. This would have put a considerable part of the army over a significant natural obstacle unobserved and cut the distance to their objectives in half. It also raised the chances of catching the enemy by surprise and gave him less time to react. Although McClellan's report indicates some thought was given to an attack against Weverton Pass, no one seems to have considered the advantages a feint here might have offered to Franklin's attack at Crampton's Gap. Couch's division, at Licksville, was perfectly situated to do this, for he was closer to Weverton Pass than he was to Crampton's Gap. McLaws was surprised that McClellan did not make any effort against Weverton. "A mere demonstration there would have made known to the garrison that McClellan's forces were coming and they 'must hold the fort,'" he wrote.[42] Action at this pass, which was closer to Harpers Ferry than Crampton's Gap, might have also caused McLaws to hold back reserves that he would otherwise have sent to reinforce defenders at the gap. Had McClellan sent Couch on this mission, he could have easily replaced him in Franklin's strike force with Sykes's division. Sykes was closer to Franklin than Couch, and Sykes had the better road on which to rendezvous with Franklin at Jefferson.

Pulling Sykes's men from the force scheduled to march on the National Road would have had the added benefit of reducing some of the traffic on that road. Although the baggage and commissary trains would be removed, McClellan still demanded that the pike accommodate an immense force of nine divisions, artillery, ambulances, and ammunition wagons. Moreover, even if well closed up, the column would stretch for a minimum of 18 miles, which meant that the head would reach the base of South Mountain before the tail started. An unreasonable march timetable also portended traffic jams and delays. Hooker's corps had to clear the city by 6 a.m., when Sykes and the reserve artillery were expected to start. Even if the 1st Corps started at daylight, with 14,000 men, artillery, and wagons it would take it at least two hours (and probably three) to clear the city. Sykes would be lucky if he could start by 7 a.m., which was when Sumner's wing was scheduled to march.

The selection of Hooker's corps to lead the march is puzzling. It must be presumed that it was to keep Burnside's Right Wing together, although two days later McClellan would have no qualms about breaking this wing up. The 1st Corps had made the longest march of any corps in the army on the 13th, between 12 and 16 miles. It left "a good many stragglers" behind in the "warm and dusty" weather and did not make camp until nightfall. Sumner's wing, however, had marched no more than 8 miles on the 13th. The men were well rested and had bivouacked west of town. They might have led the march easily, followed by Sykes, and thus provided Hooker with additional time to rest his men and collect his stragglers while he waited for his turn to start. When swiftness of movement was demanded, as it was in this situation, organizational convenience and efficiency should have given way to it.[43]

No matter who led the column from Frederick, the head of it would not arrive at the base of Turner's Gap until noon at the earliest. It would take an hour or more to deploy the leading corps into battle formation, so it could not contribute to the battle for possession of this pass until midafternoon. If the enemy defended the gap in any strength, Reno's three divisions in Middleton Valley (Rodman's division mistakenly returned to Frederick and did not rejoin the corps until the 14th) would fight alone until the 1st Corps reached them. It was unlikely that any troops besides the 1st and the 9th Corps would participate in a battle, since probably no one else would arrive in time to take part in it before sunset occurred at 6:12 p.m. The problem was twofold: there were too many troops being crowded on a single road, and they were not starting early enough. In addition, the long approach march along the National Road gave away the element of surprise and afforded the enemy ample time to react.

To divide Lee's army, McClellan needed to seize Turner's Gap quickly and cheaply, both to deny Lee a defensive locale where the advantage of position might negate a disadvantage in numbers, and to secure the army's passage over South Mountain. Yet McClellan planned no more than a reconnaissance toward the gap to determine enemy strength. He may have thought that the enemy would put up no more resistance than they had at Catoctin Pass that day. Or he might have feared that the enemy held the pass in strength, and a more aggressive move involving Reno's three 9th Corps divisions could precipitate a battle before the main body of the army was concentrated. Neither of these explanations, however, is a reasonable excuse. A swift and strong move early on the 14th would either seize Turner's Gap—for if only cavalry were defending it, as was the case at Catoctin Pass, they could not stand against even a single infantry division—or it would reveal the enemy's strength. South Mountain was a defensive position, not an offensive one. If Reno's men ran up against a large force, they were numerous enough to withdraw into the valley and hold their own until Hooker's corps came up.

Moreover, the two wings of the Federal army were imbalanced. Franklin had the minimum force possible to execute a complicated and difficult mission, while McClellan stacked the odds against Boonsboro. Although on paper Franklin had three divisions to McLaws's two, McClellan certainly knew that Couch had his division strung out for miles to watch the Potomac fords and would need most of the night to assemble his regiments. Then Couch's orders instructed him to march to Buckeystown to join Franklin, rather than take the more direct route to Burkittsville by way of Point of Rocks and Petersville, a distance of about 10 miles—approximately the same distance the 6th Corps needed to march going from Buckeystown to Burkittsville. McClellan may have selected Couch's route because of the report of a large enemy force at Petersville. If so, it was an unnecessarily cautious move. The force at Petersville could not be all that big, and McClellan's orders to Franklin indicate McClellan did not see it as a threat. McLaws, after all, only had two divisions. Sending Couch against Petersville from Point of Rocks while Franklin advanced from Jefferson would surely have unhinged whatever troops McLaws might have that were exposed there and forced them to fall back on Knoxville or Burkittsville.

With Couch unlikely to arrive in time to participate in any action on the 14th, Franklin was reduced on paper to parity with his foe, two divisions against two divisions, although Franklin would have the advantage of striking at his enemy's rear. McClellan expected much of Franklin. In approximately 12 hours of daylight he had to march 10 miles, force Crampton's Gap, "cut off, destroy, or capture McLaws's command and relieve Colonel Miles," and then, after being joined by Miles's garrison, either march north and join the attack on Boonsboro or cut off the retreat of D. H. Hill and Longstreet. It is doubtful that McClellan expected all this to be accomplished in one day, but Franklin's mission and the force he was given to complete it might have daunted even Stonewall Jackson.

Headquarters bustled with activity that night, with couriers coming and going carrying orders and dispatches and reports. Colonel Strother engaged Chief of Staff Marcy in conversation, and Marcy disclosed to him that "there was great apprehension" over Harpers Ferry. If the garrison could hold out for 48 hours (a statement that indicates McClellan thought his offensive would take two days), Marcy believed they could relieve Miles, but "he apprehended a stampede and a premature surrender."[44]

McClellan certainly shared Marcy's worry about Harpers Ferry, but to his visitors he brimmed with confidence. Brigadier General John Gibbon came by that evening, and he recalled the following about McClellan's demeanor:

[He] expressed himself freely in regard to his movements and taking from his pocket a folded paper, he said: "Here is a paper with which if I cannot whip 'Bobbie Lee,' I will be willing to go home." He spoke cheerfully and confidently and added, "I will not show you the document now but there [turning down one of the folds] is the signature [R. H. Chilton, Adjt. Gen.] and it gives the movements of every division of Lee's army. Tomorrow we will pitch into his centre and if your people will only do two good, hard days' marching I will put Lee in a position he will find hard to get out of. Castiglione will be nothing to it."[45]

McClellan may have been security conscious, but news of his having a copy of Special Orders No. 191 leaked out. Three days later the *Baltimore Sun* ran a small story about the discovery of "Rebel Order No. 119." More ominously, one of the civilians visiting headquarters was a Confederate sympathizer. Although there is no compelling evidence that this individual knew exactly what intelligence McClellan had received that day, he did learn that the Federals had come into some valuable information, and he may even have witnessed the movement of Cox's, Willcox's, and Sturgis's divisions, headed for Middletown Valley. Sometime that evening he slipped off, riding west to warn the Confederates of approaching danger.[46]

At 8:45 p.m. McClellan took a moment to send a cryptic telegram to Halleck that served more to confuse than it did to inform: "We occupy Middletown and Jefferson. The whole force of the enemy in front. They are not retreating to Virginia. Look well to Chambersburg. Shall lose no time. Will soon have a decisive battle."[47]

Shortly after this message was dispatched, a wire sent that morning by Halleck arrived. Responding to McClellan's recent correspondence regarding reinforcements and the whereabouts of the enemy's main force, Halleck advised McClellan that no reinforcements other than Porter's 5th Corps could be spared from the capital's defenses. Halleck also disapproved of how far McClellan had moved the field army from the capital. "Until you know more certainly the enemy's force south of the Potomac, you are wrong in thus uncovering the capital. I am of the opinion that the enemy will send a small column toward Pennsylvania, so as to draw your forces in that direction; then suddenly move on Washington with the forces south of the Potomac and those he may cross over. I assure you that you are wrong. The capture of this place will throw us back six months, if it should not destroy us."[48]

McClellan responded—this time more thoroughly—at 11 p.m., after the movement orders for the army's advance were finished. He opened with the biggest news. "An order from General R. E. Lee" had accidentally come "into my hands this evening." It disclosed "some of the plans of the enemy" and showed "most conclusively that the main rebel army is now before us." The authenticity of the order "is unquestionable." He related that the enemy's plan was to surround and capture the Martinsburg and Harpers Ferry garrisons, stating that this was confirmed both by the heavy firing heard from Harpers Ferry that day and the fact that "the columns took the roads specified in the order." McClellan still estimated enemy strength at "120,000 men or more," now known "to be commanded by Lee in person." Based on intelligence gleaned from sources in Frederick, McClellan confidently believed that after the capture of the garrisons Lee "intended to attempt penetrating Pennsylvania." Orders had been issued for the Army of the Potomac to march early the next morning. They would make forced marches to "endeavor to relieve Colonel Miles, but I fear, unless he makes a stout resistance, we may be too late." This was a bit disingenuous. No unit in the army had yet been ordered to make a forced march. It also reflected McClellan's scant confidence that Miles would make a stout resistance. But McClellan promised to "do everything in my power to save Miles if he still holds out."[49]

Based on this latest intelligence that he had received, McClellan believed "that there is but little probability of the enemy being in much force south of the Potomac." Responding to Halleck's comment that he underestimated the importance of Washington, McClellan wrote that he did not undervalue the need to hold the capital. He considered it "of great consequence," but not of the same consequence as the Army of the Potomac. It was on "the success of this army [that] the fate of the nation depends," and it was "for this reason that I said everything else should be made subordinate to placing this army in proper condition to meet the large rebel force in our front." There was some element of logic to this. Leaving a large force to defend the capital while the enemy massed their forces in Maryland defied sound military principles. But this statement also revealed how little political acumen McClellan had accrued. The key for any field commander was to convince his superiors to reinforce him because it was in their best interest to do so. Lee did this in persuading Davis to send him most of the Richmond garrison, arguing that he could better ensure Richmond's security if he carried the war to the enemy's frontier rather than waging it at the Confederate capital's doorstep. McClellan never had Lee's touch in dealing with his superiors.[50]

McClellan closed his lengthy message with some typical comments: "Unless General Lee has changed his plans, I expect a severe general engagement tomorrow. I feel confident that there is no rebel force immediately threatening Washington or Baltimore, but that I have the mass of their troops to contend with, and they outnumber me when united." In other words, he needed more men, and if the Army of the Potomac were defeated it was because they were outnumbered. But if the army were successful, they would have prevailed over a superior force.[51]

At midnight McClellan wrote the president. It had been a long and eventful day, but every sentence of his message danced with excitement.

I have the whole rebel force in front of me, but am confident, and no time shall be lost. I have a difficult task to perform, but with God's blessing will accomplish it. I think Lee has made a gross mistake, and will be severely punished for it. The army is in motion as rapidly as possible. I hope for a great success if the plans of the rebels remain unchanged. We have possession of the Catoctin.

I have all the plans of the rebels, and will catch them in their own trap if my men are equal to the emergency. I now feel that I can count on them as of old. All forces of Pennsylvania should be placed to co-operate at Chambersburg. My respects to Mrs. Lincoln. Received most enthusiastically by the ladies. Will send you trophies. All well, and with God's blessing will accomplish it.[52]

This told Lincoln pretty much nothing, except that his field commander was excited and confident. But even if McClellan's plan for September 14 had some shortcomings, it was still an offensive. It represented a dramatic change in his generalship from the excessive caution of the Peninsula, Second Manassas, and the advance to Frederick, and this surely pleased the president. The army approved as well. The impending offensive offered them an opportunity to avenge the summer's defeats. The pessimism that pervaded the ranks after the withdrawal from the Peninsula and the defeat at Second Manassas had slowly lifted as the army made its way across Maryland's friendly soil. In the smiles and cheers that greeted them in each village they passed through, the troops found assurance that someone believed in them and that they were fighting for a worthy cause. John Vautier, in the ranks of Hooker's 1st Corps, noted in his journal that during the march on the 13th "the men felt merry—singing most of the way . . . Oh it cheered our hearts to see the smiles of welcome bearing on us from every house by the way."[53]

The massing of the army around Frederick, with all its pomp and ceremony, boosted morale by revealing the army's muscle to all. A soldier in the green 108th New York gazed on the thousands of campfires that flickered in the night as far as they eye could see and thought it "a grand spectacle . . . the like of which is not looked upon in ages." Lieutenant Josiah Favill of the 57th New York believed the army sensed the importance of the upcoming operations. "The possibilities of a disaster to our arms at this juncture are so momentous that every man feels the necessity of doing his utmost, regardless of all personal consideration." General Alpheus Williams displayed a new assurance. He wrote to his daughter: "I have great confidence that we shall smash them terribly if they stand, more confidence than I have ever had in any movement of the war." With grim determination Favill, Williams, and their comrades of the Army of the Potomac prepared themselves for the showdown battle all knew loomed over the dark mountains.[54]

In his messages to Halleck and Lincoln, McClellan mentioned that the Confederates might have deviated from the plan outlined in Special Orders No. 191. Reports of large bodies of enemy troops at Williamsport and Hagerstown, neither of which were mentioned in the order, suggested this possibility. The Rebels had indeed made movements not laid down in the order, and they benefited McClellan. When the Army of Northern Virginia marched west from Frederick on September 10, Lee learned about a supply of flour at Hagerstown that local Unionists were hauling off to Pennsylvania to prevent it from falling into Confederate hands. He also received a report of an enemy force advancing on Hagerstown from the direction of Chambersburg. The flour was necessary to feed his men, and as Lee planned to use Hagerstown as his base of operations either to meet a Union advance over South Mountain or to invade Pennsylvania, he could not permit the enemy to occupy the town or to threaten the Williamsport ford, 5 miles to the southwest, even if the approaching force were only Pennsylvania militia. Lee did not hesitate to further divide his army or to shift the weight of his Boonsboro force to Hagerstown. Dropping off D. H. Hill's division at Boonsboro on September 11, Lee continued on to Hagerstown with Longstreet's two divisions and Evans's brigade, three battalions of the reserve artillery, the reserve ordnance train, and most of the army's commissary and quartermaster trains. Toombs's brigade of D. R. Jones's division was sent ahead to secure the city, while the rest of Longstreet's command, the trains, and the artillery camped just west of Funkstown. The next day Longstreet moved up through Hagerstown and bivouacked at the fairgrounds on the Williamsport Turnpike.[55]

Lee sensed little danger in making this additional division. In his report of the campaign he wrote, "The advance of the Federal Army was so slow at the time we left Fredericktown as to justify the belief that the reduction of Harper's Ferry would be accomplished and our troops concentrated before they would be called upon to meet it." Lee placed D. H. Hill's division at Boonsboro primarily to intercept any elements of the Harpers Ferry or Martinsburg garrisons that might elude Jackson or McLaws. Until McLaws and Jackson advanced far enough to cut off all escape routes, the enemy might attempt to slip away through Shepherdstown or along the north bank of the Potomac on the Harpers Ferry–Sharpsburg Pike. In either case, Hill was perfectly positioned at Boonsboro to cut them off. Hill could also provide Stuart with infantry support should he need it. But there were no plans to oppose the Union army's passage of South Mountain. Lee wanted to draw them west of the mountains, where they would be more vulnerable and far from their fortifications and supply depots.[56]

By the afternoon of September 12 Lee knew that the Harpers Ferry operation had fallen behind schedule. He had heard nothing from McLaws or Walker, and a dispatch from Jackson sent that morning told him that the Martinsburg garrison had abandoned their position during the night of the 11th and retired toward Harpers Ferry. At 2:30 that afternoon he sent a dispatch to Stuart, informing him of this development as well as the new deployment of their own army's forces, with D. H. Hill at Boonsboro and Longstreet at Hagerstown. "I do not wish you to retire too fast before the enemy, or to distribute your cavalry wide apart," Lee wrote, implying that Stuart's previous instructions were to observe, not necessarily to delay the enemy's advance to Frederick and beyond. Lee now needed more time to complete the Harpers Ferry operation, and he wished to prevent the Federals from divining his plans.[57]

McLaws's division was the most vulnerable force. D. H. Hill and Longstreet could withdraw to Virginia by way of Sharpsburg or Williamsport if necessary, but McLaws's escape routes were more difficult. The lack of news from McLaws caused some mild concern, since Lee did not know what progress he had made in carrying out his mission. On the morning of the 13th Lee had his military secretary, Colonel Armistead L. Long, write to McLaws, mildly admonishing him for not communicating with headquarters and expressing Lee's desire "that the object of your expedition be speedily accomplished." Lee expected that the enemy had occupied Frederick "and are following in our rear." Long advised McLaws that the Martinsburg garrison, some 2,500 or 3,000 strong, had abandoned that place and retreated to Harpers Ferry, and that Jackson was in pursuit and would be in position west of there by noon. McLaws also learned that Longstreet was at Hagerstown and D. H. Hill was in the vicinity of Boonsboro. The enemy at Frederick were within a day's march of McLaws's rear, if they moved rapidly, but if the pace they set on their approach to Frederick continued—and Lee had no reason to think it would not—then they were two to three days' march distant. Depending on how quickly the Union garrison at Harpers Ferry could be disposed of, McLaws might have to defend his rear. Therefore, Long advised McLaws, "you are particularly desired to watch well the main road from Frederick to Harper's Ferry, so as to prevent the enemy from turning your position." Long closed the message by reiterating Lee's desire for McLaws to quickly wrap up the operation and "to communicate as frequently as you can" with headquarters.[58]

By noon of the 12th, Lee had confirmation that the enemy had occupied Frederick and that their cavalry, along with infantry from Reno's corps, were pressing Stuart at Catoctin Pass along the National Road. Lee sent a communication to his cavalry commander at 12:45 p.m.

> If you find that the enemy intends more than a reconnaissance, and is too strong for your cavalry, Gen. Hill can reinforce you with a brigade of infantry and some artillery. I have as yet heard nothing from Harpers Ferry of the troops in that region. If there is a prospect of drawing the force you mention under Reno, within reach of Hill, so that he can strike at them with his whole force, do so. Keep Hill advised of any movements affecting him.[59]

This is an important and revealing message. Clearly Lee did not believe that the reported Federal advance was a significant threat if he thought a single brigade and some artillery were all that Stuart needed to check it, nor would Lee have authorized offensive action by D. H. Hill. Stuart probably reported the enemy force as cavalry and two brigades of infantry, since this is all he had been able to identify that day, and Stuart rarely either speculated or reported what he did not know to be fact. Lee remained attentive to developments in his rear, but unconcerned.

Lee's confidence received a jolt around 9 p.m., when he received a communication from Stuart. The pressure applied against him made Stuart think that the force that had pressed him back to Turner's Gap was part of a general advance by the Army of the Potomac. Minutes after this message, Lee received what he later described as an "alarming dispatch" from D. H. Hill, who reported that the campfires of a large enemy force were visible in Middletown Valley. Then, on the heels of Hill's dispatch, came another and even more worrisome report from Stuart. The Confederate sympathizer who had been present at McClellan's headquarters when the latter learned about Special Orders No. 191 had found Stuart on South Mountain about sunset. According to Ezra Carman—who unfortunately does not reveal his source—this person "did not know the character of the paper, whether it was an order to McClellan or some report from one of his corps commanders, but he knew that it was of some importance and that a rapid forward movement of the army was to be ordered." This confirmed Stuart's and Hill's reports that the enemy was advancing in some force. Longstreet had already retired for the night when Lee summoned him to his tent. Longstreet recalled that when he arrived, Lee had his map of the area spread out before him. "He told me of the reports, and asked my views," Longstreet remembered. The Georgian thought that if the enemy were at the base of South Mountain, then it was too late to march on the 14th and establish a proper defense of Turner's Gap. Instead, Longstreet "expressed the preference for concentrating D. H. Hill's and my own force behind the Antietam at Sharpsburg, where we could get together in season to make a strong defensive fight, and at the same time check McClellan's march toward Harper's Ferry."[60]

Lee listened but did not agree. First, he did not think the threat to Turner's Gap to be immediate. Longstreet remembered that Lee "held to the thought that he had ample time" to make arrangements to meet the enemy advance. Second, pulling Hill and Longstreet back to Sharpsburg would place McLaws in danger. McClellan could deploy a holding force on the Boonsboro–Sharpsburg Pike to screen Hill and Longstreet while he turned and crushed McLaws with his main force. Lee understood that defending the mountain gaps east of Boonsboro afforded the best assistance to McLaws and, if things became critical for the Georgian, kept open an escape route northward to Boonsboro. Lee also sensed that the initiative had shifted to the enemy, but he could regain it if he could check the Union advance at the passes long enough to reduce Harpers Ferry. Sharpsburg was a defensive position. To withdraw there before the enemy had even landed a blow completely surrendered the initiative and reduced Lee's options. Therefore he ordered Longstreet to ready his men to march the next morning. Longstreet would take along his entire force (minus Toombs's brigade), plus the three battalions of the reserve artillery, and march to Beaver Creek, 3 miles north of Boonsboro on the National Road. The army trains, guarded by Toombs's men, would remain at Hagerstown.[61]

Longstreet departed to make his preparations. But he found his mind "so disturbed" by Lee's strategy that he could not rest. "As I studied, the perils seemed to grow," until he finally sat down and wrote a note to Lee, appealing "again for immediate concentration at Sharpsburg." He received no answer.[62]

After his meeting with Longstreet ended, Lee was busy dictating dispatches. All went out around 10 p.m. One went to Jackson, warning him of the increased enemy activity and urging him to press matters at Harpers Ferry. A second went to D. H. Hill, instructing him to go to Turner's Gap in the morning and assist Stuart in preparing for its defense. The third went to McLaws. "General Lee directs me to say that, from reports reaching him, he believes the enemy is moving toward Harper's Ferry to relieve the force they have there. You will see, therefore, the necessity of expediting your operations as much as possible," the dispatch began. Stuart would keep McLaws informed "of the movements of the enemy." When the operations were completed, unless Jackson gave him different orders, Lee desired McLaws to march "as rapidly as possible" to Sharpsburg.[63]

Sometime after midnight Lee dictated a response to Stuart's dispatches of that evening. In one of his messages Stuart must have raised the question of whether Lee wished to defend the mountain passes or merely conduct a holding action, as Stuart had done on Catoctin Mountain. Lee replied unequivocally: "The gap must be held at all hazards until the operations at Harper's Ferry are finished." Which gap Lee meant is a question, but since Crampton's Gap was the most likely avenue of enemy advance, it is logical that he meant this gap and not Turner's Gap. But, so that Stuart would not construe this as an order to shift all of his cavalry to the south, Lee added: "You must keep me informed of the strength of the enemy's forces moving up by either route [Turner's Gap or Crampton's Gap]." Lee also did not mean his statement about defending Crampton's Gap "at all hazards" to be an order to Stuart to go there personally, but this is how the cavalryman interpreted it.[64]

The note to Stuart was preceded or followed—there is no time indicated on it, so we cannot know—by yet another dispatch to McLaws. "General Longstreet moves down this morning to occupy the Boonsborough Valley, so as to protect your flank from attacks from forces coming from Frederick, until the operations at Harper's Ferry are finished," it began. Lee once again stressed the need to push operations there "as rapidly as possible," but he had to consider the possibility of failure. In the event that Harpers Ferry was not taken and McLaws's rear was imperiled, Lee wanted him to "so arrange it that your forces may be brought up the Boonsborough Valley." He informed the Georgian that Stuart, with part of D. H. Hill's division, held Turner's Gap, and that Hampton's and Munford's brigades of cavalry were at Burkittsville to cover Crampton's Gap. There were no instructions for McLaws to reinforce the cavalry with infantry, but then Lee probably assumed that McLaws did not need to be told to protect his rear. The message closed: "If Harper's Ferry should be taken, the

road will be open to you to Sharpsburg. Around the mountains from Sharpsburg the road communicates with Boonsborough and Hagerstown." This was a
reference to the Harpers Ferry–Sharpsburg Road.[65]

Lee's pugnacity and sheer force of will are evident in his decisions and dispatches that night. Despite warnings of a major enemy offensive about to fall on
his divided army, Lee did not even contemplate adopting a conservative course,
canceling the Harpers Ferry operation and withdrawing the army to Maryland.
Instead, he made what he thought were the necessary dispositions and orders
that would deflect or check the enemy offensive so that he might regain the initiative. McLaws's vulnerability concerned him, as is evident by the three dispatches sent to that commander in the span of 24 hours, but—except for the last
message, which contained instructions in case of failure—they all exhibited determination to see the Harpers Ferry operation to a successful conclusion. The
orders to McLaws to march to Sharpsburg once the garrison was captured reflect Lee's agreement with Longstreet on the defensive merits of this position,
but the sentence in his last dispatch to McLaws—that roads from Sharpsburg
communicated with Hagerstown and Boonsboro—reveal that Lee was thinking
more of regaining the initiative than of adopting a defensive position. Sharpsburg was the ideal place to deliver troops to either point, depending on how the
situation developed.

Lee's judgment erred, however, on one important point. The decision to
move Longstreet only as far as Beaver Creek, and not until the morning of the
14th, indicates that he expected McClellan to advance with characteristic caution. Lee was no mind reader, but he had taken McClellan's measure on the Peninsula and was confident that if the Federal commander planned an offensive, it
would be conducted with his typical deliberation and no major blow would fall
on the 14th. Longstreet wrote after the war that "the hallucination that McClellan was not capable of serious work seemed to pervade our army, even to this
moment of dreadful threatening." Lee did not discount the fact that McClellan
was capable of serious work; he simply expected that McClellan's advance to
battle would be slow and methodical. Whatever influenced Lee's decision to not
march with Longstreet that night, it left D. H. Hill—and the entire Confederate
army—in grave peril, and gave a boost to the odds that McClellan might still
duplicate the feat of Castiglione.[66]

9

The Morning Battle for Fox's Gap

"My God! Be careful!"

Lee's orders to D. H. Hill directing him to assist Stuart in the defense of South Mountain arrived around midnight. They caught Hill unprepared. Since crossing the mountain at Turner's Gap two days before, on September 11, Hill had arranged his five brigades, numbering approximately 6,800 men, between Funkstown and Little Beaver Creek to watch the National Road and the fords over Antietam Creek, in order to intercept any Federals from Harpers Ferry who might try to escape the trap closing on them there. Since he had no orders to defend Turner's Gap, as there was no expectation that it would need to be defended, Hill left no troops there, but he did order Colonel Alfred Colquitt's brigade to Boonsboro on the evening of the 12th with orders to "occupy the commanding points" there. If trouble approached from east of South Mountain, Hill relied on Stuart to give him timely warning. Hill's attention, and that of his division, focused toward the west and southwest.[1]

Trouble east of South Mountain reared its head on the 13th, as Pleasonton's cavalry pushed Stuart off Catoctin Mountain and pursued him to the Middletown Valley. Stuart sent a note to alert Hill of these developments and warn him that two brigades of Union infantry were part of the pursuing force. Stuart requested that Hill "send him a brigade to check the pursuit at South Mountain." This was hardly the stuff to worry Hill, yet he responded vigorously. He ordered two brigades—Colquitt's and Brigadier General Samuel Garland's—to Turner's Gap, which was 6 miles from Boonsboro on the National Road. Shortly after dark Hill decided to pull more of his division closer to Boonsboro. He ordered Brigadier General Roswell Ripley to move his brigade, with a battery of artillery, to "the eminence immediately on the northeast of Boonsborough," and to send a regiment at daylight on the following morning to occupy Orr's Gap, 4 miles north of Turner's Gap. Lee had not relieved Hill of his duty to watch the roads from Harpers Ferry, so Hill left Brigadier General George B. Anderson's and Brigadier General Robert E. Rodes's brigades in position to watch the Antietam fords north of Little Beaver Creek for this purpose. Hill also took the precaution of ordering Anderson to have his men cook a day's rations and have them ready to march at 3:30 a.m. Given the vigor of these dispositions, it is difficult to reconcile the criticism that has been levied at Hill for his lack of preparation against the Union advance that Stuart reported.[2]

The one Alabama and four Georgia regiments that composed Colquitt's brigade were led by 38-year-old Colonel Alfred Colquitt. He had seen some staff duty as a major of volunteers in the Mexican War, but the law was his profession. He had served a term as a U.S. Congressman and was a member of the Georgia State Legislature. Colquitt was a strong advocate for secession and pushed for the extension of slavery in the western territories. His prominence won him selection as a delegate to his state's secession convention. After Georgia left the Union he took a commission as a captain, but within a month he was elected colonel of the 6th Georgia Infantry. When field service proved more than Brigadier General Gabriel Rains could stand, Colquitt took command of his brigade as the senior colonel. One of his men described Colquitt as a "brave and valiant" soldier who kept his cool in the chaos of battle. The men of the brigade were veterans, with service at Williamsburg, Seven Pines, and the Seven Days. There were approximately 1,250 in the ranks, and they were accompanied by Captain John Lane's Georgia battery of six guns in the slow, tedious climb from Boonsboro to the summit of Turner's Gap.[3]

The head of the brigade reached the gap around 4 p.m., just as Stuart came up from the Middletown Valley with the Jeff Davis Legion. Stuart paused to brief Colquitt while the infantry moved to the side of the road to allow the troopers to pass down the mountain toward Boonsboro. Lieutenant George G. Grattan, a volunteer aide on Colquitt's staff, stated that his "distinct recollection is that General Stuart reported that there were no troops following him but cavalry and that Colonel Colquitt would have no difficulty in holding the pass with his brigade." Colquitt asked if Stuart could spare two companies of cavalry for picket duty, but, Grattan recalled, "General Stuart thought it unnecessary, and declined to leave them." Actually, elements of the Jeff Davis Legion did remain in Colquitt's front until dark, when they were withdrawn. Stuart claimed he, too, remained on the mountain until dark before riding down to Boonsboro. This may be, but it does not absolve him from criticism for leaving Colquitt without cavalry. Stuart defended his decision in his report, written 17 months later, by claiming that the ground around Turner's Gap "was obviously no place for cavalry operations." Perhaps not, but it still warranted two companies for scouting and screening Colquitt's front.[4]

With Stuart's assistance, Colquitt hastily deployed his brigade to check Pleasonton's advance. He ordered Lane to move two guns to occupy a position on the eastern slope of the mountain that commanded the pike, but the rapid approach of the Union horsemen forced Colquitt to cancel the order. Lane's guns were simply "thrown rapidly into position at the most available points," while the infantry, as it came up, deployed on either side of the pike. Whether or not Colquitt deliberately displayed his regiments for the Federals to see, the show of force persuaded Pleasonton that the Confederates were on the mountain in "large force" and halted his advance along the pike. This gave Colquitt time to assess his position and the problems inherent in defending it. Colquitt learned from either Stuart or mountain locals that three other roads crossed the mountain north and south of Turner's Gap. The Old Sharpsburg Road passed the mountain a mile south of Turner's, at a gap residents called Fox's Gap or Braddock's Gap. Two local roads ascended the mountain north of Turner's Gap, one coming into the National Road at the summit of Turner's Gap, and the other joining the pike a mile west of Turner's, at a tiny village called Zittlestown. Colquitt sent strong picket details to watch all of these roads, and when he was satisfied that the Union cavalry had withdrawn from his front, he pulled the main body of his brigade back nearly to the Mountain House, an eighteenth-century building that sits on the narrow summit of Turner's Gap, leaving only a skirmish line on the eastern slope.[5]

A member of the picket detail at Fox's Gap recalled how "we could see the Yankee cavalry scouting around in every direction," but the Federals were content to observe, not pick a fight, and as night fell across the valley they withdrew out of sight. From Turner's Gap Colquitt and his men enjoyed a magnificent view of the valley below. But the number of campfires that began to appear there transformed the scene from one of tranquil beauty into cause for genuine alarm. They were, wrote Lieutenant Grattan, "far in excess of what would have been necessary for the two brigades of cavalry which General Stuart said were following him." Stuart had clearly greatly underestimated both enemy strength and the threat to Turner's Gap. Colquitt sent a courier speeding down the mountain to find Hill and convey this important news to him.[6]

It was this report from Colquitt that generated D. H. Hill's "alarming dispatch" to Lee, which, when combined with the other information he received, caused Lee to order Hill and Stuart to see to the defense of Turner's Gap. Lee's orders to Stuart forced the cavalryman to reconsider his opinion that South Mountain was "no place for cavalry operations." Sometime "before daylight" on September 14, Stuart ordered Colonel Thomas Rosser's 5th Virginia Cavalry and a section of Captain John Pelham's horse battery, which had both reached Boonsboro during the night, to occupy Fox's Gap, which Stuart thought was unguarded. It was a logical decision, since Stuart believed that Colquitt had only covered Turner's Gap, but Stuart failed to communicate to either D. H. Hill or Colquitt that he had sent some of his men to Fox's Gap. Had Stuart left Colquitt the two companies of cavalry Colquitt requested, Stuart might have known that the Georgian had posted a strong picket at Fox's and that far more than a brigade of Union cavalry were assembled in the Middletown Valley. Stuart also failed to let Hill know that he would not be assisting Hill in the defense of the two Boonsboro gaps, for Stuart had reasoned (or interpreted his orders to believe) that his personal presence was more important at Crampton's Gap, where he expected the enemy would strike their main blow at what he thought was "the weakest point of the line." Stuart's reasoning may have been sound regarding Crampton's Gap, but he added no laurels to his reputation as a cavalry commander that night. He left the defenders of the Boonsboro gaps without a cavalry screen, which they had every right to expect, and his failure to communicate and coordinate with Hill was inexcusable and led to dangerous confusion.[7]

D. H. Hill certainly took comfort in his belief that Stuart would be present to assist him in organizing a defense of Turner's Gap on the 14th. There was little else he could feel sanguine about. He had arranged his men as well as the limited information about the enemy threat to Turner's Gap permitted. But the terrain Lee ordered him to defend at the mountain gaps was unfamiliar, and Hill probably lacked maps with details about local roads. Shortly after receiving Lee's orders, Hill sent Roswell Ripley off to locate Stuart and gather all the information he could from Stuart about the mountain gaps. Why did Hill send Ripley instead of going to see Stuart in person? Perhaps he had other business to attend to, or possibly because he simply did not like Stuart (Stuart's report suggests that he did not care for Hill). Whatever the reason, it represented another Confederate command coordination failure that would have consequences in the morning.[8]

Ripley found Stuart shortly after midnight. The cavalryman expressed surprise at the request for information about "a locality where General Hill had been lying for two days with his command." Nonetheless, Stuart went over his maps of the area with Ripley and related all that he knew about the roads and terrain on the mountain, but he omitted the fact that he was leaving for Crampton's Gap in a few hours and would not be on hand to assist Hill in the morning.[9]

By the time Ripley returned to Hill's headquarters and imparted what he had learned from Stuart, there were only a few hours before sunrise. Based on Stuart's report, Hill made no changes to his dispositions. Colquitt's brigade and a battery were at Turner's Gap, and Garland's brigade with another battery had bivouacked on the western slope of the mountain and would be at the summit by daylight. Until he had personally looked at the ground and sized up the enemy threat to the gaps, Hill hesitated to commit any more of his force from the valley.[10]

Enough Federal troops to make plenty of trouble for Hill had quietly assembled during the night in the Middletown Valley. Three divisions of Major General Jesse L. Reno's 9th Corps reached the valley and bivouacked unobserved by Stuart's cavalry or Colquitt's infantry. Cox's Kanawha division of 3,544 officers and men were the closest, its two brigades making camp near Catoctin Creek west of Middletown, less than 4 miles from Turner's Gap. Brigadier General Orlando B. Willcox's 1st division, 3,316 strong, followed Cox and halted

1.5 miles east of Middletown. The campfires of one or both of these divisions are probably what Colquitt observed and what prompted his warning to D. H. Hill. Brigadier General Samuel D. Sturgis's 2nd division, approximately 3,200 strong, accompanied by corps headquarters and perhaps Burnside's wing headquarters, made camp near the western base of Catoctin Mountain. Only Rodman's 3rd division was not in the Valley. It had returned to Frederick following the reconnaissance to Jefferson. Reno sent word for Rodman to have his division on the road toward Middletown at 3 a.m. Farnsworth's cavalry brigade, after withdrawing from Colquitt's front, encamped less than 1 mile west of Cox, at the junction of the Old Sharpsburg Road and the National Road. It was a formidable force, but there were no plans to flex its muscle in the morning to seize the mountain gaps.[11]

The Federals planned nothing more than to reconnoiter the gaps on the 14th. After his encounter with Colquitt's infantry on the evening of the 13th, Pleasonton asked Burnside for infantry support for the planned reconnaissance. Burnside approved the request and referred it to Reno to make the arrangements. Reno instructed Cox to furnish Pleasonton with the necessary force in the morning, but he left the details of the operation to Cox and Pleasonton. The cavalryman stopped by Cox's tent that evening to discuss plans. Cox recalled that Pleasonton thought the enemy infantry at Turner's Gap was a rear guard, and that a single infantry brigade would be sufficient to enable his cavalry to clear the way. Cox's recollection was also clear on another point: "no battle was expected at Turner's Gap" the next morning.[12]

Pleasonton wanted Cox's 2nd Brigade for his support. Colonel George Crook commanded the brigade after Colonel Moor's capture in Frederick, and Crook was an old army friend of Pleasonton's. Cox wanted to please Pleasonton, "and not thinking it would make any difference to my brigade commanders, intimated that I would do so." But when Colonel Eliakim P. Scammon, who commanded Cox's 1st Brigade, heard of the arrangement, he objected. It was customary in both armies to rotate which brigade led the division's march each day. Crooks's had led on the 13th, so it was Scammon's turn on the 14th and he demanded his right to do so. Cox tried to explain that he had proposed the change as a courtesy to Pleasonton. Scammon was unmoved. "The point of professional honor touched him," recalled Cox. Perhaps. Scammon's brigade nicknamed him "Old Granny" for his fussiness over details and strict observance of army protocol. And he had a stain on his record he wanted to erase. An 1837 graduate of West Point, Scammon transferred to the elite topographical engineers a year later. His career with them came to an abrupt, unhappy end 19 years later while engaged in building military roads near Santa Fe, New Mexico Territory. Scammon kept poor records, and when he was unable to account for $350 in public money he was dismissed from the service for "conduct to the prejudice of good order and military discipline." This humiliation probably provided additional motivation to insist that his brigade accompany Pleasonton. Cox consented to Scammon's demand. "Crook [who Pleasonton was visiting at the time] took the decision in good stride," recalled Cox, but "Pleasonton was a little chafed, and even intimated that he claimed some right to name the officer and command to be detailed." Cox refused. Scammon's 1st Brigade would accompany Pleasonton, and they would march at 6 a.m.[13]

September 14 dawned clear and bright in Middletown Valley. As Scammon's men assembled to march, someone heard the "chime of a distant church bell," which reminded all that it was Sunday. But war's work would not rest for the Sabbath, and promptly at 6 a.m. Scammon had his brigade under arms and filing onto the National Road. Since this was only a reconnaissance, the men left their knapsacks in camp. Word had spread through the division about the disagreement with Pleasonton over which brigade would accompany the reconnaissance. Cox recalled that it "had put Scammon and his whole brigade upon their mettle, and was a case in which a generous emulation did no harm." Scammon's Ohioans were an independent-minded, aggressive group of soldiers. The brigade had been in service since the summer of 1861, and although they had seen relatively little combat, they had spent most of the war in the rugged terrain of western Virginia, and the men were veterans. Early in the Maryland Campaign they had a run-in with corps commander Jesse Reno, when soldiers of Colonel Rutherford B. Hayes's 23rd Ohio took hay from a nearby haystack to feed some artillery and cavalry horses. Orders strictly forbid such foraging, and when Reno found out he accosted and berated the men. Hayes came to his troops' defense and "in respectful language gave him my opinion of the matter." Reno calmed down and the affair ended without incident, but in camp talk afterward the men had it that someone had seen Reno put his hand on his pistol during his encounter with Hayes, at which Hayes's men picked up their weapons to defend their colonel. Nothing of the sort had actually happened, but the men did cheer Hayes when Reno rode away (which did not sit too well with the latter), which suggested that these Ohioans were not easily impressed by reputations or a general's stars.[14]

Scammon commanded a veritable task force, consisting of three infantry regiments—the 12th, the 23rd, and the 30th Ohio—who, combined, mustered some 1,455 officers and men; two troops of West Virginia Independent Cavalry; and Captain James R. McMullin's 1st Battery Ohio Light (with six 10 lb. Parrott rifles). With commendable curiosity Cox rode with them, wanting to see how Pleasonton intended to use these men. A roar of artillery from up ahead soon shattered the tranquility of the morning. Pleasonton had unlimbered the six 3-inch rifles of Captain Horatio G. Gibson's Battery C&G, 3rd U.S., and the four 20 lb. Parrotts (on loan from Burnside) of Lieutenant Samuel N. Benjamin's Battery E, 2nd U.S., on a high open hill south of the National Road, about two-thirds of a mile west of the point where the Old Sharpsburg Road leaves the pike. Pleasonton wanted them to lob some shells into Turner's Gap to flush out any enemy who might be concealed there. A response came from Lane's battery, positioned on open ground on the summit of Hill 1280 (for ease of understanding, the various hills at South Mountain will be referred to by their elevations). With two 20 lb. and three 10 lb. Parrott rifles, the Georgians thought they had both the muscle and range to duel with the Federals. But they were outgunned two to one, and Gibson's and Benjamin's guns silenced them twice. Lane then chose to move his guns to cover, rather than continue the uneven and relatively useless exchange. Between lulls, all could hear the sound of artillery fire rolling up from the direction of Harpers Ferry.[15]

As Scammon's men splashed across Catoctin Creek, Cox was astonished to find Colonel Augustus Moor standing by the roadside on the west bank of the creek. Cox rode up and asked Moor how he had come to be wandering alone along the National Road. Moor explained he had been paroled the evening before by Stuart's cavalry (which further corroborates the fact that Stuart dismissed the threat to Turner's Gap as insignificant, or he would not have paroled Moor) and was making his return to Federal lines. Cox recalled Moor's response: "'But where are you going?' said he. I answered that Scammon was going to support Pleasonton in a reconnaissance into the gap. Moor made an involuntary start, saying, 'My God! Be careful!' then checking himself, added, 'But I am paroled!' and turned away."[16]

Moor had said enough for Cox. Trouble lay ahead. He galloped after Scammon, told him what Moor had said, and added that he himself was returning to camp to bring up the 2nd Brigade. As Cox rode back along Scammon's column he paused to speak with each regimental commander, warning them "to be prepared for anything, big or little—it might be a skirmish, it might be a battle." Moving once more at a furious pace, Cox reached his division's bivouac and ordered Crook to have his brigade fall in at once and prepare to march. While the musicians sounded assembly, Cox wrote a note to Reno reporting that he believed enemy troops were in force on the mountain and that he had committed his entire division to Pleasonton's support. After sending this message off Cox rode forward to Pleasonton, finding him near the batteries shelling Turner's Gap. Pleasonton told Cox that he and Scammon agreed that the Confederates occupied Turner's Gap in some strength and that a frontal approach was unwise. Instead they had sketched out a plan to outflank the gap. While Pleasonton demonstrated with his cavalry along the National Road, Scammon would advance up the Old Sharpsburg Road to Fox's Gap and flank the defenders of Turner's Gap. Cox approved the plan, but he it made it clear that if Scammon became engaged, Cox, not Pleasonton, would direct the fight.[17]

Though more a range of large hills than a series of mountains, South Mountain nevertheless posed a significant obstacle to a nineteenth-century army. The mountain crests, described by Jacob Cox as "scattered and irregular hills

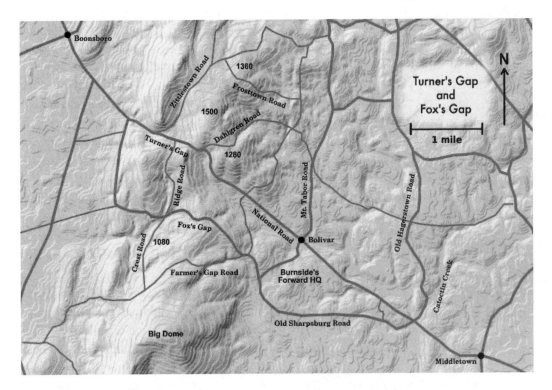

upon the high rounded surface of the mountain top," climbed to elevations ranging from 1000 feet to 1700-foot Lamb's Knoll, which stands about a mile and half south of Fox's Gap. A hardwood forest covered much of the mountain, and in some areas the woods were accompanied by a thick undergrowth of mountain laurel. Decades before, some hardy souls had hewn out farms, and there were meadows and fields in cultivation scattered about. The early farmers had discovered that this land had an abundance of granite boulders, and as they cleared the ground these were collected and used to build sturdy walls to mark fields and property boundaries.[18]

The best of the primary roads that crossed the mountain was the National Road, being "of easier grade and better engineering." The other roads on the mountain were narrow, rough, steep at certain points, and better suited for local farm traffic than that of an army. Besides the principal roads, there were other farm and logging paths that bisected the main roads and, in some instances, provided access over the mountain. For a soldier attacking or defending the area, there were several of particular importance in the vicinity of Fox's Gap. The first, known as Farmer's Gap Road—little more than a "mountain path," according to one soldier—joined the Old Sharpsburg Road where it began its ascent to Fox's Gap. This byway took a circuitous route up the mountain, first climbing in a generally west-southwest direction nearly to the summit of Hill 1100. Here it met another farm trail running south from Fox's Gap, which I shall refer to as the Crest Road. This road roughly followed the summit of Hill 1080 and ran northeast and north to Fox's Gap, three-quarters of mile distant, where it intersected the Old Sharpsburg Road. Another road, called the Ridge Road, met the Old Sharpsburg Road a few yards west of this intersection. It ran north along the mountain summit, and then along its eastern slope for a mile, until it joined the National Road at the Mountain House. Besides these farm lanes, near the point where Farmer's Gap Road and Crest Road intersected, there were two wagon paths or trails, one heading to Lamb's Knoll, the other running southwest down the west side of the mountain to the Boonsboro Valley.[19]

Three farm roads of importance were north of the National Road. The first, later called Dahlgren Road, originated near the Mountain House, but on the north side of the pike, then climbed steadily in its easterly course to the summit of Hill 1280. Here it turned north and dropped into the saddle between Hill 1280 and Hill 1500. When it reached the gorge between Hills 1280 and 1360 to the north, it turned east again and followed the direction of the gorge to the Mount Tabor Road, where a nearby collection of farm buildings had been named Frosttown. Just over a quarter mile north of the intersection of the Mount Tabor and Dahlgren roads was the Frosttown Road. It ran west along the northern side of the gorge, paralleling the Dahlgren Road along the gorge, then turned northwest and ascended the steep slopes of Hill 1360. West of the summit of that hill it met the Zittlestown Road, which connected with the National Road about a half mile west of the Mountain House. For the attacker this labyrinth of roads partially compensated for the advantage the terrain provided for the defender by offering numerous avenues of approach and multiple flanking possibilities. The defender, in turn, was obliged to spread his forces over a front extending nearly 3 miles to cover all approaches.

Following Pleasonton's suggestion, Scammon turned his brigade off the National Road across from J. Ripp's farm at 7 a.m. and followed a farm lane to the Old Sharpsburg Road. From the point where they met the Old Sharpsburg Road it was nearly 2 miles to the summit of Fox's Gap. Scammon advanced slowly. The enemy's position and strength were largely unknown, and the road's condition and steady ascent caused Scammon to order frequent halts to rest his men and keep his regiments closed up. The desultory and diversionary shelling of Turner's Gap continued during their march. Cox augmented Pleasonton's firepower with McMullin's battery and the two 20lb. Parrott rifles of Captain Seth J. Simmonds's Kentucky Light Artillery, so that 18 rifles were now concentrated together at this one point. While they waited for Scammon's reconnaissance to develop something, a courier from 9th Corps headquarters rode up to Cox with a note from Reno expressing approval of his decisions and advising Cox that Reno would support the Kanawha division with the entire corps.[20]

About a quarter mile west of Mentzer's sawmill, the gunners of a Confederate battery at Fox's Gap spotted Scammon's column and sent a shell to greet them.

It screeched over the Ohioans and struck beyond them. Scammon ordered Captain Gilmore's cavalry troop to deploy as skirmishers and advance. They jumped some Confederate skirmishers—probably of Rosser's 5th Virginia Cavalry—in the fields of the Gross farm, but the Rebels quickly melted back into a "rocky tangled woods beyond." Scammon concluded that it would be unwise to follow the direct approach to Fox's Gap along the Old Sharpsburg Road. A local farmer named John Miller, who lived north of Adam Koogle on the Old Hagerstown Road, had agreed to accompany Scammon that morning as a guide. Miller advised Scammon of Farmer's Gap Road and the opportunity it offered to flank any defenders positioned at Fox's Gap. Scammon summoned the Harvard-educated colonel of the 23rd Ohio, Rutherford B. Hayes, and ordered him to take his regiment up this road, gain the enemy flank, and attack it. Scammon estimated the Rebels had two guns with some support defending the gap. Hayes had the largest regiment in the brigade, numbering 765 officers and men, but the lack of any real idea of enemy strength and position worried him. "If I find six guns and strong support?" asked Hayes. "Take them anyhow," Scammon replied.[21]

Accompanied by John Miller, Hayes's regiment filed onto Farmer's Gap Road and slowly ascended the mountain through a pine woods. Hayes deployed Company A as skirmishers to screen his front, and Scammon sent along a small detachment of Gilmore's cavalry to provide more mobile scouts. To support Hayes's turning movement, Scammon sent Colonel Carr B. White's 12th Ohio along Farmer's Gap Road after the 23rd. While the 23rd and the 12th moved against the enemy flank, Scammon gave orders to Colonel Hugh Ewing to advance his 30th Ohio directly up the mountain toward Fox's Gap and "drive the enemy from the summit and hold it until reinforced." Scammon had composed a simple but effective plan: while Hayes and White turned the Rebel flank, Ewing would fix them in front. It was now nearly 9 a.m.[22]

D. H. Hill arose early on the 14th and reached the summit of Turner's Gap between "daylight and sunrise." A note from Stuart greeted him, explaining that the cavalryman had left for Crampton's Pass, but Stuart failed to mention that he had deposited Rosser and the 5th Virginia Cavalry and Pelham's battery at Fox's Gap before departing. Years later Hill excused Stuart as "too gallant a soldier to leave his post when a battle was imminent, and doubtless believed that there was but a small Federal force on the National Road." Stuart did believe this, but it did not absolve him of responsibility for leaving Hill without cavalry to screen or picket his front. Given his well-known disdain for cavalry, it is unlikely that Hill had such gentle words or thoughts for Stuart that morning. Hill at least found Garland's brigade and Bondurant's battery at the summit, resting along the road by the Mountain House. So far as Hill knew, his two brigades (Garland's and Colquitt's) and Lane's and Bondurant's batteries, about 2,500 infantry and 10 guns all told, were the only Confederate forces on the Mountain.[23]

A hasty examination of the ground at Turner's Gap, and probably a discussion with Colquitt, convinced Hill that two brigades were inadequate to defend the two gaps. He sent orders calling up G. B. Anderson's North Carolina brigade of 1,200 men. Hill left Ripley (minus the regiment sent to Orr's Gap) and Rodes in the valley, reluctant to withdraw them from watching the approaches from Harpers Ferry "until something more definite was known of the strength and design of the Yankees."[24]

After sending for Anderson, Hill rode forward with Colquitt to have a closer look at the approaches to Turner's Gap and inspect the Georgian's disposition of his brigade. Colquitt had picked his ground carefully. He posted seven companies of the 28th Georgia and the entire 23rd Georgia several hundred yards down the mountain from the Mountain House, on the north side of the National Road. The 28th secured its left against the steep slope of Hill 1280, "around which it was very difficult for any troops to pass." The 23rd extended the line to the National Road. A stone wall provided cover along nearly the entire frontage of both regiments. Nature had further enhanced this ready-made breastwork with a trench along the west side of the wall, created by the downhill movement of rainwater. Colonel Emory F. Best of the 23rd Georgia also observed that "a slight rise in the ground to a distance of about forty yards in front of the stone fence kept the fence from sight of the enemy." Three companies deployed as skirmishers across the front of the two regiments, one company north of and two south of the National Road. South of the pike the ground drops off sharply into a deep ravine cut by a mountain stream, so Colquitt posted his remaining regiments about 200–300 yards to the rear and southwest of the 23rd and the 28th, in the woods on the mountain slope south of the ravine. The brigade's well-trained skirmish battalion, formed from detaching one company from each regiment in the brigade, was under the command of a fine officer, Captain W. M. Arnold of the 6th Georgia. It was deployed to cover the ravine and prevent the enemy from turning the position of the 23rd and the 28th. Hill approved of Colquitt's deployment and merely advised him to extend his right to connect with Garland's brigade, which Hill planned to send to defend Fox's Gap.[25]

With no cavalry to scout his front, Colquitt could provide little information about the enemy and, according to Hill, Colquitt thought that they had withdrawn during the night. Hill was not so sure. Accompanied by his assistant adjutant general, Major J. W. Ratchford, Hill left Colquitt and rode off to have a look at the ground at Fox's Gap.[26] Hill and Ratchford almost certainly followed Ridge Road. They rode for what Hill thought was about three-quarters of a mile when they heard voices of command and the rumbling of wheels coming from the direction of the Old Sharpsburg Road at Fox's Gap. Unaware of Rosser's presence at the gap, Hill thought it was the enemy moving to turn his right. Without investigating further, the two men headed back toward Turner's Gap.

On their return they passed a cabin whose residents were standing outside, their curiosity and fear aroused by the artillery exchange between Lane's battery and Pleasonton's horse artillery. Hill paused to question the father of this mountain clan about the roads in the area. In the middle of their conversation a shell came crashing through the woods, frightening one of the Marylander's children, who began to cry. "Having a little one at home of about the same age," Hill recalled, "I could not forbear stopping a moment to say a few soothing words to the frightened child, before hurrying off to the work of death."[27]

Few men in the Army of Northern Virginia thought of Daniel Harvey Hill as the sensitive type. Most knew him as a small man with a steely glare and an acerbic personality. His men had no love for him, and even Lee harbored concerns about his administrative abilities. But no one questioned his prowess as a fighter. From his role as a junior officer in the war with Mexico to his position as a division commander in the Army of Northern Virginia, Hill was positively fearless in battle. And he stoked his battle ardor with a fierce hatred of Yankees. In referring to the enemy, he once told one of his men that "a field covered with dead is a far more gratifying sight than wounded and prisoners." If it came to a fight, Hill could always be counted on to gladly pitch in. But command and management of a battle requires more than personal courage, and Hill was about to be tested.[28]

At the Mountain House he found Samuel Garland, who was alerted by the artillery fire, with his brigade under arms and ready to march. Known as Sam to his close companions, Garland was a 31-year-old Virginia Military Institute graduate and a great-grandnephew of James Madison. Garland lost his wife to illness in the winter of 1861–1862 and the tragedy hit him hard, but he met and fell in love with a young woman of Richmond later in 1862. They were to be married, but she broke off the engagement before Garland marched north with Hill's division. While it is not known how this affected Garland, a friend of the young woman's was happy to hear the news. She thought Garland a poor match. "I have no confidence in him and few persons have," she wrote. Apparently the North Carolina soldiers of Garland's brigade thought differently. According to his cousin and commissary officer, Major Alexander B. Garland, "no General was ever more universally loved by his command . . . for no General in this or any other army, studied the interest and comfort of his officers and men more than he, and they all knew it, appreciated it and acknowledged it." Hill also had confidence in the young Virginian, for he now gave him a difficult mission.[29]

Hill's orders to Garland were to march south along Ridge Road to Fox's Gap and to hold the gap and the Old Sharpsburg Road "at all hazards." To underscore the importance of the assignment, Hill pointed out that the very safety of the army depended on holding the Federals in check. If they were able to force their way to the western side of the mountain before Lee and Longstreet came up, it might be disastrous for the Confederate army. Garland had no questions and started off immediately, "in high spirits," with his brigade and Bondurant's battery.[30]

Garland's brigade consisted of five thin North Carolina regiments, numbering approximately 1,100 officer and men. Bondurant added two 3-inch rifles and two 12 lb. howitzers for artillery support. Had Hill known the ground, the road, and trail system more fully, he would have realized how inadequate this force was for the mission he had assigned to them. The brigade had drawn new uniforms and replaced lost or damaged equipment during the respite after the Peninsula Campaign, but the heavy manpower losses all of the regiments incurred in the campaign's battles had only been partially replaced by conscripts, who represented nearly one-quarter of the brigade's strength. Most of them went to the 5th North Carolina, but they arrived shortly before the division's march north from Richmond, so they received no training. A sergeant in the 5th observed that they were so ignorant of their duties that in his regiment they could not "load a gun." But Garland was a skillful soldier, and he was sustained by generally solid regimental leadership, except in the 12th North Carolina, which was led by a young captain.[31]

Given the condition of the Ridge Road and the possibility that he might meet resistance, it is likely that it took Garland's column at least an hour to march the mile to Fox's Gap. They probably reached the gap around 7:30 a.m. As they emerged from the woods north of the gap, they discovered Rosser with his 5th Virginia Cavalry and the section of Pelham's horse battery. Rosser had not been on the mountain long and probably could tell Garland very little, other than to explain what he knew about the road network at the gap. Garland found it necessary to spread his regiments across a broad frontage to cover the different approaches. He placed the 13th and 20th North Carolina along the Ridge Road to guard the direct route along the Old Sharpsburg Road, with their right flank touching the Old Sharpsburg Road and main body fronting farmer Daniel Wise's north pasture. The left of these two regiments did not extend far enough to connect with Colquitt's right, and a 400-yard gap existed between the two brigades.[32]

Garland led the rest of his brigade south of the intersection of the Ridge, Old Sharpsburg, and Crest roads, past the farm of Daniel Wise, whose house and garden were located at the southwest corner of the intersection of the Old Sharpsburg and Crest roads. East of Wise's farmhouse, across the Crest Road, Wise maintained a four-acre pasture known afterwards as Wise's field. A rectangular woods roughly the size of Wise's field hugged its southern border, and a pie-shaped woods of slightly larger size grew along the field's eastern border. South and east of these woods were open fields, either in pasture, wheat stubble, or corn, and nearly all were separated by stone walls. Garland deployed his remaining three regiments and Bondurant's battery south of the rectangular wood, along the summit of Hill 1080. The summit was a relatively level plateau

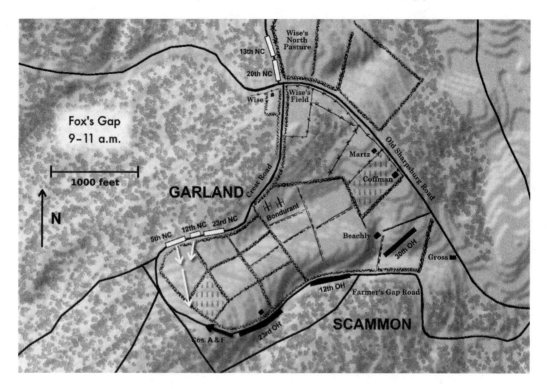

that extended approximately 40 yards east from the Crest Road before the ground dropped off and declined sharply toward the woods enclosing Farmer's Gap Road. A thick forest bordered the western side of the Crest Road.

Garland anchored his right with his largest regiment, Colonel Duncan K. McRae's 5th North Carolina, numbering over 400 effectives. They formed line along the Crest Road, near but a little north of its intersection with Farmer's Gap Road. A large cornfield stood in front of McRae's position, and to his right rose the forested slopes of Hill 1300. Rosser placed his cavalry and Pelham's guns somewhere on McRae's right, possibly where they could cover the trail leading to the west side of the mountain. Captain Shugan Snow's 12th North Carolina, counting a mere 92 muskets, formed in the Crest Road on McRae's left, and to Snow's left Colonel Daniel H. Christie deployed his 23rd North Carolina. All of the regiments enjoyed the cover of a stone wall that ran along the eastern side of the road. The space between the left of the 23rd North Carolina and the woods around Wise's field was partially filled with Bondurant's battery, which Garland ordered to be unlimbered in an open field enclosed by stone walls. After taking their position, the three infantry regiments stacked arms, broke ranks, and were allowed to rest. From right to left, the brigade's frontage covered approximately 1,300 yards. According to the tactics of the day, it should have been no more than 350 yards. There were intervals between every regiment, but the largest gap—between the left of the 23rd and the right of the

A postwar view of the intersection of the Sharpsburg Road with the Crest Road and Ridge Road at Fox's Gap. Garland's brigade arrived at the gap on the Ridge Road (*foreground*). Wise's cabin is behind the picket fence. His south pasture, across which Drayton's brigade and the 9th Corps engaged one another, is behind the post-and-rail fence. Courtesy of the Massachusetts-MOLLUS collection, USAHEC.

20th—extended a full 250 yards, although Bondurant's guns partially filled this. Garland was dangerously extended, but until the enemy displayed their force he could not concentrate his strength.[33]

After completing his deployment, Garland rode forward with McRae to reconnoiter the open ground east of the Crest Road. They were on the alert, for Bondurant had spotted an enemy column marching up the Old Sharpsburg Road and fired several shells at it. But the Federals slipped into the cover of the woods on the lower slopes of Hill 1300 and disappeared. Quiet followed, until some of Bondurant's Alabamians spotted "a few men slowly and stealthily approaching us near the north east corner of the clearing." According to John Purifoy, who served in the battery, "it did not take long to determine that they were not friends." They were skirmishers of the 30th Ohio. Bondurant sent one of his men back to the infantry to find Garland, but the general and Colonel McRae were still conducting their reconnaissance, which discovered enemy soldiers moving along Farmer's Gap Road. They were probably Company A of the 23rd Ohio. Garland thought the enemy might be attempting to use the woods to move a force across his front, in order to seize a commanding position on his flank on Hill 1300. He ordered McRae to investigate by advancing skirmishers into the woods to his regiment's right front.[34]

It was nearly 9 a.m. when McRae's skirmish line, composed of approximately 50 men, moved out, They advanced cautiously, with muskets at the ready, through the cornfield in their front and into the edge of the woods. They had gone no more than 50 steps when firing broke out. Just inside the edge of the woods they encountered Company A of the 23rd Ohio, and both sides opened fire. Garland ordered McRae to advance his entire regiment to support the skirmishers. Leaving the shelter of the Crest Road, the regiment moved downhill through the corn and entered the woods, which McRae found were so thick that "it was impossible to advance in line of battle." The woods gave way to a partial clearing, and the North Carolinians pushed across it into more woods on the opposite side. Here they observed a large force of Union infantry approaching. It was the main body of the 23rd Ohio. The North Carolinians opened fire again; several Ohioans fell and one was seized as a prisoner. But the battle quickly swung against the Confederates.[35]

Hayes had seen some element of Garland's brigade before he bumped into McRae's skirmish line, and he threw out Companies F and I as flankers to his left and right, respectively. Combined with Company A, it placed nearly 200 men in skirmish formation covering the front and flanks of the 23rd. It was elements of this skirmish line that McRae's skirmishers tangled with first. The suddenness of the engagement took Hayes by surprise. When he observed the full strength of the 5th North Carolina moving down the slope of Hill 1080 toward him, his regiment was marching by the right flank, with the right of the regiment in front, so that if Hayes simply had his regiment face right and form line, the rear rank would be in front, and the regiment inverted from its normal alignment, with the right company on the far left, the extreme left company on the far right, and so on. But there was no chance to execute the time-consuming maneuver to correct this. Hayes instead ordered his men into line to the right and hoped that his company officers and sergeants would sort things out. The underbrush and ubiquitous mountain laurel made forming any semblance of a line a challenge, even under the best of circumstances, but the regiment managed to get into some sort of order and Hayes sent them forward to meet the approaching enemy. As they pushed through the forest and reached the edge of the clearing, McRae's North Carolinians greeted them with a volley that killed and wounded several men. "I feared confusion," wrote Hayes, and he "exhorted, swore, and threatened" so as to maintain order. His men stood steady, raised their muskets, and returned the fire. The battle of South Mountain was on.[36]

Greasy gray-white smoke quickly wreathed both battle lines as they blazed away at one another. The advantage was initially with McRae, whose regiment was better formed to deliver its fire, but in some places the Ohioans did damage. Robert E. Cornwall of Company A wrote that he and his comrades "killed 8 that I see before the Regt got up to us." Yet Hayes feared his men would not stand the fire for long. "Bullets pattered about us like raindrops on the leaves," one man recalled. Then Hayes's voice was heard above the din of firing, shouting, "Men of the Twenty-third, when I tell you to charge, you must charge . . . Charge Bayonets." Raising a yell, the 23rd surged forward from the woods. The North Carolinians delivered "a cloud of bullets" into the advancing Union line but did not damage it enough to stop the blue surge. Numbers were on Hayes's side, and the conscripts in McRae's regiment became unnerved by the sight of hundreds of yelling Union soldiers with fixed bayonets charging toward them; many of them broke for the rear. The balance of the North Carolina regiment fell back to the first belt of woods and kept up the fight from this cover, while McRae raced after the broken elements of his regiment and, by "strenuous exertion of officers and veterans," managed to rally them.[37]

Hayes briefly halted his regiment to untangle his line before he ordered it forward again. McRae's veterans fought stubbornly from the cover of the belt of woods. The Federals stopped to return the fire, but the Confederates held the advantage of position and, wrote Hayes, "I soon began to fear we could not stand it." He ordered another charge. Numbers and the power of shock again carried the day. The North Carolinians were driven from the woods, through the cornfield, and up the slopes of Hill 1080. But as Hayes's men came boiling up out of the woods into the corn, they came under an accurate fire from another regiment of Confederate infantry, positioned behind a hedgerow and stone wall on the plateau of Hill 1080. This drove the Federals to seek cover behind the stone wall dividing the cornfield from the timber, but not before many men were hit. The 23rd's major, James M. Comly, recalled that "most of our loss occurred at this point."[38] Since a charge had worked with the first enemy troops he had encountered, Hayes decided to try it against this new threat. But a bullet shattered his left arm as he started to shout out the command. The shock hit him hard and forced him to lie down. He recalled afterwards:

> I laid down and was pretty comfortable. I was perhaps twenty feet behind the line of my men, and could form a pretty accurate notion of the way the fight was going. The enemy's fire was occasionally very heavy; balls passed near my face and hit the ground all around me. I could see wounded men staggering or carried to the rear; but I felt sure our men were holding their own. I listened anxiously to hear the approach of reinforcements; wondered they did not come.[39]

In addition to the fire from the front, the 23rd began to receive fire on their left flank. This may have been from dismounted troopers of Rosser's 5th Virginia seeking to help relieve the pressure on Garland's right, or it could have been from elements of the 5th North Carolina. Someone on the left of the 23rd shouted a warning about this threat, which Hayes heard. He stood up and called to Captain James L. Drake, commanding Company H, the left company, to wheel back and protect the regiment's flank. Standing made Hayes feeling woozy, so he lay down again. Nearby lay a young soldier of the 5th North Carolina, and while the battle crackled about them the two men had "a considerable talk" that Hayes recalled was "right jolly and friendly."[40]

Captain Drake pulled his company back perhaps 20 yards to face the threat to the flank, but in the din and confusion of battle the remainder of the regiment thought they were to follow suit, and all of them fell back on a line with Drake's company. The short withdrawal left Hayes lying between the lines. Major James M. Comly thought something might be amiss, and he asked Hayes if he had wanted the whole regiment to fall back. "No," replied Hayes, but he added that "if the line was now in good position to let it remain and to face the left companies as I intended."[41]

Steady firing continued for perhaps 15 to 20 minutes; then, by seemingly mutual consent, it died out and a tense quiet settled over the field. From his prone position Hayes could not see his regiment, and he feared they might have abandoned him. He called out, "Hallo, Twenty-third men, are you going to leave your colonel here for the enemy?" Six of his men immediately responded and dashed forward to rescue him. The Confederates opened fire and drove them all to cover. This acted as a signal to renew the fight, and both sides began blazing away at one another again. Lieutenant Benjamin W. Jackson of Company I then sprinted forward through the enemy fire, reached Hayes, and managed to drag or carry him back to the cover of the woods. Here a dressing was applied to his wound, and he revived enough to walk a mile under his own power to the home of Widow Koogle, where he found transportation to Middletown.[42]

The Confederates who had checked Hayes after he drove the 5th North Carolina from the woods were Colonel Daniel H. Christie's 23rd North Carolina. When the 5th became engaged, Garland ordered the 23rd and the 12th North Carolina forward as supports. The 23rd advanced about 40 yards from the Crest Road into an open field. There they took position behind a hedgerow and an old stone fence, described by one member of the regiment as "more or less dismantled by time" and "in places very low," that faced and commanded the cornfield. From this cover they were able to halt the advance of the 23rd Ohio. The 12th North Carolina, burdened with their young and inexperienced commander, Captain Shugan Snow, did not perform as well. They moved up in support of the 5th North Carolina while the latter was engaged, possibly about the time that McRae's right flank crumbled under Hayes's first charge. From their support position they loosed one wild volley. Then Snow became unglued and shouted, "Fire and fall back"; nearly half the regiment fled the field with the captain. Some 30–40 men who did not follow Snow's lead out of the fight eventually fell in with the 13th North Carolina and fought with them for the remainder of the day.[43]

After ordering McRae to probe his right front with skirmishers, Garland rode over to check on his left flank. He found things tranquil there, but the swift escalation of firing on McRae's front signaled trouble, and Garland started back for his right at a gallop. Along the way he reined up for a moment at Bondurant's battery, which was taking fire from skirmishers of the 30th Ohio. He ordered the Alabamians to limber and fall back to near Wise's cabin, then hurried off to his embattled right flank. When he arrived he ordered the 23rd and the 12th North Carolina to advance to the 5th's support. Then, when McRae's 5th North Carolina and Snow's 12th came falling back in disorder, he helped to rally McRae's men. McRae informed him of what was now obvious: it appeared that the enemy had massed a large force in the woods on the slopes of Hill 1300. McRae suggested that Bondurant shell the woods to flush them out. Garland replied that he had withdrawn Bondurant, but he agreed that the enemy's main effort appeared to be focused south of Fox's Gap, and that this front needed to be strengthened. To accomplish this he sent orders for the 13th and the 20th regiments to move south of the Old Sharpsburg Road. Garland left soon after to meet the regiments and personally position them.[44]

The 20th North Carolina led the way, followed by the 13th. Garland met them in the vicinity of the intersection of Ridge Road and the Old Sharpsburg Road. By this time skirmishers of Ewing's 30th Ohio were threatening the sector vacated by Bondurant and the woods east of Wise's south field. To parry this threat and bolster his center and right, Garland led both regiments past Wise's field and the woods south of the field. He halted the 20th North Carolina, under Colonel Alfred Iverson—a man who would later lead this same brigade to disaster at Gettysburg—along the Crest Road south of the woodlot around Wise's pasture. They faced open fields but had a limited field of fire, because the military crest was some 60 yards east of their position. But it is likely that Garland placed them here temporarily, because they were unobserved by the enemy and could serve as a reserve. Garland left the 20th in the road and went to place the 13th North Carolina. Lieutenant Colonel Thomas Ruffin Jr., an attorney and judge from Wentworth, North Carolina, commanded the 13th. Garland ordered him "to take position in an open field upon the brow of a high hill." This was to the left, and presumably to the front of Iverson, either in the same field previously occupied by Bondurant or the field north of it. Meanwhile Bondurant unlimbered his guns in the area of farmer Wise's garden, where his guns could sweep Wise's south field and some of the north field.[45]

Ruffin's regiment came under fire from Federal infantry in the woods on the slope of Hill 1300, as well as from a regiment positioned behind a rail fence "upon our left." The Federals in the woods were the 12th Ohio, while those behind the rail fence were Ewing's 30th Ohio. Ruffin's men could not see the enemy in the woods, so they directed their fire to their left front, against the 30th Ohio. "Our men were cool and fired with precision and effect," wrote Ruffin, who reported that they drove the Federals from the field. But Ewing claimed his regiment held its ground. Garland's cousin and commissary officer, Major A. B. Garland, offered evidence that this was the case, and that the fire of Ewing's regiment shook the 13th. In an October 4 letter, Major Garland wrote that Ruffin's regiment "faltered" under the enemy fire. General Garland rode forward to help steady the men. Ruffin thought that Garland exposed himself unnecessarily and "appealed to him to retire." Garland agreed, but paused to give the men "some rallying words." As he turned his horse and started back toward the Ridge Road a Union bullet struck him square in the center of the back, "and passing through the body came out two inches above the right breast, the ball lodging in the breast of his coat." Ruffin was hit in the hip at about the same time and did not see that Garland was wounded. He heard a groan and spotted his general writhing on the ground in great pain. Garland called Ruffin over and gave him his last command: "Col. I am a dead man, send for Col. McRae to take command." Four of Ruffin's men gathered Garland up in a blanket and carried his dying body from the field.[46]

The apparent ineffectiveness of his regiment's musketry caused Ruffin—who remained with his troops despite his wound—to pull his men back some 50 yards from the brow of the hill. Bondurant had his guns unlimbered near Wise's cabin by now, and they discouraged Ewing's Ohioans from following up Ruffin's withdrawal by spewing "a hail of grape" in the Yankees' direction.[47]

Meanwhile, Iverson waited for orders. Captain D. P. Halsey, Garland's assistant adjutant general, rode up and informed Iverson that Garland was dead and that McRae was in command. Iverson sent to McRae for orders and was told to "connect with the troops on my left." Afterward Iverson stated that "I knew of none to connect with as I had just passed over the ground but thinking it possible some had been thrown in between me and the turnpike," he moved off in the direction from which he had come. He marched some 200–300 yards back along the Crest Road but found no troops, although he must have gone past the 13th North Carolina. He either missed them, which seems unlikely, or forgot about them when recalling the battle later on. In any event, he turned his regiment around and "returned to the right to connect with the only troops I knew of being the 5th and 23rd N.C." McRae, who was overwhelmed by his sudden ascension to brigade command, gave Iverson no orders, and Iverson seemed at a loss as to where it was best to post his men. He apparently kept his regiment beside the Crest Road, to the 23rd North Carolina's left and rear. He described his position as "a level plateau about 100 yards wide in thick chestnut undergrowth, open fields in front sloping down steep hills, the bottom of which we could not see; in our rear a precipitous rocky, wooded descent." Iverson knew this "was a bad position for we had no range and could not kill a man until he was within sixty yards," but without instructions or a good sense of the general situation he concluded that it was the best he could manage.[48]

While Garland had been repositioning his regiments, Colonel Scammon fed the 12th Ohio into the battle. With the 23rd Ohio engaged with the Confederate right and the 30th probing their left, Scammon determined to test the

Confederate center. The 12th had arrived at the edge of the woods, on the right of the 23rd, facing the open fields climbing up to the plateau of Hill 1080. Scammon ordered the 12th's colonel, Carr B. White, to advance across this open ground and drive off what appeared to be a Confederate regiment—probably the 13th North Carolina—who were posted on the brow of the plateau some 300 yards away. White first had his regiment open fire on the enemy—this was the fire from the woods that Lieutenant Colonel Ruffin described—and then ordered his entire regiment to deploy in skirmish order. When all was set, the 12th burst out of the woods and dashed forward. The 23rd North Carolina shifted some of their fire to this new threat, which moved past their exposed left flank, but they were unable to check the 12th's advance. Ruffin had decided that the position of his 13th North Carolina was too exposed, and he withdrew as White advanced, leaving behind 15–20 dead and wounded. White's men reached the plateau of Hill 1080 and immediately came under fire, probably from the 13th North Carolina and perhaps from the 20th North Carolina as well. Some of the fire came from Confederate sharpshooters posted in trees in the woods behind Ridge Road. White ordered his men back under the plateau, where they were in defilade from the enemy fire. But their position protruded beyond their flank supports. The 23rd Ohio, on the left, remained in the woods on the northern slope of Hill 1300, and the 30th Ohio did not make a connection with the 12th's right. Until his flank supports made contact, Colonel White and his men were content to hug South Mountain's soil and wait.[49]

Well before White's 12th regiment advanced to the brow of the Hill 1080 plateau, Colonel Hugh Ewing's 30th Ohio, with its front covered by a "cloud of skirmishers," had advanced steadily up the open slopes of Hill 1080, south of the Old Sharpsburg Road, driving in a light force of Confederate skirmishers. Ewing's target was Bondurant, and as he neared the Hill 1080 plateau he had to change front to the south to attack the battery's flank. But before Ewing could reorient his front, Garland ordered Bondurant to limber his guns and withdraw, and Ewing watched his prey dash away. Minutes later Ewing observed a "large force" approaching what was then his right and rear. It was the 13th and the 20th North Carolina. Ewing quickly changed front to rear to face this new threat and became engaged in a sharp firefight with the 13th North Carolina. At some point, either before or after his engagement with the 13th, Ewing's regiment came under friendly fire from a battery in the valley that mistook them for the enemy. By the time Ewing managed to have the fire from the rear stopped, Bondurant's guns were repositioned near the Wise farm and opened with canister and shrapnel at Ewing's regiment, forcing the men to seek cover. Then he observed more Confederate infantry approaching from the direction of Turner's Gap. Ewing decided to suspend his advance and hold on to the ground he had gained near the Hill 1080 plateau "until preparations were made for a general charge."[50]

Eliakim Scammon did not yet sense that he had knocked his opponent off balance. At most points the Rebels had pulled back to better cover and positions that were difficult to assail without risking severe losses. Scammon thought some close artillery support might give him an edge, and he requested a section of guns from Cox, who ordered forward a section from McMullin's battery. According to the historian of the 12th Ohio, McMullin "at first demurred, complaining that Old Granny [Scammon's nickname] did not know what he was about." But when someone assured him that the 12th Ohio would support his guns, McMullin ordered them forward, allegedly remarking that he would "trust his 'soul' in the keeping of that regiment." First Lieutenant George L. Crome's section drew the assignment, and they went forward as far as limbers and horses could maneuver; then it became necessary for the gunners and 12th Ohio infantrymen to haul them forward by hand. Crome had two 10 lb. Parrotts, and the men pushed and pulled them uphill until they were positioned in front of the 12th Ohio, with their tubes peeking over the crest of Hill 1080. The 20th North Carolina, protected by a stone wall and thick woods, was only some 40–60 yards distant from the guns. Crome's gunners thumped double charges of canister down the gun tubes and sent the deadly charges crashing into the thicket in front, while their infantry supports rendered what help they could with small arms fire. Crome and his men served their pieces valiantly, but they were greatly exposed and Alfred Iverson moved quickly to silence the Federal guns. He ordered Captain James B. Atwell to deploy his company as skirmishers and use the cover of a stone wall that ran from the regiment's left down the mountain to gain a firing position and "kill the gunners." Atwell moved swiftly, and in minutes, Iverson recalled, "the sharp crack of his rifles told the work was being done."

Lieutenant R. B. Wilson in the 12th Ohio watched as "the men about our guns were picked off rapidly." Volunteers were called for from the ranks of the 12th, and Crome even stepped in to crew a piece. The gunners and their infantry volunteers managed to discharge only four rounds of double canister into their front before one of Atwell's riflemen dropped Crome. Lieutenant Wilson recalled that Crome had just loaded the piece he was serving himself, "and had leveled it, and was giving the command to fire to a corporal of Co C of our regiment who held the lanyard when he fell dead behind his piece as the last shot was fired." Crome was not dead yet, but he was dying. The bullet hit him near the heart and he died two hours later. His mortal wounding sapped the morale of the surviving artillerymen and infantry volunteers; they ducked for cover, leaving the guns silent. Thirty-seven years later, Lieutenant Wilson still could not shake the image of young Crome's fall: "It was a tragic scene that I shall never forget."[51]

While Crome and his men made their gallant but futile fight, Cox reinforced Scammon's foothold on the plateau of Hill 1080. The 23rd Ohio discovered an approach where they were able to crawl forward and take position on the left of the 12th Ohio. They were within 30 yards of the 23rd North Carolina, "but we were concealed by the hill," wrote one Ohioan, and their new position threatened the North Carolinians' exposed left flank. Samuel W. Compton in the 12th Ohio recalled that they were so near the rebels he "could hear them giving orders almost as plainly as our own." Crook's 2nd Brigade had come up during the opening action and formed in the woods on Hill 1300. Cox ordered Lieutenant Colonel Augustus H. Coleman's 11th Ohio, 430 strong, to protect the left flank of the 23rd Ohio. In feeling their way into position Coleman exposed his regiment's right flank and rear to a heavy fire—most likely from the 23rd North Carolina and also perhaps the 5th North Carolina—that inflicted some losses and sent the Ohioans scrambling for the cover of the woods on Hill 1300. Here they encountered "almost impenetrable" mountain laurel that threw the regiment into greater confusion. But Coleman managed to get his men out of the enemy's line of fire and into position to protect the 23rd Ohio's left flank.[52]

While Coleman maneuvered his regiment on the left of the division, Cox sent Lieutenant Colonel Melvin Clark's 36th Ohio, a huge regiment of 800 men, forward to fill a gap between the 12th and the 30th Ohio. Lieutenant Colonel Gottfried Becker's 28th Ohio, another powerful unit that was 775 men strong, formed to the 30th's right and rear to anchor the division's right flank. When the dispositions were complete, Cox had (from left to right) the 23rd, the 12th, the 36th, and the 30th, about 2,300 men, poised near the plateau of Hill 1080 and ready to assault Garland's line. It was probably close to 11:30 a.m. While the Ohio infantrymen waited for the signal to charge, some of the men amused themselves by placing their caps on their ramrods and raising them up to be perforated by Confederate marksman. The men of the 12th Ohio were confronted with a different danger. A rattlesnake crawled into their line, creating momentary terror until one man killed it with his musket.[53]

Confederate Colonel Duncan K. McRae had assumed command of Garland's brigade with considerable anxiety, later writing that "I felt all the embarrassment the situation was calculated to inspire." The brigade had contained the first enemy push, but it was evident that the Federals were in greater strength than his single brigade could handle and would renew their attack soon. He needed reinforcements if he had any hope of stopping it. He sent Captain D. P. Halsey of the brigade staff galloping to D. H. Hill with an urgent request for help.[54] To McRae's relief, Hill responded immediately. G. B. Anderson's brigade of approximately 1,200 North Carolinians had recently arrived at Turner's Gap. Hill initially had Anderson form on the Dahlgren Road north of the gap, but when he received McRae's request for reinforcements he ordered Anderson to send his 2nd and 4th regiments, about 450 men under Colonel Charles C. Tew of the 2nd regiment, to report to McRae. "We are faced to the right," recalled Lieutenant John C. Gorman of the 2nd, "and away we go up the side of the mountain [along the Ridge Road] at a double quick." What lay ahead was indicated by the many wounded from Garland's brigade encountered along the way, "limping down the mountain, trickling blood at every step." One stretcher party bore the body of Garland from the field.[55]

Colonel Tew rode ahead of his infantry to meet McRae and learn something of the situation. Tew was a solid soldier, 44 years old, and an 1846 graduate of The Citadel, the South Carolina military academy. He taught at the academy for the next 11 years before leaving to establish a military school in Hillsborough, North Carolina. McRae's first question to Tew was the date of his commission, not the sort of thing to inspire confidence in McRae's command abilities. It turned out that Tew was the senior of the two, and McRae eagerly offered him command. But Tew had no knowledge of the situation on McRae's front, or the ground, and he prudently declined. He offered instead to place his regiments wherever McRae thought best. McRae needed help at multiple points, but his dangling left flank worried him most, so he asked for Tew's regiments to take position on the left of the 13th North Carolina. With Bondurant's guns providing support, McRae hoped this measure would render his left reasonably secure.[56]

When Tew's regiments reached Fox's Gap, he posted them as requested. They became engaged at once with skirmishers of the 30th Ohio at a range of 100–200 yards and helped deter any further advance by Ewing's Ohioans. Tew could see that the left could still easily be turned by the enemy approaching over Wise's north meadow, and he sent an officer to request reinforcements from General G. B. Anderson to help fill it. Thirty minutes later Tew received orders from Anderson to "flank to the left." The place to which Anderson wanted Tew to move his regiments is not specified, but it was probably north along the Ridge Road, where they could command Wise's north meadow and would be closer to Colquitt. Tew obeyed, although it broke his regiment's connection with Ruffin's 13th North Carolina. Ruffin reported this to McRae, who sent Captain Charles Wood of the brigade staff galloping to inform D. H. Hill of Anderson's curious notion of support, "to explain to him my situation, and to request re-enforcements." With either naïve or misplaced confidence that Hill would answer the call, McRae ordered Ruffin to shift northward to maintain contact with Tew's right flank. The 13th moved off and took position along the Crest Road in front of Wise's cabin, where there was cover from the high stone walls that flanked the road. Ruffin's shift north left a gap of 250–300 yards between his right and the 20th North Carolina's left flank—space enough for half a brigade to plunge through. McRae planned to fill the gap with the 5th North Carolina, which he thought he could move from the right flank. McRae seems not to have fathomed what that would mean for the hard-pressed right flank, but it turned out not to matter. McRae had no horse (he probably gave it to one the staff officers he sent to Hill) and was moving about on foot—an exhausting experience, given the broad frontage of his brigade. By the time he reached his right, he discovered that under a previous order either he or Garland had given, the 5th regiment had advanced from the Crest Road into the open field on the right of the 23rd North Carolina, where McRae thought "it was dangerous to withdraw it."[57]

The mounting danger was readily apparent to Colonel Christie. The Federals were in his front and had arrayed a powerful force that could envelop his exposed left flank. Unaware that Garland had been mortally wounded, Christie sent his adjutant off to find him and report the 23rd's critical situation. McRae recognized Christie's exposure, but rather than adjust the position of his regiments, McRae clung to the slender hope that Hill would forward reinforcements before the enemy discovered the gaping holes in his front. Instead, it proved to be his undoing.[58]

While McRae caught his breath and hoped for help from Hill, Cox prepared to strike. The readjustment and redeployment of his divisional line was complete. The Ohioans fixed bayonets in anticipation of orders to charge. Shortly after 11:30 a.m. a signal to advance sounded. The men of the 23rd Ohio crawled on their hands and knees to the crest of the plateau in front, and then an officer shouted, "Up and at them." The men leaped to their feet and, with a "long extended yell," rushed toward the 23rd North Carolina, whose left flank was directly in their front. At nearly the same moment the 12th Ohio rose up. Just as quickly, someone shouted for them to lie down. "Never did men lie quicker even when shot," recalled Sam Compton. Everyone knew what was coming. A volley crashed from the line of the 20th North Carolina, only 40 yards away. Those few who failed to heed the order "were either killed or wounded." But the bullets passed harmlessly over the rest, and they arose swiftly and sprinted toward Iverson's line, with bayonets glinting in the sun and yells bursting from their throats. The 36th and the 30th Ohio also went in when the 23rd and the 12th did, but it was the latter two regiments who formed the main strike force of the division.[59]

"A deadly fire was poured into our ranks," wrote a member of the 23rd Ohio, when he and his comrades rushed to close with Colonel Christie's North Carolinians. Men went down, but not enough to stop the momentum of the charge. Before the Confederates could reload, the Federals were at point-blank range. They halted and, wrote one Ohioan, "gave them [23rd NC] a far more destructive volley, and then charged up on them with our bayonets." Colonel Christie, with disaster threatening to engulf his regiment, ordered a retreat. As he had feared, the heaviest blow fell on his exposed left flank, where the men of his Company E and some others from the left flank were caught in brutal hand-to-hand combat with bayonets and clubbed muskets. A bayonet thrust by one Carolinian killed Eugene L. Reynolds, the 23rd Ohio's sergeant major, but the savage struggle quickly shifted in the Federals' favor when some men found or forced a gap in the wall defended by the Confederates. The men in blue poured into the gap,

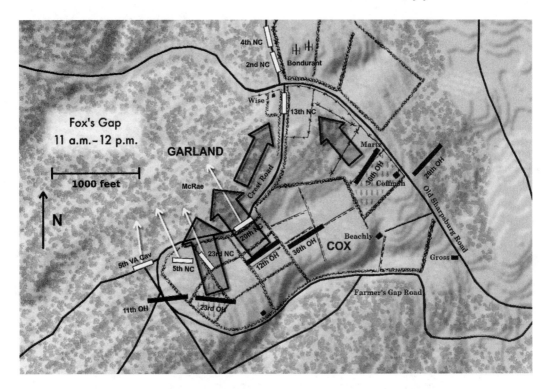

stabbing and swinging their muskets. The Confederate retreat degenerated into a rout, with the Yankees in pursuit. In the deadly running combat both the surgeon and assistant surgeon of the North Carolina regiment, not being recognized as noncombatants in the frenzy of battle, were shot and killed, and E. M. Dugand, of the nearby 5th North Carolina, watched in horror as two men of the 23rd North Carolina were run down and killed with bayonets.[60]

John Clugston, a member of the 23rd Ohio, wrote that his regiment's charge "completely routed the enemy." The left of Christie's 23rd North Carolina bore the brunt of the damage, while the right of the regiment, in company with the 5th North Carolina, streamed to the right and rear in retreat. Captain Thomas M. Garrett, now commanding the 5th North Carolina, ordered his color-bearer to halt on the Crest Road, hoping he might rally his regiment there. But a Union bullet dropped the standard bearer and the retreat stampeded on, carrying Garrett along with it. The Confederates plunged "in great disorder down the steep and bewildering mountain side" to put space between themselves and their pursuers. Losses, by Civil War standards, were not particularly high. The 5th North Carolina counted 5 killed, 10 wounded, and 33 captured, some of whom were also wounded. There were 63 casualties in the 23rd North Carolina, including 13 killed. The two regiments had exacted a terrible toll on the 23rd Ohio, which had 32 killed, 95 wounded, and 3 missing. Only two other Union regiments at South Mountain would surpass this loss.[61]

While the 23rd Ohio crushed Garland's right, the 12th Ohio smashed its center. An instant after the 20th North Carolina delivered their volley, the men of the 12th were on their feet and dashed toward the Carolinians with a "wild cry." Before the Southerners could reload, "our line was over the fence and among them with the bayonet," recalled Lieutenant R. B. Wilson. Solomon R. Smith, also in the 12th, described the action—with some exaggeration—as "a carnival of death; hell itself turned loose." The Federals discovered the gap in the Confederate line, and Iverson saw that the woods on his left flank fairly "swarmed" with Union soldiers hell-bent on his regiment's destruction. "There was nothing to do but to get away or surrender," he wrote. Most chose the former, and "fled like deer" through the woods down the western slope. Sam Compton was among their pursuers, and he wrote that "we let into their backs and did great execution." A bullet from one of Compton's comrades knocked down Jimmie Gibson of the 20th, a former student of D. H. Hill's, probably when Hill taught mathematics at Davidson College. Gibson hollered to his chum, "Texas" Dan Coleman—whose courage and great physical strength had landed him in the ambulance corps—"Great God, Dan don't leave me." Coleman stopped, and then dashed back under fire to Gibson, who now lay within 10 yards of the enemy. Coleman lifted his friend up and the two somehow managed to escape. Colonel Iverson, describing the retreat, stated that "I made terrific leaps down that mountain." Running ahead of his men, he spotted Colonel McRae. With refreshing honesty, Iverson then continued: "I must have been the fastest runner for I caught up with him and together we went to the foot of the mountain." Fred Foard, another soldier in the 20th, remembered seeing the chaplain of his regiment, "who was bounding over the tops of laurel bushes like a kangaroo." Foard heard McRae bellow at him, "Parson—Parson—God Damn it, come back here; you have been praying all your life to get to heaven and now that you have a short cut you are running away from it." Several of Iverson's men who chose to stand and fight died by the bayonet. One "bright looking young soldier" of Iverson's regiment was spared this brutal death by Lieutenant Wilson of the 12th Ohio, who seized the rifle of a man from his company "who was very greatly excited [and] was about to run his bayonet through the body of this unfortunate lad."[62]

The 20th North Carolina were broken and scattered by the Ohioans' charge. There were 7 dead, 9 wounded, and 42 missing or captured. "My regiment was scattered in every direction and it took the remainder of the day to get them together," Iverson recalled. White's 12th Ohio chased the fleeing Tarheels through the dense woods for nearly a quarter of a mile until, as an Ohio lieutenant noted, "the pursued and pursuers became scattered in the dense undergrowth." White called a halt to re-form his regiment and let his men catch their breath. They came under the fire of both canister and shell from Bondurant's battery, who attempted to render some support to their infantry comrades from their position near Wise's cabin. The fire surely caught the Ohioans' attention, but it could not save Garland's infantry from the disaster that had befallen them. The entire center and right of the Fox's Gap defense had collapsed, including Rosser's cavalry and horse artillery, who were forced to join the retreat to avoid being cut off. They withdrew to another hill west of the gap. Only the 13th North Carolina remained intact. The rest of Garland's brigade was finished as a fighting force that day.[63]

The distance between the 20th North Carolina and the 13th North Carolina was so large that Colonel Ruffin was not aware of the calamity that had overtaken the rest of the brigade. His own regiment came under attack from elements of the 30th and the 36th Ohio, whom he held at bay from his strong defensive position. But then a flank fire from the right began to bite at his line. This puzzled Ruffin, as he supposed that the rest of the brigade still extended "in one continuous line" to his right. He sent his adjutant, Lieutenant C. N. Civalier, to investigate. Civalier returned to report that "the enemy had obtained the road [Crest Road] on our right, and were coming down upon us from that direction." It was the 12th Ohio, who had turned from their pursuit of the 20th North Carolina and was moving to attack Bondurant's guns. Ruffin, thinking that his best defense was an aggressive offense, ordered a charge on the Federals in his front, which may have only been a skirmish line of the 30th Ohio, for they immediately fell back. Having cleared his front for the moment, Ruffin pulled his men back and changed front to the south to confront the advancing elements of the 12th Ohio. He ordered another charge, and again the Federals gave ground. But while engaged on his southern front, Ruffin learned that Colonel Tew had moved his regiments even farther north along the Ridge Road and that enemy soldiers, skirmishers of the 30th or the 36th Ohio, were infiltrating his rear. Ruffin ordered his regiment to about face and deal with this new threat. These Federals were easily chased away, but the 12th Ohio, who had only been temporarily checked by Ruffin's charge, came on against Ruffin's rear in greater numbers.[64]

After lying under Bondurant's artillery fire for several minutes, the 12th Ohio were ordered by Scammon to change front to the north and charge the guns, which were located about 600 yards to the 12th's right and front, near Wise's cabin. The regiment advanced through woods thick with mountain laurel, under a severe fire from the Alabama gunners. The combination of terrain and artillery fire probably played havoc with the regimental formation, which might explain their initial repulse by Ruffin's charge. But this almost certainly did not strike the full weight of the 12th, which made its way forward while Ruffin changed front to deal with the new threat to his rear. To the Confederates' surprise, Colonel White's men soon appeared at the edge of Wise's garden in the rear of both Ruffin and Bondurant. The gun crews scrambled to limber up while Ruffin's infantry fought a rearguard action. While a "severe fight" swirled about Wise's garden and cabin, Bondurant managed to extricate his guns and displaced to near G. B. Anderson's brigade in Wise's north pasture. Ruffin also managed to extricate his regiment, but not without loss. Of his 212 men, nearly one-quarter were casualties: 13 killed, 33 wounded, and 10 captured. Colonel White claimed his regiment captured a Confederate national flag and two battle flags, and that the ground "was literally covered with dead and wounded," which is surely an exaggeration. Ruffin led his command across the Old Sharpsburg Road and continued north until he met G. B. Anderson's brigade. He found D. H. Hill with Anderson. "I shall never forget the feelings of relief which I experienced when I first caught sight of you," Ruffin wrote later. "You rode up to me, and, shaking my hand, said that you had given us up for lost and did not see how it was possible for us to have escaped." Given Anderson's utter failure to render even a modicum of support to the 13th, it was indeed surprising that Ruffin had escaped, and a testament both to his handling of his regiment and their tenacity.[65]

Ruffin's withdrawal north of the Old Sharpsburg Road brought a lull to the fighting. It was nearly noon. The struggle between Garland and Cox had lasted three hours. Crumpled bodies in blue and gray lay scattered across the pastures, cornfields, and thickets, behind stone walls, along the Crest Road, and in farmer Wise's garden. Elsewhere the wounded begged for assistance, hobbled away, or were carried off the field. Sam Compton came upon a wounded North Carolinian "not over 17" who begged the Ohioan for water. "I had a scant supply," he recalled, but he handed his canteen to the injured man, who drained it. "Then the wounded rebel said wont you take a message to my mother, thus it is Mother first & Mother last. I could not deny. Tell my mother its her fault I'm here and then fell over a corpse." Soon afterward Compton came upon a dead soldier of Garland's brigade, "a husky reb" who died with both arms extended, palms up, and mouth open. Someone had placed hardtack in the Confederate's mouth and both hands. Years later Compton remembered the grim humor his comrades enjoyed at the dead soldier's expense. As they walked by the body he heard them call out such things as "Say Johnnie your [*sic*] a hog!" "You need ice not rations where you are going!" "Was that gal good looking that baked them are biskets?" "Under any circumstances men will joke," wrote Compton.[66]

Cox had effectively destroyed Garland's brigade, inflicting losses of 43 killed, 168 wounded, and 168 captured or missing—37 percent of its strength. But the North Carolinians had taken a toll of their assailants. Scammon counted 262 casualties, including 62 dead. Crook contributed 62 more casualties from the two of his regiments that were engaged. One of these statistics was Robert B. Cornwell of the 23rd Ohio. During the final charge a ball nicked his femoral artery. On October 3rd he wrote home that during the fight he had sent "14 balls after them [Confederates] and if some of them didn't do execution it was not my fault." Seven days later, on October 10th, surgeons operated and ligated

Cornwell's artery. The operation was unsuccessful, and a week later Cornwell's artery began to bleed. The surgeons arrested this and placed a tourniquet on the limb. But this, too, failed and on October 30th Cornwell's wound hemorrhaged severely. Four days later he died.[67]

As for the rest of Cox's division, three hours of uphill fighting and the nervous strain of combat had sapped the men's energy. "It was time to rest," wrote Cox. Ammunition, particularly in Scammon's brigade, probably needed to be replenished. Cox thought it prudent to let the men catch their breath and assess the situation. His victory had won Hill 1080, Hill 1300, and command of Fox's Gap, where his presence threatened the flank and rear of the defenders of Turner's Gap. But from his prisoners Cox learned that he faced D. H. Hill's division of five brigades and that Longstreet's command "was said to be near in support." Cox had destroyed one of Hill's brigades, but that still left the Confederate with a two to one advantage in brigades over Cox. There was no way he could know that Hill did not have all of his brigades on the mountain, or that Longstreet was still several miles away.

Considering the odds, Cox decided that "it seemed wise to contract our lines a little" in the event the enemy counterattacked. His right flank, which had extended across the Old Sharpsburg Road into Wise's north pasture, soon learned that this field "was no place to stay." Pelham's horse artillery, repositioned on a hill to the northwest, Bondurant's guns in Wise's north meadow, and Lane's battery above Turner's Gap all targeted the area. Cox ordered his right back into the woods south of Wise's south pasture, where they had cover and good fields of fire. The redeployment placed the 30th Ohio on the right, in the abovementioned woods, facing north or northwest, with the 28th Ohio in support. The 12th Ohio, with the 36th Ohio in support, were on their left, with the line running across the summit of Hill 1080 and into the hollow between this hill and Hill 1300, which was held by the 23rd and the 11th Ohio. Cox further strengthened his right flank with a section of 10 lb. Parrotts under Lieutenant Daniel W. Glassie of Simmonds's Battery, Kentucky Light Artillery, which were hauled forward to an open spot in the woods. Cox described his division's position when complete: "Our front was hollow, for the two wings were nearly at right angles to each other; but the flanks were strongly posted." Until the reinforcements Reno had promised came up, Cox decided to sit tight.[68]

Cox later was criticized for not pushing his division on to the Mountain House and seizing Turner's Gap. D. H. Hill advanced this fantasy in an 1886 article for *Century Magazine*, writing that after Cox defeated Garland, "there was nothing to oppose him [Cox]. My other three brigades had not come up; Colquitt could not be taken from the pike except in the last extremity." As Hill related it, in desperation he ran two guns down from the Mountain House and collected a line a "dismounted staff-officers, couriers, teamsters, and cooks" to give the appearance of infantry supports and bluff the Federals. "I do not remember ever to have experienced a greater feeling of loneliness," he wrote. It made for stirring reading, but it was pure fiction. There were no cooks or teamsters on the mountain. They were in the valley at Boonsboro, along with the other noncombatants. What stood between Cox and Turner's Gap were G. B. Anderson's brigade, the 13th North Carolina, and Bondurant's battery—1,200 to 1,300 men and four guns.[69]

Ezra A. Carman, who participated in the Maryland Campaign as a colonel of the 13th New Jersey and later was its most thorough historian, thought Cox did well. Had he pressed the advantage gained with Garland's defeat, Carman thought, "there is little room to doubt that he could have seized and held Fox's Gap and the old Sharpsburg road; but he knew nothing of the enemy's strength, did not know what he might encounter in the woods and dense thickets lying beyond the ridge road; naturally supposed that his enemy was in force to hold the position against his small division." Cox had shown that he did not lack aggression. But he was not reckless. After a three-hour fight, pressing on over rugged terrain against what was believed to be superior numbers promised potential disaster, not success. Cox intended to hold on to what his men had gained and wait for reinforcements. Then they would test the enemy again.[70]

10

Afternoon at Fox's Gap

"So little did we know of the etiquette of war"

D espite Reno's promise that he would support Cox with the entire 9th Corps, only Willcox's 1st Division was given instructions to march. Sturgis and his 2nd Division received no orders and there is no evidence that Rodman, on the march from Frederick, was encouraged to quicken his pace. The 9th Corps' inactivity is baffling, particularly in light of Reno's aggressive response to Cox's note. Perhaps Burnside interceded, as his orders were to support a reconnaissance into Turner's Gap, not force a general engagement. Burnside was not a soldier who tested the boundaries of his orders. But, to his credit, he and Reno started for the front sometime between 9 and 10 a.m. for a closer look at the situation.[1]

Willcox received his orders at about 8 a.m. His men had already breakfasted on corn, crackers, and coffee and were ready to move, but before they did, Willcox sent an aide to request directions from Cox. This officer managed to find his way to the Ohioan, but apparently more by luck than by a good sense of direction, for when he reached Cox he admitted that "he had no clear idea of the roads upon which he had traveled." Rather than try to explain roads that he himself had only a vague knowledge of, Cox suggested to the aide that Willcox should ask Pleasonton for directions. It was a simple task, but the aide proved no better at comprehending instructions than he had at finding his way, for when he returned to his division headquarters he told his chief that he should report to Pleasonton for orders instead of directions. This is precisely what Willcox did, and Pleasonton—unaware that Cox was anticipating the support of the 1st Division—suggested that Willcox move against the heights north of the National Road (presumably Hill 1280) and turn the Confederate left. This seemed like sound tactical advice to Willcox, and he marched his division west along the National Road, unaware that a glittering opportunity to solidify Cox's hold on Fox's Gap and provide the Army of the Potomac with a decided advantage in the fight for possession of the mountain gaps had been lost by an aide's failure to correctly deliver a simple message.[2]

"We advanced along the turnpike in plain view of their batteries on the right until we came within 1/2 mile of it [South Mountain] when we halted," wrote Frederick Pettit of the 100th Pennsylvania. Here Willcox ordered Colonel Thomas Welsh, commanding his leading brigade, to "attack the enemy's batteries on the right of the turnpike." Welsh ordered the 100th Pennsylvania to deploy as skirmishers and move forward along the road. Welsh led the rest of his brigade to the 100th's right, directly toward the imposing slopes of Hill 1280, in the hope that he might outflank the Rebel guns while the 100th harassed their front. Private Pettit recorded that the Confederate gunners "sent their shell among us thick and fast," and he and his comrades were forced to scurry for cover along the road bank.[3]

While Willcox deployed to attack D. H. Hill's batteries, Reno and Burnside rode up to Pleasonton's headquarters. The time is unknown, but it could not have been later than 10 a.m. When they learned that Pleasonton had sent Willcox off in the opposite direction to where Reno had intended the division to move, Reno sent a staff officer galloping to recall the 1st Division. Willcox had fortunately not moved far when Reno's messenger caught up with him. Willcox managed to extricate his men without great difficulty, although the "shot and shell flew faster than ever" during their withdrawal. Colonel Benjamin C. Christ's 1st Brigade led the way, since he had not yet deployed his regiments, and Welsh's brigade followed once it had re-formed out of range of the Confederate guns. Willcox was at last moving in the direction in which he was most needed, but the maneuvering along the National Road had cost precious time.[4]

Pleasonton's command post was in an ideal position to direct a battle for the mountain gaps. It stood just out of reach of the longest-range Confederate guns and afforded a breathtaking view across the valley to both Fox's and Turner's gaps. Fifteen months earlier, as a colonel, Burnside had led his 1st Rhode Island through Turner's Gap and paused just beyond its summit for two hours to rest his men. From that experience he surely appreciated the advantage the terrain afforded for those in possession of it, but he knew little of what the enemy might have arrayed to defend the gaps, as Cox had not yet made his haul of prisoners from Garland's brigade. According to Special Orders No. 191, both D. H. Hill's and Longstreet's "commands" were at Boonsboro, so there might be a substantial force before him. In the words of an accompanying *New York Times* correspondent, the Confederates appeared disposed "to make a vigorous stand on the mountain."

The reaction of their artillery to Willcox's movement along the National Road and the resistance Cox had encountered at Fox's Gap indicated that the enemy was present in some strength. Burnside hesitated to escalate the battle beyond committing Willcox's division to reinforce Cox. Orders went to Sturgis to prepare his division for action, but not to move yet. Rodman's division arrived in Middletown about 10 a.m., tired from their march from Frederick and their lack of sleep. They needed time to rest and prepare some food. McClellan would be up soon, and Hooker's 1st Corps was expected to begin arriving around noon. Burnside decided to wait to initiate any further action until his entire wing was concentrated.[5] Burnside might be forgiven for his conservative reaction to Cox's unexpected battle at Fox's Gap, given the intelligence about Confederate strength at Boonsboro, but Burnside's failure to move Sturgis up is inexplicable. It would have concentrated the strength of the 9th Corps and cleared Sturgis from the roadway before the 1st Corps began to arrive from Frederick.

At army headquarters outside Frederick, the Army of the Potomac's movement appeared to be on schedule. Hooker had his 1st Corps up at 3 a.m. for a breakfast of coffee and crackers, and by daylight the corps—which extended for nearly 5 miles on the road—was tramping through the streets of the city. McClellan and his staff attended to some final details for the anticipated battle. To avoid confusion, orders were issued formalizing the wing command arrangement the army had been operating under since leaving Washington. Orders were also sent to Fitz John Porter, urging him to bring his 5th Corps on "as rapidly as possible." McClellan even found time to write his wife a brief letter describing his enthusiastic reception in Frederick on the 13th and saying that "it is probable that we shall have a serious engagement today & perhaps a general battle." He was not certain the enemy would fight, but, if so, "it ought to be today or tomorrow." Then the general joined his staff for breakfast. It was about 9 a.m.[6]

As McClellan and his staff finished their meal, Major Russell galloped up from Harpers Ferry with news that shook headquarters' quiet confidence. Since leaving Harpers Ferry the previous evening, Russell had completed a dangerous and hard ride, slipping past three separate enemy picket posts, including one of some 70 men on South Mountain (probably from Colquitt's brigade), to reach Middletown, where he found Reno, who provided him with a fresh horse and sent him on to McClellan. Russell reported to the general that they had lost Maryland Heights, that the entire garrison was trapped, and that Miles estimated they could hold out for only 48 hours, which meant until September 15 or perhaps the morning of the 16th. After that, he would have no choice but to surrender.[7]

Russell's report, particularly about the loss of Maryland Heights, worried McClellan, but Miles's belief that he could maintain possession of Harpers Ferry for 48 hours was good news. McClellan expected a general engagement "today or tomorrow," the outcome of which would decide the campaign, and with it the fate of the Harpers Ferry's garrison. At 9 a.m. McClellan wired Halleck and confidently expressed the opinion that if Miles could even hold "out today I can probably save him." And, so long as Miles was able to stand fast, it kept Lee's army divided and left the odds in McClellan's favor.[8]

But to relieve Miles and crush Lee's divided army, McClellan needed his combat power up front, and the flawed planning that had placed over 50,000 troops on a single road worked against it that morning. Hooker's leading division, Meade's Pennsylvania Reserves, was on the road by 5 a.m. Sykes's division was scheduled to follow Hooker at 6:00 a.m., but the 1st Corps did not clear

Frederick until between 9 and 10 a.m. Besides the large numbers of men, wagons, guns, and animals on a single road, the ascent of Catoctin Mountain slowed the rate of march at the head of the column and led to maddening stopping and starting farther back along the column. Someone at headquarters discovered that the massive jam of troops, guns, and wagons could be relieved by redirecting Sumner's wing to the Shookstown Road (so called because it ran through the village of Shookstown, 2 miles northwest of Frederick). McClellan agreed, and at 9 a.m. he sent orders to Sumner shifting Sumner's two corps to this road. But by the time Sumner received the orders he had already pushed part of his 2nd Corps 2 miles west of Frederick along the National Road—adding to the road congestion—and had to countermarch. Sumner's troops soon discovered that the Shookstown Road was poorly suited for army traffic—"such a road you never saw—rocks & steep pitches going up & down," wrote one soldier—and the column moved at a crawl over Catoctin Mountain. A teamster with the 2nd Corps trains offered some idea of just how slowly the march proceeded when he wrote that by 5:30 p.m. they had not moved more than 2 miles from their camps.[9]

Shortly after redirecting the march of Sumner's wing, McClellan left for the front. Before he did, he asked Major Russell whether he thought he could get through to Harpers Ferry with a message for Miles. The major decided that he had used up his luck in getting out of Harpers Ferry and declined the invitation, but McClellan did not give up the hope that he might find someone willing to take the risk.[10] McClellan rode rapidly toward the front, passing the long columns of troops, guns, and trains, and reached the summit of Catoctin Pass probably shortly before 11 a.m. The view of the Middletown Valley was magnificent, and aide Colonel Strother recalled that as one, the entire party

drew rein to admire the scene which presented itself. The Valley of the Catoctin, which lay beneath us like a map unrolled, is one of the most fertile and best improved districts in Maryland. As far as the eye can reach, north and southward, it is dotted with handsome farm-houses, and pretty thriving villages, and checkered with cultivated fields and scraps of woodland, enlivened by silvery streams and traversed by fine public roads.[11]

Both Turner's Gap, 6 miles to the west, and Crampton's Gap, 8 miles to the southwest, were visible, and from both, wrote Strother, "we could hear the sullen booming of the guns, and see the white wreaths of smoke rolling up the face of the mountain." They took it in for a moment, and then McClellan urged his mount, Old Dan, down the mountain. The headquarters group swept on at a rapid gait, going past Hooker's columns—who cheered loudly when they saw who it was—to Burnside's headquarters, which were located in an orchard on the eastern edge of Middletown, where they arrived around 11:30 a.m.[12]

Burnside could offer McClellan little detailed information other than that the Rebels were present in some force and seemed disposed to make a fight for the mountain gaps, and that the present effort was to turn the Confederate right flank. Cox was just commencing his movement that swept Garland's brigade off the mountain, but he had taken some prisoners in the early fighting, and from these Burnside probably knew that it was D. H. Hill's division in front. The prisoners may have also been the source for McClellan's opinion that the "enemy were in considerable force in vicinity of Boonsborough." During McClellan and Burnside's discussion a message from Pleasonton arrived, which was largely un-intelligible in his description of the operations at Turner's and Fox's gaps, but it provided one piece of useful information from his cavalry patrols near Burkitts-ville, who reported only 1,500 cavalry and 3 guns at the village. If this was all the enemy had there, then Franklin might have an easy go of it.[13]

McClellan wrote to Franklin at 11:45 a.m., letting him know the status of operations at Turner's Gap and passing on Pleasonton's report. McClellan also advised Franklin of Major Russell's report that Miles had abandoned Maryland Heights, which heightened the urgency of the 6th Corps' operations. "Please lose no time in driving the rebel cavalry out of Burkittsville and occupying the pass," McClellan exhorted, and "continue to bear in mind the necessity of re-lieving Colonel Miles if possible."[14]

Less than an hour after this dispatch was sent, the head of Meade's division reached Middletown. As one of his Pennsylvanians recalled, the town's citizens "turned out en masse to welcome us and cheer us on our way to battle. Never was a more cordial welcome given to troops than was given to us." People ran to the side of the road or stood in doorways or windows for a look at the bronzed Union veterans, as well as to cheer them on. A profusion of U.S. flags appeared, and some of the women even tossed flowers. But what the hungry and thirsty troops appreciated most were the "bread, cakes, milk, water, fruit and tobacco" that were produced by these good people. "We felt then," wrote a member of the 2nd Pennsylvania Reserves, "for the first time during the war, that we were fighting among friends."[15]

Meade's Pennsylvanians continued through the village and across Catoctin Creek at Koogle's, where they broke ranks to rest and eat their dinner. Rufus King's 1st Division followed and halted on the east bank of the creek, while Briga-dier General James B. Ricketts's 2nd Division fell out along the turnpike east of Middletown. While his men rested from their 14-mile tramp, Hooker reported to McClellan. Besides McClellan and Burnside, he found Fitz John Porter there. Porter had two divisions trailing him: Morell's, which would reach Frederick that night; and Andrew Humphreys's, which, due to difficulties with equipment and transportation, had been delayed and had only just reached Leesboro.[16]

While McClellan welcomed the arrival of Porter, his favorite subordinate, it boded ill for Burnside. Porter probably knew that the Rhode Islander had ma-terially helped the court-martial case being assembled against Porter. During the Second Manassas Campaign Porter had written Burnside several personal letters containing stinging criticisms of Pope, bordering almost on insubordination. Burnside—thinking the information on operations in Porter's letters would be of value to his superiors, but oblivious to the possible damage he might cause Porter by forwarding letters not meant for public scrutiny—sent them on to the president and the War Department. Burnside was not a malicious man, but he lacked good judgment. By Porter's lights Burnside could not be trusted, and in the poisonous atmosphere that marked relations between the administration and McClellan, Burnside appeared to be an administration toady. It is hardly an accident that after Porter's arrival the once warm relationship between McClellan and Burnside began to deteriorate.[17]

With the 1st Corps on hand, there were now over 25,000 troops available to assault the mountain gaps. McClellan and Burnside may have discussed a general strategy to clear the mountain passes by moving against the Confederate flanks, but it is evident that the details of how this would be accomplished were left to the Right Wing commander. Sometime before 1 p.m. Burnside left to establish his forward headquarters near Pleasonton's battery position on Hill 700. Hooker departed soon after to conduct a personal reconnaissance of the approaches to the mountain north of the National Road, where it was likely his corps would attack. McClellan remained deeply concerned about Harpers Ferry. Constant artillery fire could be heard from its direction, although it was difficult to discern whether it came from Crampton's Gap or Harpers Ferry. Shortly before 1 p.m. David Strother found McClellan outside Burnside's headquarters tent, "still apprehensive in regard to Miles, and desirous of getting a messenger through to him." He sent Strother and Alan Pinkerton, his chief of secret service, into Middletown to see if they might find someone willing to carry a message to the surrounded garrison. Strother found "many willing in spirit but weak in flesh." Pinkerton may have sweetened his offer with money, for he found three individuals who agreed to try and get through. The message they carried urged Miles to hold out to the last and, if possible, to reoccupy Maryland Heights. "If you can do that, I will certainly be able to relieve you," wrote McClellan. Three copies of the order were made and the volunteer couriers departed. What happened to them is unknown, but none of them got through.[18]

In the meantime Burnside fixed on his plan of attack and began to issue the orders to set it in motion. It was a simple but effective plan: demonstrate against the enemy center while maneuvering the main strength of the 1st and the 9th Corps against their flanks. Orders were sent summoning Sturgis's division. It and Rodman's would reinforce Cox's and Willcox's at Fox's Gap. When Sturgis had cleared the road, the main body of Hooker's corps was to advance along the Old Hagerstown Road to the base of the mountain, then attack and seize the ground commanding Turner's Gap. Reno was ordered to wait until Hooker completed his maneuver and engaged the enemy; Reno was then to advance on the Confederate right, so the two attacking wings would either act like a vise to crush the Confederates or compel them to abandon the mountain. A smaller detached force from the 1st Corps would advance directly on Turner's Gap, so as to prevent the enemy from weakening its defenses there in order to meet the flanking attacks. The question was whether there was enough daylight to execute the plan successfully. Sunset arrived at 6:12 p.m. and it was dark by 7:15. Orders to the different commanders went out around 1 p.m., so they had less than six hours to move thousands of troops and artillery into position and execute an attack over difficult terrain. The failure to move the entire strength of both corps into the Middletown Valley the night before now loomed large.[19]

D. H. Hill observed the buildup of Union strength in the Middletown Valley from a lookout station near his Mountain House headquarters at Turner's Gap. He recalled, "The marching columns extended back as far as eye could see in the distance. It was a grand and glorious spectacle, and it was impossible to look at it without admiration. I had never seen so tremendous an army before and I did not see one like it afterward." The Federals had also seized a solid foothold at Fox's Gap, killed Garland, and shattered his brigade. Lee and Longstreet were en route with reinforcements, but they were still several hours away. Disaster threatened, but Hill kept his head. It would take the enemy time to deploy its large force and move against him. When they did the rugged mountain terrain would slow their advance. Hill controlled the high ground, and the forest prevented the enemy from forming an accurate idea of his strength. By deploying his precious infantry to block the easiest avenues of approach and employing a bold front Hill might keep the Union forces off balance and purchase the necessary time for Longstreet to come to his aid.[20]

The extent of the threat Hill faced revealed itself slowly over the course of the morning, which explains Hill's hesitation in calling up the full strength of his division from Boonsboro. The day before, Roswell Ripley and three of his regiments, with a battery, had been deployed northeast of Boonsboro. At 9 a.m., as Garland became engaged, Hill ordered Ripley to send his battery to Turner's Gap. Several minutes later Ripley received an urgent summons to bring his brigade to the gap, minus the 4th Georgia at Orr's Gap. Orders were probably sent to Lieutenant Colonel A. S. Cutts at the same time to send up the other two batteries of his reserve battalion: Captain G. M. Patterson's and Captain H. M. Ross's Georgia batteries. This left only Rodes's brigade near Boonsboro. They remained Hill's only security in his rear (other than picket detachments) against a possible breakout from Harpers Ferry until Longstreet arrived. "Toward noon," as the situation at Fox's Gap deteriorated, Hill could no longer afford to keep Rodes in the valley, and he sent orders summoning the Alabamians to the mountain. While he waited for these reinforcements to arrive, Hill had his artillery bang away noisily both at Cox in Fox's Gap and the Federal forces in the Middletown Valley, in order to create an impression of strength.[21]

Ripley's infantry completed their march to Turner's Gap around 1:30 p.m. Wounded soldiers from Garland's brigade trickled past them down the mountain, along with civilians fleeing their homes to escape the fighting. Ripley's three regiments had around 1,000 officers and men. He let his men fall out at the summit to catch their breath. While they rested, Rodes's 1,350 Alabamians came striding up the mountain, completing Hill's concentration. By this point Hill had learned that Stuart left Rosser's 5th Virginia cavalry and Pelham's section of horse artillery at Fox's Gap. All told, Hill had four effective brigades of infantry, the remnants of another, a small regiment of cavalry, six artillery batteries, and one section of horse artillery. It tallied to about 5,000 infantry, perhaps 200 cavalry, and 32 guns.[22]

The most immediate threat was at Fox's Gap, and Hill dispatched Ripley to this sector with orders to reinforce G. B. Anderson's brigade. Ross's and Patterson's batteries were unlimbered in open ground on the summit of Hill 1280 near Lane's battery—which, after a morning of miserable luck, had only three serviceable guns remaining—and Rodes's brigade moved up to a support position. But Hill had also situated Rodes where he could quickly deploy to cover Hill 1500, which Hill considered the key terrain of the battlefield. "If gained by the Yankees," wrote Hill, "it would give them control of the ridge commanding the turnpike. The possession of this peak was, therefore, everything to the Yankees." If the enemy moved against Hill 1500, it would be Rodes's mission to defend it.[23] Hill might delay the Federals with the force on hand, but without reinforcements he knew they would overwhelm him. The question was whether Longstreet could arrive before this occurred. "I do not remember ever to have experienced a feeling of greater loneliness," Hill recalled of that early afternoon on the mountain.[24]

Longstreet's command stirred early in their camps near Hagerstown, but as Lee did not anticipate battle that day, preparations for the march to Boonsboro were made at a leisurely pace. Soon after sunrise, as Captain William T. Owen of the 18th Virginia in Garnett's brigade later remembered, "there came tumbling along upon the bosom of the sultry air that dull heavy sound of a distant cannon." But then the firing died away. It resumed soon after, and orders were issued for the men to fill their canteens and to be prepared to march at a moment's notice. They readied themselves, but no orders to march came. The cause of the delay is unknown; neither Lee nor Longstreet offered any explanation. As the sun rose and the day warmed, Captain Owen stated that "the atmosphere becoming more rarified the sound of the distant battle seemed to recede and grew fainter and still fainter until by ten o'clock it had ceased altogether." Owen thought it was 11 a.m. when a courier came "bearing down on a mad gallop," dashing through camp "like a shooting meteor straight on toward headquarters." Minutes later drummers beat the long roll; regiments and brigades fell in and set out at a rapid pace on the road to Boonsboro. "Off we went down the long, sandy lanes with clouds of hot, suffocating dust floating around us and drifting across the fields on the road side," wrote Owen. Jones's division led, followed by Hood's, then Evans's independent brigade and the reserve artillery. So hasty was the departure that Toombs's brigade and the 11th Georgia of G. T. Anderson's brigade were left behind without orders. Given the intelligence Lee received on the night of the 13th, the level of surprise and confusion that marked the departure of Longstreet's command for Boonsboro is positively baffling.[25]

Longstreet's eight infantry brigades counted probably 7,800 effectives at the beginning of the march; five battalions of artillery and the ordnance trains accompanied them. The infantry set a blistering pace. Adjutant Robert T. Coles of the 4th Alabama recalled that the 13-mile forced march "taxed to the utmost the energies of the every man in the regiment."[26] Although the temperature that day topped out at a comfortable 73 degrees, nearly everyone remembered this as a hot and terribly dusty tramp. Captain Owen left one of the most vivid accounts.

> The march was very rapid and at times a double-quick step was kept up for 2 or 3 miles together. Men exhausted by the rapid march and overcome by the dust and heat, fell out of ranks and were left along the roadside by dozens, yet on swept the column at a tremendous pace. The rays of the sun was scorching hot and the perspiration welled out at every pore and ran down the neck and arms, and back in little rivulets; the clouds of dust settled on the face and hands and clothes until the color of the hair and face and whiskers was so changed that a soldier could hardly recognize his messmates.[27]

The grim toll that the forced march exacted is attested to by Longstreet's estimate that he carried 4,000 men into battle at South Mountain. If this is accurate then nearly 3,800 men—or almost half his strength—fell out. For those who endured and kept in the ranks it was a matter of pride that "this army made fourteen miles to the immediate vicinity of the battleground in three and a half hours—good time for a Hamiltonian horse." This works out to 4 miles per hour, a remarkable pace for such a distance. But the men might have been spared this grueling experience and arrived on the field with fuller ranks and fresher legs had Lee started the column earlier. Perhaps Longstreet's statement that "the hallucination that McClellan was not capable of serious work seemed to pervade our army" rang true.[28]

By 2:30 p.m. the first of Longstreet's dust-caked and sweat-soaked soldiers reached Boonsboro. James Simons of Major B. W. Frobel's artillery battalion observed that "the terror stricken and anxious appearance of the towns people showed that trouble was ahead." Longstreet sent word to D. H. Hill that his command was approaching and asked for a situation report. Hill's reply reached Longstreet, who was accompanied by Lee, just outside Boonsboro. Hill needed help at Turner's Gap urgently. The hurried departure from Hagerstown and swift pace of the march had left Longstreet's brigades strung out for several miles along the Old Hagerstown Road, so that they arrived gradually rather than in a compact body. The first brigade to reach Boonsboro was Brigadier General Thomas F. Drayton's, followed by Colonel G. T. Anderson's. Longstreet allowed them a short halt for the men to catch their breath and fill their canteens before ordering them both to hurry on to Turner's Gap.[29]

At 2 p.m., six hours after it had left its bivouac only 4.5 miles away, Willcox's division finally arrived at Fox's Gap. Orlando Willcox was 39, an 1847 graduate of West Point. He was a congenial fellow and made many lasting friends there, including Ambrose Burnside and George B. McClellan. Willcox left the army in 1857 to practice law in Detroit but kept active in the Michigan Militia. Four years later he led the 1st Michigan Infantry at First Manassas as its colonel. He was wounded in the arm during the battle and fell into Confederate hands, where he remained as a prisoner until he was exchanged on August 16, 1862. Four days after his exchange he was promoted to brigadier general, to date from July 21, 1861. When Isaac Stevens lost his life at Chantilly, it created a vacancy in the 9th Corps, which McClellan offered to his old friend. Though still weak from the effects of nearly a year's imprisonment, Willcox was anxious to get back to the field. Following a brief visit home, he took command of the 1st Division, joining it at Frederick. There was no special dash about Willcox; he was simply a solid, levelheaded soldier.[30]

Willcox halted his command in the Old Sharpsburg Road, about 400 yards below the summit of Fox's Gap, where the ground gave his men some cover. He found Cox's division deployed south of the road, skirmishing with G. B. Anderson's Confederates. Cox had a report of an enemy column moving toward his division's left flank, and he requested two regiments from Willcox to strengthen his line there. Willcox sent the 50th Pennsylvania, which he told an aide he considered better than two ordinary regiments, and the 8th Michigan—slightly over 800 total effectives. Probably after discussion with Cox, Willcox ordered the balance of his division to prolong the Kanawha's division's line to the right and parallel to the mountain crest. Colonel Benjamin Christ's 1st Brigade were ordered to establish the right flank of the division and deploy on the right, or north, side of the Old Sharpsburg Road. To cover their deployment and draw off the fire of the Confederate guns on Hill 1280, Willcox called up a section of Captain Asa M. Cook's 8th Massachusetts Battery and ordered it to unlimber on some level ground near the Coffman farm, on the south edge of the road. Up to this point, the Old Sharpsburg Road "was deeply gullied and very narrow . . . the banks on either side being steep and six to ten feet high." But close to Coffman's the road leveled out, which made it possible to deploy Cook's section. The guns unlimbered without difficulty and opened fire on the enemy guns a mile to the north. After four rounds, one of the guns became disabled from some cause; Cook ordered it to the rear and called up another gun to replace it.

Meanwhile, Christ's infantry, led by the very green 17th Michigan, were slowly making their way up the Old Sharpsburg Road to complete their deployment.[31]

Willcox had barely begun to deploy Christ's brigade when orders from Reno arrived, directing Willcox to form his division facing north toward the National Road, at a right angle to Cox's line. Cox was dumbfounded when he heard of it. "I can hardly think the order could have been intended to effect this," he wrote, "as the turnpike is deep between the hills there, and the enemy quite distant on the other side of the gorge." Willcox, however, had no choice but to obey, so he ordered the part of Christ's brigade that had entered the fields north of the Old Sharpsburg Road to return to the road in order to redeploy. It was at this same moment that Cook was exchanging guns to replace his disabled piece, so the narrow, sunken road was crowded with infantry and artillery vehicles. At this most opportune moment Bondurant's Alabama battery, which had remained silent and unobserved in a small field surrounded by woods immediately north of the Wise cabin and adjacent to the Old Sharpsburg Road, opened fire on Cook with canister and shell at a range of 400–500 yards. The first salvo killed one man and wounded four in Cook's artillery crews. The New Englander ordered his caissons and the disabled gun to the rear and manfully attempted to reposition his guns to respond to Bondurant. But the Alabamians had the advantage of position and surprise, and they poured iron on the Federals, forcing Cook and his men to abandon their guns and take to their heels for the nearby woods.[32]

While Cook and his gun teams looked for cover, his caisson and limber teams made a mad dash down the narrow Old Sharpsburg Road to escape Bondurant's shells and canister balls. A large part of the 17th Michigan were still in the road when the vehicles came flying toward them. Captain Gabriel Campbell of Company E recalled, "I could see the cannon balls coming bounding down the road. One came within arms length of me dashing through the head of the company just behind." The men of this company scrambled up the banks of the road to avoid the shell. So did the men in the path of Cooks's careening vehicles, and for a moment it appeared that fear and confusion might cause a stampede. The disorder seemed great enough that a Michigan officer thought that "had the enemy taken advantage of it," they might have captured Cook's abandoned guns. Skirmishers of G. B. Anderson's brigade did press down the slope so aggressively that Willcox "expected a charge to take Cook's battery." Willcox reacted swiftly and decisively. He ordered Lieutenant Colonel David Morrison's veteran 79th New York, a New York City regiment with such strong Scottish representation that they were known as the Highlanders, to deploy behind a stone wall south of the road, near Coffman's, where they could provide cover to Cook's abandoned pieces. The Highlanders executed the movement so smartly and quickly that Anderson's skirmishers halted their advance, but the Tarheels were probably also given pause by the sheer number of Federal soldiers who came swarming up from behind this single regiment.[33]

Willcox brought up the nearly 700 men of the 17th Michigan to the 79th's support. Captain Campbell recalled how Willcox had come "flying up on his horse, saying to me, 'Is this my Michigan? Form into line.'" Only three weeks before, when Willcox made his brief visit to Detroit after his release from prison, the newly formed 17th served as his escort in the city. Their colonel, William H. Withington, had been a captain in Willcox's old 1st Michigan and been captured with Willcox at First Manassas. Willcox had a special attachment to this regiment, but they were green as grass. Minutes before Bondurant opened fire, Willcox had asked Withington what his new regiment could do in the way of tactical evolutions. "We can march by a flank and load and fire, General," the colonel replied. The regiment had yet to complete even a battalion drill. They were fitted out in U.S. regular army uniforms: frock coats buttoned to the chin, Hardee hats "with a feather stuck jauntily in one side," and white gloves tucked in their belts. "A wonder we did not put them on, so little did we know of the etiquette of war," wrote Private David Lane. Yet, for what they lacked in drill, discipline, and experience, they compensated for with raw courage and enthusiasm. Officers and noncoms managed to get the regiment into a line, and it advanced into a cornfield extending south and west from Coffman's farm. This brought them in view of either Bondurant's guns or Hill's guns to the north—it is difficult to determine with certainty which set of artillery—and of G. B. Anderson's skirmishers, some of whom had filtered into the woods east of Wise's south pasture. "Here we fell on our faces," recalled Captain Campbell, while canister or shrapnel lashed their line, wounding a number of men and covering everyone with leaves from the cornstalks.[34]

Willcox praised both the 17th Michigan and 79th New York for their "coolness and firmness in rallying and changing front under a heavy fire." But he did not leave them in their exposed position for long. He revealed his force merely to deter the enemy from trying to capture Cook's guns. It was now clearly evident that Reno's orders were issued without an understanding of the situation at the front. As senior officer, Cox ordered Willcox to deploy his division where they had originally intended it to be, with Willcox extending Cox's line to the right and establishing a firm hold on the Old Sharpsburg Road. Leaving the 79th New York behind their stone wall, Willcox ordered Withington to extract his regiment from Coffman's cornfield and redeploy it in the woods north of the Old Sharpsburg Road and slightly east of Coffman's. Withington herded his greenhorns into the woods and deployed the regiment in a column of battalions, which placed five companies in the front line and five in a supporting line. Companies were mixed, and the two wings mingled together in places, but the regiment enjoyed cover in the woods and provided a numerically strong anchor to the division's right flank.[35]

While Christ's brigade adjusted its position, Colonel Thomas Welsh's 2nd Brigade deployed south of the Old Sharpsburg Road. Welsh placed the 46th

New York—287 men under Lieutenant Colonel Joseph Gerhardt—on his left, in the open fields east of the woods around Wise's south pasture and extending toward the right of Cox's division. Lieutenant Colonel John L. Linn's big 45th Pennsylvania, 694 strong, formed in the rear of the 79th New York, with their left touching the 46th and their right on the Old Sharpsburg Road. The 100th Pennsylvania, which had been delayed by the need to recall its skirmishers from the earlier advance along the National Road, were the last to arrive, and they formed in support of the 45th Pennsylvania. These movements took place under a constant harassing fire from Confederate artillery. Both Bondurant's battery and some of the guns on Hill 1280 sent a steady stream of shells at them, with a bit of canister and shrapnel from Bondurant. Fred Pettit, with the 100th Pennsylvania, found that even in the reserve line the "grape and canister flew a few feet over our heads thick and fast, but no one was hurt as we lay close to the ground." In the 17th Michigan, John Morton wrote that the "shot and shell poured down like rain bursting everywhere around us." But the woods concealed their position and the enemy fire proved more frightening than damaging, its principal success being to stampede the field officers' horses, which they had left tied to a fence in the rear of the regiment.[36]

The Confederate batteries inflicted few casualties, but they pinned down the Federals. "We lay silent and kept concealed," reported Willcox. The heavy batteries in the valley below did their best to lend support, but the range and elevation were too great to silence the Southern guns. Around 3:30 p.m. the Confederate artillery finally ceased fire, and quiet descended over Fox's Gap. Other batteries of Cutts's battalion on Hill 1280 were busily pegging away at Hooker's corps and then moving along the Old Hagerstown Road to assail the Confederate left. But all was silent at Fox's Gap. Sturgis's 2nd Division reached the base of the mountain around this time. Before they began their ascent, Reno detached the 2nd Maryland and the 6th New Hampshire from Brigadier General James Nagle's 1st Brigade and posted them near the National Road, in advance of the heavy batteries. He also dispatched half of Sturgis's artillery support—Captain Joseph C. Clark Jr.'s Battery E, 4th U.S. Artillery (four 10 lb. Parrotts)—to bolster the left of Cox's line. The balance of Sturgis's infantry, nearly 3,800 strong—accompanied by Captain George W. Durell's Battery D, Pennsylvania Light Artillery—began their slow ascent up the Old Sharpsburg Road. Once they reached Cox's and Willcox's position, there would be nearly 11,000 9th Corps soldiers massed on D. H. Hill's right flank.[37]

Around 2 p.m. McClellan joined Reno and Burnside at the latter's forward headquarters on Hill 700 to assume command of the battle. "We had as comprehensive a view of the position as could be conveniently obtained," recorded aide David Strother. "The windings of the main turnpike through cleared fields were visible from the valley to the summit." It was a panorama such as few battlefield commanders in the war ever enjoyed. Both Turner's Gap and Fox's

Gap and their approaches could be seen clearly. Only the ground where Hooker would attack was obscured. Signal communications were established with Franklin at Burkittsville, so it became possible to monitor progress there. Nearby, McMullin's, Simmond's, Gibson's, Benjamin's, and Hains's batteries, which included six 20 lb. Parrott rifles, were shelling the Confederate gun positions on Hill 1280. The rifled guns of Cutts's battalion replied vigorously, with their shells bursting "at every moment." But his guns lacked the range or were hampered by defective ammunition, for all their shells exploded short of the Union guns. By the time McClellan arrived at Burnside's headquarters, the Right Wing's attack was already in execution. Sturgis's division had started toward Fox's Gap, followed by Rodman's, and Hooker had his orders to move his corps into position to attack the Confederate left. Although McClellan would later claim that it was he who "pushed up Sturgis," ordered Hooker's turning movement, and "hurried up Sumner," the truth was that Sumner did not need prodding (he was moving as quickly as his two army corps could to get across a mountain range on the rugged Shookstown Road), and his subordinate Burnside had already taken care of the former tasks. So far as the tactical battle was concerned, the major command decisions were already made. It would now be decided by the troops and leaders at the front.[38]

D. H. Hill did not intend to wait while the enemy made their dispositions and executed their plans. He intended to knock them off balance before they could land another blow, and he thought that Fox's Gap offered the best opportunity for a spoiling attack. The Federals there had made no aggressive moves since defeating Garland, which suggested that a vigorous counterattack might drive them off the commanding ground along the Crest Road. Hill may have been unaware that Willcox had reinforced Cox; otherwise Hill might have abandoned his offensive ideas. When Roswell Ripley reported at the head of his brigade, Hill ordered him to reinforce G. B. Anderson's men at Fox's Gap and drive back the enemy threatening the pass. It is uncertain whether Ripley followed the Ridge Road, because one of his men noted in his diary that during this march they "went through some of the roughest brushwood I ever saw." But eventually they came up with Anderson, several hundred yards north of Fox's Gap. The two officers discussed the situation and decided that Anderson would redeploy his brigade in the Old Sharpsburg Road, west of the Ridge Road and facing the high ground of Hill 1080, and Ripley would form on his left. Once both brigades were in line, they would attack and attempt to dislodge Cox from the high ground south of Wise's. It was nearly 4 p.m. before the two brigades completed their redeployment, but before they stepped off D. H. Hill rode up, at the head of Drayton's and G. T. Anderson's brigades.[39]

These two brigades of D. R. Jones's division had reported to Hill at the Mountain House around 3:30 p.m. Both brigades must have been exhausted after the brutal march from Hagerstown and the rapid climb up the mountain, but they added nearly 2,000 infantry to Hill's force, with Drayton bringing up 1,300 men and Anderson 600. "I felt anxious to beat the force on my right before the Yankees made their grand attack," wrote Hill, which meant that he had to move quickly. Hill gambled that by employing his advantage of interior lines, he could reinforce Ripley's and G. B. Anderson's brigades with Drayton's and G.T. Anderson's, attack and beat the Federals on his right with this force, and then shift whatever he had available back to bolster his left before the enemy blow fell there. The nature of the terrain, the poor road network, and the physical condition of Longstreet's men, however, all stacked the odds against such tactics. So, too, did incompetent leadership, as Hill would discover.[40]

Hill personally led the two brigades to Fox's Gap, where he assembled all four brigade commanders. His orders to them were simple in concept but, as all would soon learn, quite difficult to execute. He directed Ripley and G. B. Anderson to move their brigades farther west along the Old Sharpsburg Road to make room for G. T. Anderson's and Drayton's. When all four brigades were on line, they were to advance and "sweep the woods before them." Hill entrusted command of the attack to Ripley, the senior officer, while he returned to the Mountain House to monitor the larger battle and await Longstreet. The attack plan he left for Ripley to carry out was hastily conceived, and it suffered from an imperfect understanding of the terrain, enemy strength, and position. Its accomplishment was also well beyond Roswell Ripley's capabilities.[41]

Ripley had solid credentials on paper. An 1843 West Point graduate, he had 10 years' service in the old U.S Army, including in the Mexican War, where he had earned two brevets for gallantry in action. The one blemish on his record was that he was originally a Northerner—born in Ohio and nominated to West Point from New York—but he compensated for this by settling in Charleston, South Carolina, in 1853, marrying a Charleston woman, and becoming a devoted states' rights advocate. When the war came there was no question in Ripley's mind whose army he would join. He offered his services to the Confederacy, and they gave him a command in the defenses of Charleston during the Fort Sumter crisis. Charleston's leading citizens were fond of Ripley, but his fellow soldiers were not. They found him a querulous individual. The Confederate government resolved the problem by transferring Ripley, who had been promoted to brigadier general in August 1861, to brigade command in Lee's army. His first combat, at Beaver Dam Creek, resulted in a bloody repulse, costing hundreds of casualties. He proved so cantankerous, or incompetent, or both, that later in the Seven Days campaign his entire staff, save only his assistant adjutant general, quit him in disgust. After the Seven Days battles William L. De Rosset, the colonel of the 3rd North Carolina, wrote that "it was a common subject of conversation among officers & men that Ripley was not under infantry fire during the week. We saw or heard nothing of him at Mechanicsville, Cold Harbor or Malvern Hill . . . nor was he known to be near his proper position at

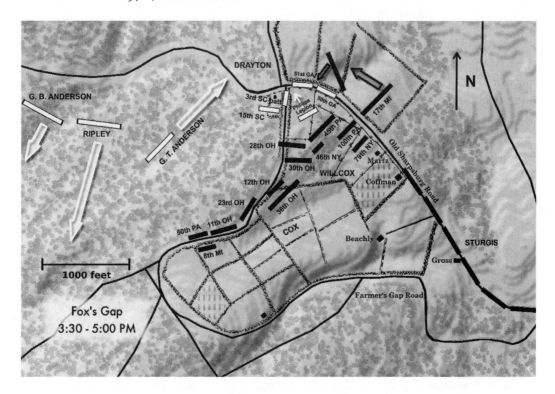

any time." Ripley's men thought he was a coward. But D. H. Hill apparently was unaware of this, although Hill would later claim that "I had feared he was either a coward or a traitor," mainly because he was "a Yankee by birth." Yet if Hill suspected Ripley of cowardice or incompetence, he surely would not have entrusted his counterattack at Fox's Gap to Ripley.[42]

Even had Ripley been a better soldier, the odds were stacked against him. He had no opportunity to reconnoiter the ground, and he had an imprecise knowledge of the enemy position and strength, since both Cox and Willcox kept most of their men under cover. Hill's vague orders to "sweep the woods before them" apparently had as their objective the recapture of the commanding ground of hills 1080 and 1300. Accomplishing this required the four brigades to execute a left wheel from the Old Sharpsburg Road uphill through a dense forest, with few features to guide the movement. Even forming the four brigades in a continuous line proved problematic. Hill thought they could use the Old Sharpsburg Road to form up for the attack, but the road curves like a lazy letter S as it descends west of Fox's Gap, which made it impossible for the four brigades to form in a continuous line in the road. The problems would probably have been surmountable with firm direction, energy, and leadership, but Ripley offered none of these.

After Hill departed for Turner's Gap, Ripley, also unaware that the Old Sharpsburg Road was not straight, ordered all four brigades to move west by the right flank far enough so that each would have room to form line of battle facing south, with the left flank of the line resting near Fox's Gap. G. B. Anderson's troops led the way, followed by Ripley's and then G. T. Anderson's. Drayton may not have understood Ripley's orders, or perhaps he did not think the other brigades were moving as far west as they did. Whatever the case, his brigade remained at Fox's Gap, and by the time Ripley and company halted their shift west, a gap of fully 300 yards had opened between G. T. Anderson's brigade and Drayton's. Since he failed to supervise the movement, Ripley was unaware of this development, so when he thought all four brigades were in position he gave orders to front left and advance. From left to right, the forces of G. T. Anderson, Ripley, and G. B. Anderson plunged into the "dense thickets" covering the western slope of the mountain, looking for a fight. Confusion ensued almost immediately. G. T. Anderson did not fully understand the plan of attack, so he had not communicated to his skirmish line that they would need to make a change of direction. When Ripley ordered the brigades to front and advance south and east, G. T. Anderson's skirmish line kept moving west or southwest, uncovering the Georgian's front and probably becoming tangled with Ripley's or G. B. Anderson's brigades. Then firing broke out, but not in front of any of the three brigades. Instead it came from their left and rear, where Drayton's brigade was.[43]

South Carolinian Thomas Fenwick Drayton was 54 years old. Although an 1828 graduate of West Point with eight years in the old U.S. Army, Drayton owed his general's rank and brigade command in part to Jefferson Davis, his good friend and old West Point classmate. Before the Civil War Drayton had enjoyed a comfortable life as a planter and as president of the Charleston and Savannah Railroad. Davis made Drayton a brigadier general and assigned him to the defense of Port Royal, South Carolina. Drayton did not do well, and there were suggestions of inefficiency from his superiors. Instead of being quietly reassigned to a noncombat post, Drayton received command of a brigade formed from South Carolina and Georgia regiments and was sent to the Virginia theater. He reached the army in time to participate in Second Manassas, where he displeased division commander D. R. Jones with a lackluster performance. Thomas Goree, an aide to Longstreet, writing after the Maryland Campaign but expressing a sentiment most likely held after Second Manassas, said that Drayton—and Goree also included Brigadier General Nathan G. Evans in this opinion—were "not worth the powder & lead it would take to kill them."[44]

Drayton commanded a brigade of three regiments (the 15th South Carolina, the 50th Georgia, and the 51st Georgia), the Georgia Phillips Legion (which amounted to a regiment), and the 3rd South Carolina Battalion, which consisted of six companies. As a brigade they had participated in only one general engagement, Second Manassas, and Drayton's caution caused them to miss the heavy fighting done by Longstreet's wing. The 50th and the 51st Georgia were raised in the late winter and early spring of 1862, and Second Manassas was their first combat experience. Drayton's other units all traced their organization to 1861 and had smelled powder in minor engagements, but they had yet to see the type of fighting they were about to experience at Fox's Gap. Rather than placing all of his regiments in the Old Sharpsburg Road, facing south, which is what Ripley desired, Drayton initially only posted the 15th South Carolina and the 3rd South Carolina Battalion in the road. The 15th were on the right, their right flank about opposite Wise's cabin. The road, particularly near the left of the line, was described as "much washed and worn down, thus giving the trooper therein stationed the advantage of first class breastworks" to any fire that might come from the direction of the woods that wrapped around Wise's south pasture. The remainder of the brigade formed at right angles to the South Carolinians, finding cover behind a stone wall along the eastern edge of Wise's north pasture. Drayton never explained his deployment, and his report, if he wrote one, did not survive, but it is clear that he did not understand how far Ripley intended to shift the other brigades to the west before they attacked. When Drayton learned of the developing gap between his right and G. T. Anderson's left, he ordered the two South Carolina units to move west far enough to enable him to move the Phillips Legion into the Old Sharpsburg Road, leaving only the two Georgia regiments to cover the flank. The enemy remained largely concealed, and Drayton gave Captain D. B. Miller's Company K of the 3rd South Carolina Battalion the unpleasant duty of probing the woods beyond the south pasture to find them.[45]

Miller's men moved across Wise's south field and observed what was probably two companies of the 45th Pennsylvania, whom Willcox had ordered forward to reconnoiter in preparation for a general advance by his division, approaching through the woods, so the Company K troops fell back to sound the alarm. Drayton, knowing that his orders were to attack and unaware of the enemy strength in his front, ordered the regiments in the Old Sharpsburg Road to advance "and drive them from the woods." At the same time he ordered the 50th and the 51st Georgia to change front south and move into the Old Sharpsburg Road, leaving only a skirmish line behind to cover the flank. Whether he intended to use them to extend his attack farther east or to support the assault of the rest of the brigade is unknown, and it was about to become a moot point. Bondurant's battery had moved from its position in the small field immediately north of the Wise cabin and the Old Sharpsburg Road, where it had fired on Cook, to a point near the northwest corner of Wise's north pasture. Therefore Drayton may have felt that Bondurant's guns and his skirmishers could cover any threat that might emerge from the woods north of Coffman's.[46]

Only the Phillips Legion made it into the woods beyond Wise's field, and this was because the woods ran closer to their front than they did to the South Carolinians. The 3rd South Carolina Battalion had only advanced partway across

Wise's field when their commander, Lieutenant Colonel George James, observed large numbers of Union troops—far more than his 160-man battalion could handle—moving up through the woods east of the pasture. James, who had been a lieutenant in the old U.S. Army before the war, quickly ordered his battalion to wheel right and take cover behind the stone wall running along the eastern side of the Crest Road. The 15th South Carolina halted their advance as well, and they sought shelter either behind the same stone wall or behind the wall on the south side of Wise's garden and in the woods west of this—the record is unclear which. The Phillips Legion traded fire with a large Union force approaching through a cornfield east of the woods, lost several men to return fire, and fell back across Wise's pasture toward the intersection of the Ridge Road and the Old Sharpsburg Road, where they were nearly fired on by the 51st Georgia. The Legion's subsequent position is something of a mystery. They may have taken position on the 3rd Battalion's left flank in the Crest Road, but some element of Drayton's brigade deployed along the Ridge Road, and it may have been the Legion. Whatever Drayton's exact deployment, his poorly directed attack had quickly collapsed in the face of powerful enemy numbers, and now his brigade hastily attempted to redeploy to meet the approaching storm.[47]

When Drayton emerged from the woods north of the Old Sharpsburg Road and maneuvered his brigade to attack the woods south and east of Wise's south pasture, Orlando Willcox was readying his 1st Division to launch their own assault. Orders from both Reno and McClellan had arrived, directing Willcox and Cox "to silence the enemy's battery at all hazards," meaning Bondurant's guns. The plan decided on by Willcox and Cox was for Cox to "hold fast my extreme left which was well advanced on and over the mountain crest," while Willcox's division swung uphill and seized the wooded ridge running north from Fox's Gap, which was along the Ridge Road. This ridge commanded Wise's north and south pasture and, therefore, Fox's Gap. To control the gap one needed possession of the ridge. Willcox planned to have the veteran 79th New York spearhead the attack with a direct assault on Bondurant—who, when Willcox made his plans, was still in the small field near Wise's—while the 17th Michigan advanced across Wise's north pasture to take the Alabama gunners in flank. The 46th New York, the 45th Pennsylvania, and the 100th Pennsylvania would all advance in support south of the Old Sharpsburg Road.[48]

Willcox personally delivered the assault orders to Lieutenant Colonel Morrison, commanding the 79th New York. Morrison drew his sword and ordered his regiment up from behind the stone wall that sheltered them. There were 312 officers and men in the regiment, but part of them were deployed as skirmishers. Their support, the 45th Pennsylvania, mustered nearly 700 men. Willcox instantly observed the disparity and asked Morrison, "Is this your regiment?" Morrison responded it was, and, sensing Willcox's concern over its numbers, added, "but if you will give me more men we'll take the battery." Willcox appreciated the grit of the colonel, but he wanted numbers up front, so he ordered the 79th to fall to the rear of Lieutenant Colonel John I. Curtin's 45th Pennsylvania, who were told to assume the front line. Curtin was made of the same fiber as Morrison. A nephew of Pennsylvania Governor Andrew Curtin, John Curtin was a civil engineer before the war, and he took to soldiering naturally. His regiment had spent most of their field service on the South Carolina coast, where they had done well, and they had only joined the 9th Corps in early August. Curtin ordered his A and K companies to the front as skirmishers, and then his voice rang out along the battle line of the other eight companies: "Attention, battalion! Shoulder arms. Forward, guide center, march!" The regiment's men scrambled to their feet, shouldered their weapons, and began to advance toward Coffman's cornfield, which extended for nearly 100 yards to the woods around Wisc's south pasture. Lieutenant Colonel David A. Leckey's 100th Pennsylvania followed in the rear as a support, the 46th New York moved en echelon on the 45th's left, and the 79th remained behind as a reserve. All told there were some 1,500 officers and men in the three assault regiments sweeping up the mountain slope toward the woods near Wise's. They were unaware of Drayton's presence, but that would not last for long.[49]

"All had become ominously silent all along the line. Not a gun was heard," recalled Eugene Beauge of the 45th's Company G. The regiment clambered over the stone wall that had covered the 79th New York, then entered Coffman's cornfield. Halfway through the corn scattered shots were heard from the woods ahead. Companies A and K had made contact with the Phillips Legion. Several bullets whined through the air overhead. Before the firing became general, Lieutenant Colonel Curtin's horse became unmanageable, refusing to leap the stone wall. While Curtin stubbornly tried to induce his horse over the wall his regiment pushed on, leaving him behind. Curtin relented, released his mount, and hurried after his regiment on foot. One of men reflected that fate had dealt Curtin a break, for "had the brute obeyed his master that day and carried him into that tempest of lead and iron the chances are that neither horse nor rider would have come out alive." Curtin reached his men and took position in front of the regiment with Colonel Thomas Welsh, who was his brigade commander and also the former regimental commander of the 45th.[50]

As the 45th Pennsylvania pushed through the cornfield they could hear their skirmishers trading fire with the Georgians of the Phillips Legion, and "minie balls began to zip through the air" above the 45th. The regiment emerged from the corn, climbed a rail fence, and entered the woods. As they did so, Confederate soldiers were seen climbing the fence on the west side of the woods, "slowly falling back, firing as they retreated." The firing had alerted the Confederate gunners on Hill 1280, and one their batteries began shelling the woods. "These missiles made sad havoc among the tree-tops scattering limbs in all directions or plowing ugly furrows in the ground," recalled Private Beauge. Amid this frightening tempest of iron, branches, and bark, Welsh and Curtain stood "as cool as if on parade" and shouted to the men, "Steady, boys, keep cool!" They did "much to allay the nervousness of the men," thought Beauge. While the regiment re-formed its ranks after crossing the fence from the cornfield and endured the shelling, several men fired at some Confederates leaving the woods on the opposite side. It proved contagious, and soon nearly the entire regiment loosed a volley that chewed up trees in its path but did little more than provide a line of smoke for the Confederate gunners to target. Officers kept shouting "Cease firing" until the musket fire finally stopped. Beauge heard Andrew Bockus in his Company G—whom Beauge characterized as "an old hunter and a good shot"—grumble, "Don't care a damn! I saw a Johnny!"[51]

Welch and Curtin ordered the regiment to the fence at the western edge of the woods. "It didn't take long to get there," according to Beauge. Reaching it, the Federals discovered Drayton's men behind the wall along the Ridge Road and in the Old Sharpsburg Road, only about 80 yards away. The Confederates immediately opened a blaze of fire that cut through the Pennsylvanians' ranks. Men dropped by the dozens up and down the line, some dead instantly, others dying, and even more with ghastly wounds that left the victims helpless on the ground or tottering off to the rear in search of medical attention. One of the latter was John Boden, a 47-year-old private in Company B, who took a ball that fractured his left arm. Boden kept the arm, but he would never use it again. Among the dead was Henry Fenton, whom Beauge remembered as "a giant in strength and fearless as a lion, shot through the heart," and George Brewster, "good natured and portly," who died in the front rank.

Bondurant's battery joined the fray, opening fire with shell and canister that struck the 45th's line at an oblique angle. "Trees and fence rails were shivered to pieces by shells and grape and canister," wrote Beauge, but the regiment grimly found what cover it could and blazed back at Drayton's line. The Union regiment carried "Harpers Ferry" smoothbore muskets with buck and ball ammunition, consisting of a round ball and three buckshot, so that each discharge sent four projectiles downrange. Multiplied by over 600 men, the 45th were sending a veritable storm of lead at Drayton's line each minute. At anything over 100 yards the muskets were inaccurate. But at 80 yards they were deadly, and many of Drayton's men were hit as they rose up from behind the stone wall or the road embankment to fire. Those who were not still had their aim affected, for none of them could expose themselves long enough to sight accurately.[52]

The 45th were soon substantially reinforced by over 700 men of the 28th Ohio, who came up through the woods on their left and opened fire. The 28th evidently exhausted their ammunition quickly—they may have used up part of their supply skirmishing earlier in the day—and Colonel Hugh Ewing's 30th Ohio relieved them. In turn Ewing's Ohioans were reinforced by Lieutenant Colonel Joseph Gerhardt's 46th New York. "With hurrah and double-quick,"

Gerhardt's New Yorkers took their place on the firing line. The battle raged around Wise's little pasture and woods. Eugene Beauge attempted to describe it. "Reports of cannon, bursting shells, musketry blended together in one continuous, deafening roar. Clouds of white-blue smoke hung over the field like a thick fog, and the air was stifling with the smell of gunpowder." So dense did the smoke become that at times it lay like a smokescreen over the field. Colonel Ewing had to order his regiment to cease fire three times, to let the smoke disperse enough so that the men could see their targets. Ewing reported with pride that although his men "were falling at every moment," they obeyed the order "cheerfully."[53]

The Union fire, particularly from the 45th Pennsylvania, took a severe toll on the 50th Georgia, part of which was caught in the open as it attempted to change front to the south and file into the Old Sharpsburg Road. "We were exposed to the most dreadful rifle and musket fire from the enemy," reported Lieutenant William O. Fleming, whose Company F occupied the extreme left of the regiment. The embankment which provided cover for most of the 50th sloped down to become level with the road in the spot where part of Fleming's company took their place in the line. The first man to fall in the company was 18-year-old Isaac Trawick. He was in reach of Fleming's arms when a bullet struck his thigh and broke the bone. "Many others soon shared his fate," wrote Fleming, including the other company lieutenant, William Dekle, who was killed. Fleming's comrades "acted nobly, loading and firing as fast as they could," but as the Federals were largely concealed in the woods, he thought that very few of their bullets "struck a Yankee." Fleming estimated that they were engaged for fully 20 minutes when suddenly a large Union regiment appeared in their rear, only some 80 yards away. It was the 17th Michigan.[54]

Soon after the 45th Pennsylvania advanced and became engaged with Drayton across Wise's south pasture, Colonel Withington's 17th Michigan were ordered to advance through the woods north of Coffman's and attack. The men received the orders to advance "with shouts of enthusiasm," having endured some 30 minutes of terrifying shelling by the Confederate artillery. The shouts alerted Drayton's skirmishers, who were along the western edge of the woods and had taken cover behind fence rails they had piled together. The Confederates opened "a sharp fire" at the advancing mass of blue; the sound reminded Captain Gabriel Campbell of "a hailstorm on the roof." The 17th responded with "tremendous shouts" and surged on unfazed, sending the skirmishers scattering and emerged into a "hollow declivity" outside the woods, where they were met "by a terrific storm of bullets" from a stone wall along the west side of the hollow. These were either more of Drayton's skirmishers or part of one of his regiments. Again the Confederate fire failed to check the 17th, who responded with their own "storm" of bullets and rushed the wall with fixed bayonets. Drayton's men positioned here did not have the numbers to contest the wall, and they fled. But as the Union regiment crossed the wall into Wise's north pasture, Bondurant's guns opened fire and "fairly swept the open field." The iron hail drove the Michiganders, in a crowded group, to the left, or south, across the Old Sharpsburg Road and into the woods, where Welch's brigade were engaged. This, Captain Campbell recalled, brought the regiment "square in front of the double lines at the lane," by which he meant the Crest Road. But the 17th were also engaging the 50th and the 51st Georgia in the Old Sharpsburg Road. The discharge of musketry from the enemy line "was a constant blaze," but Campbell noted that the Confederates were unable to take aim and "fired over us." The Michigan lads also continued to endure the fire of Bondurant's gunners, aided by the batteries on Hill 1280, who furiously shelled the woods, dropping an "abundance of branches" with their ordnance but otherwise inflicting few casualties.[55]

After several minutes of this hellish baptism of fire the shelling ceased, probably because Bondurant ran out of ammunition and withdrew, while the guns on Hill 1280 shifted to engage Hooker's 1st Corps. Colonel Withington ordered his regiment out of the woods and back to Wise's north pasture, perhaps hoping that he might dislodge the Rebels in the Old Sharpsburg Road and outflank those along the Crest Road. By this stage of the fight the regiment must have been considerably disorganized and the companies mixed up, but bullets and shells had not dampened their enthusiasm. "Their one impulse was the press forward and win," recalled Captain Campbell. As the regiment re-formed in Wise's north pasture, they came under fire from one of Drayton's regiments posted along the Ridge Road, which may have been the Phillips Legion. The 17th returned the fire and began to edge forward across the field. Their line extended beyond the flank of the Confederates in the Ridge Road, and when it became apparent to the Rebels that they could not stop the yelling mass of Yankees bearing down on them, they decamped and withdrew fighting across the small field north of Wise's and into the woods on the western slope of the mountain.[56]

Having cleared out Drayton's left flank, the 17th gradually swung around to the left, toward the stone wall running along the northern bank of the Old Sharpsburg Road. The 50th and the 51st Georgia occupied this piece of the roadbed, but they were unaware of the 17th's approach until the Federals were only 80 yards away. Lieutenant Fleming, on the left of the 50th, saw the enemy approaching and heard their officers order them to charge. "They came toward us at the charge bayonet," he wrote, but the Federals stopped when they were only 20 to 30 yards away. Fleming ordered his men to fire at them. Some did, "with some effect," but to shoot effectively at the 17th meant exposure to the Federals in the woods around Wise's south pasture. Others sought escape from the trap closing on them and crowded west along the Old Sharpsburg Road. Withington's Wolverines poured fire into the backs of the Georgians at pointblank

A postwar image, looking from Wise's north pasture toward Wise's south pasture as well as his cabin at the intersection of the Ridge Road and Crest Road with the Old Sharpsburg Road. The 50th and the 51st Georgia took cover behind the stone wall lining the Sharpsburg Road and engaged Federal soldiers in the woods south and east of the south pasture. The 17th Michigan advanced across the left foreground against the Georgians in the Sharpsburg Road. Courtesy of the Marc and Beth Storch collection.

range. "The slaughter was horrible!" wrote one officer from the 50th Georgia. "When ordered to retreat I could scarcely extricate myself from the dead and wounded around me. A man could have walked from the head of our line to the foot on their bodies." The color-bearer of the 50th was George E. Fahm. Before the regiment's entry into Maryland, Colonel William Manning, the 50th's commander, had selected a color guard of "eight of the most soldierly members of the regiment" to defend Fahm and his flag. In the Old Sharpsburg Road, seven of those eight were killed and the eighth wounded. Fahm somehow emerged unscathed, although afterward he counted 32 bullet holes in the flag, flagstaff, his clothing, cap, and blanket. If he did not have faith before that day, he certainly did afterward. "Surely God was with me in that fearful struggle," he recalled.[57]

With the Old Sharpsburg Road and the Ridge Road cleared of Confederates, Withington's troops moved toward the cover of the stone wall on the north bank of the Old Sharpsburg Road, where they opened fire on the 3rd South Carolina Battalion in the Crest Road. The left of the 17th reached the wall first, and they delivered a raking fire on the stalwart Carolinians. As more of Withington's men came up they extended the regiment's line west, enabling part of the regiment to pour a close-range, devastating enfilading fire into the Confederates. James's South Carolinians were assailed from three directions now: Cox on the right flank, Welch in their front, and the 17th Michigan on their left. Like the Georgians in the Old Sharpsburg Road, the men fell like autumn leaves. One was a private with the common name of John Jones. A bullet struck his head about an inch and a half in front of his ear, "and passed out just back of the outer angle of the right eye, destroying the globe of the right and sight of the left eye." Somehow Jones survived the wound, but he was left a cripple. His regiment and what remained of the brigade, unsupported and outnumbered, now faced utter calamity.[58]

While Drayton's brigade fought on alone, the Federals fed fresh troops into the battle. Around 4:30 p.m. Sam Sturgis's 2nd Division arrived in the rear of the 1st Division, with Rodman's 3rd Division behind them. The detritus of battle greeted Sturgis's men. "We met ambulances full of wounded, and men on stretchers being borne off the field," Lieutenant Albert Pope, of the newly raised 35th Massachusetts, noted in his diary. James M. Stone of the 21st Massachusetts recalled that his brigade halted beside a field hospital, probably either at the Coffman or the Gross farm. There were already dozens of wounded soldiers there, and many more were being carried in from the fighting. Stone saw "a pile of arms, hands, legs, feet, etc., which had been amputated," lying near the operating tables—a sobering sight for men waiting to go into battle. When the order came down the line to move forward, Stone wrote, "every man in the company was glad."[59]

The sight of freshly wounded men is often discouraging to troops advancing to battle, but one of the wounded from the 17th Michigan stirred Sturgis's men. He was a drummer, described by James Stone as "a manly little fellow, a little chap not more than fourteen or fifteen years old," who had probably gone into combat despite orders to the contrary, since drummers inevitably worked the hospitals or bore stretchers in battle. A bullet had shattered his leg, and he was being carried down from the fighting on a litter. When someone in the 21st Massachusetts asked him how things were going up ahead, the plucky lad propped himself up on his stretcher and sang out, "The 17th is doing bully." When he passed the big and very raw 9th New Hampshire, he shouted to them, "Go in, boys! They can't stand the bayonet!"[60]

Sturgis allowed his division a brief halt to pile their knapsacks and then began to deploy it. Brigadier General Edward Ferrero's 2d Brigade, over 1,700 strong, formed a line stretching across the Old Sharpsburg Road, with their left resting in Coffman's cornfield. Brigadier General James Nagle's 1st Brigade mustered only two regiments, having left the 2d Maryland and the 6th New Hampshire in the valley to support the artillery there. But the two he had—the 9th New Hampshire and the 48th Pennsylvania—were big, counting a combined strength of over 1,200 men. Both of these regiments deployed in support of Ferrero's left, in Coffman's now thoroughly trampled cornfield. The massing of nearly 3,000 men in a relatively small area caught the attention of the observant Confederate gunners on Hill 1280, and some of their pieces commenced lobbing shells at this large target. Many of the Federals had never been under fire before, and they found the shelling unnerving. It "was nearly being a serious afair with our brigade," wrote Captain James Wren of the 48th Pennsylvania. Sturgis summoned his artillery, which was Captain George W. Durell's Battery D, Pennsylvania Light Artillery (six 10 lb. Parrott rifles). Durell brought his guns up the narrow Old Sharpsburg Road at a gallop and unlimbered them near Cook's abandoned guns. The well-drilled crews swiftly cleared for action and engaged the Southern gunners in what one of Durell's men recalled as "a regular artillery duel." The Confederates had the range of Durell's position by this time, and the Pennsylvanians found the enemy fire "for a time" to be "very heavy." Confederate shells severed two limbs of trees under which the battery was positioned. One of them came down on Durell and knocked him to the ground, but the captain recovered and continued to direct the fire of his guns. The duel continued on and off until sundown. In the opinion of a soldier in the 51st Pennsylvania, which supported Durell, "the rebels got the worst of it." Perhaps, but more importantly, Durell succeeded in his primary mission—to draw the fire from the Federals' infantry.[61]

In the woods around Wise's south pasture, Welch's and Scammon's men were running low on ammunition. The 45th Pennsylvania had entered the battle with 80 rounds per man, and the regiment had fired something over 40,000 rounds of ammunition. All that lead had done damage to Drayton's men, but the Georgians and the South Carolinians, plus Confederate artillery fire, had exacted a terrible toll from the brave Pennsylvanians. The regiment had 43 dead or mortally wounded, and 91 wounded. Only one other Union regiment, the 7th Wisconsin, lost more men at South Mountain. Willcox had the 100th Pennsylvania in reserve, and he ordered them forward to relieve the 45th. Soon after that movement was carried out, the 30th Ohio and the 46th New York exhausted their cartridges. To relieve them Willcox requested help from Sturgis, and the 2nd Division commander summoned Nagle's 9th New Hampshire and the 48th Pennsylvania. The 48th had some service under their belts, but the 9th was only 20 days from home. They numbered nearly 800 officers and men, but they were really no more than a crowd of enthusiastic citizens in uniform. On the approach march to the battlefield, the regiment halted after crossing Catoctin Creek to load their muskets for the first time. "Some have never before loaded a gun, few have ever loaded with a ball cartridge, and many must be shown the whole process," wrote Edmund Lord, the regimental historian. But like the men who composed the 17th Michigan, the Granite Staters were brave and, in their ignorance of the harshness of combat, eager to participate in the fighting they heard raging up ahead.[62]

The 48th Pennsylvania moved up on the left of the 100th Pennsylvania and commenced blazing away across Wise's Field at the stone wall in front. Fred Pettit, a farm boy in the 100th, wrote a description to his parents after the fight. "We were about as far from them [Confederates] as from our corn crib to the barn. They were in a lane behind a stone fence and we were in the edge of a woods with a clear lot between us. I fired 11 shots. Most of the boys fired 15 before the rebels ran." The 9th New Hampshire arrived in the rear of the 46th New York, moments before Drayton's line collapsed. The New Yorkers were nearly out of ammunition, and the Granite Staters had double-quicked from below Coffman's farm, "sweating, and straining every nerve and muscle under the heavy loads" through Coffman's cornfield and into the smoke-filled woods to relieve them. Stray bullets struck several men as the regiment moved up toward the firing line. Afterward, it was recalled that Corporal Hiram S. Lathe of Company F was the first man wounded, struck in the knee by a stray ball as the regiment filed out of the Old Sharpsburg Road to Coffman's farm. His brother paused to extract the ball with a jackknife, bind up the wound, and carry Hiram to a surgeon, and then dashed back and rejoined the regiment before it reached the firing line. Soon after, when the regiment advanced to the relief of the 46th, Joel S. Judkins of Company A, affectionately known to the men of his company as "Uncle Joel," was seriously wounded in the thigh. The company commander called out to Judkins's nephew, Charles M. Judkins, "Charlie, take care of Uncle Joel." Charlie assisted his uncle to a nearby barn, probably Coffman's, which had been converted into a hospital. When they arrived there Uncle Joel decided he would have no sympathizing nephew doting over him and told Charlie, "Go back and give it to 'em." The regimental historian recalled that Charlie "did his best to comply with Uncle Joel's parting injunction."[63]

There were others in the 9th that were hit as they made their way to the front line, but the excitement was so great among the green soldiers that "no one minds them; no one minds the bullets now, or even the larger missiles that go screaming over their heads." Everyone strained to get into the fight. As the 9th New Hampshire came up in the rear of the 46th, Drayton's line began to fray and some of his men "are seen to rise and quickly scamper away." Orders were shouted along the Union line to fire. But 46th New York was still between the Rebels and the New Englanders. Rifles spat fire and, reported Lieutenant Colonel Gerhardt of the 46th, his men "only saved themselves by throwing themselves down on the ground." No doubt the New Yorkers had some choice words for the rookies, but the Confederates were breaking for the rear. An instant after their volley, the 9th's commander, Colonel Enoch Fellows—later described as the "first man in the state, north of Concord, to volunteer" in the war, and a veteran officer—shouted "Fix bayonets." The regiment had saber bayonets, a frightening weapon, particularly when nearly 800 excited, shouting men are carrying them attached their muskets. Fellows called out to his men, "I want every man of the Ninth New Hampshire to follow me over that wall. Now, men of the Ninth, is the time to cover yourselves in glory—or disgrace! Any man that does not cross this wall I will report to his state." The regiment poured over the wall after their colonel, yelling at the top of their lungs. "There is little thought of keeping in regimental line," recalled Edward Lord. The men cast aside anything that slowed their pursuit of Drayton's fleeing Confederates. As Lord remembered, "Blanket-rolls are flung from the shoulders; knapsacks too, the few that have been kept. Even haversacks and canteens are given a toss . . . No thought of anything but to drive, to capture, or to kill."[64]

By the time the 9th New Hampshire started to pour into Wise's south pasture, organized resistance along Drayton's line had largely collapsed under the frontal and flanking fire, and the survivors sought to escape the death trap. The 3rd South Carolina Battalion and whoever stood with them in the Crest Road were the last to give way. They had fought with great courage and stubbornness, but the flanking fire of the 17th Michigan slaughtered them. Of 160 men in the battalion, 41 were killed, 46 wounded, and 44 missing or captured—an 82 percent loss. Among the dying was brave Lieutenant Colonel George James, shot through the breast and mortally wounded. Many were brought down when they exposed themselves to get away. In the Phillips Legion, Chaplain George Smith recalled that Gus Tomlinson came to him in tears, saying, "Parson, we've been whipped; the regiment is retreating." Smith looked about and concluded that they pulled out none to soon, "for we were surrounded on all sides but west." Lieutenant Fleming recorded that his 50th Georgia retreated "in as good order as circumstances would admit of," which could mean just about anything. Drayton's assistant adjutant general, Lieutenant J. Evans Edings, summarized the action succinctly in his diary: "We got decidedly the worst." To Elisha Bracken, of the 100th Pennsylvania, Drayton's brigade "had the advantage of position but we drove them and mowed them down by the hundred."[65]

Many other regiments joined the 9th New Hampshire in the general rush toward Fox's Gap. The 46th New York, despite a lack of ammunition, went in with the 9th, and on their right the 48th, the 100th, and the 45th Pennsylvania— the latter with empty guns and fixed bayonets—poured across Wise's pasture. So did the 17th Michigan, who streamed past the Old Sharpsburg Road, the Ridge Road, the Crest Road, and through Wise's farm. They pursued Drayton's men over the mountain summit and into the woods on the west slope of the mountain, scooping up numerous prisoners in their advance. Many of these Union soldiers had never before viewed a battlefield, and they found the scene around Wise's sobering. Hundreds of dead, dying, and wounded Georgians and South Carolinians were strewn along their fighting positions. "It was horrible beyond description," wrote one man in the 9th New Hampshire, "counted no less than forty behind perhaps five rods of stone wall, most all of them shot through the head or the breast, and of all the horrid looking objects ever seen I believe they were the worst." Elisha Bracken walked over the field and found "the rebels piled. On about 10 ft. square I counted 27 dead rebs." First Lieutenant

William Bolton, in the 51st Pennsylvania of Ferrero's brigade of Sturgis's division, which came up shortly after Drayton's defeat, passed what he estimated as 50 Confederate dead in the Old Sharpsburg Road. At the summit, along the Ridge Road and wood road, he found "at least one hundred and twenty-five dead rebels laying stretched acrossed each other along the stone wall."[66]

The Federals found William P. West, a 17-year-old private in Company C of the 51st Georgia, among the wounded of Drayton's brigade. He had been hit in the left knee joint, a very painful wound. Union soldiers evacuated him to a field hospital, where a surgeon inspected the wound and said his leg needed amputation. West pleaded with the surgeon not to perform the operation, as he was willing to take his chances. The surgeon obliged. In the days that followed surgeons performed two operations on West's knee and he began to improve, but then infection set in and the young Georgian's life ebbed away until he died on October 14, exactly one month after being wounded on South Mountain. At the postmortem a "broad abscess" extending from the knee joint to the groin was found.[67]

Drayton's losses were ghastly: 206 killed or mortally wounded, 227 wounded, and 210 missing and captured. This did not include those jarred loose from their units who did not rejoin them until after Antietam, or who were picked up by Federal patrols. When the brigade held muster again, on September 17, they were minus 747 men from the previous muster of September 11. All the regiments lost heavily, but the 50th and the 51st Georgia were largely destroyed, as was the 3rd South Carolina Battalion. That night the 50th could only collect 55 effectives out of 304. Drayton had not managed his brigade well. While pinned down in the Old Sharpsburg Road, Lieutenant Fleming asked his colonel, William Manning, "why we were left in such a place," and the colonel replied that "he could not understand it." And Captain W. G. Rice, in the 3rd South Carolina Battalion, thought Drayton's decision to send his regiment across Wise's south pasture in their initial aborted attack was nothing short of "suicidal." When that attack collapsed and fell back, Drayton seemed paralyzed and failed to maneuver his brigade to deflect the devastating flank attack by the 17th Michigan. Yet in Drayton's defense, with three other Confederate brigades in the vicinity he had a right to expect some support. He received none, and the Federals were able to mass their strength and crush his brigade.[68]

The cost of beating Drayton fell principally on the 45th Pennsylvania and 17th Michigan. Their dead and wounded were liberally sprinkled in the woods facing Wise's south pasture and across Wise's north pasture, where the 17th made their charge. Between the two they counted 53 killed and 213 wounded. The other five regiments of the 1st and 2nd Divisions that were engaged added 117 extra casualties, and the 28th Ohio and 30th Ohio contributed a handful more.[69]

Drayton's defeat left a rent in the Confederate line at Fox's Gap. The three Rebel brigades in Ripley's botched attack south of the Old Sharpsburg Road were in peril of being cut off, and the approach to the Mountain House and

Turner's Gap was left undefended. Only Rosser's tiny 5th Virginia Cavalry and Pelham's two guns guarded the Old Sharpsburg Road and the route to the western base of the mountain, leading to the Confederate rear. Pelham had placed his guns in an advantageous position where they could sweep a part of the road as it descended the western slope. When Union soldiers appeared on it in pursuit of Drayton's men, Pelham opened fire and drove them to cover. But Rosser's light force could not hope to hold out against an organized attack. Fortunately for them—and the Army of Northern Virginia—the Federals were content to lick their wounds and reorganize in Wise's north and south pastures.[70]

While Drayton fought alone at Fox's Gap, Ripley's counterattack came undone in the unfamiliar terrain and dense woods on the western slope of South Mountain before it even encountered a single Union soldier. Under Ripley's weak leadership all three brigades lost contact with one another soon after pushing off from the Old Sharpsburg Road, drifting apart and losing their direction. G. T. Anderson, on the left of the line, was the first to sense something was badly awry. He heard heavy firing to his left and rear, but his own brigade had not encountered any enemy soldiers. He had also lost contact with his skirmish line and with Ripley's brigade, which should have been on his right. Anderson prudently called a halt and sent out scouts to investigate the firing as well as to find the brigade's missing skirmish line and the whereabouts of Ripley's brigade.

While G. T. Anderson waited for the scouts to return, the sounds of heavy fighting continued to his left and rear, so he concluded that his brigade, which fronted south, was facing in the wrong direction. Anderson ordered a change of front to the left to face east toward the summit of Hill 1080, and then dispatched Colonel William J. Magill's 1st Georgia Regulars as skirmishers. When Magill had completed his deployment, Anderson ordered the advance, but before it covered any distance Lieutenant W. F. Shellman, the adjutant of the 8th Georgia who had been sent to investigate the firing, returned with the startling news that the right of Drayton's brigade had been turned and driven back, and that Federal troops had penetrated to Anderson's left and rear. As if to confirm Shellman's report, a few stray Union soldiers soon wandered into Anderson's line and were made prisoners. More bad news followed. A captain Anderson had sent to request orders from Ripley returned with news—"after a long search"— that Ripley's brigade was at least a quarter mile to Anderson's right and rear. And, apparently, Ripley had no orders for Anderson. Under the circumstances, continuing the attack with his small brigade was out of the question. Saving his command became Anderson's paramount concern. He had it move by the left flank, back toward the Old Sharpsburg Road. Luckily, the direction of their march took them west of Fox's Gap, so they avoided contact with Drayton's pursuers and were able to cross the Old Sharpsburg Road, re-forming their line facing east toward the gap.[71]

G. T. Anderson had done well in extricating his brigade from danger, for it might have shared Drayton's fate had Anderson pressed on or hesitated to act. It was now well past 5 p.m., perhaps as late as 5:30 p.m., and the sun was setting. The firing at Fox's Gap had subsided, but Anderson remained ignorant of the extent of Drayton's defeat. He ordered an advance in the hope that he might find the right flank of Drayton's brigade. This movement did not proceed far before the commander of his skirmish line "called my attention to the fact that the enemy were crossing the road in considerable force on my left flank." They were the 35th Massachusetts, a large regiment, sent to probe the woods west of the Ridge Road. To prevent being cut off on his left, Anderson ordered his brigade to move by the left "diagonally to the rear," or toward Turner's Gap and in the direction of the Ridge Road. As they scrambled over the rugged mountain terrain, the hearts of those at the front of the brigade leaped with joy and relief, for they encountered Brigadier General John B. Hood's division sweeping down from the direction of the Mountain House. Anderson reported to Hood for orders and was directed to hold his position and protect Hood's left flank. Between Hood's division and Anderson's brigade, there were now 2,500 Confederate soldiers between the Federals at Fox's Gap and Turner's Gap. The rent in the Confederate line had been repaired.[72]

The presence of Hood's division meant that the last of Longstreet's command had arrived on the mountain. Accompanied by Evans's independent brigade, they brought up the rear of the column from Hagerstown. Hood rode at the rear of the rear, for he remained under arrest. The division reached Boonsboro around 3 p.m., and they hurried through the village toward the sounds of conflict on the mountain. As they marched over a stone bridge spanning a small mountain creek that crossed the National Road about a quarter mile east of the village, they observed General Lee standing in a fence corner on the west bank of the creek, holding the reins of his horse. R. W. York of the 6th North Carolina recalled that Lee's "face, clothing and everything [were] covered with that peculiarly fine dust met with in those countries where the limestone is the principal rock." As they swept by Lee, Hood's men shouted, "Give us Hood!"[73] Both moved by the men's appeal and knowing Hood's fighting qualities, Lee sent Colonel Chilton to bring Hood to him. They returned soon and Hood dismounted to meet Lee. He later described their meeting:

> I . . . soon stood in his presence, when he said: "General, here I am just upon the eve of entering into battle, and with one of my best officers under arrest. If you will merely say that you regret this occurrence, I will release you and restore you to the command of your division." I replied, "I am unable to do so, since I cannot admit or see the justness of General Evans's demand for the ambulances my men have captured. Had I been ordered to turn them over for the general use of the Army, I would cheerfully have acquiesced." He again

urged me to make some declaration expressive of regret. I answered that I could not consistently do so. Then, in a voice betraying the feeling which warmed the heart of this noble and great warrior, he said, "Well, I will suspend your arrest till the impending battle is decided."[74]

Hood then galloped to the head of his division. A cheer rose from his men: "Hurrah for General Lee! Hurray for General Hood! Go to hell Evans!" It was probably around 4:30 p.m. when Hood's two brigades, preceded by Evans's brigade, completed the arduous climb to Turner's Gap. Hood found Longstreet there. The Georgian was not encouraged by what he had encountered on the mountain. "At first sight of the situation," Longstreet recalled, "as I rode up the mountain-side, it became evident that we were not in time or sufficient force to secure our holding at Turner's Gap, and a note was sent General Lee to prepare his mind for disappointment, and give time for arrangements for retreat." Stabilizing the very fluid situation was Longstreet's top priority. When Evans's one and Hood's two brigades arrived, a single brigade—Rodes's—was all that confronted Hooker's 1st Corps, which was then forming to attack north of the National Road. Longstreet sent Evans to Rodes's support. Longstreet also initially placed Hood north of the National Road, but kept him only a short distance from the Mountain House, where he could act as a general reserve.[75]

While Longstreet assessed the situation and posted Hood's infantry, D. H. Hill established a second line of defense with Hood's three divisional artillery batteries. Hill placed Captain James Reilly's Rowan (NC) Artillery near the Mountain House, probably so his guns could sweep the gap, with explicit orders "not to fire unless he [Hill] ordered it, or our troops were driven from the mountain and passed us." Captain W. K. Bachman's German (SC) Artillery were positioned nearby in a small open field south of the National Road, where their guns also covered the gap. The position of Captain H. R. Garden's Palmetto (SC) Artillery is uncertain, but they were near the other two batteries.[76] While the gun crews made their preparations, random enemy shells dropped into the gap. James Simons of Bachman's battery noticed Longstreet near his guns and found the general's quiet courage inspiring: "Just by our battery was Gen. Longstreet with whose appearance and behavior I was very much struck—He wore a pair of slippers and sat on his horse reading a paper, his countenance unmoved by the scene of terror which was being enacted all around him. A shrapnel burst in a tree just in front of him raining down its fragments all around him, but he did not even raise his eyes from his paper, but read on with an air of utter unconcern."[77]

Less than a half hour after Hood took position north of the National Road, news of the disaster to Drayton at Fox's Gap reached Hill and Longstreet. There were still three brigades at that gap, but Hill may have learned that Ripley's attack had gone awry and that no one in either Drayton's or G. T. Anderson's brigades knew where Ripley, his brigade, or G. B. Anderson's brigade were.

There were also alarming reports that the Federals who had crushed Drayton were threatening to penetrate from Fox's Gap to the western base of the mountain. Longstreet acted at once, sending Major J. W. Fairfax of his staff with orders for Hood to move to the right immediately, with his entire division. Fairfax accompanied Hood to the National Road and then turned to go. Hood, with no knowledge of the roads, terrain, or situation at Fox's Gap, asked the major if he was not supposed to guide Hood to where he was needed. "No," responded Fairfax, "I can only say, go to the right." Equipped with these ludicrously vague instructions, Hood marched his brigades south, in column and most likely following the Ridge Road toward Fox's Gap. They encountered bits and pieces of Drayton's regiments along the way, who related the fate of their brigade and may also have provided Hood with some idea of what to expect ahead. As the division neared Fox's Gap the cheers of Union soldiers were plainly heard, and it sounded as though the enemy were moving down the western slope of the mountain. Hood led his column off the Ridge Road and marched it obliquely to the right through heavy woods, "with a view," he explained, "to get as far as possible towards the left flank of the enemy before we came in contact." Progress was slow over the rugged terrain and thick vegetation. Instead of Yankees, Hood bumped into G. T. Anderson's brigade, which Hood ordered to deploy to protect the left of his division. Then, after forming his two brigades into line of battle, Hood directed his brigade commanders, Brigadier General Evander M. Law and Colonel William T. Wofford, to have their men fix bayonets. His instructions were simple. When the Federals approached within 75 to 100 yards, he wanted both brigades to charge, knowing that the woods and falling light would provide his men with the element of surprise. Hood guided his movement toward the intersection of Ridge Road and the Old Sharpsburg Road. At that moment, about 5:30 p.m., only a half hour before sunset, the woods west of this intersection were being probed by the 35th Massachusetts, and it seemed as though the smoldering battle of Fox's Gap would soon rage fiercely again.[78]

Drayton's defeat had fractured the Confederate line at Fox's Gap, although Hood was moving quickly to make repairs, yet the Federals' 9th Corps leadership on the mountain—Cox, Sturgis, and Willcox—were more concerned about consolidating the ground won at the gap than in seeing what additional damage they might inflict by aggressively exploiting their victory. Caution played a role, but so too did fatigue, low ammunition in some units, darkness, and a lack of accurate information about enemy strength. The fierce resistance by Drayton's men sapped the energy from Willcox's division and part of Cox's and, more importantly, emptied their cartridge boxes. While they fell to the rear to await ammunition resupply, Sturgis brought up his 2nd Brigade, led by Brigadier General Edward Ferrero, to join Nagle's brigade and assume the front line. Nagle re-formed the 9th New Hampshire and the 48th Pennsylvania in the southeast portion of Wise's south pasture and placed them behind the rail fence where

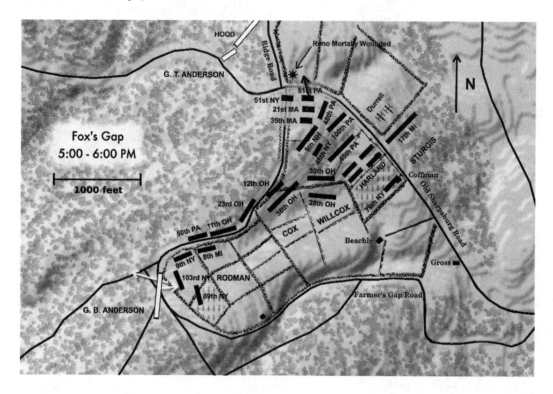

Fox's Gap
5:00 - 6:00 PM

1000 feet

the 45th Pennsylvania had fought Drayton. Ferrero's men marched up the Old Sharpsburg Road, past the scattered bodies from the 17th Michigan and piles of Confederate dead, and filed into Wise's south pasture. Here Ferrero deployed the 51st New York and the 51st Pennsylvania—both veterans of the North Carolina and Manassas campaigns—in his front line, facing Fox's Gap, with the veteran 21st Massachusetts and the rookie 35th Massachusetts behind them in column of regiments.[79]

To cover his front, Ferrero posted Captain James Wren's Company B, 48th Pennsylvania, and a detachment of the 51st New York as skirmishers. They set out "in splendid order" and passed beyond Wise's farmstead, entering the woods west of it. About 150 yards into the woods they bumped into a Confederate skirmish line, probably from G. T. Anderson's brigade. Both sides exchanged fire. The Confederates fired high, and Captain Wren wrote that some of their bullets dropped among the troops in Wise's pasture. "The old troops lay Quiet, Knowing the Contest was in the Line of skirmishers," recorded Wren, but the 9th New Hampshire "amagined that the battle had opened & the whole regiment opened fire & fired direct into my line of skirmishers in the frunt." The 9th's fire also ranged high and did no damage, but Wren could not know whether he was receiving friendly fire or if the enemy had penetrated his rear. He shouted for his company to rally to "right and left from center double-quick to the rear." The men moved rapidly, hoping to avoid a second volley. "If it was the enemy that was in our rear," wrote Wren, "better to be taken prisoner than be all Slaughtered & if it was our own troops, we would not receive thar 2nd volley." But the fire from the rear was quickly silenced, and either Willcox or Nagle ordered the 9th to redeploy in the rear of the 48th Pennsylvania, where the rookies were less likely to cause trouble.[80]

It was nearly sunset by the time the firing was stopped and the 9th New Hampshire moved to the rear line. Captain Wren and his company were ordered back out on the skirmish line with the New Yorkers from the 51st. General Ferrero wanted a reconnaissance of the woods northwest of the small field at the northern angle of Ridge Road and the Old Sharpsburg Road, and he selected the inexperienced 35th Massachusetts for this important duty, a decision that left the veterans of his brigade dumbfounded. Members of the 21st Massachusetts thought Ferrero's selection "was not only absurd but an outrage, on their first field, with their want of drill and utter fighting experience." But Colonel Edward A. Wild obeyed his orders and led his regiment of over 800 men across the Old Sharpsburg Road and the Ridge Road into what Second Lieutenant Albert A. Pope described as "the thickest woods I ever saw." The wide-eyed soldiers found the woods littered with the bodies of the dead and wounded from Drayton's brigade. They lay thickly enough that Lieutenant Pope noted that "we had to step over them and walk through rebel blood." A handful of prisoners were taken and sent to the rear.

The regiment advanced north, no doubt making a great deal of noise, until they arrived at a cart path. The path left the Ridge Road about 300 feet north of Fox's Gap and meandered northwest toward the National Road, which it intersected about 500 feet west of the Mountain House. Evidence that elements of Drayton's brigade had fled along the path could be seen in the cast-off blankets, haversacks, guns, and canteens that were found scattered along it. Wild ordered a halt here. He was more than 100 yards from his supports, the sun was setting, and with darkness descending quickly in the woods, Wild did not think it prudent to press any further with his recruits. Concluding that he had met the spirit of his orders, he commanded the regiment to fall back to the brigade. The decision surely saved his men from what would have been a disastrous encounter with Hood, whose division was rapidly sweeping through the forest toward Wild's position. Unaware of Hood's close proximity, the 35th fell back to Wise's south pasture and took position in the rear of the 21st Massachusetts.[81]

Shortly after the 35th returned from their reconnaissance, Jesse Reno rode up to Fox's Gap for a personal look at the situation. Reno had spent most of the afternoon at Burnside's headquarters, which offered a good but distant view of Fox's Gap. Around 4 p.m., when the battle with Drayton began to heat up, Reno ordered Rodman's division to march to the gap at the double-quick. This pace, according to Charles F. Johnson of the 9th New York, "of course was impracticable," for the terrain and the road's condition prohibited such rapid movements with any degree of order. Reno waited until Rodman had his division well underway, and then set out himself to visit the front. From the vantage point of Burnside's headquarters, Reno could not understand why his corps could not seize the ridge running north from Fox's Gap to Turner's Gap. "I must see to this in person," someone heard him comment to McClellan as he rode off.[82]

Reno rode in the rear of Rodman. Some stragglers from the fighting were encountered, and Reno's escort, Company G, 1st Maine Cavalry, drove them back up with their swords. But, recalled one of Rodman's men, "there were few shirkers . . . We occasionally met ambulances full of wounded and squads of prisoners marching to the rear." Cox met Rodman at the edge of the battle area and, as the senior officer on the ground, split Rodman's division. Cox remained worried about his left flank. His skirmishers had recently reported enemy activity beyond this flank, so he directed Rodman to send Colonel Harrison Fairchild's 1st Brigade to reinforce this end of the line. Colonel Edward Harland's 2nd Brigade was ordered to continue up the Old Sharpsburg Road and form in the rear of Willcox. Reno rode up after Cox had issued these orders. Cox recalled that it was "a little before sunset," which places the time at around 6 p.m. Reno inquired why the right of the corps could not seize the ridge running north toward Turner's Gap. Cox "explained that the ground there was very rough and rocky, a fortress in itself and evidently very strongly held." Cox could not have known that the reconnaissance by the 35th Massachusetts had discovered no enemy soldiers on the southern end of this ridge, and he certainly based his opinion on the substantial resistance they had thus far encountered in that direction.[83]

Reno listened to Cox's explanation and then rode forward, accompanied by two orderlies, or an orderly and a surgeon; there are differing accounts. He encountered Albert B. Cummel of the 30th Ohio, who was looking for water for his company, and asked him what troops were in front, pointing north of the Old Sharpsburg Road, in the direction of the Ridge Road, where some men could be seen moving in the woods beyond the road. Cummel replied that there were no Federal troops there, as all the Union troops were south of the Old Sharpsburg Road. Reno made no comment and continued on. He came upon Colonels Scammon and Ewing of Cox's division and congratulated them on the conduct of their troops. "Gentlemen, you have kept your brag," Reno said, referring to the incident where he had berated Cox's division for their lack of discipline, and both Scammon and Ewing had vigorously defended their men.[84]

Captain Gabriel Campbell of the 17th Michigan, with a small detachment of men from his regiment, was collecting those wounded who had fallen in the small field at the northeast corner of Ridge Road and the Old Sharpsburg Road, opposite the Wise farm. As Campbell and his men finished their work and were leaving the field, the captain observed some unarmed Confederates emerge from the woods and enter the field. He thought they were looking for dead and wounded, but then he realized that they were "pilfering from our dead as well as their own, and also gathering up arms, occasionally discharging a musket in the air." Campbell shouted at them for picking pockets and "firing at random," to which the Confederates "answered saucily." Since his men had already gone on, Campbell did not remain to banter with his enemies, but left the field through a gate at the southeast corner of the field. Here he encountered General Willcox, "who asked with some indignation what the firing meant." Campbell replied that the soldiers were Rebels who were pilfering the dead and collecting arms, and that he thought it was the beginning of a rally by them. Willcox made no response, but turned his horse and rode back toward his command at a rapid pace. Campbell continued east for perhaps 50 yards when he encountered Reno riding forward quietly with what Campbell remembered as four or five members of Reno's staff. The captain recalled that it "was now growing dusky" when he saw the corps' commander.[85]

After speaking with Scammon and Ewing, Reno continued toward Fox's Gap, riding past Ferrero's brigade in Wise's south pasture and arriving near the Wise farm. Besides Campbell, Reno encountered a few other Union soldiers in the area administering aid to the wounded, and some of them told the general that they had heard troops moving in the woods from which the 35th Massachusetts had just returned. Reno took the precaution of ordering Colonel John F. Hartranft, an excellent soldier commanding the 51st Pennsylvania, to take his regiment across the Old Sharpsburg Road and deploy it in Wise's north pasture, as well as to post a skirmish line in the woods. The Pennsylvanians moved out promptly. Captain Campbell looked back and could see Reno peering through his field glasses. Meanwhile, Companies A, F, D, I, and part of the color company, C, of the 51st had filed across the Old Sharpsburg Road into Wise's north field "when a most murderous fire of musketry was poured into them." The fire came from the woods beyond the Ridge Road. It was Hood's division. Thomas H. Parker of the 51st wrote, "It was now nearly or quite dark, but the men came to a 'front' as if by impulse, and although the enemy's position could not be exactly seen, yet their whereabouts could be near enough told by the blinding flashes of their guns." In the poor light neither side's fire was accurate, but one ball from Hood's initial volley found its mark in Reno's body. Robert West, a bugler in the 51st New York, was near him when Reno was struck. He stated that "the general reeled in his saddle, and was about to fall when some of his staff or orderlies rode up and supported him to the rear." Captain Campbell had seen that one of the horsemen in Reno's party was hit, and that some others had dismounted to catch one of the riders. When an orderly came back leading several horses, Campbell asked him what had happened. "Reno's shot," the soldier replied. A moment later a party approached Campbell, carrying the general in a blanket. The captain offered his assistance and took the middle of the blanket on the right side. No one, Campbell recalled, said a word as they hurried to the rear. At the woods east of Wise's south pasture they transferred Reno to a stretcher. General Willcox came up, and Campbell heard Reno say, "Willcox, I am killed. Shot by our own men." Reno's chief surgeon, Calvin Cutter, was with the party. He looked over at Willcox and shook his head, indicating that the wound was mortal. Under the circumstances of falling darkness and his unfamiliarity with the location of all his troops, Reno's confusion, and that of some of his staff, about who had shot Reno is understandable.[86]

The stretcher party moved on, passing Reno's West Point classmate, Sam Sturgis. Sturgis recalled that Reno spoke to him "in his characteristic cheerful manner—'Hallo, Sam, I'm dead!'" Reno's tone was so natural and firm that Sturgis did not believe his friend's wound was mortal, and he replied, "Oh no, General, not so bad as that, I hope." "Yes, yes," Reno repeated, "I'm dead—good bye!" The party continued on to the base of the mountain, where they stopped beneath a large oak tree that grew at the intersection of the Old Sharpsburg Road and a farm road that ran north to the National Road. Why they did not stop at one of the farms along the Old Sharpsburg Road is unknown, unless they were already too crowded with wounded. There was nothing Surgeon Cutter could do anyway, except stand with the other members of the general's staff in the falling dusk and watch Reno's life quickly ebb away. In a few minutes he was dead. Another surgeon who had joined the group, Thomas T. Ellis from Nagle's Brigade, recalled how "the officers of his staff exhibited the most sincere grief at his loss. Many wept over him, and vowed to avenge his death." There would be many tributes to the fallen Reno in the days to follow, but none that he would have appreciated more than Charles F. Walcott's, of the 21st Massachusetts: "There was not a member of the 21st Massachusetts who did not love him; he had always stood with his men in battle." Captain James Wren of the 48th Pennsylvania recorded a brief comment in his journal: "He was a brave & wise Genral & died without a murmur."[87]

While these tragic events were occurring, a spectacularly confusing firefight ensued between troops of Sturgis's and Hood's divisions that were scattered around Wise's fields. The first volley Hood's men delivered, in addition to hitting Reno, also wounded Colonel Edward A. Wild of the 35th Massachusetts, whose regiment occupied the support line of Ferrero's brigade. Perhaps unaware that the 51st Pennsylvania was between them and the enemy, Wild's men grabbed their weapons and began to shoot back in the direction from which they were receiving fire. Bullets zipped through the air, men cursed, and some shouted, "Cease firing!" Others were shouting "Fire! Fire!" Bedlam reigned supreme. The historian of the 51st Pennsylvania bitterly recalled how his comrades, caught between the two sets of troops firing in Wise's north field, were "getting shot down like dogs." Finally the men in the 51st New York threatened to shoot at the 35th Massachusetts unless they ceased firing. The threat worked, the 35th stopped, and Ferrero wisely pulled them back into the woods east of Wise's south field.[88]

With the fire in the rear ended, Colonel Hartranft pulled his entire regiment back from its exposed position in Wise's north field into the Old Sharpsburg Road, where they found cover behind the stone wall on its northern border. For a moment the shooting subsided. But then, on the left of the 51st Pennsylvania, the skirmishers of the 51st New York and the 48th Pennsylvania were driven in as Hood continued to probe the Federal line. "The rebel flag made its appearence," wrote Captain Wren, and the combat flared again. "The firing of the rebels was fast and furious," reported Colonel Henry Pleasants, commanding the 48th Pennsylvania, "but we returned it lively." This largely futile firefight kept up for some time, until Hood was satisfied that the enemy were present in strong force. He then ordered his men to keep up only a "desultory fire" to annoy the enemy. It was dark by this time, and since Ferrero's and Nagle's men could not see any targets, they stopped shooting, except to maintain a sputtering response to Hood's harassing fire.

The Federals had expended an enormous quantity of ammunition. The 48th Pennsylvania alone fired 60 rounds per man, or some 20,000 cartridges. Most of the lead, however, found its mark in trees. Wofford's brigade reported only 3 wounded and 2 missing. Law's brigade had 3 killed, 11 wounded, and 5 missing; but they lost a valuable officer in Lieutenant Colonel Owen K. McLemore, of the 4th Alabama. During the heaviest part of the musketry exchange, he climbed the stone fence along the Ridge Road that his men were using for cover. A bullet struck him in the shoulder, and he tumbled back into the wood road with a wound that proved mortal. Union losses were slightly heavier, due to their greater exposure and the damage done by the friendly fire incident. Nagle counted 34 wounded and 7 missing; and Ferrero had 10 dead, 83 wounded, and 23 missing, all of the latter category coming from the 35th Massachusetts. The 51st Pennsylvania remained in the Old Sharpsburg Road under off-and-on fire until 10 p.m., with 3 killed and 27 wounded. Apparently some of Hood's men were using metallic exploding bullets made of copper, for the 51st's historian complained that every one of the regiment's wounded was injured by this type of cartridge. "They exploded with a report about as loud as a pocket pistol," he wrote, "and could inflict a number of aggravating wounds" on a single soldier at each explosion. One cartridge wounded a private in 24 places.

But it was the inexperienced 35th Massachusetts who suffered the heaviest losses in Ferrero's brigade. While the veteran regiments of the brigade threw themselves on the ground when the firing started, the 35th stood up to fire, which resulted in 3 killed and 37 wounded, besides the 23 listed as missing. Among the wounded was a 21-year-old bonnet bleacher named Herbert L. Lincoln. A ball struck the right side of his head, inflicting what appeared to be no more than a nasty scalp wound. Lincoln was evacuated and eventually moved to Baltimore Hospital, where he seemed to make favorable progress. But, like so many Civil War wounds, the injury became infected, Lincoln grew delirious, and on October 9 he joined the ranks of South Mountain's dead.[89] Sturgis's men claimed victory in the firefight, but it was Hood who achieved real success. He intended nothing more than a probe to test enemy strength and to announce that the way to Turner's Gap was closed. He succeeded on both accounts with minimal loss.

While Sturgis and Hood sparred at Fox's Gap, a far bloodier drama played itself out on the extreme left flank of the Union line, where one element of Ripley's bungled counterattack finally struck a blow. Ripley's counterattack proceeded to come apart the moment it left the Old Sharpsburg Road and plunged into the dense woods on the western slope of the mountain. The consequences to Drayton's and G. T. Anderson's brigades have already been described. The other two brigades—Ripley's and G. B. Anderson's—pushed through what Major Stephen D. Thruston of the 3rd North Carolina described as "an almost impenetrable growth of ivy [mountain laurel]." Not surprisingly, the two brigades lost contact with one another. Ripley could hear the sounds of Drayton's fight at Fox's Gap, and optimistically hoped that he and G. B. Anderson would outflank the enemy opposing Drayton. But the terrain slowed their progress, and with no landmarks to guide their movement, the brigades drifted. About a half mile into the advance, Ripley's skirmish line—consisting of four companies of the 3rd North Carolina under Major Thruston, and supported by the other six companies of the 3rd under Colonel William L. De Rosset—reported "a heavy body of troops in his front" that were thought to be the enemy. De Rosset received the report from Thruston and sent it back to Ripley via his adjutant. Meanwhile, Thruston went forward in person to ascertain whether the troops in his front were friend or foe, and he discovered that they were G. B. Anderson's brigade, "deployed in a direction nearly perpendicular to my line." Having lost contact with Ripley, Anderson had come upon a mountain trail running roughly east–west and changed front to use the trail as a guide. So while Ripley was marching approximately south, G. B. Anderson, who had evidently been in front of Ripley during their advance across the mountain, now moved east and across the latter's front. Thruston sent word back about this new development and Ripley, thoroughly disoriented, made no effort to coordinate with Anderson. Instead, Ripley ordered his entire brigade to withdraw to the base of the mountain. While Ripley thus shrank from a fight, G. B. Anderson went looking for one. He was not long in finding it.[90]

To Lieutenant Colonel Ruffin of the 13th North Carolina, attached to Anderson's brigade, it was "difficult to conceive a more arduous march" than the movement across the woods thick with laurel on the slopes of Hill 1300. When they came upon the mountain trail described above, Anderson, who almost certainly was as disoriented as Ripley, but far more aggressive, decided to use the trail to lead his brigade to the enemy. While Ripley had badly mismanaged the attack and later neglected to coordinate with G. B. Anderson, Anderson himself won no laurels by not communicating or coordinating with Ripley. Using the trail, Anderson's brigade came within sight of the edge of the forest about sunset. Beyond the forest they could see a cornfield—the same one that earlier in the day the 23rd Ohio had charged through against the 23rd North Carolina. Captain E. A. Osborne of Company H, 4th North Carolina, who was commanding the brigade skirmish line, sent word back that his men could see a Union battery, supported by infantry, positioned in the corn. With more impetuosity than good sense, Anderson decided to pitch into this force, despite his ignorance of the ground and of enemy strength.[91]

The battery Captain Osborne observed was Captain Joseph C. Clark's Battery E, 4th U.S. Artillery, which had earlier been detached from Sturgis's division to strengthen the 9th Corps' left flank. The infantry supports were Colonel Harrison Fairchild's brigade of Rodman's division. Fairchild arrived only minutes before Anderson did, having been hurried to this sector by Cox, who had received a warning from Major Edward Overton, commanding the 50th Pennsylvania, that his skirmishers reported the enemy approaching in strength. The 9th New York, commanded by Lieutenant Colonel Edgar A. Kimball, led the brigade column. They formed, "as accurately as if preparing for dress parade," on the right of the stone wall the 23rd North Carolina had defended in the morning and in the rear of Clark's guns, facing west. The 103rd New York arrived next and formed on the left of the 9th, but at a right angle so that they faced south. Fairchild was placing his last regiment, the 89th New York, when, recalled David Thompson of the 9th New York, "a stir in front advised us of something unusual afoot, and the next moment the Confederates burst out of the woods and made a dash at the battery."[92]

"We were tired after climbing the mountain," recalled Benjamin B. Ross in the 4th North Carolina, "and could hardly clamor [sic] over the fence" that separated the woods from the cornfield. With barely enough energy to raise the rebel yell, the 2nd, the 4th, and the 13th North Carolina charged out of the woods and stomped through the corn toward Clark's guns. Someone wisely ordered Fairchild's New Yorkers to lie down, and a ragged volley delivered by Anderson's men passed harmlessly over their heads. Clark's gunners quickly thumped double charges of canister down the tubes of their 10 lb. Parrott rifles and then blasted the yelling Tarheels with a deadly hail of iron balls. The suddenness of the Confederate attack caused a moment of unsteadiness in the 103rd, but they held, and then the men "stood up to their work like good fellows." The 89th New York, caught in the act of deploying, halted, as if paralyzed with indecision about what to do. Major Edward Jardine of the 9th New York, in temporary command of the 89th, jumped on a stone wall and shouted at them: "Eighty-ninth New York, what in hell are you about? Continue the movement!" This steadied the men, and they rapidly moved on and began forming beside the 103rd.[93]

The height of the corn helped to conceal the New Yorkers, and their officers and sergeants managed to maintain discipline so that the men did not fire too soon and reveal their position. "After they fired the first round we rose up and let in to them," wrote Charles Croffut of the 89th. The North Carolinians were permitted to approach within 20 feet, near enough that one of Fairchild's men stated that he could see "the full intent of destruction on their faces." The deployed companies of the 89th let loose a volley of musketry that sucked the energy from the charge. The New Yorkers reloaded and kept firing as long as there was a rebel to been seen, while Clark's gunners had time to deliver more point-blank charges of double canister. "The whole earth in front of us seems torn up by grape and canister," wrote a member of the 2nd North Carolina. The flash and thunderclap of Clark's guns "seemed to frighten both parties into silence," recalled Charles F. Johnson of the 9th New York. Having discovered the enemy in far greater strength than they had imagined, Anderson's Tarheels turned and dashed helter-skelter back to the safety and cover of the woods from which they had charged only minutes before.[94]

"We retreated, each thinking that everybody had been killed but himself," noted Private Ross. The retreat degenerated into something of a stampede. Officers shouted "Halt" when the line reached the woods, "but everyone, men and officers too, were hurrying down the hill, and not one stopped until we reached the foot of the mountain," wrote Ross. Upwards of 70 dead and wounded North Carolinians littered the cornfield, the price of Anderson's rashness. Among the wounded was John McDaniels, a 25-year-old private in Company C, 2nd North Carolina. A minie ball, probably fired by someone in the 89th New York, struck him in the face and destroyed both his eyes. Besides the number of Confederate dead and wounded, the Federals collected 30 prisoners. The 89th New York absorbed the entire Union loss: 2 killed and 18 wounded. G. B. Anderson had accomplished nothing, save to prove he was more aggressive than Ripley.[95]

Following Anderson's repulse, David L. Thompson wandered out to look on the results. He left a memorable set of observations.

Before the sunlight faded, I walked over the narrow field. All around lay the Confederate dead—undersized men mostly, from the coast district of North Carolina, with sallow, hatchet faces, and clad in "butternut"—a color running all the way from a deep, coffee brown up to the whitish brown of ordinary dust. As I looked down on the poor, pinched faces, worn with marching and scant fare, all enmity died out. There was no "secession" in those rigid forms, nor in those fixed eyes staring blankly at the sky. Clearly it was not "their war." Some of our men primed their muskets from the cartridge-boxes of the dead. With this exception, each remained untouched as he had fallen. Darkness came on rapidly, and it grew very chilly. As little could be done in the way of burial, we unrolled the blankets of the dead, spread them over the bodies, and then sat down in lieu of supper, and listening to the firing, which was kept up on the right, persistently. By 9 o'clock this ceased entirely. Drawing our blankets over us, we went to sleep, lying upon our arms in line as we had stood, living Yankee and dead Confederate side by side, and indistinguishable.[96]

At Fox's Gap, cold air settled on the mountain, but fires were not permitted, due to the nearness of the enemy. A member of the 35th Massachusetts recalled that "the men were bathed in perspiration from the exertion and excitement of battle," which only accented the cold. Details were sent to the rear to bring up the blankets and coats the men had cast off before going into battle. But the rookies learned a lesson they would not forget: equipment left behind without a guard was fair game, and their blankets and coats were gone. So the men of the 35th "tried to keep warm walking about, and by turns endeavoring to catch a little sleep, lying four across four, until the welcome sun arose."[97]

Hood's division kept up its sporadic exchange of fire with Sturgis until 10 p.m., principally to cover their withdrawal back to Turner's Gap. The movement was executed so skillfully and quietly that only the most forward Union pickets suspected that the Confederates were leaving. The battle for Fox's Gap was over. Union losses in the seven brigades engaged there totaled 157 killed, 691 wounded, and 41 missing. The Confederates had also committed seven brigades, and they counted 259 killed, 466 wounded, and 418 missing. When the shooting stopped, the Federals held a slim advantage. They had undisputed possession of Hill 1080 and Hill 1300, but the long ridge running north to Turner's Gap remained in Confederate control, and Union troops were unable to penetrate to the Confederate rear along the Old Sharpsburg Road. But the Federals were well concentrated around Fox's Gap for a renewal of the fighting the next morning, while the Rebels, except for Hood, were dispersed. Tactically, the Federals beat the Confederates in each encounter, except for Hood, who managed his men well. Yet the Union army's performance was disappointing. After both Cox's hard-fought victory over Garland and the subsequent defeat of Drayton, they grew conservative and defensive minded, worrying more about where and when the Confederates would strike next than in keeping the enemy off balance by continuing to apply pressure. Cox had legitimate reasons to adopt a defensive posture in the morning, but there was less excuse for the failure to exploit Drayton's defeat later in the day.

The Confederates had little to pride themselves on, either. Garland fought ably before his fall, and Hood handled his division skillfully, but otherwise their tactical management of the battle was awful. Three brigades—Garland's, Drayton's, and G. B. Anderson's—were all beaten in detail at different points and times. The former two brigades suffered so severely that their effectiveness was largely destroyed, as would be evident three days later at Antietam. Neither of them needed to have been routed as they were. If G. B. Anderson had supported Garland more effectively, or if Ripley had managed to keep his four brigades in mutual support of one another, the heavy losses both Garland's and Drayton's brigades sustained might have been avoided.

When night fell over the living and the dead on the mountain, the living lay on their arms, ready for action at a moment's notice. The darkness was complete. There were no fires to cheer or warm the men. The damp cold aggravated the suffering of the wounded and caused the able-bodied to clutch their blankets closely—if they were fortunate enough to have them. No fires meant no food, save what a man might have in his haversack. It was, remembered Thomas Parker of the 51st Pennsylvania, a "wretched, supperless" night.[98]

11

The First Corps Attacks

"It looked like a task to storm"

It took some prodding to propel Hooker's 1st Corps into motion to execute the right hook of Burnside's double envelopment. Hooker ignored three separate commands from the Right Wing commander to put his corps into motion. Perhaps at Burnside's request, at 1 p.m. McClellan had Colonel George Ruggles, an aide-de-camp on his staff, issue orders for Hooker to move a division north of the main road and support the movement with his entire corps. Ruggles added an odd statement to the orders, "General McClellan desires you to comply with this request," as if there existed the possibility that Hooker might not do so. Burnside personally followed the bearer of these orders to see that Hooker carried them out. When he arrived Hooker was not about and Meade's division was still sprawled along the west bank of Catoctin Creek with no orders to march. By this time it was 2 p.m., and a precious hour had been lost. Burnside ordered Meade to march at once. Hooker later claimed that he had been conducting a reconnaissance, which was probably true, but it does not excuse him from being out of communication with his superiors at a critical time. Hooker rode up as Burnside was giving Meade his orders and, in a more deferential mood, discussed with Meade and Burnside the best route to follow to reach the enemy's flank. They decided that it was best to march west along the National Road to the tiny village of Bolivar, then turn north on the Mount Tabor Road and follow it until they were on the enemy flank.[1]

The coming fight would be 47-year-old Brigadier General George G. Meade's first as a division commander. He had assumed command by seniority when Major General John F. Reynolds, over the objections of McClellan and Hooker, had been ordered to Harrisburg to bring order to Pennsylvania's chaotic effort to organize a defense against a Confederate invasion. All the noise made over Reynolds's detachment offended Meade. "I considered it a reflection on my competency to command the division," he wrote to his wife. Although not an overtly ambitious man, Meade knew his business and was prideful. He had spent much of his adult life as a soldier, and served in the elite topographical engineers during the war with Mexico, service that gave him a good eye for and appreciation of terrain. Pennsylvania Governor Andrew Curtin gave Meade a brigade in the newly formed Pennsylvania Reserves early in the war, and Meade led it with skill and courage in the bloody battles of the Peninsula. He displayed evidence of his toughness when he took an ugly wound at Glendale yet returned to lead his brigade at Second Manassas before the injury had completely healed. Meade also possessed a volatile temper that did not tolerate incompetence or coward-ice. It might be said that his men and officers had confidence in him, but did not love him. On the Peninsula he had proven to be an uncommonly stubborn fighter on the defensive. Now he would demonstrate the same qualities on the attack.[2]

The Pennsylvania Reserves division that formed under Meade's eye was a unique organization in the army. Their name, Pennsylvania Reserves, origi-nated when that state, in answer to Lincoln's first call for troops in April 1861, raised more regiments than the Federal government could equip. Simon Cam-eron, then secretary of war, was a political enemy of Governor Andrew Curtin. In a largely politically motivated move intended to embarrass Curtin, Cameron refused to accept any excess militia regiments beyond what the government could properly outfit. But Curtin outmaneuvered his nemesis. The governor organized and equipped 13 regiments at state expense, dubbed them the Penn-sylvania Reserves, and provided them for use by the Federal government. The division participated in some of the heaviest fighting on the Peninsula, incur-ring 3,385 casualties. They added 611 more at Second Manassas. Such significant losses could not but impair the combat readiness of the organization. By the be-ginning of the Maryland Campaign, Meade wrote to his wife that the division "was pretty well used up, and ought, strictly speaking, to be withdrawn, reorga-nized, filled up with recruits, and put in efficient condition." Out an original complement of about 13,000 men, approximately only 4,000 effectives remained in the three brigades that assembled at the base of South Mountain. They would demonstrate in the coming fight that although reduced in numbers, their mo-rale, pluck, and determination remained undaunted.[3]

Meade promptly had his brigades formed, and they were soon tramping up the National Road, followed by the 1st Division. This division's commander, Brigadier General Rufus King, suffered from epilepsy, and field service had nearly incapacitated him. He had requested to be relieved and reassigned, and only minutes before the division received its orders to march, King's hoped-for orders reached him. He immediately turned command over to his senior briga-dier, Brigadier General John P. Hatch, a West Pointer and 17-year army veteran, who had been acting in the capacity of division commander since the latter stages of the Second Manassas Campaign, due to King's illness. King departed, his days of active field service ended, while Hatch and his four brigades moved off behind Meade. As Hatch's brigade's cleared the road, the men of Ricketts's 2nd Division rose up from their resting place alongside the National Road and filed onto the turnpike. There were probably about 13,700 men and 9 batteries of artillery in a moving column that stretched out for at least 3 miles.[4]

A 2-mile march brought Meade's Pennsylvania Reserves to Bolivar, where they turned onto the Mount Tabor Road. A march of nearly a mile along this "very rough and stony" road brought the division to the Mount Tabor church. Here, Meade moved his 1st and 2nd brigades into the fields west of the road, formed in column of regiments, and sent Captain James H. Cooper's Battery B, 1st Pennsylvania Light Artillery (four 3-inch rifles) to a nearby "high hill," which was probably Hill 727, located northeast of the house of worship. Meade initially retained his 3rd Brigade east of the Mount Tabor Road as Cooper's support.[5]

Meade's movements were closely observed by the artillerymen of Cutts's battalion on Hill 1280. When they saw the dark, dense masses of Federals beginning to form up below them, they opened fire. Evan M. Woodward in the 3rd Reserves noticed a gaggle of civilians who had tagged along with the column "to see the fun." When the first of Cutts's shells came shrieking down the mountain, the iron did no damage, but the spectacle-seeking country folk were terrified. Woodward and his comrades watched the civilians' plight with great amusement. "The children laid down upon the ground," recalled Woodward, "the women shrieked, and the men displayed wondrous agility in leaping the fences."[6]

In camp Captain Cooper's battery was notorious for its loose discipline and casual attitude toward military protocol. But in battle Cooper ran a tight ship, and his men performed superbly. They now swiftly moved into battery, unlimbered, and commenced firing shrapnel at some Confederate infantry they observed on the mountain. Cutts's guns had ceased fire after their initial salvo, and they did not respond now. While Cooper shelled the mountain, Hooker studied the ground that rose in front of his corps. To Angelo Crapsey, a rifleman in the 13th Reserves, "it looked like a task to storm." Three rugged hills—Hill 1280, Hill 1500, and Hill 1360 (from south to north)—rose steeply from the valley floor, presenting an irregularly shaped crescent front to Hooker. A deep east–west ravine cut the interior of this crescent between Hill 1360 and Hill 1280. Two roads that branched off from the Mount Tabor Road about a quarter mile apart from one another ran along each side of the ravine. The Dahlgren Road, as it is known today, hugged the base of Hill 1280 for perhaps a third of a mile before turning southwest and rapidly rising to the saddle between Hill 1280 and Hill 1500. Near the summit of Hill 1280 the road bent 90 degrees west and ambled on to the National Road. The Frosttown Road followed the steeper north side of the ravine, roughly paralleling the Dahlgren Road for about a third of a mile, then turned slightly northwest and climbed sharply until it intersected with the Zittlestown Road, which was west of Hill 1360's summit. This hilltop, most of the ravine, and the summit and northeastern slopes of Hill 1280 were under cultivation; they consisted of meadows, orchards, and cornfields, neatly set apart by the ever-present stone walls. There were some other small fields scattered about, but the rest of the ground in Hooker's front was heavily wooded, rugged, and steep. The prize—and key terrain—was Hill 1500. Its

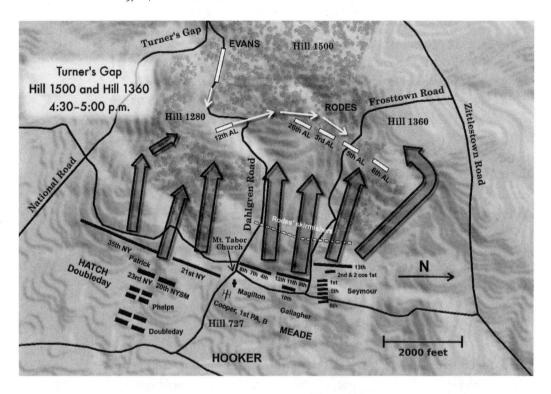

Turner's Gap

EVANS   Hill 1500

**Turner's Gap
Hill 1500 and Hill 1360
4:30–5:00 p.m.**

Hill 1280

RODES   Frosttown Road

Hill 1360

12th AL   26th AL 3rd AL   5th AL

6th AL

National Road   Dahlgren Road

Rodes' skirmishers

Mt. Tabor
Church

35th NY
Patrick

21st NY   8th 7th 4th

12th 11th 9th   13th
2nd & 2 cos 1st

HATCH
Doubleday   23rd NY 20th NYSM   1st
5th   Seymour
6th

Phelps   10th   Gallagher

Cooper, 1st PA, B   Magilton

Doubleday   Hill 727   **MEADE**

HOOKER   N

2000 feet

Zittlestown Road

possession by the Federals would render the Confederate position at Turner's
Gap untenable.[7]

Hooker observed "a strong infantry force" and some artillery arrayed across
the gorge and on Hill 1280, but he believed that they could be outflanked. It
would be an infantry show, as the nature of the ground prevented effective artillery support. Hooker planned to attack with Hatch's and Meade's divisions
up front, supported by Ricketts's. Meade's force would form the right of the 1st
Corps' assault, and to it fell the task of turning the enemy flank. Hooker ordered
the Pennsylvanian to throw out a strong skirmish line to feel for the enemy and,
at the same time, extend the right of his division to north of the Frosttown
Road. To guard the corps' flank and rear from any surprises the Confederates
might have lurking to the north, Hooker detached Meade's 3rd Reserves, under
Lt. Colonel John Clark, and sent them to a point three-quarters of a mile north
of the Mount Tabor church, on the Old Hagerstown Road. Hatch reported to
Hooker at the Mount Tabor church shortly before 4 p.m.; he was ordered to
form his division on Meade's left, deploy a strong skirmish line, and prepare
to assault Hill 1280.[8]

Meade probably first learned of the existence of the Frosttown Road during
the reconnaissance that preceded the deployment of his division. It appeared
to provide an ideal guide for the right of his division, and he ordered Brigadier
General Truman Seymour, his 1st Brigade commander, to form his brigade to

the right (north) of this road, push forward, and "feel for the enemy." According to John Burnett, a member of the 4th Reserves, Meade had "great faith" in Seymour's abilities, but the rank and file of the division "had no confidence in Gen. T. Seymour." Nonetheless, Meade had given Seymour the crucial position in the advance.[9]

Seymour ordered Colonel Hugh W. McNeil, commanding the 13th Reserves, popularly known as the Bucktails, to deploy skirmishers across the brigade front. Each man in this unique regiment wore the tail of a white-tailed deer fastened to his hat. They were armed with Sharps rifles and were crack shots with them, both of which made the Bucktails well suited for skirmish duty. McNeil placed six of his companies in skirmish order and formed his remaining four as a reserve. In the rear of McNeil's reserve companies, Seymour stacked the balance of his brigade in column of regiments, a formation where each regiment formed in line of battle, situated closely behind one another. The 2nd Reserves, reinforced with Companies A, G, and F of the 1st Reserves, formed the first line, with the 1st, the 5th, and the 6th Reserves behind them.[10]

Colonel Thomas F. Gallagher's 3rd Brigade, numbering approximately 1,110 effectives, formed south of the Frosttown Road on Seymour's left. Gallagher put the 9th, the 11th, and the 12th Reserves in line abreast (from right to left), and 10th Reserves behind them as a reserve. Meade placed his 2nd Brigade on Gallagher's left. This had been Meade's brigade before his elevation to division command, and it was now led by the senior colonel, Albert L. Magilton, a "great chum" of Meade's. The "little" colonel was a West Pointer and soldier of 18 years' service, who possessed such strong knowledge of tactics that Meade and Reynolds "were always seeking his advice." Magilton had only three of his four regiments, however, since the 3rd Reserves had been detached. To extend his front from Gallagher's left to the Dahlgren Road, Magilton was obliged to put all three regiments—the 4th, the 7th, and the 8th Reserves (from right to left)—in line abreast.[11]

Hatch's 1st Division formed for its assault on Hill 1280 south of the Dahlgren Road. Forty-year-old Brigadier General John P. Hatch may have seen the coming action as an opportunity to erase the mark on his record put there by John Pope. During the Second Manassas Campaign, Hatch had commanded one of Pope's cavalry brigades. Pope thought Hatch's performance in the early stages of the campaign poor enough that Pope relieved Hatch and reassigned him to command of an infantry brigade. Hatch did nothing in this post to impress one of his brigade commanders, the ill-humored Brigadier General Marsena Patrick, who confided to his diary only the day before South Mountain that "I am disgusted with Hatch." But Patrick grumbled about nearly everyone. Hatch was not an aggressive fighter, in the mold of a George Meade, but he was a competent soldier and had performed credibly while in temporary command of the division at Second Manassas, when Brigadier General Rufus King had fallen ill.[12]

Hatch had only three of his four brigades on hand, as Burnside had detached Hatch's largest and best brigade, that of Brigadier General John Gibbon, to use it in a demonstration on the Confederate center at Turner's Gap. This should have left Hatch with about 3,200 effectives, but it appears that he took considerably less than this into the fight. The division had suffered 1,787 battle casualties and hundreds of nonbattle losses from sickness and straggling in the Manassas Campaign. Such severe losses inevitably impair discipline and efficiency, but the morale of the division received a needed boost that very morning when they marched through Frederick. Lieutenant Sam Healy, in the 56th Pennsylvania of Abner Doubleday's brigade, wrote in his journal about how the streets of the city were festooned with the Stars and Stripes and were "thronged with ladies," all of whom (that Healy saw) "wore a joyous look and welcomed every soldier, worn out and ragged though we were." This reception, wrote Healy, "filled every breast with emotion, the weight upon those backs grew light and the step more active. We could all see now something to fight for." They departed the city with new confidence, "every man anxious to meet the rebs and felt capable of thrashing half a dozen." Yet it was ardor tinged with realism. "The eager enthusiasm of the novice had been toned down by experience," noted Captain George F. Noyes of Doubleday's staff. "The terrible scenes we had witnessed had left an ineffaceable impression; nothing but a sense of duty, the innate pride of man, and the hope that through this bloody lane might come peace and safety to the country, kept us to our duty." As they now gazed upward at the imposing mass of Hill 1280, "very few of us were burning with eagerness to charge up those heights before us," admitted Noyes, yet "there is no sign of shrinking, nor will there be, with, of course, some exceptions, when the hour for storming that height shall come."[13]

Due to the reduced strength of his division and the formidable nature of the position to be assaulted, Hatch chose a formation with depth rather than width, deploying in column of brigades with the front covered by a strong skirmish line. Two regiments of Brigadier General Marsena Patrick's brigade drew the skirmish assignment. Colonel William F. Rogers and his 21st New York were ordered to connect with Meade's division in the gorge, and the 35th New York, commanded by Colonel Newton B. Lord, extended the line toward the National Road. Patrick followed with the balance of his brigade, the 23rd New York and the 20th New York State Militia, in close support. Colonel Walter Phelps Jr.'s 1st Brigade followed 200 paces in Patrick's rear, with the regiments formed in column of division. Phelps's regiments were significantly understrength; the entire brigade mustered no more than 900 effectives, and probably less. Following Phelps in the same formation and at the same distance marched Brigadier General Abner Doubleday's 2nd Brigade, with about 1,000 officers and men.[14]

Hooker held Ricketts's 2nd Division near the Mount Tabor church, where it might support either wing of the attack. This division had also suffered heavily at Manassas, sustaining over 1,600 casualties, and its three brigades probably contained no more than 3,500 effectives. Hooker carried out his deployment with great deliberation, probably sensing that a piecemeal attack over such difficult terrain might easily be parried by the Confederates, but the order to advance was not given until between 4:30 and 5 p.m. The Confederates used every minute of this time to make their preparations to meet the Union assault.[15]

D. H. Hill initially had only Rodes's brigade of 1,350 Alabamians and the batteries of Cutts's battalion to confront Hooker's powerful force. The lean, ruggedly handsome, 31-year-old Rodes received his training at the Virginia Military Institute and had already displayed the skills of a superb soldier on the Peninsula battlefields. In the engagements there his brigade had suffered a staggering 1,669 casualties, but they emerged with unquestioned confidence in Rodes. Wrote one soldier of their commander, "he has no fear." After arriving on the mountain, Rodes had initially supported Cutts's batteries on Hill 1280. His brigade remained there for three-quarters of an hour, enduring occasional overshots from the enemy batteries firing at Cutts's guns. Rodes ordered Colonel B. B. Gayle, commanding the 12th Alabama, to post a skirmish line to the left and front to cover his flank and the approach to Hill 1280 through the gorge. The 12th apparently rotated command of skirmish details among its officers, for their very precise and exacting adjutant consulted his roster of regimental officers to determine whose turn it was. But Gayle dispensed with this formality by calling out "detail Lieutenant Park to command the skirmishers." Lieutenant Robert E. Park of Company F was a cool-headed leader, perfect for the dangers of advance skirmish duty. When he heard Gayle call out his name he reported at once for orders. They were simple: advance to the base of the mountain "and keep the enemy back as long as possible." Park had 40 men, 4 from each of the 10 companies. From his description of the terrain, Park led his party over the northern slope of Hill 1280 and posted them fronting Hooker's forming brigades, with his left resting near the gorge. "On our way down we could see the enemy, in the valley below, advancing, preceded by their dense line of skirmishers." Park dispersed his men "behind trees, rocks and bushes and cautioned them to aim well before firing.[16]

From the length of Hooker's line, it was apparent to D. H. Hill that they would easily outflank Hill 1280 and seize Hill 1360, which provided access to Hill 1500. To prevent this, Hill ordered Rodes to move his brigade across the gorge and occupy Hill 1360. Apparently neither Hill nor Rodes knew of the Zittlestown Road, for Rodes discovered it when he arrived on the hill. He immediately realized the importance of preventing the enemy from gaining possession of the road and, along with it, the Confederate rear. But to cover the road as well as defend Hill 1360, Rodes was obliged to leave a three-quarter-mile gap between his right flank and the National Road. He informed D. H. Hill of this and asked for instructions. Hill had no one to fill the space, having sent Drayton and G. T. Anderson to Fox's Gap. He anticipated more reinforcements from Longstreet, but until they arrived Hill ordered Rodes to send the 12th Alabama back to support Cutts's guns.[17]

To keep the enemy from the Zittlestown Road, it was necessary to bar their way up Hill 1360 along the Frosttown Road, and this is what Rodes proceeded to do with his four remaining regiments. The 26th Alabama held down the right of the line, with its right flank resting in the gorge. The 3rd, the 5th, and the 6th Alabama (from right to left) continued the line up the southern slope of Hill 1360, but their line did not reach quite as far as its summit. Each regiment posted skirmishers, and these extended the frontage of Lieutenant Park's small detail. The open summit of Hill 1360 offered ideal fields of fire for artillery, and Rodes sent an urgent request for some. From the enemy deployment it was evident to Rodes that they intended to assault both Hill 1360 and Hill 1280 and force their way up the gorge in between. Rodes estimated that the Union troops arrayed directly opposite his four regiments consisted of a full division (it was Meade's), which extended beyond Rodes's left flank by what he estimated to be at least a half mile. There was no real possibility of stopping such a force, but Rodes hoped that by dint of hard fighting he might check them long enough for reinforcements to come to his aid.[18]

Hooker's assault finally stepped off between 4:30 and 5 p.m. There were six brigades—with some 7,000 officers and men—in the blue waves that rolled forward. D. H. Hill watched their approach. He thought the spectacle of bluecoat soldiers "grand and sublime, but the elements of the pretty and the picturesque did not enter into it." Hatch's division, in its denser formation, presented an inviting target for artillery, and Hill shifted some of Cutts's guns around so they could shell it. The gunners fired furiously, but Hill observed in disgust that their accuracy was "the worst I ever witnessed" and "as harmless as blank-cartridge salutes in honor of a militia general." Hill desperately needed infantry if there was any chance to stop Hooker. Only minutes before Hooker's general advance began, Colonel P. F. Stevens reached the mountain summit at the head of Brigadier General Nathan Evans's South Carolina brigade, followed soon after by Hood's division. The arrival of these reinforcements relieved the 12th Alabama from duty supporting Cutts's artillery, and it hurried off to join its brigade. Hill ordered Stevens to reinforce Rodes, and he retained Hood to support the artillery and hold Hill 1280. The disaster to Drayton and the crisis at Fox's Gap, however, forced Hill to shift Hood to that point, leaving Hill 1280 without infantry.[19]

Brigadier General Nathan Evans arrived on the mountain very soon after Hood departed for Fox's Gap, and Evans proceeded to interfere with D. H. Hill's arrangements. Finding that Hood, whom Evans still considered part of his "command," had been sent to Fox's Gap, Evans decided to exert control over his own brigade, which, for unexplained reasons, he had not accompanied to the

mountain. Evans sent his assistant adjutant general, Captain A. L. Evans, galloping to overtake Colonel Stevens and order him to halt. The captain caught up
with Stevens after the latter had covered nearly a half mile toward Rodes's position. Stevens halted, but a courier from Rodes arrived nearly simultaneously
with Captain Evans, the former with an urgent request for Stevens to hurry forward. Against his better judgment the colonel instead obeyed Evans's orders.
He sent word to Rodes explaining why he had halted and dispatched a courier
to Evans requesting further instructions. While Stevens waited for a response,
Meade's division came swarming up through and along the sides of the gorge,
threatening Stevens's right flank. There was now no time to choose the most
advantageous defensive position, and Stevens hastily formed his brigade to face
the approaching onslaught. On paper it was a brigade, but in reality Stevens commanded a good-sized regiment. The whole organization contained no more
than 550 officers and men. Stevens sent the Holcombe Legion forward as skirmishers to engage the enemy advance and formed the balance of his brigade
along the "brow of the mountain side," with his left nearly joining the 26th Alabama on Rodes's right. North of the Dahlgren Road and along the slope of Hill
1500 he placed the 23rd, the 22nd, and the 18th South Carolina (from left to right).
The 17th South Carolina, under Colonel F. W. McMaster, formed south of the
road, where it anchored the brigade's right. McMaster counted his men as they
entered the fight; he had 99 muskets in the ranks. The crackle of rifles and muskets from below announced that the storm had already broken on Rodes's front
and would reach Stevens soon.[20]

The skirmish line of Colonel Hugh McNeil's Bucktails nearly covered the
entire front of Meade's division. McNeil's orders were simple: "feel the enemy."
When all was ready, he had his bugler blow the signal "Forward, march." The men
moved cautiously, carefully, scanning the rugged terrain for the enemy. "All up
the mountain side rocks and boulders abound, and here and there, stone walls,"
recorded the regimental historian. "When to these features are added heavily
wooded portions and frequent depressions in the ground itself, some idea may
be gathered of the difficulty of the task laid upon the division." To Frank Holsinger of the 8th Reserves, "so irregular was the terrain, indeed, that to keep anything like a line was next to impossible." In order to conceal themselves, Rodes's
skirmishers took full advantage of the broken terrain and the few farm buildings in Meade's path. As Lieutenant Park recalled, here they awaited "with beating hearts the sure and steady approach" of the Pennsylvanians. "Hardly had the
sound of the bugle" signaling the 13th's advance died away when McNeil's men
came under fire. Then a "storm of shell" from the guns of Cutts's battalion— or
perhaps Captain T. H. Carter's King William (Virginia) Artillery—blasted the
Bucktails' line. This was no harmless fireworks display. The shorter range meant
increased effectiveness, and this time there were casualties. "The exposure was

great, and numbers fell under the accurate fire of the shell from these guns," reported General Seymour. In Company I of McNeil's regiment a single shell wounded three men, two of them mortally.[21]

Rodes's skirmishers put up dogged resistance. Lieutenant Park estimated that his detachment had shot "at least thirty men," but it is likely that he counted those who dove for cover among those who were really hit. McNeil committed his four reserve companies to the skirmish line, as well as Companies A and B of the 1st Reserves and the right wing of the 2nd Reserves, consisting of five companies. The reinforcements provided the needed numbers to get things moving; the Bucktails rose from their cover and "with a cheer" moved forward firing. "Woe to the rebel who showed himself," wrote Captain McGee. One of those rebels was Otis Smith, a skirmisher from the 6th Alabama. He thought the enemy fire "was terrific" and commented that "the pat, pat of the bullets against the rocks sounded like hail." Smith and his comrades were forced from their points of cover, and they fell back, either up the steep, rugged slope of Hill 1360 or up the gorge toward their supports. Lieutenant Park instructed his men "to fall back slowly, and to fire from everything which would screen them from observation. I had lost only four men wounded up to this time, but six or eight more became demoralized and, despite my commands, entreaties, and threats, left me and hastily fled to the rear." With the 26 men he had remaining, Park withdrew "slowly, firing as rapidly as we could load."[22]

The Alabamians fell back fighting. A skirmisher from the 12th Alabama, writing just several days after the battle, reported, "I do not know whether I hit any body; but I took as deliberate aim as if I had been shooting at squirrels, and that with a minnie musket at very good range." Lieutenant J. J. Lake, leading Company K of the 3rd Alabama, had command of his regiment's skirmishers. He extricated them from the advancing Federals so skillfully that when he reached the main line of his regiment, Major Cullen Battle offered his compliments. Lake "lifted his cap, in recognition of the compliment," when a bullet struck him and he dropped dead at the major's feet. "He was a splendid young man," Battle lamented, "as good as he was brave."[23]

As Rodes assessed the extent and strength of the enemy moving against him, it was apparent that Seymour's brigade outflanked his left and would seize the summit of Hill 1360 unless checked. At this critical moment the 12th Alabama joined him, and Rodes inserted Colonel Gayle into line between the 3rd and the 5th Alabama, which enabled him to extend his front to counter Seymour's threat. Rodes then ordered Colonel John B. Gordon to shift his 6th Alabama farther north to cover the approaches to Hill 1360, and he partially filled the hole created by Gordon's departure with the left wing of the 5th Alabama under Major E. L. Hobson. Gordon moved rapidly. The Federals blazed away at the Alabamians but were unable to prevent them from taking what Captain McGee of the Bucktails thought was a "most advantageous position."

Both Gordon's and Hobson's men poured what Colonel R. Biddle Roberts of the 1st Reserves described as "particularly destructive" fire into the Union ranks, forcing them to seek cover and return the fire.[24] Angelo Crapsey, one of the Bucktails, described the deadly nature of the combat in a letter to a friend.

> 3 with me were posted behind a Rock. [Sgt.] Wallace Brewer & L[eslie]. L. Bard & Hero Bloom wer with me. the rebels were behind a fence & rocks Bard was wounded & Brewer helped him away & soon Bloom was shot by my side he died that night. [Delos A.] Northrup fell a few yards to the left. [William M.] Maxson fell dead within a few feet of him. Wall it was sure work I only got my face & eyes full of bark for there was a tree just on the rock thats all of this.[25]

Bard suffered a gunshot wound to his right shoulder. With Sergeant Brewer's help he was evacuated to a hospital in Frederick, where his wound was successfully operated on. But the injury left Bard a cripple, unable to use his right hand or wrist.[26]

General Seymour initially interpreted Gordon's movement as an effort to turn his right flank, so he called on Meade for help, who pulled the 10th Reserves from Colonel Gallagher's support line and sent them on the double-quick to Seymour's aid. Thinking this might not be sufficient, Meade requested additional reinforcements to bolster his flank, and Hooker sent him Brigadier General Abram Duryee's 1st Brigade, of Ricketts's division.[27]

Meanwhile, Seymour soon understood the nature of Gordon's movement and correctly determined that the Confederates were redeploying to defend the approaches to the summit of 1360. From his vantage point Seymour perceived that if he could seize the summit, his brigade could sweep southwest across the head of the gorge and ascend Hill 1500. He made his way "to the place where the fire was hottest" to find Colonel McNeil and see if they might animate the men to resume the advance. It would take something special, for the fire of the Alabamians was murderously accurate. The idea of leaving their cover and advancing over open ground in the face of such fire was, in the words of the Bucktails' historian, "enough to cause the boldest to hesitate." It did not help the situation when the color-bearer of the 1st Reserves was shot down as he came up to the firing line. A corporal of the color guard ran forward to pick up the fallen standard, but Lieutenant James M. Welch of Company K, 13th Reserves, stopped him, knowing that the attempt would only add another to the list of killed in action. The flag remained were it had fallen, a grim testament to the effectiveness of the Alabamians' resistance. The Bucktails' historian recalled that "the condition of the men was perilous. The Confederates were sheltered more adequately than the Bucktails, and were doing terrible execution." At this critical juncture Captain Edward A. Irvin, the commander of Welch's Company K, leaped to his feet and dashed in front of the firing line, shouting "Forward Bucktails, drive them from their position." Irvin had no need to prove his valor. He already had a dozen bullet holes through his clothing and equipment, and one of Gordon's men hit him with the thirteenth. It struck him in the left side of the head, passed around his neck and lodged in his chest. Irvin dropped, but his fearless act helped overcome the impasse; the men near him raised a cheer and rushed forward.[28]

Captain Irvin's bravery was one element, but it was a combination of factors, rather than the actions of a single unit, that shattered the deadlock on Hill 1360. Seymour played a role by ordering tough Colonel Joseph Fisher to hit Gordon's flank with his 5th Reserves. Fisher maneuvered his men into a position from which they delivered a raking fire on the Alabamians' position. Fisher soon had the satisfaction of seeing the Confederates "break and retreat in great disorder," which he naturally assumed was due to his regiment's musketry.[29] Although Fisher claimed credit for breaking Gordon's line, it was the simultaneous pressure on the 6th Alabama's front and flanks that compelled the Confederate regiment's retreat. Colonel Edward P. Alexander, Lee's chief of ordnance, came down from Hagerstown with Longstreet's command, climbed the mountain, and had reached a point on the eastern slope where he had a clear view of Rodes's battle and Gordon's plight. "I saw away up at my level & only about 400 yards away a heavy line of battle which had passed clear around Rodes' left flank & were now swinging around to take him in reverse," Alexander wrote. A member of the 6th Alabama observed that they fought stubbornly until "it became evident that to do so longer, would be to sacrifice the command."

Gordon managed to keep his regiment in hand and deftly extricated them from their increasingly perilous position, falling back toward Hill 1500. In Rodes's opinion Gordon handled his regiment that day with an ability that Rodes had "never heard or seen equaled during this war." But the Federals exacted some revenge for their early losses and took a severe toll from the retreating Alabamians. Among them was Otis Smith. He and three comrades had taken shelter in a covert, "protected by two large trees in front, and huge boulders on each side." When Seymour's line swept forward, Smith and his comrades attempted to crawl through thick brush to escape. "A storm of bullets poured upon us," he recalled, killing his companions and severely wounding Smith, who was taken prisoner. Also among those who had to be left behind was 18-year-old Corporal James A. Hayes of Company A, who took a bullet through the neck that lodged between his scapula and his spinal column. Hill 1360 was firmly in Union hands.[30]

While Seymour fought for possession of Hill 1360, Gallagher's and Magilton's brigades swarmed up through the gorge and along its shoulders toward the 26th and the 3rd Alabama and the right wing of the 5th Alabama. Gallagher initially moved obliquely to the right to maintain contact with Seymour's left. This brought his regiments into open ground, where they came under fire from the Confederate artillery on Hill 1280. James McQuaide was with the 9th Reserves on the right of the brigade, and he wrote that "the balls went whising over our heads but did not kill a man." Gallagher's regiments pushed on. The nature of the terrain made command and control difficult. The "line could not been seen on either side 100 yards distant," noted Sergeant Holsinger of Magilton's brigade. Except for their skirmishers, the Confederates were concealed in good cover near the base of Hill 1500, and the skirmishers made excellent use of whatever available cover they had to make a stubborn resistance.[31]

Gallagher's regiments made steady progress up the gorge, but when the 11th Reserves crossed the Frosttown Branch (the mountain stream that had, over the ages, cut the gorge) the men of the 3rd Alabama and the 12th Alabama, "strongly posted in the rocks on the mountain side," revealed themselves with a murderous volley. The 11th's commander reported that it "brought down more than half of my commissioned officers present." The Pennsylvanians took cover and returned the fire. On their right, the 9th Reserves approached the J. Haupt farm, whose buildings Captain Edward S. Ready and a group of skirmishers from the 3rd Alabama had appropriated for cover. Ready and his stout band opened fire and brought the 9th's advance to a halt. "In and around the houses, the struggle was terrific," wrote Major Battle, Ready's commander. "The gorge," he continued (with a dose of hyperbole), "had become another Thermoplylae, and Ready was its Leonidas." Lieutenant Colonel Robert Anderson commanded the 9th Reserves. He arranged his regiment behind a stone wall running parallel to his front and ordered his men to direct their full firepower on the farmhouse. Captain Richard Gustin's 12th Reserves, on the left of the brigade, came under fire as they crossed the Frosttown Branch on the 11th Reserves' left, but it was neither heavy nor accurate enough to check their advance, and Gustin's men were able to reach the woods enveloping the slopes of the mountain. "The progress was slow on account of the steepness of the hill and the rocks, logs, and brush with which the ground was covered," reported Captain A. J. Bolar of this regiment, and the firing "was incessant on both sides, the rebels yielding the ground only when routed out of their hidden positions by the balls and bayonets of our men."[32]

While the 12th Reserves fought its way up the mountain, the 9th and the 11th Reserves made no headway on their front. The Alabamians had good cover and used it efficaciously. "My men were fighting like tigers," wrote Major Battle of the 3rd Alabama. Battle's men fought so stubbornly that Rodes believed "had my line been a continuous one it could never have been forced." At one point in the firefight a bullet struck Battle's belt plate, and the force of it knocked him down. One of his men made his way over to him and asked if he had been shot. Yes, replied Battle, who thought the ball had passed through his body, leaving a mortal wound. "Well Colonel," the soldier replied, "you have got one consolation, blamed if you hav'nt had a good time in your life." He was helping Battle to his feet to assist him to the rear when it became evident that the colonel's belt buckle, not his belly, had stopped a bullet. It was not a trifling blow, but Battle had grit; he recalled that "in ten minutes I was in command again."[33]

The Alabamians got their revenge for Battle's injury when one of their bullets took Colonel Gallagher out of the fight with a severely wounded arm. Command of the 3rd Brigade fell to Lieutenant Colonel Robert Anderson of the 9th Reserves. But Anderson had his hands full on his own front, where his regiment remained stymied for nearly 20 minutes in a furious musketry battle with the 3rd Alabama. Meade, who seemed to be everywhere along his divisional front, saw that Anderson was pinned down and ordered Lieutenant Colonel Adoniram J. Warner to move his 10th Reserves to Anderson's aid. Meade had previously shifted Warner's regiment to reinforce Seymour's 1st Brigade, but before Warner reached the line of that brigade he could see that the deadlock there had broken, so Warner turned his regiment back toward his own brigade. Now, following Meade's new orders, Warner advanced his men rapidly up to the right of the 9th Reserves. As they came up to the Frosttown Branch they "received a shower of bullets from across the revine partly on our front," probably from the 12th Alabama. A number of Warner's men fell under this fire. "[We] had a splendid chance at them, and we piled them by scores," wrote one of the Alabamians.[34] Warner left a vivid account of the ensuing action.

> We opened fire, part of the men moving rapidly up under cover and firing evenly on the rebels as they showed themselves among the rocks, and a part hanging back in a way they had never done before. I saw they hesitated to enter the revine, but unsurely faltered just in the place where they were most exposed. This was the effect of the defeat at Bull Run. I did all in my power to push them rapidly forward and soon nearly all were in the revine and beyond it and the rebels were running. My horse was shot while urging the men into the revine. In a few minutes confidence took the place of hesitation and all pressed wildly forward driving the enemy from their lodgements and were fast gaining the mountainsides.[35]

The added weight from the numbers and firepower of the 10th Reserves eased the pressure on the 9th and the 11th Reserves and helped break the stalemate on their front. Captain Samuel B. Dick, who assumed command of the 9th Reserves when Anderson replaced the wounded Gallagher at brigade command, ordered his men to rush the log farmhouse from which Captain Ready and his band had made such a stout resistance. The Pennsylvanians surrounded the house and 15 Alabamians emerged to surrender. Although his regiment had expended most of its ammunition in the firefight with Ready's men, Dick sensed that the enemy were cracking and pushed his men on. This action netted many prisoners. James McQuaide of Company C wrote that he and his comrades "took fifty prisoners from behind one rock," and Captain Dick estimated that once he called a halt for his troops to re-form, he had "upwards of 100 prisoners."

Among them was a seriously wounded Captain Ready. While falling back before the 9th's advance, some of his men came upon him lying on the ground with his hands folded across his chest and unable to speak above a whisper. When they tried to move him, he told them that "there was no use" and to leave him behind.[36]

A lowly corporal helped the 11th Reserves break the impasse with the 26th and the 3rd Alabama. Samuel H. Coon of Company E was one of those individuals blessed with "great powers of mimickry." At the height of the shootout with the Alabamians, Coon "crowed lustily, like a cock uttering the note of triumph." His rooster calls so "inspirited" the men that they rose to their feet and drove the enemy back up the slopes of Hill 1500. No doubt Coon animated his comrades with his unorthodox rallying call, but dwindling ammunition in the Confederate ranks and the general collapse of Rodes's defensive front also helped the Federals.[37]

Rodes's brigade had fought with great courage, but Seymour had turned their left and now Gallagher's regiments had penetrated their front and driven in their right flank. "I renewed again, and yet again, my application for re-enforcements, but none came," wrote Rodes. There were none to send. Some guns from Captain T. H. Carter's battery came up, and Colonel Cutts dispatched a "gallant lieutenant" with several pieces from his battalion, but it was too late for artillery to play its part, and Rodes ordered them back. The only good news that reached him was a report that supports (Evans's brigade) had come up on his right. Rodes concluded "that the only chance to continue the fight was to change my front so as to face to the left," in order to confront Seymour's flanking threat. With his regiments closely engaged with the enemy at all points, effecting a change of front from facing generally east to facing north was an exceptionally difficult movement to execute. But it was Rodes's only option if he was going to keep up the fight, so he sent instructions to his regiments to fall back "up the gorge and sides of the mountain [Hill 1500]." A member of the 3rd Alabama recalled that as they carried out Rodes's orders, "no panic was visible, but a splendid resistance was made throughout the whole movement to the top of the mountain." Many did put up a "splendid resistance" during the retreat, but others did not. Rodes admitted that the 26th Alabama became "completely demoralized" around this time and the men "mingled in utter confusion" with members of Evans's brigade. This and the large haul of prisoners the 9th Reserves scooped up were evidence that while there may not have been panic, some of Rodes's men crumbled and either surrendered or left the fight.[38]

The Federals gave Rodes no respite once they had dislodged his regiments from their initial defensive positions. From Hill 1360, General Seymour saw a large field of corn extending north in the direction of Hill 1500. At the far side of the cornfield he observed Confederate soldiers—either the left wing of the 5th Alabama or the 6th Alabama—taking cover behind a stone wall. Leaving the 13th Reserves to hold Hill 1360, Seymour had the 1st, the 2nd, and the 5th Reserves, with the 6th Reserve in support, change direction to the left and assault the wall. "Put your regiment into that corn-field and hurt somebody," Seymour told Colonel Fisher as the latter passed by with his 5th Reserves. "I will, general, and I'll catch one alive for you," the colonel responded. Once again, the Alabamians fought "with great tenacity, making a stubborn resistance," but they were unable to stem the "impetuosity and determination" of the blue tide that swept through the cornfield toward them. Colonel Fisher's men made good on his brag to Seymour and netted 11 prisoners. The Rebels fell back up the slopes of Hill 1500 and Seymour's regiments pursued them, although "all order and regularity of the lines were soon destroyed" in the advance up the steep and exceedingly rugged slopes.[39]

While Seymour's and Gallagher's brigades fought their way up Hill 1500 against Rodes, Colonel Magilton's 2nd Brigade struck Evans's tiny South Carolina brigade a jarring blow. Magilton advanced with the 8th, the 7th, and the 4th Reserves in line abreast (from left to right) and encountered the same steep and rough terrain that played havoc with maintaining formations and contact between regiments in the other brigades. Bates Alexander of the 7th Reserves recalled that the ground his regiment "passed was large clear fields. But the Fourth, on our right, struck some bad little ravines, pointed hills, and stone fences." The direction of advance caused Major Silas Bailey's 8th Reserves to cross to the south side of the Dahlgren Road. They had had the good fortune to pass through a peach orchard and, not being ones to pass up a chance at fresh fruit, "all who could grabbed all [the fruit] they could in passing." The brigade soon made contact with the Holcombe Legion, which Colonel Stevens had sent out as skirmishers, and easily drove their thin line back. With fewer natural obstacles to slow their advance, the 8th and the 7th Reserves were the first to strike Stevens's main line. The blow fell first on the 17th South Carolina, which was Stevens's only regiment south of the Dahlgren Road.[40]

Having taking position only minutes before they were attacked, most of Stevens's brigade were poorly prepared to receive Magilton's assault. Only the 17th South Carolina, under Colonel F. W. McMaster, seemed to have been ready. They were one of Stevens's largest regiments, with 141 officers and men, and McMaster found them cover behind a stone fence. One of the men moving against them, Archibald F. Hill of the 8th Reserves, described the approach: "Below this [stone fence], the ground was clear; above, the face of the mountain was covered with trees and rocks." McMaster's men held off until the 8th Reserves approached to within 50 yards, when the South Carolinians blasted the Pennsylvanians with "a very destructive fire." Bailey's reserves, wrote Private Hill, raised "a wild shout" and "dashed forward—almost upward—while volley after volley was poured upon us."[41]

Moments after Stevens's right flank became engaged with Magilton's 8th Reserves, the 4th and the 7th Reserves struck Stevens's center. Captain

S. A. Durham's 23rd South Carolina, on the left center of the brigade, had moved some distance down the mountain toward the gorge and in advance of the 22nd South Carolina on its right, probably to try and render support to Rodes's right flank. Durham met the skirmishers of the Holcombe Legion falling back, followed by a swarm of Union soldiers. Durham ordered his men to lie down until the Federals came within range, when the Rebels then opened fire. The South Carolinians fought bravely, but there were not enough of them to hold the enemy off in front, and Durham observed other enemy soldiers—perhaps the 12th Reserves of Gallagher's brigade—moving toward his exposed left flank. Durham had no choice but to order a withdrawal up the mountain. In the woods on the slopes of Hill 1500, he managed to re-form his men on the left of Lieutenant Colonel T. C. Watkins's 22nd South Carolina. Both regiments fired on the 4th and the 7th Reserves, but—perhaps because they were on higher ground—they probably overshot the Pennsylvanians, for they did little damage.[42] Bates Alexander in the 7th Reserves described the situation.

> As we entered the wooded portion of the hill they opened on us with a brisk fire of musketry. They had a fine opportunity to select their targets in our line, as many of them were concealed behind trees, &c. We could not see them readily and it has often been a wonder to me that about half our line did not fall as we entered the woods. I have ever failed to understand why, &c., of the Confederates' behavior in front of our brigade that day. We marched steadily up, while they as certainly "fell away."[43]

The 22nd South Carolina fought stubbornly for some minutes, but when the adjacent 23rd South Carolina began to come apart, Watkins ordered his men to fall back. They did, with the 7th Reserves in pursuit.[44]

Shortly before tangling with the enemy, Stevens had shifted Colonel W. H. Wallace's 18th South Carolina to support Rodes's right flank. This movement placed the 18th on Stevens's left, but apparently with a wide interval between it and the 23rd South Carolina. When Wallace took position, he reported that Rodes's men were beginning to fall back. Thinking the 18th might relieve the pressure Magilton was applying, Stevens ordered the colonel to change front forward and attack the enemy flank. Wallace did so, and his men had become thoroughly engaged with the 4th Reserves when he noticed a "heavy column" of enemy soldiers, probably the 12th Reserves, advancing toward his exposed left flank, with other enemy soldiers driving Rodes's men back and threatening to gain Wallace's rear. Wallace then ordered a retreat.[45]

Meanwhile, on Stevens's right flank, Colonel McMaster's 17th South Carolina fought "persistently" against Magilton's Federals, but between the casualties and those who abandoned the fight as hopeless, McMaster found his regiment reduced to about 40 men. "It was absurd to talk of keeping the enemy back," he wrote later. "When I left I was in 200 yards of them and I never saw so many Blue Coats in my life, at one time."[46] Once they were knocked off balance,

Stevens's regiments never recovered. Lieutenant Colonel Watkins attempted to rally his 22nd South Carolina, which had fallen into "some confusion," by recklessly exposing himself and shouting to his men to rally to their colors. They responded and were re-forming when a Pennsylvanian put a bullet into Watkins's head and he fell dead in front of his men. With no small amount of understatement, Major Miel Hilton, who then assumed command of the regiment, reported that "this misfortune caused the regiment to fall into confusion." In fact, it dissolved as a fighting unit.

So, too, did the 23rd South Carolina, although a group from that regiment stuck with their commander, Captain Durham, and eventually reported to Rodes on the summit of Hill 1500, where they proved to be more of a hindrance than a help. Rodes referred to them as "South Carolina stragglers" who mingled in "utter confusion" with the 12th Alabama. Colonel Stevens was blunt in reporting the poor conduct of his command, except for the 17th South Carolina. "I am constrained to say that after once falling back I cannot commend the behavior of the men," he reported. "Some two or three bravely faced the foe, but a general lack of discipline and disregard for officers prevailed all around me." Stevens's assessment of his command's performance also revealed itself in the disparity in casualties. The South Carolinians, generally behind cover throughout, had 23 dead, 148 wounded, and 45 missing out of the 550 taken into action. Magilton, whose brigade had to advance across open ground in the early part of the fight, counted 25 dead, but only 64 wounded and 1 missing, with 50 of those casualties being incurred by just one unit, the 8th Pennsylvania. The South Carolinians' collapse might have been predicted from the lack of leadership exhibited by Evans, who left his brigade and Colonel Stevens's to fend for themselves.[47]

The disintegration of Evans's brigade left Rodes's as the sole challenge to the Union assault on Hill 1500. It was a forlorn hope that they could prevail. "My loss up to this time had been heavy in all the regiments except the Twelfth Alabama," Rodes reported. Many of Rodes's men continued to fight stubbornly, but so did Meade's Pennsylvanians, and the latter heavily outnumbered the Alabamians. And while Rodes's strength dwindled, the Federals received an infusion of fresh troops. Brigadier General Abram Duryee's 1st Brigade of Ricketts's division started forward around 5 p.m. in response to Meade's request for reinforcements to strengthen what he then thought was his threatened right flank. But by the time Duryee neared the fighting, Hill 1360 had been cleared and Seymour was wheeling his brigade to assault Hill 1500. Duryee moved into the interval between Seymour and Gallagher, placing the 105th New York and the 107th Pennsylvania in his front line with fixed bayonets, and the 97th and the 104th New York in support. They started up the "almost inaccessible" mountainside as quickly as the terrain permitted, with everyone "cheering like mad men." Lieutenant James B. Thomas of the 107th Pennsylvania wrote that Duryee kept in front, "yelling the loudest of any of us" and shouting back that "a good yell was as good as a volley when they were on the run." Holmes Burlingame, in the second line with the 104th New York, watched Duryee dash in front of his regiment at one point, climb up on one of the numerous boulders strewing the mountain, and "yell back to us 'COME ON YOU BLOODY ONE HUNDRED AND FOURTH.'" The Alabamians peppered this fresh line of Federals with musketry, but most of it went high. "The rebels being constantly on higher ground shot over us, our colors were completely riddled with bullets," recalled the 107th Pennsylvania's Henry J. Sheafer. According to 107th's commander, Captain James MacThompson, the course of their advance brought them up against Colonel B. B. Gayle's 12th Alabama, firing from behind a stone wall. The Alabamians, wrote Thompson, "delayed not the onward movement of the One hundred and Seventh a moment, but in a little while we were over the fence and among them, taking 68 prisoners." Perhaps the wall was won as easily as MacThompson claimed—the 107th only reported 12 killed or wounded—but Captain John C. Whiteside, who was with the nearby 105th New York, noted that when his regiment came under enemy fire, "we wavered and would have broken and fallen back." Whiteside, not the most humble fellow in the 1st Corps, claimed that he then drew his sword, took off his cap, stepped in front of regiment, "and called for three cheers for the Union." This, claimed Whiteside, rallied the men, and he asserted that "when I cheered they all cheered and when I advanced they advanced." If true, the incident still did not reflect well on the steadiness of the 105th, as it suffered only 3 casualties.[48]

On Duryee's right, Seymour's reserves came up against remnants of the 5th, the 6th, and the 12th Alabama, which Rodes had somehow managed to form into a defensive line. The Pennsylvanians found that on this side of the mountain the Rebels were not shooting high. As they came clambering up the slope, the 1st Reserves took a single volley that killed three officers: Lieutenant John D. Sadler, Captain Thomas P. Dwin, and Lieutenant J. H. Taylor. The same volley killed a stray dog, a setter that had accompanied Sadler from the base of the mountain, as well as the regimental mascot, "a spotted bitch that had followed the regiment through everything previous." Only a few hours earlier, Sadler had been granted a pass to visit some relatives in Middletown. When Sadler returned, he told William Jobe, a soldier in his company, that he had experienced a premonition of his death. Jobe "told him laughing that was only a revelation of a streak of superstition in a highly educated gentleman and proved nothing." But, concluded Jobe sadly, "the fact remains he was killed in the last charge of the Regt." But the reserves exacted their vengeance. "In ten minutes we were on them," wrote Jobe. "They stood for a short time when they again broke and retreated but they paid dearly for their last stand." Among those who fell was the 12th Alabama's commander, Colonel B. B. Gayle. With Duryee's and Seymour's men swarming around his regiment, Gayle reportedly drew his pistol and shouted, "We are flanked, boys, but let's die in our tracks." Gayle did, riddled with bullets. His lieutenant colonel, Samuel B. Pickens, went down as well, with a bullet in the lungs. Pickens was carried from the field by his men, but Gayle's body had to be left behind.[49]

Rodes's battered regiments fell back toward the summit of the mountain, keeping up a constant fire at their pursuers. Near the summit there was a small patch of cleared land hewn out of the rocky soil, which many of the Alabamians fell back across. They came under fire from the 7th Reserves, who had reached the eastern edge of the field. Some of the Confederates returned the volley, and a bullet struck the 7th's Colonel Henry C. Bolinger in the ankle, taking him out of the fight. Part of Duryee's men soon came up on the north side of the field and began firing. This dispersed the Alabamians, and they "disappeared in the darkness down the other slope."[50]

Companies A and B of the 6th Reserves also fired into the Confederates in the field north and west of Duryee's men. When the Rebels retreated, the two Union companies advanced to seize a rocky knob near the mountain summit. Here they encountered the 6th Alabama, the only regiment of Rodes's brigade that retained any organization. When Gordon's Alabamians checked the advance of his two forward companies, Colonel William Sinclair, the 6th Reserves' commander, reinforced them with Companies C, D, and E. They came up on the left of their comrades, then all advanced at a charge. The Confederates fell back, but only as far as a second ledge of rocks. From this strongpoint they poured "a most galling fire" into the Reserves that "caused the advance to reel under the shock and threatening its annihilation." Sinclair's regiment would tally the highest losses in Seymour's brigade, with 11 dead and 43 wounded. The 6th Alabama's stand attracted the attention of a group of stragglers that Rodes and Major Cullen Battle were trying to organize. These men joined in the fight by delivering an enfilading fire on Sinclair's companies, but it was probably neither very potent (due to their makeshift organization) nor accurate (because of the fading light). Nonetheless, it succeeded in getting the attention of Sinclair's companies, who shifted their fire to this new threat. It quickly deflated whatever defiance the makeshift command possessed, and they melted away and out of the fight, nudged along by some of Duryee's men, who came over from the engagement at the mountain meadow.[51]

By this stage of the battle confusion reigned on the mountain. Rodes's men were completely exhausted and either low on or out of ammunition. John S. Tucker, a member of the 5th Alabama, recorded in his diary that only "40 odd men" were to be found in his regiment by dark and that, in his opinion, the brigade was "cut all to pieces." This was true, except for the 6th Alabama, which somehow retained unit integrity. Darkness was rapidly closing in on the mountain, and yelling Union soldiers seemed to be everywhere. Rodes understood that his men were at the end of their tether and that Hill 1500 was lost. He ordered Gordon to pull his regiment back to a position that covered the approaches from the mountain to Turner's Gap, while he himself attempted to rally the rest of scattered elements of the brigade. As the Southern soldiers stumbled down the mountain to the gap, above them exultant Union troops celebrated their capture of Hill 1500 with cheers that "rolled down the mountain side." Rodes and his men had fought gallantly and tenaciously and, against a less determined foe, might have succeeded in checking their assault. But Meade pushed the attack relentlessly and made effective use of his superior numbers to continually turn the enemy flanks. His men drove their attack home with great determination, until they had captured the position that D. H. Hill affirmed was "everything to the Yankees."[52]

Rodes, with some help from Evans, exacted a severe toll from Meade's ranks. The Pennsylvania Reserves counted 95 killed, 296 wounded, and 1 missing. Entering the fight after the Rebels were on the jump, Duryee got off rather easily, with only 5 killed and 16 wounded. Rodes lost a quarter of his brigade: 61 dead, 157 wounded, and 204 missing or captured. When the casualties of Evans's brigade are included, the Confederates lost slightly over 600 men, nearly double what the Federals suffered.[53]

But while Meade's and Duryee's soldiers raised their parched voices in shouts of victory, the deadly crackle of musketry from the summit of Hill 1280 revealed that its possession was still in dispute.

12

The Battle for Hill 1280

"Some of you will get hurt"

Things started to go awry with the assault by Hatch's division moments after it began its advance up the slopes of Hill 1280. Colonel William F. Rogers's 21st New York and Colonel Newton B. Lord's 35th New York formed the skirmish line that covered the division's front. Rogers's orders were to extend his line to connect with Meade's skirmish line at the Dahlgren Road and tie in his left with Lord's 35th, which would continue the line in the direction of the National Road. Colonel Rogers received his orders first. He had his men drop their knapsacks and then deployed six companies as skirmishers, with the remaining four following as a reserve. Instead of obliquing his regiment to the right to connect with Meade, Rogers directed his men straight up the steep slopes, leaving a gap between his right and Meade's left. This occurred under the eye of corps commander Hooker, who ordered Hatch to fill in the space by detaching Colonel H. V. Post's 2nd U.S. Sharpshooters from Phelps's brigade.[1]

Hooker's action corrected one defect in Hatch's advance, but another arose at nearly the same time. Colonel Rogers started his regiment up the mountain before Colonel Lord had received his orders from General Patrick to deploy on the Rogers's flank. The field officers of the 35th were in poor health that day. Lord "was far from well," his lieutenant colonel was absent, and the major "had the seeds of a fever rankling in his veins" and could not accompany the regiment into action. Many of the line officers were also absent, prompting a member of the regiment to comment acidly to a hometown newspaper about both officers and men in the regiment: "Never a man falls out on the retreat, but on the advance—Oh! dear, how common it is to see men taken with the gripes." But Colonel Lord—a machinist and foundryman from Brownville, New York, in civilian life—stuck with his men. The enlisted men chose to keep their burdensome knapsacks on, having lost their previous ones several weeks earlier when they had dropped them during a movement in the Second Manassas Campaign. Lord wasted no time in deploying his men as skirmishers and ordering them forward, but the 21st New York was already out of sight, so he made an educated guess as to where its left flank should be and guided his movements on this point.[2]

General Patrick rode back from giving Lord his orders to discover that his 23rd New York and 20th New York State Militia (officially the 80th New York Infantry, but they preferred their militia designation), who were to be following the skirmishers in line of battle, had failed to start moving behind the skirmish line, which meant that neither had the rest of the division, which followed Patrick's brigade in close column. Patrick was a fussy and irascible fellow, and he set to "hurrying and pressing" both regiments. He managed to get the 23rd moving, but he complained that Colonel Theodore Gates's 20th Militia "as usual on such occasions, hung back," and that only after "much trouble" did Patrick get Gates's regiment to advance. For some reason, when Colonel Phelps, whose brigade was to follow Patrick's, received his orders to advance, Patrick's regiments had vanished from sight, so Phelps could merely speculate on the direction in which they were moving. The only thing that went smoothly in the advance was that Doubleday's brigade fell in behind Phelps with the prescribed 200-pace interval between the two brigades. For a veteran division it was a clumsy start, and things proceeded to go further astray before Hatch finally intervened and corrected them.[3]

On the skirmish line, Colonel Rogers and his New York Staters (from the Buffalo area) moved "slowly, slowly, now halting as if to listen, now crouching a while on the ground with muskets ever ready for instant service," heading across open fields that were in pasture and toward the woods that spilled down the eastern slope of the mountain. Some of them encountered an old woman, frightened out of her home and scurrying down the mountain to get out of harm's way. In an excited manner she paused to ask the grim-faced men where they were going. An officer replied they were only going up the hill. Colonel Rogers recalled her response: "'Don't you go there,' she exclaimed, waving them back with her hands. 'There are hundreds of 'em up there. Don't you go. Some of you will get hurt!' This little scene amused the boys very much, and 'Some of you will get hurt' became a standing jest."[4]

While Colonel Rogers's skirmishers warily made their way up the mountain, the 35th New York, unable to locate the left of the 21st or to fix a point on which to guide their advance, drifted to the left in the direction of the National Road, and the 23rd New York and the 20th Militia followed them, since the men of the 35th New York were the only skirmishers visible. The gradual shift of Lord's regiment left a yawning gap in the divisional skirmish line, which Patrick soon discovered. He sent orders to Lord to swing his left forward, pull his right back, and change his point of direction farther to the right. To plug the gap in the skirmish line, Patrick ordered Colonel Theodore Gates to advance his 20th Militia into the interval. To support the 35th's extended skirmish line, Patrick had Colonel Henry C. Hoffman take the right wing of his 23rd New York and move it a full quarter mile to the right to support the right of the 35th's skirmish line, while the left wing, under Lieutenant Colonel N. M. Crane, buttressed its center and right.[5]

Having corrected the drift of part of his brigade, Patrick rode off with his orderly to find the 21st New York. But Patrick's sense of direction on the mountain proved no better than Colonel Lord's, for he and his orderly managed to ride well in front of the 21st's skirmish line, which was still east of a farm lane that ran across the eastern slope of the mountain from the National Road to the Dahlgren Road. Fortunately for Patrick, his orderly was an alert and observant fellow. He caught sight of men in gray uniforms above them on the mountain and shouted a warning: "Gray Coats!" Both men instantly wheeled their horses and plunged down the mountain, followed, wrote Patrick, "by a volley from the enemy which passed over my head." The Confederates had revealed their position and given Patrick a point toward which to direct his advance. He rode back to Colonel Lord and ordered him to move his skirmish line still farther to the right, in the direction from which Patrick had drawn fire.[6]

While Patrick fretted and fumed over his brigade, Phelps's brigade came marching up the mountain and moved through the gap in Patrick's skirmish line that Patrick had ordered Colonel Gates's 20th Militia to fill. Phelps got there first. He was completely unaware that his brigade had moved in advance of the skirmish line until someone noticed that they had crossed a farm road and, perhaps, discovered that there were no friendly skirmishers in front of them. Phelps called a halt and sent an aide to notify Hatch about the cause of his delay. While they waited for Hatch to sort things out, Phelps's New Yorkers discovered that by a stroke of luck they had stopped in a field of turnips, which the men set upon. Hatch soon came tearing up the mountain—most likely in a bad humor—to investigate. He found the skirmishers of the 35th New York's right wing approaching under Patrick's orders, and Hatch ordered them in front of Phelps, whose brigade followed 30 paces in their rear, still formed in column of division. The 20th Militia, which Hatch somehow did not see in his ride to the front, had made their way across the mountain by this time and found the left of the 21st New York near the north–south farm road. Gates aligned his regiment on the 21st, and these two units resumed their climb up the mountain. The right wing of the 23rd New York—which Patrick had ordered over to support the right of the 35th New York's skirmish line—came up before Phelps's brigade had resumed its advance. Colonel Hoffman must have discovered that Hatch intended to have Phelps's men be the ones to follow the 35th's skirmishers, for Hoffman decided the services of his men were not needed there and marched his right wing back to rejoin his left wing. The whole 1st Division was finally moving in the same direction, but it was sprawled across a very broad front, extending nearly 1,000 yards.[7]

The 1st Corps soldiers had already marched nearly 14 miles that day, and the climb up the steep mountain was exhausting. Adjutant Edward Barnes of the 95th New York remembered that the mountain "rose somewhat abruptly, so much so as to render the ascent on horseback very difficult, and to require the aid of shrubs, saplings, and stumps to assist in climbing." Umberto Burnham of the 76th New York recalled that the division moved "slowly and cautiously . . . creeping through undergrowth and stumbling over rocks." The 21st New York's historian noted that the higher-elevation portion of Hill 1280 was "so broken and rocky, that a halt becomes necessary every fifteen or twenty paces, to close up and dress the line." The only reward after the arduous climb was the magnificent view of the scenic Middletown Valley. Even with death's work near at hand, many paused to admire the view. Lieutenant Samuel Healy of the 56th Pennsylvania was one. He wrote in his journal that "the finest valley I ever beheld was below us and extends as far south as the eye could reach. Middletown could be seen off to our left . . . It was a scene to make us all forget the pending battle." Another member of the division thought that the peaceful and prosperous valley "offered so strong a contrast to our present fearful business as to daguerreotype itself upon my imagination forever."[8]

While the division struggled up the mountain slopes, Colonel Phelps—who managed to stay in the saddle despite the steepness of the terrain—rode ahead to the skirmish line. "The nature of the ground afforded me an excellent opportunity to advance unobserved by the enemy," he reported. He saw Confederates "posted behind a line of fence on the summit." It was nearly 6 p.m., and the sun was slipping behind South Mountain. The struggle for possession of Hill 1280 was at hand.[9]

If Hatch had not been delayed by the various miscues that marred his division's ascent of the mountain, they might have seized Hill 1280 with scarcely a shot being fired. The Confederates who fired on Patrick, and whom Phelps had observed, beat the Federals to the summit by only a few minutes. When Hatch's division commenced its advance, between the right of Evans's brigade and the left of Colquitt's—a distance of nearly 700 yards—"there was not a single Confederate soldier to oppose the advance of General Hatch." To prevent Hatch from exploiting this interval and seizing the key terrain of Hill 1280, three brigades of Confederate soldiers made an epic march that pushed the limits of human endurance.[10]

Only three brigades of Longstreet's command remained uncommitted by the time the Federals' 1st Corps began its assault of the Confederate right. They were Colonel Micah Jenkins's South Carolinians and the two Virginia brigades of Brigadier Generals Richard Garnett and James Kemper, all from Brigadier General David R. Jones's division. After their rapid march from Hagerstown, these three brigades halted for 20 minutes along a creek—possibly Wagoner Branch, a tributary of Beaver Creek located about 2 miles west of Boonsboro—to fill canteens and rest. Lee remained near Boonsboro, where a report reached him that Union troops had forced Fox's Gap and were pushing down the western side of the mountain. Checking this advance was crucial, and Lee ordered Longstreet to send Jones's three brigades to do so. They set a rapid pace, swinging

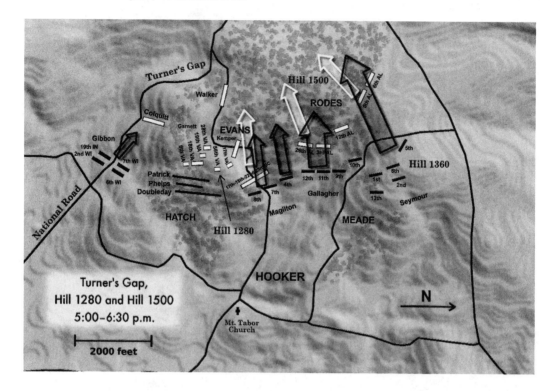

through Boonsboro and turning right on the Pleasant Valley Road, which they followed for 2 miles until they reached the Old Sharpsburg Road. Here they turned left and marched east toward Fox's Gap. As they neared the base of the mountain the firing from the gap subsided, and D. R. Jones learned that there was no enemy breakthrough—the report of one had been generated by Drayton's defeat—and the situation at Fox's Gap had been stabilized. Jones sent word of this to Longstreet and requested orders. By this time Hooker's advance had precipitated a fresh crisis, with a desperate need for infantry to fill the hole between Evans's and Colquitt's troops. Longstreet's response was for Jones to bring his brigades back to the National Road and reinforce Turner's Gap "as rapidly as possible." Jones ordered Kemper, commanding the leading brigade, to file his brigade to the left, or north, in order to regain the National Road. Jones sent Major Raphael J. Moses of his staff with orders for Garnett's and Jenkins's brigades to about face and return to the Pleasant Valley Road, which they were to follow until they reached a "path" that led to the National Road. There was some uncertainty, however, over where exactly the path was to be found. When Garnett questioned Moses on the subject, the major professed to have no idea, but he promised to ride ahead to see if he might learn something about it.[11] Kemper's Virginians reached the National Road first, contacting it only about a third of a mile from the point where they had left it earlier. They swung onto the turnpike and started the punishing climb to Turner's Gap. Discourag-

ing signs greeted the exhausted men. "Troops of the most demoralized stragglers" were making their way off the mountain, noted John Dooley of the 1st
Virginia, and there were "long lines of wounded limping down the road." Longstreet's staff strove to drive the stragglers back into the fight, and Major Moxley
Sorrel recalled that "our staff had to make sharp play with the flats of our swords
on the backs of these fellows. It tired and disgusted me." Kemper's men ignored
both the demoralized and the wounded soldiers that they passed and pressed
on up the mountain, but the physical toll of the day's marching began to be felt,
and men who were too exhausted to go on began to drop out. Longstreet, positioned near the Mountain House, watched them approaching and observed that
"the men dropped as if under severe skirmish. So manifest was it that nature was
exhausted, that no one urged them to get up and try to keep their ranks."[12]

Due to the urgency of the situation, Longstreet could allow Kemper's
dog-tired infantryman no rest when they finally reached the level space at the
summit of Turner's Gap. Meade was driving Rodes and Evans, and Hatch was
approaching unopposed up the slopes of Hill 1280. The wing commander ordered Kemper to take his regiments, now mere companies in strength, down
the Dahlgren Road to help fill the interval between Evans and Colquitt. This
required the brigade to ascend another mountain, as the Dahlgren Road climbs
steadily for nearly a half mile until it reaches the summit of Hill 1280. Without
pausing, the exhausted Virginians began the ascent. As they labored up the road
they came under observation by Durell's battery at Fox's Gap. The range was approximately 1 mile and the light was failing, but the Pennsylvanians opened fire.
Their gunnery was excellent, and their shells burst close to the Confederate
column. David Johnston of the 7th Virginia, toward the rear of the column, recalled that the Yankees "threw shot and shell thick and fast, striking the head of
the leading company of my regiment and killing one man instantly." In the 1st
Virginia, which was immediately in front of the 7th, Lieutenant Dooley wrote
that the artillery fire "sweeps every yard of the road over which we are passing,"
and the rapidly bursting shells threw the column into the "greatest confusion."
Dooley continued:

> I tell you I was frightened! These balls not content with making the ordinary
> scare, bounding over and above and among us, go crashing into the crags on
> our left, splintering into a thousand pieces large fragments of rock which
> wildly fly around our heads, and the crash resounding from ridge to ridge
> multiplies indefinitely the fearful reports and increases very much the terror
> which such missiles are wont to inspire. One shot went through a tree about
> three feet in diameter, splitting nothing but leaving a nice round smooth hole
> in the body. Another shot (I thought I saw it then) came bounding along the
> mountain side and right through out regiment. What a scatteration it made!
> John Daniels of Co. H was the only one hit.[13]

Virginia-born James L. Kemper had earned his promotion to general for his skillful handling of the 7th Virginia at Seven Pines. He was an attorney in civilian life and had served three terms in the Virginia legislature. But the military had always held an attraction for him. He entered service in the 1st Virginia Volunteers near the end of the Mexican War and was active in the Virginia Militia, attaining the rank of brigadier general in 1858. He had no combat experience before the Civil War, but his militia service and a brief exposure to field service in the Mexican War provided adequate preparation, and he proved to be a competent regimental and then brigade commander. Kemper, with his staff, now prudently rode ahead of his brigade to ascertain the situation in front and reconnoiter the ground his regiments would defend. At a point just below the summit of Hill 1280 the Dahlgren Road makes a sharp turn north and begins its descent into the gorge. Kemper reached the summit of the hill without incident and then went down the other side of the mountain on the road for perhaps 100 yards before he was fired on by Union soldiers from Magilton's brigade. Kemper quickly withdrew and sent his aide, Captain Abner C. Beckham, who had celebrated his 19th birthday three days earlier, galloping back to bring the brigade forward.[14]

Beckham arrived in the midst of bedlam caused by the flying iron of Durell's battery. "A braver young man never lived," thought Lieutenant Dooley. Beckham coolly guided the four leading regiments over the summit and out of the line of artillery fire. Kemper intended to form the main body of his brigade across the Dahlgren Road, oriented northeast toward Meade's division, which could be seen swarming over the "fields and fences and sides of the mountains." But the woods that grew on the northern and eastern slopes of Hill 1280 concerned Kemper. They provided a covered approach for Yankees to strike Kemper's right flank before Garnett or Jenkins arrived. To prevent such a surprise, Kemper ordered Colonel Montgomery Corse, commanding the 17th Virginia at the rear of his brigade, to move his regiment through a cornfield on Hill 1280's summit and up to the edge of the woods. Corse sent Lieutenant F. W. Lehew, with a company of skirmishers, into the woods, and followed them with the balance of the regiment, spread across the 100-yard-wide cornfield to the woods' edge.[15]

Kemper placed his other four regiments to face Meade's Pennsylvanians, who swarmed like a rapidly moving blue wave up the gorge and the sides of Hill 1500. Evans's brigade had been driven back by this time, and they retreated across Kemper's front, with the weight of Magilton's brigade in pursuit up the southeastern slope of Hill 1500. Some elements of the little colonel's brigade—probably part of the 8th Reserves—observed Kemper's regiments forming and opened a scattering fire on them. The 24th, the 7th, and part of the 1st Virginia (from left to right) formed first "in a body of open timber, among stones—large boulders, with some fallen timber along the line," on the left of the Dahlgren Road, the men taking "shelter as best they could" behind the available cover and trading fire with the Pennsylvanians.[16]

The balance of the 1st Virginia deployed on the right of the Dahlgren Road, and the 11th Virginia formed on their right in the above-mentioned cornfield. "Our Brigade is sent to defend a position or line which a whole Brigade might be supposed able to protect," noted Lieutenant Dooley, but the five regiments could muster "no more than 400" effectives after their punishing march. Fortunately the Federals in Kemper's immediate front were intent on pursuing Evans's and Rodes's brigades up the slopes of Hill 1500 and, apart from some skirmishing, Kemper's regiments were not seriously engaged. But the crack of muskets from Lieutenant Lehew's skirmish line on Hill 1280's eastern slope announced the approach of a new threat on the brigade's right flank: Hatch's division. Before this could develop into a crisis for Kemper, Garnett's brigade came trotting up the Dahlgren Road, hurried along by bursting shells from Durell's battery and the 20 lb. Parrotts in the valley below.[17]

The experience Garnett's brigade had in reaching the mountain summit largely mirrored Kemper's. Garnett's brigade followed Jenkins's in retracing their steps to reach the National Road. The South Carolinians had a good start on the Virginians, and Garnett reported that the former were "some distance" in front of him. Then Garnett heard musketry echoing down the mountain and, being aware of the urgency with which his men were needed, made the decision to leave the road and cut cross-country, taking the most direct route toward Turner's Gap. "This took me over rough and plowed ground up the mountain side," Garnett reported, which made for hard going for his already-weary men. The gait, recalled Captain William T. Owen of the 18th Virginia, was "a rapid trot," and fully one-half of the brigade "succumbed to the heat and over fatigue of the long hasty march."[18]

Richard B. Garnett was a man with something to prove. Virginia-born and West Point–trained, soldiering had been Garnett's life. Most of it had been with the prewar 6th U.S. Infantry, with whom he had served for 20 years. Garnett did not believe in secession, but when Virginia left the Union he followed, rising to the rank of brigadier general in the Confederate service. In the fall of 1861 he took command of Stonewall Jackson's old brigade. Like nearly everyone who served under Jackson, Garnett found him to be a difficult taskmaster. At the battle of Kernstown on March 23, 1862, Garnett's brigade was low on ammunition and facing vastly superior Union forces that threatened to cut them off. Garnett ordered a retreat, a sensible and competent decision, but it infuriated Jackson. Several days later Jackson arrested Garnett for "neglect of duty" and relieved him of command, casting a stain upon Garnett's honor and battlefield courage, a serious blow for a professional soldier. A court-martial was convened in August 1862, but the active operations against John Pope caused it to be postponed. Lee intervened at this point and ordered Garnett restored to duty, transferring him to command the brigade of George Pickett, who was recovering from a wound. Only on the battlefield could Garnett erase the disgrace of Jackson's charges. So he drove his men hard toward the sound of the guns, leaking exhausted soldiers along the way. Their cross-country jog led to an "old and broken road," where they met Captain Hugh Rose of General D. R. Jones's staff, who guided the brigade to the turnpike. By the time they reached the main road, the brigade was so winded that Garnett called a halt to let the men catch their breath. While they recovered, Jenkins's brigade, commanded by Colonel Joseph Walker, came up and formed on Garnett's right, facing the mountain. Then the command to fall in sang out; Garnett's regiments shouldered their arms and continued the steep climb up the National Road, followed in short order by Walker's South Carolinians.[19]

At the mountain summit Garnett apparently called another brief halt to close up his regiments and prepare them for action. A "rapid count" was made of the five regiments, and 407 officers and men reported present for duty. Garnett's orders were to help fill the gap on Kemper's right on Hill 1280, so Garnett led his brigade up the Dahlgren Road. By this time both Durell's gunners near Fox's Gap and observers for the Union army's heavy batteries in the valley were on the alert for any movement along this road. The light was fading fast, but they spotted the march of Garnett's column. The Union guns bucked and roared, sending shells to greet the latest visitors to the mountain. Garnett reported that the shell and shrapnel burst near the brigade "with considerable accuracy, as they had previously been practicing on other troops which had preceded mine." Some losses were suffered, but Garnett's men soon passed out of sight of the Federal gunners. One of Garnett's regimental commanders noted that the sun was setting behind "the western hills" as they arrived at the top of Hill 1280, which places their arrival around 6 p.m.[20]

At the summit Garnett found pastures studded with rock outcroppings—part of the farm of D. Rent—that extended for over 100 yards from the road to the woods along the eastern front of the mountain. Garnett hastened his regiments across this open ground, toward the woods. Colonel Eppa Hunton led the way with his 8th Virginia, its 34 officers and men no larger than an understrength company. Hunton's band dashed across the relatively level plateau and into the "thick woods." The ground descended abruptly in front them, and below they spotted Union soldiers—probably skirmishers of the 35th New York—who opened fire on them as Hunton tried to get his men into a line. The Virginians returned the fire and the Federals fell back. Meanwhile, Major George C. Cabell's 18th Virginia, 120 strong, came up on Hunton's left, forming on the edge of the woods but in a position where they had some vantage points downslope through the forest.[21] The 18th discovered that the plateau on Hill 1280's summit was still under observation by Durell's gunners, and the Virginians continued to endure a pounding by the Pennsylvanians' guns as they attempted to form line and move into position. Captain Owen described the shelling.

> While crossing the open field a battery of the enemy, located on an eminence to the front and right of us opened and poured a shower of shot and shell into

our ranks. Going on at a double quick across the field we jumped a fence, running across our course, and partly torn down, and just as the writer cleared the gap a shell struck the fence behind him with a terrific explosion, splintering and throwing the pieces of broken fence rails high in air in every direction toward the rear and placing hors de combat four of the six of his company following close on behind him.[22]

While Major Cabell formed his companies, one of his men peered down into the woods and sang out, "Major Cabell yonder is a Yankee." Cabell came over for a look, and he estimated that the Union solider was about 200 yards off—the woods here apparently had little undergrowth. Cabell shouted to him to surrender and the man appeared to be responding, but then several more Federals appeared. Then someone else on the 18th's line raised a shout—"Who ee just look at em"—and, wrote Captain Owen, "sure enough there was a skirmish line a mile long coming up the mountain side at a trot and behind was the serried ranks of column behind column coming sternly on." It was probably about this time that Hunton's muskets began to crack away. The firing quickly spread as Cabell's men opened fire and drove the bluecoat skirmishers back on their supports.[23]

Colonel John Bowie Strange's 19th Virginia followed the 18th Virginia into action. The 39-year-old Strange had been among the first group of young men to enroll at the Virginia Military Institute in 1839. Following graduation he pursued a career in education and founded the Albemarle Military Institute between 1854 and 1856, but he left the halls of academia to offer his training and service to his state when the current war began. Now he formed the 150 men of his regiment into line in the Dahlgren Road and then led them over the bordering fence and across a stubble field toward the woods. Captain William L. Wingfield's 28th Virginia came after, moving to cover the 19th's left flank. Colonel William D. Stuart's 56th Virginia, with only 80 muskets in its ranks, brought up Garnett's rear. General D. R. Jones intervened in Garnett's deployment at this point. The gap between Kemper and Garnett worried Jones, and he thought Garnett's position at the edge of the woods on Hill 1280's eastern summit was too far forward. He ordered Garnett to pull his brigade back to the woods west of the Dahlgren Road and to deploy the 56th Virginia in the cornfield on Kemper's right to help close the gap between the brigades. Garnett executed the latter command, moving Stuart's tiny 56th adjacent to Kemper's 17th Virginia, but the 56th's diminished ranks covered little ground, and a gap of nearly 200 yards remained between it and the rest of Garnett's brigade. The order to fall back to the woods west of Dahlgren Road could not be obeyed, for Garnett's regiments came into contact with Hatch's Yankees almost immediately upon reaching 1280's eastern summit, so they could not be withdrawn safely. It was sunset and the battle for control of Hill 1280 had begun.[24]

The 21st New York's skirmishers were the first of Hatch's division to near the mountaintop in any numbers. They managed to reach a point about 30 paces below the summit without drawing any fire or seeing a single enemy soldier. Colonel Rogers ordered a halt and rode forward to personally reconnoiter the ground. He found that the woods ended at the summit, with a relatively level space under cultivation beyond that. He also saw the cornfield that obscured Kemper's right. To the left, or south, of the cornfield was a large meadow, and Rogers observed a body of Confederate troops moving swiftly across it toward the stone fence at the edge of the woods. This was probably the 19th and the 28th Virginia. Rogers's skirmishers had worked their way forward, apparently without orders, and took cover along the wall dividing the field and the woods. Rogers then also called up his reserve and, joined by the 20th New York State Militia, they dashed up and joined their comrades behind the fence. They let the Virginians approach to within 100 yards and then loosed a volley that stunned the Southerners. According to C. C. Wertenbaker of the 19th Virginia, it "killed and wounded quite a number of our men." Lieutenant W. W. Wood, also of this regiment, recalled that they were hit by an enfilading fire from Durell's battery at nearly the same instant. "We were dreadfully exposed to the cross fire while the enemy was concealed behind a rock fence in our front," he wrote. Hoping that they might overpower the enemy in front, the Confederates continued to advance, "leaving the wounded as they fell." Among those who fell was Colonel Strange. Despite his wound, Strange shouted above the din of firing for his men to stand firm. His men, and perhaps the 28th Virginia, ran to a rail fence close to the enemy position, where they found some cover and returned the fire.[25]

At nearly the same moment as Rogers's and Gates's regiments opened fire, the battle exploded on their left. Preceded by skirmishers of the 35th New York, Phelps's brigade advanced through the woods to the left and rear of the 21st New York and 20th New York State Militia, and to within 80 paces of the stone fence at the woods' edge. They drew some scattered fire, perhaps from the 18th Virginia, to which the 35th's skirmishers replied. A lieutenant from the 35th worked his way far enough forward to observe a Confederate regiment, almost certainly the 56th Virginia, in a cornfield on the opposite side of the fence. He reported this information to Colonel Lord; the colonel then passed it back to General Hatch, who was accompanying Phelps's brigade. Hatch responded by commanding, "Forward those skirmishers! Forward on the First Line!" Then, recalled one of the 35th's skirmishers, "all of a sudden, a volley of bullets came over our heads from the right." The volley frightened Colonel Lord's horse; it wheeled and carried him a distance to the rear until he managed to dismount and return to the front on foot.[26]

It was the 18th Virginia who delivered the volley that checked the New Yorkers. They and the 8th Virginia had announced their presence and their determination to vigorously dispute any further advance by the Federals. Phelps immediately ordered his small brigade to deploy from column of division to line of battle, then directed an advance. General Hatch had somehow managed to remain mounted, and he urged his horse forward through Phelps's line to lead the charge. It was brave, but also reckless, yet it inspired the men of his old brigade, who raised a cheer that "could have been heard a mile away." Cabell's and Hunton's Virginians poured fire into the advancing line. The Yankees, reported Cabell, "fell back a short distance, sheltered themselves behind trees, rocks, &c., and opened a heavy fire upon us." The action that ensued, from Marsena Patrick's point of view, "was hot and heavy." With the Confederate position now fixed, Patrick drew in the balance of the 35th New York and the 23rd New York from the left and "merged them in the general line of battle."[27]

The opposing lines traded fire for nearly 15 minutes. "The conflict at the fence became desperate," reported Phelps, "many of the enemy at this time being less than 8 rods [about 45 yards] in our front." The din of musketry was deafening, and thick powder-smoke settled over the woods and the cornfield. On Garnett's left, casualties were mounting for the more exposed men of the 28th and the 19th Virginia. Captain Benjamin Brown reported that the ranks of the 19th "were thinned to such an extent as to prove a withdrawal absolutely necessary." Of the 150 men carried into action, 63 were casualties. The 28th counted 41 casualties out of their 100 effectives. The Federals' numbers and firepower had rendered the Confederates' position untenable. The 28th gave way first, falling back into the corn on the right of the 56th Virginia. The 19th followed. As the 19th retreated, 19-year-old Granville Shephard was shot and killed. His older brother Melville, a second lieutenant in B Company, instantly turned back to retrieve his sibling's body, but this was a story without a happy ending. A Union bullet killed Melville before he could reach his brother. "A truer patriot, a firmer officer, and a nobler youth is not found in our country's service," wrote his commanding officer.[28]

Despite the retreat of their flank supports, the 18th and the 8th Virginia continued to resist stoutly. But Hatch's men sensed the Rebels might now be dislodged by a general advance, and Hatch shouted for Phelps's brigade to charge. Although only a small brigade, they outnumbered the 8th and the 18th by two to one, and this time the Virginians were unable to stop them. The 18th gave way and "fled back down the hill in great confusion." This left Eppa Hunton's small band to stand alone, and they wasted no time in falling back to a fence in the rear. Cabell attempted to re-form on Hunton's left, but the retreat had scattered his regiment. "There were great gaps in our lines," wrote Captain Owen, "and the enemy outflanked us a great way upon the right and upon the left."[29]

Phelps's New Yorkers poured over the disputed stone fence and emerged from the woods into the open ground. The contest for possession of fence resulted in 20 dead, 67 wounded, and 8 missing. It also cost the division the leadership of Brigadier General Hatch, who took a serious wound in the calf during the final advance. He turned command over to Abner Doubleday and left to get medical attention. Phelps, meanwhile, pushed his brigade forward some

30 yards to "an abrupt rise of ground" where they found some cover. The colonel observed that his right extended beyond the left of the 18th or the 19th Virginia, and he ordered his right regiment, the 14th Brooklyn, to advance their right so that they could enfilade the enemy line. The 14th moved over ground littered with the dead and the wounded of the 19th Virginia. Among them was Colonel Strange. According to one account, he fired on the New Yorkers as they passed by, and an infuriated member of the 14th dispatched Strange with a bayonet thrust. The 21st New York and the 20th New York State Militia also moved forward about this time and took position along a fence bounding the northeast side of the cornfield. "We had a good position, where we could do great execution and receive little damage," wrote one member of the 20th. "The enemy were in a cornfield in front of us, where we had a clean sweep at them."[30]

Aside from these modest advances, Phelps's and Patrick's regiments made no real effort to follow up their success at the fence. Phelps's brigade had lost nearly a quarter of its strength and fired off much of its ammunition. Enemy resistance had been so stubborn that Phelps believed the enemy outnumbered him. Dusk was falling, which added to the confusion and the difficulty in coordinating movement. In the opinion of a 35th New Yorker, "we needed help." Phelps shared this opinion, and he sent his adjutant back to request that Doubleday's brigade come up. During the fight for the fence, the 2nd Brigade had deployed into line and moved up to close supporting distance of Phelps. It was the largest brigade of the three assaulting the mountain. The men had stood quietly in the ranks while the battle roared ahead of them.[31] Captain George F. Noyes, the brigade commissary officer, recalled the scene.

> The air is now full of shrieking lead, and we hear just ahead of us the cheers and yells of the opposing troops, the never ceasing rattle of musketry, and all the awful din of battle. Out of this carnival of noise and fire rushes the Adjutant of the first brigade, a noble specimen of American chivalry, exclaiming, "Our brigade cannot sustain itself much longer, as we are nearly out of ammunition. For God's sake, to the front!"[32]

Orders now rang out along the brigade line "to fix bayonets and move forward." The four regiments formed: the 76th New York, the 7th Indiana, the 95th New York, and the 56th Pennsylvania (from left to right). The entire brigade raised a "loud yell" and rushed forward. "They pushed forward so fast that it was almost impossible for the officers to keep them in line," wrote Uberto Burnham of the 76th New York.[33] Part of the 76th did not move quickly enough to suit its brave and newly promoted color sergeant, 21-year-old Charles E. Stamp of Company A. Stamp, wrote the regimental historian,

> rushed forward about a rod in advance of the Regiment, while the bullets were falling thickly around him, and, planting the flag staff firmly in the ground,

shouted, "There, come up to that!" But he made too good a mark, and before the Regiment had time to obey the order, a fatal ball pierced his forehead, and "Charley Stamp," one of the truest and best men in the Regiment, was mustered out of the army militant, and mustered into the army triumphant.[34]

Doubleday's regiments advanced to a rail fence at the woods' edge. "The broken fence was about knee high," wrote Uberto Burnham, "but seemed to give some protection." Phelps's brigade fell back through the ranks of the 2nd Brigade and re-formed downslope, where they had cover but could quickly come to Doubleday's aid if he needed help. Captain Noyes observed that "beyond this fence is an open space of about a hundred feet in depth between the fence and a cornfield, and in this space a strong force of the enemy, partially protected by rocky ledges and inequalities of the surface, forming natural rifle pits, is pressing heavily upon our position." Lieutenant Samuel Healy, the 56th Pennsylvania's adjutant, thought that "our boys were anxious to rush forward but as it was now quite dark our General [Doubleday] restrained them."

Doubleday was content to let his men trade fire with the fragmented pieces of Garnett's greatly diminished brigade. Yet the remaining Virginians fought fiercely and convinced Doubleday that he faced numbers "full four times that of my own." So the men of the 1st Brigade simply blazed away at muzzle flashes in front, or at the movements of shadowy figures darting about in the darkness. It was "too dark to see the enemy, or to locate them except by the puffs of smoke emitted from their guns," according to the 7th Indiana's historian. The result was a considerable waste of ammunition. The 56th Pennsylvania fired "over 45 rounds" and the other regiments probably did, too.[35] Had Doubleday shown even a modicum of aggressive energy, he might have swept Garnett aside, as the Confederates were barely holding on. Captain Owen related that in Garnett's ranks

> there was great confusion, and the broken ranks were hard to rally and re-form, so that had the enemy followed up closely behind they could have taken the gap but the enemy halted and this gave the Confederates time to rally and re-form in separate squads and detachments behind the rocks and fences and reopen a brisk fire. Still falling back and fighting as we retreated, we reached the fence across the field [presumably the fence along the Dahlgren Road], and although half of the brigade had disappeared the survivors made a stand along the fence and endeavored to hold the enemy back until reinforcements could be brought up.[36]

If Owen was correct, then Garnett had only about 250 men left to stand off Doubleday's 1,000 soldiers, plus elements of Patrick's four regiments. The four to one odds were precisely the opposite of what Doubleday believed them to be. But darkness was Garnett's ally, for it concealed his weakness and magnified his resistance. Doubleday, however, was not the only one with an exaggerated sense of the Confederates' strength. Captain Noyes admitted that they were "unable to form any idea of the force opposed to us," but that Garnett's men were "pressing heavily upon our position, charging gallantly two or three times, to be as gallantly repulsed before they reach the fence, and sweeping it meanwhile with sheets of fire." That 250 men could "press heavily" on over four times their numbers and "sweep" their position with "sheets of fire" is a powerful testament to the fighting prowess of the hard-core remnant of Garnett's brigade who remained in the fight, and all the more remarkable after the punishing marching they had endured that day.[37]

The push that dislodged Garnett's center and right from the edge of the woods left the right of Kemper's brigade and the 56th Virginia in Rent's cornfield largely unscathed. When Phelps's attack first struck Garnett's line, Colonel Stuart took the precaution of throwing back the right wing of his 56th Virginia to protect his flank. The corn obscured Stuart's view of the fighting, and the first he knew of Garnett's repulse was when the 28th Virginia retreated back on him through the crops. Stuart sent word to Colonel Corse, on his left, that he thought Garnett had been driven back and suggested that they fall back about 20 yards to the rear, to a fence separating the cornfield from a cleared field. Before Stuart's report reached him, Corse learned that the regiments of his brigade deployed west of the Dahlgren Road "had abandoned the left of the Eleventh [Virginia]." Then came Stuart's report. With both flanks exposed, Corse concurred with Stuart that it was time to pull out. The three regiments— the 56th, the 17th, and the 11th Virginia—fell back "in good order" to the fence on the western edge of the cornfield. They were fired on by Patrick's 21st New York and the 20th New York State Militia, as well as the 56th Pennsylvania on Doubleday's right. "We had a good position, where we could do great execution and receive little damage," wrote John McEnter of the 20th Militia. Yet it was nearly dark, and it was impossible to assess the damage being inflicted. The Virginians fought obstinately. Enos Vail, also in the 20th Militia, admitted that the Rebels "fought with great bravery." Colonel Corse reported that the three regiments under his direct control continued their fire "until long after dark" and "until nearly every cartridge was exhausted." When the men's cartridge boxes were emptied, they gathered ammunition from the dead and the wounded. The cost of their stubborn stand was high. The 56th Virginia, by virtue of their position on the right, endured the heaviest concentration of fire, with 40 killed or wounded and 5 missing out of only 80 muskets carried into action. The 17th and the 11th added 42 more casualties, but they had held the line.[38]

Although they did not feel the same weight of fire that swept the line of the three regiments under Corse's tactical control, Kemper's left fell into disorder following Garnett's retreat. John Dooley of the 1st Virginia described how the bullets from the enemy "got so entirely pranky, disorderly, and murderous in their intent" that the brigade "gave it up as a hopeless business, and came back over the brow of the hill even faster than they went up." Actually, only the 1st Virginia fell back, and Corse's believed they "abandoned" their position. Why they did so is difficult to determine, as they had only four men wounded in the action. It might have been because of a lack of firm leadership in a confusing situation. The regiment had no field officers at South Mountain and was led by Captain George F. Norton. Sergeant David Johnston claimed that his 7th Virginia did not retreat with the 1st, as Corse alleged. Johnston recalled that the enemy made "repeated but unsuccessful efforts to dislodge our men." Which group of Union soldiers attacked them is uncertain, perhaps elements of the 8th Reserves. Whoever it was, they killed 7 men in Johnston's regiment—more than any other regiment in Kemper's brigade—which lends credibility to Johnston's claim. As for the 24th Virginia, they left no record of their actions, but their reported losses of 3 wounded and 18 missing offer circumstantial evidence that they may have pulled back with the 1st Virginia.[39]

Abner Doubleday remained unaware of the Confederates' vulnerability. He believed that they "were too strongly posted and too numerous to be driven from their position," so his regiments and Patrick's blazed away into the darkness, imagining that they were holding back superior numbers. After some minutes of this, Doubleday concluded that his men's fire "was wasted against an unseen foe behind the rocks." He ordered the regiments to cease fire, then rode along the lines and instructed his officers that if the enemy advanced, the Union regiments should hold their fire until the Confederate were in short range, and then fire by rank followed by fire at will. Gradually the shooting sputtered away to silence as Doubleday's orders were passed down the line. In the tense quiet that followed, Doubleday rode along his line, peering into the darkness for any sign of an enemy advance. Movement, and perhaps the rustle of equipment and shuffling feet, caught his attention; through the darkness he made out a line of men moving "silently and swiftly" toward the left of his brigade. He permitted the Confederates to approach within 15 paces of his line when, he recalled, "I at once gave the command in a loud tone 'commence firing.'" The Rebels either heard Doubleday or knew where the Federals were, for before Doubleday's regiments could open fire the Confederates halted, knelt down, and, in the words of the 76th New York's historian, "poured a most terrible volley into our ranks." Most of the volley went high, except in the 76th New York, where it hit 18–20 men, including Colonel William P. Wainwright, who was wounded in the wrist and had his horse killed. Wainwright leaped free from his horse and repeated Doubleday's order to fire. The 76th and the other regiments of the brigade let loose what one of Wainwright's men thought was a devastating volley. The Rebels, he wrote, "will never forget that volley! They were so near that the blaze of our guns almost reached their faces." The Federals quickly rammed home another round and delivered a second volley. No more were necessary.

The Confederates withdrew, leaving their dead and wounded within 5–6 yards of the Union line.[40]

Doubleday's assailants were from Colonel Joseph Walker's South Carolina brigade. They had reached the summit of Turner's Gap at around 5 p.m. Division commander D. R. Jones initially held them as a reserve, but the pressure on Garnett forced Jones to commit them to the fight for Hill 1280. Walker hurried his thin ranks up the Dahlgren Road. Near Hill 1280's summit he deployed the 1st and the 6th South Carolina to support Garnett. Shortly after they formed and took position, Garnett's line gave way to Phelps's attack and, wrote the historian of the 1st South Carolina, "fled in great confusion to the rear." The South Carolinians held their ground, although they were under fire from Durell's battery and possibly the heavy batteries in the valley, whose "shells were now ploughing the ground at their feet or bursting in their very midst." When the Confederates saw that the Federals remained at the woods' edge after their defeat of Garnett, the two South Carolina regiments attempted to use the cover of darkness to turn Doubleday's flank. It was this advance that Doubleday observed. Their sortie was easily repulsed, but it confirmed the effectiveness of aggressive tactics, for the assault reinforced Doubleday's opinion that he was outnumbered and ensured he would remain quietly on the defensive. The cost to the 1st and the 6th South Carolina was not nearly as terrible as the men on Doubleday's line imagined; the two regiments suffered only 27 casualties.[41]

Walker's two regiments fell back to a stone wall on the right of the 8th Virginia, where they re-formed and were reinforced by Captain T. C. Beckham's 5th South Carolina. These regiments maintained a desultory fire on the enemy to cover the withdrawal of Kemper's and Garnett's scattered regiments, who were ordered to fall back to the National Road and re-form. It was a difficult retreat. By this point, Sergeant David Johnston remembered, "it was intensely dark" and everyone suffered from mind-numbing fatigue. There were also many wounded to be located and evacuated. Finding them in the inky darkness without drawing fire from the nearby enemy proved difficult. A member of the 20th New York State Militia overheard one Confederate say to a wounded comrade who was groaning loudly: "Be still, damn you, or they will shoot you again." Some of the injured either were not found or could not be reached; they were left behind to spend a cold, agonizing night on the mountain. For those wounded who were fortunate enough to be evacuated, transportation was haphazard. When no other means of conveyance could be found, Isaac Hare of the 7th Virginia, in a remarkable feat of endurance, carried comrade George Knoll, whose ankle had been fractured by a minie ball, all the way to Boonsboro on Hare's back.[42]

Once Garnett and Kemper had extricated their regiments, Walker was ordered to fall back to the Mountain House. "The men silently crept away under the protection of the rocks and gullies and marched back to their original position," recalled a South Carolinian. To cover his withdrawal as well as protect

Colquitt's rear, Walker pushed out a strong skirmish line and advanced the 2nd South Carolina Rifles along the National Road to a point east of the Mountain House. By 9 p.m., except for a few skirmishers and the wounded who could not be reached or found—and the dead—the Confederates had abandoned Hill 1280 to the Federals.[43]

The Rebels executed their retreat so quietly that Doubleday's men were unaware that they had left. It is doubtful, however, that Doubleday would have molested the withdrawal even if he had known about it. His regiments and Patrick's were low on ammunition—there being only four or five rounds per man—and exhausted. "It was as dark as a pocket, and in the confusion it was almost impossible to get any idea of our whereabouts," wrote one man. Doubleday appealed to Ricketts's division for reinforcements, and Colonel William A. Christian's 2nd Brigade was ordered forward. Doubleday reported that they "came up promptly," but Colonel Hoffman of the 23rd New York thought Christian managed things badly. Hoffman was barely able to get his regiment into a respectable line "when a brigade came up in the darkness hooting and yelling, running over everybody and throwing everything into even worse confusion than before." Lieutenant Sam Healy of the 56th Pennsylvania likewise heaped scorn on Christian's men. "They came," he wrote in his journal, "but some of the Regts. were backward about going up to the fence, the resissive we held. They were the 94th and 23rd [26th] New York. But our boys blackguarded them until they became ashamed and went up, but the heat of battle was over." Well, almost over. One final, minor act in the drama on Hill 1280 remained to be played out.[44]

When Christian's regiments came up to relieve Doubleday, the latter ordered his brigade to fall back 8 or 10 paces in the rear of Christian "in order that we might sustain him with the bayonet if necessary." Doubleday probably also wanted to get his men free of the confusion in Christian's brigade. But in delivering Doubleday's command to the 76th New York and the 7th Indiana, on Doubleday's left, a young staff officer misunderstood the instructions and directed these two regiments to fall back to the Mount Tabor church. Both regiments began to file off by the left flank, which placed them perpendicular to the rest of their brigade. As they did so, Second Lieutenant James L. Goddard of the 76th's Company F saw or heard movement in a cornfield beyond the regiment's right flank (formerly their left, but now their right, since they were moving away from the battle) and warned Colonel Wainwright. Wainwright coolly took command of both regiments and passed orders for them to form quietly into line by changing front to the rear—a tricky maneuver in pitch darkness. They nonetheless accomplished it and were soon formed into line facing south and perpendicular to the rest of their brigade. They waited silently. "The sound of the rebels stumbling over the rocks in the dark now became plainly audible to him [Wainwright]," wrote Doubleday. Exercising commendable discipline, both regiments held their fire until the Confederates were nearly on top of them. Wainwright shouted

"Fire!" and Union muskets crashed, lighting the night with a sheet of flame. The enemy quickly vanished, and the Federals imagined that they had deflected another effort to turn their flank. But this had been no more than the skirmishers of Walker's brigade, who had lost their bearings in the darkness while attempting to establish the brigade's skirmish line.[45]

This brief flare-up on the left prompted Christian's regiments to deliver several volleys into their front, although at no particular target. When the firing ceased, "three cheers were then proposed for McClellan, three for the Union and three for Doubleday," recorded Lieutenant Healy, and they were given "with a hearty will." Walker's skirmishers, "not liking our joyous feelings," greeted it with a volley, to which Christian's trigger-happy regiments instantly replied. But the firing soon sputtered out and the mountain summit lapsed back into a taut silence. Captain Noyes stated that "the excitement of our own fight is over; the woods are now so dark that objects ten feet distant are undistinguishable, and the thought of a night attack fills me with dread." While Christian's regiments fingered their triggers and peered into the dark for approaching Confederates, Doubleday's men lay down and pulled their blankets over themselves to ward off the chill descending on the mountain. Patrick found it impossible to reorganize his scattered brigade in the darkness. The 21st New York and the 20th New York State Militia remained at the fence bordering the cornfield, on Christian's right. "The night was very cold," wrote Enos Vail of the 20th. He tried to slumber, but "the ground was so cold that I could not sleep." The 23rd and the 35th New York withdrew from their position on the front line around 11 p.m. and "groped our way" down the slope of the mountain into the woods, where they, too, passed a cold and uncomfortable night.[46]

"Our own contest appears to be over for the present," penned Captain Noyes, "but we listen to the unceasing rattle of musketry on our left with great anxiety." The firing came from the direction of the National Road. One last bloody combat remained to be fought before the weapons of the two armies fell silent in the battle for Turner's Gap.[47]

13

Into Turner's Gap

"An ugly looking place to attack"

The men of Brigadier General John Gibbon's 4th Brigade of Hatch's 1st Division had "scarcely kindled" their fires for coffee on that warm September 14 afternoon when orders to fall in sang out through the division bivouac. Packs and weapons were shouldered and the brigade found their place at the rear of their division as it set out along the National Road, following Meade's Pennsylvania Reserves. They turned off with the rest of the 1st Corps on Mount Tabor Road and had marched about a mile along it when a courier from Burnside rode up with orders for Gibbon to detach both his brigade and Captain Joseph B. Campbell's Battery B, 4th U.S. Artillery (6 Napoleons), return to the National Road, and await further orders. Gibbon sent word to Hatch and then countermarched back to the National Road. At the pike the brigade turned west and followed it for nearly a half mile before Gibbon called a halt and sent back to Burnside for instructions. Burnside's intention was for Gibbon to make a "demonstration upon the enemy's center, up the main pike, as soon as the movements of Generals Hooker and Reno had sufficiently progressed." But until those larger movements developed, Gibbon was ordered to move his command south of the pike into a grass field in support of Simmonds's Kentucky battery, which was shelling the gap. Gibbon formed his brigade in two lines in double column closed in mass. The 19th Indiana and the 7th Wisconsin occupied the first line and the 2nd Wisconsin and 6th Wisconsin the second. The men loaded their weapons and then lay down to await developments. It was approximately 3 p.m.[1]

"The brigade was quiet," wrote Lieutenant Frank Haskell, aide-de-camp to Gibbon, "with no prospect of immediate work, listening and looking for what could be heard or seen." Many took note of the ground before them. "The turnpike is steep and winds up among the hills," observed Haskell. "The ground descends from both sides to the turnpike—is wooded save for a belt from one hundred fifty to three hundred yards wide on each side, and is crossed here and there with strong stone fences and abounds in good natural covers for troops— altogether an ugly looking place to attack, and held by artillery and we knew not how much infantry."[2]

It may have been the difficulty of the mission that prompted Burnside to select Gibbon and his brigade. The 35-year-old Gibbon was a rising star in the army. Although born in Philadelphia, he had grown up in North Carolina and received his appointment to West Point from that state. He graduated in 1847 and saw his share of hard service: in Florida against the Seminoles, and in the Mormon campaign. Tactics and the technical aspects of artillery—his branch of service—fascinated him; he served as an artillery instructor at West Point and authored a widely used light artillery manual. His knowledge of artillery prompted a fellow officer to rate him "a master of his profession." The war's outbreak found him a captain and commander of Battery B, 4th U.S. Artillery. The war posed a special dilemma for Gibbon. His three brothers all enlisted in the Confederate service, and his parents were Democrats and slaveholders. Yet he resisted the powerful emotional tug of family and remained loyal to the Union. To earn his star as a brigadier general of volunteers, Gibbon left his beloved battery to take command of a brigade of western regiments in May 1862.[3]

His new command consisted of one Indiana and three Wisconsin regiments. They were untested troops, save for the 2nd Wisconsin, which had fought at First Manassas. Tough and exacting, Gibbon immediately earned the dislike of his independent-minded western volunteers with his regular-army methods. But Gibbon differed from many of his fellow officers in understanding that with volunteers "the hope of reward was far more powerful than the fear of punishment." He instituted a system of rewards for achievements and, when necessary, castigation—but not harsh, regular-army physical punishment. Instead, his methods were to embarrass those who misbehaved or to hurt their pride. To instill a sense of esprit de corps in his command and set them apart from other volunteers, he had the men draw the uniform of the regular U.S. Army: frock coat, white leggings, and a black felt Hardee hat. The men grumbled over the cost of the uniform, but the Hardee hat became their mark of distinction and earned them the nickname of the Black Hat Brigade. Gibbon knew what awaited them on the battlefield, and he drilled his regiments relentlessly. One member proudly recalled: "The brigade was not excelled in the precision and accuracy of their movements by any body of troops I have ever seen, not excepting the cadets of West Point." Gibbon's training regimen paid off in the brigade's baptism of fire in the opening action of the battle of Second Manassas on August 28. Stonewall Jackson threw four brigades against them as they marched down the Warrenton Turnpike late that August afternoon. Gibbon's westerners, with the help of two regiments from Abner Doubleday's brigade, shot it out with Jackson's veterans and fought them to a bloody standstill, earning grudging admiration from Jackson for their "obstinate determination." More fighting followed in the larger battle that ensued over the next three days, and when it was over Gibbon's four regiments counted 894 casualties. The survivors had learned the value of their training and gained a new respect for Gibbon.[4]

They had also tasted the cruel reality of battle and, like other troops after their first experience in combat, had no especial desire to embrace it again. "Our one night's experience at Gainesville [on August 28] had eradicated our yearning for a fight," commented Rufus R. Dawes, the major of the 6th Wisconsin. The fates of combat had been on the minds of many in the brigade as they moved across Maryland. Veterans understood that survival rested partly on good training, discipline, and leadership, but it also depended on luck, and the more times a soldier went under fire, the less chance he had of emerging unscathed. This was surely on the mind of 7th Wisconsin Lieutenant Henry B. Young when he wrote to his wife from Frederick on September 13: "You ask what you should do if I should be killed. It is a hard question, but I have seen so many men killed and die in the last few weeks that I will give you the best advice I can. If I should be killed in battle or die while in the service, you as the wife of a 1st Lieut will draw from the government, seventeen dollars per month for five years." Similar thoughts weighed on the mind of the 6th Wisconsin's commander, Lieutenant Colonel Edward Bragg. In a letter to his wife, also written on the 13th, Bragg speculated on the prospects of his death from wounds. He had been lucky so far, he wrote, but then, reflecting on the random nature of battle, he added that "no one can tell if it be my fate to fall." Then, forgetting the sensitivities of his wife at home, he offered a cold reassurance: "My body will be sent to you."[5]

"For nearly an hour we laid upon the grassy knoll, passive spectators of the scene," recorded Major Dawes. The brigade enjoyed grandstand seating for Hooker's assault. "Two miles away on our right, long lines and heavy columns of dark blue infantry [Hatch's division] could be seen pressing up the green slopes of the mountain, their bayonets flashing like silver in the rays of the setting sun, and their banners waving in beautiful relief against the background of green," wrote Dawes. "On the left," he continued, "and along the summit of the mountain, the crash of musketry and the roar of cannon indicated that the battle was raging furiously there." Five miles to the south, the westerners could see a "lead colored cloud" hanging over Crampton's Gap, where the 6th Corps were hammering away. It was probably close to 5 p.m. when an orderly galloped up to brigade headquarters. He carried orders directly from Burnside, instructing Gibbon to advance up the turnpike, taking along as much of Campbell's battery as necessary, and attack the enemy in the gorge, dislodging him if possible, but at least moving far enough forward to complete the line of battle between Reno and Hooker. Shouted orders brought the 1,200 men of the brigade to their feet, followed by commands: "Attention, Battalion! Load at will. Shoulder arms! Forward by file right, MARCH." Grim-faced, the Wisconsin and Indiana soldiers strode forward, heading for Turner's Gap and a conflict that would earn them everlasting fame.[6]

The Georgians and Alabamians of Colonel Alfred Colquitt's brigade were awaiting Gibbon's sturdy westerners. They had been the first infantry to occupy Turner's Gap, and now would be the last to be engaged. Colquitt had spread his five regiments across a wide front to both cover the approaches to the pass and attempt to reduce the distance between his flanks and friendly forces at Fox's Gap and on Hill 1280. To defend the direct approach to Turner's Gap, Colquitt deployed Colonel William P. Barclay's 23rd Georgia and Major Tully Graybill's 28th Georgia at a sharp bend in the National Road, about 700 yards east of the Mountain House. Both regiments formed north of the pike, the 23rd with its right touching the road and the 28th extending its left to rest on "a steep cliff of the mountain." Most of the men found good cover behind a stone wall that was backed by a channel cut by rainwater rushing down the mountain, which formed a natural trench. On the extreme left of the line, where there was no wall, the men of the 28th Georgia concealed themselves in the woods on the mountainside. The ground in front of both regiments was open but "rough and rocky," and in front of the 23rd and part of the 28th it rose just enough so that an enemy approaching the Confederates' front could not see either regiment's position until they were 40 paces away.[7]

Neither regiment deployed its full firepower on line. The 23rd Georgia's Lieutenant Colonel Emory F. Best was detached with Companies B, D, E, and I to support Lane's battery. The 28th Georgia had three companies on the skirmish line: Company K covered the approaches north of the National Road, and Companies B and C, counting only 39 men combined, took cover behind a rock fence about 100 yards south of the turnpike. South of this road the ground fell away steeply to a deep ravine, through which a feeder creek that flowed into Catoctin Creek ran. About 400 yards to the right and front of these two companies "there was a thick growth of woods, with fields opening in front and around them." In these woods and in and about a nearby farmhouse, Colquitt concealed his skirmish battalion under Captain William M. Arnold, of whom a 6th Georgia soldier wrote, "a braver man never lived." Arnold's battalion consisted of Company A from each of the five regiments in the brigade, and every man was armed with a rifle. Colquitt placed Colonel L. B. Smith's 27th Georgia some 200–300 yards to the right of Arnold's battalion. The 13th Alabama and the 6th Georgia were also south of the turnpike, presumably posted along the wooded northern slopes of Hill 1080. Although necessity dictated a broad front, Colquitt anticipated that the most likely approach the enemy would follow if they assaulted the gap would be on the north side of the National Road, where 11 companies of the 23rd and the 28th Georgia awaited them.[8]

Late in the afternoon Colquitt watched "a large force" of the enemy, with skirmishers covering their front, start to move "slowly, but steadily" in his direction. It was Gibbon's brigade. With his wide frontage, Colquitt worried about his ability to stop the approaching force, and he sent a request to D. H. Hill for reinforcements, who responded that there were none to be had. Colquitt would have to make his fight with the men at hand.[9]

Gibbon deployed his brigade into battle formation as it began the ascent toward Turner's Gap. The 268 officers and men of Colonel Solomon Meredith's 19th Indiana formed into line south of the pike. Gibbon believed the 19th "had the finest material in it in the whole brigade, yet it was the worst regiment I had." He blamed this on Meredith, who, Gibbon thought, "had not the first principle of a soldier in him; he was altogether unqualified for his position." It is unclear whether this was a true assessment or the result of Gibbon's personal pique against Meredith. Big Sol Meredith stood 6 feet 7 inches tall and certainly did not lack personal courage, but he may have been deficient in the discipline and tactical acumen Gibbon expected of his regimental commanders, although there is no evidence to indicate that this was the case. Meredith's support consisted of the 200 men of the rock-solid 2nd Wisconsin, commanded by Colonel Lucius Fairchild. Gibbon considered the 2nd and the 6th Wisconsin "two of the best regiments that ever fought on any field." Fairchild formed his regiment 200 yards in the rear of the 19th, in double column at half distance, a compact formation that facilitated command and control, but which was easily deployed into battle line. Fairchild also supplied a skirmish line, consisting of his Companies B and E under Captain Wilson Colwell, to cover the 19th's advance. Colwell, a prewar banker in LaCrosse, Wisconsin, had been elected mayor of his hometown in April 1861 but chose to be a soldier instead. Captain George Otis of Company I remembered him as "one of the particularly strong men of the regiment." Colwell spread his men out in skirmish order 100 yards in advance of the 19th.[10]

The 7th and the 6th Wisconsin moved north of the pike. All the field officers of the 7th were recovering from wounds received at Manassas, so the senior captain, John B. Callis, led the regiment. Callis was North Carolina born and had been something of an adventurer before settling down in Lancaster, Wisconsin. His was the second largest regiment in the brigade, with 375 effectives, and they formed the first line. As support, Colonel Edward S. Bragg's 6th Wisconsin, the largest regiment in the brigade at 400 strong, followed in double column 200 yards to the rear. In front of these two regiments was a smooth slope checkered with orchards and, beyond the orchards, a large cornfield. Like the 2nd Wisconsin, the 6th furnished the skirmish line for the right half of the brigade. Companies B and K drew this duty. As the men dashed forward to take position, they plucked apples from the orchard they passed through and tucked them in their haversacks, which were already weighed down with 60 extra rounds of ammunition.[11]

For his artillery support, Gibbon selected Lieutenant James B. Stewart's section of Campbell's Battery B, 4th U.S. The Scottish-born Stewart was a long-time artillery veteran, having risen from the enlisted ranks to gain his commission, and Gibbon knew him well from his prewar command of the battery. Stewart moved his pair of Napoleons into the road while the infantry advanced in the fields beside him. The overcast sky gave way to sunshine, and the sun's rays "came full in the faces of the men." But it proved to be only a brief nuisance, for the sun soon began to sink behind the mountain, casting long shadows over the landscape. Steadily but cautiously, Gibbon's Black Hats moved forward.[12]

"Soon we hear the single shot of a skirmisher—another and another follow," wrote Lieutenant Haskell. They came from the 6th Wisconsin's skirmish line. After passing through the apple orchard, the Federals' skirmish line entered the cornfield, which extended for nearly a half mile along the National Road. They jumped several Georgia skirmishers in the corn, and both sides traded fire. The Georgians slipped back through the crop, with the 6th's men following warily. South of the pike the 2nd Wisconsin's skirmish line also felt fire, probably delivered by the men of Arnold's skirmish battalion. Captain Colwell's voice carried clearly over the scattered firing, shouting "Forward." But early in the fight a Confederate bullet silenced the brave captain, striking him in the left side, passing into the lower bowels, then striking his backbone and glancing forward, causing devastating internal damage. Colwell sat down and, despite the shock he no doubt experienced, managed to shout: "Advance the right; and press forward—don't give way." Then he called Sergeant Uriel P. Olin over—Olin himself would fall three days later at Antietam—and asked that he be carried to the rear. Colwell, recalled a lieutenant of his regiment, "soon expired, suffering but little pain, though expressing much solicitude for his wife."[13]

Gibbon's skirmishers pushed on, driving Colquitt's skirmishers "slowly up the mountain, fighting for every inch of ground." The courage of the skirmishers impressed Major Dawes. Watching the men of his regiment's Companies B and K, he thought that "nothing could be more gallant than the conduct of these two companies. For more than a mile of advance they played a deadly game of 'bo peep' from every log, fence, rock, knoll. They found rebels everywhere, in the barns and houses, behind the fences, in the trees, and without help or reinforcement from their battalions, they drove them back." During the course of this running fight a Confederate battery placed "well up in the gorge" opened fire on the Federals. "His shot fly wild, making a good deal of hissing, but no harm," observed Lieutenant Haskell. Stewart unlimbered his two Napoleons in the road and pumped several shells at the source of the fire. This seemed to work, for the Confederate guns fell silent, but as Gibbon's men would soon discover, the Rebels were merely changing position.[14]

Gibbon kept abreast of his infantry regiments, adjusting his position constantly so that he was "always on the highest ground where he could see the whole line." His voice could be heard clearly, always urging the men to press forward. Noticing that a strip of woods to the left of the 19th Indiana that might conceal enemy infantry, he ordered Colonel Meredith to throw out two of his companies into the woods as flank guards. Gibbon intended to "push forward rapidly and get engaged before the darkness came on." But Meredith wasted precious time when he misunderstood Gibbon's orders and ordered his entire regiment to change front forward on the left company, a maneuver that shifted his regiment's facing from west to south. It also presented his flank to the Confederate artillery at Turner's Gap. They were quick to take advantage of this opportunity and opened fire. Gibbon then sent Lieutenant Haskell galloping down to remedy Meredith's error.[15]

Southern gunnery once again proved inaccurate, or so it seemed, for they missed the 19th cleanly, but then they either got lucky or adjusted their fire. Whichever it was, they burst a shell on top of the 2nd Wisconsin, whose men lay prone on the ground while the 19th changed front. When the smoke had cleared four men were dead and three others were mangled with serious wounds. Gibbon offered the regiment no time to dwell on this bloody event, for he ordered the 2nd forward to form on the right of the 19th and extend the line to the National Road.[16]

While the 2nd moved up, Meredith correct his error, realigned his regiment, and dispatched his Company B out as flankers. When the 2nd came up and formed on his right, both regiments resumed the advance toward Turner's Gap. Up to this point resistance south of the pike had been negligible, but that changed when the skirmish line bumped up against Captain Arnold's skirmishers. Arnold's men had taken cover in a farmhouse and its outbuildings, as well as in the woods southwest of the structures. The farmhouse, which no longer exists, was south of the D. Beachley (or Buchler) farm; the latter sat at the intersection of two farm roads and the National Road, about 1 mile west of Bolivar. The buildings on the first farm were near the extreme left of the Federal line, and the fire of Arnold's men not only searched out the 2nd Wisconsin's skirmish line, but also harassed the main line of battle. Meredith sent his son to Lieutenant Stewart with a request for Stewart to shell the farmhouse and help dislodge the Confederates. Stewart thought young Meredith "the youngest and tallest, as well as the thinnest, man I ever saw." As Colonel Meredith wanted Stewart to blast a civilian residence, the lieutenant sent Meredith's lanky son back with the response that such a request must be in writing. Stewart's response displeased the colonel, and he rode over to the lieutenant, perhaps hoping that his rank and his 6-foot 7-inch frame might intimidate the Scotsman into shelling the building; it failed to budge the stubborn regular-army man, and Stewart shortly had his written order. As Stewart recalled it, he told Meredith: "You go back to your regiment and I will put a shell into the second story of that house, and about a minute after I will put another shell into the first story to catch those fellows coming down." The Napoleons were unlimbered and, true to his word, Stewart's gun crews sent their first shot smashing into the upper story of the building, causing, Meredith reported, "a general stampede of their forces from that point." No one recorded whether the second shot struck the first floor, but Stewart's iron sent Arnold's riflemen scampering to less dangerous cover. Arnold's men in the woods near the farmhouse were not so easily dislodged, however. From this cover they poured a "sharp fire" at the Federal skirmish line and brought it to a halt. Meredith led his regiment to the skirmishers' support and opened fire "at short range" on the Georgians and Alabamians. Arnold had accomplished his mission of harassing and slowing the enemy advance. But tangling with a line of battle was not a task for skirmishers, so Arnold ordered his men to fall back. The Federals followed, "cheering all the time."[17]

Meanwhile, north of the National Road, the skirmishers of the 6th Wisconsin cautiously made their way through the long cornfield paralleling the pike. They reached the end of the field just at dusk. It was marked by a stone wall, and a large pasture extended beyond the wall, "full of logs, stumps, big boulders, etc." A mature forest grew along the northern border of the pasture and extended up the slope of Hill 1280. The ground rose in the pasture, so that it was only possible to see halfway across it. What lay on the other side was not visible. The two company commanders, Lieutenants John Ticknor and Lyman B. Upham, ordered their men over the wall and into the field to find out what was there. "The field was pretty full of large stones, and now and again a huge boulder stood up and afforded both us and the enemy excellent cover," recalled John P. Sullivan of Company K. The tactics that he and his comrades employed as they moved across the pasture would be familiar to a World War II veteran: "Part of the men would fire and then rush forward while the others covered them and had at the rebels and then the rear line would pass through to the front and lay down while the other line kept up the fire, and in that way it was a steady advance." It was fire and movement, and then fire and movement once more. The men made progress until they reached the ridge in the middle of the pasture. Here enemy resistance hardened, and the Confederate skirmishers stubbornly refused to give ground. The 7th Wisconsin appeared at the edge of the cornfield, and Captain Callis ordered the regiment over the wall and into the pasture to support the skirmishers. The change from the relative cover and security of the tall, leafy crop to the open and exposed pasture tested the mettle of Callis's men. One of them, Zeb B. Russell, wrote: "Right here, my comrades, let me say to those who have faced a line of loaded rebel muskets, and say they felt no fear, that if they felt as we did in going over that last wall they did not feel brave. It was one of the hardest things we did that day, knowing that the woods were full of Southerns, and that they were going to shoot to kill."[18]

The 7th's line extended from the National Road, across the boulder-strewn pasture, to the edge of the woods on the northern border of the field—a frontage of somewhat over 100 yards. Captain Callis advanced his line to the brow of the ridge in the pasture, where he then had them lie down. The 6th Wisconsin's skirmishers cleared the 7th's front by gravitating toward the woods. Although Callis felt some scattered fire from Rebel skirmishers, he remained uncertain as to where the main enemy line lay; nevertheless, he sensed that it was close. He hesitated to move beyond the cover of the ridge, but Gibbon saw that the 7th had halted and sent a courier up to Callis with orders to advance. The captain ordered his men up and the line went forward, with the main body of the 6th Wisconsin following at a distance of 50 paces, still formed in double column.[19]

As the 7th went forward, Companies B and C of the 28th Georgia, under Captain Nehemiah Garrison, who had been lying quietly behind a stone fence south of the turnpike, revealed themselves and opened what Callis described as "a destructive enfilading fire" on his left flank. "Suddenly," recalled Major Dawes, "the seventh Wisconsin halted and opened fire." The regiment directed their fire toward Garrison's companies. Garrison also had the 2nd Wisconsin approaching his front and the 19th Indiana menacing his right. Unless reinforced, the Rebel captain knew his force would be overwhelmed. He had sent Alonzo Medlock of Company B to the 27th Georgia, which Garrison could see forming between his position and the Mountain House. "I assure you I moved as rapidly as my feet would carry me," wrote Medlock. The bullets fell around Medlock in a "perfect shower," but he survived the dash and found Lieutenant Colonel Charles T. Zachary, who had taken command of the 27th after Colonel L. B. Smith was wounded. Zachary immediately sent two companies forward to Garrison's support and followed them soon after with five or six more. Up to this point the 23rd and the 28th Georgia remained quietly behind the stone wall along the western edge of the pasture, awaiting their opportunity to strike the enemy troops, who were now within close range. Unaware that these two regiments were in his front, Captain Callis shortly presented the Georgians with a splendid target.[20]

Callis found the fire from his left so bothersome that he felt it necessary to silence it before he could advance farther, so he requested permission from Gibbon to change front to the left. Gibbon approved, and Callis executed a left half-wheel, switching the front of his regiment from west to southwest. It squarely presented his right flank to the 23rd Georgia, who suddenly leveled their muskets over the wall that had concealed them and delivered a deadly fire into the right flank of the 7th. The 28th Georgia had shifted into the woods on the northern edge of the stony field during Gibbon's approach, and they now opened fire into the backs of Callis's Badgers. "We could see a rapid spitting of musketry flashes from the woods above and in front of us, and the wounded men from the seventh began to hobble by us," recalled Major Dawes. John Gibbon's tough training now paid off. With dying men sinking to the ground and others tumbling about from bullet wounds, Callis shouted orders for the 7th to fall back to their old line, where they might face the fire of both of their assailants on a more equal footing. "They fell back as rapidly and regularly as possible under the withering fire," wrote Dawes. Nearly 50 men were hit in a matter of moments, and the 7th had been unable to return a single shot. Callis needed help, so he sent Captain Richard H. Richardson running back to the 6th Wisconsin. The captain ran up to them and yelled, "Come forward, sixth!"[21]

Colonel Edward Bragg shouted to his men over the firing from up front: "Boys you must save the Seventh." Then he commanded: "Deploy column, By the right and left flanks. Double Quick, March." This maneuver brought the right wing of the 6th into line on the right of the 7th, but the 7th's line masked Bragg's left wing. Exercising quick thinking, Bragg improvised with some innovative tactics. He ordered Dawes to take command of the right wing and open fire, while he himself led the left wing, directly behind Dawes's wing. The right wing delivered a volley into the woods that were concealing the 28th Georgia. Dawes recalled that "the roll of this wing volley had hardly ceased to reverberate" when Bragg called out: "Have your men lie down on the ground, I am going over you." As the major's men did so and proceeded to load their muskets, Bragg led the right wing over them, halted, and had his men fire a volley into the woods. Then Bragg's wing dropped to the ground to load while Dawes brought his men to their feet and moved them at the double-quick over Bragg's men, delivering yet another volley. "There were four volleys by wing given, at the word of command," recalled Dawes. "In a long experience in musketry fighting, this was the single instance I saw of other than a fire by file in battle." Although seemingly simple, this was a difficult maneuver to execute under the conditions. The Confederates had cover in the woods, and their position could only be discerned by their muzzle flashes. Smoke wreathed the fighting lines, the din of all the firing must have been deafening, and darkness was falling. All thwarted a leader's ability to command and control his troops. That Bragg and his regiment carried out a maneuver by wing was a testament to both his and Dawes's leadership and the excellent discipline of their soldiers. One of Bragg's men, Lyman Holford, remembered how "the balls flew thick and fast," and Mickey Sullivan of Company K, who was wounded and trying to hobble to the rear, recalled that "the sides of the mountain seemed in a blaze of flame." Yet Dawes noted that the men "were wild with enthusiasm" and would shout "now you thieving scoundrels, no McDowell after you now."[22]

The 6th Wisconsin's successive volleys by wing relieved the flanking fire of the 28th Georgia from the woods, but the 7th Wisconsin could still make no headway against the Georgians behind the stone wall. "All we could see of the enemy was a streak of fire as their guns were discharged," recalled Zeb Russell. The 7th blazed away at the wall, but, noted Captain Aleck Gordon Jr. of Company E, the Confederates "replied to our fire with fearful effect." One of the many casualties was Zeb Russell. He remembered firing several shots and was in the act of loading when "something struck me in the right leg. I went down of course. The first thought was, 'the limb is shot off.'" While he was down he was hit in the foot of his good leg, but his shoe took the brunt of the damage. Someone dragged him behind a large rock and tied off his wound to slow the bleeding. "As the fight went on, the wounded came back until they were stowed in behind that rock as thick as sardines in a box," wrote Russell. In the course of the fight Russell's company had 20 wounded and 1 killed. The high ratio of injured to dead might have been an indication that while the Confederates were throwing a great deal of lead in the 7th's direction, the thick smoke—combined with the fall of night—made the Georgians' aim less accurate. Yet the damage was still severe enough as bullets found their mark in faces, hips, breasts, knees, hands, wrists, sides, bowels, and arms.[23]

Gibbon was convinced by what he could see that frontal tactics would not dislodge the enemy from the wall, so he sent up orders for Colonel Bragg to move through the woods and flank the Rebels' line. This was easier said than done. Conducting a flanking movement through woods over rough, rocky ground on a steep slope with night descending was a tall order, but the little colonel quickly devised a plan. While Bragg led the left wing into the woods, Dawes's wing would cover the movement with their fire, then "advance the right wing on the skirt of the wood as rapidly as the line in the wood advanced."[24]

While the 6th and the 7th Wisconsin fought the Confederates north of the National Road, the 19th Indiana and the 2nd Wisconsin sought to clear out the Georgians south of it. The Federals came up against Captain Garrison's small command, who were busy firing into the left flank of the 7th Wisconsin, and sent a storm of bullets at the Confederates, which pinned them down and relieved the 7th of this flanking fire. Then, while the 2nd Wisconsin swept Garrison's front with musketry, Meredith sent his Companies B and G forward to flank them. The Hoosier companies found cover behind a stone wall running at right angles to the one sheltering the Georgians and "poured a deadly fire into them." Wrote Henry Marsh of Meredith's command, "the fence in which the rebles were behind ran up hill to the road so that if a bullet missed one it took another." Lead flayed Garrison's outnumbered band from front and flank. "The whole field was one sheet of fire," wrote Alonzo Medlock of Garrison's tiny force. The Confederates broke for the rear, leaving behind 11 prisoners who chose not to make the dangerous dash to safety and carrying with them the reinforcing companies of the 27th Georgia, who perceived the hopelessness of their mission and joined the retreat.[25]

Having cleared the enemy south of the pike, Colonel Fairchild ordered his 2nd Wisconsin to shift their fire to a right oblique at the 23rd Georgia. But the 2nd was on much lower ground than their target, and most of their fire passed harmlessly over the Southerners' heads. Fairchild attempted to gain more favorable results by changing front with his right wing until it was parallel to the National Road and on the flank of the 23rd. His men blazed away until their ammunition was exhausted; Fairchild then relieved them with the left wing. They, too, fired their entire ammo load. Meredith moved his 19th over, relieved the 2nd, and repeated Fairchild's tactics of firing by wings. The Hoosiers kept this up until they, too, were out of ammunition. The damage done by this storm of lead, however, was negligible. Despite the change of front, both Union regiments delivered their fire from much lower ground than the 23rd's position, and nearly all of it passed harmlessly over the Georgians' heads. Some bullets possibly landed among the combatants on Hill 1280.[26]

Both sides stubbornly stood their ground as night fell over the field. The darkness, the muzzle flashes of hundreds of muskets, and the clouds of powder-smoke created a surreal scene, which Frank Haskell evocatively captured.

> The view of this fight after dark was thrilling and grand to a high degree. The opposing lines were very close to each other—a hundred yards or less, as the advantages of ground induced deviations from straight lines to enable the men to get cover—and the fire of the infantry was incessant—Flash met flash of the opposing combatants and the frequent vollies roared and reverberated among the hills like continuous thunder; and louder than all the infantry, and with deeper flame, the well handled Napoleons of Stewart belched their iron contents over the heads of our own men, into the ranks of the enemy.[27]

Despite all the firepower Gibbon massed against them, Colquitt's 23rd and 28th Georgia clung tenaciously to their strong position. "The old 28th and 23rd met them like men and held them at bay for three long hours," wrote Major Tully Graybill of the 28th. Colquitt reported with pride, and without exaggeration, that on the front of the 23rd and the 28th "not an inch of ground was yielded." The efforts of Gibbon's Black Hats had been as gallant and courageous as possible, but they could not overcome the advantage of position held by soldiers as stubborn and brave as themselves.[28]

It was "pitch dark" by the time the 19th Indiana and the 2nd Wisconsin had exhausted their ammunition, and the combat gradually sputtered out into a tense silence. Despite tough resistance from the 28th Georgia, Colonel Bragg managed to maneuver his right wing into the woods and advance them until he thought he had extended his line around the enemy's flank. Then he sent for Dawes to bring his right wing up to reunite the regiment. "I found great difficulty in performing the maneuver," wrote Dawes, owing to the pitch-black conditions and the thick, rocky woods that his men had to make their way through. Ammunition ran dangerously low on both sides. Captain Aleck Gordon of the 7th Wisconsin wrote, "our ammunition being out, we put our last charge into our guns and laid down to await orders, which came to hold the ground at all hazards." The Georgians were in similar shape, and they, too, fixed bayonets to hold their position. But the noise Dawes's men made moving up through the woods provoked at least some of the Georgians to fire part of their precious ammunition in the right wing's direction. It killed and wounded several of the major's men, but Bragg's wing came to their comrades' relief by pouring fire at the enemy muzzle flashes. Dawes managed to complete the junction of the two wings of the regiment, and the firing gradually ceased. "We again lay down and all was still," recalled the major. Then a member of Company A, who obviously was not the brightest pupil of Wisconsin's schooling, called out loudly: "By thunder. I am out of cartridges." Some of the nearby 28th Georgians heard this; they opened fire and began to advance. "We had 'one volley' yet for them," wrote Dawes. His wing traded shots with the enemy, and it sent the Georgians ducking for cover. A taut silence ensued. Bragg then thought he heard movement on the Confederate lines; it sounded as though they were pulling out. He called for "three cheers for the Badger State," and his regiment gave them "with a will." If the Confederates had not withdrawn this might have been a foolish decision, for it gave away the 6th's position, but the response to the cheers came from beyond the hill in front, up toward the gap. Bragg requested several volunteers to investigate. They crept forward and confirmed Bragg's suspicion—the enemy had withdrawn.[29]

Gibbon's men claimed victory, since the Confederates left the field, but Colquitt had fulfilled his duty to check the enemy advance against the Confederate center. Given the enormous number of bullets Gibbon's command had fired, Colquitt's casualties were relatively light: 18 dead, 74 wounded, and 17 missing, although this loss had fallen almost wholly on the 23rd and the 28th Georgia. But Colquitt's success in delaying Gibbon did not alter the overall dismal position the Confederates were in when the fighting finally ended, and at 10 p.m. orders were quietly delivered to Graybill and Barclay to withdraw to Turner's Gap. Leaving their dead behind and collecting "all the wounded we could find in the dark," the two regiments stealthily slipped away to the summit of the mountain. It was this movement that Colonel Bragg heard.[30]

"The battle of the brigade was distinct, severe, and completely victorious," declared Lieutenant Haskell. It definitely had been distinct and severe, and Gibbon's men had exhibited superb discipline, élan, and courage. Yet they had accomplished relatively little in the face of the dreadful casualties they incurred. The list included 37 dead, 251 wounded, and 30 missing—a quarter of the brigade's strength. The 7th Wisconsin bore the heaviest number of casualties, with 11 killed, 116 wounded, and 20 missing, nearly 30 more men than Colquitt's entire loss. Even with all this bloodshed, Gibbon's attack on the Confederate center had not caused a single Rebel soldier to be shifted to this locale from another sector, although it had prevented Colquitt from reinforcing the embattled Confederate left. But, in fairness to Gibbon, his task had been a daunting one. The terrain was difficult, his room for maneuver was seriously limited, and the enemy enjoyed a well-selected and strong defensive position. That Gibbon's regiments neither flinched nor gave up the effort to drive out the enemy until

428 | To Antietam Creek

darkness ended the combat offered evidence as to why they would become known to the army as the Iron Brigade.[31]

That night on the mountain, though, no one in the unit pondered its reputation. The memory haunted Major Dawes for years. He wrote to his mother six months later about the emotionally heartbreaking experience.

> We lay down on the stony side of the mountain, not daring to go to sleep, not a cartridge in our boxes, with an order from our General to maintain our position while we had an "inch of bayonet left."

> The night was very chilly and in the wood very dark. Several of our dying comrades were begging most piteously for water, of which there was not a drop left in the regiment. I searched the whole Regt for a swallow of water for one noble fellow [Lawerance of Company I] but he died without it, there was none to be found. His efforts to say, if but one word, were painful to see. What a death that was, on the cold hard stones, in fruitless struggle to send some parting message to friends far away. Our stretcher bearers came at last and the poor suffering heroes were carried to the field hospital.[32]

Shortly before midnight, Gibbon's exhausted men were cheered by the news that they were to be relieved. The 2nd Corps had started to arrive in the vicinity of Middletown at about sunset, and Brigadier General Willis A. Gorman's 1st Brigade, 2nd Division, was sent up the mountain to replace Gibbon's, although it was nearly midnight before Gorman's regiments arrived. The 2nd and the 7th Wisconsin and the 19th Indiana all withdrew a short distance to the rear, where they drew a fresh supply of ammunition, then wrapped themselves in blankets and were soon sound asleep. The men of the 6th Wisconsin were not as fortunate. Gibbon recalled some years later that the regiment had advanced so far forward and up the side of Hill 1280, and "was in such close contact with the enemy," that Colonel Bragg thought it inadvisable to withdraw his regiment. But Gibbon's memory may have failed him here. Writing only six months after the battle, Major Dawes recalled that his regiment anxiously awaited their relief. The night was "bitter cold," and the men suffered from intense fatigue. "They only can know, who have experienced the feeling of utter prostration that succeeds the burning excitement of a battle," wrote Dawes. When no one arrived, Bragg sent a runner to Gibbon to inquire where their relief was. Gibbon sent over to Gorman for an answer but received no reply. Why Gibbon himself did not investigate is unknown, but Bragg subsequently sent his adjutant, E. P. Brooks, down to find Gorman, and Brooks offered to guide Gorman's men to the 6th's position. According to Dawes, Gorman told Brooks: "I can't send men into that woods to night. All men are cowards in the dark." So the 6th spent the frigid night on the rocky, wooded mountainside, with their dead comrades, and without water and ammunition. Six months later Dawes still seethed with anger about it, and he added his sentiments to the account of the battle he was writing for his mother: "May not Some men be cowards in the daytime!" Several days later, at Antietam, the 6th would have their chance to vent their angry feelings on Gorman's men.[33]

McClellan was among the observers of Gibbon's fight. Around 2 p.m. he had joined Burnside near the Rhode Islander's forward headquarters. It was an excellent command post, offering a sweeping vista of most of the battlefield, from Fox's Gap to Hooker's position and, wrote Colonel Strother, "we also had a good view of Franklin's operations at Burkittsville and Crampton's Gap, between three and four miles distant." McClellan observed the action of his first offensive battle with interest, but a nearby newspaper correspondent thought his bearing "almost that of a disinterested spectator, or of a general watching maneuvers." McClellan intervened in Burnside's direction of the battle only twice, once when he sent orders to Cox and Willcox to advance their line and silence Bondurant's battery and, earlier, when he ordered Hooker to send a division north of the National Road. The action from Fox's Gap to Hill 1280 was easily comprehended from McClellan's position. Hooker's advance north of Hill 1280 was more difficult to assess. To maintain communications with this element of the mountain assault, McClellan sent his chief of staff, Colonel Marcy, to accompany Hooker (or perhaps Marcy was dispatched to keep an eye on Hooker). But Marcy's presence and his communications were unnecessary, for McClellan found that he could follow Hooker's progress by the "distant muttering of musketry, which continued with little intermission until after dark, and always approaching the Gap."[34]

By sunset McClellan knew that both the 1st and the 9th Corps "had established themselves solidly in positions commanding the main pass." And despite several irresolute signal messages from Franklin (see chapter 15) that cast doubt on the 6th Corps' effort to force Crampton's Gap, it appeared that circumstances there had changed. When viewed through field glasses, the line of musketry smoke at that point seemed to be moving up the mountain. The balance of the army was completing its concentration in the Middletown Valley. Sykes's division and the reserve artillery had already reached Middletown, and the 2nd Corps, followed by the 12th, were beginning to arrive via the Shookstown Road. McClellan remained at Burnside's command post, watching Gibbon's and Colquitt's clash, until shortly after 9 p.m. He then mounted and rode to the home of Dan Koogle, located about a half mile east of Bolivar, and where army headquarters had been established. Surgeons had appropriated the residence as a temporary field hospital, and Colonel Strother recorded that the wounded lay about so thickly in the yard that it was "with difficulty that we rode through without treading on them." In one room of the house, surgeons were busy with the bloody work of dressing wounds and amputating limbs. If the shocking and disturbing scenes at the hospital bothered McClellan, he never mentioned it—which is interesting, considering the lengths to which historians have gone to prove that part of McClellan's inherent caution was a dread of incurring casualties. The general established his headquarters in "a room in which was a table, two or three chairs, and a couple of tallow-candles, without other furniture or embellishment." Here he was joined by his staff and senior officers, and they discussed the day's action. All agreed that the Army of the Potomac had captured the key terrain and inflicted heavy losses on the enemy. But the death of Reno tempered the celebration. There was no consensus about what Lee might do. "The enemy still holds the pass in front of us—Turner's Pass, and it is uncertain whether he will retire during the night, or reinforce and show fight again to-morrow," wrote Colonel Strother.[35]

At 9:40 p.m. McClellan summarized the battle for Halleck.

Major General Halleck
General-in-Chief

After a very severe engagement, the corps of Hooker and Reno have carried the heights commanding the Hagerstown road. The troops behaved magnificently. They never fought better. Franklin has been hotly engaged on the extreme left. I do not yet know the result, except that the firing indicated progress on his part. The action continued until after dark, and terminated leaving us in possession of the entire crest. It has been a glorious victory. I cannot yet tell whether the enemy will retreat during the night or appear in increased force in the morning. I am hurrying up everything from the rear, to be prepared for any eventuality. I regret to add that the gallant and able General Reno is killed.[36]

McClellan's promise that he was "hurrying up everything from the rear, to be prepared for any eventuality" was not an empty one. The 2nd and the 12th Corps were massing at Bolivar, and McClellan had ordered Richardson's division and elements of Sedgwick's from the 2nd Corps to move up in support of Hooker. Hooker received instructions to "please hold your present position at all hazards . . . Let me know at daybreak to-morrow morning the state of affairs in your vicinity." Sumner was ordered to be at Bolivar in the morning with both the balance of his corps and the 12th Corps ready for action. Fitz John Porter was directed to advance Sykes's division to Bolivar "at daylight." Morell's division, accompanied by Brigadier General Max Weber's brigade (destined to be assigned to French's division, 2nd Corps), had reached Frederick and was sent orders to march "punctually at 3 o'clock." If Lee chose to stand and fight on the 15th, McClellan intended to have the full might of his army on hand.[37]

Thanks to Jacob Cox's early initiative and aggressive generalship, McClellan had nearly won Fox's Gap and Turner's Gap cheaply and early in the day. Cox's defeat of Garland secured a solid hold on commanding ground for the Federals at Fox's Gap and opened the door to Turner's Gap. But Burnside and Reno were unaccountably slow in reinforcing Cox's success, and McClellan's order of march did not bring Hooker to the field until after Longstreet had arrived to reinforce D. H. Hill. The opportunity to divide Lee and crush him in detail slipped away, and all that was won was a tactical success. McClellan had hoped for a stunning operational victory, but his plans assured that he would not achieve one. Nonetheless, although the opportunity for a decisive victory may have eluded him, and the hope of relieving Harpers Ferry grown more distant, great possibilities remained. Lee's army—at least for the moment—continued to be widely separated, while McClellan's was now well concentrated. If Longstreet and Hill remained on South Mountain or made a run for the Potomac, they could be dealt a hard and perhaps crippling blow. And as long as Harpers Ferry held out, McLaws was trapped, and if Franklin moved with energy he might maul the Georgian's command before McLaws could escape across the Potomac. The dream of a second Castiglione had been lost, but McClellan had won the initiative. If he exploited his tactical success of September 14 with aggressive energy and unwavering determination, Harpers Ferry might still be relieved, Lee hurried ingloriously out of Maryland, and McLaws smashed badly. Lee might escape to fight another day, but his campaign and its high strategic and political hopes would be in ruins.

By the time Gibbon's and Colquitt's fight ended, the Army of the Potomac had brought 16 brigades into action, with about 24,000 effectives, against 13 Confederate brigades numbering perhaps 15,000 men. Superiority in numbers does not explain the Federals' success, which is what D. H. Hill and other Confederates claimed. The rugged terrain instead greatly favored the defender and largely offset their disadvantage in numbers. The key to the Union victories was in the superior tactical employment of their forces. At every contested point, save the encounter between Colquitt and Gibbon, Federal commanders brought a larger proportion of their troops to bear against the Southerners. Only 6 of the 13 Confederate brigades became fully engaged, while 13 of 16 Union brigades saw substantial action. Of the 6 Confederate brigades that were significantly involved in the fighting, four—Garland's, Rodes's, Evans's, and Drayton's—suffered heavy casualties and, except for Rodes, lost their effectiveness for the rest of the campaign. Garnett's brigade lost 40 percent of its strength and barely maintained its organization by nightfall. Only Colquitt's brigade inflicted greater damage than it sustained. Confederate losses totaled 410 dead, 1,0733 wounded, and 710 prisoners of war, or nearly 14 percent of their engaged forces. Union attrition was nearly equal—325 dead, 1,403 wounded, and 85 missing—but this represented only 7 percent of the Federals' engaged strength, and Gibbon's and Scammon's brigades accounted for 590 casualties, or nearly 30 percent of the total Union loss.[38]

In the opinion of William Allan, an ordnance officer with the Army of Northern Virginia and a careful and unbiased historian of his army's 1862 campaigns, the battle of South Mountain "was poorly managed by the Confederates," particularly by D. H. Hill. In Allan's judgment, "Hill's troops were badly handled. The field was not understood, and the troops not promptly put into position." But Allan was unduly harsh. Hill had made his share of errors, but in Allan's assessment of the unsuccessful outcome of the battle, it was forgotten that Hill's mission had been to watch the roads coming up from Harpers Ferry, not to defend the mountain gaps. Allen also overlooked the fact that Stuart underestimated the threat to Turner's Gap and had reassured Hill on the afternoon of the 13th that no substantial Union force threatened the mountain. Hill took more than ample precautions to respond to the threat Stuart reported by ordering two of his five brigades to South Mountain that evening. Once the threat to the mountain became clear, Hill did not delay in ordering up G. B. Anderson, Ripley, and Rodes. Hill was slow in discovering the extent of the enemy threat to Fox's Gap and, had Cox been promptly reinforced by Willcox, Hill very likely would have lost Fox's Gap that morning. But Stuart must assume the lion's share of responsibility for Hill's tardy reaction; Stuart had left Hill with virtually no cavalry, and the one small regiment Stuart did leave had no communication with Hill. Garland's defeat knocked Hill off balance. Hill made a fumbled effort to regain the initiative with a four-brigade counterattack at Fox's Gap, but he entrusted the effort to Ripley, who proved to be incompetent at managing such a large attack.[39]

Allen also neglected to take Lee to task for his failure to appreciate the seriousness of the enemy threat to his rear. The consequence of this was that Longstreet's brigades arrived too late to rectify the situation. They also suffered dreadful losses due to straggling—perhaps more than their combat losses—arriving exhausted and in piecemeal fashion. As Longstreet's forces reached the summit of the mountain they were unprepared, and then they were thrown hastily into action to respond to desperate situations. Under these circumstances it is not surprising that some of the Confederate brigades were mauled or not used effectively. When they reached the mountain summit there was precious little time to learn the ground or select the best defensive position before they were engaged. This was particularly true of D. R. Jones's brigades. The burden of responsibility for Longstreet's late arrival belonged to Lee, for he was the one who had set the time for Longstreet's march. McClellan's advance on South Mountain caught Lee unprepared and cost him the initiative. In the end, the Confederates staved off disaster due to the superb élan and tenacity of their foot soldiers, to the lateness of the day when the main Federal offensive began, and to Lady Luck.

Before Gibbon's and Colquitt's engagement subsided, Longstreet rode down the mountain to report to Lee. He had seen enough to convince him that the battle was lost. He wrote later: "At first sight of the situation, as I rode up the mountain-side, it became evident that we were not in time nor in sufficient force to secure our holding at Turner's Gap, and a note was sent General Lee to prepare his mind for disappointment, and give time for arrangements for re-treat." D. H. Hill joined Longstreet at Lee's headquarters after dark, but before 8 p.m., and the generals discussed the army's grim situation. Assessing his op-tions, and ever hopeful that he might still salvage the Harpers Ferry operation and his Maryland Campaign, Lee asked what the prospects were for continuing the fight in the morning. Longstreet deferred the question to Hill, who spoke plainly. The Federals were in heavy force on both flanks, which they could easily turn, and their artillery could (and already had on Hill 1280) bring a crossfire to bear on the Confederate position. "His explanation was too forcible to admit of further deliberation," recalled Longstreet. The condition of the men was prob-ably also discussed. Longstreet's command was exhausted, and a second day of combat might cause more brigades to come apart. With great reluctance, Lee concluded that he had no alternative but to order a retreat, and he gave orders for the two generals to assemble their men.[40]

Lee remained unaware of McLaws's situation in Pleasant Valley and of the state of things at Harpers Ferry, but he had decided that his army's situation was too precarious to remain in Maryland. McClellan had behaved with uncharac-teristic energy and taken Lee by surprise, and now Lee's divided army was in grave danger of defeat in detail unless he acted promptly to extract it. At 8 p.m. Lee dictated a dispatch to McLaws, whose command was the most imperiled. The words betrayed Lee's deep disappointment and underscored the gravity of his assessment of the army's situation. "The day has gone against us," the message read, "and this army will go by Sharpsburg and cross the river. It is necessary for you to abandon your position tonight. Send forward officers to explore the way, ascertain the best crossings of the Potomac, and, if you can find any between you and Shepherdstown, leave Shepherdstown Ford for this command." A dispatch to Jackson followed, with orders to march to Shepherdstown to cover Long-street's and D. H. Hill's withdrawal across the Potomac. By Lee's lights his Mary-land Campaign was over, and all that remained was to make good his army's escape. Orders also went to General Toombs at Hagerstown, instructing him to march immediately to Sharpsburg to secure the bridge over Antietam Creek by which Longstreet and Hill would reach the Potomac. Longstreet and Hill were ordered to start their trains, directing them across the Potomac by way of Williamsport. Security for the trains fell to the 11th Georgia of G. T. Anderson's brigade, which had been left behind at Hagerstown.[41]

At 10 p.m., while the troops on the mountain assembled to begin the retreat, Lee received more discouraging news from Colonel Thomas Munford, who was at Rohrersville. The Federals had forced Crampton's Gap and trapped McLaws in Pleasant Valley. This development wrought an important change in the stra-tegic picture. McLaws now could not join Lee by the road up Pleasant Valley through Rohrersville. Instead, he had only two known escape routes: one along the Harpers Ferry–Sharpsburg Road, passing along the west side of Maryland

Heights; the other by way of Weverton Pass to the ford at Berlin. The Weverton route was not an option, as it took McLaws on the enemy side of South Mountain and away from his supports. But there might be a way over Maryland Heights that could be discovered. However McLaws negotiated the mass of Maryland Heights—either by going around it on the Harpers Ferry–Sharpsburg Road or over it by some as-yet unknown route—it would be slow going. An immediate retreat by Longstreet and Hill to Shepherdstown would leave McLaws isolated. Lee needed to buy the Georgian some time to extricate his command. This meant a stand somewhere along the Boonsboro Pike. The best place for this appeared to be the small village of Keedysville, about 2 miles west of Boonsboro. This position shielded the vital bridge over Antietam Creek, which was less than a mile west of Keedysville; covered any possible route McLaws might find over or around Maryland Heights; and had communications with Rohrersville, where Lee knew Munford's cavalry were located. Lee changed Longstreet's and Hill's marching orders accordingly. Instead of heading to the Potomac and Virginia, they would instead make a stand at Keedysville, where Lee hoped they might draw McClellan away from McLaws. Lee made these decisions in a mere 15 minutes, for at 10:15 p.m. he responded to Munford with instructions to hold his position at Rohrersville and try and find a route over Maryland Heights and Elk Mountain for McLaws. One hour later, Lee sent new orders to McLaws. He notified the Georgian that Longstreet and Hill would halt at Keedysville, "with a view to preventing the enemy that may enter the gap at Boonsborough turnpike from cutting you off, and enabling you to make a junction with it. If you can pass to-night on the river road, by Harper's Ferry, or cross the mountain below Crampton's Gap toward Sharpsburg, let me know." Although he left the option open for McLaws to escape to Virginia by way of the lower fords on the Potomac, Lee desired him to make every possible effort to get over or around Maryland Heights and Elk Mountain to Sharpsburg, so that he might withdraw into Virginia by way of Shepherdstown and complete the concentration of the army at that point. The halt of Longstreet and Hill at Keedysville did not signal a change in Lee's decision to abandon Maryland. It was merely a temporary measure, intended only to cover McLaws's withdrawal from Pleasant Valley.[42]

There was one brief flicker of hope for the Southerners that dark and somber night. Around 11 p.m. a report reached headquarters that the Federals on the left had withdrawn. The retreat had already begun by this time, with Rodes's and Colquitt's brigades leading the way down the mountain. Although it seemed unlikely that the enemy were retreating, Lee thought it worth investigating, so he ordered a reconnaissance. This passed down the chain of command until around midnight, when Colonel P. F. Stevens, commanding Evans's battered brigade, received orders to send out a small detachment to investigate. Lieutenant W. P. Dubose, the adjutant of the Holcombe Legion, drew the hazardous mission, most likely through bad luck by happening to be on the picket line when the selection was made. Stevens provided 50 men to accompany Dubose, but the latter wisely judged that such a large force would be unable to move quietly in the pitch black that blanketed the mountain, so he set out alone. "I penetrated as far as the spot on which we had fought the day before, and becoming persuaded that there were no troops on the mountain, turned to retrace my steps," Dubose recalled. Perhaps becoming disoriented in the dark, he followed a different route on his return and walked into a picket of the 107th Pennsylvania. Dubose attempted to "hastily withdraw my pistol and compel him to surrender without firing—as I had no wish to make an alarm." But the pistol caught in Dubose's cloak and discharged. The Pennsylvanian seized the lieutenant and threw him to the ground, and his comrades were roused from their sleep by the shot. Dubose struggled to break free, but he was overcome and taken as a prisoner to Colonel Joseph W. Fisher of the 5th Reserves. Dubose's 50-man detachment heard the gunshot and the sounds of a struggle. When their lieutenant did not come back, they returned to Stevens to report that the Federals still remained. But it was old news by that time. Someone else had captured a prisoner from Sumner's 2nd Corps. Here was proof that the Federals not only were still present, but were also being reinforced. The Rebels retreat off the mountain continued.[43]

The Confederate brigades quietly assembled near the Mountain House on the summit for their departure. Randolph Shotwell, a private in the 8th Virginia, recollected that the order was to "go quietly to the rear—step easily—don't rattle your canteens—don't speak—follow your file leaders as closely as possible." Rodes's and Colquitt's brigades led the way at 11 p.m., followed by Garland's, Ripley's, and G. B. Anderson's men. These troops were surely all dead on their feet with fatigue. Shotwell eloquently described their state.

> Oh, the torture of that night. Already I had marched quite sixteen miles since dawn, including the fatiguing toil up the mountain, and, as usual, the intense excitement of the battle speedily giving way to extreme relaxation and lassitude which seemed to deprive me of the last particle of strength, rendering each step more difficult than the last. One who has never experienced the relaxation, which follows the tense excitement of a fiercely contested battle, in a young, nervous, and excitable person, can have but little idea of my real condition that night.

Drayton's battered brigade followed Hill's division, and then came Kemper's, Garnett's, and Evans's men. This left Walker's brigade at Turner's Gap, and Hood's division and G. T. Anderson's brigade at Fox's Gap; the dead and the seriously wounded were, by necessity, left to the enemy's care.[44]

Hood and G. T. Anderson remained at Fox's Gap until "about midnight." When their orders to withdraw arrived, "most of the men were fast asleep, in spite of the efforts of the officers to keep them awake." Officers and noncoms

woke them as quietly as possible and sent them off one at a time. The three brigades followed the Old Sharpsburg Road to the base of the mountain, then used
farm lanes and county roads until they struck the pike to Sharpsburg, approximately 1 mile southwest of Boonsboro, where they halted to rest.[45]

The last to leave the mountain were Walker's South Carolinians. "A cold
bleak wind" kicked up late that night, further adding to the discomfort of men
already suffering "acutely from the excessive fatigue of the day and protracted
fasting." Possibly D. R. Jones or Longstreet, or their staffs, forgot about Walker,
for he reported that his brigade did not get its orders to withdraw until "about
4 a.m." But another member of the brigade thought they withdrew at around 1
a.m. Near the base of the mountain Walker's men passed through Fitz Lee's
brigade, which had arrived in Boonsboro at 8 p.m. from their foray to Westminster and been ordered forward at 11 p.m. to cover the retreat. Fitz Lee's troopers
marched east "for over a mile" from Boonsboro; they halted in column of fours
in the road at a point that commanded the National Road as it descended from
the mountain. Fitz Lee posted his artillery here and dismounted skirmishers
on either side of the road, with mounted support behind them. While the cavalrymen made their preparations, infantrymen continued to dribble by "in
detached parties of from ten to two hundred."[46]

The Union soldiers on South Mountain were just as cold, tired, and uncomfortable as their Confederate foes. "We passed the rest of the night lying on our
arms," wrote Charles Walcott of the 21st Massachusetts. "The night was very
chilly, and our limbs were quite stiff before morning." Many of the regiments
that had been engaged during the morning and afternoon had dropped their
blankets in the rear. Now, they shivered. "I did not sleep any; it was necessary to
be awake to keep from freezing," wrote Warren Freeman of the 13th Massachusetts. William Todd of the 79th New York recalled another agony: "The groans
and cries of the wounded sounded in our ears throughout the long hours of that
weary night. Those in our immediate vicinity were relieved to the extent of our
ability, but we were obliged to keep in line and under arms till daylight, and
dared not wander far, even to give a drink of water to a tenth of those who
moaned piteously for it." Todd and his comrades may not have wandered far,
but others took advantage of the novelty of exploring a freshly won battlefield
to search for souvenirs or discover what food the haversacks of the dead might
contain. Many found a sobering and ghastly spectacle. Colonel Hugh Ewing
of the 30th Ohio came upon a pathetic scene at the spot where the 15th South
Carolina or the 3rd South Carolina Battalion had made their stand. He found
one of their officers clad in a breastplate of hardened steel, fitting closely to his
neck and shoulders, dead with a bullet through his forehead. Charles Walcott
encountered Colonel George S. James, commander of the 3rd South Carolina
Battalion. Moments before Walcott came upon James, a Union soldier had
robbed the colonel of his watch. James pretended to be dead, hoping he might

make his escape before morning. Perhaps Walcott, too, had ideas of collecting a souvenir off James, but when he found the colonel still alive he offered his assistance. James, wrote Walcott, "found himself to be growing weaker, and knew that he should die . . . he was getting very cold, I covered him with a blanket and gave him a drink of whiskey." Sometime before daylight James passed away.[47]

Uncomfortable and unpleasant as that pitch-black night was, even the lowest-ranking men in the army understood that they had won ground from the enemy.[48] It had not been the smashing victory it might have been, but it was clear enough to give a sorely needed boost to the morale of the previously dispirited Union soldiers. Colonel Adoniram Warner of the 10th Pennsylvania Reserves spoke for many in the army when he described the battle's effect on him.

> We had been baffled on the Peninsula, had been beaten and discomfited at
> Bull Run; the enemy were invading the North; All looked gloomy yet I did not
> know that I had been dispirited but the change was so glorious! The conscious-
> ness that we had by sheer hard fighting, beaten the enemy and driven him from
> his strong position filled me to overflowing and gave me confidence that we
> would finally win and the country be safe.[49]

Had Warner and his comrades known the results of the clash at Crampton's Gap, their morale would have soared even higher. There, the men of the 6th Corps had gained the most complete victory won by any troops of the Army of the Potomac in the war to date.

14

Crampton's Gap

"The best fighting that has been done in this war"

M ajor General William B. Franklin started the leading elements of his 6th Corps on the road from Jefferson to Burkittsville promptly at 5:30 a.m. The 6th Corps was a solid, veteran organization. McClellan had formed it on the Peninsula to create a position for Franklin. They saw action at Gaines' Mill and Glendale during the Seven Days battles, but were spared the Second Manassas debacle and served primarily to cover the retreat of the defeated Union forces. Having had nearly two months' respite from active campaigning, the ranks of its regiments were relatively full and the soldiers were in good condition. There were approximately 13,000 men in the six brigades that made up the two divisions of the corps, of which about 10,800 were combat effectives. The division commanders, Major General Henry Slocum and Major General William F. Smith, were both West Pointers destined for eventual corps command. The corps was equally rich in talented officers at the brigade level, with young officers like Alfred T. A. Torbert, John Newton, Joseph J. Bartlett, Winfield S. Hancock, and William T. H. Brooks. The 6th Corps' artillery consisted of seven batteries divided into two divisional battalions, or brigades, commanded by two officers who would also make their mark in the Army of the Potomac and earn a general's star: Captains Emory Upton and Romeyn B. Ayres.

One of Franklin's men recalled that the September 14 "morning was all we could ask for in regard to weather—cool and pleasant." Around 8 a.m. the head of the column arrived at the village of Jefferson, tucked in on the west side of Catoctin Mountain. After chasing off a handful of Confederate cavalry pickets, the men fell out to rest after the tiring climb over the mountain. Franklin had called a halt so that Couch's division could join him. Franklin's orders did not direct him to wait for Couch, but the passage up Catoctin Mountain probably caused the 6th Corps to become strung out, and stopping long enough for it to close up would do no harm. By 10:30 a.m. Franklin had heard nothing from Couch, so he ordered his corps to resume the march to Burkittsville.[1]

Henry Slocum's 1st Division led the march, and at the forefront of this division was Colonel Henry L. Cake's 96th Pennsylvania, slightly more than 500 strong. Cake was one of Schuylkill County's most successful businessmen in 1861 when he took a commission as colonel of the 25th Pennsylvania, a 90-day regiment. When that unit mustered out he raised the 96th, which he had now commanded for nearly a year. Cake's orders that morning were to rendezvous with a cavalry squadron (probably from the 6th Pennsylvania or the 6th U.S. Cavalry) and a section of artillery at a "designated bridge" (most likely the bridge over Catoctin Creek, west of Jefferson). The artillery never showed up but the cavalry did, and the combined force forged ahead. They turned up nothing more than a small squad of graycoat cavalry, probably from Munford's brigade, accompanied by one gun. These Rebels maintained a discreet distance until about 2 miles east of Burkittsville, where they stopped and opened fire on the Union horseman, sending them hurrying back to Colonel Cake to report a skirmish with a superior force of the enemy. Cake deployed his Companies A and F as skirmishers and, with the balance of the regiment following in support, pushed forward to pick a fight.[2]

Around noon Cake's skirmish line reached a hill about 1 mile east of and overlooking Burkittsville. The village was (and still is) a picturesque, almost New England–like community set close to the base of South Mountain, nearly midway between Crampton's Gap and Brownsville Pass. On this hill the Burkittsville–Jefferson Road intersected with a road running north–south to Broad Run Village to the north and Petersville to the South. Company A, under Captain LaMar S. Hay, went by this crossroads and down the hill, past the "fine brick mansion" of Mr. T. Barnett. Just west of Barnett's house Hay's men found a farm road running southwest. They followed this road for nearly a quarter mile until they reached a sawmill, where they halted and lay down. Meanwhile, Lieutenant John Dougherty's F Company, accompanied by the 96th's major, Lewis J. Martin, dashed into Burkittsville. Martin's orders were to work his way through the town and post a skirmish line beyond the village houses. While Dougherty's men felt their way forward, Colonel Cake led the main body of the regiment down the same road Company A had taken. Cake formed a line in the road, with his right resting on the Burkittsville–Jefferson Road, and then had the men lie down. The Confederates had remained quiet up to this point. But when Dougherty's skirmishers entered Burkittsville, the Rebels announced their presence with a greeting from two pieces of artillery. The fire proved to be no more than an annoyance, and Dougherty and Major Martin had no difficulty in posting Company F on a skirmish line within 1,000 yards of the mountain base.[3]

No citizens of Burkittsville had yet shown themselves. Cake thought the locals might provide some information about the enemy, so he sent Henry C. Boyer of Company A to "thump up" someone who might be willing to talk. Boyer went to the Barnett home and pounded on the door until "a gentleman" answered, whom Boyer took to Colonel Cake. Mr. Barnett, or whoever he was, assured Cake that Burkittsville was Union "to a man." As for the Confederates, he told Cake that there were about "4,000 infantry, several hundred cavalry and two cannons," and that "they intended to fight and did not dream of defeat." The evidence at hand seemed to confirm the Marylander's information. What appeared to be cavalry had been spotted near the summit of Crampton's Gap, and the length of the Confederate skirmish line observed at the mountain's base suggested that it screened a large force. Woods covered much of the mountainside, offering good concealment for whatever infantry supports the Southerners might have massed to defend the gap.[4]

While Cake questioned the local citizen, a staff officer rode up from the rear "with a saucy demand for something definite." Cake responded in writing that the Rebels were in force behind a stone wall running along the base of the mountain, and that they numbered not less than 4,000 infantry, a squadron of cavalry, and two guns.[5]

Shortly after noon the vanguard of Slocum's 1st Division arrived on the high ground at the Jefferson–Broad Run Village intersection. They drew some fire from Confederate artillery at Brownsville Pass, and Slocum turned his division into a field north of the Jefferson Road, where they found cover in a grove of woods and from the reverse slope of the hill. The men were allowed to break ranks and prepare their noon meal. Franklin rode up during this time, followed by Smith's 2nd Division. Franklin established the 6th Corps' headquarters in the yard of the Martin T. Shafer farm, at the edge of the grove concealing Slocum's men, and "at a point from which he could overlook the intervening valley."[6]

Franklin summoned his division and senior brigade commanders to headquarters to discuss the plan of attack. Colonel Cake also received orders to join the group, to enlighten them about what he had learned of the enemy position. Some members of the command group were of the opinion that the enemy show of force was all bluff; Slocum jested that they consisted of "four cavalrymen, two guns, and no infantry." After listening to Cake's report, Franklin deemed it prudent to gain a better idea of enemy strength before committing to a plan of attack. He ordered Cake to advance his regiment through Burkittsville toward Crampton's Gap and probe the enemy's defenses.[7]

Cake returned to his regiment and ordered them over the fence bordering the road. As they moved into the adjacent field the 96th immediately drew fire from five different enemy field pieces—two from Crampton's Gap and three from Brownsville Pass. Several solid shot struck in front of the regiment, "as though to say the Harper's Ferry road was the dead line," and Cake ordered his regiment back to the shelter of the road, where they lay down.[8]

The quick and spirited response to the advance of Cake's regiment dispelled the notion at corps headquarters that the mountain passes were lightly defended. Franklin penciled a note to McClellan at 12:30 p.m., advising the latter that "I think from appearances that we may have a heavy fight to get the pass." Slocum summoned Captain John A. Wolcott's Battery A, Maryland Light Artillery (six

3-inch ordnance rifles) to engage the Rebel gunners. Wolcott unlimbered his guns southwest of the Jefferson–Broad Run intersection and commenced a steady shelling of the Confederate firing positions.[9]

Meanwhile, the 6th Corps' brass resumed their discussion, which now focused on the best direction for and method of attack on Crampton's Gap. All agreed that artillery would play a limited role; infantry would have to carry the enemy position. This perilous duty fell to Slocum's 1st Division. Establishing the best point of attack was the subject of spirited debate. Some advocated an advance on the south side of Jefferson Road, and others argued that the approaches on the north side were more favorable. Franklin asked Slocum who would lead the assault column. Slocum responded it would be his 2nd Brigade, commanded by Colonel Joseph J. Bartlett, a 27-year-old lawyer from Binghamton, New York, and an officer of considerable ability. Since Bartlett would lead the attack, Franklin thought he should have a voice in the decision, and he summoned the colonel to headquarters.[10]

Bartlett arrived to find the headquarters' group relaxing and enjoying cigars. After some idle banter, Slocum asked Bartlett on which side of the Jefferson Road he would advance. Bartlett had a ready answer, for he had spent the time since his arrival in a thorough reconnaissance of the approaches to Crampton's Gap. "On the right," he responded. Bartlett recalled that Franklin replied, "Well gentlemen, that settles it." The point of attack would be aimed north of the Jefferson Road. The meeting broke up and the officers departed to prepare their men for action. Bartlett took this opportunity to question Slocum about the tactical formation he planned to use in the assault. Slocum replied that since Franklin had allowed Bartlett to choose the point of attack, he himself would entertain the colonel's suggestion on the assault formation. Bartlett had also considered this question, and he suggested that the division advance in column of brigades, with each brigade placing two regiments in front and two in support, and a 200-yard interval between each brigade. This would give the attack a narrow front with great depth. Bartlett further recommended that his own regiment, the 27th New York, deploy as skirmishers to screen the advance. Once the attack jumped off, Bartlett intended that it should not halt to engage in fire combat, but should instead move straight for the point on the mountain where the Burkittsville–Jefferson Road crossed Crampton's Gap. Slocum approved of the plan. All that remained was to implement it.[11]

Besides the Confederate troops, the 6th Corps would have to contend with the terrain, which afforded the defenders some important advantages. The approaches to Crampton's Gap traversed rolling farmland, crisscrossed by numerous formation-disrupting stone walls and rail fences, and the mountain rose sharply from the valley floor to nearly 1,200 feet at its highest point within the area of operations. Franklin certainly was aware of Brownsville Pass, 1 mile south of Crampton's Gap—Confederate artillery had fired on his advance from it—and understood that forcing it would cut off the defenders at Crampton's. But he probably decided against attacking here for several reasons. The road over Brownsville Pass was steep, rough, and narrow—not nearly as serviceable for army traffic as the road over Crampton's Gap. Second, the mountain was considerably steeper at Brownsville Pass than at Crampton's Gap, and more easily defended. Third, Franklin's orders included occupying Rohrersville, to interpose his corps between Lee (at Boonsboro) and McLaws. This could be accomplished more easily by forcing Crampton's Gap.

Crampton's Gap was crossed by two roads that met at its highest point. The Burkittsville Road emerged from the western end of the village and climbed the mountain in a northeasterly direction until it reached the summit, where it joined the Arnoldstown Road to pass over the gap. On the western slope the roads split again, with one descending roughly northwest toward Rohrersville, and the other running slightly southwest to the Brownsville–Rohrersville Road. The Arnoldstown Road began its ascent of the mountain about two-thirds of a mile north of the Burkittsville Road and climbed in a southwesterly direction until it reached the gap. The Mountain Church Road followed the eastern base of the mountain, departing from the Burkittsville Road a short distance west of the village and running north to and beyond the Arnoldstown Road. Stone walls flanked the Mountain Church Road for much of its length between the Arnoldstown and Burkittsville roads, offering ready-made breastworks that the Confederates used to their advantage. There was no clever way to attack Crampton's Gap. Only a frontal assault with infantry would work. In the opinion of Colonel Bartlett, it was "absolutely necessary that the first attempt should be successful or great confusion and slaughter must ensue." One element in Franklin's favor was that the Confederates would need to spread their force for nearly a mile along the Mountain Church Road to defend both the Burkittsville and Arnoldstown roads.[12]

Impressed with the natural strength of the enemy position and convinced that the Confederates held the gap in strong force, Franklin, a naturally cautious soldier under ordinary circumstances, arranged his plans for the attack with great deliberation. But the Confederates' bold front was all bluff, for at the moment the defenders of Crampton's Gap consisted of a few guns and a thin gray line with no supports.

While Franklin made his preparations to assault Crampton's Gap, 5 miles to the south of the pass, on Maryland Heights, men of Lafayette McLaws's command had nearly finished cutting a road to the summit of the Heights for artillery. Completing this road was McLaws's highest priority, and it absorbed his complete attention. There had been little activity reported elsewhere on his extended front to alert him that his rear might be threatened. McLaws had heard artillery fire to the northeast on September 13, where Hampton and Pleasonton were dueling with one another. Cavalry scouts reported that the enemy was advancing on his rear, but lookouts McLaws had posted on South Mountain did not confirm these reports, and he dismissed them as rumors. That night he received Lee's dispatch, alerting McLaws to the possibility that the Union army might be on the move from Frederick to relieve Harpers Ferry. Lee's warning elicited no special concern, for he also offered the reassurance that Stuart would keep McLaws informed of enemy movements. The Georgian felt additional comfort in knowing that he had left 4 of his 10 brigades to watch his rear: Semmes's and Parham's were in the vicinity of Crampton's Gap and Brownsville Pass (although most of Parham's was picketing Solomon's Gap), and Wright's and Pryor's were at Weverton Pass. If the enemy did move on his rear, McLaws thought Weverton was the most likely point of attack, since this pass is only about 1.5 miles from Maryland Heights, and artillery fire there could easily be heard by the Harpers Ferry garrison. Between his infantry and Stuart's screening force, McLaws was confident that there would be sufficient warning to respond to any threat that might develop.[13]

Stuart, it will be recalled, left Boonsboro early on the morning of the 14th for Crampton's Gap, which he believed to be "the weakest point of the line" in the Confederate front along the South Mountain range. When he arrived at the pass he found both Munford's and Hampton's brigades encamped in the vicinity. After Hampton's encounter with Farnsworth's horsemen on the afternoon of the 13th, both brigades passed a quiet night, and they reported no enemy activity in front that morning. Stuart pondered the situation. He still believed Crampton's Gap to be the most likely point the enemy would try to force to relieve Harpers Ferry. But Brownsville Pass and Weverton Pass were possibilities that he could not discount. He knew little of McLaws's dispositions, although he did learn that elements of Semmes's brigade occupied Brownsville Pass. But Stuart did not know if McLaws had garrisoned Weverton Pass. To be certain, he decided to send one of his two brigades there. He gave Munford—whose brigade contained only two regiments, totaling about 350–400 men—the choice of going on to the Potomac River or remaining at Crampton's Gap. Munford elected to remain—a decision he probably later regretted. Stuart left him the support of Captain R. P. Chew's Virginia horse battery, and ordered Munford to hold the gap "at all hazards." There were no infantry already at the gap, but early that morning the 16th Virginia of Colonel William A. Parham's brigade and two naval howitzers of the Portsmouth (Virginia) artillery were ordered to Crampton's Gap from their camp at Brownsville to provide support. Whether Stuart saw the small size of the infantry Semmes sent to Crampton's Gap is uncertain, but he recognized that more infantry were necessary for its defense, and he sent a note to McLaws advising him that additional reinforcements were needed. Around 11 a.m. Stuart departed for Maryland Heights, stopping at

Brownsville along the way to relay a message to Colonel E. B. Montague of the 32nd Virginia, whose force was defending Brownsville Pass, ordering Montague to hold the pass at all costs and to send for reinforcements if he was attacked.[14]

Stuart knew the ground at Harpers Ferry from his service there during John Brown's raid in 1859, and he thought he might be of help to McLaws. Reflecting back, Munford wrote that he took a dim view of Stuart's departure: "There never was any excuse for Gen Stuart being off at Maryland Heights with McLaws. He was as bad as Gen Grouchy at that battle of Ligny." Munford overstated his point, but if Stuart believed that Crampton's Gap was the most likely point where the enemy might strike, then it is difficult to defend his decision to leave this crucial position in the hands of a colonel with less than 600 defenders, and before McLaws's reinforcements arrived, while Stuart rode off to Maryland Heights to satisfy his curiosity.[15]

It is unknown when McLaws received Stuart's note requesting reinforcements for Crampton's Gap, but it was probably before noon. Around this same time McLaws may have received a message from General Semmes with news that the enemy were approaching Burkittsville, but with no comment on the Federals' strength. McLaws immediately ordered Brigadier General Howell Cobb, whose brigade was encamped at Sandy Hook, to march at once to Brownsville. McLaws also sent orders to Semmes to withdraw Parham's brigade from Solomon's Gap and have it return to Brownsville, leaving behind only a small guard to hold that gap. Semmes was also instructed that when Cobb's brigade reached Brownsville, he was to tell Cobb to take command at Crampton's Gap. Once Cobb arrived, McLaws would have three brigades of infantry, about 2,700 effectives, in place to defend Brownsville Pass or Crampton's Gap. Trusting that the cavalry would give him due warning should the enemy attack his rear in force, McLaws thought that his dispositions were more than adequate.[16]

While McLaws took action to protect his rear, Stuart—the army's outpost officer—was enjoying a meal with Brigadier General Roger Pryor. Stuart had discovered Pryor's and Wright's brigades occupying Weverton Pass, negating the need for Hampton's brigade to defend it, so the troopers were allowed to bivouac near Weverton for some needed rest. Pryor's and Wright's pickets reported no enemy activity in front. With all apparently quiet, Stuart saw no reason to decline Pryor's invitation to share lunch. Following their repast, Stuart rode with Pryor to Sandy Hook for a look at Harpers Ferry. By the time they had concluded this reconnaissance it was nearly midafternoon, and Stuart left to meet with McLaws, whom he found on Maryland Heights around 2 p.m. Soon after he arrived the sound of artillery fire from the direction of Crampton's Gap could be heard. "I felt no particular concern about it," reported McLaws, "as there were three brigades of infantry in the vicinity, besides the cavalry of Colonel Munford, and General Stuart, who was with me on the heights and had just come in from above, told me he did not believe there was more than a brigade of the enemy." Nevertheless, McLaws thought Cobb might need some stiffening, and he send Major T. S. McIntosh, his assistant adjutant general, and Major James M. Goggin, a commissary officer, to relay orders to the Georgian to hold Crampton's Gap "if he lost his last man doing it."[17]

Fortunately for McLaws, Thomas T. Munford and Paul J. Semmes, the officers defending Crampton's Gap and Brownsville Pass, were cool-headed, experienced soldiers. The 47-year-old Semmes was a Columbus, Georgia, planter with 16 years' experience in the state militia. Munford was an 1854 Virginia Military Institute graduate, who had then tried his hand as a planter in Mississippi and as a Virginia farmer. Munford was colonel of the 2nd Virginia Cavalry, serving under Jackson, in the Shenandoah Valley campaign and replaced Turner Ashby as Jackson's cavalry commander after the latter was killed. When McLaws entered Pleasant Valley on September 11 and moved against Maryland Heights, Sandy Hook, and Weverton, he left Semmes's and Parham's brigades near Brownsville to secure his rear. When Kershaw and Barksdale attacked Maryland Heights, Parham moved to cover their rear by guarding Solomon's Gap. Semmes had 868 officers and men in his four regiments, as well as two batteries, Captain Basil C. Manly's North Carolina Battery, and Captain Miles C. Macon's Fayette (Virginia) Battery. Semmes's orders were to picket Brownsville Pass with one infantry company and hold the remainder of his brigade at Brownsville. Semmes spent September 12 and 13 exploring the roads over the mountain and familiarizing himself with the ground at both mountain gaps. Throughout the 13th he heard the artillery exchanges between Stuart and Pleasonton in the Middletown Valley, rumbling steadily toward South Mountain. In the afternoon Munford's brigade arrived in Burkittsville, fending off Federal cavalry who had dogged their movement all the way from Jefferson. Given the level of enemy activity east of the mountains, Semmes took the precaution that evening of reinforcing the picket company at Brownsville Gap with Colonel Edgar B. Montague's 32nd Virginia, numbering over 286 officers and men, and a section of Manly's battery. Montague's orders were "to watch for and report any advance of the enemy."[18]

Early on the 14th Semmes ordered Major Willis C. Holt's 10th Georgia, a small regiment of only 173 effectives, to march north to a church located on the Rohrersville Road but south of the village, and picket the road. Parham's brigade arrived from Solomon's Gap around 10 a.m. The 41st Virginia remained behind to garrison the gap, leaving Parham with three very small regiments. Soon after they reached Brownsville, Semmes, perhaps unaware that Munford was already at Crampton's Gap, ordered Parham to send Major Francis D. Holliday's thin, 120-strong 16th Virginia and a section of Captain Cary F. Grimes' Portsmouth (Virginia) Battery to its defense.[19]

At nearly the same time as Parham arrived at Brownsville, Colonel Montague sighted the 6th Corps approaching from Jefferson. Montague advanced a

picket of 200 men down close to Burkittsville and deployed a line of skirmishers across his entire front, tying his left in with Munford's right at Crampton's
Gap. But as the numbers and firepower of the approaching Federals became
apparent, Montague called on Semmes for reinforcements. Semmes forwarded
the 53rd Georgia (276 men) and three rifled guns from Macon's and Magruder's
batteries. This increased Montague's strength to nearly 600 infantry and 5 guns.
With this force he put up a bold front, hoping he might deceive the enemy and
prevent them from discovering his weakness.[20]

Munford also closely watched the buildup of 6th Corps' strength. "They
were so numerous that it looked as if they were creeping out of the ground,"
recalled horse artilleryman George Neese. Munford ordered his two regiments
to the base of the mountain and deployed a skirmish line along the Mountain
Church Road. When the 16th Virginia Infantry arrived, he sent them to the
mountain base as well, posting them astride West Main Street where it con-
nects with the Mountain Church Road. Two companies took cover behind a
stone wall running south of this road junction. The rest of the regiment deployed along Mountain Church Road, finding protection behind a stone wall
along its east side. Munford dismounted his sharpshooters on the 16th's flanks.
These men, stated Munford, were "dangerous fellows, but extremely useful to
me . . . If well posted it was not safe to come within range of their rifles." Munford placed Chew's horse battery and Grimes's howitzers about halfway down
the mountain, "in the most eligible position I could find." It was a delaying
force, and nothing more. Munford desperately needed additional manpower,
and he sent a courier dashing off to order Major Holt to bring his 10th Georgia
up without delay.[21]

When the 96th Pennsylvania arrived around noon and deployed south of
Burkittsville, it initially appeared as if the fight would be for Brownsville Pass.
The Confederate guns at both gaps shelled the Federals. Manly's rifles were
principally responsible for checking the advance of the Pennsylvanians. Chew's
and Grimes's shells fell short, so Munford withdrew Chew's two rifled guns
to the summit of Crampton's Gap. Munford thought the increased elevation
improved their effectiveness. Gunner George M. Neese recalled that "our line
of fire was right over the village of Burkittsville, and completely checked their
skirmishers."

Then the Federals unlimbered Wolcott's battery, part of which attempted
to engage Chew. Neese thought the range was about 2 miles and noted that all
the enemy shells fell short. Chew responded, despite both the lack of range and
the ineffectiveness of Wolcott's fire, but Chew only succeeded in putting one of
his own rifles out of commission. Neese was one of the gunners on this piece,
and he remembered that "the mountain where we were in battery was a little
steep and my gun is a vicious little recoiler, and the recoil space of our position

was too sloping, rough, and limited for a free kick, consequently with the second shot that I fired—with a two mile range—at the Yankees my piece snapped a couple of bolts of its mounting, entirely disabling it for the day."[22] Because Franklin kept his corps concealed behind the ridge along the Broad Run Village Road, neither Munford nor Montague could form an accurate estimate of enemy strength. They also could not divine which pass the enemy intended to strike, but Munford initially thought it would be Brownsville Pass. This opinion would soon change.[23]

Around 3:30 p.m. a stir of movement north of Burkittsville attracted Munford's attention. Compact masses of Union troops suddenly emerged from a deep ravine cut by a gentle waterway known as Manor Run. The Federals deployed skirmishers and formed into line of battle with the precision of veterans, and then commenced to advance directly toward Crampton's Gap.[24]

It was over two hours since the objective and the point of the attack had been determined before Franklin's assault jumped off. Under orders to lead Slocum's assault column into position "as secretly as possible," Colonel Bartlett found a route north of Burkittsville, following a ravine carved out over the ages by a sluggish watercourse called Burkitts Run that offered cover from observation until they reached a large field Bartlett estimated to be 1,000 yards from the base of the mountain. Here the three brigades would form up for the assault. There were 13 veteran regiments in the three brigades. Slocum left the newly raised 121st New York out of the assault column as a divisional reserve. His orders to his brigade commanders were simple: advance until they had seized the crest of the mountain, then throw out a picket line.[25]

Preparations and reconnaissance for the approach march were complete around 2:30 p.m. and the division started in motion. As they set out Franklin penciled a dispatch to McClellan to report that his attack had begun and to confidently predict "that in a few minutes we will have the pass." Bartlett's 2nd Brigade led the way, minus the 96th Pennsylvania, which had been recalled but had not caught up with the brigade by the time it moved out. Brigadier General John Newton's 3rd Brigade followed, and Colonel Alfred Torbert's 2nd Brigade brought up the rear. There were nearly 5,500 infantrymen in the three brigades, and even well closed up the column probably stretched for nearly a mile. They had to march approximately 2 miles to reach their jump-off point. Between the need to carry out the movement unobserved and shift the troops cross-country, it took the column about an hour to complete the march. When the 2nd Brigade emerged from the covered ground into the open field selected to form for the assault, they were in full view of the enemy position, and Bartlett recalled that the Confederates immediately "opened all their guns bearing upon us and brought a battery from their right to ground even higher than the Pass to aid in breaking our lines." Chew's battery at Crampton's Gap opened first on the

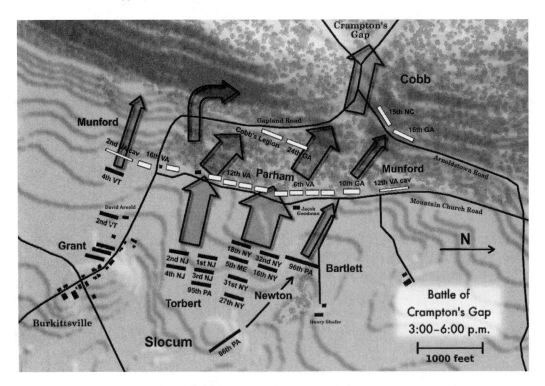

Battle of Crampton's Gap
3:00–6:00 p.m.

1000 feet

forming dark blue mass, and they were soon joined by the five rifled guns under Colonel Montague at Brownsville Pass, who, as Bartlett observed, had moved the guns several hundred yards north to bring the Union infantry into range.[26]

"The rebel shells came pouring thick and fast," noted Eugene Forbes of the 4th New Jersey from his position near the rear of the division's column. Despite the shelling, Bartlett's brigade "formed with the coolness and precision of an exhibition drill." The historian of the 5th Maine recorded with pride that "though shots were ploughing through our ranks, and shells were screaming and bursting all around us, yet not a man faltered." Lieutenant Colonel Alexander D. Adams's 27th New York (Bartlett's own regiment, and Slocum's old regiment) fanned out in a skirmish line extending for nearly a mile to screen the advance. A hundred yards in the rear of them, Lieutenant Colonel Joel S. Seaver's 16th New York and Colonel Nathaniel J. Jackson's 5th Maine formed a line of battle. Bartlett ordered the advance at quick time: 110 steps a minute, or about 110 yards a minute. Lieutenant E. P. Gould of Company E, 27th New York, was on the skirmish line and wrote that he and his men "started at almost a run," dashing across fields of clover and corn and over fences toward the base of the mountain.[27]

Observing Slocum's advance from the vantage of Brownsville Pass, for Jno. T. Parham of the 32nd Virginia "it appeared to me that the men came out of the ground—there was such a multitude of them. I never saw so many blue-coats in my life—I never have since." All of the Confederate guns were blazing away furiously at Bartlett's brigade, but their shells burst above the swiftly advancing line, which soon drew under their fire altogether.[28]

The skirmishers of the 27th New York "went at a double-quick through orchards and gardens, terrifying beast and fowls and even dogged by spiteful mastiffs and terriers." The nature of the 27th's advance brought the left and the right of their line in advance of the center, so that it resembled an arc, or bow, with the ends nearest the base of the mountain. The men on these points of the 27th's line felt the first small-arms fire, originating from the stone wall along the Mountain Church Road. William B. Westervelt described it as "a fusilade of musketry," so deadly "that we were ordered to rally by fours, halt, and wait for our line of battle to come up." As the rest of the regiment moved within range, they, too, came under fire. "Within less than thirty seconds from the time the first gun was fired, the whole line was engaged," wrote Lieutenant Gould. Lieutenant Colonel Adams, the 27th's commander, reported that the firing "was very rapid and at close range." At some points it proved deadly. William Westervelt recalled that his squad of four privates and a corporal stopped in a barnyard, "with the barn between us and the enemy." The men ran to an adjoining shed and opened a door on the west side for a look. "Our curiosity was soon satisfied," wrote Westervelt, "as we received a volley that dropped two of our squad." The majority of the 27th did not enjoy the protection of a barn or a shed; they flung themselves to the ground for cover and returned the Rebel fire as best they could.[29]

The Confederates met Bartlett's skirmish line with one that was nearly as slender. Initially it consisted only of Munford's dismounted troopers and the 120 infantrymen of the 16th Virginia. But minutes after the skirmishing commenced, Colonel William A. Parham arrived with the 6th and the 12th Virginia, and the second section of the Portsmouth (Virginia) Battery, under Lieutenant J. H. Thompson. The two infantry regiments mustered just over 200 effectives. Parham, described by one of his men as "a glorious, brave man, a good fellow and the best curser when he chose I ever heard," led his regiments down the mountain to join the fight. Close behind Parham came Major Willis Holt's 10th Georgia, adding 175 more guns to the firing line.[30]

With Holt's Georgians there were now almost 500 infantry along the mountain base, with dismounted cavalry holding the flanks of a line that extended for nearly a mile along Mountain Church Road. Counting the cavalry, there were perhaps 750 men confronting Slocum's infantry. The dismounted sharpshooters of the 2nd Virginia Cavalry formed the right of the line, finding cover behind a stone wall running south from the junction of West Main Street and the Mountain Church Road. The 16th Virginia came next, with their blocking position astride West Main Street and extending as far north as John Grams's home. The 12th Virginia filled in on the 16th's left, posting their roughly 100 men eight feet apart along the Mountain Church Road in order to cover as broad a front as possible. Next came the 6th Virginia, 120 strong, who prolonged the line to near the Jacob Goodman farm. Where the 10th Georgia initially took position is uncertain, but it was probably on the left of the 6th Virginia. A formidable stone wall paralleling the road provided good cover for parts of Munford's line, but along the 12th Virginia's front the wall stood only 8–10 inches high, with a rail fence riding over it. One of the regiment's members described the wall as only "sufficiently high to shelter a man lying flat on the ground, as we then were." Though their line was dangerously slender, the Confederates had the advantage of position, with clear fields of fire. So long as their nerve and their ammunition held out, they would be difficult to dislodge by a frontal attack. But soon after Parham had his infantry line set to his satisfaction, Major Holt received an inexplicable order from General Semmes, who seemed to have no idea of the imminent threat to Crampton's Gap. Semmes commanded Holt to take his regiment back to its post on the Rohrersville Road. Holt saw no alternative but to obey the order of his brigade commander, so he pulled his regiment out of line and started back up the mountain. There he encountered Parham, who perhaps employed some of his renowned ability for cursing and ordered Holt to return to the base of the mountain. The major agreed to do so, but he convinced Parham to let him detach two companies to picket the Rohrersville Road. Then Holt led his remaining eight companies into the Mountain Church Road, on the left of the 6th Virginia and fronting Jacob Goodman's farm buildings and the open fields beyond.[31]

On the Federal front, Bartlett's 16th New York and the 5th Maine, advancing at the double-quick, dashed over the prone skirmishers of the 27th New York to one of Henry Shafer's fence lines of stones and rails, which was about 300 yards from the Confederate position and roughly parallel to it. Even at this range the Rebels' fire was severe enough that the Union men took shelter behind the fence to return it.[32]

George Bernard of the 12th Virginia was on the receiving end of Bartlett's musketry.

> I looked through the lower rails of the fence to the front, and to my surprise discovered that the enemy were behind the stone fence just across the ploughed ground, about 250 yards distant—a fact disclosed by the flashes and puffs of white smoke darting out from the muzzles of one, two, three, and then it seemed a hundred rifles, the blaze of the guns in a second's time running down the whole length of the enemy's line posted behind the wall. It is almost needless to mention that in an instant their bullets were whistling through the rails of our fence, falling in the ploughed ground short of us, and striking the trees, stumps, logs, and rocks on the hill-side behind us.[33]

The first contact with the enemy revealed the impossibility of Bartlett's strategy not to engage in a firefight during the advance. Nor was this all. When

Bartlett looked to his rear for Newton's brigade—which, according to the plan, should have been following at 200 yards—he saw with astonishment that it trailed him by nearly 1,000 yards. Bartlett's regiments fired rapidly but with little apparent effect on the well-sheltered enemy, who kept blazing away. Bartlett's casualties began to mount steadily. "Nothing but the most undaunted courage and steadiness on the part of the two regiments forming my line maintained the fight until the arrival of the rest of the attacking column," he reported. For nearly 30 minutes Bartlett's three regiments kept up the fight by themselves. "Never did men work harder than did the noble soldiery of those two regiments," wrote George Bicknell of the 5th Maine. "Almost every man seemed angry because he could not load and fire more rapidly." But Bicknell also recalled that not every man stood the fire bravely. A recruit in his regiment, terrified by the carnage around him, dropped his musket and started for the rear at a trot. An officer attempted to stop him, but the young man was too thoroughly demoralized; he responded, "du ye 'spose I'm guine to stay here and git w-a-u-n-d-e-d?" With this statement the recruit broke into a run for the rear.[34]

By the time Newton's leading regiments arrived near Bartlett's firing line, the latter's units had spent most of their ammunition in their fruitless fusillade. Newton's first line consisted of Lieutenant Colonel George R. Myers's 18th New York and Colonel Roderick Matheson's 32nd New York. Myers's men were recruited from across the northern part of the state, from Albany to Ogdensburg. Matheson's 32nd had a more complicated and unique origin. The 38-year-old, Scottish-born Matheson had a bit of the adventurer in him, and he had abandoned the more traditional livelihoods of teaching and selling real estate to try his luck in the California gold fields. Like most, he discovered no fortune there, so he moved to San Francisco, where he seemed to find his niche. After Lincoln's election Matheson was selected to join a delegation sent to attend the president's inauguration and seek favors for California. Lincoln could offer the men no appointments, but he did encourage those with military training to travel to New York and assist in raising troops to meet the emergency. Matheson had some militia experience and accompanied the group. It was hoped that a regiment of West Coast men could be raised in the city, to be commanded by Lincoln's friend, Oregon Senator Edward D. Baker. But when only 200 men were recruited, Baker balked and refused a colonel's commission, departing instead for Philadelphia, where he would find more success raising the 1st California (later the 71st Pennsylvania). With Baker's departure, Matheson was elected colonel, and his regiment, unofficially dubbed the 1st California, was filled out with New Yorkers from across the state. Matheson shaped them into a solid fighting unit, and they saw action at First Manassas and in the Seven Days battles.[35]

As Myers's and Matheson's regiments came up, Bartlett inserted Myers's 18th into line on the right of the 16th New York, where they had the cover of a stone wall, and placed Matheson's 32nd in on the left of the 16th. As Newton's men took their place on the front line, the 16th New York and the 5th Maine fell back 20 paces, where they found some shelter from enemy fire. The 27th New York was also low on ammunition, and Bartlett ordered Lieutenant Colonel Adams to retire his regiment from the skirmish line and re-form it.[36] Minutes after Newton's 18th New York and 32nd New York reached the front, his 31st New York, under Lieutenant Colonel Francis E. Pinto, followed by Colonel Gustavus W. Town's 95th Pennsylvania, came huffing up. Pinto's New Yorkers were ordered into line on the left of the 32nd New York, while Town's Pennsylvanians formed a support line in the rear of Pinto. There were hundreds of muskets cracking now, wreathing the firing lines in smoke. Their cacophony was punctuated by the crack and boom of the Confederate artillery shells that continued to stream in.

Behind Newton's last arrivals came Torbert's New Jersey brigade. This was Philip Kearny's old brigade—men whom that demanding soldier described as the "noblest brigade in the army." But they had endured some hard knocks in the war after Kearny had left them to command a division. At Gaines' Mill they suffered a staggering 1,072 casualties, the highest of any brigade in the Union army during that battle. In the confusion attendant on the general collapse of the Union defense, nearly the entire 4th New Jersey was captured, and the 2nd regiment lost its colors. On August 27 the brigade was sent out toward Manassas Junction to investigate reports of Confederates raiding the Union supply depot there. They bumped into Stonewall Jackson's entire force and were routed, losing General George Taylor, their brigade commander, who was mortally wounded.

Command fell to Torbert, the senior colonel, an outstanding soldier with a reputation in the brigade as a tough disciplinarian. Born in Delaware and an 1855 graduate of West Point, Torbert was appointed a lieutenant in the Confederate Army, an honor he declined. The way Torbert saw it, "the United States Government has given me an education, and I should be a pretty disgraceful pupil if I used it against the country." Torbert's New Jerseyans swept "with great regularity through clover and cornfields, intersected with high wood and stone fences, being exposed the greater part of the time to the enemy's artillery fire," until they came up in the rear of Bartlett's reserve line, where they halted at the edge of a cornfield. The shelling continued and the 4th regiment suffered some casualties, but the brigade remained steady. Torbert went up toward the firing to see how his men might help, and Bartlett asked for assistance on the left of the line. The skirmishers of the 27th New York were retiring to replenish their ammunition, and Confederates of the 16th Virginia probed the void, pressing forward along Main Street toward Burkittsville so aggressively that Colonel Town of the 95th Pennsylvania thought he should change front to meet a flank attack. Torbert ordered Colonel Samuel L. Buck's 2nd New Jersey forward the fill the gap. The regiment formed into battle line, then dashed through the corn and emerged into open ground. They halted behind a rail fence near the Michael Wiener tannery on the west edge of Burkittsville and opened fire.[37]

Colonel Cake's 96th Pennsylvania followed in Torbert's path. When they arrived in sight of the front line, Henry Boyer gave testimony to the rate of fire that the thin line of Confederates were producing: "the furies of pandemonium broke loose and from the crest of South Mountain it appeared to us that from the muzzles of four or five full batteries shot and shell were rained down upon our devoted heads." Referring to an earlier jocular comment of Slocum's that only four Confederate cavalrymen and two guns were guarding the gap, the regimental sergeant major jested: "General Slocum's four cavalrymen are trying to scare us with their old rusty cannon." Cake reported to Bartlett, who directed him to take position on the extreme right of the division line. The colonel moved his regiment at the double-quick, passing over men of either the 16th New York or the 5th Maine, whom Henry Boyer stated "were buried in clover, and we stepped on some of them before we saw them." Arriving on the right of the 32nd New York, Cake ordered his men down behind the same rail fence that the New Yorkers were using for cover. Cake estimated the distance to the mountain base at 1,000 yards, about twice the actual distance, but still far enough that he instantly understood "that we could gain nothing at a stand-off fight" and that it "was evident that nothing but a rush forward would win." This was the grim conclusion that all three brigade commanders had already reached.[38]

From his command post, it appeared to Henry Slocum that the assault had bogged down in the face of heavy, accurate enemy fire. Concerned that the stone wall the rebels were using for cover might prove an "insurmountable ob-stacle" to his division, he sent an urgent request back for a battery. If musketry could not move the rebels, cannons might.[39]

Watching the action from 6th Corps' headquarters at the Martin Shafer farm, William Franklin's confidence crumbled in the face of the stubborn Confederate resistance. Franklin tapped his reserve, ordering General Smith to advance a brigade to the left of the pass. As Smith understood it, this was "to create a diversion, and, if possible, to turn the right flank of the enemy." Smith gave the mission to Brigadier General William T. H. Brooks's excellent Vermont brigade. But even before Brooks made his presence felt, Franklin's courage utterly failed him. At 5:20 p.m. he sent a message by signal to McClellan, laden with excuses for the failure he now believed would attend his corps' attack.

> I report that I have been severely engaged with the enemy for the last hour. I have two brigades in action with musketry and two others just going in. Of course I have no troops but my reserves, and Gen. Couch has not come up.

I have sent to hurry him—The force of the enemy is too great for us to take the pass to night I am afraid.

I shall await further orders here. I shall attack again in the morning without further orders.[40]

Fortunately for Franklin's reputation, his leaders were men of greater nerve and pluck, and they did not think they were whipped by a long sight.

Above the din of firing, Colonel Bartlett heard shouts and yells rolling down from the summit of Crampton's Gap. He was certain that they meant the enemy was being reinforced. This made action imperative if the Confederates were going to be dislodged from their position along the mountain base. He sought out Torbert, who agreed after a "hurried consultation" that only a united charge by the entire division could carry the enemy line. Long-range musketry had failed to budge the Rebels, and the artillery requested by Slocum had not yet arrived. The two colonels presented their plan to Newton, the senior brigade commander, who endorsed it. Apart from approving the initial strategy and ordering up artillery, Slocum had no impact on the management of the battle. From start to finish the brigade commanders directed the fight. Their challenge now was to coordinate the advance of all three brigades. It was decided that Bartlett and Torbert would separate in the center of the division and ride the length of the line in opposite directions, instructing the regimental commanders to have their men cease fire and prepare to charge at the double-quick.[41]

Torbert's New Jerseyans were ready to close with the enemy. During the firefight, several members of the 2nd jumped up on the stone wall protecting them and challenged the Confederates to come out and fight in the open. The Confederates, behind their own stone wall, simply shot them down. To fill in the space between the 2nd New Jersey and Newton's 18th New York, Torbert moved up his 1st New Jersey, but a lack of cover prevented them from moving on the same line their comrades held. The order to prepare for a charge probably met with mixed reactions. Even the simplest private understood that musketry alone had not dented the enemy's defenses, but he could also see that he and his comrades had to cross 300–400 yards of open ground to reach the Rebel line, a long distance either to double-quick or run. At the double-quick a soldier covered 165 steps, or about 165 yards, in a minute. A good Confederate rifleman could easily get off two shots in the time it took a regiment to cover 400 yards at the double-quick. It would be tough and bloody work.[42]

The musketry fire from the Federal line gradually slackened and then ceased as Torbert and Bartlett made the orders for an assault understood. The men loaded their weapons, "took an extra tug at their waist-belts," gritted their teeth, and waited for the signal to charge.[43] The cheering Bartlett had heard from the summit of Crampton's Gap did herald the arrival of Confederate

reinforcements. It was Howell Cobb's brigade, come to the rescue of their beleaguered comrades.

Camped with his brigade at Sandy Hook, Cobb received orders to march to
Brownsville at 1 p.m. from McLaws. He wasted no time in assembling his 1,341
officers and men and set off at as rapid a pace as his command could stand. The
brigade, however, was in poor physical condition. They had started the movement up from Richmond with nearly 2,000 men, but lost a third of their strength
on D. H. Hill's forced marches. Cobb was furious with Hill's management of
the march, and wrote to his wife that if a court-martial were convened to investigate, Cobb would charge Hill "with incapacity and inhumanity—and relieve
the service of as despicable a wretch, as ever disgraced any army." Their brief
stay in Maryland had not improved the diet or condition of the men, as Lieutenant H. C. Kearny of the 15th North Carolina revealed: "The men were almost exhausted from constant marching over rough roads, nearly shoeless, and
without rations, except green beef without salt and some corn." The brigade
nevertheless covered the distance to Brownsville in good time, arriving around
4 p.m. Semmes called on Cobb soon after he arrived and communicated McLaws's
instructions that Cobb should take command at Crampton's Gap and relieve
Parham's brigade. Semmes, unaccountably, was unaware that Crampton's Gap
was under attack; he still believed Brownsville Pass to be the enemy's target.
What else Semmes told Cobb is unknown, but circumstantial evidence hints
that neither Semmes nor Cobb thought it imperative that the relief take place
until it was certain which pass the enemy would move against. If Cobb marched
to Crampton's Gap at once, then—if the enemy struck Brownsville Pass—
Semmes would be without any reserves. So Cobb stayed put and Semmes left to
visit his pickets at Brownsville Pass.[44]

Howell Cobb was no dunderhead, despite the criticism heaped on him after
Crampton's Gap. The rather rotund Georgian looked out of place as a soldier,
but beneath his unimposing appearance he was a shrewd man of powerful intellect. Few men in the country could match the list of accomplishments that
he had tallied in his 47 years. Born the son of a wealthy Athens, Georgia, planter,
Cobb entered the law and politics as a young man and found his niche there. By
the time of the secession crisis he had been governor of Georgia, Speaker of the
U.S. House of Representatives, and Secretary of the Treasury under James Buchanan. Cobb was a Jacksonian Democrat, and when the Southern Democrat
and Whig parties split in the 1850s, Cobb took up the banner of the Union
Party, which pitted him against the secession-advocating Southern Rights
Party. But the rise of the Republican Party and their stand against slavery in the
territories pushed Cobb back into the Democratic Party, and the election of
the Republican candidate, Lincoln, led Cobb to advocate for secession. Such
was his standing in the South that when delegates from the seceded states gathered in Montgomery, Alabama, in February 1861, Cobb was elected president of

the provisional congress, and when the delegates went about selecting a permanent president, they viewed Cobb as a serious contender. But since this placed him in direct competition with Jefferson Davis, Cobb chose to remove his name from consideration and gave his full support to the nomination of Davis. When the guns of Fort Sumter announced that the secession crisis would be resolved by war, Cobb, despite his lack of any military training, had the courage of his convictions. He donned the Confederate gray and began recruiting the 16th Georgia Infantry. By February 1862 Cobb was promoted to brigadier general and took command of a brigade of Georgia troops, including his own 16th Georgia and his brother Tom Cobb's Georgia Legion. He did not take his responsibilities lightly, and a visitor to his camp in July 1861 reported that "for over a month Col. Cobb has been industriously training himself in the duties and discipline of the soldier, and numerous are the attestations to his rapidly acquired proficiency in the art of war which come to us through educated officers." Cobb did not lack physical courage, but he proved ill suited for a combat command. Nor did he understand the command responsibility McLaws had placed on him. "General Cobb was inexperienced enough not to realize that as ranking officer he was responsible for everything that might happen in his rear," wrote McLaws. After arriving at Brownsville, Cobb—although senior to Semmes in rank and therefore now in command of the defense of both gaps—remained in camp and made no effort to learn anything about the firing coming from over the mountain. McLaws concluded that "if he [Cobb] had had more experience as to the responsibilities which rank confers he would not have waited an hour in camp upon contingencies, but would have gone in person in advance to inform himself as to the best way to provide against misfortune."[45]

At 5 p.m. a note from Munford shook Cobb from his complacency. Munford "recommended" that Cobb march his entire command to Crampton's Gap, "as the enemy were pressing the small force he had at the gap." Cobb immediately ordered his two largest regiments, the 24th Georgia and the 15th North Carolina—770 officers and men—to march. But before they had formed up and filed onto the road to Crampton's Gap, a second note, this one from Parham, reached Cobb with news that the enemy were "pressing him hard with overwhelming numbers"; Parham appealed for all the help that could be sent. Cobb had almost certainly held back the other half of his brigade, because he still had a responsibility to support Semmes at Brownsville Pass, but the force of Parham's appeal convinced him that the enemy had made Crampton's Gap their target. He now ordered Cobb's Legion and the 16th Georgia to fall in and follow their sister regiments to Crampton's Gap. Cobb rode with them. As Cobb got the tail of his column underway, McLaws's assistant adjutant general, Major T. S. McIntosh, galloped up with orders from McLaws for Cobb to hold Crampton's Gap to the last man. Around this same time a report came from Semmes confirming that Parham and Munford were hard pressed, and Cobb's brigade was urgently needed. McLaws's orders and Semmes's message galvanized Cobb, and he set out for Crampton's Gap with "utmost dispatch."[46]

Cobb's leading regiments covered the approximately 2 miles to Crampton's Gap in a half hour, a testament to the rapid pace of their march. From the summit of the gap Cobb managed to grasp only a confused and inaccurate idea of the battle snarling below him. He believed that Parham had repulsed the enemy in the center, but that the Federals in "greatly superior numbers" threatened both Confederate flanks. Munford appeared and offered a hurried explanation of the situation; he then transferred the burden of command to the general. But there was no time for Cobb to study the fight to determine where he should deploy his brigade. Cobb deferred to Munford's judgment and knowledge of the ground and the situation, and he asked the cavalryman to post his two leading regiments where they were most needed. The men were given a moment to pile their knapsacks and blankets, and then Munford led them down the Arnoldstown Road toward the imperiled left flank. The order of regiments is a bit fuzzy here, but the evidence suggests that Lieutenant Colonel Henry P. Thomas's 16th Georgia led, followed by Lieutenant Colonel William McRae's 15th North Carolina.[47]

Ammunition was beginning to run low for the Rebels along Mountain Church Road, despite the efforts of men like Bill Andrews, driver of the ordnance wagon of the 12th Virginia, who daringly maneuvered his wagon close to the front to re-supply the men. A typical soldier could fire the full 40-round load of a cartridge box in 20 minutes of sustained firing, and nearly all the Confederate regiments along the road had been heavily engaged for more than 2 hours. Jonathan Crowe of the 12th Virginia thought he fired 60–70 rounds in the battle. Besides dwindling ammunition, fatigue had to be a factor: a man cannot load and fire a rifle or a musket for two hours, while being shot at, and not get tired. So when the 15th North Carolina and the 16th Georgia arrived with loud yells, some of the men along the Mountain Church Road assumed that the reinforcements were their relief and began to fall back. It seemed an opportune moment to do so, for the fire from the Union line had nearly ceased. But then cheering burst from the Federal line, and masses of bluecoats rose from the ground and rushed forward at the double-quick. Bartlett, Torbert, and Newton could not have picked a more fortuitous time to launch their charge.[48]

George Bernard of the 12th Virginia, who had been wounded in the leg and lay behind the slight stone wall that sheltered part of his regiment, recalled the confusion that rippled through his regiment's ranks at the sight of the onrushing Yankees.

> One of our men exclaimed, "Look yonder, boys! They are coming across the field!" Immediately upon which the command ran down our line, "Fix Bayonets,

A postwar view of the Crampton's Gap battlefield. The gap is visible to the right center. Torbert's New Jersey brigade charged across the field in the foreground against the 12th Virginia, who were sheltered behind the stone wall. Some of the buildings pictured were not present in September 1862. The buildings halfway up the mountain are along the Gapland Road. New York Monuments Commission, *In Memoriam, Henry Warner Slocum, 1826–1894* (Albany, NY: J. B. Lyon, 1904).

men! Fix Bayonets!" followed in a few seconds by another, "Fall back, men! Fall back!!" when there was a general grabbing up of guns, blankets, knapsacks, canteens, etc., and a backward movement.[49]

Torbert's brigade spearheaded the assault. He selected the 3rd and the 4th New Jersey to lead the way from their reserve position. When Torbert gave the signal, Colonel William B. Hatch, commanding the 4th New Jersey, loudly shouted "Forward, 4th Battalion; charge bayonets." Both regiments rose to their feet and, "yelling like a pack of devils," dashed forward "at a full run" past their comrades in the 1st and 2nd regiments. Torbert let them cover some 150 yards before he ordered the 1st and the 2nd New Jersey to follow as the second wave. Moments after they went forward, Newton's and Bartlett's regiments leaped up and charged toward the road, cheering loudly. "The Rebel shells came pouring thick and fast," noted Eugene Forbes of the 4th New Jersey, both from Chew's and Grimes's guns at the summit of Crampton's Gap and Manly's at Brownsville Pass, and the Confederate infantry and dismounted cavalry fired "with great rapidity" at the onrushing enemy. Although some fell to the fire, "our boys never stopped," wrote Second Lieutenant Oscar Westlake of the 3rd New Jersey. "Nothing could withstand the onset of our men," boasted Colonel Henry W. Brown of the 3rd New Jersey. Lieutenant Westlake thought the Confederates began to break and run when his regiment was 150 yards from their line. Perhaps some did, but John P. Beech of the 4th New Jersey wrote that the Rebels in his front held until the charging Federals were only 20 yards away, when "they broke and ran like sheep." The two regiments piled in behind the stone wall that minutes before had provided cover for the 16th Virginia and elements of the 12th. A furious run of nearly 400 yards left everyone panting hard, and a pause was necessary for the Union soldiers to catch their breath. Some of Parham's diehards peppered the line with musketry. "Of all the firing that I heard that was the hardest," wrote Lieutenant Westlake, with "the balls whistling around our heads like hail." John Beech concurred that the two regiments "had it pretty warm for awhile," but the other Federals returned the fire for the five minutes it took for the winded men to recover. Then someone shouted "Charge them, boys," and "Remember Manassas and Gaines' Mill." The 1st and 2nd regiments came pouring in about then, and the whole blue tide rolled over the wall and surged up the mountain. At this point the remnants of the 16th and the 12th Virginia who still resisted "broke utterly" and ran for their lives. Now it was the Federals' turn to exact revenge. "We did some good work," wrote Corporal C. C. Hall of the 1st New Jersey. "I tell you we followed them so clost they threw of[f] every thing and run and we after them it was like shooting rabits as they was running."[50]

Torbert received important flank support in his charge from Brigadier General William T. H. Brooks's Vermont brigade, which attacked south of West Main Street. When the 1st Division stalled in front of the Mountain Church Road, Franklin had committed Brooks to the action in the hope that he might relieve the pressure on Slocum's brigades. Brooks was a West Pointer with 21 years of hard service. He distinguished himself in the Mexican War, and otherwise spent most of his career on the frontier as an infantry officer. A comrade from the Mexican conflict remembered Brooks as "a true warrior," an individual "of striking countenance, physically powerful and symmetrical," and "gifted with a true military instinct." This tough regular-army man had molded his Vermonters into first-class soldiers, winning their admiration in the process. Now they followed him down Main Street and through Burkittsville in column. "We were shelled furiously" by the Confederate guns at Brownsville Pass, noted Lieutenant Charles Morey of the 2nd Vermont, but this failed to check the rush of the Green Mountain men—or the ardor of some of Burkittsville's women, who "cheered on" the boys in blue as they passed through.

The 4th Vermont under Lieutenant Colonel Charles B. Stoughton led the dash, and on the western edge of town they left Main Street and made their way through the farmyard of David Arnold's thriving farm. Arnold's "big barn" with a haystack piled up in front of it marked the western edge of his farmyard, and Stoughton's Vermonters halted behind the haystack. The enemy were most likely to be encountered beyond this, so the men waited here for the rest of the brigade to catch up. Brooks, with his staff in tow, soon joined the 4th Vermont. At this moment those Confederates who were sheltered behind a stone wall running along the mountain base "opened a brisk infantry fire" on the Vermonters that were behind Arnold's haystack and barn. Brooks noticed that they were also firing into Slocum's left flank, a problem he intended to remedy. He summoned Lieutenant Abel Parsons of his staff and sent him forward to reconnoiter the enemy position. Parsons returned to report "that the woods at the foot of the mountain were full of rebels." Brooks adjusted his position in the saddle and replied, "I don't think there are quite so many as all that." He called for Stoughton to deploy skirmishers to see if they might budge the enemy. They tried, but had "little effect." Brooks recognized that more muscle was necessary, so he ordered Stoughton to assault the wall with his entire regiment, supported by James Walbridge's 2nd Vermont.[51]

Shouted orders sent Stoughton's companies hustling out from behind the haystack and barn into a "very large open field" south and west of the structure, where they began to form into line. "We did not let the grass grow under our feet in executing this maneuver for obvious reasons," recalled John Conline. The hissing bullets fired by the Confederate infantry and dismounted cavalry, and the "very noisy shell fire" from Manly's guns, provided impetus for haste. Conline noted that Manly's guns were positioned at too high an elevation "to do anything but accidental damage," but the infantry fire "was dangerous." Even performing all their movements as quickly as possible, it took the 4th Vermont nearly 10 minutes to form their line. Orders were shouted to fix bayonets, and the regiment then swept forward, followed by the 2nd Vermont. Conline observed that before his regiment had reached the wall, "the rebels began to run singly, then in little squads of three or four, and finally, as we were about to reach the wall, they all broke pell mell up the slightly inclined open plain, from the wall to the foot of the mountain about 400 yards distant." Many of them turned to shoot at the Federals, who, once they reached the wall, returned the compliments. After firing a couple of rounds, the Union regiment climbed the wall, scooping up some 20 rebels who had sought cover behind a haystack. They then set off in pursuit, with the 2nd Vermont following in their wake. The Confederates' right flank had collapsed utterly, as had their center. But their far left was a tougher nut to crack.[52]

Minutes after Torbert's and Brooks's brigades moved against the Confederate right, Newton's and Bartlett's brigades advanced against their center and left. The earlier action had placed these two brigades in three lines. The first consisted of the 18th and the 32nd New York and the 96th Pennsylvania (from left to right). The 5th Maine and the 16th New York formed a support line, and Newton's 95th Pennsylvania and the 31st New York constituted the third line. The first line's advance was staggered, with the 96th Pennsylvania leading the way, followed by the New Yorkers on their left. The New Yorkers had the easier time of it, as the men of the 12th and the 6th Virginia, in their immediate front, fell back to avoid being outflanked by Torbert's brigade. But the 96th Pennsylvania had no such luck. They faced the 10th Georgia, who proved to be a formidable foe.[53]

Before receiving orders to charge, the men of the 96th had an opportunity to size up the ground in their front leading to the Mountain Church Road. It looked daunting, judging from Henry C. Boyer's description of it.

> Directly in front of the position . . . were three fields and three dense fence-rows of most luxuriant rubbish, of which any decent farmer would be heartily ashamed. Beyond the last field we plainly saw the rough road at the foot of the mountain . . . To our right there was a large field stretching clear to the enemy with never a tree or bush to screen a poor soldier. For a hundred yards or more next [to] the stone wall [along the Mountain Church Road] the field had been freshly plowed, but the rest of it, close up to our right flank, had a low, soggy, and dangerous appearance.[54]

After receiving orders for the attack, Colonel Cake carefully explained to his company officers the tactics he intended to employ. Lieutenants were ordered to take the ammunition from anyone who went down and distribute it to the able-bodied, "in case of a stand-up fight." Soon after Cake completed giving his instructions, they heard a loud shout and saw Torbert's brigade go storming forward. "Attention! Forward! Steady now!" rang out along the 96th's line. As Boyer later exclaimed, "Who that lived through that hour will ever forget those words?"

There were over 500 men in the 96th Pennsylvania, and their battle line extended for nearly 150 yards. Following Cake's explicit plan of attack, they rushed forward to the first fence and made their way through "the very dense growth of rubbish" that nearly obscured the wall. At the second fence they sent a thundering volley in the enemy's direction. Guns were inspected and reloaded; then the men scaled the fence and quickly re-formed. "Bursting shell now hailed around us," wrote Boyer, which hastened their advance. They moved at the double-quick to the third fence, fired a second volley, reloaded, and scrambled over that barrier. As the men formed ranks for the next rush, Colonel Cake ordered one of his two color bearers to take his flag to the extreme left of the regiment to mark the regiment's flank and prevent friendly fire from the New Yorkers he knew would be advancing there.[55]

The view from the third fence revealed more details of the approaches to the enemy position. A grass field of some 150 yards descended into a swale, which contained a cornfield some 100 yards wide. Beyond the corn a short belt of pasture intervened before the Mountain Church Road. As the regiment hastily reformed their line, Henry Boyer stated that there was an "entire cessation of infantry firing in our front." Boyer then continued: "We all believed the enemy would hold his fire until we debouched from the corn, because we felt sure that that is just what we would have done under the same circumstances." Whether it was a deliberate tactical decision by the 10th Georgia commander, Major Holt, or one forced on him due to low ammunition, this was the Confederates' intention. Cake ordered his regiment forward, issuing instructions that the men could fire at will when they entered the corn, "but only to fire at something we thought we could hit." When they reached the edge of the cornfield, "we were to break into double-quick with a cheer and take the road at all hazard."[56]

Not a single man of the regiment fell as the line swept across the first grass field to the swale. Tension mounted with each step forward. As the line entered the corn, the men commenced shooting, "but there was too much random firing," wrote Boyer. The command "Steady now! Trail arms!" was shouted and obeyed, with some men bringing their rifles to trail with the ramrods down the barrels. An instant after the nervous fusillade was brought under control, the command "Steady now! Forward, double quick!" rang out. "The rush and cheer and earthquake were simultaneous," recalled Boyer. Henry Keiser of G Company noted that as the Union soldiers emerged from the corn, "they gave us a deadly volley and a great many of our poor boys fell." Boyer remembered that 81 men were shot down in this initial volley, although such a specific number seem impossible to have been arrived at in such circumstances. Captain Jacob W. Haas stated simply: "The fire was terrific." As Boyer commented, "a shiver ran along the line that for a moment looked like flight." Then someone shouted, "Forward into the road and give them the bayonet—it is death for us to hesitate now!" With fixed bayonets the most aggressive started forward, and their example compelled the rest to follow.[57]

The Pennsylvanians crossed the narrow pasture before the Confederates who chose to make a stand could reload, but not before the Rebels fixed bayonets. A brief, savage, deadly grapple ensued in the Mountain Church Road as the Federals drove their attack home. The men of C Company, which was also the color company of the 96th, were among the first Federals to pitch into Holt's Georgians. They paid a stiff price in blood, particularly the color guard. Color Sergeant Solomon M. McMinzi, a Scotsman with 20 years in the Royal Artillery, carried the state color. Confederate balls struck his chest and shattered his thigh. He fell, but was grasping at the stone wall bordering the road to pull himself up when one of Holt's men ran his bayonet through McMinzi's body and killed him. When Private William Ortner took the flag from Mc-

Minzi, he was immediately shot. Then Color Sergeant Joseph Johnson grasped the flag, only to be felled by a shell fragment or a bullet. When Private Charles Ziegler took it from Johnson, a bullet took his life, too.

The other color drew the same reception. Its original bearer, Color Sergeant Oliver Thomas, went down with a crippling wound in his ankle. Henry Boyer remembered, perhaps incorrectly, that one color bearer received 12 bayonet wounds. Whether this particular incident was true or not, the evidence is abundant that for several moments this was a brutal, no-quarter fight. Major Lewis Martin, one of the regiment's most popular officers, also fell during the rush to the road, mortally wounded with a bullet in the head. Captain Haas entered in his diary that a Confederate who fired at him shot the top of his canteen off, with the force knocking him to the ground. Hass leaped back up, however, and managed to seize the Georgian who had shot him, making the Rebel a prisoner. "I had him in tight papers," Haas wrote.

Although the Southerners fought desperately, they were heavily outnumbered and quickly overwhelmed. Boyer stated that 12 rebels were bayoneted and killed, although the 10th Georgia counted only 6 killed or mortally wounded. "We thought we had bayoneted one hundred fifty in that road," Boyer recalled, although he noted how prone soldiers are to exaggerate the damage inflicted on the enemy. "Those . . . who were not hurt, and who seemed too much surprised to get away begged lustily for mercy," reported Colonel Cake. The initial frenzy of killing subsided quickly, and the surrender of those seeking it was accepted. Holt's survivors—those who eluded death, wounds, or capture in the road—fled up the mountain. Some 40 percent of his regiment were casualties, but they had exacted a fearful toll from the 96th Pennsylvania, which counted 20 dead and 70 wounded, the highest loss of any Union regiment at Crampton's Gap. "The officers and men behaved with great gallantry," reported Holt, "except a few who were too cowardly to go to the line of battle." Cake could also point with pride to his regiment's performance. But he wasted no time on their initial success. The Confederates were on the run, and he did not intend to let them rally. Assisted by regimental Sergeant Major John Harlan, Cake reformed his companies and resumed the advance toward Crampton's Gap.[58]

The 96th's charge completed the fracture of the original Munford-Parham line, and the remnants of it fled up the mountain. To the retreating Confederates, the Mountain Church Road seemed awash with bluecoats. The 18th and the 32nd New York arrived soon after the 96th Pennsylvania overwhelmed the 10th Georgia. The 5th Maine and several companies of the 27th New York followed in support. The 16th New York came up on the 18th New York's left, and beyond them the 95th Pennsylvania and the 31st New York were advancing in the path that Torbert's right wing had already cleared. Tactical finesse was impossible at this point. Everyone understood what was necessary: push uphill and keep the enemy on the jump. Some of Parham's and Holt's men continued to fire on the road from the cover of the woods on the mountain slope, and this caused some of Bartlett's and Newton's men to remain in the road under cover. But—like the decisive moment of the 96th's charge, when the most aggressive soldiers had propelled the regiment forward—now the boldest men drove the entire line to advance by simply starting up the mountain. Reported Lieutenant Colonel Seaver of the 16th New York, "their example encouraged others who faltered before the terrors of the enemy and steepness of the hill." From the 96th Pennsylvania on the far right to Brooks's Vermonters on the extreme left, the entire Union line was swarming up the mountain now, a seemingly irresistible mass of fighting men in blue.[59]

Just as the Confederates' Mountain Church Road line collapsed, the Rebels received a fresh infusion of reinforcements when Cobb's 24th Georgia and Cobb's Legion reached the mountain summit with 44 officers and 496 enlisted men. Given the advantage of terrain the Confederates enjoyed, such numbers might have been significant had there been time to select the most advantageous position for these men. But there was not. Torbert's regiments were pouring across David Arnold's pastures, and the line below needed support fast. Cobb again asked Munford to post his men, and the cavalryman sent them down the Gapland Road toward the imperiled right flank. It was the right move, but the situation deteriorated so rapidly that by the time these two Southern regiments were moving down the road, Torbert's New Jerseyans had shattered Parham's line and were swarming up the mountain.[60]

The 3rd and the 4th New Jersey led the surge of Torbert's brigade uphill from the Mountain Church Road, with the 1st and 2nd regiments close behind. The 2nd New Jersey may even have moved in advance of the 3rd during the climb to the Gapland Road. When Colonel Brown's 3rd New Jersey reached the road, they observed the Cobb Legion attempting to form on their right. The men of Colonel Samuel Buck's 2nd New Jersey, now past the Gapland Road and clambering toward the mountain crest, saw them as well. Buck wheeled his regiment to the right, while Brown changed front forward to get a flank fire on the Georgians. These were not neat, trim lines of men in blue conducting a textbook maneuver, however. Eugene Forbes of the 4th New Jersey related that when the brigade advanced from the Mountain Church Road, "the regiments were all broken up, and every man fighting on his own hook." But they had the advantage, since most of the brigade's manpower was on the Cobb Legion's front and flank, and they caught the Georgians in the act of forming. Men of the 3rd and the 2nd New Jersey opened a deadly flank fire, while the 4th peppered the front of the Confederate line with bullets. The Legion fell into confusion.

Then the 3rd and the 4th New Jersey charged, and the Legion, in Colonel Brown's words, "broke utterly." Theodorick B. Ruffin of Parham's 12th Virginia observed their demise, writing that they "fired one volley and scattered to the four winds." Munford affirmed Ruffin's observation, reporting that the Legion and the 24th Georgia, who formed on the Legion's left flank, "behaved badly and did not get into position before the wildest confusion commenced." Torbert's New Jerseyans pressed hard on their heels, shooting down fleeing Rebels and scooping up prisoners. It is an old adage of battle that retreating units who do not maintain a steady front suffer heavily, while their assailants lose very few men. The Legion bore out that maxim at Crampton's Gap, suffering dreadful losses of 57 killed or mortally wounded, 78 wounded, and 44 captured—a 72 percent casualty rate. Among the fallen was their commander, Lieutenant Colonel Jefferson M. Lamar, a cousin by marriage of Thomas R. Cobb, who was Howell's brother. Thomas was the normal commander of the Legion, but he was home on leave and missed the campaign. Earlier in the war Lamar had proclaimed, "I should esteem it an honor and a privilege to die for my country." He had his opportunity at Crampton's Gap, and now lay dying of his wounds. The 24th Georgia, whose line collapsed soon after the Legion's, lost 41 percent of their men. Neither regiment managed to inflict more than minor damage on their assailants.[61]

While Torbert crushed the Confederate's right flank, Cobb's 16th Georgia and the 15th North Carolina desperately attempted to check the advance of the New Yorkers and Pennsylvanians of Newton's and Bartlett's brigades. The Mountain Church Road teemed with Federal soldiers from four regiments: roughly, from left to right, the 16th, the 18th, and the 32nd New York, and the 96th Pennsylvania, although one 16th New York soldier wrote that the regiments "were not in order." After some minutes spent restoring a semblance of order, the Union line surged out of the road and into the woods covering the mountainside. Both the 18th and the 32nd New York were low on ammunition, and Major John Meginnis of the 18th called out to Colonel Bartlett that his men were out of cartridges. Bartlett responded: "Never mind, Major; push on; we have them on the run. The regiments on each side of you have got ammunition and are using it." Lieutenant Colonel Seaver of the 16th New York observed with pride how "the men fought nobly and pressed on up the steep ascent under a perfect shower of bullets."

As the Union troops pushed farther up the slope and into the woods, Seaver saw the "rebels drawn up to receive us." It was the 16th Georgia and the 15th North Carolina, formed along the Arnoldstown Road. Both regiments opened fire on the advancing Federals. Lieutenant Colonel Seaver anticipated the first volley and shouted for his men to lie down. An instant later, "down came a volley from a full regiment or more." Most of the bullets passed harmlessly over the Federals' heads. To Seaver's right the 32nd and the 18th New York were not as fortunate; or perhaps they did not hit the dirt as quickly. The Confederate fire scythed through their ranks with deadly effect. "It was here I met with my heaviest loss," lamented Lieutenant Colonel George Myers, "the fire of the enemy being well directed and fatal." Both Colonel Matheson and Major George

Lemon of the 32nd went down with mortal injuries. Despite his wound, Matheson exhorted his men, "You've got 'em, boys, push on." For a moment the New Yorkers "staggered" under the severe fire.[62]

But the check to the Union advance proved to be fleeting. As Lieutenant Colonel Myers noted, "at the command" his regiment—along with the 16th and the 32nd New York, and the 96th Pennsylvania—"immediately rushed on the enemy," firing as they advanced. "We at once observed his bullets flying high over our heads," stated Henry Boyer of the 96th. Colonel Bartlett also noticed that the Rebels were "firing over us, and our loss was very little." This, wrote Henry Boyer, "gave us renewed courage, while our aim, being uphill, was doing deadly work." One of Boyer's regimental comrades, Sergeant Andrew Anderson of Company K, dropped the 16th Georgia's color bearer, but in the ensuing excitement the 96th did not pick up the fallen colors and they were secured by another regiment. Lieutenant Colonel Seaver ordered his New Yorkers "to cover themselves and fire as rapidly as possible." This, he reported, "was done with good effect." As the full strength of the four Union regiments came on line, their firepower swelled dramatically and began to take a toll on the Georgians and the North Carolinians. Because they were firing uphill, wrote Colonel Bartlett, "each bullet must hit either a tree, a rock or a man, for they could not go over the mountain." The Confederate line wavered, and then, in the words of Lieutenant Colonel Seaver, "fled precipitously." As Clarence L. Hutchins of the 16th Georgia recalled, "it was either surrender or run over the Mt. to our left, and while quite a number surrendered, some of us preferred taking our chances, so we climbed the mountain while the Yanks hollared and fired at us when we refused to surrender." "We had them started," wrote Lieutenant Colonel Seaver, "and—they could not help it—they ran."[63]

The 15th North Carolina were outflanked on their right, a fact which lends credence to the supposition that they were on the 16th Georgia's right and had their flank exposed by the retreat of Cobb's Legion and the 24th Georgia. Some 250 of their 402 men were conscripts, without any military training, who reached the regiment immediately before its traipse north from Richmond. What they knew about maneuvering and handling their weapons they had learned on the march. It could not have been much. Lieutenant H. C. Kearney of Company E stated that the 15th's men were so focused on engaging the Federals in their front—the regiments of Bartlett's and Newton's brigades—that they were oblivious to the fact that their flank protection had disappeared. "The first knowledge we had of the situation on the right was a terrible volley of musketry from the rear and right flank, which was at first thought to be from our own troops . . . but such thoughts were dispelled by seeing the Federal flag in the rear," wrote Kearney. This volley—perhaps fired by elements of Torbert's brigade or the 95th Pennsylvania, who had joined the fray on Torbert's front and were advancing on either side of the Gapland Road—inflicted little damage, although Kearney noted that "the clothing of nearly every man bore the mark of a ball (the writer [Kearney] receiving 13 without breaking the skin), but few were hurt."[64]

Not many may have fallen in this initial fire, but it sowed disorder and quickly led to complete collapse. The regiment fled up the mountain. Not all escaped, however: 91 men of the regiment were taken prisoner, nearly all from the right five companies (A, C, E, G and I); 18 were dead; and 58 wounded. The 16th Georgia was affected even more severely, earning the melancholy distinction of suffering the single greatest loss of any regiment engaged at Crampton's Gap: 52 killed or mortally wounded, 53 wounded, and 87 captured—52 percent of their strength. An unsympathetic Lieutenant Colonel Seaver remarked in a letter the next day that "the line of our advance was marked by a train of cold and lifeless rebellious mortality, from the base to the summit of the mountain." Captain Haas of the 96th put it differently and more succinctly: "We gave them hell after we had them on the jump up the mountain."[65]

Bartlett's and Newton's regiments had indeed given the enemy hell after clearing the Mountain Church Road, but the Confederates had dealt out some damage of their own before their front collapsed. The 16th New York counted 20 dead and 41 wounded; the 18th New York, 11 dead and 41 wounded. The 96th Pennsylvania, which had lost heavily in the fight at the Mountain Church Road, was virtually unscathed in this subsequent action. Henry Boyer believed the regiment suffered only one casualty, a single wounded officer.[66]

With the defeat of Cobb's brigade, organized Confederate resistance utterly collapsed. The survivors streamed to the rear, seeking to put space between themselves and their Federal pursuers as quickly as possible. Cobb, Munford, Parham, and other officers positioned themselves at the mountain gap, near where the Arnoldstown and Gapland roads met, and risked their lives in a brave but futile attempt to rally the fleeing infantry. Major Holt was trying to form the remnants of his 10th Georgia into a line when a spent ball struck him above the left eye and bathed his face in blood. Holt turned command over to Captain P. H. Loud, but the regiment had lost nearly one-third its strength, and Loud could do no more than join in the general retreat. At one point Cobb seized a regimental standard, probably that of the 24th Georgia, in an effort to rally the knots of demoralized infantry who streamed past him, but a bullet shattered the staff in his hand. Nearby his brother-in-law, Colonel John Lamar, a volunteer aide-de-camp, went down mortally wounded.

General Semmes and his staff arrived in the midst of the collapse. He encountered "fugitives from the battle-field" as he started his ascent on the west side of Crampton's Gap, a clue that things were not going well on the other side. He endeavored to turn the fugitives back but had no success. Semmes pushed on and met troops "pouring down the road and through the woods, in great disorder." Pressing still farther, he joined Cobb at the gap and attempted to help him "in the vain attempt to rally the men." But Semmes found it "impossible to rally them so near the enemy." Munford reported more candidly on the chaos: "It would have been as useless to rally a flock of frightened sheep." Crampton's Gap was lost. The Confederates' effort was now focused on extricating the broken regiments from the mountain and building a line in the valley behind which they might be rallied.[67]

A section of the Troup (Georgia) Artillery arrived in the middle of this disaster. The rifled guns of this battery and the battery's commander, Captain Henry C. Carleton, were on Maryland Heights. The other section, under Lieutenant Henry Jennings, consisted of one 12 lb. howitzer and a Model 1841 6 lb. gun, which were named "Jennie" and "Sallie Craig" respectively. Jennings and his men had been left at Sandy Hook, but they were apparently ordered to follow Cobb's brigade when McLaws sent it to reinforce Crampton's Gap. They reached Brownsville late in the afternoon, and had already removed the harness from their horses when orders arrived to march at once to Crampton's Gap. Jennings had his two guns on the road quickly. Edgar Richardson wrote that about a mile south of the gap, "we met our men running back saying we were whipped and that our Brigade was all cut to pieces." But, continued Richardson, "we went on as fast as our horses would carry us" and reached the summit just about dusk. Here Jennings found Cobb and his staff vainly attempting to rally his broken infantry, but Richardson could see at a glance that "it was too much of a Bull Run stampede to stop them."

The 23-year-old Jennings was a fearless fellow, and he took his guns to within 100 yards of the advancing Yankees before he ordered them to unlimber. He placed the two guns at the point where the Arnoldstown Road joins the Gapland Road, which gave them both good fields of fire to cover the approaches to the summit. Fortunately for the Georgia gunners, the fading light provided some concealment and the advancing Federals were not aware of their presence until both guns opened with canister. "I fired 3 rounds at them and could see their ranks open every time," observed Richardson. Colonel Gustavus Town, commanding the 95th Pennsylvania, reported that his line "recoiled" under the fire, but only for a moment, "and then, with shouts, charged on it, firing as it [Town's regiment] advanced, the shots being directed by the flash of the artillery, as it was too dark to distinguish the gunners at that distance." John Beech and his comrades of the 4th New Jersey also felt the sting of Jennings's smoothbores. He recalled that the Confederate artillery killed and wounded "a good many of our boys," including the regimental adjutant, Lieutenant Josiah S. Studdeford, who took a canister ball that passed clear through his body.

Bartlett's and Newton's men were also targeted by one of Jennings's guns. Bartlett stated that when he emerged from the woods on the mountainside into the Arnoldstown Road, "I saw the flash of a cannon, which was within 50 yards of me, and trained toward us, the canister bursting in our very faces." The next instant the gun that fired at Bartlett limbered to the rear, passing the other gun in the section, which delivered its canister charge and repeated the same leapfrog tactic. "The last time I fired at them they were within 75 yards of my gun," wrote Edgar Richardson. "I shot at their colors and cut them down." Despite being one of Jennings's gunners' intended victims, Bartlett admired the Georgians' courage and how they handled their guns: "I cannot help giving my testimony to the skill and great bravery with which . . . the enemy's artillery retired down the road."[68]

Jennings's two guns limbered so quickly that they drew only a "scattering fire" from the surprised Federals, and it appeared that they might make good their escape. But careening down the west side of the mountain on the Gapland Road, the limber pulling "Jennie," the 12 lb. howitzer, threw a wheel. With the enemy in close pursuit, the crew were forced to run for their lives and leave behind gun, limber, and horses.[69]

The 95th Pennsylvania and the 31st New York took the lead in the pursuit from Crampton's Gap, passing their disorganized and exhausted comrades from the 18th and the 32nd New York and those elements of Bartlett's and Torbert's brigades who participated in the final push to the gap. South of Crampton's Gap, Brooks's 2nd and 4th Vermont scaled the mountain. At the summit Brooks ordered the 4th to move south and attack the Confederate artillery at Brownsville Pass, which had been so troublesome throughout the day. While the 4th worked its way south in that direction, Brooks sent the 2nd Vermont down the western slope, in an effort to cut off the Rebels who were then resisting Slocum's men at Crampton's Gap.[70]

First Lieutenant George Hooker, adjutant of the 4th Vermont, led the vanguard of his regiment's move south, following an old wagon track. Hooker was an aggressive soldier and, being mounted—remarkable, considering the terrain his horse had to negotiate—he got some distance ahead of his regiment and came upon Major Francis D. Holladay and his 16th Virginia, attempting to make their way to Brownsville Pass and safety. With great coolness of mind, Hooker bluffed the Virginians into believing that a large Union force loomed nearby and that surrender was their best option. Holladay's men were probably exhausted and a bit demoralized from the results of the fight on the Mountain Church Road, and they had seen enough Yankees earlier to give a ring of truth to Hooker's boast. They chose surrender, giving up their colors, with Holladay handing the lieutenant his sword. Hooker delivered up his bag of prisoners to a surprised but delighted Colonel Stoughton. The Vermonters claimed that they took 5 officers and 115 enlisted men, the entire engaged strength of the 16th Virginia, but the Virginians reported only 65 missing or captured, so either the Vermonters exaggerated their haul of prisoners or the 16th underreported its losses. In any event, 30 years later Hooker received a Medal of Honor for his bold exploit.[71]

The disaster that engulfed the Confederates might have been worse had not dwindling ammunition, fatigue, confusion, and darkness put the brakes on the

Union pursuit. "I never was so near worn out as I was on the 14th when I was climing the side of the mountain and my face all black with powder," wrote C. C. Hall of the 1st New Jersey to his cousin. Many of Slocum's men would have nodded in agreement. The running fight up the mountain had scattered and disorganized the regiments. "If our men had been fresh at this point, we could easily have taken the artillery and part of the baggage train, but the men were so fatigued . . . the enemy made good their escape," reported Colonel Buck. Newton's 95th Pennsylvania and the 31st New York relieved the regiments that had fought their way to the summit and led the pursuit down the western side of the mountain to Pleasant Valley. The 95th pursued the guns of the Troup Artillery and what were probably the ordnance wagons of Cobb's and Parham's brigades. The wagons escaped, helped by the guns of the Troup Artillery, but Lieutenant Jennings had to abandon his disabled gun, due to the close pursuit by the Pennsylvanians. It is uncertain whether, in the rapid fall of night, the 95th realized that this trophy, with limber and horses attached, sat abandoned in their front; before they had advanced far enough to discover it, Colonel Bartlett rode up and personally ordered the regiment to fall back to the cover of the woods on the western base of the mountain.[72]

In the dark, the Federals assembled a line along the western base of the mountain, stretching from the Gapland Road to the Rohrersville Road. Brooks's Vermont brigade anchored the left of the line, while the relatively fresh 31st New York guarded the Rohrersville Road on the right. Captain Andrew Cowan's 1st Independent New York Battery of rifled guns were brought up and unlimbered between Brooks's men and the 95th Pennsylvania. Colonel William H. Irwin's 3rd Brigade, 2nd Division, were also moved to the front, forming in close support of the Vermonters and Cowan; they contributed the 49th New York to the skirmish line. It was while establishing the skirmish line for the night that some men of the 2nd Vermont discovered the Troup Artillery's abandoned gun and limber, which they retrieved and turned over to Cowan. The regiments who had borne the brunt of the battle—Torbert's and Bartlett's brigade, and the 18th and the 32nd New York of Newton's brigade—bivouacked in the rear of this line, where they enjoyed a well-deserved chance to rest and recuperate.[73]

At the summit of the mountain, along the steep eastern slope, and at the base and its approaches, lanterns bobbed about in the darkness as Union ambulance details combed the battle area for casualties. The lanterns cast their dim light over the numerous bloody corpses in Confederate gray or Union blue, and on the groaning bodies of men too badly wounded to crawl or hobble off to the field hospitals. For many Union soldiers this was their first opportunity to explore a battlefield won by their arms. They found it sobering. "But oh! The sights—the groans, and cries for help! Who can estimate the horrors of the war; no language is adequate to describe or tongue to express the awfulness of a battle-field," penned W. E. Mattison, the assistant surgeon of the 2nd New Jersey. Mattison labored at a field hospital "with the bleeding and suffering humanity" until midnight, when he could stand no more and went out to the field with a few attendants to give water to those wounded who were not yet removed. Eugene Forbes, who survived the charge up the mountain with the 4th New Jersey, thought it "more terrible to me to go over the mountain and hear the poor wounded rebels crying for water which was almost impossible to get, and asking us to pray for them, than it was for me to face the heaviest fire we were under that day." When Forbes gave one "poor fellow" who was mortally wounded a drink from his canteen, the dying soldier "threw his arms around my neck and prayed God to bless me."[74] First Lieutenant Wilson Hopkins of the 16th New York commanded the ambulance corps of Slocum's division. He never shook the effects of that night:

> This was my first experience in gathering the wounded from a battlefield after it was won. Many have visited such a place and reported the sickening sights, but I cannot describe their ghastly realities. Later I became more familiar with such scenes, yet I can never forget that dreadful night; its horrors overshadowed all spectacles I witnessed on other battlefields, and the memory of what I there saw will remain with me to the end.[75]

There were 418 wounded in the 6th Corps, with 400 from Slocum's division. Many of the injuries were serious, for during the surge up the mountain the Confederates fired high; if their bullets hit, they frequently inflicted head wounds. In addition to the 6th Corps' disabled men, Lieutenant Hopkins's ambulance details brought in a constant stream of Confederate wounded—totaling nearly 300—until midnight, when overworked surgeons announced that they could not treat any more casualties that night. Hopkins labored on, however, gathering up some 40 more injured Confederates. He placed them in a group at the summit of Crampton's Gap and attempted to make them comfortable by building a large fire to keep them warm, as well as distributing food and water. Two able-bodied Confederates were found hiding among the rocks, and Hopkins entrusted them with watching the fire and tending to the needs of their wounded comrades. But the lieutenant's hope that these two men would be good Samaritans did not come to pass. They abandoned their helpless comrades later that night and slipped away. The fire burned out, and 6 of the 40 men died.[76]

The 6th Corps counted 113 dead, a high proportion to the number of wounded by Civil War standards. Among them was Sergeant Theodore McCoy, the best friend of the 3rd New Jersey's Lieutenant Oscar Westlake. The space between life and death was often measured in fractions of an inch. Lieutenant William H. Walling of the 16th New York had a bullet graze his nose during the action, drawing blood but inflicting no real damage. "For others I can not say as much," he wrote home. "Company D had six killed, six wounded, three mortally, one severely and two slightly." There were two men missing from the 18th New

York, which brought the total for the 6th Corps' casualties at Crampton's Gap to 533, or about 10 percent of the numbers engaged. Although it was no comfort to men like Westlake, Walling, or many others who had seen their bravest men and friends cut down, in three hours of fighting the Federals' force had escaped with relatively light losses for Civil War combat.[77]

While the ambulance details scoured the mountainside for wounded and the surgeons struggled to repair the consequences of battle, Franklin and his lieutenants took stock of their victory. In the opinion of Captain Clark Edwards of the 5th Maine, "Slocum's Div done the best fighting that has been done in this war, it is the most brilliant thing on record." While others in the army might dispute Edwards's claim of the best fighting done in the war, Crampton's Gap was the most complete victory won by any unit of the Army of the Potomac to date. The captures included 700 rifles and muskets; four colors; one gun, limber and horses; and numerous other items of equipment. In an ironic twist— and a statement on the ability of the U.S. government to equip its fighting men with the latest weapons—Colonel William B. Hatch collected enough Springfield rifled–muskets dropped by Confederate soldiers to replace the smoothbore muskets with which his regiment was armed. Nearly 400 uninjured prisoners were taken, along with 317 wounded. Burial details reported interring 150 Confederate dead, which was surely an error. Although the final Confederate death toll reached 179, it included those who died of their wounds in the days following the engagement. In terms of human damage, the 6th Corps had dealt the Confederates a hard blow indeed.[78]

After the fighting had ended, Franklin, with his division commanders Slocum and Smith, rode to the summit of Crampton's Gap, where he met with his brigade commanders. Colonel Bartlett recalled that "congratulations were generously and freely passed all around." Franklin did well to acknowledge the contribution of his brigade commanders. He owed his victory to their initiative under fire and to the courage of their men. When his resolve had crumbled, theirs had stiffened.[79]

Tactically, the battle of Crampton's Gap was the most successful engagement fought by the Army of the Potomac in the Maryland Campaign. Franklin wrote to his wife the next day that it was "one of the prettiest fights of the war & I arranged the details of it myself," a claim with which few in the 6th Corps who knew the facts would have agreed. The best that can be said of Franklin's generalship is that he at least did not call off the attack when his confidence wavered. Regarding the "details" of the attack, Franklin's biographer points out that if Colonel Bartlett's recollections were accurate—and evidence indicates that they are—then "the battle seemed to be planned more by committee than by the guiding hand of General Franklin." Franklin's principal tactical contribution to the battle was to commit Brooks's and Irwin's brigades; sound moves, but hardly the stuff of tactical genius. His decision to wait for Couch's division in the morning at Jefferson may have cost the corps a more complete victory, as well as a leg up on his orders to relieve Harpers Ferry. His collapse of will at the crisis of the battle, reflected in his 5:20 p.m. message to McClellan, spoke of a general who lacked the confidence and the mental toughness for independent command. On September 15 Franklin would confirm that he did not possess these important qualities.[80]

Henry Slocum handled the 1st Division competently, although in hindsight he erred by not thinking in terms of combined arms and supporting his infantry more closely with artillery. The true credit for the Union victory belonged to Slocum's brigade commanders and to General Brooks of Smith's division. They all displayed courage, mental toughness, tactical acumen, and a good sense of timing. Bartlett's selection of a column of brigade attack formation made a significant contribution to the Federals' success, for it allowed the division to closely concentrate its strength once they came under infantry fire. That concentration permitted the effective command and control whereby an assault in divisional strength could be organized under fire, something that might have been impossible to arrange if the brigades had attacked in line abreast. Bartlett's and Torbert's leadership was crucial in maintaining the drive up the mountain after the Mountain Church Road line cracked. To Franklin's credit, he acknowledged the contribution of his brigade commanders, recommending that Torbert and Bartlett be promoted to brigadier general, and Newton to brevet major general. The regimental officers and enlisted men also deserved credit for the day's success. They showed great élan, courage, and determination in carrying the enemy position by frontal assault—no small feat, as testified to by many a failed frontal attack during the war. These men, Colonel Bartlett observed, "never failed us when given a fair chance."[81]

Capturing Crampton's Gap was *the* crucial element in Franklin's orders, for without its possession he could not carry out any other portion of the difficult mission McClellan had given him. By securing the gap, he effectively cut McLaws off from Lee and Longstreet at Boonsboro, fulfilling that part of his orders. But he still had to relieve Harpers Ferry, and time was running out. Franklin knew of Miles's message to McClellan, reporting that the garrison would surrender on September 15 if it were not relieved. To do so meant a head-on fight with McLaws, for there were no flanking options, unless the Georgian withdrew across the Potomac River during the night. If it came to a fight, and Franklin had to believe that it probably would, he had substantial reinforcements on hand to give him numerical superiority. Couch's division, over 6,000 strong, arrived in Burkittsville around 10 p.m., raising Franklin's force to nearly 20,000.[82]

But McClellan added a new wrinkle to Franklin's orders late that night. Sometime in the early hours of September 15, Franklin received a dispatch from George D. Ruggles at army headquarters, timed at 1 a.m. It contained news of the main body's partial success at Turner's Gap, but did not answer the problem of whether the battle would be renewed there in the morning or the enemy would retreat. Since McClellan had failed to isolate Lee at Boonsboro, the possibility existed that Lee might detach a part of his force to fall on Franklin's rear by way of Rohrersville, in order to relieve McLaws. To prevent this, McClellan ordered Franklin to place a "sufficient force" at Rohrersville to hold that point should Lee attack from the north. Meanwhile, Franklin was directed to employ the rest of his command to attack and destroy McLaws's command and open communications with Miles at Harpers Ferry. "Should you succeed in opening communications with Colonel Miles, direct him to join you with his whole command, with all the guns and public property that he can carry with him," the order continued. Then Franklin was to lead the combined force north to Boonsboro, "which the commanding general intends to attack to-morrow." But, if the enemy retreated from Boonsboro toward Sharpsburg, Franklin's orders were to cut off their retreat.[83]

It is difficult to conceive how McClellan and his staff imagined that Franklin, with three divisions of infantry and no cavalry, could possibly carry out these orders in a single day. McClellan knew that Franklin faced two Confederate divisions in Pleasant Valley, which—on paper—meant that the 6th Corps did not have an overwhelming edge in manpower. Detaching a "sufficient force" to garrison Rohrersville would cut the odds down even further, and possibly paralyze the cautious commander of the 6th Corps.

Confederate management of the battle at Crampton's Gap was mixed. Munford and Parham remained cool under pressure and made the most of their slim force, first deceiving Franklin as to their true strength, and then holding five times their numbers at bay for three hours. Semmes was surprisingly uninformed about the danger to Crampton's Gap, and seemed not to comprehend what was happening there until the defense had collapsed. But his artillery, under Basil Manley, did yeoman's work in nipping at the Federals' heels throughout the afternoon with a flanking fire. Cobb took the lion's share of the blame for the disaster, much of it deserved. His failed to understand the responsibility McLaws's orders placed on him for the defense of Crampton's Gap. Holding his brigade at Brownsville to act as a reserve to reinforce either Brownsville Pass or Crampton's Gap might have been excusable, had Cobb acted vigorously and immediately established communications with Munford and Parham to learn the situation at both locations. But he remained in Brownsville for an hour, in complete ignorance of what was happening at Crampton's Gap. Had Cobb's brigade reached the gap even a half hour earlier than it did, Crampton's Gap would probably still have fallen, but a rout might have been avoided. Munford thought so, and he felt strongly enough about it to mention it in his after-action report: "Had Genl Cobb come up in time, the result might have been different."[84]

But the damage was done, a way out of the Confederates' crisis now rested on the shoulders of Lafayette McLaws. A dispatch from Semmes requesting reinforcements, received around 5 p.m., was the Georgian's first warning of trouble in his rear. McLaws immediately sent two staff officers galloping off to repeat his orders to Cobb to hold Crampton's Gap to the last man. When another note arrived, also probably from Semmes, with a "pressing demand for help," McLaws ordered Stuart to send Hampton's brigade back to Crampton's Gap. Soon after, McLaws set out to investigate the situation in person, accompanied by Stuart. They paused along the way at General Richard H. Anderson's headquarters, where they were offered some tea. McLaws's assistant adjutant general, Major T. S. McIntosh, soon arrived there with shocking news: the enemy had broken through at Crampton's Gap. McLaws ordered Anderson to have Colonel Alfred Cumming's brigade march at once for the gap; then he and Stuart galloped north to assess the damage.[85]

As McLaws and Stuart neared Brownsville, they began to encounter stragglers from the battle. Soon after dark they came upon a badly shaken Cobb. According to Stuart's aide, Heros von Borcke, Cobb rode toward them, exclaiming "Dismount, Gentlemen, dismount, if your lives are dear to you," and warning that the Federals were only some 200 yards away and approaching in overwhelming force. Ignoring Cobb's warnings, Stuart rode forward and found that Semmes had posted two of his regiments across the Brownsville Road. Using this force as a rallying point, Stuart set about collecting the fugitives from Parham's and Cobb's brigades with what his aide-de-camp, Lieutenant R. Channing Price, described as "unequalled coolness." Price found Cobb "so violently excited as to add to the confusion prevailing." Stuart managed to restore some order, and he bolstered Semmes's line with a battery that he "had accidentally met with" on the gallop up. This may have been Captain Manly's guns or Captain Macon's Richmond Artillery, recently withdrawn from Brownsville Pass. The tension relaxed slightly when no Union troops came charging out of the darkness. Stuart ordered out scouting parties, who returned to report that there were no enemy troops within 1 mile.[86]

Although the Federals had halted their pursuit, McLaws recognized that his situation was dire. His first concern was to communicate news of the disaster to Lee. He sent Lieutenant Thomas S. B. Tucker, an aide-de-camp on his staff, with a courier and a guide to find their way to army headquarters and report on the situation in Pleasant Valley. The party rode smack into a 6th Corps picket post that opened fire, killing the courier and turning Tucker and the guide back. By the time Tucker returned to report his failure, McLaws had discovered that Stuart had also sent a courier to report to Lee and planned to continue sending additional couriers at intervals to ensure that someone got through. McLaws probably also learned that Munford had alertly withdrawn his small cavalry brigade to Rohrersville, and McLaws could trust that Munford would certainly communicate with Lee. Satisfied now that Lee would learn of the loss of Crampton's Gap, McLaws turned to the immediate problem of defending his rear against the 6th Corps.[87]

476 | *To Antietam Creek*

The Georgian gave no thought to retreat. If the Harpers Ferry garrison found out that a relief force was nearby, it might prolong their resistance, with grim consequences for McLaws. It was therefore imperative that the 6th Corps be confronted as far from Harpers Ferry as possible. The fate of Lee's entire campaign in Maryland had suddenly fallen into McLaws's lap. He met the crisis with determined resolution. Thomas Munford, who believed that McLaws never received due credit for his pivotal role in the Maryland Campaign, wrote: "I am constrained to say that I believe had Pleasant Valley been under a less determined officer—had Gen. McLaws <u>flickered</u>, one moment in his trying position, the ruin of the whole army of northern Virginia was inevitable." Munford exaggerated; ruin for the entire army was not inevitable if McLaws "flickered." But if Franklin made his presence known to Miles on the 15th—before Jackson could force a surrender—there would very likely be no surrender at Harpers Ferry. McLaws would be left to conduct a difficult withdrawal, fighting against superior numbers down Pleasant Valley, through Weverton Pass, to Point of Rocks. At the least, the Maryland Campaign would end in humiliating failure; at the worst, it would mean disaster for McLaws's command.[88]

McLaws decided to make his stand against Franklin at the point where Semmes's two regiments had stood fast on the Brownsville Road and where Cobb's and Parham's brigades were rallied, about 1.5 miles south of Crampton's Gap and 3 air miles from Harpers Ferry. Besides being as far from Harpers Ferry as circumstances would permit, this position enjoyed the flank protection of South Mountain to the east and Elk Ridge to the west, forcing the Federals to confront him head on. The forces immediately on hand—or soon coming up— to man this line were Semmes's and Cumming's (Wilcox's) relatively fresh brigades, Parham's and Cobb's shattered brigades, and five batteries of artillery. Cobb mustered only 300 effectives in his four regiments, and Parham had less than that, although the 41st Virginia rejoined the brigade from Solomon's Gap during the night. McLaws also had good reason to question the combat effectiveness of these battered units. Semmes's had perhaps 750–800 effectives, and Cummings's was about 1,000. There were also six other brigades available to McLaws: Wright's and Pryor's at Weverton Pass, Armistead's and Featherston's at Sandy Hook, and Kershaw's and Barksdale's on Maryland Heights. But McLaws dared not withdraw the garrison at Weverton Pass. If things went badly, this pass afforded his only route of escape, and it was not impossible that the Federals might attack that point on the 15th. It was equally important to guard the road from Harpers Ferry to Sandy Hook, to prevent a potential breakout attempt by the Union garrison during the night. That left Kershaw's and Barksdale's men. McLaws ordered both brigades to march at once to Brownsville, leaving behind only a single regiment and a section of Read's battery to garrison the Heights and watch the Harpers Ferry–Sharpsburg Road along the western side of the mountain. McLaws gambled that the Union garrison would not risk a dash to safety along this difficult route, or be so bold as to attempt to recapture Maryland Heights. Colonel Kennon McElroy's 13th Mississippi drew the assignment of remaining behind. He sent word to McLaws "that he would guarantee possession of the heights until assistance was rendered." Kershaw and Barksdale added 1,750 officers and men, along with a section of howitzers from Read's battery and a rifled section from Carleton's battery. This raised McLaws's force to slightly over 4,000 infantry, one brigade of cavalry, and approximately 29 guns to oppose three divisions of the 6th Corps. At this moment McLaws might have quietly been thanking General Longstreet for convincing Lee to reinforce him with R. H. Anderson's division.[89]

Feeding his men posed an additional burden for McLaws. Rations had run out on September 13, and his chief of commissary had been unable to procure even one day's sustenance for the men in the limited area where his foraging parties could safely range. Many men had also worn out their shoes and were barefoot. But McLaws could solve neither dilemma until he could see his way out of his present crisis. His men would have to face Franklin on empty stomachs and, in some cases, bruised and unshod feet.[90]

Late in the night McLaws received Lee's dispatch of 8 p.m., stating that "the day has gone against us" and ordering McLaws to abandon his position and withdraw across the Potomac River. McLaws ignored the order. He later wrote:

> I determined to remain where I was, trusting to General Lee to maneuver
> General McClellan away from his position North of, and but a short distance
> away from Franklin, and leave me with no force in opposition from above but
> Franklin's command. I argued that General Lee did not know the real condi-
> tion of affairs in the valley where I was, and as it was doubtful if an officer sent
> by me to inform him would reach him, I merely wrote, and sent by carrier, that
> my position was a strong one, and I would take the risk of remaining where I
> was, and relied upon him to get me out of the difficulty I was in."

McLaws's decision took steady nerves, for he did not know how bad Lee's situation was. Nonetheless, McLaws reasoned that obedience to Lee's order would only place the Army of Northern Virginia in greater jeopardy. Events the next day would prove the soundness of McLaws's judgment.[91]

A solemn group gathered at 3 a.m. at McLaws's headquarters near Brownsville to receive instructions for the approaching day. Among them were Generals Wright and Pryor, up from Weverton Pass, and General Semmes. Captain H. L. P. King of McLaws's staff was there as well. In his diary, King entered the thoughts that most likely every man in the room felt: "Tomorrow will doubtless bring a heavy & perhaps decisive battle. A very anxious predicament. Troops ordered up . . . anxious feeling in all our bosoms. All feel that tomorrow will be a bloody day."[92]

15

Retreat from South Mountain

"God has seldom given an army a greater victory than this"

With the blanket of a moonless night to cover their movements, the exhausted soldiers of D. H. Hill's and Longstreet's commands made their way down from South Mountain into Boonsboro. All night the weary procession passed by, keeping the Unionist villagers awake with the sounds of marching feet, the rumbling of wheeled vehicles, the hoofbeats of horsemen riding swiftly on some errand, and the shouts of officers and men hunting up their regiments. More unsettling to the locals were the wounded. As John Dooley, with Kemper's brigade, recalled, "hundreds of our wounded are gathered in this little village, crowding the porches and steps of the houses and begging admittance." According to Dooley, the citizens turned them away. "They are opposed to us all along this valley, and are or pretend to be fearful of punishment from the Yankees if they befriend us in any way," he complained. The infantry and artillery turned west on the Sharpsburg Pike. Guards and patrols posted at intervals along the road tried to keep the columns moving and prevent straggling. But this effort was largely a futile exercise, as the infantry, particularly Longstreet's, were dog tired. "The men who straggled did so from inability to keep up with their comrades," wrote a member of Jenkins's brigade. "The subsistence of the army had been for the last forty-eight hours green apples and green corn. Dysentery and diarrhea prevailed in the ranks to an alarming degree." Whatever the cause, whether it was illness or exhaustion, Sergeant John Tucker of Rodes's 5th Alabama proclaimed: "Never saw so much straggling in all my life."[1]

To the frightened citizens in the village, the Confederate retreat appeared chaotic. But considering the circumstances—a pitch-black night and men broken down with exhaustion—it went quite well, although there was confusion. John Purifoy of Bondurant's battery stated that his unit and the guns of Cutts's battalions went into park during the night near the army ordnance trains and the trains of D. H. Hill's division, which were located just west of Boonsboro. The batteries filled their ammunition chests and then, "with a couch on nature's green earth," the men lay down to sleep. So acute was their exhaustion that they did not hear the wagons of the ordnance train and Hill's division depart during the night. Purifoy wrote that "all the noise and confusion of such a movement failed to disturb him and he does not remember to have been so oblivious of the passage of time as he was that night." The officers, who were equally dead to the world, arose at sunrise and discovered themselves alone and without orders; in the confusion, D. H. Hill's headquarters had overlooked giving them instructions. "I at once started moving on the Williamsport Road, with the view of making that point and crossing," wrote Lieutenant Colonel Cutts. But while his gun teams made ready to march, Cutts and Captain Bondurant galloped into Boonsboro "to see what danger my rear was in to the enemy." Along the way Cutts encountered Captain W. P. Lloyd's North Carolina battery near the road, "men asleep, horses unharnessed, &c." Cutts woke the men and ordered its captain to limber immediately and join Cutts's command on the Williamsport Turnpike. Then he and Bondurant rode into Boonsboro, where they found Fitz Lee, who ordered them to march to Sharpsburg "by the best practicable route and in as short a time as possible." Armed with the knowledge that, for the moment, their rear was covered, Bondurant and Cutts rode back and rejoined their column, now consisting of five batteries of 28 guns. They moved off on what John Purifoy described as "an exciting and rapid march" to overtake the army. Cutts understood that until they were behind the lines of friendly infantry, they were not safe. Indeed they were not, but the danger they soon encountered came from an unexpected direction.[2]

While fatigue and confusion may have played its part in D. H. Hill's headquarters leaving Bondurant's battery and Cutts's battalion behind, Roswell Ripley's inefficiency nearly deprived his brigade of two regiments. During the withdrawal from the mountain the 3rd North Carolina became separated from the rest of the brigade. Colonel De Rosset halted his regiment in a field by the side of the National Road, between Boonsboro and South Mountain, and let his men lay down to sleep. Ripley made no known effort to locate De Rosset's missing regiment, and Ripley also failed to send orders to Colonel George Doles, whose 4th Georgia had been detached from the brigade to garrison Orr's Gap. When De Rosset woke in the morning he realized that his regiment had been forgotten. De Rosset had the presence of mind to deduce that if Ripley had forgotten his regiment, the general probably had not remembered about Doles's, either, so De Rosset sent a courier galloping to recall the Georgians. De Rosset guessed right. Doles had had no orders from Ripley and did not know the army was in retreat. According to a member of Doles's regiment, "we left hurriedly, but none too soon." By the time they reached Boonsboro, the entire army had passed on and Union troops were approaching. Wrote the same soldier: "Had our notice been ten minutes later we would have been certainly cut off and captured in a body."[3]

De Rosset meanwhile encountered Hood, whose division formed the rear guard, and that officer ordered the North Carolinians to move on and overtake the army. When they finally caught up with Ripley, Captain Stephen D. Thruston of the 3rd stated: "I well remember his [Ripley's] exclamation: 'By God! I thought you were captured.'"[4] While there is little excuse for Ripley's incompetence, he probably suffered the effects of extreme fatigue, which some men can stand better than others. Colonel Edward P. Alexander recalled his own difficulties in leading the ordnance train to Williamsport. "I shall always remember that night march for my first experience in really suffering from sleepiness. I would doze on my horse until I would suddenly almost fall from the saddle, & the only relief would be to get down & walk & almost go to sleep walking." For Alexander, there were only two other nights during the entire war when he felt a similar fatigue: at Chancellorsville, and on the retreat to Appomattox. James Simons, in Garden's battery of Hood's division, described a parallel experience that night. "I frequently fell asleep on my horse and would awake by finding myself nearly falling off," he recalled. And neither Alexander nor Simons had endured the same level of activity that the infantry had.[5]

Soon after sending his 11:15 p.m. dispatch to McLaws, informing the Georgian that Longstreet and D. H. Hill would halt at Keedysville to cover his withdrawal from Pleasant Valley, General Lee climbed into an ambulance (he still could not easily manage a horse because of his injured hand) and joined the retreat. His staff rode ahead to guide the vehicle through the columns of infantry, ambulances, guns, and wagons that crowded the roadway. Around 5 a.m., about an hour before sunrise, the headquarters group reached Keedysville. It had taken nearly six hours to cover 5 miles. Lee still had received no word from McLaws, so when his party halted he dictated a fresh dispatch for him to Colonel A. L. Long.

> General: General Lee desires me to say that he sent several dispatches to you last night; he is in doubt that they have been received. We have fallen back to this place to enable you more readily to join us. You are desired to withdraw immediately from your position on Maryland Heights, and join us here. If you can't get off any other way, you must cross the mountain. The utmost dispatch is required. Should you be able to cross over to Harper's Ferry, do so and report immediately.[6]

Soon after the courier left with this dispatch, a disappointing message arrived from Colonel Munford. The cavalryman had investigated the route over Elk Ridge and reported that it would be a difficult passage for McLaws to make over the mountain. With this hopeful possibility eliminated, Lee consulted his map and reexamined the strategic situation. He had selected the position at Keedysville to cover both possible routes McLaws might use to join him: either via Elk Ridge or by the Harpers Ferry–Sharpsburg Road, which passed up the western side of Maryland Heights and crossed Antietam Creek about 2 miles southeast of Sharpsburg. With the Elk Ridge route no longer an option, Lee could retire behind Antietam Creek, at Sharpsburg. This still guarded the Harpers Ferry–Sharpsburg Road, and it was a superior defensive position to the one at Keedysville. Lee sent word back to Munford to remain at Rohrersville until morning and then rejoin the main body of the army. Lee also sent new orders to Longstreet and D. H. Hill to continue their march to Sharpsburg. This was not a reversal of Lee's decision to withdraw from Maryland. That option remained on the table and might well need to be used, but Lee had shaken off his moment of doubt, which was when he sent word to McLaws that Longstreet and Hill would retire to Virginia. Lee intended the halt behind Antietam Creek primarily to cover McLaws's withdrawal, but a slender hope still flickered that the Maryland Campaign might yet be retrieved. This depended on circumstances and individuals beyond his immediate control. Could McLaws escape from the trap in Pleasant Valley? Would Jackson complete the capture of Harpers Ferry before he marched to Shepherdstown? Would McClellan advance cautiously or aggressively from South Mountain? September 15 would tell the tale.[7]

Parts of the army were already at Sharpsburg by the time Lee made his decision. Rodes's and Colquitt's brigades, leading the march of D. H. Hill's division from South Mountain, reached Keedysville around 2 or 2:30 a.m. They halted there, posted pickets, and allowed the men to get some sleep. But an hour later Rodes received orders (whether from Hill or army headquarters is unknown) to march both brigades at once to Sharpsburg and drive out a Union cavalry force reported there. Enemy strength, where they came from, and what their purpose was were all unknown, but they represented a threat to the safety of Boteler's Ford, vital to Lee as his passage over the Potomac to Virginia, and to the army trains who were guarded by small escorts or, in some cases, had no escort at all. Rodes assembled both brigades and set out, but he was shortly overtaken by orders from Colonel Chilton that he should only send part of his force to Sharpsburg. Rodes selected the 5th and the 6th Alabama, but within a few minutes Chilton's orders were superseded by instructions from Longstreet, saying that Rodes should move on to Sharpsburg with both brigades.[8]

The two brigades reached Sharpsburg around sunrise. They found that the village was quiet, with no sign of the enemy cavalry. Pushing on rapidly through town, they may have turned south on the Harpers Ferry Road, because Rodes halted his brigade southwest of the village, probably where they could establish a blocking position astride this road. Colquitt continued on along Miller's Sawmill Road to the River Road, which led to Boteler's Ford on the Potomac River. He followed this to the W. M. Blackford farm, about 1 mile east of the ford, where his brigade bivouacked.[9]

Toombs's brigade reached Sharpsburg about an hour or an hour and a half after Rodes and Colquitt. At 10 p.m. the night before, the Georgian received orders at Hagerstown from his division commander, D. R. Jones, to march his brigade to Sharpsburg and detail the 11th Georgia of G. T. Anderson's brigade (which had remained behind at Hagerstown) to escort the trains directed to cross the Potomac River at Williamsport. Toombs marched at midnight and completed the 12-mile tramp in about 7 hours. Soon after their arrival orders caught up with Toombs from D. R. Jones, instructing Toombs to send two of his regiments to Williamsport immediately to protect the wagon trains crossing there. Toombs selected the 15th and the 17th Georgia, placing them under the command of Colonel W. T. Millican, the 15th's commander. With his men most likely cursing their bad luck, Millican led the two regiments on a hard 13-mile march to Williamsport, where he found that the trains had already passed over the Potomac. He pushed on after them, fording the river and eventually over-taking the wagons, but not before the two regiments had covered some 31 miles for the day. Commented Ivy W. Dugan of the 15th Georgia, "I leave the reader to guess whether we were tired."[10]

While D. H. Hill's division and Longstreet's command made their way toward Antietam Creek and Sharpsburg, Lee remained near Keedysville, hoping for news from McLaws. His ambulance stopped in a meadow beside the Boonsboro–Sharpsburg Pike, near the Samuel Pry farm, soon to serve as Mc-Clellan's headquarters. A local farm wife, learning that it was the famous General Lee who occupied the ambulance, sent him a hot pot of coffee. It was now shortly after 8 a.m. While Lee sipped the invigorating beverage, a courier gal-loped up with a dispatch from Stonewall Jackson addressed to Colonel Chil-ton. We can only imagine the excitement that coursed through Lee as he read its contents.

> Near Halltown
> September 14, 1862—8:15 p.m.
>
> Colonel: Through God's blessing, the advance, which commenced this evening, has been successful thus far, and I look to Him for complete success to-morrow. The advance has been directed to be resumed at dawn to-morrow morning. I am thankful that our loss has been small. Your dispatch respecting the movements of the enemy and the importance of concentration has been received. Can you not connect the headquarters of the army, by signal, with General McLaws?
>
> Respectfully,
> T. J. Jackson,
> Major General[11]

Why it had taken 12 hours for this dispatch to travel approximately 18 miles has never been explained. But it lifted Lee's spirits and infused new hope that the Maryland Campaign might still be salvaged. Jackson would surely ignore the orders to break off the siege and march to Shepherdstown with victory for him so close. If Harpers Ferry fell on the 15th, as Jackson anticipated, and Longstreet and D. H. Hill could delay McClellan, it might be possible to concentrate the army at Sharpsburg by the 16th. The odds remained long, but not impossible. Lee knew it would take McClellan all day on the 15th to move his army through the South Mountain passes, concentrate it for battle, and reconnoiter the Confederate position. The earliest McClellan could mount a major attack would be on the morning of September 16. Lee needed more time than that, but if Longstreet and Hill maintained a bold front, it might play to McClellan's innate caution and buy the necessary respite. But the risk in this reasoning was that McClellan had *not* behaved predictably on the 14th. And there were other variables over which Lee had no control. What if Jackson was delayed, or McLaws met with disaster in Pleasant Valley? But it is clear that Lee concluded he had a day to work with. The uncertainty of the situation would clear by sunset on the 15th, and he would know whether his Maryland Campaign could continue or would end in a retreat to Virginia.

While Lee calculated the risks, Garland's, Ripley's, and G. B. Anderson's brigades of D. H. Hill's division—accompanied by two of Hill's divisional batteries—passed through Keedysville and on toward Sharpsburg. They were followed by those trains that had not been sent to Virginia by way of Williamsport: the quartermaster, commissary, ordnance, and ambulance trains. Colonel Stephen D. Lee's fine battalion of reserve artillery marched with the trains, although he had cut cross-country and by farm roads from Beaver Creek to reach the Boonsboro–Sharpsburg Pike at a spot about midway between Boonsboro and Keedysville. General Lee waited for much of this long column to pass by before climbing into his ambulance and riding across Antietam Creek to the Lutheran church on the eastern edge of Sharpsburg, where he dismounted to survey the locale he had selected on which to make a stand. The church sat on the western slope of a commanding hill rising 185 feet above Antietam Creek, affording a panoramic view of nearly all the ground that would be the Antietam battlefield. The church had established a small cemetery that climbed partway up the hill and gave it its local name of Cemetery Hill. This was the southern projection of an irregular ridge that continued north of the Boonsboro–Sharpsburg Pike for nearly 700 yards and became known as Cemetery Ridge. Except for a thin belt of woods that screened Antietam Creek, the undulating landscape that spread out before Lee to the northeast, east, and southeast was clear and either under cultivation or in meadows. A mile to the north some woodlots were visible, and from Cemetery Hill the ground there appeared relatively level, although this was not the case. Good fields of fire for artillery were plentiful, as was cover to conceal troops in the natural troughs of the landscape.[12]

Lee's strategy for September 15 was simple. He would arrange his forces to command the two most accessible and direct approaches to Sharpsburg: the Middle Bridge over Antietam Creek (where the Boonsboro–Sharpsburg Pike cut across the creek); and the Rohrbach Bridge (also known as the Lower Bridge and, later, Burnside's Bridge), located about 1 mile downstream, which was crossed by the Rohrbach Bridge Road. McLaws might need this bridge to cross the Antietam if he came up along the Harpers Ferry–Sharpsburg Road, and it was the most likely point where Munford would cross from Rohrersville. There were four other crossing points that Lee chose not to contest directly, because he lacked sufficient forces to do anything more than observe them. Two were bridges, and two were fords. Of the former, the first and most important is called the Upper Bridge. It crosses the creek approximately 3 miles north of the Middle Bridge, but only about 1 mile west of Keedysville, which made it a probable avenue of approach for McClellan to use. The other bridge—the one least likely to be used by the enemy—spanned the creek at its mouth, near the Potomac River, about 2 miles south of the Rohrbach Bridge. The Harpers Ferry–Sharpsburg Road forked about a mile and a half below this bridge. The left fork crossed this lower bridge on its way to Sharpsburg, while the right fork continued north to Porterstown. The two fords were called Pry's Ford and Snavely's Ford. Pry's Ford crossed the creek a half mile below the Upper Bridge, and Snavely's Ford was situated about midway between the Rohrbach Bridge and the one at the mouth of Antietam Creek.

Lee left the tactical deployment of the infantry and artillery to Longstreet, who joined him on Cemetery Hill around 9:30 a.m. The Georgian posted D. H. Hill's three brigades along an extended front north of the Boonsboro–Sharpsburg Pike. G. B. Anderson's North Carolinians formed the right of the line, resting on the Boonsboro–Sharpsburg Pike. Ripley deployed in Anderson's rear, and Garland's battered brigade, commanded by Colonel Duncan McRae, took position nearly a half mile north of Anderson in an old sunken farm lane, facing northeast, with his left flank resting on a farm lane leading to the William Roulette farm. To fill in this wide gap, Rodes was recalled from his position southwest of town sometime that morning and placed on McRae's right, as well as at right angles to the North Carolinians, so that his brigade faced east. Colonel S. D. Lee unlimbered five of his six batteries along the crest of Cemetery Ridge, where they covered the approaches to the Middle Bridge. Of D. H. Hill's divisional artillery, only Carter's battery was placed on line, positioning its guns between Rodes's and Garland's brigades, and in Garland's front. Part of the battery pointed east, toward the creek, and part faced north. Jones's and Hardaway's batteries parked in reserve in the low ground near the Henry Piper farm.[13]

The head of D. R. Jones's division began to cross Antietam Creek around 10 a.m. These brigades were dead on their feet with fatigue. A member of Jenkins's brigade wrote that during their night march, "we were constantly stopping and then moving a few paces—that kind of marching is a great deal more tiresome than constant marching." David Johnston of the 7th Virginia, in Kemper's brigade, recalled that "having been on our feet all night, without sleep or food, save green corn or apples, placed us in no cheerful mood, but in good fighting temper." However, Johnston added that "numbers of men straggled off along the march, and even after the Antietam was crossed, in search of food." Alexander Hunter, a private in Kemper's brigade, stated that as there was no rations on hand, "squads from different companies obtained permission to forage for themselves and comrades," an open breach of Lee's strict rules against foraging. But Lee's instructions that Longstreet's ordnance and supply trains were to cross the Potomac River at Williamsport had created this desperate situation. Until they rejoined their respective commands, the men either had to forage or starve. Lee let them forage.[14]

As these troops arrived, Longstreet placed D. R. Jones's brigades south of the Boonsboro Pike, along the eastern and southeastern slope of Cemetery Hill. Kemper's, Jenkins's, and Drayton's slim brigades—literally no more than medium-sized regiments—formed the first line, between the Boonsboro Pike and the Rohrbach Bridge Road, and Garnett formed in their rear as a support. The only battery accompanying Jones's division in Maryland, Captain James S. Brown's Wise (Virginia) Artillery, unlimbered on the ridge running south and west of the Rohrbach Bridge Road, on the far right of Jones's line. Toombs and his reduced brigade of two regiments, the 2nd and the 20th Georgia—a combined force of less than 400 officers and men—drew the defense of the Rohrbach Bridge. Toombs's orders were to "occupy the most eligible position I could find on the Antietam River" near the bridge, "in order to prevent the enemy from crossing the river." Colonel Henry L. Benning of the 17th Georgia had tactical direction of the brigade, because Toombs believed that he still commanded a three-brigade division composed of his own brigade, Drayton's, and G. T. Anderson's. Benning strung his two regiments out in concealed positions along the tree-studded, steep western bank of the creek. The left of the line rested some 40–50 yards above the bridge. From here it ran south along the creek bank for nearly 200 yards, so that the Georgians' rifles could completely command the approach to the bridge along the Rohrbach Bridge Road. Benning's thin line of riflemen were supported by Captain John L. Eubank's Virginia Battery of S. D. Lee's battalion, who were equipped with two rifled guns, a howitzer, and an obsolete 6 lb. gun. Eubanks unlimbered 500 yards southwest of the bridge, on a hill that gave them a field of fire of part of the Rohrbach Bridge Road and also covered the rising ground east of the bridge.[15]

Around 11 a.m. Colonel John H. Walton's battalion of Washington Artillery, which had helped cover the Confederate army's withdrawal from South Mountain, rolled across the Middle Bridge. Walton added 16 guns in four batteries, which the Washington Artillery called companies. Longstreet posted them as they came up, placing Captain Charles W. Squires's 1st Company and Captain M. B. Miller's 3rd Company in a stubble field on the summit of Cemetery Hill, immediately south of the Boonsboro–Sharpsburg Pike (where the National Cemetery is located today), where their guns could sweep the approaches from the Middle Bridge along the Boonsboro Pike. Captain John B. Richardson's 2nd Company and Captain Benjamin F. Eshleman's 4th Company were sent across the Rohrbach Bridge Road and unlimbered in the Avey orchard, near Brown's Wise (Virginia) battery, where they covered the approaches along this road.[16]

Behind Walton's battalion came the army's rear guard: Hood's division, G. T. Anderson's brigade, and Evans's brigade. Their march was not molested, although after passing through Keedysville Hood formed a line of battle on high ground about a mile west of the town and held this position "about a half hour," perhaps to cover the crossing of Walton's battalion and some trains. After this pause the brigades filed back onto the Sharpsburg Pike and crossed the Middle Bridge around noon. Feeling no pressure of pursuit, Hood allowed the 4th Alabama, and perhaps some other regiments, to plunge into the creek for a bath and to give their filthy clothes a "partial washing." As the brigades came up, Longstreet placed Evans's on the north side of the Boonsboro–Sharpsburg Pike, on Cemetery Ridge. G. T. Anderson was directed to form in the rear of Squires's and Miller's batteries on Cemetery Hill, and Hood moved his two brigades into position on D. R. Jones's right, where they could support Richardson's, Eshleman's, and Brown's batteries. Longstreet had Colonel Walton post the guns of Hood's artillery battalion. Walton put two batteries on Cemetery Hill, on the right of Miller's battery. Captain William K. Bachman's German (South Carolina) Artillery unlimbered closest to Miller, with its guns pointed toward the Middle Bridge, while Captain James Reilly's Rowan (North Carolina) Artillery went in on Bachman's right, the muzzles of its guns aiming at the Rohrbach Bridge. Walton held Captain Hugh R. Garden's Palmetto (South Carolina) Artillery in reserve near the Avey farm, in the event the guns would be needed to repel an advance over the bridge at the mouth of the Antietam. The Macbeth (South Carolina) Artillery under Captain Robert Boyce, which was attached to Evans's brigade, also went into a reserve position on the reverse slope of Cemetery Hill, along the eastern edge of Sharpsburg.[17]

By the time the last infantry and artillery took their place along the ridges east of Sharpsburg, Lee had approximately 10,930 infantrymen and 63 guns—23 of them rifled—skillfully placed to dispute passage of the Middle or Rohrbach bridges. Longstreet deliberately posted most of the infantry in exposed positions where the Federals would see them as they came up, in the hope that a bold front might conceal the Confederates' weakness and buy some extra time.[18]

While the main body of Longstreet's and D. H. Hill's commands took up their positions outside of Sharpsburg, Lieutenant Colonel Cutts's reinforced battalion of artillery drove north from Boonsboro on the road to Williamsport, where Cutts hoped to cross the Potomac. A march of nearly 6 miles brought them near Jones' Crossroads, the intersection of the Hagerstown Turnpike and the Williamsport Pike. Here Cutts received warning of a large Union cavalry force in his front. They were actually long gone, however, having waylaid Longstreet's ordnance train shortly before dawn and made off with it to Greencastle, Pennsylvania. But Cutts knew nothing of this, and without infantry supports he dared not proceed farther, for his guns were easy prey for cavalry. He ordered his column to turn around and countermarch back toward Boonsboro. About a mile west of the village he turned off on a "settlement road which ran parallel with the Boonsboro and Sharpsburg Turnpike." Speed was not an option, for the battalion's horses were in poor condition. A detachment of Union cavalry soon hove into view, no doubt a scouting element from Farnsworth's brigade, and started in pursuit. Cutts ordered a Napoleon unlimbered and fired several shots at his pursuers, which checked them. The crew limbered the gun, drove it to the next advantageous point, unlimbered, and fired a round or two more before repeating the process once again. The game of cat-and-mouse continued until the Union troopers realized that Cutts had no supports; using their mobility the Federals swung around and drove forward to hit the Confederates' left flank. But Dame Fortune smiled on Cutts that morning, for at this critical moment a regiment of Fitz Lee's brigade appeared and drove off the bluecoats. Thomas A. Graham of Ross's Battery, recalling the event, thought that the Federals behaved too cautiously in the interval before Fitz Lee's regiment came up. "The fault was theirs [Union cavalry]," he wrote, "that the entire column of five batteries were not captured."[19]

Cutts led his battalion over the Upper Bridge to the Hagerstown Pike, where they turned south and reached Confederate lines. No one noted the time, but it was probably around 2 p.m. Lee offered his personal thanks to Cutts for preserving the 26 precious pieces of artillery under his command. Their loss would have been a hard blow to the Army of Northern Virginia, coming on the heels of the reverse at South Mountain. Cutts and his men were granted a brief respite as their reward. Lee ordered the colonel to march through Sharpsburg to the army trains' park, where Cutts's crews could replenish ammunition and refresh themselves for a return to the front. Perhaps because they were engaged longer on September 14 than Cutts's batteries, the men of Bondurant's battery were given a longer reprieve and allowed to go into park at the Stephen Grove farm for rest and refit.[20]

Around noon a courier galloped up to Lee on Cemetery Hill with a dispatch from Jackson, written at 8 a.m. that morning, announcing the surrender of the Harpers Ferry garrison and asking where Jackson's troops should be sent next. Lee's heart must have leapt, not only for the welcome news it carried, but also for Jackson's soldierly spirit—aggressive and full of fight, and ready to march wherever Lee wished. Lee ordered the news to be carried to the troops. Yet despite Jackson's victory, it still remained probable that Longstreet and D. H. Hill would need to retreat to Virginia via Boteler's Ford. In this event, Lee would need Jackson on the south side of the Potomac River, at Shepherdstown, to cover the withdrawal, and it was to this point that Lee directed him to march. Again, Lee had not abandoned the Maryland Campaign; this was merely an operationally prudent measure. McClellan and his army were the ones who would determine the course of events. If McClellan hesitated, then Jackson could be brought back over the river and Lee could effect a concentration at Sharpsburg. If McClellan pushed hard, then the Maryland Campaign would end in retreat to Virginia. Colonel Walter Taylor wrote after the war that Lee "would be guided by circumstances; he would accept battle on the north side [of the Potomac] if he could reunite his army in time, and, failing in that he would re-cross into Virginia."[21]

It would soon be evident how McClellan might behave. James Simons of Bachman's South Carolina battery thought that they had not been in position on Cemetery Hill for an hour "before heavy clouds of dust heralded the approach of the enemy." Lee knew of their approach well before this. Colonel Thomas Rosser's 5th Virginia Cavalry, with two guns of Pelham's horse artillery, covered the withdrawal of forces from Fox's Gap and moved through Boonsboro just as Fitz Lee's brigade arrived by way of the National Road. Rosser turned off on the Sharpsburg Pike, pushing numerous stragglers before him, but he did not hurry, for he wished to observe the movements of the enemy. Federal infantry made their appearance around midmorning. Rosser managed his small command well, forcing the Federals to deploy skirmishers to move him from several different positions. Throughout the morning he also kept General Lee apprised of the enemy pursuit with regular written reports. Rosser crossed the Antietam around noon, leaving a handful of skirmishers east of the stream. Since Rosser represented the only cavalry then on hand, he split his regiment, sending part of it south of the Rohrbach Bridge to picket the fords below it and the bridge at the mouth of Antietam Creek. The rest moved north, out the Hagerstown Pike, beyond the Dunker church, and down, in the direction of the Upper Bridge and Pry's Ford.[22]

An hour or two after Rosser crossed the Antietam, Colonel Thomas Munford's small brigade came clattering up from Porterstown and came over the creek at Rohrbach Bridge. Per his instructions, Munford had remained in Rohrersville until daylight, when elements of Couch's division approached; Munford then withdrew his command over Elk Ridge. Munford recalled that he found Lee with Longstreet "at a stone church or schoolhouse in or near the north of the town of Sharpsburg—on the main street." Longstreet expressed concern about his right flank, as Rosser's detachment could not possibly adequately guard the fords below the Rohrbach Bridge as well as the lower bridge at the Antietam's mouth. It was agreed to have Munford's two regiments assume this latter duty, picketing his men from Toombs's right to the mouth of the Antietam, slightly over 3 miles by the winding course of the creek. The situation was brightening for Lee, but uncertainty remained and danger still threatened. He could take some solace in the fact that Munford had extricated himself from Pleasant Valley, and Longstreet and D. H. Hill had executed their withdrawal from South Mountain with minimal loss. But Fitz Lee had not yet rejoined the main body, part of Longstreet's ordnance train had been captured by a Union cavalry force said to have escaped from Harpers Ferry, McLaws's fate remained unknown, and the might of McClellan's army were approaching along the Sharpsburg Pike. Around 2 p.m., while Lee was busy studying his maps of the region, he received a report that the advance of the Federal army was approaching. For Lee and his Maryland Campaign, the next few hours would be critical.[23]

Sometime that afternoon, 17 miles south of Sharpsburg—at Harpers Ferry— Jackson received Lee's message ordering him to march to Shepherdstown. According to Henry K. Douglas, Jackson lost no time in responding "that he would march at once, cross the river & join Gen Lee at Sharpsburg." Douglas also recalled that Jackson took Lee's dispatch, turned it over, and endorsed it with a simple sentence: "I will join you at Sharpsburg."[24]

Nine miles east of Sharpsburg, Union soldiers on South Mountain woke that morning to a heavy fog that lay like a blanket over the mountain. Captain George Noyes of Abner Doubleday's staff had spent a fitful night. Sleep "was rather nominal than real," due to frequent interruptions, a growling stomach, and damp, chill night air that army overcoats and blankets were unable to keep out.

> Our little snatches of oblivion served mainly to pass away the hours of darkness, and with the first gray of morning we were up and moving among the men. The first inquiry was, "Where are the enemy?" General Ricketts' troops still held the fence, but in front of it there were no signs of the foe; all was still, and the little interval between us and the cornfield seemed untenanted save where, through the morning mists, we could dimly discern the prostrate forms of the rebel dead.[25]

Skirmishers of Hartsuff's brigade probed down toward the Mountain House and found no enemy soldiers, but confirmation that the Rebels were gone did not come until 7 a.m.[26] Joseph Hooker, the 1st Corps commander, wasted no time in organizing a pursuit. The night before, Major General Israel B. Richardson's 1st Division of the 2nd Corps had moved up to the Mount Tabor church and been placed under Hooker's orders. Expecting a "fight or a foot race" on the morning of the 15th, Hooker ordered Richardson to ascend the mountain at daybreak on the Dahlgren Road. No one recorded the time when Richardson reached the National Road at the Mountain House, but it was probably around 7 or 7:30 a.m. "We ascended through the mists," noted Lieutenant James B. Turner, a staff officer in General Meagher's Irish Brigade, which led the division's march. Turner and his comrades found that "evidences enough of the bitterness and bravery of the conflict appeared at ever step." When Richardson arrived at the Mountain House, Hooker dispatched him "with no other instructions" than to press on down the mountain in "vigorous pursuit." Richardson was "not to engage the enemy if he overtook him," but to await Hooker's arrival. Having sent Richardson haring after the Rebels, Hooker then ordered the scattered brigades of his corps to assemble on the mountain summit and prepare their breakfast. It looked to be a foot race, and his men would need nourishment for the effort. Hooker made his way to the Mountain House, where he found a gaggle of area residents all bursting to tell someone in a blue uniform what they knew about the Rebels. There were also many Confederate stragglers, "innumerable to mention," that his men were rounding up. These proved to be a source of some information about the enemy, and Hooker penciled a note to Seth Williams to report that Longstreet's command had reinforced D. H. Hill with 15 regiments, and that Longstreet later brought up 20 more. "They are in retreat now towards Boonsboro," wrote Hooker, and added his opinion that "you may be assured that they are making for the Potomac ford at Williamsport as rapidly as possible."[27]

Some minutes later, after hearing from Boonsboro's good people, Hooker jotted a message to McClellan. "Some citizens from Boonsboro are just in & report to me that the rebel army is in a perfect panic. They have already moved from that town in a perfect panic. They [?] this is perfectly reliable."[28] As more of Boonsboro's citizens made their way to Turner's Gap and spilled their version of what they had seen during the evening, it served to confirm the impression that the Confederates were in flight. Someone swore that during the night Robert E. Lee had publicly announced that his army "must admit that they have been shockingly whipped." This played well to Hooker, who immediately forwarded it verbatim to McClellan.[29]

Hooker's first reports were in McClellan's hands before 8 a.m. McClellan had also learned that morning of Franklin's smashing success at Crampton's Gap. Early reports pointed to a "glorious and complete victory." But McClellan's initial telegram to Halleck, sent at 8 a.m., made no excessive claims. He reported Franklin's success, noted that the troops had fought well, and stated that the Confederates had retreated from Turner's Gap during the night. "I do not know where he will next be found," McClellan wrote, but "our troops are now advancing in pursuit of them."[30]

Thirty minutes later, with Hooker's subsequent reports on hand, a jubilant McClellan sent another wire to Halleck, quoting Hooker almost word for word.

I have just learned from Genl Hooker in the advance, who states that the information is perfectly reliable, that the enemy is making for Shepherdstown in a perfect panic, & that Genl Lee last night stated publicly that he must admit that they had been shockingly whipped. I am hurrying everything forward to endeavor to press their retreat to the utmost.[31]

McClellan made no empty promise this time. His headquarters were busy crafting orders, setting the army in motion after Lee's retreating forces. At 8 a.m. Colonel George D. Ruggles, McClellan's efficient aide-de-camp, drew up orders for Burnside.

> The general commanding directs you to advance with your corps upon Boonsborough by the road which you followed yesterday [Old Sharpsburg Road], to the left of the main pike. Advance as far as the intersection of the Boonsborough and Rohrersville roads. Having arrived at that point, you will place yourself in communication with the troops who shall have advanced by the main pike, and also with General Franklin if he has reached Rohrersville, being prepared to lend such assistance as may be necessary in either direction, or if required to advance upon Centreville [Keedysville] and Sharpsburg to cut off the retreat of the enemy. Headquarters and the body of the army will advance by the main pike, General Hooker on the right of the main pike. Being separated from you for the present by force of circumstances, he will, during such separation, report direct to these headquarters.
>
> I am, general, &c.,
GEORGE D. RUGGLES
Colonel and Aide-de-Camp
>
> P.S.—Hooker's corps will probably remain for some hours at the Mountain House, Richardson's division moving on in advance. Endeavor to keep the head of your column as near parallel as possible to that of Richardson. Move promptly, keeping your skirmishers well out on your front and flanks till you arrive at open ground. Gibbon is ordered to join his own corps.[32]

This was an important order, reflecting aggressive energy at headquarters. The cautions that had characterized many of McClellan's communications to his generals throughout the campaign were entirely absent. Instead, Burnside was urged to "move promptly" and be prepared to "cut off the retreat of the enemy." When the order was written was also significant. McClellan wasted no time in putting his staff to work preparing orders to organize a pursuit, something he has received little credit for from his many of detractors.

But there was also a potentially troubling aspect to the order. This was the detachment of Hooker's 1st Corps from Burnside's command. Burnside spent the night of the 14th with McClellan, and the next morning they discussed Hooker's detachment. Neither McClellan or Burnside left a record of their meeting, but Jacob Cox, who by now was the acting 9th Corps commander, remembered that Burnside left it "disturbed and grieved at the course things had taken." So far as Cox could see, there was no good reason to detach the 1st Corps. Cox accurately observed that "it was perfectly easy to advance from South Mountain upon Sharpsburg, keeping Sumner's and Burnside's commands intact." The 9th Corps and the 1st Corps could advance along roughly parallel roads from South Mountain. Why break up the wing command structure at this critical juncture of the campaign?

Ezra Carman wrote that "it is claimed that the detachment of the First Corps was at Hooker's request; this may be true, it is altogether probable, for Hooker was prone to ask such things." Whoever influenced the decision, McClellan made it official by having Seth Williams issue a special order that "temporarily suspended" the order of September 14 formally assigning Burnside to command of the Right Wing. Carman found "no sufficient reason for such action" or "any military necessity for the separation." McClellan never offered a satisfactory explanation for his decision. Burnside's performance on the 14th certainly did not warrant it. Perhaps Fitz John Porter influenced McClellan's action. Porter knew that the private letters he had written to Burnside during the Second Manassas Campaign, which Burnside had forwarded on to the president, were being used as evidence in the court-martial case building against Porter. By Porter's lights, Burnside could not be trusted and his loyalty to McClellan was questionable. "That Porter should be unfriendly to Burnside was not strange," wrote Cox. That McClellan might allow personal feelings to influence army operations at a critical point in the campaign seems utterly fantastic, but this possibility must be considered, for from the morning of the 15th on, McClellan's once-warm relations with Burnside grew markedly cooler. One of the precepts of warfare is unity of command, but McClellan set about undoing it that morning. The seeds he had sown would bear their unfortunate fruit over the next two days.[33]

Chief of Staff Marcy and Aide-de-Camp Ruggles busily crafted and dispatched orders for the corps commanders throughout the early morning. Pleasonton was ordered to assemble his cavalry and mount an immediate pursuit. This resulted in some minor confusion, for Pleasonton apparently did not know that Richardson's division had already started the pursuit. As Pleasonton's cavalry passed over the mountain summit they spotted a line of men to the west, whom they took to be the enemy. Receiving this report, Ruggles began writing orders for Sumner to move his wing to the mountain crest "and take position either to attack the enemy or defend the crest." Before he finished the first paragraph, however, a report arrived that the "enemy" line beyond the crest were friendly troops. Ruggles scrapped the order and drafted a new one, which went to Sumner at 8:45 a.m. McClellan ordered Sumner's entire wing, minus Richardson's division, to march to Boonsboro. Once Sumner reached that village, McClellan initially desired him to arrange his men for attack or defense, depending on whether he found the enemy had fled or instead had decided to make a stand. But to ensure that the aggressive "Bullhead" did not pitch in before the rest of the army was up, Sumner was ordered to consult with headquarters before engaging the enemy. While Ruggles and McClellan composed this directive, Hooker's reports continued to come in, prompting a postscript to Sumer's orders. Hooker, it read, had received reliable information that the enemy were "in a perfect panic" and making for the ford at Shepherdstown. "If upon reaching Boonsborough you find this to be the case, push on after the enemy as rapidly and far as possible, keeping your corps well in hand and doing them all the injury possible."[34]

To relieve some of the congestion along the National Road, at 9 a.m. McClellan informed Burnside that Porter's 5th Corps, which then consisted of Sykes's division and the artillery reserve, would follow the 9th Corps along the Old Sharpsburg Road. Ruggles reminded the Rhode Islander that "General McClellan desires to impress upon you the necessity for the utmost vigor in your pursuit." It could only have been minutes after this dispatch left headquarters before Seth Williams sent Burnside new orders, reflecting the rapidly changing situation. With the Rebels "retreating in disorder for the Shepherdstown Ferry," if Burnside discovered this "information to be corroborated," then McClellan "wishes you to follow the enemy up by Porterstown and Sharpsburg. Keep open your communications with Sumner, on the right, and Franklin, on the left. Take no wagons with you except your ammunition wagons and ambulances. Use effectual precautions to make it certain that your baggage wagons will be kept out of the road."[35]

Believing that the Rebels were whipped, McClellan changed Franklin's orders, which had been to send a "sufficient force" to Rohrersville and to open communications with Miles at Harpers Ferry with the remainder of his command. Now McClellan instructed Franklin to communicate with Burnside at the intersection of the Rohrersville and Boonsboro roads. If Franklin found confirmation of the report that the enemy were in retreat toward Shepherdstown, then McClellan ordered him to "push on with your whole command (cautiously and keeping up communications with Burnside) to Sharpsburg, and endeavor to fall upon the enemy and to cut off his retreat . . . In this juncture much is left by the commanding general to your judgment, trusting that you will act promptly and vigorously and complete the success thus far gained."[36]

McClellan sensed an opportunity to give Lee a hard blow, and he sought to bring the full weight of his army against the forces retreating toward the Shepherdstown Ford. His orders for the pursuit of the beaten enemy were clear and aggressive, demanding prompt action. This was a promising development, but McClellan's revised orders to Franklin raise the question of whether McClellan had abandoned the relief of the Harpers Ferry garrison to win glory by bagging a part of the Confederate army. The possibility that McClellan thought Franklin would have opened communications with Harpers Ferry by the time his 8:45 a.m. orders were received can be eliminated, since Franklin's orders contained no mention of what should be done with Harpers Ferry while the 6th Corps pursued the Confederates toward Sharpsburg. Nor did McClellan's orders consider McLaws's force in Pleasant Valley. Instead, he left Franklin in a devilish position: either of obeying his new orders and leaving Harpers Ferry to its fate, which would let McLaws withdraw without a bruise, or disregarding these orders and attempting to rescue the Union garrison.

McClellan accompanied the written orders to Sumner, Hooker, and Burnside with verbal instructions that if the enemy were overtaken on the march, "they should be attacked at once." If the enemy were found "in heavy force and in position," then the leading corps "should be placed in position for attack" but wait for the arrival of McClellan before attacking.[37] Had McClellan been fighting the campaign on a map, and had all his subordinate commanders performed with energy and good judgment, then he might have sent Lee, along with Longstreet and D. H. Hill, scurrying ingloriously across the Potomac on the 15th. But McClellan's plans went awry, due to several factors: the failure of his headquarters to ensure their implementation; a lack of energy by one key commander; and an enemy army that did not behave as it was supposed to.

McClellan's capable staff were the vital tools with which he could manage the army's advance, yet from what the record reveals, only two young aides-de-camp—Captain George A. Custer, and First Lieutenant James P. Martin—represented headquarters at the front on this vital morning. "The staff should have been out upon the road all day, full of life and all alert to prevent delays, and to keep the columns moving, to crowd the troops forward," wrote Francis A. Walker, the 2nd Army Corps' historian. Custer and Martin could report on what they observed, but they lacked the rank and authority to represent headquarters and express its will. Without this influence where it was most needed, McClellan's army lurched forward from South Mountain like a badly tuned machine.[38]

At the head of the army's advance, Israel Richardson's excellent division marched smartly down South Mountain toward Boonsboro. But behind Richardson's crisp start, movement wheezed and sputtered. Cavalry, not Richardson's infantry, were the best pursuit elements, and Hooker, waiting at the Mountain House, fretted that Pleasonton's horsemen were not yet at the front. Captain Custer was with Hooker, and at the latter's behest Custer scribbled a hasty note to McClellan's aide, Colonel Albert Colburn. Hooker had over 1,000 prisoners, Custer wrote, and "he desires me to inform the General that we can capture the entire rebel army[.] Gen. Lee (rebel) is wounded and Garland killed. Lee reports that he lost fifteen thousand men yesterday. Gen Hooker says the rebel army is completely demoralized the rebels are moving towards Shepherdstown. Boonsboro is full of rebel stragglers. Hooker has sent Richardson in pursuit (double quick) and will follow immediately. We need cavalry our cavalry has not arrived yet."[39] The cavalry—consisting only of Farnsworth's brigade and Captain John C. Tidball's Battery A, 2nd U.S. Horse Artillery—were on their way, and they may have passed the orderly carrying Custer's message on their way up the mountain. They trotted briskly past Hooker at the Mountain House and descended the mountain to overtake Richardson.[40]

Meanwhile, Hooker assembled his corps in the summit area of Turner's Gap, so they could "make a little coffee and eat their breakfasts." Before McClellan's orders arrived, the head of Sumner's column reached the gap and found the 1st Corps blocking the way. Sumner gave his men a breather while he huddled with Hooker at the Mountain House to discuss whose corps should take the lead. They agreed that it was more expedient that the 1st should lead the way. Most of that corps were on the mountain, while Sumner's two corps were strung out from the mountain summit to the valley below. George Noyes of Doubleday's division observed that the turnpike was filled with "crowded troops, artillery, and wagons," and "far down the road toward Frederick pushed on a living tide of men." But Hooker's corps was neither concentrated nor ready to march. The artillery and ammunition trains were not up, both Gibbon's and Patrick's brigades were still separated from their division, and Meade's division had not yet reached the turnpike. Gibbon recalled that he had to pass through the 2nd Corps to rejoin his division. Patrick complained that his orders were slow in arriving that morning, as well as that the movement of troops "was done very slowly." He, too, found the 2nd Corps obstructing his path.[41]

Not until 10 a.m., some three hours after Richardson commenced the pursuit of the enemy, did the 1st Corps start from the mountain. Perhaps as a nod to their performance the night before, Hooker placed Gibbon's brigade in the lead, an honor (if you can call it that) that Meade's veterans might have disputed because of their own valiant efforts. Meade's division came next, followed by Doubleday's and Ricketts's divisions. Circumstances may have played a part in determining the order of march, but if they did not, then it is unusual for Hooker to have placed the units that did the hardest fighting the night before at the head of the column. Yet the pursuit of an enemy thought to be soundly thrashed put the men in good spirits. "There is no army ration, after all, so good for troops as an occasional touch of victory," noted Lieutenant Noyes. Hooker's 3 divisions, 10 batteries, ammunition wagons, and ambulances occupied nearly 4 miles of road space, so that it was not until around noon that they had cleared the way for Sumner's column to resume its march.[42]

Hooker, at least, was moving. At Fox's Gap the 9th Corps sat motionless all morning. Between 8 and 9:30 a.m., Burnside received three communications from headquarters. Each urged a prompt advance by the 9th Corps. Cox thought that perhaps Burnside's troubled frame of mind over the dismantling of his wing "made him neglect the prompt issue of orders for moving the Ninth Corps," a weak excuse at best. Yet Burnside also deliberately delayed marching until the corps was issued rations, a decision that showed astonishingly poor judgment in light of the report from headquarters that the enemy was "demoralized" and "retreating in disorder" toward the Shepherdstown Ford. If ever a moment demanded speed and required soldiers to march at once, even on an empty stomach, this surely was one. Instead, the 9th Corps remained inert, waiting for their commissary wagons to come up.

The wait proved to be longer than expected when, due to the "stupidity of some wagon-master" or some other error, the trains took the wrong road and had to be redirected. So the clock ticked, and a hot sun rose lazily in the sky. Except for those men detailed to police the battlefield or bury the dead, the troops simply lounged about. By noon, four hours after the first orders to march were sent from headquarters, the 9th Corps still had not stirred. George Sykes's division of the 5th Corps came up the Old Sharpsburg Road at about this time, expecting a clear road ahead, but to Sykes's surprise he found the 9th Corps blocking his way. Sykes sent word of his problem back to Porter, who requested permission from headquarters to move past the 9th Corps. By this time it was 12:30 p.m. Half the day was lost. But no wrath emanated from headquarters over the delay. Instead, Colonel Ruggles sent Burnside a rather mildly worded message.

General Burnside:

GENERAL: General McClellan desires you to let General Porter's go on past you if necessary. You will then push your own command on as rapidly as possible. The general also desires to know the reason for your delay in starting this morning.

I am, general, very respectfully, your obedient servant,

GEO. D. RUGGLES,
Colonel and Aide-de-Camp[43]

While Ruggles wrote to Burnside, Chief of Staff Marcy prepared orders for Porter, giving Sykes permission to go on ahead of the 9th Corps. When these orders reached him, Sykes wasted no time in urging his division past the 9th Corps along the Old Sharpsburg Road. The combination of Sykes's movement to the front and Ruggles dispatch finally galvanized Burnside into action. After Sykes moved by, Burnside had Cox put the 9th Corps onto the road, which cut off the reserve artillery, which was following Sykes. By now it was nearly 2 p.m.—a full seven hours after the Confederates' retreat had been discovered.[44]

The delays in moving the army off South Mountain offered the men time to explore the battlefield. Although many were combat veterans, few had participated in a successful action and seen the aftermath of a battle. The new recruits typically found it unsettling and disturbing. Death for the vanquished, they learned, was dirty and squalid, shorn of honor or glory. A recruit from the 9th

New Hampshire explored the ground defended by Drayton's brigade at Fox's Gap and wrote home that "I have seen all of war I wish to. The thing is indescribable. Oh horrors!" A member of the 48th Pennsylvania and his comrades found the Old Sharpsburg Road "absolutely full of dead rebels. They lay actually two and three deep. One fellow hung on the fence opposite, an arm and leg on either side, literally riddled with bullets." They counted 40 bodies, all shot in the head or breast, within 5 rods of one another. Sergeant Robert Smith, also in the 48th, counted 105 Confederate dead in the area around Wise's farm. One "handsome, dark-haired boy" who "could not have been more than 16" caught the eye of Lieutenant Thomas H. Evans of the 12th U.S. Infantry when his regiment passed through Fox's Gap. The dead Rebel had been shot in the forehead. "His musket was in his hands, a smile upon his features, as if his last thought had been of home, parents, and heaven," recalled Evans. "There was a black silk ribbon around his neck, under his shirt, and I felt as if I should have liked to stay and bury him and that ribbon, with whatever was attached, sacredly from every prying eye." Another 9th New Hampshire man found that the features of the Southern dead "were fearfully distorted with rage, or pain, or both. This, with their dirt, long hair, and squalid uniforms, made up a spectacle such as I never wish to behold again."[45]

The spectacle of the dead—horrifying as it was—nevertheless did not deter many Union soldiers from searching through pockets, knapsacks, and haversacks for souvenirs and food. "Some made a breakfast upon the small round biscuit with which the haversacks of the dead Confederates around us were filled," recorded the historian of the 35th Massachusetts. Lieutenant Evans and a few men from his company of regulars felt differently when they inspected the haversacks of a group of Confederate prisoners being held on the mountain. "All we saw were biscuits, if they deserved that name," commented Evans. Edward Lord of the 9th New Hampshire noted that the men found "very few valuable trinkets" in the Confederates pockets and knapsacks, "though they all get searched."[46]

Burial details, which included Confederate prisoners seized during the morning and pressed into service, tended to the grim work of collecting the dead. The Union corpses were laid out in rows, wrapped in their army blankets, with their names pinned to the coverings. The work of gathering and identifying these bodies was nearly complete by the time Sykes's division came up the mountain, for Lieutenant Evans saw a large number of Union dead, arranged in three rows and covered with blankets. Those on burial detail dug into the thin, rocky soil, shoveling out an "immense shallow trench parallel to the road [Old Sharpsburg Road]" to receive the bodies. Colonel David Strother, who rode up into the gap before the burials were completed, counted 120 Union soldiers buried in this long grave. Gazing on dead comrades evokes strong emotions in soldiers. Captain James Wren noted that it "makes the [men] feel desperate towards the rebels, as many of them had brave comrades who stood in Line with them [and] was now taking thear posision in their Last Line."[47]

The Confederate dead were not interred until September 16 and 17. A Union burial detail, assisted by Confederate prisoners, carved out crude graves on the mountain and tumbled the bodies in with no ceremony. Samuel Compton of the 12th Ohio, who remained behind at Fox's Gap until the 16th, observed them at work. "The squad I saw were armed with a pick & a canteen full of whiskey. The Whiskey the most necessary of the two. The boddies had become so offensive that men could only endure it by being staggering drunk." Hard digging prompted one fellow on the detail working near Wise's farm to suggest that they dump the bodies down Wise's well. Several corpses were so deposited before Mr. Wise emerged to put a stop to the use of his well as a burial vault. But the damage was done and his well was ruined. Wise then decided to make the best of his situation, and he negotiated an agreement with the army to pay him $1 for each body buried in his well. In all, 60 corpses from Drayton's and Garland's brigades were hauled over and dumped into the well. David Strother had seen the remains of these men the day before and knew the cold, unfeeling burial that awaited them. It moved him to record in his journal the hope of all soldiers at war, "that I may die in a clean coat and be buried by my friends."[48]

The soldiers of the 1st Corps were greeted with the same macabre displays on Hill 1280 and Hill 1500 as they explored the scene of that fight. Several bold souls from Hatch's division—now Doubleday's—ventured forth at dawn into the ground defended by Garnett's brigade. Captain David Noyes, observing that these men wandered about without danger, followed them, "moved by a desire to see some of our late antagonists." Among the foremost of the fallen Confederates lay Colonel Strange, "upon his stern, determined face still lingers that look of battle, his right hand still grasps his sword." The adjutant of the 56th Pennsylvania also paused to examine Strange, who he thought "was certainly a brave man for he fell in front of his men." Several feet to Strange's left lay a young lieutenant, possibly Melville Shephard (see chapter 12), "whose very handsome face and placid expression greatly attracted me," wrote Noyes. Some of the Union men were picking up discarded equipment or souvenirs. "On returning from the left," continued Noyes, "I saw two or three kneeling and stooping around my lieutenant; hastening up, I was horrified by seeing one wretch trying to force off with his knife the plain gold ring" on the lieutenant's finger. The outraged captain drove them off. On Hill 1500 a hungry William Olcott of the 10th Pennsylvania Reserves searched the knapsacks and haversacks of the Alabamians and South Carolinians who lay nearby and was delighted to find them "generally well filled with biscuits, cold ham, etc."[49]

As they searched for food or other items, or hunted up their dead and wounded, Hooker's troops occasionally flushed out Confederate soldiers who—

either because they were disoriented, exhausted, or simply sick of soldiering—were left behind. Some men of the 6th Wisconsin found a young Georgian of Colquitt's brigade, "his face a gore of blood," who fled at their approach. Only with difficulty were they able to convince him that they were not going to kill him and thus got him to surrender. The burial detail of the 2nd Pennsylvania Reserves came upon a young soldier of Rodes's brigade who had been shot through the forehead. Although unconscious, they found the "vitality in him was strong and he swallowed water freely." Despite an obviously mortal wound, the Union soldiers still attempted to keep the young man alive. Samuel Webster of the 13th Massachusetts recorded that "Joe Kelly captured a couple of woeful looking Johnnies up in the rocks, who were afraid of being shot." The 7th Pennsylvania Reserves nabbed a Confederate major, and Lieutenant Harry Lantz entered into a good-natured debate on the war with him. "Major, you fellows may as well give in, we'll lick you anyhow, in the end," said Lantz. The plucky Confederate replied, "H'oh, that's just what we think of you." Bates Alexander, an observer of the debate, initially thought, "Major you should not thus express yourself here, nor elsewhere," but then Bates decided " 'twas O.K. as he was a Confederate and wedded to his cause as we were to ours."[50]

The physical demands of marching and fighting on September 14 left Hooker's men ravenously hungry. The commissary wagons for most brigades were unable to get forward to issue rations. The men of the 13th Massachusetts found their haversacks contained a meager two hardtack per man. So they and other 1st Corps soldiers cast covetous eyes on the few civilian dwellings on the mountain, which were nearly all abandoned by their owners during the fighting. In the opinion of the Union soldiers, that made them fair game for foraging. "As soon as the column halted the neighboring houses and gardens were ransacked for fruit and vegetables, and such other eatables as could be obtained," recorded the historian of the 83rd New York. Lieutenant Sam Moore in the 90th Pennsylvania admitted that he and his men found an abandoned house on the summit at Turner's Gap and "ransacked it," finding "plenty to eat except bread." But the pickings from foraging were slim, and most soldiers waited for rations with growling stomachs. When George Meade rode by the men of his division and inquired whether they were well supplied with ammunition, Samuel A. Dixon of the 1st Pennsylvania Reserves sang out loudly, "Yes, General plenty of ammunition but not a d——d cracker in our haversacks." Meade replied, "Well boys you must not blame me for that the wagons were ordered up but must have failed to reach you." So, except for the bolder or less scrupulous men, the 1st Corps left South Mountain with little in their bellies.[51]

Fitz Lee's cavalry brigade, the Confederate army's rear guard, waited a mile and a half east of Boonsboro for the Union pursuit to show itself. Fitz Lee had posted his men shortly after midnight. Dawn revealed that the surrounding country, cut up into farm fields with fences and stone walls, was "ground ill-suited to the operations of cavalry." But his mission was only to harass and delay the enemy, not stop them. For this purpose the ground selected served adequately. Fitz Lee placed his section of Pelham's horse artillery on a swell of ground that commanded the National Road and covered his front with dismounted skirmishers. Lieutenant Colonel John T. Thornton's 3rd Virginia Cavalry, deployed mounted on both front and flanks, supported the skirmishers. Colonel W. H. F. "Rooney" Lee's 9th Virginia formed in column along the pike a short distance to the rear of Pelham's guns, and Colonel William C. Wickham's 4th Virginia were placed back outside of Boonsboro, also in column along the pike.

As the sun poked its head above South Mountain, the Virginians observed "columns of the enemy with their bright muskets gleaming in the morning light" descending the mountain. It was Richardson's division. Thornton's skirmish line opened fire as the Federals came within range, and the bluecoat skirmishers responded. The Confederates slowly fell back before Richardson's greatly superior numbers until Pelham's guns were uncovered, which greeted the enemy with several well-placed shells, bringing their advance to a stop. The Federal column deployed into line of battle and heavily reinforced their skirmish line. Having accomplished his mission of delaying the enemy by forcing them to deploy from column to line, Fitz Lee commenced a slow withdrawal toward Boonsboro. The guns went first, followed by the 4th Virginia, then the 9th. The 3rd continued to spar with the advancing enemy, and Lieutenant George W. Beale of the 9th Virginia Cavalry recalled that several times his regiment faced about as it retired, "as if to repel a threatened charge by cavalry." But they were confronted only by slow-moving infantry—or so they thought—and the brigade made its way into Boonsboro without incident. Everyone was very weary of being in the saddle, having completed a hard ride from Westminster, Maryland, the night before and then being required to remain mounted for much of the night. When they reached Boonsboro, Rooney Lee and Wickham permitted their men to dismount—a break for both men and horses. The troopers stood by their animals or sat on the curbstones along the street, holding the bridle reins.[52]

About 1 mile outside of Boonsboro, Colonel Edward Cross, commanding the 5th New Hampshire infantry, which composed the rear guard of Richardson's division, received orders to "march to the front as soon as possible." Cross was a fearless soldier who went into battle wearing a red bandana, and his regiment excelled under his firm leadership. Richardson dubbed the 5th his Fireproofs for their fine battle record, and his confidence in them and their commander was evident to every man in the division that morning. "We went down with our canteens and traps rattling like a mule train," wrote Second Lieutenant Thomas Livermore. They dashed by the other regiments of the division, who made way for the Granite Staters and shouted encouragement: "Give 'em hell, boys!" "Hurrah for Richardson's Cavalry." Livermore added: "We learned that the honor of leading the advance had been given us in preference to the leading brigade [Irish Brigade], to their chagrin and our pride, and we took it with elated hearts." When Cross reached the head of the division he met Richardson, who told him that there were neither friendly cavalry nor artillery present. Cross's regiment would act as both. Richardson's orders were to "deploy and sweep both sides of the road."[53]

Cross sent out 8 of his 10 companies as skirmishers—4 on each side of the pike—and kept 2 companies in the center as a reserve. Richardson followed behind them with rest of his division. Cross's men dashed forward, trading shots with Fitz Lee's skirmishers, who slowly retired toward Boonsboro. As the 5th New Hampshire neared the village, Colonel Farnsworth and six companies of his tough 8th Illinois Cavalry came trotting up from the rear. The 8th had divided near the summit of South Mountain, sending four companies in the direction of Fox's Gap, probably to scout the Old Sharpsburg Road, while the rest, with Colonel Farnsworth, followed the National Road. As these latter companies descended the mountain, the regimental surgeon noted that "we found almost every house and barn converted into a hospital for the rebel soldiers." Overtaking Richardson's infantry, Farnsworth learned that Confederate cavalry were in front. It is unlikely that Richardson could offer Farnsworth an accurate estimate of enemy strength, for Fitz Lee certainly never displayed his full force to view. Nevertheless, Farnsworth concluded that his six companies could clear the way. Placing himself at the head of his command, Farnsworth ordered them forward at a charge.[54]

Farnsworth's daring caught Fitz Lee's horsemen entirely by surprise, driving their skirmish line back on Boonsboro at a gallop. Lieutenant Beale was standing beside his horse in the village when he heard someone shout "Mount! Mount!" accompanied by a "rapid fire of pistols and carbines" very close by. The command came from Rooney Lee, who saw the charging enemy horsemen and ordered his regiment to climb in the saddle and wheel about to face them. But only the officer in command of Colonel Lee's rear squadron heard the order, and the Yankees were upon him before his men could act. Lieutenant Beale recalled the chaos that ensued: "Before the men could mount and form ranks, the rear guard, retreating at full speed, dashed into our already confused columns, and in an incredibly short time the street became packed with a mass of horses and horsemen, so jammed together as to make motion impossible for most of them." Adding to the general bedlam were some of the more daring citizens of Boonsboro—Unionist to the core—who threw open their second-story windows and opened up with pistols on the mass of graycoat cavalry beneath them. When Farnsworth's troopers realized the utter confusion their charge had thrown the Confederate cavalry into, they pressed on to point-blank range and fired their pistols and carbines into the nearly helpless Southerners. "Clouds of dust enveloped everything," wrote Beale, which may have saved many of the Rebels from death or injury by obscuring the aim of the Illinois troopers.[55]

William L. Rizell of the 9th Virginia recalled that in its attempt to escape the onslaught of Farnsworth's companies, his regiment "ran back into the regiment behind us, which turned about and joined in our race, they threw the next one behind them into confusion, and the one after another, in the twinkling of a eye all five regiments [there were only three present] were panic stricken, and each horseman was rushing wildly back along the rock ribbed Pike, as if he was determined he would win the race." The 5th New Hampshire pitched into the fight as well, sending skirmishers dashing into a cornfield south of the turnpike, where they could fire at the fleeing horsemen. Some of Cross's skirmishers may have penetrated to the Boonsboro–Sharpsburg Pike and hastily thrown up an obstacle, for William Rizell stated that part of his regiment ran into a barricade across a street "behind which infantry were posted." Stone fences along the pike hemmed in Fitz Lee's horsemen, preventing them from escaping into the adjacent fields. So the routed mass of Rebel cavalrymen swept through Boonsboro and along the National Road toward Hagerstown, pursued by Farnsworth's horseman and hurried along by the bullets of the New Hampshire infantrymen. Outside of town, Fitz Lee's troopers, who were not accompanied by Lady Luck that day, came upon stones piled up in the middle of the road in preparation for road repairs. The thick dust churned up by the galloping horses—"you could cut it with a knife," wrote Rizell—masked these dangerous obstacles and "many horses blindly rushed [on them], and falling piled with their riders one on another." Other troopers, unable to see their way in the dust, ran their horses into telegraph posts and were thrown to the ground.[56]

As the rear of Fitz Lee's brigade cleared the town, Rooney Lee's horse was shot and the colonel thrown to the ground, "dazed and helpless." About 1 mile north of town a break in the stone fencing along the pike was found, and the Confederates turned into the nearby field. Officers shouted out the numbers of their regiments in an effort to restore some organization. They managed to assemble a "considerable force," which Lieutenant Colonel Richard L. T. Beale, with saber drawn, led in a countercharge against the Federals. A Hoosier trooper dropped Beale's horse within 20 yards of the Union line and the counterattack melted away. Then Captain Thomas Haynes, commanding the 9th Virginia's Company H, collected another group of troopers and led a second charge. This pressed the Union horsemen back, and even resulted in three or four Yankee prisoners. The countercharge passed by Colonel Lee, lying prostrate near the roadside. Haynes somehow managed to get Lee's wounded horse up, and he called to his colonel to mount and escape. But Lee was "so stunned and bruised as to be incapable of moving hand or foot," and before anyone could assist him the 8th Illinois came roaring up and drove Haynes and company back. Fortunately for the Rebel colonel, the Federals paid no attention to him, and he eventually recovered enough to make his way to a nearby copse of trees, where he found several other Confederate soldiers who helped him get back to his regiment by the night of the 15th.[57]

Haynes's countercharge checked the pursuit by the 8th Illinois, but Pleasonton arrived with Captain Tidball's horse battery, which unlimbered and proceeded to burst several shells near the Confederate horsemen. "The race started again," wrote William Rizell, "and this time we ran until we got tired." Fitz Lee eventually gathered a couple of color bearers to his side and rallied his thoroughly disorganized command. Finding that he had outdistanced his pursuers, Fitz Lee marched his regiments "possibly a couple of miles" along the Williamsport Turnpike before turning them off on byroads in the direction of Sharpsburg. Along the way—most likely near the Upper Bridge over the Antietam—at least one of his regiments rescued Cutts's battalion from what were probably elements of the 8th Illinois. Lieutenant Colonel William Carter of the 3rd Virginia recorded that the brigade marched to Dam No. 4 on the C&O Canal, where they turned south and proceeded along the River Road until they encountered Hood's division north of Sharpsburg. Years later, in his history of Stuart's cavalry, Henry B. McClellan generously wrote that Fitz Lee's circuitous march was designed "to draw the enemy after him." This was an unintended consequence, however. His primary purpose was to shake his persistent and aggressive pursuers. Lieutenant Colonel Carter, writing not for publication but in his diary, offered a more sober assessment: "This was an awful day for our Brigade."[58]

Fitz Lee's men had good reason to be mortified by the engagement at Boonsboro. Six companies of Union cavalry, with help from the infantry of the 5th New Hampshire, had, by aggressive action and the element of surprise, routed a fine brigade of Confederate cavalry. How Farnsworth managed to surprise Fitz Lee has never been satisfactorily explained, but a likely reason is that the Confederates let their guard down when it seemed evident that the enemy pursuit did not include cavalry. Fitz Lee did not report his losses for the battle, but George Beale wrote that the 9th Virginia Cavalry had 2 officers and 16 enlisted men killed, and 10 privates captured. According to Lieutenant Colonel Carter's tally, the 3rd Virginia's losses were 1 killed, 8 wounded, and 7 missing or captured. Pleasonton claimed 30 Confederate dead, 50 wounded, and a "very large number of prisoners, among whom were several hundred stragglers," although the latter category probably included many infantrymen rounded up by his cavalry. In the 8th Illinois Sergeant Robert McArthur was killed, 23 were wounded, and several were taken prisoner. The regiment also nearly lost their colonel. During the melee Farnsworth shot one Confederate trooper from his horse in a one-on-one encounter. Then another Virginian gave chase to the colonel and was about to strike him "a deadly blow" with his saber when one of Farnsworth's troopers shot the Rebel. The lopsided affair added further luster to the 8th's already excellent combat record, and it cleared the road to Sharpsburg for Richardson's division.[59]

Soon after the dust of the cavalry fight settled, Richardson's division tramped into Boonsboro, receiving a jubilant welcome from its citizens. Doors and windows burst open and men and women carried pails of water to their doorsteps. Richardson did not linger, but led his regiments swiftly through the tidy village and out the Sharpsburg Pike, following the trail of cast-off equipment and other debris left by the retreating soldiers of Longstreet and D. H. Hill.[60]

Around 1 p.m., nearly three hours after Richardson passed through the village, Hooker's corps entered Boonsboro. "The men took up the march in excellent spirits; the joy and satisfaction everywhere evident," noted Captain Noyes. "The jokes at the expense of the enemy flung from file to file, the very marching of the men indicated that this was not a retreat, but an actual pursuit of a flying enemy." Evidence of a Confederate defeat manifested itself the entire distance from Turner's Gap to Boonsboro. Lieutenant Noyes thought that "the western slopes of South Mountain were to-day full of straggling and demoralized rebels," and Lieutenant Sam Healy, adjutant of the 56th Pennsylvania, saw enough to jot down in his journal: "The Rebels had been completely routed." Lieutenant Frank Haskell of Gibbon's brigade wrote that the Confederates left "great numbers of their wounded, scattered by the road-side where they had been carried during the battle, or collected in barns and houses, for treatment by their medical officers." Confederate wounded filled the public buildings in Boonsboro. There appeared to be so many that to E. R. Brown of the 27th Indiana, "it seemed to us that the men in gray must be in peaceable possession of the place." During a halt in town, the men of the 12th Massachusetts discovered a large pile of knapsacks abandoned by the Confederates, which they enthusiastically ransacked for souvenirs and edibles.[61]

Prisoners were tangible evidence that things were going well. Hooker's estimate of capturing 1,000 prisoners may have been exaggerated, but a significant number were collected by the advancing Federals. Many were simply exhausted stragglers, such as the young men encountered by Adjutant Fred Hitchcock of the 130th Pennsylvania, who stated that some of them "freely expressed themselves as glad they had been captured, as they were sick of the fighting." Lieutenant Sam Moore's 90th Pennsylvania "met several squads of prisoners from 17 to fifty men in a squad" soon after they passed through Boonsboro. Hitchcock's regiment had not yet smelled powder in the war, and some of the men were awed by the numbers of prisoners passing to the rear; they inquired of a well-dressed Confederate lieutenant if there were any more Rebels left. He replied grimly that they would soon meet "plenty of Rebs." From his previous service on the Peninsula, Colonel Ezra Carman, leading the newly raised 13th New Jersey, knew something about how these Confederates fought. After watching groups of them march past his regiment, he confided to his diary: "They were lean, wiry and bony just in fighting trim. Say what you will they fight like Trojans and behave like heroes."[62]

The seemingly endless procession of Union soldiers who passed through Boonsboro did not seem to diminish the enthusiasm and benevolence of its citizens, who seemed to greet all as liberators. Major Dawes wrote that several older gentlemen from the village welcomed his regiment, which marched at the head of Hooker's column. "They hooped and 'hollared' laughed and cried without the least regard to proprieties," he recalled. One of them enthusiastically trotted along beside the regiment and exclaimed, "We've watched for you and we've prayed for you and now thank god you've come." Then he jumped on a log and kept shouting for joy. "The last I saw of him he was hurrahing and thanking God alternately," wrote Dawes. When the men reached the village, the people were standing along the roadside with food and pails of water. By the time the 12th Corps passed through later, General Alpheus Williams noted that "the whole population seemed rejoicing that we were chasing the rebels from the state." But not all were celebrating. Adjutant Hitchcock observed that many people "were sadly lamenting the destruction of almost everything that could be destroyed on and about their homes by this besome of destruction—war. Food, stock, fences, bed and bedding, etc., all gone or destroyed."[63]

McClellan remained at his headquarters in Bolivar until late morning, sending and receiving reports. At 9 a.m. he wired to General Banks in Washington that the danger to Washington from north of the Potomac had passed, and that Banks should move the greater part of his command to the south side of the river. McClellan sent a brief wire to his wife at the same time, to tell her of his great victory. A half hour later he took time to correspond with her in more detail. "How glad I am for my country that it is delivered from immediate peril," he wrote. "I am starting with the pursuit & must close this . . . If I can believe one tenth of what is reported, God has seldom given an army a greater victory than this."[64]

At 10 a.m. McClellan passed along to Halleck additional exaggerated and unsubstantiated reports from the front, offering them as authentic proof of a decisive victory. The "information this moment rec'd completely confirms the rout & demoralization of the rebel army," he wrote. "Genl. Lee reported wounded & Garland killed. Hooker alone has over a thousand prisoners. It is stated that Lee gives his loss as fifteen thousand. We are following as rapidly as the men can move."[65]

Nonetheless, there was one piece of disquieting news that morning: a report that Harpers Ferry had surrendered. McClellan hoped to hear from Franklin to either verify or refute this, but by 10 a.m. nothing had yet been received from the Pennsylvanian so McClellan decided to start forward. First, though, he planned to have a look at the battlefield for what he believed was the scene of his army's decisive triumph over the Rebels. His party took the Old Sharpsburg Road to

Fox's Gap, passing "considerable bodies" of Confederate prisoners being led to the rear and many wounded graycoats who were gathered in the shade of roadside trees for treatment. Near the summit they viewed the burial parties hewing out graves for the Union dead, who lay in rows nearby. Beyond this, scattered all across the summit and down the slope of the mountain, were strewn the Confederate dead "in all their squalor and hideous distortion." Leaving these unpleasant scenes, McClellan returned to the National Road and, passing the long columns of the 12th Corps laboring along, ascended the mountain for a look at Hooker's battlefield. His party approached a two-story farmhouse on the north side of the road that was in use as a hospital. Both the building and the yard were crowded with wounded, probably from Gibbon's brigade. McClellan reined up, dismounted, and—accompanied by General Marcy—walked among the injured lying in the grass outside the house. An eyewitness recalled how McClellan took the hands of many men, telling "them how valuable and timely a victory their bravery had won, and that he thanked them in the name of their country." He also entered the house, where the more serious cases were being treated. When McClellan emerged, "tears were trickling down his cheeks," which "he dashed away with his hand" before mounting and continuing on up the mountain. It was moments such as these that made men love McClellan.[66]

After investigating the sites of Hooker's battle, McClellan set out for Boonsboro, cantering past the long lines of troops and wagons that jammed the road. "Cheer after cheer went up," wrote Colonel Ezra Carman. "Caps flew in the air and things were noisy generally." This type of enthusiastic reception was repeated by each regiment as McClellan and his party rode by. Carman went on the state that "as he passed a long way beyond us you could hear Regiment after Regiment cheer him until the distance was so great it could not be heard." McClellan reached Boonsboro shortly after 1 p.m. and stopped at "a white house in the outskirts of the village," where he learned that yet another problem had beset the army's pursuit of the retreating Confederates. Someone had failed to guide the 12th Corps, now led by the newly arrived Major General Joseph F. K. Mansfield, onto the Sharpsburg Pike, and the head of its column had continued out the National Road toward Hagerstown. Colonel Strother was dispatched to set things aright. He found the road "so closely packed with troops and supply trains that it was impossible to turn" the column around. Mansfield could not be located, but Strother found General Alpheus Williams, who halted the column until the 12th Corps' commander arrived. When Mansfield did, he wasted no further time, ordering fences to be torn down and the column led cross-country to the Shepherdstown Pike.[67]

While Strother sorted out the army traffic, McClellan prepared a telegram to Winfield Scott, the magnificent old soldier who, only a year before, McClellan had deemed his "inveterate enemy." Yet Scott's approval clearly still mattered to McClellan. He wrote to say that the troops "behaved valiantly & gained a signal victory" in the battle of September 14, adding that Robert E. Lee commanded the Rebel forces. Now Lee's Rebels were "routed and retreating in disorder."[68]

But about the time McClellan composed his wire to Scott, fresh reports from the various fronts began to find their way to headquarters, offering evidence that perhaps the victory gained on the 14th was not as grand or as complete as McClellan wanted to believe. Franklin cast the first dose of cold water, with a report timed at 8:50 a.m.: "The enemy is drawn up in line of battle about 2 miles to our front, one brigade in sight. As soon as I am sure that Rohrersville is occupied, I shall move forward to attack the enemy. This may be two hours from now." Franklin's tone was not encouraging regarding any action, but then he added more serious news. "If Harper's Ferry has fallen—and the cessation of firing makes me fear it has—it is my opinion that I should be strongly reinforced." This implied confirmation of the earlier morning report that Harpers Ferry had surrendered. But the cessation of firing could also mean that the enemy were lifting the siege and shifting their forces, either to reinforce Lee or to cover Lee's crossing at Shepherdstown. Until he had positive verification, McClellan kept this distressing news to himself.[69]

A dispatch from the signal station at the Washington Monument on South Mountain followed Franklin's. Timed at 12:40 p.m., it read: "A line of battle—or an arrangement of troops which looks very much like it—is formed on the other side of Antietam Creek and this side of Sharpsburg. It is four times as long on the west as on the east side of the road."[70] Soon after, a note arrived from Captain Custer, who was up front with Richardson's division: "They are in full view. Their line is a perfect one about a mile and half long . . . Longstreet is in command and has forty cannon that we know of . . . We can have equally good position as they now occupy . . . We can employ all the troops you can send us."[71] More reports that the enemy was making a stand behind Antietam Creek followed. At 2:15 p.m. Hooker reached the front and wrote that the enemy were in "line of battle in open ground," but that he did not consider their position "a formidable one." He would soon change his opinion of how the enemy was situated after taking a closer look. When Sumner arrived at the front, he reported that the Rebels were "in large force" and that their line extended for a mile. "Shall I make the necessary dispositions to attack?" he asked. "And shall I attack without further orders?"[72]

Still believing the enemy to be whipped, McClellan assumed that this stand behind Antietam Creek was no more than a rear guard placed to cover the Confederate retreat over the Potomac. The same signal station that reported the enemy line of battle behind the creek also reported that there were 92 pieces of artillery (Lee's reserve artillery) accompanied by large Confederate trains moving on the Williamsport Turnpike and crossing into Virginia. If Lee had turned to offer battle, why would he be moving his artillery and his trains back to Virginia? The only logical answer was that Lee was not planning to stand and fight, but merely sought to cover his retreat across the Potomac.[73]

Addressing Franklin's situation first, McClellan wrote to the 6th Corps chief at 1:20 p.m., informing him that the 9th Corps and Sykes's division were moving on the Old Sharpsburg Road under orders to attack an enemy force reported to be at Keedysville. "I will instruct them to communicate with you at Rohrersville, and if necessary re-enforce you," he stated. The rest of the Union army was moving to Boonsboro, with one division (Richardson's) already on the main pike to Keedysville and Sharpsburg. McClellan promised to direct a portion of this division to turn south on an old road from Keedysville that forked south of the village to either Rohrersville or Porterstown, "so as to be in a position to re-enforce you or to move on Portersville [*sic*]." "Thus far our success is complete," he closed, "but let us follow it up closely, but warily. Attack whenever you see a fair chance of success. Lose no time in communicating with Sykes and Burnside."[74]

McClellan remained at his temporary headquarters outside Boonsboro through the early afternoon, waiting for an update from Franklin. How he intended to use Burnside and Sykes, and whether to divert part of Richardson's division toward Rohrersville, hinged on the situation in Pleasant Valley. Between 3 and 3:45 p.m. he received Franklin's next dispatch, sent at 11 a.m. The news was even less encouraging. Franklin claimed that the Confederate forces he faced outnumbered him two to one, and—as they were in a "very strong" position— he was requesting reinforcements.[75]

With Couch's division, Franklin had nearly 18,000 men, so if the enemy did outnumber him two to one, then they had 36,000 men in Pleasant Valley, a force not to be sneezed at. McClellan could not know that Franklin magnified the enemy force confronting him nine times beyond its actual strength, nor that the 6th Corps commander had lost his nerve in a game of bluff with Lafayette McLaws. McClellan had to act on what his commander at the front reported. With evident reluctance at diverting forces to Pleasant Valley, McClellan prepared new orders for Burnside at 3:45 p.m. "If not too late, I think you had better move on Rohrersville communicating meantime with Franklin," he wrote. "If with your assistance he can defeat the enemy in front of him, join him at once. If however, he can hold his own, march direct on Sharpsburg and co-operate with us, unless that place should be evacuated by the enemy. In that case, move at once to co-operate with Franklin." In other words, whether Burnside reinforced Franklin was entirely contingent upon the latter officer's judgment—that is, if, with the 9th Corps reinforcing him, Franklin thought he could defeat McLaws.[76]

Forty-five minutes later McClellan changed his mind about reinforcing Franklin. The catalyst may have been Sumner's report and his inquiry, "Shall I attack without further orders?" Whatever it was, McClellan now decided to hold Franklin in Pleasant Valley and use the rest of the army to crush the enemy behind Antietam Creek. Franklin's new orders, dispatched at 4:30 p.m., were to withdraw Couch's division from Rohrersville (since the main body of the army now covered Franklin's rear) and "hold your position without attacking unless you should see a very favorable opportunity." While Chief of Staff Marcy drafted Franklin's orders, Colonel Ruggles prepared Burnside's. The potential movement of the 9th Corps to Rohrersville was cancelled, and Burnside was instructed to move at once to Sharpsburg, by way of Porterstown, "to assist in the attack on the former place."[77]

Around 5 p.m. McClellan left his Boonsboro headquarters to ride forward and assume personal direction of the forces assembling in front of Antietam Creek. His spirits remained buoyant, his confidence unshaken. When Colonel Strother reported in with news of the enemy stand behind the Antietam, Mc-Clellan responded: "Your news, Colonel, is all corroborative. There we are going immediately to attack them."[78]

While McClellan spent his morning and afternoon pondering operational decisions and viewing the South Mountain battlefield, Israel B. "Dick" Richardson's division pursued the "routed" enemy from Boonsboro toward Sharpsburg. After Pleasonton's troops and Cross's 5th New Hampshire cleared Boonsboro of Rebels, Richardson wasted no time in pushing his division through town and out on the pike to Sharpsburg. The 5th New Hampshire kept the lead, with four companies deployed as skirmishers and the rest of the regiment following in support. The skirmishers scooped up 60 prisoners along the way. As Cross reported, "we might have taken more, but I had not sufficient force to secure my flanks as we marched." Pleasonton's cavalry and his horse artillery were conspicuous by their absence. What cavalry did make it to the front that morning had pursued Fitz Lee out the Hagerstown Pike, leaving Richardson with neither guns nor horsemen to support his pursuit. In Cross's opinion, "this was a great oversight." His men pushed on toward Keedysville and Sharpsburg as quickly as an infantryman can trot cross-country. Rosser's 5th Virginia Cavalry soon made their presence felt. Carbines and muskets cracked as the two lines of skirmishers sparred with one another. "We kept on for a couple of miles," wrote Cross, "my skirmish line constantly exchanging shots with the cavalry of the enemy." Cross's skirmishers cleared Keedysville and worked their way toward Antietam Creek. Shortly after noon, his advance skirmishers, who must have been exhausted from their several-mile jog across farm fields, over fences, and through woods—not to mention firing and being fired at—came to a clear hill that looked down on the tree-lined Antietam Creek and the Middle Bridge.

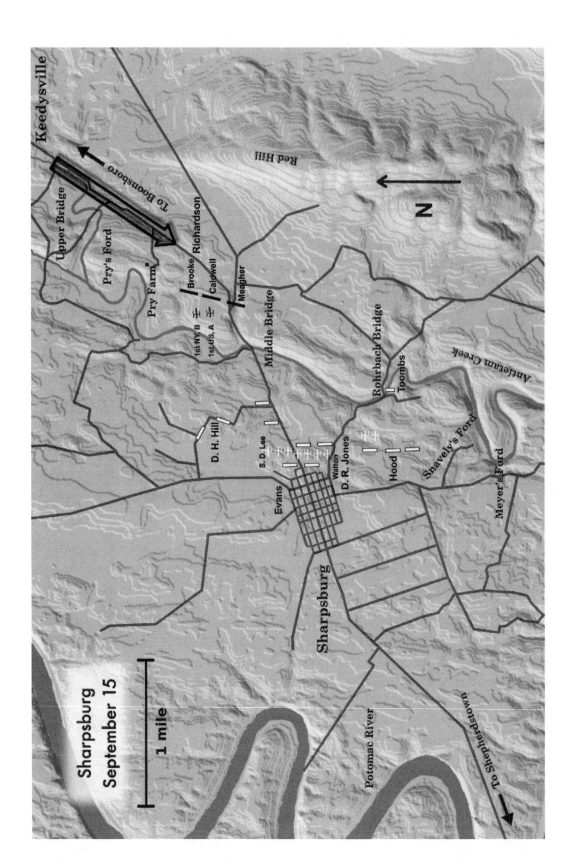

Sharpsburg
September 15

1 mile

Keedysville

Upper Bridge

Pry's Ford

To Boonsboro

Pry Farm

Brooke Richardson
Calgwell
1st NY, B
1st US, A
Meagher

Red Hill

N

Middle Bridge

D. H. Hill

S. D. Lee

Evans

Walton
D. R. Jones

Rohrbach Bridge
Toombs

Hood

Snavely's Ford

Antietam Creek

Sharpsburg

Meyer's Ford

Potomac River

To Shepherdstown

The Rebels were beyond the creek, on the ridges rising west of it, "drawn up in order of battle—their line appearing about one mile long with plenty of Artillery," wrote Colonel Cross. "They did not keep us long in suspense." There was a puff of smoke from one of the Confederate batteries, followed, recalled Lieutenant Thomas Livermore, "by the shriek of a shell." It burst above the regiment, wounding Private John Melendy. A second shell followed, and it, too, exploded above the men, who scrambled for cover. The second one flattened Livermore. "I was suddenly blind and deaf, rushing winds whirling about my head," he wrote. But the damage was temporary; Livermore regained his senses and found cover with his comrades.[79]

Southern sharpshooters also greeted the New Englanders as the rest of the regiment came up to join their skirmishers. Hood's division had left behind a rear guard of 100 men under Hood's chief of staff, Major W. H. Sellers, and it was these tough soldiers that Cross's men now encountered. The 5th New Hampshire's surgeon, Dr. William Child, must have been conspicuous, for he noted that at least half a dozen balls were fired at him, fortunately without effect. Cross had a close call himself, when a Confederate ball nicked his left shoulder strap. The Joshua Newcomer farm stood a short distance west of the Middle Bridge, with his large barn south of the pike and the house and outbuilding north of it. Newcomer's barn, in particular, provided the Confederates with excellent cover to skirmish with Cross's Yankees. The Southerners would fire, then dart behind the barn, reload, and repeat the process. One Rebel concealed himself in a bush on the east bank and fired three times at Lieutenant Ira Bronson, but missed him cleanly. Then Bronson's men identified the source of the fire and blazed away. They proved to be as inaccurate as the Confederate had been, but they managed to flush him from his cover. He dashed onto the bridge and waved his hat at his adversaries, who gave him a cheer and let him go. It was to be a rare moment of graciousness in the orgy of violence that later descended on this gentle place.[80]

Cross positioned his men in protected spots, and they continued to spar with their Rebel counterparts while the rest of Richardson's division arrived. Meagher's Irish Brigade came first. It deployed north and south of the pike, taking cover behind the ridgeline east of the Middle Bridge, where Cross's skirmishers first saw the Confederate line of battle. Caldwell's and Brooke's brigades followed, and they extended the line north of the pike on Meagher's right. "We had arrived before their [the Confederate] line of battle was complete," penned a *New York Daily Tribune* correspondent who was present with the division. "Columns were moving and deploying in all directions and positions—almost all on open ground, or ground covered only with growing corn. As a spectacle it was magnificent. As an indication that the Rebels meant to fight on this side of the river, it was hailed with delight." Officers near the correspondent estimated that the enemy strength could "not be less than forty

The Middle Bridge in September 1862. The Joshua Newcomer farm sits on either side of the Boonsboro–Shepherdstown Pike. Confederate skirmishers used the buildings for cover during the September 15 skirmishing. The ridge west of Newcomer's is where Lee initially deployed some of his infantry on the 15th. Courtesy of the Library of Congress.

thousand troops—might be eighty thousand," evidence of how deceiving a display of troops could be.[81]

Richardson had no artillery, but the Confederate guns fell silent after their initial shelling of his troops, most likely because there were no observable targets. Pleasonton came up with elements of Farnsworth's brigade soon after Richardson had completed his deployment, having made a circuitous march to reach the Boonsboro Pike from the Williamsport Turnpike. Tidball's battery accompanied Pleasonton, and Richardson—as the ranking officer on the field—promptly appropriated it. Tidball recalled of Richardson: "His combative zeal being superior to his judgment, he insisted upon my placing my guns upon an eminence and opening upon the enemy." Tidball unlimbered his six 3-inch rifles on the bluff north of the pike, in front of Caldwell's and Brooke's brigades, and began his own fusillade. "This drew the fire from four different points of their line, which was all concentrated on my battery," reported Tidball. Thankfully the range was great enough that the Confederates were unable to do much damage. Tidball's horse artillerymen held their own, and they were reinforced shortly by Captain Rufus D. Pettit's Battery D, 1st New York Light Artillery, who brought six 10 lb. Parrott rifles into line on Battery A's right. Pettit's gunners fired nearly 400 rounds throughout the on-and-off artillery exchanges of the afternoon, but, for all the noise, no one inflicted much harm. S. D. Lee, whose guns engaged Pettit and Tidball, thought nothing was accomplished other than to force the Union infantry to take cover.[82]

Hooker arrived at the front around 2 p.m. and made his way to the bluffs north of the pike for a view of the enemy position. From what troops the enemy displayed, Hooker estimated their strength at between 30,000 and 40,000 men, far more than he wished to provoke until more Federal troops came up, so he ordered Pettit's and Tidball's guns to cease fire. Hooker's party, who remained mounted, drew the attention of some Confederate artillerymen, and they sent a shell sailing over the group's heads. "They are firing at us," Hooker remarked casually, without moving from where he was. A second shot, striking closer, confirmed Hooker's comment, but he continued his reconnaissance of the enemy position and for some reason drew no more fire. Hooker correctly deduced that the enemy "were drawn up and displayed for effect." Although Hooker reported to headquarters that the enemy's position "was not a formidable one," he considered it strong enough not to "attack him in front, even after the arrival of the First Corps," and to comment to General Richardson that there were Rebels "enough on those hills to have eaten up your command at a mouthful without tasting it."[83]

Sumner, riding ahead of his corps, joined Hooker around 3 p.m. and, after conducting his own reconnaissance, sent his dispatch to headquarters, asking whether he should attack or not. While he and Hooker waited for McClellan's reply, instead of massing the troops as they came up—which these generals had been ordered to do if the enemy made a stand—they halted the column along the road a short distance beyond Keedysville. This created a colossal traffic jam, stretching back to South Mountain. Lieutenant George Breck of Battery L, 1st New York Artillery, wrote that his 1st Corps battery "lay in the road all the forenoon, which was crowded with troops and wagons. The number of wagons in our army is immense, we were about to remark equal to the number of men, but not as bad as that." The 14th Connecticut of Sumner's 2nd Corps noted that it took them 11 hours to march the 5 miles from Turner's Gap to Keedysville. A *New York Daily Tribune* reporter who was there that afternoon thought that the flow of troops to the front "was unaccountably slow. The road was good, and the ground on both sides favorable for parallel columns, but yet no considerable force arrived till nearly dark." Colonel Adoniram Warner of the 10th Pennsylvania Reserves observed that the sluggish nature of the march, combined with rising afternoon temperatures, contributed to "much straggling—more than seemed fitting for a victorious army." Even a crack unit like Gibbon's brigade was not immune. A diarist in the 2nd Wisconsin recorded that the "fatigue of the two campaigns began to tell so severely upon the regiment and of those engaged at South Mountain that 1 officer and 41 men [more than a quarter of the regiment's strength] were compelled to fall out on account of exhaustion."[84]

For most men in the 1st, the 2nd, and the 12th Corps, the afternoon wore on monotonously as they stopped and started, and then stopped again, or were finally ordered to fall out along the roadside. Shortly after 5 p.m. those men strung out along the road between Keedysville and Boonsboro heard cheering "far to the rear." Francis W. Palfrey, the 31-year-old, Harvard-educated lieutenant colonel of the 20th Massachusetts, heard the cheering "faintly at first," but it grew into a roar as it neared his regiment. The men of the 8th Pennsylvania Reserves, who were halted in Keedysville, instantly knew for whom the troops were cheering. "'That's for McClellan!' exclaimed half a dozen of OUR BOYS, in a breath," wrote one member. So it was. McClellan's ride to the front from Boonsboro had a theatrical air to it, as if he were galloping onto a grand stage to play his part. And he was. As McClellan and his large staff swept down the turnpike, the soldiers who filled the sides of the road leaped to their feet and cheered him wildly. "Such a magnificent reception as was worth living for," wrote Palfrey. On September 15, 1862, the Army of the Potomac still retained some of the innocence and enthusiastic ideals of 1861, and South Mountain upheld the boundless confidence they placed in McClellan. That September afternoon's victory still danced gloriously in the air, the end seemed in sight, and the man who, in their eyes, had delivered this all was riding to the front, waving his hat and brimming with confidence. But they would never cheer him again with the feeling they did that day. What would come in the next three days would forever dim their starry-eyed idealism. Most of them would still love McClellan and cheer him when he passed, but the army would mature on the banks of Antietam Creek; they would come to understand that the road ahead would be hard and bloody, and that their beloved general might not be the man they would follow to ultimate victory.[85]

McClellan gloried in the reception he received, but he wondered why the troops were halted along the pike instead of being massed near the front, as he had ordered. Sumner met McClellan near Keedysville and led him to the vantage point where Sumner and Hooker had previously studied the Confederate position, which was probably near the Philip Pry farm. McClellan's large staff accompanied him, as everyone was curious for a look at the Rebel position; they were soon joined by Hooker, Fitz John Porter, Burnside, Cox, and many other lesser officers. "We made a large group as we stood upon the hill," wrote Cox, "and it was not long before we attracted the enemy's attention." A puff of smoke drifted away from the muzzle of a Confederate cannon, and moments later a shell hurtled over the group. McClellan ordered everyone except Fitz John Porter to retire behind the hill for cover. He and Porter remained on the hill alone for a full 30 minutes, studying the Confederate positions and the landscape, while enemy shells whizzed by "in nervous proximity." McClellan's

coolness under fire impressed Cox, but ordering his two former wing commanders off the ridge while he kept Porter with him struck others as im-
proper, as well as a deliberate slight to the officers he shooed off. Surely it did
nothing to enhance the army's unity of command. Hooker concluded that
"should McClellan listen to the advice of Fitz John Porter," there would be no
offensive action that day.[86]

By the time McClellan and Porter completed their reconnaissance it was
just after 5:30 p.m., about a half hour before sunset. With the bulk of the army
strung out along the roads between Keedysville and South Mountain, even had
McClellan been inclined to attack—which he was not—there was not sufficient
time or daylight left to organize an offensive effort. "The first rapid survey of
the enemy's position inclined me to attack his left, but the day was far gone,"
McClellan wrote later. Hooker may have been the one to urge the movement on
the Confederate left. He had earlier sent Major David C. Houston, an engineer
officer on his staff, north along Antietam Creek to scout for fords or bridges.
Houston returned to report that there were two practicable fords, both of
which needed work on their banks to be usable, as well as a bridge a short distance north of the Samuel Pry farm and mill. But even the aggressive Hooker
agreed with McClellan that the day was too far gone to attempt any offensive
operations "without a night march through a country of which we were profoundly ignorant."[87]

McClellan gave orders that the corps should be massed and positions found
to locate batteries that could engage the Confederate guns. Hooker's 1st Corps
were ordered across the Little Antietam and bivouacked near the forks of the
Little and Big Antietam, not far from the Upper Bridge. French's and Sedgwick's divisions of Sumner's 2nd Corps formed in the rear of Richardson, with
Sedgwick north and French south of the pike. Mansfield's 12th Corps bivouacked around Nicodemus Mill, approximately 2 miles southeast of Keedysville. Sykes's division reached Porterstown about 5:30 p.m. Sykes sent Captain
John D. Wilkins's 3rd U.S. forward as skirmishers along the Boonsboro Pike to
relieve the 5th New Hampshire's skirmishers and secure the Middle Bridge over
Antietam Creek. They traded shots with the Confederate skirmishers holding
the Newcomer farm—who may still have been Major Sellers's band from Hood's
division—but after a sharp exchange of musketry the Southerners, whose mission was certainly only to harass and annoy the enemy, not hold the bridge,
withdrew and Wilkins's men dashed across and secured a bridgehead on the
Antietam's west bank.[88]

The balance of Sykes's division camped around Porterstown, protected by
the steep hills overlooking the east bank of the creek. The 9th Corps, arriving
later in the evening, bivouacked nearby, to Sykes's left rear. Moving the various
corps into their respective bivouacs after sunset and bringing up the reserve
artillery and ammunition trains consumed the entire night, and McClellan

reported that "the corps were not all in their positions until the next morning after sunrise." Pleasonton's cavalry, still consisting only of Farnsworth's brigade, did nothing in the final hours of daylight. McClellan briefly considered sending them—with some horse artillery—to Jones' Crossroads on the Hagerstown–Sharpsburg Turnpike, presumably to block this road to Confederate movement, but he decided against detaching his only cavalry force. Later in the night he learned that a detachment of 300 men of the 15th Pennsylvania Cavalry, under Captain William J. Palmer, had moved through Hagerstown to the crossroads, and that 1,300 cavalry of the Harpers Ferry garrison had escaped and ridden to Greencastle, Pennsylvania. McClellan sent orders for these troops to reinforce Palmer. Retaining Farnsworth's brigade with the main army made sense, but McClellan did not put them to work. Instead of dispatching them to probe the Confederate position and gather information about roads, bridges and fords, they were allowed to bivouac in the rear of the 2nd Corps.[89]

By 9 p.m. McClellan had confirmation that Harpers Ferry had surrendered. Men of Couch's division captured an aide of Jeb Stuart's, bearing a message from Jackson to Lee reporting that the Union garrison had surrendered at 9:30 a.m. that morning. The prisoner was taken before Franklin for questioning, and the general sent this officer under escort to McClellan that afternoon. The import of this news was clear, even to the *New York Daily Tribune* reporter, who learned the details through headquarters staff. "It releases 30,000 Rebel soldiers who will probably re-enforce the army in front of us," the journalist wrote. During the afternoon, clouds of dust were seen in the rear of the Confederate lines, and some were of the opinion that it was raised by retreating Confederate troops. But it might also have been from reinforcements arriving from Harpers Ferry. Apparently McClellan thought this plausible, for later that night he told Captain William J. Palmer, who was also acting as the chief scout for Pennsylvania Governor Curtain, that he thought Jackson had reinforced Lee that night. But McClellan certainly knew that this could not be the full enemy force that had besieged Harpers Ferry, for Franklin had reported at 3:15 p.m. that the enemy confronting him in Pleasant Valley were only then starting to withdraw. Those troops could not possibly reach Sharpsburg before sometime on September 16. But the clock was ticking. Every hour of delay allowed the enemy to recover from their defeat at South Mountain, perfect their defenses, and grow stronger through reinforcements from Harpers Ferry.[90]

If the enemy were withdrawing from Franklin's front, logic dictated there were two likely moves they—and the rest of the Confederate Harpers Ferry force—would make. The least probable would be to reinforce Lee by advancing along the Harpers Ferry–Sharpsburg Road. Although this was the shortest route to Sharpsburg, a force marching along it could easily be bottled up between the Potomac River and Elk Ridge, and the road was not a good one. It was more likely that the enemy would march to Shepherdstown, using the river to screen their movements, and then press on to Sharpsburg, if Lee did intend to make a stand there. But would Lee make a stand? McClellan's earlier confidence that Lee would retreat to Shepherdstown, founded on the report that his wagon trains were crossing to the Virginia shore, faded before the sturdy front the Confederates displayed across Antietam Creek. Yet it defied military logic that Lee would offer battle with a river at his back that had only a single ford. Prudence dictated that Lee would use the cover of night to complete his withdrawal from Maryland, but McClellan knew from the Peninsula that Lee could defy military convention. McClellan intended to ready his forces for either possibility.

But what should he do about Franklin? McClellan's final decision is puzzling. Although earlier Franklin had reported that the enemy was retreating in his front, so fast, in fact, that General William F. "Baldy" Smith's division could not catch them, McClellan was content to retain the 6th Corps in Pleasant Valley. At 4:30 p.m. he ordered Franklin to withdraw Couch's brigades at Rohrersville and have them join the rest of Franklin's corps near Brownsville. McClellan would be "satisfied if you keep the enemy in your front without anything decisive until the Sharpsburg affair is settled, when he [McClellan] will at once move troops directly to your assistance." Yet if the enemy were withdrawing from Franklin's front, what was the point of retaining three divisions in Pleasant Valley with orders to essentially sit on their hands? If Lee did intend to make a stand at Sharpsburg, then it stood the reason that he would concentrate his force there. McClellan's choice of what to do with Franklin's troops was an excessively cautious decision. Retaining a covering force to protect his communications with Frederick against a Confederate raid was sensible; keeping the entire 6th Corps in the Valley was not.[91]

At 9 p.m. McClellan wrote to Franklin again, informing him that the enemy had made a stand "in considerable force" at Sharpsburg and that "a reconnaissance will be made at daylight, and if he is found to be in position, he will be attacked." There is no evidence that McClellan had any specific plan in mind if the enemy remained, but he did direct Sumner—and probably the other corps commanders as well—to make a report at daylight on "everything that has happened during the night"; to send out reconnoitering parties "at daylight to ascertain if there is any enemy in your front, his strength, etc"; and to hold their commands "in readiness to attack the enemy early in the morning should he be found in our front at that time." An early morning attack was unlikely, given the unsettled state of the Federal army, with troops and equipment coming up all night, as well as the lack of knowledge of the enemy position and the approaches to it. But observing the hum of activity and the massing of Union muscle all about convinced the *New York Daily Tribune* correspondent that they were on the precipice of action. "A battle to-morrow is certain," he wrote, "unless the Rebels retreat. If they fight, it must be the greatest battle of the war."[92]

The Confederates *would* fight, for by sunset Lee had made up his mind to stand and offer battle at Sharpsburg. Even Lee's admirers have questioned this decision. Historian John C. Ropes called it "beyond controversy one of the boldest and most hazardous decision in his whole military career. It is in truth so bold and hazardous that one is bewildered that he should even have thought seriously of making it." Lee's chief of ordnance, Lieutenant Colonel Edward P. Alexander, later declared: "I think, it will be pronounced by military critics to be the greatest military blunder that Gen. Lee ever made." Lee had to expect that McClellan would attack on September 16. Yet during the afternoon of the 15th, William A. Owen of the Washington Artillery heard Lee express "his belief that there would not be much fighting on the morrow." Lee probably came to this conclusion for two reasons: first, the slow concentration of the Army of the Potomac across the Antietam; and second, its lack of aggressiveness. Other than seizing the Middle Bridge, which Lee never intended to contest to any great degree, the Federals neither probed nor reconnoitered anywhere else along his front. Lee could not read McClellan's mind, and the latter had surprised him at South Mountain, but Lee did know that the Pennsylvanian was a deliberate commander. There would be no hasty morning attack. McClellan would spend the morning of the 16th scrutinizing and assessing the Confederate position before attacking. But even if McClellan gave Lee until the afternoon of the 16th, the best Lee could hope for was that Jackson, with his two divisions and Walker's division, would be up by then. This would give Lee six of his nine divisions. The others three—Hill's, McLaws's, and R. H. Anderson's—could not arrive until later on the 16th, and perhaps not until the 17th. McClellan, Lee knew, had his entire army on hand, except for the 6th Corps. If McClellan attacked, in Lieutenant Colonel Alexander's opinion "a drawn battle . . . was the best *possible* outcome we could hope for!"[93]

If retreat became necessary, negotiating Boteler's Ford at Shepherdstown under pressure from the Army of the Potomac might spell the end of the Army of Northern Virginia. Lieutenant Colonel Alexander thought so, for he wrote: "A defeat would certainly involve the utter destruction of his [Lee's] army." The ford was rocky and deep, and high ground on the Maryland side offered numerous positions for the Federals' excellent rifled pieces to keep it under constant artillery fire. "This single feature of the field should have been conclusive against giving battle there," Alexander continued. "I believe that Lee would never have done so, had he ever before crossed the ford in person." Perhaps, but it is inconceivable that Lee did not have his engineers scout the ford on the 15th, when he was still contemplating a retreat, and report on its condition. Lee also took the precaution of having Pendleton place a battalion of reserve artillery to cover the ford from the Virginia side. What is more likely is that Lee acknowledged the peril the ford presented to his decision to stand at Sharpsburg, and that he made his choice to remain there in spite of it. Henry Kyd Douglas wrote in 1898 that "all battles are not fought in positions selected upon sound military principles. Wellington, Napoleon & Lee were all perfectly familiar with these principles and when they disregarded them they had strong reasons for doing so."[94] The question, then—which soldiers and historians have asked since that day—is, What were Lee's reasons for casting prudent military logic to the wind?

Unless some long-lost collection of papers in uncovered that contains Lee's rationale, the answer to this puzzle can only be an educated guess. We know that Jackson agreed with Lee's choice, for in an 1866 letter to Jackson's widow, Lee wrote that when Jackson arrived on the field "and learned my reasons for offering battle, he emphatically concurred with me."[95] But this also implies that Jackson initially questioned the wisdom of taking a stand at Sharpsburg. Lee was an opportunist, and this characteristic offers some plausible insight into his decision. Only by remaining in Maryland could Lee regain the initiative. If McClellan attacked and was defeated, or if he withdrew into a defensive position, then the Confederate campaign of maneuver into Pennsylvania might be continued. The capture of Harpers Ferry secured Lee's line of communications, and the depot at Winchester had been established with thousands of stragglers, convalescents, and conscripts assembled there, who could reinforce the Confederate army. From the Sharpsburg bridgehead, Lee could strike north along the Hagerstown Pike to Hagerstown, and then into the Cumberland Valley of Pennsylvania. McClellan would be forced to follow, and thus would be drawn farther from the fortifications of Washington and from reinforcements. Withdrawal to Virginia, the safe move, surrendered the initiative to the enemy, and it was unlikely that McClellan would not quickly guard every Potomac ford from Boteler's to Williamsport. It was only a matter of days before the Federals would reoccupy Harpers Ferry, compelling Lee to fall back up the Shenandoah Valley.

There was also the proclamation Lee made to the people of Maryland. Had the Southern army departed from Sharpsburg on the night of September 15, its words would ring hollow, and any hope of mobilizing the sympathetic element in the state would almost certainly be lost. Henry Kyd Douglas believed that by his proclamation Lee "almost pledged not to give up the state without a struggle." E. P. Alexander also thought that this declaration played a role in Lee's thought processes: "In his decision to stand his ground and fight, his attitude as a deliverer probably had a large share." Perhaps, but it is doubtful that Lee risked his army for honor's sake. Lee played for far larger stakes than the tenuous support of Marylanders' hearts and minds.[96]

Whatever reasons Lee had in making his decision to stand and fight, he was building sand castles. The combination of the physical condition of his army, a broken commissariat, and shaky logistical support inhibited his ability to exploit any repulse of the Army of the Potomac. Lee himself admitted this in his report on the campaign. Alexander wrote: "Briefly, Lee took a great risk for no chance of gain except the killing of some thousands of his enemy with the loss of, perhaps, two-thirds as many of his own men." That, noted Colonel Alexander, was a losing game for the Confederacy. But Lee had audaciously cast the die, and, if his will prevailed, then the grim and bloody climax of the Maryland Campaign would be settled beside the tranquil waters of Antietam Creek.[97]

16

The Trap Closes and a Cavalry Dash

"The fate of Harper's Ferry was sealed"

While the drama at South Mountain unfolded on September 14 and 15, Stonewall Jackson methodically and carefully closed, and then tightened, the Confederate death grip on the Union garrison at Harpers Ferry. Jackson's command spent the night of September 12 near Martinsburg, after flushing General Julius White's Federal garrison and sending it scurrying for the shelter of Harpers Ferry. At 4:30 a.m. the following morning Jackson resumed the march, with A. P. Hill's division in the lead. The column passed through Martinsburg at daylight and took the road toward Harpers Ferry. It was an unpleasant march (there were not many that were otherwise for the Confederates in the Maryland Campaign). As Captain Andrew B. Wardlaw, a commissary officer in Gregg's brigade observed, "water was very scarce on our route today & not good." At around 11 a.m. the head of the column approached the village of Halltown, about 2 miles west of the Union position on Bolivar Heights, where they encountered Federal pickets who quickly withdrew when Hill advanced a skirmish line. The area around Halltown offered a clear view of Bolivar Heights, and one of Gregg's men could see "the white lines of the enemy's tents." Captain Wardlaw jotted down in his diary that the Yankees "could be plainly seen with the naked eye drawn up in line of battle, & the gaping mouths of their cannon looked down threateningly upon us."[1]

A. P. Hill bivouacked his division just south of Halltown, while Lawton's encamped a mile north of the village, and J. R. Jones's was about 2 miles from Halltown on the road to Martinsburg, where his division formed Jackson's reserve. These movements drew some fire from the Union gunners on Bolivar Heights, but Sergeant Samuel Buck of the 13th Virginia Infantry recalled that they "did us no damage." Jackson made no response to the Federals' shots. His first concern was to learn whether McLaws and Walker were in place. Jackson searched both Maryland Heights and Loudoun Heights with a telescope, but he could not determine whether Confederates held either. The sound of fighting on Maryland Heights may have been audible; certainly the smoke from the engagement there was. Jackson summoned his signal officer, Captain Joseph L. Bartlett, and directed him to attempt to open communications by signal.

Bartlett tried but raised no response. Jackson then had no choice but to employ the more time-consuming method of couriers, each of whom had to ford a river to reach their respective destinations. To communicate with Walker, Jackson sent his topographical engineer, Jedediah Hotchkiss, and two other engineers, First Lieutenant Thomas T. L. Snead and Second Lieutenant W. G. Williamson. Hotchkiss was also ordered to help Walker establish a signal station on Loudoun Heights, while Snead and Williamson were to assist Walker in selecting positions for his artillery. Jackson appears to have been less concerned about McLaws, to whom he sent only a single courier.[2]

While Jackson waited for reports from Walker and McLaws, he used the time to make a reconnaissance of the enemy position and the approaches to Harpers Ferry. "The enemy had, by fortifications, strengthened the naturally strong position which he occupied along Bolivar Heights," Jackson reported, but he also saw that except for skirmishers, the Union line did not extend south of the Charlestown Pike into the rough, gullied terrain that led to the Shenandoah River. He certainly noted with both surprise and satisfaction that the Union commander had failed to cut down the woods on Bolivar Heights, which could provide Jackson's troops with cover should an assault become necessary.[3]

By midafternoon the distant crackle of musketry and the ribbon of smoke rising above the forest on Maryland Heights indicated that McLaws was endeavoring to gain possession of that point. Shortly after 4 p.m. a signal party from Walker's division, possibly including Hotchkiss, Snead, and Williamson, ascended Loudoun Heights and attempted to establish a station near its summit. Their activity elicited a reaction from Captain Graham's 5th New York Heavy Artillery, with its 20 lb. Parrott rifles on Camp Hill, who fired several shells at the Confederates and sent everyone scurrying for cover. But the shelling alerted Jackson to the fact that that Walker had arrived on Loudoun Heights.[4] During the night Jackson heard from both Walker and McLaws. Both had good news to report. In Walker's case he had found Loudoun Heights unoccupied by the enemy, and McLaws's advance had captured the "main heights" on Maryland Heights. The pieces were in place—albeit a day behind schedule—and now it was Jackson's task to coordinate the widely separated forces and bring the enemy to its knees.[5]

A feeling of foreboding settled on the Union garrison during the night of September 13. Nicholas DeGraff, who returned late that afternoon from the debacle on Maryland Heights with the 115th New York, recorded the emotions many felt: "Night closed in around us and found a sad company. We have accomplished nothing we know not how much we have lost or what the situation is we cannot tell." A *New York Times* reporter, trapped with the garrison, penned: "Every body retired that night, feeling that **all was lost unless reinforcements arrived**, and expected to be awoke on the morrow with the booming of artillery from the evacuated heights." The implications of Jackson's arrival and the loss of both Loudoun Heights and Maryland Heights did not sink in for some of the more inexperienced soldiers. A member of the 9th Vermont recalled that he and his comrades had no real concern about the Confederate activity they had observed on Loudoun Heights, "for it had been repeated over and over again that it was not in the range of human possibilities to get guns up those almost inaccessible heights; so we laughed at their misspent exertions."[6]

None of the senior Union commanders were laughing. They knew they were bottled up. All the key terrain, except Bolivar Heights, was in enemy hands; they had no real idea of where the Army of the Potomac was; and ammunition supplies for their long-range artillery were dwindling. Their situation was desperate. The one hope the garrison had to escape certain surrender was the Army of the Potomac. Colonel Miles had ordered Captain Russell and six of his men to slip through enemy lines after dark, find the army, and communicate Miles's grim estimate that the garrison could only hold out another 48 hours. Colonel Grimes Davis saw no reason for the cavalry to remain trapped with the infantry and artillery and share their highly probable fate. The cavalry lacked training in fighting dismounted, and Davis knew that the "horses and equipment would be of great value to the enemy if captured." He shared his thoughts with Lieutenant Colonel Hasbrouck Davis, commander of the 12th Illinois Cavalry, whom he found of like mind. Both men sought out General Julius White, the acting cavalry commander, and proposed that the cavalry be permitted to cut its way out of the trap and make contact with McClellan. White agreed to their plan and, perhaps knowing he would need all the support he could muster to persuade Miles, took the two colonels along with him to the garrison commander's headquarters to discuss the matter.[7]

The ensuing discussion considered the topic of whether the entire garrison, and not just the cavalry, should attempt to break out. Miles rejected this idea for two reasons: first, his orders did not permit him to evacuate the post; and second, the infantry and artillery would not be able to keep up with the cavalry. Miles had little enthusiasm for a cavalry-only breakout either, thinking a movement, at night, of a large column of horsemen with imprecise knowledge of enemy dispositions was both impracticable and fraught with tremendous risk. White allowed Grimes Davis to carry the argument further, and Davis pressed it passionately. "After some hesitation and sharp words," Davis wrested an agreement from Miles to issue the necessary orders for the cavalry to make the breakout attempt the following night, September 14. The question then turned to which route the column should attempt. Davis favored marching up the west bank of the Potomac as far as Kearneysville and then crossing the river at Shepherdstown, probably because it went through country his regiment had operated in and with which he himself was more familiar. Miles disapproved, sensing that there was "extreme danger in their going that way." Instead, it was agreed that the column would stand a better chance of escaping detection if they

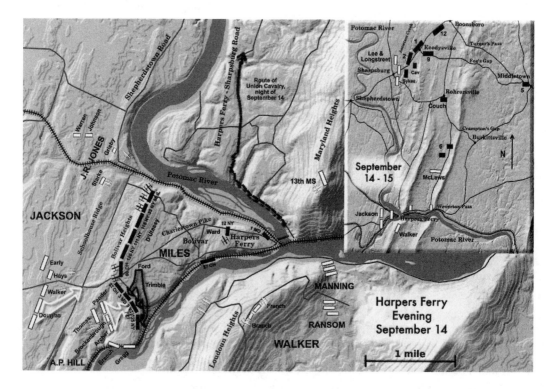

crossed the Shenandoah River at a point about a half mile upstream from its
junction with the Potomac and then strike east for Washington.[8]

One member of the Union garrison remembered that Sunday, September
14, "broke as bright and beautiful as could be wished." Except for some elements of Jackson's command in position west of Bolivar Heights, no enemy
soldiers were visible. The loss of Maryland Heights meant that those regiments
detached from the Bolivar Heights line had returned to their old positions.
With these troops back, over 5,700 infantry in Trimble's and D'Utassy's brigades occupied Bolivar Heights, stretching from the Charlestown Pike to the
northern end of the Heights, overlooking the Potomac—a distance of approximately 1 mile. They were supported by 19 guns of Rigby's, Von Sehlen's, Phillips's, and Graham's batteries. Three regiments bivouacked on the open ground
east of Bolivar Heights, as a support to the main line holding the Heights:
the 9th Vermont, the 32nd Ohio, and the 125th New York (from left to right),
just over 2,400 men in all. Miles allotted only one regiment—one of his smallest, Lieutenant Colonel Stephen Downey's 3rd Maryland Potomac Home Brigade, about 500 strong—to defend the three-quarters of a mile of rugged
ground between the Charlestown Pike and the Shenandoah River. The remaining guns of Graham's battery—two sections of Potts's battery—supported
by the unhappy 12th New York State Militia, manned the interior line of defense at Camp Hill. The vital bridges over the Potomac were guarded by the 1st

Maryland Potomac Home Brigade, the 87th Ohio, and the third section of Potts's battery.[9]

Miles's neglect of the defenses on Bolivar Heights was now keenly felt. During the night of the 13th the men of D'Utassy's brigade made efforts to improve them by felling trees on the west side of Bolivar Heights in order to create some obstacles to an enemy advance, and slight works were thrown up to protect the batteries on the right of the line. Apart from these modest efforts, the troops, in the words of the 126th New York's historian, "were entirely unprotected and shelterless."[10]

Numerous officers were deeply concerned about the length of the line Miles wished to defend on the western front. Colonel Trimble testified that he and others suggested to the colonel that the position "was so long a line, that I did not see how we could defend it, unless there was some effort made to give an advantage by throwing up breastworks and making rifle pits from the Charlestown Pike to the Shenandoah and Bolivar Heights." General White also visited Miles to recommend that they contract the line by pulling the part of the line that was south of the Charlestown Pike back to a deep ravine nearly a quarter mile east of Bolivar Heights, through which a road ran from the pike to the Shenandoah River. Miles's aide, Lieutenant Binney, recalled that White expressed the opinion that "our lines were too extended; that he thought by contracting the lines it would make the place more defensible in the case of an assault." This was what Rufus Saxton had done when Jackson threatened Harpers Ferry in the spring, but that time Jackson did not have possession of Maryland Heights and Loudoun Heights. Miles declined White's suggestion, pointing out that if he pulled the line back to the ravine the enemy could enfilade it if they placed a battery on the plateau below Loudoun Heights. Miles remained stubbornly committed to defending the Bolivar Heights line. It might have been his best option at this point, for the goal now was not to fight the enemy off, but to survive long enough to be relieved. Nonetheless, for a regular-army officer of long experience, Miles's failure to use every minute Jackson granted him to fortify and strengthen the Bolivar Heights line, clear fields of fire, and throw up any kind of obstruction in the way of the enemy was egregious.[11]

As the morning advanced, Nicholas DeGraff observed Confederate soldiers "busily occupied about something" on Loudon Heights. Captain E. H. Ripley of the 9th Vermont saw them, too, "working like beavers in batteries in two places." Colonel Cameron, commanding the 65th Illinois, also watched the activity and inquired of Colonel Miles what it meant. Incredibly, Miles responded that he did not know. Cameron expressed the opinion that the Rebels were establishing batteries, and that "we would very soon hear from them." But Miles refused to believe the enemy could haul guns up the mountain that were of heavy enough caliber to do any damage.[12]

A signal flag appeared on Loudoun Heights around 8 a.m. Captain Graham, on Camp Hill, immediately ordered his rifled guns to open fire. "We watched them uneasily as our shell crawled slowly up toward them, but never seeming to reach them," wrote Captain Ripley, "and asked each other anxiously can it be possible that they have succeeded in dragging guns up there?" Graham's fireworks burst near enough to cause Walker's signalmen to fold up their flags and withdraw to the cover of the woods, but the shelling did not dissuade Walker's artillerymen, who stubbornly continued to prepare positions for their guns. At all other points the Confederates remained quiet and out of sight, something a *Boston Evening Transcript* correspondent, trapped with the garrison, found to be oppressive: "In my thoughts I could hear them saying: 'Fire away down there, you don't disturb us. By and by our time will come.' "[13]

The continued Confederate activity on Loudon Heights prompted some Federal troops to decide on their own that it might be prudent to build up whatever cover they could. Around 10:30 a.m. men of the 9th Vermont, the 126th New York, and Rigby's battery set to work and "constructed a rude work of logs and earth, stuffing in tents, clothing, army blankets, anything that would break the force of a ball; and dug a sort of trench or line of rifle pits." But apart from this isolated burst of activity, little or nothing was done to prepare for the storm that many sensed would soon break over the garrison. Some units marched to their camps for the noon meal, or lounged about watching Graham's guns shelling Loudoun Heights. The 125th New York gathered for a worship service on the "open plain" east of Bolivar Heights, where the regiment's tents were set up.[14]

Colonel Daniel Cameron, the Scotsman commanding the 65th Illinois, was one of the few officers to suggest something aggressive. He thought that the four 12 lb. brass guns that were abandoned at the naval battery position on Maryland Heights during the evacuation on the 13th might be of good use if they were still serviceable and could be retrieved. He requested permission from his brigade commander, Colonel D'Utassy, to attempt this. The Hungarian agreed, but only if Miles would consent to the operation. Cameron asked if D'Utassy would make the request. D'Utassy did, and, by his account—which must be read with one eyebrow raised in disbelief—Miles told him that the guns were spiked and that it was no use making an effort to retrieve them. According to D'Utassy, he ignored Miles's response and assumed responsibility for leading four companies over to Maryland Heights to recover the guns. This was partly true; four companies did undertake the operation, but D'Utassy did not accompany them. Irrespective of whether it was D'Utassy or Miles who authorized it, Colonel Cameron was the one who received orders to go to Maryland Heights and, in keeping with the odd system of conducting operations with mixed commands, was directed to take two companies from his 65th Illinois and two from the 39th New York. Leadership of the expedition went not to Cameron but to his major, John Wood. The detachment assembled and set out about noon, accompanied by a wagon. Captain George H. Kennedy, also of the 65th—whose company had lost their tents, probably in the retreat from Martinsburg—asked if he could bring it along to pick up the tents retreating troops had left behind at the battery the previous day. The group ascended the mountain without incident, but they encountered a few Confederate skirmishers near the battery, who were easily driven off. The bronze guns were still there. Two were properly spiked, and two merely had a nail driven into the vent. The detachment also discovered a large quantity of artillery ammunition and concluded that it, rather than tents, should fill Captain Kennedy's wagon. They piled what they could in the vehicle and, according to Cameron, "could have loaded a great many more wagons" with what they found. Nor were the men disturbed by the enemy during the entire time they were at the naval battery site. When they had filled the wagon, they marched back to Harpers Ferry with it and the four brass guns in tow. This successful little expedition spoke to what initiative can gain. But it would be one of the few bright moments in what would be an otherwise depressing day for the Union garrison.[15]

The Confederates, meanwhile, were working industriously to put the firepower in place that would seal the fate of the Federal troops. At dawn General Walker started three 10 lb. Parrott rifles of Captain Thomas B. French's (Virginia) Battery and two 3-inch rifles, under the direction of Lieutenant M. A. Martin from Captain J. R. Branch's battery, up Loudoun Heights. The ascent was difficult, for the guns had to be hauled up by hand, and Walker later stated that he had these rifles in a masked position on the mountain by 8 a.m. This might be true, but Walker did not signal Jackson until 10:30 a.m. to report that his guns were in place and to ask whether he should wait for McLaws's to be set up before opening fire. "Wait," Jackson replied.[16]

Getting artillery into position on Maryland Heights proved to be a formidable engineering problem for McLaws. His engineers examined the mountain on September 13, after the Federals retreated, to determine the practicality of cutting a road to haul guns up the Heights. They found a steep ascent with numerous rock walls that could neither be turned nor passed without more time, tools, and equipment than were available. By pure luck, when McLaws's quartermaster, Major Abram H. McLaws (his brother and a Mexican War veteran), was making his way down the mountain to headquarters after visiting Kershaw's brigade, he discovered an old wood road by which guns could be hauled partway up the mountain. The rest of the ascent would have to be accomplished by muscle and sweat. During the night and into the morning, McLaws set details, under his brother's supervision, laboring to improve the old road. By 9 a.m. on the 14th, Major McLaws reported that the road was open as far as the ground Kershaw had captured in the fighting the previous day. But with this good news came bad. The major had discovered that the route from Kershaw's position south to the summit of the mountain was "heavily blockaded," evidently by obstacles placed there by the Federals. While the major's fatigue parties attacked this new problem, four rifled guns (three 10 lb. Parrotts and one 3-inch rifle) from Read's and Carlton's batteries started the slow ascent up the wood road. When they reached the point where it was too steep for horses to move the guns, the wheels were removed from the carriages and each piece was "lifted or pulled by long ropes to the desired position, when the guns would again be mounted." Infantrymen and artillerymen worked side by side. It was hard labor, but, wrote a prideful Mississippian, "there was no faint-heartedness among the men." Yet no amount of manpower could speed the process up, and it consumed the entire morning.[17]

On Jackson's front his signalmen continued the efforts of the previous evening to establish communications with Walker and McLaws, so Jackson could coordinate his plan to bring simultaneous artillery fire on the Federals from three directions. Captain Bartlett had his signal flag "up at daylight, and my glass bearing on Loudoun Heights after sunrise." He contacted Walker's station, but repeated efforts to raise McLaws's signal station on Maryland Heights were unsuccessful. By 7:20 a.m. Jackson lost patience with the effort and wrote out a dispatch to the Georgian, outlining his intentions.[18]

> I desire you to move forward until you get complete possession of Maryland Height[s] . . . So soon as you get your batteries all planted, let me know, as I desire, after yourself, Walker and myself have our batteries ready to open, to send a flag of truce, for the purpose of getting out the noncombatants, should the commanding officer refuse to surrender. Should we have to attack, let the work be done thoroughly; fire on the houses when necessary. The citizens can keep out of harms' way from your artillery. Demolish the place if it is occupied by the enemy, and does not surrender . . . The position in front of me is a strong one, and I desire to remain quiet, and let you and Walker draw attention from Furnace Hill [high ground west of the north end of Bolivar Heights], so that I may have the opportunity of getting possession of the hill without much loss.[19]

Jackson had devised a methodical plan to reduce the enemy garrison, which was a coordinated bombardment from three directions: his line along Schoolhouse Ridge, Walker on Loudoun Heights, and McLaws on Maryland Heights. Jackson knew the enemy would be unable to effectively respond to Walker or McLaws, due to the height advantage the Confederates enjoyed. Because of the range, Jackson knew the bombardment could not destroy the Union positions, but it would demoralize the defenders and pin them down. While the guns kept the enemy in place, Jackson intended to maneuver his infantry to seize ground on the flank of Bolivar Heights. If all went well, the combination of artillery fire and maneuver would force the enemy to surrender, saving the blood of Jackson's infantry. Time, as far as he knew, was not an issue. There had been no warning about McClellan from Lee or anyone else; hence there was no reason for Jackson to unnecessarily expose his infantry.

When the enemy's attention turned to Walker on Loudoun Heights, Jackson moved to secure Furnace Hill, dispatching Grigsby's Stonewall Brigade. This locale not only provided an excellent firing position for artillery, but also discouraged enemy movement along the Shepherdstown Pike. Grigsby's men chased off some Federal cavalry and occupied the position without loss. Soon after, Poague's and Carpenter's batteries (three 10 lb. Parrott rifles, three 3-inch ordnance rifles, and two Napoleons), moved into position there. A signal message from Walker at 10:30 a.m. stating that he was ready to fire brought Jackson back to Captain Bartlett's station. Jackson had still not heard from McLaws, whose guns on Maryland Heights were vital to the success of his plan. "I have never seen Jackson exhibit the least impatience before, but it was unmistakable to me that he was greatly worried at the delay, then inexplicable, in occupying Maryland Heights," wrote his volunteer aide-de-camp, Colonel Samuel B. French. Characteristically, Jackson forged ahead despite his worries, dictating a 130-word order for Captain Bartlett to signal to both Walker and McLaws. In substance, the message said that Jackson desired Walker's and McLaws's guns to help drive the Federals from Bolivar Heights, but not to commence firing until everyone was ready. "I will let you know when to open all the batteries," he directed. However, Jackson did permit either officer to open fire "if you should find it necessary, of which you must judge for yourself," a point that would shortly become important. He also cautioned both officers to remain vigilant against a Union advance on their rear. Jackson had probably received Lee's dispatch (sent on the night of September 13), alerting him to a possible Union advance east of South Mountain, sometime during the morning of the 14th. Most likely this is what prompted Jackson's warning, as well as what changed his mind about delaying his attack by sending a flag of truce into Harpers Ferry; there is no mention of the latter in the long signal message.[20]

It took a considerable amount of time to send an order of this length, and Jackson rode off to his left while it was being transmitted. Contact with McLaws continued to be a problem, and Bartlett could not determine whether the Georgian had received the order. The difficulty of communicating with McLaws by signal was twofold. First, McLaws's signal officer had taken ill, and Lieutenant Duncan G. Campbell, an engineer on the division's staff, had assumed these duties. How proficient Campbell was in reading signal messages is unknown, but it is unlikely that he had had the experience of the regular officer. Second, the smoke rising from the Federal guns shelling Loudoun Heights, and possibly also from fires lit to prepare the noon meal for the Federal garrison, might have obscured sight lines to Maryland Heights. But Lieutenant Campbell did manage to make contact with Walker's station on Loudoun Heights. Sometime after noon he signaled Walker with the news that enemy forces were threatening McLaws's rear. Walker immediately passed this information on to Jackson, adding that he was ready to open fire. At Jackson's signal station, Bartlett had unaccountably been left without any couriers, so he had to ride off in person to hunt down Jackson and deliver Walker's message. Jackson remained determined to deliver a coordinated bombardment, so he again denied Walker permission to open fire and ordered Bartlett to continue his efforts to communicate with McLaws. Jackson also left Lieutenant Henry K. Douglas with the captain to serve as a courier, if needed.[21]

After this interruption, when Bartlett had finished transmitting the 130-word order to Walker and McLaws, Jackson then had a 150-word operational order ready to be sent. This detailed the mission of each command. McLaws's guns were to take the Union batteries on Bolivar Heights in reverse, "and otherwise operate against him, as circumstances may justify." Walker's guns would overcome Rigby's battery on the Charleston Pike in reverse, silence a battery believed to be located on an island in the Shenandoah River, and otherwise sweep the Union position with fire. Each of Jackson's infantry divisions had an important role in his plan. He entrusted the primary element of the maneuver to his largest division and most aggressive commander, A. P. Hill. Hill's six brigades were ordered to move along the left (north) bank of the Shenandoah River, turn the Union flank, and "enter Harper's Ferry." They would be supported by Lawton's division, which would advance along the Charleston Pike—not with the intention to attack, but rather to pin the enemy in place on Bolivar Heights and prevent them from shifting troops against Hill. While Lawton demonstrated against the front of Bolivar Heights, Jackson ordered General John R. Jones to demonstrate against the Federal right with one of his four brigades and one battery—a force sufficient to keep the enemy in place, but still enable Jackson to retain the balance of Jones's division as a reserve. Jackson had seven batteries deployed along his front. Although he did not include them in his general order, Jackson's intent was that they would support the general attack by shelling the Federal forces on Bolivar Heights. It was an excellent plan. If all the pieces came together, there would not be a safe place within entire the Union position.[22]

But it was difficult to coordinate the disparate parts. Signal communications between Bartlett and McLaws again failed, and the Georgian did not receive the order. It is unlikely that Jackson did not foresee this, but it *is* surprising that he did not think to have Bartlett direct Walker's station to relay the message to McLaws, since these two stations had communications with one another.

Walker signaled back that his guns could not be brought to bear on the island in the Shenandoah, and then sent another message stating that "the enemy are advancing by Purcellville, and have possession of the passes from the valley." Jackson might have wondered what enemy could possibly be advancing by way of Purcellville, and which valley was it where the enemy held the passes. There is no record of Bartlett responding to this message, so Jackson probably dismissed the threat. Walker fretted under Jackson's insistence that he wait for McLaws to get into position before opening fire. The time was nearing 12:30 p.m., and Walker could plainly hear the sound of artillery fire in the direction of South Mountain, confirming McLaws's earlier signal that his rear was under attack. Walker later penned a rather fanciful account for *Century Magazine*, claiming that he had no doubt that the cannonading signaled the advance of the "whole Federal army." Walker could not have known this, but he was aware that the divided state of the Confederate army left it vulnerable, and that continued delay in capturing Harpers Ferry increased its peril.[23]

The Federals unknowingly helped relieve Walker's angst and triggered the Confederate bombardment. Modest activity around Walker's guns on Loudoun Heights drew renewed fire from Graham's artillery at Camp Hill. "It became necessary either to reply or withdraw our pieces," Walker reported rather lamely. Yet why had it not been incumbent on Walker to reply earlier in the morning, when the Federals shelled the crews preparing the gun emplacements? The most likely reason for Walker's action in the afternoon is that he used the window Jackson provided in his earlier 130-word order, when Jackson stated he did not wish anyone to open fire until all commands were in position, "*except you should find it necessary*" (emphasis the author's). At approximately 1 p.m., Walker decided that circumstances now required him to do so, and he ordered Captain French and Lieutenant Martin to commence firing.[24]

Captain Ripley and Major Stowell of the 9th Vermont were lying on their backs in the grass behind their regiment's tents, watching Graham's gunners attempt to shell Walker's gun positions, "when suddenly," recalled Ripley, "I saw two, three, four, half a dozen puffs of smoke burst out in the very centre of them [the Confederate position]." Both officers leaped to their feet and "clapped our hands and hurrahed in delight," thinking Graham's guns had found the range and that their shells were wreaking havoc among the Rebels. Ripley then described what happened next.

Suddenly, in the very centre of White's brigade, there was a crash, then another and another, and columns of dirt and smoke leaped into the air, as though a dozen young volcanoes had burst forth. Stowell caught the situation quicker than I, and exclaimed: "It's their guns!" In an instant the bivouac turned into the appearance of a disturbed anthill. Artillery, infantry, and cavalry were mixed in an absurd and laughable melee, as the panic increased. The rebel batteries were now in most rapid play, and as the fugitives came streaming towards us, the shells followed them with unerring practice. All at once one dropped into our camp, and Stowell sprang up with the exclamation that it was getting to be no laughing matter and we had better be taking care of ourselves.[25]

William Nichols of the 7th Rhode Island squadron recalled that the first shells from Walker's artillery "fell wide of the mark and we laughed at them." But the Confederates quickly adjusted the range and soon "pumped shell after shell in among us, killing a few horses and causing a rush for cover." John Paylor of the 111th New York observed that "some of the boys was almost scared to death" by the shelling, including himself. "Shells flying all around us made me nervously weak," he wrote. The religious services in the 125th New York's camp abruptly ended when one shell dropped in front of the colonel's tent. Fortunately it did not explode, a circumstance shared by numerous other Confederate shells. The notoriously inferior quality of Southern-manufactured fuses was frequently to blame (or to be thankful for, if one was on the receiving end). Walker's guns also fired many percussion shells, which buried themselves in the soft, sandy soil and failed to burst. But the inexperienced Union soldiers found little solace in this fact, for enough shells did explode to make the eastern slope of Bolivar Heights a dangerous place. The 125th New York bolted without order from their Sunday service to snatch their muskets from the stacks, and then they "started off at a pretty good speed for a ravine back of the hospital." Efforts to halt and form the men before they reached cover were of no avail. Recalled Charles W. Belknap of Company H: "There was no making the men hear until they were in the ravine where the companies were formed after much exertion."[26]

Most of the Union regiments positioned along Bolivar Heights were ordered to scramble over to the western side of the Heights for shelter. "No one made very slow motions in getting out of range," wrote a Vermonter, and few units maintained any order. Norman Eldred of the 111th New York stated that the men in his regiment broke ranks "and each one had found as safe a place as he could get under the fallen timber on the west side" of the Heights. Watching from his battery's position on Jackson's line, Captain Greenlee Davidson took delight in watching the Federals scurry for cover. "I never saw such consternation as there is among the Yankees," he wrote. "They are running about like a flock of frightened sheep and every sheltered gully and ravine is packed with prostrate Yankees."[27]

Shortly after 2 p.m., puffs of smoke burst forth from Maryland Heights, announcing that McLaws's four guns were joining the bombardment. "The shells from Maryland Heights we did not like at all," wrote an infantryman in the 115th New York, since the sound of a gun's discharge and its load arrived simultaneously. But, due to the range, few shells reached Bolivar Heights. Most, noted a 126th New York soldier, "exploded before they reached us, showing a fleecy white cloud with a spiteful flash in its center, and giving our boys their first experience of 'bombs bursting in air.'"[28]

Camp Hill however, was well within range of both Walker's and McLaws's guns. "Shot and shell flew in every direction, and the soldiers and civilians were compelled to seek refuge behind rocks, in houses, and elsewhere," recorded the *New York Times* correspondent. Miles's aide, Lieutenant Binney, wrote that the "shot and shell fall in every direction; houses are demolished and detonation among the hills terrible." Although the artillerymen on Camp Hill tried manfully to serve their guns and respond to their antagonists, the accuracy and speed with which the Confederate shells arrived rendered it "almost impossible to work the guns."[29]

Around 3 p.m. the defenders on Bolivar Heights observed "huge clouds of dust" rising from the west, beyond Schoolhouse Ridge. It was A. P. Hill's and Lawton's divisions, which Jackson set in motion soon after McLaws's artillery opened fire. The sound of McLaws's guns gave Jackson great joy. "I never saw his eye more brilliant than when the signal of occupation [of Maryland Heights] was made," wrote his aide, Colonel French. The more hopeful Federal soldiers on Bolivar Heights momentarily believed a relief column had raised the dust cloud. The 115th New York's Nicholas DeGraff said that they thought "it was Genl Seigle [*sic*] coming to the rescue." This elicited cheers and great enthusiasm among the men, but then Jackson's artillery ended the celebration. Two batteries opened from Schoolhouse Ridge, one where the Charleston Pike crossed it, and the other near the Shepherdstown Pike.[30] Captain Ripley—who, with his comrades in the 9th Vermont, was seeking shelter on the west slope of Bolivar Heights—recorded what happened.

> Suddenly, immediately behind us, we heard new concussions shake the earth, and to our dismay, right across the open ground where the Shepherdstown Road entered a fringe of woods, was an appallingly long bank of cannon smoke not over 1,000 yards away. We could plainly see the brass guns as they were run out of the woods. In an instant the air seemed alive with the exploding shells. We were between two fires, and there was no shelter that would protect a rabbit . . . For a space of time that seemed to me interminable we did the best we could by moving over from one slope to the other, to avoid the shell, and were miraculously preserved.[31]

One of Ripley's fellow soldiers in the 9th Vermont, W. H. Sanderson, remembered how their tough colonel, George Stannard, "used upon this occasion some pretty strong language" in speaking of the garrison commander, Colonel Miles, as Stannard rushed his men back and forth over Bolivar Heights to escape the fire from front and rear. "Whichever slope we were on, we wished it were the other one," recalled Ripley. Farther north on the Heights, Colonel D'Utassy rode coolly along the line of the 115th New York and, in his broken English, tried to reassure the frightened soldiers by advising them that the shells they heard whistling would not harm them. John H. Dye noted that just then a shell came hurtling in from Loudoun Heights, passing close by the colonel, and "it was seen that he could dodge as quick as the most expert and artful dodger we had."[32]

For all the dramatic descriptions of bursting shells, demolished houses, and exploding caissons, the Confederate bombardment inflicted few casualties and did relatively little damage. Until Jackson's artillery joined the bombardment, there were only nine Confederate guns firing. They destroyed two caissons, disabled four Union guns, and killed or wounded a handful of soldiers—good shooting, considering the range, but far from having a crippling effect. Yet the bombardment achieved two significant and critical results for the Confederates: it shook Union morale by demonstrating that there was no safe haven from enemy shells, and the ineffectual counter-battery fire of the Union guns exhausted nearly all their long-range ammunition. A *Boston Daily Evening Transcript* reporter noted that "some faint idea may be formed of the uncomfortableness of our position when each of these batteries [Jackson's] demonstrated by deeds that they could throw shot or shell over the line of troops on Bolivar Heights, while the batteries on Loudon and Maryland Heights had complete range of Camp Hill and the Plain." By the end of the afternoon the Union batteries were reduced to a total of only 36 rounds of long-range ammunition. When this was gone only canister remained. Miles might have ordered his guns to cease fire earlier to conserve their ammunition for use against an infantry assault, but this decision would have had a negative effect on the morale of his largely green infantry. Moreover, Miles did not want to invite an infantry assault on his unprepared position, manned by inexperienced soldiers. The same type of encircling artillery fire would accompany such an attack, and any experienced infantry officer knew the difficulty of forming even well-trained troops under artillery fire, let alone raw recruits. But Miles did allow a greater wastage of his precious ammunition than was necessary to sustain morale and keep the Rebels at a distance. General White, for example, watched in disgust as Potts's Ohio battery fired for nearly two hours at Maryland Heights without a single shell reaching the Confederate guns. When Miles failed to act, White rode over to him and suggested that Potts be ordered to cease firing. This shook Miles from his stupor and he did stop Potts; Miles even cautioned his other batteries not to fire unless they observed a target. But by this point the bulk of the ammunition stocks were depleted. Miles's failure to carefully manage what was perhaps his most important asset crippled the garrison and hastened its inevitable capitulation.[33]

Relief remained the garrison's only means of avoiding disaster. There had been a flicker of hope in the early afternoon, when the dust clouds raised by Jackson's infantry were rumored to be Franz Sigel coming to the rescue, but it quickly faded when Jackson's guns opened fire. New hopes were raised around 5 p.m., when the defenders on the northern end of Bolivar Heights noted that "two parallel lines of soldiers and cavalry, with sections of Batteries were seen advancing on the two roads near the Potomac." Artillery fire from the fighting at Crampton's Gap and Turner's Gap had been audible all day, and although these troops were approaching from the west, the opposite direction from which the sound of the artillery fire came, the Union defenders still held on to the possibility that they were friendly troops. Instead they soon proved to be Rebels, elements of J. R. Jones's division, moving into blocking positions astride the Shepherdstown Pike and sealing off one of the last avenues of escape for the Federals.[34]

While J. R. Jones's men advanced in full view of the Bolivar Heights defenders, A. P. Hill's division used the terrain to conceal its movement from Halltown to the Winchester and Potomac Railroad. The division followed the railroad east until Hill observed "an eminence crowning the extreme left of the enemy's line, bare of all earthwork, the only obstacles being an abatis of fallen timber." The Federals referred to this southern spur of Bolivar Heights, which extended south of the Charleston Pike, as Bull's Hill. After much prodding Miles had agreed to allow timber to be felled on it to obstruct an enemy advance. It was lightly defended by elements of the overstretched 3rd Maryland Potomac Home Brigade, some 500 men, and two companies of the 9th Vermont who reinforced them, adding about 140 more soldiers. This force was thinned out to cover a front some two-thirds of a mile long, from below Rigby's battery on the Charlestown Pike to the Shenandoah River. Hill's six brigades contained at least 4,000 men.[35]

Hill detailed three brigades to seize Bull's Hill—Pender's, Archer's, and Field's, the latter commanded by Colonel John Brockenbrough—and placed them under the direction of Brigadier General Dorsey Pender, an excellent soldier. The three units followed what General Archer described as "a by-road" roughly paralleling the base of Bolivar Heights, with their skirmishers in front. While these forces moved to secure the high ground, Hill ordered Branch's and Gregg's brigades to continue east along the railroad and, under cover of night, use the ravines "cutting the precipitous banks of the river" to establish themselves on the plateau to the left and rear of Bolivar Heights. Thomas's Georgia brigade was held in reserve to reinforce the Bull's Hill operation if necessary.[36]

A skirmish line from Archer's brigade covered Pender's advance, and—east of the farm road—they soon made contact with Downey's Marylanders and the Vermonters. Archer, whose men apparently led the column, promptly formed his regiments into line, with their left touching the road, and pressed ahead. Pender's brigade, commanded by Colonel R. H. Brewer, formed into line to Archer's left. Archer's Tennesseans and Georgians "advanced steadily, driving the enemy's pickets before us." Private Nelson Wandell of Company K, 9th Vermont, was one of those opposing them. He recalled how the Confederates advanced in good order. "We were not strong enough to withstand them again we retreated, but kept up a steady fire." Archer's men reached the crest of Bull's Hill, in full view of Rigby's battery on the turnpike. Observing the guns, Archer quickly moved his brigade to the right to gain the concealment and cover of some woods, which he hoped would also provide an approach to flank the

Union battery. But they found it a slow go. These were the woods within which Miles had reluctantly allowed his troops to fell trees, and Archer's men encountered both rough terrain and what he described as an "almost impenetrable abatis." By the time darkness fell they were a good 400 yards from the enemy guns, and Archer ordered a halt.[37]

Pender's brigade, unimpeded by any abatis and unchecked by token enemy resistance, pressed forward to within 60 yards of what Pender described as "the breastwork on the west point of Bolivar Heights," which was probably the breastwork thrown up to protect Rigby's battery. Here the Yankees' resistance stiffened.[38] When Pender's three brigades started their advance, Lieutenant Colonel Downey, whose thin line of skirmishers could do no more than harass the Confederates, sent a request for reinforcements to Colonel William Trimble. Unwilling to weaken his line further with Lawton's division moving menacingly in his front, Trimble directed Colonel Willard to lead his 125th New York from the reserve line to Downey's support. Willard was a regular-army man and a solid soldier, but the shelling had completely stampeded and demoralized his regiment of recruits, and he replied to Trimble that "it was no use to march that regiment [the 125th New York] to meet the enemy; they were so panic struck he could not hold them together to face the enemy." Trimble was forced to draw further from his reserve to help Downey, and he sent Colonel Stannard with the remaining three companies of the 9th Vermont's left wing. The line south of the pike remained dangerously undermanned, and Trimble scribbled a hasty note to headquarters requesting reinforcements. His experience with Miles had convinced him that Miles "was totally unfit for such a command," so Trimble told the orderly carrying the message to seek out General White if he could not find Miles.[39]

Trimble's precaution proved to be fortuitous, for the orderly could not discover Miles's whereabouts—which seems an odd thing in the restricted space in which the Union garrison was now confined. He did find White, but the general was sick; the orderly apparently decided not to disturb him and rode back to Trimble empty handed. Trimble promptly sent him back to White, armed with an additional note from the colonel explaining that he had no authority over any troops other than his own brigade, and reinforcements were needed on the left. This stirred White from his sickbed, and he immediately mounted and rode to Trimble's position, arriving around sunset. Miles never showed up, earning Trimble's condemnation: "He left me without any plan of defense, without any instructions, without any authority to call for re-enforcements, when the enemy were advancing upon our line, leaving me, a young officer, in a very embarrassing position."[40]

After assessing the situation, White ordered the balance of the 9th Vermont forward to support Downey's Marylanders and brought the 32nd Ohio up on the Vermonters' right. He sent his aide, Lieutenant Henry Curtis Jr., with two

24 lb. howitzers of Rigby's battery, "to run the concern." White wanted more fire-power and infantry, so he summoned Potts's battery and the 12th New York State Militia from Camp Hill. The departure of the New Yorkers stimulated Colonel Miles to action. He emerged to intercept them and order them back to their for-mer position, grumbling that he needed to maintain his interior lines. Perhaps it was just as well, for the disgruntled militiamen might have been of little real help. Miles ventured no farther toward the front that evening than Camp Hill. White, like Trimble, was left to his own devices by a commanding officer who had lost his will.[41]

Pender's North Carolinians came up against the more formidable line White had arranged and some skirmishing developed, which was described by Lieu-tenant Benjamin H. Cathey of the 16th North Carolina: "Just after dark we were assaulted by a line of battle, receiving very unexpectedly a heavy volley, but nothing daunted, we as quickly as possible returned the compliment, raised the yell and, sweeping forward, repulsed the enemy with some loss." Cathey's assail-ants were the 32nd Ohio and Rigby's two guns, one of which was found to be unserviceable. But White's aide, Lieutenant Curtis, wrote that his one remain-ing gun "banged away with their advance, bully." Curtis helped form the 32nd Ohio into line behind the gun, no easy task with the "very broken ground" they were on. It was "pitch dark" by the time Curtis had the line organized to his satis-faction. When Curtis left to withdraw his gun, Charles E. Smith, a member of the 32nd's Company I, recalled that the Rebels arose from the dark "with a yell like 10,000 demons" and advanced. Lieutenant Josiah Livingston, one of Stannard's Vermonters, wrote that "two volleys sent them back." Confusion soon reigned, with another Vermonter noting that men of his regiment were hollering, "You are shooting your own men." Both sides claimed that they drove the other back, but the truth was that neither one was interested in or could engage in a real fight in the near-absolute darkness, and after some sparring both fell back out of con-tact. Pender personally pulled back his own brigade a "short distance," as they had advanced beyond the support of either Archer or Brockenbrough.[42]

The less experienced Federal soldiers imagined that they had repulsed a Confederate attack. Instead, it was quite the opposite, as Pender had obtained his objective—the high ground south of the Charleston Pike. Although this area was lower than the Union position on Bolivar Heights, north of the Charles-ton Pike, it possessed some clear ground where artillery could deploy and good cover from which infantry could be formed to attack the flank of the Union line in the morning. Pender's advance had also caused the enemy to commit their only reliable reserve, the 32nd Ohio, and to draw the 9th Vermont from Trimble's support line.

Gregg's and Branch's brigades also gained their objectives that night. The two units slowly followed the railroad along the bank of the Shenandoah River until they arrived at a point believed to be in the rear of the Bolivar Heights line. The bluffs along the river in this area were described as "precipitous," and the North and South Carolinians had some difficulty in scaling them. "A handful of the enemy could have beaten back an army here," wrote a member of Gregg's brigade, "for it was so steep that a man could hardly carry his arms up it." There was token resistance, however. A few Union pickets were encountered, but they quickly departed. By 2 a.m. both Confederate brigades were established on the plateau southeast of Bolivar Heights. At remarkably little cost in men, A. P. Hill had maneuvered his entire division squarely on the flank of Bolivar Heights. He probably would have succeeded under any circumstances, but Miles's lack of energy and absence of command made Hill's chore decidedly easier. Only the efforts of Colonel Trimble and General White prevented Hill's brigades from securing even greater gains. But Hill could report with only modest exaggeration that by the maneuver of his division, "the fate of Harper's Ferry was sealed."[43]

Jackson waited for the outcome of Hill's advance before reporting the day's events to Lee. By 8:15 p.m. he knew enough of Hill's success to write out his well-known, four-sentence dispatch (see chapter 15), reporting that the day's advance had been successful and that he looked to God "for complete success tomorrow." A sense of urgency had descended on the operation. Although Jackson did not know of McLaws's predicament in Pleasant Valley because of the consistent failure of signal communications between Bartlett's station and Maryland Heights, he had received Lee's message—sent on the night of the 13th or the morning of the 14th—regarding enemy movements and urging a swift conclusion to the Harpers Ferry operation so that the army could reconcentrate. There would be no more chesslike maneuvers on September 15. Jackson intended to end it quickly, using the night hours to position his artillery to sweep Bolivar Heights from front, flank, and rear at first light, and then send in A. P. Hill's Light Division.[44]

Even before darkness, Jackson's artillery was in motion. A. P. Hill summoned the rifled section (10 lb. Parrott and 3-inch rifle) of Captain David McIntosh's battery at sunset, directing them to the open ground on Bull's Hill that Pender's advance had secured, only 800 yards from the enemy works on Bolivar Heights. Room was found for more guns, and Hill ordered his artillery chief, Lieutenant Colonel Lindsay Walker, to designate several gun sections and get them into position with McIntosh. Walker selected Crenshaw's four-gun battery of smoothbores (a Napoleon, a 12 lb. howitzer, and two 6 lb. guns) and two gun sections (four guns total), probably composed of rifled guns chosen from Davidson's, Pegram's, and Braxton's batteries. The gun crews were hand-picked men—the best of Walker's artillerymen. By the time the crews were assembled, horses hitched, and guns limbered, night had fallen, and the column wended its way slowly toward the front. "Presently we commenced climbing the hills," recalled Captain Davidson, "and for two hours we were scrambling up hills that we could not have pulled over in day light if our lives depended upon it." Walker's "indomitable resolution and energy" and that of his adjutant, Lieutenant John H. "Ham" Chamberlayne, helped overcome the obstacles of nature and night, and around 4 a.m. they halted the guns in a clover field on Bull's Hill, near McIntosh's location. The battery commanders were instructed to position and unlimber their guns as quietly as possible. Room could not be found for Crenshaw's smoothbores, which no doubt led to some colorful language from his gun crews, who had risked their necks only to find that they were to be left out. Walker ordered them back into a reserve position. Even without them, he had established a formidable artillery force of seven rifled guns and one Napoleon within 1,000 yards of the enemy and on their flank.[45]

Jackson's thorough reconnaissance of the terrain during the day located a shelf at the base of Loudoun Heights that offered a level platform with a direct line of fire into the rear of the Bolivar Heights line. Getting guns there was the tricky part. They would first have to cross the Shenandoah River, which could be done at Keyes' Ford, but once over the river, no road to the shelf existed. One would have to be cut during the night. Jackson was undeterred by the challenge and he ordered his artillery chief, Colonel Stapleton Crutchfield, to select 10 guns (which were probably all that would fit on the shelf) and have them in position before daylight. Crutchfield picked his guns from the batteries of Brown, Dement, Garber, and Latimer. The entire outfit rolled out after dark. Unfortunately, no one left a detailed record of this noteworthy operation, for it must have been a memorable event—crossing artillery over a river at night and then cutting a road in the darkness are not things easily forgotten. Crutchfield managed to get his guns across the Shenandoah without mishap, but then the hard work began. The artillerymen and whatever fatigue details that may have been sent along worked furiously to clear a road to the shelf to meet Jackson's demanding timetable. Sweat and muscle nearly accomplished it. Although daylight found the road unfinished, it was completed soon after, and the guns were quickly brought into position.[46]

When Crutchfield's artillery was in place, Jackson would be able to direct fire on Bolivar Heights from five directions. Walker's, McLaws's, and Crutchfield's guns would also command the open ground between Camp Hill and the Heights, preventing the enemy from reinforcing the front when A. P. Hill opened his assault. If all went well, the enemy would be pinned down and Hill's infantry would overwhelm them quickly. But Hill's foot soldiers and their supporting artillerymen did not know or understand the larger tactical picture. No one expected an easy victory. Captain Davidson, with Hill's guns on Bull's Hill, believed that "tomorrow will be a bloody day. Our division will storm the works early in the morning and will, I fear, be almost annihilated."[47]

Jackson also used the night hours to adjust his infantry dispositions, in order to seal off any possible escape available to the Union forces. The only marginal prospect left for the enemy on his front was along the Shepherdstown Pike and the B&O railroad line, both of which initially paralleled the Potomac as they led away from Harpers Ferry. To slam shut even this sliver, both Grigsby's and Starke's brigades were redeployed north and south of these two arteries. Grigsby's regiments advanced to within a half mile of Bolivar Heights' northern end, while Starke quietly moved his brigade to "within close range of the enemy's artillery" and occupied a wooded ridge overlooking the Potomac River, astride the Shepherdstown Pike.[48]

With Jackson's final adjustments, there remained only one escape route open to the Union garrison through the Confederate stranglehold: the Harpers Ferry–Sharpsburg Road, in McLaws's area of operation. Jeb Stuart warned the Georgian not to overlook its defense when he visited Maryland Heights on the afternoon of the 13th. McLaws did picket the road, contrary to Stuart's claim that he did not. But by the night of September 14, because of the emergency created by the loss of Crampton's Gap, only the 13th Mississippi remained on Maryland Heights. Its commander, Lieutenant Colonel Kennon McElroy, assured McLaws that "he would guarantee possession of the heights until assistance was rendered." These were fine words, and McElroy meant them, but his regiment contained slightly less than 200 officers and men, a veritable corporal's guard to do the work two brigades would be stretched thin to handle. McElroy positioned what was described as a "strong picket guard" on the Harpers Ferry Road. This may have been one or two companies, say 20–40 men. McLaws understood the odds when he stripped Maryland Heights of troops to fend off Franklin in Pleasant Valley, but he had little choice. "I had to take that among the other risks," he wrote years later. Franklin posed the most imminent threat. And an attempt at escape by the enemy—at night, over a river—seemed highly unlikely, particularly in light of the Federals' nonaggressive posture. If they did attempt a breakout, McLaws had Featherston's and Armistead's brigades at Sandy Hook, who could strike the vulnerable column on the march, when it was astride a river. McLaws perhaps forgot about the Union cavalry trapped within the garrison. Their mobility raised the odds of an escape attempt. But McLaws could not be strong everywhere. He posted his strength at the critical points: Pleasant Valley, Weverton Pass, and Sandy Hook. He might have pushed elements of Featherston's or Armistead's brigades up closer, to keep the pontoon bridge over the Potomac River under observation at night, but otherwise his dispositions and calculations were sound. But fate, which had treated McLaws kindly through most of the Harpers Ferry operation, abandoned him that night when the Yankees attempted the unexpected.[49]

The planned escape of the Union cavalry from Harpers Ferry suffered a setback during the day, when a reconnaissance of the ford where they intended to cross the Shenandoah River was found to be full of holes and impossible for cavalry to use. Miles, already lukewarm about the escape attempt, contemplated canceling the effort. But the cavalry commanders, particularly Grimes Davis, were not easily deterred, and they argued that a new route could be found. At one point Davis reputedly declared to Miles that "he would never surrender his force to a living person without a fight." What weight Davis's strong personality and determination had in changing Miles's mind is unknown, but the Marylander relented. According to Miles's aide, Lieutenant Binney, Miles selected the route the cavalry would take, but the process of elimination had narrowed the options to only one potentially viable choice. This was to cross the Potomac on the pontoon bridge, march north on the Harpers Ferry Road through Sharpsburg, and then go on to Pennsylvania by way of Hagerstown or Williamsport. The sound of artillery fire to the north and northeast throughout the day gave hope that the column might encounter the Army of the Potomac. But it was just as likely—indeed, more likely—that they would run into elements of the Confederate army. The risks were great, long enough that the senior colonel of the expedition, Arno Voss, commanding the 12th Illinois Cavalry, refused to embark on it without a written order from Miles. Yet the cavalry would have the element of surprise, the cover of night, and guides familiar with the country through which the column would travel.[50]

The troopers were unaware of these developments. As an old soldier, Miles well knew how quickly rumors spread through the men. Should word of the cavalry's contemplated escape reach the infantry, it might provoke a breakdown of discipline and a potential stampede. Even if it did not, it would surely cause morale to crumble. So Miles required "the greatest secrecy" from his cavalry commanders. They were not to inform their men or their subordinate officers of the plan until shortly before departure. Most of the troopers and their line officers learned what was to happen around sundown, shortly after the artillery fire ceased for the day. Sergeant Samuel Pettengill of the 7th Rhode Island squadron recalled that his commander, Major Augustus W. Corliss, shared the scheme with his men around 4 p.m., telling them that by the next morning "they would either be in Pennsylvania, or in Hell, or on the way to Richmond." Corliss also gave instructions for the horses to be groomed, the saddle girths inspected, "and for such other slight preparations as it was practicable to make." All commands were ordered to travel "in the lightest of 'light marching order'" and assemble in Harper's Ferry at 8 p.m.[51]

Seniority, and possibly personal pique, dictated command of the expedition. Although Colonel Grimes Davis was a West Point graduate and the most experienced cavalry officer in the garrison, Miles assigned command to Colonel Arno Voss, the leader of the 12th Illinois Cavalry. Voss was a German-born attorney from Chicago with prewar militia experience, but he had little real aptitude for soldiering. Less than one year later General John Buford sacked Voss, and Alfred Pleasonton, the cavalry corps' commander, endorsed Buford's action with the note that Voss "is not competent to command either a regiment or a brigade of cavalry in the field." Miles did not know Voss well, but it is inconceivable that he did not realize the difference in ability between Voss and Davis.

Miles, however, had had several run-ins with Davis, most recently over whether the cavalry would be permitted to escape. There was also the controversy concerning Lieutenant Milton Rouss of the 12th Virginia Cavalry. When Davis arrived at Harpers Ferry in late August, his orders from Miles were to engage this regiment and, specifically, to deal with Rouss and another officer who were known to be the 12th Virginia's most active officers in the area. Davis managed to capture Rouss in the first week of September, but the wily lieutenant escaped. Davis recaptured him and this time delivered him to Miles, who interrogated the lieutenant for nearly an hour before paroling him, a decision that, Lieutenant Binney admitted, caused "considerable excitement" within the garrison and, one gathers, astonishment. "There seemed to be quite a feeling of censure against Colonel Miles for it," recalled Binney. There is little doubt that one of those who shared this feeling was Davis, but whether he and Miles ever had words over it is unknown. Binney told Miles about the grumblings in the garrison over Rouss's parole, so Miles might have learned of Davis's displeasure with his decision in this way. Whatever the specific cause, Miles deliberately split hairs in the military's bureaucracy to appoint Voss as commander. Miles's rationale was that Voss's commission predated Davis's, but Davis was a regular officer and Miles could have selected him for this reason, just as Julius White, a general, deferred command at Harpers Ferry to Miles, a colonel, partially on these same grounds.[52]

Voss's orders were to assemble all commands at 8 p.m. "without baggage wagons, ambulances, or led horses"; cross the Potomac; and then march north on the Harpers Ferry–Sharpsburg Road. Troopers were instructed to leave behind their overcoats and blankets—essentially anything that might encumber their horses. Speed would be essential. The order of march placed the 1st Maryland Potomac Home Brigade Cavalry, known as Cole's Cavalry, in the lead, followed (in order) by the 12th Illinois, the 8th New York, the 7th Rhode Island squadron, and the 1st Maryland Cavalry. They would also be joined by the remnants of Captain Samuel C. Means's Loudoun (Virginia) Rangers, who followed Cole's Cavalry in the order of march. Means's company of loosely disciplined marauders had been soundly thrashed at Leesburg on September 2 by Colonel Thomas Munford's 2nd Virginia Cavalry, and they now numbered only 12 men. The entire force leaving Harpers Ferry consisted of approximately 1,594 officers and troopers. Lacking knowledge of the whereabouts of the Army of the Potomac, Miles could only give Voss general instructions "to cut his way through the enemy's line and join our army," although it was understood that Voss would march to Sharpsburg. From there, circumstances would dictate the direction of march, although, from the statement Major Corliss made to his men, Pennsylvania had been discussed as their destination.[53]

The various commands moved quietly through the darkness into Harpers Ferry, with the head of the column forming at the quartermaster's office and the rest extending up Shenandoah Street. William Luff recalled that although the "enemy was believed to be in strong force on the road chosen, and there were unknown dangers to be met in the darkness of night, it was an immense relief to be once more in motion with a chance for liberty." Men checked their saddle girths or weapons while they waited in the dark for the orders to march. Cole's battalion took the precaution of lashing their sabers to their saddles so these noisy weapons would not alert the enemy, and other regiments may have followed their example.[54]

Lieutenant Hanson Green of Company A, Cole's battalion, and Thomas Noakes, a government scout, were selected as guides. Green was "thoroughly familiar with the country" the column would pass through and a man of well-known courage. A member of the 7th Rhode Island squadron recalled Noakes as being "tall and athletic, brave and cruel, a Spartan in his indifference to physical comfort . . . a man of great prowess, and a valuable adjunct to the brigade." At 8 p.m., the designated hour, Colonel Voss reported to Miles that his men were ready to move. Miles introduced him to Green and Noakes at this point and gave Voss some verbal instructions, the nature of which Voss did not later relate. Miles, joined by General White, then rode with Voss to the head of the column. Here Miles and White bid Voss "an affectionate farewell"—both officers probably would have gladly changed places with Voss—and then the colonel quietly gave the command to march, along with orders "to keep well closed up, and follow your leaders." The latter directions were important for, as C. Armour Newcomer of Cole's battalion noted, "the night was very dark." In column of twos, and at a walk, the cavalry started across the pontoon bridge for Maryland.[55]

As the troopers edged forward, they noticed men standing on either side of the column handing something up to the horsemen. The men expected that these were probably "Christian Commissioners," handing out some form of religious material, but—to the cavalry's astonishment—they proved to be sutlers, giving away packages of tobacco. This was a surprise, for these businessmen never gave soldiers anything for free. The troopers figured that faced with having the Rebels take the tobacco when they captured Harpers Ferry, the sutlers had decided to give it away to the cavalry. "Those little tin-foil packages of tobacco were cherished during the perils of the night as a kind of 'hoc signo' for the march," remembered Samuel Pettengill. But the sutlers' sudden generosity had an ulterior motive, which soon revealed itself.[56]

Voss feared the bridge crossing: "I felt some apprehension lest the clatter of the horses' hooves should excite some suspicion of the Rebels, whose guns upon Maryland Heights commanded the bridge." But the rush of the Potomac River swallowed the sound, and the head of the column reached the Maryland bank without incident. Here the men turned left, passing between the C&O Canal and the steep side of Maryland Heights, and increased the pace of their march from a walk to a gallop. Lieutenant Luff recalled that as each company arrived on the Maryland side, it closed up into a column of fours. Perhaps the companies in his regiment did, but this formation proved impossible to achieve or maintain, due to the speed the column set, and most men recalled riding single file or in twos. It was hard enough simply keeping the column together, with the head moving at a gallop, while the pace of those crossing the bridge was a walk. "It was extremely difficult, in the darkness, to keep in touch, as one may say, with the preceding company," wrote Luff. If a company was delayed a moment in crossing the bridge, there was a good chance it would loose contact with those in front. This led to trouble early in the crossing. Company G of the 12th Illinois followed Cole's troopers across the bridge. The Marylanders must have been out of sight when the midwesterners reached the Maryland bank, for instead of turning left they turned right, toward Sandy Hook. It is surprising that no one saw fit to place a detachment at this end of the bridge to direct traffic, but it was a detail the planners had overlooked. Company G did not travel far before a group of pickets from Walker's division on the south bank of the Potomac fired at them, wounding some horses but no men. The rest of the 12th Illinois were halted while the adjutant rode after the errant company and turned them around. "This delay put too great a distance between the head of the column under Cole and our men, and it required full speed of their horses to follow," recorded the regimental chaplain.[57]

Yet another mishap occurred when the last of Voss's regiment crossed the bridge. This was Company D, which had been on detached duty. When they arrived, their captain found that his regiment was already in Maryland, and the following regiments were in the act of crossing. Rather than find a place to insert his men in the order of march, the captain pushed on over the bridge with his men strung out behind him. A party of those trailing behind, led by Sergeant Harvey Lambert and a civilian, lost track of those in front and also turned right toward Sandy Hook. They apparently had made it into the lower end of Pleasant Valley when they bumped into a Confederate camp; its occupants fired on them, wounding Lambert and driving the group back to Harpers Ferry.[58]

It took nearly 30 minutes for the 1,500 troopers to reach the Maryland side of the river. The pace of the crossing gradually accelerated, so that when the rear of the column started across the bridge the troopers' horses were moving at a trot. When the 8th New York completed its passage, the sutlers—who only minutes before had been handing out tobacco—suddenly drove their two wagons onto the bridge, inserting themselves into the column between the Davis's New Yorkers and the 7th Rhode Island squadron. There was no time to stop and deal with this development, and the sutlers were ignored. The latter soon discovered they had embarked on a perilous course, as in a moment the speed increased from a trot to a gallop. It was difficult for the troopers to keep up and simply maintain contact with their command and comrades, and the acceleration at the front of the column caused it to string out for a great distance. "It was stone dark," recalled Corporal Isaac Heysinger of the 7th Rhode Island squadron, and the only way the men could keep their direction was by the sound of the horses' hooves and the clattering of sabers (obviously some had not lashed their swords down). But in the darkness it was not always easy to discern from which direction the sounds came. Keeping up grew even harder when, about a mile from the bridge, the road turned north and ascended the precipitous slope of Elk Ridge. Heysinger stated that it was a "tremendous mountain climb, so steep that one had to grasp the horse's mane to be safe [at a gallop] from sliding back or shifting his saddle." The speed of the march and the sharp angle of the climb caused the column to spread out into a single file of horsemen. "It was now every man for himself . . . and woe to him who should lose his place," wrote William Nichols.[59]

Cole's Marylanders, at the head of the column, came upon a Confederate picket post, probably from the 13th Mississippi, who called out a challenge. Cole's men chose speed and surprise as their weapons and rode forward at a gallop. The pickets fired a few obligatory shots at the swiftly moving horsemen, missed, and then vanished into the night. The column pressed on at what William Luff described as a "killing pace." The sutlers, driving their wagons at breakneck speed, managed to keep up during the initial ascent over the shoulder of Maryland Heights. But then their luck ran out. Isaac Heysinger wrote that "perhaps one mile up this climb, with its ups and downs, the road made a sharp turn around the end of a rocky knob." In the pitch dark the sutlers came upon the turn suddenly; their galloping horses and heavy wagons were unable to negotiate it, and they plunged down the steep mountainside. Heysinger arrived on the scene of the accident moments after it had occurred. "I heard a great noise and crashing, shouts and groans, and indescribable sounds down the gorge," he wrote. But neither he nor anyone else could stop to help or investigate, as delay might mean death or capture. The sutlers were left to fend for themselves. Their fate is unknown.[60]

The column pressed north without pause, "at a hard gallop," crossing Antietam Creek near its mouth at the Antietam Iron Works and heading on to Sharpsburg, where another Confederate picket post, also surprised by the horsemen, quickly dispersed. The leading elements arrived in Sharpsburg between 11 p.m. and midnight, having covered the approximately 10 miles in just over three hours, a rate of march that indicates that everyone was not traveling at a gallop for the entire distance. "The night had now become starlight," noted William Luff, with a considerable amount of light from a waning gibbous moon that rose at 9:45 p.m. adding to the visibility. Several horsemen were observed near the entrance to the village, and a challenge sang out from them. Thinking they might be from the Army of the Potomac, some troopers from the 12th Illinois responded, "Friends of the Union." This drew a volley from the challengers, though all the bullets missed their mark. Someone ordered a charge, and the Maryland and Illinois troopers urged their mounts forward. The Confederate pickets fled east through the village and then north on the Hagerstown Pike. Meanwhile, Voss ordered a halt to allow the command, which was strung out for several miles, to close up, as well as to see whether the locals could offer any information about where the Rebel army was. The horses also needed rest and water. The extended column rapidly gathered together, and Sharpsburg's main street was soon crammed full of Union cavalry. While the commands concentrated, the Marylanders at the head of the column probed east, in the direction in which the Confederate pickets had fled. As they approached the point where the Hagerstown Pike comes into Main Street, "the darkness was suddenly illumined by a sheet of flame, and the stillness broken by a rattling volley of musketry," recalled Lieutenant Luff. Colonel Voss, with considerable exaggeration, thought "at least a hundred rifles" sent their "leaden messengers about our ears." This, no doubt, was the reserve of the force picketing Sharpsburg, although what command they were from is something of a mystery. These bullets also missed their mark, but loudly announced that trouble lay to the east. This was confirmed by a local resident who, at about the same time as the volley exploded, told Colonel Davis (8th New York) that the column was "going right into Lee's army" if it continued to march east. Exactly what else this local citizen told the Union officer is unknown, but it is highly likely that he warned the Federals that Confederates were reported to be at Hagerstown as well, a fact the people of Sharpsburg would have known by this date. This rendered the best road north, the Hagerstown Pike, too risky to travel. The guides and officers held "a hurried consultation" and decided to turn the column about and take the Mercersville Road, which runs west of and roughly parallel to the Hagerstown Pike, in the hope that this might avoid contact with any sizeable enemy force.[61]

It is evident that Noakes, who now guided the march, did not always keep to the Mercersville Road, but departed from it when necessary. Lieutenant Luff recalled they were led in "a circuitous path through lanes and by-roads, woods and fields." Corporal Henry Nichols of the 7th Rhode Island squadron remembered a "spirited dash through ravines, over creeks, fences and fields," and William McIlhenny of the 1st Maryland Potomac Home Brigade Cavalry stated that "we kept to the fields and woods, not striking a road" until nearly daylight, when they reached the Williamsport Turnpike. They rode near Dovenberger's Mill, situated at New Industry on the Potomac River, for Noakes (and perhaps Lieutenant Green) had a "friendly chat" with some of the mill workers, who gave them detailed information about the whereabouts of the Rebels in the area. The nearest Confederates were seen by their bivouac fires. Voss and Davis gathered their horsemen "close in hand" and charged into this thoroughly startled group, who were probably nothing more than a foraging party. The Rebels loosed a few shots and scrambled out of the way. Noakes led the column away from the road—the mill workers may have advised keeping clear of it—and traveled cross-country east of it to the Williamsport Turnpike, where the column emerged opposite the St. James Boys' College. The most careful student of the cavalry escape believes it was no accident that Noakes led them to this point, as it was well known that the college grounds held an excellent spring, capable of watering several regiments of cavalry. After the horses drank their fill, the column marched west for nearly a mile (whether cross-country or along the Williamsport Turnpike is unknown) before it struck the Downsville Turnpike and turned north. A march of 3 miles on this road brought them back to the Williamsport Turnpike. "It was now just in the gray of morning," recalled Lieutenant Luff, and the bivouac fires of a sizeable enemy camp in the direction of Williamsport, about a mile and a half to the west, were "plainly visible" to the Federal cavalrymen. The turnpike was empty, but the "low, rumbling sound of heavy carriage wheels" were heard approaching from the direction of Hagerstown. Scouts investigated and reported that it was a large wagon train, escorted by cavalry.[62]

Although no one mentioned that ground fog obscured visibility, it was present at South Mountain and at Harpers Ferry that morning, and it seems likely (given the weather conditions) that at least a light fog existed, which—with the limited light of early morning—probably made it difficult to discern the size of the train or strength of its escort. "We did not know but there might be a considerable body of troops as an advance guard to the wagon train," wrote Lieutenant Luff. But the weather and faint daylight also helped to mask the presence Voss's and Davis's cavalrymen. They might have used these elements to help make good their escape, but Davis—and it seems clear that by this point Davis had assumed tactical command of the cavalry—elected to use surprise and his mobility to strike a blow at the enemy.

He quickly deployed the various commands to meet the Confederates, placing most of his 8th New York north of the road, the 12th Illinois south of the pike in a body of woods, and the Marylanders and Rhode Islanders in reserve behind the 12th. A company of the 12th was moved about a quarter mile east of the main body, where they dismantled some fence panels to provide passage for their animals, and had orders to capture the rear guard of the wagon train's escort when it came up. Another detachment from the same regiment were dismounted to the left of the company that remained on horseback, at a spot where the former group could cover the turnpike with their carbines. With a squadron from his own regiment, Davis took position at the western end of his cleverly planned ambush, near an old farm lane that connected the Williamsport Turnpike with the Greencastle Pike, where he could intercept the enemy in the road. If the Rebel escort resisted, two of his regiments could strike from both sides of the pike, while the Marylanders and Rhode Islanders would be able to envelop the front and back of the column. "All was done in silence," recalled Luff, "and it was still too dark for our troopers, concealed in the timber which skirted the road, to be seen."[63]

The approaching group of vehicles that the silent Union troopers anxiously waited to pounce on was a juicer target than they could have imagined, as it was composed of Longstreet's reserve ordnance train, followed by commissary and quartermaster trains. The 11th Georgia, numbering only about 140 men, escorted the lengthy line of the latter two sets of wagons, with one-half of the regiment at the front and the other half at the rear. "The train extended for several miles, and our small force was of necessity wholly inadequate to cover the line of its movement," wrote a member of the regiment. A handful of cavalry, probably from the 3rd Virginia, escorted Longstreet's ordnance train. This part of the procession was commanded by London-born First Lieutenant Francis Dawson, who began the war as a master's mate in the Confederate Navy before transferring to the artillery and earning promotion to lieutenant. Dawson had followed Longstreet's command toward Boonsboro on September 14. Where he halted for the evening is unknown, but it was probably near Funkstown. He received orders that evening from Longstreet to move the ordnance trains to Williamsport. Dawson had his train in motion by 10 p.m., and he recalled that it was "towards morning" when he entered the Williamsport Turnpike, where he encountered a cavalry picket post; its commander "asked me to move the column as quickly as I could, and to keep the train well closed up." The lieutenant asked if there were enemy troops in the area, to which the cavalry officer said no, as "he had pickets out in every direction" and the road ahead "was entirely clear." Dawson had missed his dinner and gone without sleep for an entire day, and the thought of reaching Williamsport where food and rest awaited "seemed the summit of bliss."[64]

The concealed Union horsemen watched Dawson and a "small body of cavalry" appear over a hill that rose to their right, followed by the ordnance wagons. Worried that some trigger-happy trooper might find it hard to pass up the chance to pick off a Rebel, Colonel Davis quietly commanded, "Don't shoot, boys." The men obeyed, and when Dawson and the cavalrymen who followed behind him were nearly opposite the left of the Federal force, Davis (or someone with him) ordered them to halt. "The gloss was not yet off my uniform, and I could not suppose that such a command, shotted with a big oath, was intended for me," wrote Dawson. But then it was repeated. This time Dawson rode toward the source of the voice and "found myself at the entrance of a narrow lane," filled with men and horses stretching as far as Dawson could see in the dim morning light. Because of the poor visibility and the dust on their uniforms, Dawson could not tell that they were Federals, and he lit into the trooper who he thought had ordered him to stop. "How dare you halt an officer in this manner!" he exclaimed. Dawson recalled that the trooper answered, "Surrender and dismount! You are my prisoner!" In a slightly different version of this event,

Captain Thomas Bell of Davis's 8th New York remembered that a Rebel, who was probably Dawson, asked "What troops are these?" Davis replied, "Union troops from Harpers Ferry." When the Confederate lieutenant next asked who was speaking, Davis answered, "Colonel B. F. Davis, 8th New York Cavalry, and you are my prisoner." No matter what, exactly, was said, Dawson was captured and, according to Lieutenant Luff, "it required but a moments persuasion" to convince the cavalrymen following Dawson to dismount and surrender.

So quietly and efficiently was the advance force caught that the drivers of the wagons remained unaware of what was happening. As they came up, Union troopers halted the leading vehicles and inspected their contents, finding them "heavily loaded with ammunition." Davis ordered Captain William Frisbie, commanding Company D of Davis's regiment, to take the train to the Greencastle Pike "and run it through to that place at the rate of eight miles an hour." Frisbie was disoriented after the night march, had no idea where in Maryland he was (other than north of the Potomac River), and had never heard of Greencastle. Frisbie inquired of Davis where he might find said road and received a curt, "Find it, and be off, without delay!" Lieutenant Luff wrote that the Marylanders came to Frisbie's rescue, furnishing him with a guide, and in moments the wagons were rolling down the farm lane for the Greencastle Pike, each wagon escorted by a trooper with a drawn pistol.[65]

The Confederates farther back in the column also had no idea of what had happened. "At first the wagoners thought they [the Union cavalry] were Confederate soldiers and obeyed instructions with their usual cheerfulness," recalled the 11th Georgia's historian. Many of the teamsters were black, possibly slaves hired out to the army by their masters. The wagon master—whether of Longstreet's ordnance train or the commissary and quartermaster trains is not clear—was reported to be a Pennsylvanian. It may have been Cleggett Fitzhugh, of Franklin County, Pennsylvania, who had joined up with the Rebels only several days before and was among those captured. No one with any authority back along the Confederate column noticed at first that they were leaving the Williamsport Turnpike for a farm lane leading toward the Greencastle Pike, because other than Dawson—now a prisoner—nobody knew the area or the roads to Williamsport. The capture and redirection of the train had been executed so efficiently that there was nothing to alert anyone that anything was amiss. "But as daylight was dawning the secret soon leaked out," wrote the 11th Georgia's Kittrell Warren. Someone ran back to Captain William H. Mitchell, commanding the 11th Georgia's right wing, to sound the warning. Mitchell only had about 70 men, and whoever spoke with him apparently added that there were hundreds of enemy cavalry, for Mitchell wisely pulled his men back to link up with Major Little and the left wing. Little called for help from a cavalry escort, purported to consist of elements of the 1st Virginia Cavalry, who were following at the rear of the train, the direction from which everyone thought any threat would come. Accompanied by a section of horse artillery, the Confederate troopers galloped to the front to find the wagon thieves.[66]

By the time the Virginia cavaliers came rushing forward, the Union cavalry had cut out nearly 100 wagons: all of Longstreet's reserve ordnance train, and a good part of the commissary and quartermaster trains. "Many of the drivers rebelled against driving into captivity," recorded Lieutenant Luff, "but with a trooper on each side with drawn revolver, they had little opportunity to hesitate." With the encouragement of the gun-toting cavalrymen, who also used the flat of their sabers to nudge the horses along, the train rumbled to the Greencastle Pike and then north along it "faster than a wagon train ever moved before." Ironically, it turned out that many of the wagons were captured from the Union army in earlier battles, one being marked "1st New Hampshire Battery." A wagon or two became disabled, or was purposely ditched by its driver, but these vehicles were set on fire and did not delay the march. Once the train was safely on its way to Greencastle, Davis detailed the 1st Potomac Home Brigade Cavalry to escort the wagons there and formed the remainder of the cavalry in the rear to fend off the pursuing Confederate horsemen. Colonel Voss reported that the Rebels "sorely harassed our rear for a while," but Lieutenant Luff wrote that the Confederates' efforts were "without effect" and that the Federal troopers easily drove them back. It was essentially bloodless sparring, for if there were any casualties on either side, no one reported them.[67]

As the flying column of wagons and cavalry crossed the state line into Pennsylvania and neared Greencastle, Isaac Heysinger recalled that "we were so begrimed with dust that we actually looked more like monkeys than human beings." They also resembled Confederates, or so thought the curious civilians who emerged to find out what all the noise and clouds of dust meant. Seeing what looked like Rebels approaching, the farmers scurried toward nearby woods to hide their horses and cattle. But when it was evident that the horsemen were Union cavalry, "men, women and children" flocked out of their homes to cheer the dusty troopers and offer up "all kinds of dainty eatables and drinkables for our refreshment."[68]

The leading element of the column—which, according to one newspaper report, consisted of 50 wagons from Longstreet's reserve ordnance train—reached Greencastle around 9 a.m., 13 hours after they had begun their bold adventure from Harpers Ferry. The "wildest excitement" gripped the town as it filled with heavy army wagons, Rebel prisoners, and dust-covered but jubilant Union cavalrymen bursting to talk about their adventure and eager to accept the slices of bread thickly spread with apple butter offered to them by the town's women. Things grew ugly when Cleggett Fitzhugh was discovered among the prisoners. A crowd gathered and growled threats at the man. "Hang him!" "Shoot him!" "Kill him!" they shouted. The officers had the good sense to haul Fitzhugh away to the town jail with the other prisoners, a rough-looking set that one newspaper described as looking "as though they had never washed themselves or changed their clothes from the time they enlisted." At noon, just as things were settling down from the initial burst of excitement, the next wave of wagons—42 from the commissary and quartermaster trains—arrived, followed by the main body of the cavalry, setting off a new round of celebration.[69]

While the townspeople rejoiced and the men gobbled down the tasty things its citizens brought them to eat, Colonel Davis (or someone from the 8th New York) issued a report that made its way to William B. Wilson, who had established a U.S. Military Telegraph Department station in Greencastle several days earlier. Wilson wired Governor Curtin's office in Harrisburg with the thrilling news of the cavalry's escape from Harpers Ferry; their capture of Longstreet's ordnance train of 40 wagons, along with 40 prisoners; and a worrisome statement from Colonel Davis that "he thinks Col. Miles will surrender this morning." Davis probably had no idea of exactly how many wagons had been captured, as there had been no time make a count until they reached Greencastle, and the vehicles from the commissary and quartermaster trains had not arrived when this first telegram was sent.

Shortly after Wilson wired the message, Colonel Voss visited the telegraph office. He was probably aware that Davis had made some report, and this may have irritated him. Voss wished to make sure that, as the officer in command by order of Miles, he received credit for what had turned out to be a surprisingly successful expedition. So Voss had operator Wilson send a telegram to Middle Department commander General Wool. Voss never mentioned Davis [who had given credit to Voss in his wire, although the operator spelled his name "Boss"] and placed himself as the central figure in the affair: "By order of Colonel Miles I left it [Harpers Ferry] last evening at 8 o'clock with the cavalry, about 1500 strong, to cut my way through the enemy's lines. I succeeded in reaching this place about nine this morning." Voss reported that "over sixty wagons" and 675 prisoners were captured, and offered a strangely optimistic opinion that "Colonel Miles intends to hold the Ferry, but is anxiously looking for reinforcements."

Both reports underestimated the number of wagons captured, and Voss greatly exaggerated the number of prisoners. Someone certainly counted the number of vehicles captured or destroyed, but, if this was recorded, it has not surfaced. Claims ran from 40 to 175, but the consensus in letters and diaries written at the time or shortly after event was between 72 and 104 wagons and roughly 100 prisoners, which included the teamsters. Not a single man in the entire cavalry force had been killed. Voss reported 178 missing: all men whose horses were disabled, or who became separated from the column, or who been unable to keep up. Some of these men subsequently turned up, so how many of the 178 became prisoners of the Confederates is unknown.[70]

In the words of a Rhode Island private, it had been "a very hard ride," but it was also a successful one—beyond what anyone could have imagined when they set out from Harpers Ferry. The entire cavalry force, except those that were missing, had escaped certain capture and dealt the Rebels a blow by seizing Longstreet's ordnance train. The loss of this ammunition proved to be more of an inconvenience, rather than a serious setback for them.[71] The greater value of the expedition, however—as Stephen Starr noted—was that it offered a demonstration "of what even relatively inexperienced troops were capable of doing under resolute and competent leadership." It also provided further evidence that Union cavalry might do more than act as couriers, escorts, scouts, and sentinels; when numbers were concentrated, the troopers could be a potent offensive weapon.

Although Voss commanded the expedition and performed competently, Grimes Davis took charge when trouble loomed. He supervised the dispositions of the different commands during the capture of the Confederate trains and managed the ambush with great skill. Not a single man on either side lost his life in the affair, a remarkable fact when one considers the inexperience of the troopers with whom Davis sprung his trap. Apart from possible jealousy over who would earn credit for the expedition, which was implied in Voss's telegram to Wool, Voss and Davis must have understood one another during the escape. But without bothering to ask Voss's permission, Davis marched his regiment to Williamsport on September 16, and they then went on to join the main army near Sharpsburg on the 17th. These actions expressed Davis's opinion that whatever authority Voss had enjoyed, it expired when they reached Greencastle. Despite Voss's efforts to ensure that he would not be overlooked if any honors were distributed, the army decided that it was Davis, not Voss, who had behaved with conspicuous bravery. On September 23 McClellan wired to Halleck that Davis's management of the withdrawal of the cavalry "merits the special notice of the Government," and McClellan recommended that the Mississippian be breveted major in the regular army. Davis was awarded the brevet, but he would not survive the war. He was killed on June 9, 1863, at Brandy Station.

While the Union troopers devoured bread spread with apple butter and slapped one another's backs at their good fortune, their infantry and artillery comrades at Harpers Ferry underwent a different fate. They were suffering the humiliation of what would be the largest capitulation of U.S. soldiers in the entire war.

17

The Fall of Harpers Ferry

*"Through God's blessing, Harper's Ferry and
its garrison are to be surrendered"*

The prospects facing the garrison as the night of September 14 gave way to September 15 were grim. According to Captain Henry B. McIlvaine, the wasteful artillery exchanges on the 14th nearly exhausted the garrison's limited artillery ammunition supply. Besides what the batteries still had in their ammunition chests, McIlvaine could only scare up 36 rounds of long-range ammunition, which he divided among the pieces most in need. Some changes were made along the western front to meet the anticipated enemy assault in the morning. The 87th Ohio and a howitzer were placed along the Winchester and Potomac Railroad, in a blocking position to the left and rear of the line established during the night between the Shenandoah River and Bolivar Heights. Julius White had used the Bolivar Heights reserve to fill in this line during the night, so that now it was manned by four regiments: the 32nd Ohio, the 3rd Maryland Potomac Home Brigade, the 9th Vermont, and the 125th New York. White also strengthened the crucial hinge in the Union's western front, where the Charleston Pike crossed Bolivar Heights, with the four 3-inch rifles and two Napoleons of Potts's Ohio battery, which went into position near Rigby's battery. White wished to further reinforce the Bolivar Heights line by moving up all the remaining artillery at Camp Hill, but he learned that there were no horses or harnesses to move the guns. Apparently it did not occur to either White or Miles to order the infantry along the entire front to entrench their position. There were some rifle pits dug in a few places on the main Bolivar Heights line, but nothing seems to have been done south of the Heights. Perhaps the tools or time to build entrenchments that would protect men from artillery fire were not available, but this seems to have been an important oversight.[1]

These adjustments along the front seemed meaningless to officers whose regiments held the line between the Charlestown Pike and the Shenandoah River. They and their men listened to Jackson's artillerymen placing guns on the south bank of the Shenandoah that would enfilade their position and take Bolivar Heights in reverse. Colonel Willard, in company with Colonels Stannard and Downey, visited their brigade commander, Colonel Trimble, "in the hope that some change could be made in the disposition of the troops." But Trimble's orders from Miles allowed him no flexibility, and he sent his commanders back to their regiments with orders to defend the brigade line as it stood.[2]

While the cavalry were assembling to march on the evening of the 14th, several other regimental commanders went straight to Miles's headquarters and asked why the infantry could not join in the escape attempt. "They said they did not see the necessity of staying there and being butchered by artillery," recalled Lieutenant Binney, and the commanders spoke of either cutting their way out or surrendering, the latter suggestion presumably to avoid a slaughter. Miles listened to the men, and then explained that his orders from Halleck (which he also showed to the officers) were to hold Harpers Ferry "to the last extremity." Only when the garrison's ammunition was exhausted would Miles consider surrender or evacuation—when, of course, it could be too late to attempt the latter.[3]

Around midnight the battery commanders from Bolivar Heights—Von Sehlen, Graham, Potts, and Rigby—visited Miles. They explained what the colonel probably already knew, that the Confederates were planting batteries that would enfilade and take Bolivar Heights in reverse. Miles gave the uninspiring reply that "he expected they [the enemy] would enfilade the heights the next morning in every direction." The firing from the direction of Pleasant Valley signaled that relief was near, but even this did not stir Miles from his funk. Whether he considered shortening his line by pulling back toward Camp Hill (as Saxton had done) is unknown. Miles might have done so, but the difference between the two defensive strategies was that Saxton had still held Maryland Heights. Miles could also have reasoned that shortening his line would simply have offered the Confederates a more densely packed target at which to fire.[4]

It was a restless and anxious night for the men of the garrison. Around 9 or 10 p.m., jittery troops on the forward slope of the southern part of Bolivar Heights opened fire, probably at some Confederate scouts or skirmishers. The firing quickly spread along the line. "Soon we to [*sic*] were blazing away," recalled a member of the 115th New York. George Dawes of the 111th New York wrote to his parents that "there was nothing but a continual stream of fire pouring in upon us and a whize of musket balls flying around our heads . . . all was confusion." "Nobody seemed to know what was the matter," wrote Nicholas DeGraff of the 115th New York—or, it seems, what they were shooting at. When the firing finally ceased, the 115th found that they had two men hit, though no one could determine whether these casualties were inflicted by friendly fire or by the enemy. The 111th New York counted 2 dead and many missing, some of whom later turned out to be killed or wounded; others had simply run for their lives. Dawes wrote that some of the missing were found "about 1/2 mile from the battle field. Some had no guns[,] others threw a way their knapsacks others their haver sacks over coats and cantines. One fellow [Alexander Williams] threw away his knap sack haver sack cantine and over coat and gun and cut his belt and then run like fire for some hiding place whare the balls did not sing quite so much." Captain Benjamin Thompson, who also served in the 111th New York, recalled that during this brief engagement a private of his company complained that his rifle would not fire. Thompson inspected the weapon and extracted seven cartridges from the barrel. The first one had been inserted upside down.

Who the 111th and the 115th traded fire with is unknown. Most likely it was with skirmishers from Lawton's or J. R. Jones's divisions who either wandered too far forward in the pitch-black night or were trying to establish their line as near to the Federals as possible. Eventually everyone settled down and all became still. Gloom hung heavily over the Union lines. "The darkness of the night, with the protection it brought us, was so grateful that we wished we might always be enwrapped in it," wrote a 9th Vermonter, "so inevitable was the hopeless contest to be forced on us with the first streak of dawn."[5]

A dense fog settled in the valley during the night, so when dawn broke Yankees and Confederates alike were shrouded in mist. "But they [the fog banks] quickly rose," noted Captain Ripley of the 9th Vermont, "and stood along the mountain side, like huge drop curtains, ready to lift upon the tragedy to be enacted." What was revealed was "the dreaded sight of new batteries in the cornfield across the river." They were Crutchfield's guns. A. P. Hill's artillery on Bull's Hill was also seen. It was now shortly before 6 a.m. To Captain Greenlee Davidson, with Hill's artillery, it seemed that they had scarcely finished the difficult work of positioning their guns before the fog lifted "and exposed to my astonished view, Bolivar Heights towering above us and the guns of the enemy frowning down upon us." The moment the gunners could see to cut their fuses, shells were thumped down the gun tubes and then, recorded Davidson, "at it we went with all our might." Which guns opened first is a matter of speculation. Edward A. Moore of Poague's battery in J. R. Jones's division thought that the firing was simultaneous from all sides. The evidence points to Hill's artillery opening the cannonade, followed by Crutchfield's 10 guns on the Shenandoah River's south bank. Jones's divisional artillery also joined in, as did Lawton's artillery on Schoolhouse Ridge, astride the Charlestown Pike. McLaws's and Walker's guns opened as well, although their accuracy was entirely compromised by the fog, which clung tenaciously to the mountainsides. Walker recalled that his crews merely trained their guns "by the previous day's experience and delivered their fire through the fog," a method that might frighten the enemy but did little real damage.[6]

At the critical junction of the Bolivar Heights line, Potts's and Rigby's batteries drew the fire of A. P. Hill's, Crutchfield's, and Walker's guns, while J. R. Jones's batteries targeted the guns of Phillips, Von Sehlen, and Graham, which were clustered together at the northern end of the Federal line. The shells from Maryland Heights and Loudoun Heights added to the general mayhem by shrieking down out of the fog and bursting in the Union rear. At least 37 guns, most of them rifled, were firing on the Federals, and—depending on how many guns Lawton and J. R. Jones used beyond the three batteries Jones had in action on the left of his line—there might have been as many as 58 pieces firing, all of which were rifles or Napoleons. Against this, along the Bolivar Heights line, the Federals replied with 24 guns, only 11 of which were modern rifled pieces; 6 were Rigby's obsolete 24 lb. howitzers, with a range of only three-quarters of a mile. Rigby testified later that of the six engagements he had been in, the action at Harpers Ferry was the heaviest artillery fire he had ever experienced. None of those battles had been particularly large ones, but by the standards of 1862 it was a heavy bombardment on September 15. A provisional lieutenant serving in Von Sehlen's battery, with previous service in the Austrian artillery during the 1859 war with France, became so unnerved by the fire from the rear (either from Crutchfield's or McLaws's guns) that he bolted from the battery for cover, encouraging his men to follow. The crossfire on Rigby and Potts eventually grew so severe that both batteries were silenced and the crews were forced to seek cover. Lieutenant Henry Curtis Jr. of General White's staff was with one of these batteries, and he wrote that one shell "exploded over me, as I was directing the fire of a battery, & I never grew small so quickly in my life." When the Confederates shifted their fire to the supporting Union infantry, both crews gamely dashed back to their pieces and resumed firing, drawing the wrath of the enemy guns back on them. "The shower of shot and shell was tremendous," wrote the *Boston Daily Evening Transcript* reporter, "and the only wonder is that anyone escaped to tell the tale."[7]

The Union infantry did not escape the barrage, although how severe it was depended on where one was in the line. The 126th New York, near the left end of Bolivar Heights, was particularly hard hit. Two shells burst in succession in the ranks of Company B, killing 7 and wounding quite a few more. Another hit in Company H, beheading a lieutenant and injuring "many privates." "They could rake the whole line of our rifle pits," wrote Lieutenant Richard A. Bassett of the unlucky Company B. A veteran who endured the great cannonade at Gettysburg and many other shellings throughout the war expressed a widely shared opinion when he wrote that "it requires less nerve to face the enemy man-to-man, in the open field, than to lie down supinely while he hurls his missiles." The 9th Vermont was in a particularly trying position. "We were in a straight line between Rigby and the batteries across the Shenandoah, and in a straight line with Potts and the batteries on either side of the Charlestown Pike [Lawton's], and took much of the fire intended for each," wrote a member of the regiment. The 9th also lay in a peach orchard, the soil of which had recently been plowed, leaving it a reddish-brown color. The Vermonters made "a very conspicuous line of blue on red as seen from above," wrote Captain Ripley. To protect his men, Colonel Stannard would wait until the Confederate guns got the range of his regiment, and then he would move them forward. When the Confederates adjusted to the new position, Stannard pulled his men back to their former line. "In this way the regiment was most skillfully preserved from a heavy loss," recalled Ripley.[8]

Some units were unscathed by the bombardment. The 111th New York was one. George Dawes wrote to his parents about how "shell wer flying on every side but mostly in the woods the enemy supposing we had fell back into them but we wer just below so we escaped them." Those in the 115th New York were ordered close under the crest of Bolivar Heights and placed "in the edge of a narrow strip of woods," which offered concealment and cover. The men lay down and occupied their time "listening to the wizz & bang of bursting shells and laughing at the ridiculous evolutions of some of the more timid ones as the shriek of a shell woud sound uncomfortably near."[9]

The artillery roared for nearly 90 minutes. Despite the rain of Confederate missiles, Federal losses were relatively light. It was manifest to the Union leaders, however, that the moment the Confederate infantry advanced, and the Northerners attempted to form their men to meet them, the real slaughter would commence. "Our position was under their command," Colonel Trimble testified. "There was not a place you could lay the palm of your hand and say it was safe." The colonel offered the sober judgment that the "very moment they advanced with their infantry in such superior numbers and our men rose to engage them, we would have been swept from the very face of the earth by their artillery . . . It would have annihilated our forces on the left, and the new troops could not have been held, I do not believe by any mortal man, under such a fire." When asked how long his regiment could have held its position to meet an infantry attack while exposed to artillery, Colonel George Willard, commanding the 125th New York, answered, "I think about three minutes."[10]

Julius White recognized that the focal point of the battle was the hinge of the Bolivar Heights line on either side of the Charlestown Pike, where Potts's and Rigby's batteries were positioned. When the Confederate artillery lifted its fire, White was certain that this would be the objective of their infantry assault, and he sent orders to Camp Hill, exhorting the troops holding the interior line to reinforce this position. He also demanded a "massing of the artillery" to this strongpoint. These orders have the sound of decisive and aggressive action, qualities glaringly absent in the Union management of operations at Harpers Ferry, but they ring hollow under scrutiny. The principal infantry force available on Camp Hill was the 12th New York State Militia, not exactly a potent offensive or defensive weapon. As for the artillery, all the mobile guns—except those guarding the pontoon bridge or the approaches along the Shenandoah River—were already on the front line. But these considerations are inconsequential, for when

Miles learned of White's orders he countermanded them, because, as White later related, Miles "deemed it necessary to retain a force at the river-crossing." Miles was already defeated, but he stubbornly clung to a slender hope that relief might suddenly arrive.[11]

One by one the Union artillery forces exhausted their long-range ammunition. Phillips's and Von Sehlen's batteries fell silent first; then the 20 lb. Parrotts of the 5th New York Heavy Artillery fired their last rounds. Only Rigby's and Potts's guns remained in the fight. "Both of these sustained a heavy fire with the utmost gallantry, and replied rapidly and well," reported White. Captain Greenlee Davidson, one of the Confederate artillery commanders engaging these two batteries, agreed that they made things hot for his gun crews, writing that "shells burst in front of us, over us, around us and between the guns and everywhere near us." The Rebel guns, however, had more bark than bite. Potts and Rigby reported no casualties in the 90 minutes of firing. Davidson had one man killed, one wounded, and three horses killed, all from a single round from Potts's battery that burst directly in front of one of Davidson's caissons. He also noted that "nearly all the men at the guns were slightly bruised or received slight cuts on the face and hands from small particles of shell," an interesting comment, indicating that the Union guns were bursting their shells near their targets, but beyond the shells' lethal range.[12]

Dixon Miles was up before daylight and—accompanied by his aides, Lieutenants Binney and Willmon—rode to Bolivar Heights, arriving soon after the Confederate bombardment began. The three men left their horses on the eastern slope and made their way to the far right of the Bolivar Heights line on foot, "to see what indications there were of the enemy." Miles remained here for 15–20 minutes, observing the firing, and then he and his aides started down along the line toward the left end of the Heights. They encountered Captain Von Sehlen, who announced that his long-range ammunition was exhausted. Soon after they met Captain Phillips, who made the same report. At the center of Bolivar Heights they found General White and, according to Lieutenant Binney, Miles told the general "that the artillerists had reported that they were out of ammunition, and he [Miles] did not know what he should do; that he did not see that he could hold out any longer without the butchery and slaughter of his men, as the heights were being completely enfiladed." Binney recalled that White "did not seem inclined to recommend a surrender or anything of that sort." When White did not offer any suggestion on what should be done, Miles proposed that they raise a white handkerchief "and ask for a cessation of hostilities." White understood this to mean that Miles intended to ask for terms of surrender. White recommended that Miles call his brigade commanders together. Miles agreed and sent his aides to summon Colonels Trimble and D'Utassy.[13]

Miles, White, and the two brigade commanders met around 9 a.m., and Miles put the question of surrender to them. Trimble recognized that resistance would result in slaughter. He testified later that the "very moment they [the Confederates] advanced with their infantry in such superior numbers and our men rose to engage them, we would have been swept from the very face of the earth by their artillery, being in such close range, in full view, and taking the regiments on the flank, as would have been the case. It would have annihilated our force on the left, and the new troops could not have been held, I do not believe by any mortal man, under such a fire." Given the circumstances, Trimble believed that "there was nothing left for us but to surrender or see our men slaughtered without being able to do any public good." "We would have been morally responsible to the country for permitting it [a slaughter]," he added.

D'Utassy, not surprisingly, made the absurd suggestion that the garrison should try and cut their way out. Most likely he said this to protect his reputation, as a board of inquiry would surely look more favorably on an officer who refused surrender rather than one who embraced it too quickly. But the Hungarian's defiance faded quickly, and he soon agreed that they should seek terms "only on honorable conditions," meaning that officers retained their side arms and the men were not required to pass through the enemy's lines. White said nothing during the discussion but accepted the group's decision, and he agreed to ride out to discuss terms with the Confederates while Miles, Trimble, and Miles's staff attempted to get the Rebel batteries to cease fire.[14]

Miles, Willmon, and Binney rode to a prominent point at the northern end of Bolivar Heights and began waving their pocket handkerchiefs. Trimble rode to Rigby's battery and then onto the Charlestown Pike, attempting to signal a cease-fire from there. Miles and his aides rode south along the Heights, waving their tokens of surrender. When some infantrymen angrily questioned the raising of a white flag, Miles told them "that it was merely for a cessation of hostilities." It did not take a mental leap for any soldier to discern that this meant surrender, and the news swiftly spread throughout the garrison. Reactions varied. Some men were probably relieved, having endured a good dose of enemy artillery fire. Most however, were indignant. When Captain Rigby was ordered to take down his battery's colors he refused, declaring "that if the enemy wanted his battery and his colors they must take them." Captain Ephraim Wood, commanding Company H of the 125th New York, called for his entire company to join him and attempt to escape. Only two men, who were brothers, joined Wood, but the three succeeded in slipping through enemy lines and reaching Baltimore. Many men destroyed their muskets or bent their rammers. D'Utassy ordered Phillips and Von Sehlen to spike their guns and commanded his infantry to disable their muskets by unscrewing the nipple. He also insisted that the flags of his brigade's regiments be hidden. When Captain McGrath heard the news of surrender, he burst into tears, exclaiming, "Boys, we have got no country now." Even tough Colonel George Willard "shed tears of regret and indignation." Willard's lieutenant colonel, Levi Randall, told the regimental chaplain that "rather than have this happen, I would gladly have left my bones on this field." The men of the 125th New York tore their regimental colors into pieces and distributed them throughout the regiment. In the 9th Vermont the soldiers initially thought to wrap their colors around the waist of the color sergeant, but then they concluded that this would be the first place the rebels would look, so they, too, ripped apart their colors.[15]

When word reached the 9th Vermont's Colonel Stannard that the garrison was to be surrendered, he swore bitterly and declared that he would never surrender his regiment. He barked out orders for the men to form column and set out at the double-quick for the pontoon bridge over the Potomac. They made it as far as the head of the bridge when an aide from General White and Confederate General A. P. Hill caught up with them and ordered a halt. One Vermonter recalled that initially Stannard "refused to obey the order, but upon being impressed with the penalties which would be inflicted upon the other troops by his attempt to violate the terms of surrender, he yielded with anguish in his heart." But Stannard moved his regiment back to Bolivar Heights so slowly, allowing his men to bash their rifles against stumps and trees, that a Confederate officer, most likely Hill's aide, advised the stubborn Vermont colonel that if he did not hasten his march the Rebels would treat Stannard's regiment to a dose of "grape and canister." This finally convinced the colonel; he offered no more resistance, but marched his men back to their old position near Bolivar Heights. Stannard would have his revenge, however, less than a year later—at Gettysburg.[16]

The Confederate artillery units were slow to cease fire. Neither Walker's nor McLaws's gunners could see the white handkerchiefs of Miles and his aides through the smoke and the lingering mist. Walker finally surmised that the enemy had surrendered (most likely because Jackson's guns had stopped firing) and ordered his guns to cease fire. On Jackson's front a combination of the remnants of the morning's fog and lingering artillery smoke also made it difficult for some battery commanders to see the small tokens of surrender. Clarence A. Fonderen, a gunner in Crenshaw's battery, fired several shells into the Federal line, "owing to his not seeing the flag [of surrender]," and he was given "Hail Columbia" by Captain Crenshaw for doing so. Edward A. Moore, serving in Poague's battery, recalled that initially it was not clear that the enemy were signaling their capitulation. Miles's and his aides' handkerchiefs could not have been very large, and at another location someone flapped a tent fly to indicate surrender. Captain Poague immediately understood the meaning of the signals from the Union lines and reported to Colonel A. J. Grigsby, commander of the Stonewall Brigade, that he believed the Yankees were raising the white flag. Grigsby was a hard-bitten fellow, and Poague recalled Grigsby saying that "he could not see it and ordered me to continue firing." Poague looked again at the flag—or the tent fly—on the enemy line. "I was convinced that the white flag meant surrender and again reported what I saw and my conclusion," wrote Poague. Grigsby would have none of it and answered Poague, "Damn their eyes, give it to them." Poague did so, reluctantly, ordering his guns to fire very slowly until a courier from Jackson finally rode up with orders to cease fire. The enemy had surrendered.[17]

The Union soldiers considered the continued firing by the Confederates after the flag (or handkerchief) of surrender was raised to be "a most dastardly act." It killed one and wounded two in the 115th New York after they had marched back to their camp and drawn up into line to stack arms. It also mortally wounded Dixon Miles. He and Binney were walking down the eastern slope of Bolivar Heights to their horses when Confederate shells began to burst around them. Binney wrote that Miles said: "The enemy have opened on us again; what do they mean?" An instant later a shell burst directly behind the two men. Binney escaped unscathed, but a fragment tore the flesh entirely away from Miles's left calf and slightly wounded his right calf. Miles bled profusely, and Binney immediately applied a tourniquet and called for help. Apparently the lieutenant did not have an easy time finding volunteers to help carry Miles. The artillery fire probably deterred most from helping, but Ben Thompson marched by with his company of the 111th New York shortly after Miles went down, and Thompson recalled that the feelings against the old regular-army officer were so strong that "it was hard work to get men to help carry him." Binney eventually managed to round up six men, and they brought Miles to an ambulance.[18]

On A. P. Hill's front, his artillery had hammered Rigby's and Potts's batteries for nearly an hour when the Federal guns then fell silent. Hill ordered his pieces to cease fire, which was the signal for the infantry to advance. Pender's brigade led the way, coming to within 150 yards of the Union works, when suddenly one or both of the enemy batteries opened fire again. At this range the guns were almost certainly using canister. Pender's men took cover, and Hill ordered Pegram's and Crenshaw's pieces to limber and advance to provide closer support. The two Confederate batteries unlimbered within 400 yards of the Federals, at the edge of canister range, and commenced what Hill described as a "damaging fire." At least it looked like it was damaging, but since neither Union battery suffered a single casualty, appearances were highly deceiving. Soon a white flag was observed, probably the one raised by Trimble, and Hill immediately ordered his guns to cease fire. Hill then dispatched an aide, Lieutenant John H. Chamberlayne, to inquire whether the garrison had surrendered.[19]

Jackson observed the white flags from the schoolhouse on the Charlestown Pike. He promptly sent Lieutenant Henry Kyd Douglas, along with a courier, to investigate. According to Douglas, as he approached the Union lines he saw a group of mounted Federal soldiers riding out and learned that it was General White and his staff. Douglas rode over and introduced himself to White. "There was nothing strikingly military about his looks," recalled Douglas, although he did note that the general was superbly mounted and uniformed. White stated that he wished to see General Jackson to discuss terms of surrender. A. P. Hill rode up at about this time and went with White and Douglas to find Jackson. Douglas remembered Jackson as the "worst dressed, worst mounted, most faded and dingy-looking general he had ever seen anyone surrender to." This is a memorable image, but it was a figment of Douglas's imagination. Jackson was neither shabbily dressed nor poorly mounted. Dr. Hunter H. McGuire, Jackson's medical director, wrote that "somehow or other he [Jackson] had gotten a new hat and some good clothes in Maryland and looked very respectable." As for his horse, Jackson rode a dun-colored mount that McGuire thought cavalryman John "Grumble" Jones had given him.[20]

The interview was brief. When White asked what terms could be had, Jackson responded that the surrender must be unconditional. Having nothing to bargain with, White had no choice but to accept. Jackson directed A. P. Hill to arrange the terms of surrender and see that they were carried out. Despite his stern reputation, Jackson told Hill to extend quite liberal terms to the enemy. Officers could retain side arms and baggage, captured soldiers would be paroled, and two wagons would be lent to each regiment to haul baggage. Jackson had not suddenly softened; there were practical reasons for the terms. First, he could not spare the manpower to escort 12,000 prisoners into captivity. Second, prisoners had to be fed, and Jackson had a devil of a time finding enough food for his own men. But the loan of wagons and the terms for officers were most generous.[21]

Immediately after his meeting with White ended, Jackson composed a dispatch to Lee. Written "at near 8 a.m." (obviously no one's clocks were running on the same time, as the Federals gave the time of the surrender as 9 a.m.), it read:

> General: Through God's blessing, Harper's Ferry and its garrison are to be surrendered. As Hill's troops have borne the heaviest part in the engagement, he will be left in command until the prisoners and public property shall be disposed of, unless you direct otherwise. The other forces can move off this evening so soon as they get their rations. To what point shall they move? I write at this time in order that you may be apprised of the condition of things. You may expect to hear from me again to-day after I get more information respecting the number of prisoners, &c.
>
> Respectfully,
> T. J. Jackson,
> Major-General[22]

Jackson remained unaware of the Confederate defeat at South Mountain, as well as the fact that Lee had contemplated evacuating Maryland. Jackson's dispatch changed the course of the campaign.

For A. P. Hill's men, the Union surrender meant both a reprieve from what all expected to be a bloody assault and a chance to be the first to have a go at the booty waiting to be scooped up in the Federal camps. "You have never heard such cheering as greeted the hoisting of the white flag," wrote Captain Greenlee Davidson. "It was taken up by Regiment after Regiment and by our troops beyond the Shenandoah and Potomac until the mountains on the Maryland and Loudoun side reechoed again." Draughton S. Haynes, an enlisted man in Thomas's brigade, entered into his diary sentiments that were shared by many in his division: "How thankful we ought to feel the Yankee batteries have surrendered—the position is very strong." A member of Crenshaw's battery, who happened to have lived in Harpers Ferry before the war, despised the Yankees and delighted in their downfall. "Indeed," he wrote, "this is one of the happiest days of my life, to think that I have been instrumental in rescuing my home from the hands of the vile invaders."[23]

Captain David McIntosh and a single gun from his Pee Dee (South Carolina) Battery may have been the first Confederates of A. P. Hill's division to enter the Union lines. The captain had run one of his guns within point-blank range of Rigby's and Potts's batteries when the white flag appeared. Woods Brunson, one of the members of the gun crew, recalled that McIntosh shouted, "Limber to the front! Quick, men; let's be first in the fort." Brunson added that "no order was ever more promptly obeyed," and that a "general rush was made for the sutler stores, glory was, for the moment, forgotten and nature's demands alone heeded." Soon the infantry were pouring into the Union camps. William G. Morris of the 37th North Carolina was one of them. He "got plenty shugar & coffee, in fact almost any thing we could wish, clothing, etc." Lieutenant J. F. Caldwell of Gregg's South Carolina brigade wrote that "we fared sumptuously. In addition to meat, crackers, sugar, coffee, shoes, blankets, underclothing, &c., many of us captured horses roaming at large, on whom to transport plunder." Caldwell managed to snare two of the animals (he evidently made a fair haul), but he had to give them up to the quartermaster's department. Captain McIntosh received a Napoleon and a 3-inch rifle in exchange for two of his guns; new harnesses; and the horses of Phillips's battery to replace his thin, overworked animals. "We thought ourselves lucky," McIntosh wrote, for the Yankee horses were "fat and fine looking animals." But he would learn on the march to Sharpsburg that they lacked the toughness of the sinewy horses he gave up.[24]

As the Confederate soldiers poured through the Union camps, both sides were struck by the contrast in their uniforms and equipment. One of Pender's men stated that when his unit entered the Union lines, they found the Federal regiments drawn up in line with arms stacked. "It was quite a splendid reception," he thought, "but what a contrast! The enemy was spotlessly dressed in brand-new uniforms, shoes and buttons, and gold and silver trappings glistening in the morning sun, while we were almost naked; a great many of us without shoes, without even a faded emblem on our ragged coats to tell even rank or official command." The *New York Times* correspondent thought the Rebels a "mongrel, bare-footed crew," and that "Ireland in her worst straights [*sic*] could present no parallel, and yet they glory in their shame." White's aide, Lieutenant Henry B. Curtis Jr., described his captors as "the same miserable dirty set, as at the West, being in short, the <u>poor whites</u> of the South . . . They were rugged & shoeless and guns rusty and dirty." But Curtis was not naïve, and he did not consider the Confederates to be inferior. He thought they were "just the set to fight, having nothing to loose [*sic*] & living no better at home than in the army."[25]

Union soldiers soon realized that although the Southerners were hard looking, they were generally well behaved. "The rebels did not manifest any unseemly exultation over their success, and treated the prisoners with unexpected civility," wrote the *Boston Daily Evening Transcript* reporter who spent the siege with the Union garrison. William LeMunyon of the 126th New York agreed: "They were very dirty and lousy but they treated us well." Another member of the 126th, Lieutenant Richard Bassett, wrote that the "two armies who an hour previous were in deadly conflict might now be seen in friendly conversation and exchanges; which lasted all day. They nearly <u>all</u> traded <u>canteens</u> & made each other presents, & cut off buttons from their coats and gave to each other." Not surprisingly, however, some contact was less than positive. Colonel Sammons, commander of the 115th New York, had his magnificent black charger, which had been presented to him before leaving New York with his regiment, stolen when he went to visit Confederate headquarters. Henry Curtis Jr. noted that the Southern soldiers "stole about half the officer horses & all the niggers were claimed in two hours after our surrender."[26]

The terms of surrender permitted civilian refugees from Maryland and the Shenandoah Valley who had collected inside Union lines to be unmolested and allowed to return to their homes. But this did not apply to black people. There were nearly 1,200 negroes—many of them escaped slaves—who had sought refuge within Union lines or work with the army. All were considered escaped property and were to be seized. To his eternal credit, when Colonel Trimble heard of this he went to General Jackson and asked if this applied to blacks who were serving in noncombatant jobs with his regiments. Jackson referred him to A. P. Hill. But before he went to Hill, Trimble took the precaution of ordering all the negroes associated with the regiments in his brigade to the interior of their respective regimental areas. When Trimble finally caught up with Hill, the Confederate gave permission for all the blacks that Trimble identified as belonging to his regiments to be given passes, which was done. But the next day, when Trimble's 60th Ohio marched out from Harpers Ferry, a Confederate major attempted to separate the black men from the soldiers. Trimble drew his pistol, ordered the major aside, and saved the negroes with him from a certain return to slavery. The majority of the black people who were taken, however, were not as fortunate. A considerable number were claimed by masters who lived nearby, but many others were sent by rail to Richmond. The *Richmond Dispatch* recorded that there were men, women, and children in this group, and that they were owned (or at least reputed to be owned) by Virginians living near Harpers Ferry. The *Richmond Dispatch* observed that the negroes were being transported south because "their masters propose to offer them for sale in Richmond, not deeming them desirable servants after having associated with the Yankees."[27]

Stonewall Jackson proved to be the greatest curiosity to the Union soldiers. A member of Gregg's brigade related that the prisoners he encountered "made many of us promise to show him [Jackson] to them, if he should pass among us that day." Jackson rode into Harpers Ferry soon after his troops, accompanied by A. P. Hill, Dr. Hunter McGuire, and several staff officers. When word spread of his approach, the effect was electric. "Almost the whole mass of prisoners broke over us, rushed to the road, threw up their hats, cheered, roared, bellowed, as even Jackson's own troops had scarcely done," wrote a South Carolinian. Since contemporary Union accounts contain no reference to such a display, it is unlikely that this reaction—if it occurred at all—was widespread. Dr. McGuire, who was not prone to such exaggeration, found only that "the Yankee soldiers looked with great interest and curiosity at the general." White's aide, Lieutenant Curtis Jr., met Jackson and believed that "a more taciturn, imperturbable man, never existed. Has a perfectly unreadable countenance & never says a word even to his officers, unless necessary." Jackson did, at least, stiffly acknowledge the cheers and compliments of the captured enemy, and then rode down into Harpers Ferry, where, 14 months earlier, he had trained Virginia volunteers during the first exciting summer of the war. The war had taken a toll on Harpers Ferry, and the community Jackson looked on was now a drab, depressing place, largely deserted by its residents. He did not remain long and soon rode back to his own lines, leaving A. P. Hill behind, who set up headquarters in the building beside the one that had served as Miles's headquarters during the siege.[28]

Assessments of the Siege

The four-day operation to capture Harpers Ferry cost the combined Confederate forces slightly over 300 casualties. McLaws suffered the heaviest losses, with 213 killed or wounded. A. P. Hill reported 3 dead and 66 injured. Walker lost a handful to artillery fire, and a small number of Jackson's gunners became casualties during the engagement of September 14 and 15. In return, the Confederates killed or wounded 217 Union soldiers, along with capturing 435 officers and 12,085 enlisted men, 47 pieces of artillery, and "a vast quantity of small arms, cavalry & artillery equipment, horses, ammunition, Q.M. [quartermaster] & Comy [commissary] stores."[29]

The capture of Harpers Ferry and its garrison lost much of its glow in the bloodbath of Antietam, however. Had Lee withdrawn across the Potomac on September 15, after South Mountain, the foray into Maryland, although falling short of Lee's overall goal, would have dealt the Union a humiliating blow and possibly raised the prestige of the Confederacy in the eyes of England and France, countries that might not have understood that Lee had failed to achieve his broader strategic objectives. The Army of Northern Virginia would have returned to the South with their morale high and without the terrible losses they suffered at Sharpsburg. McClellan could only have claimed to have chased the enemy from Maryland, and his failure to rescue Harpers Ferry from capture would have eclipsed his victory at South Mountain and further shaken his already unsteady position as army commander. More importantly, without the Battle of Antietam and its patina of Union victory, Lincoln might have hesitated to issue the preliminary Emancipation Proclamation. With the escape of the enemy back into Virginia and the shame of the surrender of Harpers Ferry at the forefront of the public's mind, the timing would have been less than ideal for the president to make such a declaration. But Lee did not withdraw, for he was Lee, and he strove for something larger than merely striking the enemy a hard blow.

James I. Robertson, Stonewall Jackson's most recent biographer, believed Jackson's capture of Harpers Ferry was "in many respects . . . the most complete victory in the history of the Southern Confederacy." Surely there are none that exceeded it. Although casualties were few, Jackson inflicted a humiliating and costly defeat in terms of men (as prisoners) and material to the enemy. Since no great bloodletting resulted from it, the siege and capture of the Union garrison have not received the attention of Jackson's other campaigns and battles, but it was one of his finest moments, even if it was achieved against subpar Union leadership and green troops. At the outset of the operation he chose the boldest course, crossing the Potomac River at Williamsport instead of Sharpsburg, so that he might also destroy or capture the Martinsburg garrison. When he came up in front of the Union defenses at Harpers Ferry, he carefully husbanded his precious and exhausted infantry, instead employing maneuver and skillfully placed artillery to render the Union position on Bolivar Heights untenable. He effectively coordinated the artillery attack of Walker and McLaws— which was no easy task, given the distance between the three commands and the difficulty of communication—that utterly demoralized the enemy garrison. Tactically, it was one of Jackson's greatest achievements.[30]

But Jackson could not have captured Harpers Ferry if Walker and McLaws had not accomplished their missions. Since the Federals did not defend Loudoun Heights, Walker had an easier time of it than McLaws. Walker's most formidable obstacles were natural. He overcame these with commendable energy, wasting no time in seizing Loudoun Heights or in planting artillery on them. More will be said about McLaws later, but with multiple responsibilities assigned to him—capture Maryland Heights, seal off the enemy escape via Sandy Hook, occupy Weverton Pass, and protect his rear at Crampton's Gap and Brownsville Pass—and fewer troops than Jackson, McLaws carried out his primary mission to attack and capture Maryland Heights with vigor and skill. Had he failed to take the Heights, Harpers Ferry might not have been captured, and even it if had been, under those circumstances the cost in casualties would have been significant.

The Confederates also won at Harpers Ferry because they consistently did what Dixon Miles thought was unlikely or impossible. They carried artillery onto Loudoun Heights. They placed guns across the Shenandoah River to enfilade Bolivar Heights. And they moved through terrain south of those heights that Miles had deemed impassable.

Federal authorities acted quickly to discover how the calamitous and embarrassing defeat at Harpers Ferry had occurred. A military commission convened in Washington, D.C., in early October, and from October 4 to October 30, 1862, it heard the testimony of 44 individuals, ranging from Generals Halleck, Wool, and White; to the civilian scout Thomas Noakes; and even to the wife of an infantry company commander who had overheard a conversation between Miles and Colonel Thomas Ford. The testimony of the witnesses filled 900 pages. In most cases the commission's final report distributed blame and responsibility where it properly belonged. It concluded that Miles had displayed "incapacity, amounting almost to imbecility," which led "to the shameful surrender of this important post." Outside the commission's doors, ugly accusations circulated that Miles had been a traitor and had deliberately surrendered the post. Was he not from Baltimore, with its Confederate sympathies? Had he not paroled Confederate soldiers while the garrison was under attack, and did not one of those Confederates have a private meeting with Miles before being paroled? Treason offered a convenient explanation for Northerners who did not wish to believe the Rebels could have captured a post the press were calling "a Gibraltar."[31]

Miles had been no traitor, but White's aide, Lieutenant Henry Curtis Jr., perhaps said it best when, immediately after the surrender, he wrote that the colonel was "not competent for the command." Miles's errors were many: he did not properly use his cavalry to apprise him of McLaws's and Walker's approach; he failed to delay, harass, or impede Walker's approach to Loudoun Heights in any way; he placed an near-invalid in command of Maryland Heights, the most critical piece of terrain at Harpers Ferry, and then failed to properly supervise him; he neglected to build fortifications on Maryland Heights that were deemed necessary by his superior officer; he chose not to entrench Bolivar Heights when Jackson arrived in his front; he refused to cut down woods that blocked fields of fire along the Bolivar Heights line; he misused General White; and he exercised uninspired, unimaginative leadership throughout the siege. Yet for all his failings, with a garrison consisting primarily of green troops, Miles held out for three full days and part of a fourth against six Confederate divisions with veteran troops and leaders, and so in doing Miles gave McClellan a splendid opportunity to defeat Lee's army in detail. Reflecting years later on the events at Harpers Ferry, Julius White offered a telling observation, with which I concur.

> It has been often asserted that Harper's Ferry might have held out a day or two longer, but of those who claimed that it could have been longer held, no one has yet, so far as the writer is informed, stated how a garrison mostly of recruits under fire for the first time could have successfully defended an area of three square miles, assailed from all sides by veterans three times their number, posted with artillery, in positions commanding the whole field. The writer, with due deference, expresses the opinion that the force under Jackson could have carried the place by assault within an hour after his arrival before it, or at any time thereafter prior to the surrender, in spite of any resistance which under the circumstances could have been made.[32]

The commission also dealt severely, but justly, with Colonel Thomas Ford. Its report concluded: "It is clear to the Commission that Colonel Ford should not have been placed in command on Maryland Heights; that he conducted the defense without ability, and abandoned his position without sufficient cause, and has shown throughout such a lack of military capacity as to disqualify him, in the estimation of this Commission, for a command in the service." But Ford's good standing with the Republican Party saved him from dismissal from the service. Lincoln ordered him reinstated, but this was largely a face-saving gesture. Ford never served again. He took a position as Superintendent of Public Printing, and became a temperance leader until his death in 1868.[33]

General Julius White emerged unscathed from the commission's investigation, as did the other brigade commanders, Colonels Trimble and D'Utassy. White even earned the commission's praise for his "decided capability and courage," which was an accurate and just conclusion. Although he held several important commands subsequently, the stigma of Harpers Ferry clung to White. In July 1864, when it was rumored that he had been assigned to command a division in the 9th Corps at Petersburg, a staff officer in the division wrote: "There is a frightful story in the paper, I understand, that Gen. Julius White, the man who surrendered Harper's Ferry, has been assigned here by the War Department, but it is not believed." Through ability, White eventually changed people's opinions. The same staff officer who dreaded the possibility that White might take command of the division he served with made additional comments several days after the general did indeed assume its leadership. "I like him very much," the officer then stated. "He is a very kindly, pleasant person, rather Western, but gentlemanly and is taking hold of the Division in a very satisfactory manner."[34]

Only one combat unit was singled out for disgrace in the commission's report, the 126th New York. In the cases of Miles, Ford, White, and the other officers, the commission had been accurate and just in their findings, but their censure of the 126th's performance was unduly harsh. "The Commission calls attention to the disgraceful behavior of the One hundred and twenty-sixth New York Infantry," their report read. Had the 126th been a trained regiment, their behavior on Maryland Heights would have warranted such a judgment. But they were no more than a group of earnest civilians in uniform who performed no better and no worse than many other green regiments, either at Harpers Ferry or during the Maryland Campaign. The men of the 126th New York were incensed when they learned that they alone had been singled out from the entire garrison for bad behavior, and they requested a court of inquiry. Their request was denied, and the regiment had to endure months of public humiliation when the commission's report was published. "Our disaster was greater than in actual numbers [of casualties]," wrote one member. "It consisted of the lasting shame of the surrender, and the demoralization of our men." They and the other regiments who had surrendered at Harpers Ferry were dubbed the "Harper's Ferry cowards." Not until Gettysburg would the 126th—along with the 39th, the 111th, and the 125th New York—bury this label for good. By then the four regiments had been brigaded together and spent several months drilling and training. On July 2, 1863, they stopped the charge of one of their Maryland Heights adversaries, Barksdale's brigade, mortally wounded Barksdale, and drove his men back. Then, on July 3, they helped break Pickett's Charge. They were never called the "Harper's Ferry cowards" again.[35]

Dixon Miles died on September 16. His faithful aide, Lieutenant Binney, recorded that on his deathbed Miles said that "he had done his duty; he was an old soldier and willing to die." Binney added that Miles also talked about the failure of the Union army to relieve the garrison: "He thought the army must know of his situation, and the tremendous cannonading must have been heard by McClellan." Perhaps Miles did express these feelings, but Binney's inaccuracies in other accounts of the events at Harpers Ferry lead to a suspicion that he was not beyond inventing his colonel's near-to-last words. Following Miles's death, the old colonel's small but devoted staff transported his body to Baltimore, where he was buried on September 19.[36]

On to Sharpsburg

Precisely when Jackson received Lee's orders to march to Shepherdstown to cover the withdrawal of Longstreet and D. H. Hill is unknown, but Jackson's biographer believes that it was during the afternoon of September 15. Jackson's famous reply that he would "march at once, cross the river & join General Lee at

Sharpsburg" was in response to this message from Lee. At 3 p.m., probably soon after receipt of Lee's dispatch, Jackson ordered J. R. Jones's and Lawton's divisions to prepare two days' rations. A. P. Hill's division would remain at Harpers Ferry to superintend the parole of the Federal prisoners and remove the captured equipment and material. It took time for Jackson's brigades to issue rations and cook them, and by late afternoon only Trimble's and Lawton's brigades of Lawton's division were ready to march. They began the approximately 14-mile trek to Sharpsburg at sunset. Early's brigade did not receive its rations until late that evening, and it was midnight before they were ready for the men. An hour later, Early, accompanied by Hays's brigade and followed by J. R. Jones's division, set out for an exhausting night march. Such marches were difficult under the best circumstances, but for Jackson's poorly clothed and shod infantrymen, who had been marching or under arms since September 10, it was a punishing experience. Jackson, who never exaggerated such things, described the march as "severe."[37]

Walker's division also marched at 1 a.m. for Sharpsburg. When word reached Walker that the Union garrison had surrendered, he brought his guns and infantry down from Loudoun Heights, crossed his entire division over the Shenandoah River at Keyes' Ford, and marched to Halltown. Here he halted to obtain and cook rations and allow his men some rest. An hour after resuming their progress north, Walker's division overtook the rear of Jackson's column. Fortunately the weather that night was "warm and fair," which at least made this feature of the march bearable. About sunrise on September 16, the three divisions reached Shepherdstown and prepared to cross the Potomac River to join Lee at Sharpsburg.[38]

McLaws had a more delicate and difficult operation to conduct to rejoin Lee at Sharpsburg. He had to break contact with a powerful enemy in his rear, withdraw to the Potomac River, lead two divisions and their trains over a single pontoon bridge into Harpers Ferry, and provision his entire command before he could begin their march to Sharpsburg. He and his men's story—shortly prior to and then just after the surrender of Harpers Ferry—is central to understanding the outcome of the Maryland Campaign.

Pleasant Valley: McLaws and Franklin

A grim mood lay over the officers gathered at McLaws's headquarters in Pleasant Valley on the night of September 14. "Anxious feelings in all our bosoms," noted Captain H. L. P. King of the general's staff in his diary. Everyone anticipated that September 15 "will be a bloody day." It is doubtful that McLaws slept at all that night. Nor did many of his troops. A member of Barksdale's brigade recalled they were ordered to march from Maryland Heights at midnight, and they covered the nearly 5 miles to Brownsville at the double-quick. McLaws called his brigade commanders together at 3 a.m. to give them their orders. McLaws had assembled six brigades: the four of his own division, and Wilcox's and Parham's of R. H. Anderson's division. But of these six, two—Cobb's and Parham's—were wrecked in the fighting at Crampton's Gap and had become mere shells of their original strengths. Including the remnants of these brigades, McLaws's infantry totaled around 4,400 men on hand. It is uncertain how many batteries or guns he had, but the best estimate places it at eight batteries with 27 guns, which included 10 rifles and 11 obsolete 6 lb. smoothbores. Given the known strength of the enemy, this was hardly a force to inspire confidence, but McLaws was determined to compensate for his lack of soldiers and guns with boldness, daring, and position. The latter could not have been easy to select or occupy, since it was dark when McLaws reached the area, but Semmes and others had been around Brownsville for several days; they would have been familiar with the ground and could offer advice.

McLaws decided to make his stand south of Brownsville, where the narrow width of the valley and the lay of the land gave his artillery good fields of fire and forced the enemy to make an advance on a relatively narrow front. He placed Wilcox's, Barksdale's, and Kershaw's brigades in the first line; Parham's, Cobb's, and Semmes's in the second line; and most of the artillery near the left of the line. McLaws planned to expose enough of his infantry and artillery in the undulating terrain of the valley to hopefully fool the enemy into thinking that many more troops were tucked away in ravines and behind reverse slopes. Despite his reputation as a stolid, methodical, and somewhat plodding soldier, September 15 revealed that McLaws possessed nerves of steel and no small amount of audacity.[39]

His brigades and guns were deployed across Pleasant Valley by dawn. "Sternness was depicted on every countenance," recalled a member of the 7th South Carolina, "for we all appreciated our critical position." As daylight spread across the valley, Union pickets and some troops of Slocum's division could be seen. But the Federals had their arms stacked and were not stirring. Soon the deep-throated rumble of artillery echoed up the valley from Harpers Ferry, as the Confederate guns opened fire. "Our proximity on the Maryland side put us in position to hear the bombardment almost as audibly as if we had been with Jackson," wrote one of Wilcox's Alabamians. But even the sound of the guns failed to stir the bluecoats. "Surprise that the enemy do not attack," observed Captain H. L. P. King. McLaws was puzzled as well, commenting on this in his after-action report: "The enemy did not advance, nor did they offer any opposition to the troops taking position across the valley."[40]

Unlike McLaws, who accompanied his reinforcements to the front, William B. Franklin went to the rear on the night of September 14, returning to his headquarters at the Martin Shafer farm, east of Burkittsville. In the early morning

hours of September 15 Franklin received a dispatch from McClellan, sent at
1 a.m., with new orders, instructing him to do three things:

- Occupy the road from Rohrersville to Harpers Ferry, and place a sufficient
  force at Rohrersville to defend it from attack by the Confederate forces then
  positioned at Boonsboro.
- Open communications with Colonel Miles, "attacking and destroying such
  of the enemy as you may find in Pleasant Valley."
- Continue toward Boonsboro with his entire command, plus the Harpers
  Ferry garrison, to support the attack McClellan believed he would have to
  make in the morning. But, if the enemy had retreated toward Sharpsburg,
  Franklin would endeavor to intercept their line of retreat and cut them off.[41]

The order of McClellan's instructions is important. Franklin's first priority
was not the relief of Harpers Ferry. It was the occupation of Rohrersville, and
the road from that village to Harpers Ferry, to prevent the Confederates at
Boonsboro from reinforcing McLaws. This implied that a sizeable enemy force
was present in Franklin's rear. If Franklin attacked the Rebels that were in Pleasant Valley, and the Union troops at Rohrersville were overwhelmed by the enemy at Boonsboro, then Franklin would be caught between two Confederate
forces. McClellan's orders gave no comfort to Franklin about the enemy at
Boonsboro, other than that McClellan planned to attack them sometime on the
15th. Franklin probably wondered precisely when McClellan planned to attack,
as well as how strong the enemy was at Boonsboro. Apparently they were strong
enough for McClellan to think that they might detach a force to attack Rohrersville. The situation appeared both fluid and uncertain, and thus worrisome to
the mind of a careful soldier like William Franklin. Not surprisingly, the plan he
developed to obey McClellan's orders and exploit his corps' stunning victory of
the evening before minimized risk and maximized caution.

Those elements of General Baldy Smith's 2nd Division that were not already
at the summit of Crampton's Gap or in Pleasant Valley, as well as General Darius N. Couch's divisions, were in motion toward Pleasant Valley by 5:30 a.m.
Franklin detached one of Couch's brigades plus a battery and sent them to
occupy Rohrersville. The size of this force indicates that Franklin did not
consider the threat of attack from Boonsboro to be serious. This left him with
eight brigades of infantry and nine batteries of artillery, or about 15,000–16,000
infantry and 50 guns, a very formidable force if used effectively. As Smith's division arrived on the western side of South Mountain, it relieved Slocum's, which
Franklin had decided to be "in no condition for a fight that day," although its
losses on September 14 were only 10 percent of its effective strength and the
men's morale was high. Slocum's brigades then moved back to the summit of
Crampton's Gap and bivouacked. According to Franklin, Smith was "to begin

the movement toward Harper's Ferry," but the 2nd Division received no orders to do anything other than observe the enemy. The evidence is overwhelming that Franklin's only plan for September 15 was to see what the enemy had done during the night, and, by his own admission, he was in no hurry to do even this. Franklin did not personally cross South Mountain until 7 a.m.—an hour after daylight, four hours after Lafayette McLaws had risen to make his defensive preparations for the day, and nearly one hour after the cannonading at Harpers Ferry commenced. The firing meant that the Union garrison still held out; therefore every minute counted if they were to be rescued. Franklin had a "good view of the enemy's forces below" in Pleasant Valley as he crossed Crampton's Gap, and they seemed to be "well posted on hills stretching across the valley." Franklin met Smith at the summit, or somewhere on the western slope, and the two officers conducted a more thorough reconnaissance of the enemy's troops arrayed in front of them.[42]

McLaws's bold and clever deployment completely deceived the Union generals, and Franklin's timorous resolution sank at the sight of it. In an 1880s article for *Century Magazine*, Franklin attempted to explain his decision not to assault McLaws's line and—by default—leave Harpers Ferry to its fate.

> When I reached General Smith we made an examination of the position, and concluded that it would be suicidal to attack it. The whole breadth of the valley was occupied, and batteries swept the only approaches to the position. We estimated the force as quite as large as ours, and it was in a position which, if properly defended, would have required a much greater force than ours to have carried.[43]

Despite his dubious rationalizations, there are no possible excuses to justify Franklin's inaction. His collapse of moral courage at this moment in the campaign was—and still is—appalling. He had nearly four times the infantry strength of McLaws at hand, and 30 more guns. The situation stood squarely in Franklin's favor. The enemy troops had a river at their back, and the Harpers Ferry garrison between themselves and Jackson's forces on the Virginia shore. By 7 a.m. the guns of the garrison were still firing. Even with McLaws's line appearing far stronger than it really was, Franklin still could have aggressively probed with skirmishers to test its strength, or shelled it to alert the Harpers Ferry garrison of his position. His orders directed Franklin to attack. The timidity of the Pennsylvanian disgusted McLaws. He wrote after the war that "General Franklin had ample time on the morning of the 15th to have advanced his forces and engaged mine, which were in line, but a mile and a half distant from Crampton's Gap, and that the sound of his cannon would have been a notice to the garrison in Harper's Ferry that relief was coming." Instead Franklin, with Baldy Smith's support, convinced himself of the futility of attacking McLaws and contented himself with observing the Confederates, while less than 5 miles away the Union garrison fought a hopeless battle to stave off defeat and surrender. By 8 a.m. the firing at Harpers Ferry had ceased.[44]

Franklin did not communicate with McClellan until 8:50 a.m. He reported that his command was still closing up and that he had sent one of Couch's brigades to Rohrersville to secure the town. Only after these two things were accomplished would Franklin move to attack the enemy. Franklin also stated that he suspected Harpers Ferry had fallen; if so, he would need ample reinforcements from McClellan. Philip Kearny's harsh assessment—"Believe me, that Franklin is no soldier"—echoes loudly in the contents of this dispatch. Franklin fished for reasons to delay an attack, or even not to attack at all. First, Rohrersville must be occupied before Franklin could make an aggressive move, although the logic of this is puzzling. If the enemy at Boonsboro marched south to attempt to engage Franklin, Couch's brigade would block the road the Confederates would advance over, irrespective of whether Couch's men were at Rohrersville or marching along the road to it. Second, due to the probable surrender of Harpers Ferry, Franklin implied that an attack would be imprudent. Instead, Franklin himself should be strongly reinforced. If Franklin had asked Captain Charles Russell—who had carried Miles's message about the Harpers Ferry garrison's plight to McClellan and then ridden on to Franklin on the 15th—about the river crossing at Harpers Ferry, Franklin would have learned that only a single pontoon bridge connected Virginia with Maryland. As an experienced officer, Franklin would have known that the Confederates would consume a significant amount time in simply disarming and organizing the Union prisoners at Harpers Ferry. Any troops that were then sent to reinforce McLaws would have to cross that pontoon bridge, a slow process under the best of circumstances (it had taken the 1,500 troopers in the Union cavalry nearly 45 minutes to traverse the bridge on September 14). Time was still on Franklin's side, but he needed to act immediately. Even in the worst-case scenario—if he attacked and was repulsed—Franklin could easily have withdrawn back to Crampton's Gap; the enemy would need overwhelming numbers to drive him from there. But taking action entailed risk, and Franklin resolved to stay put, even if it meant that nearly 13,000 Union soldiers would surrender to the Confederates.[45]

Around 10 a.m. loud cheering burst forth from the Confederate lines in Pleasant Valley. The signal station on Maryland Heights had transmitted the news of the Union surrender to McLaws, who shared this at once with his brigade commanders. General William Barksdale galloped to the front of his brigade and announced the Confederate victory to each regiment. "It is unnecessary to state that the Mississippians yelled," wrote one member. J. J. McDaniel of Kershaw's brigade recalled that when Kershaw reported the surrender, "such a spontaneous burst of cheers and yells broke forth, echoing through the mountain glens." Captain H. L. P. King pulled out his diary and wrote, "Thank God!"

According to Captain William W. Blackford of Jeb Stuart's staff, a Union skirmisher, curious about what the cheering meant, called across to the Confederates: "What the hell are you fellows cheering for?" Blackford stated that "we shouted back, 'Because Harper's Ferry is gone up, G—— D—— you.'"[46]

If this news was passed along to Franklin, his only reaction was to continue to sit passively and wait for something to happen. At 11 a.m., McClellan's 8:50 a.m. dispatch (see chapter 15) reached him with news of the complete victory at South Mountain. The enemy forces at Boonsboro were in panicked retreat. If Franklin could confirm that the Confederates were moving toward the Shepherdstown Ford, McClellan now wished him to push his whole command to Sharpsburg and attempt to cut off the enemy's retreat (thus abandoning Harpers Ferry). "In this juncture much is left by the commanding general to your judgment, trusting that you will act promptly and vigorously and complete the success thus far gained."[47]

McClellan's dispatch galvanized Franklin to take up his pen and respond. The obvious problem with McClellan's orders was that if Franklin obeyed them, McLaws's force would be sitting unopposed in Pleasant Valley with the Union communications dangling in front of the enemy. Unless McLaws left, or Franklin attacked and drove him off—which was not going to happen—then McClellan's orders simply could not be acted on. But lest McClellan respond by ordering Franklin to attack McLaws, Franklin offered fresh excuses for why he should remain in the valley doing nothing. In the two hours since his previous dispatch, he had somehow concluded that he was now heavily outnumbered.

> The enemy is in large force in my front, in two lines of battle stretching across the valley, and a large column of artillery and infantry on the right of the valley looking toward Harper's Ferry. They outnumber me two to one. It will, of course, not answer to pursue the enemy under these circumstances. I shall communicate with Burnside as soon as possible. In the mean time, I shall wait here until I learn what is the prospect of re-enforcement. I have not the force to justify an attack on the force I see in front. I have had a very close view of it, and its position is very strong.[48]

McLaws's dispositions must have been remarkably clever to make his 4,400 infantry look like 25,000–30,000 men. Without firing a shot or shedding a drop of blood—with mere bluff, pluck, and nerves—-Lafayette McLaws had mentally whipped William Franklin, rendering Franklin's powerful force of 16,000 men as potent as so many campers in Pleasant Valley. In so doing, McLaws also ensured that Jackson would be undisturbed and unhurried in his dealings with the surrendered Harpers Ferry garrison and all of its equipment and supplies. Colonel Thomas Munford later asserted that McLaws never received proper credit for what he accomplished in Pleasant Valley. Had McLaws lost his nerve, or obeyed Lee's initial orders to cross the Potomac River to Virginia,

Jackson may have been forced to take Harpers Ferry by direct assault. Even more to the point, there surely would have been no Battle of Antietam.[49]

When McLaws learned that Harpers Ferry had surrendered, he immediately sent orders to General Featherston, who was positioned near Sandy Hook, to advance skirmishers to the pontoon bridge over the Potomac, or at least to go as far as they could until they were fired on. The balance of Featherston's brigade, and possibly Armistead's brigade, were ordered to march up the Pleasant Valley to join the forces confronting Franklin. Orders were also given for the trains of both divisions to be moved near the Potomac River, so that they could begin crossing to the Virginia bank the moment the way was clear. An aide-de-camp was sent to communicate with Jackson. McLaws remained at the front, where he could keep the powerful, but strangely inert enemy under observation.[50]

McLaws's aide-de-camp returned with word that Jackson wished to see the general in person. The Georgian reluctantly left his post around 1 p.m., probably still disbelieving that an enemy who had smashed McLaws's forces the day before at Crampton's Gap would then do nothing to follow up on that victory, nor relieve besieged comrades in Harpers Ferry. McLaws turned command over to General R. H. Anderson, with orders to "push the trains across the river as fast as possible and follow with the infantry when the trains were well over."[51]

Captain H. L. P. King recorded that Jackson and McLaws held a lengthy discussion when they met. McLaws suggested that if Jackson would cross his force, or part of his force, over into Maryland, they might "dispose of Franklin's command." This was precisely what Franklin feared would happen when Harpers Ferry surrendered. Ezra Carman later wrote that some of Jackson's staff officers related that Jackson discussed the idea, "and that without further orders from Lee he would have made it." This is doubtful, for without Lee's explicit blessing, it is unlikely that Jackson would have embarked on such a maneuver. Still, it is intriguing to speculate on what effect it might have had on McClellan, for such an attack would have posed a serious threat to his communications. In any event, Jackson had his orders to join Lee, so he left McLaws with characteristically simple orders to "follow him [Jackson] as soon as possible" to Sharpsburg.[52]

The generals may also have discussed McLaws's supply situation. It had been problematic, and now it was serious. The four days' worth of rations issued on September 10 were eaten by September 13. McLaws's commissary officer, Major John F. Edwards, had managed to obtain "some flour, not exceeding twenty barrels," a handful of cattle, and "some wheat," but the latter could not be ground, since the C&O Canal's banks had been cut by General Pryor's men and there was no water to run the mills along the canal. These rations fed the troops on September 14, and permitted issuing what one soldier described as "a few morsels hastily eaten" and another as "a good meal" early on the 15th. But this exhausted Edwards's supplies. When he inquired hopefully of Jackson's commissary officers about the captured stores, they replied that there were none left. Unless food to feed nearly 8,000 men and hundreds of animals could be found, McLaws faced the prospect of a 17-mile march with troops who had eaten nothing since early that morning and very little the day before. And for many of McLaws's men, in addition to short rations, they had been under arms and gone without proper sleep for four days.[53]

Around 2 p.m. R. H. Anderson quietly began to form up the brigades facing Franklin and started them down the valley, while elements of Hampton's brigade screened this delicate operation. The Yankees detected the movement, and it stirred Franklin from his torpor. He ordered General Baldy Smith to "pursue" the Rebels with a brigade and a battery, and sent along some of his cavalry (probably the 6th Pennsylvania Cavalry) to keep the enemy under observation. The rest of Franklin's large force continued to repose in the area around Crampton's Gap, waiting while their commander waffled as to what he should do. At 3 p.m. Franklin wrote out a fresh situation report for headquarters. The enemy was retreating, he wrote, with Smith's brigade and battery in pursuit. Franklin did not feel justified—under McClellan's 8:45 a.m. orders—in putting his whole command in motion toward the front, for reasons Franklin did not feel it necessary to explain; no doubt these were based on the logic that an enemy force as large as Franklin imagined McLaws's to be should not be left in Franklin's rear. Franklin also stated that he had sent a squadron of the 6th Pennsylvania Cavalry to communicate with Burnside, writing that "if they succeed in getting to him, the news from him may change my intentions." How this would change Franklin's intentions is unclear, as the circumstances that precluded him following McClellan's earlier orders still existed in Pleasant Valley. Franklin ended his dispatch with a curious statement: "I shall, however, try to carry out the spirit of your orders as nearly as possible."

What this meant is a mystery, for Franklin displayed no evidence that he intended to undertake anything more than his farcical "pursuit" of McLaws. As Franklin signed his dispatch for delivery, a courier from General Smith galloped up to headquarters with a report concerning the pursuit. Franklin then added a postscript to his message to headquarters that is at once both pitiful and hopeful: "I hear from General Smith that the enemy is drawing off through the valley too fast for him. I shall start for Sharpsburg at once." How such a supposedly large enemy force could march down the valley too fast for Smith's single brigade and battery to catch them defies explanation. But Franklin had at last promised to do *something* with his men. The 6th Corps, however, did nothing "at once," and before a single soldier stirred from his Pleasant Valley campsite, word reached Franklin that the enemy "retreat" had halted near the base of the valley and Smith's pursuit had ground to an inglorious stop.[54]

Smith's "pursuit" of the Rebels had been a sham. In fact, his brigade had left so much distance between it and the enemy that the Confederates were unaware that they were even being followed. McLaws later questioned whether there had been any pursuit at all. In 1888 he wrote:

> I am sure that the movement of my troops did not evince a disposition to avoid an engagement with General Franklin on the 15th, nor does it appear that my command, when it did move from the first line, went so fast as to prevent it being overtaken by General Smith, especially when it is known that the whole distance moved on the 15th was not over three miles, and if a pursuit was made it is strange that not one of my commanders, nor any of my staff, nor anyone else reported or mentioned that there had been seen at any time any evidence of any advance.

A soldier in Barksdale's brigade recalled that some Union cavalry "made a show of dogging the rear" of the Rebel column during their withdrawal down the valley, until a volley from the 18th Mississippi encouraged the Yankees to keep their distance. No one observed any Union infantry.[55]

McLaws formed his new defensive line across the base of Pleasant Valley, anchoring his right at Weverton Pass and his left on Maryland Heights. While the brigades took up their positions, McLaws's trains slowly rumbled over the pontoon bridge to Harpers Ferry. The bridge broke frequently from the weight of the heavy wagon traffic, resulting in numerous delays for repair. Each time the trains were halted, paroled Union prisoners anxious to get out of Harpers Ferry took the opportunity to try and cross, adding to the traffic problems and, of course, causing bridge movement, which made repairs problematic. The difficulty of McLaws's river crossing offers some notion of what a predicament he would have been in had Franklin hit him hard that morning. McLaws's trains and artillery did not complete their passage until nearly 2 a.m. Then the infantry began to cross. They were followed by elements of Hampton's cavalry, who formed the rearguard. McLaws's handling of Hampton's horsemen displeased the South Carolinian. He complained the next day to Stuart that McLaws had insisted on keeping one of Hampton's regiments "in a gap behind his [McLaws's] infantry"—either Solomon's Gap or Weverton Pass—and that they were left there until all the infantry, artillery, and trains had finished traversing the Potomac River. Moreover, McLaws had failed to communicate his movements to two squadrons Hampton had on picket east of Weverton Pass, one of which was at Berlin, Maryland. In both instances Hampton retrieved his men only through the inactivity of the enemy. "I think it proper to say that the disposition made by Genl. McLaws of my cavalry exposed one Regt. to imminent danger of being cut off, whilst the neglect to notify the two squadrons on picket made the danger to them still greater." These were important oversights by McLaws and his staff, but otherwise the withdrawal down Pleasant Valley and then the Potomac River crossing were skillfully managed.[56]

McLaws's and R. H. Anderson's infantry and artillery passed through Harpers Ferry to Halltown, where they bivouacked near the village on the morning of the 16th. The Confederate troops were worn out, disgusted, and ravenously hungry. While his men slumped down to get some rest, McLaws and his quartermaster, Major Edwards, rode to Charlestown in search of provisions. After what Edwards described as a "diligent search," a "small quantity of flour was obtained but not enough for one issue." Commissary wagons had to drive to Charlestown, load the provisions, and return, a round trip of nearly 8 miles that consumed probably four hours in travel time alone. But it could not be helped, as McLaws's command needed food before they could undertake the march to Sharpsburg. Food had delayed Stonewall Jackson's march to Lee; now it delayed two more divisions Lee desperately needed.[57]

Around 4 p.m. on September 15, Franklin received fresh orders from McClellan, which both confirmed that the 6th Corps would remain unemployed in Pleasant Valley and revealed the strategic ramifications of Franklin's failure to determine the enemy's real strength in his front. McClellan wrote that Burnside's corps and Sykes's division were moving on the Sharpsburg Pike with orders to attack an enemy force reported to be at Keedysville. "I will instruct them to communicate with you at Rohrersville, and if necessary re-enforce you," he continued. McClellan then stated that it is important to drive in the enemy in your front," yet he ensured that nothing would come of this directive by adding his familiar refrain, "but be cautious in doing so until you have some idea of his force." McClellan also informed Franklin that the 1st, the 2nd, and the 12th Corps were moving toward Boonsboro on the main pike, and McClellan promised to divert at least one division on the first road south beyond the mountains, so they would be in position either to reinforce Franklin or to continue on to Porterstown. In other words, based on Franklin's exaggerated assessment of enemy strength in Pleasant Valley, McClellan had needlessly diverted one division from the line of march to Boonsboro, and alerted an entire corps and another division to be prepared to reinforce the 6th Corps. Such was the damage done by Franklin to the Union pursuit of Lee's army from South Mountain.[58]

Franklin responded to McClellan at 4 p.m., writing that "I shall await further orders here." Franklin added that he had established communications with General Burnside, who had "nothing to communicate," and that he himself had not moved toward Sharpsburg. During that entire day, Franklin failed to pass the most important piece of intelligence on to army headquarters—perhaps because it had not been communicated to him, or because his "pursuit" of the enemy never drew near enough to find out—which was that the Confederate forces in his front had withdrawn to the base of Pleasant Valley and were apparently crossing the Potomac River to Harpers Ferry. This information was crucial for two reasons. First, it meant that the enemy's troops in Pleasant Valley were probably marching to join Lee at Sharpsburg, not hovering about to threaten McClellan's communications. Second, because of this, Franklin could leave just an observation force in the valley and march with the rest of his command to join the main army.[59]

McClellan, however, had little choice but to accept Franklin's reports from Pleasant Valley, and they profoundly—and negatively—affected McClellan's strategic decisions. Without the assurance that the enemy in Pleasant Valley had withdrawn, McClellan was compelled to leave the 6th Corps there to protect his communications. At 4:30 p.m. Chief of Staff Marcy sent Franklin new orders, directing him to withdraw Couch's brigade at Rohrersville and to do his "best to hold your position without attacking unless you should see a very favorable opportunity." McClellan, continued Marcy, "will be satisfied if you keep the enemy in your front without anything decisive until the Sharpsburg affair is settled."[60]

In sum, Lafayette McLaws is one of the pivotal—but least understood—characters of the Maryland Campaign. Perhaps no soldier did more to salvage this campaign than he did. Although Jackson deserves credit for coordinating the separate Confederate forces that compelled the surrender of Harpers Ferry, McLaws faced the hardest fighting; he was the one who seized the key terrain, ensuring that the garrison would eventually capitulate. When Franklin broke through into his rear on September 14, McLaws reacted immediately and decisively. His decision to ignore Lee's orders—which were for McLaws to withdraw into Virginia and then march to Sharpsburg on the north bank of the Potomac River—showed good judgment; the courage to follow a course of action, based on sound reasoning, other than the one ordered by his superior (who, not being in the midst of the action, was less well informed); and an appreciation of the strategic situation of his army. McLaws evinced a willingness to take calculated risks when he stripped his forces from Maryland Heights in order to make the strongest possible front against Franklin. The criticism Stuart levied at McLaws for allowing the Union cavalry to escape from Harpers Ferry is unjust. McLaws did not have sufficient troops to do everything, but he did leave a picket post to watch the Sharpsburg Pike, despite Stuart's claims that McLaws had left this road undefended. By facing down Franklin in Pleasant Valley on the 15th, McLaws sealed the fate of the Union garrison at Harpers Ferry, which provided the Confederates with their only real success in the Maryland Campaign. Then he skillfully withdrew his men down the valley and carried out a river crossing without a single casualty. McLaws's actions through September 16 had been outstanding. On September 17, he would shine again at a crucial moment on the bloody fields at Sharpsburg.

Franklin's performance stands in sharp contrast to McLaws. He had utterly failed at his test of independent command. Although he behaved adequately in putting his command into action on September 14, his nerve wavered at the critical moment in the battle. If Slocum's division had not taken matters into their own hands, the 6th Corps would not have seized Crampton's Gap that evening. Franklin, moreover, was unwilling to take any risks on September 15, despite the fact that he had orders to attack. Unless he did *something*, nearly 13,000 Union soldiers would be captured. He chose instead to imagine that the enemy outnumbered him—without ever testing their strength—and to find excuses for inaction. He permitted McLaws to withdraw from his front and cross his two Confederate divisions over the Potomac River unmolested, and then Franklin did not even bother to communicate these events to McClellan. As a result, the Army of the Potomac was deprived of Franklin's nearly 16,000 fighting men, who were left to watch a phantom force and a supposed (but no longer extant) threat to their communications, while the real enemy tramped rapidly north to join Lee at Sharpsburg. Paralyzed by his own indecision and his fear of failure, Franklin seriously undermined McClellan's strategy and handed Lee the opportunity to reconcentrate his army at Sharpsburg, allowing Lee to offer McClellan battle in Maryland at improved odds. McClellan asked Franklin for "all your intellect and the utmost activity that a general can exercise." Franklin had been found wanting on both counts, and confirmed McClellan's private opinion that "his efficiency is very little."[61]

Nevertheless, Franklin escaped the criticism he should have faced for his failures in Pleasant Valley. McClellan sheltered his favored subordinate from possible censure. In his preliminary report on the campaign, McClellan excused Franklin's inaction in Pleasant Valley on September 15 by advancing the explanation the 6th Corps' commander gave: that he had faced "a force, largely superior in numbers," because of the "shameful and premature" surrender of Harpers Ferry by its garrison. The Harpers Ferry Commission disagreed with McClellan's assessment, but they levied their criticism at McClellan, rather than at Franklin, when they concluded that McClellan "could, and should, have relieved Harper's Ferry."[62]

McClellan's plan to split the enemy in twain had seemed possible on the morning of September 15, given the success at Crampton's Gap and the Confederates' retreat from Turner's Gap and Fox's Gap. But his scheme rapidly unraveled, and Franklin's failures at both command and intelligence in Pleasant Valley loomed large in this. The opportunity to damage Lee still existed, but it was quickly slipping away.

18

September 16

"We are entirely too methodical"

September 16 dawned quietly over Antietam Creek, despite the thousands of armed men who assembled on its opposite banks and readied themselves for battle. Fog lay heavily over the course of the creek, as it had elsewhere in the area over the past few days.

McClellan: *"Attack the enemy on his left flank"*

At Army of the Potomac headquarters in Keedysville, Miles's surrender of Harpers Ferry was the topic of conversation at the breakfast mess. "This too, with Franklin's victorious columns in sight, and the booming of the guns firing a national salute in his ears!" complained Colonel Strother in his journal. The colonel might have emended his entry had he known the truth of Franklin's lethargy in Pleasant Valley. But this was not yet evident, and no one at breakfast would have questioned McClellan's assessment that the Harpers Ferry garrison's "resistance was not as stubborn as it might have been."[1]

The fog rendered it uncertain whether Lee and his army had slipped away during the night or remained in position. McClellan had instructed Sumner to hold the 2nd Corps "in readiness to attack the enemy early in the morning should he be found in our front at that time." He had also ordered Sumner to send out reconnoitering parties at daylight, "to ascertain if there is any enemy in your front his strength etc." Sumner had a scouting party out before daylight (see below), but they had not yet returned by the time McClellan sat down to breakfast. Enemy pickets were reported to have remained on the west side of Antietam Creek, but that was all the Union pickets saw. At 7 a.m. McClellan sent a brief dispatch to Halleck, advising him of the situation and adding that the Federal forces "will attack as soon as the situation of the enemy is developed." In a dispatch to Franklin written at 7:45 a.m., McClellan repeated this intention to attack if Lee had not moved off. But the quiet that prevailed across the front encouraged McClellan to think that Lee, with his main force, had prudently slipped back to Virginia during the night. McClellan reflected this hope in a telegram to Mary Ellen, sent soon after his report to Halleck: "Have reached thus far & have no doubt delivered Penna. & Maryland." To McClellan, it was unlikely that as canny a soldier as Lee would offer battle with his army divided and a river at his back—particularly after the drubbing McClellan believed he had administered to the Confederates at South Mountain.[2]

McClellan had also ordered his own reconnaissance across Antietam Creek to discover whether the enemy had departed. Either late on September 15 or very early on the 16th, Colonel Thomas Devin, commanding the 6th New York Cavalry, attached to the 9th Corps, was told to cross the Middle Bridge and probe the west bank. Unaware of these instructions, the 2nd Corps' commander, Sumner, ordered his reconnaissance for the same area, selecting four companies for the mission—chosen from the combined 61st and 64th New York—under a very tough and competent lieutenant colonel named Nelson Miles. Precisely where Devin's troopers went on the west bank and how far forward they probed is unknown. Miles's reconnaissance is better documented. He assembled his command of some 140 infantrymen at 2 a.m. and led them behind Richardson's division to the steep bluff south of the Boonsboro Pike; then he turned back, marching his command single file down the bluff to the Middle Bridge. Here the companies closed up into marching column, and they had advanced about to the center of the bridge when they heard the sound of cavalry "dashing toward us from opposit-End." Miles shouted for the approaching troopers to halt. When they failed to comply, he ordered the skirmishers at the front of his command to fire. His veteran soldiers responded instantly and delivered a volley, stopping the horsemen in their tracks. Eighteen-year-old Ephraim E. Brown, one of Miles's men, wrote that "Miles demanded in his Sharp Shrill tone what troops are you?" The response shouted back was "6th New York Cavalry. What troops are you?" Miles gave the name of his regiment and inquired by whose orders the other group had gone beyond Union lines. By McClellan's, they responded. The mistake was soon cleared up, but the failure of army headquarters to coordinate its reconnaissance with Sumner resulted in 3 troopers wounded and one horse killed. It might have been considerably worse had their limited vision at night and the slope of the bridge not caused Miles's men to fire high.[3]

The cavalry informed Miles that the enemy had withdrawn from the immediate vicinity of the bridge; this indicates that they had not, however, ventured far beyond the environs of the Joshua Newcomer farm, which was situated directly on either side of Middle Bridge. Miles and his men pushed on over the bridge and past Newcomer's farm, with the aggressive lieutenant colonel near the very front. The fog reduced visibility to no more than 15–20 feet, and the dust in the road—which probably had settled because of the moist night air—deadened the sound of the companies' footsteps. They advanced for nearly 600 yards, unchallenged by a single Confederate picket, and reached a ridge overlooking the ravine through which, north of the turnpike, the Sunken Road ran. Miles was about to go forward down the slope and into the ravine when, as Ephraim Brown recorded in his diary, "a Scared Johney came running into us from a road on our right." This road could only have been the Sunken Road, where it enters the Boonsboro Pike. Although Brown did not identify the Confederate soldier's unit, he was probably from G. B. Anderson's brigade, which was posted along the lane in this vicinity. How four companies of Federal infantry advanced so far along the turnpike without being challenged raises a question of whether some confusion existed in the Confederate command over who was responsible for picketing this ground. Nonetheless, whoever should have done so had managed it badly.[4]

The New Yorkers captured the young man, who was so frightened that, as Brown noted, "he shit his briches." The discomfiture of the Confederate had "Miles and us Boys laughing at the fun," but the pause saved them from capture. The Rebel told Miles that he was very close to the main Confederate line. While he cleaned himself up, it grew light enough for the Union soldiers to see the Confederate pickets, some of whom were observed moving along a fence line south of the road in a direction that would cut off the Federals. Miles quickly and quietly ordered his men to double-quick back to the bridge. Obscured by the fog, and moving in such a direction that nearby Rebels probably mistook them for a friendly picket detail, the detachment returned to the Middle Bridge around 6:30 a.m. without drawing a single shot.[5]

It is uncertain just when Sumner passed along the substance of Miles's report of his reconnaissance to McClellan, but it was probably after 8 a.m., since shortly before that hour McClellan sent orders for Colonel Devin to conduct another reconnaissance beyond the Middle Bridge, probing, stated Devin, "as far as they [the enemy] would let me go." Although a volunteer, Devin had seen service with the New York State Militia. He was a cool-headed leader and a superb tactician. He selected his L and M troops and set out at 8 a.m. They marched past the regulars manning the skirmish line covering the Middle Bridge and went over the bridge to the west bank. Once they were across, Devin ordered part of his command to deploy as mounted skirmishers. The New Yorkers rode forward cautiously, fanning out through the Newcomer farm and the open pasture west of it. The fog was lifting by this time, improving visibility, and as Devin's mounted skirmishers emerged into the open they were fired on by Confederate skirmishers in the Park farm's orchard, to the north. Devin thought he saw a Confederate battery "on a cornfield hill"—which was most likely Cemetery Hill—and he rode alone beyond his skirmish line to the same ridge that Miles and his infantry had reached earlier in the morning. Devin dismounted when he reached the ridge, but he had been spotted, and "they opened on me with a full battery." The fire "was so close and hot that I thought I would never get my horse away," he wrote. But he did, and then called in his skirmishers and wheeled his sections around and retired toward the Middle Bridge. As they crossed the bridge to the east bank of Antietam Creek, the same or perhaps a different battery spotted them and opened fire with solid shot and shell. This caused the head of the column to become "a little unsteady." Devin, riding at the rear, roared out in a booming voice, "The first man that trots I'll shoot." This had the desired effect, and Devin marched his companies out of range "as steady as if on parade."[6]

It was 9 a.m. (or soon after) when Devin returned from his reconnaissance. The warm September sun had burned off the fog and revealed a powerful line of Federal artillery on the ridges north and south of the Middle Bridge, on the east bank of the Antietam. Reaching elevations of 190–200 feet, the ridges offered plenty of room and excellent fields of fire for numerous batteries, and the reverse slope provided cover for the limbers, caissons, and supporting infantry. The previous evening, McClellan had ordered General Hunt to relieve Tidball's and Pettit's batteries with the heavy batteries of the artillery reserve. But the roads leading to the front from South Mountain were so jammed with troops and wagons that movement slowed to a crawl. "It is almost impossible to get to the battle-field," wrote a *New York Daily Tribune* reporter on September 16. "The road is full, such a jam was never seen in Broadway." The reserve did not reach what I shall call Pry Ridge until nearly 9 a.m. Tennessee-born Lieutenant Colonel William Hays commanded the reserve. A West Pointer, he had 22 years' service in the regular army, most of it with artillery. He placed four batteries—Taft's, Langner's, Von Kleiser's, and Wever's, together containing 16 of the army's 20 lb. Parrott rifles between them—along Pry Ridge between Pry's farm and the Middle Bridge, relieving Pettit and Tidball. South of the pike, along the southern extension of the same ridge, Lieutenant Samuel Benjamin's 2nd U.S. Battery E and Captain Stephen Weed's 5th U.S. Battery I unlimbered and cleared for action, completing a formidable line of what was now 20 of the 20 lb. Parrott rifles and four 3-inch rifles.[7]

One of these batteries targeted the Confederate artillery that had shelled Devin's retiring cavalry. This drew a response from other Confederate guns that, in turn, were engaged by all the Federal batteries along Pry Ridge. Guns thundered and shells whistled and exploded, shattering the tranquility of the morning, as well as loudly announcing that the Army of Northern Virginia had remained and was full of fight. One of the first and only casualties of this morning artillery barrage was Major Albert Arndt, commander of the 1st Battalion, 1st New York Artillery, a nearly all-German organization to which Langner's, Von Kleiser's, and Wever's batteries belonged. Arndt, described as "an experienced and excellent officer," was helping direct the fire of one of his batteries when a shell or a shell fragment mortally wounded him. His gunners partially avenged his loss by giving the Confederates a taste of the firepower that 16 massed 20 lb. Parrott rifles can produce, forcing the enemy's pieces to limber and withdraw to escape destruction.[8]

McClellan left for the front soon after breakfast, once he had completed his communications to Halleck, Franklin, and his wife. Leaving most of his staff behind at headquarters, McClellan rode south of the Boonsboro Pike to where Benjamin's battery was located, arriving soon after it took position but before the artillery duel commenced. Shortly after unlimbering, Benjamin reported firing at some groups of Confederate infantry who had revealed themselves, but this was probably before McClellan arrived. Minutes after McClellan dismounted on the ridge, however, the gunnery fight erupted. Benjamin reported that the enemy opened with 10 or 12 guns, targeting his battery and the reserve batteries aligned along Pry Ridge. *New York Daily Tribune* reporter George Smalley was present, and he stated that McClellan "found himself suddenly under a rather heavy fire." McClellan, so far as can be discerned, remained there under fire and completed his visual reconnaissance of the enemy position. As Smalley wrote, "the lines and columns that had darkened cornfields and hillcrests, had been withdrawn," and now only some artillery and a handful of infantry were visible to McClellan's field glasses. From the bluff on which Benjamin's guns sat, the terrain Lee had selected to defend was so deceptive that the Confederate position "looked like only a narrow summit fringed with woods." Smalley speculated that "it was still uncertain whether the Rebels were retreating or re-enforcing . . . as they had withdrawn nearly all their troops from view, there was only the doubtful indication of columns of dust to the rear." From the number of guns the Confederates had in action and the apparent extent of their front, McClellan thought it highly unlikely that this was some rear guard Lee had left behind to cover his withdrawal. If Lee planned to retreat, he would have done so during the night. Moreover, at various times that morning, McClellan should have received the reports from Miles's and Devin's reconnaissances, which—although they did not provide much useful intelligence—confirmed that the Rebels were still in position. Another assessment had also reached the commanding general, from scouts who had reconnoitered the Rohrbach Bridge and found it "strongly covered by riflemen" holding the steep west bank. The Confederate left appeared to rest on a "wooded eminence" north of the David Miller farm—probably the high ground around what would be called the North Woods—where McClellan may have observed elements of Fitz Lee's cavalry brigade. As McClellan stated later, "it became evident from the force of the enemy and the strength of their position that desperate fighting alone could drive them from the field."[9]

A line of hills rising south of Keedysville proffered one advantage for McClellan's position on the east bank of Antietam Creek. The first, or westernmost, range was known as Red Hill. East of Red Hill was the higher Elk Ridge, also referred to as Elk Mountain. Red Hill reached an elevation of just over 1,000 feet at its highest point and afforded a superb locale from which to observe Lee's entire position, as the view from there extended as far as the Shepherdstown Ford. Early on the morning of September 16, Lieutenant J. Gloskoski, an officer decorated for bravery on the Peninsula, and Major Albert J. Myer, the chief signal officer of the Army of the Potomac, ascended Red Hill to find a suitable site to establish a signal station. They found a point from which "we had a full view of the enemy's lines" and set up their equipment. The best observation site was a rather precarious perch in the top of a tall tree, which one of the signal officers climbed, and the best view from the tree was at a place where the officer could "only sustain himself by exertion," which apparently meant that he had all he could do to keep from falling out of it. Once this station was established, virtually any troop movement Lee attempted in daylight hours could be observed. One of Gloskoski's first reports initially lent credence to the idea that Lee was retreating across the Potomac. He signaled that "an immense train of enemy's wagons is moving on the road from Sharpsburg to Shepherdstown: they cross the Potomac and halt about a mile S. of Shepherdstown." But when the Rebel infantry and artillery in front of Sharpsburg did not stir from their positions, it became apparent that the Confederates were merely moving their trains to the Virginia bank of the river.[10]

Although the enemy had concealed their infantry and repositioned their artillery, McClellan's personal reconnaissance—combined with what he had learned from Miles, Devin, pickets, and scouts—revealed several useful pieces of information. The Confederates were positioned to contest a crossing of the Rohrbach Bridge, and their artillery could sweep the approaches to Sharpsburg from the Middle Bridge. The Upper Bridge, Pry's Ford, and Neikirk's Ford were under observation by Rebel cavalry pickets, but these locales were not directly defended and were out of range of the Confederates' artillery. The whereabouts of the enemy's flanks were not known precisely, but observation and basic map study placed their left on the high ground near the North Woods and their right at the Snavely farm, where it could cover the two crossings below the Rohrbach Bridge: Snavely's Ford and Myer's Ford. McClellan had several options open to him to assail Lee's position. The easiest to dismiss was a frontal assault from a bridgehead at Middle Bridge. It would enjoy the covering fire of the heavy guns on Pry Ridge, but then it would advance into murderous fields of fire in front of Sharpsburg, where it would be swept by Confederate artillery and small arms. Equally easy to reject was attacking the Rohrbach Bridge and then proceeding along the axis of Rohrbach Bridge Road. The enemy held superb defensive terrain on the east bank of Antietam Creek that commanded the bridge; a frontal effort to capture it would verge on madness. The two fords below the bridge, Snavely's and Myer's, offered potential opportunities to outflank the bridge defenders, and any force that crossed here would threaten the Confederate line of communications. But these fords might be contested as well, and any effort on this front would lack artillery support.

That left the Upper Bridge and Pry's Ford. McClellan had concluded from his September 15 reconnaissance that this approach, and an attack on the enemy's left, represented his best option. The Union troops could cross the Antietam unopposed, and there was ample room to maneuver large formations in the ground between Antietam Creek and the Potomac River. Once deployed, the assault forces could attack south along the axis of the Hagerstown Pike, into the flank of the enemy. Here the Federals would have the support of enfilading fire from the heavy batteries on Pry Ridge, which could have an impact on any targets from the Hagerstown Pike east. This strategy, in combination with a feint on the Confederate center and against the Rohrbach Bridge and the lower fords, had promise, as these elements would fix the defenders in place. But McClellan needed to act promptly and decisively, since every hour that he delayed raised the likelihood that Lee would receive reinforcements from Harpers Ferry. The reconnaissance on the morning of September 16 had revealed no substantial change in the enemy's position from the 15th, yet McClellan reported that he was

> compelled to spend the morning in reconnoitering the new position taken up by the enemy, examining the ground, finding fords, clearing the approaches, and hurrying up the ammunition and supply trains, which had been delayed by the rapid march of the troops over the few practicable approaches from Frederick. These had been crowded by the masses of infantry, cavalry and artillery pressing on with the hope of overtaking the enemy before he could form to resist an attack. Many of the troops were out of rations on the previous day, and a good deal of their ammunition had been expended in the severe action of the 14th.[11]

McClellan's laundry list of reasons why he could not move that morning against Lee is not altogether accurate, and it amounts to nothing more than a series of excuses. While waiting for orders to move, most of the 1st Corps regiments—who had borne all the fighting at Turner's Gap and points north—had replenished their ammunition and received rations on the morning of September 15. Burnside delayed the march of the 9th Corps to do the same thing at Fox's Gap. The 2nd, the 5th, and the 12th Corps were not engaged at South Mountain, so ammunition was not an issue for them. As for reconnoitering the new enemy position and "examining the ground," Ezra Carman observed that "from the time of McClellan's arrival on the field until Hooker's advance in the afternoon of the 16th, nothing seems to have been done with a view to an accurate determination of the Confederate position." McClellan made no use of his cavalry, other than the reconnaissance by Devin's 6th New York Cavalry. They should have driven in the Confederate cavalry pickets that had the Upper Bridge and Pry's Ford under observation, so that any crossing there would be unknown to the enemy, but this was not done. Moreover, once the Rebel cavalry pickets were forced back, the Federal troopers could have reconnoitered the approaches to the enemy left, scouted the terrain in this area, and ascertained more accurate information on the whereabouts of the Confederate left flank. This was not done, either. Nor were the cavalry used to precisely locate Snavely's Ford and Myer's Ford—something McClellan left to his topographical engineers, which would have dire consequences on September 17. Finally, part of Farnsworth's brigade could have picketed the Harpers Ferry Road, in order to give a timely warning in the highly unlikely event that any of the Confederate Harpers Ferry forces approached from this direction to threaten the Federal flank. Instead, Farnsworth's cavalry brigade remained bivouacked in the rear of Pry Ridge, largely unemployed, except to provide escorts and support to artillery batteries. McClellan conducted his own reconnaissance—as well as using his well-trained and very bright topographical engineers—but none of them ventured beyond the east bank of Antietam Creek. Events on September 17 would prove that the engineers not only failed to accurately locate Snavely's Ford, but they also failed to discover another ford above the Rohrbach Bridge.[12]

Despite McClellan's orders to Sumner to have his command in readiness "to attack the enemy early in the morning should he be found in our front at that time," it is evident from McClellan's actions that morning that he had not developed a plan for a general attack on September 16. The only other significant thing McClellan did that morning was to order Sumner to bring up Mansfield's 12th Corps from its bivouac at Nicodemus Mill. Still, McClellan understood that delay benefited the enemy and increased the odds that Lee would be reinforced by his divisions from Harpers Ferry. At 8:45 a.m. McClellan had Colonel Ruggles send a message to Sumner, urging him "to hurry up Banks' Corps." Forty-five minutes later Ruggles wrote to Sumner again, requesting him to inform McClellan "the moment the head of Mansfield's Corps comes up." McClellan evidently felt the urgency of massing his forces, yet this did not produce a plan of action. McClellan instead proceeded to ready his army for battle with great deliberation.[13]

At 9:30 a.m. McClellan visited Hooker, but neither man left a record of their conversation. McClellan planned to use Hooker's 1st Corps to spearhead an attack against the enemy left, and it is likely that he wished to speak with Hooker about the battle-readiness of Hooker's men after the fighting at South Mountain, as well as to discuss the probable routes the 1st Corps would use to reach the enemy flank. Whatever they discussed, Hooker received no orders when McClellan left around 10 a.m. to reconnoiter his left flank and visit Burnside and the 9th Corps. McClellan wrote that he carried out this reconnaissance personally, "to satisfy myself that the troops were properly posted there to secure our left flank from any attack made along the left bank of the Antietam, as well as to enable us to carry bridge no. 3 [the Rohrbach Bridge]." Clearly McClellan's faith—and confidence—in Burnside had eroded after South Mountain, for these were duties that his Right Wing commander should have attended to. McClellan was accompanied by Chief of Artillery Hunt; Captain James

C. Duane, commanding the regular engineer battalion; Colonel Albert V. Colburn, one of McClellan's favorite aides-de-camp; and two orderlies. McClellan remembered that they rode "generally in front of our pickets" and "went considerably beyond our actual and eventual left," and that they "drew the enemy's fire frequently, and developed the position of most of his batteries." Even given McClellan's penchant for embellishing the moment, it is unlikely that the party rode beyond the picket line. Nor was what he described the sort of thing an army commander should be doing, in drawing enemy fire and conducting a reconnaissance more properly carried out by cavalry or members of his staff. It simply wasted precious time.[14]

McClellan's reconnaissance revealed "that our extreme left was not well placed to cover the position against any force approaching from Harper's Ferry by the left bank of the Antietam," meaning that Burnside had not arranged the 9th Corps to McClellan's satisfaction. Since Burnside had received no known orders on the 16th to redeploy the 9th Corps, nor was he aware of McClellan's plans or of how McClellan intended to use Burnside's corps, this remark seems unjust. While arranging his left to deflect an enemy attack from the direction of Harpers Ferry may have been prudent, the prospect of this happening was small. If McClellan had questioned local citizens or used his cavalry to scout the area, he would have learned that the road up from Harpers Ferry was not suitable for heavy army traffic, and the ground along the road was unfavorable for an attack. The attackers would be compressed into a narrow front between Elk Ridge to the east and Antietam Creek to the west. McClellan did discover (which any reconnoitering officer would have, as well) "that the ground near 'Burnside's bridge' [Rohrbach Bridge] was favorable for defense on our side, and that an attack across it would lead to favorable results." The problem was with mounting a successful attack on the bridge, since a direct assault on it was a recipe for butchery. Jacob Cox stated it bluntly:

> No point of attack on the whole field was so unpromising as this. Certainly the assumption that the Ninth Corps could cross the Antietam alone at the only place on the field where the Confederates had their line immediately on the stream which must be crossed under fire by two narrow heads of column, and could then turn to the right along the high ground occupied by the hostile army before that army had been broken or seriously shaken elsewhere, is one which would hardly be made till time had dimmed the remembrance of the actual position of Lee's divisions on the field.[15]

After examining the terrain in the vicinity of the Rohrbach Bridge, McClellan rode back to see Burnside. He provided the Rhode Islander with some sketchy details of his battle plan; basically, that Hooker's 1st Corps would cross Antietam Creek that afternoon to find the Rebel left. The general attack would not begin until September 17, and Hooker would spearhead the main effort aimed at crushing the enemy's left. The 9th Corps' role would be "to create a diversion in favor of the main attack, with the hope of something more by assailing the enemy's right." In preparation for the attack, McClellan wished the 9th Corps to advance three of its four divisions, plus the Corps' artillery, to positions Mc-Clellan's staff had selected for them that were closer to the Rohrbach Bridge, and he wanted Burnside to carefully examine the approaches to the bridge, since Burnside would probably be ordered to capture it. The Corps' fourth division would constitute a reserve. "Old Burn," McClellan's friend and loyal subordinate, was being demoted. After South Mountain, Burnside thought the suspension of the wing commands and Hooker's detachment was a temporary measure, made necessary by the pursuit of what was believed to be a defeated and retreating Rebel army. Now Burnside suspected that Hooker's machinations had brought about the latter's detachment for the upcoming battle. In this he was mistaken. The decision was McClellan's, influenced by his appreciation of Hooker's pugnaciousness in an army that possessed few aggressive commanders, and possibly by McClellan's new personal distrust of Burnside. Relegating Burnside to a secondary role in the coming battle ensured that he would win no laurels in Maryland. Humiliating Burnside—by giving orders directly to Hooker, Burnside's subordinate under the wing command structure, and essentially dismantling the Right Wing—was perhaps the punishment McClellan chose to mete out for the Rhode Islander's role in the charges now pending against Fitz John Porter. In McClellan's world, Burnside had proved himself to be untrustworthy because of the latter's thoughtlessness in forwarding private letters from Porter, containing slanderous comments about John Pope and meant for Burnside's eyes only, to Lincoln and the War Department. There certainly could be no performance reasons behind the decision. Burnside had managed the battle at South Mountain competently. He had moved sluggishly from South Mountain on September 15, but in the Army of the Potomac at that time, this was hardly a reason to break apart a command structure and demote its commander. McClellan surely knew that his decision to dismantle the Right Wing bruised his old friend's feelings, yet he offered no explanation for his decision nor any clarification of a now-muddled command structure. Jacob Cox, the 9th Corps' acting commander, urged Burnside to assume command of the corps so that Cox could return to his division. It was a sensible suggestion, but Burnside refused. Cox recalled that Burnside replied that as "he had been announced as commander of the right wing of the army, composed of two corps, he was unwilling to waive his precedence or to assume that Hooker was detached for anything more than a temporary measure." This was not the spirit that wins battles, but the responsibility for delineating a clear chain of command resided with McClellan. The consequence of this particular action was an absurd and inefficient chain of command on the army's left, with a wing commander in charge of only one corps, giving orders to an acting corps commander who lacked the necessary staff to properly manage its operations.[16]

To Burnside's credit, his displeasure with his personal situation did not influence his execution of his orders. Immediately after his meeting with McClellan, Burnside issued a command, through Cox, for the 9th Corps to ready itself to march. When McClellan departed from his meeting with Burnside, he had left instructions for Captain Duane of the engineers to personally post each division, which—looking back—appears to have been an unnecessary and time-consuming duty for the senior officer of the army's engineers. Duane made the sensible suggestion that Burnside should detail three staff officers, and the captain would show them where the divisions were to be placed.[17] Cox thought that the entire situation was unnecessarily complicated.

> There was far more routine of this sort in that army than I ever saw elsewhere. Corps and division commanders should have the responsibility to protecting their own flank and in choosing ordinary camps. To depend on the general staff for this is to take away the spontaneity of the subordinate and make him perform his duty in a mechanical way. He should be told what is known of the enemy and his movements so as to be put on his guard, and should then have the freedom of judgement as to details.[18]

Earlier that day, McClellan had tasked Duane's engineers with the responsibility of locating fords across Antietam Creek. They informed Burnside and Cox that the only passable fords in the area of operations "were one between the two upper bridges[,] named [Pry's], and another about a half a mile below Burnside's [Rohrbach] bridge, in a deep bend in the stream." This locale (although it did not meet the engineers' description of it) was Snavely's Ford. Burnside and Cox did not do their own reconnaissance, trusting to the accuracy of Duane's engineers—which proved to be a costly mistake. The engineers either had not discovered Myers's Ford, below Snavely's, or they did not consider it passable (although the Confederates did); they failed to accurately locate Snavely's Ford; and they missed a ford above the Rohrbach Bridge, which would be discovered during a frantic effort to find a way to flank the bridge defenders during the battle on September 17. By that time, many a good man would be stretched out in front of the Rohrbach Bridge, either dead or wounded.[19]

After leaving Burnside, McClellan returned to the vicinity of the Pry farm. Reinforcements had arrived during his reconnaissance of the left. Major General George W. Morell's veteran division of the 5th Corps and Brigadier General Max Weber's brigade of garrison troops, assigned to the 2nd Corps, arrived at Keedysville about noon. Morell passed on through the village and bivouacked south of the Boonsboro Pike. His division, numbering three brigades with three batteries of artillery, added slightly over 5,000 officers and men to the army's strength, as well as 14 Napoleons and two 10 lb. Parrott rifles. Except for the newly organized 118th Pennsylvania and 20th Maine regiments, Morell's division contained some of the most combat-experienced veterans of the army. Weber contributed three large regiments—totaling approximately 1,800 men—who were well drilled and well equipped, but untested in battle. They were assigned to French's division.[20]

The addition of Morell's and Weber's men raised McClellan's infantry effectives to about 55,000, considerably less than the numbers McClellan is usually credited with. If artillerymen and cavalry troopers are added, then McClellan probably had 60,000–62,000 effectives. Most studies of Antietam cite McClellan's own figure of 87,000, which he gave as the army's strength in his second and more detailed report on the Maryland Campaign, but this was the number of soldiers that were present for duty, not combat effectives. In the Union army, about 17 percent of those listed as present for duty were men detailed to perform necessary noncombat jobs, such as teamsters, medical orderlies, ambulance drivers, and the like. Otherwise, McClellan expected no further reinforcements that day. He chose to leave Franklin's and Couch's divisions in Pleasant Valley, both to keep an eye on the large force Franklin had reported there and to protect the army's flank. Andrew A. Humphrey's newly formed division of Pennsylvania regiments, destined to fill out the 5th Corps by increasing it to three divisions, had not left Washington until September 14, due to logistical complications. McClellan ordered them to Frederick, to provide additional security for the army's rear.[21]

Of the 60,000 men that were available, 48,000 were in the vicinity of Keedysville. Hooker's 1st Corps was massed east of the Upper Bridge. French's and Sedgwick's divisions of the 2nd Corps were positioned on either side of the Boonsboro Pike, west of Keedysville. Mansfield's 12th Corps had marched up that morning and massed in the rear of French, near Morell's division. Richardson's and Sykes's divisions were in line in the rear of Pry Ridge, supporting the batteries on the crest of the ridge. The men were well rested, and the Army of the Potomac was ready to do battle. By noon the fog had long been dispersed and a hot sun beat down on the waiting troops. McClellan had finally determined his plan of attack. The main effort, consisting of the 1st and the 12th Corps, supported by the 2nd, would fall on the enemy left, while the 9th Corps would create a diversion "in favor of the main attack" against the Confederate right, in order to prevent Lee from shifting troops from this position over to his left. When the main attack and the 9th Corps' diversion were fully developed, McClellan planned to strike the enemy center "with any reserve I might have on hand," which meant Porter's 5th Corps.[22]

The general idea of the plan—to mass three corps against the Confederate left and pin down the enemy right with a demonstration—was sound. But its execution was amateurish, and it violated nearly every principle of successful military operations. McClellan intended to open the battle on the afternoon of September 16 by sending Hooker's 1st Corps across Antietam Creek to find and attack the Rebels' left flank. Hooker would fight alone, for McClellan had given no orders to move the 2nd or the 12th Corps to the west bank of the Antietam on the 16th. Instead, McClellan planned to conduct this movement during the night of the 16th or early on the 17th, after Hooker had developed the enemy position. This transgressed the central military tenets of surprise, mass, and maneuver. First, Hooker's advance across the Antietam on the afternoon of the 16th would sacrifice any element of surprise. Second, mass is defined as bringing a decisive force to bear on a critical point. Transferring one corps west of the Antietam while holding two others east of the creek meant that it was doubtful that mass would be achieved at the point of the main effort; this virtually guaranteed that the 1st, the 2nd, and the 12th Corps would not act in concert. Francis Palfrey observed that under McClellan's order of battle, his attacks "were far more likely to be successive than to be simultaneous." Third, by waiting until September 17 to open the main engagement, McClellan granted the Confederates more precious time to concentrate their divided forces and prepare their defenses. McClellan knew the lessons of Castiglione, but he failed to act on them when similar circumstances were presented to him. Following McClellan's reconnaissance of the left and the arrival of Morell and Weber, there was no longer any reason not to issue the necessary orders to attack. Unless Franklin were summoned from Pleasant Valley, McClellan could not increase his strength, yet every that hour he delayed before attacking the Confederates raised the prospects that Lee's numbers would go up through reinforcements received from Harpers Ferry.[23]

The objective of Hooker's mission must also be questioned. Was it a reconnaissance in force or an attack? If the latter—which is what Hooker reported that it was—then this effort had no immediate support should it encounter the enemy in superior numbers. In the opinion of Ezra Carman, it "was a blunder, in that the movement was made in the afternoon of the 16th, at an hour too late to accomplish anything before dark and serving no purpose, save to inform Lee where he was to be attacked." The entire force selected to attack Lee's left flank, with its actions well screened by cavalry, should have crossed Antietam Creek during the morning or early afternoon, while the 9th Corps demonstrated against Lee's right flank and kept the Confederates uncertain as to where the main effort would fall. Instead, it was 2 p.m. when McClellan issued orders for Hooker to bring his corps across the Antietam. Colonel Strother, McClellan's volunteer aide-de-camp, found the delay exasperating.

"It seems that we have spent the day maneuvering and studying the ground. I don't like the delay. We should have attacked on sight Monday evening, or this morning at all risks. We might then have got Lee at a disadvantage. But while we take time to concentrate he will do the same or escape. If he is here to-morrow it will be because he feels confident of his game. We are entirely too methodical." [24]

McClellan's scheme of attack also sacrificed the principles of unity of command and simplicity. No senior commander was briefed on or understood the battle plan. Although McClellan met with Hooker and Burnside and discussed operations with them, it is clear from their reports and correspondence that neither general understood the overall strategy or how their command fit into it. One historian of the campaign has suggested that McClellan deliberately did not brief his corps commanders, since he wanted Hooker to lead the attack on Lee's left. Hooker was junior in rank to both Sumner and Mansfield, so it was necessary to circumvent the seniority issue—and two corps commanders that McClellan considered to be mediocre, even on their best days—by committing Hooker first and then reinforcing him with the 12th and the 2nd Corps. In this way, as the latter two corps reached the front, Mansfield and Sumner would be obligated to ask Hooker where their divisions should go in. Thus Hooker would indirectly organize the attack of all three corps. But what if Hooker was killed or wounded? This was the rub. If he went down, the army's central engagement would fall under the direction Sumner, who did not understand the general plan of battle—an unlikely recipe for victory. This ex post facto scenario might have been true, but it is also likely that McClellan simply wanted to see what developed from Hooker's advance before he committed the 2nd and the 12th Corps to any line of action. [25]

It has often been suggested that McClellan delayed his attack because his shrank from committing his soldiers to battle, with the prospect of them dying or suffering from serious wounds. This is nonsense. But the terrible burden of command is heavier for some than it is for others. While McClellan's orders and correspondence from the morning of September 16 clearly display a resolve to attack, his excessive amount of preparation that day—the reconnaissance from the position of Benjamin's battery, the meeting with Hooker, the reconnoiter of the army's left flank, and the meeting with Burnside—all suggest a lack of confidence and a hesitation to act. This did not necessarily stem from a wish to avoid risking the lives of his men, although McClellan did care about that, but rather from a fear of potential failure. Once the army was set in motion, there could be no turning back, and with battle came the unpredictable and the un-known. Like British General Bernard Montgomery, McClellan did not like to attack until all the details were attended to. As far as possible, risks were to be minimized. McClellan planned not so much to smash his adversary as to ensure that he would not lose the battle, just as during the Seven Days he sought to save his army from the imagined Confederate hordes, rather than whip the Rebels and regain the initiative. This was his greatest shortcoming as a field general: his inability to see his intended path clearly and to take decisive action when opportunity knocked. But McClellan was not afraid to fight, as that evening and the next day would show. Hooker's marching orders including instructions to cross Antietam Creek "and attack the enemy on his left flank," and he was "at liberty to call for reinforcements as might be required." The Battle of Antietam was about to begin.[26]

Lee: "All will be well if McLaws gets out of Pleasant Valley"

Lee spent the night of September 15 camped in a small woodlot about three-quarters of a mile west of the center of Sharpsburg. On the 16th he arose early, as was his custom, and rode to Cemetery Hill, arriving sometime after daybreak. Walking among the guns of the Washington Artillery, Lee sought to find some vantage point that offered a view of the Union position, but the morning fog obscured the entire enemy line. He returned to the Boonsboro Pike and moved to a campfire, which helped shake off the chill of the cool, damp air. Earlier in the morning Lee had received the welcome news that Jackson's two divisions, followed by Walker's, had arrived at the Potomac River. A. P. Hill's division temporarily remained at Harpers Ferry—to parole the Union prisoners and remove the captured stores, weapons, and ammunition—before coming along to join the rest of the army at Sharpsburg. At the time the report Lee had received was written, McLaws still remained in Pleasant Valley, facing the enemy there, but with orders to follow Jackson as soon as possible. Knowing that three of the army's missing divisions would arrive by mid- to late morning comforted Lee, but he had hoped that his entire Harpers Ferry force, minus whatever was necessary to deal with the captured stores, would join him on September 16. Now it was doubtful whether McLaws and his two divisions could be up that day.

Lee gave vent to his anxiety when a staff officer from Longstreet rode up at sunrise and delivered a message—possibly reporting that at that point Jackson was fording the Potomac River at Shepherdstown. Lee listened carefully, and then said: "All will be well if McLaws gets out of Pleasant Valley." Lee must have felt anxious, even though he had expressed the opinion that McClellan would not attack the Confederates on the 16th. What if Lee had guessed wrong, and the Federals moved against him when the fog lifted? Had not McClellan acted with unusual energy and aggressiveness on September 14? Despite the great risks, Lee stubbornly refused to abandon his Maryland Campaign. He had already surrendered the tactical initiative to McClellan; a withdrawal to Virginia would give up the strategic initiative as well. This Lee refused to do.[27]

Lee anticipated that McClellan might attempt to turn his left, where the ground was more favorable for maneuvering large numbers of troops, by moving the Federal assault forces over Antietam Creek via the Upper Bridge and

Pry's Ford, where their crossing would be unopposed. To confront this possibility, on the evening of September 15 Lee shifted Hood's division and Stephen D. Lee's reserve battalion of artillery to fields east of the little Dunker church on the Hagerstown Pike. There were good fields of fire for Lee's guns, and they could cover an enemy approach on either the Hagerstown Pike or the Smoketown Road. This was the only major change Lee made to his dispositions. The Army of Northern Virginia was now arranged (from right to left) in the order that follows.

Munford's 2nd and 12th Virginia Cavalry watched Snavely's Ford and Meyer's Ford, as well as the bridge over the mouth of the Antietam. D. R. Jones's division continued to hold the right of the army, with its left on Cemetery Hill and its right extending along the high ridge immediately south of Sharpsburg, where it covered the approach along the Rohrbach Bridge Road. Toombs's two regiments were still deployed forward, in direct defense of the Rohrbach Bridge. G. T. Anderson's and Nathaniel Evans's small brigades were, respectively, south and north of the Boonsboro Pike on Cemetery Hill, supporting the artillery there. D. H. Hill's division continued to hold the center, with his four brigades spread across a frontage of slightly more than three-quarters of a mile, running from G. B. Anderson's brigade, which was holding down the right (astride the Boonsboro Pike), to McRae's brigade in the Sunken Lane. Hill extended his line on September 16 by recalling Colquitt's brigade from its position southwest of Sharpsburg and inserting it into the Sunken Lane on McRae's left, just west of where the Roulette farm lane enters the Sunken Lane. If Federal forces crossed at Pry's Ford or Neikirk's Ford, a likely avenue of approach would be via the Roulette farm and Roulette's lane; McRae's and Colquitt's deployment covered this. To Colquitt's left and front were Hood's two brigades and S. D. Lee's artillery battalion. Fitz Lee's cavalry brigade screened the army's left flank and kept the upper crossings over Antietam Creek under observation.

Lee gave no orders to build any form of field fortifications, which was curious, as he was an engineer by training who well understood their value. There are two possible reasons for this, besides the obvious one that soldiers in 1862 did not habitually entrench or throw up breastworks when in the presence of the enemy. First, Lee did not know where McClellan would attack. Although the left flank seemed a likely prospect, the Federals might move against his right or center. Lee anticipated a mobile defense, not a static one, and entrenching might have been a wasted effort for his exhausted soldiers. The second possibility (and the less likely of the two) is that Lee still considered a withdrawal to Virginia on the morning of the 16th if McClellan attacked before Jackson could come up. There is no evidence, however, that Lee did have this in mind.

A third scenario, advanced by Joseph Harsh in *Taken at the Flood*, is that Lee considered the option of slipping past McClellan by way of the open path to Hagerstown. Here, Lee would be able to threaten Pennsylvania and McClellan's right flank, and he could rest his army while waiting for the arrival of McLaws's divisions and A. P. Hill, when the campaign of maneuver could be resumed. Perhaps Lee did contemplate this move, but it seems unlikely that he would have attempted it until his army was fully reunited. Before then it would have been a perilous maneuver, increasing the distance between his army's main body and the one-third that was still at Harpers Ferry, with nearly the full might of the Army of the Potomac sitting squarely between them. And neither Lee's logistics nor his men were in any condition to conduct further strenuous maneuvers in the face of the enemy.

Whatever Lee's reasons for not entrenching at Sharpsburg, it was an error. McClellan granted him over 24 hours to strengthen his position with field-works, but aside from some light cover that the troops threw up on their own initiative on the day of the battle, nothing was done. Lee's infantry would pay a severe price for this on September 17.[28]

While Lee warmed himself by a campfire and fretted about McLaws, Jackson led his divisions across Boteler's Ford at Shepherdstown. Lawton's division began crossing at dawn, followed by J. R. Jones's, and then Walker's division, which had caught up with Jackson during the night. The men were dead on their feet, particularly Jackson's, and a "stream of stragglers" marked the route of their march from Harpers Ferry. An officer of the 13th Virginia recalled that in his company, "every man broke down before we got to Sharpsburg, except myself." Jackson's pride, the vaunted Stonewall Brigade, counted 250 muskets in the entire unit the next morning. A Louisiana chaplain who passed over Jackson's route on September 17 offered an evocative description. "The country was literally crowded with stragglers. Some of the men excite my sympathy, for they looked sick and broken-down but others again I looked upon with contempt, for they evidently were professional stragglers. Some of them even threw their guns in the fence corners." The chaplain noted with disgust that many officers were among their numbers. Even the artillery suffered. Colonel Crutchfield left three batteries at Harpers Ferry, "on account of their horses."[29]

The fog that obscured visibility for both armies screened Jackson's and Walker's passage over the Potomac River from the eyes of the signal station on Red Hill. The three divisions marched to within about 1 mile of Sharpsburg and bivouacked in or near the oak grove where Lee had established his headquarters. The trees shaded the completely worn out men, but the sun soon burned off the fog that had concealed them from the Union signalmen.[30]

Once the river crossing was underway, Jackson and Walker rode on ahead to report to Lee. It could not have been later than 9:30 a.m. when they reached his headquarters in the woods east of town. Lee had returned from his visit to the front to greet them. Walker expected to find Lee "anxious and careworn," but instead he appeared "calm, dignified, even cheerful." Longstreet soon joined the group, along with Jackson's division commanders. Jackson's and Walker's three divisions, though severely depleted by straggling, added 9,500 infantry and 44 guns to Lee's army, raising his total strength to approximately 20,000 infantry, about 110 guns, and two brigades of cavalry (although Munford's command hardly qualified for brigade status). Lee expressed confidence that with this force, he could hold his position until McLaws, R. H. Anderson, and A. P. Hill arrived with their divisions. During the course of the meeting, Lieutenant Colonel E. P. Alexander rode up and reported the arrival of the ordnance train at Shepherdstown, where it was distributing ammunition to the ordnance wagons of those brigades and batteries in need of resupply. The colonel looked forward to the impending battle and the part he would play in it—a view that probably few infantrymen on the line shared. But Lee dashed Alexander's hope of glory at Sharpsburg by ordering him to take whatever empty wagons he could find, go to Harpers Ferry and collect any captured ammunition that might be of use in the coming battle, and then forward it promptly. The remaining ammunition and captured guns were to be sent to Winchester. Deeply disappointed, Alexander departed to carry out his orders. Years later, having seen enough combat to satisfy anyone's thirst for battle, he observed: "I ought to consider myself lucky having escaped the chances of that day."[31]

While the generals discussed their situation, the rumble of artillery rolled back from the front. The fog had cleared, and Confederates on Cemetery Hill could see signal flags waving from Red Hill. "While we could not read the signals we knew that the devil would be to pay somewhere on our lines," wrote Sergeant W. H. Andrews of the 1st Georgia Regulars. Then one of the Confederate batteries opened fire on Devin's 6th New York Cavalry, which drew the wrath of the Federal batteries down on the Rebels. Although most of the Confederate infantry were under cover of the terrain, for unexplained reasons Drayton's hard-luck brigade was placed in an exposed position. W. H. Andrews, whose brigade—G. T. Anderson's—was on Drayton's left but behind the crest of Cemetery Hill, recalled that "every shell seemed to explode right in their ranks, where they were lying down." Confederate artillery, which was even more in the open, attracted more of the enemy's fire. Initially the Southern gunners grimly endured it, to conserve their ammunition. But around 11 a.m. Colonel Walton's patience evaporated from what he described as the "annoying" fire of the enemy. Exhibiting more emotion than good sense, Walton ordered Squires's, Bachman's, and Riley's batteries—with eight rifled guns and four Napoleons between them—to return the fire. Hearing sustained firing from his own artillery bothered Lee, for he did not want his limited ammunition supply wasted on artillery duels, and he asked Longstreet to put a stop to it.[32]

An artillery duel can be noisy, as well as spectacular to watch (provided the shells are not directed at you), but it is largely ineffective and wastes ammunition. Major B. W. Froebel, Hood's chief of artillery, kept Bachman's battery from participating in the exchange. Perhaps he even pointed out to Walton that the range was too great for his smoothbores to be effective. But Squires's and Riley's guns blazed angrily away. Froebel, who had observed them at practice, was unimpressed, judging their gunnery to be "without any perceptible result." Some shells found their mark, however. One Union veteran reported that the Confederates inflicted at least 125 casualties that day. The Southerners suffered, too, but there are no reports on the number of their losses. The people of Sharpsburg came in for their share of punishment, for Union shells that missed their mark on Cemetery Hill plunged into the town, ventilating buildings and setting several homes on fire. This was a new development in the war. Prior to Sharpsburg, battles had taken place in rural settings—Shiloh, Gaines' Mill, Manassas, Seven Pines—where damage to civilian property had been relatively minimal. Now, for the first time, a village fell within the path of the warring parties and felt the consequences.[33]

For nearly 40 minutes the guns thundered away at one another—or at any other target that invited a shell of two, which included the occasional knots of Union soldiers who wandered up to Pry Ridge for a look at the fireworks. These were invariably green soldiers anxious for a glance at a real battle. Reilly's battery exhausted its long-range ammunition during the exchange, and orders from Longstreet, which appear to have been delayed in making their way to the front, at last reached Walton, ordering him to cease fire and conserve his ammunition. Lee repeated these same orders to William M. Owen, the adjutant of Walton's Washington Artillery. During the duel, Owen had been sent out with a message for Longstreet. As Owen rode into Sharpsburg he met Lee, who was dismounted and leading his horse by its bridle, on his way toward the firing. "The shells of the enemy were falling in close proximity to him," recalled Owen, "but he seemed perfectly unconscious of danger." Lee told Owen to return with orders "to keep the artillery ammunition for the enemy's infantry only." This command, plus Longstreet's intervention, brought Walton's gun duel to a close. That it happened at all, however, did not reflect well on Walton's judgment. He certainly knew that Longstreet's ordnance train had been captured the day before by Union cavalry from Harpers Ferry, and that ammunition supplies ought to be husbanded. The Federal gunners continued their intermittent shelling through the early afternoon whenever targets presented themselves, drawing an occasional response from different Confederate batteries, but there were no more major artillery actions that day.[34]

While Lee and McClellan wrestled with questions of strategy and tactical considerations, the fighting men of the two armies waited. Once the fog burned off, the September sun beat down fiercely. Lieutenant Colonel Francis Palfrey of the 20th Massachusetts, like many others, recalled September 16 as "a terribly hot day," with "no breeze" until around 11 a.m., when the sky became overcast "and a little air stirred from time to time."[35] For most men the big artillery exchange during the morning and the other desultory shelling that went on into the afternoon provided the principal excitement. The new recruits in the Army of the Potomac, anxious to see a battle, found the artillery duel thrilling. Lieutenant Fred Hitchcock, the adjutant of the 130th Pennsylvania, in French's division of the 2nd Corps, recalled that "many of us crept to the brow of the hill [Pry's Ridge] to see the 'fun,' though we were warned that we were courting trouble in so doing." They observed a Confederate column, marching in ranks of four, come under fire of the Union batteries. Shell after shell, probably from the 20 lb. Parrott rifles, swept down on the hapless Southerners, bursting among them, killing and maiming men, and scattering those not injured. Like spectators at a sporting event, Hitchcock and his comrades set up a cheer. "We were enjoying ourselves hugely," he wrote, "until presently some additional puffs of smoke appeared from their side, followed immediately by a series of very ugly hissing, whizzing sounds, and the dropping of shells amongst our troops which changed the whole aspect of things. Our merriment and cheering were replaced by a scurrying to cover, with blanched faces on some and an ominous, thoughtful quiet over all."[36]

Even veterans were not immune from the desire to watch the show. Colonel Adoniram J. Warner of the 10th Pennsylvania Reserves wrote that "it was interesting to watch the bursting of our shells and see how near they came to 'taking the Rebs,' and our men were drawn into large crowds eagerly gazing as shell after shell was sent from our well directed guns." The Confederate gunners opened fire on these clumps of spectators, but their shells initially fell short. Before they found the range, General Meade rode up on the scene and ordered everyone back. Other units were not as fortunate. John Maycock of the 132nd Pennsylvania recorded in his diary that the first shell the Confederates fired at his sector of the field passed directly over his head and killed a soldier in the 8th Ohio. The dead man was Corporal William H. Farmer of the 8th's color guard. A member of his regiment saw the "twelve pound conical coming" moments before it struck among the color guard, who were sitting in a group near the colors. The shell did not burst when it struck the ground, but bounded up into Farmer, tearing away "the right and lower part of his sides." Farmer emitted a "few shuddering groans" and was gone. The 8th Ohio and the other regiments in the area were the victims of overshots, shells directed at the Union guns on Pry's Ridge that sailed over the intended target and dropped into the infantry massed in the rear. According to John Maycock, there were "a good many killed and wounded" by these overshots.[37]

The soldiers of the 63rd New York, an Irish Brigade regiment supporting one of the German batteries of the artillery reserve, had a particularly terrifying experience during the artillery duel. They were lying downslope in front of the battery, on the edge of a cornfield, a spot their officers may have selected to conceal the regiment from the enemy. The Southerners were hurling solid shot and shell at the supporting battery, in what one Irishman described as "an incessant cannonade." One of the shells, thought to be from a 20 lb. Parrott, struck in front of the German battery but did not explode. Instead, it began to roll down the hill directly toward the center of the regiment. "The men all saw it, but could do nothing," wrote John Dwyer. There probably was no time to get out of the way. So the shell continued to roll until it struck the foot of Sergeant Matthew Hart of Company K. "Moments of intense agony followed for every man and officer in the regiment," continued Dwyer. But Sergeant Hart and his comrades enjoyed some Irish luck. The shell's fuse was defective, and it failed to burst. "There was rejoicing in that regiment for the rest of the day," Dwyer recalled. Rejoicing, perhaps, but no one enjoyed real relief from the dread of being shredded by a shell. An 8th Ohio soldier accurately described the experience of being on the receiving end of these iron missiles: "The peculiar feeling of dread, which fills the minds of all as those screeching iron messengers of death approach, can, perhaps, be faintly described, but never realized until you have been there."[38]

Lieutenant Thomas H. Evans, commanding Company D of the 12th U.S. Infantry, was at the extreme front of the Army of the Potomac during the artillery duel. Evans's company, with others from his regiment, held a skirmish line on the west bank of the Antietam, covering the Middle Bridge. Captain Stephen Weed's Battery I, 5th U.S. Artillery, was located on the bluff directly behind Evans's unit, on the creek's east bank. Besides the danger from the significant amount of Confederate riflemen scattered across his front, Evans and his men were the recipients of numerous short rounds fired by the Southerners' artillery at Weed's guns. From what Evans could see, very few Rebel shells reached Weed's or Benjamin's batteries, but they "landed among us nicely." Nonetheless, except for some rattled nerves, Evans's company was unscathed.[39]

While casualties on both sides were relatively light, particularly in comparison with what was about to be experienced on September 17, many men reported close shaves with death or ghastly wounds received during the artillery duel. Sergeant W. H. Andrews of the 1st Georgia related that several ravenously hungry soldiers from his brigade straggled off and entered a house in Sharpsburg in search of food. To their delight they found that its residents had prepared a delicious meal (although any meal at this point qualified as delicious) and set it on the dining table, but when the artillery opened fire, the family had fled without eating. "They boys made themselves at home," quipped Andrews, sitting at the table and pitching into the food. The Georgians were enjoying themselves mightily when "a cannonball came crashing through the wall, knocked the legs from under the table, and dropped it on the floor. Needless to say that put an end to the feast."[40]

The shelling was particularly trying for the Confederates, because they were outgunned and out-ranged by the Union batteries. Sergeant Andrews recalled that to steady the nerves of the men, Longstreet rode in the rear of the batteries of the Washington Artillery on Cemetery Hill during some of the heaviest firing. "Him and his horse both seemed to be perfectly indifferent in regard to the shells that was filling the air with death and destruction," wrote Andrews. General Pendleton also rode the line under fire, as did Andrews's brigade commander, Colonel George T. "Tige" Anderson, who coolly stood and watched the Washington Artillery serve their guns. Not all stood the fire so calmly. The assistant surgeon of the 1st Georgia became panic stricken, to the amusement of the tough front-line infantrymen. Some men in the line would shout for the surgeon to run to where they lay, assuring him that it was safe. "By the time he would get there a shell would explode close to him," recalled Andrews. Then someone else would sing out that they were in a safe location, and the surgeon would dash there, only to find it as hot as the place he had just left. Eventually he sprinted off toward a small swamp to the right and rear of the regiment, with the shouts and laughter of the infantrymen following him. The foot soldiers had no pity for the surgeon's terror. "What an exhibition for a man to make of himself," observed Andrews. "Death would have been preferable to a brave man."[41] So great was the Union superiority in firepower that once the Confederate guns ceased fire, William H. Palmer, who served on General Kemper's staff, recalled that the Federal gunners "amused themselves by firing at single horsemen, or a few men, and sometimes at a single man." Such gunnery wasted ammunition, but it did have a demoralizing effect on those on the receiving end.[42]

Men might tremble in fear while under artillery fire, but when the danger passed, their thoughts invariably turned to food. This was particularly true for the Confederate army. Lee had led his army into Maryland partly to feed his troops. He had subsequently moved Longstreet's command to Hagerstown, not only to protect his communications, but also to secure the stores of provisions that locals were moving to Pennsylvania. Then difficulty in procuring anything edible delayed the march of McLaws's two divisions to Sharpsburg, and short rations weakened the men in all of the Rebel army's divisions, causing massive straggling. Not until the Appomattox Campaign would subsistence again play such a pivotal role in the Army of Northern Virginia's operations.

Lee's men who manned the line at Sharpsburg were no exception, as they, too, were very hungry, and Lee's quartermasters were having a difficult time feeding them. Alexander Hunter, a private in Kemper's brigade, recalled that "we were very tired with marching, exhausted with excitement, and savagely hungry." The men, continued Hunter, "began to grumble at being forced to fight on an empty stomach, and a long line of famine-drawn faces and gaunt figures sat there in the ranks, chewing straws merely to keep their jaws from rusting and stiffening entirely." But Hunter and his comrades had the good fortune to encounter a cow belonging to a Sharpsburg resident. Unaware of its peril, the animal had wandered close to the soldiers while grazing. "A dozen bullets crashed into her skull," related Hunter, and the beast was quickly butchered, cooked, and devoured. They even cooked and ate the tail. But most of the men on the lines were not so lucky. John W. Lokey, a Georgian in Toombs's brigade, wrote that "we had been two days without rations" on September 16, when he and some other men were detailed to go to the rear and find something for his company to eat. In Hood's division it was so bad that during the night of the 16th, Colonel Philip A. Work, commanding the 1st Texas, ordered two men from each company to gather roasting ears from the nearby cornfields to feed the regiment. O. T. Hanks was part of that group, and he thought they collected the ears from David Miller's cornfield, soon to become infamous as The Cornfield. "The lack of food placed us in no cheerful mood," recalled Sergeant Major David Johnston in Kemper's 7th Virginia, but he added that it did put the men "in good fighting temper, as hungry soldiers fight better than well fed ones."[43]

Although the Union soldiers had abundant rations, compared with their Southern adversaries, comestibles still figured prominently in their minds. Food distribution can be uneven for a force that is actively moving and engaged in combat, and not everyone in the Army of the Potomac had a full haversack. The traffic jam on the National Road had separated some units from their commissary wagons and delayed those for many others. Captain James Wren of the 48th Pennsylvania wrote that his regiment "was ordered to go into a Corn field & a potato patch which was Close by & to supply from that." Private John Vautier of the 88th Pennsylvania took matters into his own hands. He went foraging among the nearby farms and returned with half a haversack of sweet potatoes, which made "an excellent meal."

Illustrating the unevenness of the army's food distribution, the 83rd New York, a regiment in Vautier's brigade, reported that they received a full issue of rations on September 16. But the green soldiers of the 124th Pennsylvania were "very hungry," and there was no sign of their commissary wagons. When their brigade commander, Brigadier General Samuel W. Crawford, rode by, some of the men clustered around him, telling him that they were hungry and wanted their rations. With a regular's contempt for new volunteers, Crawford made some disparaging remark about the men being so many "Pennsylvania cattle" and rode away. So the Pennsylvanians did what Vautier had done—they foraged. One of their members, Private William Potts, found some shocks of wheat and shelled out enough kernels to fill his tin cup. When he returned, his comrades asked what he intended to do with the grain, and Potts replied that he would make a "rice pudding." Inquiries followed as to where he had found the wheat, and he pointed at the sheaves some distance away. "In less time than it takes to tell it, the stacks were so covered with hungry boys, it looked, in the distance, as if an immense flock of crows had lit on them," wrote Potts. The way Crawford dismissed the men's complaint about their rations did not sit well with Potts, who declared that when they went into combat, "if I was aiming at a Reb and the General got in the way, I would not stop firing on his account."[44]

Getting rations up to the front and distributed to the men took an aggressive commissary officer, and perhaps some luck. Colonel Adoniram Warner, commanding the 10th Pennsylvania Reserves, recorded that his regiment received a full ration of coffee, crackers, and fresh beef "by good management and a full stroke of [?] in the interest of order." Ammunition was typically more plentiful than food. Many Union soldiers wrote that they were issued 60–80 rounds during the day, a sign that their commanders expected a hard fight. But in such a large army, there were always those who were unprepared. When the 5th Maryland Infantry of Weber's brigade marched through Washington on its way to join the army in the field, its colonel made a requisition for ammunition for its .54-caliber Austrian rifles. Because of a temporary shortage of this type of ammunition, they were only issued 10 rounds per man. The regiment had to move on, but the colonel ordered his quartermaster to send one of the regimental wagons to another ordnance depot for additional cartridges. The quartermaster did so, but the wagon became separated from its unit and had not rejoined it by September 16. Perhaps the colonel dared not bring Weber's wrath down on him by alerting his commander to the problem, but whatever the reason, the ammunition shortage went unreported and the regiment received no additional cartridges.[45]

Around 2 p.m. on September 16, the bivouac area of Hooker's 1st Corps began to hum with activity as regiments were ordered to fall in. William Olcott and his comrades of the 10th Pennsylvania Reserves had spent the day cleaning their arms and speculating "on the events of the war." They wondered whether the Confederates would "recross the Potomac without hazarding the battle which we were confident must result so disastrously to them." Olcott and the others would have their answer soon. The regiments, brigades, and batteries of the corps—nearly 10,000 fighting men—fell into column and snaked their way toward the Upper Bridge and Antietam Creek. The Battle of Antietam was about to begin.[46]

19

Eve of Battle

"I shall not, however, soon forget that night"

After receiving his orders to cross Antietam Creek and approach the Confederate flank, Hooker issued the necessary commands to his staff to have the corps form up, and then rode to army headquarters "for any further orders" McClellan might have. Hooker disliked the idea of sending his corps alone across the Antietam to attack the Rebel flank, and he hoped McClellan would agree to commit additional troops to the movement. He also may have sought further clarification of what it was his corps was expected to accomplish. Did McClellan intend for Hooker to attack or to conduct a reconnaissance in force? The orders to probe Lee's defenses and fix the whereabouts of his flank resembled the latter, rather than the former, but Hooker, in his after-action report, stated that he was told to attack the enemy's flank. McClellan offered Hooker no clearer instructions, nor any explanation of how the 1st Corps' movement fit into the general plan, and he refused to reinforce the advance. But he did tell Hooker that he was at liberty to call for reinforcements, if he needed them, once he made contact with the enemy, and that these troops would be subject to Hooker's orders when they arrived. This was reassuring, but Hooker understood that if he ran into tough enemy resistance, any reinforcements that might start after he sent for them would not reach him until after dark. Hooker could get no more from McClellan, so he left to join his command.[1]

Hooker planned his attack based on his earlier observation of the Confederate position from the east bank of the Antietam, "my object being to gain the high ground or divide between the Potomac and Antietam Rivers, and then incline to the left, following the elevation toward the left of the rebel army." The Hagerstown Pike ran roughly along the line of this divide and provided a guide for the attack. It was a reasonable plan, given his orders and the scanty information available about the enemy position, and it enabled the 1st Corps to receive some flank support from the 20 lb. Parrott rifles on the east bank of Antietam Creek. The problem came in Hooker's execution, which was clumsily carried out.[2]

The 3rd Pennsylvania Cavalry, with Hooker and his staff riding with it, preceded the infantry and crossed at Pry's Ford. Reaching the west bank of the creek, Hooker ordered Captain Edward S. Jones's squadron, consisting of Companies C and I, to scout "directly to the westward to ascertain the location of the enemy's line of battle in that direction." Company H, under Lieutenant William E. Miller (who would win a Medal of Honor for Gettysburg) rode north to the Williamsport Turnpike to screen the infantry column, which was crossing at the Upper Bridge. Captain Jones's squadron, guided by an "old farmer," advanced over open pastures under the critical eye of Hooker, who noted that Jones's two troops were marching in column of twos. He shouted to Jones "in an emphatic manner, 'Double up those dragoons! There's a d—— site [*sic*] to do and d—— little time to do it!'" Presumably Jones promptly formed column of fours and made haste to put distance between his men and Hooker.[3]

Meanwhile Meade's division, led by Colonel Hugh McNeil's 13th Pennsylvania Reserves and Seymour's 1st Brigade, began to cross the Upper Bridge and then march north along the Williamsport Turnpike. They were delayed, for Colonel Adoniram Warner, commanding the 10th Reserves, wrote that his brigade "halted for some time just before crossing the bridge to await, I suppose the movements of those before us." The delay may have been to allow Lieutenant Miller's company to scout the road ahead. How long it lasted is uncertain, but it may have been a half hour or more. Ricketts's 2nd Division formed up to follow Meade. Doubleday, commanding the 1st Division, had received "no orders of any kind" from Hooker. Displaying initiative, Doubleday poked about and learned that the engineers had prepared Pry's Ford for crossing. He immediately marched his division there and started it through the water. Once his four brigades, numbering nearly 3,000 infantry and four batteries of artillery, were across the creek—which probably took at least an hour—Doubleday paused while he sent an aide galloping to find Hooker and ask him what he wanted the 1st Division to do. While Doubleday was waiting for orders, some bold Confederate skirmishers crept up through a nearby cornfield and managed to get "quite close to us," recalled Doubleday. They "opened a sharp fire upon myself and staff and the other mounted officers." Fortunately, the Rebels' aim was poor and no one was hit, but it warned Doubleday that the enemy was closer than he had thought. He summoned Colonel Henry A. V. Post, commanding the highly skilled 2nd U.S. Sharpshooters of Colonel Walter Phelps's brigade, and ordered him to take a detachment of his green-clad riflemen to drive off the Confederates.[4]

Doubleday soon had his orders from Hooker. He was to follow the other two divisions on the Williamsport Turnpike. Since obeying this command meant marching north, and would thus present the flank of the 1st Division to the Confederates who might be lurking in the woods visible immediately to the west, Doubleday ordered Brigadier General John Gibbon's brigade to march west of the road, where it could screen the division's vulnerable flank.[5]

The 1st Corps had followed the Williamsport Turnpike for nearly a mile—to the vicinity of the Hoffman farm—when they reached a position from which

Hooker believed he spotted the high ground near the Hagerstown Pike that he had set as the initial objective of his march. He then ordered the entire Corps to leave the road and march west in three parallel divisional columns, each division with its brigades formed in column of divisions closed in mass (i.e., each division presented a front of two companies abreast in line of battle, followed by the rest of the division in the same deployment). Meade formed the right column, Ricketts the center, and Doubleday the left. A distance of only 50 yards separated each division from the one beside it. Doubleday thought it was an unwieldy and unwise tactical formation under the circumstances. "It seemed to me that this formation was very objectionable because a sudden advance of the enemy might envelop the head of the column, in which case it would have been almost impossible for us to deploy," he observed. Sumner would use a formation that was similar in certain respects the next day with Sedgwick's division, in an attack on the West Woods. The Confederates did to Sedgwick precisely what Doubleday feared they might do to the 1st Corps, enveloping the flank of the attack column before it could fully deploy, which resulted in a bloody catastrophe. Hooker probably selected this formation because it was more easily maneuvered than a line of battle. Moreover, unlike Sedgwick, Hooker had the 3rd Pennsylvania Cavalry in front to screen his advance and provide warning of the enemy.[6]

Soon after the 1st Corps left the Williamsport Turnpike and began to move cross-country, McClellan and his staff rode up to join Hooker, for no other reason that Hooker could discern than to "see how we were progressing." Hooker, looking "fresh and game as ever," explained his movements to McClellan and again emphasized his concern over committing his single corps to the attack. In his after-action report, Hooker stated that he told McClellan, "If reinforcements were not forwarded promptly, or if another attack was not made on the enemy's right, the Rebels would eat me up." McClellan seemed unmoved, and he made no commitment to supply reinforcements, but Hooker made an impression on the commanding general. When McClellan later was at army headquarters, he ordered the 12th Corps across the Antietam. For the moment, however, McClellan rode along with Hooker until "it was gray twilight," shortly after 6 p.m. As the headquarters staff rode away, one of them—aide Colonel Strother—gazed back at Hooker, mounted on his conspicuous, tall white horse. Hooker stood out distinctly against the dark woods behind him, and Strother "was pained with a presentiment that this gallant chief would be the next victim to the fortunes of war." On his return to the east bank of Antietam Creek, McClellan rode to the Philip Pry farm and directed that his headquarters be established here. It was a good location. The bluffs immediately west of the house afforded an excellent observation point for scanning the enemy positions, and the farmhouse was centrally located for communication purposes.[7]

While the 1st Corps pushed on through meadows, cornfields, woods, and pastures toward the enemy left, the 9th Corps advanced to take up its positions near the Rohrbach Bridge. The timing of the movement was entirely coincidental with Hooker's advance, but it served to confuse Lee as to where McClellan intended to attack. Shortly after noon, McClellan had ordered Burnside to advance three of the 9th Corps' four divisions to positions near the Rohrbach Bridge. McClellan's senior engineer, Captain James C. Duane, was to select the locales. By the time Duane, accompanied by three of Burnside's aides, did this and the aides returned, it was after 3 p.m. The three divisions started forward to occupy the designated positions immediately, and Burnside rode to a nearby high point to oversee the movement. While Burnside was there, an aide-de-camp rode up and advised the Rhode Islander that McClellan "was not sure that the proper position had been indicated, and advised him [Burnside] not to hasten the movement until the aide had communicated with the general commanding." This was an irksome development. What prompted it is unknown, but a likely explanation is that McClellan was nervous about Hooker's advance and had had second thoughts about his previous orders to Burnside. Burnside reluctantly obeyed his instructions and commanded the 9th Corps to halt their advance.[8]

These new orders troubled Burnside. Before receiving them he had observed "large bodies" of Confederate troops in the distance, marching north toward Hooker. The enemy appeared to be shifting its forces to concentrate against Hooker, making it critical, in Burnside's opinion, that the 9th Corps complete their movement to stations near the Rohrbach Bridge, in order to prevent the Rebels from sending further reinforcements to their left. Burnside decided to ride to headquarters and meet personally with McClellan. When he arrived he learned that McClellan had departed to join Hooker. To Burnside's credit, he did not stand idly by and wait for the general's return. If the 9th Corps were ordered to attack in the morning, it would be vital for its divisions to be in position before nightfall, and daylight was quickly slipping away. Burnside decided to disregard the earlier instructions from McClellan's aide-de-camp to stall, and instead ordered Cox to move his three divisions to the locations Duane had selected. The movement resumed at dusk, and the sounds of fighting on Hooker's front could be distinctly heard.[9]

"It was almost dark when we got our orders," wrote Charles F. Johnson of the 9th New York. Brigadier General Isaac Rodman's division, along with those of Colonel Eliakim Scammon (formerly Cox's division) and Brigadier General Sam Sturgis, resumed their advance toward their designated positions near the Rohrbach Bridge. Colonel Jonathan B. Cumming, commanding the 20th Georgia— one of the two regiments of Toombs's brigade defending the bridge—received warning of the Federals' approach and ordered a detachment of skirmishers to cross the Antietam and harass their advance. The Georgians dashed over the bridge and took cover in a large cornfield, slightly over a quarter mile east of the bridge and about midway between the Henry Rohrbach and Noah Rohrbach farms. Someone in the 9th Corps spotted them, and Captain H. L. Devol's company of the 36th Ohio, in Crook's brigade, was ordered forward as skirmishers to engage them. Shots were exchanged, but Devol's Buckeyes swiftly flushed the Georgians from their cover and drove them back across the Rohrbach Bridge.

While Devol's Ohioans cleared the Georgians from the corn, Captain James Wren of the 48th Pennsylvania, in Nagle's brigade, was sent with a detachment of his regiment to scout the east bank of the Antietam, south of the bridge. Wren thought he and his men had reconnoitered for nearly a mile when a staff officer caught up with Wren and asked if he had seen anything. "I told him nothing except of mounted men on the opposite side of Antetam [*sic*] Crick," stated Wren. The captain took the staff officer to the place where he had spotted the mounted Confederates; they were still visible. The officer produced a set of field glasses, studied the horsemen through them, saw that one of them was riding a light-colored animal, and exclaimed, "Captain, that is Gen. Jackson & his staff. We Know him by his Cream Colored horse." Jackson was not there, so it was more likely to have been some officers or troopers of Munford's brigade, but Wren and this particular staff officer believed it was Stonewall, and they had a story to thrill comrades with that night.[10]

Other than the light skirmishing between Captain Devol's company and Colonel Cumming's Georgians, and a few shells lobbed from Captain John B. Richardson's 2nd Company of the Washington Artillery, which was located on a commanding ridge west of the bridge and southeast of Cemetery Hill, the advance of the 9th Corps was unopposed. Their objective was the reverse slopes of the hills rising east of the bridge and nearly parallel with Antietam Creek. This is not one line of highlands, but a series of uneven hills, with each line at a slightly higher elevation as the ground gradually rises toward Red Hill and Elk Ridge. McClellan and Captain Duane had chosen to position Cox's three divisions in the area around the Henry Rohrbach and Noah Rohrbach farms. A 500-foot hill, about a quarter mile north of Noah Rohrbach's, offered an ideal anchor for the left flank and a splendid artillery position. Guns here could command the Rohrbach Bridge Road, should any Confederate forces from Harpers Ferry attempt to advance along it. It also gave these same guns a clear field of fire to the bridge. Northwest of this hill, the high ground north and south of Henry Rohrbach's farm offered concealment for the infantry of Cox's divisions. Here they could remain unobserved by the Rebels guarding the bridge, and they could either be formed up to assault it if necessary or be dispatched south to outflank the bridge's defenders by crossing the Antietam at Snavely's Ford. The officers and men of the 9th Corps might have realized the various advantages the locale offered had they arrived there during daylight, but

McClellan's orders pausing the corps' movement delayed them, and they did not occupy this ground until after dark. Moreover, the night of September 16 was pitch black.[11]

The men of the 16th Connecticut recalled that it was "eight o'clock in the evening, and quite dark," when their brigade halted at Henry Rohrbach's farm. Brigadier General Israel Rodman's 3rd Division, of which the 16th Connecticut was a part, formed the left of the 9th Corps' front, and they deployed as best they could: east of Henry Rohrbach's farmhouse and east of the Porterstown Road, which ran down to the Rohrbach Bridge Road. Because it was so dark, regimental and general officers could not determine where they were with any precision, nor whether they would be concealed or exposed to enemy observation in the morning. The rolling terrain, under cultivation and crisscrossed with fences, further complicated the deployment. Colonel Harrison S. Fairchild's brigade of Rodman's division formed in Henry Rohrbach's cornfield, where Captain Devol's company had skirmished with the Georgians earlier. The stalks stood higher than a man, and as the soldiers entered it they were cautioned not to make any noise, since the enemy was thought to be close by. As the 9th New York started to go into the corn, they heard "the heavy tramp of men" coming down the hill to their left. The enemy? No one knew, so their colonel, Edgar Kimball, a quick-thinking and brave officer, ordered his regiment to fix bayonets. "The men firmly faced the expected assault," wrote Lieutenant Matthew J. Graham of the 9th New York. Someone in the 9th shouted "Halt!" several times to the approaching men, but received no reply. The strangers continued to advance through the cornfield, finally stopping only a few paces from the 9th's line, which had displayed remarkable discipline in holding their fire. This saved many lives, for the unknown men belonged to the 103rd New York, of the 9th New York's own brigade. As Graham recalled, "if they [the 103rd] had continued to advance a moment longer [they] would have received a volley from the regiment, and a terrible slaughter would have resulted."[12]

One member of the 9th New York, David L. Thompson, did not think his brigade settled into its position until 10:30 p.m., which gives a good idea of how difficult it is to deploy men for battle on unfamiliar terrain on a pitch-black night. "No lights were permitted, and all conversation was carried on in whispers," wrote Thompson. "When everything was at its darkest and stealthiest," a member of the 103rd New York, wandering through the cornfield for some unstated reason, tripped over the 9th New York's sleeping regimental dog. When he tried to avoid falling on the animal, he instead tumbled into a nearby stack of muskets, knocking them over with a clatter that rang sharply in the stillness. The muskets landed on two or three men of the 9th, startling them and sending them scrambling to their feet. This had a ripple effect that expanded through both regiments. Thompson described it as "one of those unaccountable panics often noticed in crowds, by which each man, however brave individually, merges his individuality for the moment, and surrenders to an utterly causeless fear." Order broke down and men started for the rear, or what many may have thought was the rear, for the darkness was highly disorienting. But the efforts of the officers of both regiments restored calm. The men were settled down and all returned to their positions, but the incident underscored the tension felt throughout the 9th Corps that night.[13]

Cox's Kanawha Division, commanded by Colonel Eliakim Scammon, deployed its 1st Brigade, now led by Colonel Hugh Ewing, in support of Rodman and the 9th Corps' batteries, which were located on the high ground north of Noah Rohrbach's homestead. Scammon's 2nd Brigade, under Colonel George Crook, took position north of Henry Rohrbach's farm, with the first line of hills along Antietam Creek screening their front. Jacob Cox recalled that "Crook was ordered to take the advance in crossing the bridge [Rohrbach Bridge] in case we should be ordered to attack. This selection was made by Burnside himself as a compliment to the division for the vigor of its assault at South Mountain." Either Cox was mistaken, Crook's orders were unclear, or Crook was guilty of gross negligence, for in his memoirs the colonel stated that when the Battle of Antietam opened on the morning of September 17, he was not aware that there was a bridge, let alone where it was, and—because his brigade reached its position well after dark—he did not even know where Antietam Creek was. Whether Crook's orders were unclear, or whether he received no orders other than to hold his command in readiness, he still displayed no initiative that evening to learn anything about the ground he might have to fight on in the morning.[14]

Sturgis's 2nd Division took position about a quarter mile north of Crook's brigade, with its two brigades arrayed on either side of the Porterstown Road facing south. Of the corps' artillery, only Captain Benjamin's Battery E, 2nd U.S. Artillery, consisting of four 20 lb. Parrott rifles, and Captain James Whiting's 9th New York regimental battery, with five 12 lb. Navy howitzers, were deployed. Benjamin placed his guns on high ground about 600 yards east of Henry Rohrbach's farm, in the rear of Rodman's division, and Whiting placed his howitzers on the flanks of Fairchild's brigade, apparently as a defensive precaution. The other six batteries of the corps, plus Willcox's 1st Division, were held in reserve, spending the night at various positions in the rear of the three front-line divisions. Willcox's two brigades formed in the rear of Sturgis, although most of Colonel Benjamin Christ's 1st Brigade was detached. The 79th New York was sent to guard the signal station on Red Hill, while the 28th Massachusetts and the 50th Pennsylvania marched to support some cavalry who were watching the Rohrersville Road where it crosses Elk Ridge. These dispositions completed the deployment of the 9th Corps. The intense darkness that enveloped the field during these final movements into position made it impossible to read the terrain, but the brigade and division commanders did the best they could to post their men in what seemed to be concealed positions. There was no opportunity to reconnoiter the ground they might have to fight over in the morning, or to locate the Confederate positions, or to determine the best approaches by which to attack them. McClellan's second-guessing of his earlier orders had brought about this situation, yet he would hold Burnside accountable for it. Moreover, it would be Burnside's men who would suffer the bloody consequences on September 17.[15]

When Hooker and Burnside began their respective movements, Lee, Longstreet, and Jackson were meeting in the home of Jacob A. Grove, located at the southwest corner of Sharpsburg's town square. They were studying maps of Maryland and Washington County when they heard some of Walton's guns on Cemetery Hill open fire. Soon after, news arrived that a large Union force was observed moving toward the Rohrbach Bridge. Within moments, a cavalryman rode up with a report from Stuart: the Yankees were crossing the Antietam in strength at Pry's Ford and the Upper Bridge. Both Confederate flanks were being threatened simultaneously. One movement might be a feint, but it was just as likely that the enemy was attempting a double envelopment.

Lee ordered Longstreet to confront the threat to the left flank with Hood's division. He instructed Jackson to support Hood with J. R. Jones's division and to send Lawton's division to support Toombs at the Rohrbach Bridge. Lee retained Walker's division as a general reserve until the enemy movement was more fully developed. Lady Luck had again smiled on McClellan. Purely by chance, Burnside had resumed placing the 9th Corps into position at nearly the same moment as Hooker's corps were moving cross-country toward Lee's left, causing the Confederate commander to dispatch one-third of his precious reserves to a sector McClellan had no plans to attack until the next day.[16] But McClellan's luck proved to be fleeting. Lee quickly determined that the movements of the 9th Corps were those of troops getting into position rather than planning to attack. Before Lawton had advanced his division any appreciable distance toward the army's right, his orders were countermanded and he received new instructions to follow J. R. Jones's division to the left.[17]

The 1st Corps' crossing of Antietam Creek and its subsequent movements were seen by troopers of Fitz Lee's brigade, who were screening the army's left flank. Fitz Lee had picket details on the Hagerstown Pike and the Smoketown Road, as well as at other points where they could keep the Upper Bridge and Pry's Ford under observation. The two roads were the most probable avenues the Federals would use to approach the Confederate army's left, and, since the Smoketown Road was nearer to the Antietam's crossing points, their forces were likely to appear here first. That afternoon Fitz Lee ordered his 9th Virginia Cavalry to move out along this road, beyond Hood's division, and establish a screening position. As the troopers rode past Hood's infantry, they noticed that the foot soldiers had thrown up a breastwork of "rails, logs, stones," for cover. The cavalry followed the Smoketown Road through the East Woods and

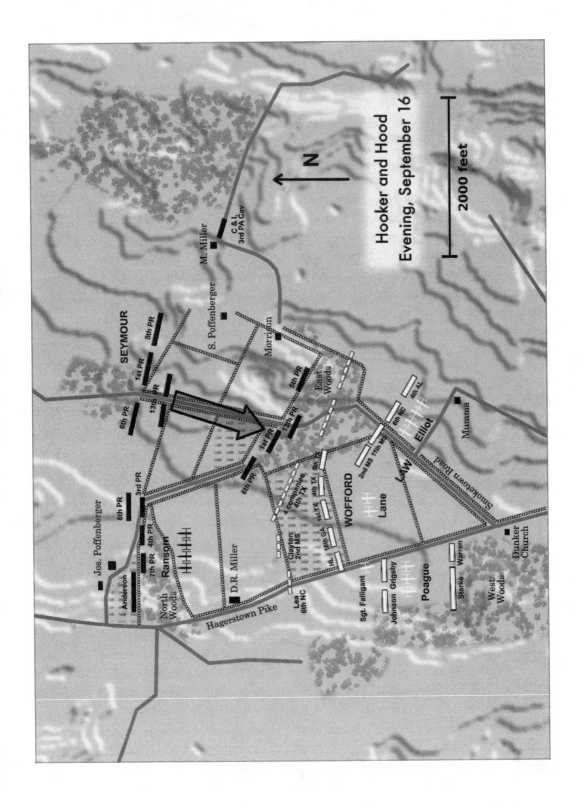

Hooker and Hood
Evening, September 16

N

2000 feet

SEYMOUR

6th PR
1st PR
5th PR
13th PR
3rd PR
8th PR
7th PR
4th PR
3rd PR
6th PR
5th PR
1st PR
3rd PR

Anderson
Jos. Poffenberger
Ransom
D.R. Miller
S. Poffenberger
Morrison
M. Miller
C & I.
3rd PA Cav

North Woods
East Woods

Hagerstown Pike

Lea
6th NC
Clayton
2nd MS
1st GA
11th GA
4th TX
4th TX
Companies
4th/7X
2nd MS
11th MS
6th NC
4th AL

WOFFORD
Lane
LAW
Elliot
Mumma

Sgt. Falligant
Johnson
Grigsby
Poague
Starke
Warren

West Woods

Dunker Church

Smoketown Road

went past them to Samuel Poffenberger's woods, some 700 yards north. Two guns, probably from Pelham's horse artillery, accompanied the regiment, and near Poffenberger's woodlot they left the road and went into position on a knoll west of the woods, where they had a field of fire due north along the Smoketown Road. They also had some concealment behind brush or bushes growing on the knoll. Lieutenant George W. Beale of the 9th Virginia recalled that the guns' position "commanded an extended view of open fields and a straight roadway [Smoketown Road] leading towards Antietam river."[18]

Beale and his comrades, situated around Sam Poffenberger's woodlot, watched the 1st Corps' approach. "Their march was regular and steady towards our position," he wrote. "Only once, where a road diverged from that on which they moved was there a halt." This was the Smoketown Road; part of the Union column Beale was observing turned down it and began to heading for his locale. Hood and Stuart were at the Dunker church when they received notice that the Federals were advancing on Fitz Lee's forward outposts. Stuart commanded Fitz Lee to ready the balance of his brigade to support the 9th Virginia, should it be necessary, and Hood ordered a powerful skirmish line to be deployed across his front. Captain Richard E. Clayton's company of the 2nd Mississippi and Captain James Lea's company of the 6th North Carolina were sent up the Hagerstown Pike and took up positions around the David Miller farm. Captain William H. Martin, with a detachment of approximately 100 men of the 4th Texas, passed through Miller's 30-acre cornfield and the pasture north of it to extend Lea's and Clayton's skirmish line east toward the Smoketown Road. They took cover behind Miller's worm fence, which separated his pasture from a freshly plowed field north of it. This furrowed ground extended for nearly 300 yards to the North Woods. Other skirmish detachments from Wofford's and Law's brigades extended Martin's skirmish line to the northern border of the East Woods, going across the Smoketown Road and then following the wood line south toward the Samuel Mumma farm. Colonel S. D. Lee bolstered the right of this long skirmish line by advancing two howitzers of Lieutenant William Elliot's South Carolina battery to a position west of the Mumma farm and near the Smoketown Road. D. H. Hill contributed Captain John Lane's battery of Cutts's battalion, which only had two serviceable pieces. Hood placed the guns in the meadow south of Miller's cornfield, about midway between the Hagerstown Pike and the Smoketown Road. Hill also sent forward a single gun, a howitzer of unknown caliber, from Captain James Blackshear's (Georgia) Battery, Cutts's battalion, under the command of Sergeant Major Robert Falligant. Falligant's crew unlimbered their piece in the Hagerstown Pike, almost due west of Lane's guns.[19]

Lieutenant William E. Miller's Company H, 3rd Pennsylvania Cavalry, led the van of Hooker's 1st Corps. When Hooker's infantry left the Williamsport Turnpike to march cross-country, Miller's company continued up the pike until they reached the Smoketown Road, where they turned south. It was possibly his company that Lieutenant Beale observed from near Sam Poffenberger's woodlot. As Miller's men made their way south along the road, they encountered Colonel Hugh McNeil, commanding the 13th Pennsylvania Reserves, or Bucktails, who were screening the advance of Meade's division. (The 13th Pennsylvania Reserves were also known as the 13th Pennsylvania Rifles, or Rifles, since they were the only regiment in their division armed entirely with Sharps rifles.) Miller recalled that "the colonel asked me where I was going. Upon my telling him that my instructions were to find the enemy, he asked me if I would not like company." Infantry, especially those armed with Sharps rifles, were handy to have around when things got dangerous, and Miller gladly accepted McNeil's offer. The colonel ordered four companies to deploy as skirmishers on either side of the Smoketown Road, in the rear of Miller's advance guard. When this was completed the advance resumed.[20]

While McNeil, Miller, and their men moved south along the Smoketown Road in search of Rebels, Hooker issued orders to his division commanders to deploy from column to assault formations. He intended to advance with his three divisions abreast of one another. Doubleday's orders were to place his right on the Hagerstown Pike and connect his left with Meade. Meade would hold the center, moving forward to occupy the East Woods and the North Woods, while Ricketts formed on his left. When they received these orders, the three divisions were still marching west in three parallel columns: Doubleday on the left, Ricketts in the center, and Meade on the right. To carry out Hooker's commands, Meade and Ricketts should have marked time while Doubleday marched ahead until he had uncovered their front; then both divisions could have changed direction to the southwest and moved toward their respective objectives. Doubleday placed himself at the head of his leading unit, Marsena Patrick's 3rd Brigade, and started his division forward, but Meade and Ricketts began to move at the same time; in their haste to execute the new maneuvers, both divisions cut between Patrick's brigade and the rest of Doubleday's division, effectively splitting the division in two. It would take "more than two hours" before Doubleday could reunited his division, and by then it was dark, which added its own complications to the 1st Division's deployment. Fortunately for Hooker, he had not met with any resistance, and his awkward handling of the 1st Corps caused no damage.[21]

Meanwhile, Lieutenant Miller's troopers, followed by the Bucktail skirmishers, continued their advance along either side of the Smoketown Road, scanning and searching the cultivated fields and woods for any sign of the enemy. There were being closely watched by the troopers of the 9th Virginia and Pelham's concealed gun crews. Lieutenant George Beale recalled that they did not reveal their position until the Federals had moved near enough "to count the buttons on their coats." Beale indulged in embellishment here, for the Federals were farther away than he claimed. Miller's Pennsylvanians saw nothing of the enemy until they reached "the lane running eastwardly to George Lyon's [Line's] farmhouse." There was a wagon path snaking through the woods south of the farmhouse, and this might be the lane to which the men of the 3rd Pennsylvania Cavalry referred. Then Pelham's gunners let loose, and probably some troopers of Beale's regiment fired their weapons at the approaching horsemen. There were no casualties listed for either side, but both the Union and the Rebel cavalrymen decided that they had done their duty. The Pennsylvanians fell back on the Bucktails, and the Virginians and horse artillerymen withdrew toward their lines. No one knew it at that moment, but the Battle of Antietam had begun.[22]

While Miller's 3rd Pennsylvania Cavalry approached the Confederates along the Smoketown Road, Captain Jones's squadron, which had departed from the main column after its initial crossing of Antietam Creek to scout in the direction of the Michael Miller farm and beyond, advanced on the southeastern corner of the East Woods. After leaving the main column near the Antietam, Jones deployed Lieutenant Willard E. Warren with the first platoon of Company C as skirmishers. Jones followed with the balance of Companies C and I, moving along the lane to Miller's farm. Warren encountered a few cavalry videttes, but they were content to merely observe the Union horsemen; these Confederates then fell back toward the East Woods. Warren reported that he did not see Lieutenant Miller's company. Captain Jones wanted to coordinate any further advance of his squadron with Miller's company, so he ordered Warren to halt where he was until Lieutenant Miller made his appearance. Apparently Warren's platoon, although mounted, was under cover, but the 2nd Platoon of Company C, commanded by Sergeant Thompson Miller, which had stopped within supporting distance of the 1st Platoon, found itself in the open. Confederate "sharpshooters"—either dismounted troopers of the 9th Virginia or skirmishers from Law's or Wofford's brigade in the East Woods—began firing at Sergeant Miller and his men. The sergeant ordered John McCoubrie, an excellent shot, to dismount and see if he might get rid of one of the bothersome Rebels. When McCoubrie did so, three other troopers in the platoon, who thought the sergeant's orders to McCoubrie preferable to sitting on a horse and making themselves a target, also dismounted. The four troopers rested their carbines on a rail fence and fired a volley at a single Confederate who stepped from behind a tree to take a shot in their direction. There is no record of whether they hit their target, but the Company I commander, Captain James W. Walsh, came tearing back from Lieutenant Warren's position, where he had ridden to see what was going on. Walsh demanded of Sergeant Miller: "Who ordered those men to dismount? This is no place for them to be off their horses!" Miller responded—with considerable logic—that he did not relish sitting on a horse presenting a target to the enemy, and besides, it did not take long for a man to mount his horse. Whatever Walsh replied is unknown, but his encounter with Sergeant Miller was cut short by the approach of Hooker and his staff.[23]

Hooker's arrival was both encouraging and disconcerting. For the line trooper who earned his living being in close contact with the enemy, it was refreshing to see a corps commander this close to the front. But for squadron commander Captain Jones, the corps commander's presence at the front most likely meant that something unpleasant was pending. Hooker waited with Jones until they could see McNeil's Bucktails and Lieutenant Miller's company coming toward them along either side of the Smoketown Road; then Hooker ordered Captain Jones to advance and drive in the enemy pickets. Jones gave this dangerous duty to Captain Walsh, who passed it along to Sergeant Miller to carry out. The sergeant's platoon contained 12–16 men, and they advanced mounted. Their route is unknown, but they may have followed the farm lane past Morrison's house. When they started forward, Lieutenant Warren, obviously a daring fellow, hastened up to join Miller, and the sergeant and lieutenant led the 2nd Platoon toward the woods at a gallop. The Confederate pickets fled at their approach, dashing into the woods. Miller, Warren, and the sergeant's troopers chased after them, bursting into the woodlot, which they discovered to be "thick with rebels." They also encountered a Confederate battery—probably Elliot's South Carolinians—coming up to them at a distance the Union horsemen recalled as being only 30 feet. The Southern gunners were probably just as surprised as the Pennsylvanians, and although they served up canister at the Yankees, they missed cleanly. So, too, did the Confederate infantry and cavalry skirmishers within the woods. "Not a single man was hit, and but one horse slightly wounded," reported the 3rd Pennsylvania Cavalry's regimental historian. Sergeant Miller, Lieutenant Warren, and the others had seen enough; they swung their mounts about and cleared out in a hurry, happy to escape without loss. They had done their duty and discovered the enemy position. Taking it was work for the infantry.[24]

At the edge of Sam Poffenberger's woods, Colonel McNeil and his Bucktails looked out on plowed fields extending on both sides of the Smoketown Road for nearly 300 yards. A small cornfield stood beyond the furrowed ground west of the road, and behind it was the East Woods. East of the road, open meadow stretched out from the plowed area to the woods. Before McNeil's skirmishers emerged from Poffenberger's woods, they came under "a raking fire" from the 4th Texas skirmishers, who were probably behind the fencing bordering the farm lane that connected Joseph Poffenberger's farm with the Smoketown Road, as well as from cavalry and infantry skirmishers strung out across Sam Poffenberger's plowed fields. The Pennsylvanians shouldered their Sharps rifles and peppered their adversaries, while McNeil summoned the balance of his regiment to strengthen his firing line. He sent four companies to the right, or west, side of the Smoketown Road, and six to the left. Their movements attracted the attention of the Confederate gunners of Rhett's and Lane's batteries, and they joined the fight with shell, shrapnel, and solid shot. But McNeil soon had his own gun support, when Captain James H. Cooper's Battery B, 1st Pennsylvania Light Artillery, came jingling up. When Rhett and Lane opened fire, McNeil's brigade commander, General Seymour, ordered Cooper to set up his guns on the knoll at the northwest corner of Sam Poffenberger's woodlot (almost exactly where Pelham's guns had been concealed earlier). Cooper's four 3-inch rifles rumbled across a meadow to their position, unlimbered, and opened fire. It was nearly sunset.[25]

General George Meade reacted quickly to the stiffening resistance his advance stirred up. He ordered Seymour to move the rest of his brigade to McNeil's support, then rode forward "to an eminence" (probably near Cooper's position), where he spotted Lane's guns, perhaps Sergeant Falligant's gun in the Hagerstown Pike as well, and the Confederate infantry in David Miller's 30-acre cornfield. To engage this force, Meade decided to extend his divisional front west, to occupy the North Woods with Magilton's and Anderson's brigades, while Seymour's brigade contended with the enemy gathered about the East Woods. Using Cooper's battery as a point of departure, Meade sent Magilton's regiments, followed by Anderson's, in column of battalions across Joseph Poffenberger's meadows toward the North Woods. Their movement was screened by eight companies of the 3rd Pennsylvania Reserves deployed as skirmishers; followed by the 4th Pennsylvania Reserves, formed in line of battle; and then by Captain Dunbar Ransom's Battery C, 5th U.S. Artillery, with its four Napoleons.[26]

The Confederates Meade had observed in David Miller's cornfield were Colonel William T. Wofford's brigade. The earlier firing from the pickets of the 9th Virginia Cavalry and Pelham's guns had alerted Hood to the proximity of the enemy, and he ordered Wofford, whose brigade lay in the pasture east of the Dunker church, to advance and meet the enemy. Wofford led his brigade to the southern border of Miller's cornfield, which he probably hoped would conceal his men from enemy observation, but, to Wofford's disgust, Sergeant Falligant's gun commenced firing just as Wofford's regiments were coming into position at the cornfield's edge. Falligant's ineffective bark gave away their position, and the responding Union guns targeted both the sergeant's single piece and Wofford's nearby infantry. Some 13 of Wofford's officers and men were wounded. Falligant and his crew fired a "half dozen shots," then limbered up and "hastily beat a retreat."[27]

Hood also gave orders for Colonel Evander M. Law to "move forward and occupy the edge of the wood [East Woods] in which the skirmishing was going on." Law's regiments were resting in the West Woods, in the rear of the Dunker church, when they received their orders. Law sent out "a heavy line of skirmishers" to cover his front, and then advanced with his regiments in line abreast along either side of the Smoketown Road. Their movement caught the attention of the Union artillerymen standing by the heavy batteries on Pry Ridge, and they opened with what a lieutenant in the 4th Alabama remembered as "a perfect tornado of bursting shells." As was so frequently the case with long-range artillery fire, it was noisy but ineffective, and there were no reports of casualties, although it undoubtedly hastened the movement of each regiment. Elliot's guns, near the Mumma farm, were also firing at Seymour's brigade to the north, and there "was such a din that the commands of the officers could with difficulty be heard." Lieutenant Robert T. Coles, adjutant of the 4th Alabama, recalled that as his regiment marched through the meadows leading toward the East Woods, he came upon a covey of quail paralyzed by the tremendous racket of the artillery. A Confederate soldier never passed up a meal, so Coles scooped up a brace of birds and dropped them into his jacket pocket.[28] Law apparently moved the 6th North Carolina and the 4th Alabama to support Elliot's guns east of the Smoketown Road, and the 2nd Mississippi and the 11th Mississippi west of the road to bolster Wofford's right flank. Dusk was fast falling over the landscape, but the struggle for possession of the East Woods had only begun.[29]

Colonel Hugh McNeil arranged his companies of 13th Pennsylvania Bucktails into a line in Sam Poffenberger's plowed fields, concentrating his strength for a renewed advance. In less than two years, the 32-year-old Scotsman had risen from private to colonel. He had never enjoyed good health, suffering from heart disease and contracting typhoid fever early in the Peninsula Campaign. But he was courageous, and he had the respect of his hard-fighting men. Behind McNeil's regiment, brigade commander Seymour arranged the 5th, the 1st, and the 6th Reserves (from left to right) into a line, and detached the 2nd Reserves to support Cooper's guns, which continued to send their shells screeching overhead. It took nearly 15 minutes to complete the deployment, so it was now 6 p.m. or later, and darkness was settling in. All the men in McNeil's regiment knew what awaited them when they emerged into Poffenberger's plowed ground. Only the approach of night offered any element of cover. McNeil understood that this was a moment demanding assertive leadership, and he provided it. Placing himself at the head of his companies east of the Smoketown Road, he ordered the regiment to charge and "drive the enemy from the woods." Company officers shouted for the double-quick. The men did the best they could, but furrowed fields are not speedily crossed. Rifles and muskets came alive from the woods in front, as well as from along the fence line west of the woods, and minies hummed in a lively chorus about the Pennsylvanians. Seventy-five yards from their objective, the regiment reached a rise of ground that offered some protection from the bullets and balls cutting through the air around them. Unable, or unwilling, to continue their advance in the face of this fire, the men threw themselves down behind this slight cover and began firing back. Elliot's South Carolina gunners thumped rounds of canister down their tubes and blasted the Bucktails' position with it. "It seemed as if they would blow us from the ground," wrote Angelo Crapsey.[30]

The 200 or so men of the Bucktails worked their Sharps rifles furiously. "We kept fireing so fast that they could not stand it," wrote Crapsey. Full darkness descended during the combat, and the 13th Pennsylvania directed its fire by the flash from the Confederate muskets. The breech-loading Sharps permitted a much greater rate of fire than did the muzzle-loading rifles and muskets carried by the Southerners, and this advantage in firepower began to make itself felt. Private Crapsey fired 70 rounds during the action; if his comrades did likewise, then the regiment fired some 14,000 rounds. Crapsey's gun grew so hot that he hesitated to load it, but he risked it nonetheless and kept "stuffing it & fireing at the flash of their guns." McNeil may have sensed that the Confederates' resistance was slackening, for after some minutes—no one recorded just how long—he ordered his men to rise and charge the dark woods. They responded, following their courageous colonel toward the trees. Within 15 yards of the woods, McNeil shouted "Forward, Bucktails, forward." As the words left his lips, a Confederate put a bullet through his heart and the colonel pitched forward, killed instantly. The death of a leader often either saps the morale of his men or enrages them. McNeil's death produced the latter effect in the Bucktails' ranks. "A mad fury seized his men," recorded the regimental historian, and they pushed on into the East Woods, blazing away at the Texas skirmishers. The angry surge of the Bucktails caused the Texans to give up some ground, but not to abandon the fight.[31]

In the East Woods, the Pennsylvanians and the Texans fired at muzzle flashes. "We got all mixed up until we hardly knew each other apart in the darkness," wrote Jonathan Stevens of the 5th Texas. The 1st Pennsylvania Reserves came to the Bucktails' support, entering the woods to their right and rear, and Colonel William Sinclair's 6th Reserves entered on the 1st's right. The weight of the numbers the 6th Reserves brought to the fight caused the skirmishers of the 4th and the 5th Texas to fall back, and Sinclair's regiment pushed through the woods to a worm fence separating it from David Miller's cornfield. Some of the 1st Reserves may have gone this far as well, for Captain James L. Lemon of the 18th Georgia wrote that his regiment "advanced through a corn field to a piece of timber where we met a force of the enemy & drove them through the woods." The Confederates' counterattack collected a handful of prisoners from the 1st and the 3rd Reserves (the 3rd were skirmishing to aid the advance of Anderson's and Magilton's brigades). Among their numbers were "some little drummer boys." The Georgians had lost their drums at Manassas, so they relieved the youngsters of their burdens. In the confusion caused by the darkness, Lemon may have thought that his regiment had pushed the Pennsylvanians from the woods, but the 6th Reserves were not evicted. Sinclair withdrew the main body of his regiment about 100 yards into the northwestern section of the woods and left a skirmish line at the worm fence.[32]

The 5th Reserves, on Seymour's left, observing that they would be exposed to the fire of Elliot's howitzers, waited for darkness to advance from Poffenberger's woods to the East Woods. They halted at a worm fence on the north edge of the woods, south of Morrison's small farm, and to the left and rear of the Bucktails. Seymour's brigade had secured a lodgment in the East Woods, but it was abundantly clear that the enemy lay ahead in strong force.[33]

While Seymour's regiments fought to gain a foothold in the East Woods, Magilton's and Anderson's brigades advanced steadily toward the North Woods. Their course took them across the southeastern corner of the Middlekauf farm and onto the Joseph Poffenberger farm. The pioneer corps (men—typically equipped with axes in addition to their rifles—who were specially detailed to demolish obstructions, build works, clear obstacles, and the like) dashed ahead to clear gaps through Middlekauf's and Poffenberger's fences. Worm fences could generally be pulled apart, but post-and-rail ones were more formidable obstacles. Bates Alexander, in the 8th Reserves, recalled that the sturdy pioneers handled these fences by chopping through the posts and letting the panels fall. Both Middlekauf and Poffenberger came out "to view the wreck and ruin" being made to their fences. They were Union men, for instead of lamenting the damage, John Burnett of the 4th Reserves recalled that they "aided us in demolishing their property as well as kindly encouraging us in our undertaking." The soldiers and the farmers did their work so well that the horses of Captain Dunbar Ransom's Battery C, 5th U.S. Artillery, stepped over the fallen fence panels "almost without flinching."[34]

The column crossed Joseph Poffenberger's meadows and the farm lane leading to the Smoketown Road, pushed through a thin field of Poffenberger's corn, and entered his woodlot, the North Woods. Resistance was negligible. Any Confederate skirmishers around Poffenberger's farm or his woods withdrew at the approach of the large mass of men. Due to the losses at South Mountain and straggling during the march to Keedysville, the two Federal brigades numbered less than 900 men each, but in the twilight they looked formidable. When the leading element of Magilton's brigade reached the south edge of the North Woods they could see Lane's battery, south of the cornfield, shelling Seymour's regiments. Magilton's leading unit was Major John Nyce's 4th Pennsylvania Reserves. Nyce got his regiment into line before anyone else and ordered the soldiers to fix bayonets. One of his men recalled that Nyce "was really a good fellow but somewhat impulsive." Battle apparently brought out his recklessness, for he intended to make a bayonet assault and capture the artillery. It apparently had not occurred to the major that the Confederates probably had infantry supports that were under cover near the battery, and that an unsupported attack was a recipe for disaster. Fortunately the cooler-headed Magilton soon arrived and promptly put a stop to Nyce's bayonet charge.[35]

Magilton arrived in the North Woods with orders from Meade to deploy his brigade into line there. He put the 3rd Reserves on his left and had their left flank snug up against Poffenberger's farm lane, about where the lane makes almost a 90-degree turn south toward the East Woods. The 4th and the 7th Reserves, respectively, extended the 3rd's line west through the North Woods, and the 8th was held in reserve. Lane's battery continued to fire while Magilton formed his line. "We could see the sparks as they flew from their muzzles and slowly fell," wrote Bates Alexander, who was in the reserve line. Due to the limited visibility and their focus on Seymour's brigade, Lane's gunners did not see Magilton or Anderson advance into the North Woods. Meade's assistant adjutant general, Captain E. C. Baird, cautioned the infantry to be quiet as they moved into position. "They don't see us and we'll just slip round by the right and capture that battery," he was heard to say. Bates Alexander related that this order never came, for moments after Baird's warning a Confederate shell "came crashing through the timber." More shells followed, along with what some thought was canister but was probably shrapnel. "Those gentlemen," noted Alexander, "had evidently received guests before this."[36]

Meade summoned Ransom's battery of regulars from where it had halted in the meadow east of Poffenberger's barn. Ransom was a North Carolinian by birth, but his family had moved to Vermont and it was from this state that he received his appointment to West Point. He had seven years in the artillery and knew his business. His four Napoleons trotted smartly up in front of Magilton, unlimbered, and cleared for action. The odds were against Lane's Georgians— already outgunned two to one against Cooper's 3-inch rifles—and Ransom increased the odds to four to one. The barrage of iron that poured in on the Confederates killed some of Lane's horses and one of Lane's lieutenants. John T. Wingfield's understated comment was that "there was some confusion" in the battery. Lane ordered his guns to limber, and they cleared out before the enemy caused greater damage. But driving off Lane brought no relief to Ransom's artillery or Magilton's and Anderson's infantry, for another Confederate battery opened fire on them from west of the Hagerstown Pike and north of the Dunker church. This was Captain William T. Poague's Rockbridge (Virginia) Artillery of J. R. Jones's division. It presence meant that Jackson had arrived to reinforce Hood's line.[37]

Stonewall Jackson reached the West Woods with J. R. Jones's division around sunset. He directed Jones to form his troops in two lines on Hood's left. Colonel A. J. Grigsby's Stonewall Brigade and Colonel Bradley T. Johnson's brigade formed the first line in a meadow west of the Hagerstown Pike, a short distance to the left and rear of Wofford's brigade and David Miller's cornfield.

Straggling had taken a severe toll on both brigades. Johnson's brigade recorded no figures for its effective strength, but it could not have been more than 300 officers and men in its three regiments and one battalion. Grigsby's brigade numbered only about 250 muskets, and perhaps 50 officers, with an average regimental strength of 75. Captain A. C. Page of the 21st Virginia went forward about 100 yards with two companies to form a skirmish line. Brigadier General William A. Starke's Louisiana brigade and Colonel E. T. H. Warren's brigade of Alabamians and Virginians formed the support line along the northeastern edge of the West Woods, about 100 yards in the rear of Grigsby and Johnson. Starke had a huge brigade by Confederate standards, numbering just under 1,000 men, but Warren's brigade was skeletal. Captain R. B. Jennings, of the brigade's 23rd Virginia, recalled that his company had only 7 effectives, and that the entire brigade "numbered all told between 75 and 100 men"—about the strength of a strong infantry company.[38]

It was while J. R. Jones's brigades quietly took their positions that Ransom's battery opened fire on Lane's guns east of the Hagerstown Pike. Jackson ordered Jones to bring up Captain William Poague's Rockbridge Artillery to respond. A prewar attorney, Poague had developed into a fine artillery officer, and his battery of two 10 lb. Parrott rifles and one Napoleon was one of the best in Jones's divisional artillery. The Virginian moved his guns up past Grigsby's and Johnson's brigades and unlimbered on a slight knoll between these units and Captain Page's skirmish line. Probably because the Federals were focused on the East Woods and Miller's cornfield, and because the twilight helped conceal the battery's movements, Poague brought his artillery up and Jones deployed his entire division unnoticed. That changed abruptly when Poague's three guns opened fire on Ransom.[39]

Lieutenant Colonel Robert Anderson's 3rd Brigade of Meade's division was moving toward the North Woods to deploy on Magilton's right when Poague opened fire. Although it is more likely that Ransom was Poague's primary target, the Southerner may have seen the Federal infantry forming to support the regulars. In any event, Anderson's Pennsylvanians were convinced that they were the Virginians' target of choice. "Just as the tenth [10th Pennsylvania Reserves] was forming over a little ridge [probably the piece of high ground immediately north of Poffenberger's farmhouse] several shot[s] struck the left of the line and shells burst rapidly and for a moment I feared lest the effect would be injurious to the steadiness of the men which I strove to maintain," wrote the 10th's commander, Colonel Adoniram Warner. Officers shouted for the double-quick, and the regiments hustled for the shelter of the North Woods. But to get there required crossing several of Poffenberger's fences, and neither the pioneers nor farmer Poffenberger had knocked paths through them. The regiment in front of Warner's, probably the 9th Reserves, did not clear these fences fast enough to suit the colonel. As he recalled, "I was not a little enraged at the imbecility manifested by the officer in command of this battalion and sent forward men to tear away the fences and hurried my men [regardless] of those in my front over the ridge and out of range of this menacing fire." It seemed to Warner that Poague's guns had "the perfect range on this spot."

A case shot from one of Poague's tubes burst near the left of Warner's regiment, causing what the colonel described as "a very amazing incident."[40] The shot burst in front of the ranks on the left of the battalion, and a missile struck the haversack of a member of Company G, went through it and his canteen and waist belt, tore his blouse, and then passed on. The man felt the shock, and an instant later felt what he supposed was blood. The soldier clasped his hands on his leg and exclaimed, "I am hit." One of his comrades asked him if he was hurt badly. "I don't know" he replied, adding that "I feels the blood running down my legs." The captain then inquired if he could walk, and directed him to the surgeon, who was not far back. On arriving there and laying bare his leg, the soldier, greatly to his surprise, found that while his canteen was perforated, his body had not been touched. In a short time he came back and approached his company, saying "O pshaw, I wasn't shot at all it was just water from the canteen that I felt on my legs."[41]

Poague's gunners worked their guns with a will, making things hot for both Meade's infantry and the artillerymen of Ransom's battery. "We lay flat on our faces and wished the short grass out of the way that we might get closer to the ground," wrote Bates Alexander. Poague's shells came "crashing, bowling and whirling through the timber," and Alexander wondered "if we would ever get of there alive." But while the infantrymen hugged the earth, they noticed their division commander, Meade, standing in front and "seemingly unconscious of danger" while observing the enemy fire. First Lieutenant John G. Simpson's Battery A, 1st Pennsylvania Light (4 Napoleons), came up during this artillery exchange, unlimbered near Cooper's battery, and joined in the fray. Under normal circumstances three Federal batteries should have sent Poague scurrying for cover, but the Virginians held their own. For nearly 20 minutes the gun duel continued. But Poague, either through superior gunnery or the better accuracy and range of his rifled pieces, soon gained an advantage over Ransom. A shell beheaded one of Ransom's sergeants, and Meade decided to spare the battery further casualties. "For God's sake take that battery out of there," an infantryman heard him command. Ransom limbered up, withdrew to the meadow east of Poffenberger's, and went into bivouac.[42]

Poague and his gunners congratulated themselves on silencing the Yankee guns. "He could not get our range somehow," the captain recalled, and most of enemy shells went over the heads of the Virginians, their fuses burning brightly in the falling dusk. But shells that do not hit their targets must land somewhere, and in Poague's case, those that missed him landed near or among J. R. Jones's infantry, who were supporting the guns. The danger depended on where one was and the spot in which a particular shell landed. Major H. J. Williams of the 5th Virginia thought that "the display was grand and comparatively harmless, except to the stragglers in the rear." Not all would have agreed with the major. John Worsham of Johnson's brigade, thinking back on this event in 1895, remembered it as the "severest shelling experienced during the war." This is probably an exaggeration, but it did leave a vivid impression. Starke's brigade lost several men to the overshots. One severed both legs of Lieutenant A. M. Gordon, the acting assistant adjutant general of the brigade, and he bled to death. Yet the casualties were very light overall, despite the number of guns firing. The enemy's shots were random—although they were intended for Poague—and inaccurate. This would not be the case on September 17, when the light would be better and the Federals' artillery would be both more plentiful and more accurate.[43]

During the artillery duel, Lawton's division arrived at the West Woods, having marched cross-country west of Sharpsburg to escape observation by the Union batteries east of Antietam Creek. They reached the woods around sunset. Enemy shells were still "flying tolerably thick." Jackson rode up and personally ordered Brigadier General Jubal Early to place his brigade so as to protect the left flank of J. R. Jones's division, as well as to coordinate this movement with Jones. Being entirely ignorant of the ground and of Jones's dispositions, Early set off to find the division commander. Between the falling darkness and the shelling this was challenging, but Early eventually located Jones "not far from where I was" and learned from him that Starke's brigade formed the division's left flank. Early brought his Virginians forward and set them along a lane—the old road to Hagerstown—running from Alfred Poffenberger's farm southeast through the West Woods and emerging immediately north of the Dunker church. This placed his brigade at nearly a 45-degree angle to Starke's brigade. Early's left rested in front of Alfred Poffenberger's farm buildings, which were outside of the West Woods, while his right extended into the woods. Soon after Early finished arranging his regiments, Brigadier General Harry T. Hays brought up his Louisiana brigade as a support. By this point, according to Early, it was "too dark to understand enough of the position to make very good dispositions," so they placed Hays's regiments as best they could in the rear of Early's line. Further adjustments would have to wait until daylight. The balance of Lawton's division—Colonel Marcellus Douglass's Georgia brigade, and Colonel James A. Walker's brigade of Alabama, North Carolina, and Virginia regiments—were held in reserve in the West Woods.[44]

As the infantry took over, Fitz Lee withdrew his brigade behind Hood's division. The 9th Virginia halted for some time in what one of its troopers recalled as "the shelter of a valley," where the shells from both sides passed over their heads. This may have been the low ground immediately east-northeast of the Dunker church, near the later position of S. D. Lee's battalion. After dark Fitz Lee moved his regiments into position to cover the army's extreme left flank. The bulk of the brigade marched to the vicinity of the Cox and Rowe farms, where they could cover the road running south from New Industry. Part of the 9th Virginia followed a guide, who lost his way in the dark and led the troopers around for quite some time before calling a halt, either because he believed he had found their destination or because he wanted them to think that he had. Their precise location is difficult to determine, but it may have been on the eastern slope of Nicodemus Heights, or perhaps on the high ground north of the lane from the Hagerstown Pike to New Industry. In either case, the men would discover in the morning that they were in full view of the artillery of Union army's 1st Corps, positioned around the Joseph Poffenberger farm. The 9th's brigade commander, Fitz Lee, seeking a place to catch a few hours' sleep, made his way up a hillside—probably Nicodemus Heights. He found a tree that offered some shelter, tied his horse to it, and lay down beneath it. A single rider soon emerged from the night. Fitz Lee said that it was Stonewall Jackson, but Jackson reportedly slept that evening on a couch at the Grove house in Sharpsburg. It may have been Jeb Stuart, who was in the vicinity late that night looking after Pelham's battery, and who rode alone. But it is also possible that Jackson subsequently left the Grove house and found a sleeping place near the front. Whoever the lone rider was, he tied up his horse by Fitz Lee's and "went to sleep near me."[45]

Major John Pelham moved his horse battery to the south slope of Nicodemus Heights around sunset. The Heights were key terrain for the Confederates, as they were out of range of the Federal batteries east of Antietam Creek and offered excellent fields of fire from David Miller's cornfield to the Joseph Poffenberger farm. Perhaps most importantly, any guns positioned here could enfilade Federal infantry advancing south along the axis of the Hagerstown Pike. The Heights reached an elevation of 500 feet, exactly the same as the center of Miller's cornfield and only 30 feet lower than the high ground north of Poffenberger's. The topography of the hill could accommodate plenty of artillery, and the reverse slope provided good cover for the limbers and caissons. Hooker took little or no notice of it, but his men would—when morning came. Pelham appreciated its value as an artillery position, which is why he moved his guns to the south side of the hill, but he did not occupy any firing positions after dark, when he could have done so unobserved. Instead, he and his men went to sleep after tending to the horses. Robert Macknall, a member of the battery, recalled that around 2 a.m. the tramp of a horse near his head woke him. Macknall demanded to know why the rider had led his horse through sleeping men. The rider replied by asking where Pelham was. Macknall instantly recognized the voice as Jeb Stuart's, so he got up and led Stuart to Pelham, who lay asleep beside a post-and-rail fence. Macknall stated that "I distinctly remember hearing him [Stuart] say to Pelham 'My dear fellow, don't you know that the corn field at the foot of the hill is full of Yankees and that you ought to have your guns in position now, for if you wait until daylight the hill will be swarming with blue coats.'" Pelham immediately awakened his crews, and they pushed their guns by hand to the crest of the hill, where they waited for daylight.[46]

While Meade's division skirmished with Hood over in the East Woods, Doubleday's and Ricketts's divisions hurried forward. Although Doubleday's division had been cut in two by the premature movement of Meade and Ricketts, Doubleday nevertheless pushed on with Brigadier General Marsena Patrick's brigade to reach the Hagerstown Pike as ordered, without waiting for the balance of his division. As the brigade crossed the Middlekauf and Joseph Poffenberger farms, they were observed by what was probably Lane's battery. One of the Confederate guns targeted this moving column. Doubleday recalled that he and his staff led the brigade, riding "in one line followed by three mounted orderlies in a row." A Confederate shell—probably a round of shrapnel—burst near the orderlies and killed their three horses, yet left the riders unscathed. Fortunately for Patrick's New Yorkers, the subsequent Confederate fire lacked the accuracy of this first round. "Our columns passed directly through a fearful storm of shot and shell," wrote a member of the 23rd New York. But although "the darting flame from the cannons, and hideous yell of the balls, together with the deafening roar of cannon made a terrible scene," only a handful of Patrick's men were wounded. The New Yorkers hustled across Poffenberger's pastures to a thin, triangular-shaped woods in the northwestern corner of Poffenberger's farm, facing the Hagerstown Pike. Patrick posted skirmishers to the front and, since the rest of the division had not yet come up, extended his picket line to the left to connect with Meade's right. Everyone felt their way around, for it was dark by the time Patrick's brigade reached the woods besides the pike. No one had a good feel for the terrain, and the occasional rifle crack from Patrick's skirmishers warned the men that the Confederates were in close proximity. This complicated the posting of pickets, and it was 10 p.m. before the picket lines were connected satisfactorily.[47]

The rest of Doubleday's division arrived in the vicinity of Joseph Poffenberger's farm buildings long after night fell. In the darkness, Lieutenant Colonel J. W. Hoffman, commanding Doubleday's 2nd Brigade, lost visual contact with Patrick's brigade and had no idea where it had gone. He made inquiries, but no one seemed to know where Patrick and Doubleday were. Hoffman finally appealed to Hooker for orders, and the corps commander ordered the Pennsylvanian "to take possession and hold a piece of wood extending along the Sharpsburg [Hagerstown] road." This turned out to be the very woods that Patrick had already occupied. With Phelps's and Gibbon's brigades following behind him, Hoffman led his brigade to the small woodlot, where he found Captain E. P. Halstead, Doubleday's assistant adjutant general. Halstead ordered Hoffman to have his brigade fill in the gap between Meade and Patrick. Hoffman eventually found his place, but not without difficulty in the pitch dark. One of his men complained to his journal later that night: "We marcht about 4 miles till after dark round through wood & fields that I canot tell ware we went."[48]

When Gibbon's and Phelps's brigades came up, Doubleday ordered them to mass in the rear of Patrick and Hoffman and act as a reserve. Gibbon's four regiments formed into column of divisions (i.e., each regiment would present a front two companies wide and five companies deep) in mass on the northern edge of Joseph Poffenberger's orchard, paralleling the Hagerstown Pike. Phelps formed his brigade in similar fashion, in an open pasture just east of the woods where Patrick had deployed. The men were not permitted to remove their equipment, and they lay down to rest on the damp ground with weapons loaded. The four batteries of the divisional artillery parked nearby, the gunners and drivers going to sleep at their posts so that they would be ready for action at a moment's notice. Both Gibbon's and Phelps's brigades massed on the western slope of what I will call Poffenberger Hill. It was the highest ground on what would be the northern part of the battlefield, reaching an elevation of approximately 530 feet. In the overwhelming darkness, no one realized that both brigades, but particularly Gibbon's, were exposed to Nicodemus Heights and Pelham's guns there. Gibbon felt anxious. From what he could discern, affairs in his division appeared to be "in a very confused and huddled up condition." The situation was no better with Meade's and Ricketts's divisions. Other than a general notion of the direction in which the Confederates lay, Hooker and his division and brigade commanders knew literally nothing about the enemy's strength and position; moreover, because everyone arrived at dusk or after dark, there was no opportunity to reconnoiter the ground that would be a battlefield in the morning. All they could do was wait for daylight.[49]

Ricketts's division halted for the night in Samuel Poffenberger's woodlot. "It was so dark that we could not see the man next to us; it was inky dark," wrote John Vautier of the 88th Pennsylvania. Men held on to one another's coats to keep together, "but much difficulty was experienced . . . in keeping the ranks properly closed." They had some consolation in the fact that the Confederates could see no better in the intense blackness. The relief for a Confederate skirmish post walked into Vautier's regiment "and innocently asked 'what Regt. this was.' They soon found out." Ricketts posted Brigadier General George L. Hartsuff's 3rd Brigade in his first line; the four regiments were deployed in line of battle astride the Smoketown Road, with the troops extending along the southern face of Poffenberger's woods and into the meadows east and west of the woods. Colonel William A. Christian's 2nd Brigade deployed on Hartsuff's left rear, with its right resting on the Smoketown Road and its left reaching east of Poffenberger's woods into one of the farmer's meadows. Duryee's 1st Brigade composed the division's reserve, and it massed in column of regiments in the woods on the west side of the Smoketown Road. The two divisional batteries— Captain Ezra W. Matthews's Battery F, 1st Pennsylvania, and Captain James

Thompson's Battery C, Pennsylvania Light Artillery—parked under cover nearby. Like the soldiers in Hooker's corps, Ricketts's men lay down to sleep in line, with their equipment on and muskets ready by their sides.[50]

In Meade's division a gap of nearly 500 yards existed between Magilton's and Seymour's brigades. Hooker filled this in by having the 3rd Pennsylvania Cavalry form along the eastern side of the Joseph Poffenberger farm lane, between the North Woods and the East Woods. One trooper recalled that the Rebels were close enough so "that we could distinctly hear them talking." The cavalrymen had orders to stand "to horse"—meaning each trooper stood beside his horse, holding its reins—a duty all found onerous. They were, from the disgusted viewpoint of that same trooper, "tired, hungry, and uncomfortable, in everybody's way, and of no earthly use, all because we were attached to an infantryman's command." Hooker detached one squadron of the 3rd Pennsylvania Cavalry, under Captain Claude White, and ordered it to picket the 1st Corps' right and rear. In giving White his orders, Hooker professed to have no information about the roads in the area, only "that he had taken position on the left flank of the enemy and wanted him [White] to move to the right and rear and use his eyes and ears so as to give him timely notice of any movement in that quarter on the part of the enemy." White was a resourceful fellow, which is probably why Hooker picked him, and he led his troopers north in the pitch-dark night to the intersection of the Williamsport and Hagerstown roads, around which he posted his main force. Along the way, White passed the Middlekauf farm lane, which connected the Hagerstown Pike with the Smoketown Road, and another road, about 600 yards south of the intersection of the Williamsport and Hagerstown roads, which also connected the pike to the Smoketown Road. Presumably he left some pickets at both of these intersections.[51]

Ezra Carman, in his history of the battle, concluded that Hooker's movement to turn the enemy left

> was barren of good results but prolific in bad ones. When darkness came and stopped his advance, he knew very little more of the enemy's position than when he crossed the Antietam. He had been ordered to turn Lee's left flank, and completed his day's work by posting his own command in such manner as to secure it from a flank attack of the enemy, a very proper thing to do, under all circumstances, but a thing not contemplated when he started; he had given Lee complete and reliable information as to McClellan's intention for the morrow.

It is an accurate assessment, although whether Hooker's movement gave away McClellan's strategy will be discussed below. But Hooker's situation and his dispositions were less than ideal to renew the battle in the morning. He did not understand the ground, the Confederates' positions, or their strength. Meade's division was spread across a front of nearly 1,500 yards, with Seymour's brigade some 600 yards forward of its nearest supports. Doubleday's division was deployed to meet an attack on the corps' right flank, not to launch an assault. Hooker bears some of the fault for the "confused and huddled up" condition of his corps that night, but McClellan's failure to begin the movement earlier—as well as to use his available cavalry to screen the movement and reconnoiter the enemy position, roads, and terrain—contributed largely to the situation.[52]

The movement of Hooker's 1st Corps to the west bank of Antietam Creek has generally been considered a blunder, in that it telegraphed to Lee where the Federals would make their main effort the next morning. But this presumes that this was the only place where McClellan could strike on September 17, which Lee knew was not the case. While Hooker's advance did alert Lee to the fact that his left would probably be attacked in the morning, he also had to consider the possibility that the 1st Corps' movement might be a feint to distract him from an assault on another part of his line, particularly his right flank, where—if the enemy pressed strongly over the Antietam—they would threaten his only viable route for a retreat into Virginia. Had Lee known McClellan's main attack would fall on his left, reason would dictate that during the night he would have shifted additional forces to oppose it. He did not. Apart from reinforcing Hood with Jackson's two divisions, the only other change Lee made to his dispositions was to have D. H. Hill extend his left flank toward Hood around sunset. Hill did this by moving Ripley's brigade from his right to a point about 150 yards south and west of the Mumma farm, where it supported Evander Law's right flank. Hill also brought up Colquitt's brigade and placed it in the Sunken Lane on the left of Garland. Skirmishers were advanced to occupy the Roulette and Clipp farm buildings. Colquitt's main body dismantled the fencing along the road, stacking the rails as breastworks or using them to build fires to roast ears of corn harvested from Piper's field. These movements left Lee's six divisions deployed with three on the left; one holding the center and one on the right below the Boonsboro Pike; and one—Walker's—in reserve, but closer to the right than the left. Lee's arrangement was weighted left but anticipated the possibility of an attack on the right.[53]

Thomas Munford's small brigade reinforced Lee during the afternoon, arriving from where they had been observing the 6th Corps near Rohrersville. With Fitz Lee guarding the army's left flank, Lee sent both of Munford's regiments to the right, where they could cover the ford at the Antietam Iron Works (at the mouth of Antietam Creek), Myer's Ford, and Snavely's Ford. Munford's third regiment, the 7th Virginia—still on detached duty with Jackson—arrived from Harpers Ferry around sunset. They crossed the Potomac at Blackford's Ford, and then marched along the C&O Canal for some distance before moving cross-country to the vicinity of Cox's farm. Someone, probably Jackson, ordered the regiment to picket the Hagerstown Pike. They marched north from Cox's, parallel with the canal; turned east to the Coffman farm; and from there passed through farm fields to the turnpike. The regiment dismounted here, and the horses were brought back to the Coffman farm, perhaps to ensure that noises from these animals did not give away their position. Captain S. B. Myers, the acting regimental commander, led the small unit north to the vicinity of Ground Squirrel Church, where he deployed them on either side of the pike, along the northern edge of the rectangular woodlot that grew around the church. Although Myers knew that he was in close proximity to the enemy, he was not aware that his command had inserted itself between Captain White's squadron of the 3rd Pennsylvania Cavalry, 600 yards to the north, and Double-day's division, a half mile to the south. They would find out come morning.[54]

Sometime that evening, Lee sent orders recalling the 15th and the 17th Georgia of Toombs's brigade, who had been sent to Williamsport to protect the trains from the marauding Harpers Ferry cavalry, as well as the five companies of the 11th Georgia, who were the train's escort. Lee did not, however, summon Colonel Brown's and Colonel Nelson's battalions of reserve artillery. Brown's battalion included five rifled guns in its armament, which were placed to guard the ferry and ford at Williamsport and the ford at Falling Waters, slightly over 4 miles below. Nelson's battalion took position below Shepherdstown to cover Blackford's Ford, a position vital to the Confederate army's security. Two factors influenced Lee's decision to leave these artillery battalions guarding the fords, but to strip them of their infantry supports. First, Lee desperately needed infantry, and he felt that the 164 or so guns he already had at Sharpsburg—plus the 55 additional guns that would arrive with McLaws, R. H. Anderson, and A. P. Hill—were sufficient. Second, Lee needed a covering force in place at Black-ford's Ford in the event that he had to withdraw, and by guarding the upper Potomac fords he ensured that Union cavalry could not penetrate his rear and threaten his communications. Another reason may also have motivated the defense of the upper fords. Lee always thought opportunistically. If he defeated McClellan's anticipated attack and the Federals assumed a defensive posture behind Antietam Creek, then the way would be open to Hagerstown and a renewal of Lee's campaign of maneuver. The combat arms at Sharpsburg could march to Hagerstown via the Hagerstown Pike. They would then rendezvous at that city with Lee's trains, fresh ammunition, and whatever reinforcements had been collected at Winchester, who would march by way of the Williamsport Ford. Lee may also have been thinking that if he were forced to retreat from Sharpsburg, he might find it possible to regain the initiative by reentering Maryland via these upper fords.[55]

If Lee pondered these possibilities on the night of September 16, it was with the knowledge that, for the moment, his campaign of maneuver was finished. The battle now pending must be won, or the entire Maryland Campaign would be over. As night blanketed the battlefield his position was strong, but it was not strongly held. Both flanks were anchored on the Potomac River, but only thin brigades of cavalry manned the anchors. The five divisions holding the

main front were greatly reduced by straggling, sickness, and—in the case of
D. H. Hill's and D. R. Jones's—casualties at South Mountain. If McLaws and
R. H. Anderson failed to arrive before morning, Lee faced possible disaster, for
he had based his decision to make a stand at Sharpsburg on the belief that he
could concentrate his army before McClellan attacked. The fate of the Army of
Northern Virginia, and possibly of the Confederacy, was literally in the hands
of the Georgian and his two divisions. Would they arrive in time? This was the
question that must have preyed on Lee most on that long and anxious evening
of September 16.[56]

McLaws's March to Sharpsburg: "Close Up! Close Up!"

As the morning wore into the afternoon on September 16, Lafayette McLaws
busied himself with trying to obtain food for his hungry men and making arrangements to have his wounded and sick moved to Charlestown. Perhaps he
felt these pressing needs were more urgent than Jackson's orders to march to
Sharpsburg "as quickly as possible," or, more likely, he believed that unless his
men were fed, many would straggle on the march in search of food. Jackson had
also delayed his own march to allow time for his divisions to cook rations.
Whatever the cause of McLaws's delay, it became a moot point when orders
from Lee reached him around 2 p.m., instructing the Georgian to march at once
to Sharpsburg. McLaws had failed to turn up even "one day's rations for my
men," but Lee's orders permitted no further delay. He returned to Halltown
and, around 3 p.m., issued orders for his and R. H. Anderson's divisions to march.
In the 7th South Carolina their commissary wagons, carrying rations, arrived
just at this moment, "which produced great joy in the Regiment." But before any
rations could be issued, the command "Fall in 7th Regiment" rang out, and the
men marched with empty stomachs. Hampton's brigade, which had covered
McLaws's and Anderson's movement across the Potomac River to Harpers Ferry,
remained near the old arsenal at the Ferry until early morning on September 17,
when they followed McLaws to Sharpsburg. But the brigade took a different
route, turning off the Shepherdstown Pike onto the road to Knott's Ford,
slightly more than a half mile below the mouth of Antietam Creek, where they
crossed the Potomac and made their way north, reaching the field at Sharpsburg between 9 and 10 a.m.[57]

Although their stomachs were grumbling, the men began the march in high
spirits. They were back on the friendly soil of Virginia, and—in their ignorance
of the general situation of Lee's army—thought they were marching toward a
well-deserved rest in the lush Shenandoah Valley after the victory at Harpers
Ferry. McLaws's route is not known with certainty, but he apparently marched
west toward Charlestown, and then turned right at Schaeffers' Crossroads to

reach the Charlestown Pike to Shepherdstown. There was a more direct route, which ran straight north from Halltown through Unionville, but this was a secondary road and McLaws may have felt that it was unsuitable for his artillery and wagons. The column went forward "at a lively gait," and as darkness began to envelop the men, they began to sing old plantation songs. A member of Barksdale's brigade recalled that they sang "Rock the Cradle, Julie," "Sallie Get Your Hoecake Done," and "We're Gwying Down the Newbury Road," among others. The column marched along happily, the men imagining the delicious foods they had heard the valley was famous for, until they reached Schaeffers' Crossroads. They turned right here, in the direction of Maryland. "As each regiment changed direction the noise of singing and jesting would cease," wrote a Mississippian. Within half an hour, this same soldier noted that "not a sound could be heard, except the tramp of the column and the din of the moving artillery."[58]

Pitch-black darkness closed in on McLaws's and R. H. Anderson's men, rendering the march all the more tedious, and the pace increased as the column continued on. Over and over again, officers shouted to their men, "Close up!' Close up!" Mounted officers ranged back and forth along the road, encouraging the men to keep moving. "The gait continued to increase, until finally all were going in a trot," recalled a Mississippian. As they plodded onward, stragglers leaked out with each mile. W. B. Judkins of the 22nd Georgia in Wright's brigade recalled that "many of the Regt. straggled out that night with many from other Regts. I was one of the stragglers, being broke down and worn out by so much hard marching." Judkins simply wandered off into some nearby woods with Gus Campbell, "who could not see at all after dark," and went to sleep, along with many others from his unit. A lieutenant in the 5th Florida wrote to his mother six days later that "about half the Regiment broke down that night," including himself. His company, he noted, went into battle on September 17 commanded by a corporal, and sergeants led most of the other companies. A member of Wilcox's brigade observed that the road "from Harper's Ferry through Sheppardstown, on to the battleground of Antietam, was crowded with the sick and straggling soldiers. Hundreds, yes thousands were barefooted." J. J. Kirkpatrick, a Mississippian with Featherston's brigade, noted tersely in his diary, "Much straggling." One of Barksdale's men wrote that hundreds of men fell out along the march. In his regiment, the 18th Mississippi, of the over 60 officers and men in his own Company C, only 16 men and 1 officer went into battle on the 17th, a noncombat loss of over 70 percent. In recalling his experiences throughout the war, this soldier remembered the night march to Sharpsburg as "one of severest ever made by infantry troops."[59]

Two miles south of Shepherdstown, McLaws called a halt and permitted his men to make camp. McLaws never explained why he halted, when his orders had clearly directed that he march posthaste to Sharpsburg, but there are two possible explanations. First, he might have been concerned about making a river crossing in the intense darkness of that night. Second, he may have wished to allow time for the large number of stragglers to catch up with their regiments. McLaws clearly reported his arrival near Shepherdstown to Lee, for shortly before midnight Captain A. P. Mason from Lee's staff rode up with orders from the commanding general. Mason informed McLaws that the "entire force" of the enemy were drawn up in line of battle; that "there must be a battle in the morning"; and that Lee's orders were for McLaws "to hasten forward" to Sharpsburg that night. One can only imagine the curses and groans that rose from the ranks of the infantry, when, shortly after midnight, McLaws ordered the column to break up the camp they had just established, fall in, and resume their march.[60] McLaws had torches lit to guide the column through the inky night. Between 2:30 and 3 a.m., the advance reached the Potomac River at Blackford's Ford. "With no unnecessary delay," the regiments waded in and started for the Maryland shore. Daylight was less than three hours away.[61]

The knowledge that McLaws was near at hand must have lifted Lee's spirits. The approach of the two additional divisions meant that he could release Walker's division to the front, where it was sorely needed. Sometime before 3 a.m. he ordered Walker to move his division to the far right of the army in order to cover Snavely's Ford and support Toombs's brigade at the Rohrbach Bridge, lending further credence to the idea that Lee believed an attack against his right flank was likely. He also sent a courier galloping to Harpers Ferry with orders for A. P. Hill to leave whatever force was necessary to remove the captured property and march with the balance of the Light Division to Sharpsburg. What had changed Lee's mind regarding Hill and Harpers Ferry is unknown. Perhaps Lee had received news that the paroling of the Union prisoners was close to completion, so that a smaller element of the division could see to the removal of the captured equipment. Franklin's timidity also probably convinced Lee that a small force could guard the Harpers Ferry crossing and protect his communications.[62]

With the river crossing underway, McLaws rode on ahead to report to Lee, while his division, followed by R. H. Anderson's, made their way across the Potomac. Had Lee's chief of staff been more efficient, he would have sent a staff officer to guide McLaws to army headquarters and given him instructions as to where the two divisions should bivouac, but such procedures were lacking in the Army of Northern Virginia, and no one was sent. McLaws had to find his own way. Being ignorant of where headquarters was located, he rode past it and through Sharpsburg without meeting anyone. "This was before sunrise, and there was not at that time, any firing, nor was there any indication of the close proximity of two contending armies," wrote McLaws. He decided to ride back and halt his command, so that he might "look around" and "find someone who could tell me where to go." As McLaws was returning to his men, he ran into Longstreet and his staff. Longstreet told him where army headquarters was and also said McLaws should have Anderson's division march through Sharpsburg to Cemetery Hill, where Anderson would receive further orders. Lee and Longstreet had probably discussed this arrangement regarding Anderson's division earlier, although in the confused organization of the Army of Northern Virginia that fall, one is never sure.

That same type of muddle led Jackson to believe that McLaws remained under his orders. When Jackson learned of the Georgian's arrival at the Potomac River, he sent McLaws an order to "go to the right" when he reached the front. McLaws wisely waited to carry out Jackson's orders until he saw Lee, whom he found in the small woodlot west of Sharpsburg. Lee was in his shirtsleeves, washing his face, when McLaws rode up and dismounted. "Well General, I am glad to see you, and have to thank you for what you have done," Lee said as he greeted McLaws, "but we have, I believe, a hard day's work before us and you must rest your men. Do not let them come quite this far, as the shells from the enemy fall about here, but halt them about 1/4 of a mile back on the road, and I will send for you when I want you." McLaws explained that he had already received orders from Jackson, and Lee responded, "Never mind that order but do as I told you, and consider yourself as specially under my orders." McLaws, therefore, would form the army reserve.[63]

Circumstances had thrown the command structure of the Army of Northern Virginia into a haphazard pattern that bore scant resemblance to the neat order of battle that appears in the *Official Records*. Jackson commanded the left, which included his two divisions, Hood's division, and Fitz Lee's brigade. Longstreet was in charge of the center and the right, consisting of D. H. Hill's, D. R. Jones's, and R. H. Anderson's divisions and Evans's independent brigade. Walker and McLaws were subject to Lee's orders. Since no one bore any allegiance to a specific corps or command yet, and the army's order of battle had been in a continual state of flux since the Seven Days, everyone seemed to take the situation in stride. But the lack of a carefully defined order of battle for the army, with clearly understood lines of authority, had caused confusion at South Mountain and at Second Manassas, and it had the potential to continue problems in the pending engagement.

The arrival of McLaws's and R. H. Anderson's divisions nearly completed Lee's concentration of his army. But doing so this rapidly cost him many men. Thousands of stragglers were left in the wake of every division that marched up from Harpers Ferry. One of Kershaw's colonels wrote that on September 18, the day after the Battle of Antietam, "at least 10,000 stragglers" rejoined the army. Some of these were not true stragglers, but soldiers who had recovered from wounds or illness and were returning to their units; they had been directed to the army's depot in Winchester. But these 10,000 men represented only those who rejoined their units. The actual number of stragglers was much greater. Lee had entered Maryland with approximately 65,000–70,000 men of all arms. When McLaws and R. H. Anderson joined him, they raised Lee's effective strength at Sharpsburg to 27,400 infantry, 3,300 artillerymen (both reserve and divisional), and about 4,500 cavalry. A. P. Hill had perhaps 4,000 in his division at Harpers Ferry. This meant that since September 2, when the Army of Northern Virginia numbered 75,000 men of all arms, 48 percent—*nearly one-half* of the army Lee had on the eve of his Maryland campaign—were absent from the ranks, with the overwhelming majority of those missing being non-battle losses. This is a staggering figure, and it is unlikely Lee's army was ever again in such dire condition, except during the Appomattox Campaign. The combination of hard marching, combat, and insufficient food pushed men past the point of endurance. Lee had pressed his army perilously close to the edge. He had to know the condition his soldiers were in—the evidence of their hunger and exhaustion was too overwhelming for him not to—but Lee was playing for high stakes, and he considered the risks, great as they were, worth the potential gain. But would there truly be a gain? Even if McClellan were repulsed, Lee's army was in no shape to renew a campaign of maneuver.[64]

The situation was so dire in Hood's division that, after the fighting with Hooker sputtered down to mere picket firing, Hood rode back to Lee and asked if Lee could "send two or more brigades to our relief, at least for the night," so that Hood's division might cook up an issue of rations they had received. For a soldier as combative as Hood to make such a request underscored the seriousness of his men's plight. In a three-day period, all the division had received was a half ration of beef and some green corn. Lee sympathized with Hood's plight, but refused to release Walker's division, which, at that hour, constituted Lee's only reserve until McLaws arrived. Lee suggested that Hood find Jackson "and endeavor to obtain assistance from him." Hood rode off and, after searching about "for a long time," located Jackson, who was lying by the root of a tree, sound asleep. "I aroused him and made known the half-starved condition of my troops," recalled Hood. Jackson assented to Hood's request; he would order Lawton's, Trimble's and Hays's brigades to relieve Hood's two brigades. Jackson, however, exacted a promise from Hood that Hood "would come to the support of these forces the moment I was called upon." Hood agreed, and then rode off into the darkness to find his division's wagons—which had been recalled from Shepherdstown—so that he could feed his men before daylight.[65]

When Walker moved his division into place on the army's far right, it completed Lee's dispositions for the coming battle. His left had 12 brigades of infantry—Jones's division, Lawton's division, Hood's division, and Ripley's and Colquitt's brigades of D. H. Hill's division—and Fitz Lee's cavalry brigade, reinforced by S. D. Lee's reserve artillery battalion. The Confederates thus had approximately 10,200 infantry and perhaps 2,000 cavalrymen to confront Hooker's 1st Corps. This represented 40 percent of the army's effective strength. D. H. Hill's three remaining brigades—about 2,800 officers and men, or 9 percent of the army's strength—held the center, supported by Cutts's reserve battalion of artillery. The right, from the Boonsboro Pike to the Potomac River, was occupied by 9 infantry brigades of D. R. Jones's division, as well as Walker's division, Evans's independent brigade, Munford's slender cavalry brigade, and the reserve artillery battalion of the Washington Artillery. In this sector, there were about 7,300 men in the infantry brigades, and Munford had perhaps 500 cavalry, representing approximately 26 percent of the Rebel army. The 10 brigades of McLaws and R. H. Anderson—23 percent of the army, or 6,963 infantry—had just arrived at the front. Based on Longstreet's orders to McLaws, Lee reinforced his right center, on Cemetery Hill, with Anderson's brigades, and McLaws formed the army reserve.

It was a balanced deployment of the Confederate forces, and it reflected both Lee's anticipation of where the enemy might strike and his uncertainty as to where McClellan would commit his main strength. The left was certain to be engaged at daylight, so Lee's strongest force was deployed there. The center posed the most difficult position for McClellan to assail, and it was the easiest to reinforce, which allowed Lee to leave it lightly defended for the moment. Lee had to be especially concerned about his right, for if this part of his line were driven in, the rest of his army might be cut off from Blackford's Ford and Virginia. Yet he could get by with committing only about one-quarter of his army to this vital sector, because the Federals had just two usable locations where they could cross Antietam Creek—at the Rohrbach Bridge and at Snavely's Ford—and both of these were closely defended. By the time the Yankees could force a crossing at either location, Lee could reinforce the defenders with R. H. Anderson's or McLaws's men. The Confederate army's overall position was a strong one, and Lee waited with assurance for the morning. "If he had had a well-equipped army of one hundred thousand men veterans at his back, he could not have appeared more composed and confident," wrote John G. Walker.[66] Lee gave battle with the conviction that his army would win the approaching fight.

McClellan's Preparations: "We might reasonably expect a violent collision at the earliest dawn"

It started to rain after dark, a "drizzling rain" that was just enough to make things uncomfortable. Hooker established the 1st Corps' headquarters at Joseph Poffenberger's farm, in the rear of Anderson's and Magilton's brigades. Outbursts of musketry punctured the quiet of the black night along his front line. Once or twice the firing escalated sharply before it subsided and then lapsed into tense stillness. Hooker visited his picket line to investigate the firing and "found that the lines of pickets of the two armies, were so near to each other as to be able to hear each other talk but were not visible to each other." Hooker's

trip to his front satisfied him "that we might reasonably expect a violent colli-
sion at the earliest dawn." He returned to Poffenberger's around 8 p.m. and sent
off a courier to army headquarters with a report "informing the Comdg. Genl
of my surroundings, and assuring him that the battle would be renewed at the
earliest dawn, and that reinforcements should be ordered forward in season to
reach me before that moment."[67]

McClellan had already taken steps to forward reinforcements. Soon after he
returned from his inspection of Hooker's movement, he had Colonel George D.
Ruggles prepare an order for Sumner, timed at 5:50 p.m.

> General: General McClellan desires you to move Mansfield's corps across
> the fords and bridge over the Antietam and to take such position as may be
> designated by General Hooker. General McClellan desires that all the artillery,
> ammunition, and everything appertaining to the corps, be gotten over without
> fail to-night, ready for action early in the morning. He also desires you to have
> the other corps of your command ready to march one hour before daylight
> to-morrow morning.[68]

Sumner reported that he received these orders "on the evening of the 16th."
After returning from his ride with Hooker, McClellan had relocated Union
army headquarters to the Philip Pry house, so there should have been very little
delay in delivering the orders to Sumner. Old "Bull Head" found them disturbing. For no good reason that Sumner could see, McClellan was breaking up
his wing command and placing half of it subject to the orders of the upstart
Hooker. This defied the most elementary rule of warfare: concentration of
force. If they were going to attack, Sumner wanted to go in with his entire
wing. Sumner may also have sensed that McClellan was working to demote
him, which indeed was the case. Sumner rode to headquarters and asked
McClellan for permission to move the 2nd Corps across the Antietam as well,
so that he might keep his entire command intact. McClellan refused, without
further comment, and he reminded the wing commander—now essentially a
corps commander again—that Sumner could not move the 2nd Corps until
ordered, and that he would not receive those orders until the morning of the
17th. On the eve of the biggest battle he had yet fought in the war, McClellan
had dismantled his command structure and sent a clear signal to both of his
senior commanders, Sumner and Burnside, that he lacked confidence in them.
This was a formula to promote suspicion and disharmony, not the cooperation
necessary to foster success.[69]

McClellan never offered an explanation for why he did not move the 2nd
Corps across the Antietam during the night, but there are some likely reasons.
One is that he wanted to keep his two corps of Peninsula veterans, the 2nd and
the 5th Corps, in reserve: either to deliver the main blow to Lee once the assault
on his right and left had forced Lee to commit his own reserves, or to form a

solid reserve should these attacks fail. If McClellan shifted the 2nd Corps to the other side of the creek, then it reduced the options for where he could commit them. Leaving the corps in place was a conservative choice. Moreover, McClellan and nearly all of his senior generals believed that Lee had numbers equal to theirs, and this assumption certainly fed their caution. Stephen Sears, on the other hand, suggests that McClellan held the 2nd Corps back because he did not want Sumner commanding the attack on Lee's left.[70]

There is probably truth in both explanations, but McClellan committed an error in not changing the deployment of the 2nd Corps on the night of September 16. His second report of the battle stated that he intended to use the corps to support the attack of the 1st and the 12th Corps. If this was the plan, then common sense should have dictated that moving the largest corps in the army over Antietam Creek during the night would save precious time. It would also help ensure that the attack would be better coordinated and more concentrated. There was plenty of ground around the Neikirk farm and the Otto Smith farm where the entire corps could have massed under cover of night; then they would have been in position to quickly follow up on any advantage or opening the attacks by the 1st and the 12th Corps might create. In addition, moving the corps to this area would not have jeopardized McClellan's desire to keep Sumner's influence over the battle to a minimum. Sumner still would have arrived after the fighting began, and thus would have needed to consult Hooker about where the 2nd Corps should go in. But by keeping Sumner's corps east of the creek, McClellan virtually guaranteed that his attack on Lee's left would be uncoordinated and successive—the type of attack that would enable Lee to use his interior lines to shift his forces to meet each blow.

Caution also dominated McClellan's handling of Franklin's 6th Corps. After the surrender of Harpers Ferry, McClellan remained leery about the Confederates still situated there, who could drive into his flank or rear. To prevent this, McClellan had taken pains to carefully post the 9th Corps to protect the army's flank and had left Franklin in Pleasant Valley to guard the rear. But Franklin's three strong divisions faced a phantom menace. The enemy in their front had departed by midafternoon on September 15, a fact Franklin had reported to McClellan. Franklin's dispatch made it plain that the Rebels were clearing out of Pleasant Valley and moving toward Harpers Ferry. Had McClellan acted boldly, he could have left Couch's large division to guard the pontoon bridge into Maryland, and marched Franklin and his remaining two divisions to Keedysville sometime around the beginning of the day on the 16th. Yet, despite additional intelligence confirming that the Confederates "were rapidly recrossing to the Virginia side by our Pontoon bridge at Harper's Ferry," McClellan hesitated to summon Franklin north. While Lee's brigades were marching furiously to complete the concentration of the Army of Northern Virginia, the commanding general of the Army of the Potomac left Franklin's 18,000 men idle in Pleasant

Valley, not even encouraging Franklin to harass or threaten whatever troops might be left at Harpers Ferry and prevent their joining Lee. In the early evening of September 16, McClellan finally changed his mind regarding Franklin and ordered him to join the main army. The orders, sent at 7:30 p.m., were written by Ruggles, and they informed the 6th Corps commander that McClellan "still desires you to occupy Maryland Heights." But if this proved impracticable, "he thinks that you had better leave a small force at your present position, and join him with the remainder of your command." These rather nebulous orders were later followed by more specific instructions. Franklin was directed to send Couch to occupy Maryland Heights, and he himself was to march to Keedysville at daylight, with his two remaining divisions.

Why was Franklin not ordered to march at once, instead of at daylight, particularly in view of the fact that McClellan believed Lee had been reinforced, so that his Confederate army equaled or exceeded the strength of the Army of the Potomac? The answer might be that it was simply McClellan following his systematic method of making war. But then his order to have Mansfield make a night march across Antietam Creek on September 16 is out of character. Or McClellan may have procrastinated in calling Franklin up from Pleasant Valley because he still thought Lee would not offer battle at Sharpsburg. On the morning of the Battle of Antietam, one of McClellan's staff officers may have reflected the thinking at headquarters. He was heard to remark during the opening fighting involving Hooker's corps that it was only a rearguard action, as "Lee was too much of a soldier to fight in that position with a river at his back." Perhaps McClellan reasoned that if Lee withdrew across the Potomac, Franklin could secure the pontoon bridge at Harpers Ferry, providing the Union army with a bridgehead into Virginia. When Hooker met stiff resistance in his probe west of Antietam Creek in the late afternoon and early evening of September 16, however, this dispelled any hope McClellan may have harbored that Lee would retreat, so he then ordered Franklin to join the main army.[71]

Whatever McClellan's thinking was, it was flawed. Franklin should have been ordered to Keedysville the night of the 15th or early on the 16th. Sharpsburg, not Harpers Ferry, was where there was a chance to strike a potentially decisive blow. Hesitation in warfare is fatal. Opportunities are often fleeting, and they must be seized vigorously. McClellan should have strained every fiber to best Lee in the competition for who could concentrate his army the fastest and then hit the enemy hard. Instead, McClellan carried out his meticulous preparations for the attack, let Lee beat him at this game, and guaranteed that there would be a costly general battle against Lee's full army on September 17. Colonel Strother's complaint—"We are entirely too methodical"—echoes loudly in all that McClellan did.[72]

For reasons unknown, Sumner did not give Mansfield orders to move his corps across the Antietam until nearly 11 p.m. The delay may have resulted from the need to determine where Mansfield was to go and who would guide him. Most of the officers and men in the 12th Corps were sound asleep when these orders arrived. "Oh, how sleepy I was, but there was no help at such times," wrote the 1st Division commander, Alpheus Williams, to his daughter. Within minutes, officers and noncoms began moving quietly through their regiments; in "subdued tones" they woke their men and ordered them to fall in. As the regiments assembled, the men were cautioned to muffle their tin cups and cooking equipment and told that there was to be no talking in the ranks. The corps formed up quickly and, with Mansfield and his headquarters staff at the front, moved softly through Keedysville. The men tramped on "through the blackest kind of darkness," turning onto the road to the Upper Bridge. What most of them remembered about this march was how quietly it was conducted. "Everything was still as death," recorded Colonel Ezra Carman in his journal. "Not a whisper was heard nor a light to be seen." Only the creaking and clinking of equipment and the tread of thousands of feet broke the silence, but in the moist air these sounds did not carry far. Mansfield led his column across the Upper Bridge, then north along the Williamsport Road for perhaps a mile before turning off into the fields and marching west. Alpheus Williams and his 1st Division followed Mansfield, but Williams complained that "it was so dark and the forests and woods so deep that I could not follow and was obliged to send ahead to stop our leaders repeatedly." A young soldier in the 102nd New York recalled that "we were halted about every 50 rods, I should judge we were feeling our way." The combination of extreme darkness and fatigue thoroughly disoriented the officers and men. "Where we went from and where we went to I haven't the least idea and can not find out," wrote Lieutenant John Gould, the adjutant of the 10th Maine, in his journal. "That we went round Robin Hood's barn I can swear to, that we stopped on ploughed land is positive and that I was sleepy and crawled under the rail fence and slept like a hog is the quintessence of truth."[73]

Williams's 1st Division reached the vicinity of George Line's farm around 1 a.m. Mansfield ordered him to halt here and assemble his brigades in column in mass. This proved to be an order more easily given than carried out. The stygian night, the need for silence, and the fact that Williams had "five new regiments who knew absolutely nothing of maneuvering" all conspired against anything being done quickly or efficiently. Meanwhile, Brigadier General George S. Greene's 2nd Division began to arrive, and Mansfield ordered them to gather up together between the Hoffman and Line farms. It took Williams "a long time" to get his division arranged in a satisfactory manner, but around 2 a.m. the men were finally settled, and Williams found a fence corner where he curled up to get what rest he could before daylight. But as often as he dozed off, fussy General Mansfield—who probably did not sleep at all that night—came by and woke him up with some new instructions. Eventually Mansfield went elsewhere—probably to keep General Greene awake—and Williams fell into a deep sleep.[74]

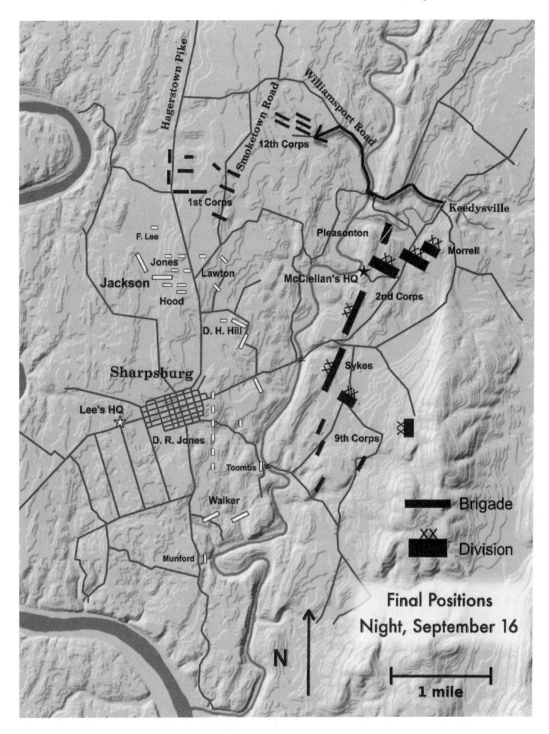

The accommodations that night were wet and uncomfortable for everyone, and downright unpleasant for several units. The regiments of Colonel Henry Stainrook's brigade made their beds on a "plowed field spred with manure." One of the soldiers, J. Porter Howard of the 111th Pennsylvania, remembered even

30 years later that it was "not a very nice place to sleep on." But, he continued, "we were tired enough to sleep almost anywhere." John H. Keatley, a new recruit in the 125th Pennsylvania, tried to snooze in George Line's big cornfield. "I did not sleep very soundly lying between two corn rows," he wrote years later. But what may have disturbed Keatley's slumber more was the frequent picket firing that could be distinctly heard from the direction of the 1st Corps, as well as the dreaded prospect that they would all "see the elephant" come morning.[75]

Only three of the 12th Corps' batteries accompanied the infantry across Antietam Creek. Two others—the batteries of the 4th and the 6th Maine—were left on the bluffs east of the Antietam to guard the approaches to the Upper Bridge. Two more—Battery F of the 4th U.S., and the 10th New York Light— apparently had not reached the front yet or had been left behind for some reason. Perhaps because of Mansfield's weakness in field artillery at the front, or because he chose to ignore McClellan's instructions not to move the 2nd Corps until ordered to do so, Sumner slipped five of the 2nd Corps' seven batteries across the creek that night and parked them near Mansfield's corps. Whatever his reasons, Sumner showed good judgment and energy, qualities rarely attributed to him at Antietam.[76]

With Mansfield's 12th Corps in position behind Hooker, McClellan completed his final dispositions for battle. The right of the army, consisting of the 1st and the 12th Corps, contained 15 brigades of infantry, totaling about 16,000 men, supported by 82 guns of the 1st, the 2nd, and the 12th Corps' artillery. It confronted a Confederate force of approximately 10,200 infantry, 2,000 cavalry, and 70 guns. These were good odds, even though the Confederates enjoyed the benefit of being on the defensive. McClellan concentrated his largest numbers in his center, which included the 2nd and the 5th Corps, totaling 15 brigades, and Pleasonton's 2 brigades of cavalry—about 24,000 infantry and perhaps 2,400 cavalry all told—supported by 110 guns of corps, cavalry, and reserve artillery. This same sector of Lee's front was his weakest, but it was also the most difficult to attack and the easiest to reinforce quickly. The 9th Corps, with 8 brigades containing almost 12,000 infantry and 47 guns, occupied the left. Lee faced them with 7,300 infantry well supported by artillery.

While McClellan enjoyed superiority in total numbers, he only had a slight edge in manpower at the two points he intended to attack first. One of the myths of the Battle of Antietam is that McClellan had an overwhelming advantage through the sheer size of his forces. Instead, the key to the impending battle rested on how each commanding general handled his reserves. Lee had 7,000 infantry in reserve, if we count R. H. Anderson's division as part of that group at the opening of the battle; McClellan had whatever percentage of the 24,000 holding his center he wished to commit. If McClellan sent his reserves in piecemeal, Lee had the manpower, the defensive position, and the benefit of interior lines to parry the blows. Had McClellan sent the 2nd Corps across Antietam

Creek on the night of the 16th, as Sumner wanted, then he would have brought 31,000 infantry in 24 brigades against Lee's 12,000 infantry and cavalry—almost three to one odds. Or, had McClellan brought the 6th Corps up on the morning of September 16, he would have had an additional 12,000 infantry in 6 brigades and 44 guns, which would again have given him almost three to one odds in infantry over Lee and enabled McClellan to greatly strengthen the attack on the right or left.[77] McClellan could still win the battle, provided that he moved his reserves at the right moment and to the place where they would produce the greatest effect. The concept is absurdly simple; executing it well is remarkably difficult.

"A Deathlike Stillness"

At the extreme front lines of the two armies, where Hooker's and Hood's men lay within speaking distance of one another, a "deathlike stillness" existed, which was only disturbed when some unlucky pickets blundered into one another, or when men, disoriented by the black night, stumbled into the enemy, generating brief outbursts of firing. In one instance, six Confederate pickets walked into the lines of Seymour's brigade; they were quietly disarmed and led to the rear. In another incident, Colonel Joseph W. Fisher, commanding the 5th Reserves, settled his men into position in the East Woods, unaware of how close the Confederates were. Fisher found a large tree slightly in front of his regiment and began to make his bed at its base. He called out in a loud voice: "If anybody wants me during the night I will be found at the foot of this big oak tree." Silence met his statement. Then, without any warning, the woods lit up with a crashing volley from nearby Rebels. Many directed their fire toward the sound of Fisher's voice, and their bullets peppered the oak. Fortunately for Fisher, he had chosen the side of the tree facing away from the Southerners, so he escaped unscathed. His men grabbed their muskets, and "it appeared as though a little battle was really going on," but the futility of such blind shooting quickly became evident and both sides ceased fire. One veteran recalled that "for the rest of the night the Col. *was not* found at the root of *that* tree."[78]

Not all of the scrapes were bloodless. Around 9 p.m., Captain Ike Turner, commanding the 5th Texas, became suspicious that the Yankees were attempting to advance their lines under cover of night. Turner ordered a detail consisting of one man from each company (there were 11 companies in the regiment) to creep forward and investigate. Jonathan Stevens was one of those men, and he recalled that "we advanced carefully along for about 300 yards through some open woods [the East Woods]—no underbrush—and the first thing we knew we were right up at the Yankee pickets." The Pennsylvanians thought Stevens and his comrades were fellow members of the Reserves, until the two groups were confronting one another at point-blank range. "Then the ball opened," wrote Stevens, "and I recall there was about the hottest fight of the war for about fifteen minutes, considering the number engaged." The Federals slipped away, leaving behind what Stevens thought were a half dozen dead. In his own group, five were killed in the shootout. Turner sent orders forward for the Texan survivors to withdraw. He was satisfied that his men had accomplished their purpose. In the frequently deadly business of setting up outposts, Turner's patrol had warned the Federals of how far forward they could place theirs.[79]

Around 10 p.m. Colonel Fisher, who had recovered from his brush with death earlier in the evening, ordered Lieutenant Hardman P. Petrikin to post a picket line of men from Companies E and I about 150 yards into the field southeast of the East Woods. Petrikin selected 12 men from each company and led them forward. Milton Laird of Company I was one of them. He remembered the night as "so dark that you could make a hole in the darkness with your finger." Laird thought Petrikin pushed on beyond 150 yards—although it must have difficult to judge distances under the circumstances—close to a worm fence that enclosed a freshly plowed field of Samuel Mumma's. Despite orders not to build fires that night, some Confederates had kindled small ones; perhaps these men were part of Colonel James Walker's brigade, which had been moved to the front and taken up a position near Mumma's. By the light of these fires, one of Petrikin's men made out soldiers lying behind the rail fence directly in front of them, and he whispered that there were Rebels in front. Petrikin ignored this warning and spread the word for his men to keep moving forward, but to be "ready for any emergency."[80]

The Confederates behind the rail fence were the 4th Alabama of Law's brigade. The regiment had been ordered forward to this advanced position around 9 p.m. "We were some distance in front of our main line, in an isolated position, on outpost duty," wrote the regimental adjutant, Robert T. Coles. The Alabamians "were completely worn out from hunger and want of sleep, and it was almost impossible to keep them awake." Most of the men tried to avoid the freshly plowed earth by lying down in the unplowed corners of the worm fence, "with their guns resting through the fence." Since the regiment was at the extreme front, the whole unit was on picket, and no other pickets were posted. Coles recalled that "everything was perfectly quiet" until around 10 p.m., when some alert men along the regiment's line heard men approaching from the direction of the enemy lines. Silently, two or three companies on the left of the 4th Alabama took their muskets in hand and waited. Tense moments followed as Lieutenant Petrikin's party came closer, until they were within 30 feet of the fence. Then someone on the Confederate line gave the order to fire. "Every gun fired at the same instant," Coles recorded. Captain William M. Robbins, the acting major of the 4th, had dozed off and was startled by the explosion of gunfire. As major, the left wing of the regiment was under his orders, and Robbins demanded to know who gave the command to fire. Some of the men told him that they had heard "a party of what must be the enemy" and shot at them.[81]

The Alabamians' volley felled five or six Pennsylvanians. The survivors fired back at the Confederates, doing no damage, and then fled in the direction from which they had advanced, leaving their dead and injured behind. In the quiet that followed the exchange of shots, Robbins and his men heard groans from the wounded men in front. Then they heard a voice from out of the darkness. It was Lieutenant Petrikin. He cried out for the "Rebel boys" to help him, as he was badly wounded and needed aid. Perhaps sensing a trap, or not liking to be called Rebels, Robbins's men did nothing. Then Petrikin pleaded for "you Southern boys" to help him, and said that he was a Federal officer of rank. Robbins responded that they would send help if Petrikin's men would not fire on his men. A gap was made in the fence, and several litter bearers crawled through. They found Petrikin, shot through the breast, as well as a badly wounded private and two or three dead Federals. Petrikin and the private were brought in, but the private died a few minutes later. The Alabamians were curious about Petrikin, as he had announced that he was an officer of rank. "They were very much disappointed when Captain Robbins informed them that he was only a Lieutenant of the 5th Pennsylvania Reserves."

Robbins made arrangements to have Petrikin taken to the rear for medical attention, but the lieutenant was certain that his wound was mortal. He pulled out his watch—"quite a fine one," recalled Robbins—and gave it to the captain, with the request that he return the watch to Petrikin's mother in Chambersburg, Pennsylvania. He also asked Robbins to "tell my comrades of the Union army for me that I died like a soldier should, doing my duty." As the stretcher party carried Petrikin away, Robbins promised him that if he lived through the coming battle and had the opportunity, he would honor Petrikin's requests. Petrikin died early the next morning. Robbins survived the battle and, true to his word, on September 18, during a local truce after the battle, he gave Petrikin's watch and his dying message to a Union officer; a thoughtful act of compassion at odds with the murderous work of September 17.[82]

Soon after the incident with Lieutenant Petrikin, Jackson's men began to relieve Hood's tired and ravenously hungry soldiers. Wofford's and Law's regiments quietly withdrew their pickets and marched back to the West Woods. Perhaps because they were essentially on the picket line, or possibly due to a staff snafu, the 4th Alabama were not relieved. Officers and men in the regiment were aware that Colonel James Walker's brigade had moved into position in their rear and bivouacked on the Mumma farm. Despite the excitement generated by the scrape with Lieutenant Petrikin's party, when things quieted down the men immediately fell asleep, although the officers made considerable efforts to try to keep them awake. "The most earnest and pathetic appeals" were made to the regimental adjutant, Robert T. Coles, to get permission "to go back and get Colonel Walker, commanding Trimble's brigade, to relieve us." Coles initially refused, claiming that Walker's men were "as much exhausted as we were." But the number of complaints the men made finally wore Coles down, and he made his way back to Walker's line. He found Walker's men sound asleep, "wrapped snugly in their blankets." He came upon Walker, sitting down, covered by his overcoat, and trying to conceal the light of a "few live coals" at his feet that were affording the colonel some modicum of warmth in the damp, chill air. Coles explained his mission and, to his great relief, Walker "very willingly consented to send one of his Georgia regiments to our relief." The Georgians— probably the 12th Georgia, which was only about 100 men strong—were awakened with much difficulty, but instead of grumbling and cursing, Coles was surprised to see the men shake and roll their blankets and then fall into line, "laughing and joking" among themselves. The exchange took place, and the 4th Alabama, no doubt thankful for the fortitude of the Georgians and grateful to be getting away from the extreme front, marched back to the West Woods, where they enjoyed a few hours' rest and some food.[83]

Jackson's relief of Hood's two brigades was otherwise completed without incident. Colonel Walker's brigade of Georgians, North Carolinians, and Alabamians formed a line of battle just north of the Mumma farm lane, in Mumma's plowed field, with the right resting on the Mumma cemetery and the left extending to—and possibly across—the Smoketown Road. On Walker's left, Colonel Marcellus Douglass's Georgia brigade relieved Wofford. Two companies of the 31st Georgia, under the command of Lieutenant W. H. Harrison, were selected to picket the brigade's front. Harrison led them about 50 feet into David Miller's cornfield and then strung out his men in a picket line extending from the East Woods through the cornfield to the Hagerstown Pike. The remainder of the 31st Georgia formed a reserve for Harrison, resting about 120 yards south of the corn. Douglass formed the main body of his brigade about 100 yards south of the 31st Georgia, extending across a grass field and a clover field. The three left regiments of the brigade—the 26th, the 38th, and the 61st Georgia—faced north toward the cornfield, while the 13th and the 60th Georgia reestablished the line toward the northeast, to both face the threat from the East Woods and extend the line toward Walker's left. The Georgians threw down the fence separating the grass and the clover fields and piled the rails for a breastwork along part of the line. In some places the men found limestone outcroppings for cover, but there was none elsewhere. What neither Douglass nor Walker realized in positioning their men in the dark is that both brigades' right flanks were exposed to the heavy Federal batteries on Antietam Creek's east bank. A deluge of Union shells would reveal this come daylight.[84]

"The quiet . . . has something of the terrible in it"

By the time the 12th Corps bivouacked for the night, there were less than four hours before the most appalling day of carnage ever seen in North America would begin. Yet all was tranquil and still, which is what no one who survived that battle ever forgot. "Everything became terrifically quiet," recalled Francis Galwey of the 8th Ohio, "for the quiet that precedes a great battle has something of the terrible in it." Major Rufus Dawes of the 6th Wisconsin, lying on Joseph Poffenberger's wet pasture, agreed: "Nothing can be more solemn than a period of silent waiting for the summons to battle, known to be impending." Fred Hitchcock, adjutant of the raw 132nd Pennsylvania, remembered that his regiment's camp "was ominously still this night. We were not allowed to sing or make any noise, nor have any fires." The orders against singing or frolicking were unnecessary, continued Hitchcock, "for there was no disposition to indulge in either." Men wrote letters home or inscribed their thoughts in their diaries. John Maycock, of Hitchcock's regiment, concluded his September 16 entry with a pious sentiment: "From this time I am Determined by the grace of God to live closer to the Lord." Colonel Richard A. Oakford, in charge of the 132nd, moved through his command, inquiring quietly of Hitchcock if his roster of men and officers was complete, for, the colonel added with a sad smile, "we shall not all be here to-morrow night."[85]

Many 2nd Corps regiments reported that they received an additional 40 rounds of ammunition during the night, increasing their load to 80 rounds. Even the greenhorns knew this meant that serious business lay ahead. Lieutenant Sebastian Duncan Jr. of the 13th New Jersey, a rookie regiment in the 12th Corps, found some solace in the fact that his regiment was in a brigade that had seen some hard fighting; even though many had been killed or wounded in those earlier engagements, "more come through safely." But Duncan had to contemplate the possibility that he might be one of the casualties, so, like thousands of other soldiers in both armies, he appealed to God for the courage to see him through the coming ordeal. "My earnest prayer is that I may do my duty," he noted in his journal. "I am willing to leave [it] in God's hands. If I come through safely I shall thank Him. If killed I hope I am prepared to meet Him."[86]

Several soldiers wrote that they slept soundly once things had quieted down, even though many had to get what rest they could with their equipment on. The men of the 35th Massachusetts formed up for the night near a large haystack, which contributed to what the regimental historian called "a luxurious bivouac." William T. Owen of the Washington Artillery found quarters in the German Reformed church in Sharpsburg, along with some surgeons "who treated us to a good supper." Owen and his comrades laid out their bedding in the chancel and "slept soundly." But the 35th Massachusetts and Owen's Louisianans were the exception. Most men in both armies spread their blankets on the ground—plowed ground, cornfields, meadows, pastures—with nothing to protect them from the drizzling rain and no fires with which to boil coffee or heat food. David Thompson and his comrades in the 9th New York mixed "our ground coffee and sugar in our hands" and ate them dry. "I think we were more easily inclined to this crude disposal of our rations from a feeling that for many of us the need of drawing them would cease forever with the following day," wrote Thompson.[87]

Moxley Sorrel of Longstreet's staff recalled that they made their beds "under thick trees," near an element of the Jeff Davis Legion's cavalry. After the night became "deadly quiet and still," a "quiver of motion" seemed to pass through the horses of the legion. A "faint sound as of a sign [*sic*]," was heard, and the horses suddenly panicked, breaking away from their picket ropes and stampeding in all directions. Sorrel and his comrades were nearly trampled in the onrush. The horses scattered across the countryside to the rear of the army, and the "troopers were all night and part of the next day recovering them."[88]

D. L. Love of the 11th Mississippi, in Hood's division, got no sleep that night. He and others from his regiment, along with details from all the other regiments in that division, were ordered to gather corn—probably from the Hauser farm or the Reel farm, which were in the rear of the West Woods—and prepare it for the men's rations. Love and his comrades found some pumpkins, too, which they liberated, and then used up the remaining time cooking the vegetables. Hood spent most of his night in the saddle, attempting to hunt down his divisional supply wagons. Despite his best efforts, and those of men like Love, rations did not reach the division until it was nearly dawn.[89]

While the soldiers of both armies made their physical and spiritual preparations for battle, the civilians of Sharpsburg and its surrounding farms waited in suspense. For two days the armies had been among them, sparring with one another. To avoid harm, many citizens were advised to leave their homes. Samuel Mumma was one; Confederate soldiers warned him on September 15 to evacuate his family. This was a difficult decision for each household that was confronted with it. Departure meant safety, but it also meant leaving behind their homes and their personal belongings with thousands of hungry soldiers nearby. Mumma and his wife Elizabeth had 11 children; a 186-acre farm planted in corn and wheat, with pastures and an orchard; as well as 200 chickens, hogs, cows, horses, sheep, turkeys, and ducks. Mumma had much to lose—everything he had worked for. But by the afternoon of the 15th, with the Federal forces arriving across Antietam Creek and the guns of the two armies firing at one another, the Mummas decided to leave, making their way to the Manor Church, about 5 miles north of Sharpsburg, where they were joined by many other farm families who had done the same thing. Some farmers, like Samuel Middlekauf and Joseph Poffenberger, remained into the evening of the 16th; these two even helped Union soldiers move across their property. Henry and Elizabeth Piper, owners of a large, prosperous farm north of Sharpsburg along the Hagerstown Pike, were strong Unionists, even though Henry, like some other farmers in the area, was a slave owner. The Pipers found themselves in a more uncomfortable position than Middlekauf and Poffenberger that night. Longstreet and D. H. Hill had established their headquarters at the Pipers' comfortable home. Piper played the gracious host—perhaps fearing that his Union sentiments might not sit too well with the Confederates—with his daughters serving the generals dinner and offering them some wine. Hill gratefully accepted and drank his glass. Longstreet initially declined, perhaps thinking Piper might have poisoned the beverage, but when he saw Hill drain his glass with no ill effects, he spoke up, saying, "Ladies, I will thank you for some of that wine." After dinner, both generals urged Piper to take his family to a safer place. Piper followed their advice. "We left everything as it was on the farm taking only the horses with us and one carriage," recalled one of Piper's daughters. In the haste and excitement of leaving, the family apparently forgot one of their female slaves, or perhaps she was afraid that they would not remember about her and leave her behind. Whatever the case, she ran out to them, crying, "Oh my God, take me along!" Piper had her walk alongside the carriage and carry the family's 6-month-old grandson. For Piper and Mumma, as well as the many other families of Sharpsburg and its surrounding farms, the personal safety of their families took precedence over all. But the decision to leave was gut wrenching. The cornfields were ripening and nearly ready for harvest. Other fields were freshly plowed, waiting to be planted in winter wheat. Orchards were bearing fruit that needed to be canned. Would the hogs, cattle, sheep, geese, chickens, and turkeys—the families' meat supply—survive? Everyone was helpless, with no chance to prevent potential calamity. The soldiers were not the only ones on whom fear and uncertainty weighed heavily that gloomy September night.[90]

In a fence corner on George Line's farm, Brigadier General Alpheus Williams tried to catch an hour or two of sleep before dawn broke. Several days later he recalled that haunting night in a letter to his daughter:

> I shall not, however, soon forget that night; so dark, so obscure, so mysterious, so uncertain; with the occasional rapid volleys of pickets and outposts, the low, solemn sound of the command as troops came into position, and withal so sleepy that there was a half-dreamy sensation about it all; but with a certain impression that the morrow was to be great with the future fate of our country. So much responsibility, so much intense, future anxiety! and yet I slept as soundly as though nothing was before me.[91]

Momentous issues were in balance from the coming battle. Though both the soldiers, who waited anxiously for the dawn, and the civilians, who huddled in fear with neighbors and in cellars, might not understand it, more than the future of the country rode on its outcome. Confederate victory would advance the cause of Southern independence and the preservation of slavery. The Federals' success would not only safeguard the Union, but would also give life to the document locked away in President Lincoln's desk. With it, the nation might yet begin down the path that led to a new birth of freedom.

ACKNOWLEDGMENTS

Researching and writing this book has been a long but rewarding journey. I never dreamed it would take me so long to complete, but working full time, raising children, and participating in the regular activities of life do not leave much time for writing. I pecked away at it, day after day, week after week, year after year, until it was done. But I did not do it alone. No one ever does. Along the path many people generously helped me.

I am deeply indebted to Tom Clemens, of Keedysville, Maryland. Tom is one of the top authorities in the country on the Maryland Campaign and, as president of the Save Historic Antietam Foundation, has done important work in helping to preserve battlefield land. He happily shared sources with me, offered sound critical advice, and promptly answered any questions I had. Marc and Beth Storch photocopied the entire Antietam Studies collection at the National Archives for me. Marc also shared items from his superb collection on the 2nd Wisconsin and pointed me to other Maryland Campaign sources he and Beth discovered in their research. Steve Stottlemeyer, an authority on the Battle of South Mountain, shared all of his research with me, an act of kindness for which I will ever be grateful. Zack Waters tracked down sources from Georgia and Florida and uncovered ones unknown to me. David Guest provided a stack of information from wartime Alabama newspapers about Alabama units in the campaign that I would never have discovered. Clarence Hollowell, of North Carolina, performed yeoman service by searching through the Southern Historical Collection at the University of North Carolina at Chapel Hill, as well as the State Archives, to find the collections relating to the Maryland Campaign. Jeff Stocker and Ed Root, in their many research forays, often found Maryland Campaign items and always shared them with me.

Mike Snyder read an early draft of the manuscript and provided comments that helped make this a better book. I am also deeply indebted to my friend Greg Coco, who passed away from cancer in 2009. Greg was a fine historian and possessed a brilliant knowledge of source material. He shared many of them with me and directed me to others. He was always my friend and a constant font of encouragement. I am grateful, too, to Brad Graham, historical documentary filmmaker, with whom I worked on an Antietam documentary. Brad has been a good friend for many years and helped me see the Maryland Campaign from different perspectives. He also guided me to John O'Grady, who created the fine maps that accompany this book. Dr. Ben Dixon of the State University of New York at Oneonta has been a longtime friend and encouraged me in this project for as long as I have known him. George Bringham, of Middletown, Maryland, formerly of the Central Maryland Heritage League, a group dedicated to preserving and protecting the South Mountain battlefield, walked with me over much of the 1st Corps and Fox's Gap battlefields, which was invaluable.

I am thankful to many of my colleagues in the National Park Service who supported me and shared source material with me through the years. From Fredericksburg-Spotsylvania National Military Park, they are Bob Krick (now retired), John Hennessy, Frank O'Reilly, Mac Wyckoff, Greg Mertz, and Don Pfanz. From Gettysburg, I count my good friend John Heiser and Eric Campbell, a fine historian who now works at Cedar Creek. Todd Bolton, at Harpers Ferry, supported and encouraged me in this project for many years. Ted Alexander and Paul Childs at Antietam were gracious hosts when I visited the park's research library; at Richmond National Battlefield, my thanks go to historian Bobby Krick.

The Confederate order of battle in the *Official Records* is incomplete, largely because of the unsettled condition of the Army of Northern Virginia in September 1862. Bob Gale filled in many blanks for me, tracking down every missing regimental commander. Among the others to whom I owe thanks are Dr. Gary Gallagher, Dr. Peter Carmichael, Dr. Carol Reardon, Dr. Keith Bohannon, John Fuller, Daryl Smoker, Gerry Gaumer, John Stoudt, Mike Phipps, Tim Smith, Scott Hahn, the late Brian Pohanka, Russell Beattie, Terry Johnston, Nicholas Picerno, Gregory Acken, John Hough, and Scott Sherlock.

The U.S. Army Heritage and Education Center (formerly the U.S. Army Military History Institute) was a gold mine of material for me. It is the finest collection of manuscripts for the Union army in the country. The staff consistently provided superb service. My especial thanks go to Dr. Richard Sommers, Dave Keough, and Louise Arnold-Friend for their generous help and assistance over the years.

I also received outstanding service from the Manuscript Division of the Library of Congress. At the National Archives, I owe thanks to archivists Mike Musick (now retired) and Trevor Plante. Musick's knowledge of the Civil War records in the archives is legendary. Once, when I visited the archives on a day he had off, the staff had to call him to help them locate the Antietam Studies collection.

Numerous other institutions assisted me along the way. They include the Connecticut Historical Society, Duke University, the Huntington Library, the Massachusetts State Historical Society, the New Jersey Historical Society, the Rutherford B. Hayes Library, the State Historical Society of Wisconsin, the Southern Historical Collection at University of North Carolina at Chapel Hill, and the Virginia Historical Society.

Bob Brugger, Senior Acquisitions Editor at the Johns Hopkins University Press, believed in this project and provided wise guidance and support that made it better. I am deeply indebted to my copyeditor, Kathleen Capels, who missed no detail and greatly strengthened the narrative. Thanks also to Terence Yorks, who checked my order of battle and saved me from some careless mistakes.

I am grateful to my parents, who encouraged and nurtured my love of history. It was my father who took me on my first visit to Antietam, sparking a lifelong interest in the campaign. Thanks also to Jason, Lindsay, and Matt, my three kids, for their love and encouragement. They grew up during the years when I wrote this book. No father was ever prouder of his children than I am. Through my son Jason, who served as an officer in the 4th Infantry Division on combat tours in Iraq and Afghanistan, I have experienced the anxiety felt by the families of the men in blue and gray who marched into Maryland in 1862, and prayed for their safe return. Lastly, I am ever thankful to my wife, Barb, for her love and never-wavering support.

Opposing Forces in the Maryland Campaign

Union Army of the Potomac
Maj. Gen. George B. McClellan, commanding

GENERAL HEADQUARTERS

Escort
Oneida (NY) Cavalry, Independent Company—Capt. Daniel P. Mann
4th U.S. Cavalry, Company A—Lt. Thomas H. McCormick
4th U.S. Cavalry, Company E—Capt. James B. McIntyre

Volunteer Engineer Brigade—Brig. Gen. Daniel P. Woodbury
15th NY—Col. John McL. Murphy
50th NY—Lt. Col. William H. Pettes

Regular Engineer Battalion—Capt. James C. Duane

Provost Guard—Maj. William H. Wood
2nd U.S. Cavalry, Companies E, F, H, & K—Capt. George A. Gordon
8th U.S. Infantry, Companies A, D, F, & G—Capt. Royal T. Frank
19th U.S. Infantry, Company G—Capt. Edmund L. Smith
19th U.S. Infantry, Company H—Capt. Henry S. Welton

Headquarters Guard—Maj. Granville O. Haller
93rd NY—Lt. Col. Benjamin C. Butler

Quartermaster's Guard
1st U.S. Cavalry, Companies B, C, H, & I—Capt. Marcus A. Reno

1ST ARMY CORPS
MAJ. GEN. JOSEPH HOOKER

2nd NY Cavalry, Companies A, B, I, & K—Capt. John E. Naylor
3rd PA Cavalry—Col. Samuel W. Owens

1st Division—Brig. Gen. Rufus King (relieved 9/14)
Brig. Gen. John P. Hatch (W 9/14)
Brig. Gen. Abner Doubleday

1st Brigade—Col. Walter Phelps Jr.
22nd NY—Lt. Col. John McKie Jr.
24th NY—Capt. John D. O'Brian
30th NY—Col. William M. Searing
84th NY (14th Brooklyn)—Maj. William H.
de Bevoise
2nd U.S. Sharpshooters—Col. Henry A. V. Post

2nd Brigade—Brig. Gen. Abner Doubleday
Col. William P. Wainwright
7th IN—Maj. Ira Grover
76th NY—Col. William P. Wainwright
Capt. John W. Young
95th NY—Maj. Edward Pye
56th PA—Lt. Col. J. William Hofmann

Artillery—Capt. J. Albert Monroe
NH Light, 1st Battery—Lt. Frederick M. Edgell
1st RI Light, Battery D—Capt. J. Albert Monroe
1st NY Light, Battery L—Capt. John A. Reynolds
4th U.S., Battery B—Capt. Joseph B. Campbell

3rd Brigade—Brig. Gen. Marsena R. Patrick
21st NY—Col. William F. Rogers
23rd NY—Col. Henry C. Hoffman
35th NY—Col. Newton B. Lord
80th NY (20th NY State Militia)—
Lt. Col. Theodore B. Gates

4th Brigade—Brig. Gen. John Gibbon
19th IN—Col. Solomon Meredith
2nd WI—Col. Lucius Fairchild
Lt. Col. Thomas S. Allen
6th WI—Lt. Col. Edward S. Bragg
7th WI—Capt. John B. Callis

2nd Division—Brig. Gen. James B. Ricketts

1st Brigade—Brig. Gen. Abram Duryee
97th NY—Maj. Charles Northrup
104th NY—Maj. Lewis C. Skinner
105th NY—Col. Howard Carroll
107th PA—Capt. James MacThompson

3rd Brigade—Brig. Gen. George L. Hartsuff
16th ME*—Col. Asa W. Wildes
12th MA—Maj. Elisha Burbank
13th MA—Maj. J. Parker Gould
83rd NY (9th Militia)—Lt. Col. William Atterbury
11th PA—Col. Richard Coulter

2nd Brigade—Col. William A. Christian
26th NY—Lt. Col. Richard H. Richardson
94th NY—Lt. Col. Calvin Littlefield
88th PA—Lt. Col. George W. Gile
90th PA—Col. Peter Lyle

Artillery
1st PA Light, Battery F—Capt. Ezra
W. Matthews
PA Light, Battery C—Capt. James Thompson

---

*Detached from the brigade on Sept. 13 to serve as a railroad guard.

3rd Division—Brig. Gen. John F. Reynolds*
Brig. Gen. George G. Meade

1st Brigade—Brig. Gen. Truman Seymour
1st PA Reserve—Col. R. Biddle Roberts
        Capt. William C. Talley
2nd PA Reserve—Capt. James N. Byrnes
5th PA Reserve—Col. Joseph W. Fisher
6th PA Reserve—Col. William Sinclair
13th PA Reserve (Bucktails)—Col. Hugh W. McNeil
        (K 9/16)
        Capt. Dennis McGee

2nd Brigade—Brig. Gen. George G. Meade
        Col. Albert L. Magilton
3rd PA Reserve—Lt. Col. John Clark
4th PA Reserve—Maj. John Nyce
7th PA Reserve—Col. Henry C. Bolinger
8th PA Reserve—Maj. Silas M. Baily

3rd Brigade—Col. Thomas F. Gallagher (W 9/14)
        Lt. Col. Robert Anderson
9th PA Reserve—Lt. Col. Robert Anderson
        Capt. Samuel B. Dick
10th PA Reserve—Col. Adoniram J. Warner
11th PA Reserve—Lt. Col. Samuel M. Jackson
12th PA Reserve—Capt. Richard Gustin

Artillery
1st PA Light, Battery A—Lt. John G. Simpson
1st PA Light, Battery B—Capt. James H. Cooper
5th U.S., Battery C—Capt. Dunbar R. Ransom

2ND ARMY CORPS
MAJ. GEN. EDWIN V. SUMNER

6th NY Cavalry, Company D—Capt. Henry W. Lyon
6th NY Cavalry, Company K—Capt. Riley Johnson

1st Division—Maj. Gen. Israel B. Richardson

1st Brigade—Brig. Gen. John C. Caldwell
5th NH—Col. Edward Cross
7th NY—Capt. Charles Brestel
61st & 64th NY—Col. Francis C. Barlow
81st PA—Maj. Boyd McKeen

2nd Brigade—Brig. Gen. Thomas F. Meagher
29th MA—Lt. Col. Joseph H. Barnes
63rd NY—Col. John Burke
69th NY—Lt. Col. James Kelly
88th NY—Lt. Col. Patrick Kelly

3rd Brigade—Col. John R. Brooke
2nd DE—Capt. David L. Stricker
52nd NY—Col. Paul Frank
57th NY—Lt. Col. Philip J. Parisen
66th NY—Capt. Julius Wehle
53rd PA—Lt. Col. Richards McMichael

Artillery
1st NY Light, Battery B—Capt. Rufus D. Pettit
4th U.S., Battery A&C—Lt. Evan Thomas

*Detached to Harrisburg, Pennsylvania, on Sept. 11.

2nd Division—Brig. Gen. John Sedgwick

1st Brigade—Brig. Gen. Willis A. Gorman
15th MA—Lt. Col. John W. Kimball
1st MN—Col. Alfred Sully
34th NY—Col. James A. Suiter
82nd NY—Col. Henry W. Hudson
MA Sharpshooters—Capt. John Saunders
MN Sharpshooters—Capt. William F. Russell

2nd Brigade—Brig. Gen. Oliver O. Howard
69th PA—Col. Joshua T. Owen
71st PA—Col. Isaac J. Wistar
72nd PA—Col. DeWitt C. Baxter
106th PA—Col. Turner G. Morehead

3rd Brigade—Brig. Gen. Napoleon J. T. Dana
19th MA—Col. Edward W. Hinks
20th MA—Col. William R. Lee
7th MI—Col. Norman J. Hall
42nd NY—Lt. Col. George N. Bornford
59th NY—Col. William Tidball

Artillery
1st RI Light, Battery A—Capt. John A. Tompkins
1st U.S., Battery I—Lt. George A. Woodruff

3rd Division—Brig. Gen. William H. French

1st Brigade—Brig. Gen. Nathan Kimball
14th IN—Col. William Harrow
8th OH—Lt. Col. Franklin Sawyer
132nd PA—Col. Richard A. Oakford
7th WV—Col. Joseph Snider

2nd Brigade—Col. Dwight Morris
14th CT—Lt. Col. Sanford H. Perkins
108th NY—Col. Oliver H. Palmer
130th PA—Col. Henry I. Zinn

3rd Brigade—Brig. Gen. Max Weber
1st DE—Col. John W. Andrews
5th MD—Maj. Leopold Blumenberg
4th NY—Lt. Col. John D. McGregor

Artillery
1st NY Light, Battery G—Capt. John D. Frank
1st RI Light, Battery B—Capt. John G. Hazard
1st RI Light, Battery G—Capt. Charles D. Owen

4TH ARMY CORPS

1st Division—Maj. Gen. Darius N. Couch

1st Brigade—Brig. Gen. Charles Devens Jr.
7th MA—Col. David A. Russell
10thMA—Col. Henry L. Eustis
36th NY—Col. William H. Brown
2nd RI—Col. Frank Wheaton

2nd Brigade—Brig. Gen. Albion P. Howe
62nd NY—Col. David J. Nevin
93rd PA—Col. James M. McCarter
98th PA—Col. John F. Ballier
102 PA—Col. Thomas A. Rowley
139th PA—Col. Frederick H. Collier

3rd Brigade—Brig. Gen. John Cochrane
65th NY—Col. Alexander Shaler
67th NY—Col. Julius W. Adams

Artillery
NY Light, 3rd Battery—Capt. William Stuart*
1st PA Light, Battery C—Capt. Jeremiah
                                        McCarthy

*Joined the division on Sept. 15.

122nd NY—Col. Silas Titus
23rd PA—Col. Thomas H. Neill
61st PA—Col. George C. Spear
82nd PA—Col. David H. Williams

1st PA Light, Battery D—Capt. Michael Hall
2nd U.S., Battery G—Lt. John H. Butler

5TH ARMY CORPS

Maj. Gen. Fitz John Porter[*]

1st Division—Maj. Gen. George W. Morell[†]

Escort
1st ME Cavalry (detachment)—Capt. George J. Summat

1st Brigade—Col. James Barnes
2nd ME—Col. Charles W. Roberts
18th MA—Lt. Col. Joseph Hayes
22nd MA—Lt. Col. William S. Tilton
1st MI—Capt. Emory W. Belton
13th NY—Col. Elisha G. Marshall
25th NY—Col. Charles A. Johnson
118th PA—Col. Charles M. Prevost
MA Sharpshooters, 2nd Company—Capt. Lewis
E. Wentworth

2nd Brigade—Brig. Gen. Charles Griffin
2nd District of Columbia—Col. Charles
M. Alexander
9th MA—Col. Patrick R. Guiney
32nd MA—Col. Francis J. Parker
4th MI—Col. Jonathan W. Childs
14th NY—Col. James McQuade
62nd PA—Col. Jacob B. Sweitzer

3rd Brigade—Col. T. B. W. Stockton
20th ME—Col. Adelbert Ames
16th MI—Col. Norval E. Welch
12th NY—Capt. William Huson
17th NY—Lt. Col. Nelson B. Bartram
44th NY—Maj. Freeman Conner
83rd PA—Capt. Orpheus S. Woodward
MI Sharpshooters, Brady's Company—Lt. Jonas H.
Titus Jr.

Artillery
MA Light, Battery C—Capt. Augustus P. Martin
1st RI Light, Battery C—Capt. Richard
Waterman
5th U.S., Battery D—Lt. Charles E. Hazlett

2nd Division—Brig. Gen. George Sykes

1st Brigade—Lt. Col. Robert C. Buchanan
3rd U.S.—Capt. John D. Wilkins
4th U.S.—Capt. Hiram Dryer
12th U.S., 1st Battalion—Capt. Matthew M. Blunt
12th U.S., 2nd Battalion—Capt. Thomas
M. Anderson

2nd Brigade—Maj. Charles S. Lovell
1st & 6th U.S.—Capt. Levi C. Bootes
2nd & 10th U.S.—Capt. John S. Poland
11th U.S.—Capt. DeL. Floyd-Jones
17th U.S.—Maj. George L. Andrews

---

[*]A 3rd Division, commanded by Brig. Gen. Andrew A. Humphreys, joined the 5th Corps on Sept. 18.
[†]Reached the army in the field on Sept. 16.

14th U.S., 1st Battalion—Capt. W. Harvey Brown
14th U.S., 2nd Battalion—Capt. David B. McKibbin

3rd Brigade—Colonel Gouverneur K. Warren
5th NY—Capt. Cleveland Winslow
10th NY—Lt. Col. John W. Marshall

Artillery
1st U.S., Battery E&G—Lt. Alanson M. Randol
5th U.S., Battery I—Capt. Stephen H. Weed
5th U.S., Battery K—Lt. William E. Van Reed

Artillery Reserve—Lt. Col. William Hays
1st Battalion NY Light, Battery A—Lt. Bernhard
              Wever
1st Battalion NY Light, Battery B—Lt. Alfred von
              Kleiser
1st Battalion NY Light, Battery C—Capt. Robert
              Langner
1st Battalion NY Light, Battery D—Capt. Charles
              Kusserow
NY Light, 5th Battery—Capt. Elijah D. Taft
1st U.S., Battery K—Capt. William M. Graham
4th U.S., Battery G—Lt. Marcus P. Miller

6TH ARMY CORPS
MAJ. GEN. WILLIAM B. FRANKLIN

Escort
6th PA Cavalry, Companies B & G—Capt. Henry P. Muirheid

1st Division—Maj. Gen. Henry W. Slocum

1st Brigade—Col. Alfred T. A. Torbert
1st NJ—Lt. Col. Mark W. Collet
2nd NJ—Col. Samuel L. Buck
3rd NJ—Col. Henry W. Brown
4th NJ—Col. William B. Hatch

2nd Brigade—Col. Joseph J. Bartlett
5th ME—Col. Nathaniel J. Jackson
16th NY—Lt. Col. Joel J. Seaver
27th NY—Lt. Col. Alexander D. Adams
96th PA—Col. Henry L. Cake

3rd Brigade—Brig. Gen. John Newton
18th NY—Lt. Col. George R. Myers
31st NY—Lt. Col. Francis E. Pinto
32nd NY—Col. Roderick Matheson (K 9/14)
          Maj. George Lemon (K 9/14)
95th PA—Col. Gustavus W. Town

Artillery—Capt. Emory Upton
MD Light, Battery A—Capt. John W. Wolcott
MA Light, Battery A—Capt. Josiah Porter
NJ Light, Battery A—Capt. William Hexamer
2nd U.S., Battery D—Lt. Edward B. Williston

2nd Division—Maj. Gen. William F. Smith

1st Brigade—Brig. Gen. Winfield S. Hancock
6th ME—Col. Hiram Burnham
43rd NY—Maj. John Wilson

2nd Brigade—Brig. Gen. William T. H. Brooks
2nd VT—Maj. James H. Walbridge
3rd VT—Col. Breed N. Hyde

49th PA—Lt. Col. William Brisbane
137th PA—Col. Henry M. Bessert
5th WI—Col. Amasa Cobb

3rd Brigade—Col. William H. Irwin
7th ME—Maj. Thomas W. Hyde
20th NY—Col. Ernest von Vegesack
33rd NY—Lt. Col. Joseph W. Corning
49th NY—Lt. Col. William C. Alberger
77th NY—Capt. Nathan S. Babcock

4th VT—Lt. Col. Charles B. Stoughton
5th VT—Col. Lewis A. Grant
6th VT—Maj. Oscar L. Tuttle

Artillery—Capt. Romeyn B. Ayres
MD Light, Battery B—Lt. Theodore J. Vanneman
NY Light, 1st Battery—Capt. Andrew Cowan
5th U.S., Battery F—Lt. Leonard Martin

9TH ARMY CORPS
MAJ. GEN. AMBROSE E. BURNSIDE[*]
MAJ. GEN. JESSE L. RENO (MW 9/14)
BRIG. GEN. JACOB D. COX

Escort
1st ME Cavalry, Company G—Capt. Zebulon B. Blethen

Unattached
6th NY Cavalry (8 companies)—Col. Thomas C. Devin
OH Cavalry, 3rd Independent Company—Lt. Jonas Seamen
3rd U.S. Artillery, Battery L&M—Capt. John Edwards Jr.

1st Division—Brig. Gen. Orlando B. Willcox

1st Brigade—Col. Benjamin C. Christ
28th MA—Capt. Andrew P. Caraher
8th MI—Lt. Col. Frank Graves[†]
17th MI—Col. William H. Withington
79th NY—Lt. Col. David Morrison
50th PA—Maj. Edward Overton

2nd Brigade—Col. Thomas Welsh
46th NY—Lt. Col. Joseph Gerhardt
45th PA—Lt. Col. John I. Curtin
100th PA—Lt. Col. David A. Leckey

Artillery
MA Light, 8th Battery—Capt. Asa M. Cook
2nd U.S., Battery E—Lt. Samuel N. Benjamin

2nd Division—Brig. Gen. Samuel D. Sturgis

1st Brigade—Brig. Gen. James Nagle
2nd MD—Lt. Col. J. Eugene Duryea
6th NH—Col. Simon G. Griffin
9th NH—Col. Enoch Q. Fellows
48th PA—Lt. Col. Joshua K. Sigfried

2nd Brigade—Brig. Gen. Edward Ferrero
21st MA—Col. William S. Clark
35th MA—Col. Edward A. Wild
51st NY—Col. Robert B. Potter
51st PA—Col. John F. Hartranft

[*]Exercised command of the Right Wing (1st and 9th Corps) until Sept. 16, when McClellan suspended the wing command structure.

[†]Transferred to the 2nd Brigade on Sept. 16.

Artillery

PA Light, Battery D—Capt. George W. Durell
4th U.S., Battery E—Capt. Joseph C. Clark

3rd Division—Brig. Gen. Isaac P. Rodman

1st Brigade—Col. Harrison S. Fairchild
9th NY—Lt. Col. Edgar A. Kimball
89th NY—Maj. Edward Jardine
103rd NY—Maj. Benjamin Ringold

2nd Brigade—Col. Edward Harland
8th CT—Lt. Col. Hiram Appelman
11th CT—Col. Henry W. Kingsbury
16th CT—Col. Francis Beach*
4th RI—Col. William H. P. Steere

Artillery

5th U.S., Battery A—Lt. Charles P. Muhlenberg

Kanawha Division—Brig. Gen. Jacob D. Cox
Brig. Gen. Eliakim P. Scammon

1st Brigade—Col. Eliakim P. Scammon
Col. Hugh Ewing
12th OH—Col. Carr B. White
23rd OH—Lt. Col. Rutherford B. Hayes (W 9/14)
Maj. James M. Comly
30th OH—Col. Hugh Ewing
Lt. Col. Theodore Jones
OH Light Artillery, 1st Battery—Capt. James
R. McMullin
WV Cavalry, Gilmore's Company—Lt. James
Abraham
WV Cavalry, Harrison's Company—Lt. Dennis Delaney

2nd Brigade—Col. Augustus Moor (captured
9/12) Col. George Crook
11th OH—Lt. Col. Augustus H. Coleman
28th OH—Lt. Col. Gottfried Becker
36th OH—Col. George Crook
Lt. Col. Melvin Clarke
Schambeck's Company, Chicago Dragoons—
Capt. Frederick Schambeck
KY Light Artillery, Simmond's Battery—
Capt. Seth J. Simmonds

12TH ARMY CORPS
MAJ. GEN. JOSEPH K. F. MANSFIELD[†]
MAJ. GEN. ALPHEUS S. WILLIAMS

Escort

1st MI Cavalry, Company L—Capt. Melvin Brewer

1st Division—Brig. Gen. Alpheus S. Williams

1st Brigade—Brig. Gen. Samuel W. Crawford
5th CT—Capt. Henry W. Daboll[‡]

3rd Brigade—Brig. Gen. George H. Gordon
27th IN—Col. Silas Colgrove

*Assigned to the brigade on Sept. 16.
[†]Assumed command of the 12th Corps on Sept. 15.
[‡]Detached at Frederick, Maryland, on Sept. 15.

10th ME—Col. George L. Beal
28th NY—Capt. William H. H. Mapes
46th PA—Col. Joseph F. Knipe
124th PA—Col. Joseph W. Hawley
125th PA—Col. Jacob Higgins
128th PA—Col. Samuel Croasdale

2nd MA—Col. George L. Andrews
13th NJ—Col. Ezra A. Carman
107th NY—Col. R. B. Van Valkenburgh
3rd WI—Col. Thomas H. Ruger

2nd Division—Brig. Gen. George S. Greene

1st Brigade—Lt. Col. Hector Tyndale
5th OH—Maj. John Collins
7th OH—Maj. Orrin J. Crane
29th OH—Lt. Theron S. Winship
66th OH—Lt. Col. Eugene Powell
28th PA—Maj. Ario Pardee Jr.

2nd Brigade—Col. Henry J. Stainrook
3rd MD—Lt. Col. Joseph M. Sudsburg
102nd NY—Lt. Col. James C. Lane
109th PA—Capt. George E. Seymour
111th PA—Maj. Thomas M. Walker

3rd Brigade—Col. William B. Goodrich
3rd DE—Maj. Arthur Maginnis
Purnell Legion (MD)—Lt. Col. Benjamin
        L. Simpson
60th NY—Lt. Col. Charles R. Brundage
78th NY—Lt. Col. Jonathan Austin

Artillery—Capt. Clermont L. Best
ME Light, 4th Battery—Capt. O'Neil
        W. Robinson
ME Light, 6th Battery—Capt. Freeman
        McGilvery
1st NY Light, Battery M—Capt. George
        W. Cothran
PA Light, Battery E—Capt. Joseph M. Knap
PA Light, Battery F—Capt. Robert B. Hampton
4th U.S., Battery F—Lt. Edward
        D. Muhlenberg

CAVALRY DIVISION—
BRIG. GEN. ALFRED PLEASONTON

1st Brigade—Maj. Charles J. Whiting
5th U.S.—Capt. Joseph H. McArthur
6th U.S.—Capt. William P. Saunders

2nd Brigade—Col. John F. Farnsworth
8th IL—Maj. William H. Medill
3rd IN—Maj. George H. Chapman
1st MA—Capt. Casper Crowninshield
8th PA—Capt. Peter Keenan

3rd Brigade—Col. Richard H. Rush
4th PA—Col. James H. Childs
6th PA—Lt. Col. C. Ross Smith

4th Brigade—Col. Andrew T. McReynolds
1st NY—Maj. Alonzo W. Adams
12th PA—Maj. James A. Congdon

Horse Artillery
2nd U.S., Battery A—Capt. John C. Tidball
2nd U.S., Battery B&L—Capt. James M. Robinson
2nd U.S., Battery M—Lt. Peter C. Hains
3rd U.S., Battery C&G—Capt. Horatio G. Gibson

Unattached Cavalry

1st ME—Col. Samuel H. Allen*

HARPERS FERRY GARRISON—COLONEL DIXON S. MILES, COMMANDING (MW 9/16) BRIG. GEN. JULIUS WHITE

1st Brigade—Colonel Frederick
      G. D'Utassy (3328)†
39th NY—Maj. Hugo Hildebrandt (545)
111th NY—Col. Jesse Segoine (981)
115th NY—Col. Simeon Sammon (985)
65th IN—Col. Daniel Cameron (817)
15th IN Battery—Capt. John Von Sehlen
      (6 3-inch rifles)

2nd Brigade—Colonel William
      H. Trimble (3613)
60th OH—Col. William H. Trimble (913)
125th NY—Col. George L. Willard (922)
126th NY—Col. Eliakim Sherrill (1031)
9th VT—Col. George J. Stannard (747)
3rd MD Potomac Home Brigade—
Lt. Col. Stephen W. Downey (546)
1st IN Battery—Capt. Silas Rigby
      (6 24 lb. howitzers)
Potts's OH Battery—Capt. Benjamin F. Potts
      (2 Napoleons, 4 3-inch rifles)

3rd Brigade—Colonel Thomas H. Ford (1332)
32nd OH—Maj. Sylvester M. Hewitt (742)
1st MD Potomac Home Brigade (battalion)—Maj.
      John A. Steiner (approx. 320)
5th NY Heavy Artillery, Company F—Capt.
      Eugene McGrath
      (2 9-inch Columbiads & 1 50 lb. Parrott)
7th Squadron RI Cavalry—Maj. Augustus
      W. Corliss (146)
1st MD Cavalry (detachment)—Capt. Charles H.
      Russell (124)

4th Brigade—Col. William G. Ward (1575)
12th NY State Militia—Col. William
      G. Ward (560)
87th OH—Col. Henry B. Banning (1015)
5th NY Heavy Artillery, Company A—Capt.
      John H. Graham (4 20 lb. Parrotts &
      2 Napoleons)

Independent (1,782)
1st MD Potomac Home Brigade—Col. William P.
      Maulsby (approx. 470)
8th NY Cavalry—Col. Benjamin F. Davis (614)
12th IL Cavalry—Lt. Col. Hasbrouck Davis (575)
1st MD Potomac Home Brigade Cavalry—Capt. Henry
      A. Cole (123)
2nd IL Artillery, Battery M—Lt. John C. Phillips
      (4 6 lb. James guns)

---

*Detached at Frederick, Maryland, on Sept. 13. Also had company detachments to 5th and 9th Corps headquarters.

†Numbers in parentheses are unit strengths as reported in *OR* 19, 1:549.

Confederate Army of Northern Virginia
Gen. Robert E. Lee, commanding

LONGSTREET'S COMMAND
MAJ. GEN. JAMES LONGSTREET

Jones's Division—Brig. Gen. David R. Jones

Toombs's Brigade—Brig. Gen. Robert Toombs

2nd GA—Lt. Col. William R. Holmes
15th GA—Col. William T. Millican
17th GA—Capt. J. A. McGregor
20th GA—Col. John B. Cumming

Drayton's Brigade—Brig. Gen. Thomas
F. Drayton
50th GA—Lt. Col. Francis Kearse
51st GA—Col. William Slaughter (?)
15th SC—Col. William D. DeSaussure
3rd SC Battalion—Lt. George S. James (K 9/14)
Maj. William G. W. Rice
Phillips Legion (GA)—Lt. Col. Robert T. Cook

Pickett's Brigade—Brig. Gen. Richard Garnett
8th VA—Col. Eppa Hunton
18th VA—Maj. George Cabell
19th VA—Col. John Strange (K 9/14)
Capt. J. L. Cochran
Lt. W. N. Wood
28th VA—Capt. William L. Wingfield
56th VA—Col. William D. Stuart

Kemper's Brigade—Brig. Gen. James Kemper
1st VA—Capt. George F. Norton
Col. William H. Palmer
7th VA—Maj. Arthur Herbert
Capt. Philip Ashby
11th VA—Maj. Adam Clement (W 9/14)
17th VA—Col. Montgomery D. Corse
24th VA—Col. William Terry

Jenkins's Brigade—Col. Joseph Walker
1st SC—Lt. Col. Daniel Livingston
2nd SC Rifles—Lt. Col. Robert Thompson
5th SC—Capt. T. C. Beckham
6th SC—Lt. Col. John Steedman
Capt. E. B. Cantey
4th SC Battalion—Lt. W. F. Field
Palmetto (SC) Sharpshooters—Capt. A. H. Foster

Anderson's Brigade—Colonel George
T. Anderson
1st GA—Col. William J. Magill
7th GA—Lt. Col. G. H. Carmical
8th GA—Col. John R. Towers
9th GA—Lt. Col. John C. L. Mounger
11th GA—Major Francis H. Little

Artillery
Wise (VA) Artillery—Capt. James S. Brown

Hood's Division—Brig. Gen. John B. Hood

Hood's Brigade—Col. William T. Wofford
18th GA—Lt. Col. Solon Ruff
1st TX—Lt. Col. Philip Work
4th TX—Lt. Col. Benjamin Carter
5th TX—Capt. Ike Turner
Hampton (SC) Legion—Lt. Col. Martin Gary

Law's Brigade—Col. Evander M. Law
4th AL—Lt. Col. Owen McLemore (MW 9–14)
Capt. Lawrence Scruggs
2nd MS—Col. John M. Stone
11th MS—Col. Philip Liddell
6th NC—Maj. Robert Webb

Artillery—Maj. Bushrod W. Frobel
German (SC) Artillery—Capt. William K. Bachman
Palmetto (SC) Artillery—Capt. Hugh R. Garden
Rowan (NC) Artillery—Capt. James Reilly

Evans's Brigade—Brig. Gen. Nathan G. Evans
Col. Peter F. Stevens

17th SC—Col. Fitz McMaster
18th SC—Col. William Wallace
22nd SC—Lt. Col. Thomas Watkins
     (MW & POW 9/14)
   Maj. Miel Hilton
23rd SC—Capt. S. A. Durham
   Lt. E. R. White
Holcombe (SC) Legion—Col. Peter Stevens
Macbeth (SC) Artillery—Capt. Robert Boyce

Anderson's Division—Maj. Gen. Richard H. Anderson

Wilcox's Brigade—Col. Alfred Cumming
8th AL—Maj. Hilary A. Herbert
9th AL—Maj. Jere Williams
10th AL—Capt. G. C. Wheatly
11th AL—Maj. John C. C. Sanders

Armistead's Brigade—Brig. Gen. Lewis
     A. Armistead
9th VA—Capt. W. J. Richardson
14th VA—Col. J. G. Hodges
38th VA—Col. Edward Edmonds
53rd VA—Capt. W. G. Pollard
57th VA—Col. David Dyer

Mahone's Brigade—Col. William A. Parham
6th VA—Capt. John Ludlow
12th VA—Lt. Col. Fielding Taylor (MW 9/14)
   Capt. John Lewellen (W 9/14)
16th VA—Maj. Francis Holladay (POW 9/14)
41st VA—Lt. Col. Joseph Minetree

Pryor's Brigade—Brig. Gen. Roger A. Pryor
14th AL—Maj. James A. Broome
2nd FL— Col. Wm. D. Ballantine
8th FL—Lt. Col. George Coppens
3rd VA—Col. Joseph Mayo
5th FL—Col. John C. Hately

Featherston's Brigade—Brig. Gen. Winfield S.
     Featherston
12th MS—Col. W. H. Taylor
16th MS—Capt. A. M. Feltus
19th MS—Col. N. W. Harris
2nd MS Battalion—Maj. William Wilson

Wright's Brigade—Brig. Ambrose R. Wright
44th AL—Lt. Col. Charles A. Derby
3rd GA—Lt. Col. Reuben Nisbet
22nd GA—Col. Robert Jones
48th GA—Col. William Gibson

Artillery—Maj. John S. Saunders
Donaldsonville (LA) Artillery—Capt. Victor Maurin
Huger's Norfolk (VA) Battery—Capt. Frank Huger
Moorman's Lynchburg (VA) Battery—Capt.
     Marcellus N. Moorman

Grimes's Portsmouth (VA) Battery—Capt. Cary F.
Grimes
Chapman's Dixie (VA) Battery—Capt. William H.
Chapman

Attached Reserve Artillery

Washington (LA) Artillery—Col. John B. Walton
1st Company—Capt. Charles W. Squires
2nd Company—Capt. John B. Richardson
3rd Company—Capt. M. B. Miller
4th Company—Capt. Benjamin F. Eshleman

Lee's Battalion—Col. Stephen D. Lee
Ashland (VA Battery—Capt. Pichegru
Woolfolk Jr.
Bedford (VA) Battery—Capt. Tyler C. Jordan
Brooks (SC) Battery—Lt. William Elliot
Eubank's (VA) Battery—Capt. John L. Eubank
Madison (LA) Battery—Capt. George V. Moody
Parker's (VA) Battery—Capt. William W. Parker

JACKSON'S COMMAND
MAJ. GEN. THOMAS J. JACKSON

Ewell's Division—Brig. Gen. Alexander R. Lawton

Lawton's Brigade—Col. Marcellus Douglass
13th GA—Capt. D. A. Kidd
26th GA—Col. Edmund Atkinson
31st GA—Lt. Col. John Crowder
38th GA—Capt. W. H. Battey
60th GA—Capt. Waters Jones
61st GA—Col. John Lamar

Trimble's Brigade—Col. James A. Walker
15th AL—Capt. Isaac Feagin
12th GA—Capt. James G. Rodgers
21st GA—Maj. Thomas C. Glover
21st NC—Capt. F. P. Miller

Early's Brigade—Brig. Gen. Jubal Early
13th VA—Capt. Frank V. Winston
25th VA—Capt. Robert Lilley
31st VA—Col. John Hoffman
44th VA—Capt. David Anderson
49th VA—Col. William Smith
52nd VA—Col. Michael Harman
58th VA—Capt. Henry W. Wingfield

Hays's Brigade—Brig. Gen. Harry T. Hays
5th LA—Col. Henry Forno
6th LA—Col. Henry Strong
7th LA—Col. Davidson Penn
8th LA—Lt. Col. Trevanion Lewis
14th LA—Col. Zebulon York

Artillery—Maj. Alfred R. Courtney
LA Guard Battery—Capt. Louis E. D'Aquin
Johnson's (VA) Battery—Capt. John R. Johnson
Staunton (VA) Battery—Lt. Asher W. Garber
Courtney (VA) Battery—Capt. Joseph W. Latimer
Chesapeake (MD) Battery—Capt. William Brown

Hill's Light Division—Maj. Gen. Ambrose P. Hill

Branch's Brigade—Brig. Gen. Lawrence O. Branch
7th NC—Col. Edward Haywood
18th NC—Lt. Col. Thomas Purdie
28th NC—Col. James H. Lane
33rd NC—Lt. Col. R. F. Hoke
37th NC—Capt. William G. Morris

Archer's Brigade—Brig. Gen. James J. Archer
5th AL Battalion—Charles Hooper
19th GA—Maj. James Neal
1st TN—Col. Peter Turney
7th TN—Maj. Sam G. Shepard
14th TN—Col. William McComb

Gregg's Brigade—Brig. Gen. Maxcy Gregg
1st SC Provisional Army—Col. David Hamilton
1st SC Rifles—Lt. Col. James M. Perrin
12th SC—Col. Dixon Barnes
13th SC—Col. Oliver E. Edwards
14th SC—Lt. Col. William D. Simpson

Field's Brigade—Col. John M. Brockenbrough
40th VA—Lt. Col. Fleet Cox
47th VA—Lt. Col. John Lyell
55th VA—Col. Francis Mallory or Capt.
    Charles Lawson
22nd VA Battalion—Maj. Edward Tayloe

Pender's Brigade—Brig. Gen. William Dorsey
    Pender
16th NC—Lt. Col. William A. Stowe
22nd NC—Maj. Christopher Cole
34th NC—Lt. Col. John L. McDowell
38th NC—Lt. Col. Robert F. Armfield

Thomas's Brigade—Col. Edward
    L. Thomas
14th GA—Col. Robert W. Folsom
35th GA—Lt. Col. Bolling Holt
45th GA—Maj. Washington L. Grace
49th GA—Lt. Col. Seaborn M. Manning

Artillery—Maj. Reuben L. Walker
Crenshaw's (VA) Battery—Capt. William G. Crenshaw
Fredericksburg (VA) Battery—Capt. Carter M. Braxton
Pee Dee (SC) Battery—Capt. David G. McIntosh
Purcell (VA) Battery—Capt. William J. Pegram
Letcher (VA) Battery—Capt. Greenlee Davidson

Jackson's Division—Brig. Gen. John R. Jones

Winder's Brigade—Col. Andrew J. Grigsby
2nd VA—Capt. Raleigh T. Colston
4th VA—Lt. Col. Robert D. Gardner
5th VA—Maj. Hazael J. Williams
27th VA—Capt. Frank C. Wilson
33rd VA—Capt. Jacob B. Golladay

Jones's Brigade—Col. Bradley T. Johnson
21st VA—Capt. A. C. Page
42nd VA—Capt. R. W. Withers
48th VA—Capt. John Candler
1st VA Battalion—Lt. Charles A. Davidson

Taliaferro's Brigade—Col. Edward T. H. Warren
47th AL—Col. James W. Jackson
48th AL—Col. James Sheffield
10th VA—Col. E. T. H. Warren
23rd VA—Lt. Col. Simeon Walton
37th VA—Lt. Col. John Terry

Starke's Brigade—Brig. Gen. William Starke
1st LA—Lt. Col. Michael Nolan
2nd LA—Col. Jesse Williams
9th LA—Col. Leroy Stafford
10th LA—Capt. Henry D. Monier
15th LA—Col. Edmund Pendleton
1st LA Battalion—Lt. Col. Marie Alfred Coppens

Artillery—Maj. Lindsay M. Shumaker
Alleghany (VA) Battery—Capt. Joseph Carpenter
Cutshaw's (VA) Battery—Capt. Wilfred E. Cutshaw
2nd Baltimore Battery—Capt. John B. Brockenbrough
Danville (VA) Battery—Capt. George W. Wooding
Lee (VA) Battery—Capt. Charles J. Raine
Rockbridge (VA) Battery—Capt. William T. Poague
Hampden (VA) Battery—Capt. William H. Caskie
Rice's (VA) Battery—Capt. William H. Rice

UNATTACHED DIVISIONS

McLaws's Division—Maj. Gen. Lafayette McLaws

Kershaw's Brigade—Brig. Gen. Joseph B. Kershaw
2nd SC—Col. John D. Kennedy
3rd SC—Col. James D. Nance
7th SC—Col. D. Wyatt Aiken
8th SC—Col. John Henagan (W 9/13)
     Lt. Col. A. J. Hoole

Semmes's Brigade—Brig. Gen. Paul J. Semmes
10th GA—Maj. Willis Holt
     Capt. P. H. Loud
53rd GA—Lt. Col. Thomas Sloan
15th VA—Maj. Emmett Morrison
32nd VA—Col. Edgar Montague

Cobb's Brigade—Brig. Gen. Howell Cobb
16th GA—Lt. Col. Henry Thomas
24th GA—Lt. Col. C. C. Sanders
15th NC—Lt. Col. William MacRae
Cobb's (GA) Legion—Lt. Col. Luther Glenn

Barksdale's Brigade—Brig. Gen. William
Barksdale
13th MS—Lt. Col. Kennon McElroy
17th MS—Lt. Col. John C. Fiser
18th MS—Maj. James C. Campbell
21st MS—Col. Benjamin Humphreys

Artillery—Maj. Col. Henry C. Cabell
Manly's (NC) Battery—Capt. Basil C. Manly
Pulaski (GA) Battery—Capt. John P. W. Read
Richmond (Fayette) Battery—Capt. Miles C. Macon
Richmond Howitzers, 1st Company—Capt. Edward S.
             McCarthy
Troup (GA) Artillery—Capt. Henry H. Carlton

Hill's Division—Maj. Gen. Daniel Harvey Hill

Ripley's Brigade—Brig. Gen. Roswell S. Ripley
4th GA—Col. George Doles
44th GA—Capt. John C. Key
1st NC—Lt. Col. Hamilton Brown
3rd NC—Col. William De Rosset

Garland's Brigade—Brig. Gen. Samuel Garland
     Jr. (K 9/14)
     Col. Duncan K. McRae
5th NC—Col. Duncan K. McRae (W 9/14)
     Capt. Thomas M. Garrett
12th NC—Capt. Shugan Snow
13th NC—Lt. Col. Thomas Ruffin Jr. (W 9/14)
20th NC—Col. Alfred Iverson
23rd NC—Col. Daniel Christie

Rodes's Brigade—Brig. Gen. Robert E. Rodes
3rd AL—Col. Cullen A. Battle
5th AL—Maj. Edwin Hobson
6th AL—Col. John B. Gordon
12th AL—Col. Bristor B. Gayle (K 9/14)
      Lt. Col. Samuel Pickens (W 9/14)
      Capt. Tucker
26th AL—Col. Edward O'Neal

Colquitt's Brigade—Col. Alfred H. Colquitt
13th AL—Col. Birkett D. Fry
6th GA—Lt. Col. James Newton
23rd GA—Col. William Barclay
27th GA—Col. Levi Smith
28th GA—Maj. Tully Graybill

Anderson's Brigade—Brig. Gen. George B.
      Anderson
2nd NC—Col. Charles C. Tew
4th NC—Col. Bryan Grimes
14th NC—Col. Risden Bennett
30th NC—Col. Francis Parker

Artillery—Maj. Scipio F. Pierson
Hardaway's (AL) Battery—Capt. Robert A.
      Hardaway
Jeff Davis (AL) Artillery—Capt. James W.
      Bondurant
Jones's (Peninsula) VA Battery—Capt. William
      B. Jones
King William (VA) Artillery—Capt. Thomas
      H. Carter

Walker's Division—Brig. Gen. John G. Walker

Walker's Brigade—Col. Van H. Manning
3rd AR—Capt. John Reedy
27th NC—Col. John R. Cooke
46th NC—Col. Edward Hall
48th NC—Col. Robert Hill
30th VA—Lt. Col. Robert Chew
French's (VA) Battery—Capt. Thomas B. French

Ransom's Brigade—Brig. Gen. Robert Ransom Jr.
24th NC—Lt. Col. John L. Harris
35th NC—Col. M. W. Ransom
49th NC—Lt. Col. Lee M. McAfee
Branch's (VA) Field Artillery—Capt. James
      Branch

Reserve Artillery—Brig. Gen. William N. Pendleton

Cutts's Battalion—Lt. Col. Allen S. Cutts
Blackshear's (GA) Battery—Capt. James
      A. Blackshear
Patterson's (GA) Battery—Capt. George
      M. Patterson
Lane's (GA) Battery—Capt. John Lane
Lloyd's (NC) Battery—Capt. W. P. Lloyd

Brown's Battalion—Col. J. Thompson Brown
Powhatan (VA) Artillery—Capt. Willis
      J. Dance
Richmond Howitzers, 2nd Company—Capt.
      D. Watson
Richmond Howitzers, 3rd Company—Capt.
      B. H. Smith Jr.
Salem (VA) Artillery—Capt. A. Hupp
Williamsburg (VA) Artillery—Capt. John
      A. Coke

Jones's Battalion—Maj. Hilary P. Jones
Morris (VA) Artillery—Capt. R. C. M. Page
Orange (VA) Artillery—Capt. Jefferson Peyton

Nelson's Battalion—Maj. William Nelson
Amherst (VA) Artillery—Capt. T. J. Kirkpatrick
Fluvanna (VA) Artillery—Capt. John Ancell

Turner's (VA) Battery—Capt. W. H. Turner

Wimbish's (VA) Battery—Capt. Abram Wimbish

Huckstep's (VA) Battery—Capt. Charles
    Huckstep

Johnson's (VA) Battery—Capt. Marmaduke
    Johnson

Milledge (GA) Battery—Capt. John Milledge

Unattached Artillery

Magruder (VA) Artillery—Capt. T. J. Page Jr.

Cavalry Division—Maj. Gen. James E. B. Stuart

Hampton's Brigade—Brig. Gen. Wade Hampton

1st NC—Col. L. S. Baker

2nd NC—Col. M. C. Butler

Cobb's (GA) Legion—Lt. Col. P. M. B. Young
    (W 9/13)
        Maj. W. G. Deloney

10th VA—Col. J. Lucius Davis

Jeff Davis (MS) Legion—Lt. Col. William
    T. Martin

Robertson's Brigade—Col. Thomas Munford

2nd VA—Lt. Col. Richard H. Burks

6th VA—Col. Thomas S. Flourney

7th VA—Capt. S. B. Myers

12th VA—Col. A. W. Harman

17th VA Cavalry Battalion—Maj. Thomas B. Massie

Lee's Brigade—Brig. Gen. Fitzhugh Lee

1st VA—Lt. Col. L. Tiernan Brien

3rd VA—Lt. Col. John T. Thornton

4th VA—Col. William Wickham

5th VA—Col. Thomas L. Rosser

9th VA—Col. W. H. F. Lee

Stuart Horse Artillery—Capt. John Pelham

Ashby (VA) Battery—Capt. R. P. Chew

"Washington" (SC) Battery—Capt. J. F. Hart

"First Stuart" (VA) Battery—Capt. J. Pelham

APPENDIX B
Strength of Union and Confederate Forces

One of the enduring images of the Maryland Campaign is that of a well fed, superbly equipped, and massive Army of the Potomac being fought to a standstill by a ragged, ill-equipped, and greatly outnumbered Army of Northern Virginia. This impression has its origin in some of the war's Lost Cause mythology, but it also crops up in the official reports of McClellan and Lee. In his second and more detailed report of the campaign, McClellan gave his strength at Antietam as 87,164, while Lee reported that he fought the battle with less than 40,000 troops. Lee wrote of his men that "nothing could surpass the determined valor with which they met the large army of the enemy, fully supplied and equipped, and the result reflects the highest credit on the officers and men engaged." Colonel Walter Taylor, of Lee's staff, made the case in his 1877 memoir that the Army of Northern Virginia fought the battle with only 35,255 men, who were "the very flower of the Army of Northern Virginia," fighting with "indomitable courage and inflexible tenacity" against odds of "one to three of their adversaries."*

That the Confederates fought with great courage and tenacity at Harpers Ferry, South Mountain, and Antietam is indisputable. But that the army had fewer than 40,000 men in its ranks by September 17, when they fought the battle of Antietam, is less a testament to the army's fortitude than a damning statement on the condition the army had been reduced to by poor discipline, hard marching, exhaustion, and the failure of the Confederacy to keep its soldiers minimally supplied with food and adequate clothing. John Owen Allen, in a 1993 master's thesis at George Mason University, conducted an in-depth study of the strengths of the opposing armies in the Second Manassas Campaign, which he derived from the muster rolls and regimental records in the National Archives. This included the strengths of the armies on September 2, the day before the Maryland Campaign officially began. What Allen learned was that the Army of Northern Virginia's aggregate strength on the eve of the campaign was 75,032 men.[†] Fifteen days later, when the army fought the Battle of Antietam, its present for duty was approximately 38,000.

---

*OR 19, 1:67, 151; Walter Taylor, *Four Years with General Lee* (New York: D. Appleton, 1877), 73.
  [†]John Owen Allen, "The Strengths of the Union and Confederate Forces at Second Manassas," master's thesis, George Mason Univ., 1993. Aggregate strength includes men present for duty,

Of the pre-campaign strength of 75,000 men, 3,107 were casualties at South Mountain, Harpers Ferry, or the other minor skirmishes. This meant that between September 2 and September 17 the army leaked approximately 34,000 stragglers, deserters, and sick, or about 45 percent of the army's strength.

While Lee publicly praised the courage of those that remained in the ranks, he privately acknowledged that the army's massive straggling had reached crisis proportions, writing President Davis four days after Antietam that the army's "present efficiency is greatly paralyzed by the loss to its ranks of the numerous stragglers," and that "a great many men belonging to the army never entered Maryland at all; many returned after getting there, while others who crossed the river kept aloof."* Lee would eventually get his straggling problem under control, and not until the Appomattox Campaign would the army again experience straggling on the scale of the Maryland Campaign.

As the statistics following reveal, the Army of the Potomac had its own problems with straggling, though not to the extent of the Army of Northern Virginia. About 28 percent of the aggregate present on September 2 were not in the ranks on September 17. The army also had about 10,000 fewer men than McClellan credited his army with. Precisely where McClellan came up with the strengths he gave in his report is something of a mystery, as the army compiled no strength returns until September 20.

Trying to arrive at accurate army strengths for the campaigns of the Civil War is generally unproductive, but in this case it is necessary for a more balanced understanding of the Maryland Campaign. These tables are not the last word on the army strengths, but rather a departure point for further study.

---

combat effectives, and men detailed to noncombat duties such as cooks, orderlies, nurses, teamsters, and the like, as well as those sick or in arrest.

*OR 19, 1:143.

Army of the Potomac, September 2–17, 1862

	Sept. 2[1]	South Mountain / Crampton's Gap Casualties K+W+M	Sept. 17[2]
Subtotal for 1st Corps—Hooker	16,536	923	10,903
			(8,619 infantry + 819 artillery = 9,438)
General staff	—	1	—
1st Division—Doubleday	5,976	495	3,931 (2,975 + 450 = 3,425)
1st Brigade—Phelps	1,102	95	(425)
2nd Brigade—Hoffman	1,298[3]	59	(829)
3rd Brigade—Patrick	1,523	23	(750)
4th Brigade—Gibbon	1,729	318	(971)
Artillery	324	—	—
2nd Division—Ricketts	5,011	35	3,674 (3,037 + 121 = 3,158)
1st Brigade—Duryee	1,574	21	—
2nd Brigade—Christian	1,417	8	—
3rd Brigade—Hartsuff	1,913	6	—
Artillery	107	—	—
3rd Division—Meade	5,549	392	3,298 (2,607 + 248 = 2,855)
1st Brigade—Seymour	1,902	171	—
2nd Brigade—Magilton	1,770	89	—
3rd Brigade—Gallagher/ Anderson	1,635	132	—
Artillery	242	—	—
Subtotal for 2nd Corps—Sumner	18,282	—	17,716 (15,208 + 859 = 16,067)
1st Division—Richardson	4,963	—	4,959 (4,029 + 246 = 4,275)
1st Brigade—Caldwell	1,551	—	1,343 est.
2nd Brigade—Meagher	1,516	—	1,343
3rd Brigade—Brooke	1,650	—	1,343 est.
Artillery	246	—	246
2nd Division—Sedgwick	6,634	—	6,274 (5,437 + 244 = 5,681)
1st Brigade—Gorman	2,027	—	1,978 (1,691)
2nd Brigade—Howard	2,650	—	2,106 (1,800)
3rd Brigade—Dana	1,713	—	(1,946[4])
Artillery	244	—	244
3rd Division—French	6,316[5]	—	6,114 (5,742)
1st Brigade—Kimball	1,751	—	1,751
2nd Brigade—Morris	2,765	—	2,563 (2,191)
3rd Brigade—Weber	1,800	—	1,800
Unattached artillery	369	—	369
Subtotal for 4th Corps	6,400[6]	—	—
1st Division—Couch	6,400	—	—
1st Brigade—Devens Jr.	n/a	—	—
2nd Brigade—Howe	n/a	—	—
3rd Brigade—Cochrane	n/a	—	—
Artillery	n/a	—	—

(continued)

	Sept. 2[1]	South Mountain / Crampton's Gap Casualties K+W+M	Sept. 17[2]
Subtotal for 5th Corps—Porter	9,589	—	9,589[7]
1st Division—Morell	6,100	—	6,100
1st Brigade—Barnes	2,020[8]	—	2,020
2nd Brigade—Griffin	2,060[9]	—	2,060
3rd Brigade—Stockton	1,675[10]	—	1,675
Artillery	345	—	345
2nd Division—Sykes	3,489[11]	—	3,489
1st Brigade—Buchanan	1,391	—	1,391
2nd Brigade—Lovell	1,288	—	1,288
3rd Brigade—Warren	523	—	523
Artillery	287	—	287
Reserve artillery—Hays	950	—	950
Subtotal for 6th Corps—Franklin	13,841	533	11,862[12]
General Staff		1	
1st Division—Slocum	6,532	513	—
1st Brigade—Torbert	1,513	172	—
2nd Brigade—Bartlett	2,744[13]	217	—
3rd Brigade—Newton	1,759	124	—
Artillery[14]	516	0	—
2nd Division—Smith	7,309	19	—
1st Brigade—Hancock	2,570[15]	0	—
2nd Brigade—Brooks	2,188	19	—
3rd Brigade—Irwin	2,164	0	(1,684)
Artillery	387	0	—
Subtotal for 9th Corps—Reno/Cox	16,621	889	14,650 (11,771 + 856 = 12,647)
General Staff		1	
1st Division—Willcox	4,785	355	3,758 (3,002 + 246 = 3,248)
1st Brigade—Christ	2,482[16]	162	—
2nd Brigade—Welsh	2,057[17]	188	—
Artillery	246	5	—
2nd Division—Sturgis	4,815	157	3,766 (3,013 + 241 = 3,254)
1st Brigade—Nagle	2,289[18]	41	—
2nd Brigade—Ferrero	2,285[19]	116	—
Artillery	241	0	—
3rd Division—Rodman	3,462	20	3,388 (2,791 + 123 = 2,914)
1st Brigade—Fairchild	1,099	20	—
2nd Brigade—Harland	2,240	0	—
Artillery	123	0	—
Kanawha Division—Cox	3,559	356	3,738 (2,985 + 246 = 3,231)
1st Brigade—Scammon	1,308	272	(980)
2nd Brigade—Moor/Crook	2,005	84	(2,005)
Artillery	246	0	246
Subtotal for 12th Corps—Mansfield	13,167	—	8,861 (7,239 + 392 = 7,631)[20]
1st Division—Williams	7,725	—	(4,735)

(continued)

Army of the Potomac, September 2–17, 1862 (*continued*)

	Sept. 2[1]	South Mountain / Crampton's Gap Casualties K+W+M	Sept. 17[2]
1st Brigade—Crawford	4,246[21]	—	(2,525)
3rd Brigade—Gordon	3,479[22]	—	(2,210)
2nd Division—Greene	5,050	—	(2,504)
1st Brigade—Tyndale	2,256	—	—
2nd Brigade—Stainrook	1,325	—	—
3rd Brigade—Goodrich	1,469	—	—
Artillery	392	—	392
Subtotal for Cavalry	4,320 + 492 = 4,812[23]	—	4,543[24]
Division—Pleasonton			
Horse artillery	492	—	—
1st Maine Cavalry	393	—	—
Total for Army of the Potomac	100,591[25]— aggregate present 83,491—present for duty	2,346	79,074—aggregate present 72,727—present for duty[26]

1. Unless otherwise noted, strengths are derived by taking the Sept. 2 strengths for the Army of Virginia and the Army of the Potomac from Allen, "Strengths," and deducting 17%. Although Allen indicates his figures are for present for duty (those men who could be carried into action), they appear to be for aggregate present, which includes noncombatants. To account for them and arrive at a reasonable estimate of present for duty, an average of 17% of the aggregate present should be deducted. The 17% is arrived at by comparing other 1862 returns for the Army of the Potomac and taking an average of present for duty compared with aggregate present.

2. Figures in parentheses are engaged strengths from Carman, chap. 23. Figures not in parentheses are estimates of aggregate present, which are arrived at by adding 17% to Carman's engaged infantry strength, and then adding the divisional artillery manpower. Artillery did not suffer the same attrition as infantry and did not detach as many soldiers to noncombat duties.

3. The estimated strength of 324 for the 7th IN is derived by averaging the strength of the other three regiments.

4. The 59th NY was added to Dana's brigade after Sept. 2. Carmen gave their engaged strength at 381.

5. For Kimball's brigade, the figures for his veteran regiments are for their strength at Antietam. Their strength at the start of the campaign was undoubtedly higher.

6. Aug. 10, 1862, return. See OR 11, 3:367.

7. Since most of the 5th Corps were not engaged at Antietam, Carman did not compile strength figures for them. The actual numbers present for duty were less than those given here.

8. Field return for Sept. 1. See OR 12, 3:795. The brigade had 1,087 present for duty. The estimated strength of 933 men for the 118th PA is derived from the average regimental strength in the Sept. 29 return of new regiments forwarded to the Army of the Potomac.

9. OR 12, 3:795. The strength of the 2nd DC is an estimate arrived at by averaging the strength of the other five regiments.

10. OR 12, 3:795. The same formula used in note 8 is applied for the 20th ME.

11. All figures are from the division's Sept. 1 return. See OR 12, 3:796.

12. Sept. 20 return. See OR 19, 2:336.

13. The strength of the 121st NY was 940. See OR, Ser. 3, 3:750. Allen gives the strength of the other regiments as 1,804.

14. Carman gave the strength of the 6th Corps artillery at 21 officers and 880 enlisted men. This gives an average of 129 men per battery.

15. The estimated strength for the 137th PA is 941. See OR, Ser. 3, 3:760. Allen gives the strength of the other four regiments as 1,637 on Sept. 1.

16. Allen's strengths plus 966 for the 17th MI. See OR, Ser. 3, 3:762.

17. Allen's strengths plus 694 for the 45th PA.

18. Allen's strengths minus 964 for the 9th NH. See OR, Ser. 3, 3:779.

19. Allen's strengths plus 1108 for the 35th MA. See OR, Ser. 3, 3:773.

20. All of the engaged strengths for the 12th Corps are drawn from Carman, chap. 23, 19-20.

21. Allen's strengths plus the 124th PA (974), the 125th PA (963), and the 128th PA (950). See OR, Ser. 3, 3:760.

22. Allen's strengths plus the 13th NJ (899) and the 107th NY (1,031). See OR, Ser. 3, 3:749, 775.

23. OR 19, 1:67. It is unclear whether this figure included horse artillery; I have assumed that it does not. This divisional strength gives an average of 393 per regiment. Based on an Aug. 10, 1862, report on the number of horses in the cavalry division, it seems likely that the strength of the division was considerably higher than 4,320 at the beginning of the campaign.

24. Sept. 20 return. See OR 19, 2:336.

25. This figure represents the entire force that reached the Army of the Potomac by Sept. 17.

26. Since no figures are available for the 5th and the 6th Corps present for duty, this amount reflects their aggregate present. It also counts the entire cavalry force, but only about one-half was present on the field by Sept. 17. The actual number of present for duty in the Army of the Potomac on Sept. 17 was probably around 70,000.

Army of Northern Virginia, September 2–17, 1862

	Sept. 2[1]	Est. present for duty at South Mtn. and Harpers Ferry[2]	Harpers Ferry or South Mtn. losses	Est. present for duty on Sept. 16–17[3]	Est. stragglers/ sick/deserters since Sept. 2
Subtotal for Jackson	20,388	14,842	69	9,235	11,076
Lawton's division	6,246	5,186	0	4,127[4]	2,119 (34%)
Lawton	1,781	—	—	—	—
Early	1,794	—	—	—	—
Hays	1,677	—	—	—	—
Trimble (Walker)	707	—	—	—	—
Lawton's artillery	287	—	—	223	—
J. R. Jones's division	5,578	3,832	0	2,094 (2043)[5]	3,476 (62%)
Grigsby	1,160	—	—	—	—
Johnson	812	—	—	—	—
Warren	1,543	—	—	—	—
Starke	1,623	—	—	—	—
J. R. Jones's artillery	440	—	—	—	—
A. P. Hill's division	8,564	5,824	69	3,014[6]	5,481 (64%)
Pender	1,596	—	—	—	—
Archer	1,149	—	—	—	—
Brockenbrough	1,336	—	—	—	—
Gregg	984	—	—	—	—
Thomas	1,205	—	—	—	—
Branch	1,754	—	—	—	—
A. P. Hill's artillery	540	—	—	—	—
Subtotal for Longstreet	24,955	17,684	1,370	10,095	13,565
D. R. Jones's division	9,034	6,563	953	3,392[7]	4,943 (55%)
Kemper	1,362	—	75	443	—
Drayton	1,464[8]	—	643[9]	465	—
Garnett	1,739	—	196	261	—
Toombs	1,221	—	0	638	—
G. T. Anderson	1,381	—	7	749	—
Jenkins	1,786	—	32	755	—
D. R. Jones's artillery	81	—	—	81	—
Hood's division	3,839	2,970	24	2,304	1,332 (35%)
Law	1,394	—	19	1,146	—
Wofford	2,177	—	5	854	—
Hood's artillery	268	—	—	304	—
Evans's brigade + artillery	1,058	550[10]	216	284 + 115 artillery	443 (42%)
R. H. Anderson's division	11,024	7,601	177	3,672 + 328 artillery	6,847 (62%)
Wilcox	1,392	—	0	—	—
Wright	1,468	—	0	—	—
Mahone	1,500	—	177	82	—
Featherston	1,565	—	0	—	—
Pryor	2,625	—	0	—	—
Armistead	2,146	—	0	—	—
R. H. Anderson's artillery	328[11]	—	—	—	—
Washington Artillery + S. D. Lee's battalion	590	—	—	596	—

(continued)

	Sept. 2[1]	Est. present for duty at South Mtn. and Harpers Ferry[2]	Harpers Ferry or South Mtn. losses	Est. present for duty on Sept. 16–17[3]	Est. stragglers/ sick/deserters since Sept. 2
Subtotal for army reserve	22,760	17,301	1,966	13,048	7,790
McLaws's division	7,759	4,432[12]	962	3,312	3,524 (45%)
Semmes	1,717	—	59	786	—
Kershaw	1,712	—	196	935	—
Barksdale	2,280	—	17	891	—
Cobb	1,631	—	690	400	—
McLaws's artillery	419	—	—	300 est.[13]	—
Walker's division	5,159	4,555	4	3,946	1,209 (23%)
Ransom	2,018	—	—	1,600	—
Walker (Manning)	2,959	—	—	2,164	—
Walker's artillery	182	—	—	182 est.	—
D. H. Hill's division	9,842	8,314	1000	5,790[14]	3,057 (31%)
Garland	2,507	—	379	756	—
G. B. Anderson	1,427	—	90	1,174	—
Ripley	2,334	—	0	1,344	—
Rodes	1,803	—	422	850	—
Colquitt	1,474	—	109	1,320	—
D. H. Hill's artillery	297	—	—	346	—
Subtotal for Stuart	5,313	5,000 est.	—	4,500	813[15] (15%)
Hampton	1,445	—	—	—	—
F. Lee	1,959	—	—	—	—
Munford	1,647[16]	—	—	—	—
Stuart's artillery	262	—	—	—	—
Reserve artillery	1,299	700 est.	0	621	678 (52%)
Total for Army of Northern Virginia	75,305	55,527	3,405	38,095	33,922 (45%)

1. Unless otherwise noted, Sept. 2 strengths are drawn from Allen, "Strengths." Allen gives the numbers as present for duty but the figures appear to be aggregate present. To account for them, on average 15% of the aggregate present should be deducted to arrive at a reasonable estimate of present for duty.

2. Estimated strengths are arrived at by taking one-half of the total number of stragglers/sick lost by a division in the entire campaign.

3. Sept. 17 strengths are from Carman, chap. 23, unless otherwise noted.

4. Includes artillery.

5. This is the strength Jones cited for his division in his report. See *OR* 19, 1:886.

6. Carman gave A. P. Hill's strength at Antietam as 2,000 enlisted men, 231 officers, and 337 artillery. Hill engaged only five brigades, leaving Thomas's at Harpers Ferry. Taking the average of five brigades with a total strength of 2,231 gives a strength of approximately 446 per brigade. This is added to Carman's figures to arrive at a full divisional strength.

7. Includes artillery, which Carman gave as 81 men.

8. Edings diary, LC. Edings was the AAG to Drayton and gave the brigade's strength on Sept. 11, 1862.

9. Graham, "Death of a Brigade," table on p. 3. Graham's figures were based on a modern study of muster roll records and include those wounded who died of their wounds. As an example of the inaccuracy of Confederate casualty statistics, Drayton's reported casualties for the entire campaign were 78 killed, 280 wounded, and 179 missing or captured.

10. Evans's strength is from Carman, chap. 23.

11. Carman, chap. 23.

12. Strength as reported in *OR* 19, 1:860-862.

13. Part of Carlton's and McCarthy's batteries were left behind at Leesburg, which accounts for the loss in manpower.

14. Includes 346 men for artillery. Carman's figures for individual brigade strengths and D. H. Hill's divisional strength do not match up.

15. This is simply the difference between Allan's Sept. 2 and Carman's Sept. 17 figures. Casualties in the various skirmishes are included in this figure.

16. Includes the 2nd VA, the 6th VA, the 7th VA, and the 12th VA Cavalry, but not the 17th VA Battalion or White's detachment.

APPENDIX C

Union and Confederate Casualties

Army of the Potomac, South Mountain, September 14, 1862

	Killed	Wounded	Captured	Total
Subtotal for 1st Corps—Hooker	167	712	44	923
Subtotal for 1st Division—Hatch (W), Doubleday	63	390	43	496
General Staff	0	1	0	1
1st Brigade	20	67	8	95
22nd NY	10	20	0	30
24th NY	1	25	0	26
30th NY	4	5	0	9
14th Brooklyn	5	15	8	28
2nd U.S. Sharpshooters	0	2	0	2
2nd Brigade	3	52	4	59
7th IN	0	12	0	12
76th NY	2	18	0	20
95th NY	0	11	1	12
56th PA	1	11	3	15
3rd Brigade	3	19	1	23
21st NY	1	3	0	4
23rd NY	0	6	0	6
35th NY	2	10	1	13
20th NYSM	—	—	—	—
4th Brigade	37	251	30	318
19th IN	9	37	7	53
2nd WI	6	19	1	26
6th WI	11	79	2	92
7th WI	11	116	20	147
Subtotal for 2nd Division—Ricketts	9	26	0	35
1st Brigade	5	16	0	21
97th NY	2	3	0	5
104th NY	0	1	0	1
105th NY	1	2	0	3
107th NY	2	10	0	12

(continued)

Army of the Potomac, South Mountain, September 14, 1862 (*continued*)

	Killed	Wounded	Captured	Total
2nd Brigade	2	6	0	8
26th NY	0	2	0	2
94th NY	2	2	0	4
90th PA	0	2	0	2
3rd Brigade	2	4	0	6
12th MA	1	1	0	2
83rd NY	1	1	0	2
11th PA	0	2	0	2
Subtotal for 3rd Division—Meade	95	296	1	392
1st Brigade	38	133	0	171
1st PA Reserves	10	30	0	40
2nd PA Reserves	5	12	0	17
5th PA Reserves	1	9	0	10
6th PA Reserves	11	43	0	54
13th PA Reserves (Bucktails)	11	39	0	50
2nd Brigade	25	63	1	89
4th PA Reserves	5	22	0	27
7th PA Reserves	5	7	0	12
8th PA Reserves	15	34	1	50
3rd Brigade	32	100	0	132
9th PA Reserves	10	33	0	43
10th PA Reserves	4	18	0	22
11th PA Reserves	12	30	0	42
12th PA Reserves	6	19	0	25
Subtotal for 9th Corps—Reno (K), Cox	157	691	41	889
Staff	1	0	0	1
Subtotal for 1st Division—Willcox	64	291	0	355
1st Brigade	26	136	0	162
28th MA	0	7	0	7
8th MI	0	8	0	8
17th MI	26	106	0	132
79th NY	0	12	0	12
50th PA	0	3	0	3
2nd Brigade	37	151	0	188
46th NY	2	7	0	9
45th PA	27	107	0	134
100th PA	8	37	0	45
8th Battery, MA Light Artillery	1	4	0	5
Subtotal for 2nd Division—Sturgis	10	117	30	157
1st Brigade	0	34	7	41
9th NH	0	23	6	29
48th PA	0	11	1	12
2nd Brigade	10	83	23	116
21st MA	0	7	0	7
35th MA	3	37	23	63

(continued)

	Killed	Wounded	Captured	Total
51st NY	4	12	0	16
51st PA	3	27	0	30
Subtotal for 3rd Division—Rodman	2	18	0	20
1st Brigade	2	18	0	20
89th NY	2	18	0	20
Subtotal for Kanawha Division—Cox	80	265	11	356
1st Brigade	63	201	8	272
12th OH	13	47	5	65
23rd OH	32	95	3	130
36th OH	17	53	0	70
1st Battery, OH Light Artillery	1	6	0	7
2nd Brigade	17	64	3	84
11th OH	7	34	3	44
28th OH	3	12	0	15
36th OJ	7	18	0	25
Subtotal Cavalry Division	1	0	0	1
Total	325	1,403	85	1,813

Army of Northern Virginia, South Mountain, September 14, 1862

	Killed	Wounded	Missing & POW	Total
Subtotal for D. H. Hill	129	453	418	1,000
Garland	43	168	168	379
G. B. Anderson	7	54	29	90
Ripley	0	0	0	0
Rodes	61	157	204	422
Colquitt	18	74	17	109
Subtotal for Longstreet	258	472	247	977
D. R. Jones's division[1]	255	458	240	953
Kemper	11	57	7	75
Drayton	206	227	210	643[2]
Garnett	35	142	19	196
G. T. Anderson	0	3	4	7
Jenkins	3	29	0	32
Hood's division	3	14	7	24
Law	3	11	5	19
Wofford	—	3	2	5
Evans's brigade	23	148	45	216
Total	410	1,073	710	2,193

1. Toombs's brigade was detached at Hagerstown and thus was not engaged.
2. Graham, "Death of a Brigade," table on p. 3.

Army of the Potomac, Crampton's Gap, September 14, 1862

	Killed	Wounded	Captured	Total
General Staff	0	1	0	1
Subtotal for 1st Division—Slocum	112	399	2	513
1st Brigade	38	134	0	172
1st NJ	7	34	0	41
2nd NJ	10	45	0	55
3rd NJ	11	29	0	40
4th NJ	10	26	0	36
2nd Brigade	50	167	0	217
5th ME	4	28	0	31
16th NY	20	41	0	61
27th NY	6	27	0	33
96th PA	20	71	0	91
3rd Brigade	24	98	2	124
18th NY	11	41	2	54
31st NY	1	3	0	4
32nd NY	11	40	0	51
95th PA	1	14	0	15
Subtotal for 2nd Division—Smith	1	18	0	19
2nd Brigade	1	18	0	19
2nd VT	0	5	0	5
3rd VT	0	0	0	0
4th VT	1	10	0	11
5th VT	0	0	0	0
6th VT	0	3	0	3
Total	113	418	2	533

Army of Northern Virginia, Crampton's Gap, September 14, 1862

	Killed	Wounded	Missing & POW	Total
Subtotal for McLaws	156	274	289	719
Semmes	3	19	37	59
Cobb	153	255	252	660
Subtotal for R. H. Anderson's division	17	49	111	177
Wilcox	—	—	—	—
Wright	—	—	—	—
Mahone	17	49	111	177
Featherston	—	—	—	—
Pryor	—	—	—	—
Munford	?	?	?	?
Total	173	323	400	896

Union, Harpers Ferry Garrison, September 12–15, 1862

	Killed	Wounded	Captured	Total
General Staff	1	0	6	7
Subtotal for 1st Brigade	5	42	3,406	3.453
39th NY	0	15	530	545
111th NY	5	6	970	981
115th NY	0	11	978	989
65th IN	0	7	810	817
15th IN Battery	0	3	118	121
Subtotal for 2nd Brigade	20	61	4,275	4,356
60th OH	2	6	905	913
125th NY	2	1	919	922
126th NY	13	42	976	1,031
9th VT	0	3	744	747
3rd MD Potomac Home Brigade	3	9	534	546
1st IN Battery	0	0	113	113
Potts's OH Battery	0	0	84	84
Subtotal for 3rd Brigade	18	67	1,738	1,823
32nd OH	10	58	674	742
1st MD PHB[1]	6	6	779	791
5th NY Heavy Artillery, Companies A & F	2	0	265	267
7th Squadron RI Cavalry	0	0	0	
1st MD Cavalry (detachment)	0	3	20	23
Subtotal for 4th Brigade	1	0	1,574	1,575
12th NY State Militia	0	0	560	560
5th NY Heavy Artillery, Company A[2]				
87th OH	1	0	1,014	1,015
Subtotal for Independents	0	2	1,521	1,523
8th NY Cavalry	0	0	92	92
1st MD Potomac Home Brigade Cavalry	0	0	0	0
12th IL Cavalry	0	2	157	159
2nd IL Artillery, Battery M	0	0	100	100
Unattached, in hospitals, etc.	0	0	1,172	1,172
Total	45	172	12,520	12,737

1. Only one battalion of this regiment was assigned to the 3rd Brigade. They sustained all the losses of the regiment. The rest of the regiment was not attached to a brigade.

2. Although Company A was attached to the 4th Brigade, its losses were combined with Company F, 5th NYHA, in the 3rd Brigade. The combined losses of both companies are noted above.

Army of Northern Virginia, Harpers Ferry Operation, September 12–15, 1862

	Killed	Wounded	Missing & POW	Total
Subtotal for Jackson	3	66	0	69
Lawton's division	0	0	0	0
Lawton (Douglass)	–	–	–	–
Early	–	–	–	–
Hays	–	–	–	–
Trimble (Walker)	–	–	–	–
J. R. Jones's division	0	0	0	0
Grigsby	–	–	–	–
Johnson	–	–	–	–
Warren	–	–	–	–
Starke	–	–	–	–
A. P. Hill's division	3	66	0	69
Pender	2	20	–	–
Archer	1	22	–	–
Brockenbrough	–	–	–	–
Gregg	0	0	0	0
Thomas	–	–	–	–
Branch	0	4	0	–
Subtotal for McLaws	35	178	0	213
Semmes	–	–	–	–
Kershaw	33	163	0	196
Barksdale	2	15	0	17
Cobb	–	–	–	–
Subtotal for Walker	1	3	0	4
Ransom	–	–	–	–
Manning	–	–	–	–
Total	39	247	0	286

ABBREVIATIONS

AAG	assistant adjutant general
ACHS	Adams County Historical Society, Gettysburg, Pennsylvania
ADAH	Alabama Department of Archives and History, Montgomery, Alabama
Antietam NB	Antietam National Battlefield, Sharpsburg, Maryland
B&L	Robert U. Johnson and Clarence C. Buel, *Battles and Leaders of the Civil War*, 4 vols. (New York: Thomas Yoseloff, 1956)
B&O	Baltimore and Ohio Railroad
BU	Boston University, Boston, Massachusetts
Carman	Ezra A. Carman, "History of the Antietam Campaign," manuscript, Library of Congress
CCW	*U.S. Congress, Report of the Joint Committee on the Conduct of the War*
C&O	Chesapeake and Ohio Canal
CV	*Confederate Veteran*
CWTI	*Civil War Times Illustrated*
DU	Duke University, Durham, North Carolina
FSNMP	Fredericksburg-Spotsylvania National Military Park, Maryland
GBM	George B. McClellan
GDAH	Georgia Department of Archives and History, Morrow, Georgia
GNMP	Gettysburg National Military Park Library, Gettysburg, Pennsylvania
HCWRT	Harrisburg Civil War Round Table Collection, USAHEC
HFC	Harpers Ferry Center, Harpers Ferry, West Virginia
HPL	Hagerstown Public Library, Hagerstown, Maryland
HL	Henry P. Huntington Library, San Marino, California
ISL	Indiana State Library, Indianapolis, Indiana
JML	Jones Memorial Library, Lynchburg, Virginia
K	killed
LC	Library of Congress, Washington, D.C.
LV	Library of Virginia, Richmond, Virginia
M	missing and captured
MDAH	Mississippi Department of Archives and History, Jackson, Mississippi
MOLLUS	Military Order of the Loyal Legion of the United States
MP	George B. McClellan Papers, LC
MW	mortally wounded

NA	National Archives, College Park, Maryland
NC Regts	Walter Clark, ed., *Histories of Several Regiments and Battalions from North Carolina in the Great War*, 5 vols. (Wendell, NC: Broadfoot, 1982)
NCSA	North Carolina State Archives, Raleigh, North Carolina
NJHS	New Jersey Historical Society, Newark, New Jersey
NT	*National Tribune*
NYPL	New York Public Library, New York, New York
NYSA	New York State Archives, Albany, New York
OCHS	Ontario County Historical Society, Ontario, New York
OR	U.S. War Department, *The War of the Rebellion: A Compilation of the Official Records of the Union and Confederate Armies*, 70 vols. (Washington, DC: U.S. Gov't. Printing Office, 1880–1901)
OR Suppl.	Janet B. Hewett, Noah A. Trudeau, and Bruce A. Suderow, eds., *Supplement to the Official Records of the Union and Confederate Armies*, 100 vols. (Wilmington, NC: Broadfoot, 1994–2001)
OSA	Ohio State Archives, Columbus, Ohio
PCHS	Potter County Historical Society, Coudersport, Pennsylvania
PHS	Providence Historical Society, Providence, Rhode Island
PMNC	Pearce Museum at Navarro College, Corsicana, Texas
POW	prisoner of war
PWP	*Philadelphia Weekly Press*
RBHL	Rutherford B. Hayes Library, Fremont, Ohio
RG	Record Group
SCSL	South Carolina State Library, Columbia, South Carolina
SHC	Southern Historical Collection, Univ. of North Carolina, Chapel Hill, North Carolina
SHSP	*Southern Historical Society Papers*
SHSW	State Historical Society of Wisconsin, Madison, Wisconsin
THC	Eugene C. Barker Texas History Center, Univ. of Texas, Austin, Texas
UM	Univ. of Michigan, Ann Arbor, Michigan
USAHEC	U.S. Army Heritage and Education Center, Carlisle, Pennsylvania
UVA	University of Virginia, Charlottesville, Virginia
VHS	Virginia Historical Society, Richmond, Virginia
W	wounded
WRHS	Western Reserve Historical Society, Cleveland, Ohio

NOTES

Introduction

1. Annette Tapert, ed., *The Brothers' War* (New York: Times Books, 1988), 85.
2. Robert E. Lee, *The Wartime Papers of R. E. Lee*, ed. Clifford Dowdey (Boston: Little, Brown, 1961), 301.

Chapter 1. The Return of McClellan

1. George B. McClellan, *The Civil War Papers of George B. McClellan*, ed. Stephen W. Sears (New York: Ticknor & Fields, 1989), 419.
2. Ibid., 421–422.
3. Jacob D. Cox, quoted in McClellan, *Civil War Papers*, 64, 68, 70; John H. Eicher and David J. Eicher, *Civil War High Commands* (Stanford, CA: Stanford Univ. Press, 2001), 371.
4. McClellan, *Civil War Papers*, 66.
5. McClellan, *Civil War Papers*, 70, 111.
6. GBM to Mary Ellen, July 27, 1861, in McClellan, *Civil War Papers*, 70.
7. Ethan S. Rafuse, *McClellan's War: The Failure of Moderation in the Struggle for the Union* (Bloomington: Indiana Univ. Press, 2005), 74–75, 83–85; GBM memorandum to Abraham Lincoln, Aug. 2, 1861, in McClellan, *Civil War Papers*, 72.
8. GBM to Mary Ellen, Aug. 15, Aug. 16, Oct. 10, and Oct. 11, 1861, in McClellan, *Civil War Papers*, 84, 85, 106–107; Stephen W. Sears, *George B. McClellan: The Young Napoleon* (New York: Ticknor & Fields, 1988), 106.
9. GBM to Winfield Scott, Aug. 8, 1861, GBM to Mary Ellen, Aug. 19, 1861, McClellan, *Civil War Papers*, 79–80, 87.
10. GBM to Mary Ellen, Sept. 6 and Nov. 17, 1861, in McClellan, *Civil War Papers*, 95, 135; Rafuse, *McClellan's War*, 144, 162; Sears, *George B. McClellan*, 133.
11. Sears, *George B. McClellan*, 138; GBM to Buell, Jan. 13, 1861, and GBM to Edwin Stanton, Feb. 3, 1862, in McClellan, *Civil War Papers*, 151–152, 164.
12. GBM to Samuel L. M. Barlow, Jan. 18, 1862, in McClellan, *Civil War Papers*, 154; Rafuse, *McClellan's War*, 173.
13. GBM to Edwin Stanton, Feb. 3, 1862, in McClellan, *Civil War Papers*, 162–171.
14. Rafuse, *McClellan's War*, 190–191; Sears, *George B. McClellan*, 157–158.
15. George B. McClellan, *McClellan's Own Story* (New York: Charles L. Webster, 1887), 195–196.
16. Sears, *George B. McClellan*, 160–161; Rafuse, *McClellan's War*, 191–192; Bruce Catton, *Terrible Swift Sword* (New York: Doubleday, 1963), 198–199.
17. James McPherson, *Battle Cry of Freedom* (New York: Random House, 1988), 424; Sears, *George B. McClellan*, 163–164; Catton, *Terrible Swift Sword*, 203.
18. Sears, *George B. McClellan*, 165–166; McClellan, *Civil War Papers*, 207.
19. See GBM to Edwin Stanton, Mar. 13, 1862, in McClellan, *Civil War Papers*, 207; Catton, *Terrible Swift Sword*, 202.

20. GBM to Edmund Stedman, Mar. 17, 1862, and GBM to Samuel L. M. Barlow, Mar. 16, 1862, in McClellan, *Civil War Papers*, 213–214; Sears, *George B. McClellan*, 169; Rafuse, *McClellan's War*, 197.

21. Catton, *Terrible Swift Sword*, 203; GBM to Samuel L. M. Barlow, Nov. 8, 1861, in McClellan, *Civil War Papers*, 128; Frederick Douglass, *Frederick Douglass: Selected Speeches and Writings*, ed. Philip S. Foner (Chicago: Lawrence Hill Books, 1999), 477.

22. GBM to Mary Ellen, Apr. 1, 1862, in McClellan, *Civil War Papers*, 223.

23. Sears, *George B. McClellan*, 170–171; Rafuse, *McClellan's War*, 202–203; Catton, *Terrible Swift Sword*, 268–269.

24. GBM to Edwin Stanton, Feb. 3, 1862, GBM to Mary Ellen, Apr. 6, 1862, and GBM to Abraham Lincoln, Apr. 5, 1862, in McClellan, *Civil War Papers*, 167, 228, 230.

25. For the problems of supplying the army, see William J. Miller, "'Scarcely Any Parallel in History': Logistics, Friction, and McClellan's Strategy for the Peninsula Campaign," in William J. Miller, ed., *The Peninsula Campaign of 1862*, 2 vols. (Campbell, CA: Savas Woodbury, 1995), 2:129–190; Stephen W. Sears, *Gates of Richmond: The Peninsula Campaign* (New York: Ticknor & Fields, 1992), 41, 43, 45.

26. Sears, *Gates of Richmond*, 45; GBM to Edwin Stanton, Apr. 11, 1862, in McClellan, *Civil War Papers*, 234.

27. Sears, *Gates of Richmond*, 43, 60–61; Edwin C. Fishel, "Pinkerton and McClellan: Who Deceived Whom?" *Civil War History* 34, no. 2 (1988): 139–140.

28. Sears, *Gates of Richmond*, 61; GBM to Abraham Lincoln, Apr. 23, 1862, GBM to Edwin Stanton, May 4, 1862, and GBM to Mary Ellen, May 8, 1862, in McClellan, *Civil War Papers*, 247, 254, 260.

29. Peter Michie, *General McClellan* (New York: D. Appleton, 1901), 257–274; GBM to Edwin Stanton, May 5, 1862, in McClellan, *Civil War Papers*, 256.

30. *OR* [Ser. 1,] [vol.] 11, [pt.] 1:614; Michie, *General McClellan*, 274–275.

31. GBM to Edwin Stanton, May 10, 1862, in McClellan, *Civil War Papers*, 260–261.

32. *B&L*, 2:218–219; GBM to Abraham Lincoln, Apr. 20, 1862, in McClellan, *Civil War Papers*, 244–245.

33. GBM to Ambrose Burnside, May 21, 1862, and GBM to Edwin Stanton, June 15, 1862, in McClellan, *Civil War Papers*, 269, 300.

34. GBM to Edwin Stanton, June 2, 1862, GBM to Abraham Lincoln, June 4, 1862, and GBM to Edwin Stanton, June 7, 1862, in McClellan, *Civil War Papers*, 286, 288, 291.

35. GBM to Mary Ellen, June 10, 1862, GBM to Abraham Lincoln, June 20, 1862, and GBM to Mary Ellen, June 22, 1862, in McClellan, *Civil War Papers*, 294, 304–305; Robert E. Lee to George W. Randolph, June 11, 1862, in Lee, *Wartime Papers*, 184.

36. Sears, *Gates of Richmond*, 189.

37. GBM to Edwin Stanton, June 25, 1862, in McClellan, *Civil War Papers*, 309–310; GBM to Edwin Stanton, June 25, 1862, in *OR* 12, 2:254.

38. For an example of the orders the corps commanders south of the Chickahominy received, see GBM to Samuel P. Heintzelman, June 25, 1862, in *OR* 12, 2:255; GBM to Randolph Marcy, June 25, 1862, in McClellan, *Civil War Papers*, 311.

39. GBM to Edwin Stanton, June 26, 1862, in McClellan, *Civil War Papers*, 317; Sears, *Gates of Richmond*, 210; McClellan, *McClellan's Own Story*, 415; Fitz John Porter, "Hanover Court House and Gaines' Mill," in *B&L*, 2:336.

40. Sears, *Gates of Richmond*, 203, 211, 215–216.

41. Joseph Harsh, *Confederate Tide Rising* (Kent, OH: Kent State Univ. Press, 1998), 91; GBM to Porter, June 27, 1862, in McClellan, *Civil War Papers*, 321; Sears, *Gates of Richmond*, 249.

42. GBM to Edwin Stanton, June 28, 1862, in McClellan, *Civil War Papers*, 322–323; Sears, *Gates of Richmond*, 251.

43. Michie, *General McClellan*, 350.

44. Ibid., 350–352; McClellan, *McClellan's Own Story*, 426.

45. Michie, *General McClellan*, 354; Sears, *Gates of Richmond*, 280–281; John T. Hubbell, "The Seven Days of George Brinton McClellan," in Gary W. Gallagher, ed., *The Richmond Campaign of 1862* (Chapel Hill: Univ. of North Carolina Press, 2000), 37.

46. GBM to John A. Dix, July 1, 1862, in McClellan, *Civil War Papers*, 329; Sears, *Gates of Richmond*, 309; Rafuse, *McClellan's War*, 228–229. The Confederates concentrated their largest army of the war to oppose McClellan. Joseph Harsh estimates the Confederate present for duty at 101,205 men, not counting the garrisons of Richmond and Petersburg (*Confederate Tide Rising*, 180–181). The June 20, 1863, returns record the Army of the Potomac's present for duty at 105,445 men, not including the troops at Fortress Monroe (*OR* 11, 3:238). The Federals had the edge in manpower, but it was small enough to be immaterial.

47. McClellan, *Civil War Papers*, 329; Philip Kearny, *Letters from the Peninsula: The Civil War Letters of General Philip Kearny*, ed. William B. Styple (Kearny, NJ: Belle Grove, 1988), 125, 128; Francis C. Barlow, *"Fear Was Not in Him": The Civil War Letters of Major General Francis C. Barlow*, ed. Christian G. Samito (New York: Fordham Univ. Press, 2004), 96–97, 99.

48. McClellan, *Civil War Papers*, 312, 323, 324–325.

49. Gideon Welles, *Diary of Gideon Welles*, 3 vols. (Boston: Houghton Mifflin, 1909–1911), 1:107.

50. GBM to Edwin Stanton, July 3, 1862, GBM to Mary Ellen, July 8, 1862, and GBM to Abraham Lincoln, July 7, 1862, in McClellan, *Civil War Papers*, 333, 344–345, 346; *OR* 11, 1:72–73; David Donald, *Lincoln* (New York: Simon & Schuster, 1995), 360.

51. Donald, *Lincoln*, 360; GBM to Mary Ellen, July 9, 1862, in McClellan, *Civil War Papers*, 348.

52. Donald, *Lincoln*, 361; GBM to Mary Ellen, July 18 and July 20, 1862, in McClellan, *Civil War Papers*, 364, 368.

53. Bruce Tap, *Over Lincoln's Shoulder: The Committee on the Conduct of the War* (Lawrence: Univ. Press of Kansas, 1998), 127; GBM to John Pope, July 7, 1862, in McClellan, *Civil War Papers*, 342–343.

54. John J. Hennessey, *Return to Bull Run: The Campaign and Battle of Second Manassas* (New York: Simon & Shuster, 1993), 9, 12–13; GBM to Mary Ellen, July 22, 1862, in McClellan, *Civil War Papers*, 368.

55. William Seward, quoted in Donald, *Lincoln*, 366. For a full discussion of Lincoln's decision to issue the Emancipation Proclamation, see Donald, *Lincoln*, 362–366, and Alan Guelzo, *Lincoln's Emancipation Proclamation* (New York: Simon & Shuster, 2004).

56. Rafuse, *McClellan's War*, 243; Eicher and Eicher, *Civil War High Commands*, 274; Catton, *Terrible Swift Sword*, 88, 306.

57. *OR* 11, 2:337–338; Rafuse, *McClellan's War*, 245; Sears, *George B. McClellan*, 239–240.

58. GBM to Henry W. Halleck, July 26, 1862, GBM to Mary Ellen, July 27 and July 29, 1862, and GBM to Samuel L. M. Barlow, July 30, 1862, in McClellan, *Civil War Papers*, 372, 374, 375, 377.

59. *OR* 11, 1:76, 80–81; Sears, *George B. McClellan*, 244; GBM to Henry W. Halleck, Aug. 4, 1862, and GBM to Joseph Hooker, Aug. 6, 1862, in McClellan, *Civil War Papers*, 383–384, 386–387.

60. *OR* 11, 1:359–360; GBM to Mary Ellen, Aug. 10, 1862, in McClellan, *Civil War Papers*, 389–390.

61. *OR* 11, 1:90–91.

62. Catton, *Terrible Swift Sword*, 391; Hennessey, *Return to Bull Run*, 30–31.

63. *OR* 11, 1:92; GBM to Mary Ellen, Aug. 21 and Aug. 23, 1862, in McClellan, *Civil War Papers*, 397, 399–400.

64. *OR* 11, 1:93–94.

65. For a detailed analysis of these operations, see Hennessy, *Return to Bull Run*.

66. McClellan, *Civil War Papers*, 406, 407; *OR* 11, 1:95; *OR* 12, 3:689–690; *OR* 11, 1:94.

67. McClellan, *Civil War Papers*, 409.

68. *OR* 12, 3:740; GBM to Mary Ellen, Aug. 28, 1862, in McClellan, *Civil War Papers*, 411. That McClellan left the meeting with this understanding is evident from his 4:10 p.m. dispatch to Halleck on the 28th. See McClellan, *Civil War Papers*, 412.

69. *OR* 12, 3:707–710.

70. McClellan, *Civil War Papers*, 416, 423–424; Sears, *George B. McClellan*, 254.

71. *OR* 12, 3:722, 723; McClellan, *Civil War Papers*, 419, 422, 423; McClellan, *McClellan's Own Story*, 520; Sears, *George B. McClellan*, 257.

72. *OR* 12, 3:741; *OR* 2:79, 80; McClellan, *McClellan's Own Story*, 525; McClellan, *Civil War Papers*, 425.

73. McClellan, *Civil War Papers*, 426, 428; Fitz John Porter to GBM, Aug. 30, 1862, in *OR* 12, 3:768–769; McClellan, *McClellan's Own Story*, 534.

74. *OR* 12, 2:83; *OR* 19, 1:37; Abraham Lincoln, quoted in Guelzo, *Lincoln's Emancipation Proclamation*, 163.

75. *OR* 19, 1:37.

76. McClellan, *McClellan's Own Story*, 535; *OR* 19, 1:37.

77. McClellan, *Civil War Papers*, 400, 428; *OR* 19, 1:37.

78. *OR* 12, 3:106; Donald, *Lincoln*, 372; Welles, *Diary of Gideon Welles*, 104–105; Abraham Lincoln, *The Collected Works of Abraham Lincoln*, ed. Roy P. Basler, 9 vols. (New Brunswick, NJ: Rutgers Univ. Press, 1953–1955), 5:404n1.

79. McClellan, *McClellan's Own Story*, 536.

80. Charles Shiels Wainwright, *A Diary of Battle: The Personal Journals of Colonel Charles S. Wainwright*, ed. Allan Nevins (Gettysburg, PA: Stan Clark Military Books, 1962), 90.

81. Rutherford B. Hayes, *Diary and Letters of Rutherford B. Hayes*, ed. Charles R. Williams, 5 vols. (Columbus: Ohio Archaeological and Historical Society, 1922–1926), 2:341.

82. Alpheus S. Williams, *From the Cannon's Mouth: The Civil War Letters of General Alpheus S. Williams*, ed. Milo M. Quaife (Detroit: Wayne State Univ. Press, 1959), 111; Edward Bragg to My Dear Wife, Sept. 13, 1862, Edward Bragg Papers, SHSW; "General Hooker's Opinion of McClellan . . . Hitherto Unpublished," *NT*, Nov. 14, 1907; Gouverneur Warren, quoted in Hennessy, *Return to Bull Run*, 471.

83. McClellan, *McClellan's Own Story*, 537; Jacob D. Cox, *Military Reminiscences of the Civil War*, 2 vols. (New York: Charles Scribner's Sons, 1900), 1:243.

84. Cox, *Military Reminiscences*, 1:243.

85. Ibid., 245. For McClellan's fanciful and largely inaccurate account of this meeting, see McClellan, *McClellan's Own Story*, 537. Also see Sears, *George B. McClellan*, 262, for Cox's comments on McClellan's account. For additional observations, see Cox, *Military Reminiscences*, 1:246.

86. Hayes, *Diary and Letters*, 2:340–341; "George Kimball to the editors of *Century Magazine*, Nov. 1887," in *B&L*, 2:550–551n; "William H. Powell to the *Century* [*Magazine*], Mar. 12, 1885," in *B&L*, 2:489–490n.

Chapter 2. The Army of Northern Virginia

1. J. Cutler Andrews, *The South Reports the Civil War* (Princeton, NJ: Princeton Univ. Press, 1970), 118.

2. Sears, *George B. McClellan*, 180.

3. Edward P. Alexander, *Fighting for the Confederacy: The Personal Recollections of General Edward Porter Alexander*, ed. Gary W. Gallagher (Chapel Hill: Univ. of North Carolina Press, 1989), 91.

4. *OR* 19, 2:590–592.

5. *OR* 19, 2:593; Frederick Maurice, *Lee's Aide-de-Camp* (Lincoln: Univ. of Nebraska Press, 2000), 147.

6. Maurice, *Lee's Aide-de-Camp*, 145–146; *OR* 19, 1:144.

7. Robert E. Lee to Jefferson Davis, Sept. 12, 1862, in *OR* 19, 2:592, 604–605. That Lee intended to enter Pennsylvania is clear from his Sept. 4 dispatch to Davis, in which he wrote: "Should the results of the expedition justify it, I intend to enter Pennsylvania, unless you should deem it unadvisable upon political or other grounds." For the pertinent section of Lee's campaign report, see *OR* 19, 1:145.

8. *OR* 19, 2:591; *OR* 19, 1:144; Edward P. Alexander, *Military Memoirs of a Confederate* (New York: Charles Scribner's Sons, 1907), 222.

9. *OR* 19, 2:600.

10. James Longstreet, *From Manassas to Appomattox* (Bloomington: Indiana Univ. Press, 1960), 201–202; *OR* 19, 2:592, 596; James Longstreet, "The Invasion of Maryland," in *B&L*, 2:663.

11. *OR* 19, 2:590, 597.

12. John H. Chamberlayne, *Ham Chamberlayne—Virginian: Letters and Papers of an Artillery Officer in the War for Southern Independence, 1861–1865* (Richmond: Dietz, 1932), 102; Thomas Elder to wife, Sept. 4, 1862, Thomas Elder Papers, VHS.

13. Thomas Elder to wife, Sept. 4, 1862, Elder Papers, VHS; William Dorsey Pender, *The General to His Lady: The Civil War Letters of William Dorsey Pender to Fanny Pender*, ed. William H. Hassler (Chapel Hill: Univ. of North Carolina Press, 1962), 173.

14. D. H. Hill, "Lee Attacks North of the Chickahominy," in *B&L*, 2:352.

15. Lafayette McLaws to wife, Sept. 4, 1862, Lafayette McLaws Papers, SHC; Jubal A. Early, *War Memoirs: Autobiographical Sketch and Narrative of the War between the States* (Philadelphia: Lippincott, 1912), 134.

16. Pender, *General to His Lady*, 179; Maurice, *Lee's Aide-De-Camp*, 33–34; *OR* 19, 2:622; *OR* 11, 3:645; *OR* 19, 1:860–861; Cadmus Wilcox to John, Sept. 26, 1862, Cadmus Wilcox Papers, LC, quoted in Joseph T. Glatthaar, *General Lee's Army* (New York: Free Press, 2008), 180.

17. Pender, *General to His Lady*, 175.

18. *OR* 12, 3:928; *OR* 19, 2:592.

19. *OR* 12, 3:945.

20. *OR* 19, 1:1019.

21. William A. Smith, *The Anson Guards, Company C, Fourteenth Regiment, North Carolina Volunteers, 1861–1865* (Wendell, NC: Broadfoot, 1978), 147.

22. D. H. Hill's division reported its strength on July 20 at 9,500, yet he only carried about 6,000 into action on Sept. 14 at South Mountain, which reflects the significant loss from straggling and illness. Parker wrote on Sept. 9 that "the stragglers are joining us slowly," indicating that many stragglers from the march from Hanover Court House did not rejoin their units before the army departed from Frederick on Sept. 10. See Michael W. Taylor, ed., *To Drive the Enemy from Southern Soil: The Letters of Col. Francis Marion Parker and the History of the 30th Regiment North Carolina Troops* (Dayton, OH: Morningside Press, 1998), 211. Also see Horace Montgomery, *Howell Cobb's Confederate Career* (Tuscaloosa, AL: Confederate, 1959), 68; Joseph Harsh, *Sounding the Shallows: A Confederate Companion for the Maryland Campaign of 1862* (Kent, OH: Kent State Univ. Press, 2000), 142.

23. According to the reckoning of Capt. William H. S. Burgwyn of the 35th NC, the division marched 59 miles in 5 days, a respectable average of nearly 12 miles a day. See William H. S. Burgwyn, *A Captain's War: The Letter and Diaries of William H. S. Burgwyn, 1861–1865*, ed. Herbert N. Schiller (Shippensburg, PA: White Mane, 1994), 15–16.

24. Constantine Hege to father, Sept. 13, 1862, Book 11, Lewis Leigh Collection, USAHEC; E. M. Dugand to Ezra A. Carman, Apr. 1892, Ezra A. Carman Papers, NYPL. Among the North Carolina regiments who recorded that they received conscripts, the following gave the number received: 1st NC—500, 3rd NC—400, 5th NC—400, 7th NC—130, 15th NC—250, 18th NC—"large number," 23rd NC—"some." All strengths are from *NC Regts*. The

3rd SC reported that they received 215 conscripts. See Mac Wyckoff, *A History of the 3rd South Carolina Infantry, 1861–1865* (Fredericksburg, VA: Sgt. Kirkland's Museum & Historical Society, 1995), 63.

25. The strength of the Army of Northern Virginia on Sept. 2 is primarily drawn from John Owen Allen, "The Strengths of the Union and Confederate Forces at Second Manassas," master's thesis, George Mason Univ., 1993. Allen's strength figures and an analysis of his methodology are available at two web pages on TOCWOC—A Civil War Blog, www.brettschulte.net/CWBlog/2005/12/15/counting-heads-looking-at-civil-war-troop-numbers-for-wargaming/ [accessed Mar. 2010], and www.brettschulte.net/CWBlog/regimental-level-orders-of-battle/regimental-level-orders-of-battle-second-bull-run-oob/ [accessed Mar. 2010]. Allen's divisional strength figures can be found in Harsh, *Sounding the Shallows*, 139, although here Allen's strength figures were rounded down or, in the case of the reserve artillery, rounded up. Also see Francis Palfrey, *The Antietam and Fredericksburg* (New York: C. Scribner's Sons, 1882), 64–65.

26. Walter H. Taylor, *Lee's Adjutant: The Wartime Letters of Colonel Walter Herron Taylor, 1862–1865*, ed. R. Lockwood Tower (Columbia: Univ. of South Carolina Press, 1995), 68, 123.

27. Ibid., 186.

28. Eicher and Eicher, *Civil War High Commands*, 352; Robert E. L. Krick, *Staff Officers in Gray* (Chapel Hill: Univ. of North Carolina Press, 2003), 216, 279; J. Boone Bartholomees, *Buff Facings and Gilt Buttons: Staff and Headquarters Operations in the Army of Northern Virginia, 1861–1865* (Columbia: Univ. of South Carolina Press, 1998), 17–33. The Adjutant General's Department was principally responsible for administration, personnel management, and strength returns, although there were many other administrative details that fell under

their responsibilities, if necessary. The Adjutant General of the Confederate Army's headquarters was in Richmond. Any officers from this office in the field, such as Chilton or Mason, were therefore AAGs, since there was only one adjutant general.

29. Krick, *Staff Officers in Gray*, 214, 283, 292–293; Tower, *Lee's Adjutant*, 42–44.

30. Chamberlayne, *Letters and Papers*, 134; G. Moxley Sorrel, *Recollections of a Confederate Staff Officer* (New York: Neale, 1905), 128; Peter S. Carmichael, "We Don't Know What on Earth to Do With Him," in Gary W. Gallagher, ed., *The Antietam Campaign* (Chapel Hill: Univ. of North Carolina Press, 1999), 259. S. D. Lee's and Richardson's battalions were assigned to Longstreet. Cutts's battalion was attached to D. H. Hill after the army left Frederick on Sept. 10.

31. Alexander, *Fighting for the Confederacy*, 60, 115.

32. Ibid., 60, 122; Jennings C. Wise, *The Long Arm of Lee: The History of the Artillery of the Army of Northern Virginia* (New York: Oxford Univ. Press, 1959), 288.

33. "Surgeons of the Confederacy: Dr. Hunter Holmes McGuire, of Virginia," *CV* 34 (Apr. 1926), 141.

34. *OR* 11, 2:501–502; *OR* 12, 3:928. Guild did not accompany the army into Maryland; he remained at Manassas to supervise the removal and care of the wounded from that battle. See *OR* 19, 2:605–606.

35. Jay Luvaas and Harold W. Nelson, *The U.S. Army War College Guide to the Battle of Antietam* (Lawrence: Univ. Press of Kansas, 1996), 265, 270; Thomas Elder to wife, Sept. 4, 1862, Elder Papers, VHS; Alexander Hunter, "The Battle of Antietam," *SHSP* 31 (1903), 40; Alexander, *Fighting for the Confederacy*, 141–142.

36. Dr. Lewis Steiner, a U.S. Sanitary Commission inspector, estimated that he observed some 3,000 blacks accompanying the Army of Northern Virginia when it left Frederick on Sept. 10. See Lewis Steiner, "Report During the Rebel Occupation of Frederick, Md.," in

Richard B. Harwell, ed., *The Union Reader* (New York: Longmans, Green, 1958), 168–169.

37. Alexander, *Military Memoirs*, 378; Henry K. Douglas, *I Rode with Stonewall* (Chapel Hill: Univ. of North Carolina Press, 1940), 254; Pender, *General to his Lady*, 171; Mary B. Chesnut, *A Dairy From Dixie* (New Haven, CT: Yale Univ. Press, 1981), 499–500.

38. Douglas S. Freeman, *Lee's Lieutenants*, 3 vols. (New York: Charles Scribner's Sons, 1970), 1:393; Thomas Munford to John C. Ropes, Dec. 7, 1897, quoted in James I. Robertson, *Stonewall Jackson: The Man, the Soldier, the Legend* (New York: MacMillan, 1997), 498.

39. Robertson, *Stonewall Jackson*, 525; Richard B. Garnett to Samuel B. Cooper, June 20, 1862, quoted in Robert K. Krick, *The Smoothbore Volley that Doomed the Confederacy* (Baton Rouge: Louisiana State Univ. Press, 2002), 49, 56.

40. Sorrel, *Recollections*, 26; Thomas J. Goree, *Longstreet's Aide: The Civil War Letters of Major Thomas J. Goree*, ed. Thomas W. Cutrer (Charlottesville: Univ. Press of Virginia, 1995), 60.

41. James Longstreet to Joseph E. Johnston, Oct. 5, 1862, quoted in Robert K. Krick, "James Longstreet and the Second Day at Gettysburg," in Gary W. Gallagher, ed., *Three Days at Gettysburg: Essays on Union and Confederate Leadership* (Kent, OH: Kent Univ. Press, 1999), 150.

42. *OR* 19, 2:643; Freeman, *Lee's Lieutenants*, 1:664–668.

43. James I. Robertson, *General A. P. Hill: The Story of a Confederate Warrior* (New York: Random House, 1987), 110.

44. Eicher and Eicher, *Civil War High Commands*, 341; Glatthaar, *General Lee's Army*, 135; Ezra Warner, *Generals in Gray* (Baton Rouge: Louisiana State Univ. Press, 1959), 175. The Battle of Brawner's Farm, on Aug. 28, 1862, is also known as the Battle of Gainesville.

45. Eicher and Eicher, *Civil War High Commands*, 602; Richard N. Current, ed., *Encyclopedia of the Confederacy*, 4 vols. (New York: Simon & Shuster, 1993), 2:866.

46. Richard McMurray, *John Bell Hood and the War for Southern Independence* (Lexington: Univ. Press of Kentucky, 1982), 49.

47. Sorrel, *Recollections*, 127; John C. Haskell, *The Haskell Memoirs*, ed. Gilbert E. Govan and James W. Livingood (New York: G. P. Putnam's Sons, 1960), 16.

48. Freeman, *Lee's Lieutenants*, 2:147.

49. Current, *Encyclopedia of the Confederacy*, 35; Micah Jenkins to wife, June 22, 1862, quoted in Glatthaar, *General Lee's Army*, 343; Sorrel, *Recollections*, 128. In his original, unpublished after-action report of Gettysburg, Cadmus Wilcox criticized Anderson for being largely ignorant of the battle his division was fighting. See Cadmus Wilcox report, July 16, 1863, Wilcox Papers, VHS.

50. Sorrel, *Recollections*, 150; Eicher and Eicher, *Civil War High Commands*, 323–324; Current, *Encyclopedia of the Confederacy*, 863–864.

51. In recalling Hill's service in Mexico, Joseph Johnston wrote to Hill after the Civil War: "You know among the young officers in Mexico you were considered to be the most fearless." See Alphonso C. Avery, "Life and Character of Lt. General D. H. Hill," *SHSP* 21 (1893), 15; Sorrel, *Recollections*, 54.

52. Jeremy F. Gilmer to My dear Loulie, Aug. 17, 1862, quoted in Robert K. Krick, "Sharpsburg's Bloody Lane," in Gallagher, *Antietam Campaign*, 225; Lee, *Wartime Papers*, 258–259; Haskell, *Haskell Memoirs*, 40: Sorrel, *Recollections*, 54.

53. Sorrel, *Recollections*, 127. Also see Eicher and Eicher, *Civil War High Commands*, 381.

54. Sorrel, *Recollections*, 129; Current, *Encyclopedia of the Confederacy*, 1677.

55. Longstreet, *From Manassas to Appomattox*, 573.

56. Lee, *Wartime Papers*, 218–220; Alexander, *Fighting for the Confederacy*, 236.

57. Robert L. Dabney, *Life and Campaigns of Lieut.-Gen. Thomas J. Jackson* (New York: Blelock, 1866), 301.

58. Henry R. Berkeley, *Four Years in the Confederate Artillery*, ed. William H. Runge (Chapel Hill: Univ. of North Carolina Press, 1961), 22, quoted in Glatthaar, *General Lee's Army*, 180.

59. Maurice, *Lee's Aide-de-Camp*, 175.

60. *OR* 19, 2:597.

61. Lewis Steiner, in J. Cutler Andrews, *The North Reports the Civil War* (Pittsburgh: Univ. of Pittsburgh Press, 1985), 166–167; George F. Noyes, *The Bivouac and the Battlefield* (New York: Harper & Bros., 1864), 161.

62. *CCW*, 38th Cong., 2nd Sess., 3 vols. (Washington, DC: Gov't. Printing Office, 1865) 1:113.

63. Douglas, *I Rode with Stonewall*, 142.

64. Joseph G. Bilby, *Civil War Firearms* (Conshohocken, PA: Combined Books, 1996), 41–86.

65. Josiah Gorgas, "Confederate Ordnance During the War," *SHSP* 12 (Jan.–Feb. 1884), 375–376; William Allan, "Reminiscences of Field Ordnance Service," *SHSP* 14 (1886), 137–140; Alexander, *Military Memoirs*, 223. Some Confederate officers, as well as some Federal officers, favored the smoothbore over the rifle. To be effective, a soldier required more training with a rifle, for at longer ranges he had to adjust his sights to hit his target. An error caused the bullet to sail over the enemies' heads or drop in front of them. Since there was little target practice afforded recruits early in the war, it is not surprising that they were less effective with rifles than with smoothbores. Once soldiers and their officers became familiar with the rifle-musket and the tactics of its effective use, they had a greater appreciation of its superiority over the smoothbore.

66. David E. Johnston, *The Story of a Confederate Boy* (Ann Arbor, MI: Univ. Microfilms, 1972), 137.

67. Hunter, "Battle of Antietam," 40.

68. Harsh, *Sounding the Shallows*, 102–103; Dabney, *Thomas J. Jackson*, 516–518. Obviously not all Confederate troops were more highly motivated than Union troops; there were Federal units that possessed equal élan and motivation.

69. E[dward] P. Alexander, "Confederate Artillery Service," *SHSP* 11 (Feb.–Mar. 1883), 99; Joseph M. Hanson, "Report on the Deployment of Artillery at Antietam," Antietam NB. Also see Alexander, *Fighting for the Confederacy*, 60; Curt Johnson and Richard C. Anderson, *Artillery Hell: The Employment of Artillery at Antietam* (College Station: Texas A&M Univ. Press, 1995), 44.

70. Alexander, "Confederate Artillery Service," 105. Arriving at precise numbers of guns in the Army of Northern Virginia in Sept. is a frustrating exercise. Pendleton's report of artillery with the army in Sept. leaves out 23 batteries that were either disbanded or consolidated after Sharpsburg. See *OR* 19, 1:835–836. The most thorough modern analysis of the artillery at Sharpsburg, Johnson and Anderson's *Artillery Hell*, fills in many of the gaps in the data, but not all.

71. For the strength of the Confederate States of America's artillery, see Hanson, "Report," Antietam NB. Also see *OR* 19, 1:835–837; Johnson and Anderson, *Artillery Hell*, 85–108.

72. Alexander, "Confederate Artillery Service," 106–108. Also see William Le Roy Broun, "The Red Artillery," *SHSP* 26 (1898), 365–375.

73. Alexander, "Confederate Artillery Service," 105.

74. Ibid., 99.

75. Ibid, 99–100; *OR* 11, 2:628.

76. *OR* 11, 2:537.

77. Alexander, "Confederate Artillery Service," 101–102; *OR* 11, 2:537.

78. Wise, *Long Arm of Lee*, 279–287. Also see *OR* 19, 1:835–836.

79. *OR* 19, 2:592. For an imperfect list of those batteries left behind in this reorganization, see *OR* 19, 1:805–808.

80. Stuart's cavalry mustered 5,277 officers and enlisted men present for duty on July 20, 1862. The return for Oct. 10 gives 5,761. See *OR* 11, 3:645; *OR* 19, 2:660. The study of Confederate

strength in Allen's master's thesis gives Stuart's cavalry as 5,664 present for duty immediately after Second Manassas. See Harsh, *Sounding the Shallows*, 139.

81. W. W. Blackford, *War Years with Jeb Stuart* (New York: Charles Scribner's Sons, 1945), 229.

82. Ibid., 246–247; George Eggleston, *A Rebel's Recollections* (Bloomington: Indiana Univ. Press, 1959), 77; John Lamb, "The Confederate Cavalry," *SHSP* 26 (1898), 261, 359. Also see H[enry] B. McClellan, *The Life and Campaigns of Major-General J. E. B. Stuart, Commander of the Cavalry of the Army of Northern Virginia* (Edison, NJ: Blue and Gray Press, 1993), 257–258.

83. Lamb, "Confederate Cavalry," 261.

84. Ibid. A good part of at least two of Munford's regiments evidently carried rifle-muskets. In a letter to Jackson in Mar. 1863, Munford indicated his troopers were armed only with pistols, but he wrote to Ezra Carman years later that his men carried rifles. See *OR* 19, 1:827; Thomas Munford to Ezra A. Carman, Dec. 19, 1894, Antietam Studies, NA. Possibly only some of Munford's companies carried rifles, but the fight they put up at Crampton's Gap indicates that many had rifles, along with their pistols.

85. R. H. Jones to wife, Sept. 5, 1862, R. H. Jones Papers, GDAH, quoted in Glatthaar, *General Lee's Army*, 163; William G. Morris to Dear Companion & Famely, Sept. 8, 1862, William G. Morris Papers, SHC; Thomas Elder to wife, Sept. 4, 1862, Elder Papers, VHS.

Chapter 3. The Army of Northern Virginia Enters Maryland

1. Early, *War Memoirs*, 134; Michael Shuler diary, LC; Jedediah Hotchkiss, *Confederate Military History*, 335–336; *OR* 19, 1:814. That Hill and McLaws marched to Leesburg on the 3rd is determined from Lafayette McLaws to wife, Sept. 4, 1862, McLaws Papers, SHC, and Jedediah Hotchkiss diary, LC. Also see Chamberlayne, *Letters and Papers*, 102. Colquitt's and Ripley's brigades were still detached from Hill and marched with the main body of the army to Dranesville on Sept. 3. See Folsom, *Heroes and Martyrs*, 55; Capt. John H. Harris diary (44th GA), GNMP.

2. William B. Howard diary, William Wombles Papers, NCSA; Hotchkiss diary, LC; George Wise, *History of the Seventeenth Virginia Infantry* (Baltimore: Kelly, Piet, 1870), 107; Dr. James R. Boulware diary (Jenkins's Brigade), LV. Longstreet's command marched about 15 miles, and Jackson's about 12 miles.

3. Lafayette McLaws to wife, Sept. 4, 1862, McLaws Papers, SHC; William H. Hill diary (13th MS), MDAH.

4. *OR* 19, 1:1019. Hill's report contains some errors. G. B. Anderson's brigade did not march until Sept. 5. The only unit that left on the 4th was Rodes's brigade. It is possible that Lee's orders to Hill were sent on the 2nd, for during the march on the 3rd, John B. Gordon announced to his regiment that they would enter Maryland the next day. See *Montgomery Weekly Advertiser*, Sept. 19, 1862.

5. *OR* 19, 1:828.

6. John Worsham, *One of Jackson's Foot Cavalry* (New York: Neale, 1912), 82; Calvin Leach diary (3rd NC), SHC.

7. Shep Pryor to Penelope, Sept. 5, 1862, Shepard Green Pryor Letters, United Daughters of the Confederacy typescripts, vol. 3, GDAH.

8. Jedediah Hotchkiss, *Make Me a Map of the Valley: The Civil War Journal of Stonewall Jackson's Topographer*, ed. Archie P. McDonald (Dallas: Southern Methodist Univ. Press, 1973), 78; James J. Kirkpatrick diary (16th MS), Eugene C. Barker Texas History Center, THC; Alexander Hunter, "A High Private's Account of the Battle of Sharpsburg," *SHSP* 12 (1884), 507.

9. Kirkpatrick diary, THC.

10. Robertson, *Stonewall Jackson*, 585. Robertson's account, citing a variety of primary sources, corrects the often cited but inaccurate account of this incident by Henry Kyd Douglas. For Douglas's account, see Douglas, *I Rode with Stonewall*, 146.

11. Douglas, *I Rode with Stonewall*, 146.

12. William A. Heirs to Darling Cousin Wes, Sept. 7, 1862, *CWTI* Collection, USAHEC; *Mobile Register and Advertiser*, Sept. 28, 1862. This edition of the *Advertiser* contained two letters, written on Sept. 8 and 9 by members of Rodes's brigade, describing the crossing in detail. Hill's report that he ordered G. B. Anderson's brigade to fire on trains opposite Berlin and sent two brigades to Cheek's Ford simply cannot be true. Accounts from Anderson's and Garland's brigades both state that they did not march until Sept. 5. See Rev. A. D. Betts, *Experience of a Confederate Chaplain, 1861–1864* (n.p., n.d.), 16, Gregory Coco Collection, GNMP; *NC Regts*, 2:217. The "Record of Events of Company E, 1st Maryland Potomac Home Brigade" states that this detachment resisted Rodes's men "until their ammunition ran out." Confederate sources indicate that the detachment made no more than a token resistance. See *OR Suppl.* 26:805.

13. *Mobile Register and Advertiser*, Sept. 28, 1862; Carman, chap. 3, 126; Otis Smith Reminiscences, Thach Papers, SHC.

14. *OR* 19, 1:1019; *OR* 19, 2:180–181.

15. Draughton S. Haynes, *Field Diary of a Confederate Soldier* (Darien, GA: Ashantilly Press, 1963), 15; Kirkpatrick diary, THC.

16. *OR* 19, 1:828.

17. Ibid., 822; Ulysses R. Brooks, ed., *Stories of the Confederacy* (Columbia, SC: State, 1912), 77. For Fitz Lee's position, see William R. Carter, *Sabres, Saddles, and Spurs*, ed. Walbrook D. Swank (Shippensburg, PA: Burd Street Press, 1998), 12.

18. Robertson, *Stonewall Jackson*, 581, 586; *OR* 19, 2:591–592. For the expression of Davis's confidence in Lee, see *OR* 11, 1:945.

19. *OR* 19, 2:592–593.

20. Harsh, *Sounding the Shallows*, 155–156; *OR* 19, 1:829, 836; *OR* 2:647–652; Berkeley, *Confederate Artillery*, 27.

21. Wise, *Seventeenth Virginia Infantry*, 108; Johnston, *Confederate Boy*, 131; letter of Alex Erwin to Brother, Sept. 15, 1862, published in the *Southern Watchman* (Athens, GA) on Oct. 1, 1862, and edited by Kurt D. Graham in *Military Images* 23, no. 2 (Sept./Oct. 2001), 36; H. C. Kendrick to parents, Sept. 15, 1862, H. C. Kendrick Papers, SHC. Charles E. DeNoon, an officer in the 41st VA, wrote on Sept. 9 from Rapidan Station that there were at least 5,000 men on the road to join the army. Many of these men were no doubt recovered sick or wounded coming up from Richmond, but some may have been stragglers and sick left behind from Manassas to Leesburg. See Charles E. DeNoon, *Charlie's Letters: The Correspondence of Charles E. DeNoon*, ed. Richard T. Couture (Farmville, VA: R. T. Couture, 1982), 83.

22. Bradley T. Johnson, "The Maryland Campaign," *SHSP* 12 (1884), 504. See Harsh, *Sounding the Shallows*, 116–124, for agricultural statistics from the 1860 census.

23. The movements for the brigades of D. H. Hill's division are drawn from Betts, *Experience of a Confederate Chaplain*, and *NC Regts*, 2:217. Further evidence that the Confederates believed they would encounter resistance is derived from Jackson's Sept. 5 dispatches to D. H. Hill and Lawrence Branch. In both messages Jackson mentions the possibility of encountering opposition. These dispatches are in *OR* 19, 2:593–594.

24. *OR* 19, 2:592.

25. Ibid.

26. Harsh, *Sounding the Shallows*, 7; Hotchkiss, *Make Me a Map*, 78. Capt. Michael Shuler of the 33rd VA recorded in his diary only that they left "very early." See Shuler diary, LC.

27. Worsham, *One of Jackson's Foot Cavalry*, 82; Pryor Letters, vol. 3, 226, GDAH; Hotchkiss,

Make Me a Map, 78; Al P. Kindberg, ed., *A Soldier from Valley Furnace* (Clairsville, OH: R&M's Home Office, 1997), 47.

28. Early, *War Memoirs*, 134; *OR* 19, 2:593; Thomas D. Boone, *History of Company F, 1st North Carolina Infantry*, 36, GNMP. Some rearguard ompanies of the 3rd NC did not cross the Potomac until Sept. 6. See Leach diary, SHC.

29. Early, *War Memoirs*, 134; Hotchkiss, *Make Me a Map*, 78.

30. *OR* 19, 2:593.

31. D. H. Hill, "The Lost Dispatch," *Land That We Love* 4 (Feb. 1868).

32. Hotchkiss, *Make Me a Map*, 78; Douglas, *I Rode with Stonewall*, 147–148. Hotchkiss thought the horse was black, but Fitz Lee agreed with Douglas that it was a "grey mare." See Jedediah Hotchkiss to Hunter McGuire, Jan. 30, 1897, Jedediah Hotchkiss Papers, LC.

33. Haynes, *Field Diary*, 15–16. Other accounts indicate that Hill's division bivouacked after midnight. See Joseph Harsh, *Taken at the Flood: Robert E. Lee and Confederate Strategy in the Maryland Campaign of 1862* (Kent, OH: Kent State Univ. Press, 1999), 88; Hotchkiss, *Make Me a Map*, 79; Early, *War Memoirs*, 134–135. The *New York Herald*, Sept. 7, 1862, contains an account of Randolph's raid, although it does not identify who the cavalry were that carried it out. It could not have been White, as he was with Jackson that night. See Carman, chap. 3, 131; *OR Suppl.* 26:810. Company G, 1st MD Potomac Home Brigade, was at Monocacy Junction. See *New York Daily Tribune*, Sept. 9, 1862, for details on the raid.

34. *OR* 19, 1:814; Heros von Borcke, *Memoirs of the Confederate War for Independence* (Gaithersburg, MD: Butternut & Blue, 1985), 182–183; Richard L. T. Beale, *History of the Ninth Virginia Cavalry* (Richmond: B. F. Johnson, 1899), 37; Brooks, *Stories of the Confederacy*, 77; *OR* 19, 2:595. The movements of Robertson's brigade are drawn from George M. Neese, *Three Years in the Confederate Horse Artillery* (New York:

Neale, 1911), 111. Neese served in Chew's battery, which habitually was attached to the Laurel Brigade, but it is not certain from Neese's account that the whole brigade marched to Leesburg that night. It may have only been his battery.

35. Von Borcke, *Memoirs*, 184; Thomas Munford memorandum book, Munford Papers, DU; Carter, *Sabres, Saddles, and Spurs*, 12; Leonard Williams to wife, Sept. 28, 1862, David G. Douglas Collection, GNMP; James K. Munnerlyn Jr. to sister, Sept. 8, 1862, James K. Munnerlyn Jr. Papers, SHC.

36. Von Borcke, *Memoirs*, 185–186. Von Borcke wrote that some Federals were killed in the engagement, but he does not give any numbers. Also see Carter, *Sabres, Saddles, and Spurs*, 12; Benjamin W. Crowninshield, *A History of the First Regiment of Massachusetts Cavalry Volunteers* (Boston: Houghton, Mifflin, 1891), 71–72; Carman, chap. 3, 129–130. For an account of this engagement, see the *New York Daily Tribune*, Sept. 10, 1862, col. 1. The correspondent wrote that Chamberlain and all his men were paroled on the 6th, and that Chamberlain had a long talk with Fitz Lee and Stuart after his capture.

37. Von Borcke, *Memoirs*, 186–187; *OR* 19, 1:822.

38. John W. Stevens, *Reminiscences of the Civil War* (Powhatan, VA: Derwent Books, 1982), 65; Thomas Elder to wife, Sept. 5, 1862, Elder Papers, VHS; Hodijah L. Meade to mother, Sept. 5, 1862, Hodijah L. Meade Papers, VHS.

39. Harwell, *Union Reader*, 159; C. E. Goldsborough, "Blue and Butternut," *NT*, Oct. 14, 1886; *OR* 19, 2:568; Carmen, chap. 3, 132; *New York Daily Tribune*, Sept. 9, 1862.

40. Douglas, *I Rode with Stonewall*, 148; Jedediah Hotchkiss to Hunter McGuire, Jan. 30, 1897, and Jedediah Hotchkiss to wife, Sept. 8, 1862, Hotchkiss Papers, LC. Hotchkiss had a low opinion of Douglas's memoir and memory. His letters to and from Hunter McGuire contain many criticisms and observations.

41. *OR* 19, 1:953, 966; Early, *War Memoirs*, 135; Steiner, "Report," 160. Goldsborough, "Blue and Butternut," also places the arrival of the first Confederate troops sometime after 9 a.m.

42. Steiner, "Report," 161.

43. Ibid.

44. *OR* 19, 1:952–953; *New York Daily Tribune*, Sept. 10, 1862, col. 2.

45. Hotchkiss, *Make Me a Map*, 79; Douglas, *I Rode with Stonewall*, 148; William M. Owen, *In Camp and Battle with the Washington Artillery* (Gaithersburg, MD: Butternut and Blue, 1982), 131.

46. Beale, *Ninth Virginia Cavalry*, 37; Carter, *Sabres, Saddles, and Spurs*, 12. Lt. Col. Carter's diary (3rd VA Cavalry) states they started "by sunrise," which meant that Hampton moved earlier. See *OR* 19, 1:118, 815; Brooks, *Stories of the Confederacy*, 78–79. Also see von Borcke, *Memoirs*, 187, although his account is incorrect in some details.

47. Von Borcke, *Memoirs*, 187–191; *OR* 19, 1:815, 822; *New York Daily Tribune*, Sept. 10, 1862, cols. 2 and 3. In separate articles the *Tribune* carried reports from Washington and Baltimore that Confederates were in "great force" at Middlebrook Mills, a rebel picket had been seen at Poplar Springs, and a guard was established within 7 miles of Westminster on Sept. 7. Although the report does not state where the picket guard was seen, it seems probable that it would have been along the Westminster Pike, a likely road a Federal force might use to approach Frederick. It also should be presumed that Stuart left a small detachment at Poolesville to observe that place.

48. Munford memorandum book, DU; Neese, *Confederate Horse Artillery*, 112–113. Munford's diary merely states he crossed the Potomac on the 6th. Neese is the source stating that they crossed at midnight and did not reach Frederick until the 7th. It is possible that Chew's battery did not march with Munford, although it normally operated with that brigade, because one of Chew's guns (the one

Neese served) had kicked loose from its mountings and needed to be repaired in Leesburg before the battery could cross the Potomac.

49. Boulware diary, LV. Boulware stated that his brigade camped within 2–3 miles of the Potomac. Also see John W. Stevens, *Reminiscences*, 66; Henry L. P. King diary, SHC.

50. Dowdy, *Wartime Papers*, 296.

51. Longstreet, "Invasion of Maryland," in *B&L*, 2:663.

52. *OR* 19, 2:596. Also see Harsh, *Taken at the Flood*, 106–107.

53. John Dooley, *John Dooley, Confederate Soldier, His War Journal*, ed. Joseph T. Durkin (Washington, DC: Georgetown Univ. Press, 1945), 24; Boulware diary, LV; Kirkpatrick diary, THC.

54. Hill diary, MDAH; King diary, SHC; Burgwyn, *Captain's War*, 16; Betts, *Experience of a Confederate Chaplain*, 16. Hood's division was still sometimes referred to as Evans's division early in the campaign. But Hood's two brigades operated as a division under his command, not Evans's, from Sept. 14 until the end of the campaign. Col. Dixon Miles, commanding the Union garrison at Harper's Ferry, reported on Sept. 6 that A. P. Hill's division was entrenching at Lovettesville, Virginia. This was G. B. Anderson's brigade. See *OR* 51, 1:794.

55. Kirkpatrick diary, THC; Hill diary, MDAH; Boulware diary, LV.

56. Burgwyn, *Captain's War*, 16; Samuel H. Walkup diary, SHC; John G. Walker, "Jackson's Capture of Harper's Ferry," in *B&L*, 2:604.

57. Carlton McCarthy, *Contributions to a History of the Richmond Howitzer Battalion* (Baltimore: Butternut and Blue, 2000), 130; David G. Martin, *The Fluvanna Artillery* (Lynchburg, VA: H. E. Howard, 1992), 48; Carmichael, "We Don't Know," 263. Pendleton's report of the campaign seems to indicate that only Cutts's and Nelson's battalions marched with him on

the 7th, but evidence indicates that Brown's battalion (commanded by Col. J. Thompson Brown) was also with him and, it must be presumed, Maj. Hilary P. Jones's battalion. See *OR* 19, 1:829.

58. Carmichael, "We Don't Know," 263.

59. Boulware diary, LV; Stevens, *War Reminiscences*, 67.

60. Owen, *In Camp and Battle*, 127; *New York Herald*, Sept. 15, 1862; Harwell, *Union Reader*, 162.

61. A *Baltimore American* story of Sept. 9, carried in the *New York Daily Tribune*, Sept. 10, 1862; Harwell, *Union Reader*, 163, 166; Greenlee Davidson, *Captain Greenlee Davidson, C.S.A., Diary and Letters, 1851–1863*, comp. Charles W. Turner (Verona, VA: McClure Press, 1975), 46; William T. Poague, *Gunner with Stonewall* (Jackson, TN: McCowat-Mercer Press, 1957), 42; Napier Bartlett, *A Soldier's Story of the War* (New Orleans: Clark & Hofeline, 1874), 129.

62. Bartlett, *Soldier's Story*, 131; Poague, *Gunner with Stonewall*, 42.

63. Ann R. Schaeffer, "Records of the Past," manuscript, privately owned by Russell H. Beatie; Goldsborough, "Blue and Butternut"; Bartlett, *Soldier's Story*, 31.

64. Richard R. Duncan, "Marylanders and the Invasion of 1862," *Civil War History* 11 (Dec. 1965), 188; Harwell, *Union Reader*, 164. It is possible that the attack on the *Examiner* was in retribution for an incident on Sept. 4, when some of the people connected with the *Citizen*, a pro-Southern newspaper in Frederick, were cheering Jeff Davis on the streets of Frederick before the Confederates arrived. Pro-Union citizens engaged in an altercation with these individuals. The Union provost guard showed up and apparently focused their law enforcement on the Southern sympathizers. One of the owners of the paper was struck with the butt end of a musket and "considerably injured." The incident was reported in the Sept. 10, 1862, edition of the *New York Daily Tribune*.

65. Hotchkiss, *Make Me a Map*, 80; Wise, *Seventeenth Virginia Infantry*, 110. Following the departure of the Confederates, the bridge was repaired within five days at a cost of less than $4,000. See Harsh, *Taken at the Flood*, 121. However, before it was repaired, McClellan was forced to unload supplies from the trains and transfer them to wagons to be hauled to the army.

66. *New York Herald*, Sept. 12, 13, and 15, 1862; Harwell, *Union Reader*, 162; Goldsborough, "Blue and Butternut."

67. *New York Herald*, Sept. 13, 1862; Harwell, *Union Reader*, 167; Goldsborough, "Blue and Butternut." The *Philadelphia Public Ledger*, Sept. 13, 1862, reported that 500 men enlisted. See Duncan, "Marylanders and the Invasion," 188–189. Also see Harsh, *Sounding the Shallows*, 158. Harsh relates that the Marylanders were enlisted into "Captain Heard's company" and assigned to the 8th VA. On Sept. 15 Lee had them all transferred to the ambulance corps. They would later become the nucleus of Company A, 2nd MD Infantry. See Harsh, *Sounding the Shallows*, 158.

68. *OR* 19, 2:601–603, 605.

69. Chamberlayne, *Letters and Papers*, 105; William Y. Mordecai to mother, Sept. 24, 1862, William Y. Mordecai Papers, VHS; Hill diary, MDAH.

70. *OR* 19, 2:597–598, 600.

71. Ibid., 602–603.

72. Ibid.

73. See Lee's dispatches to Davis on Sept. 9 and 12, 1862, in *OR* 19, 2:602–605.

74. *OR* 19, 1:913.

75. Walker, "Jackson's Capture of Harper's Ferry," in *B&L*, 2:604–606. Walker also erred in placing the date of this discussion, giving it as Sept. 8, when his report gives the date as the 9th. For a critical analysis of Walker's account, see Harsh, *Taken at the Flood*, 134–145.

76. Dabney, *Thomas J. Jackson*, 2:302. Lafayette McLaws is the source for what Lee believed

the size of the Harper's garrison to be. McLaws gave two different strengths. In an 1888 article for the *PWP*, McLaws said Lee told him it had been reported to Lee that the strength was between 7,000 and 8,000, but that Lee did not believe it was that strong. In an address before the Confederate veterans of Savannah, Georgia, however, McLaws stated that Lee told him the Union garrison was not more than 3,000 or 4,000. See Lafayette McLaws, "The Capture of Harper's Ferry," *PWP*, Sept. 5, 1888; Harsh, *Taken at the Flood*, 138.

77. Longstreet, *From Manassas to Appomattox*, 202.

78. Ibid., 202–203. Also see Longstreet, "Invasion of Maryland," in *B&L*, 2:663.

79. McLaws, "Capture of Harper's Ferry," *PWP*, Sept. 5, 1888; King diary, SHC.

80. Richard H. Anderson to D. H. Hill, Nov. 14, 1867, quoted in Joseph C. Elliott, *Lee's Noble Soldier: Richard H. Anderson* (Dayton, OH: Morningside Press, 1985), 59. Anderson did not recall the dates accurately. He told Hill that his meeting with Lee was on Sept. 8, when it was definitely on the 9th, and that Lee repeatedly told him "Harper's Ferry must be taken against Thursday evening [Sept. 11]." Special Orders No. 191 clearly indicates that Lee expected Harpers Ferry to be taken by Friday evening, Sept. 12.

81. *OR* 19, 2:603–604.

82. McLaws, "Capture of Harper's Ferry," *PWP*, Sept. 5, 1888.

83. King diary, SHC. King recorded on Sept. 11 that McLaws had two companies (one squadron) of cavalry with him.

84. McLaws, "Capture of Harper's Ferry," *PWP*, Sept. 5, 1888.

85. Gary W. Gallagher, *Lee the Soldier* (Lincoln: Univ. of Nebraska Press, 1996), 26–27. When D. H. Hill published an article in the journal *Land That We Love* in Feb. 1868, defending his role in the loss of Special Orders No. 191 and also implying that Jackson had violated his orders by moving to Harpers Ferry, Lee

reacted with some heat, remarking, "but this had all been explained to Jackson verbally, and no one could imagine that the order did not contemplate just what Jackson did." Clearly Lee and Jackson had discussed the possibility that the enemy would not behave predictably, and Jackson understood that he had the authority to move his command as he saw fit, within the spirit of the orders, to destroy or capture the Union garrisons.

86. The strength figures are derived by estimating a 20% loss due to straggling, sickness, and the like, from John Allen's Sept. 2 strength figures for the army. See appendix B for Allen's strength figures. There had been heavy straggling from the army after Sept. 2, and some 5,000 men were left behind at Leesburg, so the Sept. 2 figures are not an accurate count of the army's strength on Sept. 10.

87. D. H. Hill, "The Lost Dispatch—Letter from General D. H. Hill," *SHSP* 13 (1885), 420–423. For Maj. Ratchford's perspective, see James W. Ratchford, *Memoirs of a Confederate Staff Officer from Bethel to Bentonville*, ed. Evelyn Sieburg (Shippensburg, PA: White Mane, 1998), 24–25. Also see Chilton to D. H. Hill, June 22, 1867, D. H. Hill Papers, NCSA.

88. Hotchkiss, *Make Me a Map*, 80; Schuler diary, LC. Both of these diaries place the starting time at around 3 a.m., as does Greenlee Davidson. See Davidson, *Diary and Letters*, 47–48.

89. Lenoir Chambers, *Stonewall Jackson*, 2 vols. (New York: W. Morrow, 1959), 2:191; Douglas, *I Rode with Stonewall*, 151; Henry K. Douglas, "Stonewall Jackson in Maryland," in *B&L*, 2:622.

90. Longstreet, *From Manassas to Appomattox*, 205. See appendix B for the strength of Wilcox's three brigades.

91. J. Evans Edings diary, Edward Willis Papers, LC; Osmun Latrobe diary, Maryland Historical Society, Baltimore; Kirkpatrick diary, THC; King diary, SHC; James Shinn notes,

Edwin A. Osborne Papers, SHC. It is possible
that Edings recorded the time incorrectly, as
James Kirkpatrick, of Anderson's division,
stated that they entered Frederick at noon,
and Capt. King, with McLaws, wrote that his
division entered the city at 4:30 p.m. Whatever the precise timing, movement through
and out of the city was slow.

92. Boulware diary, LV; Dooley, *John Dooley, Confederate Soldier*, 27; Wise, *Seventeenth Virginia
Infantry*, 110.
93. Harwell, *Union Reader*, 168–169.
94. Ibid., 169–170.
95. Davidson, *Diary and Letters*, 47.

Chapter 4. The Army of the Potomac

1. Joseph W. Brown, *The Signal Corps, U.S.A., in
the War of the Rebellion* (Boston: U.S. Veteran
Signal Corps Assoc., 1896), 241; *OR* 19, 2:184–
185.
2. *OR* 19, 2:180–181; J. W. Garrett to GBM, Sept.
5, 1862, reel 31, MP.
3. In his testimony before the Committee on the
Conduct of the War, Burnside discussed the
two occasions on which Lincoln offered him
command, but he did not give a specific date.
He merely said that the meeting took place
"before the commencement of the Maryland
Campaign." See *CCW*, 37th Cong., 3rd Sess.,
3 vols. (Washington, DC: Gov't. Printing
Office, 1863), 1:650; Sears, *George B. McClellan*,
235, 264–265.
4. Welles, *Diary of Gideon Welles*, 1:116; *CCW*,
37th Cong., 3rd Sess., 1:451; *OR* 19, 1:786. Both
Lincoln and Halleck subsequently denied
responsibility for placing McClellan in command. See Earl S. Miers, *Lincoln Day by Day*
(Washington, DC: Lincoln Sesquicentennial
Commission, 1960), for Heintzelman's observation. Stephen Sears makes a persuasive
argument that Lincoln placed McClellan in
command of the army in the field on the
morning of Sept. 5, citing, among other
things, McClellan's letter to his wife that day

that opened with "again I have been called
upon to save the country." Lincoln could be
artful, but it seems odd that he would make
the decision to place McClellan in command
and then, on the same day, offer it to Burnside. Halleck also testified that the meeting
with McClellan took place "about 9 o'clock in
the morning, previous to General McClellan
leaving the city for Rockville" (*CCW*, 1:453).
McClellan left for Rockville on the 7th, and
Heintzelman saw Lincoln at McClellan's
house on the morning of the 7th. Also,
McClellan wrote his wife on the 7th that "I
leave in a couple of hours to take command of
the army in the field," which could also mean
that he had received confirmation from the
president of what McClellan had expected.
This evidence lends weight to the supposition
that Lincoln made the decision on the 7th
rather than the 5th. The other problem with
the 5th is that Burnside met with McClellan
that night and discussed the issue of command with him. If Lincoln had offered both
men command of the army on the same day,
some inkling of this should have revealed
itself during the generals' discussion. The
answer must be that he did not. Carman
believed Lincoln's meeting with McClellan
took place on Sept. 6. See Carman, chap. 4,
197.
5. Sears, *George B. McClellan*, 265; George B.
McClellan, "From the Peninsula to Antietam," in *B&L*, 2:552.
6. Carman, chap. 4, 204. Carman gives the field
army's strength as 75,800, but this includes
Morell's division, which numbered just over
5,000, and the many regiments of recruits
that reinforced the army before it took the
field. The figure of 60,000 is the approximate
strength of the army before the new regiments were added to it. For Morell's strength,
see *OR* 19, 2:195. For the army's artillery
strength, see Johnson and Anderson, *Artillery Hell*, 39. Johnson and Anderson include
with Morell's division two of the batteries,

totaling 10 guns, that were not with the field army when it first deployed.

7. Carman, chap. 4, 181; *OR* 19 2:264. These figures did not include Bayard's cavalry brigade, which, according to the returns of Sept. 20, had 1,875 present. See *OR* 19, 2:337.

8. *OR* 19, 1:101–102, 106–107, 205.

9. Henry Pearson to friend, Sept. 5, 1862, Lewis Leigh Collection, USAHEC; Uriah Parmelee to mother, Sept. 8, 1862, Samuel Spencer Parmelee Papers, DU; Marsena Patrick diary, LC.

10. Richard B. Irwin, "Washington under Banks," in *B&L*, 2:543n; Wainwright, *Diary of Battle*, 90; *OR* 11, 3:367.

11. Philip Kearny to My Dear Parker, July 31, 1862, in Kearny, *Letters from the Peninsula*, 144–145; Wainwright, *Diary of Battle*, 89.

12. G. F. R. Henderson, *The Civil War: A Soldier's View; A Collection of Civil War Writing*, ed. Jay Luvaas (Chicago: Univ. of Chicago Press, 1958), 145; *OR* 19, 2:225–227.

13. 6th Army Corps Papers, RG 393.9, NA; John Gibbon, *Personal Recollections of the Civil War* (New York: G. P. Putnam, 1928), 75.

14. Williams, *From the Cannon's Mouth*, 119; Uriah Parmelee to mother, Sept. 8, 1862, Parmelee Papers, DU; *OR* 19, 2:223–224.

15. *OR* 11, 3:380; *OR* 12, 3:781.

16. Abner Doubleday Report of Service, *U.S. Army Generals' Reports of Civil War Service*, reel 8, 13:435–436, NA; James Wren, *Captain James Wren's Diary: From New Bern to Fredericksburg*, ed. John M. Priest (Shippensburg, PA: White Main, 1990), 61.

17. Oliver O. Howard to wife, Sept. 11, 1862, Oliver O. Howard Papers, Bowdoin College, Brunswick, Maine; Charles F. Johnson, *The Long Roll* (Aurora, NY: Roycroftens, 1911), 181; Edward Bragg to My Dear Wife, Sept. 13, 1862, Bragg Papers, SHSW; Henry B. Young to Delia, Sept. 13, 1862, Henry B. Young Papers, SHSW; Williams, *From the Cannon's Mouth*, 120–121.

18. *B&L*, 2:313–315, 497–499. The 12th Corps' strength is arrived at by deducting an average of 850 men for the five new regiments attached to it in Sept. (124th PA, 125th PA, 128th PA, 13th NJ, and 107th NY) from the strength of 10,126 that McClellan gives for the corps in his second report. See *OR* 19, 2:67.

19. The strength of the new regiments is based on an estimated average strength of 850, since not all regiments were mustered with the full authorized strength of 1,000 men. For the assignment of the new regiments, see Special Orders No. 3 in *OR* 19, 2:197–198. These placements were also changed in many instances. The number of recruits is simply an estimate based on regimental histories (which indicated that the New York and Massachusetts regiments received the bulk of the recruits) and a statement of men furnished to old regiments in the field. See *OR*, Ser. 3, 2:861; Charles J. Mills, *Through Blood and Fire: The Civil War Letters of Major Charles J. Mills, 1862–1865*, ed. Gregory A. Coco (Gettysburg, PA: G. A. Coco, 1982), 24. The manpower crisis occurred as a result of an order by Secretary of War Stanton on Apr. 3, 1862, that suspended the recruiting of volunteers. The reverse on the Peninsula jolted the government, and it scrambled to assemble more manpower. On July 2, after a hurried meeting with Northern governors in New York, Lincoln issued a call for 300,000 volunteers for three years' service. But 1862 was not 1861, and the volunteers trickled in slowly. The government responded by authorizing the payment of bounties of $25 to the three-year volunteers and by passing the Militia Act of 1862. This law empowered the president to call the state militia into federal service for a period of up to nine months. On Aug. 4 the War Department called on the states for 300,000 nine-month militia troops in addition to the earlier call for 300,000. In essence the call-up was a draft, with the burden on the states rather than the federal government, for, if the states did not mobilize their militias, the gov-

ernment would step in and do it. However, the militia call-up was softened by a provision that allowed each three-year volunteer to be counted as four men against the nine-month militia quota. See J. G. Randall and David H. Donald, *The Civil War and Reconstruction* (Lexington, MA: D. C. Heath, 1969), 312–313. Also see McPherson, *Battle Cry of Freedom*, 491–492.

20. McClellan might have allowed this inefficient arrangement to exist during the Maryland Campaign because Couch may have been senior to Franklin, both men having been promoted to major general on July 4. While McClellan respected Couch, Franklin had experience as a corps commander, and McClellan went to considerable effort to keep him with the army for the campaign. Thus the 6th Corps passed through the campaign with a two-division organization.

21. *OR* 19, 1:67. McClellan gave the strength of his infantry corps as follows: 1st Corps—14,856; 2nd Corps—18,813; 6th Corps—12,300; 9th Corps—13,819; 12th Corps—10,126; and cavalry division—4,320. The two independent divisions, Sykes's from the 5th Corps and Couch's from the 4th Corps, numbered 3,820 and 7,219, respectively. The infantry corps' strength was what McClellan said was the aggregate present at Antietam. Sykes's strength was reported on Sept. 6; Couch's strength is from a Sept. 20 return. See *OR* 19, 2:195, 336. The 2nd MA, for example, carried 1,050 names on its rolls, of which 200 to 300 were detailed to noncombat duty (20%–25% of its strength). See Mills, *Through Blood and Fire*, 24.

22. *OR* 19, 2:182, 189–190.

23. Carmen, chap. 4, 205.

24. Cox, *Military Reminiscences*, 1:264; Eicher and Eicher, *Civil War High Commands*, 155; Carman, chap. 4, 217–219.

25. Eicher and Eicher, *Civil War High Commands*, 519; GBM to Mary Ellen, May 6, 1862, in McClellan, *Civil War Papers*, 257; Kearny, *Let-*

ters from the Peninsula*, 146; Wainwright, *Diary of Battle*, 264.

26. Carman, chap. 4, 206; Kearny, *Letters from the Peninsula*, 86; Wainwright, *Diary of Battle*, 66; "General Hooker's Opinion," *NT*, Nov. 14, 1907. This article contains a July 7, 1862, letter from Hooker to Hon. J. W. Nesmith commenting on McClellan's generalship.

27. GBM to Mary Ellen, Sept. 12, 1862, reel 31, MP.

28. Eicher and Eicher, *Civil War High Commands*, 243; McClellan, *McClellan's Own Story*, 138; GBM to Mary Ellen, Aug. 22, 1862, in McClellan, *Civil War Papers*, 399; Kearny, *Letters from the Peninsula*, 138.

29. John Pope, "The Second Battle of Bull Run," in *B&L*, 2:474; Williams, *From the Cannon's Mouth*, 123; Wren, *Captain James Wren's Diary*, 69.

30. Carmen, chap. 4, 223; Gibbon, *Personal Recollections*, 72–73.

31. GBM to Mary Ellen, July 27, 1861, in McClellan, *Civil War Papers*, 70.

32. GBM to Mary Ellen, Aug. 18, 1862, in McClellan, *Civil War Papers*, 396.

33. Edward W. Emerson, *Life and Letters of Charles Russell Lowell* (Port Washington, NY: Kennikat Press, 1971), 229; Worthington C. Ford, ed., *A Cycle of Adams Letters 1861–1865*, 2 vols. (New York: Kraus Reprint, 1969), 2:8.

34. Eicher and Eicher, *Civil War High Commands*, 364.

35. Michie, *General McClellan*, 102.

36. McClellan, *McClellan's Own Story*, 141.

37. Theodore Lyman, *Meade's Headquarters, 1863–1865: Letters of Colonel Theodore Lyman from the Wilderness to Appomattox*, ed. George R. Agassiz (Boston: Atlantic Monthly Press, 1922), 34; McClellan, *McClellan's Own Story*, 129.

38. *OR* 19, 1:95; *OR* 2:235; *OR*, Ser. 3, 2:798. The figures are estimates for an army of 80,000 men and around 30,000 animals. The standard daily ration was 3 pounds of food for a

soldier and 26 pounds of forage for each animal. An army wagon could haul 2,400 pounds over good roads.

39. Benjamin W. Crowninshield, "Cavalry in Virginia During the War of the Rebellion," in Military Historical Society of Massachusetts, *Civil and Mexican Wars 1861, 1846*, vol. 13 of *Papers of the Military Historical Society of Massachusetts* (Boston: Military Historical Society of Massachusetts, 1913), 26; *OR* 19, 2:225–226, 235–236.

40. Jonathan Letterman, *Medical Recollections of the Army of the Potomac* (New York: D. Appleton, 1866), 22–23.

41. Ibid., 32–35; *OR* 19, 1:106–107. The army received 200 ambulances prior to its arrival at Frederick on Sept. 12, which greatly eased the army's shortage of these vehicles.

42. McClellan, *McClellan's Own Story*, 117.

43. *CCW*, 37th Cong., 3rd Sess., 1:92; *OR* 19, 1:205.

44. Eicher and Eicher, *Civil War High Commands*, 153; Michael Phipps and John S. Peterson, *"The Devil's To Pay": Gen. John Buford, USA* (Gettysburg: Farnsworth Military Impressions, 1995), 26. According to Stephen Starr, Buford was appointed chief of cavalry on Sept. 20. See Stephen Starr, *The Union Cavalry in the Civil War*, 3 vols. (Baton Rouge: Louisiana State Univ. Press, 1979–1985), 1:313.

45. Ezra A. Carman diary, NJHS. Carman was colonel of the 13th NJ, a green regiment, but he had been a lieutenant colonel in the 7th NJ on the Peninsula. Also see Williams, *From the Cannon's Mouth*, 126; Mills, *Through Blood and Fire*, 27.

46. Mills, *Through Blood and Fire*, 24; William B. Franklin, "Notes on Crampton's Gap and Antietam," in *B&L*, 2:595. For the Sept. 1, 1862, present for duty strengths of Morell's division, 5th Corps, see *OR* 12, 3:796.

47. Carl L. David, *Arming the Union* (Port Washington, NY: Kennikat Press, 1973), 41, 61, 171.

48. Ibid., 42, 61; "Records of the Pennsylvania Reserves," 5th Army Corps Papers, RG 393.9, NA; *OR* 27, 1:370, 348, 388. Part of the problems the 118th experienced with their weapons had to do with lack of training. According to an officer in the regiment, in their excitement many of the men rammed the ball down before the powder, with predictable results. This same officer also said that they carried Belgian rifles, not Enfields. See Francis A. Donaldson, *Inside the Army of the Potomac*, ed. J. Gregory Acken (Harrisburg, PA: Stackpole Books, 1998), 133.

49. See the table in D. Scott Hartwig, "Who Would Not Be a Soldier," in Gallagher, *Antietam Campaign*, 164.

50. Starr, *Union Cavalry*, 1:240.

51. *OR* 19, 2:194.

52. George W. Cullum, *Biographical Register of the Officers and Graduates of the U.S. Military Academy from 1802 to 1867*, rev. ed., 3 vols. (New York: James Miller, 1879), 1:464–465; Allen Johnson et al., eds., *Dictionary of American Biography*, 22 vols. (New York: C. Scribner's Sons, 1946), 3:284; William H. Beach, *The First New York (Lincoln) Cavalry* (New York: Lincoln Cavalry Assoc., 1902), 19–20. The 1st's regimental history indicates that while they considered McReynolds an able officer, he was not popular with the men.

53. Starr, *Union Cavalry*, 1:313.

54. Ibid., 309n; Crowninshield, "Cavalry in Virginia," 26; *OR* 19, 1:95.

55. Hillman Hall, *History of the Sixth New York Cavalry* (Worcester, MA: Blanchard Press, 1908), 53; Henry C. Davis diary, FSNMP; *OR* 51, 1:810–811.

56. Samuel P. Bates, *History of the Pennsylvania Volunteers, 1861–5*, 14 vols. (Wilmington, NC: Broadfoot, 1993), 2:524.

57. Blackford, *War Years*, 246–247.

58. *OR* 19, 1:205; Wainwright, *Diary of Battle*, 105.

59. Edward Longacre, *The Man behind the Guns: A Biography of Henry Jackson Hunt* (South Brunswick, NJ: A. S. Barnes, 1977), 119; *OR* 19, 1:205.

60. *OR* 19, 1:205.

61. Johnson and Anderson, *Artillery Hell*, 39; Wainwright, *Diary of Battle*, 114; L. VanLoan Naiswald, *Grape and Canister* (New York: Oxford Univ. Press, 1960), 30–31.

62. Williams, *From the Cannon's Mouth*, 111; Rufus Dawes, *Service with the Sixth Wisconsin Volunteers* (Dayton, OH: Morningside Bookshop, 1984), 78.

Chapter 5. The Army of the Potomac Advances to Frederick

1. *OR* 51, 1:777. Also see *OR* 51, 1:781; GBM to Abraham Lincoln, Sept. 2, 1862, in McClellan, *Civil War Papers*, 430–431.

2. *OR* 51, 1:781, 783. McClellan's headquarters also sent similar orders to Col. Robert Williams, commanding the 1st MA Cavalry. Perhaps, when the orders to Higginson were sent, it was not known that Williams had arrived in Alexandria. In any case, it was Williams who led the two battalions into Maryland.

3. *OR* 19, 2:170–171, 174; *OR* 19, 1:38.

4. *OR* 19, 2:176, 177.

5. The 12th Corps marched at 10 a.m. See John P. Nicholson diary, HL. For the redeployment of Couch's division to Fort Ethan Allen, see "Partial History of Co. E, 2nd Regt., R. I. Vols., 1861–1864," PHS.

6. *OR* 19, 2:177–178; *OR* 51, 1:785–787.

7. *OR* 19, 1:39, 432. The 9th Corps crossed the Potomac at 9 p.m. Couch did not cross until the next morning. See "Partial History of Co. E," PHS.

8. *OR* 19, 1:118.

9. Brinkerhoff N. Miner to Nathaniel Banks, Sept. 4, 1862, reel 30, MP; *OR* 19, 2:179–181.

10. *OR* 19, 2:185.

11. *OR* 19, 2:188–189, 184–185; John W. Garrett to GBM, Sept. 5, 1862, reel 31, MP.

12. Randolph Marcy to Edwin Sumner, Darius Couch, Nathaniel Banks, Sept. 5, 1862, reel 31, MP. The 12th Corps may have subsequently been ordered to proceed as far as Dar-nestown. See Alfred Pleasonton to Randolph Marcy, *OR* 19, 2:185. Also see *OR* 19, 2:182, 184.

13. McClellan, *McClellan's Own Story*, 550; *OR* 19, 2:189.

14. *OR* 19, 2:186.

15. Ibid., 192.

16. Ibid.; Carman, chap. 5, 232; *OR* 19, 2:193–195.

17. *OR* 19, 2:186, 198.

18. *OR* 19, 2:191; *OR* 51, 1:791–793. For McClellan's correspondence with Halleck and Lincoln, see McClellan, *Civil War Papers*, 436.

19. Samuel Healy journal, privately owned, copy in GNMP; "Lt. George Breck to the *Union Advertiser*, Sept. 10, 1862," in *Union Advertiser* (Rochester, NY), Sept. 17, 1862; Joseph J. Bartlett, "Crampton's Pass," *NT*, Dec. 19, 1889.

20. John Vautier diary, USAHEC; Abram P. Smith, *History of the Seventy-Sixth Regiment New York Volunteers* (Cortland, NY: Truain, Smith, & Miles, 1876), 148.

21. Smith, *Seventy-Sixth Regiment*, 148.

22. Healy journal, GNMP; Samuel Webster diary, HL; Mat Hurlinger diary, typescript, GNMP; Cox, *Military Reminiscences*, 1:265.

23. Thomas H. Evans, "The Enemy Sullenly Held On to the City," *CWTI* (Apr. 1968), 32.

24. Webster diary, HL; Healy journal, GNMP.

25. *OR* 19, 2:211; McClellan, *Civil War Papers*, 437–438; Welles, *Diary of Gideon Welles*, 1:114–115.

26. For an example of McClellan's opinion of Banks, see GBM to Mary Ellen, May 26, 1862, in McClellan, *Civil War Papers*, 278. Also see *OR* 19, 2:202.

27. *OR* 19, 2:200–201. Also see *OR* 19, 2:211, 216.

28. *OR* 19, 2:205–206.

29. Ibid., 203. Also see Andrew G. Curtin to Edwin Stanton, 5 p.m., Sept. 7, 1862, in *OR* 19, 2: 204.

30. Abner Hard, *History of the Eighth Cavalry Regiment, Illinois Volunteers, During the Great Rebellion* (Aurora, IL: privately printed, 1868), 170–171; *OR* 19, 2:201.

31. *OR* 19, 2:201; *OR* 51, 1:798.

32. Alfred Pleasonton to GBM, 6:30 a.m., Sept. 8, 1862, reel 31, MP; *OR* 19, 2:209.

33. *OR* 19, 1:208; Alfred Pleasonton to GBM, 10:10 p.m., Sept. 8, 1862, reel 31, MP; Hall, *Sixth New York Cavalry*, 53. Also see *OR* 19, 2:211.

34. *OR* 19, 1:815, 825; H. McClellan, *Life and Campaigns*, 110–111.

35. *OR* 19, 1:208, 825; H. McClellan, *Life and Campaigns*, 111; Sgt. J. H. H. Figgat to Asher W. Harman, Feb. 14, 1886, Hotchkiss Papers, LC, in Dennis E. Frye, *12th Virginia Cavalry* (Lynchburg, VA: H. E. Howard, 1988), 14–15. Munford admitted to only 10 casualties, all in the 12th Virginia.

36. *OR* 19, 1:208, 825.

37. Alfred Pleasonton to GBM, 10:10 p.m., Sept. 8, 1862, reel 31, MP.

38. *OR* 19, 2:210–211, 213; Fitz John Porter to GBM, [no time], Sept. 8, 1862, reel 31, MP.

39. *OR* 19, 2:210–212; *OR* 51, 1:802.

40. Alfred Pleasonton to GBM, Sept. 8, 1862, reel 31, MP.

41. *OR* 19, 2:218–219; Lt. John A. DeFord to Maj. Albert J. Myer, Sept. 8, 1862, reel 31, MP. Also see Fishel, "Pinkerton and McClellan."

42. *OR* 51, 2:802–803.

43. *OR* 19, 1:208; Hard, *Eighth Cavalry Regiment*, 71.

44. Hard, *Eighth Cavalry Regiment*, 172; Frye, *12th Virginia Cavalry*, 14–15.

45. Hard, *Eighth Cavalry Regiment*, 172–173; Beale, *Ninth Virginia Cavalry*, 37–38.

46. *OR* 19, 1:208–209, 815. Stuart's report ignores the fighting on the 9th and mentions only that there was some skirmishing.

47. Alfred Pleasonton to Randolph Marcy, 7 a.m., Sept. 9, 1862, reel 31, MP.

48. *OR* 19, 1:39; *OR* 19, 2:253; Cox, *Military Reminiscences*, 1:267; McClellan, *McClellan's Own Story*, 569.

49. Alfred Pleasonton to GBM, 2:45 p.m., Sept. 9, 1862, reel 31, MP. The telegram to Porter has not been found, but his response and that of his chief of staff, Alexander Webb, to McClellan and his staff on Sept. 10 indicates that he was contacted on the 9th to investigate these reports. See *OR* 19, 2:241.

50. Alfred Pleasonton to GBM, 3:50 p.m., Sept. 9, 1862, reel 31, MP; *OR* 19, 2:230, 221–223.

51. Alfred Pleasonton to GBM, 7:30 p.m., Sept. 9, 1862, reel 31, MP; *OR* 19, 2:222–223.

52. *OR* 19, 2:219.

53. McClellan, *Civil War Papers*, 44. Also see McClellan, *McClellan's Own Story*, 555–557. Although McClellan portrayed Halleck as excessively worried about a second Confederate army south of the Potomac, he, too, was anxious about this possibility until the discovery of Special Orders No. 191 on Sept. 13.

54. *OR* 19, 2:239; *OR* 51, 1:805–809.

55. Ambrose Burnside to GBM, [no time], Sept. 10, 1862, reel 31, MP.

56. *OR* 51, 1:806–809; *OR* 19, 2:241. Couch's march to Poolesville was not suspended, since McClellan wanted Couch's division to relieve Pleasonton's cavalry, who were picketing that area. For Burnside's delay, due to the late arrival of his provision train, see Ambrose Burnside to GBM, 11 a.m., Sept. 10, 1862, reel 31, MP.

57. *OR* 51, 1:809.

58. Alfred Pleasonton to Randolph Marcy, 8:20 a.m., 10:30 a.m., 1 p.m., and 4:45 p.m., Sept. 10, 1862, reel 31, MP. Also see Hard, *Eighth Cavalry Regiment*, 174.

59. *OR* 19, 1:209; Hard, *Eighth Cavalry Regiment*, 174; Carman, chap. 5, 341; Thomas Munford to Ezra A. Carman, Dec. 14, 1894, Antietam Studies, NA. For the various dispatches relating to the Sugar Loaf operation on Sept. 10, see *OR* 51, 1:808–811. Also see Darius Couch to Randolph Marcy, 1:30 p.m. and 2:25 p.m., Sept. 10, 1862, reel 31, MP.

60. Darius Couch to Randolph Marcy, 2:25 p.m. Sept. 10, 1862, and William B. Franklin to GBM, 3:30 p.m., Sept. 10, 1862, reel 31, MP; *OR* 19, 2:238.

61. *OR* 19, 2:236–237, 241; *OR* 51, 1:810. Also see Banks's dispatch (reel 31, MP) as it was read by McClellan. The telegraph operator who received Banks's message garbled his last sentence, and when Randolph Marcy received it

at headquarters it read "the main body of the enemy is *not* between Leesburg and the mountains." Marcy wired Banks and asked him what mountains he was referring to. Banks replied that it was the Catoctin range. Banks also warned that "it seemed as if a strong force lay between Leesburg and the Catoctin. It is thought here tonight that a heavy force has crossed the river, and is in the rear of the Monocacy."

62. *OR* 19, 2:254–255. Although dated Sept. 11 in the *OR*, this was sent on Sept. 10. A copy by Gen. Marcy (reel 31, MP) is dated Sept. 10, and Halleck's reply on Sept. 13 refers to McClellan's dispatch of Sept. 10 and its reference to the capture of Washington.

63. *OR* 19, 2:254–255.

64. Ibid., 248.

65. Ibid., 234, 238–239.

66. Ibid., 234; Carman, chap. 5, 246.

67. *OR* 19, 2:247–249; Carman, chap. 5, 249.

68. *OR* 19, 2:239, 248–249.

69. Hayes, *Diary and Letters*, 2:350–351; Mills, *Through Blood and Fire*, 26; William Olcott diary, privately owned by John Croft; John Vautier journal, USAHEC; Isaac Hall, *History of the Ninety-Seventh Regiment, New York Volunteers, in the War for the Union* (Utica, NY: L. C. Childs, 1890), 83.

70. Mills, *Through Blood and Fire*, 26; Henry B. Young to Delia, Sept. 13, 1862, Young Papers, SHSW; Williams, *From the Cannon's Mouth*, 121; Bates Alexander, "Pennsylvania Reserves: That Corps' Experience During the Late War," Save the Flags Collection, USAHEC.

71. Frederick L. Hitchcock, *War from the Inside* (Philadelphia: J. B. Lippincott, 1904), 36; B. F. Blakeslee, *History of the Sixteenth Connecticut Volunteers* (Hartford, CT: Case, Lockwood, & Brainard, 1875), 9; Jonathan E. Shipman to Friend Hubbard, Sept. 14, 1862, Book 5, Lewis Leigh Collection, USAHEC.

72. Isaac O. Best, *History of the 121st New York State Infantry* (Baltimore: Butternut and Blue, 1996), 9–10.

73. Henry P. Goddard, *Fourteenth Regiment Connecticut Volunteers* (Middletown, CT: C. W. Church, 1877), 26; Best, *121st New York State Infantry*, 9–10.

74. Hitchcock, *War from the Inside*, 36–37; Sebastian Duncan Jr. letterbook, Sept. 9, 1862, NJHS.

75. Duncan Jr. letterbook, Sept. 9, 1862, NJHS; Hitchcock, *War from the Inside*, 37; Andrew N. Terhune to cousin, Sept. 9, 1862, Book 27, No. 56, Lewis Leigh Collection, USAHEC. Terhune deserted the day after the Battle of Antietam, although he did return later and served his full term of service.

76. Charles A. Fuller, *Personal Recollections of the War of 1861* (Sherburne, NY: News Job, 1906), 55; James M. Perry diary, SHSW; George A. Hussey, *History of the Ninth Regiment, N.Y.S.M.—N.G.S.N.Y.* (New York: Veterans of the Regiment, 1889), 191; Jacob Haas diary, USAHEC; Albert A. Pope diary, Gregory Coco Collection, USAHEC; Duncan Jr. letterbook, Sept. 9, 1982, NJHS.

77. Jonathan E. Shipman to Friend Hubbard, Sept. 14, 1862, USAHEC; Hayes, *Diary and Letters*, 2:347; George H. Washburn, *A Complete Military History and Record of the 108th Regiment N.Y. Volunteers from 1862 to 1864* (Rochester, NY: E. R. Andrews, 1894), 19. Why Reno referred to Hayes's men as "black sons of bitches" may have had to do with the color of the men's uniforms. Some of the Federal uniforms were such a dark blue that they almost appeared black.

78. *OR* 19, 2:226–227; Samuel W. Fiske, *Mr. Dunn Browne's Experiences in the Army: The Civil War Letters of Samuel W. Fiske*, ed. Stephen W. Sears (New York: Fordham Univ. Press, 1998), 5.

79. Washburn, *108th Regiment N.Y. Volunteers*, 106; Joseph R. C. Ward, *History of the One Hundred and Sixth Regiment, Pennsylvania Volunteers, 2d Brigade, 2d Division, 2d Corps, 1861–1865* (Philadelphia: F. McManus Jr., 1906), 84; Edward P. Tobie, *History of the First Maine*

Cavalry, 1861–1865 (Boston: Catherine H. Vanderslice (New York: Vantage Press, 1978), 97. For McClellan's dispatch to Burnside, see *OR* 51, 1:817. Burnside's response (reel 31, MP) is timed at 4 p.m. from Damascus. This dispatch is also the source stating that Sumner received a noon communication from headquarters regarding Urbana.

80. Alexander Wight diary, RBHL; Hayes, *Diary and Letters*, 2:349; *OR* 19, 2:256–257; Ambrose Burnside to GBM, 8 p.m., Sept. 11, 1862, reel 31, MP; *OR* 51, 1:809–810.

81. *OR* 19, 2:258. Munford reported no casualties in this action. See *OR* 19, 1:825. Also see Hard, *Eighth Cavalry Regiment*, 174; William B. Franklin's dispatches to GBM, reel 31, MP.

82. Lieutenant Hall to GBM, 8 p.m., Sept. 11, 1862, reel 31, MP; *OR* 19, 2:249, 266–269.

83. *OR* 19, 2:267–268, 252–253, 269, 273–274.

84. David Strother, "Personal Recollections of the War," *Harper's New Monthly Magazine* 36 (Feb. 1868), 275; William P. Saunders to Alfred Pleasonton[?], 10 a.m., Sept. 11, 1862, reel 31, MP. For McClellan's concern about Harpers Ferry and Martinsburg, see GBM to Mary Ellen, Sept. 12, 1862, in McClellan, *Civil War Papers*, 449–450.

85. *OR* 19, 1:758; *OR* 19, 2:253.

86. *OR* 19, 2:253–254; Richard B. Irwin to Seth Williams, Sept. 11, 1862, reel 31, MP. Morell's strength is in *OR* 19, 2:195. Humphrey's strength is estimated at 800 per regiment. Weber's strength is from Carman, chap. 23, 10, which he gives as 1,798 men. Halleck's message as received by McClellan is on reel 31, MP. Also see *OR* 19, 1:40. For the strength of the Washington garrison, see *OR* 19, 2:264.

87. *OR* 51, 1:814–819.

88. Ibid., 819; Alfred Pleasonton to GBM, 7 p.m., Sept. 11, 1862, and Alfred Pleasonton to Randolph Marcy, 3 p.m. [probably 3 a.m.], Sept. 12, 1862, reel 31, MP. Pleasonton's main force marched to Clarksburg as directed. McReynolds, with the elements of the 1st NY Cavalry and the 8th PA, were all ordered by Pleasonton to march to Hyattstown and then to Frederick. See Beach, *First New York (Lincoln) Cavalry*, 170.

89. *OR* 51, 1:816–817; Darius Couch to Albert Colburn, 5 p.m., Sept. 11, 1862, reel 31, MP; *OR* 19, 2:280–281.

90. Cox, *Military Reminiscences*, 1:268–269; Martin L. Sheets diary, *CWTI* Collection, USAHEC; Hall, *Sixth New York Cavalry*, 58–59; *OR* 19, 2:256–257, 272–273; Edward P. Tobie, *History* of the First Maine Cavalry, 1861–1865 (Boston: Emery & Hughes, 1887), 92. The time for Cox's arrival at New Market is in David Cunningham and W. W. Miller, eds., *Report of the Ohio Antietam Battlefield Commission* (Springfield, OH: Springfield, 1904), 88.

91. Tobie, *First Maine Cavalry*, 92; *OR* 19, 1:822; Cox, *Military Reminiscences*, 1:271; Carman, chap. 5, 354–355; Col. Hugh Ewing Report to Adjutant General, *U.S. Army Generals' Reports of Civil War Service*, reel 3, 4:182, NA.

92. *OR* 19, 1:822; Cox, *Military Reminiscences*, 1:272–273. Cox's advance entered Frederick shortly before 5:30 p.m. See GBM to Henry W. Halleck, Sept. 11, 1862, in *OR* 19, 2:271.

93. *OR* 19, 1:416, 822–823; Cox, *Military Reminiscences*, 1:272–273; Joshua H. Horton and Solomon Teverbaugh, comps., *A History of the Eleventh Regiment (Ohio Volunteer Infantry)* (Dayton, OH: W. J. Shuey, 1866), 69; Strother, "Personal Recollections," 275.

94. Cox, *Military Reminiscences*, 1:273; Harwell, *Union Reader*, 172–173; Wight diary, RBHL; Edward E. Schweitzer diary, *CWTI* Collection, USAHEC; Rutherford B. Hayes to wife, Sept. 13, 1862, in Hayes, *Diary and Letters*, 1:352.

95. *OR* 51, 1:824; *OR* 19, 2:271.

96. George G. Meade, *Life and Letters of George G. Meade*, 2 vols. (New York: Charles Scribner's Sons, 1913), 1:310; McClellan, *McClellan's Own Story*, 570–571; *OR* 19, 2:270, 271–272, 277; Alfred Pleasonton to Randolph Marcy, 3 p.m. and 9:15 p.m., Sept. 12, 1862, reel 31, MP.

97. *OR* 51, 2:823–825.

98. Ibid., 822–825.

99. *CCW*, 37th Cong., 3rd Sess., 1:439.

100. *OR* 19, 2:273.

Chapter 6. Harpers Ferry

1. National Park Service, *John Brown's Raid* (Washington, DC: U.S. Gov't. Printing Office, 1974), 12–13.

2. Miles was given command on Mar. 9. At this time the operating area of the Railroad Brigade did not extend beyond Harpers Ferry. On Mar. 29 the duties of the brigade were expanded to encompass the region from Baltimore to the western limits of the Department of the Potomac. See *OR* 12, 3:30–31. Also see Cullum, *Biographical Register*, 1:266–267.

3. Edward K. Eckert and Nicholas J. Amato, eds., *Ten Years in the Saddle: The Memoir of William Woods Averell* (San Rafael, CA: Presidio Press, 1978), 171; Sigmund Elble, "Gen. Dixon Miles," *NT*, Mar. 3, 1892.

4. Cullum, *Biographical Register*, 2:266–267; *CCW*, 37th Cong., 2nd Sess., 29–39. Miles was directed to make Harpers Ferry his headquarters on Mar. 29. See *OR* 12, 3:30–31.

5. Julius White, "The Capitulation of Harper's Ferry," in *B&L*, 2:614.

6. *OR* 12, 1:639–641. In 1892 Saxton was awarded a Medal of Honor for his defense of Harpers Ferry. Jackson's withdrawal was also influenced by the approach of Union forces under McDowell and Fremont.

7. *OR* 12, 3:378, 387, 394; *OR* 19, 1:788–789; *OR* 51, 1:397–398.

8. *OR* 19, 1:788–789; William F. Fox, ed., *New York at Gettysburg: Final Report on the Battlefield of Gettysburg*, 3 vols. (Albany, NY: J. B. Lyon, 1902), 3:1143.

9. *OR* 19, 1:691–692. Also see *OR* 51, 1:784. Miles complained that his requisitions for ordnance had not been filled.

10. *OR* 12, 3:394; *OR* 19, 1:789–791.

11. *OR* 19, 1:549, 789–790; *OR* 19, 2:174; *OR* 51, 1:765–766. Although Miles did not identify this completely raw regiment as the 111th NY, that regiment had not received their arms when they first arrived in Harpers Ferry.

12. Miles explained how dispersed his forces were in an Aug. 27 dispatch to Wool's AAG. See *OR* 51, 1:764–765.

13. *OR* 12, 2:765–768; *OR* 19, 1:533. Harpers Ferry had a strength of 8,860 infantry, 1,022 cavalry, and 585 artilleryman serving four light batteries and the naval guns on Maryland Heights. See *OR* 19, 1:549.

14. *OR* 19, 2:181, 182, 198, 218. Also see Henry B. Curtis Jr. to Lucy, Sept. 11, 1862, Henry B. Curtis Jr. Papers, USAHEC. Curtis served on White's staff, and his comments about Miles may also reflect White's negative opinion of the colonel.

15. McClellan, *McClellan's Own Story*, 549–550; *OR* 19, 2:189; Stephen Ambrose, *Halleck: Lincoln's Chief of Staff* (Baton Rouge: Louisiana State Univ. Press, 1996), 82–83.

16. *OR* 19, 2:189; *OR* 19, 1:520. For Miles's interpretation of his orders, see White, "Capitulation of Harper's Ferry," in *B&L*, 2:612.

17. *OR* 19, 1:787.

18. Ibid., 791.

19. Chester G. Hearn, *Six Years of Hell* (Baton Rouge: Louisiana State Univ. Press, 1996), 130; "Record of Court of Inquiry," cited in Hearn, *Six Years of Hell*, 130.

20. Hearn, *Six Years of Hell*, 130.

21. Ibid., 132; *OR* 19, 1:576; Julius White to Thomas Ford, Nov. 18, 1862, Series 1, General Correspondence, 1833–1916, Abraham Lincoln Papers, LC.

22. Hearn, *Six Years of Hell*, 133; *OR* 19, 2:174, 181–182.

23. *OR* 19, 1:530, 534, 716, 775, 756, 764.

24. *OR* 19, 1:533, 549, 701, 778, 791; "Consolidated Morning Report of the 3rd Brigade, Maryland Heights, Sept. 12, 1862," Returns of the Middle Department, Antietam Studies, NA. Ford claimed that the 32nd OH numbered only 400–500, but 742 men of the regiment

were surrendered. The strength of Steiner's battalion is unknown, but the total strength of his regiment was 791. If an average company was 79 men, then Steiner had nearly 240 in his battalion. Thus Ford may have had nearly 1,000 infantry, 225 cavalry, and 100 artillerymen, or about 200 more men than he claimed he had.

25. *OR* 19, 1:533, 743, 756.

26. *OR* 19, 1:533, 556; Hearn, *Six Years of Hell*, 96, 111; Carman, chap. 3, 126. A detachment of the 1st MD Potomac Home Brigade was stationed to observe Cheek's Ford, near the mouth of the Monocacy River. Col. Banning, with 200 men of his regiment (the 87th OH) and two guns from Graham's battery, were ordered to Point of Rocks on Aug. 27. See *OR* 51, 1:765–766.

27. *OR* 19, 1:764–765.

28. *OR* 19, 1:595–596, 743. There is no evidence that the trees D'Utassy recommended to have removed were ever cut down.

29. *OR* 19, 1:542, 697, 706.

30. *OR* 19, 2:180–181; *OR* 51, 1:534, 794–795; *OR* 19, 1:534.

31. *OR* 51, 1:798; *OR* 19, 1:534.

32. *OR* 19, 1:517–518; *OR* 19, 2:206.

33. *OR* 19, 1:535; *OR* 51, 1:798–799.

34. *OR* 19, 1:535, 757. Also see *OR* 51, 1:798. Although Miles reported the Loring rumor to Halleck, he did not relate it to White, which may indicate that Miles was not sure of its accuracy. See *OR* 51, 1:804, 812.

35. *OR* 19, 1:535. Also see *OR* 51, 1:804.

36. *OR* 19, 1:535, 545.

37. Ibid., 535.

38. Ibid., 535–536; *OR* 19, 2:249; Hunter McGuire to Jedediah Hotchkiss, Jan. 22, 1897, Hotchkiss Papers, LC.

39. *OR* 51, 1:812. Miles's correspondence to White was sent before he received White's dispatch about Downey's reconnaissance, but the news about Downey did not change Miles's thinking as to how the two garrisons should operate.

40. Davidson, *Diary and Letters*, 47. Davidson wrote that Jackson's command had left his quartermaster, commissary, and ordnance wagons behind at the Rappahannock River two weeks earlier, and they "have not as yet overtaken us." But other members of Jackson's command mention the presence of wagons in Maryland, so Jackson had some transportation. See James F. L. Caldwell, *The History of a Brigade of South Carolinians* (Dayton, OH: Morningside Press, 1984), 41. For the orders that wagons were to be reduced to one per regiment, see King diary, Sept. 9, 1862, SHC.

41. Shuler diary, LC; Joseph J. Norton diary, SCSL. Norton is the source stating that A. P. Hill led that day, followed by J. R. Jones and Lawton, for he wrote on the 11th that they had to wait for two divisions to pass them before starting. Also see Douglas, *I Rode with Stonewall*, 152; Douglas, "Stonewall Jackson in Maryland," in *B&L*, 2:622; *OR* 19, 1:825, 952, 953; Harsh, *Taken at the Flood*, 175.

42. Hotchkiss diary, Sept. 10, 1862, LC; Davidson, *Diary and Letters*, 48; Douglas, *I Rode with Stonewall*, 152. It took Jackson's column about 6–7 hours to march the 10.2 miles from Frederick to Middletown.

43. Davidson, *Diary and Letters*, 48.

44. Carman, chap. 6, 311. Two diarists, one in J. R. Jones's division and the other in A. P. Hill's, confirm that both of these divisions camped west of South Mountain. See Shuler diary, LC; Norton diary, SCSL. Jubal Early also agrees with Carman's placement of Lawton east of the mountains, between Middletown and Turner's Gap. See Early, *War Memoirs*, 135. According to Capt. Greenlee Davidson, it was dusk when his battery halted and went into camp. See Davidson, *Diary and Letters*, 48.

45. Douglas, *I Rode with Stonewall*, 152–154; Hunter McGuire to Jedediah Hotchkiss, Jan. 22, 1897, Hotchkiss Papers, LC; Davidson, *Diary and Letters*, 48. McGuire thought that Douglas greatly exaggerated this incident

and that Jackson was never in the danger that Douglas described.

46. Haynes, *Field Diary*, 16–17.

47. Robertson, *Stonewall Jackson*, 595.

48. Joseph Orr diary, SCHS; Schuler diary, LC; Davidson, *Diary and Letters*, 48–49. Shuler wrote that his brigade "marched at daylight." Orr related that his division waited on the roadside for three and a half hours while J. R. Jones's and Lawton's divisions passed by. Sunrise on Sept. 11 was at 5:45 a.m.

49. Capt. Davidson recorded that Hill's division reached the Potomac at 3 p.m. Since it took approximately three and a half hours for two divisions to pass Hill's division that morning, the head of the column would have reached the Potomac around 11:30 a.m. or noon. See Davidson, *Diary and Letters*, 49; Orr diary, SCHS; J. G. Morrison, "Jackson at Harper's Ferry," *PWP*, Dec. 22, 1883.

50. *OR* 19, 1:953, 966.

51. Davidson, *Diary and Letters*, 49; Norton diary, SCSL; Schuler diary, LC; Haynes, *Field Diary*, 17.

52. Henry B. Curtis Jr. to Lucy, Sept. 11, 1862, Curtis Jr. Papers, USAHEC; *OR* 19, 1:524; *OR Suppl.* 12, 2:621.

53. *OR* 19, 1:524; *OR* 51, 1:820; Henry B. Curtis Jr. to Lucy, Sept. 11, 1862, Curtis Jr. Papers, USA-HEC.

54. *OR* 19, 1:524. White reported that his brigade marched at 2 a.m. The 125th NY recorded that they left at 3 a.m. See Ezra D. Simons, *A Regimental History: The One Hundred and Twenty-Fifth New York Volunteers* (New York: Ezra D. Simons, 1888), 25. Captain Davidson claimed that the Federals left "about 80,000 pounds" of hardtack at Martinsburg. See Davidson, *Diary and Letters*, 49.

55. *OR* 19, 1:524; Simons, *Regimental History*, 27–28; *OR Suppl.* 46, 2:585.

56. Davidson, *Diary and Letters*, 49; Douglas, *I Rode with Stonewall*, 156–157; Caldwell, *History of a Brigade*, 42. Also see Hotchkiss diary, LC.

57. Douglas, *I Rode with Stonewall*, 158; Hotchkiss diary, LC.

58. One diarist recorded that they remained in Martinsburg for four hours; another said two to three hours. See Howard diary, NCSA; Norton diary, SCSL. Capt. Greenlee Davidson noted that "hundreds of the men are perfectly barefooted," and—contrary to myth and legend—soldiers were excused from duty if they were without shoes, except in the most extreme circumstances. See Davidson, *Diary and Letters*, 50.

59. Richard Lowe, *Walker's Texas Division, C.S.A.* (Baton Rouge: Louisiana State Univ. Press, 2004), 61–62; Eicher and Eicher, *Civil War High Commands*, 549.

60. For the movements of Walker's division north of the Potomac, see Walkup diary, SHC; Burgwyn, *Captain's War*, 16–17; Walker, "Jackson's Capture of Harper's Ferry," in *B&L*, 2:604–605. Walker's account is at odds with his own official report, where he states that he received orders from Lee on Sept. 9. The movements on the 9th were also not those of a division whose commander was privy to all the plans of his commander. For Walker's report, see *OR* 19, 1:912–913.

61. Harris diary, NCSA; Burgwyn, *Captain's War*, 17; Carman, chap. 6, 310. For Duffy's service record, see American Civil War Research Database, www.civilwardata.com/active/hdsquery.dll?SoldierHistory?C&119706 [members-only access].

62. Walker, "Jackson's Capture of Harper's Ferry," in *B&L*, 2:606; *OR* 19, 1:912–913; Burgwyn, *Captain's War*, 17; Robert K. Krick, *30th Virginia Infantry* (Berryville, VA: H. E. Howard, 1983), 21; Walkup diary, SHC. Walkup wrote that they left at 7 p.m. on the 10th, while Burgwyn noted the time as 7:30 p.m.

63. Krick, *30th Virginia Infantry*, 22; Walker, "Jackson's Capture of Harper's Ferry," in *B&L*, 2:607; *NC Regts*, 2:432; *OR* 19, 1:913; Walkup diary, SHC; Byrd B. Tribble, *Benjamin Cason*

Rawlings: First Virginia Volunteer for the South (Gaithersburg, MD: Butternut and Blue, 1995), 45.

64. Burgwyn, *Captain's War*, 17; *OR* 19, 1:913; Krick, *30th Virginia Infantry*, 22. The route Walker followed is not certain. Diarists in the division recorded that they marched 14–15 miles that day, which indicates that they probably marched south from the Potomac to beyond Waterford before turning west on one of the roads that made its way to Hillsborough.

65. An officer in the 35th NC noted in his diary on Sept. 13 that it was not believed that the Yankees would capitulate, but instead "would endeavor to cut their way through our brigade and not surrender." See Burgwyn, *Captain's War*, 17.

66. Robert W. Shand reminiscences, Shand Family Papers, SCSL; Hill diary, MDAH; King diary, SHC; Lafayette McLaws, "The Capture of Harper's Ferry," *PWP*, Sept. 12, 1888. McLaws complained in this article that "if I had had free scope [on the 10th] I could have reached Pleasant Valley early on the 11th and by the 12th would have had Maryland Heights." See Krick, *Staff Officers in Gray*, 194.

67. King diary, SHC; Hill diary, MDAH; Kirkpatrick diary, THC.

68. King diary, SHC; McLaws, "Capture of Harper's Ferry," *PWP*, Sept. 12, 1888; Krick, *Staff Officers in Gray*, 90.

69. King diary, SHC. King wrote that "over 100 persons," meaning civilians, were entertained by Mr. Boteler that night. Also see McLaws, "Capture of Harper's Ferry," *PWP*, Sept. 5, 1888.

70. Samuel B. Pettengill, *The College Cavaliers* (Chicago: H. McAllister, 1883), 62. Pettengill stated that the Confederates built the Lookout in 1861 as an observation post. Also see *OR* 19, 1:543, 608, 710; James D. Nance to Laura, Sept. 24, 1862, SCSL; Shand reminiscences, SCSL.

71. *OR* 19, 1:542, 601. The strength of the three companies is arrived at by taking the average company strength of the two regiments.

72. *OR* 51, 1:819.

73. *OR* 19, 1:853; Augustus D. Dickert, *History of Kershaw's Brigade* (Dayton, OH: Morningside Books, 1973), 147; McLaws, "Capture of Harper's Ferry," *PWP*, Sept. 5, 1888; George S. Bernard, *War Talks of Confederate Veterans* (Dayton, OH: Morningside Press, 1981), 41. Bernard gives the strength of the 6th VA, the 12th VA, and the 16th VA as 520, which gives an average of 173 per regiment. This average is applied to the 41st VA to arrive at a brigade strength of approximately 700.

74. *OR* 19, 1:853; King diary, SHC. It is not certain that McLaws maintained signal communication with Wright, but he probably did, since he established signals with Kershaw.

75. *OR* 19, 1:862–863; Dickert, *History of Kershaw's Brigade*, 147; J. J. McDaniel, *Diary of the Battles, Marches, and Incidents of the Seventh S. C. Regiment* (n.p., n.d.), 11; Edwin Kerrison to sister, Sept. 18, 1862, Kerrison Family Papers, SCSL; King diary, SHC. McDaniel wrote that one of the skirmish companies was from the 3rd SC. Kerrison's wartime letter indicates that it was from the 2nd SC.

76. *OR* 19, 1:601, 862; John M. Pellicano, *Conquer or Die: The 39th New York Volunteer Infantry; Garibaldi Guard* (Flushing, NY: Pellicano, 1996), 26–27, 69–70.

77. *OR* 19, 1:601, 862; King diary, SHC. Precisely where this initial skirmish took place is unknown, although it was well north of the Lookout. Hildebrandt's testimony places it somewhere on the western slope of the mountain.

78. King diary, SHC; *OR* 19, 1:601, 862–863.

79. Frank Moore, ed., *The Rebellion Record: A Diary of American Events*, 12 vols. (New York: Arno Press, 1977), 5:445. Neither Kershaw or Capt. King, whose diary is very specific about the times when skirmishes occurred during the

march south to Maryland Heights, mentioned skirmishing at 3:30 p.m., which is when the *New York Times* correspondent reported that it began. Hildebrandt's own testimony before the Harpers Ferry Commission makes it clear that he had no skirmish at that time. The only other troops that could have been involved were Hibbetts's company or elements of Company I or H of the 1st MD Potomac Home Brigade. Whoever it was, the Confederate accounts are clear that the resistance was inconsequential.

80. *OR* 19, 1:863; King diary, SHC.
81. King diary, SHC; Hill diary, MDAH; Shand reminiscences, SCSL; Mac Wyckoff, *A History of the 2nd South Carolina Infantry, 1861–1865* (Fredericksburg, VA: Sgt. Kirkland's Museum and Historical Society, 1994), 180, 185, 234.
82. *OR* 19, 1:577, 607, 672, 675; Harsh, *Sounding the Shallows*, 14; Arabella M. Willson, *Disaster, Struggle, Triumph: The Adventures of One Thousand Boys in Blue* (Albany, NY: Argus, 1870), 57. Trimble may have deliberately selected the 126th NY because he did not want to detach one of his better-trained regiments from his front, or this regiment may simply have been the most convenient one to send.
83. Willson, *Disaster, Struggle, Triumph*, 57–58; *OR* 19, 1:542, 601, 607, 672. The 126th adjutant, Samuel A. Barras, testified that "there was none of the Thirty-second Ohio there that night." But Barras's testimony implies that he remained at the Lookout, and he may not have seen the Ohio companies. Col. Ford's official report of the action states that he sent the five companies of the 32nd up the mountain with Hewitt and the 126th. No one indicates the position of the 32nd's five companies that night. It is likely that Hewitt formed them in support of the 126th at the breastwork. See *OR* 19, 1:542, 672.
84. *OR* 19, 1:601, 713.
85. Ibid., 568, 772. Hewitt never mentions that he met with Sherrill that night, but Lt. Carnes's testimony makes it clear that he did, and also

that it may have been Sherrill who ordered Hewitt to go down and see Ford and Miles in person. Unfortunately, Sherrill did not testify to the Harpers Ferry Commission because of the wound he received on Sept. 13.
86. *OR* 19, 1:543, 568. Also see *OR* 19, 1:563. Lt. Binney's account is inaccurate in several particulars. For example, there were no reinforcements sent to Maryland Heights on the 12th after the 126th New York.
87. White, "Capitulation of Harper's Ferry," in *B&L*, 2:612; *OR* 19, 1:525, 774–775.
88. *OR* 19, 1:531, 716; White, "Capitulation of Harper's Ferry," in *B&L*, 2:612.
89. *OR* 19, 1:567, 607, 672, 675. On the night of Sept. 12, when it was thought that the 126th was to go over to Maryland Heights early the next morning, Adjutant Barras was so concerned about the regiment's lack of training that he took several companies out and drilled them on loading their rifles.
90. *OR* 19, 1:542, 567–568, 601, 709, 713, 702, 727; Willson, *Disaster, Struggle, Triumph*, 57–58. Strength figures are derived from *OR* 19, 1:549. It is not certain that all the companies listed were at Ford's headquarters that night. Some were picketing approaches, but their position is not identified. An average of 80 men per company for the 126th was used.
91. *OR* 19, 1:557, 853.
92. Ibid.

Chapter 7. The Battle for Maryland Heights

1. *OR* 19, 1:601, 727; "*New York Times* Narrative," in Moore, *Rebellion Record*, 5:445.
2. *OR* 19, 1:707, 621–622.
3. Ibid, 707.
4. Ibid., 607.
5. Ibid, 601, 607, 727. For the deployment, see "*New York Times* Narrative," in Moore, *Rebellion Record*, 5:445. Participants differed on the deployment of this first line of battle and on who was present. Maj. Hildebrandt, for

instance, testified that his companies were on the extreme right. See *OR* 19, 1:601. Since the *New York Times* account was more contemporary than Hildebrandt's testimony, I have accepted it as more accurate. The approximate strengths of the units on this line are as follows: 39th NY—150, 32nd OH—140, 126th NY—560, 1st MD Potomac Home Brigade—160, 1st MD Cavalry—146.

6. *OR* 19, 1:727, 607.

7. Ibid., 607, 672, 727; King diary, SHC. King recorded that the long roll was beat at 7 a.m. and the attack developed at 7:50 a.m.

8. *OR* 19, 1:607, 727.

9. Ibid., 570, 727, 601, 607, 672, 676, 863; King diary, SHC; Wayne Mahood, *"Written in Blood": A History of the 126th New York Infantry in the Civil War* (Hightstown, NJ: Longstreet House, 1997), 36; "*New York Times* Narrative," in Moore, *Rebellion Record*, 5:445.

10. *OR* 19, 1:608, 672, 727, 728, 863; "*New York Times* Narrative," in Moore, *Rebellion Record*, 5:445; King diary, SHC; McDaniel, *Diary of the Battles*, 12; "Our Army Correspondence," *Charleston (SC) Daily Courier*, Oct. 14, 1862. Capt. Russell is the source stating that some of the 126th left the fight before Sherrill was wounded. See *OR* 19, 1:728.

11. McDaniel, *Diary of the Battles*, 12; *OR* 19, 1:608, 863.

12. *OR* 19, 1:863; "Our Army Correspondence," *Charleston (SC) Daily Courier*, Oct. 14, 1862; King diary, SHC; "*New York Times* Narrative," in Moore, *Rebellion Record*, 5:445.

13. *OR* 19, 1:568, 614.

14. Ibid., 614, 673, 728; Willson, *Disaster, Struggle, Triumph*, 59–60. Willson's passages on Maryland Heights and Harpers Ferry are a passionate, but not entirely accurate, account of what happened.

15. *OR* 19, 1:677. Barras testified that he ran back and forth to the Lookout several times during the engagement to retrieve men trying to leave the fighting, and that he saw Hewitt there "most of the time."

16. *OR* 19, 1:728, 863. It is possible that Russell included the initial attack of the 3rd SC as one of the three separate assaults. See James D. Nance to Laura, Sept. 24, 1862, SCSL. The open area in front of the Union works is described in McDaniel, *Diary of the Battles*, 12. Also see Dickert, *History of Kershaw's Brigade*, 148–149. Dickert's account is rather confused and downright incorrect in many particulars of the engagement, but it is useful for illustrating the awful carnage in the ranks of the 7th and the 8th regiments.

17. *OR* 19, 1:863, 867–868; Wyckoff, *3rd South Carolina Infantry*, 63, 283; James D. Nance to Laura, Sept. 24, 1862, SCSL; King diary, SHC; "Our Army Correspondence," *Charleston (SC) Daily Courier*, Oct. 14, 1862. One company of the 3rd was on picket duty and not engaged.

18. Willson, *Disaster, Struggle, Triumph*, 61, 66; Richard A. Bassett to Mary, Sept. 22, 1862, OCHS. Willson's statement that Sherrill's fall only emboldened the 126th is not supported by the testimony of other observers. See *OR* 19, 1:571, 608, 728, 733–734; "*New York Times* Narrative," in Moore, *Rebellion Record*, 5:445.

19. Willson, *Disaster, Struggle, Triumph*, 61. Willson writes that Companies C and D "completely foiled" the turning movement of the Confederates. The testimony of every witness before the Harpers Ferry Commission who was present at the breastwork disputes this claim.

20. *OR* 19, 1:571, 608, 614, 713, 728; "*New York Times* Narrative," in Moore, *Rebellion Record*, 5:445–446. Lt. Carnes testified but said nothing about his role in ordering the retreat. Hewitt's sworn statement was that he sent only Carnes, but Downey's testimony is clear that two messengers came up from the rear with orders to retreat. Hewitt's avowals lacked consistency. At his second appearance before the Harpers Ferry Commission, he said he ordered the troops at the breastwork to hold on as long as possible, then to retreat in good order. But he and Carnes were consis-

tent in placing the blame for the retreat on the disorder in the 126th NY, although there is no evidence from those fighting at the breastwork that the 126th withdrew before Hewitt's orders arrived.

21. For Hewitt's and Carnes's testimony, see *OR* 19, 1:566–576, 733–737, 771–774.

22. James D. Nance to Laura, Sept. 24, 1862, SCSL; *OR* 19, 1:863, 867–868; "Our Army Correspondence," *Charleston (SC) Daily Courier,* Oct. 14, 1862; King diary, SHC.

23. *OR* 19, 1:861; McDaniel, *Diary of the Battles,* 12; Wyckoff, *3rd South Carolina Infantry,* 71–72.

24. Federal losses were determined from several sources. See *OR* 19, 1:549, 568, 610, 620, 679; Frederick Phisterer, *New York in the War of the Rebellion,* 6 vols. (Albany, NY: J. B. Lyon, 1912), 4:3497, 3:2189; *OR* 19, 1:713–714, 728; King diary, SHC. For criticism of Hewitt by the 126th NY, see Willson, *Disaster, Struggle, Triumph,* 60–62, 67; *OR* 19, 1:569.

25. *OR* 19, 1:546, 707, 711.

26. *OR* 19, 1:563, 580, 625–626, 631, 645. The time when Sammon and Cameron received their orders is not known, but Sammon arrived on the mountain between 11 a.m. and 12 p.m., which would mean he received his orders before 9 a.m.

27. *OR* 19, 1:610, 645.

28. Ibid., 645.

29. Ibid., 614–615.

30. Ibid., 615, 773.

31. Ibid., 615–616.

32. Ibid., 602, 620, 691.

33. Ibid., 648, 680.

34. Ibid., 627, 695.

35. Ibid., 526, 543, 578–579, 595, 693, 719, 796. Mrs. Elizabeth Brown, the wife of a captain in the 1st MD Potomac Home Brigade, testified that she was present in the house where Binney, Miles, and Ford met. She claimed that Miles emphatically denied Ford any more reinforcements, but she also admitted that she did not hear the entire conversation between the two men. Binney did, and his

testimony that Miles conditionally agreed to send reinforcements is accepted as accurate.

36. *OR* 19, 1:617. Lt. Col. Downey thought that they could have held out on the mountain until the morning of the 14th without reinforcements.

37. Ibid., 799.

38. King diary, SHC. The *New York Times* correspondent with McGrath's battery claimed that they commenced shelling the mountain at 10 a.m., which is unlikely, since the battle at the breastwork was still going on at that time. See "*New York Times* Narrative," in Moore, *Rebellion Record,* 5:446. Also see *OR* 19, 1:615–616.

39. *OR* 19, 1:546, 707. Ford's dispatch is not timed. Pearce thought it was around 2 p.m., although he was not certain of the time.

40. *OR* 19, 1:580, 707, 729.

41. Ibid., 546.

42. Ibid., 544, 692–693, 707. Lt. Pearce's testimony implies that Miles's reply stated that further reinforcements could not be spared. McGrath's testimony indicates that Miles's order was conditional and not absolute.

43. *OR* 19, 1:618–619. Lt. Col. Downey testified that he received the order around 3 p.m., which means Ford wrote it around 2:30 p.m. or shortly thereafter.

44. *OR* 19, 1:618–619, 697, 707. No one could agree on what time the evacuation took place. Julius White, in his report dated Sept. 22, stated that it was 3:30 p.m.; the *New York Times* correspondent, at McGrath's battery, stated positively that it was 4 p.m. See "*New York Times* Narrative," in Moore, *Rebellion Record,* 5:446. Probably both White and the *Times* correspondent are correct. If Downey received his orders to retreat at 3 p.m., it was probably 3:30 p.m. before his men reached the naval battery, and it may have been 4 p.m. before McGrath's artillerymen left.

45. *OR* 19, 1:557, 576, 596. Col. Sammon of the 115th testified that he encountered Ford and Miles after coming down off the mountain

and their interview "appeared to be pleasant, very much so, as far as I could judge from their countenances." See *OR* 19, 1:627. Also see the testimony of Captain Angelo Powell, *OR* 19, 1:763.

46. Henry A. Curtis Jr. to Lucy, Sept. 18, 1862, box B-16, Gregory Coco Collection, GNMP; McLaws, "Capture of Harper's Ferry," *PWP*, Sept. 5, 1888; *OR* 19, 1:799.

47. *OR* 19, 1:863; King diary, SHC.

48. *OR* 19, 1:854, 752; McLaws, "Capture of Harper's Ferry," *PWP*, Sept. 5, 1888.

49. McLaws, "Capture of Harper's Ferry," *PWP*, Sept. 5, 1888; Bernard, *War Talks*, 25. According to Bernard, Parham's brigade was ordered to occupy Solomon's Gap on the morning of the 13th. McLaws recalled the brigade to Brownsville later in the day, but he directed that Parham leave one regiment at Solomon's Gap and send another to Crampton's Gap.

50. King diary, SHC; *OR* 19, 1:854; 2:607.

51. *OR* 19, 2:606–607.

52. McLaws, "Capture of Harper's Ferry," *PWP*, Sept. 5, 1888; Carman, chap. 6, 338.

53. King diary, SHC.

54. *Boston Evening Transcript*, Sept. 19, 1862; W. H. Scorsby, "Surrender of Harper's Ferry," *NT*, Aug. 21, 1884; G. G. Benedict, *Vermont in the Civil War*, 2 vols. (Burlington, VT: Free Press Assoc., 1886–1888), 2:192.

55. Nicholas DeGraff memoir, *CWTI* Collection, USAHEC; "*New York Times* Narrative," in Moore, *Rebellion Record*, 5:446; William H. Luff, "March of the Cavalry from Harper's Ferry, September 14, 1862," in MOLLUS, *Military Essays and Recollections: Papers Read Before the Commandery of the State of Illinois*, 4 vols. (Chicago: A. C. McClurg, 1891–1907), 1:38; White, "Capitulation of Harper's Ferry," in *B&L*, 612.

56. White, "Capitulation of Harper's Ferry," in *B&L*, 612. White is clear that this meeting took place on the night of the 13th, not the 14th. Lt. Col. Hasbrouck Davis's account supports White's, and he is the source for the

decision that "the original route proposed on Saturday was to cross the Shenandoah near Harper's Ferry." Lt. Henry Binney testified that a meeting between Miles and Davis took place on the night of the 14th, but Binney may have mixed up the dates; it is also possible that the two officers met again before the cavalry left on the 14th. Binney claimed that the meeting took place at 7 or 7:30 p.m. The cavalry marched between 8 and 9 p.m. on Sept. 14, which meant, if Binney were correct, that in only about one hour's time instructions were issued and the entire 1,500-man cavalry formed up to depart, which is impossible. Capt. Charles Russell also offered evidence of a Sept. 13 meeting, because Miles asked him that night if he thought he could guide the cavalry force out of Harpers Ferry. See *OR* 19, 1:584, 630, 720. Also see Thomas Bell, "Longstreet's Train," *NT*, July 3, 1884. Bell served in the 8th NY Cavalry and claimed to have heard the exchange of words between Davis and Miles. This is unlikely, but he may have heard about it from someone else in the regiment later.

57. *OR* 19, 1:720. The fact that Miles asked Russell whether he could guide the cavalry out of Harpers Ferry places the time of Russell's meeting with Miles after Miles had met with Davis and White.

58. *OR* 19, 1:720.

Chapter 8. September 13

1. Alfred Pleasonton to Randolph Marcy, 1:30 a.m., Sept. 13, 1862, reel 31, MP; Hard, *Eighth Cavalry Regiment*, 175; *OR* 19, 1:209; *OR* 51, 1:822–825; Beach, *First New York (Lincoln) Cavalry*, 170; Bates, *Pennsylvania Volunteers*, 2:1144; Tobie, *First Maine Cavalry*, 92; *OR Suppl.* 3, 1:524. Regarding the 12th PA, in writing their history Bates claims that they were detached to the 2nd Corps, but Pleasonton's dispatch to Marcy on the 13th states that they were to accompany McReynolds. With no other

sources about this regiment's activities, it seems likely that part of the regiment was detached and part accompanied McReynolds.

2. *OR* 19, 1:209, 416–417; Ambrose Burnside to Randolph Marcy, 1 a.m., Sept. 13, 1862, and Alfred Pleasonton to Randolph Marcy, 1:30 a.m., Sept. 13, 1862, reel 31, MP.

3. Strother, "Personal Recollections," 275; *New York Tribune*, Sept. 16, 1862; GBM to Mary Ellen, Sept. 14, 1862, reel 31, MP.

4. Strother, "Personal Recollections," 275; *OR* 19, 2:277.

5. *OR* 19, 1:209, 816, 823. Lt. Peter Hains, commanding Battery M, 2nd U.S. Artillery, gives the time the Confederates opened fire from Catoctin Mountain as 6 a.m. See *OR Suppl.* 3, 1:524; von Borcke, *Memoirs of the Confederate War for Independence*, 205.

6. *OR* 19, 1:823; McClellan, *Life and Campaigns*, 114–115; von Borcke, *Memoirs*, 205; Robert E. Lee to J. E. B. Stuart, 2:30 p.m., Sept. 12, 1862, box 2, James E. B. Stuart Papers, HL. This dispatch does not appear in the *OR*.

7. *OR* 19, 1:823; Alfred Pleasonton to Randolph Marcy, 11 a.m., Sept. 13, 1862, reel 31, MP; Cox, *Military Reminiscences*, 1:274.

8. *OR* 19, 1:817, 823. There is some discrepancy regarding the time when the Federals captured the pass. Stuart and Hampton both reported that it was 2 p.m., but Pleasonton sent a dispatch to Marcy at 1 p.m. that afternoon stating that he had cleared the pass. Since this was written at the moment it happened, with Stuart's report not written until Feb. 1864 and Hampton's in Oct. 1862, I have accepted Pleasonton's timing.

9. *OR* 19, 1:209, 817, 823. Pleasonton's report is quite sketchy and not very accurate about this engagement. See Crowninshield, *Massachusetts Cavalry Volunteers*, 74; Brooks, *Stories of the Confederacy*, 83; Ford, *Cycle of Adams Letters*, 1:186; A. C. Koogle, "Fiftieth Anniversary of South Mountain Battle," *Valley Register* (Middletown, MD), Sept. 13, 1912. Although

Confederate accounts are vague on whether they made a stand east of Middletown, it is clear from Capt. Horatio Gibson's after-action report that they did. See *OR Suppl.* 3:527–528.

10. "Destructive Fire," *Valley Register* (Middletown, MD), Sept. 13, 1862. This account states that Stuart made his headquarters at Koogle's on the night of the 12th. Also see John W. M. Long, "South Mountain Battle Events," *Valley Register* (Middletown, MD), July 7, 1922; A. C. Koogle, "Graphic Story of the War in Middletown," *Valley Register* (Middletown, MD), Sept. 13, 1912. According to Koogle's son, when his father implored Stuart not to burn the bridge, one of Stuart's staff remarked "that a man who had a son in the army fighting against them could not expect to dictate." The Confederate soldier recovering at the farm was Robert H. Alsobrook of the 1st Company, Washington Artillery. He was injured by the premature explosion of an ammunition chest during the Confederate march from Frederick to Hagerstown. Koogle asked Stuart to take the wounded Rebel, but Stuart refused because Alsobrook's injuries were too severe. A. C. Koogle, Koogle's son, who served in Battery A, 1st MD Artillery, was wounded at Antietam and recovered at his father's home, where he and Alsobrook "became quit chummy." Alsobrook recovered, was exchanged, and returned to his battery. For Alsobrook's service record, see Andrew B. Booth, *Records of Louisiana Confederate Soldiers and Louisiana Confederate Commands*, 3 vols. (New Orleans, 1920), 1:53.

11. *OR* 19, 1:817; R. Channing Price to Mother, Sept. 18, 1862, in Robert J. Trout, ed., *With Pen and Saber: The Letters and Diaries of J. E. B. Stuart's Staff Officers* (Harrisburg, PA: Stackpole Books, 1995), 99.

12. Hard, *Eighth Cavalry Regiment*, 176; Ford, *Cycle of Adams Letters*, 186–187. The 1st NC's losses are taken from W. H. Cheek to Ezra A. Carman, June 14, 1897, Antietam Studies, NA.

13. Although Pleasonton reported that the burning of the bridge did not slow him down, the historian of the 1st MA recorded that it did delay the artillery. See *OR* 19, 1:209; Crowninshield, *Massachusetts Cavalry Volunteers*, 74; Hard, *Eighth Cavalry Regiment*, 176; Timothy J. Reese, "The Cavalry Clash at Quebec Schoolhouse," *Blue and Gray Magazine* 10, no. 3 (1993), 24. Also see Reese's letter to the editor of *Blue and Gray*, correcting the location of the Quebec Schoolhouse, in *Blue and Gray Magazine* 11, no. 2 (1993), 8, 64.

14. *OR* 19, 1:824; Reese, "Quebec Schoolhouse," [10, no. 3,] 26–28, [11, no. 2.] 8, 64; Brooks, *Stories of the Confederacy*, 85–86. The precise movements of Hampton and Medill are not known, but from what evidence that does exist, it appears that Hampton's brigade followed what is now Picnic Woods Road and Medill followed the Burkittsville–Middletown Road. According to the unidentified officer who penned the account of Hampton's brigade for Brooks's *Stories of the Confederacy*, the Federals advanced against them by a road running perpendicular to the one Hampton was marching along. This would indicate that Medill turned his command west on the Quebec School Road, which connected Picnic Woods Road with the Burkittsville Road.

15. Charles N. Dawson to Mollie, Oct. 11, 1862, Steve Stottlemeyer Collection, Antietam NB.

16. *OR* 19, 1:824. The Army of the Potomac officially reported losses of 5 killed, 21 wounded, and 5 captured in the engagements at Catoctin Mountain and Middletown Valley. On Sept. 15, 1862, the *New York Tribune* reported the Union losses as 3 wounded in the Middletown skirmish and 30 killed and wounded in Medill's fight with Hampton. Also see *OR* 19, 1:204; Hard, *Eighth Cavalry Regiment*, 176; Charles N. Dawson to Mollie, Oct. 11, 1862, Steve Stottlemeyer Collection, Antietam NB.

17. Ford, *Cycle of Adams Letters*, 187–188; *OR* 19, 1:209–210; Hard, *Eighth Cavalry Regiment*, 177.

Hard relates that they captured two Confederates in the late-day reconnaissance and lost one severely wounded man.

18. *OR* 19, 1:209, 449–450, 825; Carman, chap. 7, 16. While no Union source indicates that anyone advanced on the road from Point of Rocks, Munford is clear that Federal troops advanced against him on this road. This could only have been the 6th U.S.

19. *OR* 19, 1:825; Thomas Munford, "History of 2nd Virginia Cavalry," Munford-Ellis Family Papers, DU.

20. Neese, *Confederate Horse Artillery*, 118; *OR* 19, 1:450, 825; Johnson, *Long Roll*, 182–183.

21. Johnson, *Long Roll*, 183; *OR* 19, 1:450.

22. *OR* 19, 1:825–826; Munford, "2nd Virginia Cavalry"; Carman, chap. 7, 16.

23. Carman, chap. 7, 16.

24. "Fifth Virginia Cavalry Notes, Fitz Lee's Brigade," Antietam Studies, NA; Ezra A. Carman to Thomas Rosser, May 12, 1897, Antietam Studies, RG 92, NA; *New York Tribune*, Sept. 15, 1862.

25. "Fifth Virginia Cavalry Notes," Antietam Studies, NA; Beach, *First New York (Lincoln) Cavalry*, 171; Bates, *Pennsylvania Volunteers*, 5:112; George W. Beale to Ezra A. Carman, June 6, 1894, Antietam Studies, NA.

26. Sebastian Duncan Jr. to father, Sept. 13, 1862, Carman diary, NJHS; Wilbur D. Jones, *Giants in the Cornfield: The 27th Indiana Infantry* (Shippensburg, PA: White Mane, 1997), 229.

27. Josiah Williams to *Century Magazine* editors, June 14, 1886, ISL; Silas Colgrove, "The Finding of Lee's Lost Order," in *B&L*, 2:603; Carman, chap. 7, 375; Edward R. Brown, *The Twenty-Seventh Indiana Volunteer Infantry in the War of the Rebellion* (Gaithersburg, MD: Butternut Press, 1984), 228.

28. Jones, *Giants in the Cornfield*, 229–233; Josiah Williams to *Century Magazine* editors, June 14, 1886, ISL; Colgrove, "Finding of Lee's Lost Order," in *B&L*, 2:603; Carman, chap. 7, 375–376; Brown, *Twenty-Seventh Indiana*, 228; J. Balsley, "Lee's Lost Order," *NT*, Mar. 26, 1908.

Balsley claimed that Pvt. David B. Vance was with Mitchell and Bloss when they found the order. Also see Samuel E. Pittman, "How Lee's Special Order Was Found," *NT*, June 25, 1925. General Williams's note is on reel 31, MP. There are many variations on the finding of the "lost order," and those who wish to pursue this in detail should refer to Wilbur Jones's careful examination of them in an appendix in *Giants in the Cornfield*. Josiah Williams's account of the finding agrees with Colgrove's in important details. The regiment was still in line when Mitchell found the order. Colgrove related that it was Bloss and Mitchell—he said nothing about Capt. Kop—who gave him the order and that they had wrapped it back around the cigars, which will disappoint those who hoped that the enlisted men at least were able to enjoy the cigars. Sgt. Bloss wrote that Kop accompanied him to Colgrove, but he did not say whether Mitchell also did or not. I have adopted middle ground here, contending the possibility that all three went to Colgrove.

29. Reel 41, Lincoln Papers, LC. Maurice D'Aoust discovered this important document in 2002.

30. *OR* 51, 1:829.

31. Jonathan Stowe of Sedgwick's division wrote in his diary that McClellan and Sumner reviewed them as they marched through Frederick "at noon." See Jonathan Stowe diary, *CWTI* Collection, USAHEC; Strother, "Personal Recollections," 276. Although Cox said he received orders to march at noon, he does not say when he marched or at what time he met McClellan. It may have been as late as 2 p.m., since two diarists in Cox's division wrote that they did not march until 2 p.m. See Sheets diary, USAHEC; Wight diary, RBHL. Also see Charles N. Walker and Rosemary Walker, "Diary of the War by Robt. S. Robertson," *Old Fort News* 28, no. 1 (1965), 54. Both Strother and Robertson place army headquarters on the road to the aqueduct or the reservoir. See Joseph S. C. Taber diary,

CWTI Collection, USAHEC; Freeman, *Lee's Lieutenants*, 2:718; Carman, chap. 7, 393.

32. According to the itinerary of the 1st Division, 9th Corps (Willcox's), they marched at 2 p.m. on the 13th. See *OR* 19, 1:432. But this does not agree with the diaries of some men in the division. Elisah Bracken of the 100th PA said they did not march until 5 p.m.; Ashman Ayers of the 50th PA wrote that they received orders to march at 3 p.m. and passed through Frederick at dark. See Elisha Bracken diary, Timothy Brooks Collection, USAHEC; Ashman Ayers diary, Susquehanna County Historical Society, Montrose, Pennsylvania. Capt. William Bolton of the 51st PA, in Sturgis's division, recorded in his journal that they left their bivouac near the Monocacy River "about 3 o'clock p.m." See William J. Bolton, *The Civil War Journal of Colonel William J. Bolton*, ed. Richard A. Sauers (Conshohocken, PA: Combined, 2000), 81.

33. GBM to Franklin, 6:20 p.m., Sept. 14, 1862, in *OR* 19, 1:45.

34. Ibid., 44.

35. Ibid., 45.

36. *New York Tribune*, Sept. 17, 1862, 8; Harwell, *Union Reader*, 169.

37. McClellan, *Civil War Papers*, 399; *OR* 19, 1:45.

38. *OR* 19, 1:45–46.

39. Smith's unsigned message and Franklin's signed endorsement are on reel 31, MP. Also see *OR* 51, 1:826–827.

40. *OR* 51, 1:432, 826; *OR* 19, 1:48. Sumner's orders were sent at 8:45 p.m.; Hooker's and Sykes's were sent at 11:30 p.m.

41. *OR* 51, 1:829. Pleasonton's orders were sent at 9 p.m. He received them at 5 a.m. For his reply, see Alfred Pleasonton to Randolph Marcy, 5 a.m., Sept. 14, 1862, reel 31, MP. Pleasonton's orders in the *OR* do not direct him to conduct a reconnaissance, but his official report and the memoirs of General Jacob Cox clearly show that he had such orders. See *OR* 19, 1:209–210; Cox, *Military Reminiscences*, 1:277–278.

42. McLaws, "Capture of Harper's Ferry," *PWP*, Sept. 12, 1888; Lafayette McLaws, "The Capture of Harper's Ferry," *PWP*, Sept. 19, 1888.
43. Webster diary, HL.
44. Strother, "Personal Recollections," 276–277.
45. Gibbon, *Personal Recollections*, 73.
46. *Baltimore Sun*, Sept. 16, 1862; Freeman, *Lee's Lieutenants*, 2:718, 721. It is possible that this Marylander learned that the Federals had discovered a Confederate order, but it is highly improbable that he learned it was Special Orders No. 191. Charles Marshall, one of Lee's aides, writing to D. H. Hill in 1867 on the subject, stated, "I remember perfectly that until we saw that report [McClellan's published report of the Maryland Campaign] Gen. Lee frequently expressed his inability to understand the sudden change in McClellan's tactics which took place after we left Frederick." See Stephen W. Sears, *Landscape Turned Red* (New Haven, CT: Ticknor & Fields, 1983), 351–352.
47. GBM to Henry W. Halleck, 8:45 p.m., Sept. 13, 1862, reel 31, MP. The time and date on the dispatch, as published in the *OR*, are incorrect. See *OR* 19, 2:288.
48. *OR* 19, 2:280–281.
49. Ibid., 281–282.
50. Ibid.
51. Ibid.
52. Ibid., 281.
53. Vautier journal, USAHEC.
54. Williams, *From the Cannon's Mouth*, 121; Josiah M. Favill, *The Diary of a Young Officer* (Chicago: R. R. Donnelly & Sons, 1909), 183; Washburn, *108th Regiment N.Y. Volunteers*, 19.
55. Gallagher, *Lee the Soldier*, 8, 26; *OR* 19, 1:145, 888; Latrobe diary, VHS. Not all of Longstreet's brigades arrived near Hagerstown on the 11th. Drayton's brigade of D. R. Jones's division marched only as far as Middletown that day and arrived in Hagerstown at 2:30 p.m. on the 12th. See Edings diary, LC; Harsh, *Sounding the Shallows*, 165.
56. *OR* 19, 1:145.
57. Robert E. Lee to J. E. B. Stuart, Sept. 12, 1862, box 2, Stuart Papers, HL.
58. *OR* 19, 2:606.
59. Robert E. Lee to J. E. B. Stuart, Sept. 13, 1862, box 2, Stuart Papers, HL.
60. *OR* 19, 2:606; Gallagher, *Lee the Soldier*, 8; George G. Grattan, "The Battle of Boonsboro Gap," *SHSP* 39 (1914), 36; Longstreet, *From Manassas to Appomattox*, 219–220. Lee recalled receiving Stuart's report from the Maryland civilian "soon after" both Stuart's earlier report and D. H. Hill's had been received. See Gallagher, *Lee the Soldier*, 26; Carman, chap. 7, 393. Although the evidence makes it unlikely that this citizen knew that the Federals had found Special Orders No. 191, security at McClellan's army headquarters was loose. On Sept. 16 the *Baltimore Sun* reported that a member of Col. Colgrove's regiment "found a paper purporting to be the Rebel Order No. 119 [*sic*]," and on Sept. 17 the *Baltimore American* filed a story written on Sept. 14 that "a portfolio, containing Jackson's orders, was found in the advance yesterday." If news of the lost order leaked to the Maryland press this quickly, it is not a stretch to think that a resourceful citizen could have learned this information as well.
61. Longstreet, *From Manassas to Appomattox*, 219–220. The 11th GA of Col. G. T. Anderson's brigade was also left at Hagerstown as a wagon guard.
62. Ibid., 220.
63. Carman, chap. 7, 396; D. H. Hill, "The Battle of South Mountain, or Boonsboro," in *B&L*, 2:560; *OR* 19, 2:606, 607. For some reason McLaws received the 10 p.m. dispatch from Talcott first, and the one from Long, sent that morning, second. See McLaws, "Capture of Harper's Ferry," *PWP*, Sept. 5, 1888.
64. Robert E. Lee to J. E. B. Stuart, Sept. 14, 1862, box 2, Stuart Papers, HL.
65. *OR* 19, 2:608.
66. Longstreet, *From Manassas to Appomattox*, 220. In this postwar book, Longstreet reported

that his command marched at daylight on the 14th, but more contemporaneous sources indicate that the column did not start until late morning on Sept. 14 (see chap. 10, note 25 in the present volume). Moreover, there is no evidence that Lee thought Longstreet was tardy in moving.

Chapter 9. The Morning Battle for Fox's Gap

1. *OR* 19, 1:1019; Hill, "Battle of South Mountain," in *B&L*, 2:560. In his report, D. H. Hill gave his strength at South Mountain as "less than 5,000," but this was certainly an underestimate. See appendix B for Hill's divisional strength. So far as can be determined, his brigades were deployed as follows: Garland, near Funkstown (see *NC Regts*, 1:219); Colquitt, near Boonsboro (see *OR* 19, 1:1052); G. B. Anderson, within 4 miles of Hagerstown, "in a beautiful Oak grove," which placed them at the ford at Clagett's Mill (see George Gorman, ed., "Memoirs of a Rebel," *Military Images Magazine* 3, no. 3 [Nov.–Dec. 1981], 4); Ripley, on Antietam Creek in the direction of Hagerstown (there were fords over Antietam Creek about 2 miles south of Clagett's Mill and this may have been Ripley's location—see *OR Suppl.* 3:584; Henry W. Thomas, *History of the Doles-Cook Brigade* [Atlanta: Franklin, 1903], 469); Rodes, within 6 miles of Hagerstown (see Sgt. John S. Tucker diary [5th AL], F-SNMP).

2. *OR* 19, 1:817, 1019, 1031. Garland did not march until evening. See A. B. Garland to My Dear Cousin, Oct. 4, 1862, JML; *OR Suppl.* 3:584; Edwin A. Osborne diary, SHC.

3. Eicher and Eicher, *Civil War High Commands*, 180–181; Thaddeus Russell, "Colquitt, Alfred Holt," American National Biography Online, www.anb.org/articles/05/05-00148.htm [accessed Feb. 2000, available by subscription only]; R. G. Johnson to John M. Gould, May 23, 1891, Antietam Studies, NA. Lane's arma-

ment consisted of two 20 lb. Parrott rifles, three 10 lb. Parrott rifles, and one Whitworth rifle. See Johnson and Anderson, *Artillery Hell*, 45. Colonel Emory Best of the 23rd GA recalled that they reached Turner's Gap at 4 p.m. See Col. Emory F. Best account, section A, James Longstreet Papers, DU. Colquitt left some 150 men in Boonsboro who were on picket or guard details. See Grattan, "Battle of Boonsboro Gap"; Carman, chap. 23, 32.

4. *OR Suppl.* 3:580; Grattan, "Battle of Boonsboro Gap," 34; *OR* 19, 1:817, 1052. Stuart gave the impression in his report that he dropped off the Jeff Davis Legion at Turner's Gap and the 5th VA at Fox's Gap, but he did not take these actions until early on the morning of Sept. 14, after receiving Lee's orders to assist Hill in defending Turner's Gap.

5. *OR* 19, 1:209, 1052.

6. *Central Georgian* (Sandersville, GA), Oct. 1862; *OR* 19, 1:1052; Grattan, "Battle of Boonsboro Gap," 35–36.

7. *OR* 19, 1:817; Thomas Rosser to Ezra A. Carman, May 12, 1897, Antietam Studies, NA. Rosser stated that his regiment arrived in Boonsboro "after dark." Why Rosser's cavalry and Pelham's battery moved in advance of Fitz Lee's brigade and arrived a day ahead of the rest of the brigade is not explained by either Rosser or Lee in their correspondence with Carman. According to John Allen's study of strengths in the Second Manassas Campaign, the 5th VA Cavalry had 366 officers and men present on Sept. 1. Given the service the regiment had seen in Maryland, and the detachments typical for cavalry regiments, their strength on South Mountain was considerably less than this. See Allen, "Strengths"; Hill, "Battle of South Mountain," in *B&L*, 2:561.

8. *OR* 19, 1:817.

9. Ibid. Hill never mentioned sending Ripley to Stuart in any of his published accounts of South Mountain, but it is clear from Stuart's

report that Hill did so. Freeman (in *Lee's Lieutenants*, 2:172) states that Stuart probably told Ripley about Rosser's deployment at Fox's Gap. This is unlikely, as Stuart did not receive his orders from Lee to assist Hill in the defense of the gaps until after he met with Ripley, and it was in response to these orders that he sent Rosser to Fox's Gap.

10. Grattan, "Battle of Boonsboro Gap," 35; E. M. Dugand to Ezra A. Carman, Apr. 1892, Carman Papers, NYPL.

11. Cox, *Military Reminiscences*, 1:275; OR 19, 1:427, 450.

12. Cox, *Military Reminiscences*, 1:277–278; Jacob D. Cox, "Forcing Fox's Gap and Turner's Gap," in *B&L*, 2:585; OR 19, 1:209.

13. Cox, *Military Reminiscences*, 1:278; J. E. D. Ward, *The Twelfth Ohio Volunteer Infantry* (Ripley, OH, 1864), 59. Scammon also had accomplished little in his two years' work on a road-building project near Santa Fe, which may have contributed to his dismissal. For further details, see Frank N. Schubert, "Vanguard of Expansion: Army Engineers in the Trans-Mississippi West, 1819–1879," chap. 5, www.nps.gov/history/history/online_books/shubert/chap5.htm [accessed May 2005].

14. Cox, *Military Reminiscences*, 1:278; Hayes, *Diary and Letters*, 2:347–348.

15. Sheets diary, USAHEC; OR 19, 1:210, 435–436, 461; Hugh Ewing diary, OSA.

16. Cox, *Military Reminiscences*, 1:280; Cox, "Forcing Fox's Gap," in *B&L*, 2:586. To the twentieth-century reader, Moor's refusal to provide more information when he clearly knew it is astounding, but Moor took the conditions of his parole seriously.

17. Cox, *Military Reminiscences*, 1:280–281; Cox, "Forcing Fox's Gap," in *B&L*, 2:586. Although Cox recalled that Pleasonton "cordially assented" to Cox's request to direct his division's movements if an engagement occurred, Pleasonton claimed credit for the morning's operations in his self-serving report. See OR 19, 1:210.

18. Cox, *Military Reminiscences*, 1:275; Carman, chap. 8, 432–434.

19. Cox, *Military Reminiscences*, 1:275; Hayes, *Diary and Letters*, 2:355.

20. Cox, *Military Reminiscences*, 1:281; Carman, chap. 8, 429; OR 19, 1:458, 463–464. In his report, Cox stated that only two sections of McMullin's battery unlimbered near the National Road, but McMullin's report implies that his entire battery was here. The disposition of Simmond's remaining guns is unknown until later in the morning, when a section was sent up to support the infantry.

21. Carman, chap. 8, 429; Cox, *Military Reminiscences*, 1:281; James Abraham letters and memoirs, USAHEC; Hayes, *Diary and Letters*, 2:355. Bondurant's battery and a section of Pelham's battery were in the vicinity of Fox's Gap by this time. Which one fired this shell is unknown.

22. Hayes, *Diary and Letters*, 2:355; Abraham letters and memoirs, USAHEC; OR 19, 1:461, 464. Two companies of the 12th OH were detached as skirmishers and did not move with their regiment. Their position is difficult to determine, but the best evidence suggests they may have deployed to cover the left of the 23rd OH and 12th OH in their movement up the mountain. They later came into action on the 23rd's right. See R. B. Wilson to Ezra A. Carman, July 22, 1899, Carman Papers, LC; Ewing report, *U.S. Army Generals' Reports of Civil War Service*, 4:183, NA.

23. OR 19, 1:1019; Hill, "Battle of South Mountain," in *B&L*, 2:561. Sunrise on Sept. 14 was at 5:49 a.m.

24. OR 19, 1:1019–1020; Hill, "Battle of South Mountain," in *B&L*, 2:561–562. Hill's memory failed him when he wrote that he found Colquitt "without vedettes and without information of the Federals." Colquitt may have lacked information about the enemy, but this was because Stuart left him without cavalry to gather it, and it is positively known that Colquitt posted pickets. Grattan,

Colquitt's aide, wrote that Hill's memory failed him again when he claimed to have placed Colquitt's regiments. Grattan stated that Hill made no adjustments in Colquitt's position that morning. See Grattan, "Battle of Boonsboro Gap," 38. These were not the only errors that mar Hill's account.

25. Grattan, "Battle of Boonsboro Gap," 36–37; *Central Georgian* (Sandersville, GA), Oct. 15, 1862; *OR* 19, 1:1019–1020, 1052; *OR Suppl.* 3:581.

26. Hill, "Battle of South Mountain," in *B&L*, 2:561–562.

27. Ibid., 2:562. Hill wrote that the father of the mountain family mistook him and Ratchford for Federals and that the father's responses to Hill's questions convinced the latter that the enemy was on his right.

28. Gallagher, *Lee the Soldier*, 8; Krick, "Sharpsburg's Bloody Lane," in Gallagher, *Antietam Campaign*, 226.

29. Eicher and Eicher, *Civil War High Commands*, 249; A. B. Garland to My Cousin Caroline, Oct. 4, 1862, JML; Lucy Gilmer Breckinridge, *Lucy Breckinridge of Grove Hill: The Journal of a Virginia Girl, 1862–1864*, ed. Mary D. Robertson (Columbia: Univ. of South Carolina Press, 1999), 54–55. The girl Garland was engaged to was Sallie Grattan. After learning of Garland's death, Lucy wrote, "I feel so sorry for Sallie. She loved him devotedly." I thank Richard Garland Latture for sharing these sources with me.

30. Hill, "Battle of South Mountain," in *B&L*, 2:562.

31. *OR* 19, 1:1041. Garland's brigade had suffered 844 casualties during the Seven Days fighting. See *B&L*, 2:316; E. M. Dugand to John M. Gould, Apr. 1892, Carman Papers, NYPL. A number of Federal soldiers noted that Garland's men were well uniformed. For one account, see R. B. Wilson to Ezra A. Carman, July 22, 1899, Carman Papers, LC.

32. Carman, chap. 8, 434; *OR* 19, 1:1040, 1045; Hill, "Battle of South Mountain," in *B&L*, 2:563.

33. E. M. Dugand to Ezra A. Carman, Apr. 1892, Carman Papers, NYPL. Dugand wrote to Carman that the regiment was composed of "400 conscripts." See *NC Regts*, 1:219, 627; *OR* 19, 1:1040; Hill, "Battle of South Mountain," in *B&L*, 2:563; Carman, chap. 8, 434–435; John Purifoy to Ezra A. Carman, July 15, 1899, and Aug. 7, 1900, Carman Papers, LC.

34. John Purifoy to Ezra A. Carman, Aug. 7, 1900, Carman Papers, LC; *OR* 19, 1:1040.

35. *OR* 19, 1:1040; E. M. Dugand to John M. Gould, Apr. 1892, Carman Papers, NYPL; Carman, chap. 8, 436.

36. Hayes, *Diary and Letters*, 2:355; Carman, chap. 8, 436.

37. Robert Cornwall letter, Oct. 3, 1862, USA-HEC; Charles R. Williams, *Life of Rutherford Birchard Hayes* (Boston: Houghton Mifflin, 1914), 199; *OR* 19, 1:1040; E. M. Dugand to John M. Gould, Apr. 1892, Carman Papers, NYPL; Carman, chap. 8, 436.

38. *OR* 19, 1:467, 1040.

39. Hayes, *Diary and Letters*, 2:356.

40. Ibid., 2:356–357.

41. Ibid, 2:356.

42. Ibid.; Carman, chap. 8, 437.

43. *OR* 19, 1:1040–1041; Vines E. Turner and H. Clay Wall, "23rd NCT at South Mountain," *North Carolina South Mountain News* (Summer 2001). Turner was the 23rd's adjutant and Wall was a sergeant. See *NC Regts*, 1:627.

44. John Purifoy to Ezra A. Carman, July 15, 1899, Carman Papers, LC; *OR* 19, 1:1041.

45. *OR* 19, 1:465, 1041, 1045; John Purifoy to Ezra A. Carman, Aug. 7, 1900, Carman Papers, LC. Although some accounts place the 13th NC in Wise's field, it is evident from both Ruffin's and Col. Hugh Ewing's reports that the 13th's first position, south of the Old Sharpsburg Road, was in the open ground south of the rectangular woods bordering Wise's south field. See Alfred Iverson to D. H. Hill, Aug. 23, 1885, Lilly Collection, Western Maryland Room, HPL.

46. *OR* 19, 1:469, 1046; A. B. Garland to My Cousin Caroline, Oct. 4, 1862, JML; Hill, "Battle of South Mountain," in *B&L*, 2:563–564.

47. *OR* 19, 1:469, 1046; Ewing report, *U.S. Army Generals' Reports of Civil War Service*, NA.

48. *OR* 19, 1:1041, 1045; Alfred Iverson to D. H. Hill, Aug. 23, 1885, Lilly Collection, HPL.

49. *OR* 19, 1:462, 464; Carman, chap. 8, 438; R. B. Wilson to Ezra A. Carman, July 22, 1899, Carman Papers, LC. From Lt. Col. Ruffin's report, it is evident that it was his regiment's exposure, rather than White's advance, that convinced him to withdraw. It is also apparent that White's men fired on the 13th for several minutes before they advanced.

50. *OR* 19, 1:461, 469, 1045; Ewing report, *U.S. Army Generals' Reports of Civil War Service*, NA; Ewing diary, OSA; Cunningham and Miller, *Ohio Antietam Battlefield Commission*, 77. The movements of Ewing's regiment and those of the 13th NC and the 20th NC are an example of the difficulty of reconciling conflicting reports. Both Ewing and Lt. Col. Ruffin of the 13th NC claimed that they drove one another. The Confederate reinforcements Ewing mentioned were two regiments of G. B. Anderson's brigade.

51. *OR* 19, 1:459, 462, 464; Ward, *Twelfth Ohio Volunteer Infantry*, 59; R. B. Wilson to Ezra A. Carman, July 22, 1899, Carman Papers, LC; D. H. Hill, *Bethel to Sharpsburg*, 2 vols. (Raleigh, NC: Edwards & Broughton, 1926), 1:370; Alfred Iverson to D. H. Hill, Aug. 23, 1885, Lilly Collection, HPL.

52. *OR* 19, 1:459, 472; Horton and Teverbaugh, *History of the Eleventh Regiment*, 71–72.

53. John M. Clugston diary, RBHL; *Mahoning Register* (Youngstown, OH), Oct. 9, 1862; Samuel W. Compton Papers, DU; Cox, *Military Reminiscences*, 1: 283; *OR* 19, 1:459, 472. Three companies of the 36th OH, probably about 200 men, were detached to guard some roads on the left of the division and were not present during the morning's fighting. See Lester

L. Kempfer, *The Salem Light Guard, Company G, 36th Ohio Volunteer Infantry* (Chicago: Adams Press, 1973), 87; Crook-Kennon Papers, USAHEC. The timing of actions at South Mountain is difficult to establish. Cox wrote that the fight with Garland was over by noon; hence it is reasonable to estimate that his dispositions were completed by about 11:30 a.m.

54. *OR* 19, 1:1041.

55. *OR* 19, 1:1041, 1048–1049; Gorman, "Memoirs of a Rebel," 4–5.

56. *OR* 19, 1:1041.

57. *OR* 19, 1:1041, 1046, 1049; Gorman, "Memoirs of a Rebel," 5; *NC Regts*, 2:220–221.

58. Turner and Wall, "23rd NCT at South Mountain."

59. Cox, "Forcing Fox's Gap," in *B&L*, 2:587; Cox, *Military Reminiscences*, 1:283; Clugston diary, RBHL; *Mahoning Register* (Youngstown, OH), Oct. 9, 1862; Compton Papers, DU; *OR* 19, 1:1042.

60. Clugston diary, RBHL, *Mahoning Register* (Youngstown, OH), Oct. 9, 1862: *NC Regts*, 2:221; E. M. Dugand to John M. Gould, Apr. 1892, Carman Papers, NYPL; Turner and Wall, "23rd NCT at South Mountain." Turner and Wall wrote that their regiment's retreat "was effected in great disorder."

61. Clugston diary, RBHL; *OR* 19, 1:187, 1042. Losses are compiled from Louis H. Manarin et al., eds., *North Carolina Troops, 1861–1865: A Roster* (Raleigh, NC: State Dept. of Archives and History, 1966–), 4:126–257, 7:142–245. Also see Carman, chap. 8, 505.

62. Compton Papers, DU; R. B. Wilson to Ezra A. Carman, July 22, 1899, Carman Papers, LC; *OR* 19, 1:465; Alfred Iverson to D. H. Hill, Aug. 23, 1885, Lilly Collection, HPL.

63. Manarin et al., *North Carolina Troops*, 6:432–529. The 12th NC lost 58 men, including 23 missing or captured, out of 92 effectives. Also see Benjamin Collins reminiscences (12th NC), SHC; R. B. Wilson to Ezra A. Carman, July 22, 1899, Carman Papers, LC; *OR* 19,

1:465; Hill, "Battle of South Mountain," in *B&L*, 2:566, 587.

64. *OR* 19, 1:465, 1046; Hill, "Battle of South Mountain," in *B&L*, 2:564.

65. *OR* 19, 1:465, 1046; Hill, "Battle of South Mountain," in *B&L*, 2:564. Ruffin's account in *B&L* differs in some details from his after-action report. Also see Hill, *Bethel to Sharpsburg*, 1:371; R. B. Wilson to Ezra A. Carman, July 22, 1899, Carman Papers, LC; Ward, *Twelfth Ohio Volunteer Infantry*, 59.

66. Compton Papers, DU.

67. *OR* 19, 1:465; Carman, chap. 8, 505. Carman gives Garland's losses at 49 killed, 164 wounded, and 176 captured or missing. I derived my figures from Manarin et al., *North Carolina Troops*; U.S. Surgeon General's Office, *Medical and Surgical History of the Civil War*, 12 vols. (Wilmington, NC: Broadfoot, 1990), 11:42; Robert B. Cornwell to family, Oct. 3, 1862, USAHEC.

68. Cox, *Military Reminiscences*, 1:282; *OR* 19, 1:287; Carman, chap. 8, 445–446; Cox, "Forcing Fox's Gap," in *B&L*, 2:587.

69. Hill, "Battle of South Mountain," in *B&L*, 2:566–567; *OR* 19, 1:1019–1020.

70. Carman, chap. 8, 445.

Chapter 10. *Afternoon at Fox's Gap*

1. *OR* 19, 1:441, 443, 450.

2. Cox, *Military Reminiscences*, 1:287; *OR* 19, 1:427–428.

3. Fred Pettit letter, Sept. 20, 1862, *CWTI* Collection, USAHEC; *OR* 19, 1:439.

4. Cox, *Military Reminiscences*, 1:287; Fred Pettit letter, Sept. 20, 1862, *CWTI* Collection, USAHEC; *OR* 19, 1:439.

5. *OR* 19, 1:210, 417, 450; *New York Times*, Sept. 17, 1862; William Marvel, *Burnside* (Chapel Hill: Univ. of North Carolina Press, 1991), 118. Marvel points out that Burnside passed through Turner's Gap in 1843 en route to West Point, although it is unlikely that this passage created a lasting memory. Also see Strother,

"Personal Recollections," 277; Matthew J. Graham, *The Ninth Regiment New York Volunteers* (New York, E. P. Coby, 1900), 269.

6. Henry Leib diary, CWRT, USAHEC; Andrew Jackson Elliott diary, Save the Flags Collection, USAHEC; Evan M. Woodward, *Our Campaigns* (Philadelphia: J. E. Potter, 1865), 195; *OR* 19, 1:723; *OR* 19, 2:289, 290; GBM to Mary Ellen, Sept. 14, 1862, in McClellan, *Civil War Papers*, 458.

7. *OR* 19, 1:720–723.

8. Ibid., 758.

9. Reel 31, MP; *OR* 19, 1:721; *OR* 51, 1:831; Strother, "Personal Recollections," 277. McClellan's memory surely was in error when he claimed in an 1884 letter to Francis A. Walker that Sumner had been redirected to the Shookstown Road because Hooker did not move promptly on the 14th. The evidence from diaries carried by men in the 1st Corps shows that their movement started on time and that there were no unusual delays. See Leib diary, USAHEC; Elliott diary, USAHEC; Samuel M. Jackson diary, CWRT, USAHEC. Both Leib and Jackson were in Meade's division, which led the march. Also see Samuel W. Moore diary (90th PA), Steve Stottlemeyer Collection, Antietam NB, for the timing of Rickett's division, at the tail of the corps. Since Sumner's orders to take the Shookstown Road have the annotation 9 a.m., the same time the telegram to Halleck was dispatched, it is more likely that Sumner's route of march was changed in response to Russell's report rather than by any delays Hooker might have imposed. See McClellan, *McClellan's Own Story*, 575; Charles Eager to wife, Sept. 16, 1862, book 15, Lewis Leigh Collection, USAHEC.

10. *OR* 19, 1:721. Russell also testified that McClellan sent a message to Franklin at this time, directing Franklin to hasten his operations. There is no record of a communication from McClellan to Franklin until 11:45 a.m., which McClellan sent from Middletown. If there

was an earlier verbal message to Franklin, which would have been an unusual form of delivery, there is no evidence of it.

11. Strother, "Personal Recollections," 277.

12. Ibid.

13. *OR* 19, 2:290; *OR* 51, 1:833.

14. *OR* 51, 1:833. Maj. Russell carried a written order to Franklin and thought the time was about 10 a.m., but this message could only have been this 11:45 a.m. dispatch. For Russell's testimony on this, see *OR* 19, 1:721–723.

15. Woodward, *Our Campaigns*, 195.

16. Woodward, *Our Campaigns*, 196; Healy journal, GNMP; *OR* 19, 1:265. Porter sent a dispatch to Halleck at 12:30 p.m., stating that he had arrived at Middletown. See *OR* 51, 1:832.

17. *OR* 19, 1:338. Ethan Rafuse argues that Porter did not poison the McClellan-Burnside relationship; rather, it was Burnside's poor performance on Sept. 15–17 that caused their camaraderie to degenerate. Burnside did perform poorly on Sept. 15, but he did well at South Mountain and later acted competently on Sept. 16. And McClellan had not turned against other officers whom he liked because they had not performed well; Franklin is one example. See Ethan S. Rafuse, " 'Poor Burn?' The Antietam Conspiracy That Wasn't," *Civil War History* 54, no. 2 (June 2008), 146–175.

18. Strother, "Personal Recollections," 277; GBM to Dixon Miles, 1 p.m., Sept. 14, 1862, reel 31, MP; *OR* 19, 1:45.

19. *OR* 19, 1:417. I have accepted Burnside's report of the battle as the most accurate accounting of how it developed. Hooker and McClellan both sought to discredit Burnside in their reports, but the evidence makes it clear that Burnside directed the battle. McClellan took over when he reached the front, but the battle plan was still Burnside's. McClellan's statement (in *McClellan's Own Story*, 582–583) that Burnside never came close to the battle is untrue. A *New York Tribune* reporter wrote that he observed both men together at Burnside's forward headquarters position (near the

heavy batteries) at 1 p.m., although it was probably closer to 2 p.m. See *New York Tribune*, Sept. 16, 1862; *OR* 19, 1:443. Sturgis reports that he received orders to march at 1 p.m. Meade marched at around 2 p.m., and his division had to be personally started by Burnside, who had difficulty in getting Hooker moving.

20. Hill, "Battle of South Mountain," in *B&L*, 2:564, 566.

21. *OR* 19, 1:1031, 1034; Leach diary, SHC; W[ar] B[oard] Council to General, Mar. 26, 1900, Antietam Studies, NA. The battery with Ripley was probably Capt. Robert Hardaway's Alabama battery of Hill's divisional artillery battalion.

22. *OR* 19, 1:1019–1020, 1031, 1034; Leach diary, SHC. Rodes reported that he received his orders from Hill "toward noon," but it could not have been later than 11 a.m., since his brigade reached the mountain summit sometime between 1 and 2 p.m. His brigade had a 4.5-mile march up South Mountain, and it is unlikely that he could have made this march in less than two hours.

23. *OR* 19, 1:1020, 1031, 1034; John T. Wingfield to Ezra A. Carman, Nov. 22, 1899, Antietam Studies, NA.

24. *OR* 19, 1:140; Hill, "Battle of South Mountain," in *B&L*, 2:566.

25. William T. Owen, "Battle of South Mountain," William T. Owen Papers, VHS. David Johnston of the 7th VA concurred with Owen's timing of Longstreet's departure. Johnston thought the orders to march came "just before noon." See Johnston, *Confederate Boy*, 139. In an article for *CV* (Jan. 1898), Johnston wrote that it was "about 11 a.m." when the long roll was sounded. Osmun Latrobe of Longstreet's staff recorded in his diary that the movement began at 8 a.m. See Latrobe diary, VHS. Longstreet claimed his command marched at daylight. See Longstreet, *From Manassas to Appomattox*, 220. Both of these latter start times, however, are impossible.

Several other writers stated that the march began earlier than 11 a.m., but all agree that it was a severe forced march, which a daylight start would have made unnecessary. If the column started at daylight, it could easily have reached Boonsboro by around 10 a.m. and Turner's Gap by 1 p.m. The evidence supports Owen's and Johnston's timing of the march. The late start of the march is further proof that McClellan's offensive caught Lee by surprise. Also see *OR* 19, 1:885, 888. It was D. R. Jones's intention that Toombs should remain to garrison Hagerstown and that the 11th GA should escort the divisional trains, but these orders were not conveyed to Toombs until 10 p.m. on the 14th.

26. Robert T. Coles, *From Huntsville to Appomattox: History of the 4th Alabama Infantry*, ed. Jeffery Stocker (Knoxville: Univ. of Tennessee Press, 1996), 63. The strength is apportioned as follows: Jones—4,500; Hood—2,300; Evans—1,000. The figures do not include artillerymen. See William H. Andrews, *Footprints of a Regiment: A Recollection of the 1st Georgia Regulars* (Atlanta: Longstreet Press, 1992), 73. There is some question whether Col. John Thompson Brown's battalion of the reserve artillery accompanied the march. Harsh places it at Light's Ford, near Williamsport, on the 14th. See Harsh, *Sounding the Shallows*, 83. Pendleton's report is unclear on this point. See *OR* 19, 1:829.

27. Owen, "Battle of South Mountain," VHS.

28. D. H. Hill, "Battle of South Mountain," in *B&L*, 2:577; Johnston, *Confederate Boy*, 139; Longstreet, *Manassas to Appomattox*, 220. The distance most of Longstreet's brigades covered was roughly 13 miles, which works out to a pace of approximately 3.25 miles per hour, which was still very rapid. The standard rate of march for both armies was 2 miles per hour.

29. *OR* 19, 1:839. Although Longstreet reports that he reached Boonsboro at 3 p.m., his lead-ing elements must have arrived there by around 1:30 to 2 p.m. Hill wrote that Drayton's and G. T. Anderson's brigades reached Turner's Gap at 3:30 p.m. It is possible that they could have completed the march to Turner's Gap from Boonsboro in an hour and a half if they moved at the double-quick for part of it. See Hill, "Battle of South Mountain," in *B&L*, 2:569; James Simons diary, Hood folder, Antietam Studies, NA.

30. Eicher and Eicher, *Civil War High Commands*, 570; Orlando B. Willcox, *Forgotten Valor: The Memoirs, Journals, and Civil War Letters of Orlando B. Willcox*, ed. Robert Garth Scott (Kent, OH: Kent State Univ. Press, 1999), 56–57, 346, 349.

31. *OR* 19, 1:428, 433; Cox, *Military Reminiscences*, 1:288; Lewis Crater, *History of the Fiftieth Regiment Pennsylvania Veteran Volunteers, 1861–65* (Reading, PA: Coleman, 1884), 35; Gabriel Campbell to Ezra A. Carman, Aug. 23, 1899, Antietam NB.

32. *OR* 19, 1:428, 434; Cox, *Military Reminiscences*, 1:288; Jno. Robertson, comp., *Michigan in the War* (Lansing, MI: W. S. George, 1882), 375; Carman, chap. 8, 449.

33. Robertson, *Michigan in the War*, 375; *OR* 19, 1:428, 434; Carman, chap. 8, 450; Gabriel Campbell to Ezra A. Carman, Aug. 23, 1899, Antietam NB. The Confederates were skirmishers of the 2nd and 4th NC. See Hill, "Battle of South Mountain," in *B&L*, 2:567–568. Also see Bates (*Pennsylvania Volunteers*, 1:1060), who states that the Confederates who threatened Cook's guns were North Carolinians. The 79th NY had 312 effectives.

34. Robertson, *Michigan in the War*, 375; Gabriel Campbell to Ezra A. Carman, Aug. 23, 1899, Antietam NB. Campbell thought the strength of the regiment was between 700 and 800. Also see David Lane, *A Soldier's Diary: The Story of a Volunteer* (Jackson, MI, 1905), 11; Willcox, *Forgotten Valor*, 354.

35. *OR* 19, 1:428; Carman, chap. 8, 450; William Todd, *The Seventy-Ninth Highlanders: New York*

Volunteers in the War of Rebellion, 1861–1865 (Albany, NY: Brandow, Barton, 1886), 232; Gabriel Campbell to Ezra A. Carman, Aug. 23, 1899, Antietam NB.

36. *OR* 19, 1:439–440; Carman, chap. 8, 451; Fred Pettit to parents, brothers, and sisters, Sept. 20, 1862, *CWTI* Collection, USAHEC. Pettit stated that the regiment arrived greatly exhausted and that some of the men had fallen out during the climb up the mountain. Also see John Morton to Mother, Sept. 21, 1862, USAHEC.

37. *OR* 19, 1:443, 445–446, 1020 Carman, chap. 8, 455.

38. Strother, "Personal Recollections," 277. McClellan implies that he arrived at the front earlier than 2 p.m., but the evidence supports Strother's timing. See McClellan, *McClellan's Own Story*, 577, 582–583. Also see *OR* 19, 1:50.

39. Ripley's arrival time at the Mountain House is unknown. According to a diarist in the brigade, Calvin Leach of the 1st NC, the brigade started its march at 10 a.m. and halted halfway up the mountain to shed their knapsacks and rest. Rodes passed them during this halt, evidently because he did not allow his men to stop for a rest. Given the pace of Ripley's march, I estimate that he reached Hill's headquarters around 2 p.m. See Leach diary, SHC; *OR* 19, 1:1031. In his campaign report, Hill stated that Drayton's and G. T. Anderson's brigades arrived at 3 p.m. In his article for *Century Magazine*, however, Hill revised this to "about 3:30 pm," which is more likely. See Hill, "Battle of South Mountain," in *B&L*, 2:569. A brigade could march the mile from the Mountain House to the Old Sharpsburg Road in approximately half an hour.

40. Hill, "Battle of South Mountain," in *B&L*, 2:569; *OR* 19, 1:1020–1021. Hill gave the strength of Drayton's and G. T. Anderson's brigades as 1,900 men. See *OR* 19, 1:1020. J. Evans Edings, the AAG of Drayton's brigade, recorded in his diary that the brigade had 1,464 officers and men on Sept. 11. See Edings diary, LC. According to Carman, G. T. Anderson had 597 officers and men at Antietam (minus the 11th GA, who were detached). Anderson suffered 90 casualties at South Mountain. He may have carried more than 600 into action at South Mountain, but Hill's figure may have taken into account attrition from the march from Hagerstown.

41. *OR* 19, 1:1020.

42. Johnson et al., *Dictionary of American Biography*, 25–26:626; William De Rosset to D. H. Hill, June 18, 1885, and D. H. Hill to William De Rosset, June 23, 1885, D. H. Hill Papers, LV.

43. *OR* 19, 1:908–909, 1032.

44. Johnson et al., *Dictionary of American Biography*, 5–6:446; *OR* 12, 2:579; Goree, *Longstreet's Aide*, 100.

45. Kurt Graham, "Death of a Brigade: Drayton's Brigade at Fox's Gap, September 14, 1862," *North Carolina Mountain Monument News*, Fall 2000. This is an excellent account of the action that sorts out Drayton's previously highly confusing maneuvers. Also see Dickert, *History of Kershaw's Brigade*, 174.

46. Dickert, *History of Kershaw's Brigade*, 174; Graham, "Death of a Brigade"; Carman, chap. 8, 451–452; William C. King and W. P. Derby, *Camp-Fire Sketches and Battle-Field Echoes of 61–5* (Boston: Lindsay, 1886), 147–148. It is clear from Capt. Gabriel Campbell's letter that Drayton left at least a strong skirmish line, who took cover along the western edge of the woods north of Hoffman's behind "rail stockades," which were most likely a rail fence that they tore down for cover. See Gabriel Campbell to Ezra A. Carman, Aug. 23, 1899, Antietam NB; John Purifoy to Ezra A. Carman, July 15, 1899, box 3, Carman Papers, LC. Purifoy related that they changed position from near Wise's in the afternoon, but he does not specify to where. However, Campbell's account notes that Confederate guns swept Wise's north pasture. The only place Bondurant where could have been able to sweep the pasture is if he was near its northwest corner.

47. Gabriel Campbell to Ezra A. Carman, Aug. 23, 1899, Antietam NB; John Purifoy to Ezra A. Carman, July 15, 1899, Carman Papers, LC. The position of the 15th SC is not known, other than that they were on the 3rd Battalion's right. Graham (in "Death of a Brigade") thinks the 15th SC took cover behind Wise's garden wall and the woods west of the garden. This seems possible, given that their losses were the lightest in the brigade and that Maj. Rice, in his brief history of the 3rd Battalion, does not mention any unit on their right or left. See Dickert, *History of Kershaw's Brigade*, 174. Graham does not indicate the position of the Phillips Legion after they fell back, and he places the 51st GA in the Old Sharpsburg Road. It is possible that the Legion or the 51st GA were deployed along the Ridge Road to protect the rear of the troops in the Old Sharpsburg Road, for Union accounts are clear that they confronted Confederate infantry along both the Ridge Road and the Crest Road. Capt. Frederic Swift of the 17th MI described "dense masses" of Confederate infantry along the roads at right angles to the Old Sharpsburg Road. Capt. Campbell's detailed account of the 17th's operations concurs with Swift's account. See Robertson, *Michigan in the War*, 375; Gabriel Campbell to Ezra A. Carman, Aug. 23, 1899, Antietam NB.

48. Cox, *Military Reminiscences*, 1:288; *OR* 19, 1:428.

49. Todd, *Seventy-Ninth Highlanders*, 232; Allen D. Albert, ed., *History of the Forty-Fifth Regiment Pennsylvania Veteran Volunteer Infantry* (Williamsport, PA: Grit, 1912), 52; Samuel P. Bates, *Martial Deeds of Pennsylvania* (Philadelphia: T. H. Davis, 1876), 713–714; *OR* 19, 1:428–429, 440.

50. Albert, *Forty-Fifth Regiment Pennsylvania*, 52–53.

51. Ibid.

52. Ibid, 53–54; Bates, *Pennsylvania Volunteers* 1:1060; U.S. Surgeon General's Office, *Medical and Surgical History*, 10:1004.

53. Albert, *Forty-Fifth Regiment Pennsylvania*, 53–54; *OR* 19, 1:442, 469; Ewing report, *U.S. Army Generals' Reports* of Civil War Service, NA.

54. "The Expedition into Maryland," *Savannah Republican*, in M. J. Solomon's scrapbook, DU; Frank S. Jones, *History of Decatur County, Georgia* (Spartanburg, SC: Reprint, 1980), 381. It is reasonably clear from Lt. Fleming's account that his regiment must have been in the Old Sharpsburg Road, at right angles to the rest of his brigade.

55. Robertson, *Michigan in the War*, 376; Gabriel Campbell to Ezra A. Carman, Aug. 23, 1899, Antietam NB; "Expedition into Maryland," Solomon's scrapbook, DU; Carman, chap. 8, 453.

56. Carman, chap. 8, 454; Robertson, *Michigan in the War*, 376; Gabriel Campbell to Ezra A. Carman, Aug. 23, 1899, Antietam NB.

57. Jones, *History of Decatur County*, 381; "Loss of the 50th Georgia Regiment at Antietam," in Moore, *Rebellion Record*, 6:19. The battle described in the latter source was at South Mountain, not Antietam. Also see George E. Fahm reminiscences, microfilm, Brunswick Public Library, Brunswick, Georgia.

58. Gabriel Campbell to Ezra A. Carman, Aug. 23, 1899, Antietam NB; U.S. Surgeon General's Office, *Medical and Surgical History*, 8:337.

59. Both Sturgis and his 2nd Brigade commander, General Edward Ferrero, reported that they reached the scene of action at 3:30 p.m. This seems too early; they did not enter the action until at least an hour later, as the fight with Drayton did not commence until around 4 p.m. See *OR* 19, 1:443, 448; Pope diary, USAHEC; James M. Stone, *Personal Recollections of the Civil War* (Boston: J. M. Stone, 1918), 86.

60. Stone, *Personal Recollections*, 86; Charles F. Walcott, *History of the Twenty-First Massachusetts in the War for the Preservation of the Union* (Boston: Houghton, Mifflin, 1882), 189; Edward O. Lord, *History of the Ninth Regiment New Hampshire Volunteers in the War of*

the Rebellion (Concord, MA: Republican Press, 1895), 72.

61. Lord, *Ninth Regiment New Hampshire*, 72; James Wren diary, USAHEC; Charles A. Cuffel, *Durell's Battery in the Civil War* (Philadelphia: Craig, Finley, 1900), 73. Cuffel wrote that after Durell opened fire, Cook's crews returned and retrieved their guns. Cook claims in his report that his crews returned to their guns and served them until nightfall, but this statement is not supported by any other source. See *OR* 19, 1:434.

62. William F. Fox, *Regimental Losses in the American Civil War* (Dayton, OH: Morningside Bookshop, 1985), 265; *OR* 19, 1:186; Lord, *Ninth Regiment New Hampshire*, 71.

63. Oliver C. Bobyshell, *The Forty-Eighth in the War: Being a Narrative of the Campaigns of the 48th Regiment Infantry Pennsylvania Veteran Volunteers During the War of the Rebellion* (Philadelphia: Avil, 1895), 78; Fred Pettit letter, Sept. 20, 1862, USAHEC; Lord, *Ninth Regiment New Hampshire*, 72–73, 83.

64. Lord, *Ninth Regiment New Hampshire*, 73, 78; *OR* 19, 1:442; Otis F. R. Waite, *New Hampshire in the Great Rebellion* (Clairmont, NH: Tracy, Chase, 1870), 403.

65. Albert, *Forty-Fifth Regiment Pennsylvania*, 54; Jones, *History of Decatur County*, 381; King and Derby, *Camp-Fire Sketches*, 149; Dickert, *History of Kershaw's Brigade*, 174; Edings diary, USAHEC.

66. Lord, *Ninth Regiment New Hampshire*, 78, 89, 90; *OR* 19, 1:437, 440; Bracken diary, USAHEC; Bolton, *Civil War Journal*, 81–82.

67. U.S. Surgeon General's Office, *Medical and Surgical History*, 11:382.

68. The most careful study of Drayton's losses is in Graham, "Death of a Brigade." Also see Carman, chap. 8, 505; Robertson, *Michigan in the War*, 376; Jones, *History of Decatur County*, 381; Moore, *Rebellion Record*, 6:19; Edings diary, LC. Edings gave the strength of the brigade as follows:

Sept. 11	Sept. 17
15th SC—394	15th SC—270
Phillips Legion (GA)—340	Phillips Legion (GA)—206
51st GA—259	51st GA—99
50th GA—304	50th GA—98
3rd SC Battalion—160	3rd SC Battalion—37

Also see "Expedition into Maryland," Solomon's scrapbook, DU; Dickert, *History of Kershaw's Brigade*, 174.

69. *OR* 19, 1:186–187.

70. Ibid., 1032. None of the Union accounts mention Pelham's guns. Those that detailed their actions after Drayton's defeat related that they pursued the Confederates down the western slope for some distance, capturing prisoners, but halted when they had moved too far in advance of the main body and returned to Fox's Gap. See Lord, *Ninth Regiment New Hampshire*, 73–74; Gabriel Campbell to Ezra A. Carman, Aug. 23, 1899, Antietam NB.

71. *OR* 19, 1:909. G. T. Anderson's silence about orders from Ripley implies that he received none.

72. Ibid.

73. R. W. York, "General Hood's Release from Arrest," *Our Living and Our Dead*, June 1875, 421.

74. John B. Hood, *Advance and Retreat: Personal Experiences in the United States and Confederate States Armies* (New Orleans: Hood Orphan Memorial Fund, 1880), 39–40.

75. Stevens, *Reminiscences*, 69; *OR* 19, 1:922. Hood thought his division reached the base of South Mountain at 3:30 p.m. See Hood, *Advance and Retreat*, 37; Longstreet, *Manassas to Appomattox*, 227.

76. *NC Regts*, 4:573. In his memoirs, Hood implied that all three batteries were near one another on the mountain; hence the probable location of Garden's battery.

77. Simons diary, NA.

78. Hood, *Advance and Retreat*, 40. J. B. Polley wrote that they were north of the National Road for a half hour before they moved toward Fox's Gap. See J. B. Polley, *Hood's Texas Brigade: Its Marches, Its Battles, Its Achievements* (Dayton, OH: Morningside Bookshop, 1976), 114. Also see *OR* 19, 1:922.

79. *OR* 19, 1:429, 442, 1032; Lord, *Ninth Regiment New Hampshire*, 79; Bobyshell, *Forty-Eighth in the War*, 88; Walcott, *Twenty-First Massachusetts*, 189; Thomas H. Parker, *History of the Fifty-First Regiment of P.V. and V.V.* (Philadelphia: King & Baird, 1889), 224; Regimental Assoc., *History of the Thirty-Fifth Regiment Massachusetts* (Boston: Mills, Knight, 1884), 28; Hood, *Advance and Retreat*, 40; Carman, chap. 8, 454.

80. James Wren Papers, USAHEC. One account of this action has Wren encountering the 4th NC of G. B. Anderson's brigade. The 4th struck the Union line later, on its extreme left, not on Sturgis's front. Wren probably skirmished instead with the right wing of the 1st GA Regulars, who composed G. B. Anderson's original skirmish line and sustained all of his brigade's casualties (3 wounded and 4 missing). See *OR* 19, 1:909.

81. Wren Papers, USAHEC. Wren's company may have been ordered out either before the 35th MA or at the same time; the evidence is too vague to determine which. Also see Walcott, *Twenty-First Massachusetts*, 189; Pope diary, USAHEC; Regimental Assoc., *Thirty-Fifth Regiment Massachusetts*, 28.

82. Cox, *Military Reminiscences*, 1:291; Strother, "Personal Recollections," 277; Johnson, *Long Roll*, 185.

83. Cox, *Military Reminiscences*, 1:291; Henry Little, "Reno's Death: Another Account," *NT*, Aug. 2, 1883; Johnson, *Long Roll*, 185.

84. Little, "Reno's Death"; A. B. Cummel, "Reno's Death," *NT*, Aug. 23, 1883; Ewing report, *U.S. Army Generals' Reports* of Civil War Service, NA.

85. Gabriel Campbell to Ezra A. Carman, Aug. 23, 1899, Antietam NB.

86. Little, "Reno's Death"; A. H. Wood, "How Reno Fell," *NT*, July 26, 1883; Robert West, "Reno's Death," *NT*, Aug. 2, 1883; Carman, chap. 8, 463; Parker, *Fifty-First Regiment of P.V.*, 225. Wood's account that Reno was shot by a Union soldier is not supported by other accounts of Reno's death. A careful reading of Wood's account indicates that he was not an eyewitness to Reno's wounding, but that he rode up after Reno was shot. West was an eyewitness and he wrote to the *NT* specifically to refute Wood's account. Cox wrote that Reno "had been shot down by the enemy posted among the rocks and trees." Capt. Campbell was also an eyewitness and was certain that Confederate soldiers shot Reno. See Gabriel Campbell to Ezra A. Carman, Aug. 23, 1899, Antietam NB. Also see Cox, "Forcing Fox's Gap," in *B&L*, 2:589. Given the confusion that ensued after Reno's wounding, it is understandable that there would have been some suspicion in the ranks that Reno had been struck by friendly fire. For Willcox's account, see Willcox, *Forgotten Valor*, 355.

87. Little, "Reno's Death"; Thomas T. Ellis, *Leaves from the Diary of an Army Surgeon* (New York; J. Bradburn, 1863), 258; Walcott, *Twenty-First Massachusetts*, 190; Wren Papers, USAHEC. Jacob Cox wrote of Reno's death: "It seemed to me he was hardly gone before he was brought back upon a stretcher dead." See Cox, *Military Reminiscences*, 1:291.

88. Parker, *Fifty-First Regiment of P.V.*, 225–226; Regimental Assoc., *Thirty-Fifth Regiment Massachusetts*, 29–30; Wren Papers, USAHEC.

89. *OR* 19, 1:186–187; Parker, *Fifty-First Regiment of P.V.*, 226–228; James Wren journal, USAHEC; Bobyshell, *History of the 48th Pennsylvania*, 88; Jeffery D. Stocker, *From Huntsville to Appomattox* (Univ. of Tennessee Press: Knoxville, 1996); Carman, chap. 8, 505; U.S. Surgeon General's Office, *Medical and Surgical History*, 7:160.

90. *OR Suppl.* 3:585; *OR* 19, 1:1032; William De Rosset to D. H. Hill, June 18, 1885, Hill Papers, LV; William De Rosset to S. D. Thruston, July 12, 1886, John M. Gould Papers, Dartmouth College, Hanover, New Hampshire; William L. De Rosset, "Ripley's Brigade at South Mountain," *Century Magazine*, Dec. 1886, 309.

91. *OR* 19, 1:1046; *NC Regts*, 1:245.

92. *OR* 19, 1:450; Crater, *Fiftieth Pennsylvania Veteran Volunteers*, 34; David L. Thompson, "In the Ranks to the Antietam," in *B&L*, 2:558; Johnson, *Long Roll*, 186.

93. B. B. Ross reminiscences, Lewis Leigh Collection, USAHEC; Thompson, "In the Ranks," in *B&L*, 2:558; Graham, *Ninth Regiment New York*, 271–273; Johnson, *Long Roll*, 186.

94. Charles Croffut to Mira, Sept. 28, 1863, Stone House Museum, Windsor, NY; Graham, *Ninth Regiment New York*, 271–272; Johnson, *Long Roll*, 186; Thompson, "In the Ranks," in *B&L*, 2:558; "From Our Army," NCSA; "Letter of Capt. John C. Gorman," *North Carolina Standard* (Raleigh), Oct. 1, 1862. The attack fell principally on the 89th New York, although the 103rd New York was also engaged. The right wing of the 9th New York was led by Lt. Col. Kimball to a position where they flanked the Confederate attackers but did not fire, probably because G. B. Anderson's men withdrew before they could. The 50th Pennsylvania also swung back, presumably on the right of the 9th New York, to be prepared to receive an attack. See Crater, *Fiftieth Regiment Pennsylvania Veteran Volunteers*, 34.

95. Ross reminiscences, USAHEC; U.S. Surgeon General's Office, *Medical and Surgical History*, 8:328. McDaniel survived his wound but was permanently disabled. See *OR* 19, 1:187. See appendix C for a breakdown of Confederate losses.

96. Thompson, "In the Ranks," in *B&L*, 2:558.

97. Regimental Assoc., *Thirty-Fifth Regiment Massachusetts*, 31.

98. Parker, *Fifty-First Regiment of P.V.*, 228.

Chapter 11. The First Corps Attacks

1. *OR* 19, 1:50, 214, 267, 417, 422–423. Mount Tabor Road is the current name of the road Hooker followed from the National Road.

2. Eicher and Eicher, *Civil War High Commands*, 383; Meade, *Life and Letters*, 1:310.

3. Bates, *Pennsylvania Volunteers*, 1:539–544. For casualties, see *B&L*, 2:315, 498; Meade, *Life and Letters*, 1:308. Meade indicates that the strength of the division on Sept. 14 was 4,000. See *OR* 19, 1:268.

4. *OR* 19, 1:221, 267.

5. Ibid., 267, 274; Holmes W. Burlingame letters, Steve Stottlemeyer Collection, Antietam NB.

6. Woodward, *Our Campaigns*, 198.

7. *OR* 19, 1:214, 271; Angelo Crapsey to Dear Friend, Sept. 30, 1862, PCHS.

8. *OR* 19, 1:214, 220, 267; Abner Doubleday journal, HFC; Carman, chap. 8, 466.

9. *OR* 19, 1:272; *OR* 51, 1:142, 145, 155; John W. Burnett to John M. Gould, Oct. 27, 1894, Gould Papers, Dartmouth College.

10. *OR* 19, 1:272; Woodward, *Our Campaigns*, 198; O. R. Howard Thomson and William R. Rauch, *History of the "Bucktails"* (Philadelphia: Electric, 1906), 204.

11. *OR* 19, 1:274; *OR* 51, 1:149, 153, 154; Alexander, "Pennsylvania Reserves"; John W. Burnett to John M. Gould, Oct. 27, 1894, Gould Papers, Dartmouth College. Magilton resigned after Fredericksburg and became a professor at the Philadelphia Military Academy, where they trained men who officered the United States Colored Troops. Burnett thought the army never appreciated Magilton's talents, writing that Magilton was "by slander kept a Col. of Volunteers when his abilities should have made him a Major General."

12. Marsena R. Patrick, *Inside Lincoln's Army*, ed. David S. Sparks (New York: Thomas Yoseloff, 1964), 143; Johnson et al., *Dictionary of American Biography*, 8:392–393.

13. *OR* 19, 1:222, 234, 247, 417; Healy journal, GNMP; Noyes, *Bivouac and the Battlefield*, 166–167. In two examples regarding the strength of Hatch's division, the Sept. 2 strength of the 56th PA was 350, but their commander reported that only 247 men were carried into action; and the 20th NY State Militia reported 368 present on Sept. 2, but had only 150 at Antietam on Sept. 17. See *OR* 19, 1:238, 246.

14. *OR* 19, 1:220, 221, 232, 241–242; Patrick diary, LC; Carman, chap. 8, 487.

15. *OR* 19, 1:258–259. Ricketts listed his strength at Antietam as 3,158 effectives. His Sept. 2 strength is given as 4,904 infantry, and they suffered only 35 casualties at South Mountain. A reasonable estimate places their effectives on Sept. 14 at 3,500, but the actual number may have been less.

16. Eicher and Eicher, *Civil War High Commands*, 459. For Rodes's losses on the Peninsula, see *B&L*, 2:219, 316; G. Ward Hubbs, ed., *Voices from Company D: Diaries by the Greensboro Guards, Fifth Alabama Infantry Regiment* (Athens: Univ. of Georgia Press, 2003), 90; Robert E. Park, "Diary of Capt. Robert E. Park, Twelfth Alabama Regiment," *SHSP* 1 (June 1876), 435–436.

17. *OR* 19, 1:1020, 1034; Hill, "Battle of South Mountain," in *B&L*, 2:572, 574.

18. *OR* 19, 1:1034–1035; Cullen A. Battle, "The Third Alabama Regiment," manuscript, ADAH; *South Western Baptist* (Marion, AL), Oct. 26, 1862.

19. *OR* 19, 1:941, 1020, 1034; Hill, "Battle of South Mountain," in *B&L*, 2:574; Carman, chap. 8, 469. The timing of Hooker's attack is somewhat uncertain, with various accounts placing its beginning at anywhere between 4 and 5 p.m. The preponderance of contemporary accounts give 5 p.m. as the time the advance began, although there is evidence that skirmishing started earlier. Rodes reported that he became engaged at 3 p.m., which is too early.

20. *OR* 19, 1:939, 941, 945, 947, 948, 949–950; F. W. McMaster to D. H. Hill, July 11, 1885, Hill Papers, LV.

21. Thomson & Rauch, *History of the "Bucktails,"* 204; "Dennis McGee to *Gazette*, Sept. 21, 1862," *Mauch Chunk (PA) Gazette*, Oct. 9, 1862; Woodward, *Our Campaigns*, 198; Bates, *Pennsylvania Volunteers*, 1:584; *OR* 19, 1:272, 1034–1035. Which battery provided gun support to Rodes is unknown. Also see Angelo Crapsey to Dear Friend, Sept. 30, 1862, PCHS.

22. Thomson & Rauch, *History of the "Bucktails,"* 204; Smith reminiscences, SHC; Hill, "Battle of South Mountain," in *B&L*, 2:572–573; Park, "Diary," *SHSP*, 436.

23. *South Western Baptist* (Marion, AL), Sept. 26, 1862; Battle, "Third Alabama Regiment," ADHA.

24. *OR* 19, 1:272, 1034; *OR* 51, 1:142, 155.

25. Angelo Crapsey to Dear Friend, Sept. 30, 1862, PCHS.

26. U.S. Surgeon General's Office, *Medical and Surgical History*, 10:1006.

27. *OR* 19, 1:267; James B. Casey, "The Ordeal of Adoniram Judson Warner: His 'Minutes of South Mountain and Antietam,'" *Civil War History* 28, no. 3 (Sept. 1982), 217.

28. 19, 1:267; Thomson & Rauch, *History of the "Bucktails,"* 204–205; "A Story of the War," *Valley Register* (Middletown, MD), Oct. 8, 1897. Irwin recovered and rejoined the regiment, only to be wounded again at Fredericksburg. Due to his wounds, he was discharged on May 1, 1863.

29. *OR* 19, 1:272; *OR* 51, 1:145–146; Bates, *Pennsylvania Volunteers*, 369.

30. *OR* 19, 1:1035; Alexander, *Fighting for the Confederacy*, 143; "The Sixth Alabama Regiment," *Montgomery Weekly Advertiser*, Nov. 19, 1862; Smith reminiscences, SHC; U.S. Surgeon General's Office, *Medical and Surgical History*, 8:404. Both Smith and Hayes survived their wounds.

31. *OR* 19, 1:274, 1035; James D. McQuaide letters, Sept. 22, 1862, *CWTI* Collection, USAHEC;

Battle, "Third Alabama Regiment," ADAH; *South Western Baptist* (Marion, AL), Sept. 26, 1862. A member of the 12th Alabama wrote that they took position behind a "pile of rocks."

32. *OR* 19, 1:274, 1035; *OR* 51, 1:149, 153, 154; Battle, "Third Alabama Regiment", ADAH; *South Western Baptist* (Marion, AL), Sept. 26, 1862.

33. *OR* 19, 1:1035; Battle, "Third Alabama Regiment," ADAH.

34. *OR* 19, 1:274; *OR* 51, 1:149, 153; Casey, "Ordeal of Adoniram Judson Warner," 217–218; *South Western Baptist* (Marion, AL), Sept. 26, 1862.

35. Casey, "Ordeal of Adoniram Judson Warner," 217–218; Adoniram J. Warner account of service, Save the Flags Collection, USAHMI.

36. *OR* 51, 1:149, 153; McQuaide letters, Sept. 22, 1862, *CWTI* Collection, USAHEC. Capt. Ready survived his wounds and capture. He was promoted to major and served at a conscript camp in Alabama later in the war.

37. Bates, *Pennsylvania Volunteers*, 1:850. The historian of the 11th Pennsylvania Reserves identified the soldier who "crowed" like a rooster as "Corporal Koons," who was killed in action at Fredericksburg. A search of the 11th's roster reveals no one with the surname Koons, but there was a Cpl. Samuel H. Coon in Company E. The writer may also have erred in regard to Coon's fate, as he was not killed at Fredericksburg, but survived the war.

38. *OR* 19, 1:1034–1035; Charles Forsyth, *History of the Third Alabama Regiment, C.S.A.* (Montgomery, AL; Confederate, 1866), 38.

39. *OR* 19, 1:272, 1035; Bates, *Pennsylvania Volunteers*, 1:584, 669; *OR* 51, 1:145–146. Some of the reports from Seymour's regimental commanders (in *OR* 51) indicate that they did not advance beyond Hill 1360, but it is clear from Seymour's report (in *OR* 19) that, except for the 13th Rifles, they did, and that the cornfield that Col. Fisher referenced in his report is the one Seymour described in his own report. Fisher's claim that his regiment maintained its formation "in perfect order" is certainly an exaggeration. It was impossible to maintain any semblance of a regular line while moving over the terrain his regiment covered.

40. Alexander, "Pennsylvania Reserves"; Frank Holsinger, "War Stories by 'Woodbury Kid,'" *Martinsburg (PA) Herald*, no. 113, [no date]; *OR* 19, 1:273, 941, 945.

41. *OR* 19, 1:941, 945, 947; A. F. Hill, *Our Boys: The Personal Experiences of a Soldier in the Army of the Potomac* (Philadelphia: John E. Potter, 1865), 394; Holsinger, "War Stories."

42. *OR* 19, 1:185, 942, 948–950, 1035.

43. Alexander, "Pennsylvania Reserves."

44. *OR* 19, 1:948–950; Alexander, "Pennsylvania Reserves."

45. *OR* 19, 1:947.

46. F. W. McMaster to D. H. Hill, July 11, 1885, Hill Papers, LV; *OR* 19, 1:945.

47. *OR* 19, 1:185, 942, 948–950, 1035; Carman, chap. 8, 476, 505.

48. *OR* 19, 1:261, 1034–1035; Abram Duryee account, *U.S. Army Generals' Reports of Civil War Service*, reel 4, 6:435–467, NA; Henry Sheafer account of South Mountain and Antietam, Gould Papers, Dartmouth College; James B. Thomas to Lucy, Sept. 14 or 15, 1862, privately owned by Mary W. Thomas; Holmes W. Burlingame reminiscences, Steve Stottlemeyer Collection, Antietam NB; John C. Whiteside to mother, Oct. 4, 1862, Bentley Historical Library, UM.

49. William Jobe reminiscences, ACHS; *South Western Baptist* (Marion, AL), Sept. 26, 1862; Park, "Diary," 437.

50. *OR* 19, 1:261, 1035; Duryee account, *U.S. Army Generals' Reports of Civil War Service*, NA; Henry Sheafer account, Gould Papers, Dartmouth College; Alexander, "Pennsylvania Reserves"; Hall, *Ninety-Seventh Regiment*, 87. An accurate and detailed reconstruction of the fighting near the summit of Hill 1500 is impossible, due to the confusion of the participants and the falling darkness that limited visibility.

51. Bates, *Pennsylvania Volunteers*, 1:698; Woodward, *Our Campaigns*, 199; *OR* 19, 1:1020, 1035. Cullen Battle, major of the 3rd AL, wrote that his regiment changed position "no less than seven times on that mountain, and always in perfect order." See Cullen A. Battle, *Third Alabama! The Civil War Memoirs of Brigadier General Cullen Battle, CSA*, ed. Brandon H. Beck (Tuscaloosa: Univ. of Alabama Press, 2000), 56. As good a fight as Rodes's men put up, it is impossible to believe that the 3rd executed these movements "in perfect order" under the circumstances and terrain, and Battle's statement is not supported by Rodes's own wartime report.

52. Hubbs, *Voices from Company D*, 108; Bates, *Pennsylvania Volunteers*, 1:698; Woodward, *Our Campaigns*, 199; *OR* 19, 1:1020, 1035.

53. *OR* 19, 1:185–186; Carman, chap. 8, 505.

Chapter 12. The Battle for Hill 1280

1. *OR* 19, 1:220, 241–242.

2. Ibid., 220, 221, 242; *Cazenovia (NY) Republican*, Dec. 3, 1862; *Lowville (NY) Journal and Republican*, Oct. 8, 1862. The *Cazenovia Republican* correspondent reported that the men did not remove their knapsacks because they were afraid they would lose them, as they had done at Centreville, Virginia, during the Manassas Campaign.

3. *OR* 19, 1:231, 242; Patrick diary, LC.

4. John H. Mills, *Chronicles of the Twenty-First Regiment New York State Volunteers* (Buffalo, NY: Regimental Assoc., 1887), 280.

5. *OR* 19, 1:242, 245–246; William P. Maxon [Pound Sterling, pseud.], *Campfires of the Twenty-Third: Sketches of Camp Life, Marches, and Battles of the Twenty-Third N.Y.V.* (New York: Davies and Kent, 1863), 98–99; Patrick diary, LC; Mills, *Twenty-First Regiment*, 280.

6. *OR* 19, 1:242, 245–246; Maxon, *Campfires of the Twenty-Third*, 98–99; Patrick diary, LC; Mills, *Twenty-First Regiment*, 280.

7. *OR* 19, 1:220, 231, 246. Although Hatch stated that he had Phelps deploy to the line of battle and follow 30 paces in the rear of the skirmish line, Phelps's report is clear that he remained in the column of the division until within 80 paces of the Confederates. Also see Edward L. Barnes, "The 95th New York at South Mountain," *NT*, Jan. 7, 1886; Mills, *Twenty-First Regiment*, 280; Maxon, *Campfires of the Twenty-Third*, 98–99. The 23rd's history states that their left rested about 300–400 yards from the National Road, close to the cleared fields that bordered it.

8. Barnes, "95th New York"; Umberto Burnham to parents, Sept. 18, 1862, NYSA; Healy journal, GNMP; Mills, *Twenty-First Regiment*, 280–281; Noyes, *Bivouac and the Battlefield*, 171.

9. *OR* 19, 1:231. Federal accounts of the battle are in agreement that the sun was setting before the summit of the mountain was reached.

10. Hill, "Battle of South Mountain," in *B&L*, 2:574.

11. Longstreet, *Manassas to Appomattox*, 224; *OR* 19, 1:885–886, 894.

12. Carman, chap. 8, 478; Dooley, *John Dooley, Confederate Soldier*, 35; Sorrel, *Recollections*, 101–102; Longstreet, *From Manassas to Appomattox*, 225.

13. Carman, chap. 8, 478–480. The order of battle of Kemper's brigade is derived from Carman. Also see Johnston, *Confederate Boy*, 140; Dooley, *John Dooley, Confederate Soldier*, 35–36.

14. Carman, chap. 8, 480; Dooley, *John Dooley, Confederate Soldier*, 35–36; Krick, *Staff Officers in Gray*, 71. Beckham had attended the Virginia Military Institute before the war, although it is unlikely that he had graduated when he joined Kemper's staff as a volunteer aide-de-camp. He would lose his foot at Sharpsburg three days later.

15. Carman, chap. 8, 480; Dooley, *John Dooly, Confederate Soldier*, 35, 36; *OR* 19, 1:904; *OR* 51, 2:169. It is impossible to determine precisely where Corse formed, but it seems likely that he left the road near where it turns north and

moved across what one map calls Rent's field, a square field on the mountain summit. At the eastern edge of this field, any enemy approaching the summit could be observed. This placement also helped narrow the gap between Kemper's right and Colquitt's left (although it is unlikely that Kemper knew precisely where Colquitt's left was located).

16. Carman, chap. 8, 480; Johnston, *Confederate Boy*, 140. Johnston writes that the Federals were "occupying a skirt of woods with a strip of open land between their position and ours." None of the maps drawn to document the battle show a strip of open ground in front of Kemper's left. However, a map prepared to show the operations of Burnside's Right Wing (in RG 77, F91–93, NA) does show a small rectangular field west of the D. Rent farm. This might be the strip of open ground to which Johnston refers.

17. Carman, chap. 8, 480; Johnston, *Confederate Boy*, 140; Dooley, *John Dooley, Confederate Soldier*, 36–37. Dooley wrote that his regiment formed "on the edge of a field to the right of the road and on the brow of the mountain." See *OR* 51, 2:169.

18. *OR* 19, 1:894, 906; Owen, "Battle of South Mountain," VHS.

19. *OR* 19, 1:894, 906. The incredible fortitude of these three Confederate brigades is manifest to anyone who has ever driven up the west side of South Mountain on the old National Road. How any of the men were able to make the climb and continue to fight after the other marching they had done that day is remarkable.

20. *OR* 19, 1:894, 901.

21. Ibid., 898, 899.

22. Owen, "Battle of South Mountain," VHS.

23. *OR* 19, 1:899; Owen, Battle of South Mountain," VHS.

24. *OR* 19, 1:894–895, 901, 902; *OR* 51, 2:169; William N. Wood, *Reminiscences of Big I*, ed. Bell Irvin Wiley (Jackson, TN: McCowen-Mercer Press, 1956), 35; "W. T. Strange," www.rockvil-

lemama.com/strangewt.txt [accessed May 2009].

25. Mills, *Twenty-First Regiment*, 282–283; *OR* 19, 1:246, 901; C. C. Wertenbaker to John W. Daniel, Nov. 17, 1906, John Daniel Papers, UVA; Wood, *Reminiscences of Big I*, 35–36. The 28th VA may have been in the cornfield rather than in the open meadow. Colonel Theodore Gates of the 20th NY State Militia reported that his regiment directed their fire on the enemy "who were lying behind a fence and in a cornfield." See *OR* 19, 1:246.

26. *OR* 19, 1:220, 222, 232, 242; *Cazenovia (NY) Republican*, Dec. 3, 1862; *Corning (NY) Journal*, Oct. 2, 1862. The skirmisher of the 35th might have mistaken the direction of the volley, which seems more likely to have come from his left than his right.

27. *OR* 19, 1:220, 222, 232, 242, 898–899; John Bryson, "History of the 30th NYS Volunteers," NYSA; Patrick diary, LC.

28. *OR* 19, 1:232, 895, 901; Frank E. Fields, *28th Virginia Infantry* (Lynchburg, VA: H. E. Howard, 1985), 19, 46; Ervin L. Jordan and Herbert A. Thomas, *19th Virginia Infantry* (Lynchburg, VA: H. E. Howard, 1987), 94.

29. *OR* 19, 1:898–899; Carman, chap. 8, 486; Owen, "Battle of South Mountain," VHS.

30. *OR* 19, 1:232. Hatch's wound was quite serious, and he took over a year to recover from it. See John P. Hatch report to the adjutant general, *U.S. Army Generals' Reports of Civil War Service*, reel 1, 1:873–884, NA; C. C. Wertenbaker to John W. Daniel, Nov. 6, 1906, Daniel Papers, UVA; Carman, chap. 8, 486; "John McEnter to Father, Sept. 21, 1862," *Courier* (New York, NY), Oct. 3, 1862.

31. *OR* 19, 1:220–222, 231–232. Doubleday wrote in his journal that Phelps held his ground "with some difficulty as he was greatly outnumbered." See Doubleday journal, HFC.

32. Noyes, *Bivouac and the Battlefield*, 172–173.

33. Umberto Burnham to parents, Sept. 18, 1862, NYSA.

34. Smith, *Seventy-Sixth Regiment*, 153.

35. Umberto Burnham, "South Mountain—
Maryland Campaign," *NT*, May 24, 1928;
Noyes, *Bivouac and the Battlefield*, 173; Healy
journal, GNMP; Doubleday report, *U.S. Army
Generals' Reports of Civil War Service*, NA; Wil-
liam H. Miller to sister, Sept. 19, 1862, Civil
War Misc. Collection, USAHEC; Mat. H.
Hurlinger diary, privately owned.

36. Owen, "Battle of South Mountain," VHS.

37. Noyes, *Bivouac and the Battlefield*, 173. Doubleday's men had also made a long march that
day and climbed Hill 1280. Though not as
debilitating as the experience of D. R. Jones's
brigades, Doubleday's men were certainly
tired, and fatigue most likely played a role in
their failure to press Garnett more aggressively.

38. *OR* 19, 1:234, 903–904. Also see Robert T. Bell,
11th Virginia Infantry (Lynchburg, VA: H. E.
Howard, 1985); Lee Wallace, *17th Virginia
Infantry* (Lynchburg, VA: H. E. Howard,
1990); "John McEnter to Father, Sept. 21,
1862," *Courier* (New York, NY), Oct. 3, 1862;
Enos B. Vail, *Reminiscences of a Boy in the Civil
War* (Brooklyn, NY: E. B. Vail, 1915), 82.

39. *OR* 51, 2:169; Dooley, *John Dooley, Confederate
Soldier*, 37; Johnston, *Confederate Boy*, 140. Also
see Lee Wallace, *1st Virginia Infantry* (Lynchburg, VA: H. E. Howard, 1985); David Riggs,
7th Virginia Infantry (Lynchburg, VA: H. E.
Howard, 1982), Ralph W. Gunn, *24th Virginia
Infantry* (Lynchburg, VA: H. E. Howard, 1987).

40. Doubleday journal, HFC; Doubleday report,
U.S. Army Generals' Reports of Civil War Service,
NA; Smith, *Seventy-Sixth Regiment*, 154; Barnes,
"95th New York."

41. *OR* 19, 1:906; "Memoirs of the 1st South Carolina Regiment," SCSL. The writer of this history recorded that the regiment lost 20 men
at South Mountain; Walker's report stated
that they lost 16.

42. *OR* 19, 1:895, 903, 905, 906; "John McEnter to
Father, Sept. 21, 1862," *Courier* (New York,
NY), Oct. 3, 1862; Johnston, *Confederate Boy*,
142.

43. *OR* 19, 1:906; "Memoirs of the 1st South Carolina Regiment," SCSL.

44. Doubleday journal, HFC; *Corning (NY) Journal*, Oct. 2, 1862; Maxon, *Campfires of the
Twenty-Third*, 100. Col. Hoffman wrote that
Christian's undisciplined advance "finally
terminated in a general mob, rendering it
impossible for any line to be kept in order."
Also see Healy journal, GNMP.

45. Doubleday journal, HFC; Smith, *Seventy-Sixth
Regiment*, 155.

46. Healy journal, GNMP; Noyes, *Bivouac and the
Battlefield*, 177; *OR* 19, 1:222, 242, 263. Patrick,
referring to the general waste of ammunition
by his own division and Christian's brigade,
expressed his disgust in his journal: "We
drove the enemy from the field, but a most
disgraceful scene ensued, the men firing all
their ammunition away after there was nothing to shoot." See Patrick diary, LC.

47. Noyes, *Bivouac and the Battlefield*, 177.

Chapter 13. Into Turner's Gap

1. Gibbon, *Personal Recollections*, 76; Franklin A.
Haskell, *Haskell of Gettysburg: His Life and Civil
War Papers*, ed. Frank L. Byrne and Andrew
Thomas Weaver (Madison: State Historical
Society of Wisconsin), 30–31; Rufus R. Dawes
journal, SHSW; Perry diary, SHSW.

2. Haskell, *Haskell of Gettysburg*, 31–32.

3. Dawes, *Sixth Wisconsin Volunteers*, 43; Johnson
et al., *Dictionary of American Biography*,
7–8:236–237.

4. Gibbon, *Personal Recollections*, 38; Alan Nolan,
The Iron Brigade (Ann Arbor: Historical Soci-
ety of Michigan, 1983), 51–54; Dawes, *Sixth
Wisconsin Volunteers*, 43, 45; *B&L*, 2:497.

5. Dawes, *Sixth Wisconsin Volunteers*, 70; Henry B.
Young to Delia, Sept. 13, 1862, Young Papers,
SHSW; Edward Bragg to My Dear Wife, Sept.
13, 1862, Bragg Papers, SHSW.

6. Rufus R. Dawes to mother, Mar. 1, 1863,
Dawes journal, SHSW; Haskell, *Haskell of
Gettysburg*, 32; Frank Haskell to *Wisconsin*

State Register (Portage, WI), Oct. 4, 1862, in E. B. Quiner, *E. B. Quiner Papers: Correspondence of the Wisconsin Volunteers, 1861–65,* 10 vols. (Madison: State Historical Society of Wisconsin, n.d.); Z. B. Russell, "As a Boy in the Ranks Saw It," *Milwaukee Sunday Telegraph,* Aug. 24, 1895.

7. *OR* 19, 1:1053; Grattan, "Battle of Boonsboro Gap," 36–37; *Central Georgian* (Sandersville, GA), Aug. 15, 1862.

8. *Central Georgian* (Sandersville, GA), Oct. 15, 1862; Grattan, "Battle of Boonsboro Gap," 36–37; *OR* 19, 1:1053. For the composition of the skirmish battalion and remarks on Arnold, see Sidney Lewis to John M. Gould, May 7, 1893, Antietam Studies, NA. The positioning of the 6th GA and the 13th AL is difficult to establish with any accuracy. The 6th GA's historian simply states that they were in a dense woods in a gorge of the mountain, which indicates that they were posted along the slopes of Hill 1080. See "The Sixth Georgia," Antietam Studies, NA. This account states that the 6th "was very slightly engaged, the enemy not attempting to pass our immediate front." In the "Record of Events on Muster Roll of Company D, 13th Alabama" (Antietam Studies, NA), it states that only a portion of the regiment was engaged at South Mountain. Their losses were very slight.

9. *OR* 19, 1:1053.

10. Ibid, 247, 249, 252; Haskell, *Haskell of Gettysburg,* 32; *CCW,* 37th Cong., 3rd Sess., 1:446–447; W. N. Pickerill, ed., *Indiana at Antietam: Report of the Indiana Antietam Monument Commission* (Indianapolis: Aetna Press, 1911), 107; George H. Otis, *The Second Wisconsin Infantry,* ed. Alan D. Gaff (Dayton, OH: Morningside Bookshop, 1984), 29.

11. *OR* 19, 1:253, 256; Dawes journal, SHSW.

12. Haskell, *Haskell of Gettysburg,* 33; *OR* 19, 1:247.

13. Haskell, *Haskell of Gettysburg,* 33; J. P. Sullivan, "A Private's Story," *Milwaukee Sunday Tele-*

graph, May 13, 1888; Alf Thomas letter, in Quiner, *E. B. Quiner Papers,* 2:309–312.

14. Rufus R. Dawes to mother, Mar. 1, 1863, Rufus R. Dawes Papers, SHSW; Haskell, *Haskell of Gettysburg,* 33.

15. Haskell, *Haskell of Gettysburg,* 33; Rufus R. Dawes to mother, Mar. 1, 1863, Dawes Papers, SHSW.

16. *OR* 19, 1:252; Haskell, *Haskell of Gettysburg,* 33.

17. *OR* 19, 1:249–250, 1053; James Stewart, "Short Stories," *Milwaukee Sunday Telegraph,* Jan. 26, 1895. It is commonly believed that the farmhouse was D. Beachley's or, as a map drawn up to show the positions of Burnside's command in the battle labels it, D. Buchler's. But Meredith is clear that the farmhouse was near the left end of the Federal line, which Beachley's (or Buchler's) was not. The answer is revealed in the map indicating Burnside's operations, which has a farmhouse with the initials D. B. located south of Beachley's, where today a modern house and swimming pool sit. See "The Battlefield of South Mountains Map: Showing the Positions of the Forces under the Command of Maj. Gen. A. E. Burnside," RG77, F91–93, NA.

18. Dawes journal, SHSW; Sullivan, "Private's Story"; Aleck Gordon letter, Sept. 20, 1862, in Quiner, *E. B. Quiner Papers,* 4:21; Russell, "Boy in the Ranks."

19. Aleck Gordon letter, in Quiner, *E. B. Quiner Papers,* 4:21; *OR* 19, 1:256.

20. *Central Georgian* (Sandersville, GA), Oct. 15, 1862; Dawes, *Sixth Wisconsin Volunteers,* 81; *OR* 19, 1:256.

21. Aleck Gordon letter, in Quiner, *E. B. Quiner Papers,* 4:21; Dawes journal, SHSW; Rufus R. Dawes to mother, Mar. 1, 1863, Dawes Papers, SHSW; Dawes, *Sixth Wisconsin Volunteers,* 82.

22. Rufus R. Dawes to mother, Mar. 1, 1863, Dawes journal, SHSW; Dawes, *Sixth Wisconsin Volunteers,* 82; Lyman Holford diary, Manuscript Division, LC; Mickey Sullivan, "A Pri-

vate's Story," *Milwaukee Sunday Telegraph*, May 13, 1888.

23. Rufus R. Dawes to mother, Mar. 1, 1863, Dawes Papers, SHSW; Dawes, *Sixth Wisconsin Volunteers*, 83; Aleck Gordon letter, in Quiner, *E. B. Quiner Papers*, 4:21; Russell, "Boy in the Ranks."

24. Dawes, *Sixth Wisconsin Volunteers*, 83; Rufus R. Dawes to mother, Mar. 1, 1863, Dawes Papers, SHSW; *OR* 19, 1:253–254.

25. *OR* 19, 1:250, 252. Fairchild reported that his men fired 20 rounds apiece at this point, which means that the 2nd fired over 4,000 rounds. See Henry Marsh to father, Sept. 23, 1862, Indiana Historical Society, Indianapolis, Indiana; "Army Correspondence," *Central Georgian* (Sandersville, GA), Oct. 15, 1862.

26. *OR* 19, 1:250, 252; Carman, chap. 8, 492.

27. Haskell, *Haskell of Gettysburg*, 34–35.

28. *OR* 19, 1:1053; Tully Graybill to wife, Sept. 26, 1862, Antietam NB.

29. Aleck Gordon letter, in Quiner, *E. B. Quiner Papers*, 4:21; Rufus R. Dawes to mother, Mar. 1, 1863, SHSW; Dawes, *Sixth Wisconsin Volunteers*, 83. Dawes's account in *Sixth Wisconsin Volunteers* differs in some details from his journal and his letter to his mother. I have chosen to accept his accounts that were written closer to the event. Also see *OR* 19, 1:1053.

30. Carman, chap. 8, 494, 505; *OR* 19, 1:1053. The 28th GA reported 40 killed or wounded. See Colquitt's Brigade file, Antietam Studies, NA; Tully Graybill to wife, Sept. 26, 1862, Antietam NB.

31. Haskell, *Haskell of Gettysburg*, 37; *OR* 19, 1:184.

32. Rufus R. Dawes to mother, Mar. 1, 1863, Dawes Papers, SHSW. The injured soldier was William Lawerance, who was wounded in the bowels. For more details on this incident, see Dawes, *Sixth Wisconsin Volunteers*, 84. For additional details on Lawerance's wounding and death, see George D. McDill to mother, Oct. 8, 1862, 6th WI folder, Antietam NB.

33. Gibbon, *Personal Recollections*, 77–78; Haskell to *Wisconsin State Register* (Portage, WI), in Quiner, *E. B. Quiner Papers*; *OR* 19, 1:250, 253, 257. Gorman may have arrived before midnight. Captain Callis reported that the 7th WI was relieved around 10:30 p.m. by the 15th MA. This is corroborated by the diary of Jonathan Stowe of the 15th, who recorded that they arrived on the battleground at 10:30 p.m. However, both Fairchild and Meredith stated that they were not relieved until midnight. See Stowe diary, USAHEC.; Rufus R. Dawes to mother, Mar. 1, 1863, Dawes Papers, SHSW. Also see Dawes, *Sixth Wisconsin Volunteers*, 84.

34. Strother, "Personal Recollections," 277–278; Andrews, *North Reports*, 273–274. For Marcy's communications, see reel 31, MP. According to Pvt. John Tabor of the 23rd PA, who was detached to army headquarters, McClellan sent orders to Cox (and Willcox) to advance their line and "whip the rebels from the hills" at "about 2 oclk PM." See John Tabor diary, *CWTI* Collection, USAHEC.

35. *OR* 19, 1:52–53; *OR* 51, 1:831. Koogle's residence is identified as McClellan's headquarters by "The Battlefield of South Mountains Map: Showing the Positions of the Forces under the Command of Maj. Gen. A. E. Burnside," RG77, F91–93, NA; Strother, "Personal Recollections," 278. Strother does not name any of the officers present besides Sturgis, who related the details of Reno's death, nor does he give the time of the meeting, although it is likely that it took place before McClellan's 9:40 p.m. dispatch to Halleck.

36. *OR* 19, 2:289.

37. *OR* 51, 1:831–832.

38. Carman, chap. 8, 505; *OR* 19, 1:184–187.

39. William Allan, *The Army of Northern Virginia in 1862* (Dayton, OH: Morningside Bookshop, 1984), 360.

40. Longstreet, *Manassas to Appomattox*, 227. Also see Longstreet, "Invasion of Maryland," in *B&L*, 2:666. D. H. Hill left no account of the meeting. Hood claimed that he was present,

although it may have been a later discussion that he attended. See Hood, *Advance and Retreat*, 41. The first meeting definitely took place before 8 p.m., since Lee wrote to McLaws at that time, informing him that the army would retreat.

41. *OR* 51, 2:618–619; Alexander, *Fighting for the Confederacy*, 144. Alexander wrote that he started the ordnance train after the moon came up. Also see *OR* 19, 1:888. Toombs reported that he received his orders around 10 p.m., so Lee probably sent them soon after the dispatches to McLaws and Jackson. See Carman, chap. 8, 508–509.

42. *OR* 19, 1:855; *OR* 2:608–609. Munford was the first to communicate news of the disaster at Crampton's Gap to Lee. He stated in his memorandum book that Capt. W. K. Martin reported in person to Lee. See Munford memorandum book, SHC. Also see Carman, chap. 8, 507.

43. "Notarized Statement of W. P. Dubose, Aug. 15, 1882," Division of Archives and Manuscripts, Pennsylvania Historical and Museum Commission, Harrisburg, Pennsylvania. Dubose's captor was believed to be Daniel Cronin of Company G, 107th PA. See *OR* 19, 1:140.

44. Randolph A. Shotwell, *The Papers of Randolph A. Shotwell*, ed. J. G. De Roulac Hamilton, 2 vols. (Raleigh: North Carolina Historical Commission, 1929–1931), 1:340; *OR* 19, 1:1036; Battle, "Third Alabama Regiment," ADAH; Carman, chap. 8, 513, 516; "From Our Army," *North Carolina Standard* (Raleigh), Oct. 1, 1862, 2nd NC file, Antietam NB; Stephen D. Thruston to Col. William L. De Rosset, July 28, 1886, Gould Papers, Dartmouth College; Dooley, *John Dooley, Confederate Soldier*, 38. Dooley, in Kemper's brigade, wrote that they withdrew at 11 p.m., but this may have been the time when they assembled at Turner's Gap. It was certainly later than this when they left the mountain.

45. Coles, *From Huntsville to Appomattox*, 64; Carman, chap. 8, 517.

46. *OR* 19, 1:906; "Memoirs of the 1st South Carolina Regiment," SCSL; Beale, *Ninth Virginia Cavalry*, 39; H. McClellan, *Life and Campaigns*, 124.

47. Thompson, "In the Ranks," in *B&L*, 2:558; Ewing report, *U.S. Army Generals' Reports of Civil War Service*, NA; Walcott, *Twenty-First Massachusetts*, 192; Warren H. Freeman and Eugene H. Freeman, *Letters from Two Brothers Serving in the War for the Union* (Cambridge, MA: printed for private circulation, 1871), 50–51; Todd, *Seventy-Ninth Highlanders*, 235.

48. Walcott, *Twenty-First Massachusetts*, 191.

49. Adoniram J. Warner, "Minutes of the Battle of South Mountain and Antietam," WRHS.

Chapter 14. Crampton's Gap

1. William B. Westervelt memoir, Civil War Misc. Collection, USAHEC; Peter Filbert diary, USAHEC. Filbert wrote that his regiment, the 96th PA, arrived at Jefferson at 8 a.m. Also see Joseph Bartlett, "Crampton's Pass"; *OR* 19, 1:374–375; William B. Franklin to GBM, 10:30 a.m., Sept. 14, 1862, reel 31, MP.

2. H[enry] C. Boyer, "At Crampton's Pass," *PWP*, Aug. 31, 1889, USAHEC; *OR* 19, 1:393. The "superior" force of enemy that the Union cavalry reported may have been a picket of some 200 men posted near Burkittsville by Colonel E. B. Montague of the 32nd VA, who was commanding at Brownsville Pass.

3. Boyer, "At Crampton's Pass," *PWP*; *OR* 19, 1:393.

4. Boyer, "At Crampton's Pass," *PWP*.

5. Ibid.

6. *OR* 19, 1:380, 388; Bartlett, "Crampton's Pass." Smith's 2nd Division began to arrive around 1 p.m. See *OR* 19, 1:393; Mark A. Snell, *From First to Last: The Life of Major General William B. Franklin* (New York: Fordham Press, 2002), 179.

7. Boyer, "At Crampton's Pass," *PWP*. The officers at the meeting were Franklin, Slocum,

Smith, Hancock, Newton, and Brooks. See Bartlett, "Crampton's Pass."

8. Boyer, "At Crampton's Pass," *PWP*; *OR* 19, 1:393.

9. William B. Franklin to GBM, 12:30 p.m., Sept. 14, 1862, reel 31, MP; *OR* 19, 1:375, 380.

10. *OR* 19, 1:375, 380, 388; Bartlett, "Crampton's Pass."

11. Bartlett, "Crampton's Pass."

12. *OR* 19, 1:389.

13. Ibid., 854; McLaws, "The Capture of Harper's Ferry," *PWP*, Sept. 12, 1888.

14. *OR* 19, 1:817–819, 826, 872–873, 881; Munford memorandum book, DU; Thomas Munford to Ezra A. Carman, Dec. 19, 1894, Antietam Studies, NA. Semmes reported that Parham's entire brigade was ordered to Crampton's Gap on the morning of the 14th. This is an error; only the 16th VA was sent. The remainder of Parham's brigade marched when the 6th Corps was observed by the Confederates. See *OR* 19, 1:873; Bernard, *War Talks*, 25. Timothy Reese credits the 16th VA with 118 effectives. See Timothy J. Reese, *Sealed with Their Lives: The Battle for Crampton's Gap, Burkittsville, Maryland, September 14, 1862* (Baltimore: Butternut and Blue, 1998), 298. The strength of Munford's brigade is something of a question. H. B. McClellan (in *Campaigns of Stuart's Cavalry*) gives its strength as 350 men. Yet Munford, in a postwar letter, stated that he had 550–600 men in his two regiments. See Thomas Munford to Ezra A. Carman, June 24, 1898, Antietam Studies, NA. Lewis Harman of the 12th VA Cavalry wrote to Carman that his regiment numbered 450–500 men in Maryland. See "12th Virginia Cavalry," Antietam Studies, NA. I have chosen the smallest of all these numbers, since Munford and Harman probably reported the strength of the regiments at the beginning of the campaign.

15. *OR* 19, 1:818; McClellan, *Campaigns of Stuart's Cavalry*, 118–119; Munford memorandum book, DU. Munford says that Stuart left

about one hour before the 6th Corps were seen, which would place his departure at around 11 a.m. See Thomas Munford to Ezra A. Carman, Dec. 19, 1894, Antietam Studies, NA.

16. *OR* 19, 1:854.

17. Ibid., 819, 854; von Borcke, 1:215–216.

18. *OR* 19, 1:862, 872–873, 881.

19. Ibid., 877; Bernard, *War Talks*, 25.

20. *OR* 19, 1:881, 872–873.

21. *OR* 19, 1:826; Neese, *Confederate Horse Artillery*, 120; Thomas Munford to Ezra A. Carman, Dec. 19, 1894, Antietam Studies, NA. For an unjust criticism of Munford's preparations, see Longstreet, *Manassas to Appomattox*, 230.

22. *OR* 19, 1:881; Neese, *Confederate Horse Artillery*, 121.

23. *OR* 19, 1:826.

24. Accounts vary as to the time the attack started. Bartlett thought it was 4 p.m., but Colonel Adams of the 27th NY, who led the advance, reported that it was 3:30 p.m., as did Colonel Jackson of the 5th ME. Slocum stated that it began at 3 p.m. Franklin wrote to McClellan at 2:30 p.m. that "the brigades of Slocum's division are advancing up the mountain." I have interpreted this statement to mean that the division had commenced its approach march from the Broad Run Village Road. See *OR* 19, 1:388, 390, 392. Also see William B. Franklin to GBM, 2:30 p.m., Sept. 14, 1862, reel 31, MP.

25. Bartlett, "Crampton's Pass"; *OR* 19, 1:380, 388.

26. William B. Franklin to GBM, 2:30 p.m., Sept. 14, 1862, reel 31, MP; *OR* 19, 1:380, 388, 881; Bartlett, "Crampton's Pass."

27. Bartlett, "Crampton's Pass"; *OR* 19, 1:388; Eugene Forbes, *Death Before Dishonor: The Andersonville Diary of Eugene Forbes, 4th New Jersey Infantry*, ed. William B. Styple (Kearny, NJ: Belle Grove Publishing, 1995), 22; George W. Bicknell, *History of the Fifth Regiment Maine Volunteers* (Portland, ME: Hall L. Davis, 1871), 136–137; "E. P. Gould to Friend

Allen," *Rochester (NY) Democrat and American*, Sept. 27, 1862.

28. Jno. T. Parham to George Bernard, June 6, 1892, in Bernard, *War Talks*, 43; Neese, *Confederate Horse Artillery*, 120.

29. George L. Kilmer, "McClellan's Reserves," *PWP*, July 29, 1882; "E. P. Gould to Friend Allen," *Rochester (NY) Democrat and American*, Sept. 27, 1862; Westervelt memoir, USAHEC. The farm where Westervelt sought shelter was probably David Arnold's, which was near the left of his regiment's skirmish line, and the barn would have been between the 27th NY and the Confederates.

30. *OR* 19, 1:826, 877; Bernard, *War Talks*, 25, 302.

31. *OR* 19, 1:877; Bernard, *War Talks*, 41, 302, 304. Jno. E. Crow of Company E, 12th VA, recalled that "the stone wall turned out to be a few stones on the ground, on which was built a rail fence." See Reese, *Sealed with Their Lives*, 74–75, 85.

32. *OR* 19, 1:389, 392; Bartlett, "Crampton's Pass"; Reese, *Sealed with Their Lives*, 87. Reese described the fence line the 5th ME and the 16th NY used for cover as a wall, but Bartlett referred to it as a rail fence. Part of the fence line was probably a stone-and-rider fence, which would explain why Bartlett described it as a rail fence.

33. Bernard, *War Talks*, 27. Bernard's experience is evidence that not all the Confederates enjoyed a high stone wall for cover.

34. *OR* 19, 1:389. Although in his account for the *NT* Bartlett wrote that Newton was 500 yards distant, in his official report he stated that Newton was "more than 1,000 yards" to his rear. I have accepted the latter figure, since it was written closer to the event; it is also based on Bartlett's statement that his regiments were out of ammunition when Newton's first regiments relieved his brigade. Joel Seaver of the 16th NY reported that his regiment maintained the fight for three-quarters of an hour before being relieved by Newton. Moving at the double-

quick, Newton's brigade could have covered 1,000 yards in about 10 minutes. Seaver's men could theoretically have fired 20 rounds in that time. See *OR* 19, 1:391. Newton may have been delayed, however, by Confederate artillery fire that disrupted his formation. See *OR* 19, 1:396; Bicknell, *Fifth Regiment Maine*, 137.

35. Reese, *Sealed with Their Lives*, 88–92.

36. *OR* 19, 1:389.

37. Ibid., 382, 384, 386, 388, 389, 396, 399, 400; Kearny, *Letters from the Peninsula*, 142; A. D. Slade, *A. T. A. Torbert: Southern Gentleman in Union Blue* (Dayton, OH: Morningside Press, 1992), 23.

38. *OR* 19, 1:394.

39. Ibid., 380.

40. William B. Franklin to GBM, Sept. 14, 1862, reel 31, MP; *OR* 19, 1:401.

41. *OR* 19, 1:382, 389, 396; Bartlett, "Crampton's Pass." Bartlett's *NT* account agrees with his official report but makes no mention of Newton being involved in the decision to charge. Nonetheless, as the senior brigadier on the line, Newton certainly approved the decision, and Torbert's report is clear that it was Newton who ordered him to charge.

42. Joseph Shaw, "Crampton's Gap," *NT*, Oct. 1, 1891.

43. Bartlett, "Crampton's Pass."

44. *OR* 19, 1:870, 873; Montgomery, *Howell Cobb's Confederate Career*, 68; *NC Regts*, 2:739–740. Although Cobb received orders to march at 1 p.m., it would have taken him some time to call in his pickets and assemble his regiments to march. He probably did not leave any earlier than 1:30 p.m.

45. *OR* 19, 1:870; Carman, chap. 7, 413; *Richmond Examiner*, July 31, 1861, in Freeman, *Lee's Lieutenants*, 1:160n; McLaws, "Capture of Harper's Ferry," *PWP*, Sept. 12, 1888.

46. *OR* 19, 1:826, 854, 873. Munford claimed that he sent four couriers to Cobb asking for help. Cobb's report implies that he responded to the first courier.

47. *OR* 19, 1:826, 870; *NC Regts*, 2:740. Lt. Henry
Kearney of the 15th NC maintained that his
regiment "formed on the left of the brigade,"
but Clarence Hutchins of the 16th GA
remembered that the 15th NC were on the
16th's right. Circumstantial evidence from
Kearney's account supports Hutchins's recollection. See *NC Regts*, 2:740; Clarence L.
Hutchins autobiography, *CWTI* Collection,
USAHEC. For a different interpretation of
the deployment of Cobb's regiments, see
Reese, *Sealed with Their Lives*, 127.

48. *OR* 19, 1:383, 827. Also see Bernard, *War Talks*,
28, 41, 304.

49. Bernard, *War Talks*, 28.

50. *OR* 19, 1:382–383, 386, 387; William P. Beech,
"The 1st New Jersey Brigade at Crampton's
Pass," *Grand Army Scout and Soldiers' Mail* 3,
no. 43 (Oct. 4, 1884); Bartlett, "Crampton's
Pass"; John Y. Foster, *New Jersey and the Rebel-
lion* (Newark, NJ: M. R. Dennis, 1868), 93;
William P. Beech, "Crampton's Pass," *NT*, May
8, 1884; Oscar Westlake letter, in Joseph G.
Bilby, ed., "Give My Love to All," *CWTI* 28,
no. 3 (May 1989), 39; C. C. Hall to cousin,
Sept. 15, 1862, Schoff Collection, Clements
Library, UM.

51. *OR* 19, 1:407–408; www.cclibraries.com/local
_history/MexicanWar/brookswth.htm
[accessed Oct. 2006]; Charles C. Morey diary,
USAHEC; Benedict, *Vermont in the Civil War*,
1:320–322; John Conline, "Recollections of
the Battle of Antietam and the Maryland
Campaign," in MOLLUS, *War Papers: Papers
Read Before the Commandery of the State of Michigan*, 2 vols. (Wilmington, NC: Broadfoot,
1993), 2:114.

52. Conline, "Recollections of the Battle," 115; *OR*
19, 1:408.

53. *OR* 19, 1:389, 391, 394, 396–400.

54. Henry C. Boyer, "At Crampton's Pass," *Shenandoah (PA) Evening Herald*, Sept. 2, 1886.

55. Ibid.; *OR* 19, 1:394.

56. Boyer, "At Crampton's Pass," *Shenandoah (PA)
Evening Herald*; *OR* 19, 1:394.

57. Boyer, "At Crampton's Pass," *Shenandoah (PA)
Evening Herald*; Henry Keiser diary, USAHEC;
Haas diary, USAHEC.

58. Boyer, "At Crampton's Pass," *Shenandoah (PA)
Evening Herald*; Reese, *Sealed with Their Lives*,
136, 302; Haas diary, USAHEC; *OR* 19, 1:394–
396, 877.

59. *OR* 19, 1:386, 387, 391, 398, 400; Boyer, "At
Crampton's Pass," *Shenandoah (PA) Evening
Herald*; Bartlett, "Crampton's Pass"; Newton
C. Martin, *From Bull Run to Chancellorsville:
The Story of the 16th New York Infantry* (New
York: G. P. Putnam, 1906), 170.

60. *OR* 19, 1:827, 870. Also see the report of Colonel Samuel Buck of the 2nd NH in *OR* 19,
1:384. It is evident from Buck's account that
his regiment had cleared the Mountain
Church Road and crossed the Gapland Road
before Cobb's two regiments moved down
the latter road.

61. *OR* 19, 1:384, 387, 392, 400, 861; Bernard, *War
Talks*, 41; Bartlett, "Crampton's Pass"; Reese,
Sealed with Their Lives, 116, 124. Reese has the
most detailed study of the battle's casualties.
For the losses in Cobb's brigade, see page 302
of his book.

62. *OR* 19, 1:391, 394, 398; Reese, *Sealed with
Their Lives*, 155; Joel Seaver to Colonel Howland, Sept. 15, 1862, in Martin, *Bull Run to
Chancellorsville*, 170; Bartlett, "Crampton's
Pass"; *NC Regts*, 1:740; Hutchins autobiography, *CWTI* Collection, USAHEC. Reese
contends that the 16th GA and the 24th GA
took divergent directions down the slope
from Crampton's Gap, with the 24th
ending up on the 15th NC's right and the
16th GA on Cobb's Legion's left. I did not
find evidence that supported this
disposition.

63. *OR* 19, 1:391, 394, 398; Bartlett, "Crampton's
Pass"; Boyer, "At Crampton's Pass," *Shenandoah
(PA) Evening Herald*; Martin, *Bull Run to Chan-
cellorsville*, 170; Hutchins autobiography,
CWTI Collection, USAHEC.

64. *NC Regts*, 1:740.

65. *OR* 19, 1:400, 861; Boyer, "At Crampton's Pass," *Shenandoah (PA) Evening Herald*; Reese, *Sealed with Their Lives*, 302; Joel Seaver to Colonel Howland, in Martin, *Bull Run to Chancellorsville*, 170; Haas diary, USAHEC.

66. Reese, *Sealed with Their Lives*, 301; Boyer, "At Crampton's Pass," *PWP*.

67. *OR* 19, 1:827, 870–871, 873, 877; John F. Stegeman, *These Men She Gave* (Athens: Univ. of Georgia Press, 1961), 62–63.

68. Boyer, "At Crampton's Pass," *Shenandoah (PA) Evening Herald*; *OR* 19, 1:400, 871; Stegeman, *These Men She Gave*, 62; Beech, "Crampton's Pass"; Bartlett, "Crampton's Pass."

69. Stegeman, *These Men She Gave*, 62; Shaw, "Crampton's Gap"; *OR* 19, 1:400, 408; Benedict, *Vermont in the Civil War*, 1:323.

70. *OR* 19, 1:397, 408; Benedict, *Vermont in the Civil War*, 1:323.

71. *OR* 19, 1:408; Benedict, *Vermont in the Civil War*, 1:322; Reese, *Sealed with Their Lives*, 151–152, 302. Hooker's Medal of Honor citation gives the number of Confederates who surrendered as 116. See "4th Vermont Infantry Medal of Honor," http://vermontcivilwar. org/units/4/moh.php.

72. *OR* 19, 1:385, 399, 400–401; C. C. Hall to cousin, Sept. 15, 1862, Schoff Collection, UM.

73. *OR* 19, 1:400–401, 403–404, 408, 409.

74. "From the Battlefield," *Ontario (NY) Repository*, Oct. 1, 1862; Forbes, *Death Before Dishonor*, 22–23.

75. Martin, *Bull Run to Chancellorsville*, 174.

76. Ibid., 174–175.

77. Bilby, "Give My Love," 39; Martin, *Bull Run to Chancellorsville*, 171; *OR* 19, 1:183.

78. *OR* 19, 1:377–378, 388, 861; Clark Edwards to My Dear Wife, Sept. 19, 1862; Clark Edwards Papers, PMNC; Reese, *Sealed with Their Lives*, 302. Also see Carman, chap. 7, 420.

79. Bartlett, "Crampton's Pass"; Snell, *From First to Last*, 184.

80. Snell, *From First to Last*, 184.

81. Bartlett, "Crampton's Pass."

82. *OR* 19, 1:47, 721.

83. Ibid., 47.

84. Ibid., 827.

85. Ibid., 854; King diary, SHC.

86. *OR* 19, 1:819; von Borcke, *Memoirs*, 217–218; Trout, *With Pen and Saber*, 100. Von Borcke's account has been called into question as perhaps being excessive in characterizing Cobb's demoralization, but it is consistent with Stuart's report and Price's Sept. 18 letter concerning the event.

87. *OR* 19, 1:855.

88. Thomas Munford, "The Maryland Campaign," address to the Confederate Veteran Association of Savannah, Georgia, typescript, McLaws Papers, SHC.

89. McLaws, "Capture of Harper's Ferry," *PWP*, Sept. 12, 1888; *OR* 19, 1:836, 855, 860–861.

90. McLaws, "Capture of Harper's Ferry," *PWP*, Sept. 12, 1888. Also see "Statement of John F. Edwards, Commissary Officer, McLaws' Division," Oct. 10, 1885, McLaws Papers, SHC.

91. McLaws, "Capture of Harper's Ferry," *PWP*, Sept. 12, 1888.

92. King diary, SHC.

Chapter 15. Retreat from South Mountain

1. Dooley, *John Dooley, Confederate Soldier*, 38–39. Alfred Pleasonton reported that his cavalry collected "several hundred" stragglers on Sept. 15. See *OR*, 19, 1:210. Also see "Memoirs of the 1st South Carolina Volunteer Infantry in the Confederate War for Independence," SCSL; Tucker diary, FSNMP.

2. John Purifoy to Ezra A. Carman, July 15, 1896, Carman Papers, LC; John Purifoy to Ezra A. Carman, Apr. 28, 1896, Antietam Studies, NA; "A. S. Cutts to Dr. J. William Jones, Aug. 24, 1882," *SHSP* 10 (1882), 430–431. Purifoy never mentioned the other guns of Maj. Pierson's battalion, so these batteries most likely withdrew with D. H. Hill's infantry. Lloyd's battery, the 3rd NC Artillery, (1st) Company G, was detached from Ransom's infantry brigade to serve with Cutts. Cutts may not have iden-

tified this battery in his account to save the men embarrassment. Lloyd did not run an efficient outfit. On Sept. 25, 1862, General Ransom recommended that the battery be disbanded. He reported that in Maryland it "did not fire a gun and was not exposed to fire, but succeeded in losing one gun two caissons." The battery entered Maryland with only three guns. It was disbanded on Oct. 4, 1862, along with several others, by special orders from the Army of Northern Virginia headquarters. See *OR*, 19, 1:921–922; Johnson and Anderson, *Artillery Hell*, 97–99.

3. Stephen D. Thruston to William L. De Rosset, July 28, 1886, Gould Papers, Dartmouth College; Thomas, *Doles-Cook Brigade*, 68–69.

4. Stephen D. Thruston to William L. De Rosset, July 28, 1886, Gould Papers, Dartmouth College.

5. Alexander, *Fighting for the Confederacy*, 144; Simons diary, NA. It is evident that Simons edited his wartime diary, so this is more of a reminiscence than a diary.

6. *OR* 19, 1:609–610. Although the time of the dispatch is not stated in the *OR*, Carman writes that it was written soon after Lee reached Keedysville. See Carman, chap. 10, 518. McLaws had tried to communicate with Lee by courier, but none were able to get through.

7. Carman, chap. 10, 518; *OR* 19, 1:140, 147.

8. Carman, chap. 10, 513–514; *OR* 19, 1:036. Carman states that Rodes and Colquitt reached Keedysville about 1 a.m., but this is unlikely. They had a 4- to 4.5-mile march from South Mountain to Boonsboro at night, with exhausted troops. One member of the brigade wrote that they reached Sharpsburg around sunrise, which was at 5:50 a.m. With enemy cavalry in front, the column probably did not exceed a speed of 1.5 mph from Keedysville to Sharpsburg, which meant that they left Keedysville about 3:30 a.m. Rodes reported that they halted at Keedysville for an hour after their march from Boonsboro.

Therefore Rodes and Colquitt reached Keedysville between 2 and 2:30 a.m. See *South Western Baptist* (Marion, AL), Sept. 21, 1862; *OR* 19, 1:1036.

9. *South Western Baptist* (Marion, AL), Sept. 21, 1862; George Grattan to Ezra A. Carman, Feb. 22, 1896, Antietam Studies, NA. Grattan said that Colquitt's brigade camped near Blackford's house, past Jacob's Mill. This could only have been the W. M. Blackford farm. Also see Carman, chap. 10, 514. Why Colquitt camped here and not at Boteler's Ford is evident when looking at a map. Colquitt would have posted strong pickets at the ford and at the intersection of the River Road and Miller's Sawmill Road, and Blackford's farm was equidistant from these two places.

10. Toombs reported that his brigade arrived "before daylight." See *OR* 19, 1:888. Theodore Fogle of the 2nd GA, however, in a letter written on Sept. 16, said that they arrived "about 1–1/2 hours by sun," which would be between 7:00 and 7:30 a.m. See Theodore Fogle to father & mother, Sept. 16, 1862, Emory Univ., Atlanta, Georgia; Carman, chap. 10, 509; Ivy Dugan Papers, Univ. of Georgia, Athens, Georgia.

11. *OR* 19, 1:951. This dispatch did not, as Douglas S. Freeman claimed (in *Lee's Lieutenants*, 2:196), change Lee's mind about withdrawing from Maryland. Rather, it encouraged him to try and salvage his campaign, although he understood that retreat to Virginia on the night of Sept. 15 remained a very real possibility. Jackson's dispatch announcing the surrender of Harpers Ferry, which Lee received around noon on Sept. 15, and Jackson's later reply that he would march to Sharpsburg at once, were what made up Lee's mind to remain in Maryland.

12. Carman, chap. 10, 519–520. The precise order of march of D. H. Hill's command and S. D. Lee's battalion is unknown. S. D. Lee reported that he crossed Antietam Creek at 8 a.m. He may have crossed before Hill's

brigades, for a member of Ripley's brigade wrote that they reached Sharpsburg between 9 a.m. and 10 a.m. See *OR* 19, 1:844; John C. Key to Ezra A. Carman, Sept. 29, 1897, Antietam Studies, NA.

13. Carman, chap. 10, 514, 520. Although Carman has Colquitt's brigade on Hill's divisional line on the 15th, the testimony of the brigade is that they did not rejoin the division until Sept. 16. See *OR* 19, 1:844, 1032, 1036. Ripley reported that Longstreet directed the placement of his brigade, Garland's, and G. B. Anderson's "during the temporary absence of the division commander." The reason for Hill's absence is unknown.

14. Boulware diary, LV; Johnston, *Confederate Boy*, 144; Alexander Hunter, "A High Private's Sketch of Sharpsburg," *SHSP* 11 (1883), 511; Wood, *Reminiscences of Big I*, 37.

15. *OR* 19, 1:886, 888, 907; *OR* 51, 1:161–162; Longstreet, *Manassas to Appomattox*, 233–234; Carman, chap. 10, 520–521. According to Benning, the 15th GA and the 17th GA were not detached to march to Williamsport until after he received orders to defend the Rohrbach Bridge.

16. *OR* 19, 1:848; Carman, chap. 10, 521–522; Bartlett, *Soldier's Story*, 135.

17. Carman, chap. 10, 521–522; Coles, *From Huntsville to Appomattox*, 64; Simons diary, NA.

18. See appendix B for strengths. Writers who have proposed the idea that McClellan could have attacked Lee on the 15th have no concept of the time needed to march an army of nearly 70,000 men approximately 12 miles, reconnoiter the enemy's position, issue orders, and deploy for battle. It is complicated and time consuming. If McClellan had attacked on the 15th, it would have been a piecemeal, uncoordinated effort, undertaken with little reconnaissance. Given the strength of Lee's position, it is unlikely that he could have been dislodged by such an effort.

19. "Cutts to J. William Jones," 431; Felix Callaway, *The Bloody Links* (Shreveport, LA, 1907),

42–43; Thomas A. Graham to Ezra A. Carman, Mar. 1, 1900, Antietam Studies, NA.

20. Callaway, *Bloody Links*, 34; "Cutts to J. William Jones," 431; John Purifoy to Ezra A. Carman, Apr. 28, 1896, Antietam Studies, NA; Carman, chap. 10, 524. Carman states that Cutts halted near the Dunker church, while Bondurant went on to the Grove farm. However, the testimony from Cutts's battalion is clear that they, too, parked southwest of town, at least until they had refilled their ammunition chests from the trains parked near the Potomac River.

21. Henry K. Douglas to John C. Ropes, Jan. 23, 1898, and Walter H. Taylor to John C. Ropes, Jan. 27, 1898, John C. Ropes Papers, BU.

22. Simons diary, NA; Carman, chap. 10, 523.

23. Carman, chap. 10, 523; Thomas Munford to Ezra A. Carman, Mar. 24, 1898, Antietam Studies, NA. The church Munford referred to was most likely the Lutheran Church of Sharpsburg, on the eastern edge of town.

24. Henry K. Douglas to John C. Ropes, Jan. 23, 1898, and Jan. 25, 1898, Ropes Papers, BU. In his Jan. 25 letter to Ropes, Douglas drew from his "personal recollections of the war," which he had written in 1865. Also see Douglas, "Stonewall Jackson in Maryland," in *B&L*, 2:627; Carman, chap. 10, 559. Carman believed that it was Jackson's reply that he would march to Sharpsburg that induced Lee to offer battle there, but this is unlikely. It may have encouraged Lee, but it was the inactivity of the Union army on the 15th that probably convinced Lee to hazard a stand. Douglas never made the claim that Jackson's bold reply to Lee's orders caused Lee to decide to engage McClellan at Sharpsburg.

25. Noyes, *Bivouac and the Battlefield*, 179.

26. *OR* 19, 1:268.

27. C. Dickey to One and All (2nd U.S. Sharpshooters), Nov. 23, 1862, Steve Stottlemeyer Collection, Antietam NB; Joseph G. Bilby and Stephan D. O'Neill, eds., *My Sons Were Faithful and They Fought: The Irish Brigade at Antietam;*

An Anthology (Hightstown, NJ: Longstreet House, 1997), 36–37; *OR* 19, 1:216; Carman, chap. 10, 527. Carman writes that Fitz Lee's officers said it was about sunrise when Richardson began to descend the mountain. This timing is impossible if Richardson left Mount Tabor Church at daybreak, as Hooker reports that he did. See Joseph Hooker to Seth Williams, Sept. 15, 1862, reel 31, MP. Unfortunately, Hooker did not time this dispatch. Stephen Sears thinks it was sent around 8 a.m. See McClellan, *Civil War Papers*, 462.

28. Joseph Hooker to GBM, Sept. 15, 1862, [no time], reel 31, MP.

29. *OR* 19, 2:294.

30. McClellan, *Civil War Papers*, 463; *OR* 19, 2:294.

31. GBM to Henry W. Halleck, Sept. 15, 1862, reel 31, MP. The published copy in the *OR* gives the time of this dispatch as 8 a.m., but the original shows that it was sent at 8:30 a.m. For the *OR* copy, see, *OR* 19, 2:294.

32. *OR* 51, 1:836–837.

33. Cox, *Military Reminiscences*, 1:381–383; Carman, chap. 10, 547; *OR* 19, 1:297. Also see Sears, *George B. McClellan*, 298–299. Sears writes that Porter "was a bearer of grudges." For an argument that Porter's influence on McClellan's attitude toward Burnside has been exaggerated, see Rafuse, "'Poor Burn,'" 146–175.

34. *OR* 51, 1:834–835.

35. Ibid., 1:834–836; *OR* 19, 1:295. The orders to Sumner, though, were somewhat confusing. He was informed that Richardson's division would be moving in front of Hooker "on your right," but Richardson instead followed the same road that Sumner was ordered to use.

36. *OR* 51, 1:835–836. Also see John C. Ropes to William B. Franklin, Jan. 21, 1898, and Franklin's response on Feb. 1, 1898, Ropes Papers, BU. Franklin did not recall ever receiving McClellan's 8:45 a.m. order or the one subsequently sent to him at 1:20 p.m. It is evident that either Franklin's memory failed him here or he was being disingenuous, for he sent McClellan a message at 11 a.m. stating that he

had received "your dispatch." This could only be the 8:45 a.m. orders. See *OR* 19, 1:47.

37. *OR* 19, 1:53.

38. Francis A. Walker, *History of the Second Army Corps in the Army of the Potomac*, (Gaithersburg, MD: Butternut Press, 1985), 96.

39. McClellan, *Campaigns of Stuart's Cavalry*, 124; Also see G. W. Beale, *A Lieutenant of Cavalry in Lee's Army*, Baltimore: Butternut and Blue, 1994, 44; George A. Custer to Albert Colburn, [no time], Sept. 15, 1862, reel 31, MP.

40. Pleasonton gave no time for his movement, other than he went "at daylight," and the extant accounts of Union cavalrymen offer nothing more accurate. Capt. John Tidball reported that his battery received orders on the night of the 14th to report to Bolivar at daylight. See *OR* 19, 1:210; *OR Suppl.* 3:515.

41. *OR* 19, 1:216; Gibbon, *Personal Recollections*, 79–80; Patrick diary, LC; Dawes, *Sixth Wisconsin Volunteers*, 85.

42. The source for the 1st Corps' order of march and the time of its departure is Haskell, *Haskell of Gettysburg*, 39.

43. *OR* 51, 1:837.

44. *OR* 19, 2:296; Cox, *Military Reminiscences*, 1:383; *OR* 19, 1:338. The historian of the 35th MA reported that they marched at 2 p.m.; the 36th OH wrote that they left at 3 p.m., and Matthew Graham of the 9th NY said his regiment left at 5 p.m. The order of march of the 9th Corps on Sept. 15th is unknown, but Cox wrote that his division marched in the rear.

45. Joseph Gould, *The Story of the Forty-Eighth: A Record of the Campaigns of the Forty-Eighth Regiment, Pennsylvania Veteran Volunteer Infantry* (Philadelphia: Alfred M. Slocum, 1908), 78; Lord, *Ninth Regiment New Hampshire*, 88–90; Bobyshell, *Forty-Eighth in the War*, 77. James Wren wrote in his journal that the dead Confederates he observed "ware the finest set of Rebel soldiers I ever saw, both in Muscle & in equipage." See Wren journal,

USAHEC. Also see Evans, "Enemy Sullenly Held On," 33.

46. Regimental Assoc., *Thirty-Fifth Regiment Massachusetts*, 31; Evans, "Enemy Sullenly Held On," 33; Lord, *Ninth Regiment New Hampshire*, 89.

47. Albert, *Forty-Fifth Regiment Pennsylvania*, 54; Evans, "Enemy Sullenly Held On," 33; Strother, "Personal Recollections," 279; Wren journal, USAHEC.

48. Michael Deady diary, RBHL. Deady was on the burial detail that was left behind. He recorded that the detail, apparently including Confederate POWs, numbered 75 men, and that they buried 450 Confederates over two days. Also see Compton Papers, DU; Walcott, *Twenty-First Massachusetts*, 194; Strother, "Personal Recollections," 279.

49. Noyes, *Bivouac and the Battlefield*, 179–181; Healy journal, GNMP; William Olcott letter, privately owned by John Craft.

50. Dawes, *Sixth Wisconsin Volunteers*, 85; Woodward, *Our Campaigns*, 200; Webster diary, HL; Alexander, "Pennsylvania Reserves," USAHEC.

51. Austin C. Stearns, *Three Years with Company K*, ed. Arthur A. Kent (Rutherford, NJ: Fairleigh Dickinson Univ. Press, 1976), 122; John W. Jaques, *Three Years' Campaign of the Ninth, N.Y.S.M., During the Southern Rebellion* (New York: Hilton, 1865), 191; Moore diary, Antietam NB; Charles S. McClenthen, *A Sketch of the Campaign in Virginia and Maryland from Cedar Mountain to Antietam* (Syracuse, NY: Masters & Lee, 1862), 33; Jobe reminiscences, ACHS.

52. G. W. Beale, *Lieutenant of Cavalry*, 44; Carman, chap. 10, 527–528.

53. William Child, *A History of the Fifth Regiment, New Hampshire Volunteers, in the American Civil War, 1861–1865* (Gaithersburg, MD: Ron R. Van Sickle Military Books, 1988), 118; Edward E. Cross, *Stand Firm and Fire Low: The Civil War Writings of Colonel Edward E. Cross*, ed. Walter Holden, William E. Ross, and Eliza-

beth Slomba (Hanover, NH: Univ. Press of New England, 2003), 129; Mike Pride and Mark Travis, *My Brave Boys: To War with Colonel Cross and the Fighting Fifth* (Hanover, NH: Univ. Press of New England, 2001), 124; *OR* 19, 1:287.

54. Child, *Fifth Regiment, New Hampshire*, 118; Abner Hard, *Eighth Cavalry Regiment*, 178; H. McClellan, *Life and Campaigns*, 124.

55. H. McClellan, *Life and Campaigns*, 124–125. His account is rather biased and gives the impression that Fitz Lee easily contained the Union attack, which was not the case. Neither is there any evidence that the 3rd VA turned back the initial attack of the 8th IL, as Henry McClellan claims. Also see Beale, *Ninth Virginia Cavalry*, 39; Beale, *Lieutenant of Cavalry*, 45; William L. Rizell, "The Cavalry Panic at Boonsboro," Daniel Papers, UVA. Rizell wrote that the people of Boonsboro "fired upon us at a lively rate, and from the windows of houses as well."

56. Beale, *Ninth Virginia Cavalry*, 45; G. W. Beale, "The Cavalry Fight at Boonsboro," Fitz Lee folder, Antietam Studies, LC; Rizell, "Cavalry Panic at Boonsboro," Daniel Papers, UVA.

57. Beale, "Cavalry Fight at Boonsboro," Antietam Studies, LC; Beale, *Lieutenant of Cavalry*, 45–46; Beale, *Ninth Virginia Cavalry*, 39–40; H. McClellan, *Life and Campaigns*, 126–127.

58. Beale, *Ninth Virginia Cavalry*, 39–40; Fitzhugh Lee to My Dear Sir, Feb. 15[?], 1896, Fitz Lee folder, Antietam Studies, LC; Rizell, "Cavalry Panic at Boonsboro," Daniel Papers, UVA; H. McClellan, *Life and Campaigns*, 126; Carter, *Sabres, Saddles, and Spurs*, 16.

59. Beale, *Ninth Virginia Cavalry*, 40; *OR* 19, 1:210; Hard, *Eighth Cavalry Regiment*, 179.

60. *OR* 19, 1:210; *New York Daily Tribune*, Sept. 19, 1862.

61. Noyes, *Bivouac and the Battlefield*, 183–184, 185; Healy journal, GNMP; Haskell, *Haskell of Gettysburg*, 38–39. A reporter for the *New York Daily Tribune* wrote that "all the public buildings are filled with the Rebel dying and

wounded." See *New York Daily Tribune*, Sept. 19, 1862. Also see Brown, *Twenty Seventh Indiana*, 234; Abram Dyer journal, Antietam Battlefield Board Papers, Series 707, RG 92, NA.

62. The *New York Daily Tribune* correspondent reported that 3,000–4,000 prisoners were taken on the 15th. See *New York Daily Tribune*, Sept. 19, 1862. Also see Hitchcock, *War from the Inside*, 48; Samuel W. Moore journal, Antietam NB; Bobyshell, *Forty-Eighth in the War*, 173; Carman diary, NJHS.

63. Dawes journal, SHSW; Williams, *From the Cannon's Mouth*, 124; Hitchcock, *War from the Inside*, 49; Woodward, *Our Campaigns*, 201.

64. *OR* 19, 2:294; McClellan, *Civil War Papers*, 463.

65. *OR* 19, 2:294–295.

66. Strother, "Personal Recollections," 279–280; Carman, chap. 10, 539.

67. Carman diary, NJHS; Strother, "Personal Recollections," 279–280.

68. *OR* 51, 1:836; *OR* 19, 2:295; GBM to Mary Ellen, Oct. 6, 1861, in McClellan, *Civil War Papers*, 106.

69. *OR* 51, 1:836; *OR* 19, 1:47.

70. Signal station at Washington Monument to GBM, 12:40 p.m., Sept. 15, 1862, reel 31, MP. The Washington Monument on South Mountain is a stone tower erected in 1827 in honor of George Washington by the people of Boonsboro. It still stands, within Washington Monument State Park, and offers a magnificent view of the country west of South Mountain.

71. George A. Custer to GBM, [no time], Sept. 15, 1862, reel 31, MP.

72. Joseph Hooker to Seth Williams, Sept. 15, 1862, and Edwin V. Sumner to Randolph Marcy, Sept. 15, 1862, reel 31, MP. Although Sumner did not time his dispatch, it was probably written after 3 p.m. According to a *New York Daily Tribune* correspondent, Sumner reached the front opposite Antietam Creek at that time. See *New York Daily Tribune*, Sept. 19, 1862.

73. Strother, "Personal Recollections," 280.

74. *OR* 51, 1:836.

75. Ibid.

76. Ibid., 837–838; *OR* 19, 1:47.

77. *OR* 51, 1:836, 838.

78. Strother, "Personal Recollections," 280.

79. *OR* 19, 1:287; Child, *Fifth Regiment, New Hampshire*, 118–119; Waite, *New Hampshire*, 279; Carman, chap. 10, 532; Cross, *Stand Firm and Fire Low*, 43–44; Pride and Travis, *My Brave Boys*, 125–126.

80. W. R. Hamby, "Hood's Texas Brigade at Sharpsburg," *CV* 16 (1905), 19; William Child, *Letters from a Civil War Surgeon: The Letters of Dr. William Child of the Fifth New Hampshire Volunteers* (Solon, ME: Polar Bear, 2001), 33.

81. Child, *Fifth Regiment, New Hampshire*, 119; *OR* 19, 1:293; *New York Daily Tribune*, Sept. 19, 1862; Carman, chapter 10, 533.

82. *New York Daily Tribune*, Sept. 19, 1862; Crowninshield, *Massachusetts Cavalry Volunteers*, 75; *OR Suppl.* 3:516; *OR* 19, 1:283, 844; Eugene C. Tidball, *No Disgrace to My Country: The Life of John C. Tidball* (Kent, OH: Kent State Univ. Press, 2002), 262–263. The *New York Daily Tribune* correspondent stated that Pettit had only four guns in action on the 15th. S. D. Lee reported several men slightly wounded and some horses disabled. Pettit had no casualties, and Tidball did not mention suffering any loss. See Carman, chap. 10, 533.

83. Hooker's arrival time is approximate and is based on the 2:15 p.m. dispatch he sent to McClellan. See *CCW*, 37th Cong., 3rd Sess., 1:581; *OR* 19, 1:217; *New York Daily Tribune*, Sept. 19, 1862.

84. *OR* 19, 1:29, 53–54; "George L. Breck Letters," *Union Advertiser* (Rochester, NY), Sept. 18, 1862; Charles D. Page, *History of the Fourteenth Regiment, Connecticut Vol. Infantry* (Gaithersburg, MD: R. Van Sickle Military Books, 1987), 28; *New York Daily Tribune*, Sept. 19, 1862; Casey, "Ordeal of Adoniram Judson Warner," 219; Sydney Meade journal, SHSW.

85. Palfrey, *Antietam and Fredericksburg*, 56; Hill, *Our Boys*, 399. Many soldiers wrote of McClellan's ride to the front that afternoon and described the tremendous cheering that greeted him. McClellan recalled that the men received him with the "wildest enthusiasm." See McClellan, *McClellan's Own Story*, 586.

86. McClellan, *McClellan's Own Story*, 586; Cox, *Military Reminiscences*, 1:300; Strother, "Personal Reminiscences," 280; Hooker statement to Ezra A. Carman, [no date cited], quoted in Carman, chap. 10, 542.

87. *OR* 19, 1:29, 54, 217; McClellan, *McClellan's Own Story*, 587.

88. Timothy J. Reese, *Sykes' Regular Infantry Division, 1861–1864* (Jefferson, NC: McFarland Press, 1990), 132; *OR* 19, 1:355, 356.

89. *OR* 19, 1:54, 355; *OR* 19, 2:311; Carman, chap. 10, 534, 536, 537, 542.

90. *New York Daily Tribune*, Sept. 19, 1862; *OR* 19, 2:296–297, 311.

91. *OR* 51, 1:836.

92. *OR* 19, 2:297; Albert Colburn to Sumner, [no time], Sept. 15, 1862, "Orders Received," 2nd Army Corps Papers, RG 393, NA; *New York Daily Tribune*, Sept. 19, 1862.

93. John C. Ropes, *The Story of the Civil War: A Concise Account of the War in the United States of America between 1861 and 1865*, 4 vols. (New York: G. P. Putnam's Sons, 1894–1913), 2:349; Alexander, *Fighting for the Confederacy*, 145; Owen, *In Camp and Battle*, 139; Alexander, *Military Memoirs*, 249.

94. Alexander, *Military Memoirs*, 242, 247; Henry K. Douglas to John C. Ropes, Jan. 25, 1898, Ropes Papers, BU.

95. Robert E. Lee to Mrs. Thomas J. Jackson, Jan. 25, 1866, Ropes Papers, BU.

96. Henry K. Douglas to John C. Ropes, Jan. 23, 1898, Ropes Papers, BU; Alexander, *Military Memoirs*, 225.

97. *OR* 19, 1:151; Alexander, *Military Memoirs*, 249.

Chapter 16. The Trap Closes and a Cavalry Dash

1. Shuler diary, LC. Shuler served in the Stonewall Brigade and gave the time when they marched as 4:30 a.m., so it is possible that Hill started earlier. Also see Capt. Andrew B. Wardlaw diary, USAHEC; *OR* 19, 1:953; Caldwell, *History of a Brigade*, 42.

2. *OR* 19, 1:966, 1007. The position of Jackson's division is indicated on 1st Lt. S. Howell Brown's map of Harpers Ferry and Sharpsburg, in *Official Military Atlas of the Civil War*, no. 1, plate 29. Also see Samuel D. Buck, *With the Old Confeds: Actual Experiences of a Captain in the Line* (Gaithersburg, MD: Butternut Press, 1983), 61; *OR* 19, 1:953; Robertson, *Stonewall Jackson*; Walker, "Jackson's Capture of Harper's Ferry," in *B&L*, 2:608–609; Hotchkiss diary, LC.

3. *OR* 19, 1:962, 953. The only woods that were cut along the Bolivar Heights line were south of the Charlestown Pike, in the area of what was called Bull's Hill.

4. Several Union accounts mention Walker's attempt to establish a signal station on Loudoun Heights on Sept. 13, at around 4 p.m., immediately after the evacuation of Maryland Heights. For one example, see DeGraff memoir, USAHEC.

5. The exact text of McLaws's report is not known. Jackson refers to it in his reply on Sept. 14. See *OR* 19, 2:607; *OR* 19, 1:953; *NC Regts*, 2:453.

6. DeGraff memoir, USAHEC; Moore, *Rebellion Record*, 5:446; Benedict, *Vermont in the Civil War*, 2:193. Also see William H. Nichols 3d, "Siege and Capture of Harpers Ferry," in MOLLUS, *Personal Narratives of Events in the War of the Rebellion, Being Papers Read Before the Rhode Island Soldiers and Sailors Historical Society* (Wilmington, NC: Broadfoot Publishing, 1993), 68.

7. Luff, "March of the Cavalry," 2:38; White, "Capitulation of Harper's Ferry," in *B&L*, 2:612.

8. White, "Capitulation of Harper's Ferry," in *B&L*, 2:613. White is quite clear that this meeting took place on the night of Sept. 13, not Sept. 14. Lt. Henry Binney, Miles's aide, testified that a meeting between Miles and Davis took place on the night of the 14th, but possibly Binney forgot about the Sept. 13 meeting. Lt. Col. Hasbrouck Davis's testimony before the court of inquiry supports White's account that the meeting occurred on Sept. 13. Davis is also the source of the statement that "the original route proposed on Saturday was to cross the Shenandoah near Harper's Ferry." As both White and Davis definitely were present at the meeting, while it is not certain that Binney was, their accounts carry greater weight. Moreover, Binney claimed that the meeting took place at 7 or 7:30 p.m. Since the cavalry marched on the 14th sometime between 8 and 9 p.m., Binney's assertion would not allow much time for a 1,500-man cavalry force to issue instructions, ready mounts and equipment, and assemble to march. Additional evidence that the meeting took place on the 13th comes from Maj. Charles H. Russell's testimony that on Saturday evening (Sept. 13), Miles asked him if he thought he could lead the cavalry force out of Harpers Ferry. See *OR* 19, 1:584, 630, 720. Also see Thomas Bell, "Longstreet's Train." Bell served in the 8th NY Cavalry and claimed to be privy to the words exchanged by Grimes Davis and Miles. This is unlikely, but Bell may have learned some details of their conversation at a later date.

9. Nichols, "Siege and Capture," 5:446; *OR* 19, 1:526–527, 547, 549; DeGraff memoir, USAHEC; Norman Eldred memoir, copy, GNMP. The line on Bolivar Heights was held (from left to right) by the 60th OH, the 126th NY, the 111th NY, the 115th NY, the 39th NY, and the 65th IL. Potts had four 3-inch rifles and two light 12 lb. smoothbores. The rifles were certainly on Camp Hill, and the smoothbores at the bridges.

10. Willson, *Disaster, Struggle, Triumph*, 79.

11. *OR* 19, 1:743, 606–607.

12. DeGraff memoir, USAHEC; Benedict, *Vermont in the Civil War*, 2:193; *OR* 19, 1:632.

13. DeGraff memoir, USAHEC; Benedict, *Vermont in the Civil War*, 2:193; Pettengill, *College Cavaliers*, 73; *Boston Evening Transcript*, Sept. 19, 1862.

14. Willson, *Disaster, Struggle, Triumph*, 79; Simons, *Regimental History*, 30; Norman Eldred recollections, GNMP; John Paylor diary, GNMP; Benedict, *Vermont in the Civil War*, 2:194.

15. *OR* 19, 1:596, 636–637. As D'Utassy is so self-serving, and the truth of some of his statements is questionable, I have accepted Cameron's testimony as being more accurate regarding this small operation. Capt. Eugene McGrath testified that the guns were 12-pounders. But the report by Henry McIlvaine indicates that they were two 12 lb. light howitzers and two 12-pounder guns. See *OR* 19, 1:548, 697.

16. *OR* 19, 1:913, 958; Walker, "Jackson's Capture of Harper's Ferry," in *B&L*, 2:609; *NC Regts*, 2:433.

17. McLaws, "Capture of Harper's Ferry," *PWP*, Sept. 5, 1888; *OR* 19, 1:854; *OR* 19, 2:608; Dickert, *History of Kershaw's Brigade*, 149. Although McLaws reported that work on cutting the road began early in the morning, Dickert recalled that it commenced during the night. Also see James Dinkens, "Griffith-Barksdale-Humphrey Mississippi Brigade and Its Campaigns," *SHSP* 32 (1904), 258.

18. *OR* 19, 1:953, 958. Signal communications between Jackson and McLaws were problematic throughout the siege. Also see McLaws, "Capture of Harper's Ferry," *PWP*, Sept. 5, 1888.

19. *OR* 19, 2:607.

20. *OR* 19, 1:958, 1011; Robertson, *Stonewall Jackson*, 601. In his article for *Century Magazine*, Walker recalled that he received a signal from Jackson, indicating that Jackson planned to

give the Union garrison 24 hours to remove noncombatants, after which he would carry the position by assault. Capt. Bartlett's record of signals sent from his signal station contains no such message. Both Henry K. Douglas and Bradley T. Johnson doubted the accuracy of Walker's memory. Walker's article—and Douglas's and Johnson's response—are in *B&L*, 2:609, 616, 617.

21. *OR* 19, 1:857, 958. McLaws wrote that he received only one signal message from Jackson, "and that only ordered such things to be done, as had been done long previous." See McLaws, "Capture of Harper's Ferry," *PWP*, Sept. 5, 1888. There is no time given for when Lt. Duncan signaled Walker, or Walker signaled Jackson, but it had to be around noon, for that was when McLaws learned of the threat to his rear. Since Walker opened fire at about 1 p.m., it is certain that he received Duncan's signal message well before that time.

22. *OR* 19, 1:959. Although Bartlett did not note when the operational order was sent, it definitely preceded and prompted the message from Walker's signal station, stating that "Walker cannot get position to bear on the island." According to Jackson's aide-de-camp, Lt. J. G. Morrison, the seven batteries of Jackson's command in position to fire were Poague's, Carpenter's, Braxton's, Davidson's, Crenshaw's, Latimer's, and McIntosh's. See Morrison, "Jackson at Harper's Ferry."

23. *OR* 19, 1:913; Walker, "Jackson's Capture of Harper's Ferry," in *B&L*, 2:609–610. Walker's account in *B&L* differs on several points from his official report, as well as from the series of signals that Captain Bartlett reported were exchanged between Walker's and Bartlett's stations. While there is evidence that Jackson initially did intend to ask for the surrender of Harpers Ferry, and to give the garrison time to evacuate the noncombatants (although perhaps not the 24 hours that Walker claimed—see n. 20), there is also strong evi-

dence that he abandoned this idea sometime during the morning. For a critique of Walker's statement and their own account of Jackson's intentions, see Bradley T. Johnson and Henry K. Douglas, "Stonewall Jackson's Intentions at Harper's Ferry," in *B&L*, 2:615–618.

24. *OR* 19, 1:913. In his *Century Magazine* article, Walker claimed to have maneuvered two regiments into view so that they drew the fire of the Federals, providing him with the excuse to respond. This might have happened— there seems to be no good reason for Walker to fabricate this story—but there is no other evidence to support it, and Walker's official report claims that he opened fire because the Federals began to shell his batteries, not their supporting infantry. According to Capt. Bartlett's signal log, a signal to Walker and McLaws to open fire was sent after the receipt of Walker's message that he could not get his guns to bear on the island in the Shenandoah River. Like nearly every other signal, McLaws did not receive it, and Walker had already opened fire. See *OR* 19, 1:959.

25. Benedict, *Vermont in the Civil War*, 2:194. Federal soldiers recorded a variety of different times for when the Confederates opened fire, ranging from 12:30 p.m. to 2 p.m., but there was agreement that it occurred around the time of their noon meal. The general consensus was 1 p.m., which coincides with the time in Walker's official report.

26. Nichols, "Siege and Capture," 6:69; Paylor diary, GNMP; Simons, *Regimental History*, 30; Charles Wesley Belknap journal, Civil War Misc. Collection, USAHEC.

27. W. H. Sanderson, "Harper's Ferry and Its Surrender," *NT*, Sept. 28, 1893; Eldred memoir, GNMP; Davidson, *Diary and Letters*, 51.

28. *OR* 19, 1:854; DeGraff memoir, USAHEC; Willson, *Disaster, Struggle, Triumph*, 79.

29. Moore, *Rebellion Record*, 5:447; *OR* 19, 1:538, 547.

30. *Boston Evening Transcript*, Sept. 19, 1862; DeGraff memoir, USAHEC; Willson, *Disaster,*

Struggle, Triumph, 79; *Boston Evening Transcript*, Sept. 19, 1862; Robertson, *Stonewall Jackson*, 602. According to the map prepared to accompany Lee's official report of the Maryland Campaign, the battery on the Shepherdstown Pike was Brockenbrough's MD battery (one 3-inch rifle, one 10 lb. Parrott, one Blakely rifle, and one 12 lb. howitzer). The identity of the other battery is not known. See *Official Military Atlas of the Civil War*, no. 1, plate 29.

31. Benedict, *Vermont in the Civil War*, 1:194–195.
32. Sanderson, "Harper's Ferry"; Edward H. Ripley, "Memories of the Ninth Vermont at the Tragedy of Harper's Ferry, Sept. 15, 1862," MOLLUS, *Personal Recollections of the War of the Rebellion: Addresses Delivered Before the New York Commandery of the Military Order of the Loyal Legion of the United States* (Wilmington, NC: Broadfoot Publishing, 1992), 143; John H. Dye, "Was Miles a Traitor?" *NT*, Oct. 22, 1891.
33. *OR* 19, 1:527, 549, 630, 657; *Boston Evening Transcript*, Sept. 19, 1862. General White reported that the Confederate fire disabled one 20 lb. Parrott and three other guns, but he did not specify the type of the latter artillery. Capt. Von Sehlen had one of the two caissons that were reported lost. He testified that it was a limber and contained nearly 100 rounds of ammunition, but the number of rounds indicates a caisson, not a limber. See *OR* 19, 1:664. Lt. Binney reported that four men were killed in the bombardment. The Union casualty report for the entire siege and capture lists two artillerymen killed and three wounded. See *OR* 19, 1:538, 549.
34. Willson, *Disaster, Struggle, Triumph*, 80.
35. Norton diary, SCSL; *OR* 19, 1:549, 980; Don Wickman, *"We Are Coming Father Abra'am": The History of the 9th Vermont Volunteer Infantry* (Lynchburg, VA: Schroeder, 2005), 143. A. P. Hill's route of march is documented in Lt. Brown's map in the *Official Military Atlas of the Civil War*, no. 1, plate 29.

36. *OR* 19, 1:980, 1000.
37. Ibid., 1000. Brockenbrough did not file a report, and the movements of his brigade that evening are unclear. Also see Wickman, *"We Are Coming,"* 145.
38. *OR* 19, 1:1004.
39. Ibid., 745–748; Wickman, *"We Are Coming,"* 143.
40. *OR* 19, 1:742–746.
41. Ibid., 527, 531, 538, 653.
42. Ibid., 527, 538, 1004; *NC Regts*, 1:759; C. E. Smith, "Harper's Ferry," *NT*, July 3, 1884; Wickman, *"We Are Coming,"* 145. The casualties of the 9th VT for the entire siege were three wounded. The 32nd OH had 10 men killed and 58 wounded, although most of these casualties were suffered on Maryland Heights. No one specified losses for the night action on Sept. 14.
43. Caldwell, *History of a Brigade*, 43; *OR* 19, 1:980, 985, 987. Capt. Edward Ripley's Company B of the 9th VT held the extreme left of the Union line, deploying along a bluff overlooking the Shenandoah River and the railroad. They narrowly avoided capture by Branch and Gregg, who ascended the bluff in Ripley's rear. When Ripley heard noises up on the bluff behind him, he climbed up to investigate and "found himself among the advancing rebels and our line gone." Ripley coolly gathered up his company and led them back to his regiment, following a circuitous route along the river and then doubling back. See Wickman, *"We Are Coming,"* 146.
44. *OR* 19, 1:951. It is not known at what time Jackson received Lee's dispatch or exactly when Lee sent it. It seems likely that the message went out at the same time that Lee sent similar warnings to McLaws. Jackson probably received the dispatch in mid- to late morning, since it was during this time that he changed his mind about sending in a flag of truce for noncombatants to clear out of Harpers Ferry.

45. *OR* 19, 1:980, 984; Johnson and Anderson, *Artillery Hell*, 93–94; Davidson, *Diary and Letters*, 52.

46. *OR* 19, 1:954, 962.

47. Davidson, *Diary and Letters*, 52. Also see Pender's letter to his wife, quoted earlier, in which he complained that "the other day when they thought they were going into a fight, six out [of] ten officers skulked out and did not come up until they thought all danger was over. More than half my Brigade went off the same day." It was probably written on Sept. 19 and the action was almost certainly Harpers Ferry, which underscores the dread A. P. Hill's assault troops felt about storming Bolivar Heights. See Pender, *General to His Lady*, 175.

48. *OR* 19, 1:1011, 1016.

49. McLaws, "Capture of Harper's Ferry," *PWP*, Sept. 19, 1888; *OR* 19, 1:860. The 13th MS had 210 men at the beginning of the Harpers Ferry operation and lost 11 men in skirmishing on Maryland Heights.

50. *OR* 19, 1:630; Bell, "Longstreet's Train." According to Lt. Col. Hasbrouck Davis, in his testimony during the Harpers Ferry court of inquiry, the preparations for the march had been completed when it was learned that the Shenandoah River crossing was not possible. This would place the timing after sunset, when the artillery fire ceased and the cavalry could assemble. Sunset on Sept. 14 was at about 6:15 p.m.

51. "Unofficial Report of Col. Voss," in Pettengill, *College Cavaliers*, 82; Pettengill, *College Cavaliers*, 78; Luff, "March of the Cavalry," 39.

52. Allan L. Tischler, *The History of the Harpers Ferry Cavalry Expedition, September 14 and 15, 1862* (Winchester, VA: Five Cedars Press, 1993), 20, 78, 158–159; *OR* 19, 1:738.

53. "Unofficial Report of Col. Voss," in Pettengill, *College Cavaliers*, 81; Luff, "March of the Cavalry," 39; Nichols, "Siege and Capture," 72; William McIlhenny reminiscences, *CWTI* Collection, USAHEC. There are two published copies of the order that Miles purportedly issued to Voss, one in Pettengill's book and the other in Luff's paper. The one Pettengill published was recalled from memory by Col. Voss nearly 20 years after the event. I have accepted Luff's version as the more accurate of the two, although he does not reveal his source. Luff's order of march is corroborated by McIlhenny's account, and Luff has the correct rank for Miles's aide, Lt. Reynolds, not "Capt. Reynolds," as Voss recalled. The strengths of the different commands were as follows: 1st MD Potomac Home Brigade Cavalry—124, Loudoun Rangers—12, 12th IL Cavalry—575, 8th NY Cavalry—614, 7th RI squadron—146, and 1st MD Cavalry—123+. Also see Harry W. Pfanz, *Special History Report: Troop Movement Maps, 1862, Harpers Ferry National Historical Park* (Denver: Denver Service Center, National Park Service, 1976), 46.

54. Luff, "March of the Cavalry," 40; Pettengill, *College Cavaliers*, 78; Thomas McAllister, "The Capture of Longstreet's Ammunition Train," *NT*, June 12, 1884.

55. Pettengill, *College Cavaliers*, 77; "Unofficial Report of Col. Voss," in Pettengill, *College Cavaliers*, 82; C. Armour Newcomer, *Cole's Cavalry; or, Three Years in the Saddle in the Shenandoah Valley* (Baltimore: Cushing, 1895), 43. According to Newcomer, Lt. Green had three enlisted men with him in the advance. Also see Luff, "March of the Cavalry," 40. Isaac Heysinger of the 7th RI squadron was adamant that the column was in motion "a few minutes after eight." See Isaac Heysinger, "The Cavalry Column from Harpers Ferry in the Antietam Campaign," *Morningside Notes: An Occasional Publication of Morningside Bookshop, Division of Morningside House*, Apr. 1987, 16.

56. Pettengill, *College Cavaliers*, 78–79.

57. "Unofficial Report of Col. Voss," in Pettengill, *College Cavaliers*, 82; Nichols, "Siege and Capture," 72; Luff, "March of the Cavalry," 40–41; Tischler, *Harpers Ferry Cavalry Expedition*, 137.

58. Tischler, *Harpers Ferry Cavalry Expedition*, 137. According to Voss's unofficial report, written around 1883, it was Company D that turned right and came upon the Rebel pickets, who challenged them. The captain turned his men around and rejoined the column without being fired on. However, the regimental chaplain interviewed several members of the regiment about the cavalry expedition, including Voss, in Nov. 1862, when the events were fresh in their minds, and his notes differed in several details from Voss's later report. The chaplain's account, so far as the mishaps during the crossing are concerned, is probably the more accurate recollection of what happened. Excerpts from his account can be found in Tischler, *Harpers Ferry Cavalry Expedition*, 136–139.

59. Heysinger, "Cavalry Column," 16; Nichols, "Siege and Capture," 72.

60. "Unofficial Report of Col. Voss," in Pettengill, *College Cavaliers*, 83; William McIlhenny memoir, *CWTI* Collection, USAHEC; Heysinger, "Cavalry Column," 16.

61. Thomas McAllister, "Longstreet's Ammunition Train"; Tischler, *Harpers Ferry Cavalry Expedition*, 134; Heysinger, "Cavalry Column," 8–9; Luff, "March of the Cavalry," 42; *Orleans Republican* (Albion, NY), Oct. 1, 1862, in Tischler, *Harpers Ferry Cavalry Expedition*, 128. This last was a letter from Capt. Thomas Bell of the 8th NY to his family, written on Sept. 24, 1862, that his hometown newspaper published. Although exaggerated in some details, Bell states that Davis learned in Sharpsburg that Hagerstown was occupied by Rebels. Also see "Unofficial Report of Col. Voss," in Pettengill, *College Cavaliers*, 83. Heysinger claimed that the Confederate picket post was located at the Lutheran church, and he also adamantly maintained that the command marched north along the Hagerstown Pike when it left Sharpsburg, but he is not sustained in either case by the evidence from Voss, Luff, and others. It was logical for the Southerners' picket reserve to take position near the intersection of the Hagerstown and Boonsboro roads, rather than east of Sharpsburg at the church. For a critique of Heysinger's account, see Tischler, *Harpers Ferry Cavalry Expedition*, 182–184.

62. Luff, "March of the Cavalry," 42–43; *Rock River (IL) Democrat*, Dec. 2, 1862, in Tischler, *Harpers Ferry Cavalry Expedition*, 132 (Tischler believed that the author of this unsigned article was Luff); Nichols, "Siege and Capture," 73; McIlhenny reminiscences, USAHEC; "Unofficial Report of Col. Voss," in Pettengill, *College Cavaliers*, 83–84; Tischler, *Harpers Ferry Cavalry Expedition*, 134. Also see Tischler (*Harpers Ferry Cavalry Expedition*, 53–54) for more details on his reconstruction of the route the cavalry followed from the Williamsport Turnpike to the Hagerstown Turnpike.

63. The warm days and cool nights on Sept. 14, 15, and 16 produced ground fog across the area of operations each morning. See *Rock River (IL) Democrat*, in Tischler, *Harpers Ferry Cavalry Expedition*, 132; Luff, "March of the Cavalry," 43; Col. Herbert Enderton, *The Private Journal of Abraham Joseph Warner*, cited in Tischler, *Harpers Ferry Cavalry Expedition*, 138. Also see Tischler (*Harpers Ferry Cavalry Expedition*, 101) for a description of the farm lane near the spot where Davis took position.

64. Carman, chap. 23, 26; Tischler, *Harpers Ferry Cavalry Expedition*, 99–100, 101, 105. At least six troopers of the 3rd VA Cavalry accompanied Longstreet's ordnance train. They were detached from their regiment because their horses were unserviceable. Whether they were an escort or simply accompanied the train is uncertain. See "Unofficial Report of Col. Voss," in Pettengill, *College Cavaliers*, 84; Heysinger, "Cavalry Column," 15. It is apparent from the Confederate sources that the group of vehicles encountered by the Harpers Ferry cavalry was part of a much larger train. E. P. Alexander, who was with the Confederate army's reserve ordnance train, wrote that

Davis and the cavalry "crossed our track" to capture part of Longstreet's train. Alexander also wrote that his train went over the Potomac River at Williamsport at dawn, the very time when the Union horsemen were capturing Longstreet's train. See Alexander, *Fighting for the Confederacy*, 144. Maj. F. H. Little, commanding the 11th GA, stated that the left wing of his regiment escorted D. H. Hill's commissary train; the 11th's regimental history reports noted that it did not leave Hagerstown until shortly before daylight. See *OR* 19, 1:909–910. Also see Warren Kittrell, *History of the Eleventh Georgia Volunteers* (Richmond: Smith, Bailey, 1863), 50–51.

65. Tischler, *Harpers Ferry Cavalry Expedition*, 100; *Rock River (IL) Democrat*, in Tischler, *Harpers Ferry Cavalry Expedition*, 132–133; Luff, "March of the Cavalry," 47; Bell, "Longstreet's Train"; "Unofficial Report of Col. Voss," in Pettengill, *College Cavaliers*, 85.

66. Tischler, *Harpers Ferry Cavalry Expedition*, 105; Luff, "March of the Cavalry," 45; Heysinger, "Cavalry Column," 14; *Valley Spirit* (Chambersburg, PA), Sept. 24, 1862.

67. Luff, "March of the Cavalry," 44–45; Heysinger, "Cavalry Column," 14. For evidence that it was probably the 1st MD Potomac Home Brigade Cavalry that Davis selected for escort duty, see McIlhenny reminiscences, USAHEC; McAllister, "Longstreet's Ammunition Train"; "Unofficial Report of Col. Voss," in Pettengill, *College Cavaliers*, 85.

68. Heysinger, "Cavalry Column," 14; "Unofficial Report of Col. Voss," in Pettengill, *College Cavaliers*, 85; Luff, "March of the Cavalry," 45.

69. *Valley Spirit* (Chambersburg, PA), Sept. 24, 1862; *Philadelphia Inquirer*, Sept. 16 and 17, 1862. The column in the *Philadelphia Inquirer* reported that the commissary and quartermaster wagons arrived first, followed later by those captured from Longstreet's ordnance train. Unless the former wagons passed the latter, this was impossible; it was most likely

an error made by whoever filed the report. The *Philadelphia Inquirer* column gave the time of the cavalry's arrival as 10 a.m., but a telegram from Greencastle to Gov. Curtain, reporting their arrival and details of the march from Harpers Ferry, was sent at 9 a.m. See *OR* 19, 2:305.

70. *OR* 19, 2:305. Voss's wire to Wool is in Luff, "March of the Cavalry," 47. Also see Tischler, *Harpers Ferry Cavalry Expedition*, 40–47. For the various claims about the number of wagons and prisoners captured, see Tischler, *Harpers Ferry Cavalry Expedition*, 50–53, 124–133. Lee only admitted to the loss of 45 wagons, which he also said were destroyed. See Robert E. Lee to Jefferson Davis, *OR* 19, 1:142.

71. Lee's decision to offer battle on Sept. 17 and 18 are the strongest evidence that the loss of Longstreet's ordnance train inconvenienced rather than injured the Confederates. E. P. Alexander also recalled with pride that Lee's choice to stand and fight at Antietam again on Sept. 18 showed that "in spite of distance from railroads, & of the excessive amount of fighting in the previous three weeks, his chief of ordnance [Alexander] still had plenty of ammunition at hand." See Alexander, *Fighting for the Confederacy*, 154; Starr, *Union Cavalry*, 1:308; *OR* 19, 1:802.

Chapter 17. The Fall of Harpers Ferry

1. *OR* 19, 1:531, 538, 548, 655. From the amount of firing that the Union batteries did on Sept. 15, it is evident that McIlvaine meant that there were only 36 rounds of long-range ammunition left in the garrison, besides what was in the ammunition chests.

2. Ibid., 541.

3. Ibid., 584.

4. Ibid.

5. DeGraff memoir, USAHEC; Eldred recollections, GNMP; George Dawes to family, Sept. 30, 1862, GNMP; Benjamin Thompson remi-

niscences, GNMP; Benedict, *Vermont in the Civil War*, 2:195.

6. Ripley, "Memories of the Ninth Vermont," 147; Davidson, *Diary and Letters*, 52; Edward A. Moore, *The Story of a Cannoneer under Stonewall Jackson* (New York: Neale, 1907), 142; *OR* 19, 1:914, 962. Captain Henry L. P. King of McLaws's staff recorded in his diary that he heard Jackson's guns open "before six." See King diary, SHC; Walker, "Jackson's Capture of Harper's Ferry," in *B&L*, 2:610.

7. *OR* 19, 1:650, 962; Fred W. Fout, "Miles at Harper's Ferry," *NT*, Sept. 19, 1901; Henry B. Curtis Jr. to Lucy, Sept. 18, 1862, GNMP; "The Surrender of Harper's Ferry," *Boston Daily Evening Transcript*, Sept. 19, 1862.

8. Richard A. Bassett to Mary, Sept. 22, 1862, Bassett Collection, OCHS; John D. Smith, *The History of the Nineteenth Regiment of the Maine Volunteer Infantry, 1862–1865* (Minneapolis: John D. Smith, 1909), 99; Ripley, "Memories of the Ninth Vermont," 148; Don Wickman, *"We Are Coming,"* 147.

9. George Dawes to parents, Sept. 30, 1862, GNMP; DeGraff memoir, USAHEC.

10. *OR* 19, 1:743–744, 565.

11. White, "Capitulation of Harper's Ferry," in *B&L*, 2:613. White made no mention of ordering guns or infantry to the front in his afteraction report, but there is no reason to doubt that he did send these orders.

12. *OR* 19, 1:548, 549, 527–528; Davidson, *Diary and Letters*, 53. Davidson wrote that it was a 24 lb. shell bursting in front of one of his caissons that did the damage. This could only have been from Potts's battery.

13. *OR* 19, 1:584–585.

14. Ibid., 528, 588–589, 598–599, 744; White, "Capitulation of Harper's Ferry," in *B&L*, 2:613.

15. *OR* 19, 1:585, 599, 744; Simons, *Regimental History*, 32–33; Thompson reminiscences, GNMP. Thompson wrote that "the men broke their guns against the trees as they passed them and did every ugly thing they dared." Also see

Eldred recollections, GNMP; "*New York Times* narrative," in Moore, *Rebellion Record*, 5:447; Benedict, *Vermont in the Civil War*, 2:197. The 9th destroyed only their national color. The Confederates took the state color before it could be shredded. See Wickman, *"We Are Coming,"* 150.

16. Benedict, *Vermont in the Civil War*, 2:196–197; Wickman, *"We Are Coming,"* 148–149.

17. Walker, "Jackson's Capture of Harper's Ferry," in *B&L*, 2:610; Clarence A. Fonderen, *A Brief History of the Military Career of Carpenter's Battery* (New Market, VA: Henkel, 1911), 37; Moore, *Story of a Cannoneer*, 143; Poague, *Gunner with Stonewall*, 44.

18. *OR* 19, 1:539; Thompson reminiscences, GNMP.

19. *OR* 19, 1:980, 1004.

20. Douglas, *I Rode with Stonewall*, 161–162. See Dennis E. Frye, "Riding with Stonewall," *Civil War History* 9, no. 5 (1963), 40–46, for a critical assessment of Douglas's reminiscence. Also see Hunter McGuire to Jedediah Hotchkiss, Jan. 22, 1897, Hotchkiss Papers, LC; Robertson, *Stonewall Jackson*, 604.

21. Douglas, *I Rode with Stonewall*, 162; *OR* 19, 1:980. In drawing up the surrender terms, Hill agreed to provide the Federals with two days' rations, which proved to be a considerable portion of the food Jackson captured. One of the consequences of this was that McLaws's division, which had exhausted its rations in Pleasant Valley, found none in Harpers Ferry.

22. A. L. Long, *Memoirs of Robert E. Lee* (Secaucus, NJ: Blue and Gray, 1983), 216. Long writes that Lee received Jackson's dispatch around noon, and confirmation is found in Lee's Sept. 16 letter to Davis, where he states that he had "received intelligence from General Jackson that Harper's Ferry had surrendered" before McClellan's forces arrived at Antietam Creek at 2 p.m. See *OR* 19, 1:140, 951.

23. Davidson, *Diary and Letters*, 53; Haynes, *Field Diary*, 19; Peter S. Carmichael, *The Purcell,*

Crenshaw, and Letcher Artillery (Lynchburg, VA: H. E. Howard, 1990), 95.

24. Joseph W. Brunson, *Pee Dee Light Artillery of Maxcy Gregg's (later Samuel McGowan's) Brigade, First South Carolina Volunteers (Infantry) C.S.A.*, ed. William S. Hoole (University, AL: Confederate, 1983), 19; William G. Morris to Dear Companion, Sept. 23, 1862, Morris Papers, SHC; Caldwell, *History of a Brigade*, 43; David G. McIntosh reminiscences, SHC; David G. McIntosh, "Sketch of David Gregg McIntosh while in the State and Confederate Service, from 1861–1865," in United Daughters of the Confederacy, *Treasured Reminiscences* (Columbia, SC: State, 1911), 43.

25. *NC Regts*, 1:760; Moore, *Rebellion Record*, 5:447–448; Henry B. Curtis Jr. to Lucy, Sept. 18, 1862, GNMP.

26. *Boston Daily Evening Transcript*, Sept. 19, 1862; William F. LeMunyon reminiscences, Civil War Misc. Collection, USAHEC; DeGraff memoir, GNMP; Richard A. Bassett to Mary, Sept. 22, 1862, Bassett Collection, OCHS; Henry B. Curtis Jr. to Lucy, Sept. 18, 1862, GNMP.

27. Wardlaw diary, USAHEC. Wardlaw estimated that "not less than 1200 negroes were captured." The *Richmond Dispatch* gave several different figures, ranging from 1,000 to 2,000. See *Richmond Dispatch*, Sept. 20, 1862, http://dlxs.richmond.edu/d/ddr/. Also see Pfanz, *Special History Report*, 54.

28. Moore, *Rebellion Record*, 5:447; Caldwell, *History of a Brigade*, 43; Hunter McGuire to Jedediah Hotchkiss, Feb. 8, 1897, Hotchkiss Papers, LC; Henry B. Curtis Jr. to Lucy, Sept. 18, 1862, GNMP.

29. *OR* 19, 1:548–549, 860–861, 913, 981; Wardlaw diary, USAHEC. Although Jackson reported that he captured 13,000 small arms, Lt. Binney, in a letter to the *Baltimore American*, wrote that the amount was 7,500. The actual number of serviceable or repairable Union weapons was probably in between these two

figures. See *OR* 19, 1:954; Moore, *Rebellion Record*, 5:444, 448.

30. Robertson, *Stonewall Jackson*, 606.

31. *OR* 19, 1:799; "Lt. Henry Binney to Editor of the *Boston Journal*, Sept. 27, 1862," in Moore, *Rebellion Record*, 5:444.

32. White, "Capitulation of Harper's Ferry," in *B&L*, 2:615.

33. Pfanz, *Special History Report*, 62.

34. Ibid., 63; *OR* 19, 1:798, Mills, *Through Blood and Fire*, 127, 145.

35. *OR* 19, 1:798; Willson, *Disaster, Struggle, Triumph*, 45–46, 115–116. For a thorough examination of the reorganization and redemption of the 126th NY, as well as the other regiments named, see Eric A. Campbell, "Remember Harper's Ferry," *Gettysburg Magazine* 7 (July 1992), 51–75.

36. *OR* 19, 1:540.

37. Henry K. Douglas to John C. Ropes, Jan. 23, 1899, Ropes Papers, BU. Douglas wrote to Ropes that Jackson received the correspondence in the morning. I have accepted James I. Robertson's timing. See Robertson, *Stonewall Jackson*, 606. Also see Carman, chap. 13, 19; Shuler diary, LC; *OR* 19, 1:955. Carman writes that Early and Hays overtook Lawton and Trimble during the night, and that the entire division crossed the Potomac River around sunrise, after J. R. Jones's division, which apparently took the lead during the march. See Carman, chap. 13, 19.

38. Walker, "Jackson's Capture of Harper's Ferry," in *B&L*, 2:611; Carman, chap. 13, 19; Burgwyn, *Captain's War*, 18.

39. King diary, SHC; McLaws, "Capture of Harper's Ferry," *PWP*, Sept. 12, 1888; James Dinkens, "Personal Recollections in the Confederate Army," Antietam Studies, NA.

40. Dinkens, "Personal Recollections," NA. Dinkens wrote that he could "plainly see the enemy's camp, and his guns stacked." Also see McLaws, "Capture of Harper's Ferry," *PWP*, Sept. 12, 1888; McDaniel, *Diary of the Battles*, 14; Bailey George McClelen, *I Saw the Ele-*

phant: The Civil War Experiences of Bailey George McClelen, Company D, 10th Alabama Infantry Regiment, ed. Norman E. Rourke (Shippensburg, PA: Burd Street Press, 1995), 29; King diary, SHC; *OR* 19, 1:855.

41. *OR* 19, 1:47.

42. Franklin, "Notes on Crampton's Gap," in *B&L*, 2:596. Franklin's infantry strength is arrived at by taking Franklin's numbers for Smith, which he gives as 4,500 men, and estimating Slocum's strength at 5,000 (deducting the 500 casualties that occurred on Sept. 14). Couch's strength is given at 7,219, which is those present for duty. This translates into about 6,000 combat effectives. For the number of guns, see Johnson and Anderson, *Artillery Hell*, 73, 76 (although their table does not include Walcott's Battery A, MD Light). Capt. William Stuart's 3rd Battery, NY Light (4 guns) reached Couch on Sept. 15, but no time is given for their arrival, so their numbers are not included in the strength of Franklin's battery. It is also assumed that Couch's brigade was accompanied by one of his divisional batteries, all of which had only four guns apiece. This latter information is also from Franklin, "Notes on Crampton's Gap," in *B&L*, 2:596. Also see Franklin's testimony to the Committee on the Conduct of the War in *CCW*, 37th Cong., 3rd Sess., 1:626. His explanations to the Committee are those of a man seeking to shirk his responsibility for part of the disaster that befell Harpers Ferry.

43. Franklin, "Notes on Crampton's Gap," in B&L, 2: 596.

44. McLaws, "Capture of Harper's Ferry," *PWP*, Sept. 19, 1888.

45. *OR* 19, 1:47; Philip Kearny to My Dear Parker, July 24, 1862, in Kearny, *Letters from the Peninsula*, 138.

46. *OR* 19, 1:855. Captain King's diary corroborates the time McLaws gives. See King diary, SHC. Also see Dinkens, "Griffith-Barksdale-Humphreys Mississippi Bri-gade," 259; McDaniel, *Diary of Battles*, 14; Blackford,

47. *OR* 51, 1:835–836.

48. *OR* 19, 1:47. In a letter to historian John Ropes in 1898, Franklin claimed that he did not remember the 8:45 a.m. dispatch, and that he received "no information as to the movements of other parts of the Army until late in the evening of the 16th of September." Franklin was either being disingenuous or suffering from poor memory. Since Franklin responded to McClellan's 8:45 a.m. dispatch, he clearly received it, and at 4 p.m. he communicated with General Burnside, who was then between Keedysville and Boonsboro, so Franklin's claim that he had no information about the movements of the main body before the late evening of Sept. 16 was simply not true. See William B. Franklin to John C. Ropes, Jan. 24, 1898, and Feb. 1, 1898, Ropes Papers, BU.

49. Thomas Munford, "The Maryland Campaign," McLaws Papers, SHC.

50. *OR* 19, 1:855; McLaws, "Capture of Harper's Ferry," *PWP*, Sept. 12, 1888; King diary, SHC.

51. *OR* 19, 1:855; King diary, SHC.

52. King diary, SHC; McLaws, "Capture of Harper's Ferry," *PWP*, Sept. 12, 1888; *OR* 19, 1:855; Carman, chap. 10, 581. The problem with McLaws's suggestion is that it would have created the same dilemma that confronted Franklin. Pleasant Valley, even near Crampton's Gap, is not very wide, and it is easily defended against a superior force advancing up or down the valley. But Jackson might have made things interesting had he kept McLaws in Pleasant Valley to pin down Franklin, while maneuvering his own command east of South Mountain, by way of Weverton Pass, to move against the Army of the Potomac's communications. A dangerous undertaking, to be sure, but one that would have assuredly stopped McClellan's advance from South Mountain.

53. "Statement of John F. Edwards," Oct. 10, 1885, McLaws Papers, SHC; McLaws, "Capture of Harper's Ferry," Sept. 19, 1888; McDaniel, *Diary of Battles*, 14; Shand reminiscences, SCSL. Shand stated that his regiment received rations about 7 a.m. on Sept. 15 and did not receive anything more until the night of the 17th.

54. McLaws, "Capture of Harper's Ferry," *PWP*, Sept. 12, 1888. McLaws stated that R. H. Anderson remained in his forward line "certainly until 2 p.m." before commencing the withdrawal. There is evidence that the 2nd SC, and possibly part of the 1st NC Cavalry, helped screen the withdrawal of McLaws's and R. H. Anderson's divisions. See J. M. Monie to [?]. S. Andrews, [no date], and "Carman Notes on June 14, 1897, Letter of Wm. Cheek," Hampton folder, Antietam Studies, NA. Other regiments of the brigade may have been present, but there is little documentation of their whereabouts on this day. See *OR* 19, 2:296; *OR* 51, 1:835–836.

55. McLaws, "Capture of Harper's Ferry," *PWP*, Sept. 12, 1888; Dinkens, "Griffith-Barksdale-Humphreys Mississippi Brigade," 259.

56. *OR* 19, 1:855, 857. Reports of when McLaws's infantry began crossing the pontoon bridge vary widely. McLaws reported that it was around 2 a.m., but some soldiers stated that they passed over the river during the afternoon. See Wade Hampton to J. E. B. Stuart, Sept. 16, 1862, Stuart Papers, box 2, HL.

57. "Statement of John F. Edwards," McLaws Papers, SHC.

58. *OR* 51, 1:836.

59. *OR* 19, 2:297.

60. *OR* 51, 1:836.

61. *OR* 19, 1:46; McClellan to Mary Ellen, Aug. 22, 1862, in McClellan, *Civil War Papers*, 399.

62. *OR* 19, 1:29, 800.

Chapter 18. September 16

1. Strother, "Personal Recollections," 280; *OR* 19, 2:308.

2. *OR* 19, 1:307–308; *OR* 51, 1:839; Albert Colburn to Edwin V. Sumner, Sept. 15, 1862, RG 393.2.45, NA.

3. Carman, chap. 13, 21. The strength of Miles's force is derived by averaging the strength of a company in the combined regiment. Charles Fuller gave the regimental strength as 350. If, after consolidation, it still contained 10 companies, the average was 35 each. See Fuller, *Personal Recollections*, 58; Ephraim E. Brown, *The 1862 Civil War Diary and Letters of Ephraim E. Brown, 64th New York Vol.*, ed. Patricia A. Murphy (Lakeland, FL: privately printed, n.d.), 36, 42. In an Oct. 4, 1862, letter to his uncle, Brown wrote that Miles's orders from Sumner were to drive in the Confederate pickets on the east bank of Antietam Creek. There is no extant record that McClellan ordered a reconnaissance by the 6th NY Cavalry during the night of Sept. 15, but it is evident from Brown's diary that McClellan did so.

4. Carman, Chap. 13, 21; Brown, *1862 Civil War Diary*, 36, 42.

5. Carman, chap. 13, 22; Brown, *1862 Civil War Diary*, 36, 42. Brown wrote in his diary that they reported back to Col. Barlow at 7 a.m., hence the estimate that they reached the Middle Bridge around a half hour before this.

6. Thomas Devin to unknown major, Sept. 30, 1862, Pearce Civil War Collection, PMNC. The orchard Devin wrote about does not appear on any maps of the battlefield, but it can be seen just west of the Park farm, as can part of the ridge that Devin rode up to, in a Sept. 22 photograph by James Gibson. See William Frassanito, *Antietam: The Photographic Legacy of America's Bloodiest Day* (New York: Charles Scribner's Sons, 1978), 81.

7. *New York Daily Tribune*, Sept. 17, 1862, col. 4, and Sept. 20, 1862, col. 1; *OR* 19, 1:206, 338,

342; John C. Tidball to Ezra A. Carman, Feb. 18, 1896, Antietam Studies, NA. Pettit claimed that he was relieved at 5 a.m. by a battery of 20 lb. Parrotts; Tidball thought it was 9 a.m. Tidball's timing seems more accurate.

8. *OR* 19, 1:206, 342.

9. Ibid., 29, 55, 436; *New York Daily Tribune*, Sept. 20, 1862, col. 1, 1. Benjamin must have been mistaken about the time of the prolonged artillery duel. He reported that it began at 10:30 a.m., which does not agree with other accounts.

10. *OR* 19, 1:137. Unfortunately, no one recorded the time of Gloskoski's message, although the trains they observed were probably Lee's ord-nance trains, which reached Shepherdstown in midmorning. Also see "Orders Received and Communicated," 2nd Army Corps Papers, RG 393.1.4084, NA. The wagon train was also seen by the signal station at the Wash-ington monument on South Mountain, a testa-ment to the size of the train and the power of the signal officers' telescopes. See *OR* 19, 1:122. In reporting their station positions, Federal signalmen lumped Red Hill and Elk Ridge together, but they are separate ridges. The station described as being on Elk Ridge was actually on Red Hill. For the position of this station, see *The Official Military Atlas of the Civil War*, plate 28.

11. *OR* 19, 1:55.

12. Carman, chap. 13, 24–25, and chap. 21, 25; Cox, *Military Reminiscences*, 1:342.

13. Albert Colburn to Edwin V. Sumner, Sept. 15, 1862; George Ruggles to Edwin V. Sumner, 8:45 a.m., Sept. 16, 1862, and George Ruggles to Edwin V. Sumner, 9:30 a.m., Sept. 16, 1862, RG 393.2.45, NA.

14. McClellan, *McClellan's Own Story*, 588.

15. Ibid.; Cox, *Military Reminiscences*, 1:305–307; *OR* 19, 1:31, 55, 63–64. In both his final report and his memoirs, McClellan sought to deni-grate Burnside and magnify the Rhode Islander's failures, while omitting the very real difficulties the 9th Corps faced in captur-ing the Rohrbach Bridge. McClellan's initial report of the campaign, submitted in Oct. 1862, is both less critical and more accurate in certain particulars.

16. Cox, *Military Reminiscences*, 1:305, 307, 385; *OR* 19, 1:30.

17. Cox, *Military Reminiscences*, 1:304, 385.

18. Ibid., 304.

19. Ibid., 301.

20. *OR* 19, 1:338; *OR* 51, 1:834; Carman, chap. 13, 29. For the armaments of the batteries with Morell, see Johnson and Anderson, *Artillery Hell*, 74.

21. See appendix B for the army's strength. Also see *OR* 19, 1:369.

22. *OR* 19, 1:30, 55; Carman, chap. 13, 29.

23. Palfrey, *Antietam and Fredericksburg*, 62.

24. Carman, chap. 13, 3; *OR* 19, 1:217. In his report that was published in the *OR*, Hooker gives the time he received his orders as "between 1 and 2 o'clock." But an incomplete report, also dated Nov. 8, is included among Hooker's papers at HL, and it is considerably different from the one in the *OR*. In this partial report, Hooker states that his orders were received "about two o'clock p.m." See Joseph Hooker report, Nov. 8, 1862, manuscript copy, Hooker Papers, HL. Moreover, Hooker's report in the *OR*, although dated Nov. 8, 1862, was actually submitted on July 21, 1877. He began the report on Nov. 8, 1862, but did not finish it before he returned to active duty. For safe-keeping, a member of Hooker's staff gave the draft to his brother, who was a clerk in the Treasury Department, and the staffer's brother apparently filed it away, where it remained forgotten until he later found it and sent it to Hooker in 1877. See Strother, "Personal Recollections," 281.

25. See Sears, *Landscape Turned Red*, 171.

26. Hooker report, Nov. 8, 1862, Hooker Papers, HL.

27. Carman, chap. 13, 18. Lee's disappointment that McLaws and Walker did not arrive earlier is expressed in his letter of Sept. 18

to Confederate President Davis. See *OR* 19, 2:141.

28. *OR* 19, 1:844, 923; Carman, chap. 9, 514–515; George R. Large and Joe A. Swisher, eds., *Battle of Antietam: The Official History by the Antietam Battlefield Board* (Shippensburg, PA: Burd Street Press, 1998), 40–43. For Joseph Harsh's supposition that Lee had perhaps hoped to maneuver past McClellan's flank and reach Hagerstown, see Harsh, *Taken at the Flood*, 330–335.

29. Allen, *Army of Northern Virginia*, 368; Buck, *With the Old Confeds*, 63; James P. Gannon, *Irish Rebels: Confederate Tigers; The 6th Louisiana Volunteers, 1861–1865* (Campbell, CA: Savas, 1998), 128–129; *OR* 19, 1:963, 1013.

30. Edgar M. Crutchfield diary, UVA. Crutchfield was the adjutant of the 30th VA, and he recorded that they crossed the Potomac River around daybreak. Walker confirms an early crossing, for he writes that he and Jackson started out to report to Lee around 8 a.m. See Walker, "Jackson's Capture of Harper's Ferry," in *B&L*, 2:611. The signal station on Elk Ridge sent only one known signal on Sept. 16, to report a large wagon train crossing the Potomac River from Maryland to Shepherdstown. Jackson's two divisions and Walker's division were probably already bivouacked and under cover by the time the fog had burned off.

31. John G. Walker, "Sharpsburg," in *B&L*, 2:675; Alexander, *Fighting for the Confederacy*, 148. Minus the cavalry, Lee had 107 guns. The only horse battery present was Pelham's, which had 8 guns, but whether all these guns were on the field on Sept. 16 is uncertain. See Johnson and Anderson, *Artillery Hell*, 101.

32. *OR* 19, 1:848–849; Owen, *In Camp and Battle*, 141; Andrews, *Footprints of a Regiment*, 74–75.

33. Cross, *Stand Firm and Fire Low*, 44. The 125 casualties Cross reported were all in Richardson's division. Sykes's division may have suffered some losses as well, since part of it was also supporting the Union artillery. Other Confederate batteries besides Squires's and Riley's may have participated in the exchange, or in firing at Union infantry that exposed itself from time to time on Pry Ridge, but there are no reliable reports of who these others were. See Owen, *In Camp and Battle*, 141. Origen G. Bingham of the 137th PA described Sharpsburg immediately after the battle: "It is by no means a pretty place, nearly all the houses are considerably damaged by cannon fire and shells having passed through them." See Otis G. Bingham to parents, brothers, and sisters, Sept. 1862, Civil War Misc. Collection, USAHEC.

34. *OR* 19, 1:849, 925; Owen, *In Camp and Battle*, 141.

35. Palfrey, *Antietam and Fredericksburg*, 56.

36. Hitchcock, *War from the Inside*, 51.

37. Adoniram J. Warner, "Minutes of the Battle of South Mountain and Antietam," WRHS. Warner's "minutes" were transcribed and published in 1982, although there are some minor transcription errors. See Casey, "Ordeal of Adoniram Judson Warner"; *Sandusky (OH) Daily Register*, Nov. 10, 1862.

38. Fox, *New York at Gettysburg*, 2:499; *Sandusky (OH) Daily Register*, Nov. 10, 1862.

39. Evans, "Enemy Sullenly Held On," 35.

40. Andrews, *Footprints of a Regiment*, 75.

41. Ibid., 75–76.

42. William H. Palmer to Jedediah Hotchkiss, Apr. 22, 1895, Antietam Studies, NA.

43. Hunter, "High Private's Sketch"; John W. Lokey, *My Experiences in the War Between the States* (Tishomingo, OK: John R. Lokey, 1959), 10; Philip A. Work, "The First Texas Regiment of the Texas Brigade of the Army of Northern Virginia at the Battles of Boonsboro Pass or Gap and Sharpsburg or Antietam, Maryland," typescript, Antietam NB; O. T. Hanks, "History of Captain B. F. Benton's Company, 1861–1865," Confederate Research Center, Hill College, Hillsboro, Texas; Johnston, *Confederate Boy*, 144.

44. Wren journal, USAHEC; Vautier journal, USAHEC; Hussey, *Ninth Regiment, N.Y.S.M.—*

N.Y.S.N.G., 191; Robert M. Green, *History of the One Hundred and Twenty-Fourth in the War of the Rebellion* (Philadelphia: Ware Bros., 1907), 120.

45. Casey, "Ordeal of Adoniram Judson Warner"; George R. Graham, "The Fifth Maryland at Antietam," Antietam Studies, NA.

46. William Olcott reminiscences, private collection.

Chapter 19. Eve of Battle

1. Hooker report, Nov. 8, 1862, Hooker Papers, HL. It is evident from this report that McClellan did not provide more detailed instructions to Hooker when the two met. Also see Carman, chap. 13, 31.

2. *OR* 19, 1:217.

3. Regimental History Committee, *History of the Third Pennsylvania Cavalry* (Philadelphia: Franklin, 1905), 120.

4. Warner, "Minutes of the Battle," WRHS; Doubleday report, *U.S. Army Generals' Reports of Civil War Service*, NA.

5. Doubleday report, *U.S. Army Generals' Reports of Civil War Service*, NA.

6. Carman, chap. 13, 36; Doubleday report, *U.S. Army Generals' Reports of Civil War Service*, NA.

7. McClellan, *McClellan's Own Story*, 590–591; Hooker report, Nov. 8, 1862, HL; Joseph Hooker report, July 21, 1877, manuscript copy, Hooker Papers, HL; Strother, "Personal Recollections," 280–281. McClellan's account does not agree in important details with Hooker's or Strother's, and it has a self-serving tone to it. McClellan stated that after returning from his visit to the left, he found that Hooker's preparations were not complete and he "went to hurry them in person." Hooker wrote that the corps had marched a half mile from Antietam Creek before McClellan joined them, but Ezra Carman thought that the 1st Corps had probably marched nearly a mile. There is also no con-temporary evidence that Hooker's preparations "were not complete" or that they needed to be hurried. McClellan's own report notes that Hooker's orders to march were sent at 2 p.m. Both Doubleday and Meade stated that they marched at 2 p.m. (which must be considered approximate), so no time was lost in commencing the movement. Additional evidence that McClellan rode up to Hooker after Hooker's move to turn Lee's left was well developed is found in two letters: John Burnett (4th PA Reserves) to John M. Gould, [no date], and John Burnett to John M. Gould, Oct. 27, 1894, Gould Papers, Dartmouth College. Burnett wrote that he saw McClellan while his brigade was moving across Middlekauf's or Joseph Poffenberger's farm. The time of day when Burnett claims to have seen McClellan agrees with Strother's account, which places McClellan farther forward than has generally been thought, and later in the afternoon. Burnett's is one of the few accounts from anyone in the 1st Corps who reported seeing McClellan.

8. Cox, *Military Reminiscences*, 1:384–385.

9. Ibid.

10. Johnson, *Long Roll*, 189; *OR* 51, 2:168; Carman, chap. 13, 30; Wren journal, USAHEC.

11. Carman, chap. 13, 30.

12. Blakeslee, *Sixteenth Connecticut Volunteers*, 11; Matthew J. Graham, *Ninth Regiment New York*, 280.

13. David L. Thompson, "With Burnside at Antietam," in *B&L*, 2:660.

14. Cox, *Military Reminiscences*, 1:305; George Crook autobiography, USAHEC.

15. Cox, *Military Reminiscences*, 1:304–305; *OR* 19, 1:418–419, 423–424. Also see Antietam Battlefield Board (position of troops by Gen. E. A. Carman), *Atlas of the Battlefield of Antietam*, rev. ed. (Washington, DC: Gov't. Printing Office, 1908). Carman's 1908 revised Antietam Battlefield Board map of the positions of both armies at daybreak on Sept. 17 shows Benjamin's battery in the rear of Rodman,

while Burnside stated that Benjamin was in front of Rodman. I have accepted Carman's positioning of Benjamin as correct. See Carman, chap. 13, 30.

16. Carman, chap. 13, 34; *OR* 19, 1:967.

17. *OR* 19, 1:967.

18. Carman, chap. 13, 34; Beale, *Lieutenant of Cavalry*, 46; G. W. Weedon to Ezra A. Carman, Oct. 12, 1898, Antietam Studies, NA. Beale's description of their position is rather vague. Weedon marked it on a map that accompanied his letter to Carman (the map, unfortunately, is missing). However, Carmen made a note at the bottom of Weedon's letter stating that the position Weedon indicated for the hidden guns "is at the NW corner of the S. Poffenberger woods, west of Smoketown Road, very near where Cooper's Battery came into position at night."

19. Beale, *Lieutenant of Cavalry*, 46; Carman, chap. 13, 35; Stephen D. Lee to Ezra A. Carman, Mar. 8, 1895, Antietam Studies, NA; John T. Wingfield to Ezra A. Carman, Nov. 22, 1899, Antietam Studies, NA. According to Wingfield, three of Lane's guns, including both of the battery's 20 lb. Parrotts, were "found to be useless" at South Mountain and were not placed on line at Sharpsburg. Also see Robert Falligant to Ezra A. Carman, Oct. 18, 1896, Antietam Studies, NA; Robert Falligant's map to Carman, Antietam Studies, NA.

20. Regimental History Committee, *Third Pennsylvania Cavalry*, 122; *OR* 51, 1:156.

21. Doubleday report, *U.S. Army Generals' Reports of Civil War Service*, NA. Also see *OR* 19, 1:223. The East, North, and West Woods are all postbattle names applied to farm woodlots. Since these names are so well established, they will be used throughout the text instead of the names of the farmers who owned the woodlots.

22. Regimental History Committee, *Third Pennsylvania Cavalry*, 122; Beale, *Lieutenant of Cavalry*, 47; G. W. Weedon to Ezra A. Carman, Oct. 12, 1898, NA. Weedon identified the

pieces as belonging to Stuart's horse artillery. He also was certain that the enemy soldiers who were fired on were the 3rd PA Cavalry. Carman mentions the lane through the woods south of Line's farmhouse. See Carman, chap. 13, 39. This lane does not appear on the Antietam Commission maps. Regarding the direction in which both Pelham's guns and the 9th VA fell back, Lt. George Beale wrote that "what the line of our march was as we withdrew I have little idea." See George W. Beale to Carmen, Mar. 16, 1900, Antietam Studies, NA.

23. Regimental History Committee, *Third Pennsylvania Cavalry*, 121–122.

24. Ibid., 122.

25. Carman, chap. 13, 36–37; *OR* 51, 1:156; *OR* 19, 1:269; Thomson and Rauch, *History of the "Bucktails,"* 210.

26. *OR* 19, 1:269; Josiah R. Sypher, *History of the Pennsylvania Reserve Corps* (Lancaster, PA: Elias Barr, 1865), 379.

27. *OR* 19, 1:927. It is not certain that the "little battery" referred to in the *OR* was Falligant's gun. Ezra Carman attempted to learn its identity, but without success. There is evidence that there were two other guns on this part of the field, belonging to an ad hoc force under the command of a lieutenant in the 4th VA Cavalry. See Edwin McWinn to Ezra A. Carman, July 18, 1897, Antietam Studies, NA.

28. William M. Robbins to John M. Gould, Mar. 25, 1891, Antietam Studies, NA; *OR* 19, 1:937; Carman, chap. 13, 37; Coles, *From Huntsville to Appomattox*, 65.

29. Carman, chap. 13, 37; D. L. Love to John M. Gould, Apr. 29, 1891, Gould Papers, Dartmouth College.

30. Carman, chap. 13, 38; *OR* 51, 1:147, 156; Thompson and Rauch, *History of the "Bucktails,"* 210; Bates, *Pennsylvania Volunteers*, 1:584; Angelo Crapsey to Dear Friend, Sept. 30, 1862, PCHS.

31. Angelo Crapsey to Dear Friend, Sept. 30, 1862, PCHS; Thompson and Rauch, *History of*

the "Bucktails," 210; Carman, chap. 13, 38; *OR* 51, 1:156.

32. Stevens, *Reminiscences*, 72–73; Carman, chap. 13, 38; *OR* 51, 1:143, 147; James L. Lemon diary (18th GA), Antietam NB.

33. Carman, chap. 13, 38.

34. Alexander, "Pennsylvania Reserves"; John W. Burnett to John M. Gould, Oct. 27, 1894, Gould Papers, Dartmouth College.

35. The report of the 3rd PA Reserves indicates there was no infantry resistance to their advance. See *OR* 51, 1:144; John W. Burnett to John M. Gould, [no date], Gould Papers, Dartmouth College.

36. For the deployment of these two brigades, see Antietam Battlefield Board, *Atlas of the Battlefield*, map 1; Alexander, "Pennsylvania Reserves"; John T. Wingfield to Ezra A. Carman, Nov. 22, 1899, NA.

37. John T. Wingfield to Ezra A. Carman, Nov. 22, 1899, NA; Carman, chap. 13, 40.

38. *OR* 19, 1:955, 1007, 1013; Carman, chap. 13, 41; R. P. Jennings (23rd VA) to Ezra A. Carman, Mar. 25, 1895, R. W. Withers (42nd VA) to Ezra A. Carman, Mar. 14, 1895, and John T. Worsham (21st VA) to Ezra A. Carman, Dec. 22, 1898, Antietam Studies, NA. W. E. Moore of the 1st LA thought Starke's brigade numbered 1,400–1,500 men. Given J. R. Jones's statement that his entire division did not contain over 1,600, Moore's figure cannot be correct. See "Starke's Brigade, Notes," Antietam Studies, NA. The 2nd VA was detached on Sept. 13 at Martinsburg, Virginia, and was not present with Grigsby.

39. *OR* 19, 1:1007, 1009. J. R. Jones's report is in error in placing Poague's guns in the Hagerstown Pike. For details on his position, see William T. Poague to Henry Heth, May 18, 1893, Antietam Studies, NA.

40. Warner, "Minutes of the Battle," WRHS; *OR* 51, 1:150. The 9th PA Reserves formed on Warner's left, so since Anderson's brigade was extending Magilton's line west, they would have been the regiment directly in front of Warner's 10th PA Reserves.

41. Warner, "Minutes of the Battle," WRHS.

42. Alexander, "Pennsylvania Reserves," USAHEC; Frank Holsinger [a.k.a. "Woodbury Kid"], "Being under Fire," *Martinsburg (PA) Herald*, [no date]; Carman, chap. 13, 40; Dunbar Ransom to Ezra A. Carman, Feb. 5, 1895, Antietam Studies, NA.

43. Poague, *Gunner with Stonewall*, 45; *OR* 19, 1:1009, 1012, 1016; John T. Worsham to Ezra A. Carman, May 6, 1895, Antietam Studies, NA. Several Confederate accounts mention that their units also experienced random enfilading fire from the Union batteries east of Antietam Creek.

44. *OR* 19, 1:967; Carman, chap. 13, 42. According to Jno. W. Gilkerson of the 25th VA, the 49th VA formed on Early's right, facing east toward the Hagerstown Pike, while the remainder of the brigade formed at a right angle to the 49th, presumably to the north. See Gilkerson letter, May 3, 1895, Antietam Studies, NA. The source for Early's position is Antietam Battlefield Board, *Atlas* of the Battlefield, map 1.

45. *OR* 19, 1:819. There is no evidence that Stuart placed any artillery on Nicodemus Heights during the night of Sept. 16. The guns he assembled there were gathered early on the 17th. See George W. Beale to Ezra A. Carman, June 6, 1894, Antietam Studies, NA. According to Beale, "Fitz Lee's Brigade was in motion for several hours that night, with orders to move as quietly as possible, and, misled by a blundering guide, were dismounted to rest beyond our lines, and very close to several Federal batteries." These batteries were the guns Hooker placed on the Joseph Poffenberger farm. See Carman, chap. 13, 42, 46. Charles F. Russell of the 7th VA Cavalry in Munford's brigade recalled passing a large cavalry force near Cox's farm on the evening of the 16th, which could only have been Fitz Lee's brigade. See Charles F. Russell to Ezra A.

Carman, Oct. 27, 1898, Antietam Studies, NA. Elements of Fitz Lee's brigade were detached during the night to picket various points. William L. Royall of the 9th VA Cavalry recalled that he was on picket "where I could look down from a wooded hill into the Potomac River." This may have been the northern end of Nicodemus Heights. See William L. Royall to Ezra A. Carman, Mar. 9, 1900, Antietam Studies, NA. William A. Hill of the 4th VA Cavalry wrote that his regiment supported a battery for a time (probably Elliot's) before being relieved by infantry. They then moved "to the left through a cornfield westwardly to a piece of woods." The cornfield is probably the one west of Alfred Poffenberger's, for a small woodlot was located on the western edge of this field. See William A. Hill to Ezra A. Carman, July 18, 1898, and Fitzhugh Lee to Ezra A. Carman, Feb. 18, 1898, Antietam Studies, NA. There was a small woods on the southwest slope of Nicodemus Heights, which is probably where Fitz Lee spent the night. For Jackson's whereabouts, see R. Channing Price to mother, Sept. 18, 1862, in Trout, *With Pen and Saber*, 100. John B. Hood recalled that he found Jackson sleeping under a tree as well, which raises the likelihood that Jackson may have left the Grove house during the night (see note 65).

46. *OR* 19, 1:819; Robert M. Macknall to Ezra A. Carman, Mar. 15, 1900, Antietam Studies, NA.

47. Doubleday journal, HFC; "From the 23rd Regiment," *Corning (NY) Journal*, Oct. 2, 1862; Patrick, *Inside Lincoln's Army*, 146–147.

48. *OR* 19, 1:236; Mat Hurlinger diary (56th PA), typescript, Antietam NB. Hurlinger recorded that they halted for the night around 8 p.m.

49. *OR* 19, 1:223; Gibbon, *Personal Recollections*, 80; Geo. C. Sumner to Antietam Battlefield Board, May 6, 1893, Antietam Studies, NA.

50. Vautier journal, USAHEC; Hussey, *Ninth Regiment, N.Y.S.M.—N.Y.S.N.G.*, 192; *OR* 19, 1:259. Also see Antietam Battlefield Board, *Atlas of the Battlefield*, map 1.

51. Regimental History Committee, *Third Pennsylvania Cavalry*, 123; Carman, chap. 13, 46.

52. Carman, chap. 13, 44; Gibbon, *Personal Recollections*, 80.

53. *NC Regts*, 1:184; Ben Milikin to Ezra A. Carman, Sept. 20, 1897, Antietam Studies, NA.

54. Carman, chap. 13, 46–47; Thomas Munford to Ezra A. Carman, Dec. 19, 1894, Antietam Studies, NA; Charles F. Russell to Ezra A. Carman, Oct. 27, 1898, Antietam Studies, NA.

55. Precisely when Toombs's regiments were ordered to march is unknown. Capt. T. H. Jackson, commanding the 15th GA, reported they crossed the Potomac River at Shepherdstown on the morning of Sept. 17. See *OR* 51, 2:166. This indicates that the regiments marched early on the 17th or possibly late on the night of the 16th; hence it was probably late afternoon when Lee sent orders for them to rejoin the army. For the disposition of Nelson's and Brown's battalions, see *OR* 19, 1:830. Pendleton incorrectly reported that the lower ford, which was Falling Waters, was only a mile or more below Williamsport.

56. D. R. Jones's estimated strength is 3,209, based on figures from Carman and, in the case of Jenkins's brigade, the *Charleston (SC) Mercury*, Oct. 14, 1862. Deducting the strength of Toombs's 15th GA and 17th GA, and the 11th GA of G. T. Anderson's brigade, gives the division 2,776 effectives.

57. McLaws, "Capture of Harper's Ferry," *PWP*, Sept. 19, 1888; *OR* 19, 1:857. Also see "Statement of John F. Edwards, Commissary Officer, McLaws' Division," Oct. 11, 1885, McLaws folder, Antietam Studies, NA, regarding the shortage of food and shoes in the division. McLaws may not have found any rations in Charlestown, but some of his men were fed. John T. Parham of the 32nd VA wrote that after arriving in the vicinity of Halltown, "rations were issued with instructions to cook at once." See "John T. Parham to Editor, *Times Dispatch*," *SHSP* 34 (1906), 251. A member of Barksdale's brigade recorded that they

received a ration of plain beef with no salt at 10 a.m., and "after noon we received three hardtack to the man, which was a poor return to the desperate work of the last three days." Others were not so fortunate. Robert Shand of the 2nd SC complained that "no food passed down our throats from 7 a.m. on Monday until after dark on Wednesday evening except a few apples taken from the trees on Tuesday." See Robert Shand, "Incidents in the Life of a Private Soldier," South Carolina Library, Univ. of South Carolina, Columbia, South Carolina; McDaniel, *Diary of the Battles*, 14. For Hampton's movements, see W. H. Cheek to Ezra A. Carman, Mar. 13, 1900, J. M. Monie to Ezra A. Carman, [no date], W. H. Cheek to J. M. Monie, May 28, 1897, and "Carman Notes on 2nd South Carolina Cavalry," Hampton folder, Antietam Studies, NA. To cross the C&O Canal, the brigade marched under the canal aqueduct spanning Antietam Creek.

58. Dinkens, "Griffith-Barksdale-Humphrey Mississippi Brigade," 260.

59. Ibid.; W. B. Judkins reminiscences, July 28, 1911, typescript, in possession of Zack Waters; W. B. Judkins, "Memories of a Civil War Soldier," typescript, Special Collections, Sara Hightower Regional Library, Rome, Georgia; I. M. Auld to mother, Sept. 22, 1862, Auld Papers, Putnam County Archives, Palatka, Florida; Kirkpatrick diary, THC; James Dinkins, *1861 to 1865, by an Old Johnnie: Personal Recollections and Experiences in the Confederate Army* (Dayton, OH: Morningside Bookshop, 1975), 57. Nearly every report from McLaws's division mentions heavy straggling on the march from Harpers Ferry.

60. *OR* 19, 1:857; Lafayette McLaws to Henry Heth, Dec. 13, 1894, Antietam Battlefield Board Papers, NA. According to Captain H. L. P. King, McLaws's headquarters were at Dr. Lucas's. Lucas's residence was on the road to Blackford's Ford, just east of the Shepherdstown Pike, which would mean that McLaws

did not march through Shepherdstown on his way to the ford. See King diary, SHC.

61. Lafayette McLaws to Henry Heth, Dec. 13, 1894, NA; King diary, SHC; Kirkpatrick diary, THC.

62. *OR* 19, 1:914; Walker, "Sharpsburg," in *B&L*, 2:675. There is some question as to when Walker received his orders. In his *B&L* article, he notes that Lee gave him orders at 4 p.m. to move at 3 a.m. the next morning to the right of the army. In his official report, Walker does not give a time when he received instructions from Lee, but he stated that in accordance with these orders, "at daylight the next morning I placed the division on the extreme right of our position." This implies that he received his orders during either the evening or the night before. Whenever they arrived, it appears that Lee did not want Walker to move until the commanding general was certain of McLaws's arrival time. Lee also wanted Walker to move into position under cover of darkness, to escape detection by the Union signal station on Red Hill. See *OR* 19, 1:981. A. P. Hill reported that he received his orders from Lee at 6:30 a.m., so Lee probably sent them at around 2:30 or 3 a.m.

63. *OR* 19, 1:857; Lafayette McLaws to Henry Heth, Dec. 13, 1894, NA; McLaws, "Capture of Harper's Ferry," *PWP*, Sept. 19, 1888.

64. James D. Nance to Laura, Sept. 24, 1862, SCSL. Nance's figure of 10,000 may be an underestimate. Capt. H. L. P. King of McLaws's staff recorded in his diary that after the arrival of all the stragglers, the division had more men on Sept. 18 than they had carried into action on Sept. 17. See King diary, SHC. Lt. W. W. Wood of Garnett's brigade reported that his brigade had double the force on Sept. 18 that they had on Sept. 17. See Wood, *Reminiscences of Big I*, 40. For strength figures, see appendix B. A. P. Hill's strength is an estimate. Carman gives Hill's strength in the four brigades and the artillery that he took to Sharpsburg as 2,568, which took into

account the heavy straggling on the march from Harpers Ferry.

65. Hood, *Advance and Retreat*, 42. After sending the army's trains to Shepherdstown earlier on the 16th, Lee recalled them when it became certain that McClellan would not attack before the Confederate army had completed its concentration. Hood's account lends credence to Fitz Lee's statement that Jackson slept near him, at the base of a tree (see note 45).

66. Walker, "Sharpsburg," in *B&L*, 2:675.

67. Hooker report, July 21, 1877, HL; Hooker report, Nov. 8, 1862, HL. Although Hooker had his first after-action report in hand when he wrote his subsequent report in 1877, the two differ in some details. For instance, in his November 1862 report, Hooker said that he sent a courier to McClellan at 8 p.m. His second report states that he visited the picket line of Seymour's brigade [a point on which his memory may have failed him—this was more likely the picket line of Anderson's and Magilton's brigades] at 9 p.m., then returned and sent a courier to McClellan. Since the November 1862 report was written closer to the time of the battle, I have accepted "about 8 O'clock" as the time Hooker sent his courier to McClellan. In other instances however, his 1877 report is more reliable. His 1862 report claims that he asked specifically for the 12th Corps to reinforce him, and that Sumner's corps "might follow, two hours before day." This is probably bombast, for McClellan granted Hooker no authority to select who would support him. His 1877 report notes only that he asked "that reinforcements should be ordered forward in season to reach me before that moment"; there is no mention of who the reinforcements are to be.

68. *OR* 51, 1:839.

69. *OR* 19, 1:275; Carman, chap. 13, 49.

70. For discussions on McClellan's thinking regarding the 2nd Corps, see Harsh, *Taken at the Flood*, 353. Also see Sears, *George B. McClellan*, 300–303; "Report on the Alleged Delay in Concentration of the Army of the Potomac under McClellan at Antietam," in Military Historical Society of Massachusetts, *Civil War and Miscellaneous Papers*, vol. 14 of *Papers of the Military Historical Society of Massachusetts* (Boston: Military Historical Society of Massachusetts, 1918).

71. *OR* 51, 1:839–840. Franklin's report of Oct. 7 implies that he received additional orders besides Ruggles's dispatch of 7:30 p.m. See *OR* 19, 1:376; Carman, chap. 17, 182.

72. Strother, "Personal Recollections," 281.

73. There are variety of times given by 12th Corps officers and men as to when they received orders to march, ranging from 10:30 p.m. to midnight. See Williams, *From the Cannon's Mouth*, 124; Brown, *Twenty-Seventh Indiana*, 238; Sebastian Duncan Jr. journal, NJHS; Ezra A. Carman journal, NJHS; John M. Gould, *The Civil War Journals of John Mead Gould, 1861–1866*, ed. William B. Jordan Jr. (Baltimore: Butternut and Blue, 1997), 193; Isaac Van Stumburgh to John M. Gould, Apr. 1, 1892, Gould Papers, Dartmouth College.

74. Williams, *From the Cannon's Mouth*, 125.

75. J. Porter Howard to John M. Gould, Feb. 4, 1892, John H. Keatley to John M. Gould, Nov. 18, 1892, and James Wheeler to John M. Gould, Jan. 22, 1892, Gould Papers, Dartmouth College.

76. Carman, chap. 13, 49. McClellan may have known about, and approved, Sumner's transfer of his artillery to the west bank of Antietam Creek, but Carman indicates that this was done on Sumner's own initiative.

77. The number of Confederate guns facing Hooker and Mansfield is drawn from Johnson and Anderson, *Artillery Hell*, 43–45, 100.

78. Sypher, *Pennsylvania Reserve Corps*, 379; Adoniram J. Warner, "Minutes of the Battle," WRHS.

79. Stevens, *Reminiscences*, 72–73.

80. Milton Laird, "More About Lieut. Petrikin," *NT*, Oct. 21, 1891; Milton Laird, "At the Dunker Church," *NT*, Aug. 5, 1909.

81. Coles, *From Huntsville to Appomattox*, 65–66; William M. Robbins, "What Became of Lieut. Petrikin's Watch?" *NT*, July 16, 1891. Coles maintained that acting Lt. Col. Luther H. Scruggs ordered the volley to be fired, but in Robbins's various accounts of the incident, he did not mention Scruggs and stated that only the left two or three companies fired.

82. Coles, *From Huntsville to Appomattox*, 66; Robbins, "Lieut. Petrikin's Watch"; William M. Robbins to John M. Gould, Mar. 25, 1891, Antietam Studies, NA. Robbins did eventually learn that the watch was returned to Petrikin's mother, and in the 1890s, while serving as a commissioner on the National Park Commission at Gettysburg National Military Park, he visited Petrikin's home town and met his sister, who thanked him for his kindness in honoring the request of one who in 1862 was his enemy.

83. Coles, *From Huntsville to Appomattox*, 66. A. S. Reid of the 12th GA wrote to Carman on Jan. 3, 1895, stating that in the evening his regiment moved up the Smoketown Road and "relieved troops." The correspondents of the 21st GA do not record any change of position that night. See "Accompanying Letter of A. S. Reid," Trimble folder, Antietam Studies, NA.

84. Carman, chap. 15, 56. Also see "Map Accompanying Letter of W. H. Harrison, May 24, 1895," Trimble folder, Antietam Studies, NA; "Sketch of Col. J. W. Beck [60th GA]," Lawton folder, Antietam Studies, NA; "Map Accompanying Letter of J. W. Nisbet, Jan. 10, 1895," Trimble folder, Antietam Studies, NA.

85. Thomas F. Galwey, *The Valiant Hours: Narrative of "Captain Brevet," an Irish-American in the Army of the Potomac* (Harrisburg, PA: Stackpole, 1961), 38; Dawes, *Sixth Wisconsin Volunteers*, 87; Hitchcock, *War from the Inside*, 55–56; John Maycock diary, HCWRT, USAHEC.

86. Lewis Masonheimer diary, HCWRT, USAHEC. The historian of the 14th CT recorded that his regiment received 96 cartridges at 2 a.m. on the 17th. See Page, *Fourteenth Regiment, Connecticut*, 34; Sebastian Duncan Jr. to father, Sept. 16, 1862, Duncan Papers, NJHS.

87. Owen, *In Camp and Battle*, 142; Thompson, "With Burnside at Antietam," in *B&L*, 2:660.

88. Sorrel, *Recollections*, 103–104. The Jeff Davis Legion served in Hampton's brigade. The unit Sorrel mentioned was probably on detached service as Longstreet's cavalry escort.

89. D. L. Love to John M. Gould, Apr. 27, 1891, Gould Papers, Dartmouth College; Hood, *Advance and Retreat*, 42.

90. Ted Alexander, "Destruction, Disease, and Death: The Battle of Antietam and the Sharpsburg Civilians," *Civil War Regiments* 6, no. 2 (1998), 148–149, 161; Kathleen A. Ernst, *Too Afraid to Cry: Maryland Civilians in the Antietam Campaign* (Mechanicsburg, PA: Stackpole Books, 1999), 127–128.

91. Williams, *From the Cannon's Mouth*, 125.

ESSAY ON SOURCES

The essay below provides a survey of some of the most important sources associated with the Maryland Campaign that were consulted in the preparation of this book. A full bibliography is available online at www.mdhs.org/publications/resources.

Manuscripts

One of the most important collections for the Union Army of the Potomac is the extensive George B. McClellan papers at the Library of Congress, which are also available on microfilm. While much of McClellan's correspondence was printed in the *War of the Rebellion: The Official Records of the Union and Confederate Armies*, volume 19, parts 1 and 2, McClellan's papers contain a considerable amount of daily army communications not included in the *Official Records*. The National Archives house the Antietam Studies Collection in Record Group 94. This is perhaps the most significant Antietam collection in the country. It consists of hundreds of letters, written principally to Ezra A. Carman, a veteran of the battle and the de facto historian of the Antietam Battlefield Board from 1894 to 1898. Carman sought to document the position of every regiment and battery in the Battle of Antietam and carried on an extensive correspondence with Union and Confederate veterans. Although the letters were written nearly 30 years after the battle, they are a gold mine of detailed, eyewitness accounts for the entire Maryland Campaign, as many veterans included their experiences in other parts of the campaign in their correspondence.

The majority of Ezra Carman's extensive papers are housed with the Manuscript Division of the Library of Congress, but there are also Carman collections at the New York Public Library and the New Jersey Historical Society. Carman's papers at the Library of Congress include his massive and neatly handwritten manuscript, which is indispensable for any serious study of the Maryland Campaign. This was edited and published in 2008 by Joseph Pierro as *The Maryland Campaign of 1862*. Thomas Clemens, an authority on the campaign, came out with a newly edited and annotated edition of the first half of Carman's manuscript in 2010, titled *The Maryland Campaign of September 1862*. Clemens's edition of the second half of Carman's manuscript—which covers the Battle of Antietam—will follow soon.

A Maryland Campaign–Antietam collection nearly as large as the Antietam Studies Collection is the John M. Gould Antietam Collection at Dartmouth College in Hanover,

New Hampshire. Gould was an officer in the 10th Maine, and he set out initially to establish where 12th Corps Commander Major General James K. Mansfield was mortally wounded in the battle on September 17. But Gould's correspondence with Union and Confederate veterans, which became voluminous, spilled beyond this narrow focus to cover the entire battle in the vicinity of the East Woods and Miller's cornfield. Some veterans added other details about the campaign leading up to the battle, rendering it worthwhile to examine this collection for events outside of that battle.

Among other institutions with substantial manuscript collections, two are not to be missed by anyone conducting research into the Maryland Campaign: the U.S. Army Heritage and Education Center at Carlisle, Pennsylvania, and the Southern Historical Collection at the University of North Carolina at Chapel Hill. While the USAHEC collections include manuscripts from both Union and Confederate soldiers, their holdings for soldiers of the Army of the Potomac are massive. Manuscripts relating to the Army of Northern Virginia predominate in the Southern Historical Collection, which also includes the papers of several important Confederate officers, such as D. H. Hill, Longstreet, McLaws, and William Pendleton.

Maps

The most important maps consulted for this study are in *Theater of Operations, Maryland Campaign, September 1862*, with a base map by H. W. Mattern and troop locations by Ezra Carman. This is a series of eight maps showing Union and Confederate troop positions between September 6 and 14. It is located in vault CW 242 at the Library of Congress Map Division, and it can be found online through the American Memory website, http://memory.loc.gov. Also at the LC Map Division, as well as online, is the indispensible 1908 edition of the *Atlas of the Battlefield of Antietam*, a series of 14 highly detailed maps showing troop placements for the various phases of the battle. The Crampton's Gap battle and the Fox's Gap and Turner's Gap conflicts were mapped by the army in 1872. These were published in *The Official Military Atlas of the Civil War*, which has been reprinted numerous times and is still in print through Barnes and Noble. An unpublished and significant map of the Fox's Gap and Turner's Gap battlefield is the "Battlefield of South Mountain Map: Showing the Positions of the Forces under the Command of Maj. Gen. A. E. Burnside," located in Record Group 77, F91–93, at the National Archives. It is generally more reliable than the army's 1872 map of this battlefield.

Newspapers and Periodicals

Wartime newspapers, particularly the local papers of small and midsized towns, are rich with primary source material relating to the Maryland Campaign. In this era it was not unusual for soldiers to send letters from the field to their hometown papers. Numerous small town and major city newspapers were consulted in the research for this book. Specific papers I have cited from can be found in the notes. Postwar newspapers are also a highly valuable source. One of the most important is the *National Tribune*, a Union veterans' paper started in the late 1870s that continued into the 1930s. Besides feature articles that were often written by retired officers, during the 1880s and 1890s the paper included a section titled "Picket Shots," where veterans wrote about, and frequently argued about, campaigns and battles. In the 1880s the *Philadelphia Weekly Press* ran a series of articles from former Union and Confederate officers that are quite valuable. Among the most important for the Maryland Campaign is the three-part article by Lafayette McLaws that provides many details about the operations at Harpers Ferry, Crampton's Gap, and the march up to Sharpsburg.

Within the various periodicals, the *Confederate Veteran* magazine and the *Southern Historical Society Papers* both contain considerable Confederate material relating to the Maryland Campaign. *Confederate Veteran* was not founded until the late 1890s, and while many veterans who wrote for the magazine still possessed clear recollections of the war, the Lost Cause powerfully influenced memories during the life of this magazine. Some veterans exaggerated or invented their experiences, while others suffered from poor memory, so it is a source to be used with prudence.

Published Primary and Secondary Sources

The basic building block for any serious research on the Maryland Campaign, or any military campaign of the Civil War, is *The War of the Rebellion: The Official Records of the Union and Confederate Armies*. The Maryland Campaign is covered in volume 19, parts 1 and 2 (Washington, DC, 1887). The *OR*s, as they are called, contain after-action reports of Union and Confederate officers from battery and regimental command on up to army command, and army-level correspondence. Part 1 of volume 19 also contains the full transcript of the Harpers Ferry Military Commission's investigation into the surrender of the U.S. army post there. Spanning over 260 pages, it is the single most important source for Union operations at Harpers Ferry.

The limitation of the *OR*s is that they only included reports and correspondence that the compilers had copies of. As diligent as these individuals were in acquiring Union and Confederate war records, there are missing reports (in some cases they were never submitted), and some valuable correspondence either was lost or never found its way into the records. Part of what was missed earlier, however, is included in volume 51, parts 1 and 2.

One might imagine that the importance of the Maryland Campaign and the Battle of Antietam would have produced an outpouring of books on a par with those about Gettysburg. This is not the case. The first published book-length study of the campaign was Francis Palfrey's *The Antietam and Fredericksburg* (New York, 1882). This remained the only study of the campaign until the 1965 publication of James Murfin's *Gleam of Bayonets* (Baton Rouge). Murfin's volume has since been replaced by Stephen Sears's superbly written *Landscape Turned Red* (New York, 1983) and by Joseph Harsh's *Taken at the Flood* (Kent, OH, 1998), an outstanding analysis of Confederate strategy in the campaign. Harsh also produced an indispensible companion volume, titled *Sounding the Shallows* (Kent, OH, 2000). Gary W. Gallagher edited an excellent collection of essays on the campaign in *The Antietam Campaign* (Chapel Hill, NC, 1999).

There are two modern biographies of McClellan that informed this work and represent the most thorough and balanced scholarship available on the general. These are Stephen Sears, *George B. McClellan: The Young Napoleon* (New York, 1988), and Ethan

Rafuse, *McClellan's War: The Failure of Moderation in the Struggle for the Union* (Indianapolis, 2005). Sears also edited the highly useful *Civil War Papers of George B. McClellan* (New York, 1989).

Biographies of Lee abound, but students of the Maryland Campaign should not overlook Gary Gallagher's important anthology, *Lee the Soldier* (Lincoln, NE, 1996).

For those wishing to visit the battlefield sites covered in this book, a valuable companion is Ethan Rafuse, *Antietam, South Mountain, and Harpers Ferry: A Battlefield Guide* (Lincoln, NE, 2008).

INDEX

Page numbers in boldface refer to illustrations.

Welch, Thomas, 351, 353, 355

Welles, Gideon, 7, 30, 44, 171

Wertenbaker, C. C., 406

West, Robert, 367, 733n86

West, William P., 359

Westervelt, William B., 449, 744n29

Westlake, Oscar, 459, 471–72, 745n50

West Virginia Cavalry, 305; Gilmore's Co., 309

West Woods, 608, 619, 623–24, 626, 647–48, 650, 766n21

Weverton Pass, 235, 237, 244–45, 266–68, 286, 289, 434, 443–44, 476–77, 540, 567, 578

Wheeler, Charles M., 254

White, Carr B., 309, 320, 326–28

White, Claude, 630

White, Elijah, 100–101, 178, 181

White, Julius, 163, 172, 187; agrees to cavalry escape, 523, 525, 534, 536–38, 542–43, 553, 556–58, 718n56, 753n8; arrives at Harpers Ferry, 243, 262–63, 265, 269, 521; and Harpers Ferry surrender, 560–62, 567–68; at Martinsburg, 226–27, 236; withdraws from Winchester, 209–13, 216, 218–19, 221

White Oak Swamp, Battle of, 25, 27, 54

White's Ford, 98, 102–3, 109–10, 166, 179

Whiteside, John C., 393

Whiting, Charles J., 155

Whittier, John T., 235, 239, 257

Wickham, William C., 500

Wilcox, Cadmus M., 56, 60, 128, 695n49

Wild, Edward A., 365, 368

Wilkins, John D., 515

Willard, George L., 258, 536, 553, 557, 559

Willcox, Orlando B., 303, 331–32; at Fox's Gap, 341–44, 346, 348–49, 356, 363, 365–68, 429, 432; sketch of, 340

Williams, Alexander, 555

Williams, Alpheus S., 45, 137–38, 144–45, 152, 161, 189, 192, 282–83, 294, 505–6, 642, 651, 692n82

Williams, H. J., 626

Williams, Seth, 148, 162, 284, 490, 492–93

Williamsburg, Va., Battle of, 19–20, 22, 28, 30, 74–75, 142–43, 301

Williamson, W. G., 522

Willmon, John L., 258–59, 261, 558–59

Wilson, R. B., 321, 326

Wilson, William B., 551

Winder, Charles S., 73

Wingfield, William L., 405, 623, 766n19

Wisconsin infantry regiments: 2nd, 415–16, 419–21, 423,

425–26, 513, 653; 6th, 45, 138, 161, 191, 415, 417, 419–20, 422–24, 428, 499, 649; 7th, 138, 189, 356, 415, 417, 422–28

Wise, Daniel, farm, 312, **314**, 318, 320, 323, 327, 329, 342–43, 348, 349, 352–53, **354**, 356, 358–60, 363–68, 497–98

Wise's field, 312–13, 318, 348–49, 357, 367–69, 725n45, 731n47

Withington, William H., 342, 352–53

Wofford, William T., 363, 619

Wood, Charles, 323

Wood, Ephraim, 559

Wood, John, 526

Wood, William W., 406, 769n64

Wool, John, 164–66, 171, 175, 193, 195, 208–13, 221, 243, 551–52, 567

Worsham, John, 92

Wren, James, 137, 145, 356, 364–65, 368–69, 498, 604, 610, 733n81, 749n45

Wright, Augustus R., 237, 477, 714n74

York, R. W., 361

Yorktown, Va., Siege of, 15, 17–22, 29–30, 36

Young, Henry B., 417

Young, Pierce M. B., 189, 417

Zachary, Charles T., 423

Ziegler, Charles, 463